5th edition

DEVIANT BEHAVIOR

Erich Goode

State University of New York
Stony Brook

Prentice Hall, Upper Saddle River, New Jersey 07458

Library of Congress Cataloging-in-Publication Data

Goode, Erich.
  Deviant behavior / Erich Goode. —5th ed.
    p.   cm.
  Includes bibliographical references and indexes.
  ISBN 0-13-531294-9 (case)
  1. Deviant behavior.   2. Criminal behavior.   I. Title.
HM291.G646   1997
302.5'42—dc20   96-41347
                                              CIP

Editorial director: Charlyce Jones Owen
Editor in chief: Nancy Roberts
Associate editor: Sharon Chambliss
Editorial/production supervision, interior design,
    and electronic page makeup: Mary Araneo
Editorial assistant: Pat Naturale
Marketing manager: Chaunfayta Hightower
Buyer: Mary Ann Gloriande
Cover designer: Kiwi Design

This book was set in 10/11 Times by A & A Publishing
Services, Inc., and was printed and bound by RR Donnelley &
Sons Company. The cover was printed by Phoenix Color Corp.

 © 1997, 1994, 1990, 1984, 1978 by Prentice-Hall, Inc.
Simon & Schuster/A Viacom Company
Upper Saddle River, New Jersey 07458

Printed in the United States of America

10 9 8 7 6 5 4 3 2

ISBN 0-13-531294-9

PRENTICE-HALL INTERNATIONAL (UK) LIMITED, *London*
PRENTICE-HALL OF AUSTRALIA PTY. LIMITED, *Sydney*
PRENTICE-HALL CANADA INC., *Toronto*
PRENTICE-HALL HISPANOAMERICANA, S.A., *Mexico*
PRENTICE-HALL OF INDIA PRIVATE LIMITED, *New Delhi*
PRENTICE-HALL OF JAPAN, INC., *Tokyo*
SIMON & SCHUSTER ASIA PTE. LTD., *Singapore*
EDITORA PRENTICE-HALL DO BRASIL, LTDA., *Rio de Janeiro*

CONTENTS

PREFACE

As a child in the 1920s, during her family's travels, Bronislawa Wajs, a Polish-Lithuanian Gypsy (whose nickname was Papuza, or "Doll") exchanged stolen chickens for reading lessons with her *gadje* or non-Gypsy neighbors. This is how she learned to read and write—virtually unknown among the Gypsies or Roma people at that time. But learning to read was deviant; her parents caught her with the books she was reading, she was beaten, her books were destroyed, and she was married off at 15 to an elderly and revered harpist. She led an unhappy life and, drawing on the Roma tradition, she sang and composed ballads, poems, and stories. In 1949, a Polish poet named Jerzy Ficowski heard Papuza's songs, persuaded her to write them down, and arranged to have a selection of them published. Shortly thereafter, the Eastern European governments, from Bulgaria to Poland, undertook a program of forced settlement of the nomadic Gypsies (a program that was referred to as "compulsive sedentarization"). Since Papuza had become friendly with the *gadje*, she was seen as an apologist for this despised program. Once again, Papuza had committed a deviant or punishable offense.

As her poems, songs, and stories were going to press, she rushed to the publisher and requested that they omit her material; she even begged representatives of the Polish Writers Union to intervene. "If you print these songs, I shall be skinned alive," she wrote to Ficowski. "My people shall be naked against the elements" (Fonseca, 1995, p. 87). All to whom she spoke were mystified by her request; the *gadje* could not fathom the norms of the Roma way of life, and did not understand the

seriousness of Papuza's deviant actions. She returned home and burned the remaining unpublished 300 or so songs. Papuza had done something quite literally unforgivable; she had collaborated with the *gadje*. She was summoned before the head elder of her people and was pronounced *defiled*. "The punishment was irreversible exclusion from the group." After a brief spell in a psychiatric hospital, she lived for 34 years "alone and in isolation. . . . She became her name: a doll, mute and discarded" (p. 87); she died in 1987. In the revised edition of the book containing Papuza's songs, published in 1985, editor Jerzy Ficowski proclaimed the forced settlement of the nomadic Gypsies a disastrous failure, resulting in far more harm than good.

A variety of interpretations can be read into this sad and unfortunate story. On the one hand, it is a tale of deviant behavior and the punishment of deviance. On the other, it is a story about secrecy and revelation. In a sense, it is a parable about how telling a truth may be defined and reacted to as deviant—in a sense, an unpardonable sin. The unwillingness of the Roma people to reveal anything to non-Gypsies about their lives was at that time related to their desire to preserve a way of life that threatened to crumble as a result of influences from the *gadje* world. Dissimulation to the *gadje*, and the expulsion of violators of this rule, was called upon to preserve that way of life. But it was the implementation of government policy, not revelations about Gypsy life to the *gadje*, which did the damage to Gypsy culture. Papuza's tale is one of deviance, of course, for she suffered banishment, the ultimate stigma, for her actions; her punishment demonstrates the fact that what she did was regarded as deviant in Roma eyes. In her case, her sin—her crime, if you will—was one of violating a rule of secrecy.

In different ways and dimensions, we observe negative reactions to a variety of revelations that some of us wish had remained forever in darkness. Some of us don't like violations of privacy; we feel that certain facts should not be revealed if, in the process of obtaining them, the researcher violates stipulated rules of methodological protocol, specifically, rules against disguised observation or deception in social research (Erikson, 1967; Humphreys, 1975; Goode, 1996b). To some observers, if sociologists secure information from unwitting, unsuspecting informants without their consent, they are guilty of deviant behavior.

Some don't like the fact that academics make use of popular or non-scholarly media sources, such as *The New York Times*, when writing a textbook; they claim that only sociologists with the weakest "research credentials" make extensive use of them (Babchuk and Keith, 1995). (Upon reading the article that makes this claim, my immediate reaction was, "Now wait a minute. Let me get this straight. You're telling me that *restricting* your sources is *more* scholarly, and *expanding* them is *less* scholarly?") Again, we see here a violation of the norms of scholarship held by members of some academic circles; some form of denunciation is called for in response to this deviant action.

Still others believe that sociologists cannot learn anything of value in the sexual arena by making use of the interview or questionnaire method; not only should we not even make the attempt, but researchers who do should be excoriated (Lewontin, 1994)—in a phrase, denounced as deviant.

And some observers argue that investigating the world of art by making use of any manner of counting or quantification is taboo; one critic likened a researcher who did so to a nineteenth-century autistic, who counted everything (Kimball, 1993). Again, condemnation is deemed appropriate in response to the offense.

In contrast, I am a strong proponent of the "sunshine" principle: Let's study everything we find interesting and worthwhile, hold nothing back, use whatever method that yields intellectual and theoretical pay-off, and let the chips fall where they may. But, as we see in Chapter 14, the "sunshine" principle forces us into genuine political and ideological dilemmas. Extricating ourselves from them is not an easy task. In fact, all too often, this is an impossibility. The impulse to know is more often rewarded with suffering than with serenity.

It has been nearly 20 years since the first edition of *Deviant Behavior* was published. At least one principle remains: However painful, it is better to know than not to know. My original goal was to describe and analyze in a systematic fashion what was, to me, the most fascinating of all human phenomena—the world of deviance. One of the things that made deviance so interesting, I felt, was not only the behavior itself—what persons actually do when they engage in what is commonly referred to as deviant behavior—but also what happens to them when that behavior is discovered by the more traditional, conventional members of the society. Deviance has a dual feature, I felt, and these two realms—the behavior and its condemnation—interact with each other. How can we ignore how deviance is *constructed* by a society—how it is defined, dealt with, reacted to, punished? Even physical characteristics can be regarded as deviant when looked at from the perspective of the social construction of deviance. I have continued my fascination with both deviance and social control, and their interplay, in this, the fifth edition of *Deviant Behavior*.

The study of deviant behavior is intrinsically fascinating. Nearly all of us love to look at "knavery, skulduggery, cheating, unfairness, crime, sneakiness, malingering, cutting corners, immorality, dishonesty, betrayal, graft, corruption, wickedness, and sin—in short, deviance" (Cohen, 1966, p. 1). Part of that sense is voyeuristic: We want to see things that are forbidden, excluded, hidden from our everyday gaze. Some of it stems from our sense of righteousness: We have been virtuous, yet other people have broken the rules. Are we missing out on something? Are these people gaining an unfair advantage over us? Are they engaged in filthy, loathsome behavior? Why aren't they being punished? In addition, many of us have the feeling that deviance and crime may be, by their very nature, thrilling and seductive; there may be "moral and sensual attractions in doing evil," to quote the subtitle of a recent essay on the subject (Katz, 1988).

Whatever the reason, deviance is a perennial favorite among topics of interest to most of us—and that includes undergraduates. What student would fail to find robbery, murder, rape, white collar and corporate crime, pornography, prostitution, homosexuality, alcoholism, and drug use and abuse fascinating? At the same time, instructors struggle to make a fundamental point in the study of deviance: The sociologist's attraction to the field is guided mainly by theoretical, not thrill-seeking, motives. We are interested in *rule making, rule breaking,* and *reactions* to rule breaking. What ties together the topics generally treated in studies on deviance is *social control*—the condemnation and punishment of transgressors and wrongdoers. If we find such investigations titillating and exciting, so much the better, but that is not their main purpose. The goal of any researcher, instructor, or student of deviance is an investigation of social structure and process—why and how society and social relations work, especially when violations of major rules take place.

The field of deviance studies has been wracked by numerous charges and criticisms over the decades of its existence. One is that sociologists of deviance too often focus on the scandalous, the dramatic, the sensationalistic (Gouldner, 1968; Liazos, 1972). For instance, one critic argued that sociologists of deviance devoted far too much attention to homosexuality, which presumably is representative of such "sensationalistic" forms of behavior (Liazos, 1972, pp. 106, 107)—in spite of the fact that homosexuals represent a relatively powerless minority who tend to be condemned by the heterosexual majority. Throughout the 1980s and into the 1990s, the scourge of AIDS has focused attention on homosexuality, had emphasized its deviant status, and has highlighted attitudes and behaviors on the part of the majority that many of us would regard as irrational, unjust, and oppressive. Rather than throwing light on a dark, marginal, and unimportant aspect of deviance, the study of homosexuality as deviance reveals central social processes that would otherwise remain hidden.

In fact, deviance, *including* the individuals who have been dubbed "nuts, sluts, and deviated preverts" (Liazos, 1972), is central to sociological structures and processes (Ben-Yehuda, 1985, p. 3). The subject matter of the investigation is less important than one's approach or perspective when one goes about one's investigation. (True, some behaviors are more pivotal and tell us more about how society works than others, but that must be examined in each case and cannot be assumed at the outset.) Unless one's study of deviance is mere description, without any analysis or theory, social structures and processes can be revealed through

examination of some of the traditional subject matter in the sociology of deviance (that is what is condescendingly referred to as "nuts and sluts"). The point is not to study "nuts and sluts" to the exclusion of more uplifting topics—those whose study, some critics seem to be saying, reveals the investigator's virtuousness and political correctness (such as racism, sexism, oppression, exploitation, imperialism, and so on) but to examine whatever reveals the ways wrongdoing and denunciation work. By all means, bring on the studies of corporate and white-color crime! (In fact, in the past decade or two in the study of deviance and crime, research on white-collar crime has blossomed.) To the extent that one can be sanctioned for engaging in a given form of behavior, it is deviant. And to the extent that "damaging, unethical" behavior (Liazos, 1972) is neither condemned nor formally punished, it isn't deviant, is it? (This is an interesting contradiction worthy of study!)

Too often, approaches, perspectives, and theories in the study of deviance have been taken as competitive and mutually exclusive. "If X approach is right, Y must be wrong," commentators imply. In fact, in deviance research, different aspects of almost any phenomenon are highlighted by different approaches; few perspectives seem to be directly competitive in the logical sense. In the sociology of deviance, there is no single, grand, overarching perspective that can guide our observations through the many aspects and phases of deviant behavior—no "big bang" theory. The many perspectives simply address and illuminate pieces of the puzzle, but none puts them all together into a coherent picture (Davis, 1980, p. 13; Wright, 1984, pp. v–vi). At the same time, observers too often treat deviance theories as if they were competing or mutually exclusive—as if they focused on the same questions and their differences were resolvable by examining a clear-cut data set that determines which theory is correct. Although this is true of a small number of limited theoretical approaches, much of what passes for deviance theory is incommensurable. Any thorough examination of the subject of deviance, therefore, must be eclectic and theoretically broad. This edition carries on the more eclectic tradition that was begun with the book's second edition.

This edition represents a substantial revision from the previous one. I added summaries to all the chapters. The data in all chapters have been updated. Chapter 1, the introductory chapter, is completely new; all the examples in it are new. In Chapter 2, some sections have been deleted ("Types of Relativity," "What Is Deviance? A Brief Summary?" and "Again, What Is Deviance?"), while other material ("False Accusations and Imaginary Deviance") is new. In Chapter 4, the discussion of a recent theory, self-control theory, billed as "a general theory of crime," has been added. Chapter 6 is on drug use as deviant behavior. A section, "Factors That Influence Drug Effects," has been dropped, while two boxed inserts ("Imprisonment on Drug Charges, 1979–1995" and "A Conflict Theory of Drug Abuse and Its Devastation") have been added. They reflect recent developments. The account at the end of the chapter is new. Chapter 8 has been completely restructured. Readers of the previous edition felt that I should have a chapter that focuses on sexual deviance generally, with prostitution and pornography only as types or illustrations of general principles, rather than having them serve as the basis for the entire chapter. I concurred in this suggestion; I have broadened the focus of this chapter to encompass sexual deviance generally, adding several new sections and bringing a couple of older ones back. One feature of this and the following chapter is a summary of a recent nationally representative survey of sexual behavior.

A discussion of this survey's findings on homosexuality appears in Chapter 9, as does a boxed insert, "What Is Homophobia?" as well as a new account; new developments have been added to "The World of Homosexuality: Some Recent Developments." One section and one boxed insert have been dropped. In Chapter 10, on violence, I added a boxed insert on "Criminal Homicide: From Medieval Europe to the Present," and several accounts. In Chapter 11, on property crime, I added a boxed insert on the various rational, opportunity, and routine activity theories. Chapter 12, on white collar crime, is written almost entirely from scratch. In it, I added the introduction, "Edwin Sutherland's Innovation," and the sections "What Is Criminal Law?" "Defining White-Collar Crime," "White-Collar Crime: An Overview," "Why White-Collar Crime?" and the boxed insert, "Are All White-Collar Criminals Rich and Powerful?" Only the section "A Typology of White-Collar Crime" was partly retained; it still contains some material that was written by myself, Stephen Rosoff, and Henry Pontell. All of the rest of this chapter was written by me from scratch for this edition. In Chapter 13, the boxed inserts, "Some Common Mental Disorders Listed in DSM-IV," "On Being Sane in Insane Places," and "Deinstitutionalization," are new. Except for Chapters 1, 12, and 14, this is the most thoroughly rewritten and restructured of the chapters in this book. Chapter 14, "Ideological, Ethical, and Moral Implications of Studying Deviance," is completely new.

Once again, I would like to thank the persons who agreed to supply the accounts that appear in this book. Some of these accounts began as interviews, which I transcribed, others were papers, which I edited slightly for the sake of continuity, appropriate references, and ensuring anonymity. I would also like to thank a number of graduate students who were enrolled in the two seminars I taught on deviance while I was revising this book, one during the spring of 1994, and the second during the spring of 1996. I would also like to thank the undergraduates who have taken my course on deviance and who supplied feedback to my thoughts on the subject. I am especially grateful to those who took part in the true-false quiz (fall, 1995) and those who answered the "What Is Deviance?" question (spring, 1995). They gave me very useful advice on a variety of issues. As always, I would like to thank my wife, Barbara Weinstein, and my good friend, Nachman Ben-Yehuda, for across-the-board encouragement and advice. I am grateful to Henry Pontell for reading Chapter 12 in its entirety and offering both useful comments and criticism and encouragement—knowing that it was to replace a chapter which he earlier co-authored. Gil Geis, who read parts of that chapter over Henry's shoulder, also weighed in with a few useful remarks of his own. Sharon Chambliss has been an ideal editor—firm, insistent, yet encouraging and flexible. I didn't think I had enough time to complete the revisions on time; she did, and she was right. Perhaps my greatest debt is to the sociologists who work in this area and who write such interesting and insightful works on the subject. To the inane and flatulent charge that the sociology of deviance is "dead" and deserves little aside from "an obituary" (Sumner, 1994), I offer as testimony the writings of the authors who deal with the most fascinating and turbulent subjects in the entire social science literature. Perhaps the announcement of the death of the field of the sociology of deviance, as with that of Mark Twain, was a bit, shall we say, "exaggerated."

PHOTO CREDITS

chapter 1

INTRODUCTION

Just about everyone has done something that someone else disapproves of. In fact, almost all of us have done something *we ourselves* have reservations or second thoughts about. Perhaps we've stolen something, or told a lie, or gossiped about another person in an especially nasty manner. Maybe on occasion we've gotten drunk, or high, or driven too fast, or recklessly. Have we ever worn clothes that someone else thought were out of style, offensive, or ugly? Have we belched at the dinner table, or did we ever break wind or pick our nose in public? Maybe we failed to show up for an important class or read a crucial assignment, or permitted our eyes to wander onto a neighbor's blue-book during an exam. Do we like a television program that someone else finds stupid and boring? Didn't we once date someone our parents and friends didn't like? Maybe our religious beliefs and practices don't agree with those of some other members of the society; it could be that they would regard us as too religious—or not religious enough. Politically, to some, no doubt we are too liberal, too conservative, or too much of a namby-pamby, fence-sitting, middle-of-the-roader. Does someone else consider us too tall or short, too bland-looking or exotic, too thin or heavy, too dark- or light-skinned? The number of possible ways that what we believe, or do, or are, could be judged negatively by others is almost infinite.

Humans are evaluative creatures. We continually make judgments about the behavior and the characteristics of others—and ourselves. Societies everywhere have rules governing what we may and may not do, and how we should look. Even in the same society, social groups or circles vary with respect to the judgments they pass on correct and incorrect behavior. Since the dawn of humanity, rules that dictate right and wrong behavior and characteristics have been laid down, and for that same stretch of time, many transgressors of these rules have been punished. Not everyone is able or willing to abide by these rules; in fact, *no one* abides by *all* of them *all the time*. Indeed, this is a literal impossibility, since some of these rules contradict one another. None of these rules are accepted as valid by everyone in any society in anything like a homogeneous, uniform fashion. There is in every society on earth—in some far more than in others—a certain degree of *variation* in notions of right and wrong from one person to another, one group or category to another, one subculture to another. Especially in a large, complex, urban,

multi-cultural, multi-ethnic, multi-national society such as the United States, this variation is considerable—indeed, *immense*. This means that *almost any* action or characteristic we could think of is approved in some social circles and condemned in others. Almost inevitably, we depart or deviate from *someone's* rules, simply by acting or being, since we cannot conform to *all* the different sets of rules that exist. Sociologists refer to behavior that is regarded as wrongdoing, that generates negative reactions in persons who witness or hear about it, as *deviant behavior*; disapproved-of behavior and traits, characteristics, or conditions that generate a similar condemnatory, rejection reaction in others are called *social deviance*, or simply "deviance."

Thinking about our own behavior and characteristics, should we conclude that *we are all deviants?* Does having engaged in one or more actions of which someone else disapproves—or of which we ourselves disapprove—make us *deviants?* Of course not! Clearly, we have to think of deviance as *a question of degree*. The condemnation we may have experienced, or could face, for telling a small lie is *not* the same thing as the punishment that is likely to be inflicted on us for having committed murder, the armed robbery of a bank, or the molestation of a small child. Some actions are regarded as *mildly* deviant; others are *savagely* condemned, and are seen as *seriously* deviant. We would be foolish to equate the two. In addition, some actions or traits are condemned by small, scattered numbers of people who have little or no power over others, while other actions or traits are condemned by almost everyone. Again, engaging in *trivial* and *seriously deviant* actions cannot be regarded as identical—or even remotely equivalent. At the same time, we would be remarkably unobservant if we were to miss the fact that some of the same dynamics of rejection and condemnation operate for both *milder* and *more serious* forms of deviance. As sociologists, we are interested in the full spectrum of deviance; still, it is at the *more serious* end of the spectrum on which our attention is more sharply focused. An examination of more strongly condemned behavior and characteristics tells us things that we would not see if we were to regard the full spectrum as equally deviant. No, we are *not* all deviants, but yes, all of us have engaged in behavior that *some* others don't approve of, at least *to some degree*. When it comes to deviance, even the saints are sinners—if only in the eyes of a few.

What comes to mind when you encounter the terms, "deviant" and "deviance"? To many students, and to the man and woman in the street, the terms sound distinctly evil, vile, degraded, and degenerate—perhaps even perverted. They conjure up images of wicked deeds, degenerate practices, activities of an abysmally corrupt nature. "Deviants," the popular image would hold, are perverts, junkies, murderers, child molesters, skid-row alcoholics, pimps, drag queens, sado-masochistic sex maniacs, bearded, 50-year-old, 300-pound, tatooed bikers, perhaps inmates of an insane asylum—in short, all manner of sick, twisted, violent, dangerous, corrupt, decadent people.

The first and most fundamental axiom that anyone observing, thinking about, or describing a social scene or aspect of social reality must accept is: "Things are often not what they seem" (Berger, 1963, p. 23). The public image or stereotype of deviance may bear a very loose relationship to what we would find if we were to take a closer look at it. It is the sociologist's job to take as close a look at deviants and deviance as possible. In doing this, we can assemble a more accurate, richer, and more meaningful picture if we were to adopt a *subterranean* view of it. In other words, we cannot rely on popular notions of deviance—ideas we might hold before learning much about it. Though popular myths about deviance may have an impact on the behavior and the people they incorrectly describe, they are not the very phenomenon they purport to describe. We want to look *behind* publicly approved versions of reality, see *through* official smoke screens portraying the way things are supposed to be, to understand *why* and *how* popular myths and misconceptions arise and are sustained. We need, in other words, to understand deviance itself. In the sense of being true to the phenomenon under study, our approach can be called *naturalism* (Matza, 1969, pp. 3ff.).

Although most people are able to supply concrete *examples* of deviance, at the same time, a *general* definition would be more difficult for us to come up with. In other words, though most of us know deviance when we see or come across it, we may not be able to spell out exactly what it is *in general*. Let's begin our exploration of deviance by looking at several examples, concrete instances of what some people might see as deviant behavior or characteristics. Our cast of characters includes a research team with a most decidedly peculiar method of conducting its study; a greedy and unethical business entrepreneur; a mother who suffocated her five children; a masculine, heterosexual cross-dressing 65-year-old man; a paroled serial rapist; some right-wing, anti-government paramilitary survivalists; and a violent, brutal, murderous detachment of an American-trained Salvadoran military batallion. With each case, we should keep in mind a small number of central, guiding questions: *What's deviant?* Which of the actions being described would be regarded as blameworthy? And by whom? Who is condemned, for what behavior, and by whom? What *makes* these actions an example of deviant behavior? And what is your—the reader's—reaction? Which of the actions that follow do *you* regard as deviant? Which ones do you feel are acceptable, not worthy of condemnation? Let's see.

The discovery was entirely accidental. Opening a long-locked room in Yale's Payne Whitney Gymnasium, an employee came upon a cache of thousands of extremely peculiar-looking photographs. Photograph after photograph depicted young men, nude, posed from the front, the side, and the rear. Sticking out of the back of each body was a series of what seemed to be six-inch pins. Baffled, the employee showed the photographs to the university's athletic director at the time; he, too, was mystified. He contacted Yale's officials and the mystery was solved, at least for the time being. Deciding that they no longer had any utility, and realizing that many of their subjects went on to prominent positions, the athletic director had the lot of them burned. Unbeknownst to him, however, many more survived. What was the origin of these photographs? What was their purpose? Asked one journalist (who was photographed himself, as a Yale freshman, in the mid-1960s), did these pictures represent a "scandal" or "an extreme example of academic folly?" (Rosenbaum, 1995, p. 28).

It turned out that the photographs were taken of all incoming freshmen attending some of the nation's elite undergraduate institutions, mainly the Ivy League universities, such as Yale and Princeton, and the "Seven Sister" colleges like Mount Holyoke, Smith, and Vassar, from the 1940s to the late 1960s, even into the early 1970s. They were billed as "posture photographs." The journalist who wrote about the pictures described his own experience 30 years before: "I reported to a windowless room . . . where men dressed in crisp white garments instructed me to remove all of my clothes. And then . . . they attached metal pins . . . [with] adhesive to my vertebrae at regular intervals from my neck down. I was positioned against a wall; a floodlight illuminated my pin-spiked profile and a camera captured it" (Rosenbaum, 1995, p. 28). Hardly anyone seemed to object; these photos seemed to be a "regular feature of freshman orientation week" at the institutions where they were taken. Supposedly, they were for the purpose of correcting poor posture. "Those whose pins described a too violent or erratic postural curve were required to attend remedial postural classes" (p. 28). Notables such as George Bush, president of the United States (1989–1993), George Pataki (governor of New York, elected 1995), Meryl Streep (an accomplished film actress), Hillary Rodham (First Lady of Bill Clinton, elected 1992), and Diane Sawyer (a prominent television journalist) had their nude "posture" pictures taken. Viewed from today's vantage point, the whole enterprise seems to be "pornography masquerading as science" (p. 40).

The claim that these pictures were a tool for correcting posture did not satisfy journalist Ron Rosenbaum; he decided to investigate by contacting a number of key players who are still alive. It turned out that the project had been the brainchild of W.H. Sheldon, who believed that the body is the key to one's destiny; he was the author of a famous "somatotype" theory of delinquency. Was it possible, some observers speculated, that these photographs represented an effort on Sheldon's part to locate potential deviants? A history professor at Yale, George Hersey, goes even further. He speculates that these pictures had a different purpose—eugenic. The idea of eugenics, said Hersey, was to make sure that "inferior" and "useless" humans would be either "penalized for reproducing" or "sterilized" (p. 30), while those who are "superior" should be encouraged to meet and mate—in other words, a program of "enforced better breeding" (p. 30). Could it be that getting those Ivy League men together with their female Seven Sisters counterparts was behind the photographs? Was their purpose a kind of "eugenic dating service," a "Studs" for the cultural elite (p. 31)?

Whatever their purpose, one is left to wonder how Sheldon, now deceased, could have persuaded the administrations of so many colleges to take part in the peculiar project. "What could have possessed so many elite institutions of higher education to turn their student bodies over to the practitioners of what now seems to be so dubious a science project?" (p. 56). And why did practically every freshman in every class at these institutions for a quarter of a century docilely doff his or her clothing and allow himself or herself to be photographed completely nude? (Toward the end of the program, as a consequence of objections, women were allowed to be photographed semi-nude.) Said Judith Martin, author of the "Miss Manners" column, Wellesley alumna, and subject of these strange photographs, "Why weren't we more appalled at the time?" (p. 20). To be sure, there was some opposition before the demise of the project. In 1950, an exhibit called "Atlas of Women" was planned at the University of Washington in Seattle, where Sheldon had begun to take photographs. When parents and administrators got wind of the nature of the exhibit, lawyers and university officials entered Sheldon's office and empounded the photographs and had them burned. In the 1950s, at Denison University, Sheldon's permission to rephotograph the female freshmen he had photographed the year before was denied, arguing that it would cause "insurmountable psychological problems" for some of the women (p. 56). Still, what is so remarkable about this episode is that it generated so much compliance in such high places for such a long time. Administrators and students who went along with it now shake their heads and wonder what could possibly have led them to agree to cooperate with the bizarre project.

Such an event reminds us that "skepticism is still valuable in the face of scientific certainty" (p. 56). The claims of now-discredited sciences—Rosenbaum mentions Marxian history, Freudian psychology, and Keynesian economics—suggest that perhaps some of the sciences now accepted as valid may turn out to have "little more validity than nude stick-pin somatotyping. In the Sheldon rituals, the student test subjects were naked—but it was the emperors of scientific certainty who had no clothes" (p. 56).

In 1991, Michael Carlow, a Pittsburgh native, began acquiring several local firms that were in financial difficulty. One was the D.L. Clark Company, which had made Clark candy bars for over a century. He claimed to be motivated by altruism, an example of "Pittsburghers helping Pittsburghers"; insisting that he did not need to earn a huge profit, he said he was most concerned about saving jobs. Before long, he graced the cover of

Pittsburgh magazine, which celebrated him as a "messianic hero." In February 1995, a local bank that held a major Carlow loan forced the Pittsburgh Food and Beverage Company, which owned Clark, into bankruptcy. The bank accused Carlow of a number of illegal schemes to defraud the bank, shareholders, and employees of over $30 million—startling, given the fact that for 1994, revenues generated by Pittsburgh Food totalled only $76 million. Clark employees began camping outside the factory to prevent creditors from making off with the plant's equipment. Former employees learned that their social security and credit union funds had disappeared. Carlow is currently under investigation for fraud. Said a specialist in reviving ailing companies who was hired by Pittsburgh Food: "The only difference between Michael Carlow and a holdup artist with a gun and a ski mask is that the holdup artist could never hope to get this much" (Eichenwald, 1995, p. D4).

Interestingly, Carlow and his father, Frank, had a long history of illegal practices and bad debts similar to those of which the bank accused the younger Carlow. Central to their operations, officials claimed, was what is referred to as "check kiting" schemes. The pair acquired a number of different companies; the Carlows sent checks from one company to another, drawn on different banks. There were insufficient funds to cover the checks, but by the time this was discovered, more bad checks were written. "Essentially, they were writing a furious circle of bad checks, each one covering the last" (p. D4). The Carlows' schemes, say authorities, extended to looting the pension fund of workers, acquiring and then drawing credit on credit cards for fictional managers, extracting corporate funds for personal use, defaulting on bank loans, underpaying payroll taxes, failing to acquire a bond required by law, and failing to pay penalties and fines.

In spite of the investigation into his dealings, Carlow wants to return to Pittsburgh Food. But former Clark employees say they don't want him back. Said one worker, "Michael Carlow doesn't care about anyone but himself. . . . I hope they lock him up for the rest of his life" (p. D4).

Waneta Hoyt told physicians her first child, Erik, three months old, expired after she found him barely breathing; she couldn't revive him. Her second child, James, was two years old when he called to her one morning after eating breakfast; suddenly and mysteriously, he also died. At two-and-a-half months, while feeding, Ms. Hoyt's third child, Julie, choked, turned blue, and expired. Her fourth child, Molly, and her fifth and last, Noah, both died in their cribs at three months. In 1972, a pediatrician who studied the family published an article in *Pediatrics*, arguing that the case illustrated that "crib death" or SIDS—Sudden Infant Death Syndrome—was inherited. Ms. Hoyt grieves for her departed infants. "I miss my children," she'd say, laying flowers on their graves. "They all died on me—you know, that crib disease" (Toufexis, 1994, p. 63).

Two decades later, William Fitzpatrick, district attorney of an upstate New York county, began researching the subject of infanticide for a case he was prosecuting. Linda Norton, a medical examiner, handed him the 20-year-old *Pediatrics* article. "By the way," she said, "when you read the article, you may decide you have a serial killer here" (Toufexis, 1994, p. 64). Fitzpatrick did some detective work to track down the family, identified in the article only as "H." Interrogating Ms. Hoyt, he extracted a confession; she suffocated three of her children with pillows, she said, one with a bath towel, and one against her shoulder. But after consulting with a lawyer, Ms. Hoyt recanted the confession; Fitzpatrick brought a charge of multiple counts of murder against her, the case went to trial, and she was convicted. Waneta Hoyt can expect to spend the rest of her life behind bars. Said Fitzpatrick, "We have brought to justice a killer who preyed on her own children" (p. 63).

Neil Cargile grew up on a "large estate in the rolling hills" of Nashville's most affluent, exclusive, and elite community (Berendt, 1995, p. 39). At the age of 12, he built motor scooters from parts of discarded washing machines. At 16, he built a small airplane from surplus parts from World War II materials and flew it from his back yard; eventually, he built a fleet of five such planes, all stationed in his yard. Neil Cargile played football for Vanderbilt, flew jet planes in the Navy, sailed yachts, played polo, and raced cars. He stands over six feet, is broad-shouldered, square-jawed, and moves with a "bouncy, athletic stride" (p. 42). His business—"designing, building, and operating mammoth dredges . . . used for deepening rivers and harbors and recovering diamonds and gold, often in remote parts of the globe" (pp. 39, 40). When asked why he pursues business ventures in distant lands under difficult physical circumstances,

Cargile replied that where he does business, there are no unions, no taxes, no lawyers, and no Environmental Protection Agency (p. 45). His politics—conservative Republican. Even today, at 65, Neil Cargile strikes people who meet him as "a man of action and daring" (p. 38).

Early one morning in 1990, *en route* from West Palm Beach, Cargile's small plane developed engine trouble 40 miles from his destination. Radioing the Nashville airport, Cargile was cleared for landing at a tiny airport just three miles from his location, "but just at that moment his plane started clipping the tops of trees" (p. 38). Spying a highway below, he made an emergency landing. He landed the plane's belly on the pavement, barely avoiding two oncoming vehicles; the wing of the plane caught a van, pushing it onto the median strip, where vehicle and plane came to a stop (p. 38). The airplane was a wreck, the van was slightly damaged, but no one was hurt. "Aviation officials inspecting the scene praised his skill in handling the plane" (p. 38). Sipping a drink, wearing a blue blazer, a dress shirt open at the collar, and gray slacks, and surrounded by onlookers, aviation representatives, reporters, police, and rescue personnel, Cargile seemed the model of composure. A reporter stated, "You look as though you're going to a party." He replied, "That's exactly what I *was* doing." When asked what he thought the cause of the crash was, he smiled. "I like being the center of attention" (p. 38). When his friends saw Cargile's "dapper image" on television news that evening, "they were all seized by the same incongruous thought: Thank God he wasn't wearing a dress" (p. 38).

For years, upon occasion, Neil Cargile has worn women's clothes. He receives no sexual thrill from doing it and he does not do it to be more feminine or to "get in touch" with his female side; dressed as a woman, he does not alter his voice, walk, or demeanor to appear more feminine. Cargile, twice married and the father of three, is "decidedly heterosexual" (p. 38). When asked what he feels like when he wears women's clothes, he replied, "I feel like Neil Cargile wearing a dress" (p. 44). His motivation? Plain and simple, he says, "It's fun." It's also very likely that he enjoys watching the reactions of observers. He began wearing women's clothes in public at a Halloween party at a country club in Palm Beach; dressed in a blonde wig, a red dress, and four-inch chrome heels, he came as Dolly Parton. He won first prize. Before long, Cargile began to dress in public in his hometown.

In 1979, at an annual costume party, Nashville's elite were dressed as their favorite characters in history. Cargile came in a long blonde wig and a blue dress. When asked what historic character he came as, he replied, "As Neil Cargile in a dress" (p. 39). His exploits became more frequent, more public, and more uninhibited; many were shocked, some grew to accept it. A few years ago, walking into a bar, he heard a man mutter, "Faggot." Cargile turned to the man and "as nicely as I could" said, "I'm Neil Cargile and I don't think we've met." Shaking the man's hand, he squeezed it. "Hard. I crunched. I cracked. And I kept on squeezing until his eyes bugged out and his body writhed and he let out the most pitiful gasp of pain." Added Cargile, "I haven't had any trouble with him since" (p. 42).

His current companion says that when she first heard about his predelection, she thought it was "bizarre." One evening, on a date, he showed up at her front door in a blazer, a kilt, and high heels. "I was stunned," she said (p. 42). Eventually, however, she said she stopped being embarrassed, and even encourages his hobby. "I wish he didn't cross-dress," she says, "but I won't try to change him. To me, he's a combination of Crocodile Dundee, Rambo, and Jezebel" (p. 42). He is asked how his family feels about his cross-dressing escapades. His former wife once sent him to a psychiatrist. His brother, who is a born-again Christian, strongly disapproves. His son, who is athletic, has a great deal of difficulty with it. He is asked what if his father, now deceased, had seen him in a dress. "He'd have killed me," he replies. And his mother? "She heard about it and she confronted me. She said, 'You're the best-looking man in Nashville, Neil. Why on earth would you want to dress up in women's clothes?'" His reply, he said, was: "It's fun, Mom" (p. 45).

In March 1994, California Governor Pete Wilson transferred a convicted serial rapist, Melvin Carter, to serve out his parole at a remote minimum security facility, Devil's Garden Conservation Camp, located in the northeast corner of the state. Wilson's reasoning was that the ex-convict's crimes were so heinous, and he was so notorious and incorrigible, that he should be banished from populated areas, kept "out in the wilderness someplace." A number of the 10,000 residents of Modoc county, where the facility is located, did not take kindly to the news that a convicted rapist would be paroled in their midst. In fact, Devil's Garden holds mainly drunk drivers, burglars, and drug offenders; residents of Alturas, the town closest to the facility, agreed to Devil's Garden only after they had been assured that no violent offenders would be placed there. "Things are going to get ugly now," said the mother of a young girl. "I don't think that people [around here] are going to just sit back [and do nothing]. They're going to say, 'If I see him I'll kill him.'" Photographs of Mr. Carter hang in the windows of most stores in Alturas. On a number of them, targets have been put on his forehead. On the picture that hangs in the coin-operated laundry, comments have been written: "Death becomes you!" "We all hate you!" "Stay away, Melvin or beware!" "Let's Kill Him!!!" "No, Let's Castrate Him!!!" On the marquee of the supermarket, instead of food prices, the message is spelled out: "Modoc Says No Rapist Here." A local lawyer suggests that Carter be treated so miserably when he comes to town—refusing to so much as sell him a cup of coffee—that the state has no choice but to transfer him to a facility elsewhere. Said a 20-year-old woman: "Personally, I think this man should be in a cave in the Mohave Desert." Authorities are in a quandary as to what to do with Mr. Carter. Said Lieutenant Dallas Reynolds of the California Department of Corrections, "A person goes to prison, and unless he goes to the death chamber, he's going to get out eventually, and where does he go then?" Meanwhile, authorities are keeping a close watch on Carter to ensure his safety; he is wearing an electronic device on his wrist and ankle, is under 24-hour supervision, and for now, cannot leave the camp at all (Margolick, 1994).

My own encounter with advertisements for right-wing survivalist and anti-federalist materials took place quite by accident. A peer in graduate school wrote her Ph.D. dissertation on missing persons (Weitzman, 1970, 1981). Alerted to the sociological and theoretical significance of the phenomenon, I collected several articles on the subject that, in turn, led to my tracking down and purchasing an anonymously authored pamphlet entitled, *The Paper Trip: The Hows and Whys of Getting False IDs*. I wrote a brief "boxed insert" on the subject of false identity and its implications for the social structure (Goode, 1988, pp. 90–91). An undergraduate, a citizen of another country, taking an introductory sociology course with another instructor, inquired as to how he could obtain a copy of the pamphlet; I secured one for him. As a result, I

was put on the mailing list of several purveyors of survivalist and anti-federalist material. Just as Howard Becker surmised when examining catalogues selling pictures of sado-masochistic fetishes (1963, pp. 20–21), I realized that these catalogues indicated that there are substantial numbers of Americans who either fantasize about or engage in behavior the rest of us would describe as deviant, but whose predilections are not necessarily known about. In this case, the materials for sale were not pornographic pictures, but books, pamphlets, and videotapes about, as well as equipment which enables one to take part in, a variety of paramilitary, in some cases, violent and illegal, activities.

For instance, the Paladin Press, "Publishers of the Action Library," "Your source for real-world solutions to real-world problems," issues a catalogue of 72 pages containing descriptions of hundreds of titles of books, pamphlets, and videotapes of a paramilitary nature. The descriptions of items which offer directions on how to engage in especially violent and distinctly illegal activities contain the warning, "For academic study only," or "For entertainment purposes only." A two-and-a-half page section on "Combat Shooting" advertises 20 titles, including *Principles of Quick Kill* and *The Complete Book of Combat Handgunning*. A page-and-a-half section advertises 16 titles devoted to nothing but making silencers for guns. A six-page section on "Self-Defense" includes titles such as *Kill Without Joy: The Complete How to Kill Book* ("For information and academic purposes only"). Under "Action Careers," *Drug Smuggling: The Forbidden Book* and *Gunrunning for Fun and Profit* are advertised for sale. Under "Explosives and Demolitions," there is *Improvised Explosives: How to Make Your Own*. And a five-and-a-half page section advertises publications on "New ID and Personal Freedom," including *Vanish! Disappearance Through ID Acquisition* and *How to Disappear Completely and Never Be Found*. The 80-page Delta Press catalogue includes titles such as *Successful Armed Robbery*, *Escape from Controlled Custody*, and *The Complete Book of International Smuggling*; it also sells a variety of Nazi posters from World War II. The 62-page Phoenix Systems catalogue offers for sale items such as brass knuckles ("sold for use as paperweights only"), stun guns, combat knives that shoot, fit into one's boot, slide up one's sleeve, or are so tiny that they fit into the palm of one's hand, a sword umbrella, a time bomb clock ("You'll love this very interesting conversation piece!"), smoke grenades, car door opener, pick gun ("Open locks in less than 5 seconds"), and military practice grenades ("A must for the military collector").

The bombing of a federal building in Oklahoma City in April 1995, presumably by members of an ultra-rightist "militia," resulting in the death of 169 people, should give us pause to think about the purchasers of the items advertised in these catalogues. We assume that their patronage represents an endorsement of a certain worldview. We assume, for instance, that a substantial proportion of these purchasers are opposed to the power of the federal government; believe they have the right to violate laws that others feel should be binding on all citizens; are opposed to paying taxes; and, generally, endorse the view that anyone should be allowed to do virtually anything regardless of its consequences. It is an aggressively individualistic, anti-communal, anti-federal, even anarchistic perspective. The fact that no society on earth is based on such principles, nor could any survive if more than a tiny minority acted on them, is secondary. A more important question is: Do these customers feel that they have the right to act on these views? Do they read the books and pamphlets offered in these catalogues, receive encouragement and instruction, and as a result, engage in the actions detailed therein, that is, make a silencer, install it on a pistol, and quietly kill another human being, manufacture and detonate bombs, stab a man in a knife fight, pick locks, smuggle illegal drugs, or obtain the identification of another person and "disappear forever"? We must then ask: Under what conditions *would* they engage in these actions?

In 1992, James Perry purchased a copy of *Hit Man: A Technical Manual for Contractors*, from Paladin Press. A year later, he killed Mildred Horn, her 8-year-old quadraplegic son, and his nurse. In committing the murders, Perry followed a number of instructions from the "hit man" volume, including his choice of the murder weapon, suggestions for modifying it to avoid detection, and techniques for the killings themselves. In 1993, Perry was convicted of the murders; in 1995, Lawrence Horn, Mrs. Horn's divorced husband, went on trial for contracting the murders for the family's assets. Howard Siegel, a lawyer, is suing Peder Lund, Paladin's publisher, on behalf of Horn's surviving 10-year-old daughter. "The intention of this book is to train people to become assassins and killers," he said. Lund defended his publication of these books by citing the First Amendment, or freedom of speech. Arguing that the government already has too much power over the individual's freedom, he said: "First, they take away your right to speak out. . . . Then, they take away your weapons. Then, it's up to the gray men and the thought police to tell you how to go" (Brooke, 1996).

The civil war in El Salvador produced some of the bloodiest confrontations in recent history. The violence was typically somewhat one-sided, however, since the rebels were not especially known for their viciousness; in contrast, the Salvadoran government became notorious worldwide for its atrocities. Until recently, the army had been dominated by an extremely right-wing and especially brutal faction whose members were permitted a free hand in fighting "communist agitation" in its own way—by conducting a "dirty war" against the left (Danner, 1994, p. 25). Most visible in this war were the corpses, huge piles of horribly mutilated human bodies, which were found from time to time in El Salvador. Into the flesh of some of these bodies, the signature of one or another of the country's right-wing "death squads" had been carved (pp. 25–26). The fiction was that the death squads were composed of free-lance rightist vigilantes; the reality was that they were made up almost entirely of Salvadoran Army officers, their underlings, and their hirelings. The function of these atrocious killings was: "to root out" a "leftist infection" with ruthlessness and ferocity (p. 26). As the killing continued, it became less and less selective, and more and more random. The government and the Army claimed to be in a war combatting "terrorism." Said one Army official, "we never take prisoners" (p. 42).

In 1981, the government decided to crush the guerrilla movement in the remote northern region of Morazan, nicknamed the "Red Zone"; it launched an offensive that was referred to, perhaps not facetiously, as "Operation Rescue." Government soliders told the residents of nearby areas that throughout the conflict, they would be safe and protected in El Mozote, a tiny village of a few hundred peasants of Indian ancestry. "Come to El Mozote, that's what everyone was saying," said one peasant (p. 20). Suspicious and fleeing themselves, the rebel guerrillas sent word to the peasants to flee; instead, the village's residents stayed, and nearby locals gathered there. El Mozote had attempted to perform a delicate balancing act between the rebels and the government soldiers.

They had sold food to soldiers and remained on more or less good terms with the Army. They did not support the rebels—in fact, they were more than a bit afraid of them—but, on occasion, had some minor commercial exchanges with them. In fact, the people of El Mozote were resistant to the teaching of radical priests who sided with the rebels, since a majority of the villagers were Protestants, evangelical Christians, who are known in Central America for their anti-communism. By the morning of December 8, hundreds of nearby residents had camped out in El Mozote, wherever they could find a small stretch of open space.

In the early morning hours of December 9, near a paved highway a few miles from El Mozote, an Army column came upon a retreating band of hundreds of guerrillas; among other things, they were carrying a large radio transmitter and a gasoline-powered electric generator. The band scattered into the jungle, and the soldiers fired at them. The man carrying the transmitter was fatally wounded, and the transmitter tumbled into a ravine. The next day, the military column entered El Mozote. Because the village had been bombed and strafed that morning, the residents and their guests were hiding inside. The soldiers pounded on the doors of the houses and demanded that everyone come outside and lie face-down on the dirt road. Stragglers were kicked, prodded with rifle butts, or shoved to the ground. Soon, four hundred campesinos lay face-down in the dirt while soldiers screamed questions at them: Where are the guerrillas? Where did they hide their guns? "All you sons of bitches are collaborators," an officer said. "You're going to have to pay for those bastards" (p. 63). At some point, the soldiers told the villagers to get up and return to their houses. They assumed that their lives had been spared. Night fell. They huddled in the dark; they were told they could not speak, poke a nose outside a door, or light a candle. At some point, the people were told to line up in the town square. They stood there for hours.

The sun came up. The sound of a helicopter was heard. At that point, the men were herded into a church while the women and children were taken to a large house. The helicopter touched down in the village square and disgorged a half-dozen officers. The women then heard men yelling in the church, "No! No! Don't do this to us! Don't kill us!" (p. 68). Men were lead away blindfolded, their hands bound behind them, in groups of five or six, each by a pair of soldiers; they headed in different directions. Two attempted to escape and were cut down by a blast of machine gun fire; they were beheaded with machetes. The women and the men who remained in the church were interrogated, often with a solider standing on their backs, yanking back their heads. The interrogation was perfunctory, however, indicating that the Army was aware that the peasants knew nothing whatsoever about the activities of the guerrillas.

Before long, the mass killing began. Soldiers began beheading the men in the church. All morning, all around the village, the sound of gunfire was heard. At midday, the women were told, "Now it's your turn" (p. 71). Women and girls were lead away; girls as young as 12 were raped. The smaller children remained in the house. Houses were set on fire. The skulls of children were crushed with rifle butts, their throats were slashed, or they were hanged; one child of three was thrown into the air and stabbed with a bayonet. The soldiers shot or beheaded every girl and woman they could lay their hands on. Screaming was heard in the hills for miles around. Rufina Amaya became separated from a small group of women; she hid behind a tree, almost miraculously escaping detection. She overheard one solider complaining about killing the children. His companion told him that this was a "scorched earth operation"; "we have orders to finish everyone and we have to complete our orders." Added an officer, "If we don't kill them now . . . they'll just grow up to be guerrillas. We have to take care of the job now" (p. 75). Rufina heard her children screaming for her; she crawled away and buried her face in the ground so she could "cry without anyone hearing." She vowed that if she survived, she would "tell the world" what happened that day (p. 76). At night, Rufina heard the screaming "dwindle to a few voices, and listened as it grew weaker and weaker and finally ceased" (p. 77). By the time the killing stopped, 370 peasants were killed in El Mozote; the same operation was repeated in several other nearby villages as well. In all, 767 peasants were known to have died in the Army's operation. It is possible that El Mozote was the largest massacre in modern Latin-American history (p. 10).

A few survivors, residents living in the hills and nearby villages who had been spared, and the guerrillas trickled back into the villages that had been attacked; they counted and buried the dead, who were left on the ground where they had been killed. A day after the massacre, the rebels stumbled upon

Rufina—an actual eyewitness to the killing. The rebels began making broadcasts that claimed that between 900 and 1,000 civilians had been killed in the attack. The Army disputed this statement, claiming that the only killing that took place resulted from a battle between armed guerrillas and the Army. And the rebel claim of the massacre of close to 1,000 innocent civilian dead was a lie, a product of leftist propaganda, a "guerrilla trick"; in fact, the official line continued, no more than 300 souls even lived in El Mozote. (Recall that many of the victims lived in outlying areas but had been told by the Army to come to the village for safety.)

The American government, fearing a communist takeover of the region, undermined the rebel claims and supported the Salvadoran government's version. A month after the killing in El Mozote, President Ronald Reagan sent a statement to Congress certifying that the government of El Salvador was "making a concerted and significant effort to comply with internationally recognized human rights" (p. 102). The American government's official version of what happened in and near El Mozote was that guerrillas had "established defensive positions" near the village. Knowing that government troops were about to attack, they "did nothing to remove" its residents from the line of fire; the villagers, likewise, knowing that an attack was imminent, did not attempt to leave. No evidence could be found, the government claimed, that the Army systematically killed innocent civilians in any number, and certainly not the more than 900 claimed by the rebels (p. 110). Several journalists heard about the rebel broadcasts; they traveled to the area and checked out the story, and found it substantially valid. One front-page story appeared in the *Washington Post* and another in *The New York Times*. The authors of both of these articles, Alma Guillermoprieto and Raymond Bonner, were denounced in an editorial in *The Wall Street Journal* as communist dupes. The U.S. government stood steadfastly by its version of the events, and remained silent for a dozen years. By 1992, the United States government had invested more than $4 billion in assisting El Salvador's fight against the leftist rebels; some 75,000 Salvadorans had been killed in the struggle. Finally, in February 1993, the United Nations Truth Commission released its report on human rights abuses during the Salvadoran civil war; forensic archaeologists had dug up and identified more than 700 bodies in the area of El Mozote, many of them headless, making denial impossible. And in November 1993, the Clinton administration released some 12,000 previously classified documents, a substantial number of which related specifically to El Mozote. On December 6, 1993, a long article appeared in the *New Yorker* which described the massacre in detail; an expanded book version, complete with relevant documents, was published in 1994 (Danner, 1994). Finally, the truth had come to light about El Mozote. Today, the civil war is over; the left has put down its arms. Some leftists even participate in the government, which remains, nonetheless, dominated by the right wing. While there are occasional, individual assassinations of leftists by less blatant, far more clandestine death squads, the kind of large-scale massacre that occurred at El Mozote is no longer possible. And meanwhile, the peasants in the countryside still deal with the psychological scars that have been inflicted on the survivors after a citizenry has been brutalized on a mass basis.

SUMMARY AND CONCLUSIONS

What could taking nude photographs for a pseudo-scientific project, large-scale corporate embezzlement, suffocating one's children to death, cross-dressing, being a convicted serial rapist, advertising, selling, and purchasing materials that enable one to engage in illegal, violent, or anti-government actions, and slaughtering hundreds of innocent civilians *possibly* have in common? On the surface, they seem to be a mixed and motley assemblage. Some of them involve actions undertaken by an institution, while others are actions engaged in by one or several individuals. The harm these actions cause or caused ranges from actual to potential, from the ultimate harm—death, and on a mass basis—to discomfort, embarrassment, or harm that is merely symbolic in nature. Are we putting apples and oranges into the same basket? How can we possibly group together actions that seem distinctly dissimilar, and refer to them all in the same breath, under the same rubric? Of course, things we put into a specific category do not have to be the same in *all* ways, only similar in one or more *relevant* or *significant* ways. The fact is, as different as apples and oranges seem, they are both kinds of fruit; in this respect, they differ from other physical things such as buildings and bridges, bears and wolves, diamonds and emeralds—not to mention abstract concepts or ideas such as love, honor, status, or respect. We classify things not to announce that the things which are grouped together by our classification are identical, only that they share one or more features in common. Even things that seem very dissimilar may be grouped together for certain purposes on the basis of only one or two features they share.

What the actions I've described above have in common is the fact that they all may be regarded, in one way or another, as deviant. Clearly, they are all actions that veer into the negative range of human behavior. They are actions that are highly likely to be evaluated negatively by many observers; they are, or have been, *discrediting* to the actors—*in the eyes* of a certain proportion or segment of the society. The "society" I refer to may be Western society generally, the society in which the actions take place, American society, or *any* relevant society. By "discrediting" I mean that the action itself, or the person who enacts it (whom I'll refer to as the "actor"), may be *condemned* or *stigmatized* by a substantial number of people who witness or hear about that action. (I'll refer to these potential condemners as an "audience.") Hence, *deviance* is an action that is likely to generate, or has generated, negative reactions *to* the actor *by* or *from* certain audiences.

Can one engage in deviance simply by holding certain beliefs? Of course! Let's think of "behavior" in broad terms; it's not simply a set of physical or mechanical movements, but can include what someone believes, how someone feels and thinks. *Expressing one's views* is an action, to be sure, but what counts is not the physical act of talking or writing, but *what one says* and *what that means to others*. I'll refer to holding unconventional, unorthodox, or deviant beliefs as *cognitive deviance*. This category includes unacceptable religious, political, and scientific beliefs. Try to picture what a cross section of Americans would do or say if persons they know were to tell them they believe that the world is flat. Or that they believe that the president of the United States is a space alien who is about to destroy all humans on earth and inhabit the planet with its fellow creatures. Or that Patrick Buchanan is God. Picture this cross section trying to convince their believers otherwise; imagine the impassioned rebuttal of their reasonable criticisms. Think of how you would feel about them, how you would interact with them in the future, knowing the nature of their beliefs. Isn't it reasonable to conceptualize beliefs as a kind of deviance? Yes, it is. Wouldn't

these negative reactions to the people who hold such unusual, unacceptable beliefs be very similar to those which would take place following the discovery of their participation in certain unacceptable actions, such as homosexuality, armed robbery, rape, drug addiction, alcoholism, child molestation? Of course they would. Indeed, it is entirely possible that holders of unorthodox, unacceptable beliefs have been attacked, criticized, condemned, punished—even persecuted—almost as often and almost as severely as enactors of unorthodox, unacceptable behavior. It would be a mistake to ignore unconventional beliefs—or what I'll refer to as cognitive deviance—in our exploration of deviance.

What about physical characteristics? Can someone be regarded as deviant as a result of possessing certain undesirable, involuntarily acquired physical traits or characteristics—like being extremely ugly, short, obese, disabled, or deformed? Of course! Is that fair? Of course not! But notice: It is not the *sociologist* who is being unfair here—it is the *audience* who rejects the possessor of these traits. Ask yourself: Is a disabled person treated the same way as the rest of us? Do many "abled" persons avoid the disabled socially, treat them with pity, condescension, even scorn and contempt? *To the extent that they do*, the disabled may be regarded as sociologically deviant. Is much social interaction between persons with a normal appearance and one who is disfigured strained, awkward, distant, and difficult? Haven't obese children often become an object of teasing, taunts, ridicule, harassment, and condemnation? Aren't the possessors of certain undesirable physical characteristics excluded from full social participation? Again, to the degree that these things are true, we know that we have a case of deviance on our hands. It does not matter whether we are talking about behavior, beliefs, or physical characteristics, if we have condemnation, we have deviance; it doesn't matter whether they are freely chosen or thrust upon us, again, if it results in condemnation, it is deviant. The fairness and justice of what people do is a separate matter.

Let me make another point. Given the gravity of the massacre at El Mozote, the condemnation that its perpetrators suffered was surprisingly mild—little more than the critical reports, articles, and the book published about the event and, a dozen years later, early retirement for some of them. The condemnation that the nude "posture" picture-taking enterprise generated was, likewise, surprisingly mild—at the time, a few refusals to participate, the outrage of parents and administrators which resulted in some of the pictures being burned, the eventual demise of the project and, years later, the ridicule of audiences who read about the enterprise in a newspaper article. The enterprise was condemned more *in retrospect* than at the time; such a project would not be possible today, in a more skeptical and contentious era. This example illustrates the *relativity* of deviance—what was mildly condemned in the past may be strongly so today, and vice versa. In fact, as I said, sometimes, what is praised in one time and place may even be savagely condemned in another. Our cross-dresser continues to be condemned, to be sure. Still, given his many other qualities, his friends and associates accept his eccentricity and, if they do not see his behavior as completely normal, then at least they see it as a part of his personality that is not going to go away. Members of anti-government paramilitary groups may be condemned by the majority of Americans and even investigated by authorities. And, if they do engage in illegal activities, such as the Oklahoma City bombing in 1995, they can be subject to criminal prosecution—but they have their own circles of peers, like-minded persons who agree that the federal government represents an evil conspiracy and should be resisted by whatever means possible. In other words, the condemnation of a given action may vary, again, by the group or circle of persons we are referring to. What is an act of heroism may be regarded as insanity, dangerous subversion, a crime, or thoroughly despicable behavior in another. The investigation of Michael Carlow's illegal activities is still ongoing at this time, but it is unlikely that his punishment will be as stiff as that received by most common thieves, burglars, and robbers, who steal far less. This discrepancy should intrigue us.

What do we learn from these examples? We learn that deviance is not a simple quality resting within a given action. A given act is not deviant everywhere and at all times. What *makes* a given act deviant is the way it is seen, regarded, judged, evaluated. To the sociologist, deviance does not spell out behavior that is defined by certain internally consistent features. Rather, it spells out behavior that is *reacted to* in a certain way, that is, negatively, in a condemnatory fashion—*by* designated audiences. Acts are deviant *to* certain persons or *in* certain social circles. What *defines* deviance is the actual or potential reactions that certain acts generate or are likely to generate. It is this *negative reaction* that defines a given act *as* deviant. Without that reaction, actual or potential, we do not have a case of deviance on our hands.

Our own personal reaction to these actions is both relevant and irrelevant. It is relevant in that *we* are one of many possible audiences who witness or hear or read about behavior and react to it and to the actors who engage in it. We often make the assumption that *our* reaction is representative— a small fragment—of more general societal reactions; if *we* feel that the actor should be punished for what he or she did, it is likely that *others* do, too. But, on the other hand, this is not necessarily the case. It is entirely possible that our reaction is, if not completely unique, then at least distinctive to the social circles in which we travel. Perhaps we are in a small minority. Hence, we should pay attention to our own personal reaction, but not have *too much* faith in it. It is easy to convince ourselves that the way we feel is widespread; it often comes as a surprise when we learn that our feelings toward a given action are *not* widely shared.

What is the function or purpose of a course in social deviance? Purposes are subjective, of course; two participants in the same activity may have entirely different purposes in mind. Driving a car may be an enjoyable adventure for one motorist and a means of getting from here to there for another. What is *my* purpose in this endeavor of studying, writing about, and teaching courses on deviance? To begin with, it is *not* my goal to convince students to display more sympathy for deviants. Indeed, the category, "deviant," is subjectively generated, an extremely mixed bag. It includes characters for whom I have no sympathy whatsoever. (A small sampling: rapists, racists, genocidal politicians, manufacturers who, in the ruthless pursuit of profit, kill workers, purveyors of poisonous products, mass murderers, and fanatics who blow up innocent victims to make a political point.) The "mixed bag" point is an extremely crucial one. It is not my purpose to persuade the student that "deviants" really are cuddly and are condemned unfairly and unjustly. Indeed, my morality and politics would *insist* that some deviants *do* deserve to be punished—some, in fact, far more than they usually are. My feeling about the condemnation of categories of deviants is quite beside the point and entirely separate from my goals in exploring the world of deviance.

I have three central goals or purposes in mind

in my study of and writing and teaching about deviant phenomena. For each goal, my intention is to impart a certain form of *sensibility toward* or *grasp of* the subject at hand. The first is *intellectual* understanding. The second is empathy, or *emotional* understanding. And the third, a product of the first two, is an *everyday* or *practical* understanding.

Understanding a phenomenon *intellectually* means possessing a reasonable storehouse of basic and fairly incontrovertible descriptive facts about and theoretical and analytic approaches toward it. By this I mean having a grasp of why it is the way it is—what makes it tick, so to speak—(or, at the very least, why experts think it is the way it is); having a sense of what its place in the world is; and knowing what some of its consequences are. Thus, having taken a course in the sociology of deviance, we have an obligation to know, for example, that anonymity is correlated with the commission of deviant acts, that there is no agreement among sociologists as to what the most powerful or general explanation of deviance is, and that deviant behavior is spread throughout the social class hierarchy, but that different kinds or types of deviant acts are more prevalent in some social classes than others. Having an intellectual grasp of a phenomenon means commanding the academic literature of a given subject.

Developing *empathy* is quite another story. We can grasp a field intellectually but not necessarily emotionally—and vice versa. Empathy is a *subjective*, not an *objective*, kind of understanding, having an *internal* rather than an *external* grasp of our subject. Possessing an emotional comprehension of a certain human subject means to understand it from the inside out, to possess an *actor's* or a *participant's* understanding of the behavior in question. While for an intellectual grasp of the phenomenon under study, one does not have to "*be* Caesar to *understand* Caesar," for an emotional grasp of it, it helps to be as close to Caesar as we can, to understand the world from Caesar's point of view. Empathy is *not* the same thing as *sympathy*, that is, commiserating with the trials and tribulations of someone's suffering. Empathy is getting inside the skin of a subject and seeing the world through his or her eyes. It is said that no one can truly understand another person; if taken literally, that is true. But empathy is a matter of degree, not an either-or proposition, and it is clearly a lot harder for some observers—and for some deviants—than others. And clearly, this kind of understanding is a lot different from an intellectual comprehension of one's subject.

Why is empathy important? Well, for one thing, any kind of understanding is important for its own sake; it enriches our grasp of the world to know, for example, what it feels like to have tattoos cover one's entire body, to suffer stigma as a result of weighing 300 pounds, to have one's life dominated by the ceaseless thirst for yet another alcoholic drink. But empathy is crucial for a second reason as well, one relating specifically and more narrowly to motivated behavior. Standing outside the world of the deviant often makes it impossible to understand his or her motivation for engaging in the action we are looking at. Sure, armed with intellectual understanding, we know the role of "factors," "variables," "forces," "conditions," and so on. But even after we've examined all the relevant externalistic, scientific, and statistical relationships to determine the dynamics of the behavior we've studied, we still may not be able to grasp *why* the actor did what he or she did. Some acts are beyond intellectual understanding; even after the facts are gathered, they still don't make *emotional* sense. Getting inside the skin of the actor, seeing and experiencing the world as he or she sees it, may help us grasp the motives behind the act. We *don't* have to accept the actor's reasoning as literally true to do this, only to imagine what life would be like *as if* it were true.

If we were to regard a fetus as a full-fledged human being and *if*, as a result, we were to see abortion as murder, then doesn't that make killing an abortion doctor to prevent further killings seem a great deal more acceptable? If we've convinced ourselves that society is unfair, that people become successful only to the extent that they rip off their fellow citizens, isn't it possible that this may justify stealing oneself? If we regard laws controlling business practices as mere technicalities to be ignored and skirted, and the dealings deemed illegal by those laws as harmful to no one, doesn't this make white collar crime seem more acceptable? Referring to the assumptions on which those actions are based as "rationalizations" is glib and superficial; the fact is, many deviant actors do believe them, and they do provide a motivator to their actions. Again, we don't have to accept these assumptions as literally true, but holding them, if only for the purpose of empathy, may make the actions of those who do more understandable. In the end, however, some forms of empathy may be impossible. I, for one, cannot empathize with murderers and rapists. But *to the extent that* empathy is possible, it makes the action under study more plausible, more understandable.

Our third form of understanding is *practical* in nature. I mean something quite specific by it. What I mean is that we are all citizens of a certain country, members of the world of humanity, occupants of this planet at this time. We engage in judgments about others that have consequences for their lives and ours. We are part of a public, we have opinions, we are consumers of the mass media of communication, we talk to others about our views. We will vote for certain candidates largely or partly on the basis of their views—many of which relate specifically to what they are likely to do on the issue of crime control. In fact, a large measure of the entire outlook of politicians is determined by how they see or define good and evil. Many of us will sit on a jury and help render a verdict of guilt or innocence. We will be exposed to advertising and decide which products to purchase partly on the basis of what those advertisements claim. We may take part in a social movement that attempts to change a major aspect of the society. Our relatives, friends and acquaintances, colleagues, and neighbors will engage in actions that we will make judgements on, that we will react to. We may denounce or accept someone because he or she engaged in a certain action we don't like. When I refer to a "practical" understanding of deviance, I do not mean that this course will teach students how they *should* act toward certain types of behavior. What I mean is that they should use this course to have a clearer and more informed idea of *where they stand* on certain issues. Knowing the basic facts about a certain action and its participants may give us a better grounding on which to act. This does not mean that we will always become more tolerant or accepting of deviance; indeed, as I said, it may make us even more confident about opposing it. (Of course, for some behaviors, we *may* become more accepting as a result of studying them.) What it does mean is that we will know *why* we hold the position we do; a practical grasp of our subject guarantees that we are not acting and reacting out of ignorance. In short, this type of understanding is one that looks inside *ourselves* to comprehend where we stand on this complex phenomenon that sociologists refer to as social deviance.

There is a fourth goal I have in mind, but it cannot be neatly assigned to a place in relation to the other three. In fact, it is both *central to* and *transcends* the other three. This is to emphasize the

constructed character of deviance. The fact is, when sociologists refer to a given action or a condition as deviant, we mean that its deviant quality is a result of a certain kind of *judgment* or *label* that has been applied, or would be applied, to that behavior, that condition, or their enactors or possessors—by designated audiences. By using the term, we do *not* mean that it is inherently deviant, that there is some internal, objectivistic quality that *makes* it deviant. This is the most crucial lesson the sociology of deviance teaches. Grasping its constructed nature is a central aspect of an intellectual, an emotional, and a practical understanding of deviance. Thus, when I say that homosexuality is "unacceptable," I mean that it is a *fact* that homosexuality is unacceptable *to* most audiences we could locate in this society. (Just as it is entirely acceptable to others.) I do not mean that it is unacceptable in the abstract, or unacceptable to nature or natural law, to God, to science or medicine, to the cosmos or the heavens, that is to say, in some objective, eternal, absolute fashion. It is true that some actions are more likely to attract more condemnation in the many societies around the world, that there may be some "objective" features that many deviant actions have in common. But, as we'll see, these features do not *define* deviance, they are not an aspect of its essential reality. What *defines* deviance is that it is behavior or traits that are *seen* and *judged* a certain way. *This* is the essential reality of deviance. Teaching the fact that deviance is a constructed phenomenon is likely to be the central goal of any instructor of a course in the sociology of deviance.

Appendix: True-False Quiz

Is the sociology of deviance little more than common sense? Do we already know the answers to important questions in this field even before we begin? Or are we likely to discover surprises and unexpected, *counter-intuitive* results if we were to investigate certain deviant topics empirically and in detail? For decades, sociologists have heard the (by now, tired—not to mention sexist) put-down joke that "a sociologist is someone who spends $30,000 in research money to find a whorehouse." Is it true? Do research projects in sociology generally and the sociology of deviance specifically spend money to find out what everyone already knows? To answer this question, on the first day of class, I distributed a little true-false quiz to the

148 students enrolled in my undergraduate "social deviance" course during the fall of 1995. I only asked them questions for which there were straightforward, unambiguous, more or less uncontested true or false answers. (I explained that unless otherwise indicated, these generalizations apply to the United States.) Let's look at the results. I have put an asterisk next to the correct answer.

1. Among all age categories, the *elderly* are most likely to be victimized by street crime. (a) True, 44 percent; (b) False,* 56 percent.
2. In the U.S., during national alcohol prohibition (1920–1933), alcohol consumption actually *rose*. (a) True, 70 percent; (b) False,* 30 percent.
3. The consumption of LSD by pregnant women causes significant chromosomal abnormalities in their fetuses and birth defects in their babies. (a) True, 78 percent; (b) False,* 22 percent.
4. On a statistical basis, one's likelihood of being murdered is just as high in a small town as it is in a large city. (a) True, 39 percent; False,* 61 percent.
5. Women are more likely to *attempt* suicide, but men are more likely to *commit* suicide. True,* 80 percent; False, 20 percent.
6. Throughout the world, of all men who have had a homosexual experience at least once, *only a minority of them* come to regard themselves as homosexual, shun women sexually, and engage in homosexual behavior exclusively. True,* 69 percent; False, 31 percent.
7. Since the 1970s, the number and rate of alcohol-related automobile fatalities have declined. True,* 24 percent; False, 76 percent.
8. Today, most prostitutes have AIDS or the HIV virus. True, 46 percent; False,* 54 percent.
9. In the U.S. today, most murders are *intrara-*

cial; when whites kill, they tend to kill a white person, and when Blacks kill, they tend to kill a Black person. True,* 66 percent; False, 34 percent.
10. It is *true* that persons of Irish ancestry are more likely to become alcoholics than the population in general; Irish-Americans have a significantly higher than average statistical likelihood of becoming alcoholics than is true of the American population as a whole. True,* 35 percent; False, 65 percent.

How well did my class do on this true-false quiz? Not very well at all. The average percentage of correct answers to these questions was just a shade below 50 percent (49.7 percent, to be exact). In other words, to determine what the answers were, these students would have done about as well if they had flipped a coin. To my way of thinking, the sociology of deviance is far more than common sense. Researchers in the field *do* unearth findings that are *not* common sense, not part of conventional wisdom—that are what scientists call *counter-intuitive*. Clearly, we cannot rely on what is often referred to as "intuition"—that which seems to make sense, that which is widely and popularly believed to be true—in the field of the sociology of deviance and crime. For that, we need solid, valid evidence and a willingness to accept the facts. That which "makes sense" may very well be false, and what seems to be wrong may be true. Perhaps it is time to retire the tired (again, and sexist) cliché that sociologists waste the taxpayer's money in a useless effort to find out what everybody knows—where the nearest house of prostitution is. It is entirely possible that our study of deviance may upset our notions of what's true, but encountering and grappling with intellectual surprises must be counted among the most important of all educational endeavors.

chapter 2

WHAT IS DEVIANCE?

What is it, specifically, that makes the examples in Chapter 1 instances of deviance? *Why* do they qualify? Although most of us would agree that some aspects of these cases exemplify deviance in one way or another, it is quite a bit more difficult to isolate exactly what it is that *makes* them examples of this phenomenon.

Before deciding that specific acts or conditions qualify or do not qualify as instances of deviance, it might be fruitful to step back and decide what we *mean* by deviance in the first place. What is the special quality or characteristic that certain actions or conditions have in common—which others we do *not* regard as deviance lack—that leads us to decide that they are deviant?

If asked, almost anyone can come up with a number of *examples* of what he or she regards as "deviant." From time to time, on the first day of class, I ask the students in my deviance course to define and to provide some examples of deviance. The last time I did this (spring 1995), the 134 students who were enrolled in this course were able to name an average of six concrete examples each; well over 100 separate activities or conditions were named. Drug use (59 percent of the students named it), murder (54 percent), and rape (40 percent) were the most commonly mentioned examples of deviant acts, followed by stealing or theft (37 percent), homosexuality (35 percent), alcoholism (34 percent), crime generally (22 percent), obesity (16 percent), robbery (15 percent), child abuse (13 percent), and mental illness (12 percent). However, it was much harder for these respondents to define deviance *generally*; in fact, many students did not answer this question. Although most of us can think of many *specific* examples of deviance, it is more difficult to locate the *general property or characteristic* that qualifies an act or a condition as such. According to what definition or criterion do we decide that a given phenomenon is or is not an instance of deviance? What is the defining quality that *all* such phenomena *must* have in common? Is it social disapproval? Their illegal or criminal status? That they violate certain religious or moral codes—the Ten Commandments, perhaps? That they offend God? Or some absolute, eternal law? Or do they violate someone's notion of "natural" law, law that would exist even if humans had never devised a legal code? Is deviance *unusual* behavior, behavior that only a few members of a society engage in?

Not everyone will answer these questions in the same way. For one person, the key defining element in deciding what's deviant is that if certain behavior or conditions *harm others*. A second person will say that if something *offends God*, or is a violation of certain *religious principles*, that makes it deviant. A third person will argue that it is the *criminal code* that decides: Whatever is against the law constitutes deviance. Other observers may have different criteria entirely. Our task at this point, therefore, is to spell out several of the most commonly held conceptions of deviance, eliminate those that are of little or no value, and explicate the one or ones that are most fruitful to us as researchers and students of deviance.

FIVE NAIVE, MISLEADING DEFINITIONS OF DEVIANCE

Some observers have proposed definitions of deviance that in the view of the majority of the field, are naive and misleading. Four are that deviance is defined by: (1) absolute criteria, (2) statistical rarity, (3) social and individual harm, and (4) an act's criminal status; a fifth definition insists that there can be such a thing as *positive* deviance, that deviance is not defined by its negative quality at all.

The Absolutist Definition. The first definition of deviance that most sociologists, including myself, regard as naive and misleading is the *absolutist* definition. The absolutist definition argues that the defining quality or characteristic of deviance can be found in the very nature of the act or the condition itself. It says that deviance is *instrinsic* to certain phenomena; it dwells or resides *within* them. It is God or nature—or some other absolute, eternal agent—who or that is responsible for determining what's deviant, not humans. The evil of deviance, the absolutist view holds, is part and parcel of the thing itself. If something is deviant, it is wrong now and forever, here and everywhere else. Deviance is that which is wrong *in the abstract,* regardless of how it is judged. It is an offense against the order of the universe, in the same way that adding up two and two and getting a total of five would be. Such addition would be an error now; it would have been an error in the year 1000; it will be an error in the year 3000—or, for that matter, in the year 30,000. It is an error here, in Zimbabwe, in Australia, in China, in

Brazil—and even on the moon. Something is deviant if it violates an absolute, eternal, final law. For instance, the feeling on the part of the pro-life, anti-abortion movement that abortion is an abomination and represents an act of murder is an example of the absolutist definition of deviance. Even if it were to take place in a society that accepts and condones it, abortion would still be murder, and would still be an instance of deviant behavior. According to fundamentalist Christians, homosexuality is an abomination in the eyes of God; it must be condemned at every appropriate occasion. Tolerating it would represent making a pact with evil. According to the absolutist definition, what is deviance is defined not by norms, custom, or social rules. Right and wrong exist *prior to* and *independent of* these artificial, socially and humanly created rules. What is or is not deviance, according to the absolutist view, is an *objective fact,* not an arbitrary social judgment. "Deviance is deviance is deviance," to paraphrase Gertrude Stein, an early twentieth-century writer (who actually said, "Rose is a rose is a rose is a rose").

The absolutist view is not always conservative, it must be said. In the 1960s and 1970s, many radicals, Marxists, and "critical" theorists argued that deviance should be defined not by social convention but by absolute criteria, for instance, by the fact that certain actions, inflicted by the powerful against the powerless, are harmful. Behavior that entails what these authors regarded as exploitation, oppression, sexism, racism, imperialism, and so on, were "true" forms of deviance. Focusing on behavior that is popularly regarded as bad or wrong represents a "class bias," these theorists claimed. It diverted attention away from the truly harmful, truly deviant actions that should be scrutinized instead by sociologists. Deviance is not a matter of what the members of a society think or how they feel, this school believed, since the consciousness of the ordinary citizen has been dominated by the powers that be to their own advantage. We should *redefine* deviance to refer to the harmful actions of the powerful (Liazos, 1972; Smith, 1973; Schwendinger and Schwendinger, 1975; Quinney, 1974a, 1974b, 1977, 1979, 1980).

As a result of recognizing that members of different societies practiced customs markedly different from our own, a certain measure of *cultural relativity* with respect to what is considered right and wrong came to be accepted in the social sciences. Relativity is precisely the opposite of abso-

lutism. Judgments of right and wrong, it came to be realized, varied from one place to another and from one time period to another. What is right in Tibet may be wrong in France; what was wrong in the thirteenth century may have been right in the nineteenth. Rather than regard a single standard of right and wrong as correct, many observers grew to recognize the *relativity* in deviant behavior. Today, the vast majority of sociologists of deviance regard the absolutist perspective in the study of deviance as naive and misleading. The view that there exists an absolute right and wrong independent of social custom, norms, and human judgment is now regarded as archaic. (Although, outside the field of sociology, many observers still believe it.) All sociologists have their own private views of right and wrong, of course, and for many, those views may be absolute. At the same time, pretty much all sociologists agree that judgments of deviance among different categories of people *are* relative to time and place. For instance, we may or may not believe that abortion is murder, but we would be extremely incompetent sociologists if we failed to recognize that not all members of the society in which we live agree with our view. Deviance is not *about* our private views or whether we think that such views are moral absolutes. It is about *how views of right and wrong are held and acted upon* in different societies, groups, categories, subcultures, and time periods; clearly, those views *do* vary enormously, and it is our job to take note of that variation. Notice that relativity does *not* say that judgments of what is good and bad vary and *therefore, we have no right* to make our *own* judgments. Relativity says that judgments of what is good and bad vary, and these judgments play a role in actors' and audiences' lives, depending on where they are located. We have the right to our own judgments about good and bad, but if we are studying deviance, we have to pay attention to how such judgments vary—*empirically*—through time and space.

In short, to the relativist, deviance is not bad or negative *by its very nature.* An act or a condition cannot be regarded as deviance because it supposedly violates God's law (or a law of nature). It is not even clear what that might mean, since such notions vary from one religion or society to another. Behavior is not deviant because it is immoral in some absolute sense, or intrinsically, inherently evil; again, ideas of morality and immorality, good and evil are relative to time and place. Of course, certain actions may have specific consequences, but that is a different matter altogether. And some forms of behavior are widely, nearly universally, condemned. But saying that an act is universally, or nearly universally, regarded as deviant is *not* the same thing as saying it is evil in an absolute sense. Moreover, many actions that most people would see as deviant in Western society are *not* universally regarded in this way. Many absolutists recognize that variation in judgments of deviance *exist*, but argue that any departure from their *own* version of right and wrong represents an error, objectively speaking. People make mistakes in arithmetic or grammar, but these practices are mistakes nonetheless. Likewise, people make "mistakes" in moral judgments and behavior, but that does not deny the fact that they are mistakes nonetheless. The legal or social toleration of abortion, homosexuality, and pornography has nothing to do with *the fact* of their absolute, eternal evil; God's law may or may not overlap with human law—but nonetheless, it *is* God's law (Falwell, 1981, pp. 195-205). Sociologists do not make these assumptions when they study deviant phenomena. It must be emphasized that the absolutist definition offers no guidance whatsoever to the sensitive, observant student of deviance. It may be acceptable theology, ethics, ideology, or politics, but it is very poor sociology.

The Statistical Definition. Second, some observers have naively insisted that deviance can be defined by a phenomenon's *statistical rarity*: Deviance is that which is rare, unusual, uncommon, that which departs from a statistical norm, the norm of frequency (Wilkins, 1964). Rare, uncommon phenomena are deviant; those that are common and frequent are *not* deviant.

A moment's reflection renders this definition invalid. Many statistically unusual actions or conditions are not regarded as deviant (that is, blameworthy) by anyone: being strikingly attractive, taking three showers a day, owning 30,000 books, possessing two doctoral degrees, being trilingual, shooting a roll of film a day, attending four different undergraduate institutions before receiving one's bachelor's degree, receiving more than two dozen items of mail a day, and so on. Each of these actions or conditions is fairly rare and unusual from a statistical point of view; they place one outside the average along some dimension. But none of them implies a quality that any of us would refer to as deviance. Clearly, what is deviant to us is something far more than unusualness. Deviance may overlap with rarity, but it is far more than rarity by itself. It is likely that a *correlation* exists between rarity and deviance—that extremely rare actions are more likely to be deviant than common ones—but we cannot *base* our definition of deviance on rarity.

On the other side of the coin, there are many actions or conditions that are extremely widespread, even enacted or possessed by a majority of this society, that are nonetheless widely regarded as deviant—for instance, lying, stealing, and extramarital sex. A majority, or near-majority, of us engage in one or more of these actions *at some time or another* in our lives, and hence, they are *common*; yet, these are also *widely condemned* actions, actions that many of us would refer to as deviance. If we are lied to, stolen from, or cheated on, do we shrug our shoulders and say to the offender, "That's okay, I don't mind"? Of course not! We react in some way, usually with anger, outrage, puzzlement, condemnation, or at least shunning, snubbing, or some kind of social avoidance of the offender. Certain conditions, too, are common, but widely condemned, such as being overweight; it is possible that the weight of as much as a third of the American population is heavier than a norm set by physicians as healthy. Clearly, then, statistical commonness does *not* disqualify an act or a condition from being regarded as deviance. As we'll see, there is *some* relationship between deviance and statistical rarity, but, again, statistical rarity does not *define* deviance. While *many* unusual acts and conditions are deviant, and *most* common acts and conditions are not deviant, these are nothing but generalizations, not absolutes. What we need is a quality that *defines* deviance, that is an *essential* ingredient, one that *all* deviant acts and conditions have in common and that *no* nondeviant ones possess.

Does Social Harm Define Deviance? When I ask the students enrolled in my deviance courses to locate the quality that defines deviance, a common response is that it must cause *harm* to individuals or to society. This, too, is naive and misleading. If we were to think of the many actions or conditions that readily come to mind as instances of deviance, it can be seen that many are not, by any reasonable criterion, harmful to anyone. On the other side of the coin, many conformist, conventional actions that hardly anyone regards as deviant are extremely harmful to human life. Until the AIDS crisis came along, it was difficult to imagine what was harmful about homosexuality. Most of the time, secret extramarital sex harms no one. It has not been clearly or convincingly demonstrated that the use of marijuana is medically harmful, at least, when compared with alcohol and tobacco. If the instructor of this course were to throw off his or her clothes and lecture in the nude, nearly everyone would see that as an instance of deviance, but no one would be able to explain what the direct physical harm of this act was in anything like a convincing fashion. Grabbing a steak with one's hands and tearing at it with one's teeth doesn't harm anyone, but few would regard this as normal or acceptable behavior. Clearly, deviance cannot be *defined* by harm to anyone, since it is a simple matter to think of many examples of behavior that are harmless but deviant. On the other side of the equation, we can think of actions that harm many people, but are not widely thought of as instances of deviance. Warfare has destroyed more than 100 million lives in this century, and yet, the parties responsible are rarely condemned or labeled as deviants. ("They" are always responsible—never "we.") In fact, most often, they are regarded as heroes; statues erected to them may be found in parks, plazas, and squares around the world. Industry routinely pollutes waters and the air we breathe, but is rarely held responsible for its damaging actions. Thousands of workers die on the job in the United States each year—and possibly millions worldwide—because of hazardous conditions at the work site, but the industrialists, entrepreneurs, or executives responsible for not installing safety features are rarely punished at all, and if so, almost never fined more than a few thousand dollars for such occupational violations. Clearly, many harmful actions are not widely condemned, do not come to most people's mind as examples of deviance, and the agents responsible are not held accountable for them. The conclusion seems inescapable: However harm is defined, and however deviance is defined, harm *cannot* be a defining feature of deviance. There are simply too many *harmless but deviant* actions and too many *harmful but non-deviant* actions for us to accept this criterion. Harm is a *naive, misleading* definition of deviance.

Is Deviance By Definition Criminal Behavior?
Does the same apply to our fourth possible defini-tion—crime? Does an action have to be criminal to be deviant? Once again, there are many *deviant but non-criminal* actions, although the question of the reverse, criminal but non-deviant actions, is a more complex matter. (As we'll see in the next chapter.) No one will be arrested for picking one's nose, eating steak with one's hands, shaving one's head bald, dyeing one's hair purple, or wearing a goofy grin all day long. *Eccentricity* is not a crime; being *peculiar* is not a crime. Being obese is not a crime. Being three feet tall is not a crime. By itself, being mentally ill or disordered is not a crime. Unquestionably, criminality cannot *define* deviance. Again, there are too many exceptions for us to be comfortable with this defining criterion. While most criminal actions are also deviant, many deviant actions are not criminal. The two are separate, but overlapping, dimensions.

Does "Positive Deviance" Exist?
And last, can there be any such thing as "positive deviance"? However we define deviance, clearly we are in the realm of *undesirable* behavior or conditions. Deviance implies negativity of some sort. Whatever else it is, to nearly everyone, deviance is not a good thing. When people are asked, what's deviant? their replies are almost always in the realm of the negative and the undesirable. To my mind, deviance is an *inherently invidious* concept; that is, it is offensive or repugnant *to* someone, to one or more *audiences*, even if only slightly so. In my view, a naive and misleading definition of deviance is the suggestion that good, positive, or acceptable deviance exists as well as bad, negative, or unacceptable deviance. To be sure, the concept of "positive deviance" does have its defenders (Wilkins, 1964, pp. 45–46; Dodge, 1985; Harman, 1985; Heckert, 1989; Ben-Yehuda, 1990b). Examples of "good" or "acceptable" deviance would be sainthood, being the perfect student, or being strikingly and unusually attractive. In the study of deviance, these observers complain, there has been an "exclusive fixation on the objectionable, the forbidden, the disvalued"; to see deviance exclusively as that which is "offensive, disgusting, contemptible, annoying or threatening" is overly restrictive (Dodge, 1985, p. 17).

To me, and to most sociologists of deviance, this objection makes no sense whatsoever. Good, positive, or acceptable deviance is an *oxymoron*, that is, a contradiction in terms (Sagarin, 1985). To the vast majority of sociologists, to the proverbial man and woman on the street—and the author of this book—deviance is *always and by definition* negative in nature. There is no such thing, and there *cannot* be any such thing, as good or "positive" deviance. We cannot refer to behavior or conditions that generate *positive* reactions as deviance. Certain behaviors and conditions generate negative reactions from some people or groups and positive reactions from others; this does not demonstrate the viability of the concept of positive deviance but the relativity of deviance. Certain behaviors and conditions change from being condemned at one time to positively evaluated at another time; this simply demonstrates the relativity of deviance over time, not the viability of the positive deviance notion. Certain behaviors or conditions represent "too much of a good thing," that is, such an abundant possession of a positive value (such as great intelligence, beauty, wealth, or athletic ability) that one may be condemned for it. While such claims are often exaggerated, *if* such behavior or conditions truly are condemned, again, they qualify as deviance—not positive deviance, but *deviance*, that is, behavior or conditions that attract hostility, condemnation, or punishment. In my view, all claims for the viability of the "positive deviance" concept are naive and misleading (Goode, 1991).

TWO FRUITFUL (ALTHOUGH FLAWED) DEFINITIONS OF DEVIANCE

And yet, we still have not answered the question: Wherein does the negative quality of deviance reside? Because it violates the rules of a particular society? Or because it generates punishment and condemnation? In exactly what way is deviance "bad, negative, unacceptable"? While we have looked at five naive, misleading definitions of deviance—one based on absolute criteria, one on rarity, a third on harm, a fourth on criminal status, and a fifth which permits "positive" deviance—there remain at least two that promise to spell out the phenomenon in a more fruitful fashion: the *normative* and the *reactive* definitions.

The Normative Definition of Deviance

The normative definition posits a "fly on the wall" observer, an omniscient or all-seeing sociologist with a privileged view of the behavior who classi-

fies it as deviant or conformist. This definition presumes that this observer is capable of seeing any and all actions, even if they are secret, and making accurate judgments about their deviant status in a given society. The normative definition locates the quality of deviance not in abstract actions or conditions themselves, as the absolutist definition does, but in the fact that they violate the norms of the culture or subculture in which they take place or exist. Thus, it is relativistic. According to this view, we can determine when an action or a condition is deviant by consulting the customs of a society; when it runs counter to or contradicts those customs, it is an instance of deviance. To the normative sociologist, deviance is a *formal violation of the norms*. In contemporary American society, it is the norm for a woman to weigh between 110 and 140 pounds. A woman who weighs 250 pounds has violated a weight norm, therefore, being this heavy must be regarded as deviant (Cahnman, 1968; Goode, 1996a). It is the norm for a married couple to have children; it violates that norm, and is therefore an instance of deviance, for a married couple not to have children (Miall, 1986). In a society where mainstream religions are the norm, membership in a non-standard "cult" (such as Hare Krishna, the Unification Church or the "Moonies," and Scientology) represents a form of deviance (Ward, Carter, and Perrin, 1994, pp. 403–431). When health is the norm, sickness is a form of deviance (Parsons, 1951, pp. 383ff.); when being physically and mentally abled is the norm, disability represents a form of deviance (Freidson, 1966). Deviance is defined by *the violation of a specific norm*, a rule that dictates that behavior or characteristics be a certain way.

The normative definition implies relativity. An action or condition that may be in conformity with the norm in one place or time may violate it in another. What makes a given action or condition deviant is the fact that it is a violation of the custom, rule, law, or norm *when and where it occurs*. Criticizing Islam violates custom in Iran, Saudi Arabia, and the Sudan; in the West, at least among non-Muslims, such an act is not a normative violation. Private economic enterprise violated the law of the Soviet Union of 1980; today, in the nations of the former Soviet Union, private economic enterprise is not only legal, it is encouraged by these governments. Specific actions or conditions about whose deviant status we are wondering do not have to be witnessed or judged to determine the issue.

We know what the norms are, and we can decide *in advance* whether they are violated by a given action. We know, *even before it happens* in a given case, that the behavior of a man walking down a street completely naked will qualify as an instance of deviance. We know this because we know what the norms in this society are, and they apply *generally*; we don't have to wait for each and every case to take place before we reserve our judgment as to whether they qualify as deviance. *In each instance*, we can decide *in advance* that these norms have been violated by the act of walking down the street, nude. If we know, in a certain society, that engaging in sexual activity with a partner of the same sex is regarded as wrong; when this happens, it is *automatically* an instance of deviance. (Of course, if that same act were to take place in a society where it does *not* violate the norms, it would *not* be an example of deviance. Moreover, an act may be normative in one group or category, and non-normative in another in the same society.)

In short, the normative definition locates deviance in the *discrepancy* between an act or a condition and the norms of a society, a time period, or a subculture. Something that is a violation, and therefore deviant, in one place or time may not be in another. We know what categories of behavior or conditions violate a society's norms *in advance*. We know what is deviance *in general*, that is, we know whether a given instance of behavior, or a specific example of a condition, will qualify as deviance simply by noting the discrepancy between the norm and the concrete example in question. We do not have to wait until it is judged in a specific context by a specific audience. It is proper, the normative sociologist believes, to refer to *general types of behavior* as deviant. Even if each and every specific instance of a general type does not generate actual, concrete condemnation, it is *still* deviance because of the normative violation.

Although the normative definition of deviance is the most commonly accepted one among sociologists in the study of deviance, there are some serious problems with looking at the phenomenon in this fashion. Here are three of them (Goode, 1981a, pp. 49–50).

First, the normative definition of deviance *underplays exceptions*. Talcott Parsons defines deviance normatively; it is a departure from "the normative standards which have come to be set up as the common culture" (1951, p. 206). But does a "common culture" exist with whose particulars everyone agrees? Can deviance from the dominant norms exist *alongside* of alternate, minority definitions? Is it improper to refer to deviance *from* a minority definition? The normative definition argues that deviance is defined solely by departures from the "common culture." Not everyone in a society agrees with the "common culture's" norm. The normative definition seems to be saying that there is a general *consensus* in definitions of right and wrong which are sufficiently widespread that we may ignore exceptions; deviance is defined *solely and exclusively* by an act's or a condition's departure from mainstream norms. The fact is, even the most widespread of norms will often be greeted with different and alternate definitions, and the alert sociologist of deviance must notice when and where they operate, and what their influence is.

Second, the normative definition does not adequately allow for *contingencies* or *extenuating circumstances* that alter observers' judgments as to whether a given individual or act will in fact be regarded as deviant. For instance, driving considerably over the speed limit is a violation of the norms governing driving, and will typically draw a punishment—a speeding ticket from a traffic officer. However, is this true if the driver is "transporting a seriously wounded individual to a hospital?" (Gibbs, 1972, p. 46). The extenuating circumstances of this *particular* act make it necessary for us to *reclassify* the act, *not* as an instance of deviance but of altruism and bravery. The normative view does not give sufficient importance to such contingencies; it seems to assume that the norm applies to any and all circumstances, which is clearly false.

Third, the normative definition ignores the distinction between violations of norms that generate *no* special attention or alarm and ones that cause audiences to *punish* or *condemn* the actor. For instance, a bank teller who is a petty bureaucrat, a "stickler for the rules," who "does everything by the book," is breaking a norm—the norm that dictates that he or she assist customers. Likewise, the bank robber who holds up that same teller with a gun is also violating the norm against stealing. According to the normative view, *both* individuals violate norms; hence, both are *equally* guilty of deviant behavior. In truth, the behavior of the teller does not raise alarm in the community, and he or she will not be punished for these actions, while the robber will generate a great deal of attention, concern, and other types of negative public reactions (Erikson, 1962, p. 10). Contrary to the normative definition, in reality, it is difficult to refer to both as equally deviant simply because each has violated a norm. Clearly, we are in a *qualitatively* different realm in the case of the bank robber. The normative definition of deviance fails to make important distinctions among different forms of norm violations.

The Reactive Definition

Normative theorists believe that deviance can take place or exist *in secret;* an act or a condition that nobody knows about except the violator is *no less* a violation of the norms than is an act or a condition that is witnessed and judged by others. They also believe that an act or a trait that violates a *general* norm but is met with no condemnation in a *specific* instance is deviant nonetheless. Reactive sociologists disagree with both assumptions. They adopt an *even more* radically relativistic position than the normative sociologists. The reactive perspective argues that the key characteristic of deviance may be found in *actual, concrete instances of negative reactions* to behavior, individuals, and conditions. To qualify as deviance, an act or a condition must (1) be observed or heard about and (2) generate concrete condemnation or punishment for the actor or individual. Many acts or conditions that are committed or exist are not observed by others; they never come to light in any way. Socially, *they do not exist*. They are known only to the individual who enacts or possesses them. Even acts or conditions that are known about do not necessarily result in punishment or condemnation for the individual who enacts or possesses them. According to the reactivist, *they are not examples of deviance at all*. Someone who engages in some slimy little action in a closet somewhere, whose behavior is never detected by anyone else, *has not engaged in deviance at all*. What counts to the reactivist is the *reaction*, *not* the action. In other words, reactive sociologists deny that people react to *types* of phenomena, acts, or conditions "in the abstract" (Gibbs, 1972, p. 40). It is impossible, they say, to know beforehand whether a man who admits to being a homosexual, or who is observed engaging in homosexual acts, or who makes a homosexual "pass" at a heterosexual man, will be reacted to negatively by "straight" observers (Kitsuse, 1962). It is not homosexuality per se that is reacted to, they say, but specific individuals or acts in specific situations by specific observers.

What makes an act or a condition deviant, the reactivists believe, is how it, and the individual who enacts or possesses it, are reacted to by actual people, audiences, or others who punish or condemn the individual under actual, real-life conditions. The key criterion in the reactive definition is *concrete social disapproval which is expressed against specific actions, actors, and conditions*. Reactivists argue that behavior and conditions are not deviant *unless and until* they have been condemned; the quality of deviance resides within the actual condemnation itself. There is no such thing as deviance *in advance* or *in general*. If there is no condemnation, no deviance has taken place. This means that if someone gets away with "the perfect murder" (even if the murderer *knows* that it is an act of murder), it is neither deviant nor a murder at all, because it did not result in punishment of the perpetrator. In fact, *we have no business* referring to such a killing as a "perfect murder," because it has not been *judged* as a murder by the relevant parties, that is, real-life police, prosecutors, district attorneys, judges, and juries. Deviance is that which has *already* attracted negative reactions from the relevant members of a society. There is no deviance *apart* from this negative response from the community. Deviance exists *when and only when* there is a negative reaction to an act or a condition and to the individual engaging in or possessing it by observers or others who may have heard about it. It is these negative reactions that *constitute* or *define* deviance (Pollner, 1974; Kitsuse, 1962).

Most sociologists today adopt the normative and not the reactive definition of deviance. Reactivists are in the distinct minority among researchers of deviance. There are, it must be said (as with the normative definition), both strengths and weaknesses of the reactivist definition. Here are a few problems with reactivism.

First: *It ignores secret behavior or conditions that would be reacted to as deviance, were they known to the community*. In fact, *most* deviance, and many discrediting conditions, are *not* revealed to the community; they are secret, known only to the individual who enacts or possesses them. Yet, to the reactivist, there is *no such thing* as secret deviance; it is a contradiction in terms. If we were to adopt the reactive definition of deviance, we must *give up* studying behavior and conditions enacted or possessed that do not result in detection and punishment. With respect to deviance, the professional thief whose illegal activities are never suspected by the community, or who is never apprehended by law enforcement, is *exactly the same* as the ordinary, law-abiding, conventional citizen. Many observers regard this view as erroneous and unproductive, and at least one sociologist dubbed it a "cop out" (Polsky, 1969, pp. 110–112), because it does not allow us to study vast territories of behavior *most of us* would regard as deviant. Most instances of normative violation are "off limits" to the sociologist, according to the reactivist; we cannot study them *as deviance.*

Second, the reactivist definition of deviance ignores secret behavior and conditions that *would* be reacted to as deviant, *even where the actor or the possessor knows that it would be condemned by the community at large.* In other words, the reactive definition ignores the views of the individuals who would be judged deviant, those whose behavior or conditions violate the norms. Most people who would be judged deviant by the community at large, or segments of the larger community, are *aware* of the potential reactions their behavior or condition would generate in others. They almost always disagree that they are *worthy* of punishment, but they almost always have some idea of how others *would* treat them in the event of discovery. Are these people, from the point of view of deviance, *exactly like* the conformist, the individual who does not violate the norms in some major way?

For instance, most men and women who are homosexual are not known by the members of the straight majority as gay; they "live out their lives . . . without their sexual activities ever being made a public issue." On the other hand, most are also thoroughly aware of the negative reaction that would greet the discovery that they are gay by straights; they have adopted an identity they know is saturated with public scorn (Warren and Johnson, 1972, pp. 76, 77). They are *indirect* or *symbolic* deviants, that is, they know that they would be labeled as deviants *were their identities or activities discovered.* Again, it is misleading to say that they are identical—with respect to their deviant status—to the person who would *not* be condemned for his or her sexual identity and activities by the majority. By ignoring the potential deviant's definition of the situation, the reactivist has failed at a crucial task: observing the deviant reality. In other words, the majority of sociologists of deviance support the idea that there is such a phenomenon as *secret deviance.* In *Outsiders,* Howard S. Becker (1963,

pp. 20–21) expressed surprise when he examined a huge catalogue advertising thousands of photographs of women in fetishistic, sado-masochistic poses; the dealer who sold these pictures must have a "sizeable clientele," he said. "Yet one does not run across sado-masochistic fetishists every day" (p. 21). Most sociologists find it difficult to accept this clientele as completely conventional simply because they have not been discovered or stigmatized as practitioners of non-normative sexual practices.

Third: The reactivist definition *denies the possibility that there is any predictability in the reactive process.* Reactive theorists make the assumption that the sociologist cannot predict which concrete acts or conditions will be reacted to negatively. We cannot know for certain whether a given instance of robbery, let's say, will be ignored, condemned, condoned, or praised, Let's wait until we see what observers actually do before we decide that a given act is or is not deviance, the reactivist sociologist seems to be saying, because such outcomes are too unpredictable to know in advance. But in fact, "reactions are not idiosyncratic. No one would assert, for example, that reactions to completely naked individuals strolling down a sidewalk would be indistinguishable from reactions to fully clothed individuals. Stated more generally, in all social units there is some degree of association between types of acts and types of reactions" (Gibbs, 1972, p. 43). If we followed the implications of the reactive definition to its logical conclusion, we would have to admit that we are in no position to predict whether murdering an infant in its crib or chewing gum is more likely to be regarded as deviant in real life. Both may be punished somewhere, at some time, by someone, and thus, we must reserve judgment until we see what actually happens when both are seen or heard about by real-life audiences. In contrast, most sociologists of deviance would say that to each act we can attach a certain *likelihood* or *probability* of punishment or toleration (Black and Reiss, 1970), a possibility that the reactivists seem to be denying.

Fourth, the reactivist definition *ignores the reality of victimization.* The reactive perspective ignores the fact that behavior where the actor is not apprehended or punished *may have real victims,* and that these victims' evaluation of the behavior that victimized them should be part of our definition of what's deviant. For instance, a low proportion of rapes are reported, come to public attention, and result in arrest. A woman is sexually assaulted, the man who did it is not reported and escapes detection by the police. *Does this mean that the woman was not raped?* This is precisely what the reactivists seem to be saying, but most sociologists and, my guess is, most readers of this book, would find this impossible to agree with. How do the survivors, the remaining members of the victims, and peasants in nearby areas, regard the military action in and around El Mozote that resulted in the slaughter of over 700 innocent peasants? What does it mean to say that the killers were not condemned or brought to justice? Are we truly permitted to say that *in no sense* did an act of deviance occur that fateful day? I find this difficult to accept, and so do most sociologists of deviance.

Stigma: The Discredited versus the Discreditable

One clue that the *strictly* reactive definition of deviance is unworkable can be found in the work of Erving Goffman.* In *Stigma*, Goffman identified *discrediting* information and hence, distinguished between *discredited* and *discreditable* individuals (1963, pp. 41–42). Individuals who are *discredited* have *already* been labeled as deviants; they are stigmatized, tainted, "disqualified from full social acceptance." Their deviant characteristics or behavior are known about and hence, they cannot credibly pass themselves off as anything other than individuals with a "spoiled identity." On the other hand, a *discreditable* individual possesses "undisclosed discrediting information" about himself or herself which is not known about, but who stands in danger of being found out. These are "potential" deviants in that were their status to be revealed, they stand a high likelihood of being labeled, condemned, and stigmatized.

Many potentially discrediting physical features are difficult to conceal in face-to-face encounters; they are highly visible or readily *evident* to others (pp. 48-51). Being obese or facially disfigured, for instance, is a typically discrediting characteristic because, in most social encounters, one's condi-

*Goffman is somewhat inconsistent about the parallels between stigma and deviance. On the one hand, he stated: "I do not think all deviators have enough in common to warrant a special analysis; they differ in many more ways than they are similar" (1963, p. 141). On the other hand, his detailed analysis reveals that these parallels exist, and his principal objection to deviance as a category—differences in the relative size of deviant groups—applies to stigma as well.

tion becomes readily known about and one's character and identity are swiftly discredited (p. 49). In contrast, under specific circumstances, some other physical conditions are not immediately evident, for instance, having AIDS, wearing a colostomy bag, or missing a leg. Moreover, some characteristics that are normally discrediting become visible only under certain kinds of interaction: deafness is not readily apparent unless sound is an issue, blindness cannot be detected over the phone, and so on.

In contrast to stigmatizing physical characteristics, most of which are immediately evident to others in ordinary face-to-face interaction, deviant behavior is rarely so readily discrediting. In most cases, individuals who enact deviant behavior are *discreditable* rather than *discredited*. Most homosexuals, prostitutes, ex-mental patients, alcoholics, drug abusers, and ex-convicts do not automatically reveal themselves as such by their appearance, speech, or everyday behavior. In most settings, they can "pass" as conventionals. Of course, *they* are aware of their behavior and identity; they are aware that *others* are likely to view their behavior and identity—and them—with contempt and scorn *if* their secret were to become known about. They are aware that this knowledge is likely to disqualify them from full social acceptance.

The distinction between discreditable individuals, that is, those who possess information that is *potentially* discrediting but that has not yet discredited its possessor, and those who are *already* discredited individuals, emphasizes the fact that the strict reactivist position is flawed, and that labeling by audiences cannot be taken as an absolute defining criterion of deviance. The possessor of potentially discrediting information is sociologically quite a different person from persons who possess no deviant characteristics at all and cannot be discredited or revealed to be, or to have been, deviants. While the former navigates in a social world that is likely to condemn them for what they do or are, the latter do not. These two categories of individuals lead different lives; their identities are different, they act differently, and they bear a totally different relationship to the worlds of deviance and conventionality. Simply because persons who possess potentially discrediting information have not *yet* been stigmatized or labeled does not mean that they are *exactly like* the conventional, conformist, law-abiding person, or like them in most crucial respects. As Warren and Johnson say, such individuals may be said to experience *symbolic* or *indirect* labeling (1972, p. 77). Consequently, the strict reactivist definition of deviance is flawed and must be rewritten.

A MODEST RESOLUTION OF THE DILEMMA

We are ensnared in a true dilemma here. On the one hand, it is true that we cannot know *for sure* if a given act or condition will be punished or condemned, because so many exceptions and contingencies abound, as Kitsuse (1962) argues. On that point, the reactivists are correct. On the other hand, as Gibbs (1972) points out, we *do* have some idea in advance which behavior is likely to generate punishment; sanctioning is not a random process. On that point, the normative theorists are correct. Consequently, some sort of *blend* or compromise between the normative and the reactive definitions becomes necessary.

In my view, a way out of this dilemma is to adopt a "soft" or "moderate" reactive definition of deviance, thereby avoiding the weaknesses and capitalizing on the strengths of each definition. This view, a kind of compromise between the normative and the reactive definitions would contain the following particulars (Goode, 1981a, pp. 50–51).

First, no rule is absolute. Not even the most rigid determinist can possibly expect perfect predictability to be a necessity in identifying group norms. One should be able to infer from reactions by a wide range of audiences to behavior and conditions what the norms are; if enough people punish and condemn a given phenomenon, it is fair to refer to it as a violation of the norms. Still, in specific instances, all such reactions are *probabalistic* rather than absolute; that is, something is deviant "if it falls within a class" of phenomena "for which there is a probability of negative sanctioning subsequent to its detection" (Black and Reiss, 1970, p. 63). If that probability is high, we have a clearcut case of deviance on our hands; if it is nearly zero, it is fair to say that it is not a very representative instance of deviance. If the sociologist is sufficiently perceptive, he or she will be able to discern whether the specific audience witnessing or evaluating the behavior in question will in fact judge that it belongs to that general class of behavior that has generated negative reactions in the past. But

no such prediction will, or can, be infallible. *Some* individuals will *not* react negatively to widely condemned behavior or conditions, and some *will* react negatively to behavior or conditions that are widely tolerated. There are exceptions to every generalization; however, simply because there is variation in reactions to phenomena does not mean that some reactions are more common than others.

Thus, it is necessary to make the distinction, formulated by Kenneth Plummer (1979, pp. 97–99) between *societal* and *situational* deviance. "Societal" deviance is composed of those actions and conditions that are widely recognized, in advance and in general, as being deviant. There is a high degree of consensus on the identification of certain categories of deviance. In this sense, homosexuality, robbery, being physically or mentally disabled, and transvestism are deviant. Even though specific individuals enacting or representing specific instances of these general categories may not be punished in specific situations, we all know that in general, members of this society recognize the fact that they represent serious normative violations. On the other hand, "situational" deviance does not exist as a general or abstract quality, but rather in *actual, concrete* instances of punishment and condemnation. A given individual may not be regarded as a deviant *situationally*, but may enact a category of behavior, or possess a condition which is so widely condemned that from the point of view of societal deviance, it is deviant. Such behavior is "societally" but not "situationally" deviant. Thus, in this culture, "homosexuality must be regarded as societal deviance. All members of [the] society must acknowledge (even if they strongly disagree) that homosexuality is commonly regarded as deviant. . . . Yet to acknowledge that homosexuality is societal deviance is not to acknowledge that it is situational deviance," since, in many cases, actual, concrete condemnation is lacking (Plummer, 1979, pp. 98, 99).

Second, because most behavior and conditions that would earn the actor or possessor punishment are never detected, let alone sanctioned, any reasonable observer is forced to ask the questions, "What is the *actor's* perception of how the audience feels about his or her behavior?" "How does this perception influence the actor's further behavior?" "His or her self-image?" The enactor of potentially deviant behavior, or the possessor of potentially discrediting characteristics, must operate in a sea of *imputed negative judgments* (Warren and Johnson, 1972, p. 77). The actor's sense of how others would react cannot be ignored in the equation of deviance.

And third, the reactions of audiences do not necessarily create the behavior in question out of thin air. Psychiatrists do not, all by themselves, generate mental disorder as a result of judgments of who is mentally ill. That is, they do not *create* the behavior ordinary people see as the symptoms of mental disorder: erratic behavior, "word salad" talk, and so on. They make diagnoses that often *confirm* what laypeople have been thinking all along; sometimes, their diagnoses have official standing and determine such events as commitment, medication, and so on. But what is widely referred to as "crazy behavior" and "crazy talk" is not *generated by* psychiatric labeling. Likewise, the police do not *create* criminal *acts* where they did not exist before simply by making arrests. The behavior that the police (and much of the public, it might be added) define as criminal existed *before* the official designation; however, such official actions *do impart to that behavior a specifically criminal quality*, they do designate certain actions as *officially* criminal. Although social reaction does not *create* the actual behavior that is defined as homosexuality, it does *lend to it a stigmatized status*. Further, social reaction may influence *certain* features of that activity and the lives of men and women who engage in it that would be *lacking* in the absence of negative labeling.

Can we have deviance in the absence of concrete labeling? Can conditions or behavior be regarded sociologically *as* deviance without having been observed and reacted to? We are caught in a dilemma here. If we say no, this means that we have to ignore a huge volume of phenomena that *would be* reacted to as deviance *were they to be discovered*; in fact, *most* potentially deviant behavior and conditions remain undiscovered and unpunished. On the other hand, if we say yes, this means that we contradict ourselves. If deviance is constituted or *created by* negative reactions, then "secret" deviance *cannot exist*. If it is secret, there cannot have been any negative reactions to punish the perpetrator or possessor; if there were such reactions, then it cannot be secret. If we are being truly strict about this definition, we cannot have deviance in the absence of detection and negative labeling, because that is what makes something deviant in the first place. According to several observers (Kitsuse, 1962, 1972, 1975, 1980; Pollner, 1974), deviance exists *when and only when* there is actual, concrete, real-life

condemnation. According to this line of thinking, "secret" deviance is a contradiction in terms, and "potential" deviance is a meaningless concept. Let's refer to sociologists who adhere to this definition as, "hard," "strict," or "literal" reactivists.

On the other hand, some of the sociologists who first developed the ideas that emphasized the role of labeling and social reactions in the creation and definition of deviance, notably Howard Becker and Kai Erikson, recognized (even if implicitly) the dilemma I just spelled out. Becker seems to have one foot in the strict or "hard" reactivist position and one foot in a "softer" or more moderate position that seeks a way out of the dilemma. Becker writes that it should be clear "that insofar as a scientist uses 'deviant' to refer to any rule-breaking behavior and takes his [or her] subject of study only those who have been *labeled* deviant he [or she] will be hampered by the disparities between the two categories" (1963, p. 14). In addition, Becker delineates the concept of *secret deviance* (pp. 20–22), clearly admitting that deviance can exist in the absence of literal, concrete labeling. On the other hand, Becker also writes: "We cannot know for sure whether a given act will be categorized as deviant until the response of others has occurred" (p. 14). In short, to Becker, "whether a given act is deviant or not depends *in part* on the nature of the act (that is, whether it violates some rule) and *in part* on what others do about it" (p. 14; emphasis mine).

Erikson, another sociologist who emphasized the role of social labeling and negative reactions in defining deviance, likewise endorses a compromise between the strict reactivist and what I have called a "soft" or "moderate" reactivist definition of deviance. That is, deviance can exist *as a general category* of behavior, in the *absence* of literal, concrete labeling. Erikson writes: "It is the audience which eventually determines whether or not any episode of behavior *or any class of episodes* is labeled deviant" (1964, p. 11; emphasis mine). This indicates that to Erikson, certain acts are *highly likely* to be regarded, among many or most potential audiences, as examples of a general category that is seen as deviant in nature. We can, according to this view, refer to acts *as deviance* that are likely to be so regarded *even before they are labeled as such by specific audiences*. To Erikson and Becker, then, the concept of "secret deviance" makes sense, and so does the "soft" reactivist position. This is *not* the case among the hard, strict, or more radical reactivists. In the typology Plummer laid out (1979), "moderate" reactivists believe that both societal and situational deviance exist, while the "strict" reactivist believes that only situational deviance exists, that societal deviance is a meaningless and contradictory concept.

THE MENTAL EXPERIMENT

How does the "moderate" reactivist definition of deviance direct us to what's deviant? How does it operationalize or measure deviance? If we accept or follow this definition, how do we know deviance when we see it? What constitutes a reaction that defines deviance? As we've seen, violating a norm isn't enough; it must be a certain *kind* of norm, a norm that calls for punishment, condemnation, or a negative reaction of some sort. Being fired from a job, slapped in the face, arrested, executed, socially shunned and isolated, insulted—in short, being reacted to in a negative fashion—all quality for the definition of behavior (or traits) that generated such reactions as deviance. *Whatever* generated or touched off such reactions in others who witness or hear about the behavior or trait qualifies as deviance. Some sociologists are uncomfortable about including physical characteristics within the sphere of deviance, insisting that deviance is *motivated behavior* (Parsons, 1951, p. 206; Cohen, 1966). However, the reactions of many members of the society to possessors of certain disvalued physical characteristics must be regarded as negative. If we are serious about social reactions as the quality that defines deviance, then surely *anything* that generates negative reactions can be defined as a form of deviance. The disabled, the extremely ugly, and the extremely short are reacted to by other members of the society in a condescending, pitying fashion; they are *disesteemed*, "disvalued and reacted to in a negative manner by large numbers of persons in the society" (Sagarin, 1975, p. 9). They are condemned and punished (even if only indirectly) by not being allowed to enter into normal relations with the rest of us. Hence, it is difficult to avoid the conclusion that involuntarily acquired physical traits qualify as deviance.

But remember, we need not define deviance solely and exclusively by real-life, concrete behavior. One way of answering the question, "What behavior is deviant?" is to perform a *mental experiment*. Imagine behavior being enacted in many different settings before many different audiences; imagine specific conditions being revealed to a wide range of audiences. How do these audiences react? How do they treat the individuals who enact this behavior or possess these conditions? Are they hostile and condemnatory? Neutral or tolerant? Or do they applaud and praise what they see? Imagine a mother walking past the bathroom in her home and seeing her daughter smoking crack cocaine or shooting heroin into her arm. Or a father witnessing his son fellating another young man. Or imagine seeing your best friend robbing then stabbing an 80-year-old man. Or a neighbor savagely beating a 3-year-old child. Imagine being fixed up with a blind date who weighs 300 pounds. Or being told that a friend has AIDS. Picture yourself walking into your bedroom or dorm room and seeing what you thought was your best friend making off with all your electronic equipment. What would go through your mind? What would you do? If we are perceptive, our mental experiments will sensitize us to what is deviant, that is, behavior or conditions that attract censure and punishment from numerous, or influential, people.

Audiences

In these cases, we have an action that is enacted, or a condition that is possessed, by an individual. These actions or conditions, and the individual, are evaluated—or they would be evaluated if they were to be revealed to others—by different observers, parties, or *audiences*, concrete or potential, directly or indirectly. These audiences include:

1. The actors, participants, or possessors.
2. Victims (if any).
3. Social intimates of the participants or possessors, who are not necessarily direct observers, but whose opinions the participants or possessors value greatly.
4. Direct observers, witnesses, bystanders, if any, who may impinge upon, constrain, or perhaps encourage the individual being evaluated.
5. The members of the town, village, tribe, or the general society in which the actor, possessor, and participants live, who are socially and emotionally a bit more distant or removed from the actor or possessor than his or her social intimates are.
6. Agents of formal social control, such as the

police, the courts, prison officials, welfare workers, psychiatrists, teachers, and so on.

7. The "detached" or distant observer, the person who reads or hears about the behavior or condition from such a vast social distance that the actor, participant, or possessor is not influenced by his or her judgment in any way.

Naturally, these parties, agents, or audiences may overlap some. And people who would belong in one category in one case might belong in a different one in a different case.

Considering these audiences, what makes a given activity or condition deviant? Why would it fall within the scope of our attention and interest as students of deviance? Simply for this reason: *From someone's point of view, it is regarded as reprehensible; the actor or possessor is deserving of scorn, condemnation, or punishment of some kind.* Certain parties or audiences, from the participant to the detached observer, would condemn the behavior, the condition, the actor, or the possessor, were they to come face to face with them. In determining what is deviant, it is important to identify the party judging the behavior or condition. The point is to locate the relevant audience.

"Everything Is Relative": Or Is It?

What is seen as reprehensible and worthy of punishment and scorn to one audience may be innocuous or even praiseworthy to others. Does this mean that "everything is relative," as we often hear? This sophomoric cliché is a crass simplification; it is erroneous for a number of reasons. Saying that what is regarded as deviance is a matter of judgment and evaluation, and varies from one audience to another, may appear to imply certain conclusions that aren't true. Taken literally, the "everything is relative" cliché means that *no* behavior or condition is deviant to everyone, and almost *any* phenomena may be deviant to someone. Since deviance exists only as a description of what some people believe or how they react or would react to something, almost anything could be deviant. This is literally true, but not every useful; because people and groups who react one way versus another are not equally numerous, nor are they equally powerful. Consequently, someone who enacts behavior, or possesses a characteristic that is repugnant to a small number of relatively powerless individuals stands a relatively *low* likelihood of being con-

demned, whereas someone who enacts behavior, or possesses a characteristic, that is repugnant to a large number of relatively powerful individuals is *highly* likely to be condemned. Thus, the "everything is relative" cliché is not very useful because not all acts or conditions stand the same chance of generating condemnation as deviant.

Attitudes toward and reactions to potential deviance are held and expressed by people with vastly differing degrees of power—power to have their views of what is right and wrong win out over those of other people. We are not interested in a mere patchwork mosaic of different beliefs and practices in a given society. Rather, we have to direct our attention to the *dominant moral codes*. Looking at different definitions of deviance as if they all received equal time, as if they existed side by side without impinging upon one another, as if they existed in a kind of ethical "free enterprise system" belies the *hierarchical* nature of deviance. What we have to know is *which forms of behavior and what conditions stand a high chance of earning condemnation and punishment for the individual.* Different phenomena have differing *probabilities* of exciting moral outrage in a given society. Even though these reactions vary from one audience to another, for most actions and conditions, certain reactions are a lot *more likely* than others. Thus, although it is possible, for example, to locate some people in the United States who believe that dancing is a degenerate, evil practice—probably followers of an extremely strict, orthodox, fundamentalist religious sect—our likelihood of running across them, and being subject to the punishment that flows from this belief, is extremely slim. Therefore, we can say that in the United States, dancing is *not* a deviant act. This is a shorthand way of saying that it is not deviant *to most Americans.* This does not deny, however, that to *some* people, dancing *is* a deviant practice. If we were members of a Hutterite community or an ultra-orthodox Jewish sect, we would attract condemnation if we were to dance to popular music with members of the opposite sex. Since most of us are not Hutterites or ultra-orthodox Jews, it is a simple matter to discount the minority views. But we should never make the mistake of slipping over into the assertion that the dominant view is the only one. We still have to examine the social scene or context in which the behavior or the condition we are interested in takes place or exists. If we are studying the customs of the Hutterites or ultra-orthodox Jews—or if we happened to be an adolescent growing up among them—it is *that* definition to which we would have to pay attention. Thus, some forms of behavior and some conditions may be deviant only to a tiny number of people. It is still deviance—*to those people*. And it is also not deviance to the majority. An action or condition cannot be regarded as deviant in the abstract; it is only deviant *in reference to* specific audiences. It is only out of numerical significance that we refer to, and concentrate on, *as* deviant, certain phenomena that many people consider deviant.

How many people are necessary for us to regard a given action or condition as deviant? There is no clear-cut answer to this question. If we were to answer this by saying a majority, or over 50 percent of a given society, the next logical question would have to be, how *intense* does their negative reaction have to be? People can be mildly disapproving of some phenomena while they may react in a strongly hostile fashion toward others. Also, condemnation and disapproval take many forms. Can these different faces of hostility and punishment be measured, reduced to a single dimension, to a precise score? How does a slap in the face compare with not saying hello to someone who has done something someone else does not approve of? Or gossiping about him or her? Or reporting the behavior to the police? Can an official execution by the state compare with a lynching by a mob on the street? If a wife divorces a man for something he does, something she disapproves of, is this equivalent to, or more or less serious than, his losing his job? When a man refuses to date a woman because he feels she is obese, how strongly can we weigh that negative reaction? If someone who has AIDS suddenly loses all his friends when they find out about his condition, is this more, or less, strong a reaction than if he were to be arrested for a burglary? How intense or critical is the gossip suffered by a couple who have a retarded child? The point is that all these reactions are forms of social disapproval. They vary in seriousness, but their weight varies somewhat according to the person whose behavior or condition touches off the response. Where do we draw the line and say one reaction is serious, but another isn't serious enough to qualify as condemnation or punishment? There cannot be an exact or final answer to this question. Deviance is clearly a matter of degree. People who are punished, whose behavior or condition is disapproved of, will evaluate the negative reactions of others. They will sense that disapproval is headed

their way. Deviance is just about anything that generates reactions such as these. But how serious and intense these reactions have to be to tell us we have a case of deviance on our hands is a bit arbitrary and cannot easily be measured.

Audiences: Numbers, Power, and Intensity

In the end, we are left with three dimensions that determine deviance in a society. The first is *numbers*. How many people are likely to punish a certain phenomenon defines, in part, its degree of deviance. The higher the number of people that do or will disapprove of something, the greater the likelihood of being punished for doing or possessing it, and therefore, the *more deviant* it is.

The second dimension defining deviance is *power*. The greater the power of those who disapprove of something, the higher the probability of being punished for it, and therefore, the more deviant it is. Individuals with more power have a greater ability to impose their definitions of right and wrong on others. For instance, parents who believe that the indiscriminate taking of cookies from a cookie jar is wrong are more likely to successfully impose their will on a four-year-old child than the child is to win out in his or her definition that such behavior is acceptable. A police officer has more power to sanction the actions of a homeless person than vice versa. A psychiatrist generally has more influence to define the status of the mental condition of a mental patient than the other way around.

And last, we have the *intensity* dimension. The more strongly held a belief is, the more extreme the negative reactions are to a given phenomenon, and the more severe the penalty that is likely to be touched off by that phenomenon, the more deviant it is. Although widely condemned, most of the time, picking one's nose is not likely to generate strong or intense punishment; one is not likely to be arrested or beaten up for doing it. On the other hand, certain actions touch off more extreme, more hostile reactions; they must be regarded as "more deviant." *To* a fundamentalist Christian, abortion is a form of murder; even though it is a minority opinion in the society as a whole, it is a strongly held one—*to that minority*. Hence, we must keep in mind the fact that intensity and numbers are not necessarily the same thing. By itself, the intensity dimension can often exert a powerful hold on a minority and hence, the majority may be forced to react or adjust to that definition. Even though most Americans believe that abortion should remain legally available, persons who do *not* feel so strongly about the view of most Americans, and are willing to act in a forceful manner to back up a contrary belief, can close down abortion clinics all over the country, so that now, only a small minority of physicians are willing to perform abortions (Kolata, 1990).

Just where you wish to draw the line between "more deviant" and "less deviant" is up to you. As long as we keep in mind the idea that deviance is a spectrum, a continuum, with shades of gray, and not a polarity, not a matter of black or white, we will not run into any difficulty on this point.

FALSE ACCUSATIONS AND IMAGINARY DEVIANCE

In the equation of deviance, therefore, we have the following two elements. First, *that which is negatively evaluated*. Here, I refer either to behavior or characteristics, and the person or persons being evaluated. And second, *those who are evaluating and reacting*, in other words, an "audience," either literal or potential. Do the behavior, traits, or persons being evaluated or reacted to *have to exist* for deviance to exist? For instance, what if someone did not actually commit the behavior of which he or she is accused? Here, we have what Howard Becker (1963, p. 20) refers to as the "falsely accused" deviant; in this case, the *behavior* doesn't exist but the *attribution of deviance* does. Accusations of deviance, even if falsely based, can often have a powerful impact on how the community treats the accused. There may be no difference between how a person who is falsely accused of wrongdoing and someone who actually committed the deed are treated. Of course, by itself, an accusation of deviance is not enough to discredit someone in the eyes of the community. False charges are often successfully resisted and the accused is vindicated. However, when an accusation "sticks" and the accused is stigmatized by the community, according to the reactive definition, *that person is a deviant*, albeit a "falsely accused" one. (But notice that when we use the term "falsely accused" deviant, we are assuming that *we* know that the accusation is false, even though the community doesn't.) The "falsely accused" represent an inter-

esting and theoretically important type of deviance, although my guess is, numerically, they are a great deal less common than both those who engage in "secret" deviance and those who both engage in deviance and are negatively labeled as a result.

An even more interesting type of deviance is what I'll refer to as *imaginary deviance*. Here, not only did the person not engage in the behavior of which he or she is accused, but for the most part, *the behavior does not even exist in the first place*. The entire affair is fabricated from beginning to end. In fact, there are two types of imaginary deviance: First, those of which specific, concrete parties are falsely accused, and second, those where even the supposed actors do not even exist, or at least are not specifically named. In the latter case, no specific persons are named, but the behavior is attributed to broad, vague, amorphous social entities or parties, such as "they," "the government," the rich or the poor, or persons of a different race, religion, or nationality, and so on. For such accusations to be made, the accusers need not be consciously lying. In many cases, stories about the despicable deeds of others emerge from a variety of social processes, most notably, group conflict. When emotions run high and righteous anger is unleashed, audiences often believe extremely outlandish tales on the basis of very little evidence (Shibutani, 1966; Knopf, 1975; Kapferer, 1990; Goode and Ben-Yehuda, 1994). Here, we are in the realm of rumor, gossip, panics, collective delusion, and legend, in a phrase, *collective behavior* (Goode, 1992).

A virtual treasure trove of case studies in false accusations of deviance may be found in the many urban or contemporary legends that circulate in almost all modern societies on earth. Urban or contemporary legends are empirically false, highly improbable, although widely believed tales with stereotypical elements that presumably took place in the setting of the teller, or one very much like it (Brunvand, 1981, 1984, 1986, 1989, 1993). They differ from the ordinary, run-of-the-mill or garden-variety rumor in that rumors tend to be about specific events and persons, whereas contemporary legends have an abstract, general or *cartoon-like* quality about them. What matters is not that a specific person engaged in a certain action but that a representative of a *category* of persons supposedly did so. Demonstrating that a given person did not engage in an action of which he or she is accused undermines a rumor but not a legend. Said in another way, for the believers of legends, it is enough that such a person *could have engaged* in the action in question to provide evidence for the legend to circulate. Urban or contemporary legends, like rumor, thrive on insecurity, ambiguity, uncertainty, anxiety, and credulity, gullibility, or a lack of critical faculty; in addition, they tend to be told about topics that are of importance to audiences (Rosnow, 1988, 1991; Rosnow and Fine, 1976; Goleman, 1991). Contemporary legends almost always tell a dramatic story, contain a meaningful moral or message, tap current fears, contain a grain of truth, make use of supportive local detail, and cite a credible source (Goode, 1992, pp. 325–330).

Not all urban or contemporary legends describe purported deviant behavior, but a very high proportion of them do. Very often in contemporary legends, an enemy is located against whose nefarious activities we have to guard ourselves. We are innocent victims, the legend informs us, guileless and unsuspecting; hence, the legend is a kind of *morality tale*—a wake-up call—to alert us to the danger to which we expose ourselves by being naive and trusting. They inform listeners that they are being *too good for their own good.* Not only should we be aware of the evil that is afoot under our very noses, but we should take action to make sure that others are not harmed and exploited.

Along these lines, then, we find some of the following contemporary legends which describe what can only be referred to as imaginary deviance:

• Since 1980, seemingly independently and in a number of locations around the country, accusations of satanic ritual abuse have been lodged, in many cases, against unnamed parties, in others, against specific persons, usually parents. The claim is usually made by fundamentalist Christians who believe that satanic practices are widespread and extremely threatening; supposedly, some 50,000 to 60,000 children are killed in the United States each year in such rituals. (A cautionary note: The Federal Bureau of Investigation estimates, with extremely solid evidence, that no more than 25,000 murders *of all kinds* take place in the U.S. each year.) These charges almost always emerge under one of two circumstances. First, when children are asked leading questions by prosecutors convinced in advance that the charges are true. And second, when troubled patients seek therapeutic assistance from psychiatrists who believe that all or most emotional trauma stems from childhood sexual abuse

and the patients are prodded to recall such events in their past. In both cases, initially, the party being questioned does not recall ritual abuse; however, with enough suggestion, many will oblige by agreeing with the questioner. It should be emphasized that although sexual abuse is common, especially within the bosom of the family, not a single shred of physical evidence of any kind has been turned up to document charges of satanic ritual abuse of children on a widespread basis (Victor, 1993; Hicks, 1991; Goode, 1992, pp. 337–342).

• Since the defeat and withdrawal of the United States forces in Vietnam in 1975, a legend has emerged that the Vietnamese are still holding all or a major proportion of the 2,255 American prisoners who were officially declared to be MIA, that is, Missing In Action. In this case, there are two nefarious agents who have committed evil, deviant deeds: first, obviously, the Vietnamese, and second, American politicians and the military high command, the second of whom abandoned the brave captured soldiers for expediency's sake, and lied about it afterward. This belief has generated a great deal of hostility and resentment in some quarters, provides a huge wellspring of sympathy and support for the supposed victims, and has spawned a social movement, as well as a virtual industry of buttons, pins, bracelets, T-shirts, and other paraphernalia. Several films have been based on the theme that the American forces were "stabbed in the back" by evil parties. During the war, our military "had its hands tied" by conniving politicians; hence, loyal patriots—armed to the teeth—should go back to the jungle, unfettered by schemes, deals, and bureaucracy, and rescue them. The belief, however, is almost certainly false—again, an instance of imaginary deviance. Consider the following. The number of American combattants listed as missing in the war in Vietnam is far smaller than for any previous major war. About 78,000 Americans were unaccounted for in World War II, and some 8,000 Americans were listed as officially missing in the Korean War; nearly all experts agree that the vast majority were so listed because their bodies were not recovered or identified. Almost half of the 2,255 missing in Vietnam (or 1,095) were *known* to have been killed, but their bodies were not recovered. Nearly all of the rest either crashed at sea or in the jungle, or lost contact with others in the midst of battles in the jungle. Bodies that fall in dense vegetation clearly are subject to decay and animal scavengers. The likelihood that there is even a *single* American soldier left in prison in Vietnam today (or who was held even in 1975) is very close to zero (Franklin, 1993, esp. pp. 11ff.). Once again, we have a case of imaginary deviance.

• Intergroup contact represents one of the richest of all breeding grounds of urban legends with an imaginary deviance angle. This is especially the case where one social category possesses or controls substantially more of the society's resources than another. Both subordinate and superordinate categories develop legends detailing the deviant deeds of members of the other category. These legends tend to fly especially thick and fast during periods of tension and hostility. For instance, in 1943, a series of race riots broke out in Detroit; in white communities, a rumor circulated that a white baby (in another version, a pregnant woman) was thrown off a bridge by a Black mob, and in Black communities, it was a Black baby (or a pregnant woman) who had been thrown off a bridge by a white mob (Lee and Humphrey, 1943; Knopf, 1975, pp. 55–59). In the subsequent investigation, no evidence emerged that verified either story. In the 1960s, again, during a period of civil disturbances, an even more troubling legend was circulated. It seems that a boy, accompanied by his mother, went to a changing room in a department store. The mother left the boy alone for a few minutes so that he could try on some clothes. In the interim, he was accosted by a man and castrated. (Similar legends have circulated in many societies with two or more religious, ethnic, or racial categories for thousands of years.) In the version told in the Black community, the boy was Black and the man was white; in the version told in the white community, the boy was white and the man was Black. Again, no evidence of any kind was ever located that either version actually took place (Rosenthal, 1971). Such legends express and give life to intergroup hostility, offering living proof that "they" (members of another category) are engaged in evil deeds against "us" (members of our own category), and that we should take steps to make sure that we are not harmed or exploited.

Thousands of similarly fanciful stories circulate each year in societies around the world; they are usually adapted to fit the circumstances of the local area in which they are told. These stories describe evil deeds and identify an enemy or evildoer responsible for them. Most often, the party supposedly engaged in the harmful, deviant behavior who is the subject of the legend is not a specific,

concrete person but a representative of a social category, usually one with whom the tellers and listeners of the tale have a difficult or conflictual relationship. For fundamentalist Christians, that category is satanists, or more broadly, humanists, secularists, liberals, and opponents of a strict, literalistic Christian theology and morality. For proponents of the MIA myth, that category is "the powers that be," evil politicians, and shadowy, high-level military figures who have undermined the efforts of our brave warriors, who were left to rot in the jungle for the sake of political and military expediency. For tellers and listeners of racially charged tales, the enemy is, of course, members of another racial category. In each case, supposedly, the enemy has been engaged in an activity which, evidence suggests, does not exist, in other words, such legends create imaginary deviance. And in each case, because of the emotionally charged nature of the conflict between and among groups and categories in the population, and because events have actually happened in the past which seem *very much like* the events narrated in the legend (Turner, 1993), the story is believed on the basis of little or no evidence. In other words, imaginary deviance is a case of *demonology*, which creates, identifies, and maintains enemies, persons whom we can hate so that we feel more righteous about ourselves, our beliefs, and our way of life.

ESSENTIALISM VERSUS CONSTRUCTIONISM

Perhaps, at this point, it is necessary to introduce a distinction that will run throughout the entire book. It distinguishes two entirely different ways of looking at deviance, indeed, phenomena in the world generally: *essentialism* and *constructionism*. Every form of deviance discussed in the book can be defined—and will be defined quite differently— by one or the other of these two types of thinking.

Essentialism is the view that all phenomena in the world have an indwelling "essence" that automatically and unambiguously places them in specific, more or less unchanging, categories. (Most of the ancient Greek philosophers, especially Plato and Aristotle, were essentialists.) To Plato, the task of pure knowledge or science was to discover and describe "the true [unchanging] nature of things, i.e., their hidden reality or essence" (Popper, 1963, p. 31). Essentialists are comfortable with using the terms "true" and "real" when referring to categories or their representatives. Certain inherent, unchanging characteristics define, for example, "true" alcoholism or "true" homosexuality; a certain individual is a "true" alcoholic or a "true" homosexual. Biologically inclined individuals say that a biological parent is someone's "real" parent; they do not consider an adoptive parent as a "real" parent. Essentialists believe that categories, or the question of whether certain cases or individuals belong in specific categories, is not a mere matter of definition or convention. Rather, a category is a naturally, internally consistent entity, possessing specific, syndrome-like properties that sets it apart from other, and different, categories. Scientific classifications should reflect categories that exist in nature. Thus, just as no one can mistake a diamond for a ruby or an apple for an orange, likewise, no knowledgeable observer should mistake a homosexual from a heterosexual, or vice versa (Troiden, 1988, p. 101). "Essentialists think that being a heterosexual is like having a certain blood type or being a person taller than six feet" (Stein, 1990, p. 326). For instance, two social scientists with an essentialist position assert that homosexual orientation is "biologically derived and therefore immutable, appearing in all societies at about the same rate, characterized by similar elements in different societies" (Whitam and Mathy, 1986, p. 182).

Because each phenomenon has an unchanging, indwelling, absolutely essential trait, to the essentialist, phenomena belong clearly and unambiguously in one and only one category. Thus, one encounters essentialistic thinking at work when one hears or reads: "A tomato isn't a vegetable—it's a fruit!" "Baseball isn't a sport—it's a business!" "Rape isn't sex—it's violence!" "Abortion is murder!" "Movies are not art—they are entertainment!" "Pornography isn't about sex—it's about power!" Each of these statements contains the assumption that the phenomenon it purports to describe possesses a crucial, fundamental, essential trait that defines the phenomenon in question, and dominates and *overwhelms* all other traits or characteristics.

In contrast, *constructionism* is the view that essences, or unchanging, indwelling qualities or traits (assuming they even exist in the first place) do *not* define phenomena; such qualities or traits do *not* unambiguously classify someone or something as belonging to a specific category. Moreover, for social (as opposed to natural) categories, unchanging, indwelling traits or characteristics do not exist.

Even for natural categories, nature does not classify, people do, and the many human classifications that are applied to natural phenomena differ dramatically. Different criteria are used to generate categories, these criteria being crucial or unimportant, depending on the perspective or the purposes of the observer.

Constructionists believe that categories are *social constructs*; phenomena in the world can be classified in many different ways and these different classifications are all equally valid (although not necessarily equally useful for specific purposes). No indwelling essence demands that a given phenomenon be classified in a certain way. Thus, what one gardener sees as a weed that deserves to be yanked up by the roots, another might view as an attractive, decorative plant that has a viable place in the yard. The essentialist insists that a tomato *is* a fruit—and *not* a vegetable—because that is how it is categorized botanically, or *is* a vegetable—*not* a fruit—because it is not sweet, not eaten as a dessert. To the essentialist, it *must* be one or the other—it *cannot* be both simultaneously. The essentialist insists that biological parents are one's *real* parents—*or* that adoptive parents are one's real parents: It must be *either one or the other*, it cannot be both.

In contrast, the constructionist argues that the tomato can be seen as a fruit *if* botanical criteria are deemed crucial, or a vegetable *if* culinary criteria are deemed crucial—in short, it can be *both at the same time*. Likewise, one's "real" parents can be one's natural or biological parents *or* one's adoptive parents, again, *depending on what criteria are used* to define "realness." Categories and their representatives are a matter of definition to the constructionist. Alcohol can simultaneously be a drug (if a pharmacological definition is followed) and *not* a drug (if social and legal definitions are followed). To the constructionist, definitions have no absolute, objective validity; they are meaningful *only* within the context of the criteria spelled out by a particular classification scheme. A constructionist would say, *to the extent that* a human zygote (an egg fertilized for less than two weeks), an embryo (an organism fertilized for two to eight weeks), and a fetus (an unborn organism eight or more weeks after conception) are defined as a human being, abortion is murder; but, at the same time, *to the extent that* the zygote, embryo, and fetus are *not* defined as full-fledged human beings, abortion is *not* murder. In other words, the constructionist argues that *reality depends on perspective, and perspective is to a degree arbitrary*. No one definition is definitive, final, absolute, or objective. Each is valid according to certain arbitrary and limited criteria.

Do social phenomena have inherent, unchanging "essences" that remain with them under any and all circumstances? Is it the social scientist's job to discover these essences, in effect, to reflect nature's classification scheme? Does everyone belong to a clear-cut category? Can all well-informed observers agree as to what these categories are and which individuals belong to them? Are certain definitions of things in the world correct and all others invalid and false? Is there one way—and only one way—to define social phenomena? Do we live in a pigeonhole universe?

To turn things around, is everything a matter of definition? Can we belong to one category according to a given criterion, but to an entirely different category according to a different criterion? Can we be a "homosexual" according to one definition and a "heterosexual" according to another? Is it possible to agree with the following statement: "To me, being gay is like having a tan. When you are in a gay relationship, you're gay. When you're not in a gay relationship, you're not gay" (Epstein, 1987, p. 9). Can we be Caucasian according to one racial definition, and African American according to another? Can alcohol be a drug and *not* a drug at the same time? Is the social world entirely socially constructed? Is giving someone or something a definitive label on the basis of an indwelling, unchanging quality a kind of "tyranny"? (Sagarin, 1975, pp. 144–146).

As we might expect, these questions cannot be answered definitively in a simple yes or no fashion. Suffice it to say that the majority of sociologists of deviance do *not* subscribe to the essentialist position. Most deviance specialists are *constructionists*. However, it must be added, most are not *radical* constructionists, but could be referred to as "moderate" constructionists. What I mean by this is that most do *not* believe that *everything* is a matter of definition, that there is *no* essential reality to the social world at all, that if everything and anything is simply looked at in a certain way, that is the way it is. Rather, most sociologists of deviance believe there are "limits" to social constructionism (Epstein, 1987; Goode, 1994). A 30-year-old man who has never had a sexual experience with a woman, who has had intercourse with dozens of men, and who is manifestly attracted to men, and not women, *may* be referred to as *a* homosexual—in spite of the fact that he has not had sex for a year and is not currently involved in a romantic or sexual relationship with another man. This is so because he is likely to think of himself as gay, he is likely to be defined as gay by both the gay and straight communities, he is unlikely to enter into a heterosexual relationship, and likely, if the conditions are right, to enter into a homosexual one, and his erotic attraction to men, and lack of attraction to women, are a physiological fact. Hence, it is quite reasonable to refer to this man *as a homosexual*, that is, as the possessor of a trait or characteristic that he is likely to carry around with him which remains the same in a variety of contexts, that is indwelling and fairly long-term, possibly permanent. On the other hand, many men and women *cannot* be so readily categorized one way or another. They possess a *mix* of characteristics, they are one way in one context, a different way in another, one way according to one criterion, another way according to another. Hence, though *many* people can be categorized according to some classifications, many *cannot*. In other words, sexual orientation is *not* the same thing as having a tan, but it is *also* not the same thing as possessing a certain physical trait, such as being six feet tall. (As an aside, consider the constructed nature of Epstein's example: having a tan. Many persons of African ancestry, extremely light-skinned Caucasians, as well as all albinos, cannot get a tan at all.)

Constructionism may be more relevant for certain purposes than others. The difference between the mentally disordered and individuals who are judged to be mentally normal is *not solely* a matter of definition; there *are* significant differences between the way they and "normals" act and talk. Still, psychiatric diagnoses often differ from one another and are based on criteria that are *to some degree* arbitrary. As observers of deviant behavior, it would be foolish of us to argue that individuals are referred to as alcoholics in a *completely* arbitrary fashion, that they are *just as likely* as the next person to have drunk alcohol destructively and in great quantity. Still, experts cannot agree on a definition of alcoholism, and many people classified by these different definitions end up in one category according to one definition and a different one according to another. Capricious as classification schemes may seem, belonging to certain social categories is *not* a simple matter of being classified or labeled by others, or as temporary as taking off and putting on a suit of clothing. Even though categories have an *element* of arbitrariness to them, and are very fuzzy around their boundaries, they are not *completely* arbitrary, and they are generally based on some *measure* of inherentness, that is, on *essential* criteria. This is especially the case for deviant categories and categories that are basic to one's identity. Being straight or gay is *not* the same thing as playing tennis or riding a bicycle; it is more basic to one's identity, more basic to the way others see one, and is based on inner qualities and behaviors that are more likely to endure. The fact that many individuals do not fall clearly into one category or the other does not deny the fact that most do. We should not fall into the fallacy that assumes that simply because classification schemes are generated by the human mind, not by nature, they are *completely* arbitrary, that entities classified in the same way by them are *no more likely* to have certain properties than those classified differently. This line of thinking is referred to as "vulgar nominalism" and is widely regarded as a fallacy; we should not fall victim to it. In my view, "moderate" constructionism yields the greatest benefit in the study of deviance; it will be adhered to throughout the book.

Notice that the constructionist does not deny that essences exist, that is, that certain phenomena or categories possess indwelling properties that no other phenomena or categories possess. The statement, "all dogs are mammals," is true because all animals referred to as biological dogs possess certain traits which they share in common with all other species referred to as mammals, that is, they possess fur or hair and feed its young with milk from mammary glands. Dogs' possession of these traits, in fact, *defines* them as mammals. However, once again, the term "mammal" is specific and its meaning is accepted by common agreement; the properties the possession of which define mammals are the *only* ones that are used as criteria for inclusion. Not possessing them automatically *excludes* a species from mammalhood.

Many of the terms we use to define most categories socially *very rarely* have such a precise meaning as "mammal." Most categorical nouns are used fairly imprecisely, in several senses simultaneously. Representatives of these categories possess a number of important characteristics, each of which may be relevant to different categories; two observers may refer to different qualities or characteristics to define the phenomena in question. For instance, a botanist may see a tomato as a fruit ("the developed ovary of a seed plant with its contents and accessory parts"), while the cook may see it as a vegetable—in contrast to a fruit—that is, as a botanical product that is not sweet and therefore, under most circumstances, unacceptable to eat as a dessert. Each view, each definition, is correct; neither contradicts the other; each is relevant according to different purposes and in certain contexts. The fact that both can be true simultaneously shows that essentialistic thinking *may be misleading* when examining *some* phenomena. In the same way, homosexuality may be defined in a number of different ways; different criteria may be relevant for different purposes. According to one criterion (for instance, the sex of one's sexual partners), a specific individual may be defined as homosexual; according to a different one (one's erotic preferences), one may be defined as heterosexual. Unlike "mammal," there is no single, indwelling quality that defines everyone as a homosexual in a definitive fashion. Once again, the constructionist approach seems to me to have the greatest number of strengths in the sociological study of deviance, and of its varieties. "Moderate" constructionism seems to make the most sense. It will be used throughout this book.

THE NATURE AND LOCUS OF DEVIANCE

From our discussion in this chapter, two conclusions concerning the nature and locus of deviance should be clear. First, *deviance can exist and take place anywhere, and it can be possessed and enacted by anyone.* And second, deviance is *more likely* to be possessed and enacted by *certain individuals* in *certain locations.*

Most people hold a stereotypical notion of what deviance is and who the deviant is, that is, what may be referred to as the "nuts and sluts" stereotype (Gouldner, 1968; Liazos, 1972). This is the view that the study of deviance focuses on the seamy, sensationalistic, disreputable behavior enacted by marginal, powerless, usually lower-class individuals. This stereotype is partly right and partly wrong. *A great deal* of deviance conforms to the "nuts and sluts" stereotype, especially that which is most vigorously condemned, that which is most likely to get someone in trouble. On the other hand, the "nuts and sluts" stereotype also leaves a great deal of deviance out of the picture altogether. Deviance can be *any* behavior or qualities that generate condemnation; it occurs just about anywhere and is enacted or possessed by just about anyone.

Ben-Yehuda showed that deviance occurs in science, an eminently respectable institution. Scientists sometimes plagiarize papers, fabricate data from nonexistent or uncooperative experiments, or propound theories their colleagues regard as crackpot (Ben-Yehuda, 1985, pp. 106ff., 168ff.). Deviance routinely takes place in the used car industry, where odometers are set back to show less mileage, taxes are avoided, and bribes are paid to the appropriate parties (Farberman, 1975). Deviance takes place in the bosom of the family, where violence is common, including wife battering (Gelles and Straus, 1988; Dutton, 1988), the rape of wives by husbands (Russell, 1982; Finkelhor and Yllo, 1985), and incest forcibly inflicted by older male relatives on younger females (Russell, 1986). Husbands and wives "cheat" on one another by engaging in adultery (Atwater, 1982; Lawson, 1988). Professors engage in deviance, for instance, by sexually harassing their female students (Dzeich and Weiner, 1984). Students can, of course, engage in deviance, among other things, by cheating on exams (Peyser, 1992). Corporate executives engage in white-collar crime (Coleman, 1994; Ermann and Lundman, 1992; Geis and Meier, 1995). Pharmacists fill out fraudulent prescriptions, workers steal material from the work site, automobile mechanics charge for work they didn't do, physicians perform unnecessary surgery, bill for nonexistent operations, or wildly overcharge on Medicare and Medicaid. Deviance is everywhere. It is ubiquitous. It penetrates every corner of society. It is engaged in by rich and poor alike, respectable and disreputable. It takes place in locations that are not ordinarily thought of as breeding sites for unconventionality. Deviance is a universal fixture of every sphere, locus, arena, and crevice of social life. Every place people interact with one another—or, indeed, enact behavior alone—the potential exists for someone to engage in disreputable, blameworthy behavior. Contrary to the stereotype, deviance is *not* confined to "nuts and sluts," nor do sociologists confine themselves exclusively to the study of "nuts and sluts."

On the other hand, deviance is *more likely* to exist or take place in some social locations than others. Drug addicts *routinely* engage in disreputable behavior; in fact, so much is this the case that their identity, character, indeed, their *very*

being, is likely to have been discredited among most of the more reputable they come into contact with or know. In contrast, *some* physicians—not all—engage in behavior that is likely to be viewed as reprehensible and likely to attract condemnation and punishment. The identity and character of corporate executives is rarely tainted by the revelation of malfeasance; most who are apprehended in such behavior either receive no punishment at all or receive a fine, only extremely occasionally a jail or prison sentence. While white-collar criminals *often* engage in illegal behavior and are *sometimes* convicted criminals, they are *almost never* regarded as deviants by the society at large. Though this may seem unfair, even ironic, it *is* a fact of life with which the student of deviance must grapple. Many forms of deviance committed by other respectable individuals are deviant specifically *in a particular setting*, for instance, the deviance committed by scientists discussed by Ben-Yehuda. In contrast, certain forms of street crime, certain varieties of drug use, certain kinds of sexual activities or preferences, and mental illness generally, are *widely* condemned; they discredit the offender in the *vast majority* of social circles in the society. Thus, it is glib to argue, as some do, that the field of deviance places undue emphasis on "nuts and sluts." While the investigation of deviance must look *everywhere* it exists or takes place, it is much more likely to take place in some locales than others. The traditional behaviors the field has studied are the "bread and butter," the "meat and potatoes," of deviance. *They are what arouses the most condemnation.* As such, they deserve special, although not exclusive, attention.

SUMMARY

In sum, by deviance, I mean one thing and one thing only: behavior or characteristics that some people in a society find offensive or reprehensible and that generates—or would generate if discovered—in these people disapproval, punishment, of condemnation of, or hostility toward, the actor or possessor. Deviance is behavior or conditions that are likely to get one into trouble. It is based on a judgment made by somebody. It isn't simply behavior or characteristics, or even differences between people. It is *sanctioned* differences, differences that result in any of a wide range of negative evaluations and reactions. As to whether a given phenomenon is an instance of deviance cannot be known until we know something about what specific people think and feel about it. What we have to know is *deviant to whom?* Acts, conditions, and people are *labeled* deviant. They aren't deviant according to some abstract, artificial, absolute, universal standard. Of course, some phenomena can be deviant to a small number of individuals in a given society. These phenomena are still deviant— *to those individuals.* Others can be regarded as deviant by the vast majority of the members of a society; usually, these are the phenomena sociologists study *as* deviance. Still others may generate relatively little public condemnation but have activated mechanisms of formal social control, as we'll see in the next chapter. That is, the state may attempt to control, restrain, or punish certain categories of individuals in the population. This, too, is a form of deviance, although not the only one, as some sociologists seem to imply.

The very existence of deviance implies a kind of *relationship* between behavior and conditions on the one hand and concrete or potential negative reactions from audiences on the other. Without these reactions, we do not have deviance. It is in the territory *between* the behavior and conditions and the reactions that we find the phenomenon of deviance. This definition *rejects* the validity of absolutist and statistical definitions of deviance, definitions based on the harm that behavior inflicts on the society, as well as the possibility of "positive" deviance. It insists on the fact that deviance exists when and only when behavior or traits do or would attract negative, condemnatory, or punitive reactions from a given audience.

To most people, the term "deviant" conjures up an image of individuals who are not only evil but abnormal as well; "deviance" implies that the behavior or the condition is both immoral and "sick." It must be emphasized that the sociologist does *not* use these terms in this way. "Deviance" and "deviant" are *completely nonevaluative terms.* Sociologically, they mean individuals who, or behavior and conditions which, attract widespread public scorn, condemnation, hostility, or punishment. In order to understand these phenomena, it is necessary to *purge* the terms of their automatic taint of pathology. Some forms of deviance may, in fact, be the manifestation of a disordered mind; some individuals who are regarded as deviants are mentally ill. Moreover, mental illness is *itself* a form of deviance, since the mentally ill are widely dis-

paraged. But mental pathology or disorder is not part of the *definition* of deviance. Many—most— "deviants" are psychologically quite normal, indistinguishable from the most conventional, conformist, law-abiding members of the society. The two dimensions of mental pathology and deviance are independent of one another. Mental illness is a form of deviance not because mentally ill individuals have "sick" minds, but because their condition and their behavior attracts condemnation and stigma. Once again, most deviant behavior is enacted, and most deviant conditions are possessed, by individuals who, by any conceivable measure, are perfectly "normal." Abnormality, sickness, and pathology have nothing to do with a sociological definition of deviance.

I'd like to emphasize this point even more strongly: *Referring to an action, a trait, or a person, as deviant is not pejorative.* By calling something, or someone, "deviant," we do *not* take part in the process of condemnation, we merely take note of it. We would be remarkably unobservant if we failed to notice that a given form of behavior, a given characteristic, or a specific person is, or has been, condemned. "Deviance" and "deviant" are strictly *descriptive* terms, bearing no pejorative or stigmatizing implications whatsoever.

An anecdote will illustrate my point. A few years ago, when I referred to women's liberation as a form of deviance, a young woman to whom I was talking bridled at my statement; she objected to the pejorative implications inherent in the term "deviance," arguing that women's liberationists were perfectly normal. I agreed with her point on normality, and insisted that I supported all or almost all the goals of women's liberation. But I insisted that the way the term is used by sociologists of deviance carries no stigmatizing connotations whatsoever, nor any implication of abnormality. Your understanding of the meaning of the term "deviance," I said, is archaic and obsolete. No sociologist today regards deviants as abnormal, and for no sociologist does the term "deviance" bear any negative connotation whatsoever. It means one thing and one thing only, I insisted: behavior that *is* or *would be* condemned in some quarters. Women's liberation exists to press for equal rights for women. Acknowledging that women have to fight for equal rights, and saying that women's liberation is a form of deviance, are almost exactly *the same thing.* It is *because* women do not have equal rights in American society that they have formed a movement to redress that inequity; and *for the same reason*, that movement is disparaged and stigmatized in many mainstream political circles. You and I are saying the same thing, I said, except we are using a different vocabulary. By their very nature, all nonmainstream political movements are at least somewhat deviant, otherwise they would be adopted by the institutionalized political structures and their goals would be built into the government itself. I doubt if my little speech convinced her, but my point should be clear. Deviance is *a label that others apply* and which we, as observers, take note of. We do not *endorse* the label, only observe that it is applied. Critics of this definition are confusing what is a *constructionist* definition for an *essentialist* one. By denying our right to observe that it *is* used and *does* have an impact, a critic who objects to definition of deviance would make it impossible for us to notice some extremely crucial social processes taking place under our very noses. Such a denial would, in fact, condemn us to ignorance.

Going back to the examples in Chapter 1, we are now in a much better position to answer the question of whether or not they are instances of deviance, and if so, why—and if they are not, why not? In all of them, there is a certain probability that the actor or the possessor will be condemned or punished, or already has been condemned or punished. When we refer to a type of action or condition, we have a fairly good idea in advance as to the rough likelihood that the actor or possessor will be punished, condemned, or stigmatized, given our knowledge of the audience in the picture. When we refer not to general or hypothetical behavior, but to a specific, concrete act or condition that took place or exists and was observed and reacted to, we do not have to speculate on the likelihood of condemnation by audiences—we already know how at least one audience reacted. Of course, other audiences might have reacted differently. Still, the reactions of real-life audiences tell us a great deal about deviance in general.

In retrospect, judged by today's vantage point, the peculiar, pseudo-scientific research project involving "posture" photographs initiated by W.H. Sheldon seems bizarre and blameworthy. The fact that it was rejected several times is less interesting than the fact that it was condoned and tolerated in so many places for such a long time. Hence, the question, why is a particular action condemned? is not the only question we, as students of deviance, are permitted to ask. A related question could very well be: Why *isn't* a particular action condemned?

Nearly all of us would condemn the thefts of Michael Carlow. How serious a penalty would we give him? How serious a penalty do we think he will receive? Embezzlers and corporate thieves on a grand scale rarely receive long prison sentences. Ivan Boesky and Michael Milken, the grandest of all the Wall Street felons convicted in the 1980s, served sentences lasting a year or two, and yet they committed crimes that resulted in losses of millions—possibly *billions*—of dollars for thousands of investors. In some quarters, these men are heroes, not deviants at all. An entrepreneur named John McNamara, a resident of the town in which I live, admitted to receiving over six billion dollars in loans from General Motors for vans that did not exist, of which $422 million was not returned. Mr. McNamara was sentenced to a five-year prison term, of which he will probably serve less than half (Richardson, 1996). While it is true, as we saw, that an act's criminal status does not define its deviant quality, one *form* of punishment is imprisonment. When acts have serious consequences but are not followed by serious punishment, we should be alerted to the discrepancy.

It is difficult to imagine an act more horrendous than a mother murdering her small, helpless child. We have a case of a mother who murdered five of her children, one after another. Hardly anyone would argue that these murders were not worthy of condemnation. And yet, what role did local prosecutors play? Why weren't their suspicions aroused after the demise of even the second child? And how could a pediatrician be so duped as to imagine that five children could die of a mysterious disease in this way, and publish an article in a respected journal making this argument? And where was the mother's husband in all of this killing? Aren't others responsible here, too?

Our cross-dresser, Neil Cargile, represents an interesting case from the point of view of deviance. It is true that generally speaking, if a man dresses in women's clothes (a few exceptional situations aside), he is likely to be condemned. And it is also true that many in Cargile's surroundings find his behavior offensive, truly blameworthy. In public, outside of locales where he is known, he is met with stares, derogatory remarks, derisive laughter. On the other hand, some who know him have gotten used to his peculiarity and have come to accept it—and him as well, in spite of that one peculiarity.

The fact that he has so many other positive qualities and characteristics that offset this one eccentricity is also very much in his favor. The fact that Cargile is not a deviant in any way except his habit of cross-dressing deflects, blunts, or reduces his deviant status. Is cross-dressing deviant? In most instances, sure it is. Is Neil Cargile *a* deviant? Well, in some important ways, no, he isn't. (Just as he is a deviant in some *other* crucial respects as well.) He is a more or less fully accepted member of the community in which he lives. This case shows us the complexity of the phenomenon of deviance.

What about our convicted rapist, Melvin Carter? Nearly everyone would condemn a serial rapist. His offense is so serious to many of us that we would not even want him as a resident of our community. No question about it: Melvin Carter is a deviant, and the reactions of the residents of Alturas, California demonstrate this without any ambiguity whatsoever. But are these reactions so extreme, so exaggerated, that they *themselves* qualify as an instance of deviance? After a convict "pays his debt to society," shouldn't he be permitted to have a second chance, wipe the slate clean and start all over again, with the same rights and privileges as any other citizen? On the other hand, the legal system and the informal norms of a community may differ significantly from one another; don't citizens have the right to express their outrage at particularly heinous actions? Don't they have the right to protect themselves from what they see as a clear and present danger to their safety and welfare? *Is* there any clear-cut right or wrong in this controversy?

The purchase of militaristic gear and books, pamphlets, and videotapes on how to engage in illegal, violent actions, likewise, is deviant in some quarters and it isn't in others. Members of anti-government, paramilitary organizations believe that they have the right to engage in a wide range of actions the majority feels should be illegal. If they act on these beliefs, in many cases, an arrest will follow. Some members of paramilitary "militias" keep huge stockpiles of weapons, resist paying taxes, issue racist, anti-Semitic, anti-government tracts, refuse to send their children to schools, threaten judges and police officers with violence, and occasionally, engage in violent confrontations with officials. Of course, these actions are deviant to the majority; most of us condemn them. But the fact that they are accepted, condoned, and encouraged in the social circles in which they originate should remind us of the relativity inherent in judgments of deviance.

Surely this question could also guide our thinking about the massacre at El Mozote. Here we have the horrendously brutal slaughter of more than 700 innocent Salvadoran peasants by an American-trained military unit. Why weren't the officers and commanders who were responsible brought to justice? Was it sufficient to explain, as one officer did after the event, "War is hell," and leave it at that? Is it enough to say that a dozen years after the killings, a few officers were given early retirement to appease Salvadoran leftists and America's insistence on human rights? Why were American officials silent about the killing for so long after it occurred? Was fear of a communist takeover sufficient to explain the deed? Who are the deviants here? Was the fact that no one was formally punished enough for us to say that no deviance occurred on that fateful day in El Mozote? Is there more to deviance than actual, concrete condemnation and punishment? Are there similar atrocities taking place right now around the world that are likewise encouraged, tolerated, and covered up? Do we have the right to refer to them as acts of deviance simply because we don't like them? Or is something more at work here?

The two definitions I presented in this chapter as valid (although flawed)—the normative and the reactive—possess both strengths and drawbacks. The *normative* definition posits an omniscient observer, a "fly on the wall," who witnesses a given act or trait and makes a determination as to whether the actor or possessor violates a norm of the society in which it takes place or is located. One problem is that we rarely have such a "fly on the wall"; a great deal of norm-violating behavior and traits remain unobserved and their perpetrators or possessors remain unpunished. Morever, in many cases, exceptions and extenuating circumstances transform an audience's reaction from negative to neutral. The *reactive* or *reactivist* definition argues that deviance should be defined not by a normative violation but by actual, concrete condemnatory responses from audiences. If there are no such reactions, there is no deviance. The problem is that this excludes "secret" deviance—a contradiction in terms to the reactivist—and denies that we can make predictions about which actions and traits are *likely* to elicit condemnation. Enactors of certain behaviors and possessors of certain traits know that they are likely to be condemned for them; hence, they keep them a secret. To refer to these people as completely conventional simply because that condemnation has not *in fact* occurred seems naive and misguided. Hence, our definition emphasizes the *probable* or *likely* responses from audiences as a basis for deviance. To know what's deviant, perform a "mental experiment": Imagine the public reaction to a variety of revelations. If a given revelation is negative and worthy of punishment, we have a case of deviance on our hands. I refer to a definition based on this probable or likely response as the "soft" or "moderate" reactivist definition of deviance.

One issue on which the normative and the reactivist definitions differ is the question of the *falsely accused* deviant. Is someone who has been falsely accused of wrongdoing, and who suffers community condemnation as a result, *a deviant?* The normative definition would say no, of course not; this person has not violated a norm and hence, is not a deviant. The reactivist would say, sure, this person is a "real" deviant (perhaps not a "true" deviant) because he or she has suffered "real" condemnation, "real" punishment. A witch who has been burned at the stake for "consorting with the devil" is no less dead by virtue of the fact that she is innocent. I am also very interested in what I refer to as "imaginary deviance," that is, behavior that never occurred which was supposedly enacted by people who never existed. Researchers of collective behavior have documented the existence of thousands of stories and myths—urban, contemporary, or modern legends—detailing events that never took place. For many of us, they are entertaining tales about dramatic and fanciful doings that may or may not be true. For some, they provide the basis for denouncing what they see as serious deviance. For them, these urban legends are *morality tales* or *atrocity stories* that vitalize their faith in their beliefs.

Many of the differences between various definitions of deviance center around the distinction between *essentialism* and *constructionism*. Essentialists believe that phenomena are defined by an inner, intrinsic, or inherent quality that is incontestible and that places phenomena unquestionably in a firm, unchanging category. For instance, an essentialist would say that someone "is" a homosexual in the sense that a specific gemstone "is" an emerald or a specific piece of fruit "is" an apple. In contrast, the constructionist believes that humans define phenomena according to criteria that are relevant to them; different definitions are valid according to different purposes or criteria. Something could be placed in one category according to one definition and in a different category according to another one; both could be valid for different purposes. Most sociologists adopt some version of the constructionist definition of deviance: Behavior is seen, judged, and defined differently in the various societies around the world; what is deviant in one may be conventional in another. It is this judgment that makes an act deviant, not an inner or indwelling trait or characteristic that behavior may possess which places it firmly in a deviant category. Moreover, the same applies to categories of behavior. What defines incest in one society is governed by an entirely different set of rules in other societies. A given act may be seen as murder in one setting, and as justifiable homocide in another. In fact, the very *categories* that are so important in one society in dividing up the human race ("homosexual" versus "heterosexual," for instance) may not even *exist* in another. While variation in the social construction of deviance is not infinite or completely random, for most purposes, constructionism offers a far more useful approach to the study of deviance than essentialism.

Lastly, while that which generates public outrage and the impulse to punish, condemn, or socially shun the perpetrator or possessor cluster around a fairly small number of sensationalistic actions or traits ("nuts, sluts, and deviated preverts"), we must keep in mind the fact that deviance can exist or occur in *any and all* spheres of life. Some husbands beat their wives, some executives pad their expense accounts, some professors sexually harass their female students, some physicians perform unnecessary surgery, some workers steal goods from their work site, some students cheat on exams, and so on. Deviance is not confined to the criminal underworld, the slum, the poorest neighborhoods, the most economically depressed and socially disorganized communities, the dank and dark corners or the "soft white underbelly" of our society, segments of the society we have exiled "beyond the pale." No, deviance is everywhere. It is ubiquitous. It penetrates every corner of the society, rich and poor alike. Everywhere people meet, it can and does take place. Anywhere that people do things which others don't like, we have deviance on our hands. Deviance is an ineradicable feature of social life. It is a social and cultural universal. Its study is essential to a complete understanding of social life.

chapter 3

SOCIAL CONTROL, CRIME, AND SOCIAL PROBLEMS

We now know what deviance is: A departure from a norm that upon discovery tends to generate disapproval of, punishment of, condemnation of, or hostility towards the actor or possessor by a given audience. Three concepts are often linked with deviance: social control, crime, and social problems. The linkages are strong, but they should not be exaggerated; thus, it is necessary to explore both the parallels and the differences between deviance and these closely related concepts.

DEVIANCE AND SOCIAL CONTROL

Now and throughout human history, all societies everywhere in the world have set and enforced *norms*—rules about what their members should and should not do. Norms are found everywhere. As we cast our gaze up and down the annals of time, across the world's many nations and societies, we notice that rules and norms differ, and so do the nature and severity of the punishments for violating them. *But rules and norms themselves are universal*; all societies have them, and the members of all societies enforce some of them. Of course, many—almost certainly most—norms apply to certain situations but not others. For instance, one must *not* laugh at a funeral, but one is *expected* to laugh at a comedy routine. Other norms are specific to *certain* groups but not *others*. For instance, among members of a street gang, one is expected to meet the challenge of an insult, a taunt, or a shove with an escalation in verbal and physical aggression, but among the faculty members of a university, or the physicians working in a hospital, such a response would be regarded as undignified, unprofessional, unacceptable, and improper—in a word, deviant. On the other hand, some norms apply to pretty much everyone in a given society: For instance, no one is allowed to kill a tiny baby simply because its crying is annoying. Regardless of whether a given norm applies to all situations or only some, to certain people or to all people, *everyone, everywhere* is subject to *certain* norms. To be human means being subject to the norms of the groups to which one belongs, and to those of the society in which one lives.

Although some minimal level of punishment for wrongdoing is necessary to ensure a minimal level of social order, below which societies would collapse into a "war of all against all," in which life would be, in the words of the seventeenth-century English philosopher Thomas Hobbes, "poor, solitary, nasty, brutish, and short." Actually, remarkably *few* norms are designed to condemn, punish, or protect a society or its members from injurious or predatory actions, such as rape, murder, or robbery. Most norms attempt to discourage behavior that neither directly harms anyone nor threatens the society with chaos and disorder. Most norms are intended to make a statement about what is considered by some, many, or most members of a society, to be right, good, and proper. They embody certain principles of moral correctness *independent* of what they do for the society's physical well-being. Obviously, some norms, such as "Thou shalt not murder," *do* attempt to protect a society or its individual members from physical harm, but these norms are in the minority. No one would be physically injured if some of us were to wear our clothes backwards, speak every word twice, or, as I said earlier, eat steak by grabbing it with our hands and tearing at it with our teeth. However, if any of us were to do these things, others would greet our actions with disapproval and derision. Clearly, protecting the society from acts of physical harm or disorder, chaos, and disintegration is not the only purpose for the norms and the punishment of their violators. There is implicit in norms and their enforcement a conception of favored interpretations of behavior and certain favored groups or categories who support these interpretations.

The methods that members of a society use to ensure conformity to norms are referred to as *social control*. Sociologists define social control as *efforts to ensure conformity to a norm*. Every time we do something to induce someone to engage in behavior we believe is right, we are engaged in social control; every time other people do something to induce us to engage in behavior they believe is right, they are engaged in social control. Note that social control includes "all of the processes by which people define and respond to deviant behavior" (Black, 1984, p. xi). It is formal and informal, governmental and interpersonal, blatant and subtle, and internal as well as external.

Internal social control operates through the process of *socialization*, that is, by learning and adopting the norms of a particular group or society. All people are socialized by specific *agents*. The family is, of course, the earliest agent of socialization and in attempting to inculcate in children the norms of the society, represents an agent of internal social control. Later on, schools, peers, and the mass media represent other, powerful agents of socialization; much of their socialization, again, represents efforts at internal social control. When the norms of a society are accepted as valid, they are said to be *internalized*. To the extent that internalization is successful, individuals would feel guilty if they were to engage in behavior the society or the relevant group considers wrong; thus, they refuse to do it, because they have internalized the legitimacy of the norm which condemns it. To the extent that agents of internal social control are effective, most of the members of the society do not engage in such behavior. A great deal of conformity comes about as a result of internalizing norms, values, and beliefs. We do not kill people at whom we are angry simply because we will be punished for it, but also because we genuinely feel that murder is wrong.

But it is very important to recognize that socialization is only one weapon in a huge arsenal of social control. In some way or another, socialization is *almost always* unsuccessful in instilling the "right" values in *all* of the members of the society *all* of the time. Every one of us is *incompletely* and *unsuccessfully* socialized. As a consequence, *a great deal* of social control is *coercive* and *repressive*: It is made up of the various ways we have of forcing people to do things they don't necessarily want to do. Often, many of us want, or are pressured, to move "outside the lines." When we do, and our deviance is detected, others attempt to use some form of punishment or *coercive* social control to bring us back into line.

We've all been socialized to tell the truth, but countless situations arise in the lives of all of us when we feel forced to lie. When we are caught in a lie, others will chastise or punish us, but usually, we have a convenient justification for our behavior. (Most lies come about as a consequence of the clash between two *contradictory* sets of conventional norms.) Almost all of us are socialized to be sexually and romantically attracted to partners of the opposite sex; yet, in spite of this, each year, countless individuals find that the heterosexual norm does not apply to them, and they seek partners among members of the same sex. When this is detected in individual cases, typically, social control springs into action—gossip, ridicule, persuasion, anger, disappointment, hostility, isolation. We've all learned that killing someone is unacceptable; but many males have also learned not to

back down in a confrontation with another male. When a physical altercation leads to serious injury or death, again, social control is likely to be activated, usually, arrest and criminal prosecution. When a central government is faced with a rebel uprising, the response is a form of social control: tanks, guns, and soldiers. Physical coercion is a powerful form of social control. In its classical formulation, social control was thought to be a product of harmony and consensus, a kind of natural order, a society in a state of equilibrium; here, social control was conceived of as being the *opposite* of repression and coercion (Ross, 1901, Park and Burgess, 1921; Janowitz, 1978, p. 3). Today, we recognize the fallacy of this line of thinking; we now regard repression and coercion as a *crucial* and *ineradicable* aspect or element of social control.

Most sociologists of deviance focus on *external* social control rather than internal. External social control is made up of the system of rewards and punishments persons, parties, and agents use to induce others to conform to a norm. Rewards and punishments are referred to as *sanctions*; obviously, a *positive* sanction is a reward and a *negative* sanction is a punishment. For the most part, in their examination of social control, sociologists of deviance ignore rewards or positive sanctions and focus almost exclusively on negative sanctions or punishments.*

---

*One critic dubbed the definition of social control which I presented above a "Mickey Mouse" concept (Cohen, 1985a, p. 2), altogether too broad and too bland. Like most "controlologists," he equates social control with *state* and *state-like* control, and ignores the more decentralized, informal, interpersonal forms of social control. However, if such processes are not part of social control, then *what are these processes to be called*? Some people are attempting to control the behavior of other people; if this is not social control, *then what is it*? To confine social control *exclusively* to the coercive actions of representatives filling official and semi-official positions of power makes about as much sense to me as claiming to study architecture, but confining one's investigation exclusively to buildings taller than 14 stories. Clearly, controlologists, practitioners of the "new sociology of social control," are studying a phenomenon that is quite different from what most researchers of deviance are looking at; it is not clear that their narrow focus can be justified theoretically. It is certain that informal social control is qualitatively *different* from formal and quasi-formal social control in some basic respects, but it is equally certain that *both* shape human behavior in fundamental ways, and hence, both must be examined in any consideration of deviance. For a discussion of the new sociologists of social control, see Chapter 5.

Formal and Informal Social Control

Sociologists distinguish between *formal and informal* social control. Informal social control takes place in interpersonal interaction among individuals. Some examples of informal social control include a smile, a frown, criticism and ridicule, praise, gossip and rumor, insults, denunciation, shunning someone, and efforts to embarrass someone. No doubt some things certain people do can be annoying and upsetting to others. Sometimes we feel the need to make the perpetrator aware of our annoyance. One person picks his nose; another wears tasteless, mismatched clothing; a third talks too loudly; a fourth has a habit of exaggerating and embellishing the truth. Since most people seek the approval of others they care about, they tend to adjust their behavior to avoid the disapproval of significant others by either discontinuing the offensive behavior or hiding it from public view. In other words, to the extent that we care about others and are sensitive to their behavioral cues, their efforts at social control are usually successful in influencing our behavior. On the other hand, putting people down face-to-face is not an easy proposition for most people; consequently, a substantial proportion of the informal social control that ordinary members of the society exercise is indirect, such as not associating with or gossiping about a supposed wrongdoer.

The problem here is that in large, complex societies, especially those with a substantial volume of contact among strangers, informal social control is no longer sufficient to bring about conformity to the norms. It becomes too easy to ignore how others feel about you if you do not care enough about them to be concerned about their disapproval. While agents of informal social control include just about everyone, agents of formal social control are *representatives or occupants of specific statuses in specific bureaucratic organizations*. The sanctions they apply to wrongdoers flow from their *offices* or *positions*, not from their personal relationship with the rule-violator. In fact, it sometimes happens that agents of formal social control may not even know the wrongdoers they sanction; in principle, they have no personal stake in the wrongdoers' conformity or their transgressions. It is the job of such agents to act, when transgressions occur, to bring about conformity to the formal code.

Of course, it should be said at once that informal social control may operate in formal organizations as well as formal social control; the same action may bring forth both formal *and* informal sanctions. One professional basketball player may shout at, shove, or even punch another for rough play; that is an *informal* sanction, an example of *informal social control*. A referee may call a penalty or eject a player from the game for rough play; that is *formal* social control. A drug dealer may be shunned or condemned by his neighbors; that is informal social control. That same dealer may be arrested by the police; that is formal social control. A person with mental problems may be ridiculed or avoided by his acquaintances; that is an example of informal social control. That same person may be committed to a mental hospital; here, in contrast, he is subject to formal social control. It is entirely possible for these two spheres of social control to work at cross-purposes; in principle, someone may be *rewarded* by one sphere for a given form of behavior and *punished* by the other for doing the same thing. For instance, a worker may be praised for working rapidly and efficiently, and may receive raises for it (formal social control), yet he may be condemned by his co-workers for that same behavior (informal social control). A student may be praised by the teacher and given an "A" in all her courses for working hard and performing well on exams (formal social control), yet ridiculed by her peers for such academic achievement (informal social control).

The best example of a formal code is, of course, the criminal law; agents of formal social control include the police, the courts, and the jails and prisons. These agents of law enforcement represent the premier, most well-known, and most all-encompassing of the many agents of formal social control. Law enforcement has the capacity to arrest, prosecute, convict, and imprison wrongdoers. Violations of the criminal law are referred to as crimes. More accurately, a crime is an action, if detected, that is likely to lead to arrest and prosecution. Behavior that is a violation of the criminal code but is extremely unlikely to lead to arrest (such as, in some jurisdictions, fornication, gambling, and adultery) may be referred to as "technically illegal actions." One of the more remarkable aspects of formal social control is how *informal* much of it is, that is, how much *discretion* the police have to ignore a great deal of illegal behavior that is not regarded as seriously deviant or criminal.

Somewhere between informal social control, which is based on interpersonal reactions among interacting parties, and the formal social control of the police, the courts, and the jails and prisons, lies the vast territory of *noncriminal, nonpenal bureaucratic social control*. At some point, persons are no longer subject exclusively to informal sanctioning; if the behavior becomes excessively troublesome, more formal sanctioning agents or agencies begin to step in. In other words, persons deemed difficult or problematic come under "the purview of professional controllers" (Hawkins and Tiedeman, 1975, p. 111). Representatives of bureaucracies continually enforce rules and norms that attempt to deal with "troublesome" individuals and populations. If someone engages in wrongdoing that the policy makers, administrators, and functionaries in a given bureaucratic setting regard as troublesome and problematic, they act to curb it. Such bureaucratic control agents or agencies include social workers and social welfare agencies, collection agencies, unemployment offices, psychiatrists and mental hospitals, departments of motor vehicles, civil courts, the Internal Revenue Service and other tax offices, and truant officers. Some bureaucratic agents and agencies engage in social control part of the time, while they engage in other activities not directly concerned with social control most of their working hours. For instance, school principals are mainly administrators; however, dealing with troublesome students, or keeping potentially troublesome ones in line, may also occupy much of their time. Teachers, too, are instructors for much of the day, and bureaucratic agents of social control for some of the day. Psychiatrists attempt both to heal troubled patients and attempt to ensure that they do not cause havoc in the lives of the people they interact with. In most bureaucratic agencies, there is a fuzzy line between social control and many actions that are not *explicitly* concerned with social control. The territory of social control located between informal, interpersonal social control on the one hand, and the most formal or *penal* social control on the other, represents a crucial sphere of inquiry for the study of deviance.

Unfortunately, some observers of deviance have an extremely narrow vision of social control. They focus solely and exclusively on *formal* social control and completely ignore *informal* social control (Horwitz, 1990, p. 4). The reason is that such a concentration fits in with the idea that social control is highly *centralized* and *repressive* (Meier, 1982, p.

47). If you see the way things are run as a conspiracy by a small, evil elite whose representatives attempt to dominate and exploit the mass of the people for their own narrow, selfish interests, then one is much more likely to find confirmation for one's view by looking at laws, courts, and bureaucracies than by looking at what people do *outside* a formal setting. Informal, unofficial social control is not only extremely untidy and less likely to conform to any pattern, it is also far less centralized and far less subject to elite control. Hence, the "social control" thinkers must ignore it. For them, social control *equals* state or state-like control; the rest is of no importance. When reading "social control" theorists, it is as if vast territories of human behavior simply slide away from our view, untouched by any analysis whatsoever. But in fact, *most* of the time social control is exercised, it is informal; most of the time deviance is sanctioned, the actor is sanctioned by means of informal social control. The vast majority of rule-breaking, punishable, and informally *punished* behavior is completely *ignored* by the apparatus of formal social control. Informal social control is the foundation of social life; while formal social control is, indeed, influential in shaping what we do and how we think and feel, and *must* be examined, it is exercised relatively fitfully, rarely, in a small proportion of instances of deviance. In contrast, informal social control is continually exercised in our lives; it cannot be ignored.

The equation of state or state-like control with social control generally is problematic for a number of reasons. To begin with, it's not clear who "the state" is. Members of the government? In the United States, members of the House of Representatives? The Senate? The Executive branch? The judiciary? All of the above? When a bill is passed by the legislature, are its supporters "the state"? If that same bill is defeated by a presidential veto, are its original supporters suddenly and as if by magic excluded from being members of "the state"? When a law is defeated one year but passed two years later, does the existence of the state become reconstituted?

The reports of federal commissions underscore the fanciful relationship between state control and social control. It would seem that federal commissions would represent an ideal vehicle to express the interests of the state; they receive a great deal of publicity, they are legitimated by the authority of the state, and they sometimes get translated into action.

The question is, whose interests do they actually serve, and what impact do they have in the legislative arena, on federal programs, and on public opinion? In 1971, the National Commission of Marihuana and Drug Abuse recommended the decriminalization of marijuana; during the decade of the 1970s, 11 states did so. But Richard Nixon rejected the findings of the commission and rejected the very idea of decriminalization. Were the interests of "the state" represented by the action of the 11 states that decriminalized, or the 39 that did not? Or by President Nixon's proclamations? It's not clear.

It's also not clear that in every case, the interests of "the state"—however that is defined—are served by federal commissions. In 1970, the federal Commission on Obscenity and Pornography declared that exposure to sexually explicit materials does not stimulate harmful, antisocial behavior and that all laws prohibiting their distribution to consenting adults be repealed. Again, President Nixon rejected the findings of the commission and declared that they would have no bearing on his decisions. In 1986, the Attorney General's Commission on Pornography declared that sexually explicit materials *did* stimulate harmful, antisocial behavior, and recommended that they be controlled by legal regulation. In the period of time between the first and the second pornography commission, did the interests and the make-up of "the state" change dramatically? Why the complete turnabout? Did each commission even *express* the interests of "the state"? Did either commission determine or influence public definitions of pornography as to whether it was harmful or not, wrong or not, an example of deviance or not? Did the informal mechanisms of social control with respect to pornography change as a result of this formal effort at social control? If "the state" runs the show, why can't the federal government even control the findings of its own commissions?

"The state" does exist, of course, and exercises *certain kinds* of social control. For instance, the United States military drove Iraqi forces out of Kuwait, which they had invaded and occupied; clearly, this represented an exercise of social control by the American state against the Iraqi government. It is proper, therefore, to refer to action of the U.S. government, in its exercise of the Gulf War, as state-sponsored social control because it acted *as an institution*. There are also many federal laws that are vigorously enforced by the state, that is, with the American government, again, act-

ing as an institution, a coherent entity with a unified will. However, we will find very few such examples in the annals of routine, garden varieties of deviance. For *most* forms of deviance, "the state" plays practically no role whatsoever. It's hard to figure out what "the state's" interests are and what sort of social control it exercises with respect to obesity, adultery, homosexuality, pornography, extreme ugliness, extreme shortness, eccentricity, as well as a variety of other activities and conditions that are not criminalized by the penal law. If we are to adhere to a definition of deviance that is dependent on state or state-like intervention, we are forced to ignore most activities and conditions that attract condemnation and social isolation.

It must also be emphasized that not every attempt at social control represents an effort to establish the interests of a powerful elite. It would be crude and vulgar of us to insist that efforts to define and punish deviants are little more than a conspiracy on the part of a tiny elite to dominate "the people" for its own advantage. As Downes points out, this reasoning can lead us to some extremely silly arguments. For instance: If laws are passed outlawing marijuana possession, this must mean that the use of marijuana threatens the interests of the powerful; if marijuana possession is decriminalized, this must mean that the powerful no longer fear it (1979, p. 8). If abortion is legalized, it must be in the interests of the powerful to have it legalized; if abortion were to become a criminal act once again, this must mean that the interests of the powerful are threatened by abortion. This sort of theorizing is simple-minded; such arguments amount to little more than "filling in the dots" of a theoretical outline that is already predetermined. Real-life struggles over definitions of deviance and crime are considerably more complex and difficult to unravel than this. In addition, such reasoning is fallacious because it is nonfalsifiable; there's no way to disprove or falsify an argument of this kind, since any evidence that is presented supposedly documents one's claims (Popper, 1959, pp. 40–42). While the powerful groups, segments, and classes of the society unquestionably have more influence in shaping the norms, rules, and laws of a society than the less powerful (by definition, since this is one of the ways we define and determine their power), their control is far from absolute.

In fact, the most powerful groups, segments, and classes often lose out in a given struggle over defining actions as deviant. Or their members may be sharply divided on a given issue. Or their members may not feel any differently about a given issue than the rest of the society. A great many norms and rules are of no interest at all to the most powerful classes or the ruling elite (except, of course, personally and informally). Moreover, just who "the powerful" are shifts around from one issue or question to another; on some issues, it could be the majority of the members of a society, while on others, it could be an extremely small minority which makes up less than 1 percent of the population. To equate social control exclusively with the interest of the powerful, as some have done, is extremely unrealistic. There is far more homogeneity in *characterizations* of the interests of the powerful than in their *actual* interests. Social control operates at all levels of society, and in both formal and informal contexts. It operates: in a parent's attempts to sanction a child, in one friend's comments about the clothes another is wearing, in a wife's criticisms of her husband's behavior, in a coach's pep talk to a basketball team at half-time, and in one neighbor's evaluation of the condition of the grass around another neighbor's house. Any "critical" perspective used to study deviance must deal with the fact that some, but not all, sanctions of deviant behavior are elite-initiated and/or support the interest of the elite. To take the former for the latter is to confuse the part for the whole.

Definitions of Deviance as a Political Process

Definitions of deviance are fought over. Most groups or segments of the society whose members believe strongly that a given form of behavior is wrong, immoral, and reprehensible—in a word, *deviant*—wish to do three things. First, they want to translate their belief into the formal social control apparatus, ideally, the criminal law. That is, they wish to transform their personal or private negative reactions to certain behaviors (informal social control) into punishment by the state (formal social control). To the extent that one feels that a given action should be deviant, one generally feels that it should also be criminal as well. Much of the current efforts of most social movements and social movement organizations are aimed at instituting sanctions for certain actions their members find offensive, which they judge to be harmful. That is, they wish to make sure that the perpetrators of behavior they deem to be deviant do not experience only informal sanctions for their actions, but are subject to formal sanctions as well, such as arrest and prosecution. Second, they wish to influence public opinion; they want to generate widespread support for their views, to get the public to see things the way they do, to get their definition of deviance adopted by the population at large. And third, from a pragmatic point of view, they want to seriously reduce or even eliminate the enactment of the actions they oppose.

Members of the anti-abortion, right-to-life movement believe abortion is wrong, immoral; their goal is to make it an illegal, criminal action as well, to ensure that physicians who perform abortions be imprisoned for doing so. Women Against Pornography, an anti-pornography social movement organization, wish to ensure that women who believe they have been harmed by pornography can sue its manufacturers in civil court. Members of the creationist movement believe that God created the earth, along with humans and all plant and animal life living on it, in six days roughly 10,000 years ago. Creationists want to introduce their view into the public school curriculum to challenge the prevailing evolutionist perspective. Members of the animal rights movement want to redefine the mistreatment of animal species as immoral, deviant, and criminal; they want to put an end to the suffering of animals at the hands of humans. If humans were to put themselves in the place of the animals they routinely torture and kill, they would see such actions as wrong and would stop doing them. The institutionalization of a particular interpetation of right and wrong and good and bad, in the form of formal sanctioning by bureaucratic representatives, represents a political and ideological triumph for the group or category that holds that interpretation. It informs members of other groups that this interpretation has a validity their own views lack. Once installed in the formal social control apparatus, the views on which these sanctions are based exert an ongoing influence.

DEVIANCE AND CRIME

Unfortunately, the terms "deviance" and "crime" have been used in several different ways. The term *deviance* has been used in both a broad and a narrow sense. Broadly speaking, deviance has been defined as I defined it above, that is, that which violates a norm, that which is likely to get someone in trouble or, more formally, "a class of behavior for which there is a probability of negative sanctions subsequent to its detection" (Black and Reiss, 1970, p. 63). Broadly speaking, deviance is what you are likely to be punished or condemned for. In this sense, criminal behavior is a form of deviant behavior. Crime violates one kind of norm, a law, it generates formal sanctions, which make up a type of punishment that is likely to be inflicted upon the norm-violator (Clinard and Meier, 1995, pp. 145–146).

The term *deviance*, however, has also been used in a narrower sense (Quinney, 1965; Robertson and Taylor, 1973, pp. 61–62). Rather than being seen as a particular *type* of deviance, crime has been *distinguished from* deviance; when this distinction is made, the term *deviance* takes on a somewhat different meaning from a broad category of sanctionable behavior. A crime may be defined as *a violation of formal norms* (that is, laws), whereas deviance may be defined as a violation of *informal* norms which *may or may not* be against the law.

This distinction stresses two points. First, it stresses the fact that a *law may not have widespread support*; its definition of what a crime is may not be accepted or be regarded as valid by the population of the jurisdiction in which it applies. Most Americans do not regard a Friday-night poker game among seven friends as a form of deviance; at the same time, technically, it is against the law in many jurisdictions. Premarital sex is widely practiced and has extremely widespread acceptance, and yet, in many states, "fornication" is a violation of the criminal statutes. Many "crimes" are not deviant in the sense that they are not regarded as violations of the informal norms of those living in a given society. Thus, a given action or trait may be *deviant but not criminal* (such as adultery in most states of the United States, homosexuality in nearly half the states, eccentricity, obesity, and alcoholism); *criminal but not deviant* (many forms of white-collar, corporate, and professional crime, and gambling in many jurisdictions); *both criminal and deviant* (drug dealing, murder, robbery); and *neither* criminal *nor* deviant (traditional, conventional, conforming behavior).

A second point those who distinguish between deviance and crime insist on is that a law applies to *all* the residents of a given jurisdiction (a state, a nation, or a society), *regardless* of how members of their subgroups feel about it; in contrast, an informal norm can be looked at with reference to its degree of acceptance in both the society as a whole *and* in different groups, subgroups, or categories in the population. Some categories may reject the validity of a law, but they are still subject to it; if they violate it, they may be arrested. In contrast, *within specific groups or categories*, it is *their* definition of deviance and conformity that counts. Thus, though the members of a society generally may normatively support the validity of a given law, specific subgroups within that society may reject it. Another way of saying this is that *the deviance-making and enforcement process is substantially less hierarchical than the crime-making and enforcement process*. The members of a particular subgroup are less likely to be subject to the general societal informal code than they are the formal code. Ask the members of a group whose members engage in nonconforming, unconventional activities what they think of mainstream society's view of their behavior and they are likely to shrug and say, "Who cares?" But ask them what they think with respect to the illegality of their behavior and they'll respond, "We just don't want to get arrested." The dominant *informal* code is more easily ignored and shrugged off than the *formal*, especially the *criminal*, code. Clearly, formal and informal sanctioning are very different processes; they should not be indiscriminately lumped together.

The term "crime," like the term "deviance," has been used in a variety of ways. Most contemporary criminologists agree that the first and most fundamental criterion of a crime is its *political* nature. In order to qualify as a crime, a specific statute must have been passed by the state or government calling for a penalty for its violation; in addition, specific officials, such as legislators, the police, and the courts, have been empowered to make and enforce the law, and adjudicate guilt or innocence. If this "political" quality is missing, a given action cannot be referred to as a crime; no law, no crime. Rules passed and enforced by specific private organizations, such as labor unions, clubs, faculties, and so on, cannot be referred to as laws, and their violations do not qualify as crimes (Gibbons, 1992, pp. 51–52). They do not have the coercive power of the state behind them, and they do not apply to all the citizens in a nation, as the law does. Thus, *politicality* is a necessary (but not a sufficient) criterion of a crime. To qualify as a crime, an act must be a violation of a specific criminal code, the law outlawing it must be enforced by representatives of the state and call for specific coercive penalties, and it must apply to everyone.

The problem with the use of the term "crime" is not in the fact that it must be a violation of a given legal code; nearly all criminologists agree that this is a necessary criterion. The problem comes in the *enforcement* of that legal code. As we saw, some laws are very unlikely to be enforced. Should they be referred to as crimes? What about adultery, fornication, low-stakes gambling among friends? Are they crimes? Most contemporary criminologists adopt the *probabalistic* definition spelled out above (Black and Reiss, 1970, p. 63): An act is a crime insofar as there is a significant or substantial *likelihood* or *probability* of arrest, if that act were to be detected by agents of law enforcement. We can never know *for sure* what will result in arrest and prosecution and what won't, but we *do* have a fairly good idea of the chances that various forms of behavior will result in official action.

The armed robbery of a bank, a clear-cut case of murder (especially, let's say, of a police officer), a huge cocaine or heroin transaction: From the probabalistic perspective, these are most definitely crimes. What this means is that if detected, someone enacting these forms of behavior is highly likely to be arrested and prosecuted. These are what Jackson Toby refers to as "consensus crimes" (1974; Hagan, 1991, pp. 13–14), because there is widespread consensus in Western society that they are wrong and should be against the law. There is a high degree of agreement in a given society, and in societies around the world, that these acts are *wrong* and *should be* crimes. (Of course, there may be disagreement about *which* specific acts would qualify as an instance of the general category; for instance, when is a *particular* killing a murder?) Moreover, these are the acts that are highly likely to result in arrest, if detected, on an act-for-act basis. On the other hand, the behaviors mentioned previously—adultery, fornication, low-stakes gambling—stand at the opposite end of this spectrum: They are clearly *not* crimes in the probabalistic sense, since the likelihood of arrest is extremely *small*. This means that the old cliché, "We are all criminals," is nonsense. *Many* of us commit acts that are technically against the law but *rarely* prosecuted, but relatively *few* of us engage in behavior that is *seriously* criminal and *highly* likely to result in arrest and imprisonment, and *very* few of us engage in this behavior more than a few times.

Deviance and Crime: A Rough Division of Labor

In the study of deviance and crime, American sociologists have followed a very rough division of labor. A substantial proportion, although not all, can be characterized by one of three emphases. (This classification applies much less outside the United States; for instance, Downes and Rock, 1988, look at both deviance and crime.)

The first emphasis is made up of *criminologists*, who tend to study "hard" deviance, that is, criminal behavior such as robbery, rape, murder, and burglary. This has been dubbed the so-called "Eastern" school of deviance (Ben-Yehuda, 1985, pp. 3–4), because many of its practitioners received their training, or much of its research has been conducted, or many of its researchers have been located on the East Coast of the United States, such as the University of Pennsylvania. Practitioners of this school generally adopt a natural science or positivistic model and study crime by means of official police statistics, formal interview or questionnaire studies of crime victims, or self-report crime surveys. The central issue in positivistic criminology is *etiology*, or the cause or causes of criminal behavior; "Why do they do it?" is its central concern. The work of Marvin Wolfgang exemplifies this tradition (Wolfgang, Figlio, and Sellin, 1972; Wolfgang, Thornberry, and Figlio, 1987; Tracy, Wolfgang, and Figlio, 1990).

A second emphasis also focuses on acts that are defined as crimes *by* the law, but is primarily interested in the *creation* of the law and only secondarily in the behavior defined by the law. These researchers and scholars see themselves as "radical" or "critical" sociologists of deviance. However, although they often refer to what they study as "deviance," it is clear that forms of deviance that are sanctioned informally, among approximate equals, especially those actions in which the ruling elite has little or no interest *as* a ruling class, hold no interest for them. What counts is the state's and the ruling elite's role in "controlling" deviance (Taylor, Walton, and Young, 1973, 1975; Lowman, Menzies, and Palys, 1987a; Davis and Stasz, 1990; Pfohl, 1994). As we saw, theorists of this stripe focus more or less exclusively on *formal* social control because it is seen as more concentrated in the hands of a few, is more likely to be repressive and coercive, and they assume it is motivated by the self-interest of a powerful elite class (Meier,

1982, p. 47). In contrast, informal, unofficial social control is far more decentralized and far less subject to elite domination—not the ideal platform for a critique of capitalist society. Hence, informal social control must be ignored.

A third emphasis is made up of sociologists who see themselves as studying *deviance*, as opposed to crime; they are more likely to focus on "soft" deviance. This is made up of behavior that may be technically against the law but is unlikely to lead to arrest, and is punished *mainly* informally, unofficially, interpersonally. This emphasis has been called the "Western" school (Ben-Yehuda, 1985, pp. 3–4) or the "Chicago/California" perspective (Petrunik, 1980, pp. 214ff.), because its practitioners were educated or did much of their work at the University of Chicago, Northwestern University, or the University of California at Berkeley and U.C. at San Diego. Examples of behavior that this emphasis has studied are alcoholism, marijuana use, homosexuality, mental illness, nudism, and prostitution. Practitioners of this approach are often symbolic interactionists, whose main focus is on human *meaning*, and they tend to conduct their research by means of participant observation (or anthropological field methods) and/or focused, qualitative interviews. The anthologies by Becker, *The Other Side* (1964), Adler and Adler, *Constructions of Deviance* (1994), and Rubington and Weinberg, *Deviance: The Interactionist Perspective* (1996) exemplify this approach.

Sociologists whose work is conducted within the "deviance" framework focus on a much wider range of concerns than those that are emphasized by criminologists and "critical" deviance specialists. For the most part, they regard causal analysis ("Why do they do it?") irrelevant or of marginal concern; in addition, they focus on interactions that are not necessarily between major power-wielders and deviants. They tend to investigate such issues as deviant identities, the creation of deviant categories, deviant stereotypes, learning deviant subcultures, deviant "careers," deviants' explanations for or justifications of their behavior, social adjustments by deviants to labeling and stigma, and so on. While criminologists tend to focus on criminals and what made them that way, deviance specialists usually focus on the creation and enforcement of the rules and the deviants' reactions to those rules. In addition, researchers of deviance (as opposed to crime) stress the fact that the concept includes not only voluntary behavior;

deviance can encompass involuntarily acquired physical traits and characteristics, such as disability (Freidson, 1966; Clinard and Meier, 1995, pp. 483–516), mental retardation (Edgerton, 1967), obesity (Maddox, Back, and Liederman, 1968; Cahnman, 1968; Goode, 1996), involuntary childlessness (Miall, 1986), and blindness (Scott, 1969). Criminologists do not study these characteristics because, first, possessing them is not, under most circumstances, against the law, and second, their causality lies outside the sociological and psychological realms typically studied by criminologists, that is, they are not *motivated* behavior.

This three-part characterization of deviance and crime studies into an "Eastern" school, which focuses on criminal behavior, a "critical" school, which focuses on state definitions of crime, and a "Chicago/California" school, which focuses mainly on deviance, is far from airtight. In fact, many researchers in the field cannot be put into any of these categories. It is, however, a tendency; the three categories represent "ideal types." One partial exception to this categorization is that scholars and researchers who focus on deviance (as opposed to crime) sometimes *do* study some aspects of crime, except that they look at its more informal, unofficial, interpersonal aspects. (Remember, some types of crime are both against the law and informally condemned.) Still, in studying them, they do not examine causality or etiology, as the traditional criminologists do; once again, they examine how the behavior of criminals is defined by others and, in turn, how they define their experience to themselves and to others. How do "hit men" justify and explain their gruesome deeds? (Levi, 1981). How do rapists justify and explain their sexual attacks on women? (Scully and Marolla, 1984; Scully, 1990). How is sexual assault "constructed" by the criminal justice system? (LaFree, 1989). How do persons who engage in seriously criminal acts— murder, robbery, burglary—*experience* this behavior? (Katz, 1988). Will "shaming" criminals be effective in reducing the rate of their repeat offenses? (Braithwaite, 1989). In what ways does having a criminal record stigmatize the ex-felon and deprive him of occupational opportunities? (Schwartz and Skolnick, 1964). In short, though researchers who customarily study deviance do sometimes examine crime as well, they do not usually focus on the question of etiology or cause, or on the creation of the criminal law as such, but they *do* emphasize issues such as stigma, experience, meaning, subjective definitions, the social construction of reality, and the acquisition of deviant identities.

I will observe this very rough trichotomy in this book by focusing *mainly* on deviance and only *secondarily* on crime. The application of the criminal justice system, that is, the police, the courts, and jails and prisons, is a subject for the field of criminology. (However, insofar as informal social processes influence and impinge *upon* the formal ones—which always happens, although in varying degrees—formal social control *can* be studied by the "deviance" specialist.) In the study of deviance, we are more interested in the exercise of *informal* sanctions than formal: How deviant categories are created, how individuals whose behavior is condemned are classified and reacted to *as* deviants, how they cope and deal with that social reaction, how they experience what they do. Enacting criminal behavior, of course, may generate both formal and informal sanctions. To the extent that engaging in crime generates gossip, ridicule, social shunning, and censure, and forces criminals to explain and justify their behavior, to make adjustments in their identities, deal with that condemnation, and so on, crime is a fit subject for any student of deviance. To the extent that the study of crime focuses on etiology or the machinery of the criminal justice system, there is another field that studies these matters—criminology—and dozens of textbooks that discuss these subjects. As Plummer states (1979, p. 109), the sociology of deviance is not criminology; the two fields study different (although sometimes overlapping) phenomena. While laws and their enforcement are relevant to some forms of deviance discussed in this book, they will remain somewhat in the background. For the most part, researchers of deviance are far more focused on the processes of informal social control than on the formal, and I will observe this focus. At the same time, social control operates at the formal as well as the informal, unofficial level, and how deviant populations are treated by bureaucracies is a major aspect of their field.

DEFINING DEVIANCE: PROCESS, ENTERPRISE, AND CHANGE

Norms do not drop down from the skies; they are not carved in stone, eternal truths that are so self-evident they are accepted as valid even by those who outwardly violate them. In fact, norms emerge at a particular time and place, often as a result of a dispute among contending parties. In other words, deviance does not simply exist; deviance is *produced* as a result of a specific defining process. Behavior is *deviantized* (Schur, 1980, 12f.); it is *rendered* or *made* or *judged to be* deviant. Deviance is a *construct*, not a quality inherent in certain behavior; it is *imposed on* behavior, it is behavior that has been *judged* in a certain way. There are two "deviantizing" processes; the first is a process that renders a *general category* of behavior deviant, and the second renders *specific instances* of behavior deviant. Let's look at the second process first.

Some rules are ancient and very nearly universal, such as those condemning and punishing murder, robbery, and incest. These rules define crimes which are usually referred to as "common law" or "primal" crimes. There is an extremely high degree of consensus not only in Western society but in societies around the world that such actions are deviant and should be against the law (Newman, 1976). Still, even the most ancient and universal of rules must be interpreted, and in many interpretations there is disagreement and dispute. For instance, not everyone agrees on the status of every instance of homicide (one human being killing another); in a particular instance, *is it* or *isn't it* a case of murder? Is vehicular homicide when the driver is drunk a case of murder? Some would say yes, others no. Is abortion murder? Again, there is considerable disagreement here. What about a barroom fight in which one brawler is killed—is this murder? Again, chances are, not all observers will agree. What about a "mercy killing"? The point is, even within a general category of behavior that just about everybody condemns—murder—there is disagreement, dispute, conflict, differing interpretations as to the status of specific *instances* of that general category. In other words, one deviance-rendering or deviance-judging process is *deciding whether specific, concrete instances of behavior should be regarded as deviant*, that is, as belonging to a general category everyone agrees is deviant.

But creating deviance also entails another process as well, creating norms to cover *entire categories of behavior*. Most norms do not enjoy as ancient and nearly universal a status as those prohibiting and condemning murder. In fact, norms defining entire *types* of behavior are continually evolving, continually emerging out of struggles between and among categories and groups. Many norms are continually in the process of being reformulated; some behaviors that were once condemned emerge as nondeviant, even conventional, while other behaviors that were conventional or at least nondeviant come to be seen as worthy of condemnation. Consider the newly emerging status of the following three behaviors: marijuana use, premarital sex for young women, and abortion.

Marijuana Use

During the late 1970s, the use of marijuana looked like it was becoming nondeviant, almost conventional; 11 states had dropped criminal penalties against possessing small quantities of the drug, a majority of high school students and young adults had used it and a substantial minority used it regularly, and most high school students did not disapprove of its use, did not think that occasional use of it was harmful, and favored legalizing its possession. In 1979, for example, 51 percent of high school seniors said that they had smoked marijuana during the previous year, only 45 percent said that they disapproved of marijuana being smoked regularly, only 28 percent said that the private consumption of marijuana should be against the law, and only 42 percent said that someone risked harming themselves by smoking marijuana regularly (Goode, 1993, pp. 101, 103). During the 1980s and the 1990s, the marijuana picture had changed dramatically: The use of marijuana declined, attitudes toward its use became more condemnatory, the belief that it was harmful grew, and a majority came to oppose its legalization. By 1990, only 27 percent of American high school seniors said that they had used marijuana during the previous year, 91 percent said that they disapproved of regular marijuana use, 56 percent said that private marijuana smoking should be illegal, and 78 percent said that a "great risk" of harm was entailed in smoking marijuana regularly (Johnston, O'Malley, and Bachman, 1991, pp. 42, 127, 137, 139). Moreover, in 1989 and 1990, two states (Oregon and Alaska), by popular vote, *recriminalized* the possession of small quantities of marijuana (Goode, 1993, p. 52). In short, during the 1980s and 1990s, the use of marijuana became "redeviantized." The latest surveys, however, indicate that in spite of strong norms against it, the use of marijuana began to make something of a comeback in the 1990s; between 1991 and 1995, the percentage of American high school seniors who said that they smoked marijuana during the past year increased by 11 percentage points (University of Michigan, 1995).

Thus, the deviant status of marijuana use experienced a kind of cyclical development. Early in the twentieth century, the possession and sale of marijuana were legal, very few people had heard of the drug, and few expressed disapproval of it. During the 1930s, marijuana possession and sale were criminalized, very few Americans had not heard of the drug, and in all likelihood, if asked, most would have expressed disapproval of its use. During the 1960s and 1970s, marijuana possession was decriminalized in 11 states, the use of marijuana grew to unprecedented heights, tolerance increased to the point that, it seemed, it was becoming conventional in some social circles, an almost mainstream activity. Starting roughly in 1980, the anti-marijuana backlash grew. The use of marijuana declined dramatically, tolerance toward its use declined, the decriminalization ground to a halt, and two states even *re*-criminalized its possession. In short, marijuana use and sale became, once again, an unambiguously deviant activity. (Is the use of marijuana now undergoing a shift back in the direction of greater tolerance and acceptance? This is unlikely, but it is too early to tell for sure.) Clearly, the deviant status of some activities—and marijuana use provides an excellent example—is far from permanent; it may be changeable, dynamic, in flux from decade to decade.

Teenage Sex

In the 1930s, 1940s, and 1950s, teenage sex, at least among girls, was regarded as deviant. A young woman in her teens who was known to have had intercourse, especially with more than one boy, often found herself labeled as promiscuous, a "tramp," a "slut"—in short, a deviant. Teenage sex, especially with multiple partners, was felt to be a lower-class activity, disreputable and stigmatizing; it was engaged in by a minority of high school girls. According to the classic study by Alfred Kinsey based on 1940s data, only 3 percent of American girls had intercourse by age 15, and 20 percent had done so between the ages of 16 and 20. Over half the young women who did have intercourse in those days did so with only one male partner, usually the man they married (Kinsey et al., 1953, pp. 288, 336). According to a Gallup Poll conducted as late as 1969, two-thirds of the respondents (68 percent) said that it was *wrong* "for a man and woman to have sex relations before marriage" (Gallup, 1972, p. 2216); if the question had been asked of teenagers specifically, the percentage would have been much higher.

In the 1980s and 1990s, in spite of the AIDS crisis, this changed considerably. Teenage sex became widespread, even commonplace, and widely accepted as "no big deal." In one study, half the women (49 percent) age 18 and 19 said they had more than one sex partner during the previous year; nearly half (43 percent) age 15 to 19 had had intercourse during the previous three months (Forrest, Darroch, and Singh, 1990). Less than 1 young woman in 10 who married by the mid-1980s was still a virgin, and most had had sex with partners other than, and in addition to, their future husbands. From a situation in which "nice girls don't" we have moved to a new era in which "most girls do" (Whyte, 1990, p. 26). By 1990, the average or median age of first intercourse for females had dropped to 17. In short, sexual intercourse among teenage girls moved from being a minority, condemned, even deviant, activity to a mainstream behavior—expected, accepted, and extremely widespread. While sexual promiscuity is still condemned among teens, more selective, love-oriented sex *which used to be condemned* is now acceptable. Like many activities, the deviant status of adolescent sex changed drastically from the past generations or two to today.

Defining Deviance: Grass-Roots or Elite Engineered?

Defining behavior as deviant is variable with respect to the degree to which it is *spontaneous* and *grass-roots*, or *organized* and *engineered*. Some changes in the deviant status of activities are the result of broad cultural trends, and were not the product of specific efforts by organized groups. It is unlikely that any specific organized group or groups significantly influenced the declining deviant status of teenage sex. And marijuana's *growing* deviant status is the result of a number of extremely complex forces—including efforts by some anti-drug organizations urging that the public, especially the young, avoid the drug and condemn those who use it—not the least of which is a growing conservative trend generally, which began roughly with the election of Ronald Reagan as president in 1980. (Though teenage sex may be an exception to that conservative trend, adult

sex, it seems, is not. Adults report being more cautious and conservative—and more condemnatory—concerning recreational sex than they were in the 1970s, and the fear of AIDS may have something to do with it.) However, with some behaviors, the deviance-defining process is not nearly so spontaneous or grass-roots as it was for marijuana use and teenage sex. Seeing an activity as deviant is often the outcome of the *enterprise* of "moral entrepreneurs," that is, crusaders who see an evil in the world and wish to stamp it out (Becker, 1963, pp. 147ff.). Actions they condemn and believe are wrong are not sufficiently condemned, they feel; they wish to make sure that the perpetrators of these actions are condemned, punished, prevented from engaging in their evil deeds. To that end, they band together with others who feel the same way and attempt to influence public opinion, the content of the media, legislation, educational curricula, and so on.

Abortion

A good example of a form of behavior about which there is considerable dispute and conflict is abortion. One segment of the American public defines abortion as seriously deviant and wishes it were also a crime; another segment believes abortion should be a matter of individual choice and not worthy of condemnation or punishment. Anti-abortion activists, who refer to themselves as "right-to-lifers" or "pro-lifers," regard the fetus as a human being in every sense of the word and abortion therefore as murder; they want to criminalize abortion, make it legally unavailable so that very few women will seek or have one. They regard abortion as deviant: reprehensible, contemptible, an abomination, worthy of condemnation, a violation of God's intentions and natural law. In contrast, pro-choice advocates argue that the fetus is *not* a full-fledged human being; an abortion is the removal of tissue that is part of a pregnant woman's body. Abortion, they say, should be legal, freely available, and no woman should suffer stigma, condemnation, or arrest for deciding to abort her fetus.

Abortion is an excellent example of the attempt to define an activity as deviant (or to resist that definition) by certain groups or categories. One reason why the contending parties can influence definitions of deviance and crime on the abortion issue is that the most common attitude in the United States toward the issue is *ambivalence*.

Most Americans see abortion as a "necessary evil": They are not pro-abortion, they do not take abortion lightly, and they do not stigmatize a woman who has had an abortion, but they feel it is an ugly means of dealing with an even uglier situation. A clear-cut majority of Americans believe that some form of abortion should remain legal. Only 33 percent of the respondents in a survey conducted in October 1989 by the Gallup organization of a cross section of Americans age 18 and older said that they would like to see the law legalizing abortion overturned, 61 said they would not like to see it overturned, and the rest didn't know or weren't sure (Gallup, 1990, p. 211). The poll tapped the ambivalence most Americans feel concerning the abortion issue: A majority of respondents (55 percent) said they believe that abortion "is the same thing as murdering a child." At the same time, two thirds (66 percent) *also* said abortion "is sometimes the best thing in a bad situation" (Clymer, 1986). While most Americans oppose abortion *in principle*, they accept it *in practice*. It is a painful dilemma that cannot be resolved without some violation of principles.

Americans basically divide into three factions with respect to abortion. Only a very small minority agree with the right-to-lifers in believing abortion should be *illegal under and in all circumstances*; in the 1991 Gallup Poll, this figure was 17 percent. A larger minority—roughly 32 percent in 1991—believe that abortion should remain legal (within the limitation of the first two trimesters of pregnancy) "on demand," for any reason whatsoever. And the rest in the middle, roughly half the American public (50 percent in the 1991 Gallup Poll) believe abortion should be legal under *certain* circumstances but not others (Gallup, 1992, p. 118). The last of these categories occupy an "uneasy middle ground," swinging back and forth, depending on the conditions asked about (Lacayo, 1989, p. 20). Some draw the line at risk to the woman's life; others do so at rape and incest; still others (about 40 percent) say it is acceptable if the woman is unmarried and does not want to marry the man. In addition, whether the abortion takes place during the first or the second trimester also influences respondents' answers. Neither the pro-life nor the extreme pro-choice position (abortion on demand for any reason) attracts the approval of a majority of the American public, although the vast majority do *not* want to criminalize abortion.

It is within this arena that the right-to-lifers are attempting to wage moral, ideological, and political warfare. They are struggling to win the hearts and minds of the American public, to prevent women from having abortions, to change the law so that abortion is a criminal act, to define abortion as deviance. In 1989, the American Rights Coalition, a pro-life organization based in the South, installed a billboard above the streets of Atlanta, Georgia. It advertises free legal advice to women who have suffered "emotional or physical trauma" after an abortion. A woman who calls the toll-free number listed on the billboard is directed to a lawyer who will prepare a malpractice suit against the clinic or physician who performed the abortion. Similar billboards have gone up in cities throughout the South. The Coalition's goal is to drive abortion clinics out of business and, ultimately, lower the availability and therefore the incidence of abortion (Garb, 1989). In 1989, 85 pro-life activists, members of Operation Rescue, crowded into the lobby of a building in which the office of a doctor who performs abortions is located. They confronted couples and women entering the lobby. One protester thrust the picture of a dismembered fetus at an entering woman. "Don't have an abortion," she said. "The baby inside you is a living thing." Another waved a plastic doll in the woman's face. "Don't kill your baby!" she screamed. Protesters locked arms in front of the office door. Finally, the young woman, now sobbing hysterically, left the building (Tyre, 1989). Between the late 1970s and the late 1980s, over 600 abortion clinics have been picketed by demonstrators, 134 have received harassing mail or telephone calls, over 200 have received bomb threats, 32 were actually bombed, 38 were set on fire, in two, hostages were taken, and there were 60 clinics whose personnel have received death threats (Chancer, 1989, p. 37). In the 1990s, the conflict took an even more ominous, dangerous turn: Several physicians who performed abortions were murdered by anti-abortion zealots. Over time, anti-abortion activities have become more creative and varied. "Demonstrators have passed themselves off as patients, then splashed paint in waiting rooms, dropped stink bombs or chained themselves to examining tables." In one community, "opponents set up their headquarters next door to a . . . clinic, pounded furiously on the windows and even conducted mock funerals over a septic tank" (Beck et al., 1985, p. 23). Garbage men who make pickups at abortion clinics have been confronted and asked how they feel about hauling away corpses (J. Adler, 1985). Meanwhile, the conflict continues. Ultimately, the struggle is over the belief that a given activity is, or is not, reprehensible—that is, *deviant*—and the attempt to legitimize that definition in American society generally. It is unlikely that there will be a clear-cut winner over the coming generation.

Summary

These three examples—marijuana use, teenage sex, and abortion—offer at least two lessons to the student of deviance. First, the deviant status of specific behaviors may change over time. While some activities may become less deviant to most individuals, others may become more so. Second, these changes may reflect, represent, or be influenced by the outcome of ideological or political struggles between and among specific organized groups or factions in a society, or they may reflect a more general, more or less spontaneous, "grass-roots" change in the population's attitudes toward a given activity, or they may fall somewhere in between these two extremes. Deviance is a dynamic, eternally changing affair, one whose origins must be examined rather than assumed.

DEVIANCE AND SOCIAL PROBLEMS

The field of the sociology of deviance is linked to the study of social problems in a number of important ways. Crime and deviance are typically regarded as a major type of social problem; social problems texts nearly always devote one or more chapters to crime and/or deviance; and a substantial number of scholars and researchers who study crime and deviance also study social problems, and vice versa. However, although these fields are intimately associated, they are far from identical. There are many conditions which are regarded in one way or another as social problems that are not forms of deviance—for instance, aging, the earth's shrinking ozone layer, and population problems. Likewise, many forms of deviance are not social problems, such as eccentricity and certain physical characteristics, such as short stature. It is necessary, therefore, to delineate how social problems are defined and viewed, and in what ways they differ from deviance. Social problems can be defined in one of two ways: *objectively* and *subjectively*.

The Objectivist Definition of Social Problems

In one camp, those who define social problems objectively, we find the more traditional perspective, the "objectivists," scholars and researchers who argue that what defines a social problem is the existence of an objectively determinable, concretely real damaging or threatening condition. What makes a given condition *a problem* is that it harms or endangers human life and well-being. People need not be concerned about or even aware of such conditions; what is important is that such conditions do damage to our lives in some clear-cut, nonideological fashion. Any condition that causes death or disease, which shortens life expectancy or deteriorates the quality of life on a large scale, must be defined as a social problem (Manis, 1974, 1976). Presumably, the greater the degree of objective damage or threat and the greater the number of people so damaged or threatened, the more important the social problem. According to this view, the final arbiter of the reality of social problems is the expert, armed with empirical evidence and scientific insight, not the untrained general public. To cite Manis, a proponent of the "objectivist" school: "*Social problems are those social conditions identified by scientific inquiry and values as detrimental to human well-being*" (1976, p. 25).

One variant of the objectivist model is the functionalist paradigm (which we'll discuss in the next chapter), which sees social problems largely as a product of dysfunctions (social institutions not working correctly), social disorganization, role and value conflicts, and a violation of norms. In short, social problems represent a discrepancy between what *is* and what *ought to be* (Merton and Nisbet, 1976). A second variant of this position may be found among Marxists, radicals, and some conflict theorists, who on this issue if few others, agree with the functionalists, in that they argue that what is most compelling about the study of social problems is that "objective conditions do harm to people" (Eitzen, 1984, p. 11). "I find social problems," says Eitzen, "when social arrangements prevent people from developing their full potential; when institutional barriers to racial and sexual equality exist; when educational systems are elitist; when there is economic exploitation; when there is official indifference to human suffering; and when corporations and nations create human suffering"

(1983, p. xiv, 1984, p. 11; see also Feagin, 1982, and Liazos, 1982).

In short, the objectivist definition of social problems says that a social problem is a condition that causes objective harm to the society and its members. Any condition that causes harm to a society's members is *a problem* for that society.

The Constructionist Definition of Social Problems

In the opposing camp, on the other side of the debate, representing the more avant-garde or contemporary approach, we find the "constructionists," "subjectivists," or "relativists," who argue that what makes a given condition a problem is the "collective definition" (Blumer, 1971) of a condition *as* a problem, the degree of *felt public concern* over a given condition or issue. While there are differences among the various constructionists, there is a common core to their thinking: Conditions become social problems only when they are *defined as* or *felt to be* problematic—disturbing in some way, undesirable, in need of solution or remedy. Social problems do not exist "objectively" in the same sense that a rock, a frog, or a tree exists; instead, they are *constructed by* the human mind, *called into being* or *constituted by* the definitional process (Spector and Kitsuse, 1973, 1977; Kitsuse and Spector, 1973; Schneider and Kitsuse, 1985; Schneider, 1985; Best, 1995; Miller and Holstein, 1994; Holstein and Miller, 1994). Say Spector and Kitsuse (1973, p. 5): "the existence of objective conditions does not in itself constitute social problems." Indeed, to the subjectivist, a given objective condition need not even *exist* to be defined as a problem. Witness the persecution of witches in Renaissance Europe and colonial New England (Erikson, 1966; Currie, 1968; Ben-Yehuda, 1980, 1985), the current concern of many fundamentalist Christians that satanists are kidnapping, torturing, and killing tens of thousands of children in the United States each year (Richardson, Best, Bromley, 1991; Victor, 1989, 1990, 1993; Bromley, 1992), or among a certain segment of the public, the fear of being abducted by extraterrestrials (Mack, 1995), or that extraterrestrials are already living on earth disguised as humans, infiltrating and corrupting human society (Ellis, 1988; Montgomery, 1988; Jacobs, 1992), or the almost literally impossible claim that thousands of American soldiers are still alive and being held by their Vietnamese captors, more than two decades after the conclusion of that war (Franklin, 1993).

In short, in the words of Willard Waller: "there can be no social problem without a value-judgment" (1936, p. 922). Fuller and Myers go on to state: "*Social problems are what people think they are*, and if conditions are not defined as social problems by the people involved in them, they are not problems to these people, although they may be problems to outsiders or scientists" (1941, p. 320). More contemporaneously, Spector and Kitsuse define social problems as "the activities of individuals or groups making assertions of grievances and claims with respect to some putative conditions" (1977, p. 75).

Just as to the objectivist, the reality of social problems can be measured concretely, to the constructionist, their subjective reality can be measured or concretely manifested. Four such manifestations include: (1) organized, collective efforts on the part of some members of a society to do something about, to protest, or to change, a given condition, in short, "social problems as social movements" (Mauss, 1975); (2) the introduction of bills in legislatures to criminalize the behavior and the individuals supposedly causing the condition (Becker, 1963, pp. 135ff.; Gusfield, 1963, 1967, 1981; Duster, 1970); (3) the ranking of a condition or an issue in the public's hierarchy of the most serious problems facing the country—what Manis derisively calls "the public opinion paradigm" or the *vox populi* approach (1976, pp. 18–20); and (4) public discussion of an issue in the media in the form of magazine and newspaper articles and editorials and television news stories, commentary, documentaries, and dramas (Becker, 1963, pp. 141–143; Himmelstein, 1983, pp. 152–154; Jensen, Gerber, and Babcock, 1991).

The objectivist takes public concern as a given, a background or secondary issue or focus of interest, and examines concrete threat or damage as important, problematic, and theoretically interesting. The constructionist reverses the process, and examines public concern as important, problematic, and theoretically interesting, and sets objective threat or damage in the background. It is not the objective dimension that generates subjective concern, the constructionists say, but factors external to and independent of that dimension that require explaining.

What *is* the relationship between the objective damage or threat that conditions pose or cause and the subjective concern they generate? *Do* people become upset about a given condition because they can die from it, or do altogether different forces or factors touch off their concern? Each of these two approaches can be said to have two variants.

Objectivism: Objective Damage versus Social Concern

The "naive," common-sensical, or *grass-roots* objectivist approach sees public concern as a more or less straightforward manifestation of objective harm. "The situation was so bad, people became concerned and they just had to do something about it," would be an expression of the "naive" or grass-roots objectivist point of view. Conditions that do not cause much harm do not usually generate much concern, this approach would argue; those that cause a great deal of harm tend to generate much public concern. The naive objectivist, common-sensical, or grass-roots approach to the relationship between the objectivist and the subjectivist dimensions of social problems does not generate much support among scholars in the field today, although it is very common among much of the public. The "naive" objectivists maintain that serious conditions cause great concern, and less serious conditions cause less intense concern. If this view were to prevail a great deal of the time, it would simply be too obvious and common-sensical for the researchers in any field to formulate it or seriously entertain it; the reaction would in all likelihood be, "Who cares?" It is not a particularly interesting, revealing, or strategic generalization. Moreover, as we'll see shortly, this generalization is manifestly untrue; there are too many exceptions to the "naive" objectivist's rule. It is clear that for many specific social conditions, there are vast discrepancies between these two generalizations, that is, many social conditions are objectively benign, neutral, or of trivial import but generate substantial public concern, and many extremely damaging conditions that generate little concern. Very often, common sense is wrong, and this is one example of that principle.

In contrast, the "sophisticated" objectivist admits that the objective and subjective dimensions of social problems are often out of synch with one another, that objectively serious conditions may generate little public concern, while those that harm few people often touch off a great deal. However, this approach does not find this discrepancy particularly interesting or worthy of study (Manis, 1976). Or it argues that under certain conditions, the public can be *duped* into thinking that certain conditions are less serious than they are—and others are more so—and it is the social analyst's job to make the public *aware* of the scope of damaging conditions so that something can be done about them (Liazos, 1972, 1982). Most old-fashioned Marxists and radicals fall into this camp. The "sophisticated" objectivist simply does not care very much about actual or possible discrepancies between objective harm and subjective concern; what counts to the objectivist, above all, is the fact that *harm to humans is by its very nature a social problem*—all else is of secondary interest. The fact that harm may or may not generate social concern is not an intellectual *issue* to the objectivist.

Strict versus Contextual Constructionism

The constructionists, too, divide into two schools or camps over the question of the relationship between the objective and the subjective dimensions; these two schools have been referred to as the "hard," "strict" (or radical) constructionists and the "contextual" (or moderate) constructionists.

The *strict* constructionists do not believe that there is any such thing as the "objective" dimension in the first place. By pointing to empirical, concrete damage as a definition, measure, or indicator of the objective dimension, the observer (whether scientist or member of the general public) is simply engaged in yet another "claims-making" activity, is making yet another demand that social conditions be looked at in a certain way. The strict constructionist would say that the claim, for example, that disease is a more serious problem than, say, UFO abductions is no less a social construction than the reverse. No single claim has any special status in defining reality; all are equally subjective, all are special pleadings for a certain cause, ideology, or political view; none can be referred to as "objectively" true, none can be verified outside a system of values and ideologically based assumptions. Sociologically, there is no possible way of evaluating the objective truth of *any* claims about social problems, the strict constructionist claims; all statements about objective reality are sociologically irrelevant and must be set aside (Spector and Kitsuse, 1977, pp. 76, 96). An evaluation of the seriousness of objective conditions is not the sociologist's job, the strict constructionists believe; the only permissible enterprise in the realm of social problems is to examine claims and concerns *about* those conditions (Spector and Kitsuse, 1977; Woolgar and Pawlich, 1985; Kitsuse and Schneider, 1989).

Critics of strict constructionism point out at least two problems with the perspective. First, they argue, it is practically impossible to examine claims about social conditions without referring to the empirical or concrete world. If certain claims are being made, how do we know they are being made in the first place? Who is making them? For what reasons? Are specific values or interests involved in claims-making? Who responds to these claims, why, and in what ways? Why are some audiences responsive to certain claims, while others are indifferent? Do claims-makers tailor their arguments so that they will be appealing to certain audiences? In their *own* analyses of claims-making, strict constructionists continually violate their restrictions on focusing exclusively on the claims without any reference whatsoever to the real world. In fact, such an exercise may be impossible (Best, 1994). While strict constructionists *deny* the possibility of verifying objective reality, in fact, they base their observations on hidden assumptions about the objective status of aspects of the material world.

A second problem with the strict constructionist argument is that it ignores the fact that substantial discrepancies between subjective concern and objective seriousness point to interesting sociological processes; the greater this discrepancy is, the more our scrutiny is needed (Goode, 1992, pp. 320–323). If much of the public believes a condition that causes many deaths is serious and in need of remedy, it is less likely that an explanation is necessary than if the public believes a condition that causes few deaths—or is completely nonexistent—is serious and in need of remedy. As we saw, when serious conditions are regarded as serious problems, our reaction is likely to be, "So what?" But if *imaginary* conditions are regarded as *serious* problems—or if objectively serious problems are ignored—our reaction is likely to be, "Why?" "What's behind this glaring discrepancy?" The fact that many fundamentalist Christians are concerned about the objectively nonexistent kidnapping and murder of tens of thousands of children should be intriguing to us; the fact that it is believed by some members of minority communities that certain products sold by whites harm or sterilize African-

Americans (Turner, 1993) should excite our interest. How does such a belief come to be held? We cannot become intrigued by the discrepancy between beliefs and conditions in the world unless we are permitted to study those conditions with concrete, empirical evidence. This is what the strict constructionist does not want us to investigate. The fact that many people regard illness as a major social problem is not particularly interesting, sociologically speaking; the fact that the fear of extraterrestrials has seized some otherwise normal members of society (Mack, 1995) should cause us to wonder how this fear comes about. The strict constructionist has no mechanism by which such intriguing questions can be raised in the first place.

Very few sociologists who study social problems are "strict" constructionists; "contextual" (or moderate) constructionism is the dominant perspective in the sociological study of social problems. Contextual constructionists follow a program substantially different from the "strict" constructionists (Best, 1989a, 1994). Like the strict constructionists, the contextual constructionists also focus on subjective concern as a central issue in the study of social problems. However, they argue that it *is* possible to evaluate claims of the objective seriousness of various conditions. Moreover, this school argues, it is possible to examine the *discrepancy* between objective seriousness and subjective concern. This discrepancy can be examined in at least three ways.

First, some objectively serious conditions (those which, for example, cause many deaths) generate significantly *less* public concern than conditions that are far less serious, as measured by the objective criterion of the deaths they cause. For instance, the contextualist wonders why illegal drug use has attracted an immense volume of public concern— often ranking as the nation's number one problem in public opinion polls—while some other conditions (cigarette smoking is a good example) which cause many times more deaths attract far less public attention and concern (Goode, 1993, p. 46). Consider the fact that epidemiologists estimate that roughly 430,000 Americans a year die as a result of the consumption of tobacco; it is likely that the total from illegal drug use is between a tenth and a twentieth of this figure. Why the discrepancy?

A second objective-subjective discrepancy examined by the contextual constructionist is the discrepancy that exists *over time*. A given condition's objective seriousness may remain stable over time, but the subjective concern it generates may fluctuate from period to period or even year to year. Or this concern may remain dormant at an extremely low level for decades or centuries, then suddenly burst forth as a result of a specific event, such as a series of speeches by a politician, the death of a prominent person, a highly publicized disaster or tragedy, the publication of a muckraking book or series of newspaper articles, or the outbreak of a war. In other words, the *volatility* of public concern over certain conditions, combined with the relative stability of the harm they cause, provides a clue to the importance of the social construction of social problems (Pfohl, 1977; Markle and Troyer, 1979; Troyer and Markle, 1983). For instance, since the 1970s, concern about the use of tobacco has increased massively. While still not in line with its actual harm, the fact that far more people today than a generation ago consider tobacco consumption harmful, a problem, and wish to control it, should propel us to examine the source of this upsurge.

The third way that discrepancies between the objective and subjective dimension of social problems exist is the discrepancy between the claims made by parties who wish to define social problems and what the facts say. To the contextualist, the fact that many fundamentalist Christians believe that 50,000 children or more are being kidnapped (and killed) in the United States each year, while experts place the total number of abductions of children by strangers—most of whom eventually return to their parents—at no more than a few hundred (Best, 1989b, 1990, 1995; Richardson, Best, and Bromley, 1991) is worth studying and explaining. In fact, this discrepancy between the objective and the subjective dimensions may be said to be a *central* concern for the contextual constructionist.

Along these lines, then, we learn that in the 1970s, efforts to define coffee drinking, a relatively benign activity, as a social problem emerged, and were to a certain extent successful (Troyer and Markle, 1984).

Vested interests—specifically the dairy industry—for a time during the 1930s and 1940s successfully managed to define the production, sale, and consumption of margarine as a "menace" and therefore a problem to society (Ball and Lilly, 1982).

In the 1970s, the criminal victimization of the elderly came to be seen as a major social problem, when in fact, this segment of the population is *least*

likely to be victimized by street crime (Fishman, 1978; Yin, 1980).

In the 1960s, the physical abuse of children by their parents or caretakers, which had remained a major source of death, injury, and mutilation for millennia, was "discovered," widely recognized as a social problem, and attacked as a pathological condition in need of remedy (Pfohl, 1977).

In the 1960s, poverty, previously a condition that had been ignored or swept under the rug by politicians, members of the middle class, and researchers as well, came to be seen as a condition in need of substantial attention, in part as a result of the publication of a single book, Michael Harrington's *The Other America* (1962).

It was not until the 1970s—after causing millions of deaths on the highway during the course of this century—that drunk driving came to be seen as a major problem facing the country, and movements sprang up to deal with the problem (Gusfield, 1981; Jacobs, 1989).

In short, a number of relatively harmful conditions are not defined as problems, or have existed for extremely long periods of time before being so defined, while some relatively benign conditions have at certain times and under certain conditions come to be seen by segments of the public as social problems. Clearly, then, there *is* a measure of independence between the objective and the subjective dimensions *for certain specific concrete or putative conditions*. Moreover, in each case, the process and outcome of defining a given condition as a social problem is sociologically patterned and structured, the elucidation of which is theoretically strategic. Conditions become successfully defined as social problems not at random, nor solely as a result of their objective seriousness, but because specific segments or interest groups are successful at generating, stimulating, or guiding widespread public concern about them.

It should be emphasized that the contextualists are not (primarily, at least) interested in *debunking*, that is, in disproving society's claims that certain conditions *should* or *should not* be regarded as serious social problems. Debunking is "the crudest form of constructionism" (Best, 1989c, p. 246). The contextualist constructionist's concern is mainly in understanding how definitions of social problems are generated, sustained, taken seriously, and acted upon; and how certain claims of seriousness are advanced by specific agents and reacted to, or ignored, by different audiences. Their argument is that *by themselves*, conditions do not constitute social problems; what *makes* them social problems is how they are defined and reacted to by various segments of a society. While such an investigation *may* help to reform society, this is not the contextualist's primary motivation. What such an investigation does, however, is enable us to understand how the society works, to understand society's central social processes and mechanisms, to see where we have come from and where we are going. For these reasons, most sociological social problems analysts adhere to some version of the contextual constructionist school. I include myself in this school.

SUMMARY

All societies set and enforce rules, or norms. Nearly all of us see at least some of these rules as natural, normal, and taken-for-granted. They tend to be justified on the basis of protecting the society from harm and disorder. Other ways of doing things are denounced, regarded as unnatural. Whenever someone deviates from traditional, approved practices, the members of a society, or society as an institution, attempt to bring that deviating party into line. Social control is any and all efforts to ensure conformity to a norm.

Social control encompasses a broad range of practices. Some are positive (rewards), some are negative (punishment); some are internal (mainly socialization), while others are external (for instance, imprisonment). Not all forms of punishment or condemnation represent efforts to bring deviators into line, however. It's not clear exactly what a dwarf or an extremely ugly person is supposed to do, subsequent to being humiliated, to change. Social control can also be formal and informal. Most of the social control that is exercised in reaction to violations of the rules is interpersonal or informal; admonition, criticism, gossip, laughter, anger, and ridicule represent some of the many ways that wrongdoers are reminded of their transgressions.

Nonetheless, formal social control represents an extremely important means that societies have to bring violators into line and remind the rest of the society what's right and what's wrong. The most visible and well-known mechanisms of formal social control are, of course, penal sanctions—the criminal law, the police, the courts, probation, the jails and prisons, and parole. Presumably, the more dangerous, higher-consensus violations are covered by the penal law, although it should be noted that many thousands of far from dangerous violators of low-consensus crimes are languishing in the country's prisons at the present moment. Some sociologists consider society's noncriminal, nonpenal bureaucratic agencies an extremely crucial mechanism of social control—the welfare system, family court, truant offices, unemployment agencies, civil courts, tax collection departments, and so on. Moreover, some sociologists even go so far as to restrict their notion of social control to the efforts of the state and such state-like institutions and agencies, ignoring the many mechanisms of informal social control.

Deviance and crime can be distinguished conceptually, although in reality, they are intertwined. The creation of a formal criminal code is a political act; a crime must be the violation of legislation that has been sanctioned by the state. Clearly, such a process is far more hierarchical than the mechanisms of informal social control mentioned above. By general consensus, a kind of "division of labor" has evolved among sociologists studying deviance and crime. The "Eastern" school of criminology focuses on individuals who violate the law and the processes that led them to do so. The "critical" or "radical" school of criminology (now far less prominent than in the 1970s and early 1980s) focuses on the creation of the criminal law and its enforcement. And the "Western" or "Chicago/California" school focuses on deviance rather than crime, and matters such as identity, deviant "careers," and the process of deviant socialization.

Definitions of deviance are not carved in stone, permanent for all time, but are dynamic, always in transition. They are often contested, fought and struggled over; specific factions attempt to convince the public that their views are right and that a particular practice should, or should not, be sanctioned by the state. A good example is abortion; pro-lifers wish to criminalize and deviantize the practice, while pro-choicers want to keep it legal. Both are engaged in winning the ideological and political support of a large undecided public. Whether an activity comes to be more, or less, tolerated over time may have little to do with the interests or efforts of the powers that be in a given society. In other words, the "elite engineered" model of deviance defining seems inadequate to explain a great deal of public opinion.

While deviance and social problems are related concepts, they should be distinguished. Many forms of deviance are never seen as major social problems (eccentricity, for example), while a number of social problems are not the deviant actions or conditions of rule violators (global warming, medical care, aging). Social problems can be viewed in two ways: objectivism (or essentialism) and social constructionism. Objectivism regards the existence of a social problem as an objective fact; it is measured by the concrete harm a given condition causes. In contrast, constructionism sees social "problemhood" not as an objective fact but as a matter of definition: Conditions are *constructed* into problems by being seen and dealt with in a certain way. No condition, in and of itself, is automatically a problem; it becomes a problem when it generates a certain degree of *concern* in the general public, segments of the public, or decision makers who act to do something about it. Some constructionists ("strict" constructionists) believe that all definitions of social problems are constructs and that we should not regard any of them as more definitive or objective than any other. Other constructionists ("contextual" constructionists) contrast public and institutional definitions of problemhood with empirical data on certain conditions and pay close attention to discrepancies between them. "Contextual" constructionists believe that "strict" constructionism is not a viable or possible intellectual enterprise; they are dominant in the field of social problems.

Although there are differences between the fields of study of social problems and deviance, there are strong parallels as well. In the field of deviance, labeling theory (which we'll examine shortly), and in the field of social problems, constructionism, both focus on how a given behavior or condition is *defined* and *reacted to*. Both underplay the intrinsic or objective features of the behavior or the condition and how and why it is seen, defined, and reacted to in a certain way. Just as to the labeling theorist, deviance is "what people think it is," likewise, to the constructionist, social problems are "what people think they are." In a society in which homosexuality is tolerated, homosexuality is not deviant; similarly, in a society in which there is no concern about disease, disease is not a social problem. As we'll see shortly, labeling theory is to deviance as constructionism is to social problems. The deviance specialist can learn a great deal from a study of social problems, and the student of social problems can learn a great deal from a study of deviance. The parallels are extremely strong.

chapter 4

EXPLAINING DEVIANT BEHAVIOR: CAUSAL THEORIES

Do you wonder why the men and women whose behavior was described in Chapter 1 acted the way they did? Don't you wonder why university administrators would consent to the practice of requiring all their undergraduates to be photographed in the nude to comply with what now seems a completely crackpot research program? Why a mother would murder her five children? Why a successful and affluent executive would loot and destroy one corporation after another, knowing that apprehension and arrest will almost certainly follow? What would impel an athletic and most decidedly heterosexual man nearing retirement age to dress in women's clothes? What could possibly motivate a serial rapist? How is it that thousands of the nation's citizens, calling themselves "patriots," come to have paranoid fantasies about the government usurping their rights and the United Nations invading and conquering the country—to the point where they feel they have to stockpile huge caches of weapons in anticipation of some sort of an eventual violent showdown? How could a detachment of soldiers brutally butcher over 700 innocent civilians simply because they happened to be in the vicinity of a guerrilla band?

The question, *why do they do it?* has been and continues to be asked about persons who stray beyond moral or legal boundaries. "What kind of person would do such a thing?" we ask. After all, most people cannot picture themselves complying with harebrained experiments, embezzling millions of dollars, cross-dressing, or massacring hundreds of innocent victims. What is it that influences some people to stray beyond society's normative boundaries, while most of us do not?

Over the years, many theories have been advanced to explain *rule making, rule breaking,* and *reactions to rule breaking* (Sutherland and Cressey, 1978, p. 3). Theories of deviance attempt to answer one or several of the following questions:

1. Why do they do it? (Or: Why *don't* they do it?)
2. Why is it (or isn't it) regarded as wrong?
3. Why is it (or isn't it) against the law?
4. What happens when somebody engages in it? How do other people react? And why?

The earliest theories of deviant behavior typically concentrated on the question: Why do they do it? In contrast, raising the issues of why rules and laws are made, and what accounts for reactions to breaking rules and laws, are fairly recent endeavors. (Presumably, no explanation for the origin of physical characteristics is necessary, and so they have received far less attention from deviance specialists than motivated *behavior* that is presumably deviant.) At the same time, we can recognize the difference between theories that attempt to explain why nonnormative *behavior* exists and those that focus on *reactions to* certain kinds of behavior (and conditions). In this chapter, we will focus entirely on theories of "Why do they do it?" Consequently, this *excludes* perspectives which examine *reactions* to rule breaking. And it excludes an examination of *involuntarily acquired characteristics,* such as shortness, extreme ugliness, blindness, and so on; in this chapter, I will focus exclusively on *explanations for deviant behavior.*

For a sociologist, one of the more important distinctions among different theories of wrongdoing can be made according to the *level* at which the explanation is aimed. *Micro* explanations are those that focus on *characteristics of the individual actor*, while *macro* explanations are those that focus on characteristics of *larger structural units* within which individual actors operate. *Macro* theories look at the big picture; *micro* theories look at a much smaller-scale picture. Examples of a macro structural unit would be the characteristics of the society as a whole or the communities in which people live. Thus, a macro explanation would seek to explain differences in the enactment of deviant behavior *between and among* structural units, not from one person to another. We can even locate a third level: the *meso* level, which focuses on *middle-level* units, such as a factory or a corporation. In contrast, an example of a *micro* theory would be biological or genetic explanations: Deviance is more likely to be enacted by persons who are born with a distinct genetic make-up. Personality theories, too, are micro in their focus; so are theories which argue that deviants act the way they do because of the fact that their parents did not socialize them properly. (Micro factors can *vary* in systematic ways within larger units, of course.) Micro theories argue that differences in the *characteristics of individual actors* is what explains their different rates of deviant behavior. Micro theories attempt to explain why person A is more likely to engage in deviance than person B. In contrast, macro-level theories focus on factors that affect structures, not individuals. They argue that certain kinds of *societies* or certain kinds of *neighborhoods* or *communities* generate high rates of deviance. In contrast to micro-level theories, they do not ask why person A *within the same society, neighborhood, or community* commits deviance, while person B does not. *All* persons within a given structure are subject to the *same* system-wide factor, although in varying degrees, of course. Macro theories look at *properties of the system* to explain deviance, while micro theories look at *properties of the person*. This is a major distinction among the various theories that attempt to explain deviance; it will run throughout this chapter. Meso-level theories attempt to explain where deviance is more common, let's say, in one factory or organization versus another. For meso-level theories, general societal characteristics, as well as individual differences, are secondary.

Everywhere and at all times, rules have existed. Wherever there are rules, wherever there are laws, they will be broken, even if only occasionally. Everywhere, virtuous, law-abiding, conventional members of a society wonder what leads some people to engage in acts of wrongdoing, such as adultery, blasphemy, embezzlement, theft, witchcraft, heresy, murder, incest, cowardice, treason, plagiarizing, suicide, aberrant and mentally deranged behavior, lying, and so on. Throughout history, speculation as to the cause or causes of behavior that is regarded as deviant has been a major concern of the members of cultures all over the globe. And just about everywhere, explanations and theories have been advanced as to why some members of society break its rules. Historically, the oldest explanation for deviant behavior has been *demonic possession*. For many thousands of years, evil spirits, including the devil, were thought to cause men and women to engage in socially unacceptable behavior. A half-million years ago, Stone Age humans drilled holes into the skulls of individuals who engaged in wrongdoing of some kind—who, today, would be recognized as being mentally ill—so that evil spirits could escape; indeed, this procedure was still practiced as late as the 1600s (Gallagher, 1995, p. 1). The ancient Hebrews, Egyptians, Greeks, and Romans performed rites of exorcism to cast out demonic beings dwelling in the body and soul of transgressors. In Renaissance Europe (roughly, the early 1400s to the early 1600s), hundreds of thousands of women and men were burned at the stake for "consorting" with the devil and supposedly engaging in wicked deeds as a consequence. Thus, among both the fairly well-educated and much of the mass of society, the theory of demonic possession was a dominant explanation for wrongdoing in Europe almost half a millennium ago, and in the Salem colony in Massachussetts in the 1600s (Erikson, 1966). Among intellectuals, by the 1700s in Western Europe and North America, this explanation had almost completely died out.

Of course, demonic possession has always been a belief among some segments of the public which explained deviance, and it does so today. As we saw with "imaginary deviance," some fundamentalist Christians believe that satanists are consorting with the devil—either literally or figuratively— and are abusing and murdering thousands of children in grisly rituals (Victor, 1993, 1995). In addition, although ultra-orthodox Jews' notion of the devil is much hazier and less concrete than is true for Christians, ultra-orthodox Jews in Israel and the United States (the *haredim*) nonetheless believe in the intervention of evil spirits as an explanation for wrongdoing. In a way, arguing as a self-avowed "religious socialist" or "Christian Marxist" Richard Quinney does, that American society has a high rate of crime because it lacks the proper spiritual and moral values (1980), retains something of a demonic flavor. The argument is that many Americans are deviants because they have turned from God to consort with a *metaphorical* devil. Hence, although the theory that demonic spirits are responsible for deviance has virtually disappeared among intellectuals, scholars, and sociologists of deviance, it is still held in some circles or sectors of Western society, including (a very few) sociologists.

PERSPECTIVES IN THE SOCIOLOGY OF DEVIANCE

To the man and woman in the street, "theory" has a negative connotation; it usually means wild speculation, an account for events or phenomena for which there is little or no evidence. "Theories" are usually contrasted with "facts": Facts are what have been established to be true, theories are speculations about what might be true. In contrast, in the natural sciences, the word has an entirely different meaning. To a scientist, a "theory" is not mere speculation. In fact, theories may already be established as true. To a scientist, theories possess three characteristics: First, they are *empirically verifiable,* second, they provide an *explanation* or *account for,* third, *a general class of phenomena.* "Empirically verifiable" means that a statement can be demonstrated to be true or false with the use of observable evidence; an "explanation" offers a cause-and-effect account of why something is the way it is; and if an explanation is general, it applies to *many* phenomena or events, not just a few. Newton's theory of gravitation, Darwin's theory of natural selection, and Einstein's theory of relativity represent three examples of theories. In sociology generally, and in the sociology of deviance specifically, the term "theory" is used a bit more broadly than in the natural sciences. There are, of course, sociological theories that conform to the classic scientific definition, that is, they are explanations for a general class of phenomena. For instance, arguing that attachment to conventional individuals lowers one's likelihood of committing deviant acts is an example of a theory or explanation that can be confirmed or falsified with systematic, empirical evidence. The theory is general, and it supplies a causal mechanism. Thus, it qualifies as a scientific theory because it possesses all the relevant criteria.

On the other hand, many sociological approaches are not theories in the sense I just proposed. Rather, they are *perspectives* or *theoretical orientations* toward the phenomena they examine, *paradigms* or *models* outlining in a very broad way how the world works. A perspective directs us to certain aspects of the phenomenon we wish to examine. A painter does not look at the ocean in the same way a ship captain or an oceanographer does; a poet will describe love differently from a sociologist; police officers, criminologists, and criminals are all concerned with crime, but the models of *what that phenomenon is to them* are radically different.

Most of the perspectives we will look at here and in the next chapter are not, in the strict scientific sense of the word, theories at all, even though they are widely referred to as theories among sociologists who study deviance. They are theoretical orientations, that is, they tell us what to look for, what to notice; they alert us to concepts, processes, mechanisms, and relationships that are likely to have relevance in the material world. They say, "A lot of things in the social world work this way, although often, they don't." These perspectives will not withstand rigorous, systematic operationalization or scientific testing. Robert Merton has stated, in reference to approaches to deviance: "When sociologists speak of 'theories,' they only adopt a con-

venient abbreviation. Strictly speaking, none is a theory in the exacting sense. . . . Rather, they are general theoretical orientations that indicate *kinds of sociological variables* to be taken into account in trying to understand deviance. They do not state definite relationships between sets of specific variables" (1976, p. 31). Still, they are useful in that we might often miss interesting observations if we did not look at the world through the lens of these perspectives.

Most discussions of sociological theories of deviance present them, one by one, much like different-colored eggs in a carton. They are treated as equivalents, as comparable, as covering more or less the same territory, as asking more or less the same kinds of questions, and as competing with one another. This is an erroneous view. In fact, these theories or perspectives are not at all equivalents; they do not cover the same territory or ask the same questions; and for the most part, they do not compete with or directly contradict one another. In the sociology of deviance (as in many fields of sociology), proponents of different, presumably antagonistic, schools "need never confront one another." They can "surround themselves with their own circle of followers and their own network of journals and publishers. It is quite possible for one intellectual faction to create, examine, and extend its ideas without much interference from outsiders. Challenges can be ignored. Indeed, they may never be issued." Major schools "can flourish independently and unmolested" forming "parallel intellectual universes which need never intersect" (Downes and Rock, 1988, p. 15). In this sense, then, when examining the field, we encounter a "labyrinth of deviance" (p. 2). Two other sociologists refer to different perspectives in the sociology of deviance as "ships in the night," passing one another without meaningful confrontation (Messner and Rosenfeld, 1994, p. 43).

Sociologist Nanette Davis (1980, p. 13) tells us that the various theoretical perspectives in the study of deviance should not be seen as contradictory. "To say that one theory.. . . contradicts another," she says, "is like saying that tools in a toolbox contradict one another." Instead, each can be looked at as *appropriate for a different purpose.* These theories cannot be lined up and examined as if they were different-colored eggs in a carton, as if each one dealt with precisely the same issues. Though they all look at the phenomenon of deviance, they look at different *aspects* of this phenomenon, and they approach it on their own special terms, and therefore, not at all on the terms of the other perspectives. They are not even rough equivalents, and should not be regarded as such.

Another way of saying this is that the different perspectives on the sociology of deviance and crime are *incommensurable* (Wright, 1984). Their practitioners look at different aspects of the phenomenon under study; they are concerned with different issues; they attempt to answer different questions. They use different types of evidence; they read and cite different researchers, theorists, and authors. They do not, for the most part, read the writings of practitioners of other schools and, when they do, it is only to supply them with relevant quotes to criticize and critique other practitioners' work. They think that practitioners of other schools should be concerned with their own questions and issues; when they criticize the other perspectives, they believe these criticisms are devastating, even fatal; and, for the most part, they ignore the criticisms that practitioners of other schools direct at their own school's writings, believing them to be irrelevant to a meaningful analysis of deviance.

FREE WILL AND RATIONAL CALCULATION

The first sophisticated and academically respectable perspective or theory of criminal or deviant behavior is the "free will" or classical school of criminology (Vold and Bernard, 1986, pp. 18–34); it is associated with the names of Cesare Beccaria (1738–1794), an Italian scholar, and Jeremy Bentham (1748–1832), an English jurist and philosopher, who were strongly influenced by the French rationalists, such as Rene Descartes (1596–1650), and the laissez-faire economist Adam Smith (1723–1790). The period of the eighteenth century in Europe is generally referred to as the Age of Enlightenment or the Age of Reason. (However, in spite of its impressive title, much of what eighteenth-century leaders did does not seem very "enlightened" or "reasonable" to us today!) By the 1700s, philosophers and other intellectuals had abandoned the idea of the intervention of spirits to explain worldly phenomena and, instead, concentrated on worldly forces. Rather than being seen as a result of seduction by demons, violations of rules, norms, and laws were thought to be caused by free will: a rational calculation of pleasure and pain.

Individuals choose among a number of alternative courses of action according to benefits they believe will accrue to them. They avoid activities they believe will bring them more pain than pleasure. This model, then, sees people, criminals included, as free, rational, and hedonistic. Actions that bring pleasure to a person will be enacted and continued; those that are painful will be abandoned, eighteenth-century rationalists believed. The way to ensure conformity to society's norms and laws, therefore, is to apprehend and punish offenders, thereby making the pain following a violation greater than the pleasure derived from it.

The classical school made a number of assumptions that are now recognized as false. It ignored obvious disparities in wealth and power and thereby failed to recognize forces that make certain kinds of crimes more likely among the poor and less likely among the rich. In addition, we now see that people are not completely rational in their behavior; they engage in deviance and crime for a number of reasons aside from pursuing pleasure and avoiding pain. In addition, what is pleasurable to one person may be painful to another, and vice versa. Homosexuality and heterosexuality provide relevant examples here: To someone who enjoys intercourse solely with members of the same sex, intercourse with a member of the opposite sex would not be pleasurable. Moreover, most of the time a rule or a law is violated, the offender is not caught, making the offender's calculation of pleasure and pain far more complicated than these early thinkers imagined. In addition, detection of crimes and enforcement of laws are quite often erratic, thus muddying the cost-benefit analysis the potential criminal must make. Overall, the classical school of criminology held a faulty model of human behavior.

The free will perspective has made something of a comeback in recent years in more sophisticated forms than its original version. The rationality school and the strictly economic model (Cohen, Felson, and Land, 1980; Becker, 1968; Warren, 1978; Clarke and Felson, 1995) are based on some of the classical school's basic assumptions. Unlike the classical school, these contemporary models do not encompass all crimes within their scope; they tend, instead, to focus specifically on *economic* crimes. The rational choice school argues that criminal motivation need not be considered; it is a given, that is, there are always more than enough people to go around who are motivated to break the law if it is profitable for them. Criminal behavior, it argues, is a *purposive* and *rational* means of attaining an end, that is, acquiring money more efficiently than by any other method. People act according to the *utility* that the outcome of their actions have for them. An assumption of both the rationality and the economic models is that virtually all individuals, when faced with the same constraints and alternatives, would make essentially the same choices. The rational choice model argues that crime increases to the extent that property is unguarded. It is possible that too many assumptions have to be made for the model to work. In real life, there are too many constraints and contingencies that push and pull individuals in various directions for us to assume that utility will dominate their choice of action, whether in a criminal or a law-abiding direction. Although rationality certainly enters into the crime and deviance equation, the fact that jails, prisons, and reform schools are full of young and not-so-young men (and women) who committed crimes impulsively, without planning, and got caught as a consequence, indicates that the free will factor is not a totally viable explanation. The fact is, *most* individuals who commit crimes to make money, could have earned more, in the long run, by working at a low-paying drudge job; clearly, some other explanation is necessary (Katz, 1988). At the same time—even for "irrational" actors who seek more than a concrete goal such as money—opportunity is related to the enactment of deviance. For *all* actors, the greater the perceived payoff and lower the perceived punishment, the greater the likelihood that deviance will be enacted.

THE POSITIVE SCHOOL

Among major segments of the intellectual community in Europe, the nineteenth century was characterized by a shift away from viewing human actors as rational—individuals who fully understood the causes and consequences of their actions—to seeing behavior as being determined by forces beyond their control, understanding, and rational will (McCaghy and Capron, 1994, pp. 8ff.). *Positivism*, the dominant scientific perspective in the second half of the nineteenth century, argued that the only valid information is that gathered in a strictly scientific fashion, which meets the following criteria that it is empirical, systematic, falsifiable, general, and explanatory. Nineteenth-century positivists believed that

behavior is determined or strictly caused by specific factors or forces that can be discovered and explained only by the scientist.

In the nineteenth century, the positive school assumed that deviant and criminal behavior is caused by a biological pathology or defect of some kind. Wrongdoing, such as criminal behavior, was thought to be traceable to something organically and constitutionally wrong with the offender, an inborn defect of some kind. One variety of this theory assumed that deviants were simply too feeble-minded to understand society's rules and laws, and this is why they violated them. The most well-known and influential of the nineteenth-century positivists writing on deviance and crime was Cesare Lombroso (1835–1909), an Italian physician and scholar, who argued that the physical abnormalities ("atavisms") of certain persons forced them into committing crimes. The criminal represented an evolutionary throwback to a more primitive or apelike human, according to Lombroso. Clearly, the theory was heavily influenced by Charles Darwin's theory of evolution, as spelled out in *On the Origin of Species* (1859). (However, most contemporary observers would argue that Lombroso's application of Darwinian theory represents a distortion of its central ideas.) In short, the nineteenth-century positive school of criminology argued that physical defect or pathology was the major explanation for criminal and deviant behavior. By the late 1800s and early 1900s, however, most researchers realized that physical abnormality could not explain all, or even most, deviation from laws and social norms. In fact, even Lombroso modified his own theory over the years, granting to biological pathology an increasingly smaller role, and nonbiological factors a larger and larger one. (A devastating critique of Lombroso's positivistic criminology may be found in Gould, 1981, pp. 123–143.)

Over the past generation or two, there has been something of a revival of biological and constitutional theories of deviance and crime. In the second half of the nineteenth century, biological factors were posited to represent possibly the most important single factor in crime causation; by the 1920s, with the advent of behaviorist psychology, biological factors ("nature") were relegated to an insignificant role, and learning (or "nurture") elevated to a paramount one. But beginning in the 1960s, inborn factors began to make a comeback. Of course, hardly anyone today gives them as crucial or central a role as the early or even the late Lombroso.

Still, many contemporary observers argue that biological factors play some—a *significant*—role in causing criminal behavior (for instance, Wilson and Herrnstein, 1985, pp. 69–103). This approach usually focuses on conventional street crimes, such as murder, robbery, and rape, which require risk taking and physical exertion. Thus, the biological position rests on the argument that criminal (and conventional) activities requiring risk and physical exertion are more likely to be committed by people who are more willing to take risks and are capable of greater physical exertion. Obvious candidates are men, as opposed to women, and the young, as opposed to the middle-aged and the elderly (Gove, 1985). It should not astonish us that this is so. In fact, it would be truly remarkable if it were not. More specifically, any departure from this model would require serious explaining, for instance, if women were more likely to be burglars than men, or if robbery turned out to be more commonly committed by persons over the age of 60. Of course, we do *not* find major departures from our expectation that persons who commit certain kinds of crimes—those that require risk and physical strength—are those who possess these very qualities. Still, there are *partial* departures.

For instance, if physical qualities were of such great importance, why does the proportion of women arrestees vary as much as it does from one society to another or over time? (Simon, 1975a, pp. 111–119; 1975b, pp. 89–96; Adler, 1979). Why do wives kill husbands in more than 40 percent of spousal killings in the United States, but in other Western nations, this percentage is only half that figure? (Wilson and Daly, 1992). While biological factors are not insignificant in influencing the commission of certain kinds of crime, other variables are clearly far more influential. In an advanced industrial society, physical factors count for less than they did in hunting-and-gathering and agrarian societies (Gagnon, 1971). Biological factors are always *mediated* through a social and cultural environment and must be counted as being of limited utility in explaining wrongdoing. This is especially the case when we are examining crimes for which strength and physical daring play no part.

SOCIAL PATHOLOGY

"Social pathology" is the name given to the late nineteenth-century and early twentieth-century perspective which argued that (1) *society is very much like an organism* and (2) *deviance is very much like a disease* (Mills, 1943, 1963, pp. 525–552; Davis, 1980, pp. 31–55; Rubington and Weinberg, 1995, pp. 15–51). The social pathology school abandoned physical defect as the major cause of deviance and crime. Rather, the deviant is seen as the individual who cannot or will not adjust to the laws, standards, values, or norms of mainstream, conventional society. Deviance represented the inability to fit into the normal, healthy social body, according to the social pathologists. For the most part, the most basic cause of deviant behavior specifically, and all social problems generally, is a failure of socialization.

Social pathology represented an uneasy marriage between science (or, to be more precise, pseudo-science) and moralism. The "science" (or "pseudo-science") part was evolutionary; the "moralism" part was the view that certain behaviors were inherently "bad" and others were by their very nature "good." Social pathologists saw evolution as inevitable and progressive. Its practitioners accepted the view that society was evolving slowly, steadily, and progressively toward some eventual quasi-utopian state. Certain conditions, elements, or forces disrupted this progressive evolution. Two in particular were discussed. Some persons—deviants—were seen as being unable or unwilling to adjust to conventional, mainstream society's laws, values, standards, and norms. Some people can't keep pace with society's progress; they can't contribute their fair share to the community. (Or they are so contrary and selfish, they refuse to do so.) Though evolution was something of an inevitability, progressive elements in the society can hasten this process by working to motivate regressive persons to fit into conventional society's social structure. In short, troublemakers had to be educated into middle-class morality (Rubington and Weinberg, 1995, pp. 15–20). The second condition that threatened progressive evolution and needed attention was "cultural lag." Many people are understandably bewildered by the contradictions they face when society changes as rapidly as was the case at the turn of the nineteenth century.

Most social pathologists distrusted the city. A healthy society was seen as harmonious, homogeneous, and slow-moving. In contrast, cities generated conflict, were extremely socially diverse, and subject to rapid social change. All this encouraged nonconformity and unhealthy behavior. Social pathologists saw middle-class values as normal, and those of the lower and working classes as pathological and abnormal. Deviance was seen as an almost exclusively underclass phenomenon. The solution to the adjustment problems of the poor—poverty, "vice," crime, unemployment, delinquency, alcoholism, violence—was to socialize the deviant into conventional middle-class society's values and encourage conformity to its standards of behavior.

Social pathologists had their heyday roughly between 1890 and 1920. The event that shattered their view of social change as a harmonious and progressive process was the First World War. It was so horrendous to many intellectuals that they abandoned their faith in social evolution. In addition, social change was so explosive early in the twentieth century that the evolutionary model no longer made any sense. Farms were being abandoned, rural life was being depleted. Between 1920 and 1930, the Black urban population in northern cities doubled; in 1930, one-third of the white urban population was foreign-born. Social pathologists realized that their neat, tidy, and reformist view of deviance and conformity didn't explain events exploding around them. By the end of World War I, the perspective had declined sharply among sociologists studying deviance and other social problems. Society is not really very much like an organism, and deviance cannot be regarded as anything like a disease. To argue that behavior that strays from respectability and conventionality is necessarily abnormal and pathological is to make a value judgment, not a statement of fact. The same behavior can be viewed as acceptable or immoral, depending on one's perspective. The social pathology perspective, with its emphasis on personal failure and maladjustment, the pathology of immorality, and the ideal model of small-town life, was simply inadequate to understand deviance in a complex, urban, industrial society.

TWENTIETH-CENTURY POSITIVISM: CAUSAL ANALYSIS

Twentieth-century positivism is not, strictly speaking, a theory, let alone a theory of deviant behavior. In the sense of containing specific substantive propositions gathered around a coherent, integrated explanation, positivism is not a theory at all. Instead, positivism should be looked at as a broad orientation, a perspective, a way of looking at deviant reality, a methodological *approach* to the subject.

As we saw, in nineteenth-century criminology, the "positive school" referred to the perspective which held that the major cause of criminal behavior was biological pathology. The term refers to the work of Lombroso and his followers. As we saw, today, biological pathology has not disappeared as an explanatory factor in the study of deviant and criminal behavior (Wilson and Herrnstein, 1985, pp. 69–103), but it plays a much-reduced role compared with a century ago. Thus, we must keep in mind the very clear distinction between *the positive school of criminology*, a late nineteenth-century approach having a narrow focus on biological pathology, and *contemporary positivism* in the field of criminology, a much broader orientation, only a few schools of which make much use of biological factors.

What is positivism in the social sciences? *It is the application of the strict scientific method to the study of human behavior.* The practitioners of positivism maintain that sociology and criminology are not essentially different from the natural sciences, such as biology and physics. They believe that deviance and crime can be studied in basically the same way that natural phenomena, like stars, chemicals, and ocean tides can be studied (making the necessary adjustments in research methods for the subject matter under study, naturally). The scientific method, positivists believe, can be applied equally to social and to natural phenomena.*

The positivistic approach to the study of social reality generally, and to deviance and crime specifically, is based on the following assumptions or axioms.

1. The sociologist can—and must—be objective in the study of the social world, as well as in the study of deviance and crime.
2. Social phenomena generally, and crime and deviance specifically, are *objectively real.*
3. Phenomena and events in the social world generally, and in the world of deviance and crime specifically, are *determined*, that is, linked together in a specific cause-and-effect fashion.
4. The ultimate goal of all scientific endeavor is *explanation.*

*Note that two observers (Gottfredson and Hirschi, 1990) define positivism in a somewhat different fashion: as an explanation that sees social behavior as being caused by forces specifically *beyond the actor's will*. Thus, they contrast it with the classical school, which bases its explanation on rationality and free will.

To begin with, positivistically inclined sociologists believe that they can be just as objective in their study of the social world as the physicist is in studying the social world. By employing the scientific method, the social scientist can transcend the problems of bias and subjectivity and view the world as it really and truly is. Science, the positivist says, has little or nothing to do with questions of ideology or politics (though the social scientist can *study* questions of ideology and politics—objectively). Science and ideology exist in separate worlds. Putting aside ideological and political considerations is a necessary component in scientific objectivity. One must follow the French diplomat Talleyrand (1754–1838), who said, "I do not say it is good, I do not say it is bad, I say it is the way it is."

Second, saying that deviance and crime are objectively real means that they possess certain objective characteristics that clearly distinguish them from conventional, conforming, law-abiding behavior. In other words, the many forms of deviant and/or criminal behavior share a *common thread,* a *differentiating trait* that distinguishes them from conventional, conforming, legal behavior. At the very least, each specific type of deviance or crime (such as homosexuality, robbery, drug use, adultery, mental illness, alcoholism, or homicide) shares key characteristics in common. It is the scientist who determines what deviance or crime is, and what each specific type is, by observing the behavior in question and classifying it appropriately according to its objective characteristics. The characteristics of deviant and criminal behavior *are contained within the actions themselves*. It is their possession of certain observable properties that makes them deviant or criminal in nature. Positivists argue that behavior is not deviant or criminal simply because it is labeled as such. If this were true, there would be no point in studying them as an analytic category; they would have no coherence, they would possess nothing in common except their label. Rather, positivists assert, deviant and criminal behavior are *objectively real*, just as stars and water and frogs are objectively real, there is something about them that leads the scientist to examine them together as a category. Likewise, the reality of specific *forms* of deviance exists independent of the labeling process.

The third axiom of positivism is its adherence to strict *causality* or *determinism*. This means that events in the real world happen in a cause-and-effect fashion. Things do not happen accidentally or randomly; things are the way they are because of specific forces or factors acting in a predictable, almost mechanical fashion. Factor A causes or has an impact on B; B, in turn, causes or has an impact on C; and so on. The sociological positivist argues that social factors or variables are related to one another in the same causal fashion as that which takes place in the physical world. If you deprive a tree of light and water, it will die; if you reward a rat with food for pressing a bar, it will continue to press that bar; if you mix certain chemicals, an explosion will take place. Likewise, the same cause-and-effect sequence is said to occur in the social world. Urbanization increases the crime rate; strong ties to conventional others decrease rates of deviance; anonymity increases the likelihood of committing crimes. Conditions or factors such as these cause or influence specific forms of behavior, deviance included. It is the scientist's job to locate the dynamics of the cause-and-effect sequences that exist in the world. People's behavior, to the positivist, is caused by conditions and factors. In fact, a key building block of the positivistic approach to human behavior is that it is determined, to some extent, *by forces beyond our control* (Vold and Bernard, 1986, p. 45).

The ultimate goal of all scientific endeavor is *explanation*. Why is the world the way it is? What caused it to be so? More specifically, in the sphere of deviance and crime, the positivist searches out causes for the commission and incidence of deviant and criminal behavior. Why do certain individuals, or certain categories of individuals, violate the norms and break the laws? Why do they engage in certain forms of criminal and deviant behavior, that is, what are the *causes* of rape, murder, alcoholism, mental illness, prostitution, white-collar crime, and so on? What social conditions maximize norm and law violations? Why is deviance distributed one way in one society or type of society and a very different way in others? Some positivistic approaches are *individualistic* in that they focus on the characteristics of categories of individuals who violate norms or break the law. They argue that deviants share a trait or characteristic in common— which nondeviants lack—that can be isolated, which will help provide an explanation for deviance. Other positivistic approaches are more *structural* and *sociological*. They argue that certain *deviance-inducing conditions* share a common thread, trait, or characteristic that can be discovered, which will lead to an explanation of deviance, such as urbanism, anomie, society-wide income distributions, and so on. Either way, whether individual or structural, deviance is produced by these traits or conditions in a cause-and-effect fashion, which can be discovered and explicated by the scientifically inclined sociologist of deviance and crime.

Even though positivism cannot be regarded as a theory as such, several propositions can be teased out of the work of sociologists who adopt this position (Gove, 1980a, 1980b, 1982a; Nettler, 1984; Gottfredson and Hirschi, 1990; Wolfgang, Thornberry, and Figlio, 1987; Tracy, Wolfgang, and Figlio, 1990). These propositions sound very much like the common-sense maxim, "Cream rises to the top," or, since we are examining deviant and criminal behavior, "Mud falls to the bottom." To put things simply, positivism says *people get pretty much what they deserve*. Another way of saying this is: *The relationship between action and reaction is rational and nonproblematic*. This means that two general concepts underlie these statements.

First, norms and laws represent a rational attempt to protect society from the harm that deviants and criminals inflict. Rules, norms, and laws, therefore, do not vary much from society to society; we can examine criminals and deviants to discover cross-cultural and international regularities among them. The positivist rejects the central place that relativity has in the reactive, interactionist, or labeling school's approach. (which we'll look at in the next chapter). Deviance and crime are not relative, the positivist says, or at least not nearly so relative as the interactionists claim (Newman, 1976; Rossi et al., 1974). There are strong *commonalities* in the norms and laws that societies devise to protect themselves and their members from the objective harm that deviants and criminals can inflict. Norms and laws are *taken for granted* by the positivist. To put it another way, the creation and enforcement of norms and laws are not terribly interesting or worthy of study in relation to the positivistic approach. The norms and laws that exist, positivists believe, are devised for very common-sensical and obvious reasons. Why study this process when we already know what the answers are? If the positivist were to be asked, "Why study crime?" chances are, he or she would answer more or less as follows: "I study crime not because it distresses people, but because it *hurts* people, *tears* at the fabric of society, *damages* soci-

ety in a clearly observable, objectively determinable fashion. As a general rule, crime does not distress people arbitrarily or irrationally; rather, people tend to be concerned about crime because of the objective damage it inflicts on them, their loved ones, and society as a whole. Crime has certain *objective properties*, and one of them is social harm. And, since crime has features in common, it follows that there is something distinctive about persons who engage in it or social conditions that encourage it."

The second proposition that can be found in the positivist's approach to the study of deviance and crime takes the process a step further. Not only are the laws rational and their enactment nonproblematic, but likewise, the *enforcement* of norms and laws is rational and nonproblematic. In other words, people are evaluated and judged on the basis of what they *do, not* who they are. Contingencies, positivists hold, are not an important source of labeling or stigma. Deviants and criminals are labeled *as* deviants and criminals because they violate the norms and the laws of a society, *not* because of certain secondary or ancillary characteristics they might have, such as age, race, sex, and so on (Hindelang, 1974; Cohen and Stark, 1974; Nettler, 1974, 1984). Individuals who are committed to mental institutions *really are* crazy; individuals who are arrested, in all probability, r*eally did* commit a crime; individuals who are labeled as homosexuals by the community, in most cases, *really do* share a homosexual orientation; and so on. In short, the only really important question is: *Why do they do it?*

For instance, interactionists have been concerned with the process whereby some mentally disordered individuals are regarded by the public and by psychiatrists as mentally ill, while other individuals, equally disordered, are not so regarded. In short, interactionists study the contingencies involved in being labeled mentally ill (Goffman, 1961, pp. 135ff.; Scheff, 1966, 1974a, 1974b, 1984; Lemert, 1951, pp. 387–443, 1972, pp. 246–264; Rosenhan, 1973). In contrast, the positivistic approach argues that the psychiatric diagnostic process is fairly accurate and that individuals diagnosed as mentally ill, objectively speaking, r*eally are* crazy. The role of contingencies in the diagnostic process is insignificant. What counts is how crazy someone actually is (Gove, 1980b, 1982a). In short: "Some people are more crazy than others; we can tell the difference and calling lunacy a name does not cause it" (Nettler, 1974, p. 894).

The positivistic perspective in the study of deviance and crime has sustained criticism from adherents of other approaches. First, the strict scientific approach to social reality, its critics say, ignores the crucial dimension of the *subjective experience* (Blumer, 1969, pp. 2–6, 22–23, 37, 127–139; Matza, 1969; Goode, 1975, pp. 571–576). The most important quality of all behavior, the positivist's critics say, is its *meaning to the participants*. To study deviance primarily as objective, concrete behavior is to concentrate on the superficial features of actions. Behavior viewed strictly objectively, as a set of actions classified by the scientific observer, becomes seen as mechanical movements having no relevance to how they are classified and experienced by all concerned. Looking at another person, we see one eye close for an instant; is it a "wink" or a "blink"? (Geertz, 1973, pp. 6–7). While they are almost identical actions, their *meaning* is vastly different. Positivism's critics argue that by focusing on the outward, superficial features of acts and ignoring meaning, it ignores the heart of the social process. Two actions that are superficially and mechanically similar may mean very different things to the *participants* as opposed to the individuals who *react* to the participants and what they are doing. What something is, say the subjectively oriented sociologists, is entirely dependent on how it is interpreted by the relevant audiences, including the actor. In short, "Meaning is not inherent in the act; it must be constructed" (Douglas and Waksler, 1982, p. 24). An act "is" nothing until it is categorized, conceptualized, and interpreted. It is this subjective process that locates the act as a specific instance of a general type of behavior.

In one society, incest is defined by sex with both close and very distant relatives, sometimes encompassing half the society, village, or tribe in question. In another society, incest is committed only by having sex with a very small number of relatives, including parents, siblings, grandparents, aunts and uncles by blood, and first cousins on only one parent's side (Ford and Beach, 1951, pp. 112–113). Thus, the *same* mechanical action—intercourse between partners with a specific kinship relationship with one another—in one society is regarded and reacted to as incest, and in the other, it isn't. In prison, a great deal of sexual contact between inmates is not defined as homosexual in nature. The aggressive, hyper-macho man is seen as asserting his masculinity and heterosexuality by

having sex with a receptive, submissive, or more "passive" partner, whose submission to sexual acts *is* defined as homosexual in nature (Wooden and Parker, 1982). In some societies, all the young men must engage in ritual same-sex sexual contact with grown men in order to grow up and become warriors. Contact with women is regarded as polluting and feminizing; fellating grown men is seen as obtaining their masculine essence, necessary to becoming a man (Herdt, 1981, 1987, 1988). Clearly, in such a society, the *meaning* of same-sex sexual contact is vastly different from that which prevails in prison, and in the homosexual subculture outside prison. To refer to all three as "homosexuality" is misleading, even though, again, they appear to be outwardly similar. In other words, we may know very little when we know only the objective features of an act; to know it in a truly sociological fashion, critics of positivism say, we must know it *subjectively* as well.

A second objection the more subjectively oriented theorist launches against the positivistic study of deviance is a high degree of *skepticism toward determinism*. The notion of causality is extremely complex in human behavior and may, some say, not be valid at all. To say that one factor caused or causes another cannot be determined with any real degree of precision. In the case of an automobile accident, for example, is the *cause* the fact that the driver was intoxicated, that the road was slick from a sudden downpour, the fact that the driver swerved to avoid hitting a child on a bicycle who came zooming out of a side street, the driver feeling depressed, the fact that the driver was exceeding the speed limit, or the fact that the driver was a beginner behind the wheel? Are all these factors *a* cause? Or some combination of them? Unraveling the cause or causes of a fairly simple occurrence such as a single automobile accident is an extremely problematic and difficult matter (Douglas and Waksler, 1982, pp. 27–29). How much more difficult it is to do so for a broad or general phenomenon, such as crime, homosexuality, or alcoholism, that is participated in by millions of individuals and is reacted to by even more observers. Some positivistic sociologists (Hirschi and Selvin, 1966, 1967, pp. 114–136) argue that the complexity of the social world merely makes the job of tracing causality more difficult—but not impossible. However, some critics of the idea of causality in the study of deviance argue that this means that the researcher should be extremely skeptical of the whole idea of causality in the social world. The idea that phenomena that are constructed by subjective definitions can be accounted for by objective explanations may very well be a contradiction in terms.

Third, positivists have been accused of being overly naive concerning the question of *objectivity*. Many sociologists argue that true objectivity is an impossibility. Every observer is to a degree contaminated by personal, political, and ideological sympathies. We cannot avoid taking sides, this position argues (Becker, 1967). This does not mean that there is no such thing as a "fact." But it does mean that pursuing and reporting the facts is always enmeshed in ideological and political choices. Studying street crime automatically entails ignoring and implicitly deemphasizing the importance of white-collar crime. Studying a prison from the point of view of the convicts entails accepting their view of reality as true and setting aside the view of the guards and correctional officials. Conducting research on the factors that lead to revolutions in South America may result in supplying information to repressive regimes that can be helpful to them in crushing democratic reform or revolutions. Deciding to publish a study's findings that are technically and concretely true but might be damaging to certain oppressed groups or to the cause of justice always entails making a political choice—against the people and for "science for its own sake." Choosing to publish damaging but true findings is no more "objective" than choosing to ignore, suppress, or criticize those findings. Deciding to work on atomic weaponry because one wishes to "advance scientific knowledge" also automatically entails advancing the cause of the military.

One selects sociological issues to study on the basis of subjective criteria, not simply to advance knowledge in some abstract, pure, scientific fashion. If one uses the latter argument, one is deluding oneself, for one has made a choice in a sea of political and ideological dilemmas. Choosing to study one topic instead of another, and in a certain fashion, always has political and ideological implications and consequences. One can never remove oneself from the question of morals, ideology, and politics in doing social research. And it is specifically on these issues that the positivist—claiming to seek pure, objective scientific knowledge for its own sake, uncontaminated by the constraints and circumstances of the real world—is often remarkably naive. These ethical and ideological questions are so crucial that I devote the last chapter of this

book to a more extended discussion of their implications.

All the perspectives, theories, or schools that follow in this chapter—social disorganization, anomie or strain theory, learning theory, control theory, and what is referred to as a "general" theory of crime—are positivistic in nature. That is, all apply the natural science method to social phenomena. All of these theories stress objectivity, and believe that they should be testable or falsifiable by using empirical, qualitative evidence. They all seek a general explanation of criminal behavior, and stress specific cause-and-effect sequences in generating criminal behavior. None are especially interested in the social construction of deviance, that is, the creation of the criminal law or the contingencies or accidents of the labeling process. All the statements in the paragraphs above, therefore, apply to all the theories discussed below. If there are two halves to the phenomenon of deviance—how is it defined and what causes it—these theories are concerned more or less exclusively with the second of these two halves. *Why do they do it?* positivists ask; *what causes deviance?* Let's find out what answers they give to these questions.

SOCIAL DISORGANIZATION AND THE CHICAGO SCHOOL

Just after World War I, a school of thought emerged out of research that was conducted in the city of Chicago by professors and graduate students at the University of Chicago; Chicago sociology, in fact, came to be the sociology of Chicago (Downes and Rock, 1988, p. 62). This school came to view pathological traits as being located not in the person or individual, as the positive school saw it, but in the social structure. The Chicago school argued that *entire neighborhoods* become so disorganized that adapting to them entailed engaging in certain forms of deviant behavior. Urbanization set the stage for social disorganization. As cities grew, their residents increasingly came into contact with strangers. This encouraged impersonality, social distance, and a decline in social harmony. People no longer shared the same values or cared about how others felt about them and what they did. As a city grows, its sense of community breaks down. And as social disorganization in a given neighborhood or community increases, deviant behavior increases along with it (Park, 1926; Traub and Little, 1994, pp. 53–56).

Not all neighborhoods are equally disorganized, however, and therefore, rates of deviance vary from one area, neighborhood, or community to another. Certain neighborhoods of a city "give licence to nonconforming behavior" (Suchar, 1978, p. 74). Why? What is it about certain neighborhoods that makes them hospitable to delinquency, crime, and deviant behavior? Social disorganization theorists locate the mechanism influencing nonconforming behavior in land values. Dwelling units in neighborhoods with low rental and property value are regarded as undesirable and unattractive to live in. Such dwelling units tend to attract residents with two characteristics. First, they are geographically unstable; proponents of the Chicago school referred to such neighborhoods as *zones of transition*. Residents of these areas invest little emotionally in the neighborhood, and move out as soon as they can. And second, such residents are socially, racially, and ethnically heterogeneous; hence, they do not cohere into a unified and organized community. Residents who do not sink roots into the community in which they live do not care about its fate or what happens in it; residents who are very different from one another do not care about the evaluations that others make of their behavior. Such neighborhoods are unable to develop "strong formal and informal linkages" among their residents; hence, residents find it difficult to "regulate the behavior of their fellow neighbors" and exercise the kind of social control that would discourage delinquency, crime, and deviant behavior (Bursik and Grasmick, 1993, pp. x, 7). In short, Chicago sociologists insisted that deviance varies systematically by physical and geographical *location*. Where somebody is located residentially determines the likelihood of that person committing deviant and criminal acts; the structural characteristics of a neighborhood, that is, whether it possesses the properties mentioned above, determine its crime rate. Deviance is relatively absent in certain neighborhoods and extremely frequent, even routine, in others. The Chicago school placed a heavy emphasis on *social ecology*, the view that physical spacing and social interdependence determine, or at least heavily influence, human behavior.

In the study of deviant and criminal behavior, the Chicago school, with its emphasis on social disorganization, underwent a drastic decline in influence during the 1940s. Later researchers found that poor slum neighborhoods often exhibit a high degree of cohesion and social organization (Whyte,

1943) which the Chicago school adherents failed to recognize, simply because it was different from that which prevailed in more middle-class communities. The Chicago school suffered from what came to be regarded as a middle-class bias; that is, it assumed that behavior that departed from that of comfortable, respectable, small-town folk was "disorganized." They failed to see that many socially disapproved activities are committed frequently, even as much by the affluent, middle-class members of society as by representatives of the lower and working classes. The Chicago sociologists made the erroneous assumption that deviance was almost exclusively an underclass phenomenon. They examined street prostitution without considering the middle-class call girl, the skid-row alcoholic but not the affluent drunk, the street narcotic addict but not the middle-class recreational drug user. In addition, the school has been charged with focusing too much on factual detail ("description for its own sake") and too little on theory and explanation. Indeed, some charged, there was very little connection between the Chicago school's theories and the facts its researchers turned up. Its emphasis on urban zones and social ecology was said to be only very loosely related to the detailed empirical work of most Chicago school advocates (Downes and Rock, 1988, p. 84). In addition, it was often difficult to determine which were the independent and the dependent variables in the social disorganization scheme of things, that is, what caused what. Sometimes, formulations regarded *delinquency* as a measure of *disorganization*—a classic case of a proposition being true by definition.

The social disorganization school of deviance, with its emphasis on social disorganization, had its heyday between the two world wars, roughly from 1920 to 1940. By the end of World War II, it was widely regarded as obsolete. (The interactionist theorists of the 1960s, such as Howard Becker and Erving Goffman, are sometimes referred to as the *neo-Chicagoans,* since they engaged in detailed studies of deviant behavior. However, "neo-Chicago" sociology is radically different from its "Chicago school" parent, as we'll see in the next chapter.) In 1987, a sociologist claimed that the social disorganization school "has been soundly dismissed" (Unnever, 1987, p. 845). However, in the late 1980s and early 1990s, the social disorganization school made a comeback; a substantial volume of research and writing on deviance is making use of the Chicago school's approach, concepts, and theories. Even by 1993, when two criminologists (Bursik and Grasmick, 1993, p. 29) documented the resurgence of the social disorganization perspective, they predicted that their support of its utility was "likely to elicit groans from readers" who "failed to notice" recent research and theoretical developments. One of their colleagues claimed that social disorganization was the "herpes of criminology . . . once you think it is gone for good, the symptoms flare up again" (p. 30). Although it will never regain its former dominant status in the field, social disorganization theory is experiencing a renaissance. However, to reenergize this approach, some theoretical reformulations were necessary.

What the early social disorganization theorists did not entirely grasp was the dimension of power and its relevance for their analysis. They never figured out how important decisions that were made at the top of the power structure were for the life of the community. A municipality can build a highway that cuts a community in two, destroying contact between residents in the two halves. Bridges, highways, commercial buildings, housing projects, parks, beaches, are often built in, and serve to disrupt and destroy the foundation of once-viable communities. Factories can be moved from one community to another, siphoning jobs away from the first and into the second. Tax breaks and "sweetheart" deals can be extended to builders who tear down small houses inhabited by families with modest incomes in order to build big buildings that can be afforded only by residents who are rich. Zoning ordinances and variances are designed and implemented to favor certain interests over others. They reflect the exercise of power, and they influence the lives of residents of certain neighborhoods and communities. The fact is, the fate of communities and the behavior of their residents is tied to political and economic realities. A community's ties to the municipal, state, and federal power structure was not considered by the early social disorganization theorists; it is being considered currently by theorists who, in one way or another, are looking at deviance, crime, and other phenomena in part through the lens of the social disorganization perspective (Currie, 1993; Feagin and Parker, 1990). Thus, the classic or original social disorganization perspective did not take a number of factors or developments into consideration which current research indicates are crucial in the neighborhood-crime equation. Rather than seeing these deficiencies as fatal, however, some sociologists argue that the neglected factors or developments can be *grafted onto* the social disorganization perspective to produce a still-viable approach to the study of crime, delinquency, and deviance.

The first of these is the recognition that a *reciprocal* relationship between crime and disorganization may exist. That is, a high level of crime in a community may act as an independent variable, leading to an increase in a neighborhood's lack of desirability, disorder, and economic decline, thereby affecting disorganization which, in turn, increases its crime rate (Skogan, 1986, 1990). The original Chicago school theorists did not consider the possibility that there could be a two-way street between disorganization and crime; considering that possibility strengthens the perspective. Second, the social disorganization school of the 1920s and 1930s pictured areas of a city as stable, their crime rates being a function of their desirability which, in turn, was a function of their land values. Waves of succeeding ethnic groups moved into and out of them, but their socioeconomic composition resulted from the range of economic choices available to their residents. But recent research in urban sociology has shown that areas of cities are not stable, that many experience huge swings in fortune over time; some become "gentrified," with affluent residents moving in and less affluent ones moving out, while in others, there is a decline in economic fortune (Bursik and Grasmick, 1993, pp. 49–51). And third, social disorganization theorists saw neighborhood succession as something of a natural process. They rarely if ever considered the political and economic forces outside the community and its bordering neighborhoods as relevant to its social organization (Pfohl, 1994, pp. 183ff.; Feagin and Parker, 1990). How does a community influence City Hall to act on behalf of its own interests? What national and trans-national economic developments impact on a given local community? Why do some neighborhoods lose jobs while others remain prosperous? Has the impact of deindustrialization and the resulting loss in manufacturing jobs been different in African-American communities versus those which are predominantly white? To put the matter simply: The social disorganization researchers of the 1930s did not entirely grasp the importance of the dimension of *power* and its relevance in their analysis. They didn't incorporate the idea that decisions made at the top of the power structure could drastically and dramatically impact on the life of the communities they studied and hence, the deviant and criminal behavior that took place within them.

For instance, when urban planners bisect and destroy a community with a major highway, or displace a neighborhood through urban development, they know that they can do this because this community does not have friends in City Hall, in the state capitol, or in Washington. Much of what happens in a community results from who has powerful friends, what deals have been cut, and what ties are activated. The social disorganization theories made the mistake of assuming that effective community control was a matter of factors internal to a community, or how communities articulated or related with one another. But the resources a community can, or cannot, marshall often come as much from outside as from inside the community. These and other issues have to be examined to understand how the disorganization of a community impacts on its crime rate. Again, although the earlier generation of social disorganization theorists did not raise these issues, they can be used as tools to complement or modify the theory's classic formulations rather than as weapons to critique it to death. Social disorganization is being revived, as I said, but with a sharper, tougher, power-oriented edge. The idea of community control of deviance is being given a political thrust, which it did not have in the 1930s.

In addition, many observers saw something of the same middle-class bias in the social disorganization theory's view of deviance and crime as the earlier social pathology perspective displayed. In the 1930s, there was the view that middle-class values and behavior were superior to lower- and working-class values and behavior. Single-parent families are bad for children, illegitimacy is bad, drugs are bad, prostitution is bad, immigrants have to be socialized to mainstream, middle-class American values, and so on. Much of the field reacted against these biases. (Recall that in the 1960s, some sociologists regarded certain delinquent gangs as proto-revolutionaries, fighting against the status quo. This makes one realize how opposed some sociologists of the 1960s were to the social disorganization theorists' middle-class biases.) Today, progressives are rethinking their views on how some forms of deviance and crime impact on the life of the community. Much of what the social disorganization theorists said so long ago seems to be making sense. One has only to listen to the voices of African-American politicians to appreciate what crime does to a community's viability. When the police have become corrupt and cynical, when drug dealing is blatant, intrusive, and voracious, when criminal homicide becomes the leading cause of death among young, urban Black males, when children are gunned down on the street in a cross-fire between rival gangs, when middle- and working-class people with jobs leave the community for more peaceful neighborhoods and the children who remain have few employed adult role models—it is difficult to invoke the argument that we are resorting to preachy middle-class moralism when we examine the impact of deviance and crime. These are life- and-death issues; it has become necessary to consider how crime can be kept from victimizing and destroying the community. In short, the sense of communalism, which was once regarded as a conservative value, is being revived, brushed up, and given a progressive slant. Some observers now feel the Chicago school's "bias" was right all along.

In short, in spite of the limitations of the school's original formulations, some feel, the social disorganization model "is not a hoary old framework with little relevance to modern criminology." Rather, ongoing research on recent urban developments suggests that with these suggested modifications, the future of this approach "appears to be bright and exciting" (Bursik and Grasmick, 1993, p. 59).

The Chicago school made at least two major contributions to the study of deviance in addition to its general utility as an explanation of deviance and crime. The first is that it emphasized firsthand, up-close observation of a wide range of deviance. The Chicago sociologists used the city of Chicago as their natural laboratory, studying such topics as slum neighborhoods (Zorbaugh, 1929), juvenile delinquency (Thrasher, 1927; Shaw, 1929, 1930, 1931; Shaw and McKay, 1942), mental illness (Faris and Dunham, 1939), race and ethnic relations (Drake and Cayton, 1945), alcoholism among homeless vagrants (Anderson, 1923), prostitution (Reckless, 1926, 1933), suicide (Cavan, 1928), and narcotic addiction (Dai, 1937). The work of these early researchers was marked by a distaste for what they saw and the desire to improve existing conditions. At the same time, they felt some ambivalence as well, because their emphasis was on recording what they saw in detail; their work was *empirical* in that it attempted to view their segment of the society realistically, as it really was. In this emphasis lay a certain *appreciation* for what they studied (Matza, 1969, p. 18). Chicago sociologists rejected "armchair" research, that is, writing that is conducted without any contact with the real world. Chicago sociologists insisted that to find out what society is like, it is necessary to get out of one's armchair and get into the street and study the social world as it really exists.

The second contribution of the social disorganization, or Chicago, school was *empathy:* It asked readers to imagine that deviants, delinquents, and criminals were people much like themselves (Pfohl, 1994, p. 209). Since it located the cause of deviance not in biological defect but in neighborhood dislocation, social disorganization forced us all to realize that in the tide and fortune of a changing society, we, too, could have been caught up in the process of ecological transition. Deviants are the way they are as a result of the fact that they are "disproportionally exposed to the disruptive forces of rapid social change" (p. 209). If the rest of us were to be exposed to the same forces, we might very well have ended up doing or being the same thing.

These are major contributions. As we saw, after a long period of quiescence, social disorganization theory has become, once again, a major perspective in the field of criminology (Skogan, 1990; Bursik and Grasmick, 1993). However, it must be emphasized that its generalizations apply almost exclusively to delinquency as well as the more traditional, common-law, or "primal," crimes. Its applicability to many of the forms of deviance we'll be examining is far more tenuous. For instance, does it explain homosexuality? Of course not; in fact, with homosexuality, in many ways, the causal process works in a fashion which is precisely the *opposite* of that which social disorganization theory would predict. That is, in many large cities of the world, a substantial number of homosexuals gravitate *to* certain neighborhoods whose residents are less likely to harass them than those residents of neighborhoods which they left. Thus, here, in a sense, the dependent and independent variables are reversed. (It's even possible that in low-rent districts, where crime can often gain a foothold, homosexuality would be even *less* acceptable than in more affluent communities!) And, while the concomitants of social disorganization in a given community may contribute to alcoholism, just as likely, the streets of a disorganized community become a kind of magnet for homeless alcoholics.

White-collar crime receives no illumination whatsoever from social disorganization theory, of course; in fact, it is in the more affluent and least disorganized communities that white-collar criminals are most likely to live! For their livelihood, prostitution and pornography depend on men being able to make their way *to* a specific locale in a city, unimpeded and unharmed. If the crime rate were so high in a given community that customers were frightened off, these two commercial enterprises could not survive (Prus and Irini, 1980; Cohen, 1980). And, while the most virulent forms of drug abuse and addiction can almost certainly be accounted for by a revamped version of social disorganization theory, that is, one that takes into account external political and economic factors (Currie, 1993; Goode, 1997), the more casual, recreational forms of drug use that were so common in the 1970s and early 1980s remain unexplained by the Chicago school's approach. Are any of the forms of deviance that fall under the umbrella of "cognitive" and "political" deviance explained by social disorganization? It seems unlikely. In short, the distinction I made in the previous chapter between "hard" and "soft" forms of deviance apply here: Social disorganization theory is far better at illuminating "hard" deviance, behavior that is both illegal and deviant, what is generally referred to as "street" crime. For many of the forms of deviance that are not seriously criminal, or (as with white-collar crime) which are mainly middle- and upper-class actions, the perspective is either useless or marginal. And, since it is an etiological or causal approach, it is completely irrelevant to deviant traits or characteristics. Still, within its scope, social disorganization theory remains a vital and productive approach.

ANOMIE OR STRAIN THEORY

Anomie theory was born in 1938 with the publication of Robert Merton's article, "Social Structure and Anomie" (1938). Influenced by the nineteenth-century study, *Suicide,* by French sociologist Emile Durkheim (1897/1951), Merton was struck by the insight that deviant behavior could be caused by a disturbance in the social order, which Durkheim called *anomie*. When a society's stock market crashes and its citizens suddenly experience economic depression, its suicide rate increases; however, when a society suddenly experiences economic prosperity, its suicide rate also increases. Societies undergoing rapid industrialization experience significant increases in their rates of suicide. After Italy unified in 1870 and Germany in 1871, their suicide rates increased. These changes illustrate *disruptions in the traditional social order*, resulting in a state of anomie, followed by a form of deviance—suicide. Merton assumed that states of anomie influenced the frequency of deviant behavior. He reasoned that anomie must vary from one society to another and from one group or category in the same society; consequently, their rates of deviant behavior must also vary correspondingly. He reasoned that *"social structures exert a definite pressure upon certain persons in the society to engage in non-conforming rather than conforming conduct"* (Merton, 1957, p. 132). Certain pressures, Merton argued, could produce very *unconventional* behavior from very *conventional* origins and motives. Anomie theory is also referred to as *strain* theory, because it hypothesizes that a certain kind of strain, or pressure, produces deviant behavior.

In fashioning his argument, Merton reconceptualized anomie. In fact, in many ways, his theory was almost precisely the *opposite* of Durkheim's. To Durkheim, anomie was a disruption of the social order; it was characterized by a state of normlessness, where norms no longer gripped the populace or held them in check. It is the social order that restrains our behavior and our desires, holds them in check. The norms keep deviance in check; an absence of the norms—anomie—results in deviance. When periods of anomie prevailed, the populace was no longer guided by culturally approved appetites. Unlimited greed was the rule; human desires ran rampant. People no longer had any guidelines as to what is permissible and what is not, what is possible and what is not. Their lust for anything imaginable is unleashed.

Merton's conception of anomie was very different. In his view, deviance resulted not from a too-weak hold of society's norms on actors, as Durkheim did, but from actors *following* society's norms. In addition, Merton's conception of anomie was far more specific than Durkheim's. To Merton, anomie was conceptualized as a disjunction between *culturally defined goals* and *structurally available opportunities*. Culturally defined goals are "held out as legitimate objectives for all or for diversely located members of the society" (1957, p. 132). These goals, Merton claims, are widely shared; more or less everyone in the society wishes

to attain them. Merton shared Durkheim's view that anomie was instrumental in unleashing greedy behavior—behavior that is directed at attaining goals which, under different circumstances, would not be sought. Behind both Durkheim's and Merton's conceptions of anomie was a loud and vehement voice clamoring, "I want! I want!" However, for Durkheim, what unleashed this voice was a *disruption* of the social order. For Merton, *it was the social order itself* that released this voice. Our greedy and lustful desires are actually *created* by the social and cultural order, more specifically, as I said, *the lack of congruence* between the cultural order (that says we must become materially successful) and the social and economic order (which won't give us what we have been socialized to want and expect).

What are these culturally defined goals? In Western society, including the United States, they are, of course, primarily monetary and material success. "Making it," within the scope of the American Dream, involves being affluent—rich, if possible. Everyone in this society is bombarded on all sides by messages to achieve, to succeed. And success, for the most part, means only one thing: being able to buy the best that money can buy. This is an almost universal American value, a basic goal toward which nearly everyone aspires and by which nearly everyone is evaluated. A crucial point is that not all societies are so materialistic; some place an emphasis on entirely different goals, such as spirituality, wisdom, or learning.

Every society places certain limitations on how to achieve culturally defined goals. While everyone, or nearly everyone, in our society may value wealth, it is a separate question as to how we are permitted to acquire that wealth. Groups, institutions, and societies differ in their capacity to generate material goals, and in their restrictions as to how members may reach them. For instance, beating up, bribing, or having sexual intercourse with a professor are not considered legitimate means of achieving the goal of receiving an "A" in a course. Although any one of these methods may work from time to time, the social system of higher education in America frowns on them. They are not "acceptable modes" of reaching out for the goal of a high grade in this setting.

In contrast, in another social setting, the importance of the specific means to attain a certain goal may not matter very much, the specific means may be of little or no consequence; the condemnation of certain modes may be mild or nonexistent. Some societies place an extremely heavy emphasis on attaining a given goal, but remain fairly tolerant about how one goes about attaining it. Here we have a case of "winning at any cost." Merton maintains that we have just such a situation in contemporary America. Contemporary culture "continues to be characterized by a heavy emphasis on wealth as a basic symbol of success, without a corresponding emphasis on the legitimate avenues on which to march toward this goal" (1957, p. 139). We have an acquisitive society, in which "considerations of technical expediency" rule supreme. The basic question becomes: "Which of the available procedures is most efficient in netting the culturally approved value?" (1957, p. 135). In other words, it is less important just how one makes it; the important thing, above all, is *making it* (Krim, 1961, pp. 32–38).

In contemporary America, we have a conflict between the *culture* (what people are taught to aspire to) and the *social and economic structure* (the opportunities they have to succeed). We have, in other words, a *malintegrated* society. Aspirations cannot possibly be met by the available material resources. While the aspirations of the population are unlimited, their actual chances of success are quite limited. This creates pressure to commit deviance. "It is only when a system of cultural values extols, virtually above all else, certain *common* success-goals *for the population at large* while the social structure rigorously restricts or completely closes access to approved modes of reaching these goals *for a considerable part of that same population,* that deviant behavior ensures on a large scale" (Merton, 1957, p. 134). "It is. . . . my central hypothesis," Merton wrote, "that aberrant behavior may be regarded sociologically as a symptom of disassociation between culturally prescribed aspirations and socially structured avenues for realizing these aspirations" (1957, p. 134). By itself, an ambitious monetary goal for the population will not produce a high rate of crime; by itself, the lack of opportunities to achieve that goal, likewise, does not produce a great deal of crime. It is their *combination* or *conjunction* that imparts American society with an almost uniquely, almost devastatingly, high predatory crime rate among Western societies.

How do people who are subject to these conflicting pressures adapt to or react to them? What styles of conflict resolution should we expect from dwellers witnin this type of social structure? Just what types of deviance should we predict for success-hungry Americans? Merton drew up a typology of different responses to goal attainment and legitimate versus illegitimate means of attaining these goals.

Conformity, or the *conformist* mode of adaptation, accepts both cultural values of success and the institutionalized, legitimate, or conventional means for reaching these goals. The conformist both strives for material success and chooses law-abiding ways of achieving success. This mode of adaptation is not of interest to the student of deviance except as a negative case. It is in the typology simply for the purpose of comparing it with various forms of deviance. Becoming an accountant, a physician, a lawyer, and striving for material success by becoming successful in one's profession—becoming affluent through a legal, legitimate profession, performed in a law-abiding, respectable fashion—is an example of the most common mode of adaptation: *conformity*. In fact, given the strength of the success values in this society, and given the relatively limited opportunities for genuine success for the population at large—indeed, given that most Americans *fail* to achieve their own standards of material success—it is surprising that so many Americans are conformists when it comes to enacting serious deviance. Conformity is not, in any case, deviance.

The mode of adaptation Merton called *innovation* involves accepting the goal of success but choosing to achieve it in an illegal, illegitimate, or deviant fashion. This adaptation is clearly the most interesting of all modes to Merton; he devoted more space to describing it than all the other modes combined. The innovative mode of adaptation occurs when someone has "assimilated the cultural emphasis upon the goal without internalizing the institutionalized norms governing ways and means for its attainment" (1957, p. 141). An innovative mode of adaptation to the pressures of American culture and society would encompass most types of money-making criminal activities, for example, white-collar crime, embezzlement, pickpocketing, running a confidence game, bank robbery, burglary, prostitution, and pimping.

In contrast, *ritualism* entails "the abandoning or scaling down of the lofty cultural goals of great pecuniary success and rapid social mobility," but abiding "almost compulsively by institutionalized norms" (1957, pp. 149–150). The ritualist plays it safe, plays by the book, doesn't take chances. The mode of ritualism as an adaptation to American society's heavy emphasis on success is a kind of *partial* withdrawal—an abandonment of the goal of success, but a *retention* of the *form* of doing things properly, following all the rules to the letter. In many ways, ritualism is a kind of *overconformity*. "It is, in short, the mode of adaptation of individually seeking a *private* escape from the dangers and frustrations which seem to them inherent in the competition for major goals and clinging all the more closely to the safe routines and the institutionalized norms" (p. 151). A petty bureaucrat, who insists that all rules and regulations be followed in every detail, would exemplify this mode of adaptation. In this case, the rules are adhered to, but their purpose—presumably, serving the public—has been forgotten, in fact, *subverted* by a rigid adherence to the rules.

Retreatism is a rejection of both goals and institutionalized means. It is a total cop-out, a "retreat" from the things that the society values most. Retreatists are "true aliens." "Not sharing the common frame of values, they can be included as members of the *society* (in distinction from the *population*) only in a fictional sense." In this category Merton places "some of the adaptive activities of psychotics, autists, pariahs, outcasts, vagrants, vagabonds, tramps, chronic drunkards, and drug addicts" (1957, p. 153). This mode occurs, with most who adopt it, because the individual adopts the success value, but fails to attain it (being unwilling or unable to use illegitimate means, or is a failure even after attempting to achieve success by using illegitimate means). Retreatism, in short, is brought on by repeated failure, such failure causing severe personal conflict. "The conflict is resolved by abandoning *both* precipitating elements, the goals and the means. The escape is complete, the conflict is eliminated, and the individual is asocialized" (pp. 153–154). Merton feels that this mode of adaptation is the least frequently discussed so far.

Rebellion "involves a genuine transvaluation." It is an attempt to deal with the dominant goals and means by overthrowing them altogether. While the retreatist merely rejects them and puts nothing in their place, the rebel renounces prevailing values and introduces an alternative social, political, and economic structure, one in which the current stresses and strains presumably would not exist. The act of revolution would be a clear-cut case of rebellion. Merton devotes the least attention to this mode.

The anomie theory of Robert K. Merton exerted an enormous impact on the field of the sociology of deviance for decades after its initial publication in 1938; Cole and Zuckerman (1964) list more than 80 studies published prior to 1964 that made use of the concept of anomie. (Merton's original article was expanded and reprinted as a chapter in Merton's classic *Social Theory and Social Structure* in 1949, 1957, and 1968.) In fact, it is measurably the most cited work ever written by a sociologist. At the same time, the perspective has attracted considerable criticism.

Middle-class Bias. Anomie theory, some critics say, suffers from the same middle-class bias that distorted all earlier theories of deviance: It made the assumption that lower- and working-class people commit acts of crime and deviance *in general* significantly more frequently than is true of the members of the middle class. Today, most observers readily admit that "street" crime is committed more often by individuals at or toward the bottom of the class structure than is true of those at or near the top. Yet—and here is where the problem enters—there are many criminal and deviant actions that are equally as likely, or even more likely, to be engaged in by the more affluent, prestigious, well-educated, and powerful members of society. Although official police statistics on who commits crimes show that crime is a predominantly lower-class phenomenon, it is now clear that the specific crimes that middle- and upper-middle-class people commit are those that are far less likely to result in police attention and action than are the ones that lower- and working-class individuals commit. This is especially the case for white-collar and corporate crimes—the crimes of the rich and the powerful. How can we explain the multi-million-dollar swindles perpetrated by extremely wealthy and successful traders on the stock market, for example, by the anomie scheme? Homosexuality is technically illegal in nearly half the states of the United States; it very rarely results in arrest and yet, is most decidedly deviant in most social circles. It is a form of deviance that does not vary much by social class; hence, it contradicts Merton's theory that deviance is primarily a product of status frustration.

Irrelevance of Anomie for Most Forms of Deviance. At one point, Merton claims that anomie theory "is designed to account for some, not all, forms of deviant behavior, customarily described as criminal or delinquent" (1957, p. 178). Yet in other places, he makes a case for anomie being the major cause of deviance in general. Deviance, he says, "is a symptom of disassociation between culturally prescribed aspirations and socially structured avenues for realizing these aspirations" (p. 134). Again, Merton writes, "It is *only* when" goals and means are disjunctive that "*deviant behavior ensues on a large scale*" (p. 146; my emphasis). Though Merton "is vague as to which behavior is covered by this explanation and which is not" (Clinard, 1964b, p. 19), he clearly believes that *rates* of deviance vary by degree of anomie. Consequently, though some forms of deviance may be exempt from the theory (Merton never explains which ones are, however), deviance *in general* is supposedly explained by it.

Although the malintegration between means and goals that characterizes contemporary American society will typically put pressure on many members to engage in certain forms of deviance, *most forms of deviant behavior will not be produced by the pressure of such malintegration.* Merton's theory is not an explanation of deviant behavior in general, as he claims, but a delineation of some of the possible outcomes of a certain kind of strain presumably induced by specific social and economic factors. The anomie scheme turns out to be largely *irrelevant* to *most* forms of deviant behavior. Activities such as nonaddicting recreational drug use, assault, criminal homicide, petty gambling, adultery, child molestation, the consumption of pornography, holding unconventional beliefs, and, once again, homosexuality, and so on *are completely unexplained by the anomie theory.*

Can the primary locus of the origin of mental illness truly be placed at the feet of frustrated success strivings? Did the alternate lifestyles and countercultural movements of the 1960s really arise out of the need to escape the rat race? Or did their adherents simply find them a more viable and comfortable way of living than materially successful conventionality? Did the bohemian of the 1920s, the "beat" of the 1950s, the hippie of the 1960s arise out of an "adaptive response" to the disjunction between the goals and means dictated by American society? Is financial disaster behind the alcohol consumption and destructive behavior of most alcoholics? Does the delinquent fit into the means-ends scheme at all? Are most suicides a result of the failure to achieve success values? In

1964, a team of experts argued that anomie failed to adequately account for gang delinquency (Short, 1964), mental disorder (Dunham, 1964), drug addiction (Lindesmith and Gagnon, 1964), and alcoholism (Snyder, 1964), indeed, for deviance in general (Lemert, 1964a). There are serious problems with all the forms of deviance claimed by Merton to fit into the anomie paradigm—*with the exception of innovation.* It seems almost intuitively obvious that when a culture places a heavy emphasis on a goal but far less stress on how one achieves that goal, a lot of people are going to figure out a not quite approved way of achieving it rather than stubbornly continuing to follow a thoroughly approved method that doesn't work.

Deviance: Normative Violation or Social Disapproval? Closely related to the point made about most varieties of deviant behavior is the problem that much behavior that is classified by the anomie scheme *is not really deviant at all.* If only a minor stress is placed on how one reaches the major goals in a society, then one will not be condemned for employing supposedly illegitimate means. To the extent that one's choice of the means to attain a given goal is irrelevant or morally neutral, employing those means is not a form of deviance. To the extent that choosing certain means to attain a given goal (for instance, cheating on an exam to receive an "A" in a course) is mildly disapproved of, it is an act representing only a mild form of deviance. To the extent that a technical violation of the rules generates no punitive reaction from others at all, again, are we really discussing a form of deviance? (Erikson, 1964). Merton defines deviance as the violation of institutionalized expectations. But he is really discussing a situation where formally enunciated rules exist ("don't cheat on exams"), the institutionalization of which has partly or completely broken down at the personal level. If cheating does not bring down punishment or condemnation upon the head of the cheater, then it is no longer a form of deviant behavior, regardless of what the formal rules state.

Absence of Value Consensus. Merton's theory rests on the assumption that the lust for monetary success is suffused more or less homogeneously through the society, that members of all social classes aspire, above all, to become rich—to "make it" in financial terms. Some sociologists disagree. They argue that American society is extremely heterogeneous with respect to success values (Hyman, 1953; Lemert, 1964a; Taylor, Walton, and Young, 1973, pp. 104–105). A number of different values are stressed in the many social circles and groups in this multi-cultural society. Members of the lower and working classes, they claim, tend to be satisfied with fairly modest levels of economic success; many are happy just to be able to put food on the table, pay the bills, and avoid homelessness. Among academics, professional success is relatively independent of monetary rewards. In some social circles, spiritual values, friends, an emphasis on the family, or having a good time, rank first in value. A plurality of goals is sought in a diversity of subcultural groups; Merton's emphasis on money as paramount is an inaccurate characterization of American society.

Political Naivete. Merton does not "draw out the radical policy implications of his argument" (Messner and Rosenfeld, 1994, p. 60). Granted, the source of the extraordinarily high rate of crime in American society is a disjunction between material aspirations and avenues for their attainment. Aside from reducing those aspirations, what's going to lower that rate of crime? Merton failed to spell it out: radical change, resulting in a massive redistribution of society's resources (Pfohl, 1994, pp. 288–289; Taylor, Walton, and Young, 1973, p. 101). Inequality is inherent in capitalist society, and in American society, inequality may very well reach something of a pinnacle in Western capitalism. Reduce that inequality, many argue, and the crime rate will decline correspondingly. The limited, moderate reforms that have been inspired by strain theory (Mobilization for Youth in Harlem, for instance) have done little to provide upward mobility for poor, inner-city, minority youngsters. Such programs cannot possibly alter the fact that a true socialist revolution is the only solution to American society's crippling rate of predatory crime, or so some of anomie theory's more radical critics claim.

Actually, as two supporters of anomie and chroniclers of its renaissance have astutely pointed out, this criticism is misplaced (Messner and Rosenfeld, 1994, pp. 61–62). It is true that in the United States, an undue emphasis on achievement for all, combined with limited access to avenues to success, does encourage criminal behavior for members of the lower and working classes, since they are least likely to succeed. But in a true meritocracy, where access to success would be distributed solely by ability, the pressure to commit crime would not be *eliminated* so much as *shifted* from one sector of the society to another. By expanding opportunities for the talented members of the lower rungs of the society, it is true, this segment of the society would commit crime less. On the other hand, the truly untalented and unskilled—at whatever class level—would *still* be enculturated to succeed and still be unable to do so. Hence, in such a society, someone, somewhere, will feel a strong pressure to commit crime. A democratic and equalitarian opportunity structure will simply "redistribute" crime "to different individuals" (p. 62). Sure, a true meritocracy would be a great deal *fairer* than our present system. But instituting it would *not* represent a crime control strategy. The crime problem rests in the apple, not in how it is divided up.

In the generation or two following its initial publication, anomie theory was criticized, extended, added to, and amended (Clinard, 1964a). Perhaps the two most well-known friendly additions to Merton's anomie theory have been Cohen's status frustration theory and Cloward and Ohlin's illegitimate opportunities theory. Both focus more or less exclusively on juvenile delinquency. And both represent something of a blend or synthesis between anomie or strain theory and subcultural theory, to be discussed next. Both locate the ultimate source or origin of deviance in anomie or strain. But both argue that Merton failed to understand the step that is *intermediate* between anomie and committing deviance—and that intermediate step is the creation of a delinquent subculture. Both Cohen and Cloward and Ohlin devised an explanation that accounted for that intermediate or intervening step.

Albert Cohen: Status Frustration

Albert Cohen (1955) agreed with Merton in arguing that American society indiscriminately measures members of all social classes according to a middle-class standard. And, like Merton, Cohen argued that individuals at the bottom of the class structure are less likely to be successful according to this standard; they will feel inferior and will therefore experience pressure and strain. For Merton, however, *material success* was the main focus of middle-class values; when Americans fail to achieve material and monetary success, they feel strain. In contrast, for Cohen, the failure to achieve status was the main source of strain for most individuals located in the lower and working classes.

Why are members of the lower and working classes most subject to strain? Although they are under exactly the same pressure to succeed as the middle- and upper-classes, they are less equipped and less well connected to be able to do so. The cards are stacked against the lower-class boy, Cohen argued. The status system—the one that prevails in the educational system, for example—is totally dominated by middle-class figures and middle-class values. The lower-class boy (and Cohen's theory focused almost entirely on boys) grows up in a middle-class society and is judged by a "middle-class measuring rod." Middle-class values include academic achievement, rationality, the control of physical aggression and violence, delaying gratification, wholesomeness, a respect for property, and displaying manners and courtesy toward others. In contrast, the lower-class masculine culture cultivates irrationality, impulsiveness, a display of physical aggression and violence, and carelessness with property. How can the lower-class boy possibly achieve status in a society in which everything he has learned is disvalued, and the opposite of what he has learned is specifically what generates status? It is a system in which lower-class boys are *doomed* to failure.

As a consequence of ending up at "the bottom of the heap," the lower-class boy faces a status problem: how to achieve dignity, respect, and status in such a ranking system. According to Cohen, the answer is for him to overturn the dominant, middle-class status system by regarding as bad that which middle-class society values. Everything is turned on its head. Since lower-class boys are "denied status in the respectable society because they cannot meet the criteria of the respectable status system," they value status criteria that they *can* meet (Cohen, 1955, p. 121). This entails giving free rein to violence and aggression, destroying property, freely gratifying their hedonistic impulses, failing in school—and being proud of it—being nasty, disrespectful, and impolite to others, especially middle-class authority figures. In Cohen's scheme, *the delinquent gang is a solution to the lower-class boy's problem of status frustration*. It is a way of substituting a new value system for the traditional middle-class one—a value system that has criteria by which the lower-class boy can now achieve status.

There are at least three major differences between Merton's original anomie theory and Cohen's addition to it. First, as I said above, Merton stressed the achievement of *material success,* while Cohen stressed the achievement of *status* as the key engine in generating deviant behavior.

Second, Merton's most important adaptation to the stress of anomie, innovation, is *utilitarian* in nature. That is, the lack of material success is the problem, and Merton's innovators solve that problem by going out and achieving material success in a rational, pragmatic fashion, albeit unconventionally. In contrast, Cohen stressed a *nonutilitarian* adaptation to status frustration—destroying property, failing in school, fighting, and so on. To Cohen, the stealing that the lower-class boy engages in is not a utilitarian attempt to acquire material goods, because, he believes, the boy is casual with those goods, often destroying or discarding them after they have been acquired.

The third difference between Cohen's status frustration and Merton's anomie is that Merton's scheme was atomistic or individualistic. In contrast, Cohen's theory was tightly focused on how solutions to the problem of status frustration are hammered out in a group or interactional setting. Cohen is interested in how boys devise a specifically delinquent *subculture*. (In fact, Cohen's theory belongs almost as much to the subcultural school, which I discuss next, as it does to anomie or strain theory.) For Merton, people work out adaptations to anomie more or less in isolation. He did not supply any group or interactional mechanism for working out solutions to the problem of blocked success strivings. For Cohen, it is only by experiencing status problems *in the presence of others who share the same problems that the solutions are arrived at.* By interacting with other boys who share the same status frustration, they devise or hit upon a delinquent "solution" to their problem. *This solution is the delinquent subculture.* Once devised, the delinquent subculture takes on a life of its own, and is passed down from one slightly older gang member to a slightly younger one. While the *origin* of the delinquent solution is status frustration, the *mechanism* for its promulgation is subcultural. Some observers of theories of deviance even classify Cohen's status frustration explanation of working-class delinquency as a subcultural theory (Curran and Renzetti, 1994, pp. 153ff.). The fact is, according to Cohen, it is anomie that generated the motives to fashion a delinquent subculture; hence, his theory must be regarded as a distinctively anomie or strain theory of deviance. The engine or locomotive of the theory is anomie; it is accurate to regard it as a *modification* of anomie theory. But it does make use of some subcultural ideas, so perhaps it can be seen as a *synthesis* of or *blend* between anomie and subcultural theory.

Although Cohen's status frustration theory is regarded as interesting and elegant and is often cited in the delinquency literature, today, few researchers take it seriously as an explanation of the origin of the delinquent subculture. While most observers agree that the *process* by which subcultural innovations are established is much as Cohen explained it, that is, through a sounding-out interactional process, nearly all see the *content* of the lower-class delinquent subculture in very different terms from Cohen's. There are at least two major problems with the theory.

First, it is clear that lower-class boys are not so totally wrapped up in the middle-class value system that they feel themselves to be failures as measured by it. While material success is, indeed, a widely shared American value, one that is, moreover, strongly held at or near the bottom of the class system, few of the other accompaniments of middle-class culture discussed by Cohen are of much concern to the lower-class boy. Cohen has clearly overstated the power and impact of middle-class values on the lower-class boy. Walter Miller's theory of the lower-class subculture (1958), to be discussed shortly, which posits a certain independence between lower- and middle-class subcultures, seems more accurate on this point.

The second serious, indeed fatal, flaw in Cohen's theory is that it fails completely in delineating lower-class delinquent culture as materially *nonutilitarian* and *destructive*. It is possible that Cohen's portrait was true in a previous generation, when he wrote (1955). Today, however, lower-class boys, if anything, are even more materialistic than members of the middle class. They steal (and today, sell drugs), and when they do, it is specifically to acquire material goods, such as 10-speed bikes, even cars, gold chains, watches and other jewelry, electronic gadgets, and sneakers. (When stores are looted during civil disturbances, the most popular items that are stolen are expensive sneakers.) Far from destroying or discarding them, they value them no less than their middle-class counterparts. Their orientation is clearly highly utilitarian and super-materialistic. The lower-class boy embraces and adapts some middle-class values while he simultaneously discards others. There is anything but a wholesale rejection of middle-class values in the lower-class delinquent subculture. In short, Cohen's theory of status frustration seems not to explain or characterize delinquency very well. It is entirely possible that status frustration does have a major impact on some forms of deviant behavior, but the mechanism through which it operates is quite different from the way Cohen proposed.

Cloward and Ohlin: Illegitimate Opportunities

A second major extension of Merton's anomie theory may be found in Richard Cloward and Lloyd Ohlin's *illegitimate opportunity* scheme (Cloward, 1959; Cloward and Ohlin, 1960). Cloward and Ohlin agreed with Merton in insisting that the lower and working classes have been encouraged to strive for material success. They agreed that they are more likely to find this goal blocked and frustrated, to have far more restricted access to legitimate opportunities for success, and to feel more strain because of it. And they agreed that these strains and pressures produce more deviant behavior, at least of the innovative type, on the part of members of the lower and working classes. So far, their respective theories are much the same. Where Cloward and Ohlin depart from Merton's anomie theory was in insisting that while *legitimate* opportunities for success are more accessible to the middle classes, *illegitimate* opportunities are *not* equally accessible to all lower- and working-class individuals. Merton simply assumed that all lower- and working-class individuals have equal opportunities to engage in illegal, illegitimate, criminal, and deviant activities. You want to earn money by robbing a bank? Just go out and do it! Prostitution, pimping? No problem—just find your customers! Of course, the problem is that some people may *fail* to achieve monetary success at criminal enterprises, just as some fail to become affluent at those that are legitimate; still, Merton assumed that all had equal illegitimate *opportunities* to "make it" in the deviant world.

As Cloward and Ohlin pointed out, it is not that easy to become successful in illegal, illegitimate, criminal, and deviant activities, especially innovative ones. In fact, opportunities to do so are differentially distributed; they are abundant in some neighborhoods and scarce in others. Some slums are what Cloward and Ohlin called "integrated"; that is, adult professional gangsters and criminals live and operate there and are visible, even respected, community figures. The talented, daring, ambitious youth living in such a neighborhood will be recruited from a delinquent gang that spe-

cializes in money-making crime, eventually grad-
uating to full-time, full-fledged careers in theft and
other professional crime. Thus, the first type of
delinquent gang that exists is the *criminal* subculture: those that specialize in money-making crimes.
Youths living in neighborhoods that lack such figures or organized structures cannot "make it" as
criminals; they do not have the opportunity to do so.
Such youths lack illegitimate opportunities; they
are unlikely to devise a successful, full-scale illegitimate adaptation on their own; hence, their success striving, blocked in the illegitimate realm, will
in all likelihood remain unfulfilled.

In slums where networks of gangsters, racke-
teers, and other professional criminals are lacking,
youths who feel strain to achieve have no real illegitimate opportunity to satisfy that need. So, a second type of subculture or gang that may serve to
satisfy success strivings is the *conflict* gang. Again,
such subcultures are differentially available to
lower-class youngsters. The lower-class youngster
whose aspirations for success are blocked both by
the legitimate and the illegitimate achievement
structures (or who have failed to achieve in both)
may have the opportunity to achieve status through
violence in gang warfare. The lower-class youngster who lives in a neighborhood where such gangs
do not exist, or who cannot meet the requirements
of violent activities, will be defined as a failure—
indeed, a double failure. Again, illegitimate opportunities to achieve are not available to all. Violence
can be an answer to some youngsters' otherwise
blocked achievement aspirations. But for others,
this is not an available option, owing to the lack of
illegitimate opportunities in certain neighborhoods.

Youngsters who have failed to make it in the
legitimate, law-abiding world, in the crime- and
conflict-oriented illegitimate worlds, turn to drugs.
Hence, a third subculture or type of gang that may
provide a solution for blocked aspirations is, according to Cloward and Ohlin, the so-called *retreatist*
gang. The retreatist subculture has its locus in a
drug-using gang; they "retreat" into the dreamy,
undemanding endeavor of getting high. Retreatists
are double failures because of their failure in the
legitimate and the illegitimate opportunity structures. There is nothing left for them to do but to
get high. Their aspirations are totally blocked.
Using drugs in a gang setting provides an escape
for them, a way of relieving the strain they feel for
their across-the-board catastrophic failure.

Like Cohen's theory, Cloward and Ohlin's is

more noteworthy for its theoretical innovation and
conceptual elegance than for its empirical support.
In fact, the evidence to verify the illegitimate opportunity structure explanation of delinquency has
been found to be more or less completely lacking
(Shoemaker, 1984, p. 118). The theory predicts that
blocked economic aspirations are the source of
delinquent behavior, but as a general rule, juvenile
delinquents have *lower* aspirations than nondelinquents—the opposite of what Cloward and Ohlin
predict. In addition, although many lower-class
youths do, indeed, have relatively high aspirations,
in some studies, nearly as high as middle-class
youths, most make a distinction between aspirations and realistic expectations, that is, anticipated
success, what they expect to achieve monetarily
and occupationally. Cloward and Ohlin (as well as
Merton and Cohen) assume that youths' aspirations
are what determine their involvement in illegitimate activities. In fact, what we see is that having
realistic material expectations inhibits the kind of
strain these theorists predicted would result in criminal activity. Moreover, the discrepancy between
aspiration and expectation seems to be roughly the
same for delinquents and nondelinquents.

Another problem with Cloward and Ohlin's theory is that it mistakenly assumes delinquent gangs
are specialized as to activity—theft, violence, and
drug use. Although this may have been true in the
1950s and early 1960s, it is not true today. This is
especially untrue for drugs: Nearly all delinquent
gangs use illegal drugs, although in varying degrees.
Some delinquent gangs are devoted more or less
entirely to stealing, and engage in violence only
when they have to; others are more focused on violence, and steal intermittently, on impulse. Moreover, gangs that are heavily involved in drug use
always do a great deal of stealing. And when stealing becomes common, this *almost inevitably* entails
an escalation in violence. *Most* delinquent gangs
steal, do drugs, *and* engage in violence. Cloward
and Ohlin's characterization of gang specialization
is largely a fantasy. Gangs, for the most part, do
not specialize as the theory predicts.

Anomie Theory into the 1990s and Beyond

As we saw, Merton's "Social Structure and
Anomie" (1938) is the most frequently cited single article in the history of sociology; in the 1950s
and 1960s, anomie theory was the most frequently

used theoretical tradition in the study of deviance and crime (Cole and Zuckerman, 1964; Cole, 1975). But by the late 1960s, the perspective underwent a sharp decline in influence, and during the 1970s and early-to-mid-1980s, it seemed as if it would disappear from the field altogether, tossed onto the "dustbin of history." In 1978, in a detailed appraisal of theories of deviance, crime, and delinquency, Ruth Kornhauser stated: "Strain models are disconfirmed" (p. 253). She advised that sociologists seeking an explanation of delinquency, crime, and deviance forget anomie theory and turn their attention elsewhere (p. 180). But, as with social disorganization theory, some time in the late 1980s to the early 1990s, anomie theory underwent a renaissance. Some of the most potent of the theory's criticisms have been answered (to the satisfaction of some observers, although not to others), while other, less serious ones, have been ignored, and still others have prompted a revamping or reformulation of anomie theory. As with the social disorganization framework, anomie or strain theory will never recapture its former glory as the field's preeminent approach to the study of deviance. However, judging by a recent rebirth in research and writing adopting the theory as a lens with which to examine deviant phenomena, it remains as vital as ever (Messner and Rosenfeld, 1994). In 1995, a substantial volume of papers, each in its own way praising the anomie approach, was published bearing the title, *The Legacy of Anomie Theory* (Adler and Laufer, 1995). While it has its detractors, the anomie theory is being born again; it is not likely to go away any time soon.

DIFFERENTIAL ASSOCIATION: LEARNING THEORY

In 1939, in the third edition of a criminology textbook written by sociologist Edwin Sutherland (1883–1950), a major theory of deviance was propounded for the first time (Sutherland, 1939). It was called the theory of *differential association,* and it has become one of a small number of important perspectives in the field. Sutherland set for himself two somewhat different but overlapping tasks. The first was to explain what he referred to as *differential group organization:* why crime rates vary among different groups of people, why a criminal tradition was endemic in certain social circles. The second task was to explain why some *individ-uals* engage in crime more than other individuals. Unfortunately, Sutherland did not develop his ideas on differential group organization in much detail. In contrast, he did spell out the individual processes behind criminality fully and in detail, and this is his theory of differential association.

The first and most fundamental proposition of the theory of differential association states that criminal behavior, and by extension, deviance as well, is *learned.* This proposition was directed against biological theories which assert that crime is caused by genetic, metabolic, or anatomical defects, and against the view that criminal behavior is hit upon accidentally or through independent invention. Hardly anyone, Sutherland asserted, stumbles upon or dreams up a way to break the law; this must be passed on from one person to another in a genuine learning process. The theory of differential association also opposed the view that mental illness or an abnormal, pathological personality is a major causal factor in the commission of criminal behavior. Rather, Sutherland argued, crime is learned in a straightforward, essentially normal fashion, no different from the way in which members of American society learn to speak English or brush their teeth.

A second proposition of the theory of differential association is that criminal behavior, and again, by extension, deviance as well, must be learned through face-to-face interaction between people who are close or intimate with one another. People are not persuaded to engage in criminal behavior as a result of reading a book or a newspaper, seeing a movie, or (today, as opposed to 1939) watching television. Criminal knowledge, skills, sentiments, values, traditions, and motives are all passed down as a result of *interpersonal*—not impersonal—means. Two major factors that intensify this process are *priority* and *intensity.* The earlier in one's life one is exposed to attitudes and values (which Sutherland called "definitions") favorable to committing crimes, the greater the likelihood that one will in fact commit crime. And the closer and more intimate the friends, relatives, and acquaintances that endorse committing crime, likewise, the more swayed one will be to break the law.

Sutherland's theory, then, argued that people who embark upon engaging in criminal behavior *differentially associate* with individuals who endorse violations of the law. Notice that the theory does not say that one needs to associate with actual criminals to end up breaking the law oneself, only that one should be more heavily exposed to *definitions* favorable to criminal actions. One can be exposed to law-abiding definitions emanating from criminals and criminal definitions emanating from law-abiding individuals (though, of course, it usually works the other way around). Still, as most of us know, "actions speak louder than words," and one wonders how much more of an impact the example of criminal actions has than criminal words.

In sum, Sutherland's theory of differential association holds that a person becomes delinquent or criminal because definitions favorable to the violation of the law exceed definitions unfavorable to the violation of the law. The key to this process is the *ratio* between definitions favorable to the violation of the law to definitions that are unfavorable. When favorable definitions exceed unfavorable ones, an individual will turn to crime (Conklin, 1995, p. 256).

The theory of differential association has been criticized for being vague and untestable (Sutherland and Cressey, 1978, p. 91; Gibbons, 1992, pp. 179–180; Conklin, 1995, p. 257). Later efforts to refine and operationalize the theory (Burgess and Akers, 1966; DeFleur and Quinney, 1966) have not been entirely successful in rescuing it from imprecision. Exactly how would a researcher measure this ratio of favorable to unfavorable definitions of violations of the law? And exactly how could "favorable" and "unfavorable" be indicated or measured? Even one of the theory's staunchest defenders admits that Sutherland's formulation of the differential association process "is not precise enough to stimulate rigorous empirical test" (Cressey, 1960, p. 57).

A great deal of research and anecdotal evidence demonstrates that much crime is, indeed, learned in intimate social settings. However, it seems at least as overly ambitious to assume that all criminal behavior is learned in a straightforward fashion as it is to assume that all noncriminal behavior is learned. Many actions, criminal and noncriminal alike, are invented anew by individuals in similar situations. For instance, adolescents need not learn how to masturbate from other adolescents (although many, possibly most, do); many discover the activity as a result of exploring their own bodies. All behavior is not learned, at least not directly. Much of it, deviant or otherwise, may be devised in relative isolation. There is a great deal of independent invention of certain forms of deviance, delin-

quency, and crime. The human mind is, after all, almost infinitely creative. The idea to do something and its eventual enactment almost always have a cultural or learning *foundation*, but the entire process was not necessarily learned in detail. One can, either by oneself or in the company of an equally untutored individual, "put the pieces together."

For instance, when I discuss learning theory, I am often asked by members of my deviance courses whether a preadolescent boy and girl untutored as to its how and why, suddenly isolated on a deserted island, would get around to having sex. My answer is, of course they would. First, they have learned, again, enough of a cultural *foundation* relative to sex to be able to get to the act itself: the attractiveness of the opposite sex, the desirability of physical closeness and affection, hugging and kissing, the fact that nudity has something to do with sex, and so on. And, of course, biological drives and anatomical factors would take over at a certain point. (On the other hand, newborn infants put into the same situation would not only *not* come to have sex, but, even if they were provided with food, would not even mature mentally or psychologically to the point that they could walk, talk, or interact with one another, because they have not been provided with the necessary cultural foundation for these basic and supposedly instinctual acts.) Thus, one can enact certain behaviors *in the absence of learning or by learning about those behaviors oneself;* learning may take one to a certain point, after which creativity and imagination take over. Any learning theory that requires that one learn positive values *about the precise behavior itself* must therefore be incomplete and deficient. Any learning theory that includes all the other factors that go into human behavior, such as biological drives, the pleasure principle, and so on, is likely to be so vague as to be tautology—true by definition.

Many criminal activities do not fit the differential association model at all: check forgery (Lemert, 1953, 1958, 1972, pp. 150–182), embezzlement (Cressey, 1953), child molestation (McCaghy, 1967, 1968), wartime black-market violations (Clinard, 1952), as well as certain crimes of passion (Katz, 1988), and crimes involving psychiatric compulsion (such as kleptomania). While for many deviant and criminal activities, learning may assist their enactment, they do not cause them. In addition, many forms of deviance and crime are not approved of by a majority of the people who engage in them, such as mental illness, alcoholism, and child molestation. Consequently, they could not be learned in anything like the fashion that Sutherland suggests. That is, one may learn *about*, say, mental illness or alcoholism, but one hardly ever learns that they are activities or states one should emulate. While it is true that much criminal and deviant behavior is learned, much of it is not. As a partial theory, differential association is valuable. As a complete or general theory, it is overly ambitious. Rather than a theory that explains all crime, delinquency, and deviance, differential association should instead be regarded as a concept that helps us to understand a particular *process* that some rule breakers go through and some do not.

Learning is not necessarily a *cause* of much deviant behavior, although learning is *involved* in the process of becoming deviant. That is, in the process of becoming absorbed in certain deviant roles, one learns *about* that role, just as one does in more conventional roles. One learns what is expected of one if one is to be a prostitute, say, or a homosexual; one learns the prostitute or homosexual role. This is not, however, to say that the learning process causes one to *become* a prostitute or a homosexual. Rather, *in becoming* a prostitute or a homosexual, one is involved in a learning process—quite a different matter. At times, Sutherland's theory seems to confuse a *process* for a *mechanism*.

Sutherland's theory of differential association has been revamped by contemporary theorists and cast into a behaviorist or social learning framework (Burgess and Akers, 1966; Akers, 1985, pp. 40–52). This perspective attempts to explain the deviance learning process in terms of *operant conditioning*. That is, people are rewarded or reinforced for certain behavior by others and are punished for engaging in different behavior; people will learn deviant behavior to the extent that rewards follow their engaging in deviance. In deviant groups or circles, one is rewarded for engaging in deviance; in conventional groups or circles, one is rewarded for engaging in conventionality and punished for deviance. Thus, to the extent that one is involved in deviant groups or circles, one will engage in deviance. This contemporary version of Sutherland's theory is more sophisticated than the original and attempts to deal with the objections to it addressed by some of its critics. However, social learning or behaviorist theory has been attacked for ignoring social, structural, and economic factors, for being unable to explain why certain things are rewarding or reinforcing to some people and not to others, and for not being a real theory but a tautology or a statement that is simply true by definition. (That is, when examined closely, it seems to say, people like to do what they like to do.) While learning is a major aspect of all sociological theories or perspectives regarding deviance, behaviorism, as a total theory, does not have a substantial following among sociologists of deviance.

The idea that crime, delinquency, and deviant behavior is learned in a direct, straightforward fashion within certain social circles has been explored and elaborated by a number of researchers. One extension of Sutherland's theory of differential association is the "culture transmission" paradigm set forth by Walter Miller, an anthropologist (1958). Sutherland's version of learning theory locates the mechanism of acquiring deviant norms, values, and practices mainly in one's closest peers, and mainly in youth, adolescence, and even adulthood. In contrast, Miller's locates that mechanism as beginning with birth, in the family. In effect, Miller argues, a major sector of the society learns to become delinquent from their parents and other relatives, from the neighborhood, and from their class peers. Miller's theory locates a site of criminogenic values specifically in the lower class, arguing that gang delinquency is a direct by-product of lower-class culture. "The lower class way of life," he writes, "is characterized by a set of focal concerns—areas or issues which command widespread and persistent attention and a high degree of emotional involvement" (1958, p. 6). These "focal concerns" are trouble, toughness, smartness, excitement, fate, and autonomy. Each concern pressures young lower-class males into direct contact with the law and agents of law enforcement. For instance, an emphasis on toughness often leads to a desire to demonstrate one's masculinity by engaging in fights, assaultive behavior, and belligerent confrontations with the police. A desire for thrills, fast-paced excitement, and danger make "hanging out," gambling, fighting, bar hopping, and heavy drinking appealing. Miller argued that simply by being a participating member of the lower-class subculture, one "automatically violates certain legal norms" (1958, p. 18). One is expected to break the law in many situations (which would call for law-abiding behavior for middle-class members of society). Lower-class culture, Miller writes, "is a distinctive tradition many centuries old with an integrity of its own," and that tradition includes the routine violation of the criminal law (p. 19). Miller's argument is that lower-class adolescents "get into trouble because they are faithful to cultural standards learned from their parents" (Empey, 1982, p. 199).

A number of critics have questioned Miller's analysis. Some researchers find that self-reported delinquent behavior does not vary significantly by social class at all; they argue that lower- and working-class adolescents are no more likely to engage in illegal and delinquent acts than are middle-class youths (Tittle, Villemez, and Smith, 1978; Tittle and Meier, 1990). However, the studies that show no, or very little, difference between the classes in delinquent behavior are *self-report* studies; that is, they are based on asking people if they engaged in certain kinds of behavior. And, although self-report studies on deviant and criminal behavior generally are fairly valid and reliable, researchers must know how to interpret their findings. In the studies that show no differences in delinquent behavior between socioeconomic strata, the problem is that most did not distinguish among *degrees of seriousness* of delinquent acts as well as *frequency of their commission* (O'Brien, 1985, pp. 63–79). While it is possible that middle-class youths have no higher rates of *trivial* delinquent offenses, lower- and working-class adolescents certainly *do* have significantly higher rates of *more serious* delinquent acts, and they tend to engage more frequently in those acts they do commit (Elliott and Ageton, 1980). The "no difference" hypothesis does not seem to hold up after all; serious acts of delinquency and crime are far more likely to be committed by members of the lower and working classes. Thus, Miller's hypothesis that lower-class culture is a "generating milieu" for delinquent and criminal behavior probably does have some basis in fact. The argument that lower-class males are no more delinquent than those from the middle classes is clearly based on a serious methodological fallacy.

However, even if lower-class adolescent delinquent and criminal behaviors were more prevalent and frequent than were those of the middle class, this still would not explain why a fairly *low* proportion of lower- and working-class boys are involved in serious violations of the law. Miller's theory *overexplains*: If we were to follow its implications strictly, we would predict that all lower-class adolescents are delinquent, a clearly false assertion. Moreover, some argue, the supposed "focal concerns" that Miller claims characterize lower-class culture seem to be just as much a feature of middle-class culture and values (Valentine, 1968, pp. 135–138; Hirschi, 1969, pp. 212ff.). Many observers do not find Miller's "culture transmission" theory entirely convincing. On the other hand, Miller performed a service to the field by emphasizing the crucial importance of learning, and that of social class, in the commission of delinquent, criminal, and deviant behavior.

CONTROL THEORY

Control theory is a major explanatory paradigm in the fields of deviance behavior and criminology. Control theorists see their perspective as a critique of and a replacement for both anomie theory and the subcultural or learning approaches. For instance, one study found that youths who did poorly in school and who were least concerned about it, that is, who suffered *least* from the "strain" that anomie theory refers to—had the *highest* rates of delinquency (Hirschi, 1969, pp. 124–126). Likewise, youths who were *least* attached to peers, contrary to Cohen, Cloward and Ohlin, and the subcultural approaches, were the *most* likely to commit delinquent acts (pp. 159–161). However, one important consideration about control theory is that it has been far more often used in the study of delinquency (Nye, 1958; Hirschi, 1969; Wiatrowski, Griswold, and Roberts, 1981; Agnew, 1985) than in the study of deviance or crime generally.

Control theory is often regarded as a "micro" or an individualistic version of disorganization theory, which offers a more "macro" or structural approach (Messner and Rosenfeld, 1994, pp. 53–55). While most theories ask, why do they do it? that is, what processes *encourage* deviant behavior, control theory turns the question around and asks, why *don't* they do it? In other words, control theory assumes that engaging in deviance is not problematic, that if *left to our own devices*, all of us would deviate from the rules of society. In fact, control theorists believe that deviance is *inherently attractive*. Under most circumstances, we are encouraged to break the rules; deviance-making processes are strong, obvious, and common-sensical. Why shouldn't we lie and steal, if they are what get us what we want? Why not hang out on street corners, get drunk, and throw bottles through windows—it's so much fun! This approach takes for granted the allure of deviance, crime, and delinquency. What has to be explained, control theorists argue, is why most people *don't* engage in deviance, why they don't engage in delinquent behavior, why they don't break the law and engage in a life of crime. What causes deviant behavior, they say, is the *absence* of the social control that causes conformity and conventional behavior. Most of us do not engage in deviant or criminal acts because of strong bonds with or ties to conventional, mainstream social institutions. If these bonds are weak or broken, we will be released from society's rules and will be free to deviate. It is not so much deviants' ties to an unconventional group or subculture that attracts them to deviant behavior, but their *lack* of ties with the conforming, mainstream, law-abiding culture; this frees them to engage in deviance.

Control theory would predict that to the extent that a person has a *stake in conformity*, he or she will tend not to break the law and risk losing that stake; to the extent that a person lacks that stake in conformity, he or she will be willing to violate the law (Toby, 1957). Thus, jobs, especially satisfying, high-paying jobs, may act as something of a deterrent to crime. (It should be pointed out, however, that in the most important statement spelling out control theory, *Causes of Delinquency*, Travis Hirschi found few class differences in delinquency.) Attending college, likewise, represents a stake or investment that many students are not willing to risk losing. Being married and having a family, too, will discourage criminal behavior to the extent that arrest may undermine the stability of married life. Everyone knows that *some* crime is committed by the employed, by college students, by married persons with families. But control theory would predict that there are *major differences* in the crime rates of the employed versus the unemployed, college students versus their noncollege-age peers, and married parents versus the unmarried. A partial confirmation of control theory was achieved by a study that found that *employed* wife beaters who were arrested had a significantly lower rate of repeat offenses than those who had not been arrested, whereas *unemployed* wife beaters who were arrested did not differ in their rate of repeat offenses from those who had not been arrested. In this case, deterrence was *conditional* on employment. The logic is that a man who has a job is less likely to risk losing it as a result of hitting his wife and getting arrested again than one who has no job and

hence, little to lose by being arrested again (Sherman et al., 1992). To the extent that a society or a neighborhood is able to invest its citizens or residents with a stake worth protecting, it will have lower rates of crime; to the extent that it is unable to invest that stake in its citizens or residents, its crime rate will be correspondingly higher. Home ownership, for instance, can act as a deterrent to crime, as can organizational and community involvement. A society with many citizens who have nothing to lose is a society with a high crime rate.

Of course, delinquency, deviance, and criminal behavior are matters of degree. Nearly all of us engage in *some* deviant and criminal acts at least once in our lives. Control theory does not state that individuals with strong ties to conventional society are absolutely *insulated* from deviance, that they will *never* engage in *any* deviant or criminal action, regardless of how mildly unconventional it is. It does, however, assert that both deviance and social control are matters of degree: The more attached we are to conventional society, the lower the likelihood of engaging in behavior that violates its values and norms. A strong bond to conventionality does not absolutely insulate us from mildly deviant behavior, but it does make it less likely.

Control theory has four basic components: *attachment, commitment, involvement,* and *belief.* The more *attached* we are to conventional others—parents, teachers, clergy, employers, and so on; the more *committed* we are to conventional institutions—family, school, religion, work; the more *involved* we are in conventional activities—familial, educational, religious, occupational; and the more deeply we *believe* in the norms of conventional institutions—family, school, religion, and occupation—the less likely it is that we will violate society's norms and engage in deviant behavior. Deviance is "contained" by bonds with or attachments to conventional people, institutions, activities, and beliefs. The stronger these bonds or attachments, the more conventional one's behavior. If they are strong, deviance and crime are unlikely (Hirschi, 1969, pp. 83ff.).

The theory works a great deal better for some behaviors than others. Many of the activities that control theorists see as natural, recreational, and requiring no special explanation, are part and parcel of relatively minor delinquencies. But what about more seriously aggressive and violent behavior, such as murder, robbery, and rape? Are they part of the same constellation of acts that if left to our own devices and in the absence of simple societal controls, we all would engage in? It's difficult to envision that the same logic applies (Vold and Bernard, 1986, p. 246). In fact, there may be a very good reason why the vast majority of the research applying control theory has been self-report surveys of relatively minor delinquencies among youths: It works best for them. As we saw, such studies run into a serious roadblock. Hirschi's 1969 study found few class differences in rates of delinquency. There is a good reason why. The most important crimes, those that criminologists are most interested in (murder, robbery, and rape) tend to be relatively rare. The least important crimes are sufficiently common to make a self-report possible. The less common the behavior, the more difficult it is to study by means of self-report surveys, since so few of the sample will have engaged in them, especially within a recent time frame. Hence, control theorists are a bit like the drunk who is searching for his keys, not in the dark, where he has lost them, but in the light, where he can see better. In spite of this restriction, control theory represents one of the more powerful approaches we have to explain crime, deviance, and especially delinquency.

A GENERAL THEORY OF CRIME: SELF-CONTROL THEORY

Michael Gottfredson and Travis Hirschi have devised what they refer to as *a general theory of crime* (1990), that is, force or fraud in pursuit of self-interest (p. 15). The authors claim that their theory applies to any and all crimes, regardless of type: white-collar and corporate crime, embezzlement, murder, robbery, rape, the illegal sale of drugs, underage drinking, burglary, shoplifting, indeed, any and all illegal actions. In fact, in their view, their theory is even more general than that, since it is an explanation of actions that may not even be against the law or entail inflicting force or committing fraud against a victim. More properly, it is a general theory of deviance, and includes, besides crime, what used to be referred to as "sin," a variety of self-indulgent actions (like smoking, getting high or drunk, and, one might suppose, even being a couch potato), and reckless behavior which has a high likelihood of resulting in accidents, such as driving dangerously fast or preferring a motor-

cycle to a car. (Unfortunately, although the authors are meticulous about defining crime, they never define what they mean by deviance, a serious drawback.) Their theory, they say, represents a combination or synthesis of theories that stress the factors present in the immediate or "proximate" situation of the criminal action that determine or influence its *enactment* (which they refer to as "crime") and those background or "distal" factors that determine or influence the *tendency* to commit crime (which they term *criminality*).

The origin of crime, Gottfredson and Hirschi say, is *low self-control,* which in turn, results from inadequate, ineffective, and inconsistent socialization by parents early in childhood. Parents who breed delinquent and criminal offspring lack affection for them, fail to monitor their behavior, fail to recognize when they are committing deviant acts, and fail to control wrongdoing. What makes crime especially attractive to people who lack self-control? Criminal acts, Gottfredson and Hirschi say, are characterized by the fact that they provide *immediate* and *easy* or *simple* gratification of desires (p. 89). "They provide money without work, sex without courtship, revenge without court delays" (p. 89). People who lack self-control "tend to lack diligence, tenacity, or persistence in a course of action" (p. 89). In addition, criminal acts are "*exciting, risky, or thrilling,*" crime provides, in the typical case, "*few or meager long-term benefits,*" it requires "*little skill or planning,*" and often results in "*pain or discomfort for the victim*" (p. 89). As a result of the last of these characteristics, people with low self-control and hence, frequent enactors of criminal behavior, tend to be "self-centered, indifferent, or insensitive to the suffering and needs of others (p. 89), although they may also "discover the immediate and easy rewards of charm and generosity" (p. 90).

Since crime entails "the pursuit of immediate pleasure," it follows that "people lacking in self-control will also tend to pursue immediate pleasures that are *not* criminal: They will tend to smoke, drink, use drugs, gamble, have children out of wedlock, and engage in illicit sex" (p. 90). Some crimes entail not so much pleasure but an attempt at relief from irritation or discomfort, such as physically abusing a crying child or beating up a taunting stranger in a bar. People with low self-control have little tolerance for frustration and little skill at dealing with difficult circumstances verbally or by applying complex, difficult-to-master solutions.

"In short, people who lack self-control will tend to be impulsive, insensitive, physical (as opposed to mental), risk-taking, short-sighted, and nonverbal, and they will therefore tend to engage in criminal and analogous acts" (p. 90).

Their general theory of crime, Gottfredson and Hirschi argue, is both consistent with the facts of criminal behavior and contradicts the bulk of mainstream criminological theories. The authors are not modest either about the reach of their theory or its devastating implications for competing explanations. They insist that their general theory of crime *cannot* be reconciled with other theories; instead, they insist, it must of necessity *destroy* them. In fact, even Hirschi's own control theory (discussed above), formulated a quarter of a century ago, is abandoned. More specifically, it is *specified* in that according to the control theory, the *social* controls that Hirschi saw previously as central he now views as secondary to the *internal* controls developed in childhood. Now, life circumstances such as marriage, employment, and home ownership, so crucial to control theory, are rejected as irrelevant, having little or no independent impact on crime. After all, how can someone with low self-control maintain a marriage, keep a job, or buy a house? They lack emotional and psychic wherewithal—the self-control—to do what has to be done even to be *subject* to external or social controls. It is self-control that determines social control, not the other way around, Hirschi now argues.

The problem with the theories of crime that are now dominant in criminology, Gottfredson and Hirschi argue, is that they are inconsistent with the evidence. Strain or anomie theory "predicts that offenders will have high long-term aspirations and low long-term expectations," but that turns out to be false; "people committing criminal acts tend to have lower aspirations than others," while, among offenders, "expectations for future success tend to be unrealistically high" (p. 162). In anomie theory, crime is a long-term, indirect solution to current life circumstances, whereas, in reality, Gottfredson and Hirschi say, crime is an impulsive act which provides immediate, short-term, and rather skimpy rewards. Criminals lack the skills, diligence, and persistence necessary for the deviant "adaptations" spelled out by Merton. True, some criminals do possess these qualities, and do engage in these adaptations, but strain does not explain the incidence or rate of criminal behavior as a whole, since most of it is petty, impulsive, and immediate. Like-

wise, the many varieties of learning theory (such as differential association theory, subculture theory, and culture transmission and, by extension, labeling and conflict theory, to be discussed in the next chapter) should be rejected as being inconsistent with the facts, Gottfredson and Hirschi argue. All such theories make the assumption that deviants engage in deviance as a result of a positive learning experience, that is, *they learn the value* of engaging in deviance and crime. In fact, one does *not* learn to engage in crime, since no learning is required. Criminal acts are simple, common-sensical, immediate, concrete, and result in instant gratification. Neither motivation nor skill to commit them are problematic; criminals are, in fact, simply doing what comes naturally. What causes such behavior is not the *presence* of something—learning—but the *absence* of something—self-control. Learning theories simply fail utterly and completely to explain criminal, deviant, and delinquent behavior, Gottfredson and Hirschi argue.

More generally, they reject the idea that crime is *social* behavior (in fact, it is more accurate to refer to it as *asocial* in nature), that it is *learned* behavior ("when in fact no learning is required"), that the tendency to commit it can be an *inherited* trait (when it is clearly acquired, through childhood experiences), that it is *economic* behavior (when, in fact, "it is uneconomical behavior outside the labor force"). To be plain about it, they reject all other explanations of criminal behavior except their own (p. 75); only a lack of self-control is truly consistent with the facts of crime. Gottfredson and Hirschi contemptuously reject any effort to integrate their own theory with the explanations they so roundly destroyed—with one or two exceptions.

Not all persons who exhibit low self-control commit crime; self-control merely *predisposes* someone to commit crime. What determines which persons who are predisposed to commit crime will actually do so? In a word, opportunity. Hence, any explanation which focuses on the *patterning* and *distribution* of criminal opportunities—although incomplete—is consistent with the facts, Gottfredson and Hirschi argue. Their approach is an attempt to revitalize classical, free-will, or rational-choice theory, mentioned early in this chapter, as half the crime equation. The contemporary version of the classic approach to crime, referred to as opportunity theory, the routine activity approach, or rational choice theory (Cohen and Felson, 1979; Felson, 1987; Clarke and Felson, 1995), argues that

Table 4.1 Explanatory Theories of Deviant Behavior

Theory	Explanatory Factor	Origin	Key Theorists
Demonic possession	Consorting with evil spirits	prehistoric	—
The free will or "classical" school	A rational calculation of pleasure, risk, and pain	1700s	Cesare Beccaria
Ninteenth-century positivism	Biological defects or "atavisms"	1870s–1880s	Cesare Lombroso
Social pathology	Inadequate socialization	1890s	many
Social disorganization	Community disorganization	1920s	Robert Park Clifford Shaw Robert Faris
Anomie or strain theory	Disjunction between means and goals	1938	Robert Merton Albert Cohen Richard Cloward Lloyd Ohlin
Differential association	Deviant socialization	1939	Edwin Sutherland
Culture transmission	Deviant socialization	1958	Walter Miller
Control theory	Absence of bonds to conventional society	1950s–1960s	Jackson Toby Ivan Nye Travis Hirschi
Self-control theory	Impulsiveness, lack of self-control, due to inadequate socialization	1980s–1990s	Michael Gottfredson Travis Hirschi

crime can take place to the extent that a *motivated offender* has access to a "suitable target" (such as money and valuables) which lacks a "capable guardian." Routine activity theorists emphasize the factors of *proximity*, *accessibility*, and *reward* (Hough, 1987). They *assume* or *take for granted* a motivated offender—the criminal—since there will always be an abundant supply of them to go around; instead, they focus on the necessary preconditions for the commission of the crime. The assumption that crime is the most rational means to acquire property is abandoned, however, since Gottfredson and Hirschi argue that most crimes do not net the offender much in the way of goods or cash. Nonetheless, they say, opportunity is a crucial element in the crime equation. (Not in *criminality*, or the individual *propensity* to commit crime, but in crime, that is, in the likelihood that criminal *actions* will take place.) While incomplete, Gottfredson and Hirschi say, a theory which focuses on opportunity is consistent with self-control theory. Moreover, they say, both are necessary for a complete explanation of criminal behavior (1990, pp. 22–23; 1987). In addition, they argue, social disorganization theory is both consistent with classical theory and consistent with the facts of crime; the inability

of a community to monitor the behavior of its residents' complements, and is similar to, parallel parental incompetence (1990, pp. 81–82).

As might be expected, self-control theory has met with mixed reactions. Strain theorists argue that social strain and anomie are indeed significant causal precursors to criminal behavior. For instance, the aggressiveness and anger that many criminals exhibit when committing their crimes is far more than a lack of self-restraint; only strain theory explains it, they say (Agnew, 1995, p. 125). Some learning theorists argue that a lack of self-control is a basic component or element of the deviant learning process (Akers, 1991), hence, they say, learning theory *subsumes*, or swallows up, self-control theory. Labeling or interactionist theorists (such as myself) see in Gottfredson and Hirschi's portrayal of labeling theory a distorted caricature rather than an accurate, nuanced portrait (1990, pp. 76, 113, 147, 159). Certainly, the reductionistic, mechanistic, either-or logic Gottfredson and Hirschi display in their theorizing has led some observers to believe that they may have missed crucial subtleties in characterizing and explaining human behavior (Lynch and Groves, 1995, pp. 372–378). One critic takes Gottfredson and Hirschi to task for selectively reading the data, focusing on those that seem to confirm their theory and ignoring those that would damage it (Polk, 1991). It is too early to assess the validity of self-control theory in anything like a definitive fashion. Chances are, contrary to its claims, bits and pieces of it will be incorporated into mainstream criminology and deviance theory, while its global, blanket—perhaps overblown—critiques of rival theories will be taken far less seriously. The fact is that it is likely that Gottfredson and Hirschi have not offered a "general theory" of crime and deviance, but an important piece of the puzzle.

SUMMARY

Whenever some members of a society engage in what others regard as wrongdoing, the latter wonder why the former do it. Explanations for violating society's rules are as ancient as human existence. Historically, the most ancient of such explanations was demonic possession—the influence of the devil or evil spirits.

By the 1700s, intellectuals and the educated sectors of Western society no longer believed that the intervention of evil spirits caused people to violate the norms or the law. The eighteenth century in Europe was referred to as The Age of Reason. Hence, it makes sense that it was in this era that an explanation for crime arose which focused on humans as reasonable and rational actors, exercising their free will and guided by the pursuit of pleasure and the avoidance of pain.

With the publication of Charles Darwin's *On the Origin of Species* in 1859, more deterministic forces were seen as being at work in the crime equation. The positive school argued that criminal behavior is caused by inborn defects or "atavisms," whose possessors are genetic throwbacks to a more primitive stage in the evolutonary process. In short, criminals are biologically inferior to law-abiding segments of society; it is the possession of inferior traits or characteristics that causes them to engage in criminal behavior. Biological determinism had its heyday in the second half of the nineteenth century and the first few years of the twentieth; by the 1920s, it had suffered a sharp decline in influence. However, in the 1960s, biological reasoning was revived in a much-qualified form. Although far less influential today than a century ago, some researchers nontheless think that biological factors play a significant role in contributing to the etiology of criminal behavior.

Between the turn of the century and roughly 1920 or thereabouts, some sociologists saw deviance from the social pathology perspective. Social pathology abandoned the idea of direct biological causality, but argued by using a biological analogy. Society is much like an organism and deviance is much like a disease. Deviants are social and moral defectives who can't or won't fit into the healthy social "body."

But during the 1920s, this perspective was abandoned by sociologists, who came to see the community rather than the individual as the source of norm violations. Some neighborhoods are unstable by virtue of their undesirability. As a result, residents are heterogeneous (and hence, often strangers to one another) and do not sink roots into the community. In such neighborhoods, wrongdoing is common, since residents cannot or do not monitor or control normative and legal violations. In sum, deviance varies systematically by ecological location. The social disorganization school was the dominant perspective in academic sociology between the 1920s and the 1940s. After World War II, it suffered a serious decline in importance and influence. Although it never regained its former glory, roughly by 1990, the social disorganization school experienced a dramatic renaissance. Today, numerous researchers are conducting studies which are guided or inspired by the social disorganization perspective.

Anomie theory is distinctive by virtue of the fact that it had its origin (except for the work of Emile Durkheim, who had something very different in mind) in a single article by a single sociologist: Robert K. Merton's "Social Structure and Anomie," published in 1938. Merton argued that in the United States, deviance was a product of a disjunction or contradiction between the culture, whose norms urged material and financial success for all members of the society, and the social and economic structure, which granted high levels of success only to some. This condition produces a state of stress or *anomie*. As a result of failing in the traditional sectors of the society, those who were left behind were forced into one of an array of deviant "adaptations." This theory did not receive a great deal of attention until the appearance of a book, more than a decade and a half later, by Albert K. Cohen, *Delinquent Boys*, at which point, the theory began to inspire an entire generation of deviance specialists. Merton's 1938 article is the most often cited single article in the history of sociology, and during the late 1950s and the 1960s, the anomie perspective was the most often used approach in the study of deviance. But in the 1970s, the approach underwent a sharp decline in influence; in 1978, in a review of theories of deviance and delinquency, Ruth Kornhauser declared that anomie theory had been "disconfirmed." However, as with nearly all perspectives in this field, anomie theory experienced a strong rebirth, roughly beginning in 1990. Today, once again, it is the focus of vigorous commentary and research.

Learning theories encompass a variety of perspectives, all of which center around the idea that deviance, delinquency, and crime are learned in a fairly straightforward fashion. By being isolated from mainstream society and its definition of deviance, and integrated into unconventional groups, one learns deviant values, beliefs, and norms and thus engages in deviant behavior. Two varieties of this approach include the theory of differential association, devised by Edwin Sutherland in 1939, and culture transmission theory, which was systematized by the anthropologist Walter Miller in 1958. As with all other perspectives in the field, learning theory has been attacked, defended, amended, and added to.

Control theory takes strong issue with both anomie and learning theory. Deviants do not have to be stressed into committing deviance, nor does anyone have to learn to become a deviant. Indeed, what requires explaining, say the control theorists, is conformity. Deviance is readily understandable, common-sensical, and nonproblematic. In fact, left to their own devices, everyone would deviate from the norms: It's easier, more fun, and it is effective in getting the actor what is desired, than is true of conformity. The important question is not, why do we commit deviance? Instead, it is, why *don't* we commit deviance? The factor or variable that control theorists have isolated as the explanation is that people engage in conventional behavior to the extent that they are involved with and attached to conventional others, activities, and beliefs. To the extent that we have an investment or stake in conventionality, we will engage in conventional behavior. To the extent that we don't, we will engage in deviance.

In 1990, a major theory of deviance made its appearance: "a general theory of crime." It is based on several tenets of control theory (as well as clas-

sic, free-will, or rationalistic theory), but it breaks with it in its lack of stress on *current* conventional attachments. People violate norms and the law because they lack self-control; they tend to be insensitive, self-centered, impulsive, relatively unintelligent; they lack a long-range perspective, can't deal with frustration, and require immediate gratification. And they lack self-control because they were subject to inadequate, inconsistent, and ineffective socialization by their parents or other caregivers. Self-control theory is one of the few perspectives whose advocates argue that all other perspectives (except for rational choice and social disorganization) are completely incompatible with the facts of crime. Its advocates set out to destroy all now-dominant approaches to deviance and crime. As might be expected, self-control theory has met with a mixed reception.

Today, no single perspective or approach is dominant in the study of deviance. As we can see, all of the approaches discussed in this chapter are concerned entirely on *an explanation of deviant behavior*. In this sense, they are all positivistic, or "scientific" in their general approach. In the next chapter, we'll look at theories that are up to a very different task, in a sense, looking at the opposite side of the deviance coin. Instead of attempting to explain why deviant behavior is enacted, for the most part, they ask about the nature and operation of *definitions* of deviance and the exercise of *social control*. Instead of asking why deviance is enacted, they wonder about why deviance is conceptualized and defined a certain way, and how and why certain behaviors, traits, and persons are caught up in the web of punishment and condemnation. Although this enterprise is less traditional, less likely to be thought about by the man and woman in the street, it is every bit as rewarding and potentially enlightening as those which ask why some of us deviate. No examination of deviance is complete without an investigation of the nature, social roots, and the exercise of social control.

Before we proceed to the next chapter, however, I must issue a most emphatic warning. The perspectives we are about to examine are largely focused on how the society or segments of the society define and deal with deviance and deviants. One major aspect (although not all) of this focus is social control: the attempt to deal with, treat, rein in, reduce, or eliminate the incidence of the behavior defined as deviant. The term, "social control," represents a constructionist approach to deviance.

Unfortunately, two theories we looked at in this chapter share names that are very similar to this social control emphasis—"social control" theory and "self-control" theory. I must emphasize that they are *not* theories of social control in the sense that I'll be using the term in Chapter 5, that is, they are not constructionist in their approach. They are etiological and essentialist theories. They do not examine social control as problematic, that is, as the subject to be investigated. They ask: *Why do some persons engage in deviant behavior?* They do *not* ask: *Why social control?* Don't be confused by the similarity in their names. Their approaches are completely different; they share little else with the perspectives discussed in Chapter 5 *aside from* their names.

Another absolutely crucial qualification. These "social control" or constructionist theories are most emphatically *not* about, let's say, how the police, prison officials, psychiatrists, teachers, and so on can improve their effectiveness in "controlling" norm violators. It does not attempt to offer advice about how to *engage* in social control; instead, it attempts to *understand* the processes of social control. The job of these theorists is to show how social control is a sociological—and human—endeavor rather than simply a rational means of dealing with an important and troubling technical problem, much like, let's say, how we can cure cancer. If anything, the facts are the reverse: Social control theorists offer a critical and faultfinding perspective on the how and why of society's efforts to deal with deviance and crime. One aspect of their job is to show how social and how fallible the enterprise of social control is. Let's look at what they are up to.

chapter 5

CONDEMNATION AND PUNISHMENT: PERSPECTIVES ON RULES AND THEIR ENFORCEMENT

The perspectives and approaches that were discussed in Chapter 4 attempt to explain the occurrence, enactment, and/or distribution of deviant or criminal behavior. They are concerned with the factors that lead certain persons to break the rules or that result in acts of deviance being more common in certain societies, or under certain conditions, than others. These perspectives focus on the question, "Why do they do it?" (Or, in the case of social control theory, "Why *don't* they do it?") Some emphasize micro or individual characteristics, such as biological positivism, learning theory or differential association, and control and self-control theory. Others emphasize the macro or broader social structural conditions that generate deviant behavior, such as social disorganization and anomie theory. Still, all attempt to provide an explanation for *why deviant behavior is enacted*—why some people engage in it, why residents of some communities are more likely to engage in it, why some societies and historical time periods generate more of it than others. These perspectives see deviance *as a type of action*.

A very different orientation is provided by approaches that ask about *the rules and their enforcement* rather than their violation. Here, rather than seeing deviance as an action, these perspectives see rules as an *infraction*. That is, the focus is on what *makes* certain actions infractions, why rules are made in the first place, who makes the rules, why *certain kinds* of rules are made, why certain *persons* or *types of persons* are apprehended and punished, and what *consequences* rule making and rule enforcement have. This approach turns the focus of attention around; now, instead of the spotlight being on the rule violator, or on the conditions that make for rule violation, it is on the society and the groups in the society that *make and enforce the rules*. The theoretical schools that adopt this perspective include: functionalism, labeling or interactionist theory, conflict theory, feminist theory, and "controlology," or the new sociology of social control. Some approaches (such as conflict theory and feminism) contain an explanatory thrust (their "minor" mode) but focus largely on the generation of the rules and their enforcement (their "major" mode).

The *functionalist* approach to deviance is an early perspective that put forth two arguments. First, certain behaviors harm society and its members; hence, they must be prohibited in order for a society to survive. Second, some behaviors that are widely condemned are actually functional or beneficial in their effects in that they protect certain mainstream values and institutions and therefore, the society as a whole. *Labeling* or *interactionist* theory focuses on rule making and, especially, *reactions to* rule breaking. It deals mainly with the question, "What happens to people *after* they have been singled out, identified, and defined as deviants?" This school shifts its attention to "the important role of social definitions and negative sanctions" (Traub and Little, 1994, pp. 289, 290). *Conflict theory* deals with the question of making the rules, especially the criminal law. Why is certain behavior outlawed? And why is other, often even more damaging behavior, *not* outlawed? Conflict theory focuses its attention on the role of powerful groups and classes in the formation and enforcement of the criminal law. The powerful are able to make sure that laws and rules favorable to their own interests, and possibly deterimental to the interests of other, less powerful groups and classes, are institutionalized. Marxism, radical sociology, critical theory, or the "new" criminology, which are (in varying ways and to different degrees) variants of conflict theory, also focus on the role of the powerful in making and enforcing the rules, especially the laws, but emphasize the economic dimension, that is, how the capitalist class maintains its interests in capitalist society (Sheley, 1995). *Feminist theory* is also a variety of conflict theory, focusing specifically on the role of sex and gender in deviance and crime: How do men express and maintain their dominance by defining and enforcing certain actions as deviant and criminal? Why does patriarchy exist, whose functions does it serve, and what impact does it have on deviance and social control? (Daly and Chesney-Lind, 1988). "*Controlology*," or "the new sociology of social control," is the view that social control is state or state-like control, and that in order to understand the nature of deviance and control, it is necessary to understand how the state and its allies control troublesome populations (Scull, 1988; Cohen, 1985; Lowman, Menzies, and Palys, 1987).

FUNCTIONALISM

Functionalism is a general term that has been used in a variety of fields, including architecture, philosophy, psychology, and sociology. In its most general meaning, functionalism refers to the view that phenomena are to be understood by their consequences. *Intention* or *motive* is explained by *interest*, and interest, in turn, is explained by *outcome*, according to the functionalist. Answering the question, *"Who profits?"* simultaneously answers the questions: *How and why did this occur?* In short, *functions indicate interests.* For instance, if the consequence of the passage of a law is beneficial to the ruling elite, that elite must have engineered the passage of that law. If a social custom has a beneficial effect on a society, the members of that society must have *done* something to keep that custom alive. If a custom survives for centuries, it must serve a *function* for the members of the society. When we refer to functions, we are referring to consequences that explain motives, even if those motives may not be clear to the participants. A function is an outcome in which a reason may be found for its existence. In sociology, a functionalist examines the consequences an institution or practice has and, from them, speculates about the part they play in the functioning and interests of a society or segments of that society.

In sociology, the term "functionalism" (also referred to as "structural-functionalism") may be distinguished from *functionalist thinking*. The approach that is referred to as functionalism is associated with a type of reasoning which is narrower than functionist thinking in general. Functionists typically answer the question, "Who profits?" by saying "The society *as a whole* profits." In contrast, functionalist *thinking* looks for specific individuals, social segments, categories, or groups who may profit at the expense of others, who may lose. But the basic reasoning process for both is the same.

Emile Durkheim (1858–1917), the first academic sociologist, is seen as the most important precursor to twentieth-century American functionalism. Durkheim believed the members of a society possessed a "collective conscience" (or, sometimes, "collective consciousness"); his work was focused on the causes and consequences of societal cohesion. In his early writing (1893/1933), Durkheim pictured crime as pathological and negative in its impact, although he saw the *punishment* of crime as having a beneficial impact. However, soon after, he quickly saw crime as "functional" for the society (1895/1938). An entirely crime-free society is an impossibility, Durkheim said, because even in a society of saints, the slightest transgression will generate punishment and condemnation

(1895/1938, pp. 68–69). The punishment of crime firms up the "moral boundaries" of most societies; upstanding citizens "wax indignant" about the criminal and, in so doing, reaffirm the moral correctness of conventional norms and values. Crime, therefore, is useful, it is necessary; it has a part to play in social life. Moreover, Durkheim argued, in crime there are the seeds of social change. Too much conformity produces a society that "would too easily congeal into an immutable form" (p. 71). Crime is "an anticipation of future morality—a step toward what will be" (p. 71). Durkheim offended conventional, common-sensical thinking by arguing that *crime is good for society!*

Durkheim had a powerful impact on the thinking of Talcott Parsons (1902–1979), who is regarded as structural-functionalism's founder and, at one time, its most prominent spokesperson. Functionalism asked the basic question, "How is social order possible?" The answer it gives is that societies, in a more or less unintended, nonconscious fashion, have protected themselves over the years by prohibiting harmful activities (that is, those that threaten their survival) and encouraging beneficial ones (that is, those that maximize societal survival). Social customs and institutions that persist over time tend to be those that are good for society because they serve one of these two functions (Parsons, 1951; Davis, 1949; Davis, 1937; Davis and Moore, 1945). That is, the *positive consequences* of certain institutions (those which have a beneficial impact) cause the members of the society to preserve and maintain them.

Deviance, according to the functionalists, can be either beneficial ("functional") or harmful ("dysfunctional") to the society as a whole. Certain activities will promote social stability, integration, and cohesion, and are therefore functional. Others, by their very nature, will generate hostility, discord, and conflict among the members of a society and will thereby make the society more unstable and less viable; they are dysfunctional in nature. Certain taboos will be more or less universal around the world, because the activities they prohibit will inherently sow the seeds of conflict. Specific activities will be regarded as deviant everywhere because they threaten the social order. Incest, for example, creates competition and conflict between and among family members, pitting one against another for the affection of fellow family members. The roles of family members and lovers are in conflict with one another; hence, incest, which makes the family a less stable and less viable institution, is tabooed just about everywhere (Davis, 1949, pp. 401–404). Note that the impact of a given practice or institution is examined according to its effect on the society *as a whole*, as a unit or *total social system*. Functionalists tended to focus on functions for *total societies* rather than units, groups, or classes within societies. (Although, in principle, by following the logic of functionalist thinking— as opposed to functionalism—one could theorize about the functions of certain institutions and practices *for designated segments of the society*. As we'll see, this is what conflict theorists have done, although, for the most part, functionalists have not.)

However, the main contribution of the functionalists lies not in their analyses showing that certain forms of deviance are harmful, or dysfunctional, and their prohibition is therefore beneficial, or positively functional, to society. Rather, functionalism represented an advance over previous ways of looking at deviance in large part because it stressed that certain forms of deviance have a *positive* or *integrative* impact on society. "Overwhelmingly," functionalists "stressed the functions—not the dysfunctions—of deviant" behavior (Matza, 1969, p. 55). Of course, often, most of the members of a society will not recognize, be aware of, or admit these effects, positive or negative; they may be hidden, unacknowledged, or in functionalist terminology, they may be *latent* consequences of deviance.

Deviance, the functionalists argued, is often beneficial for society, a kind of "blessing in disguise," a kind of "cloud with a silver lining." For example, Kingsley Davis (1937, 1971, 1976) argued that prostitution serves a positive function for society: "Enabling a small number of women to take care of the needs of a large number of men, it is the most convenient sexual outlet for armies and the legions of strangers, perverts, and physically repulsive in our midst. It performs a role which apparently no other institution fully performs" (1971, p. 351). By diverting the sexual interest and energy of a large number of "disreputable" women and away from "respectable" women, Davis argued, the traditional family is preserved and society benefits as a consequence. Prostitution "provides males with a sexual outlet that has limited liability," it produces "no emotional interference with other roles. In this way, the contraband act presents no threat to institutionalized relations" (N. Davis, 1980, p. 104). Robert Merton, probably the most prominent func-

tionalist sociologist writing today, argued that deviant institutions often serve positive functions. For instance, political bossism and the local party machine of the 1930s, although corrupt, inefficient, nepotistic, favoristic, and deeply involved in criminal activity, fulfilled the crucial function *"of humanizing and personalizing all manner of assistance* to those in need" (1957, p. 74). This solidifies the neighborhood and strengthens the society as a whole. Daniel Bell (1961) argued that organized crime served a useful purpose for the society: It provided a "ladder of social mobility" for talented, ambitious sons of immigrants who would otherwise be knocking at legitimate occupational doors. Even social conflict, while frequently condemned and often disruptive, may serve unrecognized, positive, integrative social functions (Coser, 1956). In an essay that is more functionalist than interactionist, Kai Erikson says that deviance "may itself be, in controlled quantities, an important condition for *preserving* stability" (1964, p. 15).

The positive contribution that the *punishment* of deviance makes to the society is at least as important as that made by deviant behavior itself. The punishment of a criminal represents a "ritual expression" of group sentiment; it upholds "the institutionalized values which the criminal has violated. This ritual expression serves to consolidate those sentiments and above all to strengthen them in that part of the population which has positive but latent motivations to the deviance being punished" (Parsons, 1951, p. 310). Punishment represents "a kind of declaration" that "you are either with us or against us." "A good deal of it therefore is not directed at the criminal himself, but at others who potentially might become criminals" (p. 310). In short, deviance and crime provide a resource for the society, a means of affirming society's mainstream values, because in the periodic punishment of criminals, the conventional but seducible members of society are reminded of the righteousness of law-abiding behavior and the evil of breaking the law. As Erikson says, public hangings went out of vogue with the institutionalization of the mass media. In a sense, publicizing the punishment of deviants and criminals in the news serves the same function as hanging them in the public square: Everyone can see what happens to wrongdoers. In a functionalist sense, "morality and immorality meet at the public scaffold" (Erikson, 1966, p. 12).

Functionalism made three contributions to the study of deviance (Matza, 1969, pp. 31–37, 53–62,

73–80). First, it emphasized the *complexity* of the relationship between conventionality and deviance. Second, it *purged the automatic implication of pathology* from the field. And third, it emphasized an *appreciation* for deviance.

Where earlier perspectives saw deviance as almost inevitably producing *undesirable* effects on a society, functionalists argued that the effects that nearly everyone recognized as desirable often flowed from deviance. Where earlier perspectives saw deviance as *untenable*, a phenomenon that could (and should) be gotten rid of through firm and authoritarian intervention, functionalists argued that deviance provided a tenable, viable way of life for many members of society. The *persistence* of certain forms of deviance, such as prostitution— the fact that it has existed everywhere, throughout history—indicates that it makes positive contributions for both the members of society that engage in it and for the society as a whole. Where earlier perspectives saw a *disjunction* between deviance and conventionality, a yawning chasm separating the "good guys" from the "bad guys," functionalists pictured a *continuity* between them. Deviance, the functionalists argued, *shades off into* conventional behavior. Much of what ordinary, law-abiding folk think and do borders on, but usually doesn't quite become, deviance. There is deviance *in miniature* in the most conventional of behavior, and an *incipient* or *potential* deviant in even the most conformist of souls. We should look at deviance in *linear* terms rather than in either-or, black-or-white terms. There is an *unbroken continuum* between the respectable and the disreputable. A clear break between them simply does not exist. The relationship between vice and virtue is *devious* rather than simple, *continuous* rather than dichotomous (Matza, 1969, pp. 74, 77).

Functionalists offered insight into why rules— and therefore deviance—exist in the first place, as well as into some of the major consequences of deviant behavior. Historically, it was the first major perspective to argue that deviance is not necessarily a result of an undesirable or abnormal condition and that it does not always produce negative consequences. Deviance is, in fact, part and parcel of the normal functioning of any society.

At the same time, the functionalist perspective suffered sustained and, in the view of many critics, fatal criticism (Gouldner, 1970). Functionalism was accused of justifying the status quo, of falsely arguing that we live in "the best of all possible worlds,"

of being incapable of analyzing or predicting social change, of glossing over and ignoring conflict between groups and social classes, as well as failing to take note of, indeed, even justifying, profound differences in power and wealth, and the implications these have for deviant behavior. An example of the narrowness of its approach can be seen in its analysis of prostitution (Davis, 1937). Functionalists assumed that because prostitution was beneficial for the traditional patriarchal family, it was therefore beneficial *for the society as a whole*. As feminists came to argue, what is good for the traditional male-dominant family may very well *oppress, repress,* and *be harmful to* women.

Functionalism incorrectly assumed a unity and homogeneity of interests among different groups and categories in the society; later conflict and feminist approaches assume much more diversity and heterogeneity. A given institution may be beneficial to one group or segment of the society *at the expense of another.* While functionalists paid lip-service, in principle, to the notion of functional diversity (Merton, 1957, pp. 25–30, 38–46), in their concrete analyses (for instance, Davis and Moore, 1945; Davis, 1937; Merton, 1957, p. 74; Parsons, 1951, p. 310), they focused on the impact of institutions and on the behavior of society *as a whole.* Functionalism was prominent in sociology generally from the 1940s to the early 1960s. (It never became a dominant perspective in the study of deviance.) In the field of the sociology of deviance, the functionalist argument was briefly revived with Kai Erikson's historical study, *Wayward Puritans* (1966), which argued that crime was functional for colonial Puritan society. But this book, although highly regarded, could not stem the decline of the perspective's influence in sociology, and by the 1970s, functionalism went into total eclipse. Nonetheless, in the 1980s, a perspective whose practitioners refer to themselves as *neo-functionalists* emerged (Alexander, 1985), giving the field a kind of mini-revival. Functionalism is currently in disrepute in sociology. It is an almost obligatory ritual for instructors of introductory sociology to demolish functionalism (Downes and Rock, 1988, p. 88). Still, as some observers point out, even though *functionalism* has all but disappeared from the field, *functionalist thinking* is still very much alive. There is an implicit or "tacit but perfectly virile functionalism still lurking in much of the sociology of deviance" (Downes and Rock, 1988, p. 110). For instance, nearly all Marxists, radicals, conflict theorists, feminists, and contrololologists argue that functions indicate interests—the cornerstone of functionalist thinking.

LABELING OR INTERACTIONIST THEORY

In the 1960s, a small group of researchers produced a small body of work that came to be looked upon as a more or less unified perspective that is widely referred to as *labeling theory*. Two of the major labeling theorists, Becker (1973, p. 178) and Kitsuse (1972, p. 233) reject both the term "labeling" and the title "theory" as a valid description of their perspective. Both prefer the term "the interactionist approach" (Becker, 1973, pp. 181, 183; Kitsuse, 1972, p. 235). Their approach, they explain, is not, strictly speaking, a theory—that is, a general explanation for why deviance occurs in the first place—and the term, "labeling," they say, implies too simple-minded a connection between stigma and its outcomes. Unfortunately, in the field of deviance, the perspective is widely known as "labeling theory." I will refer to it both as the labeling *and* the interactionist approach, and I will use the terms "theory," "approach," "model," "school," "paradigm," and "perspective" more or less interchangeably.

The definition of deviance that the members of this school adopt is the reactive or *reactivist* definition spelled out in Chapter 2. Some labeling theorists prefer the "hard" or "strict" reactive definition (Kitsuse, 1962), and some the "soft" or "moderate" one (Erikson, 1962), but all adopt *some* version of the reactive definition. Labeling theory was built on the work and writings of two principal precursors: Frank Tannenbaum (1938) and Edwin Lemert (1951). The first, Tannenbaum, cannot be regarded as a member of the labeling school, since he wrote so long ago, had no firsthand contact with its other proponents, and did not work out the implications of his early insights. Tannenbaum can be regarded as the "grandfather" of labeling theory. The second, Lemert, is much closer in time to current labeling theorists, is a sociologist (while Tannenbaum was a historian of Latin America), and wrote in a much more sophisticated fashion than did Tannenbaum. Some of Lemert's writing is squarely in the labeling tradition, and some criticizes it sharply. Lemert may be regarded as the "godfather" of labeling theory.

Labeling theory grew out of a more general perspective in sociology: *symbolic interactionism*. This approach is based on "three simple premises." First, people act on the basis of the *meaning* that things have for them. Second, this meaning grows out of *interaction* with others, especially intimate others. And third, meaning is continually modified by *interpretation* (Blumer, 1969, p. 2). These three principles—meaning, interaction, and interpretation—form the core of symbolic interactionism and, likewise, labeling theory. People are not robots, interactionists are saying; they are active and creative in how they see and act on things in the world. People are not simple "products" of their upbringing or socialization, or of their environment, but arrive at what they think, how they feel, and what they do through a dynamic, creative process. Men are not automatically patriarchal and sexist simply because they grew up as men in a patriarchal, sexist society; they continually reinterpret what they have been taught in the light of their everyday lives. Pornography does not have the same impact on all viewers, even all male viewers; the meaning of pornography is mediated through the defining and reactive filter of each viewer in a particular interactive setting. Drug use patterns—even the use of one specific drug or drug type—are not a simple product of the inherent properties of drugs themselves. How people use drugs depends on who they are and how these drugs are woven into their lives. In short, all behavior, deviance included, is an interactional product; its properties and impact cannot be known until we understand how it is defined, conceptualized, interpreted, apprehended, and evaluated; in short, what it *means* to participants and relevant observers alike. Labeling theory is not a separate theory at all, but an application of symbolic interactionism to deviant phenomena.

Labeling Theory: The Precursors

The year 1938 marked the publication of a book written by Frank Tannenbaum, a professor of history and a Latin American specialist; it was entitled *Crime and the Community*. Tannenbaum argued that in a slum area, nearly all boys engage in a wide range of mischievous, sometimes technically illegal behavior—getting into fights, skipping school, stealing apples, and throwing rocks at windows. These actions, perfectly normal and taken for granted by the boys themselves, are typically regarded as deviant and criminal by the authorities—teachers, the police, and the courts. In an effort to curtail this behavior, the police apprehend and punish some of these boys. If the boys persist in this behavior, they will be sent to reform school. However, punishment does not always put an end to these activities. In fact, it often has the ironic effect of escalating the seriousness of the deeds that these boys commit. Arrest and incarceration will typically result in the community regarding a boy as not merely mischievous, but as incorrigible—a budding criminal. By being treated as a delinquent and forced to associate with slightly older and more experienced young criminals in reform school, the troublemaker comes to see himself as a true delinquent.

Tannenbaum was the first observer of deviance to focus more on reactions to behavior than on the behavior itself. He argued, in fact, that the key factor in escalating an individual's behavior from mildly to seriously deviant was the punishment he or she received. It is possible that Tannenbaum did not believe that punishment always and inevitably resulted in this escalation process, but he certainly wrote as if he believed it.

About a dozen years after the publication of Tannenbaum's *Crime and the Community* (1938), a textbook with the inappropriate and anachronistic title *Social Pathology* appeared (1951). Written by sociologist Edwin Lemert, it pursued Tannenbaum's insights, but with considerably more sophistication, complexity, and detail. Lemert distinguished between *primary* and *secondary* deviation. Primary deviation is simply the enactment of deviant behavior itself—any form of it. Lemert argued that primary deviation is *polygenetic* (1951, pp. 75–76, 1972, pp. 62–63), that is, it is caused by a wide range of factors. For instance, someone may come to drink heavily because of a variety of reasons: the death of a loved one, a business failure, belonging to a group whose members call for heavy drinking, and so on. In fact, Lemert asserted, the original cause or causes of a particular form of deviance is not especially important. What counts is the social reaction *to* the behavior from others.

Secondary deviation occurs when the individual who enacts deviant behavior deals with the problems created by social reactions to his or her primary deviations (1951, p. 76). "The secondary deviant, as opposed to his actions, is a person whose life and identity are organized around the facts of deviance" (1972, p. 63). In other words, when someone is singled out, stigmatized, condemned,

or isolated for engaging in deviant behavior, it becomes necessary to *deal with* and *manage* this social reaction in certain ways. One begins to see oneself in a certain way, one defines oneself in different terms, adopts different roles, associates with different individuals. Being stigmatized forces one to become a deviant, to engage in secondary deviation. It should be said that Lemert recognized that not all primary deviation results in punishment or condemnation. Some communities or social circles display more "tolerance" for rule-breaking behavior than others (1951, pp. 57–58). When primary deviation results in punishment, however, the individuals engaging in it tend to be stigmatized, shunned, and socially isolated. They are forced into social groups or circles of other individuals who are also stigmatized. This isolation from mainstream, conventional society reinforces the individual's commitment to these unconventional, deviant groups and circles and to the deviant behavior itself.

Lemert, like Tannenbaum, emphasized the ironic consequences of condemning and punishing rule breakers; it can make further deviance more likely. However, Lemert, unlike Tannenbaum, discussed both sides of this process. One possible outcome of negative social reaction to primary deviation is to "eliminate the variant behavior" altogether. Certain radical or revolutionary groups in Europe "have at times been ruthlessly hunted down and destroyed." In the United States, the practice of polygyny, or multiple marriages, "was stamped out" (1951, p. 63). Although the repression of deviance can result in its elimination, the ironic effect of strengthening it and making it more likely has captured far more attention from labeling theorists over the years. As with the functionalist perspective, the labeling theorists wished to be original, and one way of doing that was to attack common sense, to put forth an argument that contradicts what is commonly known or thought to be true (M. Davis, 1971).

Although Lemert is often mentioned as a member of the labeling or interactionist school (Plummer [1979, p. 86] says that only the name of Becker is more often mentioned than Lemert's as a representative labeling theorist), I prefer to think of him as its "godfather" rather than a member in good standing. Lemert has in fact distanced himself from the labeling or interactionist school by vigorously criticizing what he sees as its excesses (including an assertion which I myself made). Lemert has rejected what may very well be the key idea in any reactive perspective in the study of deviance: that the relationship between action and reaction is problematic. In counterpoint, Lemert invokes the "objective aspects of deviance" and "values universal in nature" (1972, p. 22). Labeling theory, he asserts, suffers from "extreme subjectivism," a biased "underdog perspective, reflecting sympathy for the victim and antipathy for the establishment," and distorts "by magnifying the exploitative and arbitrary features of the societal reaction." More important, Lemert argues, labeling theory "leaves little or no place for human choice" at any level of interaction (1974, p. 459). And lastly, it fails to recognize or take note of "dissensus within the dominant group," or that claims made by groups other than the dominant group must often be acknowledged and honored (p. 460). While he strongly influenced the thinking of this perspective, given these critical remarks, it is difficult to think of Lemert as a member in good standing of the labeling school.

Labeling Theory: The Main Points

In addition to Tannenbaum and Lemert (whom I see as *precursors* to the labeling or interactionist theory of deviance), most observers regard Howard Becker (1963, 1964), John Kitsuse (1962), and Kai Erikson (1962, 1966) as labeling theory's main proponents. (As I said, in *Wayward Puritans,* Erikson's analysis is primarily functionalist in its orientation, not interactionist, although a number of the key statements in the first chapter of that book, 1962, 1964, 1966, pp. 3–29, are largely within the interactionist framework.) Although Becker (1973) and Kitsuse (1972, 1975, 1980) later elaborated their original formulations, for the most part, what is now known as labeling theory was spelled out in the short span of time between 1962 and 1966. It should be said that although labeling theorists have been depicted by most commentators, particularly critics, as consistent in their views, in reality, they represent a diverse group of thinkers (Goode, 1975, p. 570; Plummer, 1979, p. 87). For instance, as I said in Chapter 2, some, like Kitsuse (1962) hold a "hard," or strict, reactivist definition of deviance, while others, such as Becker and Erikson, are more "moderate" reactivists. Still, there are some ideas these theorists do have in common. Almost as important, they are *regarded* as a school whose representatives agree about deviance in nearly every detail. Thus, labeling or interaction-

ist theory can be discussed as a more-or-less unified school or perspective in the study of deviance.

According to Becker (1973, pp. 177–208, 1981) and Kitsuse (1972, 1980), labeling theory is not so much an explanation for why certain individuals engage in deviant behavior as it is a perspective whose main insight tells us that the labeling process is crucial and cannot be ignored. Labeling "theory" is not so much a theory as it is an orientation, a "useful set of problems" centered around the origins and consequences of labeling (Plummer, 1979, pp. 88, 90). The labeling approach shifts attention away from the traditional question, "Why do they do it?" to a focus on how and why judgments of deviance come to be made and what their consequences are. Why are certain acts condemned at one time and in one place, but tolerated at another time, in another place? Why does one person do something and get away "scott free," while another does the same thing and is severely punished for it? What happens when someone is caught violating a rule and is stigmatized for it? What consequences does the stigma have for that individual's subseqent behavior? (McCaghy and Capron, 1994, pp. 94ff.). What is the difference between enacting rule-breaking behavior, which does not result in getting caught, and enacting that same behavior, and being publicly denounced for it? These are some of the major issues with which labeling theorists have been concerned.

Labeling or interactionist theorists, as I pointed out earlier, are occasionally referred to as "neo-Chicagoans" (Matza, 1969, pp. 33ff.). They *depart* from the Chicago sociology tradition in deemphasizing social disorganization as a cause of deviant behavior. In fact, the labeling theorists are not interested in the issue of the etiology of deviance at all; following Lemert, they argue that deviant behavior is polygenetic, that is, it has many causes. *One* possible outcome of being labeled or stigmatized as a deviant is a strengthening of one's commitment to a deviant identity and further deviant behavior. But they do not attempt to explain the occurrence of deviant behavior, as the proponents of the original Chicago school did. However, the "neo-Chicagoans" do *follow* in that tradition in emphasizing up-close, detailed ethnographic studies of deviant circles, groups, and subcultures. That is, in order to understand the phenomenon of deviance, they say, it is necessary to go out into the street and talk to the individuals who break the laws and norms, to get into the natural habitat of the deviant and understand how he or she lives. It will not do, they say, to receive one's views of deviance from books, from the vantage point of one's comfortable armchair, from studies that entail one-shot interviews with thousands of respondents which are then analyzed by means of complex, arcane statistics. One must immerse oneself in the everyday lives of deviants, get as close to the phenomena under study as possible, nose-to-nose with your subjects, so to speak. Anthropological ethnography is a cornerstone of the interactionist's research methods.

Compared with the other perspectives, the interactionist or labeling perspective has emphasized the following concepts in the drama of deviance: *relativity, the construction of moral meanings and definitions, the inner world of deviance, labeling and stigma, audiences, contingencies, reflexivity, and the "stickiness" of labels* and *the self-fulfilling prophecy.*

Relativity. The most important characteristic of an act, labeling theorists say, is how a society, or its major segments, view it, and how people react to such behavior and to someone who enacts it. Behavior is not deviant in itself; it only becomes deviant when it is seen and reacted to in a society. Is adultery deviant? Not in some societies, such as the Lepcha of Sikkim, a tiny state in northern India. The Lepcha tolerate and even encourage adultery (Gorer, 1967). In other societies, such as Saudi Arabia, adultery is most decidedly deviant; the female partner, if caught engaging in it, is likely to be severely punished, and in principle, in some areas, could even be put to death (Minai, 1981, p. 115). What is crucial here is not the nature of the act itself, which represents the same outward action in both places, but the *meaning* of the action to those who evaluate it, and the actual or potential reactions by others to the act and its perpetrators.

It might seem that this is a noncontroversial and universally accepted notion, that every sociologist agrees that definitions of right and wrong vary from one society to another (Merton, 1971, p. 827). This is not entirely true. Some approaches are more likely to emphasize the universals in deviance than the variation or relativity. Functionalism, for instance, has argued that some actions are more likely to be punished—that is, regarded as deviant—more or less universally, in societies and cultures around the world, because they are *dysfunctional.* Consequently, tolerating them would

lead to their widespread enactment and hence, a weaker, less cohesive, less viable society. Incest is just such an act: Cultures almost everywhere prohibit incest because it undermines the foundation of the society: the family (Davis, 1949, pp. 401–404, 1976, p. 226). Likewise, certain actions are highly likely to be regarded as crimes in nearly all societies with a penal code because they are inherently harmful; any society that did not discourage them by outlawing and penalizing them would be seriously jeopardized (Newman, 1976). Moreover, even though some types of acts (such as the unprovoked killing of a member of the society or group) are condemned everywhere and at all times, exactly which *specific* acts fall into a deviant category and hence, qualify as worthy of condemnation, vary a great deal. In the Middle East, the murder of Arabs by Jews may be seen as heroic—not deviant—among some Jews (but not others), while the murder of Jews by Arabs, likewise, may be praised, not condemned, among some Arabs (Cowell, 1994; Greenberg, 1995). The recognition of this fact varies considerably among sociological perspectives. Hence, though most other perspectives are, at most, only *moderately* relativistic in that they are more likely to stress the universals in deviance and crime—that is, the similarities from one moral code to another—the labeling perspective may be referred to as much more *radically* relativistic in that it is more likely to emphasize differences, that is, the variation or relativity in moral and legal codes from one society to another.

In addition, the labeling or interactionist approach emphasizes relativity from one group, subculture, or individual to another *within the same society.* For instance, some social circles approve of marijuana use, while others condemn it (Becker, 1963, pp. 70, 72–78). Some individuals condemn homosexuality, while others do not (Kitsuse, 1962). Dance musicians regard the music they are hired to play, which their "square" audiences request, as inferior to the jazz they themselves prefer (Becker, 1963, pp. 89–91). Heroin addicts see themselves, in many important respects, as superior to "conventional, middle-class society" (Finestone, 1964). We will almost always be able to locate certain circles of individuals who tolerate or accept forms of behavior that are widely or more typically condemned. Some of these circles are, of course, practitioners of deviance themselves. But others are made up of individuals who, although they do not practice the behavior in question, do not condemn those who do, either. Relativity from one group to another is a crucial element in the labeling theorist's approach. It underscores the distinction, made by Plummer and stressed here in Chapter 2, between *societal* and *situational* deviance (1979, pp. 97–99). That is, an act or type of act may be widely condemned in a given society, according to that society's "abstract meaning systems," although *in a specific situation,* that condemnation may not have in fact taken place. Research has shown that although some variation does exist, the degree of agreement in the same society about what should be condemned is quite high (Rossi et al., 1974; Klaus and Kalish, 1984). Again, this becomes a question of emphasis: Labeling theorists emphasize the variation; adherents of most other perspectives emphasize the agreement. And once again, labeling theory emerges as the more radically relativistic position. Far from being trivial and unoriginal, the labeling or interactionist perspective can be seen as bucking the tide of mainstream consensus.

Audiences. The labeling process is generated by *audiences*. An audience is an individual or any number of individuals who observe and evaluate an act, a condition, or an individual. An audience could be one's friends, relatives, or neighbors, co-workers, the police, teachers, a psychiatrist, bystanders or observers—even oneself, for you can be an observer and an evaluator of your own behavior or condition (Becker, 1963, p. 31; Rotenberg, 1974). It is the *audience* which determines whether something or someone is deviant: no audience, no labeling, therefore, no deviance. However, an audience need not *directly* view an act, condition, or person; audiences can witness behavior or conditions "indirectly," that is, they can hear or be told about someone's behavior or condition, or they can simply have a negative or condemnatory attitude toward a class or category of behavior: "The critical variable in the study of deviance . . . is the social audience rather than the individual actor, since it is the audience which eventually determines whether or not any episode of behavior *or any class of episodes* is labeled deviant" (Erikson, 1964, p. 11; my emphasis). In other words, audiences can evaluate *categories* of deviance and stand ready to condemn them, even before they have actually witnessed specific, concrete cases of these categories.

This means that no act is deviant in the abstract, independent of the actual or potential reactions of audiences. Behavior is deviant only *to* specific audiences. Deviance is not a property contained in specific actions (although certain kinds of actions are more likely to be condemned than others in a wide range of settings). Rather, deviance is a *relational* or *transactional* term that spells out a certain kind of *relationship* between an act and specific audiences. This relationship, in effect, says that members of audiences A, B, and C are likely to find this behavior or condition offensive and may wish to punish the perpetrators or possessors, even though most of audiences X, Y, and Z are unlikely to have this reaction. Thus, *to* audiences A, B, and C, a specific form of behavior or type of trait are deviant; *to* audiences X, Y, and Z, they are not. Again, the question, "Is this behavior deviant?" cannot be answered until we specify the specific audiences that are evaluating and reacting to them. Moreover, members of audiences may *express* their condemnation in certain situations but not others.

Some audiences include the following. First, society at large (Schur, 1971, p. 12). It can be said, for instance, that a majority of the American public finds adulterous sex morally unacceptable and therefore deviant. They are likely to voice condemnation of the adulterer, although in most instances, that condemnation is likely to be fairly mild. The widespread acceptance of this view leads us to say that in American society as a whole, adultery is regarded as a form of deviance. A second audience are the *significant others* of the potentially labeled individual (Schur, 1971, pp. 12–13), that is, those people with which one interacts most frequently and intimately, and with whom one has a close relationship and whose opinions one values. It could be, for instance, that in your social circle, sex by a married person with someone other than one's spouse is perfectly acceptable. Thus, to the audience of *your* significant others, adultery is *not* deviant; you will not be condemned by them for such an action. On the other hand, in *my* significant social circle, let's say, adultery is an abomination, a sin of the highest magnitude, one that if known about, will stigmatize an individual who engages in it and make him or her an outcast. Thus, to the audience of my significant others, adultery is most decidedly deviant. And a third type of possible audience are official and organizational agents of social control (Schur, 1971, p. 13). Can you get into some kind of *formal* or *official* trouble for engaging in and getting caught at the behavior? Can you be arrested for it? Can you be committed to a mental hospital? Lose certain benefits or rights?

In most law enforcement agencies, at least in the United States, adultery is not a legitimate cause for arrest. Thus, to the audience of agents of formal social control, adultery is not deviant. Thus, whether an act is deviant or not depends on the audience which does or would evaluate the act. Without specifying real-life audiences, the question of an act's or a trait's deviance is meaningless.

The Construction of Moral Meanings and Definitions. Acts or traits are not intrinsically deviant. They can be, and usually are, looked upon and judged in various ways. How does a particular type of behavior or characteristic come to be regarded as morally undesirable, deviant, worthy of generating condemnation? Moral meanings are *constructed*. Notions of wrong and right come to be defined over time within specific social and cultural contexts. They arise out of specific processes and structures. As we saw in Chapter 3, at one time in the United States, marijuana use was not condemned; it was a morally neutral activity. By the 1930s, however, its use came to be defined as deviant. Why? What causes an activity to be defined as deviant? What processes and structures collaborate to generate the construction of a negative moral meaning and definition with respect to this particular activity, marijuana use? What led to a relaxation of this negative definition in the 1970s? And a strengthening of the view of marijuana use as morally unacceptable during the 1980s and 1990s?

Although there are many factors that play a role in the construction of moral meanings, labeling theorists have stressed two: *moral entrepreneurs* and *social status and power*.

First, if *moral enterpreneurs*—persuasive, legitimate, active, credible, figures—launch a campaign to discredit an activity, it stands a high chance of being widely regarded as wrong or immoral, in a word, deviant (Becker, 1963, pp. 147–163). Just such a process took place in the 1930s with marijuana (Becker, 1963, pp. 135–147). In the 1980s, antidrug sentiment was revived, with First Lady Nancy Reagan acting as a "moral entrepreneur" (Goode, 1993, p. 53).

A second factor facilitating the definition of an activity or condition as deviant is the *social status and power* of individuals who engage in an activity, and that of those who condemn it (Becker, 1963, pp. 15–18, 145; Lofland, 1969, p. 14). Relatively low-status, powerless individuals are more likely to find their activities or traits defined as morally unacceptable—deviant—than those who have a higher status and more power. In the 1930s, for instance, marijuana was more likely to be used by racial and ethnic minorities, the young, and jazz musicians—all politically marginal social categories—than by the mainstream. This made it easier for moral entrepreneurs to categorize their behavior as morally undesirable and therefore deviant.

The Inner World of Deviance. One major endeavor of the labeling theorist is the attempt to understand the *inner world* of deviance. As I said above, interactionism stresses the ethnographic, anthropological, or participant observation research method: hanging around the individuals under study, observing them in their natural habitat, getting as close to the activity of interest as possible. This means attempting to understand the deviant world *as the deviant lives and understands it.* For instance, how do homosexuals see and define their behavior? What is their attitude about being gay? How do they experience being homosexual? How do they look upon the "straight" world? What is the construction of *their* moral meaning like? How do they define right and wrong with respect to sexuality? What does it feel like to be a member of a minority whose members are looked down upon by the straight majority? To know how the world of homosexuality is lived, it is necessary to enter that world and listen to and observe those who actually live in it.

It makes sense that there is a certain "compatibility" in interactionism's view of deviance as stigma and its practice of participant observational research techniques (Downes and Rock, 1988, p. 169). After all, if one, and one's behavior, are condemned, one is likely to draw together into "small, bounded social worlds" of similarly condemned individuals. "Heroin-users, thieves, and prostitutes may draw themselves apart [from mainstream society], seeking those who share common problems, experiences, and solutions" (p. 169). In such groupings, one makes oneself available for study by the interactionist who uses anthropological field techniques. To the extent that stigmatized individuals do not gather together in such social groupings, they are not amenable to study by means of this research technique.

It has sometimes been said that interactionism is focused more or less exclusively on the definers and labelers of deviance, that the deviant is secondary, a passive cipher who merely responds but does not act, who becomes a product of how he or she is defined (Gouldner, 1968). Nothing can be further from the truth. Interactionism is *fascinated* by the details of the lives of individuals and groups defined as deviant. It emphasizes how *creative* and *diverse* reactions to being so defined are, how *incapable* powerful deviance-definers are in imposing their will and conceptions on deviants, how *active* deviants are in creating their own definitions and conceptions, how truly *complex* the lives of deviants are, and how totally *ignorant* outsiders are of these lives until they enter them and make the effort to find out about them. Inspect the primary documents of the labeling school, for instance, Becker's *Outsiders* (1963) and the articles making up his anthology, *The Other Side* (1964). The first includes detailed ethnographies of jazz musicians and marijuana smokers, their lives, their inner worlds, how they see and define things, how they carve out a meaningful social existence in the face of mainstream opposition to their way of seeing and doing things. The second, a collection of articles, again, details the lives of those within a specific deviant scene, circle, or group: for instance, heroin addiction (Ray, 1964; Finestone, 1964), physician narcotic addiction (Winick, 1964), homosexual prostitution (Reiss, 1964), check forging (Lemert, 1964b), mental illness (Sampson et al., 1964), gambling (Zola, 1964). All the *articles* reflect an interactionist approach in that they represent *detailed descriptions of an insider's view;* they all attempt to get at "the inner world of deviance." The same can be said for the more recent, second-, third-, or fourth-generation interactionists, the theoretical descendants of the original labeling theorists. (For a representative sampling, see Adler and Adler, 1994; Kelly, 1995; Rubington and Weinberg, 1995.)

Labeling and Stigma. The key elements in the deviance process are labeling and stigmatizing. This entails two steps. First, an *activity* (or condition) is labeled deviant, and second, a specific *individual* is labeled as *a* deviant. In these two labeling processes, if no one labels something or someone deviant, *no deviance exists.* An act cannot be deviant in the abstract; it must be defined as such by the members of a society or a group *as* deviant, it must be *labeled* as morally wrong. Likewise, a person cannot be regarded as a deviant until this labeling process takes place.

Labeling involves attaching a *stigmatizing* definition to an activity, a condition, or a behavior. Stigma is a stain, a sign of reproach or social undesirability, an indication to the world that one has been singled out as a shameful, morally discredited human being. Someone who has been stigmatized is a "marked" person; he or she has a "spoiled identity." (Although, interestingly enough, Erving Goffman, who wrote a classic book on stigma that strongly influenced the labeling theorists [1963, p. 141], stated: "I do not think all deviators have enough in common to warrant a special analysis.") A stigmatized person is one who has been labeled a deviant. Once someone has been so discredited, relations with conventional, respectable others become difficult, strained, problematic. In other words, "being caught and branded as a deviant has important consequences for one's further participation and self-image. . . . Committing the improper act and being publicly caught at it places [the individual] in a new status. He [or she] has been revealed as a different kind of person from the kind he [or she] was supposed to be. He [or she] is labeled a 'fairy,' 'dope fiend,' 'nut,' or 'lunatic,' and treated accordingly" (Becker, 1963, p. 31, 32). Becker cites the case of a young Trobriand Islander who had been having an affair with his cousin. Such incestuous liaisons were strongly condemned in that society; the couple's behavior, though known about and disapproved of, did not generate any concrete reaction. The problem began when the young woman's former lover, resentful at having been jilted, publicly denounced the incestuous pair. At that point, the young man, now publicly labeled and stigmatized, committed suicide (Becker, 1963, pp. 10–11; Malinowski, 1926, pp. 77–80).

So crucial is this labeling process that in some respects, it does not much matter whether or not someone who has been stigmatized has actually engaged in the behavior of which he or she is accused. In the light of labeling theory, *falsely accused* deviants—if the accusations stick—are still deviants (Becker, 1963, p. 20). In many important respects, they resemble individuals who really *do* commit acts that violate the rules. For example, women and men burned at the stake for the crime of witchcraft in the fifteenth and sixteenth centuries were deviants in the eyes of the authorities and the community (Currie, 1968; Ben-Yehuda, 1980), even though they clearly did not engage in a pact with the devil. Two day-care workers are stigmatized in a certain community for, let's say, the sexual molestation of young children. One did it and the other didn't. Labeling theory would hold that these two individuals will share important experiences and characteristics in common, *by virtue of that labeling process alone,* even though they are poles apart with respect to having committed the behavior of which they were accused. While their lives are unlikely to be *identical* simply because both are seen by the community as deviants, the similarities they share are likely to be revealing.

As we saw in Chapter 2, labeling theorists are split down the middle with respect to whether a class or category of behavior or characteristics can be regarded as deviant *in the absence of* the labeling of specific enactors or possessors. In other words, can someone who engages in behavior that is widely condemned—such as homosexuality, crack cocaine abuse, or robbery—be said to engage in "deviant behavior" without having actually been caught and punished? Can someone who is infected with the HIV virus or AIDS—a condition that no one except himself or herself and a few medical specialists knows about—be regarded as having a "deviant" condition? Erikson (1964, p. 11, 1966, p. 13) refers to a "class of episodes" as deviant, indicating that a category of behavior can be labeled even though someone who engages in it may not be labeled. Becker, (1963, pp. 14, 19, 20–21) waffles on the issue. In some places, he implies this is possible; in other places, he seems to say it is not. For instance, he refers to "secret deviance" (pp. 20–21). Clearly, these are acts that are unlabeled in the concrete instance. But if deviance is *defined* by labeling, how can something be deviant *in the absence of labeling?* The only way is for a *specific, concrete* act to be sufficiently similar to a *class* of acts that is *generally* condemned. In contrast, Kitsuse (1962) is entirely consistent on the issue: Until and unless a specific, concrete individual engaging in a specific, concrete act is caught and punished, *we cannot refer to deviance at all.* No punishment, no deviance, period. To Kitsuse, a class of behavior—for example, homosexuality—cannot be regarded as deviant. Only specific instances of it, which have in fact been detected and their perpetrators punished, can be so regarded.

Once again, this problem is resolved by Plummer's distinction between *societal* deviance and *situational* deviance (1979, p. 98). "Societal" deviance is made up of widely condemned categories or classes of behavior. It would be difficult to argue that robbery, homosexuality, transvestism,

or adultery per se are not regarded by a high proportion of Americans as censurable, deplorable behavior, even though, in some specific instances, individuals who engage in them and are detected doing them are not condemned. The fact is that one is far more likely to be stigmatized than praised for engaging in them. For most people, they are not acceptable or "normal" behavior. One need not agree with this judgment, or its appropriateness, justice, or fairness, to recognize that it exists and is widely accepted.

In contrast, "situational" deviance ignores such a broad consensus and examines only concrete negative judgments of behavior, traits, and individuals *in specific contexts.* Not all alcoholics are condemned for their excessive drinking by all who face them; there are likely to be specific situations and contexts in which they interact with individuals who do *not* condemn them, where the majority judgement is *not* followed. Looking at situational deviance focuses exclusively on judgments of deviance in real-life, micro-interactional settings (Plummer, 1979, p. 98).

Thus, among the early labeling theorists, Kitsuse believes that societal deviance *does not exist;* the only legitimate form of deviance is *situational* deviance. Erikson admits that both societal and situational deviance exist. And, in places, Becker implies that societal deviance exists, and in other places, he suggests that *only* cases of situational deviance constitute legitimate examples of deviant behavior. As we saw earlier, this distinction between "societal" and "situational" deviance parallels Goffman's distinction between having a *discreditable* and a *discredited* identity. Someone with "discrediting" information that is not known by others has a *discreditable* identity; they are likely to conceal that information from others and engage in "passing" as "normal." Were others to find out about that information, one is likely to be condemned, denounced, stigmatized, labeled a deviant, in short, one's identity will be *discredited.* Thus, the "secret deviant" is an individual with a *discreditable identity,* who possesses a guilty (or "dirty") secret: discrediting information, which is concealed, enabling him or her to pass as a conventional person in a conventional world.

Contingencies. Not everyone who violates a rule or a law will be criticized, condemned, or punished by those who witness or hear about the deed (Kitsuse, 1962; Becker, 1963, pp. 11–13; Erikson,

1964, pp. 10, 12). Labeling theorists argue that rule breakers are not punished or condemned *simply* because they have violated society's rules. Actions or traits that are regarded as deviant to most people in a society may be tolerated by certain individuals or groups within it, or in a number of situations or contexts. Ideas about what behavior should be tolerated or punished are not necessarily held in common by all members of a large, complex society. In other words, we should not expect homogeneity and uniformity in what is regarded as deviant. Even when people disapprove of a given class of behavior in general, or specific, concrete instances of it, they do not always condemn or punish those who engage in it (Becker, 1963, p. 12; Kitsuse, 1962). Condemnation may not be relevant in a specific situation or interaction; every moment in the relations between a homosexual and a disapproving "straight" person need *not* be saturated with disapproval on the part of the latter for us to nonetheless say that he or she disapproves of homosexuality and homosexuals. Moreover, *who* the deviant actor or possessor of a deviant trait *is* often makes a difference, which we saw in the discussion on different kinds of relativity in Chapter 2. One may voice disapproval to the perpetrator when one discovers the adultery of a friend or a peer; however, one is likely to keep that disapproval hidden when it is one's boss who is the guilty party.

A contingency is a seemingly incidental or accidental feature of an event or a phenomenon which nonetheless exerts a significant impact; it is a supposedly chance factor which determines an outcome. In the world of deviance, a contingency is anything that logically *shouldn't* influence the labeling process, but *actually does.* Two people are mentally disordered. One lives in a rural area very far from a state mental hospital, a second lives very near one. The first is able to live out his life among people who tolerate him and his behavior, and he is never institutionalized. The second, in contrast, is institutionalized (Goffman, 1961, p. 135). In this case, the distance one lives from a mental hospital is a contingency. One theorist even went so far as to argue that it is possible to say that "mental patients suffer distinctly not from mental illness, but from contingencies" (Goffman, 1961, p. 135).

The "Saints" are a gang composed mainly of middle-class adolescent boys. The "Roughnecks" are a gang made up of lower- and working-class boys. Both engage, more or less equally, in a variety of delinquent activities. None of the Saints is

ever arrested for the crimes or delinquencies they have committed; when apprehended, they are taken home to their parents and given a stern warning. In contrast, all of the Roughnecks have been arrested, some of them frequently. Here, the *socioeconomic status* of their parents is a contingency determining whether or not they get arrested (Chambliss, 1973).

One specific type of contingency is what is referred to as *ancillary* or *auxiliary characteristics.* These are all the seemingly secondary characteristics or traits, such as power and status, which shouldn't influence the labeling process, but actually do. As a general rule, the greater the prestige and power of the deviator, the greater the likelihood that he or she will be able to avoid or resist being stigmatized as a deviant. The less prestige and power the deviator has, the higher the likelihood of being successfully stigmatized or negatively labeled. In short, the application of the label "deviant" is strongly influenced by factors that lie outside deviant behavior itself. Other ancillary, auxiliary, or secondary traits or characteristics include appearance, age, sex, and race. At times, they exert an influence on the labeling process. Labeling theorists emphasize the role that ancillary characteristics play as contingencies in the labeling process. As we saw in Chapter 4, positivists are much less likely to stress the role of contingencies in the criminal-defining process.

Reflexivity. Reflexivity means looking at ourselves in part through the eyes of others. It is what is widely referred to, although too mechanistically, as the "looking-glass self." Labeling theory is based on a seemingly simple but fundamental observation: "We see ourselves through the eyes of others, and when others see us in a certain way, at least for long enough or sufficiently powerfully, their views are sure to have some effect" (Glassner, 1982, p. 71). Being stigmatized by others is certainly not the only factor that influences what people do in the drama of deviance, but it is a crucial one. In addition, not everyone who enacts behavior that would be punished if it were discovered is caught—nor, for that matter, punished. Nor do all people who enact certain behavior care what the majority thinks of them or their behavior; they may be focused more or less exclusively on the views of their own circle or group. At the same time, nearly all people who violate society's major norms know that they are likely to be punished, condemned, stigmatized, and labeled as deviants if they were to be discovered. Thus, they move around in a world in which they are aware that their identities and behavior are potentially punishable. They may be able to *partially* insulate themselves in circles or groups whose members would tolerate what they do or who they are, but nearly all have to navigate in the "straight" or mainstream world from time to time. In other words, both direct *and* indirect, or concrete *and* symbolic labeling operate in the world of deviance (Warren and Johnson, 1972, pp. 76-77). "Indirect" or "symbolic" labeling is the awareness by a deviance-enactor that his or her behavior is saturated with public scorn, his or her identity is potentially discreditable, that he or she *would be* stigmatized if discovered. People who violate norms have to deal with the probable and potential, as well as the actual and concrete, reactions of the respectable, conventional, law-abiding majority. All violators of major norms must at least ask themselves, "How would others react to me and my behavior?" If the answer is, "They will punish me," then the rule breaker must try to avoid detection, remain within deviant or minority circles, or be prepared for being punished, condemned, and stigmatized.

The "Stickiness" of Labels and the Self-Fulfulling Prophecy. Labeling theorists argue that stigmatizing someone as a socially and morally undesirable character has important consequences for that person's further rule breaking. Under certain circumstances, being labeled may intensify one's commitment to a deviant identity and contribute to further deviant behavior. Some conventional, law-abiding citizens believe "once a deviant, always a deviant." Someone who has been stigmatized and labeled "is ushered into the deviant position by a decisive and often dramatic ceremony, yet is retired from it with hardly a word of public notice." As a result, the deviant is given "no proper licence to resume a normal life in the community. Nothing has happened to cancel out the stigma imposed upon him" or her. The original judgment "is still in effect." The conforming members of a society tend to be "reluctant to accept the returning deviant on an entirely equal footing" (Erikson, 1964, p. 16, 17).

Deviant labels tend to be "sticky"; the community tends to stereotype someone as, above all and most importantly, a deviant. When someone is identified as a deviant, the community asks, "What kind

of person would break such an important rule?" The answer that is given is "one who is different from the rest of us, who cannot or will not act as a moral being and therefore might break other important rules" (Becker, 1963, p. 34). Deviant labeling is widely regarded as a quality that is "in" the person, an attribute that is carried wherever he or she goes; therefore, it is permanent or at least long-lasting. Deviant behavior is said to be caused by an indwelling, essentialistic trait; it is not seen as accidental or trivial, but a fixture of the individual. Once a deviant label has been attached, it is difficult to shake. Ex-convicts find it difficult to find legitimate employment upon their release from prison (Schwartz and Skolnick, 1964); once psychiatrists make a diagnosis of mental illness, hardly any amount of contrary evidence can dislodge their faith in it (Rosenhan, 1973); ex-mental patients are carefully scrutinized for odd, eccentric, or bizarre behavior; a young woman who is seen as sexually promiscuous (the label may or may not have been earned as a result of her actual behavior) will, in all likelihood, continue to be so viewed until she leaves the community.

Such stigmatizing and stereotyping tends to deny to deviants "the ordinary means of carrying on the routines of everyday life open to most people. Because of this denial, the deviant must of necessity develop illegitimate routines" (Becker, 1963, p. 35). As a consequence, the labeling process may actually increase the deviant's further commitment to deviant behavior. It may limit conventional options and opportunities, strengthen a deviant identity, and maximize participation in a deviant group. Labeling someone, thus, may become "a self-fulfilling prophecy" (Becker, 1963, p. 34) in that *someone becomes what he or she is accused of being*, even though that original accusation may have been false (Merton, 1948, 1957, pp. 421–436; Jones, 1977; Jones, 1986). The ex-con will be seen as dishonest and thus will find it impossible to get a straight job, and will return to a life of crime; the ex-mental patient will be defined as "still crazy," and buckle under the strain of having to prove he or she is normal; the sexually permissive young woman may find the only reason why boys will want to date her is for short-term sexual gratification, and so she ends up satisfying their demands.

Nonetheless, contrary to the stereotype about labeling theory (N. Davis, 1980, p. 199), interactionists are careful to point out that negative labeling does *not* always or inevitably have this self-fulfilling outcome. "Obviously," says Becker, "everyone caught in one deviant act and labeled a deviant does not move inevitably toward greater deviance" (Becker, 1963, p. 36). Indeed, such labeling could very well "stamp out," repress, or cause a discontinuation of the deviant behavior that was punished, as is often the case with marijuana use (Becker, 1955, 1963, p. 59), political radicalism in Europe, and polygyny (a man having several wives) in Utah (Lemert, 1951, p. 63). Still, the more interesting prediction, and the one on which labeling theorists have focused, is that social control will lead to an intensification of the commitment to deviance, not a discontinuation of it.

It is important to emphasize that labels, stereotypes, and definitions of deviance are always in a state of flux. It is almost certain that many of the public conceptions of deviance that were widely held when labeling theorists were writing, are now quite different. For instance, in the 1950s and early 1960s, when Becker wrote about marijuana use, it was regarded as a serious form of deviance (1953, 1955, 1963, pp. 41–78), one that often disqualified the known user from normal interaction in polite company. Although there is more condemnation of marijuana use today than there was in the late 1970s, its seriousness as deviance has considerably diminished from the 1950s and early 1960s. The condemnation by the nonusing public has softened and the stereotypes they hold of use and users are more realistic. As a result, the capacity of the ex-user to cast off a stigmatizing label is almost certainly far greater than was true in past generations. (Still, recall that in 1985, a Supreme Court nominee, Douglas Ginzberg, was disqualified for having smoked marijuana more than a decade before; and in 1992, the Democratic candidate for president, Bill Clinton, in describing a marijuana-smoking episode of 20 years in the past, felt sufficiently pressured about it to claim that he "didn't inhale.") Likewise, ridicule and stigma of the mentally ill and ex-mentally ill has diminished since the heyday of interactionist writings on the subject (Goffman, 1961, 1963; Scheff, 1966). The label of ex-mental patient is far less "sticky" today than it was in the past; being mentally ill is certainly seen as a far less irreversible condition. Today, it seems likely that the label of mental patient does not necessarily carry over into the future of former mental patients if over time their behavior does not correspond to the label. If former mental patients can act relatively normal, they probably can shed their label and live a normal life (Cockerham, 1996, pp. 259–272). Just as conceptions of deviance are relative to time and place, so is the degree of "stickiness" of deviant labels.

Criticisms of Labeling Theory

Perhaps what is most remarkable about labeling theory is not so much what it says but what has been said about it. If we were to examine only the original texts, that is, those that have attracted the majority of the citations—Lemert's book (1951), a forerunner to labeling theory, one book and an anthology by Becker (1963, 1964), one article by Kitsuse (1962), included in Becker's anthology, one article by Erikson (1962), also included, and a book by Erikson (1966), whose theoretical foundation is functionalism, not interactionism—we would find that they have attracted commentary running into hundreds of works. There are few examples in the history of sociology of so much having been written about so little. (Anomie theory represents an even more spectacular case.) Moreover, the bulk of this commentary on labeling theory has been negative. It represents, in the words of one defender of the perspective, "a major industry of criticism" (Plummer, 1979, p. 119). If these critiques had died out by now, it might indicate that labeling theory had been refuted, discredited, and was no longer valid or useful. In fact, these comments, criticisms, and critiques continue to be written and published, suggesting that the theory may resonate with meaningful themes in the sociology of deviance (Conover, 1976, p. 229). Although the perspective is often charged with being "moribund" (Manning, 1975), it is interesting that its insights have provided the inspiration for a substantial body of recent work (for instance, LaFree, 1989; Braithwaite, 1989; Link et al., 1989; most of the selections in Kelly, 1993, Adler and Adler, 1994, and Rubington and Weinberg, 1996).

Many contemporary observers agree that labeling theory's shift away from an exclusive emphasis on questions of the causality and etiology of deviance to broader concerns, including the issue of judgments of deviance, is all to the good. At the same time, the perspective has encountered a great deal of criticism from a wide variety of sources.

Perhaps the most common criticism of labeling theory—and it has come from sociologists working in the positivist tradition—is that it is not a theory at all. It does not explain the etiology or cause of acts such as rape, criminal homicide, homosexuality, robbery, drug addiction, child molestation, and so on. Instead, its critics charge, it is only concerned with *reactions to* these acts, not why they occur in the first place. Social scientists with a positivistic orientation want to know, *"Why do they do it?"* On this issue, they say, labeling theory is silent, in fact, useless (Gibbs, 1966, pp. 11–12, 1972, p. 44; Hirschi, 1973, pp. 168–169; Clinard and Meier, 1989, p. 96). Labeling "does not create the behavior in the first place" (Akers, 1968, 1985, p. 81). Therefore, these critics charge, the perspective cannot account for why the behavior was enacted; it is, in short, inadequate with respect to the most basic requirement of any theory—explanation.

Labeling theorists actually agree that their perspective does not deal with the question of etiology or cause. In fact, they say, labeling theory was never intended to be an explanation of primary deviation (Kitsuse, 1972, p. 236; Becker, 1973, p. 179), or why people engage in deviant behavior initially. In the words of Becker, the original proponents of labeling theory "did not pose solutions to the etiologic question." This sentiment was captured early on by Lemert's observation that primary deviation is "polygenetic," and its causality of no special significance. Labeling theorists agree that the perspective should not be thought of as an explanatory theory in the strict sense. Rather, it is an orientation, a perspective that guides the social scientist to interesting processes, variables, and observations. Thus, the criticisms along these lines are, for the most part, irrelevant and misguided. Critics are insisting that labeling theory should do something its proponents never set out to do in the first place.

A second commonly leveled criticism is that the act of labeling does not inevitably produce an intensification of the actor's commitment to deviance, deviant behavior, or a deviant identity. Critics often charge that punishment is frequently effective; it causes wrongdoers to give up rule breaking and return to conventionality (Mankoff, 1971; Akers, 1985, pp. 30–32; Gove, 1982b; Bordua, 1967). In addition, some critics aver, it is possible for individuals to engage in rule-breaking behavior *prior to* or *in the absence of* labeling or stigma (Scull, 1972, p. 284). In other words, a career of enacting certain forms of behavior can develop *in the absence of labeling* (Clinard and Meier, 1995, pp. 121–128). Many, perhaps most, individuals who engage in deviant behavior, even routinely, are never apprehended, stigmatized, or labeled, and yet they continue the behavior in question (Warren and Johnson, 1972).

However, as we saw earlier, labeling theorists concur with this line of commentary, too. The perspective never asserted that labeling necessarily produces further deviant behavior. Nor is labeling necessary for primary deviance to take place or be continued over time. The theory's critics are confusing labeling theory's emphasis on deviant *labels* which judge certain actions to be instances of deviance with the *behavior* to which the labels refer. Moreover, as I explained earlier, Lemert pointed out that a number of practices (the two examples he provided were political radicalism and polygyny) were "stamped out" rather than stimulated by social control (1951, p. 63). Becker, too, emphasized that pursuing a deviant path may be facilitated best by an *absence* of social control; being apprehended and condemned for engaging in deviant behavior often results in a *discontinuation* of the practice. For instance, Becker pointed out, the marijuana smoker must learn to "contend with the powerful forces of social control" in order to continue the use of this drug (1955, 1963, p. 59). When nonusers punish or apply sanctions to the user, the latter may simply decide to give up the grass. These sanctions often have the effect of rendering the activity "distasteful," "inexpedient," or "immoral," and users are pressured to become nonusers. The user can continue only if he or she is able to render these sanctions ineffective (1963, pp. 60–62). Social control, then, *according to labeling theorists,* may actually function to *prevent* some deviant behavior. The view that is claimed for labeling theorists—that they argued that everyone who is labeled inevitably moves toward greater deviance—although widespread, is clearly erroneous. It is a view of the perspective that has been "vulgarized into a narrow theory"; it attributes to labeling theorists a position they simply did not support (Plummer, 1979, p. 89).

Another criticism, usually stemming from critics holding a radical or Marxist approach, argues that labeling theory solidifies the rule of the powerful and thereby assists in the oppression of powerless groups. More broadly, labeling theory contributes to oppression, exploitation, imperialism, racism, and sexism (Gouldner, 1968; Smith, 1973; Thio, 1973). It does this in two ways. First, by concentrating on the condemned and stigmatized behavior of powerless individuals—"nuts, sluts, and deviated preverts" (Liazos, 1972), that is, the dramatic and "immoral" varieties of deviance that capture the conventional imagination and outrage the general public. And secondly, as a consequence, it ignores the truly dangerous and damaging individuals and forms of behavior, "the unethical, illegal, and destructive actions of powerful individuals, groups, and institutions in our society" (Liazos, 1972, p. 111). Here, Marxists would include the exploitation of workers by factory owners and managers; manufacturers selling shoddy, dangerous mechandise to the public; employers denying qualified workers jobs on the basis of their sex or race; owners and managers failing to install safety devices in mines and factories, killing workers as a result; industrialists polluting the atmosphere with factory waste; and so on. Why haven't the labeling theorists studied actions such as these? such critics ask. Why have they concentrated on the mentally ill, the sexually unconventional, drug users, and skid-row alcoholics, in short, individuals who are socially marginal and politically powerless, who are acted upon but who have relatively little impact on society? Why haven't the labeling theorists concentrated on the real villains, the manipulators, the high-level capitalist criminals—the business elite?

This line of criticism can be addressed in at least two ways. First, it is true that sociologists identified as belonging to the labeling school have not investigated the destructive actions of the powerful in society. The forms of behavior that radicals, conflict theorists, Marxists, and feminists study, and urge that practitioners of other perspectives study, those that they criticize labelists for ignoring—oppression, exploitation, racism, sexism, imperialism, and so on—certainly do more harm to human life than deviant behavior generally. But the reason for this is quite simple and, within the labeling approach, obvious: They have not studied them because *they are not seriously deviant,* that is, they are not condemned by the public to the same degree as those actions that labeling theorists *have* studied are condemned. Like the functionalists, labeling theory stresses *irony*: It is ironic that behavior such as obviously destructive acts are not generally regarded as deviant. Many of us, no doubt, feel that such behavior *should* be condemned by the public. And yet, deviance is behavior that is widely condemned; a study of deviance is not *about* oppression and exploitation. (Except insofar as it is also condemned.) It is *about* condemnation and punishment, and behavior and traits that generate condemnation and punishment. To put the matter another way: To the extent that oppression and exploitation are *not* condemned or punished, they are *not* forms of deviance; to the extent that they *are* condemned or punished, they *are* forms of deviance. Oppression and exploitation vary independently of deviance; they cannot be equated by decree. Certainly they can be studied, but in most cases, not under the rubric of deviance. The plain fact is that most of the forms of oppression and exploitation that radicals and Marxists denounce *are simply not condemned very much by the members of the society.* Therefore, they do not qualify as acts of deviance. When they become condemned, labeling theorists will study them. The growing denunciation of a variety of crimes and unethical acts by the powerful (for instance, pollution, sexual harassment by executives, corporate crimes) should stimulate an interest in them *as* deviance by sociologists. However, this is a fairly recent development, and postdates the work of the original labeling theorists.

To be condemned is to be disvalued; to be disvalued is to be rendered powerless. One cannot be a respectable business executive engaging in actions that are widely seen as "just business" and be regarded as a deviant at the same time. *"The study of deviance is the study of devalued groups, and devalued groups are groups which lack status and privilege."* A sociology of deviance "which does not focus centrally on powerless groups is likely to be a very odd sociology of deviance" (Plummer, 1979, p. 110). The radicals and Marxists want it both ways, as Edwin Lemert points out; they "call for sociologists to stigmatize the oppressor instead of their victims." In so doing, they contradict themselves "by insisting that high-ranking persons are deviants even though they admittedly hold the power indispensable to defining deviance" (Liazos, 1972; Lemert, 1974, p. 462). The fact is, logically, one *can't* have it both ways. If high-level, damaging, unethical behavior *can* be defined as deviance, then the powerful do *not* have the most influence in defining deviance; if definitions of deviance are deflected away from their actions to those of the powerless, then clearly, the definitions of the powerful have to be taken into account. The radical and Marxist criticism of labeling theory founders on the shoals of a fatal contradiction.

A closely related criticism is that labeling theorists failed to take the role of *power* into account in the study of deviance. It is true that interactionists *mentioned* power in the deviance-defining process (for instance, Becker, 1963, pp. 15-18); however, for the most part, power is an *implied* or *taken for granted* rather than a truly *examined* factor. It is not enough to invoke the role of "moral entrepreneurs" in the passage of legislation, as Becker did in his analysis of the Marihuana Tax Act of 1937 (pp. 135–146). Power must be understood *in detail* and *in general*. *Exactly how* is power translated into the deviance-defining process? How is it wielded, how is it resisted? *Who prevails* in a dispute over what and who is deviant? *Under what conditions* are definitions created by the powerful successful, and under what conditions are they successfully *resisted*? What role does the state play in this process? Are there types of deviance in which the state plays a more substantial role than others? Questions such as these could be multiplied almost endlessly; they emphasize the fact that for the labeling theorists, power was a hazy, amorphous, and poorly understood concept, very much in need of systematic analysis. The very fact that labeling theorists invoked the crucial importance of power provided a critique of more traditional perspectives toward deviance, principally positivism and anomie theory. However, the fact that they did not follow up on these invocations provides a critique of their own work, even on its own terms. The failure of interactionists to study the role of power, systematically and in detail, is perhaps its major shortcoming.

And last, one problem that many observers have with the implications of the labeling perspective is a moral one: its laissez-faire or "live and let live" approach to deviance and crime. It seems to extend a hand of tolerance and acceptance—indeed, *appreciation* (Matza, 1969)—toward all manner of disvalued, harmful activities. Labeling theory's stance seems to be that harm, like deviance, is in the eye of the beholder. It's all a matter of definition as to whether a given form of behavior is harmful or not. When first formulated in the 1960s, labeling theory seemed quite radical. Its message was that the individuals who are condemned, ridiculed, persecuted, even arrested and imprisoned should not be the primary focus of attention. Instead, it said, we should take a hard look at the condemners, the persecutors, the self-righteous framers and enforcers of the law. Perhaps, labeling theorists seemed to be saying, deviants aren't nearly so harmful to society as conventional, law-abiding folk have said.

Maybe deviants are a problem to society just because a lot of people *think* they are a problem. The epigraph to Howard Becker's *Outsiders* (1963) is taken from William Faulkner's *As I Lay Dying*, which read, in part: "It's like it ain't so much what a fellow does, but the way the majority of folks looking at him when he does it." The clear implication seemed to be that the "problem" of deviance would disappear if we were to simply accept a wider range of unconventional behavior.

From today's vantage point, it is clear that this approach works better for some forms of behavior than others. If we do not condemn the jazz musician and the marijuana smoker (two examples of deviants in Becker's *Outsiders*), the homosexual (the subject of Kitsuse's classic article), and the Puritan law-breaker (Erikson's focus of attention), what about the rapist and murderer? The man who beats his wife and children to a bloody pulp? Or racists who rove in gangs and beat up African-Americans whom they catch walking in predominantly white neighborhoods? The chronic drunk who speeds, runs a red light, and plows into another car, killing an entire family? Are they condemned simply because of society's misplaced prejudices and biases? Should the mantle of tolerance be extended to cover them too?

In the early 1960s, it may have seemed extremely important that we understand how labeling and stigmatizing work to discredit perfectly harmless behavior, traits, and individuals. Today, it is equally important to recognize that *deviance may have real victims*. Not all deviance is harmful, it must be emphasized. But by the same token, not all deviance is harmless, either. The labeling theorists served an important service in the 1960s by showing that condemnation does not necessarily fall on the most harmful actions or the most harmful members of a society. At the same time, taking this argument to its logical extreme can imply that *all* deviants are misunderstood and mistreated, that *all* condemnation is irrational and based on erroneous preconceptions, and that in a sense, deviants are *always* society's victims (Goode, 1994). Clearly, no labeling theorists meant to say this, but their focus of attention on "soft" deviance to the exclusion of "hard" deviance (Ben-Yehuda, 1985, pp. 2, 3) seemed to imply this. (See Marcia Millman's essay, [1975, pp. 266-274] on how, in labeling theorists' studies of deviance—the work of Goffman being a major exception—*suffering* tends to be neglected.) Today, we know better and can take the labeling perspective for what it is: a flawed, incomplete, only partial look at an important, controversial phenomenon.

Labeling theory's influence has declined sharply since its heyday, which can be dated roughly from the mid-1960s to the mid-1970s. At that time, it was one of the most influential, most frequently cited perspectives in the study of deviance. This was especially so among the field's younger scholars and researchers, who yearned for a fresh, unconventional, and radically different way of looking at deviance. As I said above, it was widely and vigorously attacked, and many of these criticisms stuck. Eventually, much of the field recognized its inadequacies, and moved on to other perspectives, or sharply modified or adapted interactionist or labeling insights (Link et al., 1989; Braithwaite, 1989; LaFree, 1989). Today, there is no single approach or paradigm which dominates the field in the way that the Chicago school did in the 1920s or that labeling theory did circa 1970. What we see today is diversity, fragmentation, and "theoretical confusion" (Scull, 1988, p. 685). While the practitioners of a variety of perspectives attacked labeling theory for its inadequacies, no single perspective has managed to succeed "in establishing an alternative orientation to the field that [has] commanded wide assent" (p. 685). In spite of the criticisms, the labeling school left an enduring legacy to the field that even its critics make use of, albeit, for the most part, implicitly. Today, it is clear that while as a total approach to deviance, labeling *theory* is inadequate and incomplete, labeling *processes* take place in all deviance, and deserve a prominent place in its study.

CONFLICT THEORY

Social scientists can be divided according to how much *consensus* or *conflict* they see in contemporary society. Talcott Parsons, for instance, saw deviance as "a disturbance of the equilibrium of the interactive system" (1951, p. 250); in other words, harmony is the rule, and a disruption of that harmony calls for steps to reestablish peace and tranquility. The members of a society are socialized to behave properly; most of them accept the central values and norms of their society, and act accordingly; a few are improperly or inadequately socialized, or for some reason, the components of the social system are improperly integrated;

deviance ensues, disrupting the social order; forces act to restore society to its former state of equilibrium (Parsons, 1951, Chapter VII). This is a *consensus* view of society: Most people agree on the central values in a given society, disagreement causes disruption, disorder, and disequilibrium and a societal need to repair the damage that they inflict.

Consensus thinking is based on three principles. First, the values and beliefs of the members of a society are more or less consistent with one another; there is a high degree of consensus about basic or core values. In sociology, this view is likely to have been influenced by the thinking of French sociologist Emile Durkheim (1858–1917), who believed that societies possessed a "collective conscience," or a shared sense of morality. In other words, most people agree with one another about the most basic and important values.

Second, consensus thinkers argue that in advanced industrial societies, the members of the socety tend to be *interdependent*. They need one another to get along, each is doing something essential to the lives of others (Durkheim, 1933, pp. 111ff.).

And third, consensus theorists tend to see social life as fairly harmonious, and societies as more or less cohesive and stable. Societies display a kind of inherent and unconscious wisdom. As we saw, many social institutions that might seem destructive and repressive actually turn out to benefit the society as a whole, such as social stratification (Davis and Moore, 1945; Davis, 1949, pp. 366–368), prostitution (K. Davis, 1937, 1971), deviance and crime (Merton, 1957, pp. 78–80; Bell, 1961, pp. 127–150; Hawkins and Waller, 1936), and even conflict itself (Coser, 1956). The functionalists discussed at the beginning of this chapter are a good example of consensus theorists. All consensus theorists—functionalists included—agree that conflict exists, and has a crucial impact on the society; however, for the consensus theorist, much conflict turns out to serve a broader, long-range agenda: reintegrating the society as a whole, making it more cohesive, stable, and viable (Coser, 1956).

In contrast, conflict theorists do not see a great deal of consensus, harmony, or cohesion in contemporary society. They see groups with competing and clashing interests and values. They see struggles between and among categories, sectors, groups, and classes in the society, with winners and losers resulting from the outcome of these struggles. Most social institutions, they argue, do not benefit the society as a whole. Rather, they benefit some groups *at the expense of* others. Conflict theorists envision the resources of the society as being distributed according to a "zero sum game," that is, they are of a fixed size, and whatever is distributed to one faction or category is taken away from another. They argue against the functionalists' analysis of stratification as benefiting the society as a whole. In contrast, the conflict theorists argue, stratification benefits only the rich and the powerful *at the expense of* the poor and the weak. Moreover, it is to the advantage of the rich and the powerful to have the disadvantaged *believe* stratification is for the good of the entire society; that way, the disadvantaged will be less likely to threaten the interests and privileges of the rich. Likewise, the conflict theorists argue, prostitution does not benefit the society as a whole; it benefits representatives of groups—mainly men—who profit from society's patriarchal institutions.

Conflict theorists stress that institutions, changes, and behavior tend to have a very different impact on the various classes, categories, and groups in a society; what helps one may very well harm another, and vice versa. And the interests of one often clash or contradict those of another. Some groups are helped most by keeping things the way they are, by the status quo; others have an interest in radical change. No phenomenon has the same impact on all social categories equally. On many issues, there is no common ground, no plan that would help everyone, no unified or homogeneous unit—society as a whole—that would be helped or hurt by any institution, change, or behavior. What helps one group takes away from another, and vice versa. Even stability and cohesion may be repressive, for they may prevent change and a redistribution of resources, thereby helping the advantaged and hurting the disadvantaged. Many of the very institutions the functionalists saw as "functional" for the society as a whole repress and exploit less advantaged groups and categories, such as women, African-Americans, and the working class.

Groups struggle to have their own definitions of right and wrong enacted into law. They key word here is *hegemony*, or dominance: Groups struggle to legitimate their own special interests and views and to discredit and nullify the influence of those of competing groups. For instance, pro- and anti-abortionists hold rallies and demonstrations and lobby in Washington and in state capitols to get laws passed, have laws taken off the books, or keep existing laws on the books. Each side is struggling for dominance or hegemony, struggling to have its own views translated into law and public opinion. Such is the order of the day, according to the conflict theorist, who sees a constant struggle among competing groups in contemporary society.

Perhaps the most conflict-oriented of all the conflict theorists are the Marxists. Their ideas are somewhat distinct and different from the non-Marxist conflict theorists. Conflict theorists who do not work within the Marxist paradigm are often called *interest group theorists* (Orcutt, 1983, pp. 311, 316–322), or *pluralistic conflict theorists* (Pfohl, 1994, pp. 428–431; Sheley, 1995, pp. 46ff.). I will use the terms conflict theory, interest group theory, and pluralistic conflict theory more or less interchangeably, and will refer to Marxist theory as partly separate from this tradition. While the Marxists, obviously, draw their inspiration from the writings of Karl Marx (1818–1883) and his followers, the non-Marxist conflict theorists are more likely to have been influenced by the writings of Max Weber (1864–1920).

The central issue for all conflict-oriented criminologists is the emergence and enforcement of norms, rules, and especially, laws. How do laws get passed? Which groups manage to get their own special interests and views enacted into laws? Who profits by the passage of laws? Which laws are enforced, and which are passed but never enforced—and why? Why are certain activities regarded as deviant while others are regarded as conventional by the members of a given society?

The answer provided by the conflict approach is that laws, rules, and norms grow out of a power struggle between and among interest groups, factions, and social classes. The most powerful group or groups in society are the ones who are successful in having their own special views of right and wrong accepted by the society as a whole and formulated into the criminal law. Likewise, the enforcement of the law represents the application of power against the powerless by the powerful.

Conflict theorists explicitly reject two commonly held views concerning the law. The first is, of course, the *consensus* view that the law is a "reflection of the social consciousness of a society," that laws make up a "barometer of the moral and social thinking of a community" (Friedman, 1964, p. 143), that the law reflects "the will of the people." Instead, conflict theorists argue that public views on what is regarded as conventional or deviant, law-abiding or criminal, vary strikingly from group to group in a large, complex society. Even where consensus exists on a given issue as to what should be against the law, the conflict theorist asks *how* and *why* that consensus is achieved (Turk, 1980, pp. 83–84; Chambliss, 1976, p. 3). For most issues, there is no majority consensus, only different views held by different social groups. The point of view held by the most powerful of these groups tends to be the one that becomes law.

The second widely held view that conflict theory rejects is that laws are passed and enforced to protect the society as a whole, to protect all classes and groups more or less equally. The conflict theorist argues that laws do not protect the rights, interests, and well-being of the many, but rather the interests of the few. There is no such thing as "the society as a whole," the conflict theorist would argue. Societies are broken up into segments, sectors, classes, groups, or categories that have very different interests. Very few laws have an equal impact on all segments of society equally. For instance, the earliest laws of vagrancy in England were passed to protect the interests of the wealthiest and most powerful members of English society: the landowners in the 1300s and the merchant class in the 1500s (Chambliss, 1964). The laws of theft in England, again, were interpreted by the courts in the 1400s as a means of protecting the property of merchants, the emerging powerful class at that time, a class the Crown needed to protect and curry favor with (Hall, 1952). The laws regulating the quality of meat sold to the public in the 1920s were supported by, and served the interests of, the largest meat packers (Kolko, 1963).

It is true that legal systems attempt to cloak the special interest character of the law by invoking "the common good." A crime is said to represent an offense against "the state," against "the people." Indeed, some laws *do* serve the common good, as the three above examples attest. Still, this was not necessarily why the law was passed in the first place, and it does not account for the fact that a given law does not have an equal impact on everyone, and every social category, in a given society. For instance, laws against theft—admittedly, widely, practically universally, endorsed by the public—protect the interests of people who possess property far more than those who do not. If you own nothing, you have nothing to lose to theft.

Conflict theorists do not see laws as an expression of a broad consensus or as an altruistic desire to protect a large number of the members of a society from objective, clear, and present danger. Rather, they are the embodiment of the beliefs, lifestyle, and/or economic interests of certain segments of the society. Thus, the law is a means of forcing one group's beliefs and way of life onto the rest of the society. Laws are passed and enforced not because they protect society in general, or because many people believe in their moral correctness, but because they uphold the ideological or material interests of a certain sector of society. This serves to stop certain people from doing what others consider evil, undesirable, or unprofitable, or to make them do something that others consider good, desirable, or profitable. The passage of a law represents the triumph of a point of view or an ideology associated with a particular group, social category, or organization, even if that law is not enforced.

Conflict theorists also emphasize the role that power and status play in the enforcement process. (A point also emphasized by the labeling theorists, as we saw.) That is, even for the same offense, apprehension is more likely to lead to more serious punishment for the person who commands less power and a higher ranking in the socioeconomic status system; for juveniles, especially, this extends to the parents of offenders. We've cited the example of two juvenile gangs, the "Saints" and the "Roughnecks," whose members were accorded very different treatment at the hands of local law enforcement. The "Saints," whose parents had respectable, relatively powerful upper-middle-class occupational positions, were treated far more leniently by law enforcement than the "Roughnecks," whose parents were lower- and working-class. None of the "Saints" had ever been arrested, while all of the "Roughnecks" had, and most of them, on numerous occasions; yet, their offenses, and the frequency with which they had been committed, were quite comparable (Chambliss, 1973). A tenet of the conflict perspective is that not only does the *law* define actions as illegal in conformity with the interests of the most powerful segments of the society, but the *enforcement* of the law is also unequal in that in any society, it reflects the distribution of power.

In addition to being interested in the passage and enforcement of criminal laws, conflict theorists also examine—although to a far lesser extent—the question of the *causes* of criminal behavior. These are the etiological concerns discussed in

Chapter 4. What causes criminal behavior according to the conflict perspective? To be succinct about it, conflict theorists would answer this question by pointing to the *nature of the society* on which we are focusing and the classes or categories in them. Conflict theorists generally would argue that inequalities in power and income cause certain types of criminal behavior; Marxists, for instance, would say that *capitalist society is criminogenic*, that the exploitation of the working class by the capitalist class or ruling elite causes certain kinds of crime to take place.

The conflict theorist is careful to point out that the issue is not explaining criminal behavior as such, but explaining forms of behavior that have *a high likelihood of being defined as criminal.* What forms of behavior are these? The behavior of the poor and the powerless stand a higher likelihood of being defined as crimes, while the behavior of the rich and the powerful stand a considerably lower likelihood as being so defined. Thus the violent, predatory actions that the poorer strata are more likely to commit are those actions that tend to be criminalized and enforced, while the harmful, unethical corporate actions of the wealthier strata are not as likely to be defined as crimes, and if they are, tend not to lead to arrest, and are not as often studied by the criminologist. Thus, when someone asks, "What causes criminal behavior?" he or she almost invariably means, "What causes people to engage in a particular *type* of illegal behavior?" namely, street crimes such as robbery, rape, and murder.

It seems almost intuitively obvious that being at the bottom of the heap economically in a highly stratified society will lead to many problems of living, which in turn, make certain actions more likely, most notably, street crimes. In a society in which money is the measure of a person, if one has no money, one will be more likely to seek to obtain it through illegal means than someone who already has a great deal of money. To put things another way, the affluent are unlikely to engage in money-making actions that have a high likelihood of leading to arrest and imprisonment, although they may engage in technically illegal, and largely unenforced, actions. Very few wealthy executives or heart surgeons grab a gun and hold up a liquor store; if they already earn half a million dollars a year—why should they? In addition, if one faces countless problems, many of them economic, in just getting through each day, it seems obvious that

anger and rage will occasionally erupt into violence. If a person has a great deal of money, power, and status, again, it seems almost intuitively obvious that he or she is less likely to feel a sense of frustration and rage, and hence, engage in violence. The conflict theorist has no problem looking at the origins of crime within the class structure. Indeed, if the "no class difference" approach discussed in Chapter 4 were correct, that is, that there were no differences among the class levels in the commission of street crime, it would imply that the indignities of social class are not great, that being at the bottom of the class structure does not generate major problems for lower-status occupants, and that the class system is relatively free of conflict. This conclusion is exactly the *opposite* of that held by the conflict theorists (Mankoff, 1980, pp. 141–142).

Conflict theorists also find that sharp *economic inequality* is associated with a high rate of crime. In the United States, cities with the greatest economic inequality between rich and poor and Black and white are those with the highest rates of street crime, especially violent crimes (Currie and Skolnick, 1984, p. 441; Currie, 1985, pp. 144–179). Likewise, in nations around the world, countries with the greatest measure of inequality between rich and poor tend to have the highest rates of street crime and violence (Braithwaite and Braithwaite, 1980). In the welfare states of Western Europe, which show fairly small economic differences between rich and poor, crime rates are fairly low. In the United States, with the greatest economic differences between rich and poor, crime rates are much higher. And in economically developing Third World nations, especially those in which the traditional culture has been seriously disrupted, crime rates are higher still. "The evidence for a strong association between inequality and crime is overwhelming" (Currie, 1985, p. 146).

As I said earlier, Marxism is a brand of conflict theory. However, Marxism holds to a number of special and distinct assumptions that are unique to itself. Conflict or interest group theorists agree with Marxists on a number of points. Marxists also say that the criminal law is the creation of the most powerful segments of a society. They agree that the interests of the powerful tend to get translated into, and are protected by, the criminal law. They agree that a consensus rarely prevails with respect to behavior the public feels should be criminalized; in any case, if such a consensus should prevail, it is rarely the principal reason why the law is passed in the first place. Moreover, Marxists agree that criminalizing certain forms of behavior rarely protects the interests of the society as a whole. Rather, some segments will profit, while others may be hurt by the passage and enforcement of many laws. Laws and their enforcement rarely have a uniformly positive—or uniformly negative—impact on all classes or segments in any society.

These two schools of thought part company on a number of crucial points, however. In contrast to Marxists, non-Marxist conflict theorists argue as follows.

Not All Important Conflicts Are between Economic Classes. Marxists regard the economy as paramount, of central importance, and conflicts between the economic haves (the bourgeoisie or capitalist class) and the economic have-nots (the proletariat, the working class) as the primary determinant of social change in a capitalist society. In contrast, the conflict theorists, following Max Weber, regard the economic institution as one of several crucial dimensions in a society. The question of which institution influences which others— whether it is religion influencing the economy, the family influencing politics, the economy influencing education, and so on—depends on the issue and the circumstances in question, and the society we are studying. Not only can the various institutions influence one another, but also, the world of ideas can influence the material world and vice versa. Ideas are "codeterminant" with economic forces (Hinch, 1983, 1984). In Marx's scheme, the material world is paramount, and the ideational world, the world of ideas (religion, politics, art, a system of criminal justice, and so on) is dependent on it, caused by it, rests upon it but is not an equal with it. For example, Max Weber's theory, expressed in *The Protestant Ethic and the Spirit of Capitalism* (1904/1930), that religious ideas could have been influential in generating industrial capitalism, is almost universally rejected by Marxists because it gives the world of ideas equal power with the material or economic sphere. Non-Marxist conflict theorists do not see one sphere as dominant, while Marxists most emphatically do.

Interest group theorists insist that there are sources of conflict that cannot be traced directly to economic and social class factors. For instance, during the 1920s, a series of unusually harsh laws was passed in Canada criminalizing opium possession. Anyone convicted of selling or giving narcotics to a minor was to receive a mandatory whipping. Convicted narcotics offenders were denied the appeals usually extended to other convicted offenders. In searching for narcotics, the police were given the "drastic right to search" certain establishments, a right not normally extended to the majority of suspects. It turns out that the brunt of this narcotics legislation was directed at the Chinese minority, who were suspected of passing on their supposed opium-smoking habit to whites. Majority whites were not, for the most part, engaged in an economic struggle with Chinese-Canadians. Many members of the white majority, however, did hold racist beliefs about the Chinese, a factor that found its way into the drug laws passed at the time. Here, we have a struggle not between social classes, but different racial groups (Cook, 1970; but also see Small [Cook], 1978). While Marxists place class and economic struggles at the center of the passage and enforcement of the criminal law, for the conflict theorists, such struggles are only one among a wide variety of conflicts that are relevant to the criminologist and deviance specialist.

Some Conflicts Are Over Symbolic Issues. Marxists insist that struggles between and among classes and factions in capitalist society are typically "rational" and relate to the distribution of resources and economic power and their maintenance or change. Non-Marxist conflict theorists insist that while many issues are of this type, a substantial proportion is over questions that can be classified as "symbolic" or "irrational." That is, they have more to do with matters of status than with power or economic interests.

For instance, compare the Marxist with the conflict analysis of the passage and the demise of national alcohol prohibition (1920–1933). Some Marxists believe Prohibition succeeded because the business class thought that outlawing alcohol would produce more efficient, productive, and profitable workers. Prohibition eventually failed because the business class finally realized it bred disrespect for the law among the working class, which would generalize to all laws, making their rule over the working class tenuous, and their profits would thereby be threatened (Rumbarger, 1989).

Conflict theorists have a somewhat different take on Prohibition. Both the ratification of the law, the Volstead Act, and its eventual repeal can be explained by power differences between segments in the population with differing views of right and wrong. Early in the twentieth century, rural dwellers, Southerners, and the "old" middle class consisting of prosperous farmers, local business merchants, white, Anglo-Saxon Protestants, and native-born Americans of native-born parentage wielded a great deal of power in American politics relative to their numbers in the population. And these segments favored Prohibition. They tended to regard total abstinence from alcohol as respectable, a sign of virtue; they felt that drinking was distinctly disreputable, in fact, deviant. The triumph of Prohibition represented the triumph of a certain lifestyle and the moral virtue of the groups that bore that lifestyle. "Some of the deepest struggles in American politics have emerged over issues which are not directly related to economic divisions in society" (Gusfield, 1963, p. 13).

By the 1930s, Prohibition was widely regarded as a failure. Why? The segments of the population that came to exert more power in national politics than earlier in the century consisted mainly of urban dwellers, non-Protestant ethnics—mostly Italian and Irish Catholics and Jews—as well as residents of the Northeast, immigrants, and sons and daughters of immigrants. Among these segments in the American population, abstention from drinking was seen as no particular virtue. They tended to favor moderate drinking. opposed Prohibition, and supported its repeal. Prohibition was repealed *not* because it didn't "work," according to conflict theorists, but because the groups that supported it lost power, and those that opposed it became significantly more influential in the political process. Prohibition served a symbolic function: It asserted that the groups who favored it and whose lifestyle it affirmed were dominant and respectable, and that those whose lifestyle it criminalized were disreputable. When Prohibition was in effect, conservative, rural, WASPs were told, your beliefs are law, your lifestyle is dominant, you are legitimate—and all other groups are less than respectable. When Prohibition was repealed, drinkers—the supporters of repeal—were then told, you are respectable, your lifestyle is legitimate, acceptable, nondeviant. Prohibition and its repeal were as much about a struggle over status as anything else.

In short, to many conflict theorists, the law has a symbolic function. "Public affirmation of a norm through . . . government action expresses the public worth of one subculture vis-à-vis others. . . . It

demonstrates which cultures have legitimacy and public domination, and which do not. Accordingly, it enhances the social status of groups carrying the affirmed culture and degrades groups carrying that which is condemned as deviant" (Gusfield, 1967, p. 175). To a non-Marxist conflict theorist, many issues pertaining to deviance and crime, to norms and laws, may have little to do with rational, instrumental, economic questions, but may be *symbolic* in nature. In contrast, the Marxist tends to look for economic conflict, particularly class struggle, behind the important issues of the day. (For a *Marxist*—as opposed to a conflict—analysis of the rise and fall of Prohibition, see Rumbarger, 1989.)

Deviance and Crime Will Exist, and Will Continue to Exist, in Socialist Societies. Conflict and rule breaking are omnipresent and universal; they will exist and flourish everywhere, even in a socialist society. Interest group theorists, following Max Weber, tend to emphasize the continuities and similarities between capitalism and socialism. In contrast, Marxists emphasize the differences. Some of the more "vulgar" or simple-minded Marxists insist that crime and deviance will not exist at all under "true" socialism, that they are solely a product of the ills of capitalism. Marxists with a more complex view of how the world works argue that crime and deviance will exist, although they will be drastically reduced under socialism. All brands of Marxism contain a strain of utopianism. That is, they all believe that when capitalism is overthrown and abolished and the age of socialism is ushered in, society will look a lot better than it does today. Many of society's basic problems will be solved, or at least ameliorated. Capitalism is based on a competitive, exploitative ethic, with individuals, groups, and classes struggling with one another to obtain more resources for themselves, stealing from others to line their own pockets. This competitive, exploitative ethic, many Marxists believe, lends an atmosphere of opposition, hostility, conflict, and brutality to life in capitalist society which in turn stimulates high rates of crimes such as robbery, murder, and rape. (For one such argument pertaining to rape, see Schwendinger and Schwendinger, 1983.) In addition, under capitalism, certain relatively harmless activities, such as homosexuality, are stigmatized. In contrast, laws discrediting and criminalizing harmless minority activities will not be necessary and will not exist. Severe conflict between and among groups, so rife and deep-seated under capitalism, will subside when true socialism is installed.

Non-Marxist theorists disagree. They argue that conflict is endemic to all social relations. Transforming a society's economic base from private to public hands will not eliminate conflict, violence, or differences in conceptions of what should and should not be a crime. Crime and deviance are probably ineradicable features of all societies, capitalist or socialist. For instance, the high rate of alcoholism that existed in pre-1917 czarist Russia remained throughout the period of the communist Soviet Union, and remains today in Russia, after the collapse of communism. The heavy consumption of alcohol among Russians has nothing to do with which political/economic regime has been in power, but rather it has to do with a culture that places a strong emphasis on heavy drinking. True, certain actions are and will be considerably more common or likely in some societies than others, but the nature of a society's economic base has nothing to do with most of them. Socialism, most conflict theorists insist, will not eliminate, or probably even drastically reduce, the incidence of deviance or crime or the impulse to legitimate norms, pass laws, stigmatize the deviant, or arrest and punish the lawbreaker. Of course, if a society's laws are drastically different, its crimes will be different, too. For instance, in some socialist societies, buying and selling for a profit is or was illegal; clearly, such economic crimes do not exist under capitalism. But a society's legal and normative structure is not likely to change much under socialism, most interest group theorists insist. Much the same forms of deviance and crime that exist under capitalism will remain under socialism, should some future socialist system be instituted.

For a century, beginning with the writings of Karl Marx (1818–1883), many of the brightest minds in the world were focused on the question of how, why, and when capitalism would collapse. They considered the demise of capitalism so self-evident that hardly any of them ever wondered about the demise of socialism. The fact that socialism, not capitalism, collapsed in Europe, retreated in Latin America, and has been seriously compromised in China—all within the space of a few short years—must have been a stunning blow to Marxist thinkers everywhere. In the field of the study of deviance, these developments have discouraged traditional Marxist thinking. Marxism's decline began at least

a half-dozen years before the surprising disintegration of Marxist regimes in the late 1980s and early 1990s, but the latter development further discredited Marxism as academically respectable.

Many of the Marxist and radical sociologists who wrote in the 1970s on deviance and crime have drastically altered their thinking on the subject. Richard Quinney, for instance, has turned to Zen Buddhism in fashioning what he refers to as a "peace and social justice" perspective on crime (Quinney, 1986; Quinney and Wildeman, 1991), an approach that would be anathema to any traditional Marxist. Jock Young, one of the original "new" criminologists, is working on an approach he refers to as "left realism" (Lea and Young, 1984; Jones, MacLean, and Young, 1986), which emphasizes ways of protecting citizens from predatory street crime and reforming means of administering the criminal justice system, again, a reformist approach that would have been thought unacceptable, even reactionary, by Marxists of an earlier generation—an early 1970s Jock Young included.

The number of Marxist criminologists who, today, remain steadfast to the principles they espoused a generation ago is small. This is not to say that all or even most of the ideas of Marxist or radical criminology have been discredited. Certainly social class is central to crime and its control. Certainly some features of capitalist society encourage certain crimes. Certainly the street crime of the poor is enforced and prosecuted more vigorously than the corporate crime of the rich and the powerful. Certainly one's ideology has *something* to do with one's approach to crime and the research one conducts, and the latter *may* have political or ideological implications or consequences. Marxist criminology certainly had a positive impact on the field. However, in the long run, as an all-embracing perspective, most researchers realized that it was of limited utility, and they focused on other approaches. Two are feminism and the "new" sociology of social control.

FEMINISM

Until a generation or so ago, most Western intellectuals viewed the world through two related biases: *Eurocentrism* and *androcentrism*. Eurocentrism is the view that the world revolves around European—that is, Western, including North American—society and culture, that all other societies and cultures should be evaluated according to how well they measure up to the European yardstick. It is only in the past 25 or 30 years that serious efforts have been undertaken to incorporate African, Asian, and Native-American perspectives into the social sciences, history, philosophy, literature, and art. Is the study of the sociology of deviance Eurocentric? This is entirely possible, as some African-American scholars and researchers have argued (Russell, 1992; Covington, 1995). *Androcentrism* is a male-centered bias. It is the view that men are the center of the universe and women are at the periphery of the action. Women take on relevance only insofar as they relate to men and their activities. The androcentric bias in the study of deviance and crime began to be subject to criticism only in the late 1960s; these critiques are having an impact on the way sociologists view the phenomenon of deviance. And it is *feminism* that launched this assault on androcentrism.

There is no single universally agreed-upon definition of feminism. However, perhaps the definition that might win broadest acceptance is this one: Feminism is the perspective that stresses the fact that "women experience subordination on the basis of their sex" (Gelsthorpe and Morris, 1988, p. 224). Social scientists refer to "sex"—as distinguished from "sexual behavior"—as a biological characteristic of men and women, consisting of hormones, genitals, and secondary sex characteristics. In contrast, "gender" refers to the psychological and cultural reality of the way men and women are treated (that is, "sex roles") and how they are shaped by that treatment. Thus, feminism argues that men and women are typically treated as *representatives* or *embodiments of sexual categories*; men are usually dominant in this process, and women, subordinate. Feminists are concerned with uncovering the origins and functions of this unequal treatment, and seek to bring about a more sexually equalitarian society. For feminists, the enemy is *patriarchy*—institutions of male dominance; it is patriarchy that is responsible for the oppression of women, and it is patriarchy which must be analyzed, critiqued, and eliminated. Feminists often begin their analysis with an examination of how a given field has studied a phenomenon in the past, because this typically serves to justify patriarchy; this usually entails uncovering the sexist biases of more traditional approaches.

In 1968, Frances Heidensohn, a young British sociologist, noted that the "deviance of women" was one area that has been "most notably ignored in [the] sociological literature." At first glance, she said, this seems understandable; after all, in comparison with men, women "have low rates of participation in deviant activities." Such a defense might seem to be a reasonable explanation for the field's concentration on men, Heidensohn writes, "but not the almost total *exclusion*" of studies on female deviance and crime (Heidensohn, 1968, pp. 160, 161, 162; see also Smart, 1976). The exceptions to this rule, she argues, show that women are not only virtually invisible in the field of criminology and deviance studies, but they hold a peculiar and skewed place in its literature as well. Some very early work on crime argued that women criminals were "atavistic and hysterical," that their criminality was a product of biological abnormality (Lombroso and Ferro, 1916; Smart, 1976, pp. 31–37). A later perspective argued that women engaged in criminal behavior just as often as men; however, they weren't detected as often, because of their distinctively feminine trait of deceitfulness (Pollak, 1950; Heidensohn, 1968, pp. 165-166; Smart, 1976, pp. 46–53). Finally, the deviance of females was seen as an extension of the "focal concerns" of the female role; men are pressured into committing crimes that result from the need to succeed in the occupational and financial realms, while women are pressured into committing crimes that result from the need to succeed in the sexual and marital realms—which means prostitution and sexual delinquency (Cohen, 1955, pp. 44-48, 137–147; Heidensohn, 1968, pp. 166–168). At present, Heidensohn says, "we barely possess the basic components for an initial analysis of the deviance of women. These are lonely, uncharted seas of human behaviour." What is needed to remedy this marginal, distorted image of female deviance is a "crash programme of research" (pp. 170–171).

The neglect of women in the field of criminology and deviance studies is not only characteristic of the traditional approaches. It also marked the more contemporary perspectives, such as labeling or interactionist theory and radical or Marxist theory. In an insightful analysis of the role of women in studies on deviance, Marcia Millman (1975) argues that in much of the writings by labeling theorists, men appear as interesting, adventurous deviants who lead exciting lives, while women are depicted as boring, conventional, nagging drudges who attempt to rein in the wilder side of the men in their lives. While deviants are depicted with understanding and empathy in interactionist research, it is almost always *men* who are engaged in the deviance that is focused on, while *women* play a marginal, passive, inhibitory role. It was not until the 1980s that the implications of labeling theory were fully spelled out for the involvement of women in deviance (Schur, 1984).

Critical, radical, or Marxist criminology was no better in its analysis of women's role in deviance and crime than the more conventional perspectives. As one feminist analysis of criminological theory pointed out, there is *not one word* about women in Taylor, Walton, and Young's treatise on the "new" criminology, and Quinney, a major self-designated Marxist of the 1970s, "is all but blind to the distinctions between conditions of males and females in capitalist society"; these authors "thoroughly scrutinize and criticize theoretical criminology, yet they never notice the limited applicability of these theories to women" (Leonard, 1982, p. 176). The sexism lurking in earlier writings can be illustrated by an aside made by Alvin Gouldner, critic of traditional sociology, especially functionalism, and author of a well-known critique of the interactionist approach to deviance (1968), who, in arguing that the sexual lives of sociologists may influence their work, remarked: "For example, it is my strong but undocumented impression that when some sociologists change their work interests, problems, or styles, they also change mistresses or wives" (1970, p. 57).

Three main points can be made about the depiction of women in writings on deviance prior to the 1960s and 1970s. (These generalizations apply even today, although to a far lesser extent.) The first is, as we saw, that women represented a minor theme in these writings. They were studied less, appeared less often as subjects of attention, remained marginal, secondary, almost invisible. The study of women and deviance suffers from "a problem of omission"; women have been "largely overlooked in the literature" (Millman, 1975, p. 265).

Second, the study of deviance reflects "a male-biased view" (Millman, 1975, p. 265). Not only was the deviance of women less often studied, when it was, it was nearly always *specialized* deviance; the deviance of men was deviance *in general,* the deviance of women was *women's* deviance. In a chapter entitled "The Criminality of Women," which appeared in a textbook that was eventually published in multiple editions, Walter Reckless (1950, p. 116) argued that the criminal behavior of

women should not be considered "in the same order of phenomena as crime in general," meaning the criminal behavior of men. Unlike men, in committing crimes, women are deceitful (p. 122), kill by administering poison (p. 121), throw acid in the face of a victim, "usually an unfaithful lover" (p. 122), and are prone to "make false accusations of a sexual nature" (p. 123). In short, the *forms* of deviance and crime women engage in are said to be very different from those that men commit. The three specific forms of deviance that have attracted attention from the field are shoplifting, mental illness, and prostitution. While women do play a majority role in the first of these, at least an equal role in the second, and the overwhelmingly dominant role in the last of them, they *do* commit a far wider range of deviant actions than these, their participation in deviance *has* been stereotyped in the literature, and men's deviance is *not* deviance "in general," as some observers have claimed.

And third, the role of women *as victims* of crime and deviance was underplayed until recently. This was especially the case with respect to rape, domestic assault, and sexual harassment. It was not until the 1970s, when feminist scholars began a systematic examination of the ways women are brutalized and exploited by men, did deviant and criminal actions such as rape (Brownmiller, 1975), wife battering (Martin, 1976), and sexual harassment (MacKinnon, 1979) find a significant place in the literature on deviance and crime, and the suffering inflicted on women at the hands of men given sufficient attention. In the 1980s, a number of radicals recognized that the question of women as victims of crime created "enormous theoretical problems for the radical paradigm in criminology" (Jones, Maclean, and Young, 1986, p. 3; Gelsthorpe and Morris, 1988, p. 233). Specifically, feminist research on female victims of crime has brought home to certain radicals "the limits of the romantic conception of crime and the criminal" (Matthews and Young, 1986, p. 2; Gelsthorpe and Morris, 1988, pp. 232–233). While it is true that men are significantly more likely to be the victims of crime than women, for some crimes (such as the three I just mentioned), the sex ratio is *overwhelmingly* in the other direction. Moreover, women suffer certain crimes *specifically* because of their relatively powerless position relative to that of men. In short, women victims of crime have been "hidden from history" (Summers, 1981).

Prior to the 1970s, then, sociology and the other

disciplines have been "unable to explain adequately the phenomenon of women and crime. Theories that are frequently hailed as explanations of human behavior are, in fact, discussions of male behavior and male criminality." These theories and explanations "are biased to the core, riddled with assumptions that relate to male—not female—reality. Theoretical criminology is sexist because it unwittingly focuses on the activities, interests, and values of men, while ignoring a comparable analysis of women." Any acceptable theoretical framework must either "incorporate an understanding of both male and female behavior" or, alternatively, explain exactly *why* and *how* it applies specifically or more forcefully to either women or men (Leonard, 1982, p. 181; for additional critical summaries of the classic literature on female crime, see Klein, 1973; Naffine, 1981, 1987; Mann, 1984, Chapters 3, 4, 5; Heidensohn, 1985, pp. 146–154). In the words of French philosopher and writer Simone de Beauvoir, in Western society, man is the "subject," the "absolute," while woman is "the Other" (1953).

Leonard warns that the classic approaches in the study of deviance cannot provide an adequate analysis of women and crime on their own. Since they were constructed with men in mind, any reexamination of past theories of deviance must be "approached with a solid grounding in feminist understandings of the role of women in contemporary society." Otherwise, she says, they will succumb to the "partial and distorted" portraits of the past (1982, p. 190). Such a grounding would examine differences in power relations between men and women, a thorough examination of sex roles and their historical origins and contemporary functions, the part women play in the family, and their role in the marketplace (pp. 188, 190). Although Leonard has not provided that analysis herself, she has pointed the way to such an analysis.

The position of women relative to deviance and crime is very different in at least one major way from that of other oppressed, relatively powerless categories, such as African-Americans and members of the lower and working classes. For the most part, the tendency to engage in a variety of street crime is negatively related to power and income: The lower the power and income of a given category, the greater the likelihood that its members will engage in acts traditionally regarded as crimes. With women, we see precisely the opposite tendency: A category that is less powerful and less affluent than men engages in street crime at a strikingly lower level than men. So different are women from the general pattern that they pose a serious challenge to radical and Marxist thinking about crime. If crime is a "rational" response to oppression in capitalist society, why are women so disinclined to commit crimes? What makes them different? If the ruling elite use the criminal law to control troublesome categories and classes, why is it so rarely applied to women? If crime can be seen as a primitive means by which the less powerful struggle against oppression, why are women so often the *victims* of these struggles? In short, a systematic analysis of women's role in deviance, crime, and the law would require a serious modification of radical criminology's assertions. Indeed, this may be precisely why radical criminologists failed to deal with the issue of women and crime for so long.

A great deal of what has been written about women and crime has focused on *etiology*—that is, *why* women have such a strikingly lower rate of crime than men. (See Gottfredson and Hirschi [1990, pp. 144–149] for an empirical summary of this literature.) In the last two decades, the question of whether the gender gap in crime is closing or not, likewise, has occupied the attention of a number of criminologists, that is, whether there is a "new female offender" unleashed by female emancipation (Adler, 1975; Simon, 1975a, 1975b). For the most part, this research shows that with respect to crimes of violence, women are *not* becoming more like men, but with respect to less serious property crimes and white-collar crimes, the male-female crime gap may be narrowing somewhat. In other words, most contemporary observers believe that the evidence shows the "new female offender" is more myth than reality (Steffensmeier, 1978; Steffensmeier and Cobb, 1981; Austin, 1982; Gora, 1982; Simpson, 1989, p. 610). Another angle of the etiological question is that *patriarchy*, or male dominance, *is criminogenic*. What causes crime, at least, crime against women? Patriarchy causes crime. Hence, feminism has not ignored the etiological question; it has, however, not been feminism's principal thrust. At least as interesting, however, is the question of the social control of female deviance and crime relative to that of men. This can be divided into three parts: first, the treatment of women versus men at the hands of the criminal justice system; second, the informal labeling of women versus men as deviants; and third, the treatment of male offenders against female victims by the criminal justice system.

A central thesis of the conflict, radical, and labeling theories is that social control is related to *power*; members of less powerful categories in the society are treated more harshly at the hands of the criminal justice system. Although these perspectives do not mention women, they might very well have predicted that for the same offense, women are more likely to be arrested, and more likely to receive longer jail or prison sentences. For a long period of time, traditional criminology put forth the opposite hypothesis, the so-called "chivalry" or "leniency" thesis that women are treated less severely by the criminal justice system, that they are arrested less on the same evidence for the same offense, that they are charged and convicted less, and that they are less likely to serve a jail or prison sentence and, if they do serve, receive shorter sentences. (See, for instance, Pollack, 1950.) More recently, some observers have argued the opposite thesis, that criminal justice discriminates against women, that as the members of a minority, women are more likely to be convicted and serve a long term of incarceration (Temin, 1973).

As we might expect, making precise comparisons between the crimes that men and women commit and their sentences is not easy. For one thing, women are strikingly less likely than men to have a lengthy record of prior convictions, and this is a major determinant of sentencing. Second, even for the same offense, there are likely to be more mitigating factors at work for women than for men. For instance, men sometimes murder strangers, while women almost never do, and thus the sentences of male murderers are likely to be harsher than those for women killers, on average, since killers of strangers receive longer sentences than murderers of intimates. Women killers are far more often provoked by abuse at the hands of a male partner, a factor which may mitigate (although often does not excuse) their sentence. Women very, very rarely commit armed robbery, but when they do, it is usually in the company of a male companion; thus, when they are sentenced, they can often claim some measure of coercion. Factors such as these point to complexities in the sex criminal-sentencing picture; even what seems on the surface to be "the same" offense is *not* the same to the criminal justice system. Still, when all the evidence is accumulated and evaluated, neither the leniency nor the discrimination model seems to hold up.

Statistically speaking, for the same offenses, all things being equal, women and men receive and serve roughly the same sentences (Simon and Landis, 1991; Daly, 1995). It is entirely likely that a search for overt discrimination against women in the criminal justice system will not be productive for feminist criminology. What we see, for the most part, is equality rather than discrimination.

In contrast, the realm of *informal* social control reveals strong differentials in treatment of female versus male deviance. For many conditions or behaviors, women are held to a more exacting standard, and are more likely to be criticized, denounced, or stigmatized if they stray from it. For instance, women are evaluated more strictly and harshly for not conforming to most appearance norms; their appearance is scrutinized more exactingly and they are more likely to be punished for not living up to an abstract ideal of how one must look. Women must conform more closely to specific standards of beauty, for instance, or suffer the consequences (Freedman, 1986). Women are criticized and stigmatized more harshly for each pound they are overweight than are men; in fact, the weight at which one is labeled "overweight" is strongly sex-linked (Kaplan, 1980, p. 6; Schur, 1984, pp. 70–72). Women are more likely to be evaluated negatively for having sex at an early age, for having sex in loveless relationships, and for having sex with too many partners than is true of men (Klassen, Williams, and Levitt, 1989, pp. 18, 25–50); in some communities, such women are stigmatized, earn a reputation for being sexually promiscuous, and attract lewd, lascivious, degrading, and sometimes violent reactions from men. Women are more likely to be punished for a departure from a variety of sex role norms and expectations (Schur, 1984, pp. 51ff.). Although men, too, are criticized for straying from sex role expectations, the roles they are allowed to play without penalty are much wider and more varied than is true for women. The list of such discriminations is extremely long: For many conditions or behaviors, women are more likely to be labeled as deviants if they violate widely held norms than is true for men. This differential treatment is central to a feminist or female-centered perspective on deviance. Why do these norms exist? Whose interests do they serve? What functions do they play in contemporary society? Can they be changed, and if so, how? Any feminist perspective on deviance must address questions such as these.

Lastly, the treatment of male victimizers of women by the criminal justice system reveals valuable insight into deviance and social control. Rape has been analyzed as a means of controlling women; it serves to keep women in their place (Brownmiller, 1975). Until the 1970s, rape was a seriously understudied crime. Fearing that they would be shamed, stigmatized, and blamed for the man's attack on her, fewer than half of female victims of sexual assault report the crime to the police. In most cases—especially where the attack was by an acquaintance—prosecution of the offender is not pursued with a great deal of enthusiasm (Estrich, 1987). In other words, women are often victimized several times after the rape: informally, through public stigma, and formally, through a discriminatory criminal justice system. Much the same applies to wife battering. Until recently (and even today, in most jurisdictions), the beating by a man of his wife was completely ignored by the criminal justice system; wives seeking justice were told that their beating was a private matter, not an issue for police intervention. Beginning in the late 1970s, a number of jurisdictions passed and enforced laws making spouse beating a crime. Police were dispatched when called about domestic disputes; if they determined that an assault took place, an arrest was made. The results of these efforts have been mixed. The findings from one early study (Sherman and Berk, 1984) indicated that arrest was effective; arrested husbands were less likely to continue to beat their wives than nonarrested husbands. However, later studies have not produced such encouraging results (Dunford, Huizinga, and Elliott, 1990; Sherman, et al., 1991). It turns out that arresting wife beaters is highly contingent on the employment of the husband. *Employed* wife beaters who are arrested are far less likely to repeat their abuse than those who are not arrested, but arrested *unemployed* wife beaters, if anything, are *more* likely to repeat their crimes (Sherman et al., 1992). It is entirely likely that the picture of widespread police nonintervention in cases of wife beating is not going to change very much in the foreseeable future. Sexual harassment represents a third area in which women are abused, subordinated, and humiliated by the unethical, deviant, and even criminal actions of men, where an insufficient response by social control reveals the workings of a male-dominated power structure (MacKinnon, 1979; Friedman, Boumil, and Taylor, 1992).

A feminist approach to deviance and crime did not exist more than a generation ago; the perspective is young and still in the process of development. Perhaps it is too early to say that *a* feminist criminology of the sociology of deviance exists as a coherent and unified approach. Perhaps it is more appropriate to refer to feminism*s,* or feminist criminolog*ies,* or feminist perspectives within criminology (Gelsthorpe and Morris, 1988, p. 227). There are, at the very least, liberal, radical, and socialist varieties of feminism. Incomplete as the perspective is, however, it shows great promise to enrich and inform the discipline. No approach that treats the behavior of less than half the population as if it were behavior in general can claim to be adequate or valid. The fields of criminology and deviance studies have a long way to go before they fully incorporate the insights of feminism into the way they look at their subject matter. It is possible that feminism may have a more revolutionary impact on the field than that of any other perspective we've examined. Feminism forces us to think about sex biases and how they distort our views of deviance, crime, the law, and the criminal justice system. These biases are deep and pervasive. Confronting and overcoming them makes us better sociologists, criminologists, and students of deviance, and, just perhaps, more capable of changing society for the better.

CONTROLOLOGY OR THE NEW SOCIOLOGY OF SOCIAL CONTROL

The last and most recent perspective in the field of deviance we shall consider is *controlology* (Ditton, 1979) or "the new sociology of social control" (Scull, 1988, p. 685). Like feminism, controlology was stimulated by the perceived deficiencies of Marxist sociology; in fact, one early work adopting a controlology perspective was subtitled "Beyond the New Criminology" (Ditton, 1979). The new sociology of social control emerged in the late 1970s and early 1980s, and is associated with the names of Nanette Davis (Davis and Anderson, 1983; Davis and Stasz, 1990), Stanley Cohen (1985a, 1985b; Cohen and Scull, 1983), David Garland (1985, 1990; Garland and Young, 1983), and John Lowman (Lowman, Menzies and Palys, 1987a; Lowman et al., 1986). Because of theoretical differences, it *excludes* such prominent sociologists whose work focuses on social control as Jack Gibbs (1981, 1989), Donald Black (1984), and Black's disciple, Horwitz (1990). To the new sociologists of social control, Gibbs, Black, and Horwitz entertain far too broad a conception of social control, one that is not focused specifically on the formal social control that emanates from the state and state-like institutions. In addition, Gibbs's, Black's, and Horwitz's adoption of the natural science model—positivism—and along with it, their adherence to a value-free stance, disqualifies them from the controlology fraternity. Far from seeing their own research as value-free, the new sociologists of social control see their work as a radical critique of existing society, one that will help usher in a more humane and just one.

The central concern of the new sociology of social control is captured in a fishing analogy advanced by one controlologist, Stanley Cohen:

Imagine that the entrance to the deviancy control system is something like a gigantic fishing net. Strange and complex in its appearance and movements, the net is cast by an army of different fishermen and fisherwomen working all day and even into the night according to more or less known rules and routines, subject to more or less authority and control from above, knowing more or less what the other is doing. Society is the ocean—vast, troubled and full of uncharted currents, rocks and other hazards. Deviants are the fish (Cohen, 1985a, pp. 41–42).

Of course, as we are reminded, the analogy does not work perfectly; deviants are not literally cleaned, packed, cooked, and eaten. They are kept alive (usually) and processed "(shall we say punished, treated, corrected?)"; after they have been processed, they are thrown back into the sea—now tagged and labeled—occasionally to swim free for the rest of their lives, or, "more frequently, they might be swept up into the net again. This might happen over and over. Some wretched creatures spend their whole lives being endlessly cycled and recycled, caught, processed and thrown back" (Cohen, 1985a, p. 42). The operation of this net, and the "recycling industry which controls it," is the subject matter of the new sociology of social control.

The spiritual father of the "new sociology of social control" is Michel Foucault, a French philosopher.* In the early 1960s, Foucault pub-

lished a work that was to be translated into English as *Madness and Civilization* (1967). Its central idea was that the brutal repression of the prison was replaced by a new, different, seemingly enlightened, more subtly repressive entity, the mental institution. Social control, it seems, need not be overtly and brutally repressive to be effective, but may repress through reason, persuasion, and scientific authority.

Even more important was the work that was translated into English as *Discipline and Punish* in 1979 (Foucault, 1979). In this later work, Foucault extended his idea of enlightened but repressive social control. The centerpiece of traditional social control was torture and execution; it was aimed at destroying or mutilating the offender's body. Traditional means of punishment were fitful and sporadic rather than continual and ongoing. Public confessions, torture, and execution created spectacle, but increasingly, they were ineffective; eventually, crowds came not to be seized by the terror of the scaffold but to protest the injustice of the punishment. In the end, public executions produced disorder and protest, not fear and compliance.

With the growing importance of portable commercial property in the 1700s, the merchant class needed a stable, predictable means of protecting their investments from the predatory activities of the lower classes. The traditional means of punishment had to be replaced with a system of control that was more effective, certain, comprehensive, and which operated all the time. The traditional prison was used to detain suspected offenders before their trials or executions. It was only in the second half of the eighteenth century that the modern prison became a location specifically for the incarceration and punishment of the offender. This

---

*Some observers argue that an author's theories can be explained by his or her personal life, biography, and location in the social structure. In Foucault's own words: "The key to the personal poetic attitude of the philosopher is not to be sought

in his ideas . . . but rather in his philosophy-as-life, his philosophical life, his ethos." Thus, perhaps it would be worthwhile to refer to a few biographical facts that might shed some light on his theory or approach. Foucault died of AIDS in 1984 at the age of 57. He was fascinated by and frequently participated in anonymous, promiscuous homosexual encounters, including sadomasochistic practices. In addition, he experimented with a wide range of illegal psychoactive drugs, and saw them as a pathway to insight, creativity, and freedom. One wonders whether his views of social control are related to the restrictions he felt conventional society placed on his own sexual and personal expression. For instance, he resented the fact that he was not able to give full expression to his unconventional desires in France, where he was well-known, as opposed to Brazil and the United States, where he was less readily recognizable. See Miller, 1992, 1993, for biographical details on Foucault's life.

new prison system, Foucault believed, revealed the special character of a new age. Jeremy Bentham (1748–1832), British philosopher, reformer, and utilitarian, came up with a plan for a modern prison; it was designed so that a small number of guards could observe a large number of inmates; he called this arrangement the *panopticon*. It was Foucault's belief that the central thrust in history was the evolution from traditional society, where *the many observe the few* (as was true in public spectacles, such as executions) to modern society, where *the few observe the many* (as in the modern prison, with its panopticon). Foucault believed that Bentham's panopticon was typical, characteristic, or *paradigmatic* of modern society in general; the panoptic principle had become generalized and imitated throughout the entire society. We live, Foucault believed, in a society that is bent on observing and controlling its citizens in a wide range of contexts. In a sense, then, modern society has become one gigantic, monstrous, extended panopticon.

Foucault has become one of the most influential and fashionable intellectuals of the second half of the twentieth century. He has many disciples; his ideas are widely cited and have spawned a virtual industry of commentary and development. His writings have influenced thinking in a dozen disciplines. To a critical, thinking, empirically minded individual, the Foucault craze must seem puzzling, for his ideas are shot through with fatal flaws, specious reasoning, and factually incorrect statements. While his analysis is more philosophical, literary, and metaphorical than empirical and social-scientific, he does make statements which, he claims, have real-world referents. Thus, he must be judged on the empirical and explanatory adequacy of his writings. On these grounds, the work of Foucault, at least in *Discipline and Punish*, is for the most part incorrect, inadequate, and misleading.

A first-rate critique of *Discipline and Punish* has been written by David Garland (1990, pp. 157–175), a sociologist who has, in fact, made use of some of its ideas (Garland, 1985; Garland and Young, 1983). Much of Foucault's historical analysis, Garland writes, has been found faulty and inaccurate. Public torture, mutilation, and execution had begun to decline in importance in Europe as early as 1600, over a century and a half before Foucault's argument requires (Garland, 1990, p. 158). Imprisonment as a form of punishment, as opposed to detention in prison while awaiting trial or execution, had been in widespread use in the 1600s, again, more than a century before Foucault claims, which contradicts his argument (p. 158). The "scaffold riots," which Foucault argues were essential in the shift away from public executions were, in fact, far rarer than he claims; disorder at public hangings was always a risk—long before Foucault argues they began to pose a threat to authorities—and, in any case, it was no reason for abandoning the practice (p. 159). A close analysis of historical documents left by prison reformers demonstrates that benevolent motives, often fueled by religious conviction, often lay behind the shift away from the cruel treatment of prisoners in the late 1700s and early 1800s, a factor Foucault discounts (p. 159). While more humane treatment is often compatible with greater control, the first cannot simply be reduced to the second, as Foucault does (p. 159). And Jeremy Bentham's panopticon prison was a failure—it was never even built; Foucault is fascinated by the *image* of the panopticon rather than its actual execution, which never took place (p. 171).

As a general rule, Foucault takes *thought* and *discourse* as a reality, as indicative of the way things are—in a sense, even more real than actions—a serious flaw to the empirical social scientist. In fact, modern prisons are not even remotely like Bentham's panopticon. (Except when prisoners are in the yard and the guards are in the gun towers—the kind of naked repression Foucault argued had died out by the second half of the 1700s.) In general, Foucault takes consequences, including unintended ones, as if they were intended by the powerful actors on the scene, indeed, a direct outcome of their motives (Garland, 1990, p. 165). Foucault ignores all countervailing forces that operate to limit the control of the exercise of power; there is no political opposition in his scheme (p. 167), which makes his analysis a crude caricature, not a serious depiction of social reality. He nearly always presents the control *potential* of the powers that be as the *reality* (p. 168). And, for all its claims to being a political understanding of modern society, *Discipline and Punish* presents a "strangely apolitical" analysis (p. 170): There is no motive to power—only more power, more discipline, more control. Why and for what purposes power is wielded is never fully explained. Lastly, Foucault writes as if a society is possible without power; he is against power per se (pp. 173–174). He never presents an alternative system, one that can operate with the humane, enlightened exercise of power; to Foucault, in the context of modern society, "humane" and "enlightened" mean only one thing: insidious attempts at greater and more effective control. The fact is, a society cannot exist unless some measure of power and control is exercised by some citizens over others. Foucault's critique of power and control in modern society makes no sense in the absence of a feasible alternative. In fact, Foucault's alternative is a utopia that does not—and cannot—exist, more fantasy than reality. As serious social science, *Discipline and Punish* is fatally flawed.

No matter that Foucault's assertions in *Discipline and Punish* are mostly incorrect; this book provided an inspiration for a new perspective in the sociology of deviance and crime. This new perspective must stand or fall on its own terms; even if Foucault's analysis is deficient, in principle, his followers could be inspired to construct their own, entirely valid, theoretical edifice. Although the central themes of controlology or the new sociology of social control were initially developed to some degree independent of Foucault, his work does provide the perspective's most powerful inspiration. The central ideas in the new sociology of social control are these.

First, *social control is problematic; it should not* be treated as a given. By that, controlologists mean it is not produced "naturally" by the "invisible hand of society" but rather is "consciously fashioned by the visible hand of definable organizations, groups, and classes" (Scull, 1988, p. 686). We cannot assume, as the functionalists seemed to do, that society will be wise enough to preserve institutions and practices that serve the whole in the best possible way by sanctioning what is harmful and encouraging what is beneficial. Social control, as it is practiced, is *not* a product of a broad, widely shared social "need" or the workings of "functional prerequisites," in functionalist terminology. Instead, the controlologists say, social control is *imposed* by specific social entities, usually for their own benefit, and often at the expense of individuals, categories, and groups who are controlled. To put the matter another way, punishment is a *political tactic* practiced by the powerful in their exercise of control over individuals, groups, and categories who make trouble for them.

Second, social control is typically *coercive, repressive,* and *far from benign.* (Even though it typically appears as a "velvet glove" rather than an "iron fist.") Traditional criminologists have taken social control generally and the system of corrections specifically as society's reactive means of self-protection, a system that is understandable, necessary, and beneficial. (Even though, to liberal criminologists, the existing system of corrections should be reformed.) In the hands of the controlologists, social control takes on a more sinister and repressive function: to restrain troublesome populations. It is, says one observer, "within the state's power to manipulate, dominate and constrain that we discover the secrets of social control in the modern age" (Spitzer, 1987, p. 56). The purpose of psychiatry is not to heal but to control; the purpose of the welfare system is not to provide a safety net for the poor but to control; the purpose of education is not to teach but to control; the purpose of the mass media is not to inform but to control; and so on. And when segments of the population under institutional control are perceived as no longer threatening and in need of direct control, they are *dumped out of the system* (Scull, 1977, 1984a).

Third, *social control is coterminous with state or state-like control.* More specifically, a number of organizations, agencies, or institutions are now performing the function of social control *on behalf of* or *in the service of* the state. These include social welfare organizations, psychiatrists and psychiatric agencies, professional organizations, hospitals, clinics, mental health organizations, and so on. It is the contention of the controlologists that state control has been assumed by civil society; activities that were once performed by the state have been taken over by these seemingly autonomous, often private, organizations, agencies, and institutions. Troublesome populations can now be controlled on a wide range of fronts by a wide range of agencies; essentially the same clients are circulated and recirculated among them. Even institutions which seem to have little or nothing to do with the control of deviance, such as the mass media of communications, are involved in controlling through defining and shaping public opinion, and influencing how deviants are to be dealt with (Ericson, Baranek, and Chan, 1987, 1989, 1991). "The original compact methods of discipline are . . . being broken up and made more flexible as they circulate into the new 'regional outposts' of the control network" (Cohen, 1985a, p. 111).

Fourth, the social control appararatus is *unified* and *coherent.* The subsystems "fit together" into interrelated, functionally equivalent parts. The phenomenon of interlocking agencies and institutions working to control troublesome populations may be referred to as *transcarceration* (Lowman, Menzies, and Palys, 1987). Foucault refers to this "transscarceral" system as "the carceral archipelago" (1979, p. 298), an obvious reference to Aleksander Solzhenitsyn's description of the Soviet prison camps, *The Gulag Archipelago* (1974, 1975). The "carceral archipelago transported" the punitive approach "from the penal institution to the entire social body" (Foucault, 1979, p. 298). Controlologists point to a "peno-juridical, mental health, welfare and tutelage complex" in which "power structures can be examined only by appreciating cross-institutional arrangements and dynamics" (Lowman, Menzies, and Palys, 1987b, p. 9).

Although he is a Marxist, not a social control theorist, Steven Spitzer (1975) made a distinction between two types of "problem populations" that has proven to be useful, at least implicitly, by the new sociologists of social control, the distinction between *social junk* and *social dynamite* (pp. 645–646). "Social junk" is made up of those individuals who represent "a costly yet relatively harmless burden to society." They include the aged, the handicapped, the mentally ill, and the mentally retarded (p. 645). In contrast, "social dynamite" is made up of "politically volatile" individuals. Social junk is dealt with through welfare and social service agencies, while social dynamite is likely to be handled by more active and reactive agencies, such as the police, the courts, jails, and prisons. Social junk is "dumped," that is, given a minimum of care with a minimum of expenditure of resources, while social dynamite is isolated, segregated, and if need be, incarcerated. The membership in these two categories shifts around from time to time, depending on the economic and social circumstances of the period. For instance, the welfare poor, homosexuals, alcoholics, and "problem children" have been treated at times as social junk, and at times as social dynamite (p. 646). From the point of view of the theorists of social control, society's problem is *neutralizing* and *defusing* potential social dynamite, that is, monitoring, controlling, and managing their behavior by means of ancillary state-like agencies so that they do not *have* to be arrested and incarcerated, that is, making sure they do not *become* "social dynamite." In Cohen's terms (1985a, pp. 270–272), a system of *inclusion* (controlling deviants in our midst) supplements the system of *exclusion* (that is, isolating and incarcerating them). Once again, the "velvet glove" may be more effective than the "iron fist."

The new sociology of social control is still evolving; it may look very different a decade from now. At the same time, its practitioners have a clear conception of deviance and social control, and the version they have advanced must be evaluated on the basis of its current state of development.

Certainly the insight that in modern society, a number of organizations and agencies operate *in place of* and *on behalf of* the state represents an advance over a vulgar and simple-minded Marxism that argues that the capitalist state is monolithically centralized and serves a single function: preservation of the status quo (Quinney, 1974a). One must be impressed with the variety and range of people-processing institutions and agencies in modern society, many of them designed to deal with or handle the behavior of troublesome individuals and groups (Hawkins and Tiedeman, 1975). No one can doubt that some of the functionaries who work for these agencies are often uncaring and insensitive. Especially in the inner cities, where these agencies are simply overwhelmed with the sheer volume of clients, we see the community being shortchanged. But most of these problems stem not from *too much control* but from *too few resources*. Once again, modern society is unprecedented in the number, variety, and almost ubiquitousness of organizations, agencies, and institutions that perform state-like functions, who operate in place of and on behalf of the state. And social control is one of their functions. In most cases, from the clients' perspective, that may not even be their main function. It seems almost inconceivable that such welfare and service institutions are approached *primarily*, even *exclusively*, as agencies of social control. Clients themselves more often see these institutions as a shield to protect them rather than a net to catch them.

It is one thing to say that the state and state-like agencies have been left out of more traditional analyses of deviance and crime. For instance, Cohen (1985b, p. 717) complains that Donald Black's approach to social control is "constructed as if the modern state does not exist." However, it is an altogether different matter to pretend that the only social control worthy of the name is formal social control, that a broad perspective toward social control, which includes formal and informal social control, is a "Mickey Mouse concept" (Cohen,

1985a, p. 2). In effect, pretending that interpersonal social control does not operate, does not influence deviant and criminal behavior. As I said earlier, a criminologist focusing exclusively on formal social control is a bit like someone writing the history of architecture by focusing exclusively on buildings higher than 14 stories tall. In fact, the new sociology of social control is not interested in social control per se. It is interested in how the state and its allied organizations and institutions control deviant behavior, that is, the actions of populations who are troublesome for elites. In fact, to the controlologist, it doesn't much matter *what* "troublesome populations" do—their behavior is irrelevant—what counts is the response of agents in power. What we get is an exaggerated, almost simple-minded caricature of labeling theory, but with social control artificially equated with formal (or semi-formal) social control. The new sociology of social control turns out to be an extremely narrow view of both deviance and social control.

Anyone who has studied or explored the world of deviance and crime in an intimate, up-close fashion must be struck by three essential facts that contradict the model proposed by the new sociology of social control. First, far from looking anything like a fishing net, agencies of formal and semi-formal social control are extremely erratic, fitful, and *inefficient*. Let's return to Cohen's fishing analogy (1985a, pp. 41–42). While Cohen admits that the analogy can be "occasionally quite misleading," the differences he points out are *literal* (for instance, agents of social control do not actually *eat* deviants) and not *substantive* ones. What we see in the real world is far from a tightly meshed wide net, in fact, it is an extremely loosely meshed net whose borders are unclear. Individuals who engage in deviant and criminal behavior engage in *countless* sanctionable actions without encountering formal social control. One study found that in a one-year period, 1,000 Miami drug abusers committed over 300,000 crimes, but were arrested only 1,300 times; crimes led to arrest less than one-half of 1 percent of the time (Inciardi, 1986, pp. 127, 129, 1992). One researcher of homosexuality estimated that there are roughly *six million* homosexual acts for every 20 convictions (Hoffman, 1968, p. 91). (Over half the states in the U.S. have repealed their laws outlawing homosexual acts.) Residents of neighborhoods infested with crack and heroin sales want *more* social control, not less, and charge the police with negligence, a lack of vigilance, a lack of concern for their plight. The likelihood that someone arrested on a felony charge resulting in police prosecution will be sent to prison is roughly one in seven (Boland et al., 1990). One must be struck by the utter *contempt* and *disdain* many deviants and criminals feel toward agents and agencies of social control.

A second basic fact represents the opposite side of the coin: While it is true that a very low proportion of offenders are caught and processed, it is also true that the number and proportion of offenders who are incarcerated is increasing hugely in the United States. To reiterate, Foucault and his followers argued that the kind of social control that evolved in modern society increasingly *underplayed* physical punishments that were directed at the offender's body and emphasized treatment, rehabilitation, and resocialization, which invaded the offender's mind and soul. Yet, in at least one important respect, what we see is precisely the opposite; in penology, increasingly, rehabilitation is being abandoned in favor of physical punishment. "Lock 'em up and throw away the key" has become the watchword. Between 1970 and 1980, the American prison population doubled, from 200,000 to 400,000; between 1980 and 1990, it doubled again, to 800,000. Today, it is over one million (this does not count jail inmates). Between 1980 and 1994, the rate of incarceration jumped from 139 per 100,000 in the population to 375. In many ways, with respect to how criminal offenders have been treated over the past quarter-century or so, we have moved *away from* the "velvet glove" Foucault referred to and more *toward* an "iron fist" policy.

Interestingly, in some crucial respects, another form of deviance presents almost precisely the *opposite* picture. After 1955, the mentally ill began to be released from insane asylums in record numbers. In that year, there were 560,000 residents in publicly funded mental hospitals; at last count, this number stood at 80,000. Essentially, these patients are being "dumped" into the community, with little in the way of treatment except pills. Although some observers argue that this policy verifies the new sociology of social control perspective (Scull, 1984a), it seems difficult to argue that two *opposite* trends—incarcerating *more* criminal offenders and incarcerating *fewer* mental patients—simultaneously provide evidence for the same explanation. (Are criminals "social dynamite" and the mentally ill, "social junk"?) More likely, systems of social control are not guided by a single master plan or guiding principle these theorists propose. Instead, different sectors of social control operate to some degree under their own logic, each with its own specific, concrete exigencies and dynamics. An approach which offers partial explanations for different forms of deviance is anathema to the vaster ambitions of the new sociology of social control, which seeks to identify one master plan for all forms of deviance.

Instead of a systematic, unrelenting system of formal social control, what we see is one that is fitful and erratic, one that fails to detect, capture, or punish most deviants until one victimizes the wrong person, or victimizes once too often, or victimizes a bit too blatantly, and is apprehended, judged, and punished. Felons have to be convicted two, three, or four times before they are sent to prison (Boland, et al., 1990). Still, even though the American criminal justice system system is considerably less harsh than any social control model of it holds, it is moving in a *more* punitive direction over time—the opposite of Foucault's speculation. Prison officials are abandoning the efficacy of treatment and reform and simply holding convicted felons who are serving increasingly longer sentences. Over time, the "iron fist" is replacing the "velvet glove": We are moving "from the therapeutic to the punitive state"; the rationale of the criminal justice system is increasingly "much more likely to be punishment than reform or cure" (Sykes and Cullen, 1992, pp. 482–485). Thus, the new sociologists of social control are deficient in their analysis of formal social control in characterizing the criminal justice system overall (it is less punitive than their analyses hold), and in characterizing its direction (it is becoming more punitive over time, not less).

To be fair, the primary focus of the contrologists is not on the criminal justice system, but on how policelike functions have been taken over by allied agencies, organizations, and institutions. But if their characterization of how the *principal* agency of formal social control actually operates is so far off the mark, one wonders about their analysis of the allied ones. And what we actually see in public and semi-autonomous "social control" institutions—such as hospitals, psychiatric clinics, social welfare agencies, social services—is a much more *reciprocal* and *interactional* dynamic than the social control model suggests: overwhelmed functionaries attempting to engage in limited, patch-up assistance, and clients attempting to "work" the system

to their best advantage. The fishing analogy utterly and completely fails to capture the true relationship between the allied agencies of deviance and social control.

Most individuals who engage in behavior widely regarded as deviant slip through the fishing net. Most homosexuals (without HIV or AIDS) not only never get arrested, as we saw, they are never dealt with *as* homosexuals, by *any* semi-formal agency of social control. The same may be said of most adulterers (unless a spouse forces them to seek family therapy), consumers of pornography, adult pornographic actors and models, most alcoholics (unless they are arrested or are forced to seek treatment), petty thieves, white-collar criminals, drug users, in fact, *most* enactors of *most* of the deviant behavior discussed in this book. The contrologist will object, claiming that if these individuals are not dealt with by semi-formal agencies of social control, they are simply not "troublesome populations." They may be *deviant* in the *informal* sense, but not in the formal or semi-formal sense of the word. But isn't this something of a tautology? That is, deviance is *defined* as that which generates action by formal and semi-formal agencies of social control and, at the same time, it is taken as *problematic*, something *which must be explained,* that is, *why* these agencies react to certain categories *as* troublesome. That which is assumed to be true cannot also be taken as an intellectual puzzle.

One basic question that the new sociologists of social control have not been able to answer is: What would a society look like *without* social control? Another is: What would a *humane* system of social control look like? A third is: Within the constraints set by resources, the economy, budgets, political exigencies, and the raw material with which agents of social control have to work, how could a system of social control be set up in existing society that would have more beneficial than harmful effects? In my view, theorists of this school have not even addressed these or kindred issues, indicating the sketchy, preliminary state of the contrology agenda.

The new sociologists of social control yearn (as many of the rest of us do) for a more humane public bureaucracy; for a truly effective means of separating "hard" offenders who are likely to wreak genuine harm on others from "soft" offenders who pose no real threat to anyone; for mechanisms that incorporate marginal populations into the social mainstream without passing judgment on their differences; for a society that appreciates human diversity and maximizes human dignity, that controls as little as is feasible; for a society that passes and enforces as few laws as is possible and feasible; for one that gives ordinary citizens maximum voice in their own destiny; for one in which the psychiatrically troubled can receive treatment based on their needs, not on society's need to control their troublesome behavior; for a truly civil society in which people, especially those in power, truly care about the welfare of others. It is not clear, however, what is going to bring any of this about. The new sociologists are to be commended for emphasizing that human values play a major role in how and why a subject is studied. Most of them study deviance because they wish to challenge the evils of modern society and help effect a more humane, reciprocal system of social control. Whether their analyses will accomplish these goals remains to be seen. The new sociology of social control is not a balanced, systematic analysis of deviance and social control. Perhaps it was not meant to be. It does, however, represent a worthwhile recent addition to the field, one that deserves attention and encouragement.

SUMMARY

The other side of the coin of the etiological quest ("Why do they do it?") is the focus on the structure and dynamics of *social control:* definitions of deviance, the rules, and their enforcement.

The earliest perspective to undertake a serious examination of rules and their enforcement was functionalism. The approach and concerns of functionalism could be broken down into two parts: first, those that were common-sensical and second, those that violated common sense. Into the first category fell a concern as to why certain behaviors (such as incest) have been widely condemned, and what part the punishment of offenders plays in the functioning of societies and groups. Into the second concern fell the question of why certain deviant practices (such as prostitution) endure, and in a sense, seem to be encouraged by the very institutions that have been designed to eliminate them. Such practices endure, functionalists argue, because they make a contribution to the stability and viability of the society. Rather than undermining the society, they represent a valuable resource; it is in

the interest of the society to ensure their survival because, in fact, they help the society to survive. Functionalists were the first approach or perspective to argue that deviance was not necessarily a pathological phenomenon.

The labeling or interactionist perspective had its roots in the work of two precursors, Frank Tannenbaum and Edwin Lemert, who shifted their attention away from the etiology of deviance, crime, and delinquency to an examination of what implications punishment has on the deviators' identities and the enactment of their further deviance. The labeling theorists of the 1960s (who never approved of the title, "labeing theory," to apply to their approach, preferring instead the term, "the interactionist perspective") stressed the relativity of deviance from one time and place to another; the social construction of moral meanings and definitions; the inner or subjective world of the deviant; the impact of labeling and stigma on the person so labeled; the role of audiences in defining deviance; the role of contingencies, such as ancillary characteristics in influencing the labeling process; the reflexive or the "looking-glass self"; the "stickiness" of labels; and the self-fulfilling prophecy. Although a number of its insights have been incorporated into the mainstream of the field as a whole, the labeling approach to deviance nonetheless remains controversial.

Conflict theory overlaps with the labeling approach but contrasts with functionalism on a number of key points. Conflict theory sees struggles between and among classes and categories in society, with winners and losers resulting from the outcome of these struggles. Advocates of this perspective (contrary to functionalists) stress the fact that the interests of one faction or segment of the society often conflict with or contradict those of another; what helps one may hurt another, and vice versa. For instance, the institution of prostitution may reinforce male power and help to oppress women; social stratification may be good for the rich and harmful to the poor. Classes and categories attempt to establish dominance or hegemony over others to maintain their interests. The criminal law, for instance, may help to reinforce the rule of the ruling elite and assist in exploiting or oppressing the poorest segments of the society. Marxists may be seen as a distinct variety of conflict theory. Although Marxism's influence in intellectual circles has plummeted in the past decade or two, some Marxist sociologists of deviance and crime remain.

Marxists stress the economic dimension and underplay nearly all other factors in evaluating crime and its control.

Feminists hold that women are subordinated as a result of their sex; it is their intention to eliminate *androcentrism* (a male-centered bias), *patriarchy* (male supremacy), and *sexism* (prejudice and discrimination against women). Feminist sociologists argue that earlier researchers displayed male biases in neglecting the deviance and crime of women; they looked at the few crimes that they did examine in a distinctly skewed, biased fashion; and they neglected the victimization of women by male-initiated acts of deviance and crime. Moreover, feminists stress, the issue of the social control of female versus male deviance and crime is a neglected topic and should be examined. Do female offenders receive harsher sentences at the hands of the criminal justice system? Is women's deviance treated more punitively in *informal* social control? Are male victimizers of women (in acts of rape, wife battering, and sexual harassment) treated leniently by the agents of formal and informal social control? These and other questions have occupied feminist students of deviance and crime since the late 1960s.

Lastly, a perspective that has come to be referred to as the "new" sociology of social control has emerged in the past decade or two. Inspired by the work of philosopher Michel Foucault, these "contrologists" are concerned with some of the more repressive features of social control in modern society. While more enlightened and less physically punitive, social control in the industrial age has come to be a far more effective surveillance, control, and punishing apparatus than was true in the past. A variety of institutions, agencies, and organizations that are technically separate or semi-autonomous from the state or government are becoming unified into a giant prisonlike "transcarceral" system. The "new" sociology of social control calls attention to dimensions and processes that may be crucial and have not been adequately studied by other perspectives. The approach is still in the process of evolution.

It is possible that a Black-oriented or Afrocentric sociology of crime and deviance is in its very beginning stages (Russell, 1992). Such a perspective would argue that the laws and their enforcement are systematically biased against African-Americans (Mann, 1993; Duster, 1995). To fully understand the exercise of social control, it is necessary to grasp the role it plays in the life of the Black community, as well as in suppressing Black demands for justice and equality. The systematic denial of equal power and resources to African-Americans is central to an adequate understanding of Black crime and deviance, as well as the control of that crime and deviance in the United States (Rose and McClain, 1990; Oliver, 1994; Tonry, 1995; Covington, 1995).

The rules and their enforcement cannot be assumed or taken for granted. A variety of perspectives have taken this side of the equation as problematic and worthy of study. Less concerned with etiology or the causes of deviance itself, functionalism, labeling theory, conflict theory, feminism, and the "new" sociology of social control have tried to understand why certain definitions of deviance emerge and why they are enforced. While they do not deny the validity or importance of etiological or positivistic theories of deviance, these theories do limit their scope. They insist that no study of deviance can be complete without understanding the origin and dynamics of social control. They are worthy of our attention.

chapter 6

DRUG USE AS DEVIANT BEHAVIOR

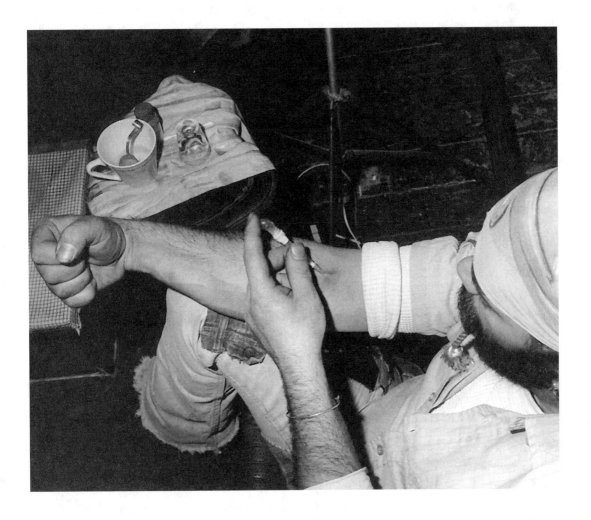

"Execute Drug Dealers, Mayor Says," "Brutal Gangs Wage War of Terror," "Flood of Drugs—A Losing Battle," "Surge of Violence Linked to Narcotics," "War on Drugs Shifting to Street," "Drug Violence Erodes a Neighborhood," "Drug Production Soars"—these and other headlines like them fairly scream out the public's anxiety over the drug abuse issue.

These newspaper headlines tap a certain *fear* and *concern* felt by the public about drug abuse. (More specifically, they tap the fear and concern that journalists, editors, and newspaper publishers *believe* the public feels.) Drug use, like every existing social condition, has a *subjective* dimension: the public's feeling or attitude about it, what is believed about it, what the public, or segments of the public do, or want to do about it, and the public's feelings, attitudes, and beliefs about the individuals who engage in it.

Likewise, drug use and abuse has an *objective* side: what drugs do to humans who use them, how widely and frequently they are used, what kind of an impact they have on the society.

As we might expect, as with most other behaviors, conditions, and issues, the subjective and the objective sides of drug use overlap extremely imperfectly. That is, fear and concern may be great about behavior and conditions that are not especially threatening or damaging, and they may be minimal about others that are objectively very threatening or damaging. Moreover, these two dimensions—the subjective and the objective—may be out of synch with one another over time, with concern rising when damage from drug abuse is dropping, and declining when it rises. It is wise, when investigating deviant behavior and conditions, to keep the subjective and the objective dimensions separate in one's mind. Regarding a given condition or behavior *as* deviance or *as* a social problem (the subjective dimension) may be completely unrelated to the physical or psychological damage it does (the objective dimension).

Fear of and concern about the threat of drug use and abuse have waxed and waned over the years in the United States. One measure of that fear and concern is the number and content of news stories on the subject. In the 1930s, hundreds of sensationalistic newspaper and magazine articles were published nationally which detailed the supposed horrors of marijuana use. In the 1940s and 1950s, such stories declined sharply in number and stridency. In the second half of the 1960s, literally

thousands of news accounts were published and broadcast on LSD's capacity to make users go crazy and do dangerous things to themselves and others. In the early 1970s, heroin was in the news. By the mid-1970s, the media had quieted down on the drug front. But the mid- to late-1980s witnessed a rebirth—indeed, something of an explosion—of public concern over the use and abuse of illegal drugs. For instance, between the early and the mid-1980s, the number of articles on the subject of drug abuse published in all the popular national magazines that are indexed by *The Reader's Guide to Periodical Literature* multiplied approximately eight times. In the single year between 1985 and 1986, the number increased more than two and a half times, from 103 to 280. Clearly, although it had been building up in the two or three years prior, 1986 was the year that drug use and abuse fairly *exploded* as a social problem in the United States. However, into the 1990s, this concern, although it remains high, had declined significantly.

Another measure of the subjective or fear dimension is the public's designation of a given condition or behavior as a serious problem. Each year, and during some years, several times during the year, the Gallup Poll asks a sample of the public what they regard as the "number one problem facing the nation today." As with the articles published in *The Reader's Guide*, the Gallup Poll provides a very rough measure of subjective public concern over a given condition at a particular time. The public's concern over drug abuse rose and fell twice between the early 1970s and the early 1990s. In February 1973, 20 percent of the respondents in the Gallup Poll felt that drug abuse was the nation's number one problem. However, between that date and 1985, the percentage mentioning drug abuse as the country's most serious problem was so low that it did not even appear among the top half-dozen problems. During 1985 and into January 1986, between 2 and 3 percent of the American public mentioned drug abuse as the country's most important problem; in April 1986, in a set of parallel polls conducted by *The New York Times* and CBS News, again, 2 percent mentioned drugs as the country's number one problem. In a July 1986 Gallup Poll, the figure was 8 percent; in an August *Times*/CBS poll, the figure was 13 percent. The figure continued to increase throughout the remainder of the 1980s until, in September 1989, a whopping 64 percent of the respondents in a *Times*/CBS poll said that drugs constituted the most important issue facing the country at that time. This response represents one of the most intense preoccupations by the American public on the drug issue in polling history.

The September 1989 figure proved to be the pinnacle of public concern about drugs; it is unlikely that a figure of such magnitude will ever be achieved for drug abuse again. After that, said one media expert, intense public concern simply "went away" (Oreskes, 1990). By November 1989, according to a *Times*/CBS poll, the figure had slipped to 38 percent; in July 1990, 18 percent; in August 1990, only 10 percent (Kagay, 1990; Oreskes, 1990; Shenon, 1990b). Between November 1990 and December 1991, this figure remained in the 8 to 12 percent range, and between March 1992 and August 1994, it had dipped slightly into the 6 to 8 percent range. (For these figures, see George Gallup, Jr., *The Gallup Poll: Public Opinion*, Wilmington, Del.: Scholarly Resources, for the relevant years.)

What we saw during the late 1980s, then, was period of *intense* public fear of and concern about drug use and abuse. It was so intense that observers referred to it as a drug "scare" or "moral panic" (Goode, 1990b; Goode and Ben-Yehuda, 1994; Reinarman, 1994; Reinarman and Levine, 1995; see also Kerr, 1986b; Jensen, Gerber, and Babcock, 1991; Ben-Yehuda, 1986). A *moral panic* is an intense, widespread, explosively upsurging feeling on the part of the public that something is terribly wrong in their society because of the moral failure of a specific group of individuals, a subpopulation that has been defined as the enemy, a "folk devil" (Cohen, 1972). In short, a category of people has been *deviantized* (Schur, 1980). This is precisely what happened with drug use and abuse between 1986 and 1989. During this period, American society was undergoing something of a moral panic about drug use; drug abusers were defined, even more intensely than was true in the past, as deviants. Of course, drug use was seen as deviant before 1986, and continues to be so regarded today, but the *intensity* of this feeling reached something of an apex during that relatively brief three-year period.

This does not necessarily mean that objectively speaking, drug use ceased to be a problem in the United States by the late 1980s and early 1990s. In fact, by some indicators, such as drug overdoses, the drug problem actually increased in seriousness in the late 1980s (Goode, 1990). But the important point is this: Moral panics and the fear of and concern about a given behavior or condition do not emerge solely as a result of public awareness of an objective threat. There are usually far more serious conditions or more dangerous behaviors that attract little or no concern than those generated during a given moral panic. In fact, as a rule, the public has an extremely hazy notion of how threatening or damaging certain conditions or forms of behavior are, and the world of drug abuse is no exception. Why is illegal drug use, including the illicit use of prescription drugs, a source of far more public concern than the use of legal drugs (alcohol and tobacco cigarettes), when the former kills no more than 25,000 or so Americans, while the latter kills over 600,000? Why are illegal drug users deviants, while legal drug users are not? There may be concrete reasons for this greater concern that relate to the concrete, objective, or real-world impact of illegal drugs as opposed to legal drugs. Perhaps it is based, in part, on the fact that the victims of illegal drugs are *younger* than the victims of alcohol and tobacco, and hence, far more years of life are lost per death. Perhaps there is the feeling that drug dealers destroy communities and corrupt law enforcement in a way that is quite unlike the way that purveyors of legal drugs work. (Of course, a drug's legal status may have a great deal to do with why this happens.) There may very well be a wide range of objectivistic factors influencing this relationship. But the fact remains, legal drugs kill perhaps 20 times as many Americans as illegal drugs do, yet Americans are *far* more concerned about illegal drug abuse than legal. This paradox is central to any examination of drug use as a form of deviance. As a general rule, the public formulates judgments about the seriousness of certain conditions, behaviors, and issues, and regards certain behaviors as deviant, on the basis of criteria that are to some degree *independent* of estimates of their objective harm. In fact, the public's estimates of the objective harm of specific conditions, behaviors, and issues are extremely faulty, and influenced by a wide range of extraneous factors (Slovic, Fischoff, and Lichtenstein, 1980; Slovic, Layman, and Flynn, 1991; Erikson, 1990).

Humans have ingested drugs for thousands of years. Alcohol was consumed in Stone Age societies, even before the fashioning of metals. Strands from a marijuana plant have been found by archaeologists embedded in Chinese pottery thousands of years old. Statues of figures depicted chewing coca leaves, which contain cocaine, have been dug

Imprisonment on Drug Charges: 1979–1995

Some extremely disturbing trends have been taking place recently in America's criminal justice system. More specifically, the laws and the courts are producing rates of incarceration for drug offenders that are historically unprecedented. Today, there are well over a million inmates in state and federal prisons in the United States, and between 400,000 and 500,000 incarcerated in local jails. (Prisons hold convicted felons, that is, persons convicted of serious crimes, whereas jails hold suspects and defendants awaiting trial and persons convicted of misdemeanors, or minor crimes.) Between 1970 and 1995, the number of prison inmates increased by over five times; the *rate* of incarceration in the United States more than *tripled* during that same period. It might be assumed that this increase is mainly due to increases in rates of violent offenses, such as murder, rape, and robbery. This assumption would be entirely mistaken. Actually, since the early 1980s, rates of violent crime have declined slightly. There are two reasons why there are so many more inmates in prisons in the United States today as compared with the past decade or two. The first is that increasingly, inmates are being held for a longer portion of their sentence. In the past, a convicted felon drawing a seven-year sentence would expect to serve a two-and-a-half to three-year sentence. Today, that sentence would stretch to four and even five years. Lawmakers are putting pressure on prisons to ensure that offenders serve at least half of their sentences; many conservative politicians are aiming for full-term sentences.

The second reason why there are so many more inmates in prison today as compared with the 1970s and 1980s is that today, compared with the past, a conviction on a drug offense is *much* more likely to result in incarceration. Consider the following facts:

• In 1980, only 25 percent of all inmates in federal prisons were incarcerated for a drug offense (about 6,100 out of 24,300); in 1994, this was 61 percent (58,200 out of 95,000). To put the matter another way, while the total federal inmate population increased less than four times between 1980 and 1994, the number of drug offenders increased over nine times.

• Drug offenders convicted in the federal system who were released from prison in 1992 served an average of 33 months; in contrast, those who were *sentenced* in 1992 *must* serve at least 70 months prior to release—a sentence that is more than twice as long.

• In 1980, drug offenders made up only 7 percent of new commitments to state prisons (8,800 out of 131,200); in 1992, they comprised 30 percent (101,600 out of 334,300)—more than a quadrupling. On the other side of the coin, in 1980, violent offenders made up 47 percent of all new commitments to state prisons, while in 1992, this was only 28 percent. Thus, while drug offenders make up an *increasing* proportion of state prisoners, the proportion of *violent* offenders is decreasing over time. The *number* of new admissions to state prisons increased *almost 12 times* in the same number of years.

Changes in the law and in commitment practices with respect to drug violations have had the most serious impact on women and on African-Americans. Consider the following facts.

• In 1979, 20 percent of all female federal prisoners were drug offenders; in 1993, this was 68 percent. In 1979, there were a total of 228 incarcerated female federal drug violators; in 1993, this number was 5,243—an increase of 23 times! In 1979, there were 1,181 women in state prisons on drug violations; in 1993, this was 12,633, more than a tenfold increase. In 1979, only 11 percent of new female admissions to federal prison were drug offenders, while by 1992, this was 40 percent.

• For African-Americans, the dramatic shift in the way drug offenses are dealt with by the criminal justice system expresses itself most blatantly in the distinction the law makes between *powdered* and *crack* cocaine. While only 27 percent of *powdered* cocaine defendants in federal courts are African-Americans, 88 percent of federal *crack* cocaine defendants are Black. Yet, the law stipulates that to draw a five-year sentence in federal court, one need only possess *one-one-hundredth* as much crack as powdered cocaine—five versus 500 grams. Regardless of the law's *intent*, its *result* is to put more Black drug offenders behind bars than white, and for longer sentences. Over the past five years, while the number of white drug violators in state prisons has doubled, the number of African-Americans has multiplied five times.

Source: The Lindesmith Center, "Drug Prohibition and the U.S. Prison System," 1996.

up from South American graves which predate the arrival of Columbus by hundreds of years. Significant numbers of nearly every society on Earth have used one or more drugs to achieve certain desired physical or mental states. Drug use comes close to being a universal, both worldwide and throughout history; it is possible that the Eskimos, or Inuit, are the only society in the world whose members have never used mind-altering substances (Weil, 1972). Most of the time drugs are used, it is in a culturally appropriate and approved manner (Edgerton, 1976, p. 57). Sometimes, drug use is regarded as unacceptable to its more conventional members: The wrong drug is taken, it is taken too often, or under the wrong circumstances, or it is taken with undesirable consequences. In that case, we have an instance of deviant behavior.

WHAT IS DRUG USE?

Before we embark on an exploration of the territory of drug use as deviant behavior, we must answer a deceptively simple question: What is drug use in the first place? Most of us assume the term "drug" refers to a set of substances with clearly identifiable chemical properties or biological effects. It is a common belief that specific characteristics are *intrinsic to* or *dwell within* the substances that are called drugs, that is, drugs must *be* or *do* something that makes them part of a clearly delineated natural entity. This could be called the "objectivistic" or "essentialist" definition of what a drug is: The property of "drug-ness" exists in a state of nature; it is independent of human judgment. For instance, a drug may be defined as a chemical substance that heals sick bodies. Another objectivistic definition defines drugs by their *psychoactivity*, that is, their capacity to influence the workings of the mind—mood, feeling, emotion, thinking, cognition, how people see, perceive, experience the world. In short, if an organism ingests it, will it become high or intoxicated? Objectivistic definitions assume that drugs are used to the extent that they have specific properties or characteristics, that is, physicians prescribe drugs that heal for that purpose, users take drugs which get them high for that purpose, and so on. It is the objective properties that determine what people do *with* drugs, this definition assumes.

In contrast, a *subjectivistic* definition focuses not on what drugs *do*, that is, what concrete effects

they have, but how drugs are *seen*: evaluated, judged, defined, regarded, dealt with, treated, reacted to—or socially *constructed*. The subjectivistic definition would define drugs by the fact that these substances are *thought to be* drugs, by the fact that their possession and sale are *against the law*, by the fact that they are talked about, thought about, and looked upon *as* drugs. Ask a cross section of the public to name a half-dozen "drugs." Ask people to provide an example of drug "users." The users of *which* substances are offered as examples? Find out about the substances whose possession and sale result in arrest and imprisonment. Ask researchers and therapists to discuss the issue of drug "treatment." Which substances show up a lot on these lists, in these discussions—in this "discourse"? Subjectively, *this is what defines what drugs are*. Constructionist definitions of drugs assume a certain *independence* between their objective properties and how they are defined, seen, and dealt with. For instance, they would argue, it is not *only* the most harmful drugs whose possession and sale are against the law, it is not *only* the most medically efficacious that are used by physicians to heal the body and the mind.

The point is that some substances may be a drug according to one of the objectivistic definitions, but not according to the subjectivistic definition. Subjectively speaking, it is the specific *aspect* or *dimension* of chemical substances in which we are interested that defines them *as* drugs, not the simple chemical properties or pharmacological effects the substances have. The constructionist definition argues that when we speak or write of drugs, we are referring to a *social* and *linguistic* category of phenomena, not to an internally consistent natural, objective, chemical or pharmacological category. This does not mean that drug effects are imaginary, that people just think that they occur, that there is no such thing as objective or "real" drug effects. The effects are quite real; we just have to consider them important enough to pay attention to and use as the basis for our definition. If we were to define drugs by their objective psychoactive or mind-altering property, penicillin would not be a drug, and alcohol would be. On the other hand, penicillin is used in medical treatment, while currently, for the most part, alcohol is not (although it was at one time). The subjectivistic definition, therefore, emphasizes that whether a given chemical substance is a drug or not is, in part, in the eye of the beholder.

A CLASSIFICATION OF DRUGS AND THEIR EFFECTS

There are many ways of looking at drug effects. For our purposes, the most important is the distinction between those that are psychoactive, that is, that influence the workings of the mind, and those that are not. Drugs that are psychoactive tend to be taken for recreational purposes, that is, to get high; their use tends to attract condemnation, and their users may become deviants. In contrast, drugs that do not influence the workings of the mind are not taken for the purpose of getting high and their users do not attract a deviant label. Another crucial distinction is between effects that may be referred to as "objective" and those that are "subjective" in nature. *Objective* effects can be perceived and measured by an external observer. Examples would be heartbeat rate and pupillary dilation. Here, it does not matter what the user *thinks* or *says* happens; what happens is what external observers actually see, if need be, aided with mechanical instruments or monitors. *Subjective* effects are experienced internally by the user and can be known to those who do not take the drug themselves only in a secondhand fashion, by means of verbal reports from users or, even more indirectly, from the behavior of users. It must be emphasized that this is a somewhat *different* use of the term, "subjective" than the one I just used; unfortunately, both usages are in common currency. Used in this sense, "subjective" does *not* refer to a social construction or a reaction. More properly, this use of the term means *experiential:* Its reality is confined to how the person having a certain experience *feels.* Psychoactive drugs have an experiential or "subjective" dimension: They make users feel a certain way. We can't always measure this directly, the way we can measure heartbeat rate; here, for the most part, we have to rely on descriptions of users which detail how they feel. Both objective and subjective effects are equally "real"; however, subjective effects are more difficult to study, although they are usually more interesting—at least to the sociologist.

It must also be recognized that a variety of factors influence drug effects. *Dose,* or how much is taken, is one such factor; some drugs may have mild effects when taken in small doses, and much more powerful ones when larger doses are taken. *How* a drug is taken, or *route of administration,* is also crucial. Injected intravenously or smoked,

drugs tend to have a stronger, more immediate effect; swallowed, their effects will be weaker, more muted, much slower to take place. *Experienced* users will manifest somewhat different effects from drug *novices; expectations* of what effects a drug will have may influence the effects themselves; the *setting* in which a drug is taken, likewise, may alter drug experiences; whether a drug is *mixed,* or taken simultaneously with other drugs will also determine the effects it has. All in all, a wide range of factors and dimensions influence or determine the effects drugs have.

All classifications of drugs and their effects are at least a bit misleading. A drug does not "belong" together with other drugs in a certain category and apart from others as a result of an edict from reality, science, or medicine. In fact, humans *construct* drug classifications. We latch onto certain traits, characteristics, or effects as a relevant basis for a classification scheme. One of the basic principles in pharmacology, the science that studies drug effects, is that *all drugs have multiple effects.* There is no drug with a single effect. This means that one effect of a given drug will lead a scientist to place it in one category, while a second effect of that same drug will cause another scientist to place it in an altogether different category. Which scientist is right? In which category does the drug "belong"? The answer is that it depends on what is of interest to the observer; it does not depend solely on the objective characteristics of the substance.

Still, while drug classifications are fuzzy around the edges, the picture is not totally without a certain pattern. Several drugs classified in one way do have some—although not all—properties and effects in common; these properties and effects are quite different from those possessed by drugs that are put in a different category. So, classify we must, for as misleading as classification is, it is also necessary; the human mind thinks in terms of categories. (For two drug classifications, see Ray and Ksir, 1996, and Julien, 1995.)

Almost all the drugs in which we are interested are psychoactive. However, psychoactive drugs have a vast range of different effects; the drugs that cause these many effects must be classified. One way of classifying drugs is to look at their effects on the central nervous system (CNS), that is, the brain and the spinal cord. Some drugs directly stimulate or speed up signals passing through the CNS; others depress or slow down these signals; still others have little or no impact on the speed of CNS signals; and lastly, some have a complex and contradictory effect.

Central nervous system *stimulants* produce arousal, alertness, even excitation; they inhibit fatigue and lethargy. Stimulants speed up signals passing through the CNS. Examples include cocaine and amphetamine, of course, and caffeine, nicotine, and Ritalin.

Depressants have the opposite effect: They inhibit, slow down, retard, or *depress* signals passing through the central nervous system. There are two basic types of CNS depressants. The first is the *analgesics*, which inhibit mainly one principle action of the CNS—the perception of pain. For the purposes of the observer of deviant behavior, the most important type of analgesics are the *narcotics*. This category includes opium and its various derivatives: morphine, heroin, codeine. It also includes the various synthetic and semi-synthetic narcotics, called *opioids* (or "opiumlike" drugs), such as Percodan, methadone, and meperidine (or Demerol). All narcotics are also physically addicting, that is, they generate a physical dependency upon regular, long-term use. There are also several nonnarcotic drugs that have some of the narcotics' pain-killing properties, but do not induce dependence, mental clouding, and euphoria. Nonnarcotic analgesics include aspirin, ibuprofen, Tylenol (acetaminophen), Talwin, and Darvon. As might be expected, nonnarcotic analgesics are far less potent painkillers than the narcotics.

Unlike narcotics, which have a depressive effect principally on one bodily function—the perception of pain—*general depressants*, while not effective painkillers, have a depressive effect on a *wide range* of body organs and functions. They tend to induce relaxation, inhibit anxiety, and at higher doses, result in drowsiness and, eventually, sleep. The most well-known of the general depressants is alcohol, which is known to scientists as ethyl alcohol or ethanol. Other examples include sedatives (or sedative-hypnotics), such as barbiturates and methaqualone (once sold under brand names like Quaalude and Sopor), and tranquilizers, such as Valium and Librium. In sufficiently high doses, general depressants induce mental clouding, drowsiness, and physical dependence; an overdose can produce unconsciousness, coma, and even death.

Hallucinogens (also referred to as psychedelics) have effects on the central nervous system that cannot be reduced to a simple stimulation-depression continuum. These are the drugs that induce *profound sensory alterations*. They occupy their own unique and distinct category and include LSD, peyote and mescaline, and psilocybin or "magic mushrooms" ("'shrooms"). The principal effect of the hallucinogens is not, as might be expected from their name, the inducement of hallucinations, but extreme psychoactivity, a loosening of the imagination and an intensification of emotional states. MDMA, or ecstasy, is sometimes referred to as a hallucinogen, but it does not produce sensory alterations; a more accurate term to describe it would be "empathogen," that is, capable of inducing empathy or an emotional identification with others. Most recent classifications of hallucinogens include a drug called PCP, or Sernyl, once referred to as "angel dust." Used as an animal tranquilizer, this drug has almost none of the properties associated with hallucinogens, such as dramatic sensory transformations. I prefer to classify it as a sedative with paradoxical and unpredictable effects.

Marijuana has, at different times, been classified as a depressant, a stimulant, and as late as the 1970s, a hallucinogen. Most observers nowadays feel that it belongs in a category by itself.

THE EXTENT OF DRUG USE IN THE UNITED STATES

There are four fairly readily identifiable types or categories of drug use in the United States: (1) medical or *legal/instrumental* use, (2) *legal recreational* use, (3) *illegal instrumental* use, and (4) *illegal recreational* use.

Medical Use

Medical use includes the use of drugs, called *prescription* drugs or *pharmaceuticals*, that are prescribed by physicians to patients and taken within the context of medical therapy, as well as the use of the less potent over-the-counter (OTC) drugs purchased by the general public directly off the shelf, without the need for a prescription. Roughly two billion prescriptions are written for drugs in the United States each year, about half of which are new prescriptions and the other half refills. Roughly one in seven prescription drugs is psychoactive; psychoactive drugs influence mood, emotion, and other mental processes. The majority act more or less entirely on the body rather than on the mind. In the 1990s, prescription drugs made up well over

$40 billion a year industry in the U.S. at the retail level. OTC drugs, for the most part, are not significantly psychoactive, do not produce a strong dependency, and have a fairly low level of toxicity, that is, it is fairly difficult to overdose on them; they are hardly ever taken for recreational purposes. Examples include aspirin, No-Doz, Sominex, Allerest, and Dexatrim. In 1995, the annual retail sales of OTC drugs in the U.S. totaled $15 billion. The medical use of prescription and OTC drugs is not regarded as deviant by most Americans. These drugs can be abused or misused, of course. Unscrupulous physicians can overprescribe pharmaceutical drugs, particularly those that are psychoactive, for patients who seek their effects; such practices were extremely common in the 1960s and 1970s. Aspirin and acetaminophen (Tylenol) are responsible for hundreds of overdose deaths in the country each year (mainly either children accidentally ingesting them, or intentional suicides), and thousands more nonfatal overdoses. Still, the vast majority of prescription and OTC drug use is safe, conventional, ethical, legal, and most decidedly nondeviant.

With some notable exceptions, the use of psychoactive prescription drugs has been declining during the past generation. For the majority of legal psychoactive prescription drugs on record, the number of prescriptions written in the 1990s is significantly lower than that written in the 1970s. For instance, roughly *one-fifteenth* as many barbiturate prescriptions, and *one-seventh* as many amphetamine prescriptions are being written today as was true 20 to 25 years ago. (Dexedrine is an exception, since it is being prescribed in the absence of Benzedrine, which is no longer prescribed at all.) In 1985, methaqualone, a sedative, was discontinued altogether as a prescription drug. The decline in the number of prescriptions written for psychoactive pharmaceuticals is not counter-balanced by an increase in the number or the size of the doses prescribed because, for most prescription drugs, these have also declined as well.

The decline in prescription drug use in the past two decades is one of the most remarkable and significant of all the changes that have taken place on the drug scene in this country. This decline has come about as an indirect consequence of drug manufacturers' aggressive marketing strategy in convincing physicians to adopt pharmaceuticals with insufficient testing and to over prescribe them for their patients, which has resulted in numerous adverse medical consequences, including physical dependence, death by overdose, and the diversion of these drugs into street recreational use. Because of the negative publicity that resulted from both medical misuse and overuse and street use, pressure was put on the medical establishment to reduce the practice of over prescribing psychoactive pharmaceuticals. For instance, in the 1960s and 1970s, amphetamines were widely prescribed by physicians to combat obesity. (Many of these patients were adolescents, and most were only slightly overweight, if at all.) Today, because of such abuses and their attendant medical consequences, prescribing amphetamines for obesity has been brought to a virtual halt. Methaqualone (whose trade name in the U.S. was Quaalude), hugely prescribed in the 1970s and widely used on the street—once billed as an aphrodisiac, the "love drug"—is not being prescribed at all today. In short, over prescribing came to be defined as deviant behavior by the medical fraternity. As a consequence, the excesses of the 1960s and 1970s were brought under control by both formal and informal sanctions, including the arrest of physicians who continued to overprescribe. In contrast, the number of prescriptions for *non*-psychoactive drugs is stable, even increasing a bit, because ours is an aging population, and as people grow older, their need for medication tends to increase. But the use of mood-altering medical drugs is declining over time.

Halcion and Prozac, two prescription drugs whose use, in contrast, *increased* between the late 1980s and early 1990s, offer an instructive morality tale to the student of deviance.

Prozac is a mood elevator, that is, a drug designed to combat depression; introduced on the market in 1987 by Eli Lilly, it quickly became the nation's number one selling anti-depressant, with nearly a million prescriptions written per month. Between 1988, its first full year of commercial availability, and 1990, its sales increased by more than five times. In its earliest years of use, the drug seemed to be a promising treatment for depression (Cowley et al., 1990). As its popularity increased, however, anecdotal horror stories detailing the destructive behavior of Prozac patients—including self-mutilation, suicide, violence, and murder—began to mount. Some of these patients ("Prozac survivors") have sued Lilly for multi-million-dollar damages, and some who have murdered have claimed in court "the drug made me do it" (the so-called "Prozac defense"). Lilly claims that some untoward behavior is to be expected of a certain proportion of depressed patients, whether or not they take Prozac; in Lilly's clinical studies, patients taking the drug displayed fewer suicidal tendencies than those not taking it (Cowley et al., 1991). In spite of the negative publicity surrounding Prozac, the majority of physicians who prescribe the drug, and most patients who take it, remain staunch supporters. Some observers have claimed that there is a Prozac "culture," whose members sing its praises at every opportunity (Cowley, 1994; Kramer, 1993). In 1994, Prozac was the nation's ninth most frequently prescribed pharmaceutical, and its most popular anti-depressant, by far (Goode, 1997); in 1995, it ranked thirteenth. Clearly, the negative media coverage of this drug has not discouraged many physicians from prescribing it.

In 1982, the Food and Drug Administration (FDA) approved the sale of the sedative-hypnotic Halcion in the United States by its manufacturer, Upjohn. In 1983, Halcion was marketed and, within a short period of time, it became the best-selling sedative on the market, with seven million prescriptions filled in the U.S. each year; in 1991, 8 percent of Upjohn's $2.5 billion in sales worldwide derived from Halcion. In the late 1980s and early 1990s, the President of the United States, George Bush, used it. However, soon after physicians began prescribing Halcion, they began noticing peculiar things happening to their patients. A Utah woman taking the drug shot her mother eight times and placed a birthday card in her dead mother's hand; she claimed the drug made her do it. Patients reported symptoms of paranoia, depression, nervousness, and an obsession with suicide. Termination of the use of the drug usually resulted in a cessation of the symptoms. One physician, Ian Oswald, working on behalf of patients who were suing the company, began reanalyzing the data Upjohn submitted to the FDA and claimed that some of the results of the studies were falsified. Upjohn's spokespersons admit that mistakes were made in some of these experiments, but they say that there was no pattern of falsification. The implication that Halcion was responsible for untoward reactions in depressive patients, Upjohn claims, is false and misleading, since many of them would have felt and done the same things without the drug (Kolata, 1992a, 1992b). One observer concludes that Halcion is a drug that has been shown to cause

"extreme and frightening side effects in a small number of people if taken in large quantities for extended periods of time" (Byron, 1992, p. 18). As a result of the unfavorable publicity about the drug and its effects, Halcion's sales have gone "into a tailspin. Physicians simply don't want to take the risk of prescribing the drug any more" (Byron, 1992, p. 18). In 1994 and 1995, Halcion was not even on the list of the nation's 200 most often prescribed pharmaceutical drugs.

Legal Recreational Use

Legal recreational use is the legal use of psychoactive substances to achieve a certain mental or psychic state by the user. The most commonly used legal recreational drugs in the United States are alcohol, tobacco cigarettes, and caffeine. In each case, a mood-altering substance is consumed in part to achieve a specific, desired mental or psychic state. Of course, not every instance of use of these drugs is purely for pleasure or euphoria. Still, they are consumed for a desired psychic state. Coffee drinkers do not achieve a high with their morning cup, but they do use caffeine as a "pick-me-up" to achieve a mentally alert state, a slight "buzz" to begin the day. Thus, coffee drinking can be described as both recreational and instrumental. Many—perhaps most—cigarette smokers are driven to smoke by a compulsive craving at least as much as by the pleasure achieved by inhaling a psychoactive drug; still, the two dimensions are far from mutually exclusive. If smokers do not achieve a true high, then at least they achieve a psychic state that is more pleasurable to them than abstinence.

According to the 1994 National Household Survey of the general population, sponsored by the U.S. Department of Health and Human Services, just over half (54 percent) of the sample, roughly 113 million Americans age 12 and older, said that they drank alcohol within the past month, and were therefore defined as "current" drinkers. Just over a fifth (22 percent) of American youth age 12 to 17 reported consuming an alcoholic beverage within the past 30 days, as did nearly two-thirds (63 percent) of young adults age 18 to 25 and a very slightly higher proportion (65 percent) of older adults age 26 to 34; only a bit more than half of those age 35 and older (54 percent) said that they were "current" drinkers, that is, that they had drunk alcohol in the past 30 days. Not quite three Americans in 10 age 12 and older (29 percent), or 60 million individuals, can be considered current users of cigarettes (Health and Human Services, 1995a). These figures represent significant declines from those of the 1980s, which, in turn, were smaller than was true of the late 1970s. However, they represent a significant upturn between the early to the mid-1990s.

Thus, the extent of legal recreational drug use is immense. (Although it declines—and rises— unevenly over time.) With the exception of caffeine, the most popular legal recreational drug is alcohol, which is used by a majority of the adult American population. Even tobacco, the second most commonly consumed legal recreational drug (again, with the exception of caffeine products), is used by more individuals *than are all illegal recreational drugs combined*. In fact, of all drugs, tobacco, in the form of cigarettes, *is used most frequently*. Smokers use their drug of choice 10, 20, 30, or 40— or more—times a day, whereas the vast majority of drinkers do not use alcohol that much during an entire week. Clearly, in the total picture of drug use, legal recreational use looms extremely large.

At the same time, the moderate use of the legal recreational drugs, alcohol and tobacco, by adults is not typically considered a form of deviant behavior in most quarters of American society. We'll look at the deviant use of alcohol in the next chapter in more detail. However, in a nutshell, the use of the legal drugs may be considered in a discussion on deviance for the following reasons. First, the *excessive* and *inappropriate* use of alcohol—which overlaps heavily with the condition referred to as alcoholism—*is* regarded as deviance. Second, the use of alcohol *by minors* is against the law, and is condemned in most social circles. Third, alcohol is often used *in conjunction with* a great deal of criminal and violent behavior, which is deviant. Fourth, the sale of alcohol has been outlawed once in this country's history, during Prohibition (1920–1933); in addition, the use of alcohol is both deviant and criminal in some other countries (such as Iran and Saudi Arabia), even to this day. Fifth, both in the past and currently, efforts have been instituted to criminalize and *deviantize* the sale, possession, and use of tobacco cigarettes (Troyer and Markle, 1983); at the present time, these efforts are escalating. They tell us a great deal about the circumstances under which certain definitions of deviance are constructed and enforced. And last, as we'll see, there are more arrests (though not more imprisonments) on alcohol-related charges in the United States than on illegal drug-related charges. In 1994, according to the Federal Bureau of Investigation, arrests for drug abuse violations totaled 1.1 million. But there were 1.5 million arrests for driving while under the influence of alcohol, half a million for violations of the liquor laws, and three quarters of a million for public intoxication. Whenever law enforcement swings into action, we have a case of deviance on our hands.

Illegal Instrumental Use

Illegal instrumental use includes taking various drugs without benefit of prescription for some instrumental purpose, such as driving a truck nonstop for long distances, studying for exams through the night, calming feelings of anxiety, improving athletic performance, and so on. Individuals who purchase pharmaceutical drugs illegally, without a physician's prescription, do not think of themselves as "real" drug users. They do not seek a high or intoxication, but rather a goal of which most conventional members of society approve. These users regard their behavior as only technically illegal and, therefore, not criminal in nature, and decidedly nondeviant. They do not make a sharp distinction between the use of legal over-the-counter drugs and the use of pharmaceuticals without a prescription; both are for the purpose of attaining a psychic or physical state which permits them to achieve a given socially approved end. In our society, however, using psychoactive pharmaceuticals without benefit of a physician's prescription happens to be illegal and, in some quarters, deviant as well.

Illegal Recreational Use

It is in the realm of illegal recreational use that we encounter our most harshly condemned instances of deviant drug use. The illegal drug trade is an enormous economic enterprise, variously estimated to represent a $40 to $100 billion a year business in the United States (Johnston, 1991; Lang, 1986). In 1993, the White House Office of National Drug Control Policy estimated illegal drug sales in the United States at $50 billion for that year. Whichever

Table 6.1 Drug Use among High School Seniors, 1980–1994

	Lifetime Prevalence		Percent Using: Annual Prevalence		30-Day Prevalence	
	1980	1994	1980	1994	1980	1994
Marijuana	60	38	49	31	34	19
LSD	9	11	7	7	2	3
Cocaine	16	6	12	4	5	2
Heroin	1.1	1.2	0.5	0.6	0.2	0.3
Stimulants	26	16	21	9	12	4
Sedatives	15	7	10	4	4	2
Any Illicit Drug	65	46	53	36	37	22
Alcohol	93	80	88	73	72	50
Cigarettes	71	62	—	—	31	31

—indicates figures not tabulated.
Stimulants "adjusted" for 1994.
Source: Johnston, O'Malley, and Bachman, 1995a, pp. 78–82.

figure is correct, clearly, a great deal of money is spent on illegal drugs in the United States, certainly tens of billions of dollars a year. And these huge sums represent a correspondingly huge demand for illicit drugs.

The Health and Human Services National Household Survey cited above found that in 1994, about a third of the American population age 12 and above (34 percent), 72 million individuals, said that they had tried at least one illegal drug one or

Table 6.2 Drug Use among College Students, 1980–1994

	Lifetime Prevalence		Percent Using: Annual Prevalence		30-Day Prevalence	
	1980	1994	1980	1994	1980	1994
Marijuana	65	42	51	28	34	14
LSD	10	11	6	5	1.4	1.6
Cocaine	22	6	17	3	7	1
Heroin	0.9	0.6	0.4	0.1	0.3	*
Stimulants	30	10	22	4	13	2
Barbiturates	8	4	3	2	1	0.4
Any Illicit Drug	69	46	56	31	38	15
Alcohol	94	91	91	87	82	72
Cigarettes	—	—	36	39	26	25

—indicates figures not tabulated.
Stimulants "adjusted" for 1994.
*indicates figure too low to be meaningfully presented in table.
Source: Johnston, O'Malley, and Bachman, 1995b, pp.160–162.

Table 6.3 Drug Use in General Population, 1994

	Ever Used	Used Past Year	Used Past Month
Percent using:			
Marijuana	31	9	5
Cocaine	10	2	0.7
Crack	2	0.6	0.2
Hallucinogens	9	1	0.5
Stimulants	5	0.7	0.3
Sedatives	3	0.4	0.1
Any Illicit Drugs	34	11	6
Alcohol	84	67	54
Cigarettes	73	32	29

Source: HHS, 1995a, pp. 19, 25, 31, 37, 49, 61, 67, 85, 91.

more times in their lives; one American in 10, 11 percent of the population or 22.6 million Americans, had done so within the past year; and 6 percent, some 12.5 million, had used an illicit drug within the past 30 days, and can be regarded as "current" users. As we might expect, of all age categories, young adults age 18 to 25 were most likely to have used illegal drugs in the past year, or the past 30 days, 26-to-34-year-olds were next most likely, youths age 12 to 17 slightly less likely, and individuals age 35 and older were least likely (Health and Human Services, 1995a).

The most frequently used illegal drug in America is, as we might expect, marijuana; a third of all Americans age 12 and older (31 percent) have at least tried it, and 4.8 percent (10 million individuals) used it within the past month. For cocaine, the next most popular illicit drug, 10.4 percent of all adult Americans (21.8 million people) have at least tried it. Almost any general survey on drug use is least useful for the light it sheds on *heavy* users (since they are less likely to be at a fixed residence and hence, cannot be located to be interviewed) rather than nonusers and lighter users; still, the Health and Human Services National Household Survey estimated that less than 1 percent (1.4 million) of the American population said that they used cocaine in the past month. Crack cocaine, a highly publicized drug, was used, ever, by only 2 percent of Americans, and only 0.2 percent, or half a mil-

lion, said that they had used it in the past month. (The National Household Survey is almost certainly least useful for estimating the drug consumption of heavy users of crack and heroin, again, because of the problem of locating them.) The other drugs and drug types—hallucinogens, stimulants, analgesics, tranquilizers, and sedatives—fall into the 2 to 9 percent "ever" range and the 0.1 to 0.7 percent "used in the past month" range. Heroin, like crack, a well-known and highly publicized illegal drug, was used by too few Americans for its percentages to be statistically valid (Health and Human Services, 1995a). A study of drug use among high school seniors, college students, and young adults not in high school or college (the "Monitoring the Future" survey) found much the same picture with respect to illegal drug use, except that their level of use was slightly higher than for the population as a whole (Johnston, O'Malley, and Bachman, 1994a, 1994b; Michigan, University of, News and Information Services, 1995). Whatever the drug, as a source of illegal and deviant behavior, drug use is formidable and impressive. At the same time, as we'll see shortly, the use of nearly all illegal drugs declined significantly after the late 1970s. Moreover, use is not nearly as high as many sensational media stories claim. And illicit drug use is considerably lower than the use of alcohol and tobacco.

Both legal and illegal drugs vary considerably in user loyalty, or continued use. Some drugs are much more likely to be "stuck with"; others are more likely to be used episodically or infrequently, or to be abandoned after a period of experimentation. As a general rule, *legal* drugs tend to be used much more on a continued basis *while illegal* drugs tend to be used more infrequently, and are more likely to be given up after a period of time (Goode, 1993, 1997; Sandwijk, Cohen, and Musterd, 1991, pp. 20–21, 25). Of all drugs, legal or illegal, *alcohol* attracts the greatest user loyalty; just over six Americans in 10 who said that they ever drank, even once, drank within the past month. For cigarettes, only a third (36 percent) of all at-least one-time smokers are still smoking. For illegal drugs, marijuana tends to be "stuck with" the longest— 15 percent of all Americans, and 34 percent of all high school seniors, who have at least tried the drug are still "current" users. Of all drugs, legal or illegal, users are *least* likely to "stick with" heroin (only 3 percent of all at-least one-time users took it

A Conflict Theory of Drug Abuse and its Devastation

There is a wide range of theories or explanations of drug use and abuse to choose from, the most important and widely cited of which I discuss in another publication (Goode, 1993, pp. 64–86). Most of these theories address a fairly narrow or limited range of phenomena, for instance, only addiction but not experimentation (or the reverse), only addicting drugs but not drugs which are not addicting, only alcohol but not illegal drugs, only factors which explain individual differences in drug use but not differences between and among members of larger categories, groups, or structures. However, one theory, although also limited, attempts to explain the aspect of drug use in which most of us are interested—the heavy, chronic, compulsive abuse of heroin and crack cocaine. It is focused on the larger, broader, or "structural" level; in other words, it does not address the issue of why specific individuals within these broader structures are more likely to become abusive users of these drugs than others. Still, it is a crucial piece of the drug puzzle and deserves elaboration. It is closest to the etiological strain of "conflict" theory discussed in Chapter 5, although there are elements of social disorganization theory (which was discussed in Chapter 4) in it as well. This conflict theory of drug abuse is endorsed by a number of radical and liberal sociologists and criminologists and by some Black or African-American political leaders, such as Reverend Jesse Jackson and Representative Charles Rangel, and to some extent the Nation of Islam. However, its value as a theory or explanation of drug abuse for us should rest exclusively on its empirical validity and not its ideological resonance for a particular political position. This theory also has the support of a substantial number of social scientists who are interested in the impact of the larger political and economic factors on the lives of residents of inner cities (Currie, 1993; Bourgois, 1995).

The "conflict" theory of drug abuse argues that the chronic use of heroin and crack cocaine is strongly related to race and social class. It is not race per se that has anything to do with drug abuse, but a combination of factors that are statistically related to race, and to which members of all racial and ethnic groups are subject. A significantly higher proportion of lower- and working-class minority males abuse the hard drugs as a result of structural factors: poverty, economic dependence, lack of economic opportunity, unemployment, underemployment, low-paying, dead-end jobs, economic hopelessness, deteri-oration of the community, and community and individual powerlessness. All these factors combine in a society with a generally high level of affluence, where the rich are very rich, and evidence of their riches is flaunted through the media and other vehicles, a level of affluence that is almost completely unattainable by the majority, especially the poor. (Practically the sole exception being, significantly enough, the sale of illegal drugs.) To some extent, these conditions have always prevailed. However, there are several distinctive features about the contemporary situation that did not prevail in the past. What makes today different from the past are two economic developments and a third factor which is a consequence of these developments.

First, over the past generation, economic opportunities for the relatively unskilled, uneducated segment of the working class have been disappearing. As late as the early 1970s, it was still possible for substantial numbers of heads of families with low levels of skill and education to support a family with a job they could obtain and earn enough to lift their income above the poverty level and live a modest, almost comfortable way of life. This is much less likely to be true today; far fewer family heads can earn enough to support a family and avoid slipping into poverty. The moderately paying semi-skilled or unskilled jobs are disappearing. Increasingly, a higher and higher proportion of the jobs available to the unskilled and uneducated segments of the economy are dead-end, poverty-level, minimum-wage jobs. In other words, the bottom third or so of the economic structure is being dismantled and its occupants are becoming increasingly impoverished.

As a consequence, the poor are getting poorer. Ironically, at the same time, the rich are getting richer. It is a cliché that this is the case; we even have a popular saying which states precisely that. However, this has *not* been the case until 1973; in fact, between the end of the Second World War (1945) and 1973, as the economy improved, the income of all segments of the economy improved correspondingly and more or less equally. For the past 20 or 25 years, in contrast, American society is becoming increasingly polarized with respect to income. This is not only a racial development; in fact, the income gap between whites and African-Americans has not changed much in the past two decades or so. What *has* changed is that among both Blacks and whites independently, the rich are getting richer and the poor are getting poorer. That is, the income gap between whites and Blacks among married couples, both of whom work year-round, is declining, but the size of the minority residents of inner cities—the so-called "underclass"—is increasing; the latter category is sinking deeper and deeper into poverty. (For a detailed exposition on this development, see Cassidy, 1995.) Thus, while the income difference between the races is not increasing, the income difference between the top and bottom economic layers of American society most decidedly is growing. In short, the poor are getting poorer, and a substantial proportion of the poorest segments of the society are inner-city African-Americans.

And third, a consequence of the economic decline of the bottom segment of the income hierarchy is that the neighborhoods in which poor people, particularly poor minority people, live are collapsing, becoming politically impotent and structurally disorganized, increasingly incapable of mounting an assault against the incursions of crime and drug dealing. The ties of such communities with the federal government and City Hall have weakened, they have less and less political influence. Criminals and drug dealers are capable of establishing a beachhead and prospering in poorer neighborhoods, whereas in the more powerful, more affluent neighborhoods, they would be uprooted and kicked out. The difference is that structurally, affluent neighborhoods have more political clout, and individually, are made up of residents with more optimism and an activist orientation. Recent economic developments produce a feeling of hopelessness, alienation, anomie, and depression among poor, especially minority residents of the inner cities. In short, declining incomes have generated declining power, which in turn, causes an inability to deal with and activate the processes that can overcome the consequences of a wide range of harmful conditions.

These three developments make drug abuse and drug dealing especially attractive. Drug abuse works because it alleviates and even obliterates feelings of hopelessness, despair, and anguish. It generates a small oasis of excitement and fantasy and a hierarchy of respect and prestige in the lives of the impoverished and alienated. Drug dealing is attractive because there are very few legal opportunities for poor, inner-city minority youths to earn a respectable sum of money. A counterculture or subculture of drug abuse may flourish as an alternative to the hopelessness and despair of the reality of everyday life. Ironically, the very avenue that seems to offer a kind of rebellion against the oppressive conditions in which

the poor and impotent live makes it even likelier that they cannot escape them (Bourgois, 1995). This "conflict" explanation of drug abuse is a *macro* theory, of course; it looks at structural factors, the big picture, the overarching conditions to which the society as a whole, and major segments of it, are exposed. The theory is weak , however, in between the "macro" and the "micro" level. After all, only a small proportion of minority youth become destructively and abusively involved with heroin and cocaine. In other words, the micro level is not a simple reflection of the macro level. What the theory cannot do is to predict *which* inner-city youths will abuse drugs.

This theory contains an additional component which is that there are really two forms of illegal drug use: one encompassing a broad spectrum of the class structure, including the middle and upper-middle class, and the second, mainly attracting the so-called underclass, the poor, urban dwellers of inner cities. The first sector of drug users is made up of casual, experimental, once-in-a-while users, who take drugs once or twice a week, usually on weekends; these may be referred to as *recreational* users. This type of drug use is caused by a variety of factors: unconventionality, a thirst for adventure, risk taking, hedonism, tolerance for deviance, willingness to break the law, and so on. A relatively low proportion of these drug users progress to more serious, abusive levels of use; moreover, a relatively low proportion use heroin or crack cocaine, at least on more than a very small number of occasions. The second type of drug user is, as I said above, motivated by despair, hopelessness, alienation, poverty, and community disintegration. In this type of user, use becomes abuse fairly readily, quickly, and with greater certainty; drug use tends to become more compulsive, virulent, and harmful to both the person who uses and to the community in which he or she lives.

To the conflict theorist, the solution to the drug problem is clear, if difficult: a restructuring of the society, the economy, and the communities in which we live. The economy has to be stimulated and rebuilt, meaningful jobs have to be created for all segments and layers of the society, the economic pie has to be divided up more equitably than it is now, inequality has to decline. Communities have to be rebuilt, political institutions have to be more responsive to all communities, and not simply those that are affluent and powerful. The key to the latter is empowerment: Members of all communities must be imbued with the sense that they can work together to achieve common goals, that when they work together, such goals are in fact attainable. Most conservatives would reject the conflict thesis, both as an explanation of drug use and abuse and as a suggestion for solving the drug problem. Conservatives agree that poor people use drugs more than affluent persons. But they disagree as to the cause of this relationship. Poor people don't use drugs more because of their misery and alienation. Instead, the conservative says, poor people are poor because they can't cope with the problems of the society, because they are lazy and incompetent—that's why they occupy the bottom rungs of the society. They are poor *and* they use drugs because they are incompetent, unambitious, not very bright, and they just want to have a good time They are hedonistic and self-indulgent. The same explanation for why they are poor also applies to their higher levels of drug abuse.

Which of these two explanations strikes you as more plausible?

Source: Adapted from Goode, 1997.

---

in the past month) and the hallucinogens (4 percent) (Health and Human Services, 1994a, 1994b; Johnston, O'Malley, and Bachman, 1994a, 1994b).

MARIJUANA

The Effects of Marijuana

Technically, what is referred to as marijuana is not a drug, but a vegetal substance containing an extraordinary range of chemicals. What is sold on the street in the United States as marijuana is made up of the dried leaves and flowering tops of the *Cannabis sativa* plant. Hashish, which is far less commonly sold in the U.S., contains only the resin and flowering tops of the cannabis plant, with no leaves; it is typically, although not always, more potent than marijuana itself. The cannabis plant contains hundreds of chemicals, of which over 60, called cannabinoids, are unique to itself. The primary psychoactive agent in marijuana is tetrahydrocannabinol, or THC for short. It is generally agreed that it is the THC that gets the user high. Poor quality street marijuana may contain as little as 1 percent THC; extremely potent strains may contain as much as 10 percent.

In considering the effects of any drug, "acute" and "chronic" effects must be distinguished. "Acute" effects take place under the influence of the drug, within the context of immediate use. "Chronic" effects take place over the long run, after an extended period of use. Marijuana causes an increased heartbeat rate, redness of the eyes, and dryness of the mouth; these are acute effects. In addition, motor coordination is impaired, raising the possibility of an increased risk of automobile fatalities under the influence. Short-term memory also deteriorates under the influence; one has a harder time remembering things that have just happened or that one just said. These are acute effects.

In contrast, *chronic* effects take place not during the immediate context of a given episode of use, when the user is under the influence, but over the long run, after a considerable period of use. Examples of chronic effects would be cirrhosis of the liver, after heavy, long-term consumption of alcohol, and lung cancer, after heavy, long-term cigarette smoking.

One of the interesting things about the use of drugs whose use is regarded as deviant is that in different periods of history, different claims are made as to their harmful effects. In the 1930s, newspaper and magazine stories alleged that marijuana caused users to go crazy, engage in promiscuous sex, and commit violent acts. Today, these claims are hardly ever made, even by the strongest anti-marijuana propagandists. It is not the *acute* or short-term effects of marijuana that attract the most critics today, but the *chronic* or long-term effects. Instead, today, it is feared that the long-term use of marijuana will prove to be medically damaging. Even so, these effects remain controversial.

Perhaps it is a cop-out to say that the jury is still out on the marijuana medical question. One should keep in mind the fact that no drug is *completely* safe. There is no chemical substance, no drug, no activity known to humankind, that is completely without harm to anyone who has ever used or engaged in it. *Some* damage can be found with the ingestion of every drug on earth, that is, in some people, at some time. As we saw, aspirin, one of the safest drugs known, causes hundreds of deaths a year in the United States. So the question for a given drug should *not* be: Can *some* damage be found if we look hard enough? After all, one can die of an "overdose" of water; it's called drowning, a source of thousands of deaths in the United States each year. Does that mean that water is a dangerous and damaging substance? Of course not. Thus, with the use of any drug, the question should be: What is the *likelihood* of damage—both acute and chronic—in a wide range of situations and instances of use? Moreover, when assessing studies that claim to show damage caused by one drug or another, we would want to have an ingredient that is essential to all scientific research: *replication*. That is, studies are often conducted whose findings are not duplicated by any later researchers; to a scientist, a study that lacks replication lacks confirmation and thus, lacks validity. If other scientists can't come up with the same findings using the same methods, scientists reason, perhaps they aren't valid, perhaps the first study was flawed, faulty, invalid. A number of studies have produced findings that indicate that marijuana may be harmful to the brain, male testosterone levels, white blood cells, chromosomes, female reproductive system, and so on. (These studies are summarized in one-sided discussions in Mann, 1985, and Jones and Lovinger, 1985.) However, these studies remain controversial, because every one of these findings is matched by one or more others that document the fact that marijuana does *not* have this effect (Goode, 1993, pp. 198–200). The only medical pathology that has been independently confirmed by several researchers and is unmatched by non-pathological findings is impairment to the functioning of the lungs. Heavy, long-term marijuana use decreases the lung's capacity to take in, utilize, and expel air. Daily marijuana use leads to lung damage similar to that resulting from heavy cigarette smoking. Moreover, it must be emphasized, the use of marijuana is *correlated* with a wide range of undesirable associated factors, such as a lower level of academic achievement; however, direct causality has yet to be established.

What about the drug's subjective effects, that is, what it feels like to experience the marijuana high or intoxication? After all, the subjective effects are why the drug is used in the first place. Marijuana is used, overwhelmingly, because individuals who use it want to get high and because they like the feelings associated with being high. Individuals who have unpleasant experiences under the influence tend to discontinue their use of the drug. A number of interview studies have been conducted on the subjective effects of marijuana (for instance, Goode, 1970; Tart, 1971). Feeling more relaxed, more peaceful is an extremely common description of the marijuana experience. Almost as many say that they felt more aroused, their senses felt more "turned on," that they were more physically sensitive. Not all of the effects users describe are judged to be pleasurable—in my study, for instance, 15 percent said that they often felt paranoid—but most of the effects tend to be experienced as pleasurable and positive in nature. What is the impression conveyed by the many studies on marijuana use and intoxication? The most obvious and dominant impression is that users overwhelmingly describe their marijuana experience in favorable and pleasurable terms; in short, most users, most of the time, enjoy what they feel when they get high. A second impression is that marijuana use is a distinctly recreational activity. The vast majority of the effects reported by users are whimsical in nature—happy, silly, euphoric, relaxed, hedonistic, sensual, foolish, and decidedly nonserious. Moreover, marijuana is commonly used in conjunction with pleasurable activities—eating, sex, listening to music, watching a movie or television, attending a party, socializing, and so on. The most common episodes for most marijuana smokers are specifically these recreational moments. The high is deliberately sought as a means of intensifying enjoyable experiences. The drug tends not to be used during more serious moments, such as studying or reading. Moreover, serious activities are usually felt to be *impaired* while the user is high. For instance, in my study, two-thirds who had read while high said that their ability to read something was worsened under the influence (Goode, 1970). Still, a certain proportion, a small minority of marijuana users, possibly as little as 5 percent, become so compulsively involved with the drug that they use it more or less all the time. For them, intellectual and motor functions are diminished; they tend to have problems navigating their way through the day, and are regarded as deviant both among the nonusing majority and among more casual marijuana users.

Marijuana Use in the United States, 1960–1990s

In 1960, less than 1 percent of youths age 12 to 17, less than 5 percent of young adults age 18 to 25, and less than one-half of 1 percent of all adults over the age of 25, had at least tried marijuana; in 1967, these figures had nearly quadrupled to over 5 percent for youths and over 15 percent to young adults (Miller and Cisin, 1980, pp. 13–16). The percent trying and using marijuana increased throughout the decade from the late 1960s to the late 1970s, and reached its peak roughly in 1979, when nearly a third of youths age 12 to 17 (31 percent), two-thirds of young adults age 18 to 25 (68 percent), and 20 percent of older adults over the age of 25, had tried marijuana; use in the past year was 24 percent, 47 percent, and 9 percent respectively for these three groups. In addition, according to the high school study, in 1979, slightly over half (51 percent) of high school seniors said that they had used marijuana during the previous year. That year, 1979, represented the historical high-tide mark for marijuana use in the United States; after that, use dropped off sharply, declining throughout the 1980s. In 1990, only 11 percent of 12-to-17-year-olds said that they had used marijuana during the past year (versus 24 percent for 1979); for young adults age 18 to 25, the figure was 25 percent (versus 47 percent for 1979); and for adults above the age of 25, it was 32 percent (versus 38 percent for 1979). Likewise, for high school seniors, between 1979 and 1990, lifetime prevalence declined from 27 to 51 percent; annual prevalence declined from 51 to 27 percent; and use in the past 30 days, from 14 to 37 percent. Declines in college marijuana use were comparable. There is no doubt whatsoever that the use of marijuana between the 1970s and 1990 became significantly, even strikingly, less common (Michigan, University of, Information and News Services, 1995).

What is happening in the 1990s? Though the 1979–1990 decline is real and significant, sometime in the early 1990s, marijuana use began to reverse its direction and rise again. In 1992, 22 percent of high school seniors said that they used marijuana at least once during the past year; in 1995, this was 35 percent. For use in the past 30 days, the comparable figures were 14 and 24 percent (Michigan, University of, News and Information Services, 1995). While the figures for the general population do not show as impressive an increase into the 1990s, the marijuana figures for the mid-1990s are nonetheless higher than for the early 1990s (Health and Human Services, 1995a). A second qualification: Today, marijuana use is *far more* common today than it was in the early, even the late, 1960s. While use has declined significantly in the past two decades, it grew so much during the 1960s and 1970s that marijuana use would have to decline far, far more dramatically than it did in the 1979–1990 period to reach the *vastly* lower figures of the 1960s. Given its rise in the 1990s, this is unlikely to take place during the remainder of this century, or even over the course of the next two decades. The fact is that as a recreational activity, a sizable volume of marijuana use seems to be *entrenched* in American society.

Marijuana Use as Deviance and Crime

The use and the criminal status of marijuana have had a remarkable and extremely complicated history in the United States. In the 1920s, very few Americans had even heard of marijuana or even knew anyone who used it and, consequently, very few thought of it as deviant. Until well into this century, the few who did know of the drug thought of it as a kind of medicinal herb; George Washington grew it on his plantation, probably for this purpose. During the decade of the 1930s, however, marijuana became the subject of hundreds of sensationalistic newspaper and magazine articles. The drug was dubbed the "killer weed," the "weed of madness," a "sex-crazing drug menace," the "burning weed of hell," a "gloomy monster of destruction." Journalists and propagandists allowed an almost unlimited rein to the lurid side of their imagination on the marijuana question. Every conceivable evil was concocted concerning the effects of this drug, the principal ones being insanity, sexual promiscuity, and violence. A popular film distributed in the 1930s, *Reefer Madness*, illustrates this "marijuana causes you to go crazy, become promiscuous, and want to kill people" theme; in the past few years, it has been shown a number of times to promarijuana audiences, who find it so ludicrous as to be hilarious.

By 1937, partly as a result of the hysterical publicity surrounding the use of marijuana, laws criminalizing its possession and sale were passed in every state and at the federal level as well. Several observers argue that racial discrimination against Mexican-Americans was one of the principal reasons for the white majority public's belief in the drug's evil effects, as well as the swiftness with which these laws were passed (Musto, 1987, p. 219, 245). The majority of the states that passed the earliest antimarijuana laws were western states with the largest concentration of Mexican-American populations. At times, an activity can be condemned, even criminalized, less as a result of a sober assessment of its objective impact than because of the majority feeling about the group that is thought to practice it.

Marijuana remained completely illegal and deviant throughout the late 1930s, the 1940s, and 1950s. In the 1960s, as we saw, the popularity of this drug increased dramatically. Along with this increase in use came the widespread awareness that it was not simply the poor or members of minority groups, but the sons and daughters of affluent, influential, middle-class folk who used it. Marijuana acquired a mantle of, if not respectability or conventionality, then at least not complete deviance either. Attitudes began to soften and, in the 1970s, 11 states comprising one-third of the U.S. population decriminalized the possession of small quantities of marijuana. Then, beginning roughly with the election of Ronald Reagan as president in 1980, the tolerant sentiment toward marijuana that had been growing during the 1960s and 1970s dissipated, and a new, more condemnatory mood set in. No states decriminalized marijuana possession after 1980 and, in fact, in popular referenda held in 1989 and 1990, two—Oregon and Alaska—recriminalized the possession of marijuana. Increasingly, the public saw the drug as dangerous and a decreasing proportion of Americans, as we saw, actually used it. The tide had been reversed: Marijuana, its possession, use, and sale, had become deviant once again. For certain activities, deviance and crime display something of a cyclical pattern.

One measure or indicator of the growing deviant status of marijuana use is the growing percentage of high school students who say that marijuana use should be illegal, that the regular use of marijuana is harmful, that they disapprove of regular marijuana use. In 1979, a poll of high school seniors showed that only a fairly small minority (28 percent) believed that adults should be arrested for smoking marijuana in private; less than half (42 percent) believed that someone who smoked marijuana "regularly" risked harming themselves; and

less than a majority (45 percent) disapproved of the occasional use of marijuana. What happened roughly after 1980 was truly remarkable. Between 1979 and 1990, belief among high school students that private marijuana use should be illegal increased from 28 to 56 percent; between 1979 and 1990, the belief that one risks harming oneself by smoking marijuana regularly increased from 42 to 78 percent; and the percent saying that they disapproved of the occasional use of marijuana increased from 45 to 81 percent (Johnston, O'Malley, and Bachman, 1994a). The same pattern prevails in this study for college students and young adults not in college (1994b). In short, marijuana use came to be seen as *more deviant* over the course of the 1979–1990 period. In the sense of supporting the arrest and imprisonment of users, believing that regular use is medically dangerous, and disapproving of regular use, America's high school seniors moved *away from* seeing marijuana use as conventional, acceptable, safe, and ordinary *to* seeing it as unconventional, unacceptable, dangerous, and out of the ordinary—in short, as deviant. However, as with the increase in marijuana use among young Americans into the 1990s which we discussed earlier, we also observe a slight but significant increase in support for legalization, and a decline in the belief that marijuana is harmful and in disapproval of use of the drug after 1990. For instance, disapproval by high school seniors of adults age 18 and older smoking marijuana was 70 percent in 1992 and only a bare majority, 57 percent, in 1995 (Michigan, University of, News and Information Services, 1995). Thus, it is possible that the trends that continued throughout the 1980s turned around in the 1990s; today, marijuana use is slightly *less* deviant than it was in the early 1990s.

During the 1920s, marijuana use was practically unknown to most Americans; during the 1930s, it became publicized, illegal, and deviant; during the 1940s and 1950s, it remained illegal and deviant, but was not widely mentioned in the media; during the 1960s and 1970s, it grew dramatically, its deviant status diminished, and during the 1970s, its illegal status was terminated in some states; during the 1980s and 1990s, it declined dramatically, its deviant status grew and, in two jurisdictions, its illegal status was reinstated. These shifts demonstrate that the deviant and criminal status of an activity is a dynamic, labile affair, one that is usually accompanied by changes in the social, political, and economic landscape. And, just as activities can become *more* deviant and *more* criminal over time, likewise, they can become less so. Historically, we are witnessing fluctuations in the deviant and criminal status of marijuana use, possession, and sale. The most substantial change was the huge, unprecedented increase in the use of marijuana, and a corresponding decline in its deviant status, throughout the 1960s and 1970s. The decline in its use, and the increase in condemning it that took place throughout the 1980s did not come close to offsetting the earlier changes. During the 1990s, again, we see a shift in the wind. What these more recent changes will portend for the new millennium can only be guessed at now.

HALLUCINOGENIC DRUGS

Hallucinogenic drugs are those that produce severe "dislocations of consciousness" (Lingeman, 1974, pp. 91–92), that act on the nervous system to produce significant perceptual changes (O'Brien and Cohen, 1984, p. 114). There are many hallucinogenic drugs, but most are not very widely used; nearly all hallucinogenic drug use is with LSD. Psylocybin mushrooms (or "'shrooms"), and among devotees of the Native-American Church, the peyote cactus (which contains mescaline), are also used in some social circles. As we saw, ecstasy (or MDMA) is commonly referred to as a hallucinogen, but it produces almost none of the profound perceptual changes caused by LSD and the other psychedelics. Some experts prefer the term *empathogen* for ecstasy, that is, it stimulates the capacity to empathize or identify with others. When I refer to hallucinogens, I will be referring mainly to LSD. In the 1960s, hallucinogens were commonly referred to as "psychedelics," a term which implied that the mind is "made manifest"—or works better than ordinarily—under the influence. Today, the term "psychedelic" is used less frequently among drug experts than "hallucinogen."

It is in the mental, psychic, and "subjective" realm that the effects of LSD and the other hallucinogens have their most profound, dramatic, and interesting effects. Experiences take on an exaggerated emotional significance under the influence. Moreover, huge, emotional mood swings tend to dominate an "acid" trip. On the other hand, in spite of their name, hallucinogens typically do not generate full-blown hallucinations, that is, cause users to see things in the concrete world they know

"aren't there." More often, they will have experiences or visions they know are a product of the drug, that is, they are in their minds rather than a reality that is located "out there" in the material world. (These visions may be referred to as "virtual" hallucinations.) Many users will experience *synesthesia*, or the translation of one sense into another, that is, "hearing" color and "seeing" sounds. Many LSD users, under the influence, experience the world as in flux, fluid, dynamic, wobbling, flowing. The effects of LSD are experienced as *vastly* more incapacitating than those of marijuana (depending on the dose, of course); many users imagine that they can cope (drive a car, converse, interact with others, especially parents and the police) on marijuana, whereas very few will say that they can do so at the peak of the LSD trip. In spite of the sensationalistic media reports, very, very few users of hallucinogens experience a psychotic outbreak sufficiently serious as to require hospitalization. Such reports reached their peak in the 1960s (when use was actually quite low) and declined after that.

Psychedelic drugs have been used for thousands of years: psilocybin, or the so-called "magic" mushrooms, by Indians in Mexico and Central America, the peyote cactus by the Indians of northern Mexico, the Amanita (or "fly agaric") mushroom among the indigenous Siberian population, the mandrake root among pre-Christian Europeans, to name only a few (Schultes and Hofmann, 1979). In 1938, a Swiss chemist named Albert Hofmann discovered the chemical that was later to be called LSD; he did not experiment with it until 1943, when he ingested a minuscule quantity of the substance himself. He experienced an extraordinary and intense "play of colors," a sense of timelessness, depersonalization, a loss of control, and fears of "going crazy." The early researchers on LSD thought the drug might be the key to unlock the secrets of mental illness, especially schizophrenia. Later, they found that the differences between the LSD experience and schizophrenia outweighed the similarities, and this line of research was abandoned. In the 1950s, an English writer named Aldous Huxley, author of the classic novel, *Brave New World*, took mescaline (the psychoactive ingredient in the peyote cactus) and wrote about his experiences in a slim, poetic volume, *The Doors of Perception*. Huxley drew the parallel with insanity, of course, but he added a new dimension not previously discussed. Psychedelic drugs, he claimed, could bring about a view of reality that washes away the encrustation of years of rigid socialization and programming. These drugs, Huxley argued, enable us to see reality without culture's blinders—reality "as it really is." Taking psychedelic drugs can bring about a kind of transcendence, much like religious insight.

Huxley's book was read by Timothy Leary, a Ph.D. in psychology and lecturer at Harvard University. Leary took a dose of psilocybin and had a "visionary voyage." Soon after, he began a series of experiments which entailed administering the drug to convicts, theology students, and undergraduates; he claimed the drug "changed their lives for the better." Many authorities felt that the experiments were casually administered, lacked sufficient safeguards, and were aimed mainly at proselytizing. Leary brushed off such concern as so much "hysteria" that was hampering his research. In the spring of 1963, Leary was fired from his job at Harvard, an event which touched off national headline stories. In the decade prior to Leary's firing, fewer than a dozen articles had been published in the national magazines indexed by *The Reader's Guide to Popular Literature*. (Excluding *Science*, which is not really a popular magazine.) The number of these articles exploded after the Leary incident; publicity surrounding his firing focused an intense public glare on the use of LSD and the hallucinogens.

Prior to 1967, nearly all the articles focused on the drug's supposedly bizarre effects, especially those that seemed to indicate that it caused users to go insane. The effects of LSD were described as "nightmarish"; "terror and indescribable fear" were considered common, even typical experiences under the influence. *Life* magazine ran a cover story in its March 25, 1966 issue entitled "The Exploding Threat of the Mind Drug that Got Out of Control." *Time* magazine ran a feature essay on LSD emphasizing the "freaking out" angle. "Under the influence of LSD," the story declared, "nonswimmers think they can swim, and others think they can fly. One young man tried to stop a car . . . and was killed. A magazine salesman became convinced he was the Messiah. A college dropout committed suicide by slashing his arm and bleeding to death in a field of lilies." Psychic terror, uncontrollable impulses, violence, an unconcern for one's own safety, psychotic episodes, delusions, and hallucinations formed the fare of the bulk of the early news stories on the use of LSD. On March 17,

1967, an article was published in the prestigious journal *Science*, which seemed to indicate that LSD damaged chromosomes (Cohen, Marinello, and Back, 1967). The media immediately surmised that the drug would cause birth defects; this wave of media hysteria was not quite as intense or as long-lasting as that touched off by the "insanity" angle, but it did convince much of the public—some users included—that the drug was uniquely and powerfully damaging and dangerous. An article that appeared in the *Saturday Evening Post* (Davison, 1967) was perhaps typical. It explained that "if you take LSD, even once, your children may be born malformed or retarded" and that "new research finds it's causing genetic damage that poses a threat of havoc now and appalling abnormalities for generations yet unborn." As I said earlier, scientists learned soon after that the whole issue was a false alarm; in the doses taken on the street, LSD is an extremely weak mutagen or gene-altering agent, and extremely unlikely to cause birth defects (Dishotsky et al., 1971).

In the 1960s, LSD use appeared to many to pose *a uniquely deviant potential*. In 1966, the New Jersey Narcotic Drug Study Commission declared LSD to be "the greatest threat facing the country today" (Brecher et al., 1972, p. 369). And yet, this hysteria and fear evaporated in what was probably record time. Today, the use of hallucinogens is no longer a public issue, at least not apart from the use of illegal drugs generally. LSD has been absorbed into the morass of drug taking in general—less seriously regarded than crack and heroin use, but more so than marijuana. LSD never really materialized into the threat to the society that many observers and critics (or, for that matter, its supporters) claimed it would. The drastic, dramatic, cosmic, philosophical, and religious claims originally made for the LSD experience now seem an artifact of an antiquated age. The psychedelic movement—whose members glorified the drug as a highway to a startlingly new vision, perhaps a new way of life for the society as a whole—never made up a majority of even regular users in the 1960s, and simply disappeared. The conventional majority's fear that users would go crazy, drop out, or overturn the social order never came to pass. LSD became simply yet another drug taken upon occasion by multiple drug users for the same hedonistic, recreational reason they took other drugs—to get high.

One of the most remarkable aspects about the use of LSD and the other hallucinogens is how *episodically* or *sporadically* they have been taken. In fact, of all drugs or drug types ingested currently in the United States, among the universe of everyone who has taken the drug at least once, very nearly the *lowest* percentage are still *current* or *recent* users. Of all at-least one-time users, only one out of 25 (or 4 percent) took it in the previous month; this is in contrast to 60 percent for consumers of alcohol, 25 percent for smokers of tobacco, and 15 percent or so for marijuana users (Health and Human Services, 1994a, 1994b; Johnston, O'Malley, and Bachman, 1994a, 1994b; Sandwijk, Cohen, and Musterd, 1991, pp. 20–21, 25). LSD is simply not a drug that is taken very often, even among users.

Perhaps the second most remarkable fact about the use of LSD is (as I hinted above) that its incidence does not correspond to the historical stereotype. The myth is that the use of LSD and the other psychedelics exploded in the 1960s and subsided soon thereafter, and has remained at a fairly low level since then. For instance, two drug experts state (without supplying evidence) that "LSD seems to have reached a peak during 1967 and 1968, after which it tapered off" (Ray and Ksir, 1993, p. 330). The fact is that the use of LSD was extremely *low* (although climbing) in the 1960s; it reached something of a peak in the 1970s; it declined into the 1980s; and it has remained at a fairly stable level for the past 20 years or so. In 1967, according to a Gallup Poll, only 1 percent of American college students (in all likelihood, the category that was *most* likely to have taken the drug at that time) said that they had tried LSD, even once; by 1969, this figure had grown to 4 percent. But by 1970, this had increased to 14 percent, and by 1971, 18 percent. In other words, precisely at a time when media attention to LSD had dropped off, its use was mushrooming. In 1980, the lifetime prevalence figure among high school seniors for LSD was 9 percent; by 1985, this had declined slightly to 7.5 percent; in 1990, it was 8 percent; and in 1995, it was 12 percent (Michigan, University of, News and Information Services, 1995). For college students and noncollege young adults, the trend lines are similar. Thus, although LSD and the psychedelics are used extremely *episodically* by those who use them, their use has not disappeared; it is possible that as many young people use LSD today as was true a generation ago.

The use of LSD in the United States should teach us some very important lessons about the perception of social problems and the imputation of deviance to an activity. First, the public hysteria generated over an activity or condition may be totally disproportionate to its objective threat to the society. Some activities or conditions attract considerably more than their fair share of public hysteria, while others attract far less. Second, media attention does not necessarily reflect how common or frequent an activity is; some commonly enacted behaviors receive little or no media attention, while some rare or infrequent activities receive a great deal. Media attention to an activity could very well *increase* at a time when it is declining in frequency, or *decline* when its frequency is increasing. Third, it is likely that people base their notions of the frequency or commonness of conditions or behaviors, and the threat they pose to the society, more on how *well-known* they are than on the objective, concrete facts of the matter. In many ways, a study of LSD is more instructive for what it tells us about deviance in general than about what it tells us specifically about drug use.

COCAINE AND CRACK

Cocaine is a stimulant. Its most commonly described effect is exhilaration, elation, euphoria, a voluptuous, joyous feeling. Probably the second most frequently described effect by users is confidence, a sensation of mastery in what one is and does. And third, users most commonly report a burst of increased energy, the suppression of fatigue, a stimulation of the capacity to continue physical and mental activity more intensely and for a longer than normal period of time. In the nineteenth century, before its effects were fully understood, cocaine was used by physicians for a variety of ills, ailments, and complaints: first, to offset fatigue and depression, later, to cure morphine addiction. Today, one of its very few medical uses is as a local anesthetic, that is, to kill pain when applied topically to delicate tissue and organs, such as the eye or the gums. The earliest papers of Sigmund Freud were devoted to singing the praises of this drug; when he became dependent on it, he realized his mistake (Byck, 1974; Ashley, 1975, pp. 21–28). At the end of the nineteenth and the beginning of the twentieth centuries, cocaine, like morphine and opium, was a major ingredient in many patent medicines. In fact, cocaine was an ingredient in many "soft" drinks—including Coca-Cola—until 1903, when it was deleted because of pressure applied "by Southerners who feared blacks' getting cocaine in any form" (Ashley, 1975, p. 46).

A major reason for the criminalization of cocaine after the turn of the twentieth century, many observers feel, was racism. Although there is no evidence whatsoever which indicates that African-Americans were any more likely to use cocaine than whites, or that those who did were any more likely to become dangerous or violent under the influence, the fear among many whites that both were the case may have been responsible for bringing the drug under state and federal control. Numerous articles were published just after the turn of the century which made the claim that cocaine stimulated violent behavior among Blacks. In 1903, the *New York Tribune* quoted one Colonel J.W. Watson of Georgia to the effect that "many of the horrible crimes committed in the southern states by the colored people can be traced to the cocaine habit." A Dr. Christopher Koch, in an article which appeared in the Literary Digest in 1914, asserted that "most of the attacks upon white women of the South are a direct result of a cocaine-crazed Negro brain." *The New York Times* published an article in 1914 entitled "Negro Cocaine Fiends Are a New Southern Menace," which detailed the "race menace" and "hitherto inoffensive" Blacks "running amuck in a cocaine frenzy" (summarized in Ashley, 1975, pp. 66–73; Grinspoon and Bakalar, 1976, pp. 38–40).

"All the elements needed to ensure cocaine's outlaw status were present by the first years of the twentieth century: It had become widely used as a pleasure drug . . . ; it had become identified with [groups that were] despised or poorly regarded [by middle-class whites]. . . . [that is], blacks, lower-class whites, and criminals; and it had not . . . become identified with the elite, thus losing what little chance it had of weathering the storm" (Ashley, 1975, p. 74). By the time of the passage of the Harrison Act in 1914, which included cocaine as a "narcotic" (which, as we saw, pharmacologically, it is not), 46 states had already passed state laws attempting to control cocaine. (Only 29 had done so for opiates, such as morphine, opium, and heroin by that time.) This indicates that cocaine was seen at that time as a serious drug problem. It is entirely likely that a major reason for the criminalization of cocaine was racial hostility toward African-Americans by the dominant white majority.

Most experts argue that the use of cocaine

declined sharply during the 1920s, and remained at an extremely low level until the 1960s. The increase in cocaine use during that decade and into the 1970s paralleled that of marijuana use, although on a much smaller scale. Although no systematic, nationally representative surveys were conducted on drug use in the United States until 1972, one 1979 study "reconstructed" estimates for the 1960s based on dates interviewees gave for when they began drug use (Miller and Cisin, 1980). This study estimated that only 1 percent of all Americans who were 18 to 25 in 1960 had used cocaine even once in their lifetime; by 1967, this had doubled. In 1972, when a full-scale survey was conducted, this lifetime prevalence figure stood at 8 percent, and in 1979, it was 27 percent (p. 17). According to the National Household Survey, the figures for at-least one-time use declined significantly into the 1980s and 1990s: 1985, 24 percent; 1991, 18 percent; 1994, 10 percent (Health and Human Services, 1995a). The trend lines for younger and older age categories, specifically for college and high school students, and noncollege young adults, as well as for use in the past year and the past month, show a similar pattern, although for each of these categories, the figure is at a somewhat different level of incidence (Johnston, O'Malley, and Bachman, 1994a, 1994b; Michigan, University of, Information Services, 1995; Health and Human Services, 1995a).

The point is this: Practically all surveys show a decline in the use of cocaine in the general population over time since the late 1970s. This sounds encouraging, but yearly, even monthly, use may not present a serious problem to the society. Even the once-or-twice-daily use of cocaine is not intrinsically harmful to the user, nor does such a level of use pose an unambiguous threat to the nonusing majority. What most expert observers are most concerned about is the problems posed by cocaine *addicts*—the frequent, chronic, heavy, compulsive abusers who stand a high likelihood of causing medical damage to themselves as a result of overdoses and heavy use, and victimizing others in the form of property crime and violence. The problem is that such users, as I said, are extremely difficult to locate. What indicators we do have, however, indicate a trend line that is not nearly so encouraging as that for casual use. While casual, recreational use of cocaine *has* declined in the past decade or two, it is possible that the heavy, chronic abuse of the drug has actually increased. What we see is something of a *polarization* in cocaine use, with the *least* involved (and least criminal and least deviant) user *most* likely to give up the drug, and the *most* involved (and most criminal and deviant) abuser *least* likely to abstain. Abusers who are most likely to harm themselves and victimize others are also most likely to stick with cocaine over an extended period of time.

One indicator of this increase comes from a program that is referred to by its acronym, DAWN, the Drug Abuse Warning Network. DAWN is a federal data-collection program that plots two drug-related events over time: nonfatal drug-related emergency room admissions, and medical examiner reports on lethal drug-related deaths. While there are many reasons why these figures would change over time (including changes in drug potency, trends with respect to taking different drugs simultaneously and taking drugs via different routes of administration, and an aging addict population), one reason is the change in the number of very heavy abusers, resulting in changes in the medical problems they exhibit. Between 1990 and 1993, the number of cocaine-related emergency room episodes increased 34 percent, from 80,000 to 123,000, and the number of cocaine-related deaths recorded in medical examiner reports increased 36 percent, from about 2,500 to 3,900 (Health and Human Services, 1991a, 1991b, 1993a, 1993b, 1994c, 1995c). In short, patterns that hold for occasional or even regular users may not be valid for heavy, frequent, compulsive abusers. In fact, what

Table 6.4 Emergency Room Data, Acute Drug-Related Emergencies

	1990		1993	
	Number of Drug Mentions	*Percent of Total Episodes*	*Number of Drug Mentions*	*Percent of Total Episodes*
Cocaine	80,355	22	123,300	26
Heroin/Morphine	33,884	9	63,000	13
Alcohol-in-Combination	115,162	31	141,773*	33*

TOTAL DRUG EPISODES, 1990: 371,208
TOTAL DRUG EPISODES, 1993: 466,900

*1993 alcohol-in-combination figures taken from 1992 data; 1993 data not available at this time.
Note: Data sources not completely standardized with respect to years.
Source: Adapted from Health and Human Services, 1991a, p.34, and "Preliminary Estimates from the Drug Abuse Warning Network," Substance Abuse and Mental Health Services Administration, Office of Applied Studies, December 1994; 1993 figures provisional.

Table 6.5 Medical Examiner Data, Acute Drug-Related Death

	1990		1993	
	Number of Drug Mentions	*Percent of Total Episodes*	*Number of Drug Mentions*	*Percent of Total Episodes*
Cocaine	2,483	43	3,910	46
Heroin/Morphine	1,976	34	3,805	45
Alcohol-in-Combination	2,304	40	3,444	40

TOTAL DRUG EPISODES, 1990: 5,830
TOTAL DRUG EPISODES, 1993: 8,541

Note: Data sources not completely standardized with respect to year.
Source: Adapted from Health and Human Services, 1991b, p.16, 1995c, p.16.

we see with cocaine is that while relatively *infrequent* use has been declining in the past few years, relatively *frequent* use may have increased.

In its powdered form, cocaine is usually sniffed, or snorted, that is, inhaled sharply through a nostril. Often, the drug is chopped on a smooth surface, then it is arranged in the form of a fine line; the user snorts each line up one nostril per line with a tiny tube, such as a short, chopped-off soda straw or a rolled-up bill. Some users prefer to scoop up the powder with a tiny spoon (or a long fingernail), place it adjacent to the nostril, and then snort it. Snorting cocaine is slower, less efficient, less reinforcing, and less intensely pleasurable than smoking it. Perhaps nine users out of 10 will snort cocaine most of the time that they use it. Until 1985 or 1986, pure cocaine, in the form of "freebase," was smoked. After 1986, crack became the cocaine substance that was smoked. Crack is an impure crystalline precipitate which results from heating cocaine with baking soda; it contains only 30 percent or so cocaine. The difference between powered cocaine and crack is mainly in the route of administration, or the way these substances are taken. Taking powdered cocaine intranasally produces a high that takes roughly three minutes to occur and lasts perhaps 30 minutes. There is no real "rush" or intense orgasmlike explosion of pleasure. Injected, the rush will take only 12 to 15 seconds to appear, and it is described as vastly more voluptuous feeling than the high that occurs when cocaine is snorted. When cocaine is smoked, in the form of freebase or crack, the onset of the drug's impact is even faster, a matter of six to eight seconds, and the intense, orgasmlike high or rush lasts for perhaps two minutes, followed by an afterglow that lasts 10 to 20 minutes. The euphoria achieved in this experience is extreme—in the terms of the behaviorist psychologist, it is highly *reinforcing*—and, often, this impels the users to want to take the drug over and over again.

However, to say that smoked crack cocaine is highly reinforcing, more so in fact than almost any other drug, is *not* to say that most users become chronic abusers. As with nearly every newly introduced drug, sensationalistic exaggeration in the media accompanies its widespread use. In the mid-1980s, newspaper headlines and television reports implied that all teenagers in the country had used crack or were in imminent danger of doing so, that every community nationwide had been saturated by the drug. The reality is not nearly so terrifying.

The first year the "Monitoring the Future" study asked about crack (1987), only 5 percent of high school seniors questioned said that they had used crack even once in their lives; in 1995, this was 3 percent (Michigan, University of, News and Information Services, 1995). The figures for annual and 30-day prevalence are much lower. (Unfortunately, high school dropouts, whose crack use is likely to be considerably higher, could not be included in this survey.)

Just as the incidence or frequency of crack use was exaggerated by the media, the drug's demonic addictive power was sensationalized as well. A June 16, 1986 story in *Newsweek* claimed that using crack immediately impelled the user into "an inferno of craving and despair." "Try it once and you're hooked!" "Once you start, you can't stop!" These and other slogans were repeated so often that they seemed to take on a life of their own. In fact, they are a serious distortion of reality. Crack may be among the most reinforcing drugs we know, and it is possible that a compulsive pattern of abuse builds more rapidly than for any other known, widely used drug. Still, only a fairly small minority of users take the drug compulsively and destructively. In one Miami study of over 300 heavily involved drug users age 12 to 17, 96 percent of whom had taken crack at least once and 87 percent of whom used it regularly, only a minority, 30 percent, used it daily, and half used it weekly or more but not daily. A majority of even the daily users limited their use to one or two "hits"—"hardly an indication of compulsive and uncontrollable use. Although there were compulsive users of crack in the Miami sample, they represented an extremely small minority" (Inciardi, 1987, p. 484). While there is unquestionably a certain *risk* of dependence in smoking crack, the hellish experiences that were described in the media in the 1980s did not typify what most users went through when they took this drug. Once again, drug users are often characterized as extreme deviants by the media, a characterization that assumes a reality in the way drug users are pictured by much of the public.

A good example of the way that cocaine and crack use was demonized in the media is provided by the "crack babies" phenomenon of the late 1980s and early 1990s. In his *Folk Devils and Moral Panics*, Stanley Cohen (1972, pp. 77–85) refers to the process of *sensitization* in the early stages of a moral panic, that is, "the reinterpretation of neutral or ambiguous stimuli as potentially or actually deviant"

(p. 77). Thus, a familiar, nondeviant source that causes a certain measure of harm does not generate much concern, while an unfamiliar, deviant source that causes the same level of harm will touch off a *firestorm* of concern, fear, and hostility. We already saw the sensitization process at work in the 1960s with LSD: Panic reactions were interpreted as an epidemic of psychotic episodes; peculiar-looking chromosomes drawn from one mental patient who was administered LSD were interpreted as a future tidal wave of malformed, abnormal children.

The findings of the initial studies on children born to cocaine-dependent mothers were extremely pessimistic. Babies whose mothers were exposed to crack and powdered cocaine during pregnancy, compared with those whose mothers were not exposed to the drug, were more likely to be born premature, have a lower birth weight, have smaller heads, suffer seizures, have genital and urinary tract abnormalities, suffer poor motor ability, have brain lesions, and exhibit behavioral aberrations, such as impulsivity, moodiness, and lower responsiveness (Chasnoff et al., 1989). Findings such as these were picked up by the mass media with great speed and transmitted to the general public; within a short period of time, it became an established fact that crack babies made up a major medical and psychiatric problem for the country; it is possible, some argued, that they could never be cured. Crack babies could very well become a catastrophe of monumental proportions. William Bennett, then federal drug "czar," claimed that 375,000 crack babies annually were being born in the United States in the late 1980s—one out of 10 births!—a figure that was echoed by *Washington Post* columnist Jack Anderson and *New York Times* editor A.M. Rosenthal (Gieringer, 1990, p. 4). Claimed one reporter, in a major and widely quoted article published in *Time* magazine, the medical care of crack babies will cost society 13 times as much as normal babies. There is fear, she said, that these children will become "an unmanageable multitude of disturbed and disruptive youth, fear that they will be a lost generation" (Toufexis, 1991, p. 56). A Pulitzer Prize-winning columnist describes the crack baby crisis in the following dramatic, heart-wrenching words: "The bright room is filled with baby misery; babies born months too soon; babies weighing little more than a hardcover book; babies that look like wizened old men in the last stage of a terminal illness, wrinkled skin clinging to chicken bones; babies who do not cry because their mouths are full of tubes. . . . The reason is crack" (Quindlen, 1990).

It was not until the early 1990s that enough medical evidence was assembled to indicate that the crack baby "syndrome" was, in all probability, mythical in nature (Neuspiel et al., 1991; Richardson and Day, 1991; Coles, 1991). The problem with the early research on the babies of mothers who had used cocaine and crack was that there were no *controls*. Most of these women also drank alcohol, some heavily, and medical science has documented at least one damaging outcome of heavy drinking by the expectant mother: the fetal alcohol syndrome. Likewise, no controls were applied for smoking, which is associated with low birth weight in infants, nutritional and medical condition of the mother, medical attention (receiving checkups, following the advice of one's physician—indeed, even seeing a physician at all during one's pregnancy), and so on. In other words, factors that vary with cocaine use are known to determine poorer infant outcomes; mothers who smoke crack and use powdered cocaine are more likely to engage in other behaviors that correlate with poorer infant health. Is it the cocaine or these other factors that cause these poorer outcomes? Expectant mothers who use cocaine are more likely to get sexually transmitted diseases; such mothers are less likely to eat a nutritious, balanced diet, get regular checkups, and so on. Were these factors at work in their childrens' poorer health? Or was it the independent effect of the cocaine itself that produced these medical problems?

When the influence of these other factors was held constant, "it becomes clear that cocaine use per se does not affect infant outcomes. Rather, the lifestyle and covariates of cocaine use combine to affect the infant's status." Currently, medical opinion leans toward the view that "the effects of prenatal cocaine exposure that have been reported to date reflect the impact of polydrug use and a disadvantaged lifestyle, rather than the effects of cocaine" (Richardson, 1992, pp. 11–12). In short, it is entirely possible that the crack babies issue is a "hysteria driven" rather than a "fact driven" syndrome. In the late 1980s and the early 1990s, the public, the media, and even the medical profession, were sensitized to believing in the harmful effects of cocaine on newborns with scanty, skimpy evidence; at the same time, the possible influence of the more conventional factors were normalized and ignored. Such processes are characteristic of the moral panic; it is in the moral panic that hostility to and condemnation of deviant behavior and deviant actors are invigorated, intensified, reaffirmed.

HEROIN AND THE NARCOTICS

Of all well-known drugs or drug types, heroin ranks lowest in popularity. Assuming the polls are reasonably accurate, only a shade over 1 percent of the American population has even tried heroin, and a fraction of that figure has used it, even once, in the past month (Health and Human Services, 1994a, p. 49). The percentages for high school students are almost identical to those for the general population (Michigan, University of, News and Information Services, 1995). Remember, however, that school surveys do not interview dropouts, and they are less likely to interview infrequent than regular school attenders, and it is almost certain that dropouts and truants are significantly more likely to have used heroin. In addition, studies of the general population are based on households; homeless people and the incarcerated do not live in households; and the chances are that they are more likely to use heroin than members of stable households. All things considered, however, heroin nonetheless ranks extremely low on America's list of the illicit drugs that are most likely to be used.

The question that then arises is: Why study heroin use at all? If, compared with marijuana, cocaine, and the hallucinogens, it is used with such rarity, why study it at all? Why discuss it in a general overview of drug use and abuse as a form of deviance? One answer is that until the advent of crack in the mid-1980s, heroin use, and especially addiction, has been the most *deviant* form of drug use in the public mind. It is usually regarded as the *ultimate* or *most serious* form of drug use known. In addition, although many users take heroin once, twice, a dozen times, and abstain from it from then on, and many use it occasionally, or, if regularly, confine their use to weekends or special occasions, still, a very substantial number of heroin users become addicts. As we saw, LSD is a drug that is taken by many Americans, of whom an extremely *tiny* proportion use it with any regularity. In contrast, heroin involves a far higher proportion of users in frequent, compulsive, abusive, and harmful use. Most estimates of the number of narcotic addicts in the United States hover in the half a million range; it is possible that according to a more generous definition, there may be as many as a million American heroin addicts. (It must be stressed that defining just who is an addict is not so obvious or straightforward as might be supposed.) In contrast, practically no one is an LSD "addict."

One reason why heroin is such an important drug for sociologists to study (aside from its strongly negative image in the public's mind) is that its use seems to generate social problems of great seriousness and magnitude. This is not merely a matter of socially or subjectively *constructing* a problem in a certain way; objectively speaking, heroin causes a great deal of damage to users and nonusing victims. As we've already seen, it is clear that alcohol and tobacco kill more Americans than the illegal drugs. Still, among the *illicit* drugs, heroin ranks at or near the top in objective seriousness. Heroin causes a great deal of *medical* damage. Heroin ranks second (after cocaine) in DAWN's medical examiners reports, figuring in over four out of 10 (or 45 percent) of all lethal drug-related deaths; it ranked third in nonlethal emergency room episodes as well. Considering that heroin may be used one-tenth as often as cocaine, its contribution to the overdose figures is truly remarkable. It is possible that on an episode-by-episode basis, heroin is the most dangerous of all well-known drugs. Momentarily, we'll have to consider whether it is the *direct action of the drug*, or the way the legal system *deals with* heroin users, that causes such extensive medical havoc. But clearly, *given the way that heroin is currently used*, its contribution to medical harm justifies attention to its use as sociologically important.

Another reason why a study of heroin is crucial in any course on deviance is that the potency of the drug sold on the street has been increasing dramatically over the past decade. Through the 1960s and 1970s, the heroin available on the street at the retail level had remained stable at only 3 to 5 percent pure; the rest was made up of relatively inert and nonpsychoactive fillers such as mannitol, lactose, and quinine. In 1986, however, the New York City police were confiscating heroin with a purity of 30 to 70 percent. Much of this was co-called "China White" heroin, derived from opium grown in Southeast Asia and imported from Hong Kong by ethnic Chinese. Between the early and the late 1980s, the percentage of "China White" on the streets of New York City grew from 3 to 70 percent. Today, a packet of heroin purchased on the streets of our large cities averages 50 to 60 percent.

Currently, a substantially greater range of ethnic and national groups is importing heroin than was true in the past; partly as a consequence, it is being imported from a far greater range of countries of origin. (Although perhaps three-quarters originates from the "Golden Triangle" of Southeast Asia, mainly Burma, now referred to as Myanmar.) The drug's hugely abundant supply has brought its purity up and its price down. During the 1990s, the collapse of the Soviet Union served to expand the countries of origin of heroin to include the central Asian republics. Given the diversity of its origins, halting heroin distribution by stamping out the drug at its source seems a fool's errand.

Some reports indicate that into the mid-to-late 1990s, while heroin use in the general population remains low, the heavy or abusive use of heroin among a small minority may be on the upswing. Certainly, the increase in DAWN's figures on lethal and nonlethal overdoses suggest increases in heavy use and abuse. (A second possible explanation: an aging addict population, leading to more deaths and medical complications. A third explanation: the increase in the potency of heroin has lead to more overdoses.) Between 1990 and 1993 alone, nationwide, heroin-related visits to emergency rooms have nearly doubled, from 33,900 to 63,000 (Health and Human Services, 1995c), while lethal drug-related overdoses in which heroin was present increased during that same period from 1,976 to 3,805 (Health and Human Services, 1991, 1995c). Applications to drug treatment programs, likewise, have increased significantly in the past three years. Some journalistic reports suggest that the use of heroin in chic, trendy, "fast lane" clubs and scenes and among the more avant-garde professions, such as fashion and the arts, may be increasing (Gabriel, 1994). In 1994, River Phoenix, a young actor, died of a multiple drug overdose and was found to have had morphine in his bloodstream (heroin breaks down into morphine in the body), and the same year, Kurt Cobain, a rock star, committed suicide; morphine was also found in his body. Today, heroin is far more likely to be smoked (or, more properly, it is heated and its vapors are inhaled, a practice that was once referred to as "chasing the dragon") or sniffed than was true in the past. The fear of needles—and of AIDS—kept many middle-class druggies away from heroin; with an increase in the popularity of these other methods, this barrier has been dissolved.

A History of Narcotic Addiction

Narcotic addiction did not emerge anew out of the drug-using generation of the 1960s; in fact, it was extremely widespread even before heroin existed. (Heroin was first introduced in 1898.) However, most narcotic addiction in the 1800s was not recreational, not for the purpose of getting high. It was a result of medicinal use. Early in the nineteenth century, morphine was chemically isolated from opium; a practical hypodermic needle was devised in 1854. Morphine was, and still is, used extensively in medicine; it is an extremely effective painkiller. Opium and morphine (and cocaine as well) were ingredients in some 50,000 different patent medicines that were sold openly and legally in the United States before 1914. These concoctions and nostrums had little to recommend in the way of healing power; they were panaceas, quack "cures" that were hawked by unethical and ignorant purveyors for any and all ailments. But they were painkillers; they numbed one of the most troubling symptoms of disease. And since many diseases cure themselves, often these morphine-based patent medicines were thought to work. They were used for teething pains, menstrual cramps, toothaches, insomnia, nervousness, depression, rheumatism, athlete's foot, diarrhea, dysentery, consumption, even baldness and the common cold. And they were available, legally and without prescription, almost everywhere: pharmacies and drugstores, by physicians, in grocery and general stores, in book shops, by tobacconists, in department stores, through mail-order catalogues, and from traveling medicine shows. Nineteenth-century America was truly a "dope fiend's paradise" (Brecher et al., 1972, p. 3).

Unfortunately, for a substantial proportion of medical users, after the disease passed, the patient was left with a physical dependence. It is impossible to estimate with any degree of accuracy just how many medical addicts nineteenth century patent medicines created. (Even today, with vastly more accurate information, no exact figure can be arrived at.) Records kept at the time were extremely unreliable and unsystematic; in fact, the very concept of addiction was not clearly understood. Estimates range from a low of 100,000 to a high of several million. In 1919, the Treasury Department issued a report claiming that roughly a million persons were addicted to narcotics at the turn of the century. Other estimates, based on extrapolations from local surveys, range from less than a quarter of a million (Terry and Pellens, 1928) to just under half a million (Kolb and DuMez, 1924). The American population was only 75 million in 1900 (it is over 260 million today), so that even adopting the modest 250,000 figure gives us a narcotic addiction rate then that was significantly higher than it is today.

Medical addicts at the turn of the century were, for the most part, respectable folk. The heavy users of patent medicines were disproportionately drawn from the middle and upper-middle classes (Brecher et al., 1972, p. 18). Although a substantial proportion of criminals did use narcotics—mostly they smoked opium—the vast majority of users of narcotics took drugs for medical reasons, and they were not involved in a life of crime. A century ago, there was no necessary connection between the heavy, chronic use of narcotics and criminal behavior. The addict was not a deviant, an outsider, or an outcast. He or she usually carried on conventional, everyday activities—marriage, a family, a job, conventional friendships, an education—and was not cut off from polite society, as tends to be the case today. In the nineteenth century, the addict was seen as a sick person in need of medical attention, a helpless victim, but not a criminal or a deviant. The public didn't approve of drug addiction, but it was considered an unfortunate affliction rather than a manifestation of immorality and depravity; addicts were pitied rather than scorned. There was little or no stigmatization of the addict before the turn of the nineteenth century. Moreover, there was no *subculture* of addiction: Addicts did not associate with one another because of their drug habits; they did not behave differently from nonaddicts; there was nothing particularly remarkable about them except for their addiction (Terry and Pellens, 1928; Lindesmith, 1965, 1968; Duster, 1970; Griffin, 1976; Musto, 1987).

In addition, the nineteenth-century addict was more likely to be a woman than a man, the reverse of today's picture. In studies conducted at the time, roughly two-thirds of the medical addicts surveyed were female. Users tended to be middle-aged rather than young (Brecher et al., 1972, p. 18). Blacks were underrepresented among addicts then, again, the reverse of the contemporary scene. And in the past, users were not drawn mainly from large cities but from the entire rural-urban spectrum. In short, the narcotic addict population of a century ago was almost totally different in nearly every respect from the addict of today.

In December of 1914, Congress passed the Harrison Act. It required that everyone who sold or dispensed narcotics to register with the Treasury Department, pay taxes, and keep a record of all drug-related transactions. In addition, it banned the sale of all over-the-counter narcotics (along with cocaine, which the law arbitrarily defined as a narcotic). Initially, the law was not intended to criminalize medical addicts, and seemed to permit the sale of narcotics via prescription, if they were written "in the course" of the physician's "professional practice," "for legitimate purpose," and "prescribed in good faith." Many physicians interpreted maintaining addicts on narcotics and keeping them away from the agony of withdrawal as part of legitimate, acceptable medical practice. However, after 1914, the police began arresting addicts and physicians who wrote prescriptions for drugs containing narcotics. The legal appeals went all the way to the Supreme Court. In a series of Supreme Court cases between 1919 and 1922, it was decided that maintenance of the addict on narcotics was not a part of legitimate medical practice; "the court ruled that such prescriptions were illegal regardless of the purpose the doctor may have had" (Lindesmith, 1965, p. 6). According to one estimate, in the dozen years following the passage of the Harrison Act, roughly 25,000 physicians—one out of 10 of all the physicians in the country!—were arrested for issuing prescriptions for narcotic drugs to addicts. Roughly 3,000 actually served a jail or prison sentence for this new crime. Fairly quickly, most physicians abandoned treatment of narcotic addicts, leaving them to fend for themselves. By the mid-1920s, addicts began to be arrested in substantial numbers (Lindesmith, 1965, p. 143).

Although the criminalization of addiction almost certainly reduced the size of the addict population, most estimates hold, it also had another effect: the generation of an addict subculture, a criminal class that had barely existed previously. Some criminals smoked opium, but the number was tiny; most addicts, as we saw, were medical addicts. What the law and its enforcement did was to forge a link between addiction and crime. The addict was a criminal, first by definition, by purchasing and possessing an illegal substance, and second, by virtue of having to commit crime to secure expensive drugs. It was the criminalization of addiction that created addicts as a special and distinctive group, and it is the subcultural aspect of addiction that gives addicts their recruiting power. The majority of medical addicts probably did give up their habit when narcotics became criminalized, but some turned to the emerging addict subculture for their drugs, and committed crimes to pay for them.

The criminalization of heroin addiction also influences or determines another crucial facet of heroin use: the medical harm the drug inflicts on users. Earlier, we saw that on a dose-for-dose basis, heroin is an extremely dangerous drug, far more so, for example, than is true of cocaine, a far more widely used drug. The question I raised was whether the overdoses of narcotic addicts and users we see in such abundant numbers are a result of the direct or intrinsic action of the drug or a product of our legal system. What I am about to say is going to sound contradictory, but many things that are true seem to be false, at least on a superficial level. The fact is that overdosing aside, heroin, like all of the narcotics, is an extremely *safe* drug. Unlike alcohol, tobacco, and many prescription drugs, the continued use of or addiction to heroin does not harm bodily tissue in any way. Even a lifetime of heroin addiction does not do damage to any tissue or organ of the body (Ball and Urbaitis, 1970; Isbell, 1966; Wikler, 1968). But heroin addicts do die in great numbers, about two out of every 100 per year (Goldstein, 1994, p. 241), a huge death rate. (The same is true of Great Britain, which has instituted a less punitive and more treatment-oriented drug policy than is true of the United States.) Most die of overdoses and the rest die of more long-term addiction-related diseases, such as AIDS, hepatitis, infection from unsterile needles, and suicide, homicide, and, ironically, alcoholism (Goldstein, 1994, p. 241). If addicts were administered standard doses of medically pure heroin, using sterile needles, and lived a healthful lifestyle, in principle, they could live lives that were as long and as healthy, on average, as the population as a whole. Heroin-related deaths are a *secondary* rather than an intrinsic or direct feature of addiction.

Heroin Addiction and Dependence

Everyone knows that heroin is an addictive drug, certainly one of the most addictive drugs known. In addition, it is common knowledge that heroin addicts are "enslaved" by their habit; they commit money-making crimes to pay for the drug they take so they can continue their addiction and avoid the agony of withdrawal. They have to take heroin just to remain normal. And since heroin is illegal, it is difficult to obtain and costly to buy; because of this, it is profitable for the underworld to sell it. Like most pieces of conventional wisdom, this picture isn't entirely accurate.

There are many theories as to why addicts continue to use heroin, in spite of the many painful and life-threatening experiences they have as a result of taking the drug, and even after many episodes of "kicking" the drug habit. Two of these theories are based on the mechanism of *reinforcement,* or the rewards subsequent to a given act. *Positive* reinforcement theories explain the continued use of heroin by the pleasurable sensations that come with using the drug. *Negative* reinforcement theories explain continued heroin use by the avoidance of pain that taking heroin produces. Which of these two theories explains heroin use, abuse, and addiction better?

The argument invoking negative reinforcement goes more or less like this. Initially, the use of heroin may not be pleasurable at all. In time, the user learns how to take heroin and how to interpret its effects, so that its use is pleasurable. In the first few weeks or months of use, pleasure is a major motivating force in continuing to use heroin; this period could be called the "honeymoon" phase. However, the user gradually becomes physically dependent on the drug, usually without realizing it. Because of the tolerance mechanism, the user, in order to continue receiving pleasure, must increase the doses of the drug; eventually, physical addiction takes place. At some point, the attainment of euphoria becomes problematic, for all practical purposes, an unreachable goal. If use is discontinued, painful withdrawal symptoms wrack the addict's body. But even though addicted, the user is not yet a true addict, because withdrawal, though painful, may not necessarily be associated in the user's mind with taking the drug. To become a true addict, the user must, first, recognize that continued administration of heroin has produced physical dependence; second, that discontinuing the heroin use produces agony and pain; and third, that taking heroin *will alleviate painful withdrawal distress.* It is this dramatic, three-step process that fixes in the individual's mind the need to keep taking narcotics. This is what makes an addict a true addict.

According to Alfred Lindesmith (1947, 1968), the earliest proponent of this theory:

The critical experience in the fixation process is not the positive euphoria produced by the drug but rather the relief of the pain that inevitably appears when a physically dependent person stops using the drug. The experience becomes critical, however, only when an additional indispensable element in the situation is taken into account, namely a cognitive one. The individual not only must experience withdrawal distress but must realize that his [or her] distress is produced by the interruption of prior regular use of the drug. (1968, p. 8)

In short, "The perception of withdrawal symptoms as being due to the absence of opiates will generate a *burning* desire for the drug" (Sutter, 1966, p. 195).

In contrast, the positive reinforcement theory holds that the majority of drug users, abusers, and addicts continue to take the drugs because of their "extremely potent reinforcing effects" (McAuliffe and Gordon, 1980, p. 138); that is, because of the intense pleasure they generate. According to positive reinforcement theory, continued, compulsive drug use, heroin included, does not require that the user be physically addicted; users take drugs day after day, year after year, because of their positive reinforcing effects, because they derive intense pleasure from doing so. Why don't all people who experiment with a given drug become compulsively involved with it? Many drug users are reinforced—that is, they experience euphoria—from their very first drug experience onward, and the more they use the more intense the sensation and the greater the motivation to continue. There are, therefore, individual differences in the reinforcement value of a given drug or of drugs in general.

Which explains heroin addiction better—the negative or the positive reinforcement theory?

The negative reinforcement theory holds that the pleasure addicts derive from the administration of heroin declines over time; it becomes harder and harder to get high—to the point where euphoria is no longer a factor. The primary motivation in continued use is the reinforcement heroin offers in alleviating pain. Recent evidence, however, suggests that addicts and other compulsive drug abusers do, in fact, experience euphoria, and that this is a major factor in their continued drug use. In one study of addicts, all of whom used heroin at least once a day, 98 percent of the sample said that they got high or experienced euphoria at least once a month,

and 42 percent got high *every day.* For nearly all respondents in this study, euphoria was consciously desired and sought. In fact, 93 percent said that they wanted to be high at least once a day, and 60 percent wanted to be high *all the time* (McAuliffe and Gordon, 1974, p. 807). Clearly, most heavy, compulsive heroin users continue to seek, and many in fact achieve, euphoria; its attainment is a major motivating force behind their continued use.

These two perspectives may not be as far apart as they seem. In fact, there are two quite different types of addicts, the behavior of each ruled by a distinctly different mechanism: the *maintainers* and the *euphoria seekers.* The maintainer takes just enough heroin to avert withdrawal distress. Some addicts lack the financial resources, and are insufficiently willing to engage in a life of crime, to obtain enough heroin to attain euphoria. They are simply staving off the agony of withdrawal, "nursing" their habit along. To achieve the high they really want would require taking such a substantial quantity of the drug that their lives would be utterly and completely transformed. They would have to work very hard and run a substantial risk of danger and arrest to do so. Not all users want to commit crimes, and certainly not to live a life of crime, to get high; not all think the chances of arrest are worth threatening such valued features of their lives as their jobs, family, and freedom. They prefer to "maintain" a habit over risking what they have in order to achieve euphoria. They have retained most of their ties with conventional society, and "let loose only periodically" (McAuliffe and Gordon, 1974, p. 822).

In contrast, the pleasure-seeking addict takes narcotics in sufficient quantities and at sufficiently frequent intervals to achieve euphoria. Such a habit is extremely expensive, and typically requires illegal activity to support it. In addition, the lifestyle of the euphoria-seeking addict is sufficiently disruptive that a legal job is usually not feasible; he or she must resort to criminal activity instead. It is also difficult for the nonaddict to fit in with and be capable of tolerating the addict's lifestyle, so that marriage and a family are typically not possible—or are, at best, extremely chancy propositions. Further since heavy opiate use depresses the sexual urge, intimate relations with the opposite sex are difficult.

In short, the euphoria-seeking addict has sacrificed conventional activities and commitments for the hedonistic pursuit of pleasure; and to engage in this pursuit, a commitment to a deviant and criminal lifestyle is necessary. Such sacrifices make no sense "if they were directed solely toward reducing withdrawal symptoms, which could be accomplished with much less effort, as every addict knows. . . . *For it is the frequency of euphoria, more than anything else, that stratifies the addict social system."* In the addict subculture, the greater the success in achieving euphoria, the greater the prestige. "In this sense, hard-core addicts are the true elite, and the addict stratification system itself points to the fundamental importance of euphoria" (McAuliffe and Gordon, 1974, p. 828).

In short, the negative reinforcement theory works better for the maintainer-addict, while the positive reinforcement theory works better for the euphoria-seeking addict. Which theory works best depends entirely on how much heroin the addict takes and what motivation is the primary mover in his or her actions.

Since positive reinforcement is the major reason why many heroin addicts use narcotics, it forces us to face an extremely crucial point: The line between addiction and use is not sharp or clearcut. If positive reinforcement is a (possibly *the*) driving force behind most dependence, then it does not much matter whether users are technically addicted for them to be long-term, compulsive users. Many users continue taking heroin because they have been powerfully rewarded with repeated administrations of the drug over a long period of time. They *have* to take heroin because their bodies are attuned to the euphoria they have experienced. They aren't necessarily physically dependent on heroin—that is, they wouldn't undergo withdrawal symptoms if they stopped—but the psychological dependency is just as strong as if they were. Dependency is a *linear* dimension, a spectrum, not an either-or proposition. Physical dependency or addiction is simply the end or extreme point of a continuum.

This conclusion is verified by a study of some 200 New York heroin abusers (Johnson et al., 1985), which found that doing what one has to do to survive is a common theme in heroin users' lives. Most of the "addicts" in this study were not addicted in the physical sense. They were psychologically and behaviorally dependent on heroin; they used it as much as they could, week after week, and their lives pretty much revolved around procuring the money to pay for it, getting the drug itself, and using it. Most regular users of heroin are not addicted in the strictly physiological sense; that is, they would not suffer painful withdrawal symptoms if they were to discontinue use. Most regular, even compulsive, users of heroin take their drug often, but not necessarily several times a day, day in and day out, in classic junkie fashion. Instead, they use twice one day, once the next, not at all for three days, four times the day after that, and so on. The classic junkie may be a relative rarity compared with the number of nonaddicted compulsive heroin abusers. It is likely that the 500,000 figure commonly quoted for the number of addicts in the United States includes many technically nonaddicted heroin abusers rather than only addicts who are physically dependent on heroin.

This means that most "addicts," that is, most compulsive heroin abusers, are not driven by the need to avoid withdrawal. The popular image of the addict being impelled by the physiological drive to avoid withdrawal symptoms ("I need a fix") is highly likely to be a myth. Psychological dependence is every bit as powerful a drive as—and may even be more powerful than—physiological dependence. The heroin abusers in the study of Johnson and his colleagues (1985) *do* "need a fix." But for the most part, they do not need it to avoid withdrawal, since most of them are not taking enough heroin or any other narcotic sufficiently frequently, or in large enough doses, to be physically dependent.

Is experimenting with heroin an automatic ticket to addiction or even compulsive abuse? Does trying and then using heroin always lead to physical or even psychological dependence? Is there any such thing as a "recreational" heroin user? Is there any such thing as "controlled" opiate use? The heroin users I've just described are compulsive users; their lives revolve around the drug, and they would take more of it if they could. But is there a different heroin user who takes the drug on a regular but noncompulsive basis—that is, on a fairly *controlled* basis? Until fairly recently, it was not recognized that controlled opiate use was possible; one was considered either an addict or an abstainer. Recent research suggests the occasional yet regular controlled user of narcotic drugs is more common than the addict. The term used in the world of street narcotic use to describe this limited use is "chippying" or "chipping": to fool around with heroin, to use it once in a while or even more often without getting hooked, without developing a true habit. How common is this pattern of heroin use?

We all recognize that the controlled use of alcohol is possible—it is in fact the majority pattern. Most drinkers are moderate in their consumption of alcohol and do not become alcoholics. Alcohol, as we will see in Chapter 7, is every bit as dependency-producing—is as physically addicting—as the narcotics. How much and how often people in a given society use a certain drug, including alcohol, and what proportion are physically dependent on it are not a simple function of the pharmacological properties of the drug itself, but depend in part on the people—their culture and society—using the drug. For instance, in the United States roughly during the 1800 to 1840 period, about *three* times as much alcohol was consumed per capita as is true today (Lender and Martin, 1987, pp. 205–206)—same drug, different rules, different patterns of use, and differing proportions of alcoholics in the population. It is the people who take drugs, not the drugs themselves, that control people. All drug use is surrounded by values and rules of conduct; these values and rules spell out sanctions—penalties for misuse and rewards for proper use—and these values, rules, and sanctions have an impact on how drugs are actually used. Some of these values may be societywide and some may be distinctive to special groups or subcultures within the larger society. All have an impact on the behavior of the members of the culture or subculture who take them seriously.

Is it really possible to use heroin or any of the other opiates on a moderate or controlled basis? One study (Zinberg, 1984) located a number of controlled opiate users and examined their patterns of use—what made them distinctive, how they accomplished this seemingly impossible feat. They had been using opiate drugs on a controlled basis for an average of four and a half years. For the year preceding the study, about a quarter (23 percent) used opiates sporadically, or less than once a month; a third (36 percent) used one to three times a month; and four in ten (41 percent) used twice a week. None used daily or more. Their pattern of use and the length of time they had sustained this pattern showed "without question that controlled use can be stable" (1984, p. 69).

It might be objected that stable, nonaddicted opiate users have simply not yet reached the stage

in their drug careers when use inevitably becomes uncontrolled and compulsive. This objection is easily countered by comparing the length of time of the opiate use of the controlled users with the length of time of the addicts in the sample of this same study; they were not substantially different. In addition, most compulsive users and addicts had never had a period of controlled use. And third, the length of time these controlled users had been taking narcotics represents ample time for them to have developed an addiction or a pattern of compulsive use (Zinberg, 1984, pp. 69–70). Clearly, controlled use is a stable pattern for a significant proportion of narcotics users; experimentation or moderate use does not necessarily or inevitably turn into compulsive use or addiction. Addiction is a phenomenon that must be understood in its own right. At the same time, without more information, we cannot be sure exactly how typical or frequent controlled use is.

This study also compared and contrasted the patterns of use that characterized controlled users of narcotics with compulsive users and found interesting differences. They did not differ in their route of administration—for example, snorting versus intravenous injection—or personal acquaintance with someone who died of an opiate overdose. They *did* differ from controlled users in that, they (1) rarely used more than once a day; (2) often kept opiates on hand for a period of use without immediately using them; (3) tended to avoid using opiates in the company of known addicts; (4) tended not to use opiates to alleviate depression; (5) rarely or never used opiates on a "binge" or a "spree"; (6) usually knew their opiate source or dealer personally; (7) usually used opiates for recreation or relaxation; and (8) tended not to use opiates to "escape" from the difficulties of everyday life (Zinberg, 1984, pp. 69–81).

In short, some users of opiates manage to set rules for themselves—norms—and stick to them; for them, regular use does not necessarily lead to compulsive use or addiction. Again, it is the people who take drugs, not the drugs themselves that control people; in many ways, patterns of drug use are determined more by *who* takes the drugs than by the intrinsic characteristics of the drugs themselves—by what the drugs *are,* in some abstract sense. In fact, what drugs "are" is determined by how they are used and what happens to whomever uses them; and, in turn, this is determined by just who it is that uses them in the first place. If we forget the social and personal dimensions of drug use, we are distorting its fundamental reality.

LEGALIZE DRUGS?

In the latter half of the 1980s, a drastic and unusual proposal to solve some of the disastrous consequences of illicit drug use and abuse has become popular in some circles: to *legalize* all or most currently illegal drugs. Taking the profit out of drug sales and making drugs more or less readily available, this view holds, would sharply reduce the crime, violence, and devastation that have taken place in many urban neighborhoods as a result of drug use and abuse (Gonzales, 1985; Nadelmann, 1988, 1989; Kerr, 1988; Church et al., 1988; Hamill, 1988). This proposal has no realistic hope of becoming law, so the debate it has stirred up is in many ways a theoretical exercise, not one based on anything likely to happen. Still, since this argument is taken seriously among some observers, it is worthwhile to respond to it.

The fatal flaw in the prolegalization argument is that drug use is almost certain to increase after legalization, but the impact of legalization is likely to be variable, depending on the drug. It would be least for marijuana: Studies suggest that in the states in which small-quantity marijuana possession is not a crime (there are 9), decriminalization has not resulted in an increase in use (Cuskey, Berger, and Richardson, 1978; Single, 1981; Johnston, 1980). There are probably three reasons for this: (1) a condition of near-saturation has been reached for marijuana; nearly everyone who wants to use already does; (2) the odds of being arrested on marijuana possession charges are extremely slim (there are some 400,000 marijuana arrest in the United States each year—but, annually, well over 25 million Americans who use); and (3) the effects of marijuana are pleasant, but not as immensely reinforcing as those of some drugs (heroin and cocaine, for example). The legalization, and thus the ready availability, of marijuana would have a greater impact than mere decriminalization, but not much.

Cocaine is altogether different. As we saw, cocaine is an *immensely* reinforcing drug, both for animals and for humans; it is, in fact, the most reinforcing drug known. It offers so much pleasure—direct, immediate, sensuous pleasure, unmitigated

by learning—that it is reasonable to expect many more users would be attracted to it if it were legally available. In a 1994 national survey, just under a million and a half Americans took cocaine in the past month and were therefore defined as "regular" users; it is possible that one in 10 of these are compulsive, uncontrolled users. In contrast, 113 million Americans drank alcohol during the previous month, of whom, again, roughly one in 10 is a compulsive, uncontrolled drinker; they could be called alcoholics. Doesn't it make sense that we should expect at least as many compulsive cocaine users as alcoholics if cocaine were readily available?—in fact, certainly more, since alcohol is far less reinforcing and far more of an acquired taste. Can we afford to have more than 10 million cocaine addicts in our midst?

Even the medical control and dispensation of heroin are unwise. For the most part, they have been phased out in England, and there are some 50,000 unregistered addicts there—a huge explosion of addiction during the 1980s. The reason maintenance programs cannot be successful in eliminating addiction is that the primary motive addicts have in using narcotics is euphoria. They want that orgasmlike rush coursing through their veins, and that is one thing maintenance programs do not supply. Maintenance programs appeal mainly to the older, burnt-out, used-up addicts who have a couple of decades of addiction behind them. On the other hand, giving junkies exactly what they want can only balloon the number of heroin addicts.

Drug profits do not create drug users and abusers; eliminating drug profits will not diminish the number of users or the quantity of use; quite the reverse. It will eliminate *some* drug-related problems, as its proponents suggest—the murders, much of the crime, many of the medical maladies of junkies. It is society's choice as to which we want: a relatively small number of sick, violent, criminal addicts or a much larger number of healthier, less violent, and less criminal addicts. Most Americans would choose the former.

The current somewhat punitive policy has not worked because it has not eliminated drug use and abuse. But it has worked in at least one extremely crucial respect: *containment*. It has kept certain highly reinforcing drugs out of the hands of millions of Americans who would otherwise become involved with them. Actually, there is no politically acceptable, nondrastic means of eliminating or

---

Does the American Public Want to Legalize Drugs?

In 1988, in a nationwide poll conducted by ABC News, nine out of 10 Americans said they rejected the legalization of currently illegal drugs. Over half (51 percent) said they believed that legalization would lead to increased drug use; 11 percent said use would decrease; and 38 percent said it would make no difference. Legalization was favored for marijuana somewhat more often (25 percent of those polled) than for cocaine (7 percent) and heroin (6 percent), but for no drug did the prolegalization sentiment even remotely approach a majority. By a margin of two to one, those polled believed that legalization would lead to an increase in crime: 47 versus 23 percent.

Source: The New York Times, September 15, 1988, p. 26.

---

sharply reducing drug use in the United States. Viewed in that light, current policies have worked, in their clumsy, limited, even damaging way. Clearly some medium-scale reforms would work better, but any major change on the scale of outright legalization is likely to be a disaster.

SUMMARY

Drug use has both an objective and a subjective side; that is, it has certain concrete, measurable consequences and generates a certain level of public concern as well. These two dimensions, the objective and the subjective, overlap extremely imperfectly. By this I mean that the *magnitude* of public concern is not always an accurate reflection of the degree of danger or damage represented by drug abuse. Often, there is great concern at a time when the harmful effects of drug abuse are declining and, contrarily, concern is often relatively low when these drug effects are on the rise. In addition, the specific drug that attracts public concern has shifted over time, from marijuana in the 1930s, LSD in the 1960s, heroin in the early 1970s, and crack cocaine in the later 1980s. Sociologists refer to a period in which concern over a given condition, such as drug abuse, is intense and disproportionate to its concrete danger, a *moral panic*. In a moral panic, a specific agent is held responsible for the condition or threat—a *folk devil*. Humans have ingested psychoactive or mind-altering substances for thousands of years. Drug use is very close to being a human universal the world over in that nearly all cultures use psychoactive substances. Sometimes, the wrong substance is ingested, it is taken too often, or under the wrong circumstances, or with undesirable con-

sequences. In such cases, we have instances of deviant behavior.

Most definitions of drugs have focused on the objective or concrete properties of substances. However, the fact is that no such property exists such that *all* substances that are referred to as drugs share it and, in turn, *no* substances that are *not* called drugs do not. In contrast, a *subjective* definition of drugs recognizes that though substances that are referred to as drugs do share certain properties in common, they do so only within specific contexts. In other words, some substances referred to as drugs are psychoactive; some are not. Some "drugs" are useful as medicine; some are not. Some are taken for the purpose of getting high; some are not. Some are addicting; some are not. The possession of some drugs is illegal; some drugs are completely legal. Each of these dimensions defines "drug-ness," but only in certain contexts. No single objective or concrete quality covers all substances that are known as drugs; each is useful in a limited fashion. Thus, the subjective definition emphasizes that whether a given chemical substance is a drug or not is in part in the eye of the beholder.

Since all drugs have multiple effects, they may be classified in different ways, according to different criteria. Still, by focusing on a limited number of effects, certain drug classifications have come to be widely accepted as standard. One classification, useful for psychoactive drugs, focuses on the effect of substances on the central nervous system, or brain and spinal column. *Depressants* retard or "obtund" signals passing through the central nervous system. Two types include *general depressants,* which inhibit a wide range of functions and organs of the body, and *narcotics,* which act more specifically on dulling the brain's perception of pain. Narcotics are popularly known as "painkillers." Narcotics also produce euphoria and all are addicting. *Hallucinogens* (or "psychedelics") produce profound alterations in perception, especially those of a visual nature. Most classifications put marijuana into a distinct and separate category.

Four types of categories of drug use may be distinguished: legal medical, or instrumental use; legal recreational use; illegal instrumental use; and illegal recreational use. In the past two or three decades, with a few exceptions, psychoactive prescription drug use has declined sharply. Legal recreational drug use (mainly the use of tobacco and alcohol) has declined as well. Illegal instrumental use—for instance, taking amphetamines to stay up all night to study for an exam—represents a substantial part of the drug picture. It is the illegal recreational use of drugs—taking psychoactive substances for fun, that is for the purpose of getting high—that defines the drug problem for most of the public. Studies show a huge increase in illegal drug use between the early 1960s and the late 1970s; 1979 or 1980 represented the peak year for the use of most illegal drugs. Marijuana use has gone through several drastic changes as an illegal and deviant activity. In earlier centuries, marijuana was used as a medicine. Early in the twentieth century, the recreational use of marijuana was not well-known; users were rarely condemned as a separate category of deviants. During the 1930s, numerous articles in popular magazines and newspapers created something of a marijuana scare or panic; in that decade, possession and sale of the drug became a crime in all states of the United States and at the federal level as well. Harmful medical effects of marijuana have been asserted but never fully documented; the jury is still out on this question. In the United States, during the 1960s and 1970s, marijuana use became much more common, more accepted, and less deviant, and the drug was decriminalized in 11 states. Since 1980, the decriminalization movement has been halted and use has become less acceptable and more deviant.

Hallucinogens or psychedelics include LSD as their most well-known representative. During the 1960s, a LSD scare or panic erupted. Users were said to suffer temporary insanity and irreparable chromosomal damage. The first effect is now regarded with suspicion by experts, while the second has been entirely discounted. LSD use has not disappeared; if anything, it has stabilized over the past decade or two. LSD is taken extremely sporadically, with great infrequency. It very rarely becomes a drug of serious, heavy, or chronic abuse.

Although an ingredient in some medicines and beverages, for recreational purposes, cocaine was never a drug of widespread popularity in the United States until the 1970s. Cocaine was criminalized, along with narcotics, in the aftermath of the Harrison Act. In the 1980s, a new form of cocaine, "crack," became popular. Crack is smoked and thus produces an intense and extremely rapid high. Never widespread in the country as a whole, crack quickly became popular among poor, inner-city, minority youth. Crack use, while far from safe, was demonized by the media; its harmful effects were hugely exaggerated. Babies born to cocaine-dependent mothers were said to be permanently disabled mentally and physically. In fact, it is now clear that their medical problems are due more to the lifestyle of their mothers than the effects of cocaine per se. In other words, the fear that crack will severely harm the fetuses of dependent mothers was a "fear-driven" rather than a "fact-driven" syndrome. Crack abuse became another in a long line of drug panics.

Heroin is perhaps the least popular of all widely known drugs in America. As it is used, it is also one of the most dangerous. (Although, interestingly, if used in a medically controlled fashion, heroin does not harm the body at all!) Considering the small number of heroin users in the United States, an astonishingly high number of addicts die of heroin overdoses and other related ailments. It is possible that this has as much do with the legal situation as the effects of the drug itself. During the 1980s, heroin sold illegally on the street became increasingly pure and abundant. It is now imported from a much wider range of sources than was true in the past. In the nineteenth century, most narcotic addiction resulted from medical misuse; recreational use and addiction remained low. Medical addicts were for the most part respectable folk; there was only a rudimentary narcotic addict subculture and addicts were not considered deviants. The Harrison Act of 1914 required the registration of sales of narcotics; it seemed to permit prescription medical use, but later Supreme Court interpretations struck this down. By the mid-1920s, narcotic addicts began to be arrested in large numbers. As a result, a criminal addict subculture was generated.

There are a number of theories which attempt to explain narcotic addiction. Some emphasize the avoidance of withdrawal as the significant causal factor; others emphasize the pursuit of intoxication or euphoria. It is now clear that a substantial number of narcotic addicts are motivated by the pursuit of euphoria. Indeed, contemporary researchers believe that positive reinforcement is almost certainly a more potent motivator for addiction than the avoidance of withdrawal. The question of the legalization of the currently illegal drugs has emerged during the second half of the 1980s with great vigor. Legalization advocates claim that the current system of penalizing addicts and sellers is a failure and that their proposal will cure or improve society's drug problem. Opponents argue that the current system is not as much of a failure as its critics claim and that the cure would be worse than the disease. Penalizing drug possession and sale probably does contain or keep drug use and abuse from growing. In any case, since the overwhelming majority of the public opposes drug legalization, it is not likely to become law any time in the foreseeable future.

ACCOUNT: ONE UNDERGRADUATE'S INVOLVEMENT WITH ILLEGAL DRUGS

This account was written by a college student.

I was raised in an upper-middle class family, the third of four children. My parents were strong practicing Catholics; I went to parochial school for six years, and received religious instruction for another six years. I loved it. I thought of Christ as my personal friend. I went to Mass often, became very close to our parish priest, and maintained a relationship with my sixth grade teacher, a nun. I wanted to become a nun myself. However, my parents did not want me to make the choice of entering a convent until I had completed college. I decided to attend a Jesuit college, assuming that the atmosphere there would be conducive to my life's dream.

Before attending college, I spent the summer with my sister and brother-in-law in South Dakota, taking care of their baby. I quickly fell into the lifestyle of the people I met there. Even though I was underage, I went out drinking every night. Mainly, I ran around with the college kids from the university nearby. I had a grand time. I drank in bars; if the owners knew I was underage, they told me to be on the lookout for cops. No problem. My sister and brother-in-law tried to grow marijuana, without any luck as it turns out. Even though my sister told me how great it would be to smoke grass, secretly, I was very relieved that it never grew. I knew it was wrong. In high school, I knew kids who smoked grass

and drank at someone's house when their parents were away. These things seemed bad to me, dangerous, illegal, and risky. The fact that I drank didn't seem like a contradiction to me. That summer, I also became sexually active. Still, it seemed OK, since I was sure I was going to marry my boyfriend. At some point, I realized that I had thrown away my chance to become a nun.

When I went to college, once again, I wrapped myself in the protection of being "good." I still had a fearful distrust of marijuana. I believed that hard drugs were used only in the ghettos of large cities, or among people who had no morals or backbone, people who were amoral. I would never associate with such depraved, pathetic souls. True, I did take "speed" the summer after my first year of college, but it was for more or less therapeutic reasons: to keep my weight in check and make my job seem less boring. And my source had been my dentist. So I didn't define it as deviant at all, and I didn't see any harm in it.

For my second year of college, I transferred to a large state university. At first, I lived off campus in an apartment with two girls I didn't even know initially. My neighbors were two guys who were fine, upstanding, wealthy, "good old boys"; it turns out, they were also very active in the drug scene. Since my roommates were boring, straight arrow types, I spent a great deal of time with my far more interesting neighbors. It was amazing! These guys had a lifestyle I had never seen before. One night, they offered me hashish. I was ready to refuse, but on the first hit, I had an incredible explosion of ribboning heat and color shooting up through my head and behind my eyes; it flew with equal intensity down through my legs to my toes. These guys did speed, too, and they turned me on to black beauties, which was great, because I needed something to pull me through nights of cramming for tests. I had began to ignore my schoolwork, so anything that helped me at least get a passing grade was welcome. The following semester, I decided to move into the dorms. What an experience! It seemed that everyone smoked dope, drank, and did other drugs as well. I became engaged to a straight arrow redneck type, Mr. Navy ROTC himself. We drank together; that was allowed. At the time, I dabbled in pot and took an occasional hit of speed—for studying, of course. I began to become involved with radical hippie-types and drug users; I also began reading some unconventional, alternative culture-type books. Well, Mr. Navy didn't like the riffraff I was hanging out with or the stuff I was reading; he saw all this as subversive, unpatriotic, and deviant. We had an argument about it, and he beat me up. Another time, he objected to a book I was reading, and he hit me again. I gave him back his diamond ring and called off the engagement. I would not allow myself to become a victim of abuse. Besides, he was interfering with my budding and enjoyable new lifestyle.

I quit school and began working for a psychiatrist. I moved into a house that needed a great deal of work; to fix the house and work, I had to sleep very little. The shrink received drug samples in the mail, which I stole. I also stole his old PDR [Physician's Desk Reference] when his new one arrived. I thought it might come in handy one day. After five months, I was fired.

My neighbors were heroin users. They also seemed to have had access to just about everything else. They offered to get me what I wanted. They also invited me to try heroin with them. But what I saw simply didn't appeal to me. I liked the effect of speed. It made me feel in control. I'd talk incessantly or become so absorbed in a project, I couldn't tear myself away. I began seeing Mark. He and I did speed together. Often, Anne, a girl I met in the dorms, joined us. I re-enrolled in school, though I was put on academic probation. I had no steady income; I'd work enough to pay the rent and buy beer and speed. We reached the point where we'd plan speed weekends. Mark and I only dropped speed, but Anne, I soon found out, was doing something else. One day, she called and asked if I might be interested in "partaking intravenously," as she put it. I was intrigued. I was astounded. I was shocked. In my mind, at that time, I hadn't really done anything dangerous. After all, I had refused the chance to do heroin. To me, needles meant the gutter—they were disgusting. I refused, but told her that if she wanted to do it, it was OK with me. Our "date" was still on.

The night came. Mark and I went to Anne's house and sat around the kitchen table. He and I dropped our hits of speed as planned. I watched Anne closely as she went through her preparations. It seemed like a ritual to me. I held the top of her arm. She pumped up her vein, swabbed it with alcohol-soaked cotton, took the syringe, and inserted the needle in her vein. She pulled out the plunger, and some blood flowed into the syringe; then she depressed the plunger and shot up. She told me to let go of her arm, and she pulled the needle out and bent her arm up. Her lips became red, she breathed a little heavier, and she smiled. I kept watching her. I decided that I had changed my mind, and asked her if I could take a hit. She looked at me and said sure. Mark wasn't interested, and I felt glad; I didn't really want to share this experience with him. I was ready.

I had good veins; my heroin using friends told me I was wasting my veins by not shooting. I held my arm. Anne dabbed the vein with the cotton and asked if I was sure, then asked if I was ready. I said yes. I was scared, but I was also thrilled with anticipation. But more than that, this was shooting speed—a new realm for me. By shooting, I had become willing to throw caution to the wind, I was risking everything in my life as I had known it. She inserted the needle, and I felt it hit my vein. She pulled back the plunger, and I saw my own blood flow into the syringe. She slowly depressed the plunger, and I relaxed my fist. I felt a welling in my chest and throat, almost as if my stomach was rising to my mouth. Then my head and my whole body was overtaken with an inde-

scribable feeling. I felt wonderful, incredible. I had never felt anything like this before. I knew with almost absolute certainty that I'd do this again.

But how could we get a hold of more speed? I had the PDR, so we could look up the necessary terminology to write the script. But how could we get our hands on the prescription forms? I made an appointment with my physician for a gynecological exam. While I waited in the examining room, I spotted and took a prescription pad. We now had everything we needed to get all the speed we wanted. By this time, Mark had decided to join us in shooting up. We took turns going to different pharmacies and presenting our forged scripts. If a druggist became suspicious and picked up the phone, we left immediately. Most of the time, we got what we wanted.

The ritual of preparing the pills for use was becoming almost as important as taking the stuff. I sterilized the water. We got 60 pills in a vial. I poured them into a mortar, and crushed them with a pestle. The longer I soaked them in water and the finer I crushed them, the greater the strength of each dose. Usually, what we got in one vial gave us two potent "hits" each. On a typical run, we'd shoot up every six to eight hours, using two or three vials of pills. I divided everything up. I felt I had to in charge—I wanted to make sure I got what I needed. I administered my own shots and Mark's, and sometimes Anne wanted me to do her, too. I was good at it. I never left a mark on anyone. I got a rush just by shooting someone up. And I was always the last to go.

Although I didn't do speed every day, my thoughts were totally preoccupied with doing it. I had no steady job. I had dropped out of school. I shoplifted. I lost a tremendous amount of weight. I went for days without eating or sleeping. I became something of a recluse, avoiding almost everyone except Mark and Anne. Even though I denied that anything was wrong, I struggled with conflicting feelings. I was depressed, sometimes paranoid. Coming down from the speed became a dreadful, painful, and even frightening experience. To insulate myself from this feeling, I drank, took Valium, and even, when it was available, acid. I also baked brownies with marijuana, dropped mescaline, and even, once in a while, cocaine. But what I wanted to do most of all was shoot speed. Speed was my thing. So I began shooting it on my own, while Anne and Mark slept. My tolerance was building up, and I became more and more reluctant to share it equally. I needed more and more. But coming down became scary, nightmarish. I hallucinated, I heard voices. My life was a disorganized mess. I began selling speed to friends in a city some distance away. On one trip, after no sleep for three or four days, while driving home, at night, in the rain, I began hallucinating. I slowed down to 35, but the visions kept haunting me. Finally, I pulled over to the side of the road, and every few miles, at each rest stop, each gas station along the way, I called Mark, I called Anne, I called anyone I could think of. No one was home. I barely crawled the rest of the way home, slipped into bed, cried and shook, and finally passed out.

Still, I had to keep chasing that high. I persuaded Mark to cop some more for me. He went to a pharmacy in a nearby city. The last time we went there, the pharmacist picked up the phone, so we had decided it wasn't safe. Still, I wanted the speed, so I made him take a chance. He was arrested on the spot, taken to the station house, and charged with illegally attempting to obtain a controlled substance. Fortunately, he managed to arrange a plea-bargain; he was on probation for two years, finished law school, and was allowed to take the bar exam. He's now a practicing attorney. He could have turned me in, but he didn't. Remember, I stole the prescription pad from my doctor, I wrote the scripts, including the one he used when he was busted—and I was the one who sent him out to get a hold of some speed for me. Still, he remained silent about me. After he made bail and was released from jail, we no longer saw each other. Did I stop doing speed? Did I give up drugs? Not right away. I was a wreck. Nothing made any sense. I was overwhelmed with despair, frightened to continue my almost suicidal life, yet even more frightened to terminate it. I just couldn't get out of it. One night, while tripping on acid, I called my sister, who now lived in Canada, and asked if I could visit her for a while. I sold my car, bought a one-way plane ticket, packed up my clothes, took my dog, locked up the house, and embarked on the next stage of my life's journey. That ended my love affair with speed, with illegal drugs, and with a self-destructive lifestyle.

chapter 7

ALCOHOL USE AND ALCOHOLISM

With respect to its impact on the workings of the mind, alcohol is a drug in precisely the same sense that LSD, heroin, and cocaine are: It is *psychoactive*. Second, likewise, in the sense that alcohol is used largely for its effects on the drinker, it is a drug in the same sense that marijuana and cocaine are, that is, it is a *recreational* drug. And third, with respect to its capacity to induce a *physical dependence* in the drinker, alcohol is also a drug in the same way that heroin, cocaine, and the barbiturates are: Alcohol is "addicting," it is physically dependency-producing, that is, it generates severe withdrawal symptoms when the heavy, long-term drinker discontinues its use. In fact (cigarette smoking aside), alcoholism is by far our most common form of drug addiction. Estimates hold that there are roughly 10 million alcoholics in the United States. In contrast, there are only half a million or so heroin addicts. The typical drug addict, then, is an alcoholic, not a street junkie. In that a sizable minority of drinkers display a pattern of *behavioral dependence*—they continue to drink heavily in spite of the social cost to themselves and to others whom they care for—alcohol is a drug no different from cocaine, amphetamines, and heroin. In the bodily sense, then, *all drinkers are drug users*. Thus, there is no biochemical aspect of drinking that is qualitatively different from what most of us regard as "drug use." In fact, as one medical researcher declares: "Alcohol is the only addictive drug that dangerously alters behavior yet at the same time is freely and legally available without a prescription. As it is so widely used, it represents the most serious addiction problem for our society" (Goldstein, 1994, p. 121).

There are three ways in which alcohol *cannot* be regarded as a drug, however: First, much, possibly most, of the public does not *consider* alcohol a drug; consequently, second, most Americans do not regard drinking as a form of deviance; and third, under most circumstances, the sale and purchase of alcohol is not a crime. Almost any adult may buy it in almost any jurisdiction in the country. This chapter will consider some of the similarities and differences between alcohol and the substances that are universally regarded as drugs and what relevance these similarities and differences have for human behavior.

If alcohol is not a drug in the definitional or constructionist sense, if its possession and sale are legal, and if its use is not deviant, why study it in a course on deviance? If drinking is conventional,

law-abiding behavior, does it really belong in a textbook on deviance? The answer is a most emphatic yes. Why? As we saw in the last chapter, there are several very good reasons why we should look at the consumption of alcohol, a legal and conventional activity in the United States, in the context of deviance. Let's review them.

First, the *heavy* consumption of alcohol—alcoholism—is considered deviant, or reprehensible, in nearly all societies on earth. Second, the norms in this and all other societies spell out not only *how much* drinking is acceptable and unacceptable, but they also spell out appropriate and inappropriate *occasions* or *situations* for imbibing alcohol. Drinking and getting tipsy may be acceptable at a New Year's Eve party, but not while lecturing in front of a class. Third, while alcohol may be a legal drug, it is illegal to buy, sell, and consume it *under certain circumstances*. In fact, as we saw, in the United States, more alcohol-related arrests take place each year than arrests for the possession and sale of illegal drugs: For 1994, there were 1.1 million for drug abuse violations, but 1.5 million for driving while under the influence, half a million for violations of the liquor laws (mainly the sale of alcohol to minors), and three-quarters of a million for drunkenness. (Almost none of these arrests result in incarceration, it must be said—in sharp contrast to drug arrests.) Fourth, many criminal, deviant, and violent acts—murder and rape most notably—are so often committed under the influence of alcohol that some researchers believe that drinking may be a *cause* of them. Fifth, the possession, sale, and use of alcohol have been legally controlled at different times in different societies; for instance, they are illegal and deviant in orthodox Muslim countries, such as Iran and Saudi Arabia, and in the United States during Prohibition, the sale of alcohol actually was illegal. Sixth, in a country so diverse and heterogeneous as the United States, *some* social circles may be found in which the consumption of alcohol is regarded as deviant—among traditional Mormons, for example, or strict fundamentalist Christians. And last, the fact that alcohol possesses many objective characteristics in common with the illegal drugs indicates that the constructionists are correct: There is often a yawning chasm between an activity's concrete or objective properties, characteristics, and consequences and its *legal status* and *image* in the public mind.

Alcohol has an ancient and checkered history. Fermentation was one of the earliest of human discoveries, dating back to the Stone Age. Alcohol emerges spontaneously from the fermented sugar in overripe fruit; the starch in grains and other food substances also readily converts to sugar and from there to alcohol. Because the process of fermentation is so simple and basic, the discovery of alcohol by humans was bound to be early. Alcohol consumption, in all probability, began when a prehistoric human consumed fermented fruit and experienced its effect. It is also no accident that alcohol's "remarkable and seemingly magical properties as the ability to induce euphoria, sedation, intoxication and narcosis" (Health, Education, and Welfare, 1971, p. 5) and its "great capacity for alleviating pain, relieving tension and worry, and producing a pleasurable sense of well-being, relaxation, conviviality, and good will toward others" (Straus, 1976, p. 184), have made it an almost universally acceptable beverage. Consequently, humans have been ingesting beverages containing alcohol for at least 10,000 years. Therefore, it is (coffee excepted) the most widely used drug in existence—ubiquitous, almost omnipresent the world over.

Actually, what is usually referred to as "alcohol" is one of a whole family of alcohols. Pharmacologists call it *ethyl alcohol* or *ethanol*. Other representatives of the alcohol family include wood alcohol (methyl alcohol) and rubbing alcohol (isopropyl alcohol), which are outright poisons, even in small quantities. It is therefore no accident that ethyl alcohol, the most pleasant and one of the least toxic of all the alcohols, has come to be identified with the general term. I will refer to ethyl alcohol simply as "alcohol."

Societies differ vastly in their average level of alcohol consumption. What proportion of their members drink at all, and how much each drinker consumes on the average, varies enormously from one nation or society to another, and even from one group to another within a country or a society. In addition, as we've seen, every society that has some acquaintance with alcohol has devised institutionalized rules for the proper and improper consumption of alcohol. There is, then, intersocietal variation both on the behavioral and the normative levels. Although biochemical "effects" of alcohol, both short-term and over the long run, do exist, most of them can be mitigated or drastically altered by the belief in and observance of these cultural rules. The extent to which intoxication leads to troublesome, harmful, or deviant behavior varies considerably from society to society. In many places,

alcohol use poses no problem to the society according to almost anyone's definition; the drug is consumed in moderation and is associated with no untoward behavior. In other places, alcohol use has been catastrophic by any conceivable standard. The overall impact of alcohol, then, is not determined solely by the biochemical features of the drug itself, but by their *relationship* to the characteristics of the people drinking it. This is not to say that alcohol can have *any* effect the members of a society expect it to have. There is a great deal of latitude in alcohol's effects, but it is a latitude that lies within certain boundaries.

As with illegal drugs, the effects of alcohol can be divided into short-term or *acute* effects, that is, effects while the drinker is under the influence, and long-range, or *chronic* effects. Even this breakdown is crude. The acute effects can be further subdivided into those that rest within the "objective" or strictly physiological and sensorimotor realms; the realm of behavior under the influence, called "drunken comportment"; and the "subjective" realm, or what it feels like to be drunk, how the intoxication is experienced. The sensorimotor effects are fairly specific and easily measured in mechanical and mental performance, such as motor coordination, memory, and the ability to achieve a given score on certain psychological tests. Drunken comportment in contrast, refers to the vast spectrum of free-ranging, real-life behavior: what people do with and to one another while under the influence. An example of a sensorimotor effect would be driving more poorly under the influence; drunken comportment might refer to whether or not one even gets into a car while one is drunk in the first place. The long-range effects can be divided, at the very least, into *medical* effects and *behavioral* effects—what happens to one's daily life after ingesting certain quantities of alcohol over a lengthy period of time.

ACUTE EFFECTS OF ALCOHOL

The potency of alcoholic beverages is measured by the percent of alcohol (sometimes referred to as "absolute," that is, *pure* alcohol) they contain. Pure ethyl alcohol is 100 percent "absolute" alcohol. Beer contains about 4 percent. Wine is about 12 percent; it is the most potent drink we can concoct through the natural fermentation process. ("Fortified" wine, in which alcohol is added to the natural substance, is legally set as no higher than 20 percent alcohol. The wines that skid row alcoholics drink are usually "fortified." Sherry is a wine fortified with brandy.) However, the process of distillation (boiling, condensing, and recovering the more volatile, alcohol-potent vapor from the original fluid, and adding an appropriate quantity of water) produces drinks like Scotch, vodka, gin, rum, and tequila that are about 40 to 50 percent alcohol, or 80 to 100 "proof." Consequently, in order to consume roughly an ounce of absolute alcohol, someone would have to drink two 12-ounce cans of beer, or one 8-ounce glass of wine, or a mixed drink containing about two to 2 1/2 ounces of Scotch or gin. According to *the rule of equivalency*—which states that the effects of alcohol are determined principally by the volume of pure alcohol that is drunk, rather than the type of

Table 7.1 Alcohol Intake and Blood-Alcohol Level (BAL) (for a 150-pound individual in one hour of drinking)

Absolute Alcohol (ounces)	Beverage Intake	BAL (grams/100 milliliters)
½	1 can beer	.025
	1 glass wine	
	1 oz. distilled spirits	
1	2 cans beer	.05
	2 glasses wine	
	2 oz. distilled spirits	
2	4 cans beer	.10
	4 glasses wine	
	4 oz. distilled spirits	
3	6 cans beer	.15
	6 glasses wine	
	6 oz. distilled spirits	
4	8 cans beer	.20
	8 glasses wine	
	8 oz. distilled spirits	
5	10 cans beer	.25
	10 glasses wine	
	10 oz. distilled spirits	

Note: The less someone weighs, the higher the BAL, other things being equal; the more someone weighs, the lower the BAL. Given the same level of alcohol consumption, the BAL of males is significantly lower than that of females. *Source:* Simplified from Ray and Ksir, 1996, p. 223.

drink itself—these drinks would be roughly equal in strength, and would have approximately the same effects on one's body.

Alcohol, when it enters the body, is translated into what pharmacologists call *blood alcohol concentration* (BAC), or *blood alcohol level* (BAL). This corresponds fairly closely to the percent of one's blood that is made up of alcohol after it is ingested; a given BAC or BAL level has been described as "bathing the brain" in a given alcohol concentration (Goldstein, 1994, p. 121). There is a relationship between blood-alcohol concentration and what we do under the influence. The effects of alcohol are, to a large degree, dose-related: With some variation, the more that is drunk, the greater the effect.

The effects of alcohol are influenced by many factors. Some of them are directly physiological. Since alcohol registers its impact via the bloodstream, the *size* of the drinker influences blood-alcohol concentration; the presence of food and water in the stomach; the speed at which one drinks; the presence of carbonation in an alcoholic beverage; and lastly, sex or gender. (Women, apparently, are more sensitive to the effects of alcohol, and manifest effects at lower doses, or greater effects at the same dosage, than is true of men.) In addition, as with practically all drugs, alcohol builds up pharmacological *tolerance:* It takes more alcohol to achieve a given effect in a regular drinker than in an abstainer, more in a heavy drinker than in an infrequent drinker.

Alcohol's strictly physiological effects include cellular dehydration (a major reason for a hangover the day after), gastric irritation (which may lead to an upset stomach after drinking too much), vasodilation (an increase of blood flow through the capillaries), a lowering of body temperature (though the surface of the skin does become flushed, creating an illusion of greater body warmth), some anesthesia, and a depression of many functions and activities of organs of the body, especially the central nervous system. Alcohol also disorganizes and impairs the ability of the brain to process and use information and hence, impairs many "perceptual, cognitive, and motor skills" needed for coordination and decision making. One ounce of alcohol consumed in less than an hour will result in a blood-alcohol concentration of roughly .05 percent in a person of average size. This produces in most people a mild euphoria, a diminution of anxiety, fear, and tension, a corresponding increase in self-confidence and, usually, what is called a "release" of inhibitions. Decreased fear also typically results in a greater willingness to take risks; this effect has been demonstrated in laboratory animals. Alcohol is, for most people, at low doses, a mild sedative and a tranquilizer. This is by no means universally the case, however. There are many people for whom alcohol ingestion results in paranoia, distrust, heightened anxiety, and even hostility. These "effects," however, typically occur, when they do, at moderate to high doses.

Alcohol's effects on motor performance are familiar to us all: clumsiness; an unsteady gait; an inability to stand or walk straight; slurred speech. One's accuracy and consistency in performing mechanical activities decline dramatically as blood-alcohol concentration increases. And the more complex, the more abstract, and the more unfamiliar the task, the sharper the decline. The most noteworthy example is the ability to drive an automobile. It is crystal-clear that drinking, even moderately, deteriorates the ability to drive, and contributes to highway fatalities. How intoxicated does one have to be to lose the ability to perform mechanical tasks? What does one's blood-alcohol level have to be to display a significant decline in motor coordination? And how many drinks does this represent? The answers depend on a number of factors, as I just said, experience with alcohol being crucial. It is true that seasoned drinkers can handle themselves better at the same blood-alcohol level than novices, but experienced drinkers are typically far too overconfident about their ability to function while under the influence. In fact, since alcohol tends to dull anxiety and tension, drunk drivers typically think they perform better than they actually do—and are surprised, even incredulous, when their ineptitude is demonstrated to them—so that the problem becomes more than a simple deterioration in mechanical ability. All drinkers experience a loss of motor skills at a certain point, and it occurs at a fairly low BAC. However, many drivers are quite willing to get behind the wheel while intoxicated: As we saw, according to the FBI's *Uniform Crime Reports*, in the United States in 1994, there were 1.5 million arrests for drunk driving.

There is a kind of "zone" within which alcohol impairment occurs. At about the .03 percent blood-alcohol level, some very inexperienced and particularly susceptible individuals will display a significant decline in the ability to perform a wide range of tasks. The Federal Aviation Administration (FAA) sets a .04 percent BAC as representing an alcohol-influenced condition, and prohibits pilots from flying at this level of intoxication. This is slightly less than two typical drinks. (Ross and Ross, 1990, found that only a third of the pilots questioned were even aware of this .04 rule; Modell and Mounts, 1990, recommend that the allowable BAC level for pilots be lowered to .01.) At the .10 level, even the most hardened, experienced, and resistant drinker will exhibit some impairment in coordination; this is four typical alcoholic drinks. Most states set a BAL of .10 as constituting legal intoxication—a far too conservative a level, in the view of most experts. Zador (1991) estimates that compared with someone who is sober, a driver with a BAC between .02 and .04 has a 1.4 increased chance of having a fatal single-vehicle crash. This risk increases to *11 times* for the driver with a BAC between .05 and .09, *48 times* at the .10 to .14 level, and *385 times* for drivers with a BAC over .15! The risk increases even more sharply among younger drivers and for females. (Although both categories are *much* less likely to be intoxicated and behind the wheel than males and adult drivers and hence, are less likely to cause a fatal alcohol-related accident. Here, clearly, we have to distinguish between *absolute numbers*—there are many more males and adults who drink and drive than females and teenagers—and *the likelihood of harmful consequences*—females and teenagers are more likely to have an accident if they drive while they are drunk.)

Motor-vehicle crashes are the leading cause of "nonnatural" death in the United States; they account for more fatal injuries than any other type of accident. The National Highway Traffic Safety Administration monitors the proportion of drivers involved in fatal crashes by blood alcohol concentration. In 1982, 39 percent of all drivers involved in a fatal car crash had a BAC of .01 or higher; 30 percent measured .10 or higher. (The latter figure is obviously a subset of the former.) This dropped every year since then; by 1994, those drivers with a BAC of .01 or higher made up only 25 percent of the total, and those who were at the .10 level or above represented only one-fifth of the total (19 percent). The National Highway Traffic Safety Administration also reported that 60 percent of fatally injured drivers of motorcycles had a BAC of .10 or higher; for fatally injured drivers of heavy trucks, this was only 20 percent. Even pedestrians vastly increase their chances of being killed by an automobile—more than fivefold!—if they are intoxicated. A third of pedestrian fatalities in one study had a BAC of .15 or higher, whereas only 6 percent of the control group randomly selected at the same time and place were this intoxicated (Brodie, 1973, p. 32).

Motor vehicles are not the only source of fatal alcohol-related accidents. In fact, alcohol use has been "empirically linked to an array of serious and fatal injuries" (Health and Human Services, 1994a, p. 234). Coroners' reports permit the *empirical* link between recent alcohol consumption and death to be made in a more or less definitive fashion, although the *causal* link is likely to be much thornier. In other words, the presence of alcohol in the victim's body is relatively easy to establish. However, whether the alcohol *caused* the victim's death is much more difficult to nail down, since controls are not applied in some studies, and there is no clear-cut or widely agreed-upon standard by which we may establish the fact of causality. Goodman et al. (1991) examined the death certificates of over 15,000 cases of intentional (suicide and murder) and unintentional (or accidental) victims to determine alcohol's role in their demise. A quarter of the suicide victims, a third of the homicide victims, and nearly four out of 10 of the homicide victims tested at the .10 BAC level. Another study (Smith et al., 1989) turned up similar results— BACs testing .10 were 27 percent for suicides, 52 percent for homicides, and 40 percent for accident victims. Only 8 percent of persons who died of natural causes tested at this level. Alcohol was significantly more likely to be present in the bodies of male than female victims. One study examined a thousand consecutive violent or accidental deaths in New York City in 1972. A BAC of .10 or higher was found in a third of all victims—33 percent for victims of falls, 44 percent for vehicular drivers or passengers, and 32 percent for pedestrians (Haberman and Baden, 1974). Numerous studies (Combes-Orme et al., 1983; Abel and Zeidenberg, 1985; Goodman et al., 1986) show that close to half of all homicide *victims* were drinking at the time they were killed, and one-third had a BAC of .10 or higher. Adding it all up, one estimate holds that in 1980 alone, alcohol was responsible for nearly 60,000 premature deaths from accidents (38,000), suicides (8,000), homicides, (12,000), and other nondisease-related sources (Ravenholt, 1984; Health and Human Services, 1987, 1990).

Beyond the .15 blood-alcohol level, one's ability to function plummets. At the .20 level, the drinker is somewhat dazed, confused, and distinctly uncoordinated; any movement at all becomes risky and problematic. Driving is extremely hazardous. At the .30 level, any response to the stimuli of the outside world becomes an insurmountable chore. One's ability to perceive and comprehend what is happening is reduced to a bare minimum. At the .40 level, most people pass out and lose consciousness, this is regarded as the lethal dose or LD50—the point at which half of all drinkers die from an overdose. At .50 percent, if the drinker is still alive, he or she has entered a coma, from which he or she can be aroused only with the greatest difficulty, even with stimulant drugs. At .60 percent, overdoses are increasingly common; death occurs as a result of the inhibition and paralysis of the respiratory centers. Almost anyone whose blood is .80 percent alcohol will die; it is considered the LD100 for humans.

ALCOHOL AND VIOLENCE

One of the most consistently documented generalizations in the alcohol literature is the relationship between alcohol intoxication and the commission of violent acts (Pernanen, 1991; Parker, 1995). The empirical evidence linking alcohol with violence is overwhelming, convincing, and incontrovertible. Worldwide, alcohol is *by far* the drug that is most likely to be implicated in violent crimes. A *majority* of persons who commit violent offenses are under the influence of alcohol at the time of the offense. The *descriptive* or *empirical* connection is so consistent that it cannot be challenged. On the other hand, as I explained earlier, a *causal* or *etiological* connection is more difficult to establish. Does alcohol *cause* drinkers to engage in violent, dangerous, criminal behavior? Or is some other causal mechanism at work here? For instance, caffeine and tobacco aside, alcohol is the most frequently used drug in existence; it is possible that alcohol consumption is empirically connected to behavior of *all* kinds—violent and nonviolent, criminal, and law-abiding. By that fact alone, even if it played no causal role whatsoever, we should expect alcohol to be consumed in conjunction with many violent acts. (Just as, say, coffee or soft drinks would be, since they are drunk so much in so many contexts, including before the commission of violent acts.) In addition, alcohol is most frequently consumed at the very *times* and *places* that a great deal of violence is committed: in bars, for instance, where males are heavily congregated, on Friday and Saturday nights. To establish the causal connection between alcohol and violence, we'd have to do more than simply establish the frequency with which violent offenders are intoxicated at the time of their offense.

Criminal Homicide

As with violence generally, descriptively speaking, alcohol is strongly correlated with criminal homicide. Persons who are under the influence have a strikingly higher likelihood of killing others than do persons who are not under the influence. One classic study reported that in 60 percent of all murders, the killer had been drinking prior to the attack on the victim (Wolfgang, 1958). A later study, conducted in Chicago, found the figure to be 53 percent (Voss and Hepburn, 1968). In a study of Scottish killers, 58 percent of the males (but only 30 percent of the females) were intoxicated at the time of their offense (Gillies, 1976). In Finland, 66 percent of the perpetrators of criminal homicide were described as having been under the influence at the time of the killing (Virkkunen, 1974). The same generalization holds true for a number of national and cultural settings and social contexts (Tinklenberg, 1973, pp. 247–248; Giesbrecht et al., 1989). This is an empirically indisputable relationship; alcohol is implicated in an extremely high proportion of all homicides, both in the United States and internationally. Wieczorek and his colleagues (Wieczorek, Welte, and Abel, 1990) interviewed nearly 1,000 convicted homicide offenders and found that a third of the respondents were under the influence of alcohol alone at the time of committing their homicides; 13 percent drank alcohol in combination with one or more illegal drugs; and only 7 percent used some other drug or drugs alone. The researchers estimated that alcohol was "directly implicated" in roughly half of all criminal homicides. Interestingly, in spite of the public image of illegal drugs being intimately related to lethal violence, not only are killers less likely to be under the influence of an illegal drug at the time of their violent offenses than alcohol, but drug *intoxication* is rarely implicated in lethal violence, while drug *selling* frequently is (Goldstein, 1985; Goldstein et al., 1989; Parker, 1995, xiii).

It might seem almost paradoxical, but one of the ways that the violence of alcohol-intoxicated persons has been studied has been through an examination of the *victims* of violence, more specifically, homicide victims. At first glance, it might seem that this line of analysis would represent an example of "blaming the victim." Still, in order to understand how the intoxication of murder *victims* represents an important source of information concerning the intoxication of their killers, it is necessary to understand the dynamics of the most common criminal homicide. Although it sometimes—even often—happens that a completely innocent victim is murdered by a marauding killer who selects his (very, very rarely, her) victim almost at random, in truth, a high proportion of murderers and victims, and the actions of a high proportion of murder victims, actually make a contribution to their own demise. In many altercations, it is a 50-50 proposition as to who ends up being the killer and who ends up being the victim. Often, the fact that the future victim is drunk will contribute to his or her death as a result of a range of mechanisms, such as being selected by the offender as a victim, being more willing to engage in a potentially dangerous situation, getting into an altercation, struggling with the offender, even initiating violence against the eventual killer.

It must be emphasized that this generalization—that the victims of violence are often themselves engaged in violence just before they are killed—applies *only* to assault and homicide. It would be ludicrous to argue that rape, another violent crime, can be characterized in the same fashion. Women are not attempting to rape men when *they* are raped; at that moment, they are concerned with survival and avoiding being raped. The generalization that violence is frequently an interactive affair applies *only* in situations in which two combatants are engaged in *similar* and *reciprocal* acts of violence against one another. It should also be emphasized that though this pattern applies to many male-on-male killings, killings *by* males *of* females—or the less common killings *by* females *of* males—have a very different pattern and dynamic. In the latter, victim precipitation, broadly understood, figures heavily; in the former cases, we do not have two approximately equal combatants but a more one-sided, bullying encounter, whose outcome cannot be predicted by considering the concept of precipitation.

In any case, an extraordinarily high proportion

of murder victims are under the influence at the time of their deaths. In one study (Abel, 1987), over four out of 10 homicide victims (45 percent) had some detectable level of alcohol in their blood. In another, conducted in New York City, the figure was 42 percent; over a quarter, or 27 percent, had a level of .10 percent or above, which constitutes legal drunkenness in almost all states (Haberman and Baden, 1978, p. 80). In another study, in Los Angeles, for murder victims, the figures were 46 percent for any detectable level and 30 percent for the .10 percent blood-alcohol level and above (Goodman et al., 1986). In the Finnish study cited above (Virkkunen, 1974), the *victims* of criminal homicide were slightly more likely to have been under the influence of alcohol (68 percent) than the perpetrators (66 percent)! In the Scottish study referred to above, 42 percent of the victims of the male killers and 32 percent of the victims of the female killers were intoxicated at the time of their deaths (Gillies, 1976). Welte and Abel (1989) argue that the fact that alcohol is *most* likely to be present in the victims in stabbing homicides, homicides that take place on Saturday night, and homicides that happen in bars, indicates that alcohol plays the most prominent role in homicides that emerge more or less spontaneously out of personal disputes, through a process that has been referred to as *selective disinhibition* (Parker, 1995).

Aggravated and Sexual Assault

Since alcohol intoxication is strongly correlated with criminal homicide, we might expect the same to be true for assault, because it is illegal and results in serious bodily injury. In this expectation, we are not disappointed. In a survey of jail inmates conducted by the U.S. Department of Justice, 62 percent said that they had used alcohol prior to committing the crime of assault (Baunach, 1985). In one study of assaults by adolescent males that resulted in damage to the victims, 55 percent of the assailants described themselves as being under the influence of alcohol at the time of the offense (Tinklenberg et al., 1981). Wifebeating is a type of assault, and it, too, is related to the consumption of alcohol. The probability of physical abuse by husbands against wives increases as the frequency and amount of alcohol consumed increases (Bland and Orn, 1985; Kantor and Straus, 1987; Van Hasselt, Morrison, and Bellack, 1985).

Sexual assault, including rape, is significantly more likely when the offender is under the influence of alcohol. The study conducted by the Institute for Sex Research (the "Kinsey Institute") on convicted, incarcerated sex offenders indicated that alcohol plays a significant role in sexual violence. In about 40 percent of all acts of male sexual aggression against adult women (mostly rape and attempted rape), the offender was classified as drunk. In two-thirds of all aggressive sexual offenses against young girls, or the molestation of a female child, the offender was drunk (Gebhard et al., 1965, pp. 761–763, 813). Another study found that 45 percent of the men arrested on the charge of rape had a blood-alcohol concentration of .10 percent or higher (Shupe, 1954). In a Canadian study, statements by the accused, the victims, and the police indicated that in 63 percent of the rapes that were reported to the police, the attacker was under the influence of alcohol. Significantly, the victim was more likely to have been injured when alcohol was present than when it was absent (Johnson, Gibson, and Linden, 1978). After eliciting, then reading, "detailed autobiographies" of convicted California rapists, a psychiatrist inferred that 50 percent of them had been drinking at the time of their offense and that 35 percent were alcoholics (Rada, 1975). The same psychiatrist examined a sample of child molesters and found that 49 percent had been drinking at the time of the commission of the offense; 34 percent were judged to have been drinking heavily (Rada, 1976). The link between alcohol and sexual assault seems indisputable.

Alcohol and Violence: Exploring the Causal Links

Clearly, the empirical link between alcohol consumption and violence is strong; it is, in fact, beyond question. However, as we all know, simple correlation does not demonstrate causality. What *produces* this massive and powerful link? What is the causal *mechanism* underlying the fact that alcohol is so often found in violent episodes? Is the alcohol/violence nexus, in Goldstein's terminology (1985) *pharmacological* in origin? Nowadays, few researchers refer to "cause" when they discuss the effect of alcohol on violence; they are more likely to use the term "contributing factor" or even "determinant" (Wolfgang, 1981). Still, alcohol does have pharmacological actions that *potentiate* behavior and *incline* persons, or *categories* of persons or *specific* persons, in a certain direction, under certain circumstances.

Alcohol can act on aggression and violence in two ways—*directly* and *indirectly*: directly by heightening or stimulating "aggression centers" in the brain, or indirectly as a result of lowering inhibitions. In the United States and elsewhere, in a wide range of social settings, alcohol does act to lower inhibitions and heighten impulsivity. Experiments on both animals and humans, in both real-life and artificial conditions, demonstrate that fear is reduced under the influence; subjects take risks they would not take when sober. By removing social and other barriers to violence, alcohol, at least in the settings in which it is consumed, may encourage violence. More directly, in experimental situations, alcohol has been shown to heighten interpersonal aggression in social situations, but only in individuals with a background of arguments, aggressive acts, and low self-control (Boyatzis, 1975). In one study, among assaultive juveniles, marijuana was used as often as alcohol and in much the same settings, but its role in assault was found to be significantly less prominent (Tinklenberg et al., 1981). Hence, it is not simply who uses a drug, how often, or in what settings that determine its association with violence; this indicates that these two drugs seem to have entirely different effects. After all the qualifications are made, the strength of alcohol's association seems to be so strong and consistent that it is difficult to believe that it is not in some sense causal, or pharmacological, in nature.

At the same time, it must be recognized that although the correlation between alcohol use, especially heavy use, and violence is strong, significant, and quite consistent, drinking is only one of a number of factors involved in the commission of violence. Alcohol consumption can be looked at as "but a link in the overall chain of events that produce violent crime" (Walfish and Blount, 1989, pp. 371–372)—a link, "but a link" nonetheless. In fact, it is far from the most important factor in the violence picture. To sum things up, the following points must be stressed. First, alcohol use, especially heavy use, is empirically correlated with committing a wide range of violent acts, including murder, aggravated assault, wifebeating, and rape. And second, alcohol's impact on violence, indeed, on all human behavior, is *mediated* or strongly influenced by social context, setting, and cultural definition (MacAndrew and Edgerton, 1969; Room and Collins, 1983). In short: "The circumstances of drinking produce greater changes in behavior than the alcohol does" (Carpenter and Armenti, 1972, p. 540). Third, *most* violence *cannot* be ascribed to alcohol and must be explained by other factors, such as institutional and ideological support for violence in certain settings (Kantor and Straus, 1987; Gelles and Straus, 1988, pp. 44–48). And last, when all the necessary qualifications have been registered, in all likelihood, alcohol is a causal factor in at least a *portion* of the violence that takes place; in this sense, violence can be said to be a direct effect of (or "caused by") the alcohol itself. When all is said and done, though, in many societies, alcohol intoxication does not result in violence (MacAndrew and Edgerton, 1969). In the United States, it *is* associated with a great deal of violence. In fact, so much is this the case that it is fair to say that *in this society*, alcohol's role is a causal one—*guided* or *encouraged* by our attitudes and cultural norms and the settings in which drinking takes place, but causal nonetheless.

ALCOHOL CONSUMPTION AND CONTROL IN THE UNITED STATES

Alcohol consumption should be interesting and instructive to any student of human behavior for a variety of reasons. For one thing, legal controls have been applied to the manufacture and sale of alcoholic substances, with mixed results. Moreover, the use of alcohol has been regarded as respectable during most of the nation's history, indeed, to refuse to drink has been seen as unacceptable, unfashionable, even slightly deviant. Yet during the period between roughly 1850 and 1920, drinking declined sharply in popularity and a substantial proportion of American society disapproved of it on principle. Perhaps equally important, "respectable" Americans were *most* likely to oppose alcohol consumption; the less prestigious, less affluent, and less powerful social and ethnic groups tended to be more favorably inclined toward drinking. The dominant attitude of conventional Americans was that moderate drinking was not possible: One either abstained altogether or became an incurable alcoholic—there was no in-between territory.

The Early History of Alcohol in the United States

Alcohol has had a fascinating cyclical history in America. The Native Americans who greeted Columbus brewed and drank beer. (They were not, however, acquainted with distilled spirits.) The Puritans, although remembered for an abhorrence of sensual and physical pleasures, arrived on the shores of New England with ample supplies of beer, wine, and hard liquor. The *Arbella*, which arrived in the Boston area only a few years after the *Mayflower*, "set sail with three times as much beer as water, along with 10,000 gallons of wine." In addition, most settlers brought along a supply of distilled spirits as well. "So liquor was more than a luxury in the colonial mind; it was a necessity to be kept close at hand" (Lender and Martin, 1987, p. 2). Increase Mather, a Puritan minister of some distinction and the author of *Woe to Drunkards* (1673), while warning against overindulgence said, "Drink is in itself a good creature of God, and to be received with thankfulness." Drinking "constituted a central facet of colonial life. Indeed, two of the key characteristics of early drinking patterns were frequency and quantity. Simply stated, most settlers drank often and abundantly" (Lender and Martin, 1987, p. 9).

Drinking in colonial America was "utilitarian, with high alcohol consumption a normal part of personal and community habits." Beer and cider were common at mealtime, with children often partaking; collective tasks, like clearing a field, were typically accompanied by a public cask. Farmers usually took a jug into the fields with them each morning. Employers often gave their employees liquor on the job. Political candidates usually "treated" the electorate to alcoholic beverages, including at polling places on election days. The Continental Army supplied its troops with a daily ration of four ounces of rum, when it was available, or whiskey. In short, drinking was extremely common in seventeenth- and eighteenth-century America, considerably more common than it is today. Estimates put the per capita alcohol consumption for all Americans age 15 and older in 1790, when the first national census was taken, at 5.8 gallons of absolute alcohol per year, more than twice its present level (Lender and Martin, 1987, pp. 9–10, 20; Levine and Reinarman, 1992; Miron and Zweibel, 1991).

Drinking in seventeenth- and eighteenth-century America was rarely considered a serious social problem; in fact, there was a remarkable lack of anxiety about it. While heavy drinking and even alcoholism certainly existed, most drinkers consumed alcohol in a family or a community setting, and strong social norms kept excessive drinking within acceptable bounds, and prevented unacceptable and potentially dangerous behavior under the influence from getting out of hand. Drinking, though heavy by today's standards, was fairly well socially controlled. "As the colonial period drew to a close, most Americans still held to the traditional view of drinking as a positive social and personal good" (Lender and Martin, 1987, p. 34).

High as alcohol consumption was at the turn of the eighteenth century, it actually rose significantly into the nineteenth—from 5.8 gallons of absolute alcohol per person age 15 and older per year in 1790 to 7.1 in 1830. Moreover, the proportion of the alcohol consumed in the form of distilled spirits, in contrast to beer and wine, was 40 percent in 1790, in 1830, it was 60 percent. Said one observer in 1814, "the quantity of ardent spirits" consumed in the United States at that time "surpasses belief." Drinking "had reached unparalleled levels." The notion "that alcohol was necessary for health remained firmly fixed. It was common to down a glass of whiskey or other spirits before breakfast . . . instead of taking coffee or tea breaks." Americans customarily took breaks at eleven and four for a few pulls on the jug. "Even school children took their sip of whiskey, the morning and afternoon glasses being considered 'absolutely indispensible to man and boy.'" Distilled spirits "were a basic part of the diet—most people thought that whiskey was as essential as bread." In the early nineteenth century, "the idea that the problem drinker could cause serious social disruption had occurred to relatively few people; drinking behavior, even when disruptive, remained largely a matter of individual choice" (Lender and Martin, 1987, pp. 46, 47, 53, 205).

Reacting to these apparent excesses, the temperance movement began to take shape. Perhaps the most influential of the early advocates of prohibition, who wrote when he was but a voice in the wilderness, was Benjamin Rush, Philadelphia physician, signer of the Declaration of Independence, surgeon general of the Continental Army, and author of *An Inquiry into the Effects of Ardent Spirits on the Human Mind and Body* (1784). Rush challenged the conventional view that drinking was an unmixed good. Rush did not condemn drinking per se, only heavy, uncontrolled drinking, nor did he condemn alcoholic beverages per se—his primary target was hard liquor. "Consumed in quantity over the years," he wrote, distilled spirits "could destroy a person's health and even cause death." Rush was the first scientist or physician to label alcoholism a disease characterized by progressively more serious stages; in addition, it was accompanied, he said, by addiction. Rush felt that community constraints on drinking in eighteenth-century America had broken down, destroying drinkers' lives, families, and ability to function as breadwinners and citizens.

Enter the Temperance Movement

Although he conveyed a powerful sense of urgency, Rush was not optimistic about reform. However, he had friends who were influential in religious affairs, and "he had sown the seeds of reform movements to come." The first temperance society was founded in 1808, and by 1811, the temperance movement, uniting a number of scattered and independent organizations, was formed. In 1826, the American Society for the Promotion of Temperance (later called the American Temperance Society) was founded. Initially, the society, like Dr. Rush, preached the gospel of moderation. It "helped organize local units, sent lecturers into the field, distributed literature (including Rush's *Inquiry*), and served as a clearinghouse for movement information." Within three years, more than 200 state and local antiliquor organizations were active. By 1830, temperance reform "constituted a burgeoning national movement" (Lender and Martin, 1987, p. 68).

By the 1830s, the adherents of total abstinence carried the day in the movement. The Temperance Society boasted 1.5 million members who proselytized righteously for their cause. Employers stopped supplying liquor on the job. Politicians ceased being so free and easy and "treating" their constituency and supporters to alcohol. An extremely effective tactic of the temperance movement was to influence local and county politicians to refuse granting licenses to taverns, undercutting major centers of heavy drinking. Although the movement lost some steam before and during the Civil War, while more pressing matters were settled, the 1870s and 1880s witnessed a rebirth of even prohibitionist activity.

Alcohol consumption plummeted between 1830 (7.1 gallons of absolute alcohol per person age 15 and older per year) and 1840 (3.1 gallons). Between 1850 and 1900, alcohol consumption remained, with decade-to-decade fluctuations, at about 2 gallons per year for every adult age 15 and older in the population; between 1901 and 1915, it was about 2.5, and between 1916 and 1920, when Prohibition began, just under two gallons (Lender and Martin, 1987, p. 205). Even before 1920, a number of states outlawed the sale of alcohol.

National Alcohol Prohibition (1920–1933)

The Volstead Act, bringing about a complete national prohibition of the sale of alcohol, was ratified in 1919, and took effect in 1920. After its passage, the author of the Volstead Act, Senator Morris Sheppard, representing the state of Texas, uttered the classic statement: "There is as much chance of repealing the Eighteenth Amendment as there is for a hummingbird to fly to the planet Mars with the Washington Monument tied to its tail." But by 1933, Prohibition had been declared a failure and was abandoned as a social experiment. (The Eighteenth Amendment is the only one ever to be repealed in American constitutional history.) What happened in the historically brief intervening fifteen years? More specifically, why was Prohibition regarded as a failure? What brought about its downfall? A number of factors have been suggested.

It must be realized that most alcohol prohibitionists were extremely naive both about the feasibility of enforcement and the impact the Volstead Act would have on drinking and on reducing the problems associated with drinking. Many Americans believed the law would automatically bring about a sharp reduction in drinking, compliance would be nearly universal, and drunkenness and its associated maladies would be a thing of the past. Billy Sunday, one of the most famous preachers of the time, delivered a sermon on the passage of the Eighteenth Amendment to an audience of 10,000 souls which declared: "The reign of tears is over. The slums will soon be a memory. We will turn our prisons into factories and our jails into storehouses and corncribs. Men will walk upright now, women will smile, and the children will laugh. Hell will be forever for rent" (Kobler, 1973, p. 12). Obviously, nothing like this took place. Prohibition is now regarded as a catastrophic failure. Why did it fail—and precisely in what ways did it fail?

Perhaps one of the best-known sociological explanations for the demise of Prohibition was that it was the outcome of a *status struggle*. Many forms of behavior that become criminalized pose no direct threat in any way to their practitioners, nor to the other members of a society. But they may be considered deviant by the self-righteous, morally indignant conventionals. The struggle between alcohol drinkers and Prohibitionists in the years before the passage of the Volstead Act can be looked at primarily as a struggle between status groups and lifestyles. Supporters of Prohibition were primarily rural dwellers, native-born members of native-born parentage, either white-collar, middle-class, or owners of farms, and overwhelmingly Protestant. Opponents of Prohibition were far more likely to be urban dwellers, immigrants or the sons and daughters of immigrants, manual laborers, and Catholic. "Prohibition stood as a symbol of the general system of ascetic behavior with which the Protestant middle classes had been identified" (Gusfield, 1963, p. 124).

A number of historical changes took place during the twentieth century that directly impinged upon the issue of alcohol and Prohibition. First, the old Protestant middle class suffered a serious decline in prestige as a social group. Second, urban dwellers, Catholics, the non-Anglo-Saxon ethnics, all secured far more political power than they had held previously. Third, the "new" middle class rose in numbers, in power, and in status. The urban cosmopolitan, college-educated, technically trained executive working for a nationally based corporation became the symbol of the middle class. The old-time locally based entrepreneur lost hold on the American consciousness as the model representative of the middle class. *And it was specifically this "new" middle class that abandoned abstinence and took to recreational drinking.* The Volstead Act was passed because abstinence was identified with a prestigious and powerful group in American society. Prohibition failed because it was the powerful, prestigious middle class that abandoned abstinence as a legitimate and respectable way of life. Temperance ceased to be necessary to a respectable life; its symbolic connection with respectability was severed. (Gusfield, 1963, pp. 111–138.)

A very different explanation is offered by another conflict perspective, Marxism. Some observers argue that the business elites in the late nineteenth and early twentieth centuries played a major role not only in Prohibition but also in its demise. Capitalists were major supporters of temperance movements, this line of reasoning goes, and exerted a major influence on Prohibition legislation because they believed that alcohol consumption produced bad workers. "Employers believed that workers who did not drink were usually more efficient, orderly, disciplined, easier to manage and control, and less likely to make trouble on the job than workers who did drink" (Levine, 1989, p. xi). Rather than seeing the cutting edge of the temperance movement steming from rural, conservative segments of society, this Marxist or "power elite" argument sees the supporters of Prohibition as being urban, well-educated, industrial, and northern (Rumbarger, 1989). "Wealthy businessmen supported Prohibition because they thought it would reduce crime and other social problems; make workers more efficient, productive and disciplined; and eliminate the saloon as a center of working-class social and political life. To many businessmen at the time, Prohibition seemed like a good deal" (Levine, 1985, p. 105). This same argument has been applied to the failure of Prohibition as well (Levine, 1983, 1985; Levine and Reinarman, 1992). The effects of Prohibition were clear. The law was "massively and openly violated"; this "raised a new specter: Prohibition, many came to believe, undermined respect for all law, including property law," which "frightened many of the rich and powerful. . . . Those with wealth and power increasingly supported repeal in part because they felt they needed to do something to raise public morale and show that the government was in some way responsive to popular pressure in a terrible depression." Prohibition was causing workers "to further distrust and resent government." As a result of the legalization of the sale of alcohol especially beer, workers "would feel better about government" and their minds would be taken "off their troubles" (Levine and Reinarman, 1992).

By the time repeal took place, the idea of Prohibition had become so unpopular that the population of no area of the country wanted to retain the Volstead Act. A study conducted in 1932 by a magazine of the time, the *Literary Digest*, found that adults favoring the retention of Prohibition ranged from a scant 19 percent in the populous, urban northern states of New York, New Jersey, and Pennsylvania to 41 percent in the rural Bible-belt southern states of Mississippi, Alabama, Tennessee, and Kentucky. Thirty-nine states actually voted on the repeal of the Prohibition in 1933. Repeal carried by three to one (15 million for, 5 million against). Again, as with the *Literary Digest* poll, in northern, urban, and heavily Catholic states of New York, New Jersey, and Rhode Island, repeal was chosen by more than 80 percent of the voters. But in rural, Protestant southern states like Alabama, Arkansas, and Tennessee, the vote was between 50 and 60 percent for repeal. Only in North and South Carolina did a majority vote to retain Prohibition.

Did Prohibition "Work"?

We've all learned that Prohibition was a catastrophic failure, perhaps the least successful effort to control behavior in the nation's history. Many of us even believe that alcohol consumption rose during this period—after all, we say, outlawing an activity will only encourage people to engage in it. In fact, the truth is exactly the opposite from this gem of conventional wisdom: All indications point to the fact that alcohol consumption declined significantly, although not drastically, during Prohibition, and rose once legal restrictions were lifted.

Of course, we do not have hard data on alcohol consumption between 1920 and 1933; since sales were illegal, no official record of them was kept. We must, therefore, make inferences about use by relying on more indirect indicators of alcohol consumption. One such indicator is the incidence of cirrhosis of the liver, which is very closely correlated with alcohol consumption in the population. The rate of death from cirrhosis of the liver remained between 12 and 17 per 100,000 in the population each year between 1900 and 1919. But it dropped to between 7 and 9 per 100,000 in the 1920s and early 1930s, a reduction of almost half. In the mid-1930s, it began it rise again (Grant, Noble, and Malin, 1986). By piecing together a number of different indicators, several observers (Levine and Reinarman, 1992; Rorabaugh, 1979; Warburton, 1932; Miron and Zweibel, 1991) place the alcohol consumption in the United States between the turn of the nineteenth century and the year before Prohibition took place (1920) at about

2.5 gallons per person age 15 and older—2.3 for 1905, 2.6 for 1910, and 2.4 for 1915. Estimates during Prohibition place it roughly at just under a gallon of alcohol (0.90) per person per year (Lender and Martin, 1987, p. 205).

Why do many people believe that drinking increased rather than decreased during Prohibition? That's not hard to answer: It's a much more entertaining and interesting story. We tend to focus on "speak-easies" and honky-tonks, jazz clubs, secret passwords, bathtub gin, silver hip flasks, Al Capone, gang warfare, corruption, payoffs, a few honest, crusading crime fighters—all of this is exciting stuff. It sticks in our minds. We tend to exaggerate the frequency of the unusual and underplay that of the routine, the everyday. We assume that most people were engaged in these exciting alcohol-related activities that we've heard so much about. People living in a given age often think nearly everyone who lived at a different time was engaged in that period's most memorable and noteworthy activities. In contrast, the truth about Prohibition is fairly unexciting. In general, most Americans did not drink during Prohibition, and those who did drank significantly less, and less often, than they did before or after.

However, before we conclude that Prohibition actually "worked" to reduce alcohol consumption, and that similar legal restrictions on currently illegal drugs are also working and should be retained, let us review both the other effects that Prohibition wrought and legal alternatives to outright prohibition.

For starters, making the sale of alcohol legally unavailable shifted consumption from less to more potent beverages (Morgan, 1991). Between 1900 and 1920, beer, a low-alcohol beverage, was the source of more than half the alcohol consumed in the United States; during Prohibition, the bulk of the alcohol consumed in this country shifted in the direction of distilled spirits, a beverage that contains between 40 and 50 percent alcohol. The reason is not hard to discern: It was much more profitable to sell and distribute illegal distilled spirits during Prohibition than beer. Beer is far bulkier, less easily stored, transported, and hidden, than distilled spirits. Moreover, large-scale beer bottling and refrigeration developed only in the 1930s, after repeal (Levine and Reinarman, 1992); in the 1920s, beer spoiled quickly, while distilled spirits could be stored indefinitely. Thus, distilled spirits distributed illegally, in far greater volume than beer, and were far more widely available; hence, drinking habits shifted from the less to the more potent beverage. In addition, the consumption of wine, two to three times as potent as beer, also increased during Prohibition. As a result, even though less absolute alcohol was drunk between 1920 and 1933, greater volumes of more potent and potentially dangerous substances were consumed.

Second, during Prohibition, more toxic, adulterated, contaminated, and dangerous substances were consumed as a substitute for ethyl alcohol, often with disastrous consequences. Morgan (1991) cites the example of a medicinal tonic, "Jake," a Jamaica ginger extract containing 75 percent alcohol, marketed and sold to skirt the Prohibition laws. In 1930, some half a million two-ounce bottles of this substance were shipped a month. In January and February 1930, a new and improved "Jake" was formulated and sold; by March, in the cities in which this product was sold, 50,000 people were found to have been permanently paralyzed by the adulterant, tricresyl phosphate (TCP); "Jake" was found to have been responsible. No history of Prohibition is complete without a consideration of the more harmful substances that were consumed as substitutes for ethyl alcohol.

And third, as we all know, organized crime received a huge boost from Prohibition. The sale of illegal alcohol proved to be the major source of revenue for high-level gangsters during the 1920s; this entrenched their power in the nation's largest cities as no other single legal change has ever done. However, as Levine and Reinarman point out, although organized crime was heavily involved with the distribution of alcoholic beverages during Prohibition, much, perhaps most, of the volume of alcohol produced, distributed, and consumed at that time originated from small-scale operations. Family wineries and stills, self-certified priests, rabbis, and ministers, distributing "sacramental wine," station wagons, as well as lobster boats, pleasure boats, and fishing boats taking trips to Canada, prescriptions containing alcohol written by physicians and sold by pharmacies, over-the-counter concoctions with a high alcohol content—these were the major sources of beverages contaning alcohol during Prohibition, at least outside the major cities. It is entirely possible that Prohibition actually "decentralized and democratized [alcohol] production and distribution"; as a general rule, prohibitionist policies "increase the number and types of people involved in illicit production and distribution" (Levine and Reinarman, 1992).

What Is the Lesson of Prohibition?

What is the lesson of Prohibition? The small reduction in alcohol consumption was clearly bought at an extremely high price. The latest Gallup Poll (1994) indicates that only one American in five (21 percent) favors a return to national alcohol prohibition. Not only are the side-effects of this policy too costly, but experience shows us that less repressive alternative policies may work even better. During Prohibition, the liquor industry was completely unregulated. Its representatives "sold whatever they wanted, to whomever they wanted, at whatever price they wanted. They decorated as they wished, provided whatever food or entertainment they wished. Producers made alcohol in any strength they wanted, in any way they wanted." They were "not regulated by any government agency. During Prohibition, the liquor industry was probably the freest large industry in America" (Levine and Reinarman, 1992).

At the very end of Prohibition, a plan for alcohol control was laid out in the so-called "Rockefeller Report," *Toward Liquor Control*, by Raymond Fosdick and Albert Scott (1933). This report offered two alternative proposals for state control of the sale and distribution of alcoholic beverages—government-owned liquor stores and a licensing system. For both plans, it was proposed, state agencies would have jurisdiction over matters pertaining to the sale of alcoholic beverages. For instance, control laws attempted to moderate drinking by specifying, for on-premises establishments, such matters as the distance of an establishment to a church or a school, how many feet of kitchen space and how many food preparation workers it must have, number and location of entrances, times of the day and days of the week during which sales may take place, whether customers may sit at a long bar or must sit in booths or at tables, the ratio of chair seating to bar seating, and so on (Levine, 1983, 1985; Levine and Reinarman, 1992). For the most part, such restrictions are obeyed, since a liquor license tends to be extremely profitable, and are not seen by customers as unduly restrictive.

Such controls, some believe, kept alcohol consumption at a fairly low level following Prohibition; moreover, their impact, according to some observers, shows that when psychoactive substances are legal but controlled, their use will tend to be moderate, and their sale will not be associated with the damaging side-effects that criminalization causes—such as organized crime, gangland killings, the consumption of harmful adulterated, or more potent, substitutes. The lesson of Prohibition, some say, is that criminalization is harmful to society; in contrast, decriminalization *with* government controls, they say, works to keep substance abuse a "domesticated" public phenomenon, under surveillance, and in check (Levine and Reinarman, 1992).

Alcohol Consumption Today

Today, Americans age 14 or older consume an average of 2.3 gallons of absolute alcohol per person per year, according to the National Institute for Alcohol Abuse and Alcoholism (Williams, Clem, and Dufor, 1994, p. 15). This is a fairly "hard" or reliable statistic because it is based on sales and not simply what people *say* they drink. This figure is called "apparent" alcohol consumption, because not every drop of the alcohol that is purchased is actually drunk during a given year; some of it may just sit on a shelf for years. Moreover, some of the alcohol that is consumed may be purchased abroad, some may be manufactured at home or by "moonshiners," and thus, will not be legally recorded. Still, the figures on alcohol sales are very close to actual consumption levels. In any case, 2.3 gallons of absolute alcohol per year works out to just under 1 ounce of absolute alcohol per person age 14 or older per day. Of course, some people drink a lot more than this, some less, and some not at all. Roughly one-third of all Americans are more or less total abstainers. Thus it makes sense to tabulate the quantity of alcohol consumed specifically *for drinkers*, and leave abstainers out of the picture altogether. Adult drinkers consume about 1.5 ounces of absolute alcohol per day. This represents three 12-ounce bottles or cans of beer *or* three eight-ounce glasses of wine *or* three drinks of hard liquor per day for every drinking adolescent and adult in the country.

Sometime between roughly 1980 and about 1990, the American population became somewhat more moderate in its use of psychoactive substances: We saw earlier that the use of illegal drugs declined significantly between 1979 and 1990. More or less the same has been true of the use of alcohol. (The difference: Most forms of illegal drug use have risen since the early 1990s, whereas alcohol consumption continues to decline.) The use of alcohol rose, with some fluctuation, from the end of Prohibition, in 1933, (an average of 0.97 gallons of absolute alcohol per person was purchased in 1934) to 1980 (2.76 gallons) and, as we saw, declined after that. It is likely that this downward trend will continue for the foreseeable future.

Recorded yearly alcohol sales can be backed up with information on the proportion of the American population who say they drink. Every year or so, the Gallup Poll asks a sample of Americans the following question: "Do you have occasion to use alcoholic beverages such as liquor, wine, or beer, or are you a total abstainer?" This question was first asked in 1939, when 58 percent defined themselves as drinkers, 42 percent as abstainers. In 1947, 63 percent said that they drank; the percentage rose steadily throughout the 1950s and 1960s, and reached a peak of 71 percent in 1976 and 1978. Today, just under two-thirds of Gallup's sample (65 percent) say that they "have occasion to use alcoholic beverages." The Health and Human Services National Household Survey I cited so often in the chapter on drugs (Health and Human Services, 1994a, 1994b) also contains information on alcohol consumption. The questions the National Household Survey asks are a bit different from Gallup's; they are more specific about the time periods in which the alcohol consumption took place, that is, has the respondent *ever* drunk alcohol, drank it within the past *year* and within the past *month*. There has been a noticeable decline in self-reported alcohol consumption between 1985 and 1993 for all ages. The fact that the self-report figures on alcohol consumption corroborate the sales figures lends confidence to their validity.

For youths aged 12 to 17, between 1979 and 1985, the proportion who had *ever* taken a drink dropped from to 70 to 55 percent; by 1993, this had dropped again to 41 percent. For those who drank in the past *30 days*, the figure stood at 37 percent; in 1985, it was 31 percent, and in 1993, only 18 percent. For young adults age 18 to 25, the corresponding "ever" figures declined from 95 to 92 to 87 percent, and the corresponding "30 day" figure, from 76 to 71 to 59 percent. Clearly, then, the National Household Survey, like the sales figures, shows a significant decline in alcohol consumption during the 1980s and into the 1990s. The trend must be regarded as real and not the artifact of one particular study or measuring device.

One significant development that influenced this trend is the fact that by the late 1980s, all states in the United States (except Louisiana) had instituted a 21-year-old drinking age, while in 1979, only fourteen had such a law. Although conventional wisdom says that young people will find a way to drink in spite of legal restrictions (Ravo, 1987), the same fallacy applies here as to the claims that Prohibition produced a rise in the use of alcohol: When legal controls exist and are enforced, drinking will decline significantly; although many will break the law, enough will comply to bring down the average level of alcohol consumption significantly. According to one study, a year after New York State raised its drinking age to 21, alcohol purchases among 16- to 20-year-olds declined by 50 percent and use itself declined by 21 percent. When the legal age was 18, 25 percent of 17-year-olds, and 20 percent of 16-year-olds said that they had purchased alcohol during the previous month. When the drinking age was raised to 21, more than a quarter of the 19- and 20-year-olds surveyed said that they had purchased alcohol within the last month; but only 9 percent of the 18-year-olds, 14 percent of the 17-year-olds, and 6 percent of the 16-year-olds said that they had done so. The same systematic tendency toward a decline prevailed for use and, other studies indicate, the same pattern holds for the country generally (Kolbert, 1987).

In short, the claim that under 21-year-olds are drinking at least as much as, if not more than, they did since the 21-year-old drinking age limit was imposed is not born out by the evidence. The annual high school survey conducted by the University of Michigan's Institute for Social Research verifies what other systematic studies tell us. The annual prevalence for alcohol for high school seniors stood at 88 percent in 1979; in 1995, it was 74 percent. The 30-day prevalence was 72 percent in 1979 and by 1995, it was 51 percent. For the study's college subsample, the annual prevalence dropped only 4 percentage points between 1980 (when the first survey of college students was conducted) and 1993—91 versus 87 percent—but the decline in the 30-day prevalence was a bit more substantial, from 82 to 72 percent (Johnston, O'Malley, and Bachman, 1994a, 1994b, 1995). Given the weight of the evidence, it seems foolish to deny the decline in alcohol consumption by adolescents and young adults—indeed, for the population as a whole—in the past half-generation or so.

However, the under-21 drinking law does not affect the 21-and-over crowd, and yet during the period after 1980, there were also declines in alcohol consumption of the population as a whole. The simple fact is that fewer people are drinking today than was true a decade or two ago, and among those who drink, a higher proportion are drinking less when they do drink, and less frequently as well. The same pattern prevails with drinking as with illicit drugs: Fewer Americans are using psychoactive drugs nowadays than they were a generation ago. But why is this happening? Why the decline in both legal and illegal drug use—why the decline in psychoactive drug use generally? A number of reasons have been suggested: an increased awareness of the risks that drug use, alcohol included, entails; the trend toward health and fitness; the more generally conservative political and social climate. These explanations do not apply only to the United States, as the National Institute on Alcohol Abuse and Alcoholism pointed out in its latest report, *Alcohol and Health*, the same downward trend we see in the United States is also true of Canada and Western Europe generally.

The decline in drinking in the population generally, and for teenagers specifically, along with stricter law enforcement with respect to drinking and driving, have translated into a significant decline in alcohol-related deaths in auto accidents. The National Highway Traffic Safety Administration estimated, as I said above, that a significantly lower percentage of all drivers in a fatal automobile accident today have a BAL of .10 or higher than was true 10 or 20 years ago. In 1982, the administration estimated, 16,790 drunk drivers were involved in fatal crashes, whereas the figure for 1985, with more total cars on the road, was 14,650. A survey by Louis Harris in 1983 found that 32 percent of those questioned said that they had driven a car after drinking during the past year; by 1986, this figure had declined to 26 percent. In Minnesota, random roadside checks indicated that roughly 5 percent of all drivers on the road at night were legally drunk in 1976; in 1986, the figure was 2.5 percent. In that same state, in 1976, only 14,000 drivers lost their licenses in connection with alcohol-related offenses; in 1986, the figure was more than 45,000. Clearly, the result of increased police enforcement of the drunk-driving laws has been to reduce the number and proportion of drunks on the road, and consequently, alcohol-related deaths. However, such actions have mainly had an impact on the more moderate social drinkers. Heavy drinkers and alcoholics are undeterred by the crack-down; as a result, a higher proportion of alcoholics are now being arrested on the road than in the past. Said a Maine highway official, "We're getting into the hard-core alcoholics now. Before, they bagged social drinkers, and the heavy drinkers got by. . . . Now that social drinkers aren't out there, the alcoholics are getting caught" (Malcolm, 1987).

WHO DRINKS? WHO DOESN'T?

Just as interesting as the overall figures on alcohol consumption and their changes over time is the group-to-group variation in drinking. Who drinks and who doesn't? Are certain groups or categories significantly and consistently more likely to drink than others?

There are at least two crucial measures of alcohol consumption: drinking at all, and drinking to excess. Drinking varies dramatically from one category in the population to another; likewise, drinking heavily, compulsively, and abusively—that is, to excess—likewise varies along sociological lines. We might expect that categories in the population that have a high proportion of drinkers (and, contrarily, a low proportion of abstainers) would also rank high in the likelihood that their members are alcoholics, that is, drink to excess. The opposite side of the coin should be expected as well: The lower the proportion of drinkers in a social category, the lower the likelihood that the members of that category will be abusive drinkers. This is not always the case, however; some groups in the population have extraordinarily high proportions of drinkers but low proportions of alcoholics, while other groups are more likely to abstain, but its drinkers are more likely to drink compulsively and abusively (Armor, Polich, and Stambul, 1976). Let's see how this relationship works with one dimension, social class or socioeconomic status (SES), which is usually measured by income, occupation, and/or education. SES demonstrates an extremely complicated relationship with drinking.

As a general rule, in the Western world, including the United States, the higher the social class or SES, the *greater* the likelihood of drinking at all: As we've seen, the Gallup Poll asks a question on whether respondents "have occasion" to use alcohol. In 1994, more college graduates (80 percent) said that they had than respondents with no college at all (58 percent). In a like fashion, respon-

dents living in households with an income of $75,000 and over were significantly more likely to "have occasion" to drink alcoholic beverages (85 percent) than those living in households with incomes of under $20,000 (54 percent). A considerably higher proportion of respondents in the Gallup Poll with some education beyond college said that they drank an alcoholic beverage in the last 24 hours (48 percent) than was true of respondents with no college education (27 percent). Clearly, then, drinking, and drinking regularly, is strongly related to education. The same applies to income: Nearly half of the Gallup Poll respondents with incomes $75,000 and higher said that they drank in the past day (45 percent), while only a fifth of those with an income under $20,000 (18 percent) said so. Clearly, then, there is a strong and powerful correlation between drinking and education, drinking and income, drinking and social class in general. The higher the SES the greater the chances that someone will drink.

However, this relationship makes an interesting flip-flop when it comes to drinking *to excess* or *getting into trouble* as a result of drinking. When these same respondents were asked, if they planned to "cut down or quit drinking within the next year," between twice and three times the proportion of less educated (33 percent) and lower income respondents (34 percent) said yes than was true of more educated (15 percent) and higher income respondents (12 percent). When they were asked, "Has drinking ever been a cause of trouble in your family?" the same pattern was revealed: A higher proportion of the less educated (30 percent) and lower income (31 percent) said yes than was true of the more educated (20 percent) and higher income (17 percent) categories. Clearly, while high-SES people are more likely to drink, they are also less likely to get into trouble for drinking, while for lower-SES individuals, the reverse is true.

Also interesting: Support for "a law forbidding the sale" of all alcoholic beverages "throughout the nation"—in short, a return to Prohibition—varies *inversely* by education and income. The higher the level of education and income, the lower the support for Prohibition; the lower the level of education and income, the higher the support for Prohibition. In Gallup's 1994 poll, only 7 percent of the respondents with a postgraduate education favored a national law forbidding the sale of alcoholic beverages, but 25 percent of those with no college education did so. Likewise, only 5 percent of respondents earning $75,000 and over favored such a law, while 29 percent of the respondents who earned under $20,000 did so. (These figures were not presented in the 1994 edition of *The Gallup Poll*; I would like to thank Maura Strausberg of the Gallup organization for granting me access to them.)

The Catholic-Protestant difference in drinking tends to be large nationally. (Although much of the difference is a product of factors that correlate with religion, such as region, race, and rural-urban residence.) In the Louis Harris poll (Armor, Polich, and Stambul, 1976, pp. 53–62), 42 percent of the Protestants were total abstainers, nearly twice as high a figure as for the Catholic respondents (22 percent). This statistic was also backed up by the Gallup Poll: 60 percent of Protestants said that they drank, and 78 percent of Catholics did so. The majority of Southern Baptists, a highly abstemious denomination, said that they were abstainers—only 45 percent drank at all. However, interestingly, Southern Baptists were also more likely to get into trouble for drinking, possibly indicating a lower degree of acceptance of any level of drinking whatsoever in the Southern Baptist milieu.

Gender or sex, too, correlates strongly with drinking. In fact, of all variables, perhaps gender correlates most strongly with alcohol consumption. Men are consistently more likely to drink than women, and men drink more when they do drink. In the 1994 Gallup Poll, more men (70 percent) than women (61 percent) said that they "had occasion" to drink alcoholic beverages. But, even more strikingly, the proportion of regular, or daily to almost daily drinkers among men is twice that among women—33 versus 17 percent.

Age, too, is strongly correlated with drinking. In the National Household Survey, only 18 percent of the 12- to 18-year-olds said that they drank within the past month; this shot up to 59 percent for the young adults age 18 to 25; increased only slightly for the 26- to 34-year-olds (63 percent); and it decreased somewhat for the older adults 35 and older (49 percent). Other studies show that drinking peaks in the late 20s—age 25 to 29—and declines slowly throughout middle age, and declines fairly steeply into old age.

Drinking's correlation with race and ethnicity has been studied extensively and in detail, and clear-cut differences among groups remain in spite of generations of assimilation (Greeley, McCready, and Theisen, 1980; Cahalan and Room, 1974;

Health and Human Services, 1987a, pp. 18–20; Health Education, and Welfare, 1971, pp. 23–25). Consistently, individuals of the following ethnic backgrounds are highly likely to drink: Irish, Italians, Jews, northern WASPs (White Anglo-Saxon Protestants), Slavs, Scandinavians, and Germans. Members of the following ethnic groups are more likely to be abstainers and not drink at all: Blacks, Latins, Southern WASPs, and Asians.

Among all ethnic groups, the Irish rank near the top in their likelihood of drinking a great deal, and getting into trouble when they do drink. In one study (Health, Education, and Welfare, 1971), fully a third of individuals with an Irish-born father were defined as heavy drinkers, far higher than the proportions of any other category. In another study (Greeley, McCready, and Theilson, 1980, pp. 9–10), Irish-Americans were most likely to drink two or more times per week (42 percent versus 15 percent for Italians and Jews and 24 percent for WASPs), and most likely to drink three or more drinks at a sitting (33 percent versus 11 percent for Jews, 14 percent for Italians, and 24 percent for WASPs). Another study (Cahalan and Room, 1974) devised several measures of heavy drinking and getting into trouble as a result of drinking. Jews were extremely unlikely not to drink at all (only 8 percent were abstainers), but they were also extremely unlikely to drink heavily or to get into trouble as a result of drinking. Irish and Italian Catholics had almost exactly the same proportion of drinkers (only 4 and 5 percent abstainers respectively). But Irish-Americans were far more likely to drink heavily and to get into trouble when they drank (Cahalan and Room, 1974, p. 101). Clearly, some alcohol-related aspect of Irish culture seems to be preserved even after several generations of residence in the United States. In a survey of 22 countries by the Gallup organization, a majority of the Irish surveyed (51 percent) answered yes to the question "Do you sometimes drink more than you think you should?" The average for respondents from all countries was 29 percent, and it was 32 percent for residents of the United States.

ALCOHOLISM

When asked how many alcoholics there are in the United States, researcher Michael Hilton (1989) offers three entirely different answers. The first answer he gives is: "I can't answer your question because it is based on a false premise." The question assumes that alcoholism is a condition that one has or doesn't have, and that the population can readily be divided into alcoholics and nonalcoholics. Alcoholism is both made up of a series of dimensions and a continuum, and at no point can we accurately and unambiguously separate the sheep from the goats.

The second answer Hilton gives is that the alcoholic is chemically and behaviorally dependent on alcohol; if an individual answers yes to three or more out of 13 questions about alcohol dependence, he or she can be said to be an alcoholic—or at least, a "problem drinker." According to this criterion, 8.2 million Americans (5.7 million men and 2.5 million women) are alcoholics. But if he had made the definition more restrictive and decided that four or more items on this scale defined the alcoholic, then only 5.2 million would have been so designated; if he had made it less restrictive and used two or more items to define the alcoholic, 13 million would have been so designated. "The point is that any estimate I give you depends on where I draw the line" (Hilton, 1989, p. 459).

The third answer he gives is that there are 10.4 million alcoholics in the United States, since that is the estimate given by the National Institute on Alcohol Abuse and Alcoholism.

The field's inability to pin down the number of alcoholics in the United States underlines the socially defined nature of all social phenomena, emphasizes the yawning chasm between how experts see a field and how the general public sees it, and stresses the controversial nature of the field of alcoholism research. It should be mentioned that the fourth edition of the American Psychiatric Association's *Diagnostic and Statistical Manual of Mental Disorders*, or DSM-IV (1994), does not even mention *alcoholism* at all; instead, the relevant alcohol use disorders discussed are "alcohol dependence" and "alcohol abuse," presumably, categories that are a bit easier to pin down.

The writings and research on alcoholism are controversial, contradictory, and confusing. Most of the major and pressing questions as yet have no definitive answers. Is alcoholism a disease? Can recovered or recovering alcoholics drink in a moderate, controlled fashion? On what criteria should a definition of alcoholism be based? Can the cause of alcoholism be located primarily in the substance, alcohol itself, or in the characteristics of the drinker? Is biological make-up a major component

in the etiology of alcoholism? For any imaginable answer to these questions, there are fervent supporters and critics. Very little is conclusively agreed upon in this field.

Alcoholism: Four Commonly Used Definitions

There are four common definitions of or criteria for alcoholism (Schuckit, 1985, p. 5). First, the *quantity* and *frequency* of alcohol consumed (DeLindt and Schmidt, 1971): Alcoholics are individuals who drink a substantial quantity of alcohol over a period of time. Second, *psychological dependence* (see the essays in Blane and Leonard, 1987): Someone is an alcoholic if he or she "needs" alcohol psychologically, cannot function without it, suffers extreme discomfort and anxiety if deprived of it under specific circumstances. Third, *physical dependence:* Someone is an alcoholic to the extent that he or she would suffer *withdrawal symptoms* upon discontinuation of drinking (Mendelson and Mello, 1985, pp. 265–269). And fourth, the life-problems definition (Schuckit, 1984): Whoever drinks and incurs "serious life difficulties" as a consequence—divorce, being fired from a job, being arrested, facing community censure, harming one's health, being accident-prone, and so on—and continues to drink in spite of it, is an alcoholic.

Each of these definitions poses serious problems, and has been criticized for its deficiencies.

Defining alcoholism by the quantity of alcohol consumed, say, 15 centiliters, or about five ounces per day, has the drawback that the same amount of alcohol may be relatively innocuous for one person (a healthy 28-year-old) but harmful to another (an ill 68-year-old). Further, someone may drink no alcohol at all, but have the potential for developing a pattern of heavy consumption subsequent to taking up drinking. Is this individual to be regarded as exactly the same animal with respect to alcohol as the abstainer whose potential alcohol experience is likely to be positive and moderate? And lastly, some drinkers consume alcohol in binges; they drink heavily for two or three weeks, or a month, abstain for weeks at a time, and then, once again, begin drinking for a time. Their yearly average may not appear to be excessive, but when examined closely, their pattern of consumption qualifies them as alcoholics.

Psychological dependence has been criticized

for being vague and difficult to test. Questions supposedly tapping the "signs" of alcoholism include "Do your friends drink less alcohol than you do?" "Do you drink to lose shyness and build self-confidence?" "Do you occasionally drink heavily after a disappointment, a quarrel, or when the boss gives you a hard time?" "Are there certain occasions when you feel uncomfortable if alcohol is not available?" A yes answer to these and similar questions is supposedly a sign that one is dependent on alcohol—and therefore an alcoholic. The problem is that many moderate drinkers could also give a yes answer to such questions. Psychological dependence on alcohol is extremely difficult to pin down; in the words of one expert, "determination of this attribute is very subjective" (Schuckit, 1985, p. 5).

The physical dependence or withdrawal criterion of alcoholism is an absolutely certain sign of the condition—but it is far too restrictive. Indeed, anyone who is physically dependent on alcohol must be regarded as an alcoholic by any reasonable definition, but many other drinkers who would also be called alcoholics are not physically dependent on the drug. The physical dependence criterion is far too narrow and limited to be useful.

The life-problems definition is dubious because it is contingent on the nature of one's social milieu, as we saw in the previous section. In some areas, one can get into a great deal of trouble with an extremely moderate amount of alcohol consumption, as for example, in contemporary Iran or in a fundamentalist Christian community. On the other hand, many communities and cultures worldwide tolerate extremely high levels of alcohol consumption, and "cushion" the drinker from many serious problems and consequences that drinking may entail elsewhere. Moreover, medical complications consequent to high levels of drinking appear on a statistical, rather than an absolute basis. Not all heavy drinkers develop cirrhosis of the liver; is one who does an alcoholic and one who drinks just as much, but doesn't contract the disease, not an alcoholic?

Alcoholism is one of those phenomena that is difficult to define, but most experts would say that they "know one when they see one." The four above criteria overlap in practice; most drinkers encompassed by one definition will also be encompassed by at least one of the others. A clear, reliable, and valid definition is far more important for theoretical purposes than for practical or clinical reasons.

Can Alcoholics Learn to Drink Moderately?

Perhaps the bitterest controversy in the field of alcohol research in the last decade has been the question of whether or not recovered or recovering alcoholics can drink in moderation after treatment. The controversy has, in fact, spilled over into the courts and scientific review panels in both Canada and the United States, as one team of researchers accused other investigators of scientific fraud, and filed a $96 million lawsuit against them for their study and its results. While the lawsuit and the charges of fraud were dropped or dismissed (Maltby, 1982; Boffey, 1982, 1984), the debate rages on.

On one side of the controversy stand researchers who argue that formerly heavy drinkers and problem drinkers, and even a substantial proportion of victims of severe alcoholism, can learn to drink sensibly, in moderation, and in a controlled fashion. Uncontrolled, heavy, damaging drinking, they contend, is a *reversible behavioral disorder;* behavior that is learned can be unlearned, at least, in a substantial proportion of cases. These researchers do not claim that all alcoholics can drink moderately—some say one in ten, others say a majority—but that controlled drinking is not only possible, but a feasible long-term treatment goal for many alcoholics. This approach is especially likely to be endorsed in Europe (Boffey, 1983; Heather and Robertson, 1981) and in Canada (Sobell and Sobell, 1978, 1984), although a few American researchers accept it as well (Armor, Polich, and Stampul, 1976; Polich, Armor, and Braiker, 1980).

On the other side, the more traditional and orthodox approach, and the one most likely to be adopted in the United States, is that alcoholics are incapable of drinking in a controlled, moderate fashion; the only possible alternative is total abstinence (Pendery, Maltzman, and West, 1982). Alcoholism, say the advocates of this position, is an *irreversible disease;* the alcoholic is sick, and *cannot* return to drinking. The National Institute on Alcohol Abuse and Alcoholism (NIAAA) has consistently adhered to the view that "abstinence is the appropriate goal of alcohol treatment." In a 1981 report to Congress, the NIAAA stated that "while a substantial minority of alcoholics are capable of engaging in controlled drinking for a short period of time, it is difficult to predict in advance who they are and it is not likely that they can control their drinking over the long run" (Boffey, 1983, p. C7).

The abstinence-only school argues that studies showing the possibility of controlled drinking are flawed because they rely on self-reports of drinking by alcoholics, who lie notoriously about their alcohol consumption; they select heavy drinkers and problem drinkers, but not true alcoholics as subjects (so-called gamma, or physically dependent alcoholics); they do not use a long enough follow-up period to determine whether their subjects have relapsed into dangerous drinking behavior; they have been careless about following up their subjects and often fail to record the disastrous lives these individuals are leading, even the fact that some of their subjects have died of alcoholism. (Pendery, Maltzman, and West, 1982, summarize most of these points.) These objections, say the abstinence-only faction, render misleading, indeed, valueless, the results of studies showing that controlled drinking is possible.

Some of these objections are valid for some of the controlled-drinking studies that have been conducted. However, enough such studies have been done without these flaws to make it clear that some alcoholics can drink in a moderate, controlled, nonproblem fashion. The only question is the size of this category. Is it one in 10, as a report by the National Academy of Sciences suggested in 1980? Or six out of 10, as others argue? (Boffey, 1983, summarizes several of these studies.) Perhaps future research will yield better data than we have today.

In one study, alcoholics were studied four years after their release from a variety of federal treatment programs. These programs were not geared specifically toward training recovered alcoholics to drink sensibly, so its results must be taken as a conservative estimate. More than half of the nearly 1,000 subjects in the study (54 percent) were still drinking heavily enough to be considered problem drinkers. More than a quarter (28 percent) had abstained completely from alcohol during the six months prior to the study, and thus fit the "abstention-only" model. The remainder, a bit less than a fifth (18 percent), were drinking in a more or less moderate or "nonproblem" fashion, half drinking an average of 3 ounces of absolute alcohol per day; the other half, less than 2 ounces per day (Polich, Armor, and Braiker, 1980, p. 51).

Abandoning the "abstention-only" model for

treated alcoholics—even if they constitute only a substantial minority—represents something of a revolution in thinking about the subject. If the notion of the alcoholic's inevitable "irreversible impairment" when drinking has to be abandoned, then the very idea of alcoholism as a disease must also be questioned, and the notion of alcoholism as a modifiable behavior has to be introduced (Heather and Robertson, 1981, pp. 247–248). Given the fundamental systems of thought on which these two assumptions are based—the medical model and the learning-theory model of alcoholism—it is likely that this controversy will be with us for some time to come.

SUMMARY

Objectively speaking, alcohol is a drug; it is psychoactive, it is taken for its effects on the mind, it is physically and psychologically addictive, and it can cause a lethal overdose. In fact, again, judging strictly on the basis of objectivistic criteria, alcohol (along with tobacco cigarettes) represents this society's most serious drug problem. But *subjectively*, alcohol is not a drug at all, that is, its possession and sale are legal and it is not *regarded* as a drug by much of the public. Although alcohol is a legal substance and its use conventional in most quarters, its use is deviant under certain circumstances: Its heavy use is condemned, its use at all is against the law under some conditions, and in some social circles, regarded as non-normative as well. Hence, its study in a course on deviance is important. The use of alcohol dates back thousands, possibly tens of thousands, of years—longer ago than the fashioning of metals. Nearly every society on earth makes use of alcohol; at the same time, the way it is used varies from one society to another. In some societies, its use has become a serious problem; in others, moderation is overwhelmingly the rule.

Alcohol's effects are closely related to the concentration of alcohol in the bloodstream. Perhaps its most well-known effect is discoordination, which results in a substantial increase in the likelihood of an accident and death while engaged in a wide range of activities. Violence, too, is associated with intoxication, although the causal dynamics here are not altogether clear.

In North America, the use of alcohol stretches

back to the earliest days of human habitation. The Indians who greeted Columbus brewed and drank beer. The Puritans brought ample supplies of beer, wine, and distilled spirits to this continent in their sailing ships. Drinking in colonial America was substantial; in 1790, when records were first kept, the per capita consumption of alcohol was over twice as high as is true today. Alcohol consumption actually increased into the early years of the ninteenth century. However, by then, the temperance movement had begun to lobby for moderation, and later, abstinence, and its efforts helped to bring alcohol consumption to much lower levels by the time Prohibition took effect in 1920. In spite of public mythology, indirect evidence suggests that alcohol consumption actually declined substantially during Prohibition. However, it did have some extremely noxious effects, including a shift to more potent beverages, some deaths and medical harm from ingesting poisonous alcohol substitutes, and providing organized crime with a lucrative enterprise. With the decline of power of rural, native-born White Anglo-Saxon Protestants and the rise of social and ethnic groups and categories who supported repeal, Prohibition was terminated in 1933. In the years immediately following Prohibition, drinking was moderate, but it increased gradually until roughly 1980, where it stood at 2.76 gallons of absolute alcohol for the American population age 14 and older. Since 1980, the use of alcohol has been declining on a year-by-year basis; it now stands at about 2.3 gallons per year per teenager or adult. Though some observers claim that the 21-year-and-older law has stimulated drinking among teenagers, the evidence suggests lower teenage alcohol use after the law than before. Drunk driving and auto fatalities under the influence have decreased as well, both for teenagers and for the population as a whole.

The consumption of alcohol is distributed unevenly in the population, with some groups and categories drinking significantly more than others. As a general rule, drinking is *positively* related to social class or socioeconomic status (SES)—the higher the level of income, education, and occupational prestige, the greater the likelihood that someone will drink. However, though upper SES persons tend to drink, they are highly likely to do so moderately. The lower the SES, the lower the likelihood that someone will drink, but the higher the likelihood that he or she will drink heavily and abusively. Catholics are more likely to drink than Protestants; Jews and persons of Italian descent are more likely to drink than most other ethnic groups—but they usually drink moderately. Irish-Americans are both more likely to drink than other ethnic categories, but also to do so heavily. African-Americans are statistically much more likely than whites to be abstainers. Men are more likely to drink than women and men who drink, have a higher likelihood of doing so in greater volume. Of all age groups, young adults under the age of 35 are most likely to drink; the likelihood of drinking declines with age.

Alcoholism seems not to be susceptible to a widely agreed upon definition; instead, experts in the field have provided at least four, based on *quantity* and *frequency* of alcohol consumed; *psychological dependence*; physical dependence; and whether the drinker experiences *serious life difficulties* as a result of consuming alcohol. A sharp, protracted controversy continues over whether alcoholics can learn to drink moderately and nondestructively. One side argues that alcohol is a reversible behavior disorder and that a substantial proportion can unlearn their alcohol habits and drink sanely and noncompulsively. The other side (the "abstinence-only" school) argues that true alcoholics are incapable of drinking wisely; for them, true abstinence is the only acceptable treatment.

ACCOUNT: ALCOHOLISM

The contributor of this account is an electrician in his forties.

I started drinking when I was about 12. I used to go out with a bunch of other guys and we'd find some wino from the neighborhood and we'd give him a half a dollar and have him go into a store and get four or five quarts of beer. Then we'd go to the park and we'd drink there. Most of the guys, when they'd fill up, they'd leave and go home. But with me and maybe one or two other guys, if there was something left, we'd drink it up. Or if it was gone, I'd try to go out and get some more. Most of the time I'd get drunk. I'd do this at least once-twice a week, usually more. My whole social life was drinking. I'd just hang around guys who drank. Or I'd be with girls who had baby-sitting jobs. I'd go with them and drink the booze that was around the house. During this time, I'd black out quite a bit. Later, the next day or something, I'd be told the funny and not-so-funny things I did when I was drunk—and I wouldn't even remember. I'd climb a pole or a tree, or I'd wind up getting in a fight, or getting nasty, and I wouldn't remember any of it. I didn't know it at the time, but I was having blackouts.

When I was 16, I forged my birth certificate and I enlisted in the Army. They found out after four months and I got a minority discharge. Right after my discharge, I got drunk one night and stole a car. I wasn't aware of stealing the car. In fact, I wasn't even aware I was in a car. I woke up when I smashed into the rear end of a police car waiting for a red light. The cops got out and asked me for my license and registration. I didn't have it. No license, no registration, I was driving a stolen car, and I had smashed into a police car. They put me in a juvenile detention home for three or four weeks. When I turned 17, I enlisted in the Air Force for four years.

For most of the time I was in the Air Force, I'd drink whenever I could. I drank a lot. The booze was plentiful. I'd drink maybe four-five times a week, probably. Like a fifth of Seagram's or if it was beer, maybe twenty-four bottles or cans. I'd drink from five in the afternoon to two or three in the morning. I used to get in a lot of fights. I got one court-martial. I drank like that until the age of 25. Basically I was a periodic drinker for most of this time. I'd drink for four or five weeks, and then I'd quit for a week, and then I'd drink again. During this time, I got married. I'd stay out all night and I'd drink. I'd drink rather than pay my bills just to feed my drinking habit. Relations with my wife were strained, to say the least. If she tried to admonish me, I'd say, "I drank before I knew you and I'll probably die drinking." I never thought it was a problem. I thought the problem was with my wife, not me.

I was getting into a lot of car accidents. I'd wake up in a smashed-up car and not remember where I was. I had one really major car accident and that's when I swore off alcohol, for good, I thought. It was only for five-and-a-half years. And after all that time, when I picked up the first drink, it was just like it was before. I drank a beer at 10 A.M. and I kept drinking all day, till late into the evening, until I passed out on my brother's living room floor. I went right back into my periodic drinking pattern. I'd go for a few weeks and then give up for a week or two. And then I'd try to see if I could drink one or two drinks, and I could, that night, and then I'd go back the next night and drink till I had another blackout. This got worse and worse for the next eight and a half years. It came to the point where I no longer wanted to go out and have a drink. Then, I *needed* it, just to clear the cobwebs out. It got to be where it was a hopeless thing. When I picked up one drink, there was no telling what would happen—where I'd go, what I'd do, who I'd end up with.

The last three years of my drinking were almost daily—there were no off days, I did nothing but drink. I'd work only a couple of days a week. My relationship with my wife was gone by then—she was just beaten down by it. The emotional turbulence in the lives of my six children was tremendous. A lot of pain was involved

there. My teenage daughter would have to answer the phone, and it would be some woman I had wound up with—I would just go somewhere and the next day, I'd find myself with someone. My kids had to deal with that. I was never a father to my children. I just didn't bother coming home. And when I did, I'd get into an argument with my wife about the whole thing, and I'd want to go out and drink again. I'd wake up with guilt and remorse, and want to drink to drown it out.

One night, I sat down at my kitchen table and started going into a crying jag. I knew I was in trouble. The bottom had fallen out. My wife was in Al-Anon, which is an organization for the relatives of alcoholics. She suggested that I go to AA. She even dialed the phone for me. I went to a meeting that night. I listened to three speakers, and I thought they were nuts. I couldn't wait to get out of there and get a drink—which is what I did. I drank for three more months. That was the pits. I knew my life was really messed up. So I stayed off the booze for ten months. Still, my mind wasn't functioning properly. I couldn't concentrate, I couldn't work on the job. I'd work fifteen hours a day just to wear myself out. My marriage had fallen apart. I was still miserable. See, I was fighting it. I had quit drinking on my own, and I thought I was a self-sufficient person. I now realize I wasn't. So once again my wife suggested that I go to another AA meeting and I went. I sat down and talked to some people I could talk to. This fellow shared his life with me. I realized that I wasn't unique, that I wasn't a freak. I came to see that I could have a decent life without booze, and that it was alcohol that was causing my problems. I saw that I had the choice of destroying the rest of my life or staying sober. I could have ended up on the Bowery or killing someone. That day was my last drink—August 13, nine years ago.

I lost my wife and kids. I lost a house. My business was down the drain. I was $40,000 in debt in back taxes and bills. I owed everybody. I even owed the garbage man—he wouldn't come and pick up my garbage. If I heard the phone ring I wouldn't want to pick it up. I was afraid it was another bill collector. At the age of 38, I woke up and found out what life was all about.

In the beginning, I went to a lot of AA meetings. For three and a half years, I went to an AA meeting almost every day. I had a lot to work on. I had to learn to live with some kind of humility and self-acceptance. My life took a complete turnaround. Everything is right in my life now. I'm out of debt. I can put in a full day's work. I'm a respectable person. I've gotten remarried. Today I feel good about my life.

If I were to give someone advice, I'd say, if you see the road signs coming down the pike, use them. When you pick up a few drinks and you can't tell what's going to happen—don't drink. Drinking robbed me of any kind of relationship with anybody. I didn't know what it was like to be with somebody because I didn't know who I was. The only social occasions I wanted to go to was where booze was going to be served. If there was no booze, I didn't go. So if booze is pulling you away from what's out there, don't drink. I didn't care about the consequences of my drinking—sickness, the accidents, the fights, the destruction of my marriage, causing my kids nothing but misery. That's another sign: If you drink and don't care what happens, you're in trouble. And another thing. When I drank, I thought I was the person I wanted to be. It increased my self-confidence. I could always blame somebody else for what went wrong, put everything off on the external world. It wasn't me, it was everybody else. If I'd get something bad off somebody, I'd just go away from the people who were bothering me about my drinking and I'd go to another bar and drink there. If you can't be who you are without drinking, don't drink. If you need booze to cover up your problems,

don't drink. If you have to change your circle of friends because of your drinking, you need help.

In my heart I knew I didn't want to drink. But I suppressed it. I pushed it down. And what made it possible for me to do that—was drinking. I say these things not just to talk about my life. I would like to share my life with other people to help someone. I'd like someone to learn from my life. If they can't handle it, stay away from it. That's what I would tell them—don't drink.

The last thing I want to say is the most important—in fact, it's the point of the whole thing: I couldn't have stopped drinking without God's help. I could never stop drinking before. Only when I asked God for sobriety, to be relieved of the obsession to drink, was I able to quit. It was God who gave me the strength to stay sober. (From the author's files.)

chapter 8

HETEROSEXUAL DEVIANCE

There is perhaps no area of human life in which a contrast between essentialism and constructionism is starker and more glaring than sexual behavior. The *essentialist* position sees sexuality as an instinct or powerful drive that demands fulfillment, an independent and powerful force, much like a riderless horse. Sexual satisfaction can be sublimated, repressed, or rerouted, of course. However, according to one's perspective, this sublimation can be *productive*—indeed, the sublimation of the sexual drive is said to be one requirement for the development of higher civilization (Freud, 1961)—or *damaging*, that is, unfulfilled sexual demands can lead to neuroses, corruption, and violence (Marcuse, 1966). For the sexual conservative, sex is a strong temptation to engage in evil that must be resisted; for the sexual libertine, sex is a delicious garden of delight that should not be denied. But whether it is satisfied or repressed, both perspectives agree that the sex drive is nagging, pressing, importunate, and powerful. It is *there*; it exists prior to human consciousness, a natural force in the world that has to be reckoned or grappled with. The human diversity we see in sexual expression the world over is simply a veneer that is overlaid, and rests uneasily upon, the raging, bubbling, seething force of raw, universal animal sexual energy. This *physiological* or *hydraulic* model of sexuality—that sees the sex drive as an unstoppable force of nature much like the flow of water—is spelled out in the work of Sigmund Freud; some version of it dominates the thinking of much of the general public.

A completely different view of sex is offered by *constructionism*, which overlaps heavily with the symbolic interactionist approach. (Recall that labeling theory, spelled out in Chapter 5, stands squarely within this tradition.) Constructionism asks questions about the *construction* and *imputation* of *meaning*. (Gagnon and Simon, 1973, and Plummer, 1975, 1982, offer an exposition of this position.) Instead of assuming beforehand that we already know what phenomena in the world bear a sexual meaning, symbolic interactionists ask *how sexuality itself is constructed*. What *is* sexuality? How is the category put together? What is included in it, what's excluded? What are the meanings that are attached to it? These meanings vary from person to person, from setting to setting, from one social circle to another, from one culture or society to another, and so on. Symbolic interactionists insist that behaviors or phenomena that are superficially, mechanically, and outwardly the same—that are *formally* the same to an external observer—can bear radically different meanings to the participants. At the same time, radically different actions or phenomena, examined externally and mechanically, can bear very *similar* meanings to observers or participants. What is sexual to one person may be totally lacking in sexual content or meaning to another. An enema, for instance, or a family playing volleyball in the nude at a nudist colony, may be sexual to one observer or participant and not another. Is a vaginal examination by a gynecologist "sexual" in meaning? Is a stripper engaged in a "sexual" act when she removes her costume, or, for that matter, a male stripper, when he dances nude before an all-female audience? Their audiences may think so, and many become suitably aroused; however, these performers may be going through the motions, utterly unmoved by their acts. Sexual meaning is *read* or *infused into* things or behaviors in the world; it does not lie there, inert, ready to be noticed and picked up, much as we might reach down and pick up a rock.

Consider the following roster of behaviors, all which may be regarded as "sexual" by some actors or observers but not by many others:

When a child plays with his genitals, is this "sexual"? When a person excretes is this sexual? When a man kisses another publicly, is this sexual? When a couple are naked together, is this sexual? When a girl takes her clothes off in public, is this sexual? When a lavatory attendant wipes down a toilet seat, is this sexual? When a boy has an erection climbing a tree, is this sexual? When a morgue attendant touches a dead body, is this sexual? When a social worker assists her client, is this sexual? When a man and woman copulate out of curiosity or out of duty, is this sexual? The list could be considerably extended. . . .Most of the situations above could be defined as sexual by [some] members [of the society]; they need not be. Sexual meanings are not universal absolutes, but ambiguous and problematic categories (Plummer, 1975, p. 31).

Even more dramatically, consider the vastly different meanings that different participants "read into" what is essentially much the same sexual action, described below:

Imagine, if you will, a panel of matched penises entering an equal number of matched or randomized vaginas; the penises entering an equal number of thrusts, all simultaneously achieve orgasms of equal magnitude, and all withdraw at the same time, leaving all vaginas in an equal state of indifference. What can we possibly know of the character of any of these acts? Or and of the involved actors? Let me suggest, if I may, some reasonable candidates for this panel: (a) a lower-class male, having a mild sensual experience, though glowing with the anticipation of the homosocial [same-gender non-sexual friendship] acknowledgement he will receive as long as the vagina did not belong to his wife; (b) an upper-middle-class male crushed by his inability to bring his partner to orgasm; (c) a male achieving unusual orgasmic heights because his partner is a prostitute or someone else of equally degraded erotic status; (d) a stereotyped Victorian couple "doing their thing"—or is it "his thing"?—or possibly, natives of contemporary rural Ireland; (e) a husband fulfilling his marital obligations while dreaming dreams of muscular young truck drivers; (f) a couple performing an act of sexual initiation in the back seat of a VW (Simon, 1973, p. 64).

A crucial point to be made is that sexual activities should not be translated in an automatic, glib, superficial, and mechanical fashion from one culture or social context to another. If actions that are *outwardly* similar are *experienced* in radically different ways, does that mean they are "the same" in other, more crucial ways? Can same-gender sexual behavior in ancient Greece, where it was accepted, even expected, if one male was older and the other was an adolescent, and the older male had sex with women as well, be equated with same-gender sexual behavior in the contemporary United States, where it is stigmatized, the partners tend to be age peers, and is not typically accompanied by heterosexual activity? In Eskimo (or Inuit) society, a custom exists of husbands offering their wives sexually to male guests; in the contemporary United States, in some social circles, married couples "swap" or "swing" or engage in "co-marital" sex. Are these two practices very similar to, or very different from, one another? The point is that vastly different *meanings* are attached to genital activity, depending on the social context in which they take place. (Indeed, much behavior that is not even *initially* genital in nature may *generate* a genital response, so symbolic or constructed is this thing we refer to as sex.) And vastly different actions can be interpreted as having a sexual content or meaning. The meaning does not arise automatically from the nature of the act; it is the meaning that *makes* the act sexual in nature.

In the classic Freudian formulation, "everything is sexual." (But recall Freud's famous and oft-quoted—attributed—statement, "Sometimes a cigar is just a cigar.") That is, much of what we do in ordinary, everyday life is a symbolic representation or a stand-in for sex. A big, fancy sports car or motorcycle symbolizes or represents a fear by its owner that he is insufficiently masculine, that his penis is too small. Aggressively achieving in the corporate world symbolizes the urge to dominate others sexually, to capture and rape them. Camaraderie or strong male fellowship symbolizes strong homosexual impulses. Collecting things symbolizes the lust to save or keep one's feces, so cruelly taken away when one was an infant—essentially, Freud believed, sexual and erotic in meaning.

In contrast, the symbolic interactionists turn the equation completely around and argue that far from the social world being in the service of sexuality, in contrast, *sexuality is in the service of the social world*. Sexuality does not shape our social conduct, social meanings give shape to our sexuality (Plummer, 1982, p. 232). There is no necessary hidden sexual message lurking behind every item of our social lives; instead, each and every item in our sexual behavior has an overt and readily discernible social dynamic motivating or underlying it. We are sexual because we are social; it is social life that *creates*, *motivates*, and *shapes* our sexuality. Some men seduce women to gain the admiration of their peers; in prison, sex acts as a power broker, a source of masculinity and affection (Gagnon and Simon, 1973, p. 258); one teenage girl dates many boys in search of admiration and respect, another dates very few, seeking the boy of her dreams; the prostitute has intercourse in pursuit of cash; the health faddist has sex as part of a rigid schedule of vitamins, exercise, and fat-free foods. In each case, "sexual experiences are constructed from social motives and settings" (Plummer, 1982, p. 233).

Constructionists make extensive use of the concept of *sexual scripts* in their understanding of sexual behavior (Simon and Gagnon, 1984, 1986). Actors follow "scripts" in their pursuit of sexual lines of action. However, far from assuming that actors follow "scripts" in a literal, line-by-line, scene-by-scene rendering, much as an actor in a play or film might do, the constructionist use of this metaphor allows for far more improvisation in real life. There are at least three varieties of scripts that guide human sexual life: (1) cultural scenarios; (2) interpersonal scripts; and (3) intrapsychic scripting. Cultural scenarios are the "instructional guides" that exist at the level of collective life" (Simon and Gagnon, 1984, p. 53, 1986, p. 98).

Though "too abstract" to guide behavior under any and all conditions, they provide broad outlines for appropriate behavior. We learn from these cultural scenarios, broadly speaking, what sexual behaviors are acceptable and unacceptable and with whom and under what circumstances sex may take place. However, there are plenty of blank spaces in cultural scenarios; interpersonal scripts fill in many of the blanks, permitting the actor to turn from acting in a play with parts written by another (that is, the culture) to "being a partial script writer or adapter shaping the materials of relevant cultural scenarios into scripts for behavior in particular contexts" (p. 53). Still, interpersonal scripts are always constrained by real partners in the concrete world; the script one writes must always be in collaboration with others, and entails certain do's and don'ts that must be observed. Hence, one's capacity to improvise is constrained by the actions and reactions of one's role partners. Such constraints do not apply to intrapsychic scripting, which enables the actor to "reorganize" reality, to create "a private world of wishes and desires" (p. 53). The more diverse the society, the more varied and diverse are the scripts that operate to guide our sexual behavior.

But the symbolic interactionist or constructionist position goes considerably beyond the insight that understanding symbolic meaning and personal scripting is necessary to understand sexual behavior. It argues further that not only is the very *category* of sexuality constructed, in addition, a specific *evaluative* meaning is read into it as well. By "evaluative" I mean that sexual categories are rendered "good" or "bad," that is, conventional and norm-abiding, or deviant, in violation of the norms—through the construction process. For instance, not only are the categories "homosexual" and "heterosexual" constructed (and in some societies, they are not even constructed at all!), and constructed at different points in different societies, but they are *infused with positive or negative meanings*. Each is regarded in a certain way—as "abnormal" or "normal," "evil" or "acceptable," "an offense in God's eyes," or a "tolerable practice," "repulsive" or "straight, boring, vanilla sex," "liberating" or "repressive," an "alternative lifestyle" or "conformist," "nonhierarchical" or "patriarchal," "compulsive" or "freely chosen"—depending on the society or social circle rendering the judgment. It is these social definitions to which we have to pay close attention; they are what social deviance is

built upon. Different forms of sexual expression do not bring with them an automatic response or evaluation; they do not drop down from the skies as a reaction to their essence or basic reality. What *creates* the phenomenon of deviance is these reactions; they are variable in societies the world over, from one historical time period to another, and from one social circle or context to another in the same society. It is the construction process that is the very stuff of deviance.

Of all areas of deviance, it is perhaps in the sphere of sexual deviance that the idea of sickness and pathology has been and remains most prominent. Historically, the imputation of pathology has been part and parcel of the construction process in the study of deviance. Until the 1970s, the vast majority of research and writing on nonnormative sex cast it beyond the pale of normality. Sexual deviants, these early researchers and authors said, are distinctly *not like the rest of us*. When the term, "sexual deviant" is used to describe someone, the image that comes to mind is someone who is impelled to act as a result of uncontrollable, unfathomable, and distinctly abnormal, motives; someone whose behavior is freakish, fetishistic, and far-out. Certainly, the term *sexual deviant* would include sadism (being aroused as a result of inflicting pain); masochism (being aroused through receiving pain); transvestism, or receiving a sexual thrill through cross-dressing; the practice of sexual stimulation through asphyxia (denying one's body of oxygen by choking or strangulating oneself to the point of near-unconsciousness); sexual activity with prepubescent children (pedophilia); voyeurism (the habitual peeping into windows to see others undressing or engaged in sex); exhibitionism (displaying oneself sexually to nonconsenting others); frotteurism, or rubbing against a nonconsenting person; sex with nonhuman objects, such as animals (bestiality); "kinky" sex, that is, engaging in what others would regard as highly bizarre and unusual sexual practices. The fourth edition of the American Psychiatric Association's *Diagnostic and Statistical Manual of Mental Disorders* (DSM-IV) discusses sexual "disorders" such as these (1994, pp. 522–532).

Although DSM-IV's list of sexual disorders would qualify, without question, as sociologically deviant sexual behavior, they also represent *extreme versions* of what is in fact a *continuum* or *dimension*. The *full range* of sociologically deviant sexual behavior, although by definition condemned, is considerably more mundane or *ordinary* than these extreme and spectacular cases. It seems especially necessary to remind ourselves when discussing sexual behavior that deviance refers specifically to *socially disapproved* behavior and characteristics—and to these only. It includes no taint of pathology or disorder whatsoever, no implication of harm; it does not assume that we are discussing the *more extreme* end of a continuum that runs from mildly to extremely deviant. Practitioners of certain forms of deviance will often respond to the term by saying: "We're not deviants! There's nothing sick or wrong with what we do!" A sociologist would respond by asking if these persons *do* or *would* receive negative, punitive, or condemnatory reactions from others as a result of what they do. "What would your parents do or say if they found out? Your friends, acquaintances, fellow students, teachers, your boss, co-workers, relatives, neighbors—the general public?" If the answer is that their reactions are likely to be negative, that they would condemn or socially reject you, ridicule or gossip about you, punish or humiliate you, then we have a clear-cut case of deviance on our hands; if not, we don't.

Let's put the matter another way: *Psychological* and *social* (or sociological) deviance are not the same thing. They delineate two separate and independent dimensions. They overlap, of course; the chances are that nearly all cases of *psychological* deviance would qualify as *sociological* deviance. But the reverse is not the case. Psychologically, sexual deviance implies a *disorder*, a *dysfunction*; socially and sociologically, sexual deviance simply refers to a violation of norms and a subsequently high likelihood of condemnation. No disorder and no dysfunction is implied. What violates the norms in a given society may in fact be quite normal psychologically (although it may not). What is accepted, practiced, and even encouraged in one society may be savagely condemned and harshly punished in another. What is a normative violation at one time may be the norm at another. Again, because the link between sexual deviance and psychological abnormality is so strong in many observers' minds, we have to be reminded of their conceptual independence.

In fact, psychologically, some quite "functional" and "nondisordered" sexual behaviors have been condemned at certain times and places—including here and now. Consider the fact that homosexuality does not appear in DSM-IV's catalogue of sexual disorders (1994); before 1973, however, it did. Consider the fact that as late as the 1960s, some psychiatrists attempted to pathologize premarital sex (Levin, 1968). Consider the fact that in the past, sexual equality between men and women, likewise, has been regarded as a sign of a disorder (Ginsberg et al., 1972; Bettelheim, 1971). Again, I'd like to emphasize that *condemnation* is not the same thing as *disorder; punishment* is not the same thing as *dysfunction*. (And remember, too, that which is regarded as a disorder or a dysfunction at one time may be accepted as normal at another time.) For something to qualify as social deviance, all that is necessary is that it be condemned in some social quarters or circles, and this may include behavior that clinical psychologists and psychiatrists agree is quite normal. No doubt some forms of sexual deviance harm others, or the actors involved, or are the product of a clinically disordered or abormal psyche; the majority do not. Many practitioners of sexual deviance—homosexuals and prostitutes perhaps especially—will insist that they are not "deviants," meaning, of course, that they are psychologically normal. Yet they will agree that much of the public views them as somewhat less than respectable. It is easy to become ensnared in a squabble about what words mean. Reminding ourselves that sociologically, "deviant" simply means "unconventional" and "likely to be condemned" will put us back on the right track.

SEXUAL BEHAVIOR AND CUSTOM AROUND THE WORLD

Is sex an instinct? Is what we do sexually dictated by our biological inheritance? Are certain activities prohibited, or regarded as deviant, because they are harmful—because they threaten the survival of the species? Contrarily, are certain acts approved and encouraged simply or largely because they maximize our survival? Evolutionary biologists insist that this is indeed true. But if the answers to these questions were "yes," it would be the case that sexual custom and practice would be fairly standard the world over. Sexual behavior is not random the world over. Looking from society to society, it is clear that some acts are highly likely to be prohibited, while others tend to be approved. Clearly, customs do not run riot in infinite diversity. At the same time, there is considerable variation from one society to another as to which sexual acts are condemned and which ones are customary and frequently practiced.

To examine this issue, it would be instructive to examine two starkly discrepant examples: societies in which sex and sexual deviance are vastly and radically different. Mangaia is a small island community in Polynesia, in the South Pacific. Inis Beag is another small island, off the coast of Ireland. These two communities represent the extremes of sexual permissiveness and repression. If we were to see human sexuality as a biological constant, it would be extremely difficult to explain the massive differences we observe in what people do sexually. (The patterns I'm about to describe may not exist today; they prevailed when the anthropologists who wrote their reports on them did their research. Still, at the time these societies were studied, they represented empirical examples of sexual practices in two real-life locales.) It is necessary to examine the rich fabric of social life for the explanation of this variation, not the more-or-less standard biological equipment we all bring to the sexual arena. It is an axiom in science that we cannot explain a variable with a constant.

Inis Beag (Messenger, 1971) is one of the most sexually repressed societies on earth. Sex is rarely discussed; it is a subject that causes embarrassment if, for some reason, it arises. There is almost no known sexual diversity of any kind on the island; there is no premarital or extramarital sex of any kind—that is known about, at any rate. *Any* departure from marital, man-on-top intercourse is considered distinctly deviant. There seems to be no instruction on menstruation or pregnancy by the mother to her daughter. The general feeling by the islanders is that for women, sex is a burden that has to be endured. Women are not told that they can enjoy sex. In fact, the author of the study, John Messenger, an anthropologist, claims that the female orgasm is unknown. The men of the island feel that engaging in intercourse is physically debilitating, that it drains one of one's "vital bodily fluids." Magazines such as *Time* and *Life* are considered pornographic and are denounced from the pulpit by the local priest.

There seem to be almost no opportunities at all to engage in sex outside a marital context, and even relatively few to engage in it even *within* marriage! In Inis Beag, as in Ireland in general, marriage takes place quite late for the man, at age 46, on the average. And a high proportion (about a third) never marry at all. There is little interaction between the sexes; men interact almost exclusively with other men, and women almost exclusively with other women. A sharp dichotomy is drawn; any crossing over the gender barrier is viewed with suspicion and distrust. Gestures of affection and love are discouraged, and are rare, even in private. Foreplay in intercourse between spouses is limited to kissing and some fondling. The husband nearly always initiates the act. There is only one coital position known. The woman who enjoys sex is looked down upon and considered a "bad" woman; no "good" woman in Inis Beag enjoys it, or at least claims to. There is very little nudity in intercourse (or at all, for that matter). Husbands and wives have sex in long undergarments that unbutton at the appropriate places. The man achieves orgasm quickly and just as quickly falls asleep.

The islanders abhor nudity. They don't even wash nude: Washing is limited to sponging off furtively a few key spots on one's body. (The anthropologist's wife caused extreme embarrassment and consternation when she walked into a room when a man had just finished washing; the man's feet were bare. He ran out of the room, put his shoes on in another room, walked back with his shoes on, saying, "Ah, it's good to have your clothes on!") One mother physically attacked a mainland nurse for sponging off her son's bare chest. Sailors have been known to drown because they couldn't swim; they couldn't swim because it wasn't the custom to go onto a beach—or anywhere else, for that matter—dressed in clothing as scanty as a bathing suit.

The contrast with Mangaia (Marshall, 1971) could not possibly be more extreme. Sex appears to be the main and central concern on the island of Mangaia. In folk tales and songs, sex is the dominant theme. (On Inis Beag, the anthropologist caused much blushing and averting of eyes when he sang a song he had written which contained the line, "I am dreaming perhaps of a beautiful mate." Judging from the reaction, it was very possibly the most risqué line ever heard on Inis Beag.) Intercourse among adolescents and young adults takes place without much prior interaction. Copulation precedes affection. The main emphasis on sex in Mangaia is the ability of the male to engage in sexual intercourse vigorously for long periods of time a number of times a night. Mangaians say that a good man can hold off his orgasm for 15 minutes to half an hour, allowing the woman to have as many as half a dozen orgasms. The longer the man can continue, the greater will be his prestige. Performances are rated, and men are rated on the basis of the performances they turn in. Any man who ejaculates too soon is thought not to want to please his partner. So sex is put on a very competitive plane. A young woman will tell her companion for the night that her lover of the night before stimulated her so that she had five orgasms; this will encourage her current young man to try for six.

Oral and anal intercourse are common. Homosexuality and bestiality are not unknown, but are extremely uncommon. Out of wedlock births are common; although the unmarried woman with children has less prestige than the woman who is married, the condemnation of the unmarried woman is comparatively mild. Young women are discouraged from having sex with too many men, and are reminded not to make themselves sexually too readily available to men. But the point at which these judgments are made is considerably more lenient than in Western society. The average quantity of sex that the typical Mangaian couple engages in is prodigious by American standards. Here, married couples in their twenties have sex an average of two or three times a week (Michael et al., 1994, p. 116; Laumann et al., 1994). In Mangaia, it is three times a night, seven nights a week. Naturally, the amount of sexual activity declines with age, but it still remains considerably above the amount here at any age. In fact, the middle-aged Mangaian couple engages in intercourse more than the American couple in their twenties.

What should be clear is that many of the phenomena that we might assume to be biological functions, such as the frequency of intercourse and the experience of orgasm in the woman, are learned, and not innate in the human organism. (They may have a biological *basis* or *potential*, but whether this is manifested in real life is determined by the culture, not biology.) Even something so seemingly dictated by our bodies as what arouses us sexually is shaped by our sociocultural environment. For instance, on the whole, American males are more interested in and turned on by the female breast than is true of males of other societies. "The Mangaian," writes Donald Marshall, the anthropologist who studied the sexual customs and practices of this society, "is completely flabbergasted at the American . . . male's [sexual] interest in the female breast, for the Polynesian considers this organ to be of interest only to a hungry baby. Yet, the Mangaian male is as fully concerned with the size,

shape, and consistency of the mons veneris"—that pad of fatty tissue in the female pubic region— "as is the American male with the size, shape, and consistency of the female bust" (Marshall, 1971, p. 110). Interestingly, Marshall did not report on what portion of the *male* anatomy Mangaian females found sexually inticing.

In a nutshell, sexual behavior, sexual custom, and sexual deviance are not dictated by—certainly not *exclusively* by—the body's anatomical, hormonal, or genetic characteristics, but the society and culture in which humans live. These biological factors and forces *potentiate* sexual behavior, but they do not dictate specifically how sexual behavior in a particular locale will manifest itself. The sex drive is highly labile, variable, and susceptible to a variety of forms of expression. It may be nurtured, it may be inhibited, it may be maximized or minimized, but exactly how its expression is shaped is a social and cultural, not a biological, matter.

It is something of a cliché that sexual deviance is "relative" to time and place: Behavior that is condemned in one place at one time may be tolerated or encouraged in another. Cliché or not, it is most decidedly true. (Remember, again, the sexual customs of these societies prevailed when they were studied by anthropologists, which may have been decades in the past. Today, these societies may be quite different. Still, when they were studied, they represent a page in the book of human diversity.) Among the Pokot of East Africa, "a woman who does not enjoy sex is called deviant" (Edgerton, 1976, p. 48). Yet only a few hundred miles to the south, the Gusii present exactly the opposite picture; among the Gusii, sexual hostility between men and women is institutionalized, and "Gusii women who enjoy sex are seen as deviant" (Edgerton, 1976, p. 48; LeVine, 1959).

Among the Azande of East Africa, young warriors are sent to live with one another in bachelor barracks during years of military service. They are forbidden to marry at this time, and sexual behavior with younger boys is both common and approved. When they return to their villages, they eventually marry, their early experience having had no impact whatsoever on their sexual preferences (Evans-Pritchard, 1970). Among the Sambia of New Guinea, at the age of seven to 10, boys are segregated in their own villages from women and girls and initiated into an all-male society, where they remain for the next 10 to 15 years. During that time, they exclusively engage in homosexual behav-

---

The Readiness of Men versus Women to Engage in Sex with Strangers

Psychologists Russell Clark and Elaine Hatfield conducted an experiment which was designed to determine the likelihood that a stranger who was approached and asked for a date would be willing to comply (Clark and Hatfield, 1981; Hatfield and Sprecher, 1986, pp. 136–137). College men and women who were judged to range in appearance from "slightly unattractive" to "slightly attractive" were selected to act as confederates or accomplices in the experiment. They were asked to approach attractive males and females of the opposite sex in public and ask them one of three questions: (1) "Would you go out with me tonight?" (2) "Would you come over to my apartment tonight?" or (3) "Would you go to bed with me tonight?"

Surprisingly, more than half of the men and women who were approached agreed to go out on a date with a complete stranger. If the requestor was a male, 56 percent of the women he approached agreed to a date that night; if the requestor was a female, 50 percent agreed. Interestingly, as the level of intimacy of the request *increased*, the percent of women who agreed *decreased*, while, for men, the percent *increased*. Only 6 percent of the women who were approached agreed to go to the male requestor's apartment that night, and *not one* agreed to go to bed with him. On the other hand, almost seven out of 10 of the men who were approached (69 percent) agreed to go to the female requestor's apartment, and three-quarters (75 percent) agreed to go to bed with her! The verbal responses to the sexual request were as revealing as these percentages. Even many of the men who said that they wouldn't were apologetic; they said things like, "I'm married," or "I'm going with someone," or "I can't tonight, but tomorrow would be fine." In contrast, the women reacted by saying "You've got to be kidding," or "What is wrong with you—leave me alone!" (Clark and Hatfield, 1981; Hatfield and Sprecher, 1986, p. 137).

This experiment clearly shows that men are *vastly* more likely to be ready, willing, and eager to have casual sex with a complete stranger than is true of women. To put the matter another way, what would be a deviant sexual act—hopping into bed with a complete stranger—if enacted by women seems to be an act of conformity among men. And, very possibly, what is an act of conformity among women (turning down a stranger's invitation for sex) may well be an instance of deviance if enacted by a man!

---

ior, first as the fellator (or insertee), later as the fellated (or insertor), role. It is believed that boys can only become men through this ritual, both as a result of avoiding the polluting and feminizing influence of their mothers, and because the semen of the older males infuses the male essence into these boys, making it possible for them to grow into fierce warriors. Every Sambian boy, without exception, is initiated into the warrior cult through this ceremonial practice (Herdt, 1981, 1987). The contrast with the military in the United States could not be more extreme. Although here, homosexual behavior in the military is widespread, it is far from tolerated. It is considered deviant, and can be a cause for a dishonorable discharge.

In the same way that sexual standards vary from one society to another, they also change over time. It is clear that many forms of behavior that were once vigorously condemned a few generations ago or even a decade or two ago are now widely tolerated. It is important that premarital intercourse is growing both in frequency and acceptance; there is a declining condemnation of the practice and persons who engage in it. In short, premarital intercourse—under specified conditions—has lost its deviant status for the society as a whole. (Though it remains deviant in some minority circles.) A Gallup Poll conducted in 1969 showed that the clear majority of the respondents in the study, two-thirds (68 percent), agreed with the statement that premarital sex is "wrong." The same question asked by the Gallup organization in 1973 elicited only a 48 percent minority which agreed with the statement. The younger respondents, under 30 years old, were very unlikely to agree that premarital intercourse was wrong (29 percent), while the older respondents, age 50 and older, were far more likely to agree (64 percent). This age gradation suggests that the condemnation of premarital sex is a dying view. In the 1990s, in what was perhaps the most complete sex survey ever conducted, a team of researchers found that only 20 percent of a sample of Americans agreed with the slightly stronger proposition which stated that premarital sex "is always wrong" (Michael et al., 1994, p. 234; Laumann et al., 1994).

There is, then, both cultural and historical variation in judgments concerning what constitutes sexual deviance. Likewise, there exists a strong *actor* relativity: *Who* is condemned as a consequence of having committed certain acts varies enormously. Although the Azande warriors mentioned above could engage in homosexual liaisons while living in sex-segregated barracks, the women in Azande society are "not granted comparable privileges" (Edgerton, 1976, p. 49). Among the Azande, wives in polygamous households headed by an aging man are typically sexually neglected; they often form lesbian relationships. Men look upon such relationships "with revulsion," and if they are discovered, the women could be put to death (Edgerton, 1976, p. 49; Evans-Pritchard, 1970).

Likewise, in the societies of the world that condemn premarital intercourse, most do so only for the women, and nearly all of the rest do so more strongly for the women. This is referred to as a *double standard*. In studies on the subject, attitudes toward sexual behaviors of all types, premarital intercourse included, vary significantly according to *whose* behavior is being evaluated. In one study of "sex and morality" in the United States, it was found that the premarital intercourse of females was judged more negatively than that of males; teenagers engaging in premarital sex were judged more negatively than adults; and males and females engaging in sex outside of marriage *who were not in love* were judged more negatively than those who were in love. The nonmarital sex that the highest percentage of the population regards it as "always wrong" or "almost always wrong" is that engaged in by *the teenage girl who is not in love;* the nonmarital sex that is thought wrong by the *lowest* percentage is *the adult male who is in love* (Klassen, Williams, Levitt, 1989, pp. 388–389). Hence, premarital sex is evaluated in a radically different fashion by audiences, according to the *sex and age* of the actor and the *emotional intensity and duration* of the relationship under consideration. In a like fashion, a 12-year-old prostitute is more strongly condemned than a 22-year-old prostitute; again, *who* the actor is will temper the evaluation of his or her behavior by most audiences.

In short, what is or is not sexual deviance varies from one society or culture to another, from one historical time period to another, and according to who is enacting the behavior in question. What is condemned is not universal, but culture-specific, actor-specific, and situation-specific.

WHAT CONSTITUTES SEXUAL DEVIANCE?

The human being is capable of sexual arousal and satisfaction by means of a wide range of different activities. Alone of all animals in creation, human sexual drives and enactment can be completely separated from simple biological reproduction. We are the only beings on earth who have sex for fun. Think of the many ways by which humans seek and obtain sexual gratification, one author (Buckner, 1971, p. 7) suggests: "homosexuality, fetishism, necrophilia, pedophilia, masturbation, oral intercourse, anal intercourse, oral-genital and oral-anal intercourse, bestiality, heterosexuality, voyeurism, exhibitionism, clusterfucks [orgies], masochism, and sadism, to name only the more direct methods." One feminist who (Rodmell, 1981, p. 153) criticized me for citing Buckner's list of potential sources of sexual gratification claims that while many men partake in these "unusual, bizarre sexual practices," very few women do so, or at least, do so willingly, without being forced or pressured by men. Thus, she says, the list ignores the *power differentials* between men and women in such activities, that is, that participation in them presupposes a mutual consent which is, in fact, actually lacking in our society. But the fact that *some* of them *are* unusual and rarely practiced—by men *or* women—is precisely the point, isn't it? There are a wide range of cultural and social reasons (the capacity of women to resist men's suggestions or importunings to engage in "unusual, bizarre" sexual practices included) *why* men and women actually engage in a fairly narrow sexual repertory, in comparison with the potentiality that faces them. Almost none of us anywhere, male *or* female, engage in the range of sexual behaviors of which we are capable. Some of the activities Buckner lists above are prohibited (such as orgies, necrophilia, pedophilia, and sadomasochism), while others are accepted and even encouraged (heterosexuality). Moreover, the same acts are tolerated and condemned, depending on historical and social location (for instance, oral sex, homosexuality, masturbation). The fact that a political dimension is one of these reasons *strengthens* my point, it does not diminish it. What is it about certain forms of sexual behavior that attracts public hostility in the Western world today? Why are they regarded as deviant? Why are some forms vastly less frequently practiced than others? Why are they regarded as deviant in one locale more than in another, why certain actors more than others? These are questions that any sensitive observer of the sexual scene must address.

One observer (Wheeler, 1960) has isolated four main dimensions of aspects of sexual behavior that our laws are designed to govern. Although laws represent an extremely imperfect reflection of attitudes and morality, it happens that some of the same dimensions are relevant to sexual deviance as to sex crimes. What *makes* a sexual act deviant, by extension, is an *inappropriateness relative to one or another of the following dimensions:* (1) the degree of consent, or one aspect of the *how* question; (2) the nature of the sexual object, or the *who* and *what* question; (3) the nature of the sex act, another aspect of the *how* question; and (4) the *setting* in which the sex act occurs, or the *where* question.

Rape, which is regarded by most expert observers as more an act of violence than a type of sexual behavior, and which is discussed in some detail in a later chapter on violence, is deviant along dimension (1)—*consent* on the part of the woman is lacking; force, violence, or the threat of violence is used to obtain sexual intercourse.

All societies on earth proscribe certain sex partners as unacceptable, and sex with them as deviant—dimension (2), or *nature of the sex partner*. The number of sex partners who are regarded as inappropriate for all members of societies around the world is enormous. In addition, all societies deem certain partners for designated persons off-limits, while those partners may be acceptable for other persons. In our society, close relatives may not have sex with one another (again, the *who* question); if they do, it is automatically an instance of deviance. The same applies to members of the same sex, strangers, partners who are married to someone else, or anyone except our spouse if we are married, and so on. Adults may not have sex with underage minors; Catholic priests may not have sex with anyone; on many university campuses, professors should not have sex with students; psychiatrists may not have sex with their patients; and so on. Many of these restrictions pertain to the relationship we have (or don't have) with certain persons—brothers and sisters, strangers, and so on. Dimension (2), the nature of the sexual partner, also includes nonhuman sex objects, such as animals or sex dolls. (This is the *what* rather than the *who* question.)

"Kinky" sex, encompassing dimension (3)—the nature of the sex act, or the *how* question—represents a broad umbrella. It is made up of sexual behavior that is unusual and bizarre to many people, constituting what used to be referred to as "perversions." Some people receive a sexual charge out of receiving an enema; this is regarded as "kinky." Others like to be tied up when they have sex, or to tie their partner up; this too may be referred to as "kinky." Sadomasochistic practices (giving or receiving pain during the sex act) likewise fall under the *how* umbrella of dimension (3). Some acts that were once considered kinky or perverted are now more likely to be accepted and considered normal today—for instance, oral and anal sex. (Still, consider the fact that in the 1990s, 16 states of the United States still have heterosexual "sodomy" laws on the books which outlaw oral and/or anal sex between consenting male and female adult partners.) "Kinky" sex is condemned or considered deviant specifically because what is done—the nature of the act—is considered weird, unwholesome, and worthy of condemnation. Another sexual activity that is widely controlled—by custom, if not by law—in Western society is masturbation. Adolescent boys and girls are admonished not to "touch" themselves, and adults are very rarely willing to discuss their participation in it, even to their close friends.

And lastly, some people find sex in public and semi-public places exciting and practice it because they have a certain chance of being discovered by others (Karpel, 1975; Farr, 1976). Pushed to its extreme form, this is referred to as exhibitionism, and it is regarded as deviance because of dimension (4), the *where* question—sex in an inappropriate setting. Judging from the sexual fantasies (of many men, at least) that researchers have elicited from respondents, sex in an inappropriate setting excites the imagination of a substantial number of the members of this society.

There are other dimensions that are not covered by the law or are less strongly governed by law than by custom that nonetheless dictate the inappropriateness of certain sexual behaviors. To begin with, there is the *how often* question: The desire for sex that is widely deemed *too often* may court the charge of being a "sex addict" (Carnes, 1983) or being "sexually compulsive" (Levine and Troiden, 1988). On the other hand, desiring or having sex *not often enough* may result in being labeled "impotent" or "frigid." Next, there is the *when* question; a wide range of cross-cultural taboos attend intercourse at certain times (Paige, 1977), such as during pregnancy (63 percent of all societies), menstruation (73 percent), and the postpartum period (95 percent). Generally, sex at *too young* an age, even if the partners are the same age, generates condemnation and punishment among conventional others, parents especially. Not uncommonly, too, persons who are deemed too *old* will experience some negative, often condescending, reactions from others—often their own children! Sex with *too many* partners (a pattern that is conventionally referred to as "promiscuity," a loaded and sexist term) will attract chastisement, although more often for women than men, and more often homosexual than heterosexual men. Sex with too many persons in the same place at the same time (called an "orgy") likewise is regarded as a deviant practice by much of the public. Watching others have sex or undress (voyeurism or "peeping") is deviant and under certain circumstances illegal as well. As we saw, exposing one's sex organs to an unwilling audience (exhibitionism), too, qualifies as an unconventional sex act, and is illegal as well. Selling, acting in or posing for, making, or in some quarters, purchasing and consuming material that is widely regarded as pornographic is widely regarded as deviant. And selling and buying sexual favors is a clear-cut instance of sexual deviance in most people's eyes; prostitution is one of the more widely known and condemned forms of sexual deviance.

The sociologist has an enormous variety and range of deviant sexual activities from which to choose as subjects for study. How is this selection made? Sociologists of deviance are generally interested in two quite different dimensions of behavior which guide their selection of specific activities for study. The first would be the *degree of outrage* touched off in others. Some acts are sure-fire instances of deviance, necrophilia, for instance (having sex with a corpse). Many people would become very upset if they were to apprehend or hear about someone they know engaging in it. As a general rule, the more deviant a given form of behavior, the greater the likelihood that it will be of interest to a sociologist of deviance. Looking at the other end of the spectrum, some forms of behav-

ior may not be interesting to a sociologist studying deviance because they are not regarded as deviant enough, for instance, premarital intercourse. Here, the condemnation directed at the participants tends to be relatively mild or even absent in most social circles; for the most part, it has lost its deviant quality. What is of interest to the sociologist of deviance is the *dynamic* quality of acts, that is, those which once attracted condemnation but that now attract far less, or none. But as a *current* instance of deviance, acts that are only very *mildly* deviant, or deviant only under certain circumstances, are not terribly compelling to the sociologist of deviance as subjects worthy of study.

However, to a sociologist, a second dimension comes into play as well; this is how *common* the activity is, how frequently it is practiced, what its incidence is in the general population. Some behavior clearly qualifies as deviance; it is widely thought of as the product of a degenerate mind. It is behavior enacted by a person well worthy of condemnation. But it may be so rarely practiced that it would be thought of by sociologists as marginal and exotic; once again, necrophilia, or the erotic attraction to dead persons, would constitute an example. Practitioners of such a practice are likely to be studied by the clinical psychologist or psychiatrist, not the sociologist. How many participants make an act "common"? How few make it "rare" and statistically unusual? We can't decide these questions with any exactitude, but in general, sociologists do not study extremely uncommon forms of behavior. Generally, the types of behavior that attract the interests of sociologists are either widely practiced enough for the conventional public to have heard of and to have formed an opinion on; or they generate a *social structure*, that is, a web or network of interacting persons who play specified roles and relate to one another on a stable, predictable, ongoing basis (Gagnon and Simon, 1967, pp. 9–10; Prus and Irini, 1980).

As a general rule, the more "extreme," deviant, or strongly condemned an act is, the *rarer* it is, the less frequently it is practiced and the smaller the number of people who engage in it (Wilkins, 1964, p. 46). *Mildly* deviant behavior (for example, premarital intercourse) is extremely common, and often the rule. *More strongly* condemned behavior (such as adultery) is less frequently practiced. And *much more strongly* condemned behavior (say, extreme sadomasochistic practices) are rarer still. Behavior that is regarded as an instance of *extreme* deviance, that excludes its practitioners from all or nearly all respectable social company (as I said above, necrophilia), is engaged in by minuscule numbers of participants. Of course, for any form of behavior, some members of the society will become more outraged by certain activities and their participants than will others, but society-wide, generally speaking, deviance and frequency are related to one another in an inverse fashion.

The forms of heterosexual deviance that are most frequently studied by sociologists would include prostitution, pornography, and extramarital sex, including "swinging," or co-marital sex. Premarital sex is studied in part, as I said above, because it represents an example of an activity that has lost its deviant status. Recently, sexual harassment has been studied as well, although there is some disagreement as to just where it should be categorized. In many ways, it is similar to rape, a form of violence. For women, by its very nature, it contains no sexual significance; even for the man, the exercise of power and domination over a woman seems to be the dominant motive. In addition, homosexuality has attracted a great deal of attention from sociologists, since it possesses both the characteristics I just discussed, that is, it is both widely known about, therefore forming a distinct deviant role in the minds of the straight majority, and it is also strongly condemned. Homosexuality will be discussed in the next chapter.

A MAJOR NATIONALLY REPRESENTATIVE SEX SURVEY FOR THE 1990s

How do we gather information on sexual behavior and attitudes? Some observers argue that we can't, that this realm of human life is simply too secretive and controversial to study (Lewontin, 1995). Still others argue that we *shouldn't* study sex, that sexual behavior should be a world apart, a sphere that should be protected from the probing, prying gaze of the social scientist; conservative Senator Jesse Helms exemplifies this position, as we'll see. (This argument reminds one of the objections the Romanies or Gypsies have to self-disclosure, a fact we discovered in the Preface.) Fortunately, a substantial number of social scientists have ignored these objections, forged ahead anyway, and tried to bring the world of sex into the clear light of day for all to see and understand.

Ken Plummer (1982) classifies sex research into four "main traditions": the *clinical* tradition of Freud and the psychoanalysts, psychiatrists, and clinical psychologists; the *social bookkeeping* tradition of Alfred Kinsey and other survey takers; the *experimental* method of Masters and Johnson and many other psychologists; and the *descriptive/ethnographic/symbolic interactionist* tradition of anthropologists and participant observation sociologists, including Plummer himself. Although Freud's reputation has suffered a virtual eclipse in psychology and the social sciences (Webster, 1995; Gray, 1993; Crews, 1995)—it lives on in the field of literary criticsm, where statements are insulated from empirical falsification—the clinical tradition is nonetheless alive and well in the study of sexual behavior, as are the other three traditions as well. However, each is appropriate for understanding somewhat different questions. It is impossible to understand how widespread a given practice is by putting a couple into a room, attaching electrodes to their bodies, asking them to make love, and measuring their physical responses, as the Masters and Johnson research team did (1966, 1970, 1979). On the other hand, to cross-check a man's response to a question about whether he finds forcing a woman to have sex arousing, some psychologists have found that measuring their arousal patterns in a laboratory valid and reliable (Malamuth, 1981; Malamuth, Check, and Briere, 1986).

The "social bookkeeping" method of studying sexual behavior, too, has its strengths and weaknesses. We already know some of its weaknesses; the symbolic interactionist model, which guides the approach of many sociologists of deviance, finds "social bookkeeping" deficient in most respects (Plummer, 1982). It must be emphasized, however, that because tabulations of sexual behavior lack the dimension of what these behaviors *mean* to their participants—the dimension stressed by symbolic interactionists and constructionists— does *not* imply that they are without sociological significance or value. To begin with, behaviors summed up by such tallies are the *products* of symbolic processes. We know, for instance, that people meet sex partners in much the same way that they meet romantic and marital partners. (We'll have more to say about this point momentarily.) And to have reached that conclusion, some social "bookkeeping" is necessary. We don't know in advance just what a given act means for *each and every* participant, but we can make inferences about what their behavior is likely to mean *to the majority* in that society, since we know the prevailing norms and attitudes relevant to the behavior in question. In short, we know the social and cultural sea in which participants in certain behaviors navigate and hence, can infer something about these behaviors' meaning to them.

In addition, *some* "social bookkeeping" is necessary for knowing a wide range of crucial facts. For instance, we know that the HIV/AIDS virus is far more likely to be transmitted to the extent that sex partners are anonymous and large in number. Without accurate tallies of who does what with whom, we would be in the dark about this important fact. If wanted to know the likelihood that unmarried teenagers will become pregnant and either have an abortion or bear out-of-wedlock children, again, some social bookkeeping is necessary.

And last, only through "social bookkeeping" can we discover *correlations* or *relationships* with key factors or variables that *do* bear symbolic meaning. We don't necessarily know how person A "constructs" the meaning of having sex with only one partner during the past year, or how person B "constructs" the meaning of having sex with 100, but through a survey, we *can* determine that monogamously married partners are much more likely to say that they are more satisfied with their sex lives than unmarried persons who "sleep around." A sexual encounter between a man and a woman often means different things to these two partners, and we don't know this until we try to understand their explanations on their own terms. At the same time, social bookkeeping or poll taking enables us to see, in a systematic fashion, differences between the sexes not only in how they construct meanings but also in objective, concrete behavior. For instance, men are twice as likely to masturbate than women. Again, by itself, this is only a mildly interesting fact; linked with the internal dimensions in which the symbolic interactionists and constructionists are interested, such a concrete datum takes on significance. All of this is a preamble to saying that in spite of their limitations, surveys and polls ("social bookkeeping") do have great value in the study of sexual behavior.

In 1987, an agency of the federal government sent out a request for researchers to submit proposals to conduct a survey of sexual practices as a means of understanding ways to combat the spread of the AIDS virus. A team of researchers, based principally at the University of Chicago, submit-

ted a proposal that was accepted and funded. However, in 1991, ultraconservative Senator Jesse Helms got wind of the project and successfully lobbied to have its funding cut off. The research team managed to secure funding from private sources. Although the sample size was a great deal smaller than originally intended, the research team managed to conduct the study without political interference. Nearly 3,500 adults age 18 to 59 were interviewed nationwide; they represented an accurate cross section of the country in that age range. The study, conducted by Edward Laumann, John Gagnon, Robert Michael, and Stuart Michaels, was published as a scholarly monograph, *The Social Organization of Sexuality* (1994). A briefer volume, *Sex in America*, written for a popular audience, was coauthored with the science and medical writer, Gina Kolata (Michael et al., 1994).

The results of the study turned out to be surprising in that the sexual behavior of the American population turned out to be a great deal more *conservative* and *conventional* than almost anyone, the researchers included, had expected. Perhaps the most consistent finding, one that ran throughout all aspects of the study, was that whether or not marriage was the aim of the relationship, people usually have sex with partners who are similar to themselves in age, race and ethnicity, and socioeconomic status, especially education. There are three reasons for this, the authors argue. First, even *meeting* someone takes place within social boundaries. The fact is that one rarely interacts with a random cross section of the population. Social relations are constrained by religious membership, neighborhood or community residence, school or occupational setting, friendship networks, and so on. Statistically speaking, the people one runs into in one's social circles and settings are likely to be similar to oneself. And it is in these circles and settings that one meets romantic and dating—and sexual—partners. Second, "stakeholders," that is, third parties—parents, relatives, peers, co-workers, friends, acquaintances, associates in one's social networks—are likely to put pressure on one to date within certain social boundaries. And the more serious the relationship, the more intense that pressure is. And third, similarity makes compatibility more likely which, in turn, makes liking and intimacy more likely. Sharing the same social background or characteristics is far more likely to lead to a sexual and romantic and, eventually, marital relationship than having a different background or characteristics. "Like has sex with like" is a far more accurate and realistic aphorism than "opposites attract."

In addition to the conventionality of the avenues through which partners met and from which they drew their "pool" of sexual candidates, there was the conventionality of the behavior itself. More than eight Americans in 10 had had sex with either no partners (12 percent) or only one partner (71 percent) in the past year; only 3 percent had had sex with five or more partners. Since the age of 18, not quite six in 10 (59 percent) had had sex with four or fewer partners; only 9 percent said that they had had sex with more than 20 partners in their lifetime. Three-quarters of the married men (75 percent) and 85 percent of the women said that they had been sexually faithful to their spouses during the course of their marriages. Among married persons, 94 percent said that they were faithful during the past year. The study's data on homosexual behavior were even more surprising, given a widespread assumption in many quarters that one out of every 10 Americans is gay. Only 2.8 percent of the men in the sample, and 1.4 percent of the women, identified themselves as homosexual or bisexual. Only 2 percent of the men and the women said that they had had sex with a same-gender partner in the past year; only 5.3 percent of the men, and 3.5 percent of the women said that they had done so since the age of 18; only 9 percent of the men and 4 percent of the women said that they had done so since the onset of puberty. These figures are a fraction of those that were obtained by the famous "Kinsey Reports" of roughly 50 years earlier (Kinsey et al., 1948, 1953), which were based on very skewed or biased samples of the American population. In short, regardless of how we feel about the "social bookkeeping" tradition of sex research, clearly it has something to offer any inquiring observer of the subject.

A third set of findings that the media and the public (and the researchers) found surprising related to sexual *frequency*, which was considerably lower than many observers had anticipated. Only one-third of the sample (34 percent) had sex as often as twice a week; of that total, only 8 percent said that they had sex as often as four or more times a week. One out 10 of the men in their fifties (11 percent), and three out of 10 of the women of that age (30 percent) did not have sex *at all* during the past year. Perhaps even more surprising, the *married* members of this sample were significantly

more likely than the single members to have had sex twice a week or more (41 versus 23 percent); however, cohabiting partners, who were living together but unmarried, were even more likely to have had sex this often (56 percent). In addition, the marrieds were most likely to report being physically and emotionally pleased with their sex and its frequency. The image of the wild, free, and easy sex lives of the "swinging singles" received a serious body blow from the findings of this study.

And a fourth set of findings pertained to the sexual *activities* that were most appealing to the sample. Traditional penile-vaginal sex turned out to be the only sexual activity that was almost universally appealing: 84 percent of the men and 77 percent of the women said that it was "very" appealing to them. Moreover, 80 percent of the sample said that *every* time they had sex during the past year, they had vaginal sex. Just under half (45 percent) of the men and just over a quarter (27 percent) of the women said that they found watching their partner undress "very" appealing; the same proportion said that receiving oral sex was very appealing to them. Of the remaining sex acts, only giving oral sex (34 for the men, 17 percent for the women) was appealing for a substantial proportion of the sample. All the other activities attracted only a tiny fraction of these figures. For instance, only 4 percent of the men (and only 1 percent of the women) said that having sex with a stranger was very appealing to them. All in all, the activities the respondents said they found appealing were quite traditional and conventional. Unusual, far-out, or "deviant" activities attracted very, very few positive evaluations.

How much confidence can we have in the findings of this survey? Some observers have criticized the study because they assumed that respondents would lie about their sex lives, for instance, that men would exaggerate the extent of their sexual behavior, while women would minimize it. Some critics claimed that many people simply forget about a great deal of what they do sexually, and hence, leave it out of their answers to an interviewer. It is too early to tell whether the results of this study can be taken as definitive; it will be a while before its validity will be sorted out by later researchers. Nonetheless, it is certainly the best survey ever conducted on sexual behavior in the United States. Its answers are as close to what we'll get to the true picture of sexual behavior for some time to come. The fact that the researchers used a variety of techniques to cross-check the respondents' answers (asking the same question twice, in different parts of the survey, in different ways, or having respondents fill out a questionnaire for especially touchy and sensitive subjects) gives us more confidence that the answers they received are accurate. And the fact that similar surveys have been conducted elsewhere—in Britain (Johnson et al., 1992, 1994; Wellings et al., 1994) and France (Spira et al., 1992, 1993), for instance—and have reached similar conclusions for a number of behaviors, again imparts confidence to the study's conclusions.

PROSTITUTION

Pornography and prostitution are both widely condemned and fairly widely practiced (although less so than public stereotypes hold, as we'll see), which makes them reasonable subjects for sociologists to investigate. Moreover, they are also instructive for the sociologist of deviance to study because with both, in this society, we experience a certain *ambivalence* toward them, that is, they are simultaneously tolerated and condemned, although not always by the same individuals or segments of society. And as we saw, both are also sociologically crucial to study because both generate a *social structure* (Gagnon and Simon, 1967, pp. 9–11), that is, a network of persons whose actions are patterned, predictable, normatively governed, and routinized. With both, specific individuals in particular positions are expected to do certain things, and for the most part, they actually do them. People in the social structures of prostitution and pornography have commitments, obligations, mutual expectations, individuals with whom they have more or less ongoing reciprocal relations; there is a "community" of prostitution (Prus and Irini, 1980), just as there is a community of pornography.

Both prostitution and pornography entail not simply a number of isolated, scattered individuals, each doing his or her own thing, or even sets of isolated pairs of individuals doing his or her own thing together, but a *social organization* surrounding both activities. Prostitution and pornography are both, in a sense, social *institutions*. In prostitution, these participating individuals involved in the social structure include not only the prostitute and her customer but also, at the very least, other prostitutes, pimps, the police and judges, hotel owners, clerks, and bellboys, landlords, and madams. The actors on the stage of pornography include

male and female actors or models, producers, photographers, camera and sound persons, customers, viewers, and purchasers of the pornographic material, distributors, owners, and employees of the retail stores or shops that sell, rent, or distribute the material. Thus, one of the more interesting aspects of these two forms of sexual deviance is that they are a product of a number of people acting more or less together to produce an institution or a form of behavior that is widely condemned and socially disvalued.

Prostitution is most often defined as the more or less indiscriminate granting of sexual favors for money or other things of value. However, constructionists emphasize that *how prostitution is defined* is not a simple concrete or objective fact. Some actions that qualify under this definition may not be regarded as prostitution in some quarters. Is a "sex surrogate"—a person, usually a woman, who assists a sexually dysfunctional client or patient of a therapist to become sexually effectual—a prostitute? The patient, the therapist, and the surrogate would never refer to such an action as prostitution, even though it technically often involves sex for pay. (Some prostitutes might even regard *themselves* as sex therapists, since they may help men to enjoy sex more!) At the same time, many observers have in fact labeled what sexual surrogates do as prostitution (Szasz, 1976, p. 21; Gold, 1976). Is the exchange of sex for crack cocaine an instance of prostitution? Many observers would most emphatically agree that it is, but most participants refer to it as *survival sex* rather than prostitution (McCoy, Miles, and Inciardi, 1995). If a call girl has a small list of only a few dozen clients—or if the mistress of a wealthy man has only one—is what she is engaging in prostitution? After all, with each, the "more or less indiscriminate" element of our definition is lacking. Still, many, probably most, observers would regard such behavior as prostitution. Does it make a difference if what is exchanged for sex is "things of value" and not money? If a car, a fur coat, or a diamond ring qualifies, what about dinner and a movie? Help with a woman's career? In ancient Babylonia, India, and Greece, a class of religious or temple prostitutes flourished; they were required to have sex under ritualized occasions, but they did not do so for material gain (K. Davis, 1971, pp. 267–270). Was this practice an instance of prostitution?

Again, what is or is not prostitution—what specific acts are included and which ones are excluded—is not a matter of their objective, concrete, or essential reality, but in large part *how we construct our categories*. The point is that there is no clear-cut behavioral category into which an unambiguous set of acts can be neatly pigeonholed as "prostitution," while all others are neatly excluded. Many actions clearly qualify, but as with all categories, prostitution is fuzzy around the edges; some observers or audiences will see a given action as prostitution, while others will not. There is some arbitrariness in what acts are included and which ones are excluded. In any discussion of the subject, we must remind ourselves that we are examining a socially constructed, not a natural, category. Still, most sociological studies of prostitution have focused on those forms that are fairly clear-cut, about which there are consistent rather than diverse designations.

Prostitution is a very well-known and notorious form of heterosexual deviance; it often ranks high on the lists supplied by audiences when they are asked for examples of deviant behavior. Several deviance textbooks (Thio, 1995, pp. 188–220; Ward, Carter, and Perrin, 1994, pp. 245–275) devote an entire chapter to prostitution. Objectively speaking, however, among males, prostitution represents a fairly small and declining source of sexual behavior. The American sex survey I discussed earlier in the chapter (Laumann et al., 1994; Michael et al., 1994) found that only 16 percent of the male respondents said that they had *ever* paid for sex, even once in their lives (Michael et al., 1994, p. 63). The proportion of men whose first sexual intercourse was with a prostitute declined from 7 percent of the men in their forties and fifties to 1.5 percent for those who were in their late teens to early twenties (p. 95). Very few of the men in their study— just six out of a thousand—visit prostitutes at least once a year (p. 213). The French sex survey arrived at precisely the same conclusion. Only 3 percent of the men in their sample had had sex with a prostitute in the past five years. As with the American survey, the oldest age cateogry (45–69) was *most* likely to have done so at least once in their lives (10 percent), while the youngest age category (20–24) was the *least* likely, only 2 percent (Spira et al., 1992, p. 408). The British sex survey's findings paralleled those conducted in the United States and France. In Britain, the proportion of men who have ever had sex with a prostitute varies inversely with age (p. 137), that is, the youngest (16-24) male respondents were *least* likely ever to have sex with

a prostitute (2 percent) and the oldest respondents (45-59) were *most* likely to have done so (10 percent). Only 2 percent of the entire sample had done so, even once, in the past five years (p. 137). This difference cannot be explained by the fact that older men have lived a longer period of time and hence, have had more experiences by that fact alone, since they were more likely to have had sex with prostitutes even when they were the same age as the younger men are now. Clearly, then, with respect to its incidence, sex with a prostitute is a fairly *minor* and *declining* source of sexual behavior for most men. At the same time, it does represent an interesting and revealing type or form of heterosexual deviance (Johnson et al., 1994).

Prostitutes can be male or female; they can sell sex favors to same- or opposite-sex customers. However, in terms of frequency, there are far more female prostitutes selling sexual favors to male customers than all other forms combined. In a sexist society, women can more readily earn a high income selling sexual favors than engaging in most other economic enterprises. Where women are treated as sex objects, where their chances for achievement are at least partially blocked in other areas, and where men can easily separate sex from affection, the institution of prostitution will flourish.

In many ways, rather than being an outright rejection of conventional society, prostitution is an extension and a reflection of conventional values, activities, and institutions. Prostitution upholds and reflects at least four basic values of American society. One is the double standard by which men and women are judged by two separate sets of sexual rules. Women who sell their bodies (or even who have sex with a substantial number of men) are far more often regarded as "tramps," "sluts," and "whores," earning widespread public scorn, while men who purchase sexual favors (or who sleep with many women) are socially and morally acceptable, even respectable. (This is changing, however; men who are apprehended by the police either soliciting an undercover officer or in the act of sex with a prostitute may suffer great embarrassment as a result of the ensuing publicity, as the English actor, Hugh Grant, discovered in 1995, or even jail time, as the convicted statutory rapist, Joey Buttafuoco, found out the same year.) The double standard necessitates the existence of a relatively small number of women who sexually service a very large number of men. The lust of men finds its outlet in "bad" women, outcast women—prostitutes. They are condemned; they are deviant. They are, according to this ideology, markedly different from the virtuous wives, mothers, and sisters who comprise the population of "good" women, the conventional women who tolerate the animal nature of their men, their husbands, brothers, and sons.

The institution of prostitution also affirms the *commercial money-making ethic* of a capitalist society. Engaging in sex, like selling used cars, is a commercial transaction. Women, like cars, are salable commodities. The sign of a true capitalist economy is that human relations become reduced to cash transactions. The basic reason why much human contact takes place is that someone expects to profit from it in a monetary sense.

Third, our economy is based on *alienated labor:* Workers are engaged in jobs they do not enjoy, jobs that are simply a means of keeping them alive, jobs with no enjoyment in them, little more than drudge labor. A society whose members expect and demand work that enriches them would not have the forms of prostitution that manifest themselves in our society.

The fourth feature of this society that encourages or nurtures prostitution is the *devaluation of women*. What they do is not held in the same regard as what men do. Women receive their reward primarily through men; their role is secondary—to serve men. Many men find it difficult to regard women as fully human, whether they are mothers or whores. Prostitution is the outward manifestation of a male-dominated society: an institution that caters to the desires and delusions of men, which exploits women and keeps them in their place.

The institution of prostitution, then, rests on and grows out of the double standard, the commercial ethic, alienated labor, and the inferior, secondary status of women. As such, it reflects and upholds the status quo rather than challenges or undermines it. Prostitution is not the manifestation of a true permissive society but of a restrictive, repressive one. While it is true that in severely sexually repressive societies, prostitution is rare, it would also be rare in a society in which true sexual freedom prevails. In fact, sexual repression and prostitution seem to go hand in hand. "I see it as a symptom. . . . of the kind of sex we have here now," a former prostitute writes. "I think as long as you're going to have compulsive marriage and compulsive families, you're going to have prostitu-

tion.. . . . Monogamy and prostitution go together" (Millett, 1973, pp. 50, 51). The motives of the customers who frequent prostitutes demonstrates this fact.

The Prostitute's Clients

The simple fact is that prostitution is based on many men paying for the sexual favors of usually anonymous women which they are unable to obtain noncommercially, in ordinary human relationships with women. These men are sexually deprived, not sexually free. As we've seen from the three nationally representative sex surveys, middle-aged men are overrepresented among the clients of prostitutes. The British sex survey found that widowed, separated, and divorced men are most likely to have had sex with a prostitute (14 percent), men who cohabit with their partners next most likely (9 percent), then married men (7 percent), and least likely are single men (4 percent), although this may in part reflect age differences (Johnson et al., 1994, p. 137). The American picture is almost certainly quite similar. And, since just over six out of 10 males age 18 and over in the population are married, this means that *most* of the customers of prostitutes are married, in all likelihood, in the United States as well as Great Britain. Their visits to prostitutes indicates that their marriages are sexually unsatisfying in some way. Perhaps their wives are less than enthusiastic about performing certain sex acts that these men desire, such as fellatio. Or perhaps these men feel guilty about demanding such acts of their wives—who, after all, are "good" women—but not of a "bad" woman, a whore.

It may be that these men are incapable of asking, or even unwilling to ask, their wives to perform or take part in certain acts *they themselves* consider deviant and "dirty." If their wives were to agree to the behavior they want, according to their standards, this would demean them in their eyes. They wouldn't want their wives to engage in "immoral" sexual acts, because they believe in the sexual double standard. One prostitute described a somewhat unusual act one of her customers wanted to try out (one, he discovered, that didn't turn him on at all, and which he abandoned midway into the act for ordinary intercourse). She says:

He absolutely could not try this with his wife. . . . [The] wives might be horny to try it, but the whole marriage scene—husbands and wives just don't open up this way to each other. And this man, I have a feeling he would be disappointed if he would do this with his wife and she went along with it. I think he probably has a certain amount of contempt for me because I will do these things, but I'm a whore, I'm supposed to do these things. He wouldn't be so pleased if his wife were in this position, and he had contempt for her. He wants her, if not on a pedestal, at least a long ways from being a hooker (Wells, 1970, p. 111).

Said another prostitute: "These men [Johns] couldn't have their wives do these things [that prostitutes do] because their wives might think that there's something wrong with them, and they would want a divorce. Some guys just can't get turned on by normal sex. This is the only way they can get off" (Zausner, 1986, p. 61).

Perhaps these men have not paid too much sexual attention to their wives, and consequently, they have become turned off by their husband's lackluster performances. Or perhaps because their wives have begun to expect sexual satisfaction—which these men feel inadequate and inept to provide—they seek the company of women who will put on a show of faking orgasms to bolster the sagging male ego. Men do not feel it as necessary to apologize to a prostitute for their inability as a lover.

Perhaps these men have become successful in their careers and have become persuaded that they are "worth" much more on the sexual marketplace than their wives are. In the equation of a sexist society, a man's desirability is largely tied in with his success, particularly in the economic sphere; a woman's desirability tends to be measured by her surface physical attributes. Prostitution is one social institution designed to handle this disparity.

Perhaps the client is starved for companionship and intimacy, for someone with whom he can say absolutely anything without fear or embarrassment. Many men do not have an "anything goes" relationship with a woman, any woman. They may be trapped in verbal, emotional, and behavioral games of masculinity that involve bragging, lying, and pretending invulnerability. The prostitute's room may serve as a kind of confessional. As Wayland Young says about the prostitute, "Listening, next to fucking, is the thing she does most of" (1966, p. 142).

There are men who simply prefer sex for pay, because they want things emotionally clean, neat, and uninvolved. "Prostitution is much less of a pressured interaction" than conventional courtship, says

psychiatrist Joshua Golden. "A prostitute is a complete and total stranger," says Warren Farrell, author of *The Myth of Male Power*. For a man, "the prostitute has the promise of being quick, easy. The contract is clear." Adds Gilbert Geis, a criminologist, the ease of the encounter is its major appeal. "No fuss, no muss. Sometimes men don't have the energy to be romantic and social—they want to be indifferent" (Anonymous, 1995).

Of course, these do not exhaust all the customers' reasons for visiting a prostitute. There are many men who travel a great deal—sailors, salesmen, truck drivers—and are frequently in a town in which they are strangers. Or there are men who work in an area that is located far from an even-sexed population, such as lumberjacks, members of the armed forces, oil workers, and so on. Rather than face the prospect of an empty hotel room or all-male companionship, or the unlikely success of a "one night stand," they seek out the services of a prostitute. Some men have just recently moved to a new location and have not yet found female companionship. There are physically deformed or handicapped men who, as a result of rejection or fear of rejection, turn to prostitutes for sex and the semblance of companionship.

And there are what are referred to as "kinkies," men whose sexual interests are so bizarre that it would be almost impossible to locate women whom they would not have to pay to agree to their requests. (Or men who are too ashamed to ask their wives or lovers to take part in them.) Sadomasochism, with the man as the "submissive" partner and the woman as the "dominant" partner, is probably the most commonly requested form of "kinky" sex prostitutes encounter. Various fetishes also make their appearance, with clients dressed in women's clothes, a fixation on overcoats, articles of rubber and leather, feathers, high heels, nylon stockings, and so on. Nearly all prostitutes, if they have been plying their trade for a significant length of time, encounter kinkies. Xaviera Hollander, author of several books on her experiences as a prostitute, classifies "freaks" into, first, "sadists and masochists, who need to inflict pain or have it inflicted," and second, "weirdos, or sickies, whose preference is for more subtle, way-out fantasy." A freak, Ms. Hollander writes, is basically anyone who needs degradation, humiliation, or punishment to achieve erotic gratification (1972, p. 208).

How Do Prostitutes Feel about Their Work?

Many conventional men imagine that the prostitute is attracted to the profession because she enjoys sex and wants as much of it as she can get. This is male mythology, plain and simple. Said one prostitute about another woman, "Sandra would be no good" as a prostitute. "She likes men and she enjoys fucking" (Young, 1966, p. 131). Participants in the prostitution scene—prostitutes themselves, pimps, madams, everyone, that is, except for customers—will almost universally say that the woman's enjoyment of intercourse, on those extremely rare occasions when it does occur, actually gets in her way, it does not make her a more effective prostitute. This is true both of the specific sex act and of sex with customers generally. One woman, Joyce, a prostitute, explains it this way:

I would say that nothing could prompt me to have an orgasm or even become excited with a John. . . . I doubt that I would be able to manage it.. . . . I will pretend to be excited, and to come at the moment he comes, but if I really got excited I would be all involved with myself, and the timing would be thrown off, and actually he wouldn't have as good a time as if I were faking it. It's funny to think of, but he gets more for his money if it's a fake than if he were to get the real thing (Wells, 1970, p. 139).

A woman who does enjoy sex with her customers does not make a good prostitute, according to those who are acquainted with this institution firsthand. Instead of thinking about the most effective way of making money at the job, such a woman would be doing things for her own pleasure and enjoyment. For instance, if she met a man who pleased her in bed, she would want to stay with him a protracted length of time, thereby extending their turnaround time and hence cutting down on how much she can earn. Or she would allow a man to perform oral sex on her, which is time-consuming; it is not considered a money-making activity in the trade. It is relevant only insofar as it pleases the customer and induces him to pay more. If a woman treats it as an avenue to her pleasure, she is being a poor businesswoman. "It's terrible if they enjoy their work," says Silky the pimp. "I think that anyone who would love it has a problem" (Gootman and Mekelburg, 1973, p. 32). When asked if prostitutes have a touch of "nymphoma-

nia" in them, Sheri, a madam, replies, "No, definitely not. A nymphomaniac couldn't make it in this business for a number of reasons. For one, she likes sex too much to use it for financial gain. For another, she is constantly thinking, 'Maybe this is finally the man who is going to help me reach *my* climax.' Consequently, she is totally worthless in the profession" (Wolman, 1973, p. 111). A prostitute who is concerned with her own enjoyment is contemptuously referred to by others on the scene as a "come freak."

The fact is that few prostitutes enjoy their work. While the major inducement is money, the major "unpleasantry," according to one study, is having to engage in sex with their customers (Gray, 1973, p. 411). Most look upon having sex with many strangers with distaste; most disdainfully view the men with whom they have sex. "Usually I can't stand tricks," one prostitute explains. "It's sex with tricks I hate. Sex is horrible. Just horrible. I used to be able to stand it, but now I close my eyes and keep thinking it's a dog fucking me. It's just disgusting. If I didn't have a strong mind, I would go off— crazy. . . . When I get a guy up to the apartment, I get the money and then I light a cigarette and put it in the ashtray. I clean the guy off and fuck. When the cigarette burns out, I know the time is up" (Hall, 1972, pp. 100, 102). A prostitute named "Juicy" puts the matter bluntly and plainly: "I never enjoy sex while I'm working. I'm only interested in one thing, money" (Zausner, 1986, p. 43).

The reasons for this attitude are not hard to fathom. It is extremely difficult, if not impossible, to develop a positive and affectionate attitude toward hundreds of strangers while engaging in the most intimate act possible with them. Prostitutes feel that commercial sex is a gruesome mockery of the love relationship. Nearly everyone in this society, regardless of how cynical they may become, has been taught, and still to some extent believe in, the romantic ideal. Where tenderness, affection, even passion, are absent in behavior that we've learned is supposed to be dominated by these qualities, it becomes an embittering experience. When this is multiplied hundreds of times over, the result can be positively numbing.

"One day and then another day, and all the days are the same. It's just one thing after another, one man after another. I see this endless parade of penises. Coming at me. Just an endless parade of marching penises," one prostitute explains. Eventually, she says, she just thinks of the customer "as a penis with a body attached." The only way to deal with this alienating experience, she explains, is to remain absolutely "detached. Removed. Miles and miles away" (Wells, 1970, pp. 88, 92, 97).

A woman interviewed by Kate Millett, feminist author of *Sexual Politics*, explains her reactions to her former life as a prostitute. "The worst thing about prostitution is that you're obliged not only to sell sex only, but your humanity. That's the worst part of it: that what you're selling is your human dignity." This woman, an ex-prostitute (now a psychologist with a Ph.D.), tells us that the specific aspect of sex for sale was only one part of the indignity; mainly it was "being a bought person," having to play at a charade of being polite, agreeable, and charming to men who were unappealing and odious to her. "That's the most humiliating thing," she says, "having to agree with them all the time because you're bought." It is true that other professions also require a certain prostitution of the soul, such as being agreeable to a boss whom one does not respect, selling products that people don't really need, being friendly to rude, insensitive customers. "But there's a special indignity in prostitution," this woman explains, "as if sex were dirty and men can only enjoy it with someone *low*. It involves a kind of disdain, and a kind of triumph over another human being" (Millett, 1973, pp. 57, 58).

The prostitute typically harbors even more contempt for her client than he for her. The term "trick" expresses this contempt: Her customer has been "tricked" out of his money, his dignity, and his manhood—the very things he has tried so hard to demonstrate. He has been deceived into thinking of himself as sexually potent and desirable at the very moment he is being relieved of his money. The prostitute usually thinks of her customer as basically stupid; he believes practically everything she tells him. "The hardest thing to learn is the vulnerability of the man. You have to make yourself believe that this man is stupid enough to believe anything you tell him. And he is" (Hall, 1972, p. 59). The prostitute feels that she sees the John *as he really is*, but he sees only the social facade of her— the illusion she constructs in order to part him from his money. He is doubly contemptible, first, for being "tricked" out of his money, and second, for believing in the phony act the prostitute devised to take it.

How Do Women Become Prostitutes?

A great deal of research on prostitution has attempted to answer the question of what factors are associated with entering "the life." Poverty or an economically deprived background is one of the most commonly cited of such factors. It is no doubt true that street prostitutes are more likely to have been recruited from the poorer segments of the society (Hoigard and Finstad, 1992), but that has to be qualified. There are many women who are not, and never were, poor, and who become prostitutes. The street prostitute with a working- or lower-class background is far more visible than the middle-class, college-educated call girl. The former's visibility makes it easier for her to be both arrested and studied. As a result, the sociologist may underestimate the number of women who stem from a middle-class background (who are far more likely to end up being only semi-visible call girls) and to exaggerate the number of women who come from a lower- or working-class background (who are more likely to end up working on the street, and to be highly visible). Furthermore, relatively affluent women may be more likely to engage in activities that very few observers would label or enumerate as acts of actual prostitution, but which are outwardly similar to it in many ways, like marrying for money or receiving gifts, entertainment, wining and dining in exchange for intercourse. The last chapter in Gail Sheehy's (1973) book on prostitution is entitled "The Ultimate Trick"; it chronicles one woman's climb to great wealth through the wise and shrewd use of her body.

Another factor that the available research links with prostitution is sexual contact with many partners on a superficial basis at a relatively early age (Hoigard and Finstad, 1992). Nanette Davis, in an exploratory study of 30 prostitutes selected from three correctional institutions (1971), characterizes the process of drifting from casual sex with many boys (often referred to as "promiscuity") at an early age to the young woman's first few acts of prostitution. The average age of first intercourse for Davis's women was 13.6. Petting experiences were almost entirely absent; their first sexual contacts typically involved intercourse right from the beginning. And for 28 out of the 30, that first experience was felt as either distasteful or meaningless. The average age of this sample's first experience of prostitution was 17.3. What happened during the three or four years in between? This is described as a "preliminary period of vague, floating promiscuity," of an "increasing irrelation to society" (Young, 1966, p. 132). All except two of Davis's sample of jailed women reported that they had been regarded by parents, teachers, and neighbors as troublemakers, slow learners, and misfits, in short, even before they became prostitutes they were seen as deviants. As adolescents, all except seven had been confined to a juvenile home or training facility for truancy, incorrigibility, or sexual delinquency. Davis speculates that this process of typing and labeling is a contributing condition that facilitates the emergence of a deviant identity: "In the interactional process with significant others . . . the girl achieves an identity of one who is different. She is expected to behave in unconventional ways" (N. Davis, 1971, p. 303; see also Hoigard and Finstad, 1992). One small measure of this is that girls who were confined to a training school engaged in acts of prostitution for the first time at a significantly earlier age than nontraining school girls, at 15.8 versus 21.3 years of age.

Many studies indicate that a very high proportion of women who become prostitutes were the victims of incestuous sex with their fathers or stepfathers, violence within their families and/or rape or other coerced sex at an early age (James and Meyerding, 1977; Rosenblum, 1975; Pines and Silbert, 1983; Zausner, 1986). Early victimization seems to figure prominently in the lives of prostitutes. It is likely that these experiences contribute to a young woman's loss of self-esteem, to a view of herself as "sexually debased," the inevitable target of sexual exploitation and objectification. Rather than turn her negative feelings on her oppressors, some victims turn them inwardly, feeling somehow responsible for their victimization.

Many sensational articles have been published that claim that a high proportion of young women who become prostitutes enter the life as a result of being forced against their will by being beaten, tortured, and raped by pimps (Tomlinson, 1981; Adams, 1981). It would be a mistake to think that this *never* occurs. In fact, coerced prostitution is fairly common in a number of poor, Third World countries (perhaps Thailand is the most well-known instance); it even takes place within the borders of the United States. In the latter case, women in poor, Third World countries will be offered free passage to the U.S. in exchange for a job here; they may not know that the offer comes from a criminal gang. Upon entering the country, they may be informed that the job is prostitution; they are told that they must work for a stipulated period of time to pay off their debt for the transportation. Such enterprises are difficult to combat, even in the United States, because of threats made against the women by persons who profit from their employment. They may be held virtual prisoners for years until they have paid off their indebtedness. In 1995, one such enterprise was broken up as a result of several raids by New York City inspectors; the madam of the brothel, which catered more or less exclusively to Asian men, testified for the prosecution in exchange for immunity, detailing its operation. The prostitutes had been "bought," that is, the entrepreneurs, including the madam, had paid a certain sum of money for their passage; in exchange, they "owed" a certain period of service, that is, sex with a certain number of men. In addition, they owed a certain sum of money for their room and board, again, which was paid off through sex with a specific number of men. Such enterprises are not unusual in the United States; rarely are they broken up by arrest and information gathered on their operations.

Forced prostitution is much more common outside the borders of the United States. It is often—perhaps even usually—in conjunction with the prostitution of children. Observers have noted a sharp increase in the incidence of prostitution in Asia among children under the age of 15 or 16. Poverty has always fueled the prostitution of children and young adolescents. What has been different over the past one or two decades, however, is that three factors have emerged, converged, and pushed the practice to unprecedented heights. The first is the AIDS crisis. Customers fear infection and believe that young teenagers—especially virgins—are unlikely to carry the infectious virus; hence, they will request them specifically. Ironically, the second is the worldwide spread of affluence, or to be more precise, the spread of *symbols* or *manifestations* of affluence even to the remotest corners of the globe. The parents of a 14-year-old girl living in a tiny village in northern Thailand, only recently supplied with electric power, may decide that they cannot live without a television set and will "sell" her to a recruiting agent into virtual bondage. Although the TV set was not the cause of her being forced into prostitution, acquiring expensive goods has become an impetus for unscrupulous parents to force their children into sexual bondage. And the third factor contributing to the recent explosion of child prostitution is the huge increase in tourism to certain "wide open" Asian locations, most notably Bangkok. The Thai government is unwilling to step in and attempt to control this trade because Thailand earns more foreign currency from tourism than from any other source, including rice (Miller, 1995). Not all or even most of the prostitution in Asia is forced (but see Barry, 1995, for a contrary position), although given the extreme poverty of certain provinces in Thailand, the Philippines, India, and other East Asian countries, it would be difficult to make a sharp distinction between "forced" and "voluntary" prostitution—and children are certainly in the minority among Asian prostitutes. Still, a substantial proportion of prostitution in Asia is forced in the most literal sense of the word, and a substantial proportion of Asian prostitutes are under the age of 15 or 16 (Robinson, 1993; Kempton, 1992; Simons, 1994; Hornblower, 1993). Hence, the view that prostitution is very rarely a result of threats or brutality by a pimp must be qualified so as to encompass a fairly specific set of contexts. It certainly is one of the factors that explains how some women in some locales become prostitutes. In the United States, typically, "charm, flattery, the promise of money, protection, companionship, and emotional closeness are enough to initiate girls into the world of prostitution" (Bracey, 1979, p. 23).

It would be foolish to think that a single generalization can serve as a universal explanation as to why some women become prostitutes, especially given the fact that it is a practice that flourishes in extremely diverse social and cultural settings. No single factor can possibly explain prostitution everywhere for all women. But many women do go through one or several of a fairly limited set of common experiences. There are many different *paths* to prostitution, but one experience is fairly widespread. This is the process of *deviance neutralization*. We do know for sure that prostitution is a form of deviance; nearly all girls grow up learning that prostitution is disvalued, worthy of condemnation. Most women who eventually become prostitutes at one time looked down upon the practice and the women who engaged in it. For most, it was an undesirable thing to do and to be. It is a widely condemned activity. Even if they or persons in their milieu did not share that view, at the very least, they were *aware* of its deviant status. So, for women to become prostitutes, at least willingly, it is necessary for them to look upon prostitution with enough favor to allow

themselves to participate in it. In other words, in their own minds, they have to neutralize the stigma attached to prostitutes and prostitution. They have to reconcile something of a positive and desirable self-image with their participation in an activity that they look upon with scorn. (Another possibility is that they maintain a negative self-image and participate in prostitution because of it. However, the available sociological studies on prostitution do not favor this interpretation, as we'll see momentarily.)

Deviance neutralization takes place among participants in a variety of deviant activities: juvenile delinquents (Sykes and Matza, 1957), rapists (Scully, 1990; Scully and Marolla, 1984, 1985), child molesters (McCaghy, 1967, 1968), professional hit men (Levi, 1981), homosexuals (Dank, 1971; Troiden, 1979, 1988), embezzlers (Cressey, 1953), white-collar and corporate criminals (Benson, 1985), psychotherapists who have sex with patients (Pogrebin, Poole, and Martinez, 1992), and so on. In the study by Nanette Davis on how some women became prostitutes, few of the women launched themselves directly from a few initial acts of prostitution into a full-time career of selling sex. For a majority (21 out of 30), there was a transitional stage involving occasional acts of prostitution, a zigzag pattern of vacillation between deviant and conventional lives and identities. Conventional attachments have not yet been given up or denied; their self-definition as prostitutes is delayed, not easily or smoothly incorporated into their sense of self. There seems to be something of an internal struggle taking place. During this period of vacillation, attempts are made to adopt the deviant identity without self-condemnation. What is needed to progress further is a successful effort to *normalize* prostitution (N. Davis, 1971, p. 312). Processes of accommodation take place to incorporate a once-condemned publicly deviant status into one's self-conception. The movement into accepting selling sex as a vocation (p. 315) is made only as a result of resolving this stuggle over self-acceptance, this problem of maintaining self-respect. To do this, an emphasis is placed on the desirability of other values—those from which prostitutes can attain achievement—mainly monetary success. Another weapon in the stigma neutralization armament is the idea that straight people are to be looked upon with increasing distaste. "I can't cope with square people," (p. 316) the prostitute will say to herself. "All the square people I meet are pale. You get hooked on this life and nothing else satisfies you" (Hall, 1972, p. 176). What we see is something of a twofold process: the normalization of engaging in acts of prostitution, and the denial of the legitimacy and validity of conventional behavior and values. Prostitutes "develop a set of beliefs which counteract the social anathema attached to their way of life" (Jackman et al., 1963). Facilitating this process is an identification with the criminal or "hustler" lifestyle and seeking out, or falling into the company of, persons who reward and who believe in deviant, unconventional values.

Many women are initiated into prostitution over a period of time through a step-by-step process. They do something that bothers their conscience only slightly, something that demands that they redefine themselves, revise their self-image in a deviant direction. This permits them to participate in another act that they see as a bit more deviant, something that they ordinarily would condemn slightly more strenuously. But their attitude has already been revised toward that behavior because they've taken part in something that really wasn't radically different from it. Eventually, they step over into a realm they themselves have to admit is truly deviant. Many of us engage in actions that could be seen, even by ourselves, as similar to prostitution. Men may act obsequious or ingratiating to a boss for career advancement, or even spend eight hours a day at a job they detest. Some women may flirt with or act charming to persons they aren't fond of because these people can help them. The line between completely pure, morally impeccable behavior and outright prostitution becomes blurred by many ethically marginal actions. The steps from one to the other may be quite small and almost imperceptible. Some people are not able to draw a clear line in the sand.

One woman, Bernice, explains her initiation into prostitution in the following manner. She worked as a model for a garment manufacturer who was married and had four children. She had an affair with him that "eventually sputtered to an end." One afternoon, she and a number of models, modeled a line of clothes for several buyers for a chain of Midwestern clothing stores. Later, her boss came to her and told her that one of them expressed an interest in her. "Look," he said, "this fellow thinks you're really beautiful, and he'd like to go out with you. You do what you want to do, but if you want to go out with him—well, it might be good for business" (Wells, 1970, p. 29). She asked her boss to point

the man out, and Bernice decided that he was "not bad looking." She says that she didn't think "about any sex part to it. Not immediately." But while on the date, she realized that if the man liked her, he would naturally want to make love to her. "Here I was actually going out on a date with a John, that's what it really amounted to, and I didn't see it in those terms at all" (p. 30).

She did go out on a date with the man, and she slept with him. After coming to work the next day, her boss took her aside and gave her an envelope with a sum of money in it. Bernice was shocked. "I asked him what kind of girl he thought I was. Can you imagine a line like that? But that's what I said." Her boss looked chagrined. He explained that she had "showed this fellow a good time, and maybe he'll be grateful in the future." Her boss explained that he had given her presents in the past—why not now? "It's funny," Bernice remarked, "how you won't mind doing something, but you will mind the name, the label." The next occasion, a week later, her boss set up a date with another buyer. She knew this time that she would get extra money for it, plus the next day off. And she was not naive this time; she knew that sex would be involved. So she gradually began accepting dates with buyers, working for the same boss. And later, some were buyers and some weren't— some were just friends of her boss. And later still, she began accepting dates from these buyers on her own, independent of arrangements her boss had set up—and was paid for it. Finally, her boss told her that it would be a good idea if she stopped coming to work altogether and concentrated entirely on being "available if someone wanted to see her."

At each step, Bernice said, "I would keep being amazed at the way I could just shrug off the changes I was going through. . . . And I look at myself in the mirror, and I'm amazed to see that I'm still me" (Wells, 1970, pp. 33–34).

Prostitution and AIDS

It might seem reasonable to assume that a major reason for the wildfire spread of the AIDS virus in the 1980s and 1990s has been sexual encounters between prostitutes and their customers. The logic makes a great deal of sense. For one thing, in a number of countries, this is true. One recent study of 1,000 prostitutes in Nairobi, Kenya, found that 85 percent were infected with the AIDS virus (Lambert, 1988, p. B5). Much the same picture holds for Asia (Robinson, 1993, p. 493). However, in contrast, in the United States, only a small minority of prostitutes who are not intravenous drug users or the sex partners of IV drug users are infected with HIV or AIDS. In one study of prostitutes in eight areas around the country, 13 percent tested positive for the AIDS virus. The figure was 21 percent for the self-admitted needle-using drug takers and only 5 percent for those who denied injecting drugs; most of the latter had had drug-using sex partners (Lambert, 1988, p. B5). This same conclusion has been reached in a number of studies on AIDS in prostitutes (Wallace, 1989). In one study, out of 78 call girls, only one tested HIV-positive, and she had a history of IV drug use (Seidlin et al., 1988).

There are at least two reasons why AIDS is rarely spread from prostitutes to customers in the United States, aside from the relatively low rate of infection among prostitutes. (And recall, too, that a fairly small proportion of the male population resorts to sex with prostitutes.) The first is that nearly all prostitutes use condoms nowadays. (All of the prostitutes interviewed by Zausner, 1986, stated that they insist that their customers use condoms for all sex acts, including fellatio and even masturbation.) Infection is considerably less likely if a condom is used. A second reason why such infection is fairly uncommon is that heterosexual intercourse, both vaginal and oral, is not an efficient spreader of the AIDS virus. The chance of contracting AIDS in a single sexual encounter with someone who is infected is roughly one in 500. Using a condom brings this risk down to nearly zero. One-time sexual intercourse without a condom with a partner who is not in a high-risk category but whose infection status is unknown carries a risk of infection of one in five million, or "about the same as the risk of being killed in a traffic accident while driving ten miles on the way to that sexual encounter" (Boffey, 1988a, p. A18).

Although prostitution cannot be dismissed as a potential future source of AIDS—especially given what we know about the tragic experience in other countries—in the United States, for now, prostitution is not a major, or even much of a minor, source of AIDS.

As with all generalizations, this one must be qualified. As I said at the beginning of this section, some sexual actions are not clear-cut instances of prostitution; they may be a significant source of the spread of the HIV virus, but not defined as pros-

titution per se. It turns out that a type of *prostitution-like* behavior *does* contribute to the AIDS picture: sex-for-crack exchanges. While men are significantly more likely to *possess and sell* crack—men control the *distribution* of the drug—women are at least as likely to *use* it as men. Since crack is a drug that acts over an extremely short duration, a habitual user may take it a number of times a day—a minority of users, as we saw in the drug chapter, although nonetheless a significant minority. The only possible way for most poor women to use crack on a regular basis is to trade sex for crack (Inciardi, 1989; McCoy, Miles, and Inciardi, 1995). Since sex is a frequent accompaniment of crack use in crack dens and condom use is rare, this paves the way for widespread HIV contamination. In one study, a comparison was made between two categories of drug users: those who used crack and those who did not. One-quarter of the crack-using women in the sample said that they had traded sex for drugs, whereas less than 3 percent of the noncrack drug-using women said that they had. The crack-using group had had sex with 13.6 men during the previous month, while the noncrack drug-using group averaged only 1.6. As we might expect, HIV infection was significantly higher, twice as high, for the crack users, 20 percent versus 11 percent (McCoy, Miles, and Inciardi, 1995; McCoy and Inciardi, 1995, p. 101). Clearly, crack use puts women at considerable risk for contracting the HIV virus (McCoy and Inciardi, 1995, p. 101), and sex-for-crack exchanges represent one major reason for this vulnerability. Again, these women are not technically prostitutes, but they are engaging in sex for things of value—that is, crack—and they do increase the likelihood of the spread of AIDS. At the same time, most are not professional prostitutes, who are far more likely to protect themselves and their clients by taking certain precautions to prevent the spread of AIDS.

PORNOGRAPHY

There are strong parallels between pornography and prostitution. In fact, the word "pornography" stems from the ancient Greek and literally means writings about prostitutes or harlots. For the most part, both prostitution and pornography entail the use of women's bodies for men's pleasure. Both cater largely, almost overwhelmingly, to the desires of men; that is, most customers of prostitutes are men, most consumers of pornography are men. Both institutions are, for the most part, based on alienated labor: women pretending to enjoy themselves while engaged in activities they find distasteful or, at best, neutral. (As Marx said, much the same also applies to most men and women who work at licit jobs in a capitalist society.) Both prostitution and pornography grow out of women's inferior status; both entail treating women as objects. In both prostitution and pornography, equality is usually absent: They represent the expression of a certain kind of power of one individual, or category of individuals, over another.

What Is Pornography?

As with every other form of behavior, the definitional question must be answered before an intelligent discussion can follow. One problem is that pornography has always been a battleground of controversy, as we'll see shortly. On one side of the controversy, pornography is opposed and criticized by conservatives and moralists (Hudson, 1986), and, since the 1970s, by the antipornography faction of feminism (Lederer, 1982), called Women Against Pornography (or WAP). As we've seen with other types of deviant behavior, in any area where controversy is intense, even defining the relevant phenomena can be a problem.

Most antipornography feminists make a clear distinction between "erotica," which some claim to regard as good, and pornography, which everyone ought to recognize as bad. Erotica is the representation of "a sexual encounter between adult persons which is characterized by mutual respect" (Longino, 1982, p. 28), mutual affection, desire between equals, while, in contrast, pornography is sexually explicit material which entails "clear force, or an unequal power that spells coercion . . . , no sense of equal choice or equal power" (Steinem, 1982, p. 23). Interestingly, antipornography advocates very seldom offer concrete examples of erotica.

According to some observers, this distinction between erotica and pornography "sounds promising, but it doesn't hold up." Erotica, which is literature or pictures containing sexual themes, may actually be used for pornographic purposes. In fact, the term "erotica" is widely used as a euphemism for "classy porn." If it is expressed in "literary language" or if it takes the form of esthetically pleasing photographs or videos, and is used and

consumed by the educated, by members of the upper-middle class, it is called erotica; if it is esthetically trashy and "can't pretend to any purpose" except sexual arousal, it is called pornography— by its very nature "smut." The "erotica-versus-porn" distinction evades the "question of how porn is *used*. It endorses the portrayal of sex as we might like it to be and condemns the portrayal of sex as it too often is, whether in action or in fantasy. But if pornography is to arouse, it must appeal to the feelings we have, not those by some utopian standard we ought to have. . . . In practice, attempts to sort out good erotica from bad porn inevitably come down to 'What turns me on is erotic; what turns you on is pornographic.'" (Willis, 1983, p. 463).

In short, as Gagnon and Simon observe, the category pornography "is as elusive as mercury" (1973, p. 281). Thus, rather than insisting on a single definition of pornography as valid, it makes more sense to isolate several *dimensions* that capture specific angles or aspects of the phenomenon. Since some observers will see as pornography works that others would regard as innocuous or even innocent of sexual meaning, it becomes necessary to determine *how pornography is defined by different audiences*. At least three different definitions could be used:

1. The *functional* definition: *works consumed for the purpose of sexual excitation*. This definition looks at material from the point of view of the *consumers* of the material, and primarily in terms of their use of it, and the responses it generates in them.
2. The *labeling* definition: *works that much of the public thinks of as obscene*—that is, material which, it is believed, excites "lustful" thoughts and which is therefore sexually vulgar, offensive, shameful, and disgusting. This definition looks at pornography from the point of view of the disapproving public, or segments of the public.
3. *The* genre *definition: works that are created primarily for the purpose of arousing the lust of an audience or customers and that conform to a narrow and distinct formula*. The genre definition takes the point of view of the *creators* and the *producers* of pornographic works (who, in turn, are trying to figure out what the audience wants). They assemble, manufacture, and sell commercialized sex; they want to turn on the largest number of men possible, and want to make a profit doing it.

These definitions lead us to two inescapable conclusions: (1) *Something may be pornographic in one sense, but not in another.* (2) *Something may be pornographic to some people, but not to others.*

Any meaningful look at pornography must necessarily be relativistic. Some works can arouse sexual excitation in one individual but not in another; many people are sexually bored and unresponsive to material that others become wildly excited by. Most men are not sexually excited by pictures of women being bound and gagged, dressed in uniforms or leather attire, wearing masks or spike heels, or brandishing whips On the other hand, a minority of men are so wildly turned on by such photographs that an entire industry is based on supplying them to customers (Becker, 1963, pp. 20–21). In addition, standards as to what is pornographic change over time. In the pre-*Playboy* era, when photographs of nude women were more difficult to obtain than they are today, many young men found photographs of bare-breasted "native" women in the pages of *National Geographic* to be extremely arousing and used them in conjunction with masturbation. Today, with more revealing and explicit material far more readily available, adolescents rarely find these pictures exciting, and rarely use them for the purpose of masturbation. Thus, in the past, such pictures *were* pornographic to many adolescents; today, they are not. The pictures haven't changed very much, but the reponses to them have.

Can great works of art be pornographic? Of course: *Insofar as they are offensive to some*, and *insofar as they are used for the purpose of arousal and masturbation*, they *are* clear-cut instances of pornography. To the extent that neither is true, they are not pornographic. The categories "work of art" and "pornographic" do not inhabit separate worlds; they overlap and cross-cut one another (Peckham, 1969). In 1814, a painting of a nude woman, entitled *Venus*, by Diego Velasquez (1599-1660)—one of the greatest painters who ever lived—was described by a Spanish Inquisitor General as "obscene." In 1914, while hanging in the National Gallery of London, this work was slashed by a feminist demonstrator because she regarded it as obscene (Troutman, 1965, p. 42). Thus, *to this Inquisitor General*, and *to this early feminist*, Velasquez's *Venus* was obscene—a pornographic painting. The fact that it would not be so regarded by hardly anyone today does not detract from the fact that it *was* so regarded at one time by some

observers. To select an even more extreme example, the antiporn feminist Susan Griffin labels as pornographic the works of the German painter Franz Marc (1880–1916)—work which is utterly devoid of sexual content—a judgment nearly all art historians and critics, not to mention ordinary, run-of-the-mill appreciators of art, would find totally baffling, indeed, outright bizarre (see Griffin, 1981, pp. 4, 8ff.). To focus on our second dimension, the fact that many artworks are not only sexually exciting, but have been used for the purpose of sexual arousal—specifically masturbation—can be verified by interviewing any number of sensual men and women of artistic taste.

Our last definition of pornography—the genre definition—looks at works from a different angle. Anyone who is in the business of supplying material which is used for the purpose of sexual arousal must have some sense of what it is that turns customers on; if not, they will go out of business. Thus, producers and manufacturers of sexually explicit material rely on formulas and conventions that they believe will arouse consumers and stimulate them to purchase the product in question. However, rather than there being a single convention, there are a number of them, each catering to the tastes of different *segments* of the pornography market.

What might be regarded as "classy" or middle-class "soft core" photographic pornography is one such convention; the pages of *Playboy* and *Penthouse* supply examples here. If these magazines were to violate the canons spelled out by the genre, their readers would be disappointed, and their sales would suffer. The women whose photographs appear in the pages of these magazines are overwhelmingly young—late teens to middle twenties. They are, in conventional terms, extremely attractive. Blemishes on their faces and bodies do not appear. They tend to be slim and long-legged, and in recent years, have busts of a certain size (not too small, not too large). Nearly all are white. All are, or seem to be, middle class—"the girl next door." These women are photographed in a variety of poses with respect to undress: some of the shots show them fully clothed, some depict partial nudity, and some are of complete nudity. The conventions ruling their fully nude photographs are fairly clear-cut and detailed. For instance, while pubic hair has been allowed since 1970, pictures flaunting the woman's inner labia are not acceptable in "classy" soft-core photographs. Men sporting an erection never appear in these pictures; in fact, most of them, at least in the main pictorials, the centerfolds, are of the women alone, very rarely with a nude male accompaniment. And overt violence hardly ever appears in the photographs in these magazines (though it may in their cartoons or stories). These are some of the current conventions that guide middle-class "soft-core" photographic pornography. (The canons for working-class soft-core pornographic photographs, exemplified by those that appear in *Hustler*, are somewhat different.)

"Hard-core" pornography is an altogether different convention. In hard core, sexual explicitness reigns supreme. Hard core contains sex and little else; its sex is out in the open, leaving little or nothing to the imagination. Erections bloom like flowers in springtime; intercourse is depicted explicitly, as are anal and oral sex. To pander to the sexual cravings of a large number of men, it is necessary to get to sex fairly quickly, without much ado. The proportion of explicit sex relative to everything else is extremely high in hard-core genre pornography. The ratio of photographs or footage depicting total nudity to those depicting clothed subjects is extremely high. Within hard core, there are a variety of genres. *Mainstream* hard core focuses on activities that many, if not most, couples are likely to engage in, such as intercourse, fellatio, cunnilingus, and anal sex. But there are deviations from this genre as well; minority sexual expressions find their way into pornographic fare in the form of "golden showers," sex with animals, S&M (sadomasochism), sex with amputees, sex with children, and so on. Each form of sexual expression, however repugnant to most of us, has generated pornography that is produced, distributed, and sold to an audience which wants it to look a certain way.

These, then, are the outlines of pornography. What effects does it have on the viewer, the reader, the consumer?

The Effects of Pornography: Definitions and Concepts

What happens to people who read or view pornography? What effects does it have? While dozens of possible effects could be studied, in recent years, most research and commentary on the subject have focused on aggression and violence. Specifically: Does exposure to pornography stimulate men to become more violent in their behavior toward women, that is, to be more likely to engage in rape and other forms of assault, including mutilation,

torture, and murder? There are at least three possible models with respect to the effects of pornography on male aggression against women. The first is the *catharsis* theory; the second is the imitation or *modeling* theory (McCormack, 1978); and the third is the *no effects* theory.

The catharsis theory, which is widely regarded as obsolete nowadays, is that pornography acts as a kind of "safety valve," permitting men to express "antisocial" sexual impulses harmlessly. Pornography arouses the viewer sexually; by satisfying this arousal through masturbation, there is less sexual energy left over for aggressive encounters with the women in the man's life (Polsky, 1969, pp. 183–200; a similar argument has also been applied to prostitution: Davis, 1937). While masturbation is a frequent, indeed, practically universal accompaniment to exposure to pornography among men, by no means do such experiences exhaust the consumer's total output of sexual energy. Indeed, it is entirely possible that following such masturbatory episodes, the consumer of pornography will then go out and seek to sexually aggress against women. Moreover, violence against women need not express itself exclusively in the act of rape; other forms of violence are entirely possible. Indeed, many rapists are totally or partially impotent when they attack women. The catharsis model is based on two completely fallacious assumptions: first, that rape is mainly, even exclusively, a sexual act, and only secondarily an act of violence; and second, that each man has a more or less finite and fixed quantity of sexual energy that is partially used up by exposure to pornography. (This is referred to as the "zero-sum" model and with pornography, as in most areas of life, it is fallacious.)

The imitation or *modeling* theory argues that viewers of porn imitate or model their behavior after what they have read about in books and seen in pictures and on the screen. Pornography, the advocates of this approach claim, stimulates unwholesome impulses that might otherwise rest dormant in the male. In pornography, women are treated as sexual objects to be exploited and debased. According to the proponents of this school, the message in pornography is not sexual liberation; it is that in sexual encounters, women should be subordinated, humiliated, dehumanized, degraded, injured, raped, and mutilated. In pornography, women are depicted as creatures who enjoy and invite all of these things; in real life, men who are exposed to this message will treat women in the same manner that they see women being treated in pornographic depictions.

In the 1970s and 1980s, the modeling approach received a great deal of support from a segment or wing of the women's liberation movement (Griffin, 1981; Lederer, 1982; Dworkin, 1981). Pornography, according to this view, is "the ideology of cultural sadism" (Barry, 1984, pp. 205–252), "the undiluted essence of anti-female propaganda" (Brownmiller, 1975, p. 394). In the words of the principal slogan that feminists chant at antipornography rallies: "Pornography is the theory; rape is the practice" (Morgan, 1982). The feminist view adds a *political* domension to the imitation model: Pornography specifically and explicitly serves the function of defining women as "dirty whores" so that men can better keep them in a subservient position in real life; pornography reflects, reinforces, and stimulates hostility, aggression, and violence in men against women, who become terrorized by the assaults that result. What pornography is "about," say some feminists, is men subjugating and dominating women, and women being held in a subservient position; what pornography is about, they say, is *power* (MacKinnon, 1987, pp. 146–153, 1993).

The *no effects* theory holds that the evidence does not support the contention that pornography causes men to become more aggressive or violent towards women. Some adherents of this model hold that the evidence is insufficiently compelling or is conflicting; others hold that the evidence is fairly strong—but in a "no effects" direction: Men specifically do *not* become more violent towards women after being exposed to pornography.

Perhaps a clear-cut and fruitful distinction than that between pornography and erotica is one that could be made between sexually explicit materials that *contain* violent images and those that do *not*. It might be assumed that such a distinction would be easy to make, that everyone would agree as to what violence is and which specific images contain it and which ones do not. *Most* pornography contains *no* clear-cut, overt violence, just depictions of nude women, or nude couples engaged in various consensual sexual acts; it would be "hard to make a convincing case that such images are violent" (Rubin, 1984, p. 298). Not all observers agree, however. Some feminists argue that since we live in a sexist society in which women are not free to do what they wish, *all* sexually explicit images of women produced by and for men, are *by their very*

nature violent (Dworkin, 1981, 1982c, pp. 286–287).*

---

*In fact, perhaps the most influential antipornography feminist, Andrea Dworkin, regards *all heterosexual intercourse*, by its very nature, as "penetration," an invasion, an act of mutilation, domination, humiliation, and brutality (Dworkin, 1987). Which raises the inevitable question, if all consensual heterosexual intercourse is by its very nature a brutal act of violation and subjugation, *then how does it differ from rape?* As feminist Ellen Willis (1983, pp. 464–465) says: "If all manifestations of patriarchal sexuality are violent, then opposition to violence cannot explain why pornography . . . should be singled out as a target. Besides, such reductionism allows women no basis for distinguishing between consensual heterosexuality and rape." To feminists such as Dworkin, "In a patriarchy, all sex with men is pornographic" (Willis, 1983, p. 465). And if there's no difference between ordinary heterosexual intercourse and rape, then what does one mean when one says that pornography causes rape and violence? In an age when nearly all feminists are making a clear distinction between consensual intercourse and rape, one of their principal and most outspoken spokespersons is doing exactly the opposite—claiming that consensual intercourse and rape are basically the same thing. To Dworkin, the male sexual urge is fueled by hostility toward the woman and the need to commit violence against her. Dworkin has written: "Men love death. In everything they make, they hollow out a central place for death. . . . Men especially love murder. In art they celebrate it, and in life they commit it" (1982a, p. 141). She has also said: "sex and murder are fused in the male consciousness, so that the one without the imminent possibility of the other is unthinkable and impossible." The "annihilation of women is the source of meaning and identity for men. . . . The fact is that the process of killing . . . is the prime sexual act for men in reality and/or in imagination" (1982c, pp. 288–289). Ms. Dworkin's theory to explain why men "need" pornography—and why it is inevitably linked to murder—is twofold. First, "the sons" (younger men, presumably), because they fear anal rape, "phallic power," and being murdered by their fathers, "bonded with the fathers who had tried to kill them. Only in this alliance could they make certain that they would not again be bound on the altar for sacrifice." (Her documentation for this assertion is the biblical story of Abraham and Isaac.) And second, having experienced episodes of impotence and waning virility, and feeling rage because of it, they wished to "revenge themselves on the women who had left them." The conclusion: "The perfect vehicle for forging this alliance was pornography" (Dworkin, 1982a, p. 146). It is not clear what one should make of this bizarre and deranged theory, nor if it was even meant to be taken seriously in the first place. It is a literary, not a scientific theory, more metaphorical than empirical. It violates most of the criteria for meaningful, serious, systematic, scientific thinking spelled out in Chapter 4. Whether her theories are deranged or not, however, Ms. Dworkin has had a great deal of influence on feminist thinking about pornography, and she and her writings have received the endorsement of a number of important feminist leaders, authors, and spokespersons. In addition, she has spearheaded a drive to change the pornography laws, and her efforts are at least partly based on these deranged musings. Thus, she and her writings, however bizarre and easily dismissed, deserve attention.

Given this approach, it is not clear exactly how we could make any kind of meaningful distinction between violent and nonviolent sexually explicit material. By means of this definitional trick, one is able thereby to define all sexually explicit images as violent, because they do not depict perfect reciprocity. For instance, a *Playboy* centerfold is defined as "violent" because it is a photograph of a nude woman which is purchased and ogled by young men who use it for masturbatory purposes, without any possible reciprocity on the woman's part. Of course, that is not how most people would define violence, but this is how the Women Against Pornography feminists define it. The next step that Women Against Pornography take in this definitional process is to present slide shows of women who are bound, gagged, and tortured in pornography, claiming that this is what pornography is all "about." Again, this is a definitional trick, since very little pornography depicts such sadomasochism.

Of course, not everyone shares the view that no such distinction between violent and nonviolent pornography should be made; in fact, even most feminists would reject it. Feminists can be divided into the antipornography position outlined above and a "pro-sex" or "anticensorship" position. (For a "pro-sex" feminist position, see Snitow, Stansell, and Thompson, 1983 and Vance, 1984.) In fact, one anthology of feminist writings on pornography, entitled *Caught Looking*, (Ellis et al., 1988) is replete with pornographic photographs from the front cover to the back. Pat Califia (1994), most decidedly a feminist, defends not only pornography but lesbian S&M practices, and lustily attacks antiporn advocates such as Dworkin and MacKinnon. So, perhaps we can make a distinction between sexually explicit material that would be *widely* and *conventionally* regarded as violent and sexually explicit material that would *not* be so regarded. The presence of *overt, clearly ascertainable, widely agreed-upon* violence is what defines pornographic material for us as violent. (We'll let the philosophers answer the question of whether or not a picture of a nude woman, intrinsically and by its very nature, implies violence.) For example, in one study of pornography, violence was defined as "rape, sadomasochism or exploitative/coercive sexual relations" (Scott and Cuvelier, 1987a, p. 535). To us, as sociologists, to define an image as violent, we have to be able to see concrete violence, and others have to see it as

well; we cannot simply define violence into existence.

Defining pornography as violent if it contains fairly explicit and widely agreed-upon acts of violence allows us to determine in an objective fashion the proportion of pornography that is violent versus that which is not. Defined specifically and concretely, it can be said that violence tends to be fairly rare in sexually explicit material. One study (Scott and Cuvelier, 1987a, 1987b) found that the ratio of violent pictorials to all pictorials in *Playboy* between 1954 to 1983 was 8.6 per thousand; the ratio in total pages was 0.78 per thousand pages. The Attorney General's Commission on Pornography (Hudson, 1986), an antipornography document, conducted a study which examined the imagery in sexually explicit material, but refused to report its findings; as the American Civil Liberties Union reveals, only 0.6 percent of the material the commission examined contained "force, violence, or weapons" (Lynn, 1986, p. 42). My own examination of advertisements for 500 pornographic videos shows that about 4 percent of these ads describe scenes of simulated rape or forced sex, and 11 percent describe sadomasochism, domination, or humiliation. (Slightly more ads featuring domination depict men being dominated by women than the other way around.) Thus, while violence in pornography is not *extremely* rare, it is *relatively* so; it is far from typical. Interestingly enough, one study (Palys, 1986) found that the most hard-core or sexually explicit ("Triple X") videos contained *less* violence, and depicted more egalitarian and mutual sexual behavior than "adult" videos that were *less* sexually explicit. Films and videos containing the most extreme and brutal violence—so-called "slasher" movies—are *almost never* sexually explicit, and typically receive an "R" rating.

It is often asserted that over time, nonviolent pornography is becoming "old hat," passé, boring to most consumers, and that violent pornography is becoming far more widespread (Longino, 1982, pp. 31–32; Smith, 1976; Malamuth and Spinner, 1980). In fact, recent tabulations (Scott and Cuvelier, 1987a, 1987b; Donnerstein, Linz and Penrod, 1987, pp. 88-93) have shown that this is not the case. If anything, there was something of an increase in the proportion of violent pornography from the early to the late 1970s, and a decrease since then. There is almost certainly an increase in the *total volume* of violent pornography since the early 1970s, because there has been an increase in the total volume of pornography overall. Still, it is important to make a distinction between violent pornography and the nonviolent kind; to have some sense of how common violent pornography is; and to understand the impact that both violent and non-violent pornography have on male consumers of the material.

The Effects of Pornography: Research Findings

Does viewing violent sexually explicit material cause men to become more violent toward women? Does sexually explicit material by itself, without any violent imagery, cause men to become more violent toward women? Does material depicting violence itself, with no sexually explicit images, cause men to to act more violently towards women?

How do we study this question? Clearly, social scientists cannot show pornographic films or videos to men, and then follow them around to see if they engage in aggressive or violent acts against women in real life. Sociologist Michael Kimmel (1993) summarizes the studies that have raised the question according to three types of research techniques: first, studies of the porn consumption of sex offenders; second, laboratory studies which expose male volunteers to pornography; and third, "aggregate" studies of porn consumption and rates of rape in different locales. Sex offenders show no higher rates of porn consumption than is true of the male population at large; even if they did consume more pornography, however, the causal link would still be problematic. The same applies to aggregate studies. Rates of rape tend to be higher in regions with higher circulations of men's magazines such as *Field and Stream* and *Rifleman*; again, causality is difficult to demonstrate (Baron and Straus, 1989; Gentry, 1991).

The way that studies on this issue are usually conducted is to look at certain types of aggressive behavior in a laboratory setting. There are at least three problems with this type of research. First, the men who are in these experiments are not necessarily the men, or even the *kinds* of men, who actually purchase pornography in real life, and on whom the effects of this material are most relevant; the effects of pornography may be significantly different for these two sets of men. Second, the behavior of men in the immediate setting of the laboratory may not necessarily carry over into everyday life. And third, some aggression against

women could be noted in these experiments simply because, in them, young men are being sexually aroused by explicit material, but are not afforded the opportunity to satisfy their arousal, resulting in some frustration.

Nonetheless, experimental conditions may be the most practical way to study this question. Moreover, research has shown that there is a strong correlation between men's behavior in laboratory experiments and their behavior in everyday life (Donnerstein, Linz, and Penrod, 1987, pp. 101–103, 111; Malamuth, Check, and Briere, 1986). Clearly, such research affords a *clue* to what kind of an effect violent and nonviolent pornography may have on how men treat women.

Since a certain proportion of pornography—as we saw, a minority—contains explicit violence, we should be interested in the question of whether it is the sexually explicit nature of pornography, or its violence, that produces any of the effects on viewers that we might observe. So, first: Does viewing sexually *explicit* but *nonviolent* pornography cause men to become more aggressive or violent toward women?

The relationship between viewing *nonviolent but sexually explicit* material and acting violently toward women is extremely complex. Sapolsky (1984, pp. 86–95) summarized ten studies which researched this relationship; the conclusions of some of these studies supported the "hostility-aggression" hypothesis, while those of others did not. In addition, several studies have been conducted since then (Donnerstein, Linz and Penrod, 1987, pp. 38–73), with equally inconclusive results. At this point, the best generalization that we could form about this relationship is that "there is not enough evidence from laboratory experiments to conclude that exposure to nonviolent pornography leads to increases in aggression against women under most circumstances." Moreover, the "research outside the laboratory is even less conclusive" (Donnerstein, Linz, and Penrod, 1987, pp. 72, 73). As a general rule, when such inconsistent results are obtained in research, the hypothesized effect tends to be weak and appears only under certain conditions and only in some individuals. Clearly, sexual explicitness in pornography, by itself, is not a major determinant of male aggression against women, indeed, if it is a determinant at all.

The violence depicted in some pornography (again, a minority genre) is an altogether different matter. It is possible to state conclusively that

Sex in America: Masturbation and Erotica

The "Sex in America" survey discussed in this chapter (see "A Major Nationally Representative Sex Survey for the 1990s") asked its respondents a number of questions on their use of pornography and related erotic materials and, along with it, their practice of masturbation (Laumann et al., 1994, pp. 134–145; Michael et al., 1994, pp. 155–168). Erotica is used overwhelmingly as an aid in masturbation. Unlike sex with a partner, which is the *public* world of sex, the consumption of erotic materials in the pursuit of masturbation is a *private* world, a world of *fantasy* (Michael et al., 1994, p. 155). While masturbation is common among teenagers, especially boys, it is clear from this study that a substantial proportion of the population continues to masturbate as they grow older. Over the past year, roughly 60 percent of the men in the sample and 40 percent of the women said that they had masturbated in the past year. One man in four and one woman in 10 said that they masturbate at least once a week (p. 158). The researchers asked respondents whether they had purchased or paid for a number of "autoerotic materials" in the past year. Nearly a quarter of the men (23 percent) and one out of 10 of the women (11 percent) had rented an X-rated movie or video during the past 12 months; 41 percent of the men and 16 percent of the women had purchased, rented, or paid for at least some autoerotic material during that time (Laumann et al., 1994, p. 135; Michael et al., 1994, p. 157).

Two common-sensical and widely held theories come to mind with respect to erotica and/or masturbation. One relates mainly to pornography and focuses mainly on its *consequences*, while the other relates mainly to masturbation and focuses mainly on its *cause*. As we saw, some militant feminists insist that porn causes violence against women. This study did not, and in all likelihood, could not test the proposition that when men are exposed to pornographic material, they become more violent toward women. A resolution of that issue necessitates quite different evidence from that which this sex survey gathered.

In the nineteenth century, it was widely believed, indeed, many medical books asserted, that masturbation was not only evil but physically harmful as well. Today, few of us believe that; however, a commonly held and homespun theory points to the likely *cause* of masturbation. Conventional wisdom on the question rests on a *zero-sum* conception of sexuality: Masturbation is a *substitute outlet* for the sexually deprived. It is specifically persons who have little or no sex with partners who are likely to resort to masturbation; when one has sex, one does not need to masturbate. As it turns out, in this survey, conventional wisdom is completely incorrect. In fact, the opposite is the case: It was the respondents who were *most* sexually active with partners who were *most* likely to consume pornography and masturbate. Masturbators (and consumers of pornography) tend to be the people who are most interested in sex, most likely to engage in a wide range of sexual practices, and most sexually active overall—"not the sexual loners that popular imagery depicts" (p. 157). Conclude the authors of this study: "masturbation is not a substitute for those who are sexually deprived, but rather it is an activity that stimulates and is stimulated by other sexual behavior" (p. 165). In short, "higher levels of autoeroticism are associated with higher levels of partners' sexual activity. Men do not masturbate to compensate for the lack of a partner, and women without partners are actually less likely to masturbate." Far from representing a compensation for sexual deprivation, self-stimulation with erotic materials provides "imaginative tutelage in a diversity of sexual scripts"; it is strongly related to engaging not only in *more* partnered sex but also in a wider *range* of partnered sexual activities, such as oral and anal sex (Laumann et al., p. 137). Once again, common sense provides an extremely inaccurate guide to social reality.

"exposure to violent pornography will increase aggression against women"; in addition, "it also plays a part in changing the way men think about women" (Donnerstein, Linz, and Penrod, 1987, p. xi), that is, believing more strongly in rape myths (such as the view that all women yearn to be raped), becoming more tolerant and accepting of rape and other violent acts against women, and believing that rapists should receive more lenient punishment, or no punishment at all.

In one experiment, men who watched films depicting sexual violence were more likely to administer more electrical shocks to partners than were those who watched nonviolent sexual films. In addition, the former administered more shocks specifically to women than the latter did (Donnerstein, 1981; Sullivan, 1980; Goleman, 1984). Another study asked 120 male undergraduate volunteers to rate the essays written by partners in an experiment (who were actually confederates of the researcher); they were also instructed to administer shocks to their partners for writing a poor essay. Once again, viewing films depicting violent sex increased the likelihood of administering more shocks and ones of greater intensity (Baron and Bell, 1977). A third study tested the connection between viewing acts of violence against women and attitudes toward this violence by showing matched groups of students two different types of films: one depicting male aggressive sexual behavior and the second containing no violence at all. A week later, the students in the study filled out a questionnaire. Men who had seen the violent movies, compared with those who had not, were significantly more likely to believe myths about rape (for instance, that women have an unconscious wish to be raped) and to hold more positive attitudes toward aggression against, and the domination of, women (Malamuth and Check, 1981).

In short, "violent pornography can increase aggression against women in a laboratory situation" and can change men's attitudes toward women for the worse (Donnerstein, Linz, and Penrod, 1987, pp. 96, 100). It has this effect, first, because it presents "the idea that women find sexual violence arousing," second, because it *desensitizes* the viewer to violence through repeated exposure, and third because it initiates the process of *misattribution*, that is, by linking sexually explicit images with violence, the viewer is aroused and misattributes his arousal to the violence, not the sex, thereby associating the two (Donnerstein, Linz, and Penrod, 1987, pp. 88, 112ff.). Significantly enough, however, depictions of violence against women *devoid of sexual content* or containing only mildly sexually explicit depictions also tend to increase men's aggression and hostility toward women every bit as much, or nearly as much, as violence *with* sexual content. Violence "against women need not occur in a pornographic or sexually explicit context to have a negative effect on viewer attitudes and behavior" (Donnerstein, Linz, and Penrod, 1987, p. 112).

Does pornography cause rape? Most observers would agree that the results of the available research remain "inconclusive" (Kimmel, 1993, p. 8). In the experimental laboratory, depictions of violence against women elevate the likelihood that men will act more aggressively toward women, but this is true whether the material contains sexual content or not. Exposure to sexually explicit material depicting consensual sex does not seem to have this same effect. In short, if there is a culprit in this drama, it is depictions of violence, not explicit sex. The antiporn militants seem to have chosen the wrong target; the material that is more likely to cause the effects they impute to pornography would be the gruesomely violent and hugely popular "splatter" or "slasher" films. Given its feeble impact on men (aside from its capacity to arouse them sexually), the question of why porn was selected as a crucial target by a wing of feminism as the basis for female oppression should be interesting for the curious and inquiring constructionist.

SEXUAL HARASSMENT

Sexual harassment entails one or more attacks based on a person's sex or gender. These attacks need not specifically involve the element of actual or intended sexual behavior (although they often do); the essential element that defines sexual harassment is that someone is being *attacked*, *persecuted*, and/or *discriminated against* as a result of his or her membership in a particular sexual category. Although, in theory, men can be the victims of sexual harassment, the vast majority of such cases entail men victimizing women. A policy statement released by the State University of New York at Stony Brook claims that 90 percent of sexual harassment cases entail a man victimizing a woman; 9 percent involve a man victimizing a man; and in only 1 percent of such cases does a woman harass a man. Even today, men tend overwhelmingly to hold power and authority over women, and sexual harassment represents an unjust use of power by one person over another. Thus here, I will focus more or less exclusively on male-female sexual harassment. Since sexual behavior is not the defining element of sexual harassment, it may not belong in a chapter on sexual behavior. Perhaps it is more appropriately discussed as a form of violence; consequently, it sould be discussed in Chapter 10. At the same time, the most well-publicized cases of sexual harassment usually entail some element of sexual behavior: unwanted sexual advances, inappropriate lewd remarks, proposed or actual exchanges of sex for job security or advancement (referred to as "quid pro quo" sexual harassment), and so on. Sexual harassment is as ancient as humankind, but it is only recently that it has been defined in its more routine forms as both illegal and an instance of deviance.

There are two forms of sexual harassment: *legally actionable* sexual harassment, and forms of sexual harassment that are *not* legally actionable. "Legally actionable" means that the behavior can form the basis of a lawsuit; as a result of being harassed, a woman can file a grievance in court and win some form of compensation. If a woman walks down the street and a man makes lewd and obscene remarks to her, that's sexual harassment, but at this writing, it is not legally actionable; she cannot take the man to court and win a settlement. She has been wronged—that is, attacked in some way—but not *legally* wronged. In contrast, cases of legally actionable sexual harassment involve attacks upon women on the basis of their sex *in an occupational or educational setting*. The Equal Employment Opportunity Commission (EEOC), a federal agency, in its "Guidelines on Discrimination Because of Sex," states:

Unwelcome sexual advances, requests for sexual favors and other verbal or physical conduct of a sexual nature constitute sexual harassment when (1) submission to such conduct is made either explicitly or implicitly a term or condition of an individual's employment, (2) submission to or rejection of such conduct by an individual is used as the basis for employment decisions affecting such individual, or (3) such conduct has the purpose or effect of unreasonably interfering with an individual's work performance or creating an intimidating, hostile, or offensive working environment.

As can be seen, sexual harassment has come to be regarded as a form of discrimination, a violation of the victim's civil rights. Typically, in a case of sexual harassment, a woman is being denied her rights under the law solely or exclusively because she is a woman. She risks being dismissed, she cannot advance in her profession, in her work setting, she has been made to feel insecure or unsafe *because of her sex*. As a result of being a woman, she cannot earn a living on the same footing as a man.

Sexual harassment also exists in nonworkplace settings that are nonetheless job-related, mainly the educational sphere. If a professor demands sex from a student for a certain grade, that is sexual harassment; it is unprofessional, unethical, illegal—and deviant. If a professor makes lewd and obscene remarks privately to a student or in the classroom, dwells on her physical attributes, makes unwanted sexual advances toward a student, stares or leers at or ogles a student's body—these are all instances of sexual harassment. They interfere with or make it difficult or impossible for a female student to pursue an education and hence, a career. It is a form of discrimination, a denial of the student's civil rights.

Sexual harassment is extremely common in American society. According to a survey conducted in 1988 of over 20,000 federal employees, 42 percent of the female workers said that they had experienced at least one episode of sexual harassment on the job *during the previous two years* (Brownmiller and Alexander, 1992, p. 71). In a survey conducted by *The New York Times*, nearly four out of 10 women questioned (38 percent) said that they had been "the object of sexual advances, propositions, or unwanted sexual discussions from men who supervise you or can affect your position at work." Nearly nine out of 10 of these women who were the object of sexual harassment did not report the incident at the time (Kolbert, 1991, p. A17). As I said, in the United States, on-the-job sexual harassment is legally actionable. In 1990, a former worker for the District of Columbia's Department of Administrative Services won a $300,000 verdict, charging that her former supervisor had threatened to fire her if she would not have sex with him; a single mother with two children, she submitted to his demands. In 1991, a Long Beach, California police department employee received a $1.4 million settlement after demonstrating that her fellow officers told graphic sex stories in her presence, kept pornographic magazines at work, and urinated in her presence. In 1989, a billing clerk who worked for an airline catering service won a $625,000 jury verdict in a suit which alleged that her manager had made sexual comments, required women at work to wear high heels so that he could "admire their legs," and suggested that women in the office show him "a good time" (Lewin, 1991).

Although sexual harassment received a certain amount of attention during and after the late 1970s (Farley, 1978; MacKinnon, 1979), it was not until the Senate confirmation hearings regarding the appointment of Judge Clarence Thomas to a Supreme Court seat in 1991 that awareness of the problem reached very nearly the entire American public. During these hearings, Anita Hill, formerly a legal staff member for Judge Thomas, described incidents that took place a decade before, in which Judge Thomas allegedly discussed with Ms. Hill pornographic films he had seen, pressed her for dates, and on one occasion, mentioned that he had seen a pubic hair in her drink. Another witness and former Thomas subordinate, who was not asked to appear at the confirmation hearings, claimed that Judge Thomas asked her about her breast size. An especially dramatic and revealing aspect of these hearings was that all 14 of the senators questioning Judge Thomas were white, middle-aged males. A number of observers speculated that this fact, as well as the public knowledge of the sexual escapades of at least one member of the committee, led to a tentative and far-from-probing questioning of Judge Thomas, a politically conservative African-American. While Judge Thomas was confirmed by the Senate for the Supreme Court (by a very narrow margin), the American public became aware of the issue of sexual harassment as never before in this country's history. According to one journalist, although Judge Thomas was nominated to the Supreme Court, the hearings "were a triumph" for both Anita Hill and the cause of women's rights (Taylor, 1991).

It is something of a cliché that sexual harassment is solely and exclusively "about" power, that its function is to humiliate women, keep them powerless and in fear, in a subservient position. (For a discussion of the distinction between sexual harassment as "power" versus "lust," see Goleman, 1991a). A great deal—in fact, the overwhelming majority—of sexual harassment does serve this function, whether consciously or nonconsciously. Examples of this are lewd and obscene remarks or gestures made to women by superiors or even by a substantial number of male co-workers to females on the job, the open display of nude photographs in a work setting, comments focusing on the woman's physical features, and so on. Such acts are not *sexual* in the more specific meaning of the word; that is, they are not intended as an overture or invitation to a sexual encounter or relationship. Plainly and simply, they are designed to "put a woman in her place," to vulgarize her presence on the job, to intimidate her, to make her feel cheap, insecure, an object of derision, an unwelcome presence in the workplace. They remind a woman that although she works with men, she can be taunted, humiliated, debased; through sexual harassment, men are calling attention to their sexuality. In a setting in which her qualifications as a worker should be

emphasized, such actions remind her that she is not only a woman before she is a worker, she is a woman who may be subject at men's will to their lewd derision. It reminds the female worker either that she does not belong on the job, or belongs only in a marginalized, subordinate, debased position. An indicator that sexual harassment serves this function is provided by a study that shows that women who enter traditionally male jobs are subjected to significantly more harassment than women who work in traditionally female jobs. Says Louise Fitzgerald, a researcher of sexual harassment, in these cases: "Men see women as invading a masculine environment. . . . They're trying to scare women off a male preserve" (Goleman, 1991a, p. C12).

At the same time, the sexual function for *some* instances of sexual harassment cannot be dismissed. Dr. Fitzgerald estimates that roughly a quarter of cases of sexual harassment are "botched seductions" in which the man "is trying to get someone into bed" (Goleman, 1991a, pp. C1, C12). The claim that sexual harassment is "about" power, solely and exclusively, represents a confusion over what "about" means. Power is certainly an element in *all* cases of sexual harassment, and in all such cases, women are extremely likely to *experience* being vulnerable and powerless. In these senses, sexual harassment is "about" power. On the other hand, observers argue that *by its very nature*, men engage in sexual harassment primarily to keep women in a subservient position. This is not necessarily the primary motive or intention in all such cases. In fact, there are at least two separate motives at work in cases of unwanted sexual advances. In a certain proportion, men in a position of authority use their power as an instrument; their power is a *means* of sexual conquest. Although sexual harassment has accurately been referred to as a subtle form of rape (Goleman, 1991a, p. C1), men who abuse their power to gain sexual access simply see their authority over women as an instrument in their arsenal of seduction; it is a means of "getting laid." For them, authority is much like good looks, money, youth, or charm; it gets them what they want. In fact, for many, since they lack good looks, youth, and charm, power serves as a substitute for these valued commodities. For them, sexual harassment is "about" sex; power is merely an instrument. For other men, sex and power are intertwined. The fact that they hold power over women is *itself* erotic to them. What sex *means* for them is control over

The Decline of Sexual Harassment in Law Firms?

A survey was conducted on sexual harassment among 2,000 lawyers at 12 large law firms around the country. They were asked whether they had experienced any of the following kinds of "unwelcome sexual advances" in the office during the previous year. As we might expect, the percentage who replied "yes" to the questions varied strongly by sex: Women were many times more likely to have experienced sexual harassment than men. The figures uncovered by this survey were revealing, especially given the claim that the attention paid to sexual harassment recently has all but eliminated the practice. The percent of "yes" responses varied according to the specific type of behavior asked about:

Sexual teasing, jokes, remarks, or questions: Women, 43 percent; men, 9 percent
Pressure for dates: Women, 7 percent; men, 0 percent
Letters, phone calls, cartoons, materials of a sexual nature: women, 9 percent; men, 1 percent
Sexually suggestive looks or gestures: Women, 29 percent; men, 3 percent
Deliberate touching, pinching, leaning over, cornering: Women, 26 percent; men, 7 percent

Pressure for sexual favors: Women, 3 percent; men, 0 percent
Actual or attempted sexual assault: Women, 0.25 percent; men, 0 percent *

There is no baseline by which to compare these figures with practices in the past, since no precisely comparable study was conducted. A quarter century ago, only 4 percent of all lawyers were women. Today, roughly a quarter of all lawyers, and nearly half of law school students, are women. A law firm that attracts negative publicity in a civil harassment suit is certain to become known as a place that is inhospitable to women, one which talented, aspiring female lawyers will choose to avoid; when that happens, says a spokesperson for a large law firm, "well, your recruitment efforts will be dead" (Slade, 1994). With such strong economic and business incentives at stake, it is very likely that law firms will be forced to "clean up their act."

*Source: Slade, 1994.

---

another human being. For these men, lust and power are inseparable; they are part and parcel of one another. For them, what fuels lust *is* power. To say that sexual harassment is "about" power and not sex ignores the basic fact that for some men, power and sex are inseparable.

Thus, usually, sexual harassment *is* "about" power rather than sex. Sometimes (in perhaps a quarter of all cases), sexual harassment is primarily "about" sex. This does *not* mean that power can be conveniently forgotten however, for even in these cases, power is a crucial element. In some of these cases, power is an avenue possibly leading to sexual access; power is an instrument to get sex. And in other cases, power and sex are so intricately and densely interconnected that for men who harass, they are essentially the same thing: The exercise of power is an erotic experience, and sexual behavior inevitably represents the exercise of power. In these cases, assigning a primary motive to the behavior of such men is futile and meaningless. Sexual harassment is merely the stage on which these forces play themselves out.

SUMMARY

Throughout this book, I have emphasized the difference between how constructionists and essentialists view deviant phenomena. The essentialist sees sex as a drive that exists to some degree independent of and prior to socialization—a kind of "riderless horse"—that demands fulfillment. In contrast, the symbolic interactionist perspective, which overlaps heavily with constructionism, argues two points. One, sex is *constructed* by the society and social context through the *imputation of meaning*. And two, the sex drive itself is largely a *product* of human contact. In many ways, constructionists and symbolic interactionists stand at the opposite end of a spectrum from Freudian psychology—one of a variety of essentialistic approaches to sex—which argues that sex is lurking behind even the most mundane of social phenomena. In contrast, the constructionists and symbolic interactionists argue that social dynamics are lurking behind all things sexual; sexuality is *in the service of* the social world. Sexuality does not shape our social conduct so much as social meanings *give shape to* our sexuality. We are sexual *because* we are social; it is social life that *creates, motivates and shapes* our sexuality.

All humans on earth are both given, and play an active part in writing, sexual scripts. The broadest of these are *cultural scenarios*, which instruct all people in a given society on what to do and what not to do in the sexual arena. However, these cultural scenarios have a lot of "blank spaces"; they are too broad and lacking in specificity to dictate what parts we are to play at every instance of our lives. Hence, we also collaborate in the writing of a second kind of script, an *interpersonal script*, with our interacting partners, which spells out appropriate roles and parts to play with those partners. And third, our intrapsychic scripting, or personal, idiosyncratic scenarios, permit us to play out in an imaginative fashion "a private world of wishes and desires."

The construction process applies not only to infusing phenomena and behavior specifically with *sexual* meaning, but also applies to filling the content of "sexual" definitions with a certain type of evaluation—positive, negative, or neutral, "normal" or "abnormal," conventional or deviant. As with scripts, these evaluations operate on the societal, the interpersonal, and the intrapsychic levels. How deviance is socially constructed is central to any understanding of sexual behavior. It is likely that sexual deviance is more likely to be regarded as "sick," abnormal, and pathological than any other type of deviance. A central feature in the psychiatrist's and the psychologist's conception of sexual deviance is *dysfunction* or *disorder*, an undesirable condition in need of treating or curing. However, the notions of dysfunction and disorder are alien to the sociologist's, particularly the constructionist's, notion of sexual deviance. Sociologically, what defines sexual deviance, as with all varieties of deviance, is that it is *nonnormative* and *likely to result in the condemnation of the actor*. No implication of dysfunction or disorder whatsoever is implied. Hence, the sociological conception of sexual deviance overlaps extremely imperfectly with the psychiatric and psychological conceptions.

Anthropologists and other social scientists have examined sexual customs and behavior the world over. What is tolerated and even encouraged in one locale may be savagely denounced and harshly punished in another. Knowing this insulates us from assuming that it is our genes or hormones or anatomy that determine what we do sexually. To illustrate this point, I contrast sexual behavior and custom in two sharply divergent societies, Inis Beag, an extremely sexually repressive society, and Mangaia, an extremely permissive one. Moreover, not only do sexual customs, attitudes, and reactions to sexual behavior vary enormously from society to society, they also vary historically in the same society. Moreover, *who the actor is* makes a huge difference in the judgments that audiences render of the actor's behavior.

A variety of dimensions determine judgments of deviance with respect to behavior in the sexual arena. Several include degree of consent, who (or what) the sexual object or partner is, specifically what behavior is engaged in, where it takes place, who engages in the sex act, how often, when, with how many partners, and so on. These dimensions proscribe or render deviant a substantial number of sexual acts. The sociologist of deviance decides which sexual acts should be studied according to these criteria: How strongly a given behavior is condemned (some acts are not deviant enough), how frequently it is enacted (some acts are not common enough), whether it makes up a category that is well-known enough to be a form of deviance in the public's mind (some acts are not conceptualized as a deviant category, and some are too obscure to be thought about or condemned), and whether it generates a social structure (some acts are enacted by scattered, isolated individuals).

In 1992, a major study of sexual behavior was conducted by a team of social scientists, mainly at the University of Chicago; parallel studies were conducted in Great Britain and France. While the survey method tends to be long on "social bookkeeping" and short on questions of symbolic meaning, finding out what people actually *do* sexually provides us with valuable information about social deviance. The results of this study, published in 1994, paint an extremely conservative and conventional portrait of sex in America, compared with both the public stereotype and the findings turned up by the Kinsey surveys 40 or 50 years ago. This survey's difference with the Kinsey study is likely to be the fact that Kinsey's sample was skewed or biased, while the sample the survey conducted in the 1990s was representative of the nation as a whole. The recent survey found that sex partners find each other through traditional avenues (friends, work, school, and so on), and have sex with partners who are very similar to themselves with respect to key social factors (age, education, ethnicity, and so on). In addition, their sexual behavior tends to be traditional: Most had had sex with only one partner during the past year, very few had had sex with more than a small handful of partners over their lifetimes, marital partners tended to be faithful to one another, and very, very few Americans identified themselves as homosexual or bisexual. A very small proportion of the sample had had sex with someone of the same gender, even once, since the age of 18 (5.3 percent for the men and 3.5 percent for the women). Moreover, overall, reported sex took place fairly infrequently—less than two times per week; the most conventional sexual activity (penile-vaginal intercourse) was the most appealing of all sexual acts for the overwhelming majority of the sample.

Prostitution is one of several sexual behaviors that have been studied extensively by sociologists of deviance. Actually, the nationally representative survey of sex in America, and parallel surveys in Britain and France, demonstrate that prostitution is a fairly small and declining sexual outlet for heterosexual men. Nonetheless, it remains a sociologically interesting and revealing practice. In many ways, prostitution upholds and is an extension, rather than an outright rejection, of many mainstream values: the sexual double standard, the commercial ethic, alienated labor, and a devaluation of women. In spite of one stereotype of prostitutes as nymphomaniacs, who enter "the life" to get as much sex as they can, very few prostitutes enjoy their work. Street prostitutes are certainly drawn mainly from the ranks of the lower and working classes; however, call girls, who are less often studied, are almost certainly far more likely to come from a more middle-class background. Rape, sexual abuse, and sexual exploitation are frequently found in the backgrounds of prostitutes. In the United States, women are rarely forced by pimps to become prostitutes. However, this must be qualified, since a number of operations which cater mainly to men from poor, Third World countries have been uncovered here. Moreover, in some Asian countries, the forced prostitution of adolescents and even preadolescent girls is not uncommon.

Pornography has been defined in a number of different ways. Rather than regarding one definition and one alone as paramount, the constructionist regards each as appropriate for different purposes. The *functionalist* definition sees pornography as defined by whether materials are used for the purpose of sexual excitation. The *labeling* definition sees pornography as it is defined by the public or segments of the public. And the *genre* definition regards as pornographic these materials which fit a standard formula, or set of formulas, presented by the industry. This diversity implies that a given set of materials can be seen as pornographic by one definition and as not pornographic by another.

The question that seems to dominate much of the debate on pornography is whether it causes men to become violent toward women. Does pornography cause rape? The *catharsis* model, regarded as discredited, argues that men's consumption of porn *reduces* sexual energy and hence, aggression toward women. The *modeling* or *imitation* theory, which argues that men who consume porn become more aggressive and violent toward women, is adopted by sexual conservatives and a militant wing of feminism. The *no effects* model sees little change in men's behavior as a result of exposure to pornography. The debate has become highly politicized. In fact, some feminists feel that pornography *is itself* a political issue, that is, that the very *function* or *purpose* of porn is political: to terrorize and intimidate women to become less militant, more docile, and less feminist. Experiments indicate that while *violent* porn does seem to stimulate men to become more aggressive toward women in an experimental or laboratory situation, the same is true of material that depicts violence toward women which is *lacking* in sexual content. In contrast, sexually explicit material which depicts consensual sex does not have this effect, or does so weakly or inconsistently. It seems to be the violence, not the sexual explicitness, which influences this elevation in male aggressiveness toward women that is observed in the laboratory.

Sexual harassment is defined as creating a climate of intimidation in the workplace or educational arena that produces discrimination on the basis of sex or gender. The vast majority of such cases entail a male in a position of power who is harassing a female in a subordinate position. In the vast majority of such cases, sexual harassment is not "about" sex, but the exercise of power: to keep women in their place, to remind them that they do not really belong where they are working and that they are sexual beings before they are co-workers. Examples would be obscene comments, sexual jokes, comments about a woman's body parts, and photographs of naked women in the work site. It is possible that as many as a quarter of cases of sexual harassment are specifically "about" sex; they represent a botched seduction of an underling by a superordinate. However, in all cases of harassment, whether power or sex is the motive, power always plays a central role. For some men, power is an aphrodisiac: The way they express their sexuality is *through* the exercise of power. Hence, power is *never* absent from *any* case of sexual harassment.

ACCOUNT: INTERVIEW WITH A PORNOGRAPHER

The informant is 30 years old and works in the entertainment industry. I am the interviewer. ("Q" indicates my questions; "A" indicates the answers the respondent gave to my questions.)

Q: Why don't you tell me a little bit about this movie that you made.

A: I feel, like many men, that I've been treated badly by women and that the more I try to be nice to them, the more license it gives them to treat me worse. And I think many men feel this way. Basically, the idea of the movie was to concentrate on the damsel in distress: girls tied up, girls being knocked around, spat upon, kicked around, punched, beaten up. The movie is a soft-core kind of a pornography, a soft X rather than a hard X: There's no nudity. In my movie, women are terrorized. Women are not fucked in the movie at all—they're *fucked over*. Every scene has a woman being taken advantage of against her will, forced to do something sexual, like a striptease or suck a dildo or take a punch. It's an exploitation movie. The idea is to appeal to the darker side of the prurient interest of men. I think more exciting than naked girls and stuff like that is the resistance—you know, the rape fantasy, forcing a girl against her will. That's a more striking screen image than the touching, sensitive love story, which I find terribly boring. Another thing is, they're all women in the movie. There are no men in the film, not even an off-screen voice of a man.

Q: Give me a typical scene, a couple of scenes.

A: Okay, one typical scene is a woman who is dressed for the Governor's Ball comes to the door: full evening gown, red, very nice and tight and clinging; bouffant hairdo; long white gloves; too much make-up; big, long earrings. She goes to the door and a lady cop bursts in the door, knocking her down, throwing up her skirt so you can see her legs and all that. Before the woman can protest, she's tied up and frisked, with the hands passing all over her, underneath the skirt. The victim is not enjoying it at all, but the lady cop's

enjoying herself tremendously, much the same way a lascivious man cop would. So the lady cop talks about how much she digs it and then she frisks her, ties her up, spanks her, accuses her of some ridiculous crime, like selling heroin to kindergarten kids, before she discovers, ahhah! big surprise—that she's got the wrong woman. The cop turns aside and goes. "Hey, don't tell her, but I knew it all the time." She turns back and says, "Sorry, lady—these things happen," and she walks out. That's one of the scenes in the movie.

Q: What about another one?

A: Another one involves what I call the CARLA—Computerized Anthropomorphic Responding Love Automaton: C-A-R-L-A. One of the first uses that somebody will consider in making robots, artificial people is, you know, the sex dolls. Similar to the sort of thing that you buy in Times Square and blow up, except *infinitely* more sophisticated. This is a device, a machine, that any man will be proud to own. In the office, it never forgets appointments. It never shows up late. It's completely reliable, 100 percent efficient. Also, it can be a personal bodyguard. It has faster reflexes than a real person. Somebody pulls out a gun and points it at you, it steps in front of you. It's 10 times stronger than a real girl. It can easily double as jack for your car, but its real purpose of course is to jack up your spirits. At home, it's the perfect housekeeper and the equivalent of a master chef. And, of course, at your leisure, it can be programmed to have any kind of sexual response you want. You can program it to occasionally give you a hard time. And if it gives you too bad a time, you can knock it around and not have any fears of hurting anybody, 'cuz it's not a body, it's a *thing*. It can be programmed so that, like, 15 to 20 times a year, it won't let you fuck it no matter what you do. You can take your frustrations out on her. It's the perfect wife. Not only that, but the longer it lives with you, the more hip it becomes to your personal idiosyncrasies, so the longer you own the machine, the more personal it becomes to you. So after a while, it'll put real women out of business.

Q: Was it hard to get women to act in this movie?

A: It was a big problem at first. I jerked around for a long time trying to ask women that I knew personally or guys who knew women that they could turn me on to. They'd get three or four pages into the script and they'd, like, run screaming into the night. Well, not literally, but figuratively. I'd have to stop and change the subject and then forget all about it.

Q: What do you think they were reacting against?

A: Well, the dialogue is actually what they were turned off about it, because the dialogue is one long, non-stop profanity. You never hear girls talking like that, at least, not unless they're, like, in the bathroom with themselves or something. But the thing was, when I found the right medium to advertise for actresses, I had no trouble whatsoever getting girls to act in the film. I had many more women than I needed. I realized that the type of woman I would have to use would have to be a regular actress. I simply approached them as an actress-type gig. I said, this is an exploitation film, but here's the criteria: There's a lot of profanity and so on. And for them, it was strictly a job.

Q: Do you think that this profanity that's in your movie is what's appealing to some men who would [go to] a movie?

A: I don't *think* it's appealing to some men—I *know* it's appealing to *a great many men.*

Q: Dirty talk?

A: *Absolutely!* The most popular pornographic film ever made was a movie called *Talk Dirty to Me.* That's what the boys'll buy.

Q: How do you think women would react to your movie?

A: Most women wouldn't go for this type of stuff. I think most women would watch the movie I made for a few seconds before they put their fist through the screen. Even most so-called levelheaded or even-tempered women would be *deeply offended* by this film. Actually, the feminists wrote my script for me. Everything that they complain about is *just* what I wanted to put in the movie. The last bit, the bit about the CARLA, is where women are *literally reduced* to sexual toys for the pleasure and amusement of men. I mean, that's the bottom rung of the ladder, that's as low as you can go.

Q: If you were to tell somebody about this movie, like a friend, or a woman you met in a bar or something, what would you say?

A: I wouldn't necessarily discuss my project with just anybody that I'd meet. You see, I'm pretty closed-mouthed about my private life, and I consider this my private life. It's something hot for me to jerk off to in the middle of the night, 'cuz I *love* pornography. With me, it's the last drug I'll give up after Coca-Cola. Its very much like a drug for me. I hafta have it, and quite a bit of it. Usually the stuff that's available is weak. It gets me very high, but only for a short time. And then I need more. I never get any of the good stuff. So I decided I could do it better.

Q: So what you're saying is that there's a personal connection between your own tastes and what gets you excited and what you're doing to make money.

A: Absolutely. There's no way I can say that I'm coldly detached from the whole thing. No. I picked this particular subject and topic because I knew it would have to be something that I liked and something that would, you know, turn me on, too.

Q: Well, one time I was at your house and you had this stack of, um, bondage magazines. Looking at those magazines is what turns you on?

A: Yeah. Ever since I was a kid, maybe 15. It's only in bondage magazines and a few other specialized magazines that you get women in glasses, women in lingerie, skirts, costumes, uniforms—*anything.* What's suggested in the bondage magazines is that somebody's being taken advantage of or somebody using their body to take advantage of a situation. In some of these magazines, with the pure bondage, women strive to be, like, expressionless on their face. You get the very, very beautiful women in the absolute, strict bondage. The face, and the expressions, even when one woman's tying up another one, would be completely blank, or eyes closed. Never struggling against the bonds, only *in bondage.*

Q: That's interesting. I think; well, I guess most men, if they wanted to jerk off, they'd want to look at a picture of a woman who's completely naked.

A: How can you say that about most men? Most of the guys I hang out with, all they ever talk about is kink. *High* heels (bangs on the table), *make*up (bang), *lip*stick (bang), *ear*rings (bang), *slit* skirts (bang). Yeah, man. Absolutely.

Q: Okay, so how does this carry over into your personal life?

A: It doesn't. I never get a chance to tie up any of the women that I go out with. They'd think I was nuts and wouldn't go out with me. So I pretty much stick with the fantasy.

Q: Interesting. What would you do if you met a woman who'd go along with it? Would that make it more exciting than the pictures?

A: Gee, it's hard to say. There's a real danger in realizing your fantasies. I'm pretty happy the way it is now. Occasionally, I think almost anybody gets a little rough in their lovemaking. It's a very loving kind of a thing. You understand that what I'm talking about in bondage and lovemaking is not beating people up or anything like that, but it's, like, tying your girlfriend to a chair while you feel her up, or tying her to a chair while you fuck her in the face, or tying her to the bed while you make love to her, or something like that. It can be stimulating, it can be a turn on. I think a lot of men have it in the back of their minds, even the most civilized and gentlemanly of men, that, one or two times, when, boy, if I could have given that bitch a good (slaps his hands together) *crack*, boy, I sure would'a felt a lot better! And believe me, I'm not a physical person or anything; I've never been in a fight in a bar. It's the monsters from the id. That's why we have laws and religion—we're all monsters in our subconscious. And women, the most liberated of women, will wink at the boss to get by a tough situation. And when it comes to that, *so much* for your ERA. Women will still occasionally use their physical attractiveness to take advantage of a situation. Don't you agree?

Q: I think that there's a certain proportion of women who don't do it at all.

A: (Angrily.) *Bullshit!* Oh, well, the ones that are physically unattractive, yeah.

Q: I've met a number of women who are beyond this stuff.

A: Unless you spend your entire life with all of those women, you can't say that. Because maybe they would never do it to you. Maybe with you, they know that intellect or wit or charm will work a lot better.

Q: So you think this feeling of, like, hostility toward women gets translated into a certain kind of sex act?

A: (Loudly, almost shouting.) *Am I the first guy to tell you that there's a lot of hostility involved in male sexuality?*

Q: I'm getting you to spell it out. I'm being naive on purpose. It's an interviewer's tactic.

A: Oh, I see. I'm being manipulated. That's okay; manipulate away, man.

Q: So what I'm asking is whether you see a connection between this feeling of hostility that you sometimes feel toward women and the type of sexual acts that you were describing before involving bondage and things like that—do you see any connection there?

A: It's pretty obvious, really. There's an old, established connection between sex and violence. You have only to look as close as the animal kingdom. Attacking and biting each other is part of the courtship and mating ritual. So there's really no reason why it shouldn't extend to *Homo sapiens* as well. Basically, there's still that hunter-killer thing there. All we have to do is walk down the street and see the hickeys on people's necks and scratches on people's backs and stuff and then you have exactly what it is I'm talking about. This fetish thing, though, I'm appealing to what would be probably a very small minority of men. But such guys would be willing to pay for it as long as they could get what they wanted.

Q: Did you ever work these routines into your actual lovemaking?

A: No. Let me tell you more about the movie than about my personal life. (From the author's files.)

ACCOUNT: ENCOUNTER WITH PORNOGRAPHY

The informant is a 40-year-old writer. His reaction to an experience in a Times Square pornography parlor was quite different from the attitude described by the first informant.

I had a meeting with one of my publishers in an office on Fifth Avenue in the forties, and after that one was over, I had a couple hours to kill before my next appointment, so I decided to wander around Times Square and check out the scene. I had seen a couple of porno movies before, and I had seen hookers propositioning customers in various parts of the city, but nothing I had ever witnessed prepared me for what I saw that day. I walked into the biggest porno parlor on 42nd Street and started looking around. As far as I could tell, there were three activities going on there.

The first was the booths. You step in, close the door, face a small screen, and insert a quarter into a slot and watch a few minutes of a crude, grainy, scratchy, silent porno movie. When the time is up, the screen goes dead. You can keep watching one till the end, paying another quarter each time the movie stops, or you can move on to another booth and watch a different movie. Outside of each booth on the door, there's a still shot depicting the movie's main theme—bestiality, bondage, a woman with huge breasts, a man with a huge penis, a sex scene between a Black and a white person, and so on. To give you some idea of what goes on in these booths, there were several men walking around the place, with mop and pail in hand, cleaning up what the guys had left behind on the walls and the floors of the booths. Leaving a booth, I passed by an employee who had just made change for a customer. He turned to me and smiled and said, "I don't know what that guy had on his hand, but it was wet and sticky." Okay, these, movies were pretty much what you'd expect—sleazy porn.

The second thing that was going on there was that there were scantily clad women wandering around the halls of this joint asking the men to join them in four-by-four glass stalls, where they'd draw the blinds and do whatever it is that they do. I imagine it's all negotiable—the activity and the amount the man pays. All that was was prostitution in glass stalls, so I wasn't all that shocked by that, either.

Upstairs, there were more booths, just like the porno booths, but with no pictures on the doors. Loud rock music was playing inside, on the other side of the back wall of the booths. You step in and close the door. Facing you is a small window maybe one foot wide and two feet high, covered by some sort of a yellow shield. You put a quarter in a slot, and the shield lifts up, and you find yourself staring into a room occupied by maybe five or six women, completely naked, sort of swaying to the music. The thing is, when the shield lifts up, there's no pane on the window—the shield was the pane—so you can just reach right into the room where the women are swaying to the music. And it's not just you, but there's maybe 10 other guys staring into the room from the other booths.

A woman came over to me, stood right in front of the open window, and asked, "Would you like to touch me?" I was stunned—shocked, really. I'm not sure why. It all seemed so raw, vulgar and, well, *dirty*. I shook my head and she wandered off, looking for other potential customers. Four or five of the other guys in the booths reached their hands into the room, grabbing the women, clutching their breasts, fingering their vaginas, stroking them all over, as they bobbed and swayed to the music.

To me—and this is going to sound *melodramatic* or something—it seemed like a vision of *hell*. The lights were bright and harsh, the music was blaring, and all these men were reaching through these small windows to fondle women who were clutching huge wads of one-dollar bills, as they bobbed up and down to the music, pretending, in a halfhearted way, to be enjoying themselves.

After a few minutes, the yellow shield closed, and I left the booth, walked down the stairs and out onto 42nd Street, feeling sick. I kept thinking: This whole thing is so *degrading,* why would anyone, man or woman, want to do something like that? Does that make me a prude? I don't know. All I know is, that scene made me feel that the human body and spirit were being degraded. (From the author's files.)

chapter 9

MALE AND FEMALE HOMOSEXUALITY

Dexter Amend is the coroner of Spokane County, Washington. Recently, when an 11-year-old boy died in a fire, Dr. Amend asked the boy's parents if their son had ever had a homosexual experience; when a nine-year-old girl was found bludgeoned and strangled to death, he implied, without evidence, that a homosexual had sexually assaulted and killed her. "It's a crime that we don't expose the homosexual community," Dr. Amend stated in a television interview. "I'd like to see the homosexual lifestyle be condemned for what it is in terms of its raping innocent lives," he added (Egan, 1996). In China, most physicians regard homosexuality as a mental illness; homosexuals are given shock treatments, or herbal medicines that induce vomiting, to reduce their desire for members of the same gender. Says Gao Caiqin, a pioneer in the study of sexual behavior in China, "After being cured, they are very, very grateful, and they are in tears as they hug us in gratitude" (Kristof, 1990). Penny Culliton, a teacher in a rural New Hampshire high school, was dismissed in the middle of a school year for distributing novels with homosexual characters. The school board claims that professionalism is the issue, not homosexuality, since Ms. Culliton did not request permission from them in advance, before distributing the books. On the other hand, in the past, she has not had to do so for any books aside from textbooks. Says a representative of her union, the National Educational Association, "If these books were about any other subject than homosexuality, Penny Culliton would not have been fired." The day after her dismissal, 40 students held a protest demonstration. "I think we can handle reading a book," said a sophomore (Dunlap, 1995).

Considering how frequently homosexual acts are engaged in, and how common male and female homosexuals are in the population, the depth of public misconceptions concerning both should be astonishing. In one of the most popular books on sex ever published, *Everything You Wanted to Know About Sex But Were Afraid to Ask*, physician David Reuben displays his abysmal ignorance on the subject of homosexuality, parading myth and misconception as truth. Lesbians, Dr. Reuben claims, commonly use a dildo, or artificial phallus, "held in place with an elastic harness," so that "an unreasonable facsimile of heterosexual intercourse is possible" (1969, p. 218). Male homosexuals, he writes, because they "find their man-to-man sex unfulfilling," frequently masturbate while forcing a carrot or cucumber, lubricated with vegetable oil, into their anus, or have intercourse with a melon, a cantelope, or, "where it is available," a papaya (1969, pp. 129, 142, 147). It is not altogether clear just how Dr. Reuben gathered this information; it is at any rate, nonsense, although instructive of the prevailing ignorance on the subject. Although some lesbians do engage in dildo sex (Byron, 1985; Califia, 1994, pp. 175, 217), it is a small minority phenomenon. And my guess is that having intercourse with fruit (and here, a watermelon seems a likely target!) is more common among heterosexual than homosexual males.

HOW MANY HOMOSEXUALS ARE THERE? A RECENT SURVEY

The same study that uncovered such surprisingly conservative figures on heterosexual behavior (Michael et al., 1994; Laumann et al., 1994) also asked questions on homosexual behavior and related phenomena. For most observers, the surprising news this study provided was the remarkably *low* level of homosexuality that was uncovered. Many gay spokespersons cite a "one in ten" figure for the proportion of homosexuals in the American population. It is possible that this figure was derived from Kinsey's pioneering studies on sexual behavior in America a half-century or more ago (Kinsey et al., 1948, 1953). Kinsey did not state that one out of 10 Americans are homosexuals, however. His research team stated that roughly one out of 10 American *men* (not women) had *only* homosexual experiences for *any* three-year period during their adulthood. Moreover, Kinsey's study was not based on a randomized sample of the American population; instead, it was a "catch-as-catch-can" sample that did not accurately reflect the characteristics of the population as a whole. Among other flaws, Kinsey deliberately oversampled men with homosexual experiences. Still, the "one in ten" figure continues to be cited.

It must be recognized that there is likely to be a political angle to the findings a survey on homosexuality may turn up. The goals of gay political activists are furthered by the finding that there are *many* homosexuals in the population, since this means that politicians cannot ignore a major segment of their constituency, and must take their interests and demands into account. After all, greater numbers translate into greater power. On the other hand, a conservative agenda is likely to be furthered by the discovery that there are *few* homosexuals in the population. If that were the case, it may be concluded that homosexuality represents only the perverted practice of a minuscule minority that should not be tolerated by the rest of us. The smaller the number of Americans who engage in homosexuality, the more plausible the claim that the vast majority of us "would never dream of indulging in such behavior" (Michael et al., 1994, p. 171). Or so a conservative stance would reason.

In truth, the prevalence of homosexuality in America depends very much on what it means in the first place, how it is defined, and what questions one feels are important to ask to establish its reality. In short, in the realm of homosexuality, as in all areas of social life, the constructionist perspective assumes central importance. To be plain about it, there is no single criterion, measure, or indicator that unambiguously defines someone as a homosexual. Is identifying oneself as a homosexual an infallible definition of who is gay? In the "Sex in America" study, only 2.8 percent of the men and 1.4 percent of the women said that they consider themselves as homosexual or bisexual (Laumann et al., 1994, p. 297; Michael et al., 1994, p. 176). About 6 percent of the men said that they were attracted to persons of the same gender, and 4 percent said that they found the thought of sex with someone of the same gender appealing; for women, these figures were 4 and 5.5 percent, respectively. Only 2 percent of both men and women said that they had had sex with someone of the same gender *during the past year;* 5 percent of the men and 4 percent of the women had had homosexual sex *since the age of 18;* and 9 percent of the men but 4 percent of the women had done so *since puberty* (Laumann et al., 1994, pp. 295–297; Michael et al., 1994, pp. 174–175). These figures depart so drastically from the conventional "one in ten" wisdom that the study has been vilified in a wide range of publications. Yet, interestingly, roughly the same results have been uncovered in parallel studies in Britain (Johnson et al., 1992, 1994; Wellings et al., 1994) and France (Spira et al., 1992, 1993).

If we take these findings as an approximate measure of homosexual desire, attraction, behavior, and identification in the population, we are forced to three inescapable conclusions.

The first is that there is *no* single infallible measure of homosexuality, as some essentialistic researchers have claimed (Whitam, 1977; Whitam

and Mathy, 1986; Socarides, 1978; Bieber et al., 1962). Again, how many homosexuals there "are" in the population depends on what we mean by homosexuality and on the questions we ask to determine its reality. Desire is not the same thing as behavior, and neither overlap very well with sexual self-identification. In short, homosexual sex is *multidimensional.*

The second conclusion we are forced to make when we examine the result of careful, systematic sex surveys is that male and female homosexual expression are markedly different. Homosexuality is a distinctly "gendered" experience; men and women have dramatically different homosexual "styles." Many more males act on homosexual desires than females, especially from the onset of adolescence to the age of 18. In contrast, many more women who experience homosexual attraction and desire do not act on them. Among women, if all the respondents in this survey with one or more homosexual dimensions or components (that is, behavior, desire, and self-identification) were put together in a single category, the *majority* (59 percent) would be made up of those who have experienced a homosexual desire *without* engaging in homosexual sex *or* regarding themselves as lesbians (Laumann et al., 1994, p. 299). Among females, there is much less adolescent homosexual sex than among males. Almost all the women who had homosexual sex after the onset of puberty also had homosexual sex into adulhood. In contrast, almost twice as many males had homosexual sex after the onset of puberty as continued to have homosexual sex after the age of 18. In other words, males act on their homosexual impulses earlier in their lives and with much less inhibition; many of them experiment with homosexual behavior in adolescence, and then give it up. In contrast, women engage in homosexual behavior for the first time much later in their lives, and a substantial proportion feel homosexual attraction and desire without engaging in homosexual behavior.

Just as important for our purposes as the *multidimensionality* of homosexual sex and the distinctively different male and female *expressions* of homosexuality is the *size* of the figures turned up by the "Sex in America" survey. They are *much* lower than the figures turned up by Kinsey's research team a half a century ago (Kinsey et al., 1948, 1953), much lower than many commonly assumed figures on the magnitude of all measures of homosexuality, and much lower than the figures that are

Ritual Homosexuality Among the Sambia of New Guinea

New Guinea is a large island north of Australia and southeast of Southeast Asia; the eastern half of the island is called Papua New Guinea. Formerly a protectorate of Australia, Papua New Guinea is now an independent country. Until fairly recently, most of the cultures of New Guinea were extremely warlike and had engaged in combat with their neighbors for centuries. The former colonial Australian government banned traditional warfare that took place among tribes in their territory, and, for the most part, its efforts were successful.

Sambia society, like most of New Guinea, is based on warfare; in spite of the ban on fighting among their traditional enemies, every Sambia man regards himself as a warrior who stands ready to engage in lethal combat if necessary. As a general rule, warrior societies are profoundly misogynist—that is, based on hostility toward women and the inherent superiority of men. As with nearly all societies based on warfare, the contrast between male and female is the foundation of Sambian beliefs and practices. The men fear their loss of strength and virility—what they regard as their masculinity. Masculinity, Sambia men believe, is easily depleted; it must be constantly renewed through ritual. Women contaminate and weaken boys, prevailing Sambia beliefs hold; they must be protected and envigorated by adult men. The key to infusing masculinity into young boys is ritual homosexuality.

From age 7 to 10, Sambia boys are separated from the women and children of their village and initiated into an all-male society, located in its own exclusive hamlet, where the boys remain for the next 10 to 15 years. During that time, they regularly engage in homosexual activities, "first as the fellator (insertee) and then as the older fellated (insertor)." At marriage, which takes place between the ages of 18 and 25, youths are bisexual, engaging in sex with both initiated boys and women. With the advent of fatherhood, when a Sambian man's wife gives birth to his first child, all homosexual activities cease; he becomes exclusively heterosexual. However, when the new cycle of initiating boys into the all-male cult begins, he engages in ritual homosexuality with the new crop of boys (Herdt, 1987, p. 6). Adult men never have sex with other men, and their homosexuality with boys and adolescents is usually dominated by its ritual significance. Some Sambian men continue to have sex with adolescents, a deviant practice there, but always as the insertor, never as the fellator. Fellating boys "is strictly forbidden, is immoral, and whould be regarded as unspeakably unmanly" (Herdt, 1981, p. 252).

In American society, in contrast, *most* of the homosexual behavior between older and much younger males takes place with the older male acting as the fellator and the younger man, the insertor. In contrast to the prevailing (and mistaken) view that predominates in the United States, the Sambia do not see homosexuality as a denial of masculinity; in fact, to them, it is "the only means through which it is attained" (Herdt, 1987, p. 10). The male body is seen to be incapable of manufacturing its own semen; it must be externally acquired and renewed. Fellatio is the concrete means by which boys attain semen and, therefore, their strength and masculinity. Prior to initiation into the warrior cult, boys are seen as being polluted by their mothers and, therefore, soft and weak. For boys to reach puberty requires semen, which, in turn, requires the cult initiations based on homosexual practices. Without exception, every single Sambian man is initiated into the cult; there are no exceptions. "No Sambia man exists who is uninitiated" (Herdt, 1987, p. 111), and this includes a mentally retarded man, another who is regarded as mentally ill, and a third who is blind.

The Sambia do not see homosexuals as effeminate; in fact, there are no effeminate homosexuals among the Sambia. More specifically, in Sambia, there are very few homosexuals as such; there are boys and young men who, following custom, practice exclusive homosexual relationships for more than a decade, then practice bisexuality for a time, and then, finally, are exclusively heterosexual. In short, although behavior we would see as homosexual exists among the Sambia—behavior between two males that entails genital arousal—*homosexuality as we know it* is not a feature of this behavior. It is not stigmatized; in fact, to engage in *anything but* this behavior during a certain period of the Sambian male's life is savagely stigmatized. It is not part of a homosexual role; in fact, it does not separate the enactors from those who are not, since all males engage in homosexual behavior. There is no homosexual subculture among the Sambia; all men are part of the all-male villages for their adolescence, and no men are in their adulthood. The practice does not lead to a lifetime of homosexual behavior; in fact, it leads to bisexuality, which, in turn, leads to heterosexuality. In short, in nearly all respects, this behavior, which we call homosexuality, contrasts almost violently with homosexuality in Western society. It is so different, in fact, that it is difficult to regard the two as belonging to the same category.

often cited by gay activists. It is possible that this misperception arises from the fact that most observers of and commentators on homosexuality reside in the nation's largest cities and their suburbs, where homosexuality is vastly more common, rather than in its small towns and rural areas, where it is exceedingly rare. Indeed, the percent identifying themselves as homosexuals or bisexuals varies from 9 percent in the country's 12 largest central cities to 1 percent in rural areas (Michael et al., 1994, p. 178). Since urban dwellers are both more likely to live in areas with a substantial homosexual minority and more likely to publish or publicly comment on estimates of the extent of homosexuality, they are, first, likely to misperceive this extent because of their milieu and second, more likely to have their misperception promulgated and accepted as an accurate reflection of the reality. But again, if we are to trust these findings, homosexuality is *vastly* less common than conventional wisdom has it. And, once again, the fact that much the same figures were turned up in separate but related studies in Britain and France lends some confidence to these findings. As with so many other social phenomena, perception and reality may be miles apart.

THE WORLD OF HOMOSEXUALITY: SOME RECENT DEVELOPMENTS

In the past decade or so, several crucial and relatively novel developments have hit the world of homosexuality. In addition, several conditions that have prevailed for generations have shifted gears and increased in intensity. Some of these developments and conditions include the following.

• *Outing.* In March 1990, soon after the death of magazine publisher, multimillionaire, media celebrity, and father of four grown sons, Malcolm Forbes, a homosexual news magazine located in New York City, *OutWeek*, published a cover story by its feature story editor, Michaelangelo Signorile, entitled "The Secret Gay Life of Malcolm Forbes." Although gossip had circulated about Forbes's "secret gay life" for some time, it had never been discussed in the media before. That article marked the beginning of the phenomenon of "outing"—the exposure, against their will, of the fact that certain supposed heterosexuals secretly are practicing homosexuals. The exposure is provided by known homosexuals. (Since Forbes was

dead, some considered his secret life fair game; since his exposure, however, "outing" has been extended to the living as well.) Some gays consider "outing" an outrageous invasion of their privacy; others approve of the practice on principle, arguing that secrecy about sexual orientation hurts all gays and lesbians and helps to maintain a stigmatizing, oppressive system. In contrast to secrecy, the latter faction claims "outing" provides young homosexuals with positive role models, demonstrating that there are many successful, famous men and women who are gay and lesbian. A middle ground, and probably the majority opinion in the gay community, is adopted by observers who feel that outing is ethically justified when specific closet homosexuals engage in behavior that is harmful to homosexuals. Examples of such acceptable targets include Father Bruce Ritter, a Catholic priest who was dismissed from his position at Covenant House because he had sex with adolescent boys, but who nonetheless publicly condemned homosexuality, and Roy Cohn, a powerful, ultra-conservative New York lawyer who died of AIDS but who spent much of his life making anti-homosexual statements.

• *Queer Nation.* Early in 1990, a group of homosexual activists in New York City called a meeting to discuss the issue of homophobia, or the hatred of homosexuals in feeling, word, and deed. A social movement sprang out of that meeting. Their goal was to express their homosexuality without being harassed, abused, attacked, or beaten. Their solution was to engage in active and aggressive confrontation with representatives of institutions that they saw as oppressive. No more apologizing, retreating, or explaining; "let yourself get angry" they exclaim, "it's time to fight back!" Its leaders chose the name "Queer Nation" because the term "queer" has aggressive, "in your face" connotations, because it is "one of the most freighted symbols of oppression" (Trebay, 1990, p. 37), because it makes polite, liberal heterosexuals and assimilationist homosexuals uncomfortable, and because it refers equally to men and women. (In contrast, "gay" is used almost exclusively to refer to male homosexuals.) "You can't say much that's going to hurt a queer who already calls herself one," explains one activist (p. 37). The motto of Queer Nation is: "We're here. We're queer. Get used to it." To that end, Queer Nation engages in militant demonstrations, protests, marches, campaigns, while wearing bottons and T-shirts with militant slogans (such as "Queer Nation—Get Used to It" and "Action=Life"). Queer Nation runs neighborhood patrols, pickets the homes of politicians who vote against gay rights, and engages in the nonviolent "occupation" of bars, business offices, and meetings whose patrons, executives, participants, or members are felt to harm homosexuals.

• *Queer Theory.* At the Lesbian and Gay Studies Conference in 1991, critic Arlene Stein presented a paper entitled "Sisters and Queers: The Decentering of Lesbian Feminism." Stein argued that "queer" is a better term than "lesbian" because it "emphasizes what can't be assimilated" (Warner, 1992, p. 18). In the same year, a journal devoted to discussions of homosexual culture, *differences*, published an issue entitled "Queer Theory: Lesbian and Gay Sexualities." Queer theory had been launched. Like "queer nation," the term "queer theory" tends to be offensive to straight liberals and assimilationist homosexuals. "Queer" emphasizes the apartness and differentness of gays and lesbians. "You can't eliminate queerness, says queer theory, or screen it out" (p. 19). The reality we see grows out of our sex and sexual orientation. Queer theory is an affirmation that for thousands of years, history and literature have been seen through the perspective of heterosexual males; *gendering* history and literature—uncovering the patriarchal, heterosexist biases in past intellectual enterprises—will enable us to cast off oppressive structures and liberate our true nature, enable us to be who we really are. The heterosexual reality, queer theorists say, is constrained, compulsive, conventional, repressive, exploitative; the homosexual reality is loose, free, wild, unfettered, and liberative. By adopting an unconventional, nonstandard, nontraditional sexual identity and expression, homosexuals are throwing off the chains of gender oppression and domination and are subverting patriarchy. (Some queer theorists even reject the idea of adopting a sexual identity at all, insisting on being available to any and all sexual experiences, regardless of their classification.) Queer theorists want "to emphasize the queerness of queers" (p. 19). They reject the idea that being homosexual is an alternative to being straight, parallel to it in every way (p. 19). Being gay or lesbian is a qualitatively different reality, not a parallel, sanitized alternative. Have fun, make trouble, be bold, confuse and terrorize the enemy, fight back, overturn the system, reject domination, oppression, and the tyanny of labels—these are some of the tenets of queer theory. At present, nearly all who call themselves queer

theorists are academics teaching in English, humanities, or film departments.

• *Legal changes.* In 1990, three states (Texas, Kentucky, and Michigan) repealed their laws outlawing homosexual practices. Today, in 28 states, homosexual practices are legal; six outlaw certain "deviate" practices (referred to as "sodomy")—mainly anal and oral sex—but only among same-sex partners; and 16 outlaw anal and/or oral sex for both heterosexual and homosexual sex partners (London, 1990). While arrests rarely take place, they are an ever-present reality in states in which certain acts are criminalized. Since they are by definition violating the law, many rights can be taken away from persons who are known homosexuals, such as adoption of children and the right to practice certain professions, including medicine, the law, the clergy, and teaching.

In addition, at the present time, 87 cities or counties have passed ordinances prohibiting discrimination on the basis of sexual orientation. Nine states (California, Connecticut, Hawaii, Massachussetts, Minnesota, New Jersey, Rhode Island, Vermont, and Wisconsin) also extend legal civil rights protection to gays. Elsewhere, such legislation has been defeated, or the political climate has been so hostile to it that it has never been proposed. In fact, some jurisdictions (the City of Cincinnati, for instance) specifically *prohibit* laws from being passed which protect homosexuals from discrimination. Nationally, a majority of Americans favor the passage of equal-rights laws protecting homosexuals against job discrimination by a margin of almost two to one—62 percent in favor, 32 percent opposed. However, two-thirds (65 percent) also believe that "too much attention is being paid" to the issue of homosexual rights (65 percent), and less than half say that they would vote for a homosexual candidate (48 percent), allow their child to watch a TV program with a homosexual character in it (46 percent), attend religious services presided over by gay clergy (42 percent), allow their child to attend a preschool that had homosexual staff members (42 percent), and see a homosexual doctor (39 percent). In fact, most Americans oppose discrimination against gays, but admit they would practice it themselves (Henry, 1994, pp. 58, 59).

• *Etiology.* Many homosexuals claim that they have no more choice in becoming gay than heterosexuals did in being straight. The awareness of same-sex attraction (for men, at any rate) comes so early in life and, for many homosexuals, is so strong that it seems almost inconceivable that there is no genetic or hormonal component in its etiology or cause. In 1991 and 1992 and again in 1995, in three separate studies by different teams of researchers, anatomical differences were located in the brains of homosexuals and heterosexuals (Angier, 1991, 1992; Nimmons, 1994; Watson and Shapiro, 1995). In addition, a psychologist and a psychiatrist found a strikingly higher proportion of brothers of identical twins of homosexual men (52 percent) to be gay themselves than was true of fraternal brothers (22 percent) and genetically unrelated adopted brothers (11 percent); this study argued for a possible genetic origin of homosexuality (Bailey and Pillard, 1991). In 1993, a team of geneticists located a "shared stretch" of genetic material that homosexual brothers have in common; they claim that there is a 99.5 percent certainty that there is a gene or set of genes that predisposes men to become homosexual (Pool, 1993; Angier, 1993; Hamer et al., 1993). By now, a substantial literature has accumulated on the issue of the biological etiology of homosexuality (LeVay, 1995; Hamer and Copeland, 1995).

However, it must be stressed that the biological origin of homosexuality is controversial. Two of the brain studies relied on the organs of deceased AIDS patients who were known to have engaged in homosexual relations; it is possible that the disease generated the difference the scientists observed, not the homosexuality. In addition, correlation does not demonstrate causality; it is entirely possible that engaging in certain sexual practices triggers biological processes that influence cerebral structures. Moreover, it is not known in what way the areas of the brain where differences were observed have to do with sexual orientation. Even the team that found similar genetic material in homosexual brothers are cautious about their findings. Nonetheless, some observers, scientists and laypersons alike, do take the research seriously and believe that it indicates that inborn biological processes may determine or influence sexual orientation. Some gay activists have endorsed the findings, arguing that they show how unjust society's condemnation of homosexuality is. If sexual orientation is an inborn condition and not a choice, how can homosexuals be condemned for behavior over which they have no control? Other gay activists reject this argument, claiming the reasons *why* one seeks the companionship of same-sex partners should be irrelevant (Massa, 1991; Talan,

1991). In any case, possessors of a number of congenital conditions—for example, dwarfism, Downs' Syndrome, albinism—which are widely regarded as undesirable do attract condemnation and scorn, so the involuntary character of homosexuality is quite beside the point. Meanwhile, the controversy continues.

• *Family Values.* During the 1992 presidential campaign, homosexuality became an issue as never before in the nation's history; "for the first time, the Presidential candidates are engaging in open debate over sharply different views on gay rights" (Schmalz, 1992, p. A1). The 1992 Republican party platform unambiguously expressed opposition to civil rights statutes which mentioned sexual preference status as defining a protected minority. Arriving at the Republican National Convention in Houston in August, President Bush attacked his Democratic opponents with a sexual innuendo, stating: "They give new meaning to the words, *closet liberal.*" Bush also seemed to hint that his opponent, Governor Clinton, might be a "swishy-decorator type" by saying in reference to his opponent's confidence about being elected and taking up residence in the White House, "I half expected, when I went over to the Oval Office, to find him over there measuring the drapes" (Taylor, 1992, p. 25).

In his speech at the Republican National Convention in support of Bush's candidacy, reactionary, far-right former presidential candidate Patrick Buchanan lashed out at the Democrat's support of homosexual rights several times. Sneered Buchanan, "a militant leader of the homosexual rights movement could rise at that [Democratic] convention and exhault, 'Bill Clinton and Al Gore [Democratic presidential and vice-presidential candidates, respectively] represent the most pro-lesbian and pro-gay ticket in history.' And so they do." Buchanan likened Clinton and Gore and their followers to sexual deviants who pretended to be normal. "Like many of you last month," Buchanan said, "I watched that giant masquerade ball at Madison Square Garden [the Democratic National Convention] where 20,000 radicals and liberals came dressed up as moderates and centrists—the greatest single exhibition of cross-dressing in American political history" (Taylor, 1992, pp. 25, 26). The antihomosexual theme of the 1992 GOP convention was best expressed by a candidate holding a poster for a *Newsweek* photographer: "Family Rights Forever: 'Gay' Rights Never!" These attacks were part of a larger strategy to portray the Republicans as strong—and the Democrats as weak—on traditional "family values." Exactly what that meant wasn't clear; at the Republican convention, Bush's wife Barbara claimed it meant whatever one understood by it. Whatever it meant, it most decidedly did not embrace homosexuality.

At the same time, the "family values" theme proved to lack appeal to the majority of voters, who were more concerned about basic, meat-and-potatoes issues such as jobs and the economy. Well before the election, it was clear that the "family values" theme was appealing only to the Republican party's conservative right wing, and represented something of a liability with more mainstream voters. In September, *The New York Times* ran a front page story with the headlines, "Bush Tries to Recoup From Harsh Tone on 'Values'" (Rosenthal, 1992). Its central message was that for most voters, a stress on "family values" backfired for the Republicans; most voters were simply not buying it. The outcome of the election, that is, Bush's defeat and Clinton's victory, indicated that a substantial number of American voters rejected the "family values" theme and instead were concerned with more fundamental issues. For Democrats, "It's the economy, stupid!" became the watchword of the 1992 election campaign. The 1996 Republican presidential campaign has been much more subdued with respect to the "family values" theme, including homosexuality. Senator Bob Dole, the Republican candidate, rarely mentioned it, and minority gadfly candidate Patrick Buchanan, who eventually bowed out of the race, focused his attention mainly on abortion and illegal immigration.

However, where the "family values" theme failed to catch fire in the *national* election of 1992, it was, and remains, absolutely central in hundreds of *local* elections. Fundamentalist Christian candidates won in 40 percent of the 500 races they entered which were monitored by People for the American Way, a liberal lobbying group opposed to the intrusion of the religious right into mainstream politics. Ralph Reed, head of the Christian Coalition, a politically oriented religious-right organization, in describing the 1992 elections, said, "at school boards and at the state legislative level we had big, tremendous victories" (Mydans, 1992, p. 9). These elected officials support "family values," which means that they are *opposed* to a pro-choice position on abortion, laws guaranteeing women's rights and homosexual rights, sex education in the schools, and *in favor of* prayer in the schools, the

teaching of creationism, the teaching of sexual abstinence, and removing certain offensive books from school libraries. Of all political arenas, successful "family values" candidates are most likely to have a substantial impact on local school boards. The "family values" theme will prove to be troublesome for the lives of many homosexuals across the country well into the twenty-first century.

• *Gays in the Military?* Although most high-ranking military officials (as well as the majority of the rank-and-file in the armed services) reject permitting known homosexuals to enter or remain in military service, the election of a moderate-to-liberal Democratic president in 1992 opened the possiblity that this policy might change. In the decade before 1992, more than 15,000 homosexuals were dismissed from the American military. While "tens of thousands" of homosexuals serve in the 1.8 million member armed forces at present, "they keep their sexual orientation secret" (Cushman, 1992). In the absence of an outright ban, some military officials claim, homosexuals might "openly display their homosexuality, possibly undermining morale and discipline." On the other hand, soon after he was elected and before he took office, Bill Clinton, following up on a campaign pledge, stated in a press conference that he was committed to lifting the ban on homosexuals in the military. He did, however, emphasize that he would "consult with a lot of people about what our options are, including people who may disagree with me about the ultimate merits" (Cushman, 1992). The upshot of Clinton's consultation proved to be discouraging to change. He came up with the "don't ask, don't tell" compromise, which made neither gays nor conservatives happy. The fact is that many homosexuals in the military are being asked about their orientation—as well as their parents, their friends, and their therapists. In the fiscal year ending October 1995, the three services discharged 488 military personnel for homosexuality, an increase of 17 percent from the previous year (Shenon, 1995, p. 1). Clearly, Clinton misjudged the depth and strength of the opposition to openly homosexual personnel serving in the armed forces. Currently, the issue of gays in the military has reached something of a stalemate, with neither side pushing for a clear-cut resolution. In 1996, a federal appeals court upheld the legality of Clinton's "don't ask, don't tell" policy.

• *Gay Bashing*. In 1990, two women embraced on a street corner in New York City's Greenwich Village; a dozen teenagers taunted then punched the two women, knocking them down, then kicked them as they lay on the pavement (Hayes, 1990). Scrawled across a homosexual rights leaflet were the words: "I Kill Faggots!" and "Death to Faggots!" The leaflet was mailed back to the organization's office. A T-shirt in Queens displayed a picture of a hatchet, with the words, "Fag Swatter" printed directly below. In 1991, a Syracuse fraternity was suspended for distributing T-shirts that condoned violence against homosexuals. The front of the shirts announced, "Homophobic and proud of it!" The back said: "Club Faggots Not Seals!" Depicted was a muscled crow (the fraternity's symbol), holding a spike-studded club, standing next to a prone, clearly unconscious figure. Next to the figure, a seal hoisted a mug of beer ("Anti-Homosexual T-Shirts Prompt Suspension of Syracuse Fraternity," *The New York Times*, June 26, 1001, p. B4). In the early morning of July 2, 1990, three young men, hunting for "a drug dealer or a drug addict or a homo out cruising," encountered and lured a known homosexual man into an isolated schoolyard and beat him with a hammer and a beer bottle before stabbing him to death. The killer admitted that he had stabbed his victim "because he was gay" (Stanley, 1991). Homosexuals have been described as "the most violently attacked community in America" (Hentoff, 1990, p. 24).

While "gay bashing"—the physical attack on men and women specifically because their assailants think they are homosexuals or recognize them as such—has been common for some time, many experts believe that in the 1990s, this violent practice is on the rise. In a survey of five cities, the National Gay and Lesbian Task Force Policy Institute found that antihomosexual violence increased between 1989 and 1990 by over 40 percent, and from 1990 to 1991 by over 30 percent. The number of documented antigay murders increased, the institute said, from three to eight in the 1990–1991 period (Broznan, 1991; "Attacks on U.S. Homosexuals Held Alarmingly Widespread" and "Anti-Gay Crimes Are Reported on Rise in 5 Cities," *The New York Times*, June 8, 1989, March 20, 1992). The same pattern is claimed for Great Britain (Rule, 1990).

• *Gay Marriage?* Perhaps the most recent battleground is over the question of state recognition of gay marriages. A court case in Hawaii opened the possibility that by the end of 1997, same-sex marriages may be legal in that state. Some conservatives envision a future when gay couples can fly to Hawaii and return with a legal marriage license. Currently, 19 states are considering legislation to *deny* government recognition to gay marriages that have tken place in that or any state; South Dakota and Utah have already enacted such legislation. (Such laws have failed to pass in three states.) A clear majority of the American public (64 percent) *oppose* legal homosexual marriages; only 31 percent approve (Henry, 1994, p. 58). Legal, state-recognized same-sex marital unions, says a lawyer working for a fundamentalist Christian interest group, "strikes at the very core of who we are as a people. . . . Marriage defined as a man and a woman has been around more than 6,000 years and has served most cultures well" (Dunlap, 1996). In opposition, a gay activist says, "the government . . . has allowed the legislation of hate and the creation of a second-class citizen. This second-class citizen is defined by love." The battle is likely to be fierce, and to continue until well into the twenty-first century.

HOMOSEXUALITY: ESSENTIALISM VERSUS CONSTRUCTIONISM

There are two basic ways to view the reality of homosexuality: the *essentialist* model and the *social constructionist* model (Goode, 1981, pp. 58f.; Plummer, 1981a, pp. 54f.; Troiden, 1988, pp. 101–122; Greenberg, 1988). Most psychiatrists and other physicians, many psychologists, a few sociologists, and for the most part, the man and woman on the street, see homosexuality from the viewpoint of the essentialist model. Most sociologists and anthropologists, and some psychologists, see the reality of homosexuality through the prism of the social constructionist model.

The essentialist argues that homosexuality, like heterosexuality, is a natural, universal category that exists independent of culture, time, or situation. It exists *a priori* or *before* it is defined by any particular society; it is a *pregiven* entity, much like stars, frogs, or orchids. Homosexuality is a concretely real phenomenon with more or less identical basic properties the world over. Just as "a rose is a rose is a rose," to the essentialist, a homosexual is a homosexual is a homosexual, a specific type of being, identifiable by means of hard, reliable measures or indicators. Somewhere lurking within each homosexual are clear-cut manifestations of his or her homosexuality. Every scientifically informed observer should agree as to the exact nature of someone's sexual classification. It is nature that accurately divides the human world into homosexuals and heterosexuals, not members of the culture, the subculture, or the particular scene in which these humans live and act. In this sense, homosexuals and heterosexuals are as clearly distinguishable from one another as apples and oranges or rubies and diamonds (Troiden, 1988, p. 101). Essentialists typically apply the disease analogy to homosexuality and see it much like a *condition* that one "has." In medicine, for example, experts diagnose patients to determine whether they have cancer, diabetes, or an ulcer; likewise, experts can determine whether someone "has" homosexuality in the same way. (The difference is that homosexuality is usually regarded by essentialists as a condition that *saturates* the person, one that is thoroughly and completely "in" someone, whereas diseases are generally seen as external invasions, not an aspect of someone's "true," indwelling self.) Many homosexuals also view homosexuality as an indwelling, essentialistic trait, although they do not see it as pathological. Instead, it is *different from*, although not *inferior to*, heterosexuality, much like left-handedness. For instance, homosexuals will say, "When I *discovered* I was gay . . ." as if it had been there all along, waiting to be discovered, in much the same way that one would pick an apple off a tree.

Essentialists regard the fundamental reality of homosexuality as residing in *sexual orientation*, sexual *preference*, or sexual *feelings*. To them, sexual behavior is secondary; what counts is erotic desire. Some men and women have sex with persons of the same gender in contexts that call for it, in prison, for instance, or in some societies in ritualistic contexts. Likewise, some men and women have sex mainly or exclusively with members of the opposite gender, but lust after same-sex partners, for example, "closet" gays who are married and keep their desires hidden. Essentialists are concerned with the question of whether or not someone is a "true" homosexual or a "pseudo" homosexual (Socarides, 1978, pp. 100–101). Someone who engages in situational homosexuality may not be a "true" homosexual, that is, does not have the homosexual's fundamental motivation or etiology,

or display the homosexual's essential traits, while, contrarily, someone who never engages in homosexual behavior may actually be a "true" homosexual, because he or she harbors those traits. What is crucial about homosexuality to the essentialist is the etiology of sexual orientation, that is, what *causes* someone to prefer same-sex partners. Little else is of any consequence about the phenomenon of homosexuality (Whitam, 1977, 1983; Whitam and Mathy, 1986).

In contrast, the social constructionist believes that homosexuality is *not* a concrete, universally agreed-upon reality, but a phenomenon that exists because of the way it is defined socially, culturally, and situationally. What homosexuality "is," social constructionists argue, is what collectivities believe it to be. Constructionists talk about the "invention" and the "social construction" of homosexuality and heterosexuality (Greenberg, 1988; Katz, 1995). This does not mean that they do not regognize that same-gender (and opposite-gender) sex *existed* prior to its recognition. What they are interested in, however, is the *recognition* or *creation* of separate categories of humanity which are based on sexual orientation, as well as separate treatment based on that fact. The "essential reality" of the gender aspect of sex is not a constant or a universal, but varies according to the settings within which it appears. There are no definitive, absolute criteria for what homosexuality "is" or who "is" a homosexual. Rather, there are *dimensions* of homosexuality, which are regarded as crucial in defining its reality; those dimensions vary in importance from one society or culture to another, one social context to another, or one historical time period to another. Likewise, the *content* of homosexuality varies enormously; the norms, values, and practices that are accepted among homosexuals which are characteristic in one time and place are absent in others. In other words, "being" a homosexual is experienced differently, according to the social context within which it takes place. And what it means to "be" a homosexual also varies considerably: It is a savagely stigmatized category at one time and in one place, tolerated in another, encouraged in a third, and required in a fourth. Indeed, prior to the modern world, even the very categories, homosexual and heterosexual, *did not exist*.

The constructivist argues that homosexuality can be looked at as a social *role* (McIntosh, 1968; Goode, 1981b; Weeks, Plummer, and McIntosh,

1981), that is, a set of norms, beliefs, and practices that one learns as a member of a particular culture or subculture. In some societies, this role is lacking; same-gender sexual contact appears, and may even be extremely common, but there is no such thing as homosexuality as such—no such role as a homosexual. In other societies, some men and women are called homosexuals and are expected to do, and not to do, certain things; if not, they are punished, both by others called homosexuals and by the heterosexual majority. And in the many contexts in which the role exists, homosexuality manifests itself differently: here, one set of rules, and there, a different set. Same-gender sexual behavior does not assume universal outlines everywhere. In ancient Greece, adult males who made love with individuals of the same gender did not choose other adult men as partners, but adolescent boys. And both adult and adolescent males were expected to marry, have sex with women, and raise children (Dover, 1978; Hoffman, 1980). In the United States, adult male homosexuals have sex with one another and rarely have sex with women once they decide that they are gay; here and today, homosexuality and heterosexuality are seen as mutually exclusive, one precluding the other. Both institutions, of ancient Greece and the United States, are called homosexuality, and they are similar in that same-gender sex is involved, but what homosexuality *means* and how it is *experienced* in these two settings is radically different.

Among the Sambia (Herdt, 1987), as we see in the boxed insert, same-gender sex is required of *every single male* for a period of 10 to 15 years. In contrast, in the United States, the straight majority prefers that *no one* engage in homosexual behavior, and most Americans look on homosexuals with contempt. In prison, men who act as the aggressor or insertor in sex with other men are regarded as supremely heterosexual; men who act out or who are forced to play the passive or insertee role are regarded as girlish, effeminate, weak, and therefore homosexual (Wooden and Parker, 1982). On pirate ships, likewise, very masculine and otherwise heterosexual males would have sex with smaller, younger, less macho men; not only did they not see themselves as homosexual, they did not even regard what they were doing as homosexual sex (Burg, 1984). The social constructionist would argue that what homosexuality "is" is how it is regarded and defined in its many contexts. In prison it is the insertee who is regarded as homosexual, not the insertor; most people who have no knowledge of sex in prisons would see both as engaging in homosexual behavior. What the Sambia do would be seen by most Americans as homosexual in nature, even though the Sambian would define as homosexual only same-gender sexual contact taking place outside a ritualistic context. To the social constructivist, there is no universal essence that defines the reality of homosexuality, only these varying culturally, socially, situationally, and historically based definitions.

In a sense, the argument between the essentialists and the constructionists is one not only about what is true but *what is crucial to look at;* in this sense, they are not talking *to* but talking *past* one another. Phenomena that constructionists regard as important and interesting are dismissed by essentialists as irrelevant and trivial. Essentialists focus on sexual preference, as I said; in contrast, constructionists examine a wide range of phenomena revolving around same-gender sexual contact. Says one essentialist: "Homosexuality is . . . a sexual orientation and no useful purpose can be served by regarding it as anything else" (Whitam, 1977, p. 2). In other words, it matters not that men and women who are "truly" heterosexual have homosexual sex in prison, that supremely masculine men—pirates, warriors, bandits—have often engaged in homosexual acts when they are in exclusively same-gender company, but are otherwise exclusively heterosexual. To the essentialist, it is irrelevant that the content of the homosexual role or subculture varies so much from one society to another, that "homosexuals" are bisexual in their behavior in one place and exclusively homosexual in another, that in some societies, boys and adolescent men are expected to be, and are, exclusively homosexual in their behavior for a substantial stretch of their lives in ritual contexts, and then, as adults, are exclusively heterosexual—*none of this matters*. To the essentialist, there is one thing and one thing only that is of any consequence: sexual preference. Everything else is an exercise in obscurantism and irrelevancy. The reality of homosexuality is exhausted by a single dimension or criterion. To discuss anything else on the same level is to confuse what is secondary with what is primary (Goode, 1981b, p. 59). Thus, because of this disagreement concerning what is important, there is no possibility of resolving the argument between the essentialists and the constructionists. It is a semantic and definitional issue that has no conceivable solution.

HOMOSEXUALITY AS DEVIANCE

Recall that our definition of deviance conveys no negative or pejorative overtones whatsoever. It does *not* mean immoral, sick, unnatural, or pathological. It is necessary to issue this reminder because the public seems to stick to the obsolete and sociologically invalid meaning of the term *deviance* in relation to homosexuality more than for any other form of behavior. Roughly halfway through a course in deviant behavior that I taught recently, a student used the term *deviance* in the pathological sense to apply to homosexuals. I was thunderstruck. I asked how, after my elaborate explanations as to the meaning of the term, she could use it in such an antiquated sense. She replied that the term just seemed to her to apply to homosexuality because, in spite of what I said, she regarded it as unnatural. No amount of evidence could persuade her otherwise. At the other end of the spectrum, soon after the publication of a previous edition of this book, I received a half-dozen letters from a self-proclaimed gay activist in the Midwest who claimed that my classifying homosexuality as a form of deviance implied that it was unnatural and pathological. Again, no amount of attempts at persuasion on the subject would alter his position. So let's be clear about this: Homosexuality is a form of deviant behavior because most members of this society do not approve of it, and because this disapproval takes the form of condemnation and punishment of homosexuals and strained, difficult relations between straights and gays.

Homosexual behavior, desires, and a homosexual identity and orientation are deviant; they typically attract *sexual stigma* (Plummer, 1975; Troiden, 1988, pp. 52–57). How do we know this? How exactly can we measure the deviant status of homosexuality? What clear-cut indicators or manifestations of homosexuality's deviant status do we have? What can we point to which will permit us to *see* that homosexuality is a form of deviant behavior?

In some ways, homosexuality provides an almost perfect or "ideal" model for what deviance is all about. (There are ways that the status of homosexuality departs from this deviant ideal, which we'll look at momentarily.) In many social circles, homosexual practices are regarded as an abomination: People who are known to engage in them are treated as outcasts. Wisely, most who do so keep the fact hidden from the heterosexuals whom they know. The prohibition against homosexual behavior, for Westerners, stretches back to the story of Sodom and Gomorrah in the book of Genesis, cities destroyed by the wrath of God because their citizens practiced "unnatural" acts. Typically, parents consider the question, "Would you want your son or daughter to become one?" with trepidation and fright. Many jobs are closed to known homosexuals, especially those that involve dealings with children or the national security or that demand respectability and conventionality. Some of the most derogatory words in the English language address themselves to known or suspected homosexuals: "faggot," "queer," "punk," "cocksucker," and "fairy" would be examples. In 1994, when asked, "Are homosexual relations between consenting adults morally wrong?" a majority of a sample of respondents (53 percent) said yes—exactly the same figure as was elicited by the same question in 1978 (Henry, 1994, p. 57); four in 10 (41 percent) said no. Any activity regarded as "morally wrong" by a majority of the public is almost by definition a form of deviance to a sociologist.

One civil liberties lawyer compared the public hostility against homosexuals (called "homophobia") with the persecution of Jews in Nazi Germany (Glasser, 1975). It is not widely known that in spite of the fact that many high-ranking Nazi officials were homosexuals (Bleuel, 1974), many thousands of male homosexuals were arrested for their sexual orientation (lesbians were spared this fate), put into concentration camps, forced to wear their badge of stigma—the pink triangle—castrated, and even killed (Rector, 1981; Plant, 1986). One civil libertarian estimates the total number of homosexuals who died in Nazi camps at a quarter of a million (Glasser, 1975), while a historian more conservatively estimates that the figure is closer to 5,000 to 15,000 (Plant, 1986). Although even a roughly accurate figure is probably impossible to ascertain, it is clear that at times, homosexuals have been savagely persecuted.

American public opinion is also strongly negative concerning homosexuals and homosexuality. In a study based on a nationally representative sample, two-thirds of all respondents regarded homosexuality as "very much obscene and vulgar," two-thirds said that they have never liked homosexuals, two-thirds said that homosexuals should never be allowed to practice medicine or enter government service, three-quarters said that they should be prohibited from being judges, school teachers, and ministers. A clear majority disapproved of decriminalizing homosexual acts. Nearly half agreed that "homosexuality is a social corruption which can cause the downfall of civilization" (Levitt and Klassen, 1974).

We might be tempted to argue that recent changes in public opinion have reduced the intensity of some of these feelings, but alas, for the most part, this is not the case; if anything, most Americans have a more negative feeling toward homosexuals and homosexuality that was true in the recent past. Each year, Gallup Polls have been conducted on the American public's attitudes toward homosexuals and homosexuality; one question the Gallup organization frequently asks is: "Do you think homosexual relations between consenting adults should or should not be legal?" In 1982, 45 percent of those questioned said that homosexual relations should be legal, while 39 percent said that they should not. This gave a slight edge to the liberal, tolerant, accepting position. But in only five years, in Gallup's 1987 poll, American sentiment had turned against homosexuality: 33 percent said that homosexual relations should be legal (a drop of 12 percentage points), while a clear majority, 55 percent, said that they should not be legal (a rise of 16 percentage points). The 1987 poll represented the first time that a majority of the American public opposed the legalization of homosexuality. In these polls, there was a clear-cut relationship between education and attitudes toward the legalization of homosexual relations, with better-educated individuals being far more likely to favor making or keeping them legal, and less well-educated individuals favoring making or keeping them illegal. In 1987, 53 percent of college-educated respondents said that homosexual relations should be legal; 36 percent said that they should not be legal. Support for the "should be legal" position declined, and support for the "should not be legal" position rose among less well educated respondents. Only 21 percent of the respondents with less than a high school education said that homosexual relations should be legal, while nearly two-thirds (65 percent) said that they should not be legal.

Public opinion favoring the criminalization of homosexuality is only one out of a vast array of concrete measures, indicators, and manifestations of the deviant status of a same-gender sexual orientation. Nearly everywhere we turn, we are reminded of the homosexual's second-class citizenship; nearly everywhere, heterosexuality is expected, preferred, favored, taken for granted, regarded as superior. Homosexuals are unwelcome in many quarters. They tend to be regarded as morally inferior, looked down upon, made fun of, stigmatized, in a word, they are seen as deviants by the straight majority.

When the issue of a male homosexual teaching adolescent boys is considered, most heterosexuals will raise the question of whether he will seduce his students. (Most Americans wish to restrict homosexuals' access to the teaching profession more than for any other occupation.) The fact that this possibility holds at least equally for male heterosexual teachers of adolescent girls rarely enters the minds of most heterosexuals; somehow, they will say, homosexuals are "different."

Lesbian mothers are often asked if they "brainwash" their daughters to become lesbians. The fact is that heterosexuals are engaged in an almost daily, nonconscious campaign to "brainwash" their children to become heterosexuals. In any case, the evidence from empirical research suggests that children raised by lesbian mothers are just as likely to grow up to be heterosexual as those raised by mothers who are heterosexual (Gutis, 1987).

When the question of repealing the laws against homosexual acts is debated, a cry often goes up that this will open the doors to homosexual assaults upon young boys. Consider this diatribe published in the *Humbard Christian Report* in 1972 (not 1872!): "Here in Youngstown, we are shocked by a terrible crime against a young boy by a sex pervert which resulted in the boy's murder, yet our lawmakers passed a bill legalizing this crime . . . ! What insanity! This is giving a green light to more and worse sex crimes. This is bringing out into the open what the law and moral standards have always condemned. . . . This bill, if it passes the Senate, will open a Pandora's box of crime and filth unparalleled in the history of the United States" (Petras, 1973, p. 102). Why one case of sexual violence by a man against a boy is any more typical of homosexuality in general than one case of a heterosexual rape-murder is of heterosexuality in general is not clear. But the fact that this equation is taken seriously in some circles emphasizes that the same rules of logic do not apply to the same forms of behavior for many heterosexuals.

When he asked a sample of respondents to name persons they regarded as deviant, Simmons (1965) found that the most common response (49 percent) was "homosexuals." Of all the deviant groups listed, the sample was most intolerant of homosexuals, and wanted to place the greatest social distance between themselves and homosexuals. ("Lesbians" were next most rejected group.) The characteristics attributed to homosexuals were by far the most negative and consistently stereotyped: 72 percent of the sample said that homosexuals were "sexually abnormal," 52 percent felt that they were "perverted," and 40 percent said that they were "mentally ill" (Simmons, 1969, pp. 28, 33). When I asked the undergraduates enrolled in one of my recent courses on deviance which forms of behavior came to mind as examples of deviance, homosexuality was fourth most often mentioned, after murder, rape, and theft; for over a third of the class (35 percent), homosexuality spontaneously came to mind as a form of deviance.

Even today, many—perhaps most—practicing psychiatrists and psychotherapists feel that homosexuality is, in and of itself, a form of emotional illness, or at the very least a *manifestation* of an emotional illness. Perhaps for no other form of deviant behavior is there so strong an urge on the part of scientific researchers and clinicians to *pathologize* homosexuality. It is clear that for homosexuality, scientific and medical stigmatization is strong and widespread. The pathology perspective seems to be most clearly exemplified by professional writings on homosexuality. Albert Ellis, a clinical psychologist, states "every gay person I've seen is . . . pretty nutty. . . . I think that 50 percent of them are borderline psychotics" (Karlen, 1971, p. 223). Ellis's mentor, Eli Siegel, founder of the therapeutic school of "Aesthetic Realism," stigmatizes all homosexuality by claiming—without presenting a shred of evidence—that its fundamental cause is contempt for everything outside of oneself (Reiss, 1986).

In spite of the American Psychiatric Association's 1973 ruling that homosexuality is not in itself a sign of a mental disorder, many psychiatrists and other therapists continue to adhere to the view that homosexuality is pathological. In 1977, the journal *Medical Aspects of Human Sexuality* distributed questionnaires to psychiatrists on the issue of homosexuality. Two-thirds of the respondents of this survey (69 percent) answered "yes" to the question, "Is homosexuality usually a pathological adptation (as opposed to a normal variation)?" Seven in 10 agreed with the statement, "Are homosexuals' problems in living a result of personal problems more than stigmatization?" And a clear-cut majority (60 percent) believed that homosexual men are "generally less capable than heterosexual men of mature, loving relationships." Slightly less (55 percent) believed the same of lesbians when compared with heterosexual women (Lief, 1977). It is unlikely that these attitudes have changed substantially in recent years.

In 1979, the House of Bishops of the Episcopal Church voted overwhelmingly to ban homosexuals from becoming Episcopal priests. Voting 99 to 34, the ecclesiastical body declared: "We affirm the traditional teaching of the Church on marriage, marital fidelity and sexual chastity as the standard of Christian morality. Candidates for ordination are expected to conform to this standard. Therefore we believe that it is not appropriate for this church to ordain a practicing homosexual (Sheppard, 1979). In 1988, the primary policy-making body of the United Methodist Church voted to retain its standard that homosexuality is "incompatible with Christian teaching" and therefore a bar to the ordained ministry. Motions to change the church's position were rejected by two-thirds of the voting delegates. A similar proportion voted to keep the church's current prohibition on using church funds for projects advocating the acceptance of homosexuality (Steinfels, 1988). Renwick Jackson was a popular, well-liked, and often-praised Congregational minister tending to a Long Island flock; in 1994, he had been given an extension on his contract, which ran into 1997. On the last day of 1994, he performed a wedding ceremony legitimating the union of a lesbian couple. Some members of the congregation were outraged. Meetings were held to determine Reverend Jackson's tenure at the church. Tempers flared; chairs were thrown; members screamed at one another; some stalked out of the meeting. A vote was held, and by a margin of 84 to 76, it was decided that Reverend Jackson be fired. One member, though he saw the minister as "a very liberal and progressive fellow," nonetheless said, "the lesbian issue pushed it [matters] over the edge, and many people in the congregation became disenchanted with him" (McQuiston, 1995). In January 1996, Lakeshore Avenue Baptist Church of Oakland, California, with a long history of progressive activism, announced that it would welcome homosexuals without teaching that homosexuality is sinful. Shortly thereafter, the American Baptist Churches of the West, the organization of which Lakeshore had been a member, voted to expel Lakewood from its ranks. Two Lutheran churches in San Francisco were expelled from their denomination for appointing self-declared homosexuals as pastors (Niebuhr, 1996).

"Sodomy" is defined as "unnatural" copulation; it refers most particularly to anal sex, although some definitions include oral sex as well. (A disparaging term to refer to homosexuals is "sodomite.") Clearly, both heterosexual and homosexual sex can entail "sodomy"; although the term does not refer exclusively to homosexual actions, typically, the implication is that sodomy is what homosexuals engage in. Sodomy is a crime in 22 states of the United States; in 16 of these, the act may be either heterosexual or homosexual, and in four, the law refers specifically to homosexual actions. In Georgia, an antisodomy state, oral or anal sex between any two people, heterosexual or homosexual, is a crime. In Atlanta, in August 1982, a police officer, armed with a search warrant, and after being admitted to Michael Hardwick's place of residence in an investigation of a public drunkenness offense, noticed through the crack in a door that was ajar that the man was having oral sex with another man. The officer promptly arrested Hardwick, who contested the constitutionality of Georgia's sodomy law all the way to the Supreme Court.

In 1986, in a five-to-four decision, the Court decided that the state's antisodomy laws are constitutional, that a state may legally prohibit sodomy among homosexuals, even if it is practiced among consenting adults in the privacy of their own homes. Individuals engaging in homosexual acts, the Court declared, do not enjoy the right of privacy accorded those who practice more conventional sexual behavior. The majority opinion declared that the argument claiming that individuals have the right to practice homosexual relations is "insupportable" and "facetious." To give homosexuals the "fundamental right to engage in homosexual sodomy," wrote Justice Byron White, is something that the Court was "quite unwilling to do." Laws against homosexual acts, he said, have "ancient roots" and therefore should not be tampered with (Greenhouse, 1986; Taylor, 1986; White, 1986).

Of course, the sodomy laws are very rarely enforced; hardly anyone is ever arrested in the United States for this crime. In fact, Hardwick was not convicted of sodomy, but he chose to challenge the law's constitutionality so that it would be striken from the books, not so that he would escape punishment. At the same time, the sodomy laws do spill over into other crucial areas. For instance, custody and adoption: Social welfare agencies cannot award custody or the adoption of a child by a household in which one or more biological or potential surrogate parents are engaging in actions that are specifically criminal. This means that in nearly half of the states of the United States, the custody or adoption of a child cannot by law be awarded to a known homosexual. In addition, professional licenses that are granted to candidates on the basis of their "good moral character" could be denied because of their practice of a criminal act. The Supreme Court case could also "impede counseling and research into AIDS," license police harassment of gays, and slow the advance of homosexual rights. Said one spokesman for a homosexual rights organization of the court ruling, "It's a major disaster from our point of view." Said the Reverend Jerry Falwell, a fundamentalist minister, "The highest court . . . has issued a clear statement that perverted moral behavior is not accepted practice in this country" (Rohter, 1986).

In May 1981, a 19-year-old University of California at Los Angeles student, Timothy Curran, was expelled as an adult leader in a California Boy Scout troop because a newspaper photograph depicted him attending a local dance with a male date. Mr. Curran attended the dance as a homosexual to make a political statement. A spokesperson for the Boy Scouts of America stated that as a homosexual, Mr. Curran "was not a good moral example to be emulated by younger scouts." (This episode was reported by the Combined News Services and appeared in newspapers on May 1, 1981.)

Thus, all around us, we see countless indicators of homosexuality's deviant status. Most heterosexuals want to keep or make homosexual acts illegal, indeed, in nearly half the states of the United States, they *are* illegal, a long-standing tradition recently upheld by the highest court in the land. Homosexuals are readily and spontaneously thought of when heterosexuals are asked to provide examples of deviants. Many, perhaps most, psychiatrists and practitioners of other therapeutic traditions regard homosexuality as abnormal, a pathological condition. Being a homosexual has been grounds

What Is Homophobia?

"Homophobia" is the term experts use to refer to prejudicial attitudes against and negative feelings toward homosexuals, which often manifest themselves in the form of overt discrimination or other hostile acts. Homophobia covers a broad spectrum, from unreflective negative attitudes at one end to outright anger and hostility—sometimes culminating in violent incidents of "gay bashing"—at the other. Sociologists and psychologists who study the phenomenon liken such attitudes and feelings to racism, anti-Semitism, and sexism. Just as a racist claims not to hate Blacks irrationally, but on the basis of their presumed characteristics, homophobes will claim that their sentiments rest on a rational foundation. They are not biased against gays any more than gays deserve, they will claim. They will cite religion, science, medicine, nature, or some other seemingly reasonable source for their negative feelings. For instance, fundamentalist Christians claim that their antihomosexual stance stems from religious principle, not from prejudice; homosexuality is an abomination in God's eyes, they will say. But the fact is that homophobes dislike gays, feel contempt for them, feel that they *deserve* contempt. Homophobes feel self-righteous in these feelings. Clearly, more than simple religious prohibition is behind these hostile feelings, however; the Bible forbids many practices, such as usury (or taking interest on a loan) and trespassing on holy property, but hardly anyone harbors the same hostile feelings toward bankers and trespassers as they do toward homosexuals. The Bible states that the rich cannot enter the gates of heaven, and that adulterous women should be stoned to death, yet fundamentalist Christians do not support these teachings. Clearly, there is something of a *selective interpretation* of the holy text here. Something more than theology is afoot in the hostility of some fundamentalist Christians toward homosexuality; what is it?

Homophobia has its roots in the view that homosexuals represent a threat to one's moral universe. Gregory Herek, a psychologist, says that homophobes see gays and lesbians "as a litmus test" for being a decent, moral person; one's own values become reaffirmed through hostility toward homosexuals. Bob Altemeyer, another psychologist and researcher of homophobia, says that homophobes "see homosexuality as a sign that society is disintegrating. . . . Their self-righteousness makes them feel they are acting morally when they attack homosexuals." Homophobia is difficult to change; this is especially the case if it is based on a religious justification. Facts become selectively interpreted to filter out neutral or positive messages about homosexuals and reinterpreted to see something negative. In a classic study by psychologist Mark Snyder, the more homophobic the subject, the more negatively he or she interpreted the biographical details of "Betty K.," a hypothetical woman, if they were informed that she is a lesbian; in contrast, homophobic subjects who were told beforehand that "Betty K." is heterosexual did not see anything negative in these same details. Dr. Herek cites the opposition of homophobes to homosexuals being teachers because they might sexually molest children as a case in point; when informed that the vast majority of child molesters are heterosexual, homophobes do not change their minds on the question. Homophobes are victims of simplistic, stereotypical antigay thinking that is difficult to change. In addition, some homophobes, mainly adolescent boys and young men, hate gays because they feel insecure and defensive about their own sexuality. By hating and attacking gay men, they can reassure themselves that they are not gay, but supremely masculine (Goleman, 1990).

for dismissal from a leadership position in the Boy Scouts, exclusion from ordination as a priest or minister, expulsion from the armed services (Egan, 1988), being deemed unfit for adoption (Dullea, 1988) or for gaining custody of one's own children (Gutis, 1987). And gangs of youths, to demonstrate what they see as their manhood, beat up homosexuals. In other words, homosexuality provides us with an almost perfect example of a deviant status. Being publicly known as a homosexual in the United States today almost inevitably entails attracting hostility and stigma, being condemned and punished, in short, being labeled as a deviant.

Given the widespread hostility, fear, and denunciation that faces known homosexuals, it should come as no surprise that most keep their sexual identity hidden from heterosexuals. Contrary to popular stereotypes, most gays, male or female, are not readily detected by straights as gay. Their sexual orientation is probably known to their gay friends, but is hidden from the heterosexual community. Much of what the homosexual does—and this is true of most self-admitted "deviants"—involves deception, play acting, information control, and an elaborate *presentation of self* to the outside world (Goffman, 1959, 1963, pp. 41ff.). Typically, homosexuals must negotiate, navigate, and interact in a world of (usually correct) *imputed hostility* (Warren and Johnson, 1972, pp. 76–78).

Most homosexuals keep their sexual preferences hidden even from the heterosexuals to whom they are close. In one study of male homosexuals, only slightly more than a quarter of the sample (27 percent) said that their mothers "definitely know" that they are homosexual; only one-fifth of the fathers of these respondents said that their fathers definitely know. Half of the mothers, they said, do "not seem to know or suspect," and this was true of 62 percent of the fathers. Just under half of the respondent's sisters (48 percent) and brothers (48 percent) definitely did not know. *Only 10 percent of the respondents said that most of their heterosexual friends know*, and half (52 percent) said that "only a few" know or suspect. One in 10 (11 percent) said that *none* of their heterosexual friends know about their sexual orientation (Weinberg and Williams, 1974, p. 105).

When asked, "From how many heterosexuals do you try to conceal your homosexuality?" 30 percent said *all*, and 38 percent said *most*; only one in 10 said "only a few" (10 percent) or "none" (9 percent). This secrecy and deception is based on a solid foundation. These male homosexuals sense that homosexuality is saturated with public scorn. Only 7.5 percent of this study's sample of male homosexuals said that "most heterosexuals in general" would feel tolerant and accepting of their homosexuality; the figure was only 29 percent for most of their heterosexual friends of the same sex; and it was roughly half (53 percent) for their "best friend of the same sex" (Weinberg and Williams, 1974, p. 106). A quarter of this sample (26 percent) said that "most people" feel *disgusted or repelled* by homosexuals, while an additional four out of 10 said that most people simply "dislike" homosexuals.

Given the strong suspicion of, discrimination against, and even hostility toward homosexuals, many observers view homosexuals as one of a number of *oppressed minority groups* (Humphreys,

1972; Adam, 1978, pp. 24–27; Yearwood and Weinberg, 1979) whose members are in the process of struggling to obtain civil rights granted to the majority. Hatred of homosexuals is called "homophobia" (Lumby, 1979), and is considered no different from racism, sexism, anti-Semitism, or an irrational prejudice against any other group or category in a society. (But see Plummer's qualifications of the homophobia concept, 1981b, pp. 61ff.) Homosexuals are discriminated against in hiring, gay spokespersons insist, excluded from housing in certain areas, sometimes attacked by gangs of youths who need fear no reprisals for their acts of violence (this is called "gay bashing"), avoided socially by many respectable, conventional members of society, and often deprived of honest portrayals in the mass media. It is difficult to argue that while they are not perfect, the parallels between minority status for racial and ethnic groups and that for being homosexual are not extremely strong. In any case, hostility toward homosexuals is one of the reasons why this identity, orientation, and behavior are studied in a course on deviance.

HOMOSEXUALITY AS DEVIANCE: SOME AMBIGUITIES

There is no doubt that homosexuality is a form of deviance. Any behavior, identity, or characteristic that generates such public condemnation is by definition a form of deviance. At the same time, there are aspects of homosexuality that run in the opposite direction, which contradict its generally deviant character. To begin with, although the general status, homosexual, is widely condemned by the heterosexual public, the majority of homosexuals, as individuals, are not themselves condemned. In fact, the quality of homosexual "deviantness" stems not from direct face-to-face condemnation, but from *symbolic stigma* (Warren, 1974, p. 146) or what might be called *indirect labeling*. Second, in spite of the Supreme Court's anachronistic 1986 ruling, over half the states have repealed their laws against homosexual acts. (The first of these was Illinois, in 1961.) In addition, very few men (and no women) are ever arrested for committing homosexual acts in private. Almost all such arrests take place when men solicit the attention of the wrong men in public places. One observer estimated that there are approximately 6 million acts for every 20 convictions for homosexuality (Hoffman, 1968, p.

91). Of course, any estimate of this type is bound to be chancy, but it should be clear that in terms of the enormity of the ratio of apprehended to unapprehended culprits, homosexuals are far ahead of marijuana users.

Another factor that makes homosexuality a less than clear-cut case of deviance is that the United States is almost alone among the nations of the Western world in keeping the statutes against sodomy and other homosexual acts on the law books. Alfred Kinsey said nearly four decades ago that the citizens of practically no European nation "have become as disturbed over male homosexuality as we have here in the United States" (1953, p. 477); the statement applies with equal force today. Moreover, engaging in homosexual behavior is morally neutral in most of the societies of the world. A survey of 76 societies found that in 49 of them (64 percent), "homosexual activities of one sort or another are considered normal and socially acceptable for certain members of the community" (Ford and Beach, 1951, p. 130). Indeed, in some societies, homosexual behavior is not only tolerated, it is encouraged, even expected, and not only for some members of the society, but for *all* of its male members. (See the boxed insert on the Sambia.) Of course, the fact that it is accepted elsewhere does not make homosexuality any the less deviant here. It merely underscores my earlier point concerning the relative and subjective nature of judgments and evaluations of human behavior.

In addition, not all of the heterosexual majority accepts the traditional definition of homosexuality as immoral and depraved. Many see homsexuality as a variant of normal sexual expression, with no particular moral significance. Although it is true that *all* homosexuals would face condemnation by at least *some*, indeed most of the "straights" in their lives were they to reveal their orientation to everyone they knew, it is also true that *some* of their heterosexual peers accept homosexuality and homosexuals without qualms and problems. This means that while declaring oneself as a homosexual often, probably usually, results in censure from the straight majority, this is not always the case. It is almost certain, for instance, that a publicly proclaimed homosexual could not get elected president of the United States, at least, not for the foreseeable future. Yet, a tiny handful of openly gay politicians have gotten elected to public office in recent years. For instance, in 1983, Gerry Studds, a Massachussetts Democrat, acknowledged his

homosexuality after disclosures revealed that he had had a sexual relationship with a teenage page in the House of Representatives; Congressman Studds was re-elected six times since his admission. Clearly, a majority of his constituency did not hold such negative views of homosexuality that this revelation damaged his candidacy.

An acceptance of homosexuality in some social circles does not mean that it is not a form of deviance to the majority of the members of our society. It just means that some people can be found who feel otherwise. A very different case is presented by Robert Bauman, a conservative Republican congressman from Maryland, who did not enjoy the same fate as Congressman Studds. In 1980, his homosexual behavior and orientation were revealed to the voters of his district, who promptly voted him out of office. Former Congressman Bauman also lost his wife, his family, his house, and "most of his powerful friends." He published his memoirs in a book, *The Gentleman From Maryland: The Conscience of a Conservative*. Said Bauman, "I might have been Speaker of the House—who knows. . . . Instead, I'll be remembered for different things" (Leersen, 1986).

HOMOSEXUALITY AND AIDS

AIDS—Acquired Immunity Deficiency Syndrome—was not diagnosed until 1981, and the virus, HIV, which causes the disease was not isolated until 1983. An average of slightly more than 10 years passes between the time a person contracts HIV until he or she contracts a full-blown case of AIDS. Once diagnosed with AIDS, most die within two years. Although HIV infection is clearly a necessary condition for contracting AIDS, it is important to distinguish HIV infection from contracting AIDS; some persons infected with HIV have lived for 15 years or more without succumbing to the disease itself. In fact, most persons who carry the HIV virus look and feel healthy. AIDS does not kill its victims directly, but by weakening the body's immune system, that is, its capacity to fight off diseases; as a result, illnesses a healthy body can withstand are often fatal for the AIDS patient.

HIV is communicated from an infected person through the exchange of bodily fluids. For all practical purposes, this means anal or vaginal (or possibly oral) intercourse, or the exchange of contaminated blood. Contaminated blood can pass from the body of an infected to an uninfected person as a result of a blood transfusion or through an intravenous injection; a pregnant woman can also infect her fetus, since HIV can pass through the placental barrier. Intravenous injection with a needle contaminated with infected blood is an extremely efficient means of transmitting the virus; anal intercourse is less so but more efficient than vaginal intercourse. It seems to be the case that intercourse with a number of different partners, some of whom are infected, is riskier than intercourse with only one partner who is infected. It is not known for certain where the HIV virus originated; it may have existed and remained undiagnosed for decades. One theory, that it began in Central Africa as a result of a monkey biting a human, has now been discredited. Another theory, that white scientists developed the virus to infect and destroy persons of African descent, cannot be supported with any credible evidence. The fact is that rampantly virulent viruses mutate naturally and spontaneously from time to time; they need no assistance from diabolical human agents.

In the United States, almost all the earliest AIDS cases were homosexual men who received the HIV virus through anal intercourse. Initially, it was known as the "gay plague." Over time, the proportion of those diagnosed as having AIDS who were homosexual has declined, while those who were intravenous drug users has grown. Of all persons diagnosed with AIDS in 1993 (the majority of whom were infected in the early to mid-1980s) half were gay men who engaged in anal sex; a quarter were intravenous drug users; 10 percent were heterosexuals who did not inject drugs; and the remainder were either hemophiliacs or homosexuals *and* IV drug users. In contrast, among all persons who were *new* HIV infections in 1994, only a quarter were homosexual men; half were IV drug users; and a quarter were heterosexuals who did not inject drugs. (Hemophilia has ceased to be a source of new infections in the United States, since donated blood is carefully monitored for HIV.) Hence, drug addiction is a growing source of HIV infection, and homosexual sex is a declining one. The majority of the *heterosexuals* who became newly infected with HIV in 1994 were women who had sex with men who injected drugs. And of these, most were infected during crack binges or sex-for-crack exchanges with addicts (Kolata, 1995). In

the past decade, a minuscule number and proportion of persons have been infected *aside from* male homosexuals and bisexuals, IV drug users, sex partners of IV drug users, and children of infected mothers. As we'll see in more detail shortly, the late 1980s fear that AIDS would invade every social circle in America (Masters, Johnson, and Kolodny, 1988) has not materialized, according to the most recent evidence.

One of the most puzzling features of HIV transmission is its huge variability from one locale to another. More specifically, in industrialized countries, such as the United States and Western Europe, it is most often transmitted in one of two ways—through homosexual anal intercourse, and through the IV administration of drugs. In contrast, in nonindustrialized Third World countries, especially Africa and to a lesser extent, Southeast Asia, it is transmitted mainly through heterosexual intercourse. In the United States, there are two AIDS epidemics: among whites, an epidemic among homosexuals, and among racial minorities, an epidemic among drug addicts. Although this pattern has changed somewhat in the past three years or so with the increase of heterosexual transmission among crack addicts, nonetheless, even today, the majority of HIV carriers are either homosexuals or drug addicts. In Africa and Asia, the vast majority of HIV-infected persons are neither homosexual nor drug addicts; the male-female ratio on these continents is roughly 50-50, with slightly more females infected. Why heterosexual intercourse is transmitted so much more readily in Africa and Asia than in industrialized societies is not fully understood. It is possible that the higher rate of condom use in the industrialized world, and the higher rate of genital infection and poorer health care in Third World countries may account for a large portion of the difference.

Worldwide, the picture looks like this. In North America (mainly the United States), there are between 600,000 and as many as a million persons infected with HIV. It is possible that in Latin America and the Caribbean, there are as many as two million infected persons, in Western Europe, perhaps a half a million, in Eastern Europe and central Asia, some 50,000, in North Africa and the Middle East, about 100,000, in East Asia and the Pacific, 50,000, and in Australia and New Zealand, roughly 25,000. It is in Africa south of the Sahara and in Southeast Asia where the greatest number of cases are located. In 1994, UNESCO estimated that there are 11 million persons infected with HIV in sub-Sahara Africa and 3 million in Southeast Asia (Merson, 1995). A later estimate for Asia made by the World Health Organization placed the total at 12 million HIV infections by the year 2000; without a cure, perhaps 10 million Asians will die of AIDS by the year 2015 (Shenon, 1996, p. 8). In the worst hit areas of Africa, as much as one-quarter of the population of many villages is infected and now dying of the disease.

Media attention focused on a given subject indicates a measure of public concern about it. In 1981, no articles on AIDS appeared in major newspapers or weekly news magazines published in the United States. In 1982, there were 27, and in 1983, the number jumped to 343. Attention focused on the subject mounted until 1987, when a grand total of 4,125 articles appeared nationally. Between 1988 and 1994, roughly 3,000 newspaper and magazine articles were published annually in the United States on the subject of AIDS ("AIDS and the Press," *Time*, August 22, 1994; the 1994 figure is a projection). This tally demonstrates two important points. One, public concern about AIDS, like the disease itself, is extremely recent. And two, that concern grew at an explosive rate in the mid-to-late 1980s, and remains at an extremely high level to this day.

AIDS is an extremely frightening disease in many ways. The fact is that it is always fatal, it is extremely recent, the number of cases is growing rapidly, and the total number of victims may reach staggering totals. In addition, although the total numbers are much lower than for cancer and heart disease, AIDS victims tend to be young and hence the number of *years of life lost* per victim are much greater than for the nation's top killers. Experts estimate that nearly as many years of life are lost to AIDS as to accident and cancer, and substantially more are lost to AIDS than to heart disease (Eckholm, 1992).

Taken by themselves, these facts ought to frighten anyone. On the other hand, there are much less frightening features of AIDS as well, the most important being that it is extremely *difficult* to contract the disease. The AIDS virus lives for only a very short period of time outside the body, and it is not very communicable. You can't get AIDS by being bitten by a mosquito or from a toilet seat, or being in the same room as, shaking hands with,

touching or hugging, kissing, drinking out of the same glass as, being sneezed on by, swimming in the same pool as, or eating food prepared by, someone who is infected with it. As far as experts are able to tell, the only way someone can contract the AIDS virus is through an exchange of bodily fluids with someone who carries it. Practically speaking, this means that the disease can be contracted in only one of four ways: receiving contaminated blood through a transfusion; injecting oneself or being injected with a needle previously contaminated by a carrier; having sex, especially anal sex, with someone carrying the virus; and being born to an AIDS-contaminated mother. A tiny number of health workers, including at least one physician, have become infected as a result of being stuck with a needle contaminated with the AIDS virus. And a tiny number of patients may have become infected by one or more health workers. And, as we saw in the last chapter, vaginal intercourse is an extremely inefficient means of spreading AIDS. Said a science writer, the chance of picking up the AIDS virus from a partner in a singles bar "is about the same as the chance of winning the jackpot in a state lottery." The likelihood that a non-drug-using heterosexual who is not a hemophiliac, and who has only non-drug-using heterosexual partners who are not hemophiliacs, will get AIDS over a lifetime is less than the chance of being struck by lightning; such a person is 200 times more likely to die in an automobile accident than to get AIDS, and 1,000 times more likely to be murdered (Langone, 1985, p. 31). The chance of contracting the virus from a random heterosexual encounter is one in five million. This is the same as the chance of dying in a car accident if one drives 10 miles to a date, yet hardly anyone worries enough about dying in an automobile accident to prevent them from driving.

Although the picture has improved slightly, many Americans retain an extremely distorted view of how communicable the HIV virus is. A federally sponsored study on "AIDS knowledge and attitudes" was conducted in 1992 (Schoenborn, Marsh, and Hardy, 1994). The percent of respondents who said that it is either "very likely" or "somewhat likely" that "a person will get AIDS or the AIDS virus infection from" the following sources was: "working near someone with the AIDS virus," 7 percent; "eating in a restaurant where the cook has the AIDS virus," 24 percent; "sharing plates, forks, or glasses with someone who has the AIDS virus," 27 percent; "using public toilets," 17 percent; "being coughed or sneezed on by someone who has the AIDS virus," 27 percent; and "being bitten by mosquitoes or other insects," 25 percent.

In addition to a substantially overblown conception of the likelihood of contracting AIDS on the part of much of the public, Americans are also highly likely to *stigmatize* AIDS victims. While over three-quarters of the respondents of the Gallup Poll said that AIDS sufferers should be treated with "compassion" (78 percent), nearly half (48 percent) said that they should be allowed to live in the community "normally," and only a minority (33 percent) said that employers have the right to dismiss an employee because that person has AIDS. A substantial proportion, at the same time, displayed more punitive and condemnatory attitudes toward AIDS victims. Over half (51 percent) agreed with the statement, "In general, it's people's own fault if they get AIDS." Nearly half (42 percent) said "I sometimes think that AIDS is a punishment for the decline in moral standards." And a whopping six in 10 (60 percent) said, "People with the AIDS virus should be made to carry a card to this effect." A substantial minority (43 percent) said that they plan not to associate with people they "suspect might have AIDS"; this figure was exactly 50 percent for males; and for the youngest age group, 18 to 29, it was a staggering 60 percent! As many nonhomosexual, non-drug-using AIDS sufferers have found out, this stigma is not confined to deviant minorities (Schmalz, 1988; Hilts, 1990, 1992; Barringer, 1991).

It should come as no surprise that the negative sentiments held by much of the American public toward AIDS sufferers that emerges in these polls and interview studies have also expressed themselves in numerous discriminatory and even hostile incidents. In New York City, a physician who treats AIDS patients was evicted from his office by the building's co-op board. Said the doctor, "People in the building didn't like AIDS patients walking through the lobby." In New Orleans, a writer was fired from his editing job after publishing an article discussing his own suspected case of AIDS. "They just walked in and said, 'Get the hell out,'" he recalls. In Indiana, Ryan White, age 13, a hemophiliac and an AIDS patient, was not allowed to attend the seventh grade; school officials, fearing contamination of the other pupils, did not want the youngster in class. Said the superintendent, "What

are you going to do about someone chewing pencils or sneezing or swimming in the pool?" A 1985 *Time* magazine story noted that "AIDS victims are treated like lepers even by some in the medical community. Ambulance workers in several cities have refused to transport desperately ill patients to hospitals. Hospital orderlies are reluctant to clean their rooms. Nurses are wary. . . . In St. Louis and New York, undertakers have refused to embalm the remains of patients." Even in the face of the horror of their medical problems, many AIDS sufferers say that the most painful aspect of their condition is the stigma, rejection, and social isolation that they experience (Wallis et al., 1985, p. 45).

In 1994, *Newsweek* magazine polled American public opinion on the impact of AIDS on attitudes toward homosexuals. Respondents were asked: "Has the AIDS epidemic made you more or less sympathetic toward gays?" Their answers were almost evenly divided: 38 percent said more sympathetic; 31 percent said less; and the remaining 31 percent said either the same or they weren't sure (February 14, 1994, p. 45). Some negative feeling toward homosexuals has increased since the advent of AIDS, at least among a substantial minority. One "openly homosexual faculty member" at a conservative southern religiously affiliated university (Southern Methodist University) attended a public debate held by the SMU student senate on the question of whether the Gay/Lesbian Student Support Organization should be recognized. "In the glare of television cameras, homosexuals (including, presumably, the dozens of us present, both students and faculty) were compared to rapists, thieves and robbers. We were portrayed as sinners and liars. The group would serve as a student-faculty sex club, a vehicle for orgies and recruitment." Worst of all, said a speaker, homosexuals were "disease-carrying, sexual deviants"; because of AIDS, "the health—the very lives—of every person on campus would be at risk." In the midst of the debate, when the point on AIDS was raised, one young man shouted out, "Now we can shoot you" (Beauchamp, 1983).

Until the late 1960s, homosexual behavior tended to be furtive and clandestine. There were very few open gays, and for most, meeting other homosexuals for sexual contact was a proposition fraught with guilt and fear. Gay bars existed, to be sure, especially in large cities, but they were subject to periodic busts, and hence, public exposure. Then, on one summer night in 1969, at a bar in Manhattan's Greenwich Village called the Stonewall Inn, this changed dramatically. The police initiated a raid against the patrons of the Stonewall. In the past, gays would have passively accepted being arrested. On this particular night, the clientele of this particular bar resisted, and that touched off a riot, and the riot, in turn, some say, "gave birth to a social cause and sexual style." One outcome of the Stonewall riot was an active, open gay civil rights movement. And another was a more open sexual style among gay men. Homosexual promiscuity became more acceptable, less furtive, more militant. "When liberation came along," said one homosexual spokesman, "there was a proliferation of what we already had, more bars, bigger bars. What gay men wanted was easy anonymous sex with no attachments." Throughout the 1970s, "extreme sexual activity" was regarded as legitimate by a certain segment of the male homosexual community (Norman, 1983, p. B8).

AIDS has changed all this. To be plain about it, promiscuous sex is no longer so openly tolerated or encouraged in the gay community; the proportion of homosexual men who engage in casual pickups has declined precipitously. Steam baths, once the locus of an enormous volume of casual, anonymous sex, have either been closed down by local health departments or gone out of business as a result of lack of patronage. Most of the notorious sadomasochistic bars featuring on-the-premises back-room sex—the Mine Shaft and the Anvil in Manhattan were examples—have been closed down, gone out of business, closed their back rooms, or gone underground. One study conducted in San Francisco by representatives of Atlanta's Centers for Disease Control showed that in the four months preceding the interview, the average number of "nonsteady" sex partners among gay males, that is, those with whom the individual had sexual contact just once or twice and not again, dropped from 16 in 1978 to 3 in 1984 to only one in 1985. Between 1978 and 1985, 90 percent of this sample reduced the number of their nonsteady sex partners. The exposure risk from receptive oral sexual contact dropped by 68 percent, and the exposure risk from receptive anal-genital contact dropped by 96 percent (Doll et al., 1987). Clearly, promiscuous sex and "at risk" sexual behavior have declined sharply and significantly among gay males in recent years. The majority of gays, said a gay activist, are "no longer willing to play Russian roulette. Safer sex and monogamous relationships

have taken root" (Clarke et al., 1985). Psychologist Stephen Morin reported that one-fifth as many homosexual men were engaging in sex with multiple partners in 1985 as compared with 1983 (Gelman et al., 1985, p. 29). In a survey of 500 gay men living in San Francisco in 1985, 81 percent reported that they were monogamous or celibate; just a year before, the comparable figure was 69 percent; the proportion saying that they had had more than one sexual partner during the previous month declined from 49 percent in the 1984 survey to 36 percent in 1985. Commenting on the drastic change that AIDS has had on the sex lives of gay men, one homosexual spokesperson said: "The party's over" (Clarke et al., 1985).

The AIDS epidemic illustrates many of the central principles that inform this book. In the earliest days of the epidemic, conservative politicians and fundamentalist Christian spokespersons claimed that AIDS was divine retribution against homosexuals for practices that are an abomination in the eyes of God. (Why this retribution did not strike lesbians, or why it struck persons who did not engage in such practices, such as hemophiliacs, was not explained.) On the other side of the controversy, homosexual militants claimed that AIDS was a myth invented by straight propagandists to dissuade gays from engaging in disapproved sexual behavior (Shilts, 1987). Much of the mainstream public reasoned that AIDS sufferers have "only themselves to blame" for contracting the disease; since they were infected as a result of freely chosen behavior, and that is most decidedly deviant, many Americans found it difficult to support federal funding for AIDS treatment and research. Thus, spokespersons faced a serious problem, namely, a lack of empathy for and identification with AIDS victims. In response, AIDS campaigners did two things. First, they created the "blameless" AIDS victim, the sufferer who did nothing to contract the disease: the hemophiliac, the recipient of tainted blood, the faithful wife, the child born to an infected mother. And second, the point was made that literally *anyone* could contract HIV, that AIDS is not simply a gay disease or an affliction of IV drug users. Indeed, quite respectable people can contract the dread disease through ordinary heterosexual intercourse. "AIDS is everyone's disease" was the message; "protect yourself—anyone can get it" was the watchword. AIDS is spreading rapidly to all social categories in the population, this message warned (Masters, Johnson, and Kolodny, 1988).

The intention of propagandists and educators in stressing that anyone can get the disease that we all ought to protect ourselves, and that we all ought to support federal funding for research and treatment is praiseworthy. However, the fact is that the *odds* or *statistical chances* of contracting HIV are *vastly* different as a result of engaging in different sexual practices, and for different segments of the population. In fact, AIDS is *not* spreading rapidly outside a small number of delimited social categories. According to the panel put together by the National Research Council, "many geographical areas and strata of the population are virtually untouched by the epidemic," and are extremely likely to remain so. In contrast, "certain confined areas and populations have been devastated [by it] and are likely to continue to be" (Michael et al., 1994, p. 201). An uninfected person engaging in a single act of unprotected penile-vaginal intercourse with an infected person has roughly a one in 500 chance of being infected with HIV. (Of course, if the number of sex acts increases, the odds increase correspondingly.) This chance drops to nearly zero if a latex condom is used properly (p. 203). It is "all but inconceivable that infected members of middle-class Americans will start an epidemic going in the general population" (p. 214). Sexual contacts "between infected and uninfected groups are too infrequent, and the few people who do become infected in this way have too few partners and their partners have too few partners to start an epidemic" (p. 215). In short, AIDS "is likely to remain confined to exactly the risk groups where it began: gay men and intravenous drug users. We are convinced that there is not and very unlikely ever will be a heterosexual AIDS epidemic in this country" (p. 216). The National Research Council emphasizes that in the name of decency and compassion, all Americans ought to support treatment and research to find a cure for AIDS, but it is counterproductive to pretend we are all equally at risk when that is simply false (pp. 217–218).

COMING OUT

The term "coming out" does not have a precise meaning in the gay world; in fact, it has several meanings. One is to decide that one is, in fact, a homosexual—to accept a homosexual *identity* for oneself. Another meaning of the term is to make a public disclosure of one's homosexuality among other homosexuals, to "come out of the closet." And a third meaning is to participate in the homosexual subculture. Hooker (1965, p. 99) and Gagnon and Simon (1973, pp. 143–145) define "coming out" as including self-identity and public exploration of the homosexual community. Dank (1971) uses the term to mean "identifying oneself as being homosexual"; this self-identification, he writes "may or may not occur in a social context in which other gay people are present" (1971, p. 181). One aspect of "coming out," then, is *accepting a homosexual identity* (Troiden, 1979, 1988, p. 35ff; Plummer, 1975; Cass, 1979, 1984; Pons, 1978). Regarding oneself as gay—in the vocabulary of some, recognizing that one *is* a homosexual—is not something that happens automatically. Translating the erotic feelings one holds for others of the same sex, or translating same-gender sexual behavior that one has experienced, is a long, often difficult and socially patterned process.

There is a considerable independence between engaging in homosexual behavior—and even recognizing that what one is doing is, in fact, "homosexual" behavior—and adopting a homosexual identity. Dank (1971) reports a six-year interval between a person's awareness of his first same-gender sexual arousal and the decision that he is a homosexual. Homosexuality is not an orientation that one learns directly from one's parents, or from any other agency of childhood socialization. Nearly everything one learns from the heterosexual majority about homosexuality is negative. It is such an uncomplimentary image that no one would want to embrace it. In fact, not only is the homosexual role saturated with stigma, but so is homosexual behavior and erotic desires toward someone of the same gender. Consequently, very few young people who do actually feel sexual desires toward members of the same sex will identify these desires as specifically "homosexual." In addition, very few who engage in homosexual behavior will, at its initial inception, define it as "homosexual." So the first two processes that must take place for men and women who eventually say to themselves, "I am a homosexual," is that their *desires* and their *experiences* must be specified as, essentially, homosexual in nature.

Initially, such experiences will be defined away as adolescent horseplay rather than as a prelude to adult homosexuality. (In fact, this is usually actually the case: what they do usually *is* adolescent horseplay.) Such desires will be seen as "a passing phase," a "childhood crush," meaningless and not indicative of anything in general. The public stereotype of homosexuality is so denigrating and unattractive in our society that, most young people will reason, no self-respecting human being would want to be identified with the label. What someone who feels homosexual desires or who derives pleasure from homosexual contact will say is something like, "I know that homosexuality is an ugly, dirty thing, so this can't be a homosexual experience, since it feels good and I like this person." Identification of gay experiences will bring about a crushing feeling of guilt, a sense that "there's something wrong with me." Consequently, their gayness must be explained away. "I started to realize that I felt a sexual attraction for other men. . . . I passed the attraction off as being due to the circumstances—the loneliness and the need for female companionship," explains a man who was enlisted in the military service at the time. "I rationalized my feelings as indicating . . . deep friendship. . . . The possibility that I might be gay terrified me" (Troiden, 1977).

Once experiences and feelings have been identified as homosexual in nature, the next step is seeing oneself as homosexual. Just as it is possible to say to oneself, "Yes, I lied, but I'm not a liar," or "I did get drunk last night, it's true, but I'm not an alcoholic," likewise, many men and woman can (and do) say, "I had a homosexual experience, but I'm not a homosexual." Being a homosexual is condemned in our society far more than is engaging in homosexual acts. Being a homosexual means, to most of us, adopting the homosexual role, of being saturated through and through with a stigmatizing and shameful identity. An act is what one *does*; it is possible to distance oneself from it. But an identity is what one *is*: Distancing oneself is impossible in every sense of the word. It is part of one's *essence*, the core of one's being. So this is a very basic step. Seeing one's experiences as homosexual is a necessary but not a sufficient condition for seeing oneself as gay. It is only one step, far from the final one. At some point, men and women begin to "suspect" that they might be gay. Being continually *aroused* by members of one's own sex is one element in this process. Having homosexual fantasies also ushers in the process. And engaging in homosexual activities—and especially enjoying it, in spite of the guilt that often accompanies it—also will commonly cause one to question one's sexual orientation. But remember,

probably most men and women have had sexual desires toward a member of their own sex at least once, most have had same-gender sexual fantasies, and at least a significant minority of both sexes have had homosexual experiences. But only a tiny proportion of this total comes to see himself or herself as being *a* homosexual. What, then, precipitates the gays out from the straights?

The answer is a combination of several things. One is *a persistent lack of erotic and/or emotional interest in the opposite sex*. Second is the continuing failure of one's ability to explain away one's homosexuality. Third is having a deep, significant, meaningful homosexual experience with someone whom one respects and loves. Fourth is having an intimate, particularly one who is gay, explain to one that one *is*, in fact, gay. And last is dramatically realizing that there are many attractive, desirable, "normal" men or women—who don't fit one's preconception of the homosexual—who are gay. In some as yet unknown combination, these factors come together to bring someone who *suspects* that he or she is gay to gradually *accept* and *incorporate* it into his or her identity. Being introduced to a particular homosexual scene in which one meets large numbers of desirable, attractive people who destroy the public stereotype of what it means to be gay—that there are many like-minded individuals—can be particularly electrifying.

I knew that there were homosexuals, queers and what not; I had read some books, and I was resigned to the fact that I was a foul, dirty person, but I wasn't actually calling myself a homosexual yet. . . . I went to this guy's house and there was nothing going on, and I asked him, "Where is some action?" and he said, "There is a bar down the way." And the time I really caught myself coming out is the time I walked into this bar and saw a whole crowd of groovy, groovy guys. And I said to myself, there was the realization, that not all gay men are dirty old men or idiots, silly queens, but there are some just normal-looking and acting people, as far as I could see. I saw gay society and I said, "Wow, I'm home" (Dank, 1971, p. 187).

What is necessary is for the individual to be able to neutralize the stereotype of what it means to be a homosexual—to "change . . . the meaning of the cognitive category homosexual before they can place themselves in the category" (Dank, 1971, p. 189). Homosexuality must be seen as a morally and psychiatrically neutral or even desirable status. A vocabulary of motives has to be adopted that places one's actions and status in the realm of normalcy—even if this interpretation is rejected among the heterosexual majority: "Being a homosexual does not label a person as sick or mentally ill. In every other capacity I am as normal or more normal than straight people. Just because I happen to like strawberry ice cream and they like vanilla, doesn't make them right or me right" (Dank, 1971, p. 190). In short, what is at stake here is the individual's sense of esteem and self-worth. And this necessitates "an entire transformation in the meaning to the concept of homosexual for the subject." In the words of one subject, "I had always thought of them as dirty old men that preyed on 10, 11, 12-year-old kids, and I found out that they weren't all that way. . . . It was a relief for me 'cause I found out that I wasn't so different from many other people. . . . I thought I was mentally ill. Now I accept it as a way of life, and I don't consider it a mental illness. . . . I consider myself an outcast from general society, but not mentally ill" (Dank, 1971, p. 191).

I met a straight guy when I was in college. . . . As our friendship developed, I realized that I was falling in love with him and that I had never cared for anyone as deeply as I cared for him. . . . One night we were out drinking with a bunch of guys at a college bar. We both got rather high and when we returned to the dorm I went with him to his room. It was the beginning of a very beautiful night. I walked over to him, put my arms around him, and kissed him. He reciprocated. We eventually masturbated each other to orgasm. He is now married and has a family. This incident led to a fateful resignation that I was irrevocably gay. Due to the beauty of the experience. . . . I was able to rid myself of any doubts that I had regarding my being a homosexual as negating the possibility of being a good person (Troiden, 1977).

Heterosexual conceptions of homosexuality not only define it in negative terms; they also make a "big deal" out of it. As men and women who gradually come to the realization that they are gay begin to "come out," they also come to see that being gay is not the "big deal" they have been taught it is. One male homosexual explained it to me in the following words: "Before you come out, you see being gay as this huge, monstrous thing. In fact, the sexual side of being gay is no more a big deal in one's life than it is for straight people." So not only does the homosexual neutralize the stigma of being gay in his or her vocabulary of motives, he or she also minimizes its *weight*. It assumes manageable proportions.

DIFFERENCES BETWEEN MALE AND FEMALE HOMOSEXUALS

Heterosexuals tend to view aspects of the life of the homosexual more or less in its entirety as stemming from its uniquely homosexual character. The homosexual's gender choice is a "prepossessing concern" on the part of nonhomosexuals (Gagnon and Simon, 1973, p. 137). Many heterosexuals forget that what homosexuals are and do may have nothing to do with their sexual preferences. Actually, although there are parallels between male and female homosexuals by virtue of the fact that their behavior and their character are widely condemned by "straights," and by virtue of the fact that they are alienated from many mainstream institutions, actually, the differences between them are in many ways far more striking. In most crucial respects, the lesbian is more similar to her heterosexual sister than she is to the male homosexual. Consequently, the differences between male and female homosexuals should be instructive.

Perhaps the most striking difference between male homosexuals and lesbians has to do with the nature of their sexual—and emotional—relationships. Typically, the male homosexual has had intercourse with many partners on a relatively anonymous, impersonal basis. In a reanalysis of the original Kinsey data, two researchers show about half of the male homosexuals in the sample reported that 60 percent or more of their sexual partners were men with whom they had had sex *only once*. And for four-fifths of the sample, their longest homosexual affair had lasted less than a year (Gagnon and Simon, 1973, p. 139, 140). Every study that has ever been conducted on the subject has found that male homosexuals tend to be extremely promiscuous. (Not every one is, and many are involved in long-term monogamous relationships, but the general tendency is difficult to deny.) In a study I was involved in, 23 percent of the sample said that they had had intercourse with 500 or more partners; the point at which the category designating respondents who had slept with the *least* number of partners was drawn at under 100 partners (Goode and Troiden, 1979). Another study found that 43 percent of the white male homosexuals and 33 percent of the Black homosexuals said that they had had 500 or more homosexual partners; 79 percent of the whites and 51 percent of the Blacks said that more than half of their partners were strangers (Bell and Weinberg, 1978, p. 308).

Lesbians, in contrast, tend to have fewer sexual relationships, the relationships tend to last much longer, and both partners tend to be far more romantically involved than is true for male homosexuals. In the Kinsey volume on women, it was found that the number of sexual partners that homosexual and heterosexual women had been involved with was most identical—for both, about half had had sex with only *one* partner, and a bit over 10 percent had had sex with six or more partners (Kinsey et al., 1953, p. 336, 492). No doubt for both groups the figure is different today, but the male-female differences are still marked. In a much more recent comparison between male and female homosexuals (with heterosexual controls) the same basic pattern was uncovered. Nearly all the male homosexuals (94 percent) had had sex with 10 or more partners, but this was true of only a tiny minority of the lesbians (15 percent). Although only one of the male homosexuals in the sample had had sexual contact with three or fewer partners, this was true of 30 percent of the lesbians and 60 percent of the heterosexual women (Saghir and Robins, 1973, pp. 59, 229). Another way of saying this is that female homosexuals tend to be more interested in much more of the *total person* of their sex partners. For them, sex is more than just sex. Their more romantic and intense commitment inclines them to be concerned with all aspects of their partner's personality and being. Most heterosexuals—particularly men—fixate on, and exaggerate the importance of, the specifically sexual side of lesbianism. In fact, lesbians see their orientation as primarily a *romantic* matter, a holistic approach toward women, a lifestyle, a way of being. The sexual side is only one facet of that lifestyle. Male homosexuals, in contrast, tend to be far more interested in their sex partners specifically *as* sex partners. There is, in fact, a more intense *genital fixation* for male homosexuals.

The comparative number, intensity, and duration of their relationships also has a reflection in the twin phenomena of *cruising* and the *locales* of sexual activity (Delph, 1978). Male homosexuals, especially those who live in large, urban areas, are often "on the lookout for some action." Between a third and a half of the adult male homosexuals in one study, depending on their age, customarily had sex both in public and private settings. In comparison, "no homosexual women ever engaged in sexual activity in a public place" (Saghir and Robins, 1973, p. 236).

Cruising as a purposeful activity aimed primarily at finding sexual partners is a very different behavior when practiced by the homosexual women compared to the homosexual men. . . . Cruising among the men is an intense activity involving a multiplicity of places and hangouts, many of them public facilities like parks, beaches, movie houses, streets, bars and numerous other locales. Among the homosexual women, cruising of public places is almost nonexistent and, when it occurs, it is usually done within the framework of a socially acceptable setting. To find a sex partner, the homosexual women usually embark on establishing a relationship over a period of weeks or months before any sexual contact occurs (Saghir and Robins, 1973, p. 234).

Male homosexuals are typically much more impatient and wish to start (and end) the sexual side of the relationship at the first meeting.

Perhaps the two locales that represent an extreme version of the impersonal sex that characterizes many homosexual encounters are certain steam baths and public urinals in large cities, which acquire a reputation for places that are frequented by men interested in quick, easy, impersonal sex. (Not all—or even most—of the men that visit the "tea rooms" are self-admitted homosexuals, remember.) In the baths, one gay author explains, "verbal foreplay is rare" and "the accent is on genitalia. . . . Romance is removed from the sex act and is reduced to lust." One bath house attempted to cater to lesbians, in addition to male homosexuals. "Instead of zeroing in on each other, the women preferred to chat in the television lounge. There was hardly any stalking, very little sex transpired. After a month, the place reverted to an all-male policy." The sex that goes on in the baths involves men who are, "like the extras in *Quo Vadis.* . . , faceless and nameless" (Bell, 1976). One sociologist observed sexual encounters between men in public restrooms. Of 50 such encounters on which he took notes, in only 15 of these was there any exchange of words *at all* between partners, so impersonal were they (Humphreys, 1970, p. 12).

It is true that sex in public places like "tea rooms" (public urinals) and the baths represents the most impersonal of all homosexual encounters that could be engaged in. But it is also true that such encounters are almost totally absent among lesbians. The willingness of many male homosexuals to engage in completely impersonal sex with many other men marks them off from lesbians in a distinct fashion. Entire institutions are supported by the casual sex of male homosexuals. The gay bar, for instance, is primarily for the purpose of meeting and picking up new sex partners. "A gay bar where you couldn't pick anyone up would stay in business around a day and a half," a gay man explained to me. This is not true of lesbian bars—lesbian bars are primarily for the purpose of social-izing with friends—and it is true of only a minority of bars where heterosexuals mingle. But it is also true that cruising and promiscuity among gay males *is a distinctly male phenomenon.* It is not specific to *gay* males. Were heterosexual females as willing to engage in casual sex as men are, then the world of heterosexuality would be as marked by casual sex as the world of male homosexuality. It is only because most heterosexual females keep the cruis-ing tendencies of heterosexual males in check that heterosexuality is not marked by the volume of casual sex that prevails among male homosexuals.

Male homosexuals also begin their sexual activ-ity much earlier in their lives than female homo-sexuals. When asked about the age of the "onset" of mutual masturbation, 60 percent of a sample of male homosexuals said that it began at age 13 or earlier; only 15 percent said age 20 or older. For fellatio, 24 percent began it at age 13 or younger, and 32 percent said 20 or older. But for lesbians, the percentage saying that the onset of mutual gen-ital stimulation was at age 13 or younger was only 9 percent; 51 percent said 20 or older. For cun-nilingus, it was 2 percent at age 13 or younger, and 72 percent age 20 or older (Saghir and Robins, 1973, pp. 51, 219, 221).

Lesbians have also had a great deal more *het-erosexual* contact than male homosexuals have. In one study, slightly under half (48 percent) of the male homosexuals said they had had intercourse with a woman, but over three-quarters of the female homosexuals (79 percent) said they had had inter-course with a man at least once. In fact, the les-bians were more likely to have had heterosexual intercourse than the *heterosexual* women were—79 percent versus 58 percent (Saghir and Robins, 1973, pp. 88, 246). Of those women who did have intercourse, about the same proportion said that they had had it with five or more men—69 percent for lesbians and 60 percent for the heterosexual women. As many homosexual as heterosexual women had been maritally proposed to by a man (Saghir and Robins, 1973, p. 250), a fact that resoundingly refutes the notion that lesbians are, in some way, "failed" women with respect to their sexual desirability to men.

Goode and Haber (1977) found that college women who had had at least one homosexual expe-rience (not necessarily self-admitted lesbians) were strikingly more likely to have had intercourse than women without homosexual experience; they were also more likely to have had intercourse with a larger number of male partners. The median num-ber of men that the homosexually experienced women had had intercourse with was 5, and the mean was 7.4; for the homosexually inexperienced women, these figures were 2 and 3.6. They also tended to have been more heterosexually *preco-cious,* that is, they had had intercourse for the first time between a year and a year and a half younger in their lives. The two groups of women did differ significantly on the dimension of the experience of loveless heterosexual relationships in which they had intercourse, the enjoyment of fellatio, and the source of their most pleasurable orgasm. Women who had had homosexual experience were far more likely to have ever had intercourse with a man they were not in love with—80 percent versus 53 per-cent. They were less likely to say that they usually enjoyed fellating a man (20 percent versus 46 per-cent), and more likely to say that they usually did not enjoy it (27 percent versus 8 percent). And they were less likely to say that the source of their most pleasurable orgasm was intercourse with a man (21 percent versus 52 percent).*

What these and other women who eventually say to themselves, "I am a lesbian" are highly likely to have at least given men a try sexually. Relatively few were totally turned off to men sexually even before they engaged in heterosexual intercourse. For the majority of lesbians, their awareness of their lack of sexual, erotic, and emotional interest in men comes from *their experiences with men,* and not their prior and relatively fixed notions of what men are like in the absence of that experi-ence. With the awareness that they are gay, lesbians will eventually lose interest in men and stop having intercourse with them. After their early twenties,

---

*Using a variety of indicators, Goode and Haber surmised that the women with at least some homosexual experience formed a very mixed group. Some could be called sexual "adventurers," and their experiences with other women were simply one out of a number of viable sexual experiences that they wished to try—and actually did try. It is out of this group that women who come to see themselves as bisexuals will emerge. And others will eventually decide they are lesbians and will abandon intercourse with men altogether as a viable option for them.

heterosexual contact among homosexual women drops off sharply. But generally this does not occur until they have sexually experimented with men.

This pattern is in strong contrast to homosexual men, who are far less likely to have had intercourse with women, especially with a number of women. This pattern emerges in part because male homosexuals come to see themselves as gay much earlier in their lives than female homosexuals do. And in part it is due to the fact that even today, the male is expected to take the initiative sexually, and heterosexual males tend to be more sexually aggressive and even insensitive than heterosexual women; they are more likely not to "take no for an answer." Consequently, they will sometimes pressure women to have intercourse with them, women who may be only half-interested.

This leads us to another difference between homosexual men and women: their *public image* in the straight majority's eyes. There is considerably less fear and hostility on the part of the heterosexual majority toward the lesbian than toward the male homosexual. (At least this is true in contemporary America. Anthropological data indicate that in many other societies there is more outrage at female homosexuality than male.) The reasons for this are complicated. To begin with, the prevailing sexist attitude dictates that the lesbian simply hasn't met the right man yet, that she can be converted to heterosexuality by an aggressive, expert lover. (And many men fantasize that they could be that lover!) They see the lesbian as a challenge, a test to their manhood, a potential means of demonstrating their virility. They think of lesbianism as a primarily *sexual* orientation rather than a whole emotional approach to men and women.

To many heterosexual males, the lesbian is actually erotic—at least, the stereotype is, since most of them would not know a lesbian if they met one. Scenes of two or more women making love (or pretending to) with one another comprise a high proportion of pornographic fare, and prostitutes are often employed to put on a lesbian lovemaking scene by Johns, for whom such scenes are highly stimulating. Heterosexual women typically find lesbians a puzzlement, but not a threat. (And they typically ask lesbians questions about their *emotional* life far more than about its specifically *sexual* side, which is the side men are so curious about.)

Yet both male and female heterosexuals seem unusually threatened by male homosexuals. Perhaps both sense a threat to what they see as the very basis of manhood. Or perhaps both think that they can easily envision what male homosexuals do in bed, but they cannot conjure up a comparable image of what lesbians do. Perhaps, too, in our chauvinistic tradition, it is considered degrading for a male—the dominant sex—to play the role of the subordinate sex, by playing at femininity. (Of course, remember, there is no inherent link between femininity and male homosexuality, but most straights don't know this. They feel that the androgynous male lowers his status more than the androgynous female does—toward whom a kind of begrudging respect must be extended.) In addition, since the male homosexual's style is so much more conspicuous, more blatant, and more public, and the lesbian's is more low-key, unobtrusive, less overt, and obvious, he comes to the public eye more and consequently is available for, and attracts, more public condemnation. All of this is not to say that female homosexuals do not meet with widespread and strong disapproval, denunciation, and hostility from the straight majority. Indeed they do. But it does not have quite the savagery that the male homosexual faces. But notice: It is primarily because of *sexism* that this is the case. It is only because the dominant heterosexual male does not take lesbianism seriously that it is not condemned to the same degree as male homosexuality. Ironically, it may be the case that the more seriously lesbianism is taken by heterosexuals the greater the threat they will see from it, and consequently, the more they will condemn and sanction those who practice it.

SUMMARY

Sociologists study homosexuality as a form of deviance because, in Western society, homosexuals tend to be denigrated, scorned, punished, and stigmatized. Stereotypes about gays and lesbians are widely held, deeply entrenched in the culture, and influence the thinking of heterosexuals toward homosexuals. In its most extreme form, negative attitudes and feelings express themselves in open hostility, even violence. Thus, what *makes* homosexuality a form of deviance is the social rejection that homosexuals receive at the hands of the straight majority. Public opinion that supports the view that homosexuality is immoral and should be against the law is widespread, and the number of people who hold this view approaches or surpasses a majority of the population. Gays cannot work in certain occupations; antihomosexual attitudes are part and parcel of the theological doctrine of certain denominations; homosexual practices are against the law in 22 states; many psychiatrists and clinical psychologists view homosexuality as the manifestation of a mental disorder; in certain jurisdictions, homosexuals may not adopt children. It is clear that *homophobia* is common and deeply entrenched in American society.

Homosexuals are far from a perfect case of a despised, condemned category, however; there are "ambiguities" in homosexuality's deviant status. Most homosexuals are not spotted and condemned as gay in most settings; hardly any men, and no women, are ever arrested for homosexual practices; in just about all other Western societies, homosexuality is less strongly condemned than in the United States; and in certain social circles, heterosexuals do not condemn or denigrate gays. Homophobia represents a continuum rather than a black-or-white affair. Still, even though not all heterosexuals condemn gays, all homosexuals would face condemnation by *some* heterosexuals in their midst were their sexual orientation to become known. Thus, although homosexuality represents a less-than-perfect example of deviance, it is a clear-cut instance nonetheless.

Several studies on sexual practices, desires, and identification have been conducted in recent years. One, the "Sex in America" survey, indicates that homosexual behavior is far less common than has been previously assumed. Only 2.8 percent of American men, and 1.4 percent of women, consider themselves homosexuals or bisexual, and only 2 percent of both categories say that they have had sex with someone of the same gender in the past year. The fact that quite different measures of homosexuality, based on identification, behavior, and desire, yielded quite different answers concerning the extent of homosexuality in the population indicates that there may be no single definitive indicator of homosexuality. In short, homosexuality is a *multidimensional* matter. Roughly the same results were obtained in parallel studies in Britain and France.

In the past decade or so, a number of developments worthy of note have hit the world of homosexuality. The morality of *outing*, or the deliberate exposure of persons known to be homosexual in the gay community but not to the world at large,

is a hotly debated topic. "Queer" is a term used by some militant gays to express a confrontational, "in your face" style of homosexuality. "Queer theory" is a field of studies that cropped up in the early 1990s that stresses the gendered quality of history and literature, as well as the patriarchal quality of past scholarship. Homosexual practices remain illegal in 22 states; homosexual civil rights bills have been defeated almost everywhere; the legality of homosexual marriages may become a new political battleground. On the etiological front, a number of scientists claim to have discovered evidence that suggests that a predisposition to homosexuality may be genetic in origin. In 1992, candidate Bill Clinton made abolishing the ban on gays in the military a plank in his presidential platform; once elected, he discovered how difficult effecting such a change was. Currently, the issue is stalemated.

Homosexuality may be viewed through one of two perspectives: *essentialism* and *constructionism*. Essentialism sees homosexuality as a clear-cut, natural, pregiven, concretely real entity, a kind of *condition;* identifying it is much like picking an apple off a tree. In contrast, constructionists see homosexuality as a social creation, a category that is a cultural product, not a clearly identifiable entity. In fact, they argue, it is only in the past several centuries that "homosexual" and "heterosexual" even existed as categories; they are *invented*, not natural, categories. Homosexual and heterosexual *behavior* has always existed, of course, but dividing up the world into categories with the labels "homosexual" and "heterosexual" is a fairly recent cultural invention. *What it means* to to be homosexual, likewise, is a cultural creation. However, it cannot be validly argued that heterosexuality and homosexuality are mere labels that can be attached and discarded at will; being straight or gay is not like playing tennis, riding a bicycle, or getting a tan. Surely there are *limits* to the reach of constructionism.

AIDS was discovered and diagnosed in the early 1980s; it is caused by a virus, the human immunovirus, or HIV. HIV is transmitted through bodily fluids, almost exclusively blood and semen. This means that it can be communicated through vaginal or anal sex, receiving, or using a needle tainted with, contaminated blood, or being born of an infected mother. Initially, almost all AIDS cases were homosexuals; over time, the proportion who received the virus through anal-penile sex has been declining, while the proportion who did so through injection of a drug is increasing. Today, roughly half of all *new* HIV diagnoses are intravenous drug users; a quarter are homosexuals or bisexuals; and a quarter are heterosexual partners of IV drug addicts or children born to AIDS-infected mothers. Experts now believe that AIDS is extremely unlikely to become widespread in the heterosexual, non-drug-using majority. AIDS victims tend to be stigmatized, regardless of the origin of the disease. Almost as many people say that the AIDS epidemic has made them less tolerant of gays as those who say it has made them more so.

Coming out, or accepting oneself as gay, is a sociologically patterned process. To be able to say to oneself, "I am a homosexual," it is necessary to neutralize the stigma adhering to homosexuality and to oneself as a result of adopting a homosexual identity.

To most heterosexuals, the category "homosexual" is a dominant prepossession. It obliterates all other features or characteristics of a person; homosexuality is a *master trait*. However, a major axis of difference among homosexuals is gender; the differences between male and female homosexuals are more substantial than their similarities. In fact, lesbians and heterosexual women share many more characteristics with one another than the first share with male homosexuals and the second with straight males. In spite of the inhibiting impact of the AIDS epidemic, male homosexuals are far, far more likely to have sex with multiple partners than is true of lesbians, who tend to have fewer, longer, more stable relationships. In addition, male homosexuals come to an awareness of their sexual orientation far earlier in their lives.

ACCOUNT: ADOPTING A HOMOSEXUAL IDENTITY

The contributor of this account is a 35-year-old male social scientist.

The term "coming out" has many meanings. As used here, the word refers to the decision to label oneself as homosexual. I shall describe below how I came to see myself as "being" homosexual in the sense of an identity. For me (and for many other homosexuals), coming out was confusing and difficult for a number of reasons.

First, I found it difficult to identify my feelings as homosexual due to my involvement with sports. I was a very athletic and sports-minded child. I boxed; played football, basketball, and baseball; ran cross-country and track; skied, swam, and bowled; hunted, fished, and water skied. I was also active in scouting. I was an Eagle scout and earned the bronze, silver, and gold palms. Since I had been taught that "queers" were girlish, incompetent at sports, and unable to rough it in the wilderness, I found it nearly impossible to view my emerging sexual interests as homosexual.

Another reason I found it hard to see myself as gay had to do with my experiences with women. I liked women very much. I enjoyed their company and like many adolescents I dated frequently. By the time I was 16, my sexual experiences with women had included petting (above and below the waist, clothed and unclothed), intercourse, and oral sex both ways. Inaccurate stereotypes held by certain segments of Anglo-American society led me to believe that gay males hated women and were repulsed by the idea of sexual contact with them. It never entered my mind that someone could desire men sexually without disliking women. So I reasoned I could not be homosexual because I liked women, was not repulsed by them sexually, and had never had a homosexual experience. One aspect of sex with women, however, bothered me quite a bit. Although I enjoyed very much the physical release of orgasm during lovemaking with them, I never felt totally involved with them in an emotional sense. Instead, I felt distanced, removed, and detached from the lovemaking experience, as if I were viewing it from a great distance through the lens of a telescope. This sense of alienation led me to conclude that I was sexually different, but not homosexual.

Inaccurate knowledge about homosexuality and homosexuals also prevented me from labeling myself as homosexual. I thought that all male homosexuals were of two types: the masculine homosexual, who spent most of his time preying on young boys foolish enough to wander unescorted into public toilets, or the effeminate homosexual, who dressed like a woman and pranced the streets, shrieking and simpering, limp wrists aflutter. To make matters worse, I also thought that homosexuals were mentally ill, unhappy, suicidal, insane, or turned on by young boys. I was unable to conceive of myself as homosexual. As far as I could tell, there existed no points of similarity between myself and homosexual males. Although I knew I was sexually attracted to other men, I wrote such feelings off as reflecting a phase of development I would soon outgrow or bisexual tendencies. I thought that I was the only person in the world who felt this way. In short, I felt very much alone with a very terrible secret.

I decided that I was homosexual and defined myself as such once I began to meet homosexual males through mutual heterosexual friends. Initially, my mind was blown. I could not believe my eyes, or my other senses, for that matter. I mean, here I was meeting good-looking, masculine-acting and successful gay males; men who bore scant resemblance to the negative stereotypes I had assimilated and internalized while growing up. More important, these men were decent people—thoughtful, kind, funny, intelligent, and accepting.

Sex was different too. Not so much physically, but emotionally. During lovemaking with other men, I was not plagued by the sense of detachment that had marred my heterosexual encounters. Instead, I felt vitally involved and integrated on a number of levels. In addition, I had always worried that if I were gay I would never find anyone to love and grow with over the years. Accordingly, I was shocked and delighted to learn that most homosexual males are not just interested in sex; that many desire and enter into love affairs with other men, with some relationships lasting a protracted duration.

Positive social encounters of this sort forced me to revise my attitudes and opinions radically regarding homosexuality and homosexuals. I realized that homosexuality did not preclude the possibility of being happy, well adjusted, masculine, and successful. For me, this realization dramatically marked the outset of a new way of life. Exposure to gay institutions and the opportunity to assimilate gay culture left me convinced that I had made the right choice in opting for a homosexual lifestyle. Would I return to heterosexuality if given the opportunity? Not a chance! (From the author's files.)

ACCOUNT: HOMOSEXUALITY

The author of this account is an office administrator in her late twenties.

When I was growing up, I regarded homosexuality as repulsive. The thought of two females or two males together sexually just didn't make any sense to me. For starters, the parts don't fit! I was under the impression that it was unnatural for two people of the same gender to be together sexually. Even science taught us that opposites attract and likes repel. But as I grew a little older, homosexuality seemed less and less unnatural to me. When I was in junior high school, it no longer seemed repulsive to me, but I still never thought I would be involved in it one day. I could accept the fact that other people chose to live their lives that way. They were happy, and that's what was important. I just never imagined that it could make me happy.

Actually, I grew up around homosexuality. I was always interested in sports and loved to play on teams. Starting in the seventh grade, I played in a summer softball league. Many of the players in this league were homosexuals. So what? I was there to play softball and as long as they kept their preference to themselves, I didn't care what they did. I found out that even some of my friends were involved in homosexuality. It bothered me at first to find this out, but I got over it. I feel that if I had not grown up around homosexuality, I never would have experienced the homosexual feelings I had.

Another big influence for me was my strong feelings for friendships. I liked to get very close to my friends. When I was a senior in high school, I met Sally. We didn't become really close until my first year in college, though. Sally was a lot of fun to be around. We seemed to be interested in the same things. We were both involved in sports, so we often ran into one another at the gym. We both liked to roller skate, and so we ended up going skating together twice a week. We were great buddies. Also, Sally is a very caring person and would do just about anything for someone. She is an especially good person to talk to. She's a good listener and she always seems to know the right thing to say. I always felt comfortable around her. It was no wonder when I did experience homosexual feelings in myself, they were for Sally.

I had been involved in a relationship with a man for over two years, and it was time for it to end. I just wasn't happy with him any more. I had become too dependent, and thought that if I ever did let go, I would be all alone. This thought made me afraid. I needed someone to talk to, and Sally was there. She listened, commented, and above all, she helped me see that I wouldn't be alone if I did let go of this relationship. The next night, she came by again and we talked some more. This time, when she left, she gave me a big hug. She said that I looked like I needed it. She made me feel very comfortable.

Right after she left, I saw my boyfriend. He told me he never wanted to see me again. So when I left, I called Sally. I told her what happened, and she came over right away and picked me up. We went to the beach and sat there for hours. She held me in her arms the whole time we were there. I felt very secure and wished we didn't have to leave. My feelings for her grew, but I still wasn't sure what to do about them.

We spent a great deal of time together. All I could think about was Sally. My only problem was whether or not to let her know how I felt about her. We sat on the beach at night and talked. I wanted to tell her exactly how I felt, but I was just too afraid. Even though she held me close that night, I couldn't be sure if there was anything else behind it, or if she just knew I needed someone to be close to, and so she comforted me. Everything up until this point had happened very naturally between us, so I decided just to continue to be natural with her. I couldn't hide how I felt any longer. The night before her birthday, we took a walk on the beach. I asked her what time it was. It was a few minutes past midnight, the day of her birthday. I looked at her, wished her a happy birthday, and then I kissed her. I realized that she was also attracted to me. I told her that I loved her, and we let nature take its course. I was overwhelmed when she told me that she loved me, too. It all seemed very natural. The two of us just came together and we've been together ever since.

The first decision I had to make was whether or not to be open to others about our relationship. At first, I didn't want anybody to know or even to see us together. It would be just between Sally and me. I told myself that I would never go into a gay bar because people who know us would see us there. And for the first couple of months, we did keep it to ourselves. Eventually, some other people did find out, but it wasn't a problem because they were homosexuals, too. We all ended up becoming good friends. This was nice because we could hang out together and more or less be ourselves. We didn't have to hide our feelings. It doesn't seem fair that homosexuals have to keep their feelings inside when they are in public. We are two people who are very much in love with one another, but we can't show it unless we are alone or among homosexuals. That's the main reason why I like to go to gay bars now. It is the one place where we can openly show our affection for one another. . . .

There's a common belief about homosexuality I can't agree with. This is the belief that homosexuals only like people of the same gender. When people began finding out I was seeing Sally, their first reaction was, "How could you like girls that way?" Well, I don't "like" girls that way. I fell in love with Sally, a person—and not her gender. With me, I fall in love with the person first, and only then do I consider their gender. When someone is called gay, it gives me the impression that the person is only interested in people of the same gender and thinks of heterosexual relations as repulsive. I don't like to be referred to as gay. I prefer to be considered as a homosexual *right now*. I am sexually attracted to and romantically involved with a person of the same gender now—Sally. The only unanswered question in my mind now is whether or not I will always be a homosexual. I don't know for sure if my relationship with Sally is going to last. I do know that if it doesn't work out, the next person I fall in love with could very well be a man. It could also be another woman. . . .

I think the high point of homosexuality for me is the equality in the relationship. There is a certain degree of equality that is not found in the majority of heterosexual relationships. No one partner is expected to call the other up first, to pay for everything, to drive the car, or to pick the other one up. In a homosexual relationship, all this is shared. In most marriages, the man works full-time while the woman stays home to cook and clean. In a homosexual relationship, both parties usually work, and everything is split fifty-fifty. This equality even applies to making love. When a man and a woman make love, the man usually plays the active role and the female, the passive one. I'm not saying that in a heterosexual relationship, equality in these things doesn't exist. I'm simply saying that it just doesn't happen as much as it does in homosexual relations.

I've never been as happy as I am now, and I'm happy because of whom I'm with. I love everything about Sally. She is always there when I need her and she's always ready to help me out. I do not feel I'm missing out on anything because I'm not with a man. The only part that

makes me unhappy is that homosexuality is not accepted by society. I sometimes wish I could tell my family how I feel about Sally. I know they wouldn't accept it, but I do want them to share in my happiness.

A major question in my mind right now is whether or not I'll ever get married. I think I wonder about it so much because of my parents and because of society's expectations. Ever since I was little, I was always told that you grow up, you meet someone nice, and you get married and start a family. I don't know what's going to happen, but right now I don't see marriage in my future. I'm happy with Sally, so why should I be looking any further for a partner? Sally and I have many common interests and we enjoy being together. We are two very compatible people. There is a high degree of giving and sharing. We understand and trust one another very much. I am happy with Sally; in fact, I couldn't be happier. My relationship with Sally has really made a difference in my life. We are very good together, but we have both kept our identities. I can always be myself, and she can always be herself. We are best friends, something that is not very common in most heterosexual couples. I like having the person I'm in love with as my best friend. . .

Sometimes I wish I knew where my life was going. I often wonder about marriage and having children; but at this point, I really don't have much to say about either one. I only wish society could accept homosexuals. Why can't society simply accept it when two people of the same gender fall in love? My feeling is that if two people are happy together, no one should care who they are. Sally and I are happier than most heterosexual couples. The feelings we share are not any different from those that are shared in a heterosexual relationship. Love is love, and there should not be any restrictions on who can share it and who can't. Why should we have to hide our beautiful relationship from others? Is that fair?

ACCOUNT: MY SEXUAL ODYSSEY, 1985–1995

I'm telling you these things and I don't want to be judged. Just listen to me and have an open mind. For a person to judge me, they're no better than I am, I'm just more honest. I will tell you many things that will curl your toes. You may not believe them, but this is the truth. The story starts in my childhood. My coming out was a long, difficult process. I was afraid of my own sexuality. As long as I can remember, when I saw older boys, when I saw the band of their underwear, I became aroused. I didn't even know what the word "aroused" meant. They were feelings I was told were bad; I knew that this undertaking was not considered normal. All through junior high school and high school, I always had a fondness for looking at men. I loved the showers, I loved the locker rooms. I remember looking at the boys and thinking how beautiful they were. And I wanted to touch them. The first time I saw a naked man, I was so turned on. These feelings were just too much for me to control. All through high school I was called names, but I never did anything sexual. My first sexual escapade was with the high school custodian. I didn't even do anything, I just watched him play with himself.

When I was 19 years old, I went to a beauty school to be a male hairdresser. There was this guy at work, Tony, who was a hairdresser, who was really hot. I really wanted him. I was afraid to do anything with him, I was so guilt-ridden. I would shake uncontrollably with anxiety and nerves. I was so nervous I'd start to shiver, I couldn't stop. People used to say things to me about being gay, like, you're gay, or are you gay? And I would run and hide, and I would get angry. I was angry at them, but I was really angry at myself. I couldn't deal with myself, I couldn't deal with my feelings, my sexuality. It wasn't until about 10 years ago that I finally came to terms with myself about being gay.

Throughout my teens and much of my twenties, I was a closet homosexual. I had a fascination with picking up hitchhikers. I used to proposition them for sex. I would touch them and sometimes they would respond in a negative way, and sometimes in a positive way. I think it was the edge. Yeah, it was always the edge, the risk of being turned down or it becoming violent, that was exciting for me. Sometime in my twenties, I picked up a hitchhiker. He told me about "park and ride." I couldn't believe what he told me. He said there was a parking lot nearby where you could park your car, and men simply drove up to you and asked if you wanted to have sex. I was amazed; I had passed this spot a thousand times and had no idea what went on there. I drove there, very nervous and insecure, and parked my car. An older man drove up and propositioned me. He said shocking things, things he wanted to do with me. Terrified, I left there *fast*. But later, I came back—again and again. I got a lot of attention, and I loved it. I was new bait, I was new meat, I was *trade*. I was something people wanted, something they needed. It was quite a fun-seeking thing for me. It was addictive; I was really addicted to it for a very long time. Being chosen and wanted and desired, having all this attention lavished on me, was like a drug I wanted to keep on taking. I used to go there and get picked up by men, and they would do things to me and I would do things to them. You see, I had a weight problem when I was younger; I was sure that girls were not attracted to me because I was overweight. When I went to "park and ride," I was thin. When I lost weight, I realized that weight that had nothing to do with my not going out with women. The more in shape I became, the more I was attracted to men. The sex at "park and ride" was phenomenal. I saw a diverse bunch of men, from all walks of life, all shapes and sizes, colors, and social class backgrounds. Some of these men I never saw again, and

some I became friends with. It was amazing. The "cookie jar" was full, and my hunger could not be sated.

The gay men who go to bars and clubs—they never go to "park and ride," and they never speak to men who do. You try to approach them, they'll give you a dirty look, as if they are superior to you. Did they forget one thing? We were all little boys at one time; all gay men were lonely and verbally and physically abused when we were young. Now that we're all adults, we should bond together and be friends. Where is their sense of community and solidarity? There's a lot of discrimination and prejudice among gays. This is sad. We ought to have an open mind. We're all different, but we're also all alike.

I met a married police officer at "park and ride." He enjoyed his experience with me so much, he wanted to see me again. He came up to me when I was mowing my lawn and said, "I remembered how to get to your house." We continue to see each other. He still sees me, he still calls. He claims he is straight; he has some pretty strict rules about what we can and can't do. He sticks to me doing oral sex on him, with a few other things thrown in. I've done all kinds of things to him. And I've taken him to heights. But he won't reciprocate because he feels he's not gay. The only exception was when I paid him—which is like a joke! He said, if you pay me, I'll let you do whatever you want. We have this running game that he's trade. I've been with him a lot, I've done a lot to him, and he really likes it. *He* discovered *me*, and he followed *me* home. Why should I pay him? I'm out of the closet and I can do what I want. I have to laugh when he tells me he's really straight.

I see these married men all the time. They commute to and from the City; between three and seven, they return from their jobs and pull off the highway with their minivans and baby seats and signs that read, "Baby On Board." My friends and I call them the "commuter special." I ask them, "Where does your wife think you are?" Their answer is, "I tell her I'm working overtime, or stuck in traffic, or working out in the gym." They come to "park and ride" and act superior to everyone else. They are incredibly picky about who they have sex with, and they always seem to get what they want. The hypocrisy is just so overwhelming, people are so fake and so bourgeois. Many of them want you to perform oral sex on them without a condom—and they are married! Most straight men want unsafe, risky sex, while gay men—who are seen as the deviants—don't want it. You would be amazed at the kind of sex they have! I really feel sorry for their wives. They go home and their wives say, "Don't use a condom, I'm on birth control." They think they are not at risk because their husband is monogamous. They imagine the worst thing that could happen is that their husband has an affair with another woman. The fact is, it is harder to transmit HIV from a woman to a man; it's a lot easier from a man to a man. A lot of them come to "park and ride" under the influence of some chemical substance and perform all kinds of sex acts there. I truly believe that with chemical abuse comes impairment and the loss of judgment and inhibitions. People become more true to who they really are under the influence.

I've had sex with a lot of married men, men with girl-friends, men who think they are straight. The escapades I've had with these men is just unbelievable. I've had sex with a carpenter. I've had sex with someone in every school in an entire school district. One was a security guard. I love the game, I love the edge. I like playing head games, I like coming on to men, I love teasing them. I had sex with the cable man, I've had sex with the garage man, I've had sex with the refrigerator repairman, the appliance man, service men, gas station men. I bought a vacuum cleaner just to have sex with the salesman. The guy who's living with me, the reason I met him was through car detailing. I've had sex with so many differ-ent service men, electricians, carpenters. And it's really, really hot. Most of them said they were straight.

I am discriminated against constantly because I am gay, act gay, and sound gay. But I wouldn't trade my life for a lie. Being out is so much healthier and more posi-tive to my mental health. The closet is such a lonely place to be. You can't tell certain people about your experi-ences, the places you go, the people you know. We live in a homophobic society; in the closet, you have to be ashamed of yourself and whom you associate with. If you haven't come out, people who discover you are gay have a great hold over you. If they see you with someone who is gay, or see you in a place that is a known gay hangout, they have the power to hurt you, threaten your job, your relations with friends, things like that. It's very difficult to suppress your true emotions and expressions of affection toward friends and lovers. This is harmful and destructive. Many gays who don't come out and can't accept themselves as they are end up abusing alco-hol. There's a lot of substance abuse among gays. When they are impaired, gay men do and say things they would not normally do or say; they put themselves at risk. When they come to terms with themselves and their sexuality, most of them manage to moderate their drinking and their abuse of drugs. Unfortunately, some don't.

At some point, I discovered gay life in the City—in particular, the West Village. I also discovered a sense of identity, a whole new world of people, fashion, music, clubs, culture, glamor, glitter, nightlife, as well as a sense of belonging. We got into punk, New Wave, and androg-yny. Back home, in the suburbs, even among gays, we would have been stared at and made fun of. In Manhat-tan, we fit right in, no one even noticed us. One night, my friend Tim, a drag queen, and Rocco, a Gypsy, a Boy George wannabe, and his Spanish boyfriend, José, and I walked into this club in the meatpacking district, near the river. We blended right in. The music was phenom-enal, the people were phenomenal. I walked into the bathroom and the next thing I knew, this Black man was all over me. It happened so fast, it was really hot. This was the first time I experienced tearoom sex in a club. I couldn't believe something like this could happen with-out my looking for it. This would never happen in a club in the suburbs.

When the weather was warm, we'd also go to the piers under the West Side Highway and hang out, "bug out" to the music. It was a wonderful experience, all these men with different backgrounds just being free, creative, and open. You met people who were into androgyny, you met "he-shes," you'd meet transvestites. It was incredible. We discovered that by the piers, men hung out and cruised in cars, just like they did in "park and ride." One night, my friend Rocco and I picked up a wealthy foreign doctor who begged and pleaded for us to demoralize, degrade, and dominate him verbally and physically. He'd even pay us. Everything was so open and free, it was mind-blowing.

The first time I walked into a leather bar near the West Side Highway, I saw a man suspended from the ceiling, hanging from chains, from his wrists and ankles, wearing nothing but a leather hood and jock strap. He had his nipples pierced, with chains running through them. I was scared yet turned on by what I saw. Every-thing is really underground. You can only get in if you wear leather. In leather bars, you get young boys, you get big men who are called "bears," they're heavy and they're hairy, and you get muscle queens—these were very masculine men with huge muscles, big burly guys who look, act, and sound straight. There's all kinds of spanking. I loved it. I still go back. Down by the West Side Highway, there are these two leather bars that are within 100 feet of each other, and you go back and forth. There's dungeons that you can go into and there's back rooms and alcoves. The muscle bars are, like, I've been propositioned, I've been taken to people's places, I've done things with them. Some of them are into S&M, into torture, into genital torture. There's a place which is really into heavy bondage, it's in the West Village, and it's funny, it's in the meatpacking district, huh, meat, you know, trade. You can't get in unless you wear rubber or you wear a uniform, like a cop.

Then there are the sex clubs. There's one club that *opens* at three, four in the morning. They serve no alco-hol. One night, I saw a young man being spanked by an ugly, old man. The young man was so turned on he reached an orgasm without having his penis touched. I couldn't believe what I saw. I said to my friend, Rocco, "What's going on? Where the hell are we?" He said, "Get over it, bitch, this is a lot better than back home." I was amazed yet scared. There are lots of different sex clubs. One we went to, it was an underground club with a little light S&M. You could check your clothes at the door. All this took place in someone's apartment. Another one, in a high-rise building in Manhattan, double secu-rity, you have to be buzzed in. It's so discreet, so secretive. You have to have passes to get in, you have to know what magazines to buy to find out about them. This club was extremely secretive. We walked in, a man was lying face down on a pool table, with his hands and feet in each corner pocket; there were cheese and crackers all over his body. The idea was, you were supposed to eat them off his body, as if he were an appetizer. The whole thing, it was nothing but a glorified orgy, a jerk-off party. There are all these little rooms, and they shave your head, they're into body shaving, they're into piercing. It's these crowded little rooms, and people all push and shove and everyone starts to touch each other, hundreds of men in a small area, pushing and shoving, and everyone is touching and moving, and groping and pulling, and everyone starts yanking off their clothes, and everyone starts having sex, and it's just massive amounts of group sex. There's no anal sex, and people are not supposed to perform oral sex, but many of them do. It's just hot and sweaty, and it's really just unbelievable. This would never happen in the suburbs. These places have gone underground since the mayor closed them down. Everytime it goes underground, it just pops up somewhere else.

There are all kinds of clubs. There are foot fetish clubs, there's clubs for men that are hairy, there are men who have a thing for uncircumcised penises, there are men who have a thing for having a *small* penis. All these little organizations are for certain kinds of stimulations and titillations. I personally think some of them are kind of on the bizarre side, but who am I to judge other people, right?

There are the parks. One night, Rocco—who's something of an adventurer—said to me, "Come on, let's go for a ride." We ended up in Central Park. I had never been to Central Park even in the daytime. To me, it was a scary place in the middle of the night. Well, you wouldn't believe it. This place was packed wall-to-wall with men cruising for sex. A man came up to me and said, "I'll give you $50 if you let me touch your hairy chest and back and then urinate on me." I couldn't believe what I was hearing! I was dumbfounded. No way!

And the baths. Most of them are closed because of the AIDS epidemic. Some of them are open illegally. But one night, I went to an underground bath. The place opened at midnight. It was in a high-rise building, on the top floor. We were buzzed in—there were all sorts of security precautions. It cost $40 to get into the club. There were many naked men on cots, in saunas, in steam rooms. This sort of thing goes on, even today.

The movies. One night, my friend and I went to a popular movie house, I won't tell you the name. We met the stereotypical old man in a raincoat. And the young man, and the middle-aged man—and so on and so forth. A married man propositioned me. He wanted me to go to his apartment. He'd give me $100. I screamed at him, "What do you think I am—a prostitute!" I wouldn't do it.

You can also go on trips. Vacations. I went to Mexico with a gay travel group. Many rich and beautiful men came along. The adventure was unbelievable—lavish parties, fashionable men, great music, and wall-to-wall partying. The men were the cream of the crop, with muscle men, body-builders, pretty boys, LA queens, New York City punk and grunge, men from Texas and Southern states dressed in Western wear, men from Canada. It was a week-long orgy. On another trip, I attended a "Winter White" party in Palm Springs. Even before I got out of the airport, I saw rich, old queens, driving Rolls-Royce convertibles. All this affluence, all these rich, old men. I met a guy at the airport who looked extremely manly, but when he spoke, he had such a high voice, we both began laughing. He had 10 suitcases for four days, and I had seven. Queens don't travel light. You never know when you might need some special outfit—leather, flannel, just the right costume. So the trip was off to a good start. Everything was glamorous. Fabulous music. Affluence everywhere, nonstop parties, cream of the crop men—and nonstop sex. Men having sex in hot tubs, sex in saunas, sex at parties, sex in the clubs. Gay men everywhere—in the sun and having fun. I met a rich doctor from Beverly Hills driving a Porsche, a male dancer with a body to die for, and a boy who looked exactly like a girl, a fabulous drag queen. This was a great adventure! It's amazing to see all these gay people together, out and about, not caring what straight people thought.

Summers on Fire Island! Such beautiful beaches, lots of affluence, fabulous houses, openly gay communities, the landscape, nature—the deer come right up to you. One Fourth of July, two friends and I went to Cherry Grove. Most of the people come from Manhattan and Europe, very cosmopolitan. My friends and I were dancing and having such a good time, we got so carried away, we lost track of the time. We missed the last ferry, so we were trapped there till six in the morning. We decided to walk to the next community, the Pines, along the boardwalk—maybe a later ferry left from there. But the boardwalk ended, and in the woods, in the dark, we discovered the infamous "Meatrack"—an ongoing, all-night orgy. We didn't know, in this period of safe sex, that this sort of thing went on. Here we were in the woods, in the dark, with a lot of naked, muscular men. Shouldn't we worry about Lyme Disease, poison ivy, AIDS? Well, we decided to join in. They performed all kinds of sex acts, both giving and receiving. In fact, we became the center of attention. It was quite a turn-on.

I'm going to talk about situational sex. Sex in cars, sex in stores, sex in department store bathrooms. This is really cool. What you do is, you get a shopping bag and you go into the store, and you go into a stall with another man. You can sit on the toilet and put your legs up, and he pretends he's peeing, and nobody knows that there's two guys in the stall. There's sex in airports, sex on a plane, sex on a train, sex in a bus station. That's what I call situational sex.

In this era of supposedly safe sex, a lot of not-so-safe sex is going on. I think that during the beginning of the

AIDS scare, a lot of men and a lot of places became more conservative. AIDS declined for a while. It seems that many men have started to move in another direction, almost like backsliding to the practices of the pre-AIDS era. Especially the young men, they think that nothing can happen to them, they think they are invincible. Some day, there will be a world free of prejudice and discrimination, and a world free of disease. I hope I will be there to see and enjoy it, and relish the moment.

The author of this account is a social worker in his thirties.

chapter **10**

VIOLENT BEHAVIOR

We all know what violence is, and we all condemn it: true or false? On the surface, it might seem that defining violence would generate less controversy than is true of any other form of deviance. We might assume that what constitutes violence is obvious and nonideological. Everyone knows what it is and nobody likes it. This is at best a half-truth. It is probably true that we would get a fairly high level of agreement concerning what constitutes violence if we were to show films or videotapes of certain behavior and ask an audience to rate just how much violence is taking place on the screen. After all, inflicting a stab wound or throwing a punch at someone's jaw are not easily classified as friendly acts. But notice: The behavior that is being evaluated in these hypothetical examples would be stripped of their social and personal context. More to the point, a great number of harmful actions are likely to be regarded as violent by some observers but not others; some of this variation can be traceable to their ideological and political orientation.

The term "violence" contains the implication that actions so characterized are illegitimate, deviant, worthy of condemnation. Consequently, many people refuse to label as violent those actions of which they approve, however much damage they may inflict. For instance, in the months following the civil disturbances touched off by the "not guilty" verdict in the trials of four Los Angeles police officers who were accused of excessive brutality in the beating of motorist Rodney King, I heard several observers refer to the rioters as "freedom fighters." These actions constituted an uprising, they said; these actions were not violent, but were a reasonable and legitimate reaction to oppression. Most Americans—even a majority who deplored the court's decision—did not agree with this assessment, and regarded the disturbances as yet another sorry chapter in urban violence and decay. The point is that most of us disapprove of certain actions that kill or harm people or destroy property, and we refer to them as violence. Other acts that produce the same damage and loss of life, but of which we approve, we do not label as violent. In short, violence has, in part, a political and ideological character. "The kinds of acts that become classified as violent, and, equally important, those that do not become so classified, vary according to who provides the definition" (Skolnick et al., 1969, p. 4). This might seem extremely peculiar; violence is a hard, concrete fact, how can it "vary" at all?

For instance, consider the behavior some have referred to as *covert, institutional* violence. Racism, sexism, and the indignities of prejudice based on social class are examples of this type of violence. The denial of a job to a qualified woman because of her sex, the refusal of a landlord to rent an apartment to a Black family simply because of their race, the unwillingness of the government to institute policies that would result in more equitable distribution of income are examples of "institutional" violence, according to some observers. That is, they hurt, damage, or violate, but would not appear on most people's lists of examples of violent acts. Violence, these observers say, means that a person is violated in some way. There is harm done to a person's body, dignity, autonomy, freedom (Liazos, 1972).

Is abortion a form of violence? Is extracting a fetus from a woman's body the same as murdering a baby? Americans are split on the issue; some regard abortion as the removal of unwanted tissue, while others regard it as an act of extreme violence, literally as murder, essentially no different from gunning down someone on the street. Is killing in a declared war a violent act or not? The extreme pacifist sees warfare as the same as murder; the patriot does not regard killing in wartime as a violent act, but regards this killing as only brave fighters doing what they must for their country. There is no way of resolving these conflicting positions, however we feel about these views. They are real, they determine how some people define violence, and they often provide the basis for how some people interact with individuals whose actions are defined by these views.

Clearly, as students of deviant behavior, we must pay close attention to the manner in which behavior is seen and classified by the members of a society. What is or is not regarded as an act of violence—and as a consequence, labeled as deviance—is not solely dependent on the damage inflicted by the act. Rather, what leads observers to think of an act as an instance of violence depends on what they see as legitimate or illegitimate, justified or unjustified, excusable or inexcusable actions taken by one person or set of persons against another person or persons. At the same time, while a huge universe of actions remains controversial, there is unquestionably a solid core of actions that nearly all observers would regard as violent. Thus, we must pay attention to both the variations and the universals in defining violence.

VIOLENCE: A CROSS-CULTURAL PERSPECTIVE

Since the 1960s, some of the once-moribund biological theories claiming that human behavior is genetically determined have undergone a renaissance. This has been particularly true of explanations for violence, aggression, and homicide. Humans killing one another, it is claimed, is the manifestation of a drive to inflict harm on others. It is a *natural* drive, some say, a kind of instinct, similar in strength to the need for food, water, and sex. "Man is a predator whose natural instinct is to kill" declares Robert Ardrey, a popularizer of this view (1961, p. 316). A school of social science called *sociobiology* (Wilson, 1975, 1978, 1984) seems to endorse this view. Humans, says one sociological adherent of this school, are "genetically programmed" to kill; they have a "natural penchant for violence" (Van den Berghe, 1978, p. 175).

One serious problem with the theory that violence is innate and biologically programmed in humans is that it is far from universal; in fact, the incidence of serious physically violent behavior varies wildly from one society to another. And, it varies within the same society, from one group, social category, subculture, and geographical area to another. There are hunting and gathering and peasant societies in which violence is practically if not literally unknown. In Margaret Mead's classic study, *Sex and Temperament in Three Primitive Societies*, the Arapesh of New Guinea are described as cooperative, unaggressive, responsive to the needs of others, mild-mannered, passive, nurturant, contented, and secure. When Mead studied them, violence was simply not known among the Arapesh. On the other hand, Mead also described the Mundugumor, a nearby tribe, as ruthless, aggressive, undisciplined, insecure, disgruntled, hostile, and very violent. How can we account for these differences with an explanation that invokes some universal, innate characteristic for committing violence against one's fellow humans? The Tasaday, a tiny isolated band living in caves deep in the Philippine rain forest, are never angry, hostile, or aggressive with one another. Incidentally, some observers argue that the Tasaday are not the primitive, isolated people that others claimed them to be (Mydans, 1988; Molony, 1988). Regardless of who they are, the Tasaday are a peaceful people. Among them, there is no fighting, no punishment of children, and virtually no conflict or even disagree-

ment among themselves. The Tasaday do not even have words or concepts for what we would call "weapons," "war," "murder," "enemies," or "fighting" (Nance, 1975, pp. 19–20, 129, 130, 444). The Lepcha of Sikkhim (Gorer, 1967) and the pygmies of the Ituri rain forest of Central Africa (Turnbull, 1962) are two other peoples whose members exhibit practically no serious violence toward one another.

Societies in which gentleness and nonviolence are the rule provide two object lessons for any observer of violence and its relation to human behavior generally. The first is that it is unlikely that violence is innate or instinctual because it is not universal; peoples everywhere are not uniformly, necessarily, or inevitably violent. Any proponent of the genetic school of violence would have to explain *why*, in many societies the world over, violence is rare or nonexistent. And the second lesson is that the rate, incidence, and occurrence of violence the world over varies enormously. Violent behavior is a variable, not a constant. It is present in *degrees*. These basic, hard facts suggest that violence is culturally learned and sustained, and not inborn or instinctual.

Another problem with the view that violence is instinctual is the very basic fact that every society designates legitimate and illegitimate *targets* of violence; just what these targets are varies from society to society. Violence, including its most extreme form, homicide, which takes place among members of certain tribal societies acquires a starkly different coloration from that which prevails in a unified nation-state with a formally administered, bureaucratically controlled legal system. Here, the issue is just *who* can be killed with impunity. Some peoples are peaceful regardless of whom they come into contact. However, many others regard people who are not members of their tribe as not fully human. Among some societies (but not others) this means that nonmembers can be robbed, raped, or killed with absolutely no pangs of conscience whatsoever. One anthropologist writes, with perhaps a bit of exaggeration, "For most of humanity, the tribe is the unit within which killing is considered murder, and outside of which killing may be a proof of manhood and bravery, a pleasure and a duty. . . . Man, as a species, has no inhibitions against killing his fellow man who did not belong to the same pack, however the pack may be defined, and often gets intense pleasure and a sense of pride from doing so" (Gorer, 1966). A good example of this principle is the Kaingang of Brazil. Their members never kill one another; in 200 years of oral history, only one instance of an intratribal homicide took place. On the other hand, their violence against other tribes, and that of those tribes against them, has decimated their numbers to almost total obliteration (Henry, 1941).

With the institutionalization of the modern nation-state, the willful killing of all fellow citizens, regardless of their tribal status, came to be defined as off-limits, illegitimate, illegal—deviant. Permissible, willful killing was permitted only when the victim was a member of a different nation-state from one's own, and then, only in the course of an activity the killer's political leaders defined as warfare.

If it were true that the will to commit violence is caused by a strong and more or less unmodifiable instinct, we would expect a fairly high and standard rate of violence from one society, nation, and period of history to another. The differences would have to be explained by extenuating circumstances. Instead, what we see is immense variation for all of these comparisons. It is difficult to understand how the manifestation of an inborn instinct could be subject to as much variation as we actually observe.

FAMILY VIOLENCE

A nation whose members fear assaults from strangers on city streets may be surprised to learn that violence in the home at the hands of family members is far more common. Relative to their numbers in the population, violence inflicted by family members is hundreds of thousands of times more common than that inflicted by strangers. In fact, even in absolute terms, a person is more likely to be assaulted or killed by a family member than by a stranger. In the words of two experts on family violence: "The family is society's most violent institution, with the two exceptions of the police and the military" (Gelles and Straus, 1988).

If you punch or hit a stranger with an object and inflict severe bodily injury on that person, this is referred to as *assault*. It is a serious crime, and you can be arrested for it. If you do the same thing to your child or spouse, the chances are high (although diminishing) that it will be ignored by the police and the courts. It is a peculiar fact that violence among family members, when it does not result in death, is relatively lightly regarded by the legal system as well as by the public. If a wife appears

before the police bruised, battered, and bleeding, a common response will be, "It's not a Police Department thing. . . . It's really a family thing. You'll have to go to Family Court. . . . There's nothing I can do" (Maitland, 1976). Family violence is all too often not regarded as a crime at all, unless it results in death, and is routinely treated with great leniency. One attorney who specializes in marital cases, Emily Jane Goodman, puts it this way: "In essence, nothing is done about this type of crime. . . . A man can assault his wife with relative impunity and walk down the street and assault a stranger and be arrested. It is the only crime in which marital status dictates how it is treated" (Maitland, 1976).

The same holds for the public's attitudes. In a study of responses by a population sample to a list of offenses whose "seriousness" was rated; in its ranking, one is seen as the most serious offense, while the one that was ranked 140 was the least serious. This study found that violent acts among intimates were less harshly evaluated than when the acts took place among strangers. Beating up a spouse ranked 91 in seriousness out of a total of 140 offenses; beating up a stranger ranked 64. The forcible rape of a stranger in a park was ranked 13; the forcible rape of one's former spouse was ranked 62nd (Rossi et al., 1974). However, again, when the violence resulted in death, intimacy did not soften the judgment of the seriousness of the act. The same holds for violence inflicted on children by parents; the "battered child" syndrome is common yet often ignored by authorities and lightly regarded by the police (Van Stolk, 1972). As with wife battering, however, attitudes are changing, and the official response, slow to change, will eventually catch up with changing attitudes. A study of 300 homicides in Houston found that "the severity of the penalty for killers correlates inversely with the degree of intimacy between killer and victim." Of all killers of relatives, 61 percent "escaped any form of legal penalty"; this was true of 53 percent of killers of friends and associates and 36 percent of strangers (Lundsgaarde, 1977, p. 16). Although this has been changing in recent years, as a general rule, the closer the relationship between victim and attacker, the greater the public tolerance for violence. To put the matter another way, violence inflicted against a stranger is regarded as much more deviant than violence against an intimate. This apparent anomaly is worth exploring.

Under what circumstances is family violence

regarded as deviant and criminal? And what factors are related to its incidence? Let's examine two serious and common types of family violence: *wife beating* and *incest*.

Wife Beating

Although a national survey found that violence inflicted on husbands by wives is as common as violence inflicted on wives by husbands (Straus, Gelles, and Steinmetz, 1980, pp. 36–38; Dutton, 1988, p. 190), I will concentrate here on the latter. This is not because of a double standard that dictates that the injury of a woman is more serious than that of a man. Rather, there is evidence that shows that the beatings of husbands by wives is significantly less serious than are those of wives by husbands. In this same nationally representative survey, it was found that: (1) husbands have higher rates of the most *dangerous* and *injurious forms* of violence; (2) abuse by a husband usually does more damage than abuse by a wife—in part because the husband is apt to be larger, stronger, and better trained in violence; (3) husband violence against wives is more likely to be *repeated*; (4) a higher proportion of the wife's violence against the husband is in *self-defense*; (5) a fairly high proportion of the violence inflicted on women (roughly one-quarter) takes place when they are pregnant; (6) women are more likely to be economically dependent on men and to have fewer alternatives to putting up with the beatings (Straus, Gelles, and Steinmetz, 1980, pp. 43–44; Gelles, 1987). Because of these factors, I will concentrate on wife-beating by husbands.

Asking a nationally representative sample of Americans about various violent acts which couples inflict on one another turned up the following findings. About 7 percent said that they had thrown something at their spouse in the past year; 16 percent said that this had happened at least once in their marriage. Seven percent said that they had slapped their spouse last year; 18 percent said that this had happened at least once. Thirteen percent shoved, pushed, or grabbed their spouse during the previous year; 24 percent said that this had happened once during their marriage. During the past year, 1.5 percent said, they had beaten up their spouse; 5 percent said that this had never happened. And .5 percent said that they had used a knife or a gun on their spouse (most of this entailed menacing and threatening); 4 percent said that this had

happened at least once during the course of their marriage (Straus, Gelles, and Steinmetz, 1980, pp. 33–34). This places the total at close to *two million* Americans who had at some time faced a husband or wife wielding a gun or a knife, and slightly more than this figure who had been beaten up by his or her spouse. The researchers who conducted this survey state that these figures probably *underestimate* the volume of violence that takes place in the American family, partly because of shame, guilt, or faulty recall, or because the families in this study are all intact and hence, display relatively *low* levels of violence. Other research shows that couples who have divorced or separated have *higher* rates of violence than those that are intact. The authors estimate that the rate of violence for American families is probably roughly double what these figures reveal (1980, pp. 35–36).

In short, the marriage license seems to be something of a "hitting license." Violence may very well be "built into the very structure of the society and the family itself" (Straus, Gelles, and Steinmetz, 1980, p. 44). There is an unacknowledged norm that hitting is acceptable. Overall, about a third of all American couples experience a violent incident every year, and two-thirds do so at least once in the marriage. One-eighth of all couples who were interviewed admitted that at least some time during their marriage there had been an act of violence which could have caused serious injury to the spouse, an act that qualifies as the crime of assault. Translating these figures into rates of assault, this works out to a national rate of 6,100 per 100,000 in the population per year for American couples generally; the rate of assault reported to the police and officially recorded by the FBI is only 280 per 100,000 in the population per year. In other words, if serious family violence were recorded as assault, the rate of aggravated assault in the United States would increase *by over 20 times* (1980, pp. 48, 49).

Why does such a high level of family violence exist? More specifically, what factors are related to wife beating by husbands? What variables are related to the likelihood that husbands will slap or punch their wives or strike them with an object? What kind of man beats his wife? There are at least two distinctly different types of factors related to the incidence of wife beating; they correspond to the "macro" and the "micro" levels of explanations or theories which I discussed in Chapter 4: those factors that characterize American society generally, that all American couples have in common, and those that distinguish some couples from others.

The factors that all American couples have in common relate to the structural and cultural institutions we all are exposed to, principal among them is *patriarchy*. Patriarchy is the view, carried out in practice, that the man should automatically exert power and authority over the woman, that the home "belongs" to the man, that the woman must endure whatever abuse or punishment is inflicted on her by her husband. It is difficult to argue with the fact that the sexist or patriarchal character of American society contributes to wife beating (Gelles, 1979, pp. 18–19). Where the man is the sole financial support of the family, he is more likely to think he has the right to do whatever he wants to, to whomever lives in the household he supports. Culturally, this view has an ancient history. Historically, wives have been seen as men's property. The term, "rule of thumb," stems from English common law, which regarded it as the husband's right to beat his wife with a stick no bigger around than the circumference of his thumb.

But the simple fact is that not all couples accept patriarchy or sexism as valid. This is a question of degree, not an absolute rule. While living in a society with sexist or patriarchal institutions encourages wife beating generally, many—most— husbands living in societies with patriarchal institutions do not beat their wives. What distinguishes those who do from those who do not?

Unemployment dramatically increases the likelihood of violence in the home. Unemployed men are twice as likely to act violently toward their wives as are men who are employed full-time. And men who are employed only part time are three times as likely to be wife beaters as are the men who are employed full-time (Straus, Gelles, and Steinmetz, 1980, p. 150).

Poverty is also related to wife beating. It is erroneous to assume that family violence is exclusively or even primarily a lower-class phenomenon. However, wife beating is *statistically* more common in the poorest homes (O'Brien, 1975). Husbands living in families in the lowest income bracket are about six times as likely to beat their wives as are those who live in families in the most affluent income category (Straus, Gelles, and Steinmetz, 1980, p. 148). Poverty is associated with feelings of failure and powerlessness in a wide range of areas of life, and the husband's frustrations are often translated into violence against the wife. Ultimately,

wife beating can be traced to the unequal distribution of wealth in American society and to an economic structure that severely restricts access to achievement and success. We've already learned that since the early 1970s, social and economic inequality have been increasing in the Western, industrialized world; the rich are getting richer while the poor are getting poorer (Cassidy, 1995). Thus, assuming that all other factors remain the same, it seems to make sense to predict an increase in family violence over time.

Stress, too, is related to violence against wives. As stress within the family increases so does wife beating. The greater the number of extremely stressful events in a couple's life (in the study, 18 were mentioned, for instance, trouble with the boss, the death of a loved one, sickness), the greater the likelihood that the husband will beat his wife (Straus, Gelles, Steinmetz, 1980, pp. 183–185; Linsky and Straus, 1986).

And last, wife beating is much more common in homes where power is concentrated in the hands of the husband; the least amount of wife beating occurs where the household is democratic with respect to power and authority. Violence is a means of asserting or legitimating a dominant position. The greater the sharing of decisions, the lower the likelihood that husbands will inflict violence against wives (Straus, Gelles, and Steinmetz, 1980, pp. 193–196).

One common-sensical question many observers ask about wife beating is why the woman "puts up with" it. There is a hint of "blaming the victim" reasoning behind this question—it's her fault that she's beaten, there must be something wrong with her to stay in such a relationship. Some observers have even assumed that a woman subconsciously wishes to be beaten. An Ann Landers column states: "According to the experts, a man who gets his jollies beating up a woman can always find someone who will tolerate it and they are both sick" (quoted in Langley and Levy, 1977, p. 123). Actually, "the experts" say no such thing; today, experts *reject* the notion that either the husband *or* the wife in such a relationship is sick; the contemporary view argues that the wife does *not* wish to be beaten, whether consciously or subconsciously, but by and large is a victim of circumstances (Dutton, 1994; Martin, 1976). Nonetheless, the question remains: Why does a woman stay in a marriage in which her husband beats her? After all, some wives *do* leave abusive husbands. Refusing to ask the question fails to recognize a difference between wives who remain and those who leave. Moreover, some wives react to violence with corresponding violence, while others do not (Browne, 1987); why?

As with the issue of what factors lead husbands to beat their wives, the question of what leads wives to stay with husbands who beat them can be answered by examining two different sets of factors. The first set is the "macro" factors that all couples in the same society have in common. The second set consists of the more "micro" factors that distinguish different couples from one another. In the first set, we must include the patriarchal institutions that pervade American society. In the second set, we must include, at the very least, degrees of violence, the resources the wife commands, and her childhood experiences with physical abuse.

In a sexist and patriarchal society, women are socialized to think of themselves as powerless and dependent, a condition psychologists refer to as "learned helplessness" (Walker, 1979, pp. 42–54). The "very fact of being a woman, more specifically a married woman, automatically creates a situation of powerlessness" (1979, p. 51). Again, this is a factor rather than an absolute; still, in a patriarchy, most women are taught that they take on value only in relation to how specific men interact with them. Patriarchy trains women to be passive. These cultural values, many laws pertaining to marriage, attitudes of the community, the unwillingness of the police or the courts to do much about abuse, "all these teach women that they have no direct control over the circumstances of their lives" (1979, p. 52). For the most part, the cultural, social, and economic institutions of this society conspire to convey a message to the wife that she had best endure the physical abuse to which she is subjected by her husband.

And yet, many—in all likelihood most—women who are married to a violent man will seek outside assistance or in the long run terminate the relationship altogether rather than put up with severe, prolonged abuse. This shows either that the "macro" factors pertaining to the institutions of patriarchy make up only one of a number of factors playing a role here, or that patriarchy may not be as deeply entrenched in American society as is true in societies in which women are even *more* likely to remain in a violent, abusive marriage. (If we had data on this issue, we could settle the question; unfortunately, we do not.) What are the more "micro" or individual factors that distinguish the

women, or categories of women, who stay from those who leave?

Degree of violence is one distinguishing factor. As a general rule, the more severe and extended the violence is, the greater the likelihood that the woman will seek outside assistance or intervention from a relevant agency, and the greater the likelihood that she will leave or divorce her abusive husband. One study (Gelles, 1976, 1987) coded the severity of violence on a 10-point scale, and found that the "mean violence severity" inflicted on wives who did not seek outside intervention was 2.1, whereas it was over twice as high, 4.6, for wives who did go outside the home to secure assistance from a relevant agency; the score was 5.1 for wives who divorced or separated from their husbands. Only 42 percent of the women who had been struck once in the marriage sought outside intervention, whereas 83 percent of those who had been struck at least once a week obtained a divorce, became separated, called the police, or went to a social service agency. Clearly, *most* women are not willing to put up with absolutely *any* level of violence, a fact which shows that by itself, patriarchy is an inadequate explanation. The more severe the violence, the smaller the percentage of women who stay in an abusive relationship.

Second, the fewer the resources at the woman's command and the more "entrapped" she is in the marriage, the more reluctant she is to seek outside intervention or to leave her husband. The greater her education, the greater the likelihood she will seek the help of an agency or leave her husband. Her employment is also important here: Women who are employed, that is, who are not totally economically dependent on their husbands and can support themselves and their children, are much less willing to submit passively to their husband's physical abuse and are much more likely to seek outside help or leave him. This suggests that full employment for wives would increase their options, decrease their dependence, and assist many who are in bad marriages to terminate them.

And third, it is clear that women who were themselves physically abused as children, principally by their fathers, are more likely to have been socialized to accept such abuse as normal and natural, and hence are more likely to stay in an abusive marriage. There is something of a *generational continuity* here: Abuse breeds abuse. Women who did not have to put up with such treatment are far more likely to see it as outside the norm, deviant, unacceptable, and intolerable, and are more likely to leave their husbands when they begin beating them.

Is law enforcement able to intervene and make a difference? Above, we saw that law enforcement is reluctant to treat wife beating as a criminal matter. But changes are afoot. Prior to the late 1970s and early 1980s, nearly every police department in the country routinely ignored complaints of wife beating, treating it as a family rather than a criminal matter. In 1981, the Minneapolis Police Department began an experiment to determine which of three responses to complaints of domestic assault would be most effective in reducing their incidence: advice, ordering the suspect to leave the premises for eight hours, or arrest. The experiment clearly demonstrated the superior deterrent effect of arrest; within a six-month period, 37 percent of the advised suspects, 33 percent of the suspects ordered off the premises, but only 19 percent of the arrested suspects committed another assault or another crime against the women who lodged the original complaints (Sherman and Berk, 1984).

The results of this experiment were surprising even to experienced police officers, who typically saw such arrests as futile and bothersome. In fact, simply calling the police, even if they do not make an arrest, has something of a deterrent effect. A nationwide study that compared women who called the police after being assaulted by their spouses with those who did not call the police revealed that fewer callers (15 percent) were reassaulted within six months than were those who did not call (41 percent). While calling did not eliminate the likelihood of being assaulted again, it did reduce a woman's chances of being revictimized (Langan and Innes, 1986). As a result of the findings of these and other such studies, for the police in some jurisdictions, "domestic violence is no longer low priority" (Nix, 1986). Said the former Police Commissioner Benjamin Ward of the New York City Police Department, "We have made enforcing the law against batterers a top priority. . . . I know that one of the most effective methods of dealing with domestic violence is to arrest the batterers. Every arrest sends a clear message that violence in the home is just as criminal as violence in the streets" (Bohlen, 1988). Arrests in domestic violence cases in New York City quadrupled between 1984 and 1988. Statistics in Suffolk County, a suburb of New York City, are an indication of the recent policy of arresting batterers. In all of 1987, the police made a total of only 126 arrests for domestic violence; between March 28 and November 11, 1988, they made over 1,000 arrests on this charge (Brasley, 1988). However, it is possible that decades will pass before the policy of arresting wife beaters will be instituted in jurisdictions all over the country.

Unfortunately, the initial success of these early experiments was not matched by later studies, which showed few differences between arrested and nonarrested wife-battering husbands and live-in companions in their later offense rates (Dunford, Huizinga, and Elliott, 1990; Sherman et al., 1991; Sherman and Smith, 1992; Pate and Hamilton, 1992; Berk et al., 1992). To be more specific about the later findings, *unemployed* arrested battering husbands *increased* their post-arrest battering, while *employed* arrested battering husbands *decreased* it. This suggests that men with a low stake in conformity are undeterred from their domestic violence as a consequence of deviance labeling, while those with a higher stake were deterred from deviance through negative labeling (Sherman and Smith, 1992).

Incest

It might seem surprising to include incest as a type of family violence. Superficially, it might seem that it is a nonviolent form of behavior, deviant in most quarters, to be sure, but nonviolent nonetheless. Moreover, incest has sometimes been referred to as "the last taboo," the last remaining activity that will eventually be tolerated with the growth of sexual freedom. In fact, contemporary thinking does not regard the tolerance of incest as a form of sexual freedom. The taboos regarding it are not the same sort as those that condemn homosexuality, premarital sex, and consensual adultery. It is now recognized that incest grows out of sexual *repression*, not sexual freedom, and that it is distinctly a form of violence.

To grasp this point, it becomes necessary to distinguish between incest that is initiated by an older relative against a considerably younger one from those cases which take place between age equals. Children have been taught to respect and obey their parents; obedience by the daughter is especially stressed, more so than by the son, and particularly obedience to the father more so than to the mother. In addition, children look to parents for moral guidance (Forward and Buck, 1978, p. 21). This makes it inconceivable that any sexual act initiated by the father could be willingly complied with by a minor daughter. Any passive acceptance by her of her father's sexual advances must be regarded as a product of coercion, intimidation, and fear—not free choice. Moreover, given the great disparity between the physical size, authority, and knowledge and sophistication of adults versus children, it is simply not possible for a child to consent to a sexual relationship with an adult (Finkelhor, 1979, p. 52). Since one study found that the average age of female sexual victims was a few months over 10 years old (1979, p. 60), it is clear that father-daughter incest typically entails adult-child experiences. As a result, intimidation, not free choice, dominates in cases of father-daughter incest. Since freedom, not coercion, is the main ingredient of sexual liberation, incest cannot be an instance of sexual liberation.

The distinction between incest that takes place between age equals and that which is initiated by a considerably older relative against a younger one emphasizes that incest per se must be distinguished from *sexual victimization*. By its very nature, sex between children and adults constitutes victimization. Operationally, one study (Finkelhor, 1979, p. 56) defined sexual victimization as sex between a child and an adolescent five or more years older, and sex between a young adolescent and an adult partner 10 or more years older. (Most of this did not entail vaginal intercourse, it must be stated; most entailed touching and fondling, some exhibitionism and, more rarely, oral sex. Intercourse with a young child is likely to result in severe tissue trauma, medical care, and hence, discovery.) Not all of these cases entailed incest, but many did. For the girls, 43 percent of the cases were with a family member; for the boys, this was 17 percent. Likewise, not all cases of incest entailed sexual victimization—two five-year-old cousins playing "doctor," for instance. In this same study, 23 percent of the boys and 28 percent of the girls had had at least one incestuous experience, of which only 10 percent crossed generational lines (1979, p. 87). However, we must keep in mind that a very high proportion of incestuous contacts entail some measure of coercion or intimidation of a slightly younger sister or female cousin by an older brother or male cousin. Nonetheless, sexual victimization and incest must be regarded as *overlapping but distinct* phenomena.

The exploitative, victimizing nature of adult-child sexual contacts can be seen in the contrast between father-daughter and mother-son incest. The simple fact is that women generally, and mothers specifically, hardly ever initiate overtly sexual acts with children, male or female. The cases of mother-son incest that do take place are so rare as to constitute an anomaly, a sociological and psychiatric curiosity. In fact, little boys are much more likely to be sexually victimized by their fathers and stepfathers than by their mothers and stepmothers. Why? The overwhelming predominance of male cross-generational incest and sexual victimization over female (by roughly 30 times!) is explained by the institution of patriarchy, many observers argue (Herman and Hirschman, 1977; Herman, 1981; Janeway, 1981). Incest takes place because men are dominant in this society so that many feel entitled to use children (women more so, of course) for their sexual satisfaction and pleasure. Patriarchal culture teaches males that their will should be unopposed, that others exist to serve and service them. Historically, the father has had more or less uncontested power to do with his daughter as he wishes.

As long as fathers dominate their families, they will have the power to make sexual use of their children. Most fathers will choose not to exert this power; but as long as the prerogative is implicitly granted to all men, some men will use it. . . . As long as fathers rule but do not nurture, as long as mothers nurture but do not rule, the conditions favoring the development of father-daughter incest will prevail (Herman, 1981, pp. 202, 206).

Of course, as we saw in the discussion on wife beating, the "macro" factor, patriarchy, takes us only so far. The fact is that most fathers do not molest their daughters; what distinguishes those who do from those who do not?

Although brother-sister incest does not contain the same element of disparity in authority, physical size, and obviously age as father-daughter incest does, nonetheless, a very high proportion of such cases entail a brother who is five or more years older than his sister; hence, it is a case of sexual victimization as it is commonly defined. In one study, nearly a third of the cases of sibling incest entailed literal physical coercion (Finkelhor, 1979, p. 90). In another study (Russell, 1986, p. 276), the *average* age disparity between brothers and sisters was seven years: 17.9 for the brother and 10.7 for the sister. (But as we'll see below, this study focused specifically on incestuous *abuse*, hence, it excluded the more equalitarian experiences.) The age dis-

The Incest-Survivor Machine

Incestuous sex inflicted on a younger relative by an older one is a horrifying crime, one that often has damaging and long-lasting consequences for the victim. This crime is real, but it has been ignored for centuries. One indicator that our society is becoming more enlightened and progressive is the fact that this crime is being brought into the light and its perpetrators held accountable for their abusive actions.

At the same time, the recognition of incest has had at least one ugly and bizarre byproduct: the "incest-survivor machine" (Tavris, 1993), a virtual industry whose advocates make the following claims: (1) Any memory of abuse or abuse-like acts inflicted on you in the past is valid; (2) any psychological dysfunction in your present life is probably a sign that you were abused; (3) if you don't recall having been abused, you probably were anyway, and you are repressing its memory, since sexual abuse is practically universal; (4) if you weren't abused in childhood, you probably were in infancy; (5) if you weren't abused in this life, chances are, you were abused in a *previous* life; (6) incest survivors should buy books that make these claims, and seek solace in the company of other abuse survivors, but should not attempt to create major social change to ensure that the conditions for abuse are not perpetuated, since such abuse is inevitable anyway. (Tavris, 1993, cites Blume, 1990, and Bass and Davis, 1988, among others, as examples of this genre.)

In a way, the "incest-survivor machine" cheapens and trivializes the real sexual victimization of genuine victims, because if everyone is a victim then no one is. It fobs off as real that which is fraudulent, equating imagined experiences with real ones. Research shows that many of our most strongly held memories simply never happened in real life (Loftus, 1979; Baker, 1992). Vague feelings of dissatisfaction, powerlessness, inferiority, or shame cannot be taken as symptoms of incest without more concrete information. The inability to recall having been a victim of incest as a child is by no means a sure-fire indicator that one is repressing such a memory. In any case, incest is far from universal, as we see in this chapter. Depending on the study, between 15 and 30 percent of individuals in this society report childhood incest victimization. *Infant*, as opposed to childhood, sexual abuse is *extremely* rare. (I leave it to the reader to decide whether statements about incestuous abuse in one's *past* lives are meaningful!) And in order to do something concrete and meaningful about incest victimization, real changes—for instance, in the relative distribution of power between men and women—have to be made; simply making supposed incest victims feel better about their lives does not attack the root of the problem. According to Tavris:

> Contemporary incest-survivor books encourage women to incorporate the language of victimhood and survival into the sole organizing narrative of their identity. It becomes their major story, and its moral rarely goes farther than 'Join a group and talk about your feelings.' Such stories soothe women temporarily while allowing everyone else to go free. That is why these stories are so popular. If the victim can fix herself, nothing has to change (1993, p. 17).

crepancy, the degree of coercion, and the impact of brother-sister incest (in this study, almost half of the sisters in brother-sister cases never married) led the author to write, "the notion that brother-sister incest is usually a harmless, mutual interaction is seriously wrong" (Russell, 1986, p. 289).

What forms of incest are most common? Who is usually the victim? One study of sexual victimization found that 19 percent of the women and 9 percent of the men surveyed said that they had been sexually victimized as children (Finkelhor, 1979, pp. 53, 58). Of the 151 women in this study who reported an incestuous experience, five were with a father and two with a stepfather; of the 60 men in the study who had had at least one incestuous experience, none was with a mother, father, or stepfather. For the girls, incest with a brother was most common (72 out of 151) and with a male cousin next most common (48). With the boys, incest with a female cousin (33 out of 60) was most common, a sister next (16), and a homosexual relation with a brother close behind (15). In this study, girls were twice as likely to be victimized by an older sexual aggressor as boys. And father-daughter incest made up only 3 percent of all the cases of incest the women had experienced. Brother-sister incest appears to be extremely common; it made up half of all the cases of incest and 94 percent of the cases that took place within the nuclear family (1979, p. 87). Far more cases of father-daughter incest come to the attention of authorities, of course, which indicates that they may be more traumatic for the family than are cases of brother-sister incest. This also indicates that the will of the patriarchal male may be a great deal less unopposed than some militant feminists claim.

Another study of incest, focusing specifically on incestuous abuse, tells a different story. Defining incestuous abuse as an attempted or completed physical act of a sexual nature, perpetrated by a relative five or more years older, that took place before the victim was 18, or an unwanted act initiated by a relative less than five years older, Russell found that *uncles* made up the largest category of abuse perpetrators (25 percent), with fathers next most common (24 percent), of whom slightly less than two-thirds (14 percent) were biological fathers and slightly less than one-third (8 percent) were stepfathers (the rest were adoptive fathers). Next in line were male cousins (16 percent) and brothers (14 percent) (Russell, 1986, p. 217). It is possible that the difference between the Finkelhor and the Russell studies is the delineation of their respective areas of inquiry: Finkelhor was interested in incest, in sexual abuse or victimization, and in the overlap between the two, whereas Russell focused specifically on *abusive* incest. Not all cases of brother-sister incest were abusive (Russell excluded them), whereas all cases of father-daughter incest were abusive. Thus, their tallies of the respective contribution made by each category of relatives are likely to be discrepant.

One dramatic axis of difference here is between fathers and stepfathers. In Russell's study, relative to their numbers, stepfathers were *seven times* more likely to sexually abuse their stepdaughters as biological fathers were to abuse their daughters (17 versus 2 percent). *One-sixth* of all the women in her sample who had stepfathers as a "principal figure" in childhood were sexually abused by them by the age of 14 (Russell, 1986, p. 234). Moreover, they were more likely to have been abused by other relatives as well than was true of the girls who grew up exclusively with their fathers. In addition, of those fathers and stepfathers who did abuse their daughters, stepfathers were over three times as likely to have abused their stepdaughters 20 or more times (41 percent) as biological fathers (12 percent), and only one-third as likely to have done so only once (18 versus 48 percent). So pronounced was this tendency of stepfathers to sexually victimize their stepdaughters that Russell suggests

divorced mothers "be more careful in their evaluation" of potential husbands than many women have been in the past. More generally, she suggests that strengthening the mother-daughter bond will help protect daughters from abuse by male relatives (1986, p. 269).

Russell, who terms father-daughter incest "the supreme betrayal," states the case bluntly: *"Not a single case of father-daughter incest was reported to be positive in its entirety"* (1986, p. 44). In her study, the women who were victims of father-daughter sexual abuse were twice as likely to report being "extremely upset" by the experience as was true of the combined other categories of victims of abusive incest (p. 231); it was the most traumatic form of incestuous abuse. Twice as many such victims report "great long-term effects" than was true of the sample as a whole. Moreover, fathers (mainly stepfathers) were more likely to impose vaginal intercourse on their victims than were all other categories of incest perpetrators, 18 versus 6 percent (p. 231); to have abused their victims a greater number of times (11 or more), 38 versus 12 percent (again, this was mainly stepfathers); and they were far more likely to have used physical force (p. 232). Moreover, fathers and stepfathers were more than a decade older than the combined average ages of all other categories of abusers. And in 86 percent of all father-abuser cases, they were the principal economic providers of the family, which made their power all the more entrenched. In all, an empirical examination of father-daughter incest paints a very grim picture indeed.

The destructiveness of father-daughter incest is revealed by its dynamics. In addition to an authoritarian, domineering father, a combination of factors relating to the wife and mother is causally related here: If the mother is deceased, ill, an alcoholic, or incapacitated in some way, or if she and her daughter are significantly estranged, the likelihood of incest increases significantly (Finkelhor, 1979, pp. 124–127; Herman and Hirschman, 1977; Herman, 1981). This incapacity often results in the daughter stepping in and assuming the mother's household duties and becoming a kind of "surrogate wife." One observer argues that such "distortions of family role" betray the daughter's trust and prevent her movement toward growth, maturity, independence, and autonomy (Janeway, 1981, p. 81). Father-daughter incest is not only generated out of malfunctioning family relations, as well as a sexist, patriarchal culture, but, in addition, this critic observes, it also has devastating consequences for the daughter. Some of the costs of incest include the following.

First, there is the cost of "the experience of exploitation, of seduction by a powerful person to whom affection is owed. Will affection always be tainted, afterward, by the expectation of exploitation, of manipulation, of blackmail?" (p. 81).

The second cost entails entering into a terrible and destructive secret with the father. Even though the vast majority of girls who are forced to endure incest with their fathers find the experience repellent, they are typically intimidated into a pact of secrecy. This creates tension and tends to be destructive of relations among all members of the family.

Third, the girl usually enters into a kind of unholy alliance with the father against the mother, which results in "the sacrifice of female connections to one another in patriarchal loyalties to the male. Incest often culminates in cultivating competition between female generations or between sisters, one of whom sees herself as the loved and favored one" (p. 81).

And fourth, there is the cost of the "establishment of the girl's perception of herself as a sexual being, instead of a complete person who can enjoy and control sex as she wishes, and can also enter into other sorts of relationships as she chooses: nonsexual relationships of friendship with either sex, of shared work, of continuing, cross-generational respect" (p. 81).

In short, it is difficult to see adult-child sexual victimization generally, and father-daughter incest specifically, as anything but a form of violence against the child. In many cases, its impact is even more devastating than actual, overt physical violence, such as frequent beatings (Wyatt, Newcomb, and Riederle, 1993). A significant part of this devastation stems, oddly enough, from feelings of guilt. The girl often—even typically—feels that somehow she *provoked* her father's attention. Even more traumatic than simply being physically assaulted by a complete stranger for no reason at all is passively acquiescing to an act with a powerful and loved figure that is a mockery of love and affection. The girl is made to feel *responsible* for the incest; most victims later report that this was one of its most troubling aspects. A simple act of assault can be externalized; the attacker can be seen as a monster. But an act in which the victim is made to feel responsible—however inaccurate this percep-

tion may be—and in which there is some degree of technical complicity is far more psychologically damaging. The true mark of an oppressive institution can be found in the cooperation the victim extends to his or her oppression.

FORCIBLE RAPE

Considering the gravity of rape as a social problem by almost any conceivable measure, it is surprising how little was written on the subject until the past generation or so. Until the 1960s, the psychoanalytic view of Sigmund Freud that women were masochists who yearned to be raped tended to dominate the subject (Abrahamsen, 1960; Horney, 1935, reprinted 1973). It was not until the 1970s that feminists such as Susan Griffin (1971), Susan Brownmiller (1975), and Diana Russell (1975) turned the field around by arguing that women are systematically victimized by men through the practice of rape. Since these early writings, the feminist perspective has illuminated the subject; it remains the most important approach to the subject, the one against which all others may be measured.

It must be emphasized that rape is discussed in a chapter on violence, not one on sexual behavior; the fact that rape is primarily a violent rather than a sexual act is one of feminism's many insights into the subject. This has become common wisdom in sociology for nearly two decades. Rape is an assault; it employs force, violence, or the threat of violence. This is not to say that sex is not involved in any way whatsoever, after all, there is a difference between beating a woman and sexually assaulting her. If there were no difference, acts of rape would be classified as assault, and rape would not exist as a separate category. To be technical about it, in rape there is genital contact, or an attempt to effect genital contact, while there is no such element in assault itself. Instead of seeing rape as sexual, one observer sees rape as a *pseudosexual* act, one that is motivated more by hostility and the urge to exercise power than by passion (Groth, 1979, p. 2).

However, we must be very clear and precise about exactly *what is meant* by the statement that rape is a violent act. Legally, rape entails the use of force, violence, or the threat of violence. Thus, rape is *always* and *by definition* a violent act. Rape is *never* free of its violent character. Even if one or another party (say, the rapist, or men—or women—who might share the rapist's view on the subject) did not regard a specific rape as violent, what *defines* or *constitutes* it as a rape is that it is *by its very nature* against the victim's will, and therefore violent.

However, as Scully says, the arguments that stress the violent and aggressive character of rape will often "disclaim that sex plays any part in rape at all" (1990, p. 142). The fact that rape is—always, by definition, and by its very nature—violent, does not mean that it cannot be *other* things as well. The "rape isn't about sex—it's about violence" cliché is a bit too simplistic for sociological purposes; it sets up a false dichotomy which assumes that rape is "about" *either* violence *or* sex, it cannot be "about" both. This formulation adopts the essentialistic perspective which, as we saw in Chapter 9, is incapable of illuminating many deviant phenomena. It assumes that there is one and only one way of looking at rape, that there is an inner concrete or objective "essence" contained by rape—violence—that manifests itself to all reasonable and unbiased observers under any and all circumstances. *And that this essence precludes other, very different, essences, such as sex, whose essence is mutual consent; since that act lacks this essence, it cannot by definition be "true" or "real" sex. But as we've already seen so often, the same phenomenon can be seen, defined, or experienced in different ways; what is rape to the woman and to the law *may* be sex to the man. This does not mean that it is any less violent and therefore not rape; what it does mean is that it may be experienced differently by the rapist.

There are at least three different ways that rape can be sex *in addition to* being violence. First, for some men, violence and sex are fused (Bart, 1991); second, for many men, rape is instrumental in gaining sexual access to otherwise unattainable women (Scully, 1990, pp. 142–144); and third, for some men, rape is a sexual adventure (pp. 155–158).

As some feminists have pointed out (Bart, 1991), for some men (Bart might say for *all* men), *violence against women has become sexualized.* That is, to them, there is something erotic and sexually exciting about inflicting violence upon women. To their victims, of course, there is nothing erotic or sexual about the experience. But to these men, however, rape is sexual *because* it is a form of violence, that is, because they are inflicting violence upon a woman. To these men, sex and violence do not exist

in separate worlds; to the contrary, they are fused. There is hardly a more potent condemnation of the sexist and patriarchal values embedded in Western society than the fact that for a substantial proportion of the male population, violence against women is eroticized. Some who repeat the "rape isn't about sex—it's about violence" cliché seem unaware of the fact that for some men, rape *is* sexual and therefore a powerful validation of the feminist perspective.

A second problem with the "rape isn't about sex—it's about violence" formulation is that for many men, rape represents a means of sexual access. Rape is instrumental. It gets the offender what he wants: sexual intercourse with women who are, or a particular woman who is, otherwise unattainable. For these men, sex is the primary motive; they may even imagine that their female victims desired and enjoyed the attack. For these men, rape was not "about" violence because they did not imagine that what they did was particularly violent. "When a woman is unwilling or seems unavailable for sex, men can use rape to seize what is not offered" (Scully, 1990, p. 143). The fact that some men are able to continue believing this in the face of what ought to be contrary evidence—the woman's resistance—once again demonstrates the validity of the feminist position which argues that, in this society women's needs, desires, and motives count for very little.

A third problem with the either-or position, "rape isn't about sex—it's about violence," is demonstrated in the motives of the men for whom rape is "recreation and adventure" (p. 155); for them, "the element of danger" makes rape "all the more exciting" (p. 157). For them, rape is "more exciting" than "a normal sexual encounter" because it involves "forcing a stranger" (p. 158). Said one convicted rapist: "After rape, I always felt like I had just conquered something, like I had just ridden the bull at Gilley's" (p. 158). The primary motive for these men is not violence but adventure; they do not necessarily seek the humiliation of women but the thrill of doing something illegal, out of the ordinary, something that courts "the element of danger" (p. 157).

To repeat: Saying that the motives which drive men—some men—to rape *may* entail elements other than violence against, and humiliation of, their victims but does *not* deny that rape is a violent act. Rape *always* and *by definition* entails force, violence, or the threat of violence; therefore, rape is *always* violent. In addition, rape almost always entails inflicting psychological harm on the victim; at the very least, it is experienced by the victim as humiliating and debasing. In addition, rape often (although not necessarily) physically harms the victim as well. But rapists, as with every other behavioral category, make up a mixed motivational bag, and violence does not represent the primary motive of *all* of them, even though they always engage in a violent act when they rape. Thus, the *act* is always (that is, by definition) violent, though the *motive* need not be (although it often is).

The Federal Bureau of Investigation (FBI, 1995, p. 23) defines rape as the "carnal knowledge of a female forcibly and against her will." The FBI also includes attempted (as contrasted with "completed") rape in its classification. In the latest tally at this writing (1994, published 1995), 87 percent of rapes in the United States reported to the police were classified as "completed" rapes, while the remainder were seen by the police as "attempts or assaults to commit forcible rape." (In many of these cases, a rape attempt was made, but the man did not have an erection sufficient for penetration.) As we might expect, the total number of rapes tallied by the FBI from the police departments all over the country (in 1994, about 102,000) represent only a fraction of those that actually took place. We'll see why so few rapes are reported to the police very shortly.

It is important to note that while rape is defined specifically and concretely by the FBI at this time, as Randall and Rose (1984, p. 49) point out, the definition of rape is dynamic; in the future, it may encompass elements such as: a wider range of coerced sexual acts beyond simply intercourse (such as oral sex); psychological, economic, and vocational, in addition to physical, coercion; an elimination of spousal immunity in all states of the United States; and a broadening of the gender of the attacker and the victim to include female-male, male-male, and female-female rapes. In short, the FBI's definition of rape may be quite different a generation from now.

It should also be pointed out that the FBI follows current ideology and law in excluding *statutory* rapes from its definition of rape. When discussing the subject of forcible rape, I am often asked by students, "Isn't that redundant? Aren't *all* rapes forcible?" The answer is yes and no. The fact is that most instances of statutory rape would not be regarded as forcible by most of us. Originally, the

law assumed that below a certain age (which varies from one jurisdiction to another), a woman—or in this case, a girl—should be considered incompetent to consent to sexual intercourse. Thus, by definition, *any* intercourse with her by an adult constitutes rape. In practice, however, law enforcement treats, and the courts prosecute, perpetrators of statutory and forcible rape in two entirely different ways. The statutory rape category confuses two distinctly different phenomena: the first, rape in legal name only, and the second, essentially no different than forcible rape. If the offender is 18 and the young woman who consents to have intercourse with him is 17, in the strict legal sense of the term, this would be a case of statutory rape in a number of states, but it would not be so regarded by the police, by the courts, by the general public, or even by a majority of feminists. Most of us would feel that this should not be regarded as statutory rape at all. On the other hand, if the female is below a certain age, the question of her consent becomes irrelevant, and all would regard intercourse with her by an adult as rape, indeed, *even if she consents*, as *forcible* rape. For instance, in New York State, intercourse with a girl who is less than 11 years old is first-degree rape and is a Class B felony. Nearly everyone would agree that a 10-year-old girl is not competent to grant sexual consent; consequently, any intercourse with her is *automatically* rape. Again, consent is the issue. Thus there are parallels and differences between statutory and forcible rape.

We should keep in mind that the FBI's definition of rape includes the phrase "against her will." There have been instances of men raping women without using technical force: Either trickery was involved, or the woman, although an adult, was not capable of granting consent. Hence, some acts of intercourse qualify as rape which have been "against her will," even though technically, force was not used. Consensual sex with a mentally retarded or a mentally ill woman will be regarded as rape because she, like the 10-year-old girl, is incompetent to decide to consent to have intercourse. Having sex with a sleeping woman qualifies as rape. The same applies in principle (although rarely in real life) to having intercourse with a woman who is under the influence of alcohol or drugs. Likewise, using certain kinds of deception to have sex may qualify as rape. Men have been convicted of rape after crawling into bed with a woman in the dark, pretending to be her husband. Thus, the determining element here is not force (although by itself, force indicates a lack of consent on the woman's part) but that the intercourse is not desired, that it is *against her will*. Force is simply one among a number of criteria determining whether the sexual contact was desired by the woman or not.

There is one last definitional issue. The law recognizes only rape *by* a man *of* a woman. There are, of course, other kinds of rape. In prison, the rape of men by men is extremely common (Wooden and Parker, 1982). To the law, this would be assault or sodomy—not rape. In addition, in principle, it is possible for a woman to rape a man. (In 1987, for example, New York State amended its statutes to include the rape of a man by a woman.) Most of us, however, correctly recognize the extreme rarity of such acts. Men tend to be larger and stronger than women, as well as better trained in the use of weapons, including their own hands and feet, and are socialized to be more aggressive, even violent. Traditionally, women are more likely to have been taught to be passive in the face of male aggression; thus, rape (at least outside prison) is *almost always* an act of violence perpetrated *by* a man *against* a woman.

Defining Rape by Audiences

Even if we settled the above definitional issues and problems, we would still have a great deal of controversy concerning what is and what is not rape. Two persons could watch a videotape or hear a description of exactly the same act, and one would regard it as an instance of rape and the other wouldn't. Many men are genuinely astonished when they are accused of rape; they assume that what happened was consensual and not a crime. This does not mean that we cannot settle the issue of what rape is legally. In fact, the law is quite specific concerning its definition of rape. What it means is that social, cultural, group, and individual conceptions vary as to just what constitutes rape (Klemmack and Klemmack, 1976; Estrich, 1987; Bourque, 1989). What rape *is thought to be* is partly a matter of definition. Some might argue that introducing the subjective dimension into considerations of rape denies its objective reality and suggests the possibility that if someone thinks an instance of sexual aggression isn't rape, then it isn't "really" rape. Nothing could be further from the truth. In fact, one of the more frightening features

of rape is the discrepancy between its objective reality in the law and subjectivistic judgments and definitions of what it is by different audiences and individuals. According to the objectivistic definition spelled out by the FBI, hundreds of thousands of women and girls are raped each year in the United States. Yet, subjectively, many of them are not *regarded* as victims of rape. What we have here is a striking contradiction between how the law defines rape ("the carnal knowledge of a female forcibly and against her will") and how many people judge concrete cases *that actually qualify as rape* according to the law. As a result, it is absolutely necessary to examine *how rape is seen, defined, and judged by audiences*.

To understand rape and the judgments as to what constitutes rape, it is necessary to recognize that there is a *spectrum* or *continuum* of judgments. At one end, we have judgments that are extremely *exclusive*, that is, they are very narrow, the definition is very strict. Very few acts of sexual aggression by men against women are judged as rape. At the other end, we have judgments that are very *inclusive*, that is, they are extremely generous, very broad, and which include *many* acts as rape.

Perhaps the most extremely exclusive definition would be held by rapists, many of whom believe, in effect, that rape does not exist, that all or nearly all charges of rape are false. One convicted rapist expressed this view when he denied the existence of rape on the grounds that "if a woman don't want to be raped, you are not going to rape her." Rape is when a woman says, said another convicted rapist, "No, you're not going to get it and you're going to have to beat me senseless to where I can't fight you" (Williams and Nielson, 1979, p. 131). An extremely minuscule number of acts of intercourse against a woman's will would qualify as rape by this extremely narrow definition, which sees men as having nearly unlimited sexual access to women, regardless of their resistance, and women as having no rights at all, only the choice between death or being beaten unconscious on the one hand and being assaulted on the other. In one study of convicted, incarcerated rapists (Scully and Marolla, 1984), nearly a third said that they had sex with their victims but denied that it was rape. "As long as the victim survived without major physical injury," these men believed, "a rape had not taken place" (p. 535). One rapist, who pulled a knife on his victim, then hit her "as hard as I would a man" said: "I shouldn't have all this time [length of his prison sentence] for going to bed with a broad" (p. 537).

At the other end of the spectrum, equally as extreme, is the completely *inclusive* definition, held by some radical, militant, lesbian feminist separatists, who believe that *all* intercourse between men and women, however consensual it may appear on the surface, represents an assault, an act of aggression, an invasion, a violation, in a word, rape. Men exercise power over women—*every* man has power over *every* woman—and consequently, no relationship between any man and any woman can be freely chosen by the woman. Consequently, *all* heterosexual sex is coerced, that is, it is not freely chosen by the woman and hence, qualifies as rape. Heterosexual sex is, *by its very nature, tainted* by patriarchy, *saturated* with its sexist essence. In a patriarchal society, women are brainwashed to think that they want male companionship and all that goes with it. In a truly equalitarian society, no woman would want to have sex with any man. (It must be emphasized that most feminists do not endorse this view; it is the expression of a small minority among militant feminists.)

Both the extremely exclusive view, held by some rapists, and the extremely inclusive view, held by some radical feminist separatists, represent small minority views. Very few Americans would agree with them. Between these two extremes, we will find the *moderately exclusive* and the *moderately inclusive* definitions, which together encompass the views of the overwhelming majority of the American populace.

The moderately exclusive definition tends to be held by sexual and sex- and gender-role *traditionalists* and *conservatives*. Persons who hold to the moderately exclusive definition believe that a woman's place is in the home, that she must have a man to protect her from the advances of other men. If she puts herself in a vulnerable position, this view holds, such as going to bars, acting flirtatiously or seductively, going alone to a man's apartment and allowing one in hers, wearing "provocative" clothing, dating a number of men, hitchhiking, or walking on the street alone at night, or even remaining single too long, well, perhaps she is responsible for provoking men's sexually aggressive behavior, maybe she provokes men into forcing intercourse on her. In fact, maybe she wanted it all along, maybe it wasn't force at all. This definition does not see many acts of coercive intercourse as rape because it does not accept the view that women should have the freedom, especially the sexual freedom, that is granted to me. This view is summed up in the saying, "Nice girls don't get raped." In other words, if women don't engage in all these sexually provocative activities, they won't bring on men's sexual attention in the first place. The corollary of this saying is that if a woman is raped, maybe she wasn't so nice after all. It is possible that some version of this definition is held by a majority of the American public. It is possible, in other words, that most Americans hold a moderately exclusive definition of rape. Many, perhaps most, Americans—to a degree and under a number of circumstances—will blame a woman for a sexual attack against her. They restrict their notion of what constitutes rape to a relatively narrow set of acts.

The *moderately inclusive* definition tends to be held by sexual and sex- and gender-role *liberals*. They believe that a woman has the right of sexual determination, the right to choose where she wants to go and with whom she wants to go. Thus, she cannot be blamed for an attack against her. If a woman makes it clear she is not interested in a man's advances, and he persists, then he is forcing himself on her; she is being coerced, the act takes place against her will, and it is a case of rape. Moderate inclusionists feel women should not have to be "protected" by a man to live a life free of assault. She has the same rights as a man to go where and when she wants. And she has the right of control over her own body, choosing with whom to have sex and with whom to not. Men have no right to force her to do anything sexual; if they do, it's rape. Men do not have the right to pin a woman's shoulders down, twist her arm, force her legs open, physically restrain her, jam an elbow into her windpipe, or do *anything* to physically overpower or coerce her, in order to have intercourse with her. If they do, it's rape. The moderately inclusive definition is probably held by a minority, albeit a substantial minority, of the American public.

The absolutely central importance of this continuum becomes clear when we examine their role in subjective judgments of rape made by three crucial audiences: *the general public, the criminal justice system*, including the police, and *victims of rape*.

One study (Klemmack and Klemmack, 1976) distributed questionnaires to and conducted interviews with 208 randomly selected women residing in an Alabama city. The respondents were presented with seven situations and asked to state whether they believed that rape had occurred. Each situation entailed forced intercourse; therefore, legally, each represented a case of rape. Yet, *only 54 percent* of their responses indicated that they believed that rape had occurred. Even in a case in which a woman was accosted in a parking lot, beaten, dragged away, and sexually assaulted, only 92 percent agreed it was rape. (One is tempted to ask, if that isn't a case of rape, *what is?*)

There are at least two sets of factors that influence someone's decision to see acts of sexual aggression by a man against a woman as rape. The first set has to do with the *characteristics of the respondents* who make these judgments. And the second set has to do with the nature of the act, more specifically, the nature of the *relationship* and the *interaction* between the aggressor and the victim.

In this study (Klemmack and Klemmack, 1976), the higher the level of education of the respondent, the greater the tendency to judge that a rape had occurred, that is, the greater the likelihood that the respondent holds an *inclusionist* definition of rape. Respondents who were highly educated were more likely to judge an act of sexual assault or aggression as an instance of rape than less well-educated respondents. Second, women who held paying jobs outside the home were more likely to make this judgment than women who did not work for a living, that is, whose full-time job was being a homemaker. Third, respondents who were tolerant and accepting of sex before marriage also classified more acts of forced intercourse as rape than did the respondents who did not approve of sex before marriage. And last, respondents who held a conservative, conventional, traditional view of women's role were less likely to see rape in these actions. Women who believed that "a woman's place is in the home" also believed that if a woman is assaulted, it might have been her fault, because she shouldn't have been where she was attacked in the first place. Consequently, they often feel the assault against her wasn't really a case of rape. These respondents seem to be saying that a woman has no right to place herself in a vulnerable position. If she does, she brings unwanted sexually aggressive actions on herself. The respondents who did not see these actions as rape—all of them, let's remember, are defined *legally* as rape—refused to see women as free and independent, with rights and privileges to go where they wished and do what they wanted. In contrast, the respondents who

believed that women have the right to sexual, economic, and physical equality, independence, and freedom were far less likely to blame the woman for sexual aggression directed against her by a man; they were significantly more likely to blame the man for his actions; and were much more likely to define such acts as instances of rape.

The second set of factors that influenced a respondent's likelihood of classifying an act as rape is related to the relationship between the victim and her attacker, and the nature of their interaction just prior to the assault. The more intimacy that exists, the lower the likelihood that a given action will be categorized as rape by observers in general, not just those with more traditional views. "If any relationship is known to exist between the victim and the accused, no matter how casual, the proportion of those who consider the event rape drops to less than 50 percent" (Klemmack and Klemmack, 1976, p. 144). This holds especially for a woman who once had a sexual relationship with her attacker. If a former husband or lover attacks a woman and forces her to have intercourse with him, against her will, only a small proportion of observers will regard that as a legitimate instance of rape. It is almost as if these observers are saying that once a woman has granted sexual access to a man willingly, she has no right to refuse him that access in the future. According to a high proportion of observers, an act of sexual aggression or assault by him against her is not a serious matter. In dealing with the issue of rape, the student is forced to grapple with difficult issues such as these.

Judgments made by the criminal justice system—the police, prosecutors, and the courts—reflect the same discrepancy between what rape is legally (or "objectively") and how it is defined by various audiences. Each year in the United States, hundreds of thousands of women are victims of coerced intercourse—they are raped, according to the legal definition—who are not *regarded* as having been raped by the criminal justice system. Sexual violence inflicted against women is tolerated by the criminal justice system under certain circumstances. To understand how this happens, it is necessary to grasp the distinction between two kinds of rape—*simple* and *aggravated* rape. These categories correspond roughly, but not perfectly, with *acquaintance* and *stranger* rape (Estrich, 1987, pp. 4ff.).

Simple rape is forced sexual intercourse in which there is little overt, clear-cut violence (that is, there is no weapon and no beating), there is a single assailant, and he has some prior relationship with the victim. Aggravated rape—to the law, "aggravated" means serious—is defined by overt violence (a weapon and/or a beating), or multiple assailants, or no prior relationship between victim and assailant. The American criminal justice system is schizophrenic about rape. Even though by law there is only one kind of rape, the way that sexual violence is prosecuted—or not prosecuted—makes us realize that in fact there seem to be two kinds of rape: simple and aggravated rape, as spelled out above.

If our definition of rape is limited to aggravated cases, then rape "is a relatively rare event, is reported to the police more than most crimes, and is addressed aggressively by the police." On the other hand, if the cases of simple rape are included, "then rape emerges as a far more common, vastly underreported, and dramatically ignored problem" (Estrich, 1987, p. 10).

Almost no one "has any difficulty recognizing the classic, traditional rape—the stranger with a gun at the throat of his victim forcing intercourse on pain of death—as just that" (Estrich, 1987, p. 13). In such cases, victims usually report the crime to the police, who record it as a crime, and undertake an investigation to discover and apprehend the perpetrator. If the offender is caught and the evidence against him is compelling, he will be indicted and prosecuted. It is likely that he will be convicted. Given our system of plea bargaining, the likelihood is high that he will be convicted on a less serious charge than rape; nonetheless, there is a better than even chance that he will serve jail or prison time for the offense.

On the other hand, when the case is one of simple rape—say, when a man has forced himself on a woman he knows, especially in a dating situation, when he is in her apartment, or she in his, willingly and voluntarily, and when there is no overt violence and no weapon—the criminal justice outcome is almost always different. Women who are victims of such attacks rarely report them to the police. If they do, the police are not likely to pursue the case or sometimes even to officially record it as a rape. Even if by some accident the suspect is arrested, he is very unlikely to be indicted. If he is, the case is unlikely to go to trial. If it does, he is not likely to be convicted. And if he is, he is unlikely to go to jail or prison. In a classic experimental study of juries, Kalven and Zeisel (1966) found that juries were four times as likely to convict in cases of aggravated rape as in cases of simple rape. In New York, 24 percent of the rape complaints in acquaintance cases were designated as "unfounded" by the police, that is, judged to be without merit and not officially recorded, while this was true of only 5 percent of all rape complaints in stranger cases (Chappell and Singer, 1977). A study of decisions made about cases brought to the district attorney's office revealed that only 7 percent of the acquaintance cases led to indictments, while this was true of 33 percent of all stranger cases (Estrich, 1987, pp. 18, 114).

Clearly, a number of factors go into the making of these decisions by the criminal justice system. Nonetheless, acquaintance is one major factor. It influences the determination of whether or not a crime has taken place, indeed, whether or not a woman has been raped. Notice that the criteria used to pursue, or to fail to pursue, a case are completely *extralegal*. That is, *they have nothing to do with the law*. Even though the cases that are brought to the attention of a prosecutor's office nearly always qualify, legally and objectively, as rape, they will be pursued or dismissed on the basis of *subjective* or *cultural* criteria concerning what audiences *regard* to be instances of rape. Again, we see a huge discrepancy between the objective definition of rape and judgments of its reality in specific cases.

The crucial importance of the subjective dimension becomes even clearer when we look at definitions of rape *used by the victims themselves*. Research indicates that the *majority* of women who are victims of forced intercourse *do not see themselves as having been raped!* Any time a man coerces, forces, or threatens violence against a woman in order to have sex with her, it is rape. But most women who are so coerced, forced, or threatened do not define themselves as the victims of rape. One study asked 595 undergraduates at a large Eastern university several questions about rape and forced intercourse. One question read: "Have you ever been forced to have sexual intercourse when you did not want to because some degree of physical force was used (e.g., twisting your arm, holding you down, etc.)?" Sixteen percent of the sample answered this question in the affirmative. But when they were asked, "Have you ever been raped?" only *2 percent* said yes. (In addition, not all of those who said yes to the second question also said yes to the first.) In other words, only about one out of seven of the women (or 15 percent) who said that they had been forced to have intercourse saw themselves as having been raped! For most of them, there was a failure to perceive forced sex *as* rape. "There seems to be a tremendous confusion among these victims regarding their experiences and their legal rights. They were legally raped but they do not understand this behavior to be rape, or they are not willing to define it as such" (Parrot and Allen, 1984, p. 18). Clearly, here again, the patriarchal values of this society excuse the violence and force men use against women as justified and acceptable. So ingrained are these values that they are held, to a degree, even by the very women who have been the victims of that violence or force.

Blaming the Victim

As we saw, many men are genuinely astonished when they are accused of raping a woman with whom they just had sex. These men feel that their behavior constituted an appropriate response to their interactions with the woman. They do not believe that what they did should be regarded as wrong by anyone. They feel they are taking what is rightfully theirs. They feel they have managed to maneuver the woman into a situation in which sexual aggression was inevitable. In one interview study of prison inmates who had been convicted of rape, a majority felt that *all* accusations of rape are false (Williams and Nielson, 1979, p. 131). These men, the authors state, did not recognize a woman's right or need to control her body and her choice of sex partners. Her resistance was not taken seriously, they felt, because she did not have the same rights as a man.

For instance, many men feel a woman who allows herself to be picked up while she is hitchhiking has made herself available for sexual intercourse. The same applies to a woman who accompanies a man to his apartment, or who willingly goes to his: By doing this, they feel that she has automatically consented to have intercourse. Again, they feel that her resistance is irrelevant. If raped, they would say, she "got what was coming." Her resistance, they would maintain, is for display, to convince the man, vainly, they are respectable. Two feminist authors comment on this attitude: "Rape does not apply to a woman who falls outside the limits of respectability; she is just a free lay" (Medea and Thompson, 1974, p. 45). These men do not "see" that an instance of rape has taken place because they do not draw a sharp line between rape and consensual intercourse. To them, the fact that they have managed to have sex with a woman at all is what counts. They have "scored," resistance or no resistance. To them, women are objects to be used in pursuit of their own private sexual gratification. The will and the desire of women are relevant only insofar as they permit these men to manipulate women into situations in which exploitation and abuse are facilitated.

The fact is that *rape grows out of masculine contempt for women.* Many men feel sexual aggression against certain women is justified because these men see women as objects of exploitation. These men do not consider what they do as rape because for them, the mistreatment of women is routine and deeply ingrained. Perhaps more than any other single fact, knowing that rape is interpreted differently by different observers, and differently by men and women, reveals and emphasizes the sexism that is so firmly entrenched in this society.

The majority of rapists, according to a study by the Institute for Sex Research, "may be succinctly described as . . . men who take what they want, whether money, material, or women" (Gebhard et al., 1965, p. 205). Their sex offenses are a byproduct of their general inclination to seek a goal without being particularly concerned with how they obtained it. The notion that a man should be able to grab what he wants, that it is up to the woman to realize this and not put herself in a vulnerable situation, is a fixture in the mind of many members of our society. Even some women believe in this view. Said one rape victim, "I thought women couldn't be raped" (Russell, 1975, p. 19). Their view is, "It can't happen to me—I'm a *good* girl!" This view places the primary burden of responsibility on the woman and excuses the man for his natural, normal passion. This sexist attitude is most decidedly reflected in our male-dominated system of justice. Judges will often refuse to convict a man of rape if they feel there is any complicity on the woman's part, and complicity is defined in extremely broad terms. This bias is referred to as *blaming the victim* (Ryan, 1976).

A substantial volume of the literature on rape has examined the role of the victim. We'll see shortly in the discussion of homicide that in a significant proportion of cases of murder—perhaps as many as a quarter—victim precipitation is deemed to be a determining factor in the dynamics and causality of the act. Some theorists and researchers have suggested that rape, too, might be victim-precipitated (Mendelsohn, 1963). In a study of 646 cases of rape reported to the Philadelphia police, one sociologist claims that about one in five (19 percent) were victim-precipitated (Amir, 1971b, pp. 259–271). This was defined as "those rape situations in which the victim actually, or so it was deemed, agreed to sexual relations but retracted before the actual act or did not react strongly enough when the suggestion was made to the offender" (1971b, p. 266). In a later study of hitch-hiking rapes, the same researcher saw *all* cases of rape that take place while the woman is hitchhiking as victim-precipitated, "in which the victim's behavior contributes to her victimization." This report states, "Subconciously, many of those who hitchhike may be reacting to the thrill gained from deliberately challenging a potentially dangerous situation" (Nelson and Amir, 1975, p. 48).

The notion of the victim's "precipitation" in her own rape has been couched within an ideological framework. Feminists correctly point out that the woman "provoking" a man into raping her is a male-centered notion. Few criminologists would claim that the victim of a robbery "provoked" the robber into committing the crime (Brownmiller, 1975, pp. 383–384). They also rightly argue that the current definitions as to what constitutes victim "precipitation" are overly broad. Brownmiller (1975, p. 355) takes Amir (1971b) to task for adhering to a concept of victim precipitation that is "generous to the rapists." On the other hand, as Amir stresses, rape is not "a wholly and genuinely random affair." Feminists acknowledge this by issuing survival handbooks on "how to avoid entrapment" (Medea and Thompson, 1974) that inform women about "what they must do to protect themselves" (Connell and Wilson, 1974). Consequently, it is possible to discuss factors relating to the woman—who she is, what she does—without making the claim that she "provoked" her own rape. Factors statistically related to rape should not be considered precipitation. Some women stand greater or lesser likelihoods of being raped, just as there are varying statistical chances for different men and women to be robbed. It is an element of some feminist thinking that *any* woman can be raped, that *all* women, in the broad sense of the term, are victims of rape. While it is true that any and all women *could be* raped, statistically speaking, certain women are *far more likely* to be the victims of rape than others, and these likelihoods are a function of factors such as age, race, socioeconomic status, what women do, where they go, and so on. The statement that all women have an *equal* likelihood of being rape victims is empirically false.

Perhaps at this point it is useful to distinguish between *blame* and *cause,* or *causality* (Felson, 1991). Blame implies moral wrong; it stains a particular agent, individual, or group with a kind of stigma, implying that it or they acted in a deviant fashion. In light of this, women are *never* to blame for being raped; *they* did not engage in a moral wrong by becoming victims of sexual assault. Regardless of the rhetoric an offender might use in attempting to deflect blame onto the woman, the man is *always* to blame for the rape, *regardless* of what that woman did prior to the attack. On the other hand, it is possible that the behavior of some rape victims is causally related in certain ways to their victimization. While women have a legal and moral right to the same physical and social mobility as men—to go wherever they want and whenever they wish—it must also be said that being in certain places at certain times may place women in jeopardy with respect to being raped. My guess is that women who frequent bars where large numbers of young males congregate are statistically more likely to be assaulted than those who do not; those who date many men they know only slightly more than those who do not; and so on. While many rapes are completely "out of the blue," so to speak, and take place when an unknown offender attacks a woman, say, in her own home, some are statistically related to actions in which women engage that place them at risk. Once again: The offender is *always* to blame for a sexual assault; the woman is *never* to blame. However, the causal sequence behind some rapes begins with certain actions the woman initiates.

The concept of victim precipitation, however, is an altogether different matter. Victim precipitation implies a certain set of causal dynamics that simply do not exist. In fact, I believe the entire concept of victim precipitation in regard to rape is completely meaningless. It is not that I believe its role has been exaggerated, for instance, that Amir's 19 percent figure is somewhat inflated. It is that I believe the concept of victim-precipitated rape is a worthless, misleading, and sexist notion to begin with. It should be discarded altogether from the sociological lexicon.

Recall what Amir's definition of victim precipitation was with reference to rape: the victim agreed to have intercourse, *or so it seemed to the rapist,* and then changed her mind or did not put up a sufficient show of resistance. This notion is based on a number of ideologically based and highly questionable assumptions. The first is that the woman does not have the right to change her mind about intercourse. Once she has indicated any interest at all, she bears a contractual obligation to complete the act. It further assumes that the man's desires are overwhelming and uncontrollable. Once he has the prospect of a sexual conquest dangled before his eyes—and penis—a mechanism is automatically triggered that makes intercourse—if necessary, by force—inevitable. This too is specious. Most men are highly capable of controlling their lust. Further, by indicating that it is the *man's* definition of the situation that counts and not the woman's, the notion of victim precipitation negates what might seem to be a reasonable source for defining when a rape has taken place: the victim herself. After all, rape is the violation of the life, the body space, and the autonomy of a woman. According to the male-centered notion of precipitation, the woman is responsible for displaying a sufficiently high level of resistance, but *it is the man who defines what that level is.* Thus, the concept of victim precipitation in rape is mired in an unresolvable contradiction.

Rape is one of the very few forms of deviance where the victim is stigmatized almost as much as—and in some cases, even more than—the perpetrator. *She* is often tainted with the stigma of the crime *against her.* A woman who was raped states, "After that, it was all downhill. None of the girls were allowed to have me in their homes, and the boys used to stare at me on the street when I walked to school. I was left with a reputation that followed me throughout high school" (Brownmiller, 1975, p. 364).

Some Myths and Truths

Rape is one of the most difficult of all human activities to study because most of the time it isn't reported, even in cases that qualify objectively. There is a huge gray area of cases where many observers would have differing views as to whether they qualify as rape. As we saw, our society harbors a dominant belief that might be called "schizophrenic" with respect to rape. On the one hand, many believe that "nice girls don't get raped," that

the woman, if she is attacked, must have somehow provoked the attack. On the other hand, another dominant belief is maintained, one that is equally as unrealistic—yet totally contradictory but usually believed by the very same people. This myth states: Rape is a rare, unusual, isolated act, perpetrated by deranged, psychotic men on women who are total strangers to them. Violence, according to this view, is a standard fixture of rapes; murder is a frequent accompaniment. It seems that to view a woman as a rape victim, we have to construct her in our mind as totally innocent and totally victimized by an insane and perverted monster. Actually murder is extremely rare in rape, contributing to a fraction of 1 percent of all rapes. In its Uniform Crime Reports, the FBI tallied only 78 rape-murders for the United States during 1994, down from 152 for 1990. (In contrast, there were over 2,000 murders stemming from a robbery; over 1,200 that were classified as stemming from the "narcotic drug laws," and over 1,100 that were deemed "juvenile gang killings.") Of course, *any* case of murder—or rape—is too many, but as a numerical feature in the rape picture, murder is insignificant.

Knowing that most cases of forced intercourse by men against women are not even regarded as rape *by the victims of such acts themselves* points to the extreme difficulty of estimating how frequently rape takes place in the population. On the one hand, we have some idea of how common the classic or aggravated rapes are from victimization data. On the other hand, the far more numerous cases of "simple" rape are not only unlikely to be reported, victims don't even tell an interviewer about them because they don't regard themselves as having been raped. Numerous researchers (for instance, Johnson, 1980; Koss and Oros, 1982; Russell, 1982a; Russell and Howell, 1983) have attempted to estimate the incidence of rape in the general population, and all admit that it is a difficult, tricky issue.

The image of the lone, mad, rare, and violent stalker of women as the typical rapist is fallacious for a number of reasons. First, rape is a more frequent act than official records indicate. Imagine three circles (see Figure 10.1). The outer circle (Figure 10.1c) represents all cases that would qualify as rape in the legal sense, that is, cases of forced intercourse. We've already seen that an extremely high proportion of cases of forced intercourse are not even regarded as rape by the victims themselves (Parrot and Allen, 1984). Consequently, the outer

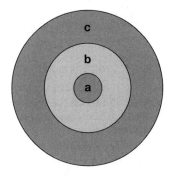

Figure 10.1 Actual Rape versus Judgments of Rape. (c) All cases of actual rape, that is, forced intercourse—which therefore qualify as rape in the legal sense. (b) All cases of forced intercourse which are judged by the woman to have been instances of rape. (a) All cases of forced intercourse which are judged by the woman to have been instances of rape that are reported to the police.

circle is extremely large. A much smaller circle within this larger one represents cases in which the women who had intercourse forced upon them judge that they have, indeed, been raped (Figure 10.1b). The smallest circle (Figure 10.1a) represents those cases where these women not only have been raped, believe that they have, but have also reported the incident to the police.

The FBI tallied a total of 102,096 reported rapes in the United States in 1994. Of these, 87 percent, as we saw, were defined as "rapes by force," while the remainder were rape attempts where no genital penetration technically took place. The rate of reported rape was 41.1 per 100,000 in the population for 1994. Clearly, a more meaningful population base would include only women—or females—and not the entire population. Hence, the rate of rape victimization should be twice as high. Focusing only on cases where the woman judges herself to have been raped, what proportion of the total number of women who were raped in 1994 reported that fact to the police?

The United States Department of Justice sponsors a biannual study of crime victimization; there are roughly 60,000 households included in its sample. These victimization surveys are probably the most accurate, valid, and complete studies of the rates of criminal offenses we have. A report which summarized the findings from the surveys that were conducted between 1987 and 1991 found

that the annual rate of rape victimization for the female population was 1.3 per 1,000 (0.6 for "completed" rapes and 0.7 for "attempted" rapes), or 130 per 100,000 (Bachman, 1994, p. 2). This figure was significantly, but not strikingly, higher than the figure turned up by the FBI's tally of reported rapes for 1994, which was 41 per 100,000 for the population as a whole, and thus, roughly 80 per 100,000 for the female half of the population. In fact, compared with the FBI's total number of 102,000 rapes for 1994, victimization surveys estimate a total of 130,000 per year for 1987–1991. It is entirely likely that a certain proportion of women who were raped will not admit that fact to an interviewer in a victimization survey. Nonetheless, victimization surveys do bring us closer to the actual number and rate of rape than police or FBI figures do.

The rise in officially reported rapes from 17,000 in 1960 to over 100,000 in 1994 (actually, the number declined a bit between the early to the mid-1990s) may or may not represent a rise in the actual incidence of rape. The rise may be due mostly to a greater willingness of women to report rape than was true in the past, which is another way of saying that there is a growing refusal by women to be passive victims of male sexual aggression. Many more women are willing to subject themselves to the potential humiliation that reporting rape often entails. Perhaps women's definition of rape is changing. They may be less willing to accept masculine sexual aggression as routine and normal. This makes rape reporting more common because more male sexual behavior is judged to be rape. The greater the pride and self-confidence that exists among women the greater the likelihood that male sexual aggression against them will be both mentally and officially recorded as rape. The lower this sentiment is, the greater the likelihood that women will walk away from masculine aggression and think, "Was I raped? I'm not sure. Maybe I did provoke it," and the less likely that they will report it to the police. But it's also possible that male sexual aggression itself is increasing; no one can say for sure.

Not only do police figures give us an extremely misleading view of the *extent* of rape, they also present a biased view of the *nature* of the rapes that take place. Although it is difficult to avoid using data on rapes that are known to the police—for this is one of the very few sources of data we have—scattered studies based on interviews or questionnaires yield a very different picture. Pauline Bart (1975) demonstrates that there are systematic differences between the kinds of rapes that are reported to the police and those that are never reported, except to the researcher. She found in her analysis of 1,000 questionnaires which were distributed at women's centers (clearly, not a true cross section of rape victims) that about 70 percent of her rape victims did not report the offense to the police. As important, the 30 percent that made up the cases that were reported were quite different in important respects from the unreported, hidden 70 percent. For one thing, the older the woman, the greater the likelihood that she reported the rape; the younger the woman at the time that the rape occurred, the lower the likelihood that she reported it. In the victimization survey mentioned above (Bachman, 1994, p. 3), the rate of rape victimization peaked in the early twenties (52.1 per 1,000), was second highest in the teenage years (31.1 per 1,000), and next highest in the 25- to 34-year-old category (28.5). It dropped for the middle-age years, 34 to 49 (18.5), dropped again in the 50- to 64-year-old category (7.8), and declined again in the 65 and older age range (3.5). Although some observers wish to argue that a woman of *any* age can be raped (which is true), the fact is that the statistical likelihood of rape victimization is *strongly* correlated with age.

The Bart study also found that rapes that occurred recently, that is, four or fewer years before the survey was conducted, were far more likely to have been reported than those that occurred in the more distant past. This suggests that the increases in recorded rapes that have taken place in the past generation or so are at least partly a function of the greater willingness of victims of rape to report the offense to the police.

The greater her acquaintance with the attacker, the lower the likelihood that she will report a rape incident to the police (Bart, 1975). Stranger rapes are far more likely to be reported to the police than are rapes by friends, relatives, and even acquaintances. This means that rapes known to the police tend to be biased in the direction of, and tend to overstate, stranger rapes.

And last, Bart's study indicates that highly educated women with professional occupations tend to report cases of rape far more often than women who are less well educated and who have non-professional occupations. It is entirely possible that in real life, the incidence of lower- and working-class rape victims is even higher than it appears in official statistics. In any case, the rate of rape victimization, as revealed by the Justice Department's biannual victimization survey, shows an extremely strong relationship to socioeconomic status (Bachman, 1994, p. 3). The lowest income category had a rate of rape victimization that was nearly three times that of the highest income category (42.9 versus 15.1 per 1,000).

It is possible that a stimulus to the change in reporting rape by women in the past generation or so can be attributed to the institution of female-administered rape squads in large cities to whom victims can report their cases. As I said earlier, in the past, many women who have reported the offense to the police have been met with a disbelieving, unfriendly, and at times even contemptuous response, if the circumstances of the case did not fit the proper image. However, police*women*, many rape victims say, tend to be far more sympathetic. The difference is so basic as to extend to whether the police believe the woman's story or not. To be officially recorded as a rape, a case has to be "founded," that is, believed by the police. One study conducted a number of years ago estimated that roughly 50 percent of all rape cases were unfounded, that is, the police did not believe the woman's report that she was, in fact, raped (King, 1968). This has certainly changed in recent years. The FBI's Uniform Crime Reports estimates that 8 percent of reported cases are (or become) "unfounded." And yet, when New York City instituted a special sex crimes analysis unit consisting of policewomen, cases deemed by them to be "false charges," that is, that were "unfounded," dropped to 2 percent, "a figure that corresponds to the rate of false reports for other violent crimes" (Brownmiller, 1975, p. 387). Clearly, women police officers are far more likely to believe the word of another woman, while men are less likely to do so. This phenomenon of "unfounding" cases that come to the attention of the police—that are reported but not recorded—actually lowers the official percentage of rapes that take place between intimates. (Remember, if a rape case is unfounded, this does not mean that it did not occur, only that the police did not regard it as a legitimate instance of rape.) If a woman has had consensual intercourse with a man previously and refuses to do so on a later occasion, the police are likely to look upon her report of it as rape with disfavor and in all likelihood will unfound the case. The greater the degree of intimacy between victim and rapist, the greater the likelihood that the case will be unfounded by the police. In an unpublished study of rape cases in Memphis, Brenda Brown writes: "The closeness of the relationship was a frequently used reason for categorizing cases as unfounded." Knowing their cases are likely to be dismissed out of hand, women who have been raped by an intimate will be far less likely to report their experience to the police. (For an excellent study of how rape is handled by the criminal justice system, see LaFree, 1989.)

Men Who Rape

Different theories of rape pose different questions. Some ask why the activity of rape exists in the first place, why men, as a category, so often rape women, as a category. Others ask about differences among various social units, such as variations from one country to another, or subcultural differences. Still others focus on the characteristics of rapists and ask what causes some men to rape while others do not. Each specific question or type of question asks for a certain kind of information, and excludes other kinds from its attention. Too often, observers argue from a single theory or perspective, pretending that no other is valid, that if theirs is correct, all others must be wrong. Too often, the issue has been framed as if there were one and only one way of addressing rape.

One otherwise remarkable book divides explanations or models of rape into two, "psychopathological" and "feminist/sociocultural" (Scully, 1990, pp. 37–41, 58–59). Scully claims that the "feminist/sociocultural model . . . locates the predisposition for sexual violence in the gender imbalance of power in patricarchical societies" (p. 7). In support of this position, Pauline Bart, in a dust-jacket blurb, claims the book's central thrust takes the focus away from "why some men rape" to to one which asks, "in a society where dominance and subordination are eroticized, why don't all men rape?" One would be led (erroneously) to conclude from this simplistic reasoning that rape is an exclusively sociocultural product and that all men would rape if they had the opportunity. But dominance and subordination are not erotic for all, or possibly most, men, and most men do not rape. By Bart's reasoning, all men *ought to* rape; if this is false, does that demonstrate the falsity of the sociocultural explanation?

There are other ways of conceptualizing theories of rape. To begin with, as a category that contrasts with the "feminist/sociocultural" model, the "psychopathological" theory is far too narrow: It is clear that most rapists are not mentally ill; rapists may have different personalities from nonrapists without being sick or pathological; second, some explanations can account for a subcategory of rapists, while other explanations may account for a different one; and third, there may be other theories or models that help explain the phenomenon. The reasoning behind either-or thinking about rape is that if the psychopathological explanation is wrong, the sociocultural one must be correct. The plain and simple fact is that rape is *not* an exclusively sociocultural phenomenon. No culture is a seamless, unified whole. All members of all cultures are exposed to, and learn, different strands of an elaborate, complex mix of cultural teachings. There is practically no value or norm that is swallowed whole by all members of any society. While the eroticization of dominance and subordination exists in our society, as it does in many others, this is not necessarily a cultural strand that is picked up and adopted by all, or even most, of its male members. One observer takes this view to the logical extreme by asserting in a book on rape: "All men are socialized towards an aggressive masculinity and encouraged to see women as inferior to themselves"; thus, she claims, all men are capable of rape, the only missing element is an "individual man's decision to become a rapist" (Roberts, 1989, p. 28). Such a naive and twisted perspective is likely to encourage very little understanding, although it may provide handy political slogans. A crude cultural determinism makes no more sense than any other form of rigid, simplistic determinism. To say that rapists "have reached the apex of the sexual violence continuum" (Scully, 1990, p. 59) isn't enough. The question is, "Why?"

Contemporary research indicates that different men have different motives for rape; even an individual man's motives may be mixed. Moreover, in specific cases, accidental, situational, and opportunistic factors are often at work which discourage motivated potential rapists from carrying out their attack and encourage those who are only moderately motivated to complete theirs. It is entirely likely that instead of some explanations being right and others wrong, what is more likely is that each explanation may be more valid for some rapists than others. At the same time, certain other theories of rape may be entirely invalid.

Any complete theory of rape must answer five very different sets of questions. Each question refers to a different dimension or factor: the *structural*, the *cultural*, the *subcultural*, the *situational*, and the *individual*. While separating them in real life is problematic, they can be distinguished in principle

The *structural* dimension refers to the broader social structures in which all of us are located. Why does rape vary from one social structure to another? Such a question would lead us to investigate differences in rates of rape among different societies, countries, and historical time periods, different cities, industrial versus agrarian societies, urban versus rural areas, socialist versus capitalist societies, and so on. Does living in a state of society-wide anomie increase the likelihood that men will rape women? Does extreme income inequality, or racism, or social disorganization have an impact on whether men commit sexual violence against women? Does the sex ratio in a society or region influence rape? These and other structural conditions have been posited as possible causes or factors in the rape equation.

Cultural and subcultural dimensions refer to the attitudes, values, and norms that are held by men in some societies, nationalities, categories, or groups within a given society or nation. Independent of the social structure, norms governing acceptable and unacceptable levels of masculine aggression and violence toward women are differentially socialized into the young in different societies and categories. Are Arapesh men socialized into different ways of treating women from men growing up among the Mundugumor? Are Swedish men different from American men in this respect? In the United States, did young men growing up in the 1950s and 1960s learn a different pattern of sexual interacting with women than the generation which grew up in the 1970s and 1980s? Do racial differences exist in respect to rape? Are there differences in regard to rape among men located at different socieconomic levels? Cultural and subcultural differences in beliefs, values, attitudes, and norms relevant to sexual aggression and violence exist, and they are sometimes striking; it is inconceivable that they do not play a role in overt behavior.

The fourth or situational dimension points to the physical or social situations or contexts in which

men and women are located. The "routine activities" perspective on crime emphasizes opportunities. It argues that if there is a convergence of motivated offenders and undefended "suitable targets," the likelihood of criminal behavior is increased (Cohen and Felson, 1979). For instance, robbers and rapists are more likely to victimize individuals who are alone than those who are in the company of others; structures that are unoccupied are more likely to be burglarized than those that are occupied (over 90 percent of all burglaries take place in unoccupied structures); engaging in activities outside the home at night, as opposed to staying at home, increases the likelihood of being victimized by a crime, and so on. The situational dimension predicts that victimization will take place to the extent that motivated offenders encounter contexts or opportunities in which they may obtain that which they value without being effectively resisted or apprehended.

And the fifth dimension might be referred to as the *individual* or personality factor: Even in the same society and within the same social categories, why do some men rape while others do not? Most men do not rape; what distinguishes those who do from those who do not? Do some men, independent of the broader cultural and social values and contexts in which they are located, have certain idiosyncratic experiences in their backgrounds that incline them to sexually assault women? Did they, for example, have difficult or disordered relations with their mothers or fathers? Were they abused as children? Do they have poor self-esteem, a low sense of self-worth? Were they more, or less, likely to have had sisters? Are men who rape more impulsive, less empathetic, more narcissistic, and more domineering than men who do not? Do significant personality differences exist between rapists and nonrapists, and are these differences related to their relative rape "proclivities"?

Countless theories have been advanced to explain rape. Nearly all operate on a single level. Some are individual, some structural, some are social, and a few are situational. The theory that "all men are rapists" clearly cannot explain variation of any kind; the fact that some men rape and some do not, or that rape is more common in some categories or structures than others, cannot be addressed by this approach. The theory that rape is a simple manifestation of sexist values deeply embedded in this society misses the fact that once again, some men rape and most do not. The theory that rape is little more than an action caused by men with a particular personality structure cannot deal with the fact that rates of rape vary enormously from one social structure and social category to another. Different perspectives should be thought of as complementary rather than competing and mutually exclusive.

There are four basic perspectives toward or explanations of rape: the *psychopathological*, the *psychological*, the *cultural*, and the *subcultural*. I find it difficult to take two clearly erroneous theories that have some currency nowadays very seriously: the sociobiological and the radical feminist separatist theories. The sociobiological theory of rape claims that the fittest and most evolutionarily successful males rape women to impregnate them and perpetuate their own genes; or, in contrast, rapists cannot attract and impregnate women within a normative relationship, and so must impregnate them by force to perpetuate their genes. The radical feminist separatist theory argues that men rape because they are men, because they have penises, and because "all men are rapists." (For a discussion of the former, see Ellis, 1989; for a critique of the latter, see Schwendinger and Schwendinger, 1983, pp. 77–88.) As for the "routine activities" perspective, I take it as a given that more opportunities to engage in rape by men who are so motivated increases the likelihood that they will do so. The psychopathology and the psychological theories stress the individual or personality factor or dimension, the cultural and subcultural theories stresses factors of the same name.

The psychopathological theory of rape argues that rapists are "sick," that there is a serious illness or pathology in the personalities of rapists. These are men who experienced disordered family relations as children, who are unable to resolve their hatred and hostility toward their mothers (and fathers) and who, as a consequence, take revenge by brutalizing and humiliating contemporary substitute targets. This approach sees rape as alien to the society in which it takes place. It views rapists as enacting behavior that is contrary to the central values of the culture of which they are a part. They are acting out of the dictates of a relatively rare mental illness which distinguishes them from more typical representatives of their society. (For a moderate and sophisticated version of the psychopathological approach, see Groth, 1979.) It is clear that this perspective cannot explain the actions of *most* rapists. Most rapists are, in fact, depress-

ingly "normal." Most are able to function in the everyday world—attend school, hold down jobs, interact with others in a conventional fashion. As an explanation for the *typical* or *most common* rapist, the psychopathological theory is clearly wrong. At the same time, the more *violent* and *brutal* the rape, the greater the likelihood that personality pathology comes into play; the further away from ordinary male-female courtship in this society a given rape is, the greater the likelihood that it was perpetrated by a man motivated by psychopathological forces.

The psychological theory or perspective toward rape holds that the personalities of rapists are not so much sick as they are *different* from those of men who do not rape. Some observers have leapt from the fact that rapists tend to be "normal" to the conclusion that rapists and nonrapists are not different in any way. This is a completely erroneous conclusion. It is clear that even as cultural, structural, social, and situational factors operate, individual differences can be seen as well. These explanations should not be seen as contradictory.

Neil Malamuth (1981), a psychologist, employed a scale that ran from one (not at all likely) to five (very likely) to inquire as to whether male undergraduates would rape a woman if they knew they would not be caught. Over a third of Malamuth's sample (35 percent) said that there was *some* likelihood—that is, they were categorized as two's through five's—while the remainder of the sample (65 percent) said that there was no likelihood at all that they would rape a woman even if they would not be caught. (The proportion saying that there was at least some likelihood rose to just over 50 percent if the wording of the question was changed from *raping* a woman to forcing her to have intercourse, which, as we've already seen, though legally the same thing, has fewer negative connotations for most people.)

Malamuth was interested in whether it was possible to measure individuals along a scale of rape "proclivity"—that is, the likelihood that they would actually rape a woman—and whether simply asking men would accurately and validly tap into this dimension. (Obviously, men could lie in their answers to such a direct question; thus to the skeptic, we may simply be measuring the tendency to tell the truth rather than the tendency to rape!) What Malamuth found was that the tendency to give a "likely" response to the question is part of a whole cluster of dimensions and measures that indeed reflect the tendency to rape. He compared respondents in his college sample who were one's, on the one hand, and the two's through five's, on the other, with a third group of individuals—convicted rapists. Men who are in prison for the crime of rape have, in all likelihood, actually *engaged* in the behavior that is being *predicted* for the others. If the two's through five's are more similar to the one's in a number of crucial respects, then asking men directly about their likelihood of committing rape will not turn out to be particularly revealing. On the other hand, if the two's through five's are more similar to the convicted rapists, then the chances are high that we have a strong clue as to their respective rape "proclivities."

In all important respects, what Malamuth found was that the college men who said there was some likelihood they would rape a woman (the two's through five's) were significantly more similar to the convicted rapists than they were to the college men who said there was no likelihood (the one's). The two's through five's, *like* the convicted rapists and *unlike* the one's, were more likely to believe in rape myths, that is, that women yearn to be raped, that if a woman was raped, she was "asking for it," that women enjoy being raped, and so on. Second, like the rapists and unlike the one's, they were likely to have said that they personally have used force against women in the past in order to have had intercourse with them, and may do so again in the future. And third, like the rapists and unlike the one's, they were highly likely to be sexually aroused by listening to tapes depicting a woman being raped and hating it. Although it is easy to lie on a questionnaire, "the penis doesn't lie," that is, it is difficult to fake having, or not having, an erection in a study on sexual arousal. Malamuth argues that his findings suggest that the answers men give to a direct question asking about the likelihood of their raping a woman provide a good indicator of their propensity or proclivity to rape in real life (1981, p. 153).

Another researcher, Howard Barbaree (1990; Barbaree and Marshall, 1991), also a psychologist, detected strong differences between the personalities of rapists and nonrapists. Like Malamuth, Barbaree used a "penile plethysmograph," a kind of doughnut-shaped device, to measure blood flow to the penis—and therefore sexual arousal—as the man views or listens to certain scenes. For most men, being exposed to a depiction of an encounter where the man is forcing a woman to have sex,

where the woman is in distress or pain, "dampens the arousal by about 50 percent compared to arousal levels during a scene of consenting lovemaking. . . . Ordinarily violence inhibits sexual arousal in men. . . . A blood flow loss of 50 percent means a man would not be able to penetrate a woman" (Goleman, 1991b, p. C10). And as the men continued to be exposed to the depictions of forced sex in these experiments, the arousal of most of them continued to decline over time. (The findings of this experiment refute the contention of some feminists that all or most men in Western society find the domination and humiliation of women sexually arousing.) However, this was *not* true of convicted rapists. Not only was their blood flow loss far smaller than was true of the nonincarcerated volunteers in the experiment, in roughly 10 percent of the rapists, their arousal levels were actually *greater* for the forced sex scenes than they were for those that entailed consensual sex. While an erect penis is not necessary for attempted rape, it is for completed rape. Clearly, the men who were aroused by these forced-sex depictions were markedly different from those who were not. If the eroticization of domination is a basic value in this society, why do we see these striking differences? It seems reasonable to assume that personality differences help explain them. Once again, a naive cultural determinism fails as a complete explanation of rape. Sexual responsiveness alone is not a *sufficient* indicator of being a rapist; however, such responsiveness is *necessary* for most rapes.

After summarizing the available literature and their own research, a team of psychologists (Malamuth, Heavey, and Linz, 1992), present a powerful and persuasive perspective they refer to as the "interactional model." It argues that for a male to commit an act of sexual aggression against a woman, several factors must converge; rape represents the *confluence* of these factors: (1) sexual arousal at the sexual assault of women; (2) anger or hostility toward women; (3) attitudes supporting violence and aggression toward women; and (4) impersonal, promiscuous sex. These factors "interact" with one another. When presented with an available opportunity, a male who ranks high on a scale of these four dimensions is substantially more likely to rape a woman than the male who ranks low on such a scale.

Once again, men who are sexually aroused at the sight and sound of a woman being assaulted are vastly likelier to find such arousal cues an impetus to act in a similar fashion. And again, though this is far from the only determinant of who is a rapist, in combination with other factors, it acts to facilitate such behavior. Likewise, hostility toward women—while not an infallible clue to men's behavior—serves to remove inhibitions against acting when the victim is clearly suffering. Men vary considerably in their support of force, violence, and aggression against women; certain attitudes play an important role in contributing to neutralizing the prohibitions against injuring or forcing others that most accept as valid. And lastly, some men are attracted to impersonal, promiscuous sex—sex with a substantial number of women with whom they are only superficially acquainted. It is possible that this dimension is itself dependent on prior, more fundamental factors, such as seeing sex primarily in terms of power which, it is theorized, may be more characteristic of sexually promiscuous men. Once again, by itself, this dimension does not determine rape; in conjunction with the others, it serves to facilitate aggressive, coercive, violent sexual behavior.

These four factors may be referred to as *proximate* causes of sexual aggression against women, that is, they stand near, next to, or immediately prior to the physical act of rape; they motivate or disinhibit some men to inflict sexual violence or aggressive actions against women. But what forces or factors encourage these orientations? Malamuth and his collaborators (Malamuth, Heavey, and Linz, 1992) locate a number of earlier, prior, or more *distal* factors: being abused as a child, especially sexually, experiencing poor, conflictual, violence-ridden parent-child interactions, and observing violence between parents stand out as some of the more influential of such factors. Of course, these factors are far from necessary in generating the constellation of dimensions that characterize many rapists. They facilitate, but do not dictate, the process. Children who grow up with such conflictual backgrounds are *far likelier* to be characterized by this constellation, but other factors may contribute to their backgrounds as well. Malamuth et al. also argue that a specific subculture, the delinquent subculture, acts as an intermediary between early conflictual experiences and the later, four-part constellation discussed above. A subculture of delinquent peers may contribute to the development of these attitudes and traits. Youngsters are socialized by the delinquent subculture; it may exaggerate certain incipient atti-

tudes they already have, in miniature, at a fairly young age. "Subcultures and societies that regard qualities such as power, risk-taking, toughness, dominance, aggressiveness, 'honor defending' and competitiveness as 'masculine' may breed individuals hostile to qualities associated with 'femininity.' For these men 'aggressive courtship' and sexual conquest may be a critical component of 'being good at being a man.' Men who have internalized these characteristics are more likely to be controlling and aggressive toward women in sexual and non-sexual situations" (Malamuth, Heavey, and Linz, 1992). Sanday (1990) suggests that college fraternities facilitate much the same socialization process.

It must be emphasized that the individual, psychological, or personality model does *not* contradict the cultural or subcultural model. The two, in fact, should be looked at as complementary. Proponents of the "feminist/sociocultural" model discussed at the beginning of the section on rape often argue that men do not have to neutralize inhibitions against violence toward women, such violence is already a basic value in American society. Stated in this form, the argument is false; mainstream American values do not support, condone, or encourage violence against women to the point of rape. What they do support, in varying degrees, is masculine dominance over women which, *if taken to a logical and behavioral extreme*, can find an outlet in rape. Saying that rape has a cultural component and that sexual assault is an exaggeration of conventional American values and behavior *does not imply* that there is no difference between conventional and deviant sexual aggression, or that "all men are rapists," or that there are no detectable differences between men who rape and those who do not, or that unmodified, mainstream American values directly encourage or stimulate the rape of women by men. Just as violence is a cultural value for some American males, not all men are violent to the point of homicide or even assault. Cultural values are adapted, shaped, transformed, or ignored by each individual living in a society. In American society, clearly, there is a continuum that begins with men at one end who are most sexually aggressive to those at the other end who are the least aggressive. To say that all American men are equally sexually aggressive would be to make a crude, simplistic, and erroneous statement.

In many ways, rape is the polar extreme of a number of American values. Although most of us regard the rapist as a deviant, and rape itself as deviant behavior, in fact, the kinds of violent sexual attacks upon women that are perceived by the law and by members of the society as rape are the end product of much that many of us value in somewhat diluted form. We expect the man to take the initiative and to be somewhat aggressive in matters both sexual and nonsexual. Many of us believe that the woman is indecisive in making up her mind and often needs the assistance of a man to "help" her along. To many men, "no" means "maybe" or "later" or even "yes." Female autonomy and independence are disvalued, frowned upon, discouraged—even punished. Many men (and women as well!) feel women have no right to be in certain places at certain times; their adventurousness, they will say, makes these women deserving of rape. A double standard of morality is encouraged. An inevitable corollary is that there exist "good" women (who are never raped) and "bad" women (who are the legitimate targets of male sexual aggression). A society that discourages women from seeking their own destiny, freedom, and autonomy, from wanting to have some of the mobility and privileges that men enjoy, will be one that will excuse certain forms of rape as justified or provoked by the woman. "The propagandists for male supremacy broadcast that it is women who cause rape by being unchaste or in the wrong place at the wrong time—in essence, by behaving as though they were free" (Griffin, 1971, p. 33). But once again: Mainstream American cultural values do not directly encourage men to rape women; they may (for some men) provide *raw material* which can be used to justify hostile, exploitative attitudes and behavior against women. By themselves, they dictate no specific rape-related behavior.

Are rapists different from the majority of males in the population who do not rape? The available studies (Abel et al., 1978, 1980; Groth, 1979; Malamuth, 1981; Malamuth, Heavey, and Linz, 1992; Barbaree, 1990; Barbaree and Marshall, 1991) demonstrate most emphatically that they are marked off by significant and striking differences. Once again, this should not be taken as a refutation of the "cultural" view that sees rape as the exaggeration of mainstream positively valued attitudes and behavior held and practiced among most men. Rape represents the end point of a continuum of valuing the domination of women, which exists *in a more watered-down version* in the general society. Rape is perhaps the most extreme version of a man's act

of dominating and exploiting a woman. Only a minority of men resort to this extreme; most do it in more subtle and socially approved ways.

Each of these four theories or explanations best accounts for a different category of rape or rapist. The more that rapes depart from what is considered conventional or "normal" male-female courtship, the greater the likelihood that the psychopathological and the psychological perspectives are relevant in explaining them. The more that rapes conform to what is considered conventional or "normal" male-female courtship, the greater the likelihood that the cultural perspective is relevant in explaining them. "Aggravated" rapes are highly likely to be committed by men with personalities that depart from the norm; "sadistic" rapes, as a polar extreme of aggravated rapes, stand a substantial likelihood as having been committed by men with personalities so different from the norm that many psychiatrists and clinical psychologists would classify them as abnormal. On the other hand, "simple" rapes—ones that entail no overt violence, no weapon, a single assailant, and an assault of a woman by a man who is acquainted with her—are far more likely to be explainable by the cultural dimension. Subcultural explanations probably lie somewhere in between psychological and cultural theories. As Sanday (1990) says, an all-male subculture—such as that found in fraternities—may cultivate and socialize values, norms, and behavior that legitimate sexual assaults against women. Some of these assaults may be aggravated assaults in that they often involve multiple assailants. The same may be said of delinquent gangs (Malamuth, Heavey, and Linz, 1992). Some masculine subcultures also socialize their members to be even more aggressive in courtship than the mainstream norms allow. Hence, when such norms are acted out, they can be said to have a subcultural basis.

CRIMINAL HOMICIDE

Most of us have a stereotype of what a typical homicide looks like and what the typical killer looks like. Our dread of the act and the actor is deep-seated and intense. Few activities can generate as much horror in us as taking another person's life. It would seem that homicide is a form of deviance par excellence. It is said that murder is the one universally criminal, universally deviant, universally punished human act; the taboo against murder, many believe, is a true universal.

In fact, matters are not quite so simple. To begin with, it is extremely misleading to refer to murder as a universally tabooed act. The fact is that to refer to a killing as murder *already* classifies it as a deviant act. Calling an act "murder" is a judgment, not a fact. If we were to use the more neutral term, "homicide," we'd see this clearly. The term "homicide" refers broadly to the killing—any killing—of one human being by another. Whether it is an instance of murder, or is seen as something else— an act of heroism, negligence, as excusable, an accident, or whatever—is for audiences and observers to make social and legal judgments about. Homicide and murder are no exception to our rule that in order to be regarded as deviant, audiences or observers have to make a certain *judgment* about a certain form of behavior.

Forms of Homicide

There are two basic forms of homicide, *criminal* and *noncriminal*. And within each of these broad categories there are subtypes. Each legal jurisdiction—each nation, state, or province—has a somewhat different (but hugely overlapping, of course) classification of homicide. And in each individual case, extenuating circumstances render an act a legal instance of one or another category, depending on who did it, to whom, why, when, where, and so on. In other words, a very hard, concrete, basic, and seemingly indisputable fact—taking a human life—is judged very differently, is subjectively evaluated and put into vastly different categories according to how it is seen by observers and audiences surrounding the killer and the victim.

Another matter to keep in mind is the fact that the killer may be convicted by a court on a charge that is quite different from the original act or even the original charge. Instead, convictions are the outcome of various factors that relate to the resources of the criminal justice system. One person may have intentionally caused the death of another (in most jurisdictions, this is murder), but after the case winds its way through the maze of the district attorney's office, and is presented to a grand jury, evaluated by the prosecutor, discussed by the defense attorney, and makes its way to the court, the charge may very well have been reduced to manslaughter, an unintentional, although criminal, act of homicide. In New York State (as well as elsewhere in the United States), roughly eight out of 10 homicide cases result in "plea bargaining," or the exchange of a lighter sentence and charge for a certain conviction.

Two basic forms of noncriminal homicide are *excusable* and *justifiable* homicide. Excusable homicide is an accident. If somebody jumps in front of your car and you run him over, that would be excusable homicide. Justifiable homicide is a killing that results from the dictates of a legal demand, such as a police officer shooting a fleeing felon. *Self-defense* is also a form of noncriminal homicide. Thus, although the death of a human being is an indisputable biological and medical fact, exactly how the killing is perceived and classified is highly variable and subject to endless debate. So one thing we should keep in mind is just *how* homicides are categorized, and *why*. Are the so-called "assisted suicides" of "death doctor" Jack Kevorkian criminal or noncriminal—murder or acts of mercy? This is for the courts to decide. How much force constitutes "reasonable" force necessary for an officer to subdue a suspect? The police kill roughly five times as many suspects as suspects do police officers; these police killings are rarely judged to be criminal in nature. Are they justifiable? Again, here, the courts decide. Is the killing of civilians in warfare by enemy soldiers justifiable or criminally prosecutable? Are the zygote, embryo, and fetus full-fledged human beings and hence, all abortions murder? Or are they unwanted tissue which is expelled from a woman's body? Once again, the question is answered by the law, the criminal justice system, and the courts. But in addition, we all have our own opinions on the matter. And whatever that opinion is, it is the result of a certain *judgment* which is made about the termination of human life. Making a judgment one way or another will transform a given act, in the blink of an eye, from criminal to noncriminal behavior, and vice versa.

How criminal homicide is classified varies somewhat from one jurisdiction to another. In New York State, there are three basic forms of criminal homicide. The first is murder, of which there are, again, three basic varieties. Murder is defined as intentionally causing the death of another, that is, *premeditated* murder, having "malice aforethought"; or killing someone in the course of committing a felony, such as a burglary or a robbery (the so-called "felony murder"); or demonstrating a "depraved indifference for human life," also referred to as "reckless endangerment," by wantonly and recklessly endangering the lives of others, such as plowing a car into a crowd while driving 90 miles an hour. There are two degrees of *manslaughter*. The first is "voluntary," or first-degree, manslaughter, in which a death resulted from an act that reasonably could have been expected to produce it, where one person had the "intent to cause severe injury to another." "Involuntary," or second-degree, manslaughter is where the act is less directly related to the outcome, where there was no intention to cause severe injury to the victim. Perhaps hitting someone over the head with a baseball bat in a fight might be seen as second-degree or "involuntary" manslaughter, while stabbing them with a knife would be deemed first-degree or "voluntary" manslaughter. In addition, there is another charge of criminal homicide termed "criminally negligent homicide." In most cases, this refers to the reckless or negligent operation of a motor vehicle.

A basic question we have to ask here is: *What sorts of killings qualify as criminal?* When does a homicide—simply a killing of one person by another—come to be seen as an instance of murder, manslaughter, or a noncriminal category? When we read that the FBI tallied a bit over 23,000 criminal homicides (which included murder and non-negligent manslaughter) in the United States in 1994, we should ask ourselves: *Which* killings of one human being by another were put into this figure? And which ones were *excluded?* Orthodox Catholics and fundamentalist Christians believe abortion is murder. If all abortions were suddenly classified as murder, the murder rate would sky-rocket (there are between one and one-and-a-half million abortions in the United States each year), not because people began being more violent toward one another, but because the classification scheme that defines murder is changed. An absolute pacifist would see all killings, including those that take place in warfare, as murder. If killings in warfare were classified and recorded as murder, the incidence of murder—and any explanation for why murder occurs—would have to be drastically revised. What about the killing of civilians suspected of subversive activities in Central and South America—should they be classified as murder? The fact is that the vast majority of the killings had the blessing of the government and were never included in the murder figures. What about the million or so Cambodians who were killed in the 1970s by the Pol Pot regime—were they murders?

Why were they never officially recorded as such? The genocides that took place in the 1990s in Rwanda and Burundi—Hutus killing Tutsis, Tutsis killing Hutus: Again, were these criminal or non-criminal acts? Will the willful killings of civilians by the respective military forces in Bosnia ever by prosecuted?

The point should be clear: *The taking of human life is tolerated, even encouraged, under certain circumstances. Some* killings are not seen by certain observers as murder, as criminal, or as deviant. They are permitted, again, even encouraged—indeed, ordered—by governments, leaders, or organizations for a variety of reasons. Human life has never been an absolute value in this or in any society in human history. What is evaluated as murder, as criminal homicide, or as a deviant form of killing is the result of a socially and culturally based judgment.

Some Myths About Murder

There are several clear-cut, sharply etched popular stereotypes of what the typical murder looks like and who the typical murderer is. (From now on, I'll refer to all criminal homicides as "murder" or "homicide" out of convenience.) All phenomena in the world have a certain size and shape in the public imagination. Murder occupies a substantial space and tends to take on a certain form. In the popular mind, there are several images or stereotypes of murder. One would be the murder mystery murder: premeditated, calculated, executed in cold blood, a "whodunnit" murder. The second would be that which occurs as a consequence of a felony, such as a rape, a robbery, or a burglary, where the offender panics, or intentionally kills after getting what he wants. A third stereotype is that of a psychotic killer who goes berserk, slaughtering a dozen innocent people who just happen to be in the vicinity. Perhaps a fourth is the serial killer, who stalks his victims, one by one, and keeps killing until he is caught. A fifth might be a gang-land slaying, the planned execution of a professional criminal who made the wrong move with the wrong party. And last, a variation on the fifth stereotype, is the drug-related killing: the execution, often in public, of someone who has muscled into the territory of, cheated, short-changed, or somehow crossed a drug dealer.

The first thing we should notice about murder is that it occurs far less than do many other causes of death that very rarely impose themselves on our minds. Diseases are, of course, vastly more common as a cause of death than murder; in the United States, there are over 350,000 deaths a year from cardiovascular diseases. Roughly 90,000 deaths a year take place as a result of a variety of accidents, over 40,000 of which are auto fatalities. Roughly 30,000 Americans a year take their own lives. Thus, clearly, the 23,000 criminal homicides which occur annually do not loom nearly so large from a quantitative point of view. However, our "mental map" of murder is far larger and more expansive than the actual incidence of it warrants. It ranks high in subjective importance and emotional impact. It is prominent in the news and in our conversations; it captures our imagination; it ranks high in our concerns. We *fear* it far more than these other sources of death. From a constructionist point of view, it looms much larger on the horizon. The contrast between its *subjective* and *objective* importance should strike us as interesting.

There is another significant point about the "mental map" of murder: Its *nature* or *configuration* is very different from what most of us imagine. Our image of how it happens—its dynamics, who does it and why—is extremely inaccurate. According to the FBI, roughly half the time, murder takes place between intimates; 12 percent of the time, the killer and victim were related, and 35 percent of the time, they were acquainted. (Thirteen percent of the time, it was known that they were strangers, and 40 percent of the time, the relationship between killer and killed was unknown—in all likelihood, most of these were strangers to one another.) The fact that so many killings take place between persons known to one another rules out the mass murder and the felony murder as the *typical* criminal homicide. In addition, murder is nearly always unplanned, which rules out the murder mystery murder, the gangland slaying, and the serial killing as typical. It is true that felony murder, which takes place between strangers, is more common in large cities than in smaller communities, and it is also true that such killings are on the rise. Consider the fact that 10 percent of all murders, 2,072 of them for 1994, take place during a robbery—a sizeable percentage of the murder picture. (This is only two-tenths of 1 percent of all robberies, however.) But nonetheless, the majority of all killings take place between people who are well-known to one another, and are typically spontaneous, arising out of the seeming demands of immediate situations. Another

commonly held myth is that murder frequently, even typically, occurs between persons of different races. The fact is that criminal homicide is overwhelmingly *intra*racial, that is, it tends to take place between people who share racial characteristics.

Let's examine the reality of murder.

Relationships

The FBI tallies and publishes extremely detailed information on murder, more specifically, on the circumstances of the killing and the relationship between killer and victim. The FBI deemed that roughly 4,000 of the 23,000 murders that took place in the United States in 1994 were felony murders; as we've seen, half of these, over 2,000 of all murders, stemmed from robbery alone, just under one murder in 10. Just under 12,000 of these murders, not quite half, were judged to be "other than felony type," and about 6,000 had an "unknown" origin. There were two sniper attacks, 22 killings of children by baby sitters, 111 gangland killings, 1,157 juvenile gang killings, 132 deaths from arson, 53 murders that stemmed from motor vehicle theft, and so on.

Over time, as I said, the felony murder is becoming more common. Still, the FBI determined that half of all killers knew their victims. (Again, in four out of 10 murder cases, their relationship was unknown; chances are that they were strangers to one another.) The significance of this figure can be appreciated by considering the fact that in a population of roughly 265 million, almost all of them are strangers to us; the number of people we know is an extremely tiny number—a few hundred, perhaps a few thousand. Hence, relative to their numbers in the population, people who know one another are vastly more likely to kill one another than strangers are. Clearly, intimacy is closely related to murder. In fact, it can be said that the more intimate we are with someone the greater the likelihood that we will kill, or be killed by, that person. This relationship is one of the most thoroughly documented in the entire social science literature (Goldstein, 1986, pp. 80–82; Daly and Wilson, 1988, pp. 17ff.; Nettler, 1982).

Why are intimates so much more likely to kill one another than strangers? We could probably come up with many elaborate explanations for this strong relationship, as psychoanalysts have over the years—that there is an element of hate in all love, that we are really killing ourselves when we kill a loved one, and so on—but the most fundamental if obvious explanation is that we are *with* family members and other intimates more than strangers. We are also likely to engage in a wide range of activities with intimates—have breakfast, lunch, and dinner with them, talk to them, make purchases with them, drive in cars with them, engage in recreational activities with them—in short, to do all sorts of things with them, including kill them. We just don't *interact* with strangers all that much and, consequently, we don't do too many things with them, including kill them. "Perhaps the most powerful if crude answer," to the question of why we kill and are killed by intimates "is that they are *there*. . . . We are all within easy striking distance of our friends and spouses, for a goodly part of the time" (W.J. Goode, 1973, p. 148).

We should not, however, fall into the trap of thinking that because intimates, especially family members, are substantially more likely to kill us than strangers, based on their numbers in the population, that the home is an extremely unsafe place to be from the standpoint of being murdered. Although a very high proportion of all homicides take place in the home, we also spend a great deal of time there. That does not mean that the home is an unsafe place to be, on a minute-by-minute basis. Three legal scholars make precisely this error when writing about our physical safety, they state: "A person is safer in Central Park at three o'clock in the morning than in his or her bedroom" (Zimring, Mukherjee, and van Winkle, 1983, p. 910). Here, these researchers have confused frequency relative to other forms of homicide with frequency relative to the total amount of time spent with the family. On an hour-by-hour, minute-by-minute basis, being with the family is extremely *safe*, whereas being in Central Park at 3 A.M. is extremely *unsafe*. Far more people are killed driving a car than training elephants, but on an event-by-event basis, training elephants is far more dangerous than getting behind a wheel of a car.

Perhaps as important an explanation of why intimates are highly likely to be involved in homicides is that *intimacy means emotion*. And emotions are volatile and easily ignited. The more intense the emotion, the greater the chances that hostility will be released—*in addition to* love. We "are violent toward our intimates—friends, lovers, spouses—because few others can anger us so much. As they are a main source of our pleasure, they are equally

a main source of frustration and hurt" (W.J. Goode, 1973, pp. 148–149).

Race

An extension of the "intimacy" dynamic between victims and slayers is the fact that, as I mentioned above, murders are overwhelmingly intraracial: Whites tend to kill whites, and Blacks tend to kill Blacks. When a white person is killed, his or her slayer is usually white; when an African-American is killed, his or her slayer is usually African-American. And when a white person kills, he or she usually kills a white person; when an African-American kills, he or she usually kills an African-American. It is true that the interracial factor is stronger in large cities than in smaller towns, and it is also true that interracial killings have been on the rise over time. But even today, and even in the nation's largest cities, intraracial killings are the rule. It makes sense: People who know one another stand a higher likelihood of killing one another than people who are more socially and emotionally distant. People tend to be more intimate with persons of the same race, and more distant from persons of different races. Consequently, persons of the same race also kill one another with greater frequency than persons of different races. People of the same race interact more with one another; they spend more time with one another; they are emotionally more important to one another; they tend to marry one another; and so on.

In the FBI's annual statistics on murder, for 1994, in cases where the killer was apprehended, where there was only one killer and one victim, where the race of both killer and victim was known, just under 50 percent of all murder victims were white, just over 50 percent were Black. (Hispan-

Table 10.1 Race of Victim and Killer (1994)

| | | Killer | |
		Percentage White	Percentage Black	Total
Victim	White	85	14	5,235
	Black	6	94	5,443

Source: Adapted from the Federal Bureau of Investigation, *Crime in the United States, 1994*, p. 17. Includes only white and Black victims and killers, single killers of single victims, and cases that resulted in arrest.

Table 10.2 Race of Victim and Killer (1994)

		Victim		
		Percentage White	Percentage Black	Total
Killer	White	93	7	4,782
	Black	13	87	5,896

Source: FBI, 1995, p. 17. Same qualifications as for Table 10.1.

Table 10.3 Gender of Victim and Killer (1994)

		Killer		
		Percentage Male	Percentage Female	Total
Victim	Male	88	12	8,216
	Female	90	10	2,771

Source: FBI, 1995, p. 17. Includes only single killers of single victims who have been arrested.

ics not of African descent are counted by the FBI as white.) Excluding members of other racial categories, 85 percent of all white victims were killed by a white person, and 94 percent of all Black victims were killed by African-Americans. (The same generalization holds if we focus exclusively on persons of Hispanic ethnicity; in over eight out of 10 murders of a person of Hispanic descent, his or her killer is also Hispanic.) Overwhelmingly, when someone is murdered, he or she is killed by someone of his or her own race. Even when we consider multiple killings, the same generalization applies; almost 90 percent of all the multiple killers of a Black victim are Black, and nearly three-quarters of all the multiple killers of a white victim are white. The intraracial character of murder in all multiracial societies is one of the most abundantly documented of all relationships in the criminology literature.

Sex or Gender

The matter of sex or gender and homicide is much more complicated than it is with race. In 1994, there were just under 11,000 murders in the United States in which the killer was apprehended by the police, there was a single assailant and a single victim, and the sex of both killer and victim was known and recorded. Almost exactly three-quarters of the victims were men, one-quarter were women; just under nine out of 10 of the killers were men (89 percent), just over one out of 10 were women (11 percent). Although persons of the same race tend to both kill and be killed by members of the same race, the same is not true with sex or gender. When a man is killed, he tends to have been killed by a man: Just under nine out of 10 (88 percent) of the slightly more than 8,000 *male* victims were killed by a man. In addition, when a man *kills*, he tends to kill a man: Of the just under 10,000 male killers, three-quarters (74 percent) chose a male victim. However, when women kill or are killed, the situation is drastically different. When a woman *kills*, she usually kills a man, not a woman: Eight out of 10 (78 percent) of the victims of female killers are men. And when a woman *is killed,* she is almost always killed by a man: 90 percent of the 2,771 *female* victims were killed by a man. In other words, male killers loom much larger in the fewer killings in which women are victims, and male victims loom larger in the fewer killings women commit.

Perhaps the main reason why women kill a man when they do kill is that a substantial proportion of them are defending themselves against physical abuse. Battered women kill men rather than women because it is men who are battering them, not women, and murder seems the only avenue of escape from abuse (Browne, 1987; Gillespie, 1989). If a woman kills a man who is beating her, we might make the assumption that this is self-defense, not murder, and that under such circumstances, a jury would acquit her. This assumption falls into what one researcher (Ewing, 1987) has dubbed a "media myth." Among the 100 cases he examined of women who killed their batterers, "nine pleaded guilty to homicide charges, three entered pleas of

Table 10.4 Gender of Victim and Killer (1994)

		Victim		
		Percentage Male	Percentage Female	Total
Killer	Male	74	26	9,741
	Female	78	22	1,246

Source: FBI, 1995, p. 17. Same qualifications as for Table 10.3.

not guilty by reason of insanity, and three had the charges dropped before trial. The remaining 85 women all went to trial claiming self-defense. Sixty-three were convicted of various forms of criminal homicide. Twelve of these women were sentenced to life in prison. The others received sentences ranging from four years probation . . . to 25 years in prison. Seventeen women received prison sentences potentially in excess of ten years" (Ewing, 1987, p. 3).

Why are so many battered women who kill their batterers convicted and imprisoned in spite of the strength of the evidence supporting their abuse? All these women had been beaten not merely once but numerous times, often seriously. All had been subjected to severe psychological abuse and humiliation as well. In a substantial number of these cases (41), these women's husbands threatened to kill them; many of these women had contacted the police repeatedly. However, the problem with a self-defense plea was that in a majority of these cases (about two-thirds), the women did not kill their husbands during an incident of physical abuse but some time *after* one. Only a third killed their batterers while they were attacking them. In at least 18 cases, "the killing took place while the batterer was asleep or nearly asleep" (Ewing, 1987, p. 5). Thus, the majority of women who kill their husbands are nearly always arrested for murder or manslaughter, are usually charged with one of these crimes, and are usually convicted of one of them. Though this practice seems unjust, the killings by these women appear as criminal homicides on official tabulations.

Mann (1996) is not entirely persuaded by the "battered woman syndrome" defense. She argues that the profile of her killers argues against the usual "learned helplessness" orientation. In more than half of her cases, some premeditation existed before the killing; few of them were in any immediate danger; almost all of them could have left their husband or lover without harm to themselves. Nearly half of her sample of killers had a criminal arrest record, including 30 percent who had been arrested for one or more violent crimes. All of these facts, Mann says, "belies a suggestion that they were either helpless or afraid of their victims" (p. 171). However, Mann also states that some evidence points in the opposite direction. Killers of lovers and husbands claimed self-defense three times as often as killers of persons with whom the killers had no domestic relationship, and of the for-mer, over eight out of 10 were deemed "victim precipitated," where the victims initiated the spiral of violence against them. The victims of domestic murders were more likely to have had a prior arrest record, a violent history, and to have been drinking prior to their demise. Actually, says Mann, the criminal justice system recognizes such possible extenuating circumstances, since female killers of men with whom they shared a domestic relationship were less likely to have been charged with murder, less likely to have been convicted of murder, more likely to have received no prison time at all, and of those who did receive prison, more likely to have received a sentence of less than 10 years (p. 172). Thus, it is possible that in spite of the complexity of these cases, increasingly, some measure of clemency is creeping into the criminal justice system when domestic battering is an issue.

Socioeconomic Status

Criminal homicides are not committed equally frequently by members of all social classes. Murder is very strongly related to socioeconomic status or social class. The acts American society and its legal system call murder are far more likely to be committed by the poor and the powerless, the uneducated, the unemployed, and the underemployed. No matter how much we tinker around with the definition of what murder is (with the exception of wars, accidents, abortions, auto fatalities, and so on), even after we have taken account of the inadequacies of officially recorded statistics, and no matter how we define social class, the same ineradicable fact remains: The lower the social class, the higher the likelihood of committing murder. The higher the socioeconomic status the lower the likelihood that someone will commit murder. It is still true that the rich and the powerful start wars, manufacture unsafe products, fail to protect their workers' lives, pollute the environment—all of which, added together, kill more people than ordinary, run-of-the-mill murders. Almost certainly the rich and the powerful are indirectly *responsible* for a larger loss of life than are the poor and the powerless. But after all of these qualifications are registered, we are still left with a far greater rate of ordinary murder at the bottom of the class structure.

One year, *The New York Times* computed a precinct-by-precinct homicide rate for New York City for 1972, along with the median family income for each police precinct (Burnham, 1973a). Of the

37 precincts in the bottom half in terms of family income, two-thirds (68 percent) had a homicide rate of 25 or higher per 100,000 in the population for that year. Of the 34 precincts in the top half in terms of median family income, only 3 (or 9 percent) had a homicide rate this high. The precinct with the sixth lowest family income, Manhattan's 28th precinct in central Harlem, had a homicide rate of 203, New York's highest. The homicide rate of the city's wealthiest precinct, Manhattan's 19th precinct, the so-called "silk stocking" district, ranked fifty-seventh out of 71 precincts—4 per 100,000, one fiftieth as high as that of its highest-ranking precinct. (Killers cross precinct lines fairly infrequently, and when they do, it is residents of poorer precincts who leave their neighborhoods and kill residents of wealthier precincts.) Certainly there is more to the homicide picture than income, but it cannot be doubted that the economic factor is massively evident in killing and being killed at the hands of others. Poor people are likely to be both the *victims* of violent crime and its perpetrators.

It is not sheer poverty or material want, by itself, that influences the frequency with which poor people murder one another, however. The residents of central Harlem are more affluent by far, than, say, the residents of Zaire or Nepal. White southerners (who have a very high rate of criminal homicide) are vastly more affluent than are the citizens of Egypt or the People's Republic of China (both of whose rate of homicide is low). It is probably true that homicide is more common among the least affluent segments within a given society or nation. It is possible that poorer people in much of the world are more likely to be members of or participants in what is referred to as the "subculture of violence" (Wolfgang and Ferracuti, 1967).

The Subculture of Violence

Among some segments of many societies of the world, group norms call for, and even demand, violence in face-to-face situations in which one's honor, manhood, and dignity have been challenged. Often, these situations are interpreted extremely broadly, that is, while most men will let certain incidents pass without a response, others—those who share in the subculture of violence—consider them demanding or calling for a certain kind of reaction. Most of us accept an apology from someone who steps on our foot; some of us do not, consider this an affront to our dignity, and react with a shove or a punch. It would be considered shameful for many men to ignore an insult or seeming insult, to let a demeaning comment go by without what is considered an appropriate response, to allow another man to question one's masculinity, courage, status. This is especially true if one is in the company of others with whom one is close. Certain situations, then, come to be defined as requiring an aggressive and, eventually, a violent response. A male is expected to defend his *machismo*. Not only is a ready resort to violence *not* seen as illicit, a restraint from using violence under these circumstances would be experienced as frustrating, ego-deflating, even degrading. But notice: The subculture of violence theory does not argue that these men positively value violence in and of itself, under any and all conditions. *Most* situations are not regarded as legitimate arenas within which one may aggress against others. Moreover, certain others are not considered legitimate targets of one's aggression. But where it is crucial to establish and maintain an image of masculinity in the eyes of other men, where one's masculinity is felt to be continually under attack, and where aggression and masculinity are closely linked, the quick resort to violent acts will be relatively common. In contrast, where men are most secure in their manhood, and where virility does not have to be demonstrated by physically aggressive acts, violence—and homicide—will be far less common. But where physical confrontation and combat are seen as the key to manhood, much ordinary masculine aggression will escalate into killing.

The subculture of violence thesis requires that *both* parties—the killer and his victim—accept the legitimacy of violence as a demonstration of their manhood for this ethos to have a significant impact on the incidence of homicide. In most violent killings, there is a personal interplay, a true interactional dynamic. It is out of this basic framework that the idea of the *victim-precipitated* homicide emerged. In an early theoretical work, Hans von Hentig (1948) discussed what he referred to as the "duet frame of crime." A later study verified this insight. Piecing together police and coroner's reports, sociologist Marvin Wolfgang (1958) concluded that roughly a quarter of the criminal homicides he investigated could be classified as victim-precipitated. By that he meant those killings "in which the victim is a direct, positive precipitator in the crime. The role of the victim is characterized by his having been the first in the homicide drama to use physical force directed against his subsequent slayer. The victim-precipitated cases are those in which the victim was the first to show and use a deadly weapon, to strike a blow in an altercation—in short, the first to commence the interplay or resort to physical violence" (Wolfgang, 1958, p. 252). The killing escalated from, or began with, actions initiated *by the victim.* As it turns out, it was blind luck, differences in strength, a superior weapon, or skill in using that weapon, which determined who was the slayer and who was the victim.

Here is one indication of this fact: In a very high proportion of criminal homicides, in a number of crucial respects, the killer and his victim look remarkably alike. In one study conducted by the New York City Police Department in 1977, of the 1,622 homicide victims killed in that city in 1976, it was discovered that over half (53 percent) of the *victims* had prior arrest records. This was true of three-quarters (77 percent) of the arrestees. Almost the same number of victims (35) as suspects (40) had been arrested previously for the charge of murder. Almost half of the victims were found with "detectable levels of alcohol, narcotics, or both, in their blood at the time of death." In addition, about four-fifths of the victims (82 percent) were male; 90 percent of the suspected killers were male. In not quite four-fifths of the cases (79 percent) the victim and the arrested suspects were of the same race. More than half of the victims were killed by friends or acquaintances in an argument or dispute (Buder, 1977). But let's keep *blame* and *cause* separate: It would be obscene to *blame* homicide victims for their violent demise at the hands of another. On the other hand, a great deal of evidence suggests that in a substantial proportion (though far from a majority) of all cases of criminal homicide, the behavior of the victim actually *contributed* to his demise.

Often, homicide escalates from an argument, a fight, or an altercation. The line between what is legally classified as "aggravated assault" and homicide is simply whether the victim died or not. Assault and homicide are often the same crime with a different outcome. One criminologist argues that "aggravated assault is really a first cousin of murder" (Reckless, 1973, p. 186). It is the fate of the victim rather than the behavior of the assailant that distinguishes them. Generally, and with only a small exaggeration, homicide is an act of aggravated assault in which the victim died. In fact, one shift that has taken place over the past two generations or so is that many seriously wounded assault victims who *would have* died in the past now live because of improved medical care and the speed with which they are rushed to a hospital. Many of the same acts that were committed in the past now result in a completely different outcome because of a change that has *nothing to do* with the incidents of violent behavior.

In many nations around the world and in some social circles in the United States, matters of family honor rank high among the reasons for generating the homicidal impulse. In rural Sardinia and Sicily, there are some families among whom practically all the adult males have been killed in feuds and vendettas originating decades ago over matters that to outsiders seem trivial—a slap, an insult, a stolen sheep, boundary disputes, a broken promise. It is not uncommon, even today, in the most remote regions of these provinces, for a godfather to give a shotgun as a baptismal gift to a male child. Local custom and the code of honor are rigidly enforced; mainland Italian law is seen as remote, nonbinding, at times even meddlesome. Murders do not occur because the killer acts *in opposition to* the dictates of his community. Exactly the reverse is true: He would be an outcast if he did *not* kill under certain circumstances. Custom *demands* murder when it can cleanse the family name. Sicilian and Sardinian killers tend to have no guilt feelings about their offense, they are not rejected by their families—indeed, they are supported by them—they are "devoid of psychopathologies," and seem to be conventional and "normal" within the confines of their community's definition (Ferracuti, Lazari, and Wolfgang, 1973). Far from being the psychoanalytic monster with a weak superego that some psychiatrists make murderers out to be, if anything, the subcultural killer seems to be *more* powerfully bound by his conscience than any other category of killer. Where the culture or the subculture demand it, the murderer does not suffer from being "abnormal," but from being *super*normal! But let's be sure we understand the limitations of this theory. It does not apply to murder *in general.* It only refers to killings that are called for *in response to* a wrong perceived by the culture or subculture. A Sicilian who murders his mother because he was written out of her will would be *violating* the dictates of his culture, not following them. Again, participants in the subculture of violence consider a violent reponse legitimate *only under very specific circumstances.*

Criminal Homicide: From Medieval Europe to the Present

Several assumptions about criminal homicide have guided generations of criminologists. Two are that murder was far less common in the past than it is today and that it was far less common in rural areas than in cities. The impulse to kill one another, prevailing expert opinion holds, is a product of fairly recent developments: industrialization, urbanization, heterogeneity, social and geographical mobility, anonymity, crowding, alienation, and anomie. Societies in the past, and especially those segments of them which were located in rural sectors, were relatively homogeneous, undifferentiated, simple, stable, slow-moving, cohesive, intimate, compassionate, community-oriented, and familistic—all characteristics that *inhibit* the violent taking of the life of a fellow member of the society.

Recent historical research has called these assumptions into question. At a conference held in Atlanta by the Social Science History Association, several historians presented systematic, detailed findings that independently demonstrated that in a number of different locales, the rate of criminal homicide was extremely high in past centuries, and it is entirely possible that it was higher in rural areas than in cities.

All historians have to contend with the fact that data is much sparcer, more difficult to come by, and far less systematic than comparable currently available information. With respect to homicide, there is no data source even remotely equivalent to the Uniform Crime Reports for earlier centuries. Consequently, scholars must tediously and painstakingly piece together old court records, coroner's reports, and work with complex estimates of the population. Intimidating as the prospect is, a number of historians have taken on the task. The results surprised even them.

At the Atlanta conference, Pieter Spierenberg, a Dutch scholar, presented data which showed that the homicide rate in Amsterdam dropped from 47 per 100,000 in the mid-1400s to between 1 and 1.5 per 100,000 in the early 1800s.

Lawrence Stone estimated that in the 1340s, the annual rate of homicide in Oxford was 110 per 100,000; in London in the early 1400s, it stood at between 36 to 52 per 100,000 in the population. (By way of comparison, it is 25 in New York City, and 9 for the United States as a whole.) Roger Lane calculated that the rate of criminal homicide in Philadelphia fell from 4 per 100,000 in the 1850s to 2.2 in the 1890s.

Why the decline? These scholars suggest several reasons. Disputes in earlier times centered around many of the same issues they do today. "Insults to honor were taken seriously," explains historian Barbara Hannawalt about medieval England, "and violence was the accepted method of settling disputes, since the king's courts were slow, expensive and corrupt." All peasants carried a knife and a quarterstaff, or heavy herding stick. "Given the lack of sanitation at the time, even simple knife wounds could prove deadly." Why would such violent disputes decline in frequency over time? Many scholars suggest the influence of the "civilizing process," a concept proposed by sociologist Norbert Elias, who argued that manners and matters of mutual consideration, as well as the restraining influence of the state, spread from the cities to rural areas over time. In part, in earlier times, the rural areas were simply too distant from the cities for their populace to be restrained either by the norms of this civilizing process or by the social control of the state. Two major forces which brought all areas under the restraining norms of polite society were the factories and the schools. As people began to work in factories, "their behavior was restrained by the foreman and the whistle"; in addition, in the United States in the nineteenth century, public schools acted as "agents of social control," as did comparable institutions, such as Sunday schools and the YMCA. Eventually, through this restraining influence, we learned to control our violent impulses and settle our quarrels verbally rather than physically (Butterfield, 1994).

Here is another qualification: We have to be very careful about how we use the term "subculture." It is legitimate when we compare Sardinia and Sicily with mainland Italy and to a much lesser degree when we compare the American North with the South. In these cases, males learn how, why, and when to be violent in much the same way they learn to drive on the right side of the road or speak their native language. However, when we are discussing class and racial differences within the same nation and region, we run into a somewhat different phenomenon. Our society, for example, disvalues people who work with their hands. Even more strongly, it stigmatizes being poor, being unemployed, being materially insecure. Being at the bottom of the heap is ego-deflating. Even before one has gone about one's daily rounds and interacted with anyone, one's manhood is called into question by being a socially and culturally disvalued human being. Being a member of what is seen as the lower class, by itself, will generate frustration and anger. Often, one will strike out not at the agents that are responsible for one's position in life, but at those who are close at hand. If professors, say, or business executives, were to be unemployed for long periods of time, on the edge of economic disaster with no hope of improvement, the chances are that their feelings of security and competency, and their low likelihood of committing violent acts, might very well dissipate. It is entirely possible that they would see many more occasions as legitimate for the expression of their violence. Engaging in violence is not something they have learned directly; it is not "subcultural" in this sense. Rather, it is a response to their *immediate life circumstances.* And, unlike the commonly accepted understanding of subcultures, which are stable after a certain point in one's life, it is dependent on what one's life is like.

Jack Katz (1988ff.) sees the typical homicide as *righteous slaughter*, a killing that represents an "impassioned attempt" to reclaim positive value in a negative situation. Righteous slaughter is seen by killers as *defending their rights.* They attempt to restore dignity by obliterating the source of their humiliation, in this case, the victim. Through the victim's annihilation, the killer's dignity and respect are restored and redeemed. The humiliation they feel—for a variety of reasons—becomes intolerable; it is an affirmation of their impotence in the face of mockery. "The experience of public degradation carries the fear of bearing the stigma of disgrace eternally" (p. 24). The attacker believes that he or she (usually, as we've seen, a "he") has no option but to strike out and obliterate the source of his or her tormenter. Continuing to live with the pain of humiliation is intolerable; the killing makes it possible to live, to draw the clean breath of life, regardless of the consequences. The feeling of righteousness makes it possible to believe that one has been wronged and engage in an act that involves taking another human being's life and may entail a lengthy prison sentence. "Righteousness is not the product of rage; it is the essential stepping stone from humiliation to rage" (p. 23); "humiliation and rage are both experienced as aggressive powers reaching into the soul" (p. 27). Katz believes that killers who claim "I *had* to do it" are not exagger-

ating; violence is seen by them as defending their rights, as a necessary action that through the death of another, makes it possible for them to continue living.

SUMMARY

Although a great deal of violent behavior is regarded as deviant, much of it is tolerated, condoned, even encouraged. Moreover, as the constructionist perspective would predict, *what violence is* varies from one observer to another. We tend to regard as violence those harmful acts that have a motive of which we disapprove; we are less likely to regard as violence those actions intended to achieve a goal of which we approve. Clearly, violence is partly a matter of definition.

Violence is extremely common in the family; wife battering and incest provide two instances of this principle. If spousal abuse were included in the FBI's figures on assault, its incidence would increase by over 20 times. Patriarchy lies at the core of wife battering. In addition, unemployment, poverty, and stress are closely related. Arrests of wife batterers have not proven to reduce the incidence of this crime significantly. Incest is a form of child abuse; most children experience it as a form of violence against them. Father-daughter incest is especially traumatic and destructive.

Prior to the 1970s, the dominant perspective toward rape argued that women are masochistic and yearn to be raped. More recent research has refuted this contention. Today, rape is likely to be seen as a form of violence rather than a sexual act. At the same time, as a number of feminists have shown, it may be both. That is, rape is by its very nature a violent act, but for some men, violence against women is eroticized.

As with all phenomena, rape has a constructionist side. That is, it is "defined" differently by different audiences. Though the law is clear in defining rape as forced sex, a substantial number of observers do not regard many instances of forced sex *as* rape. There is a spectrum from an inclusionist view (many instances of forced sex are seen as rape) to an exclusionist view (few instances of forced sex are seen as rape). Women with a higher education, who work outside the home, and who hold liberal views of sex and sex-roles tend to have more inclusionist views of rape; less well-educated women, those who are full-time homemakers, and who are more conservative and traditional with respect to sex and sex-roles tend to have a more exclusionist view. In addition, most audiences modify their view that a given instance of forced sex is rape according to the relationship that exists between a woman and her attacker. Many women who have been forced to have intercourse by a man do not regard themselves as having been raped, since the experience did not correspond to a classic or stereotypic model of rape.

Research shows that "aggravated" rape (more than one attacker, overt violence, the use of a weapon, *or* no prior relationship between the victim and her attacker) tends to be prosecuted by the criminal justice system fairly vigorously in comparison with other crimes. In contrast, "simple" rape (one attacker, no overt violence, no weapon, *and* a prior relationship between the victim and her attacker) tends to be prosecuted strikingly less vigorously.

Some observers have argued that because most rapists are psychologically normal (and hence, the psychopathological theory of rape is invalid as an explanation of rape in general), there are no personality differences between rapists and nonrapists. Actually, men differ strikingly from one another in their likelihood of being aroused by depictions of women being raped. There is, in other words, a rape "proclivity" that can be measured experimentally. To account for rape, cultural, subcultural, personality, and situational factors would have to be explored.

The taking of human life is tolerated under certain circumstances and condemned under others; what is regarded as a criminal homicide varies from one time period and place to another. A number of stereotypes and myths circulate about criminal homicide. One is that murder tends to be premeditated; in fact, murder is nearly always spontaneous and spur-of-the-moment. Murder usually takes place among intimates. In fact, the closer one is to someone, the greater the likelihood that he or she will either kill or be killed by that person. In the United States, murder is strongly intraracial; that is, overwhelmingly, whites tend to be killed by whites, and Blacks tend to be killed by Blacks. Men are much more likely to kill than women; in addition, they are also more likely to be the victims of murder than women. Men tend to be killed by men, and women tend also to be killed by men. The fewer killings that women commit are often within the context of being battered by a man and retaliating. Murder is strongly related to socioeconomic status; the majority of murders are committed by lower- and working-class persons. Many sociologists believe that murder grows out of a subculture of violence; responding to aggression with escalating violence is called for under certain circumstances. In a substantial proportion of all cases of criminal homicide, the difference between being the victim or the killer depends on which one was stronger, more ruthless, or had the superior weapon or the skill to use it.

ACCOUNT: ACQUAINTANCE RAPE

This account was contributed by a 21-year-old college student. She describes being raped by her date.

In the middle of one of my classes, someone I had met recently named Ed flew a paper airplane at me asking if I'd like to go to dinner with him. I thought it was a cute gesture, but refused the date after class, since I had to study. Ed asked me out about five times during the next two weeks, but each time I would say no. The older women in the class had been observing his persistence, and one of them finally said to me: "He seems like such a nice boy. Why don't you go out on a date with him? If you don't have a good time, don't go out with him again. No harm done." That Thursday night I agreed to go out with him and gave him my number.

That Saturday night Ed came to pick me up in my dorm room. I was quite excited and even glad I had decided to go out with him. All my roommates and friends loved him. Ed was 6 feet 4 inches tall, muscular, had light brown hair and deep blue eyes, and a great personality. He was very clean-cut and very conservative looking; he looked like Mr. All-American. Boy, would my Mom and Dad have been glad to meet him.

The evening progressed well. We went to dinner at a local restaurant; I was amazed at how easily Ed could converse with me; I seemed to know his whole life story by the end of the evening. After dinner, Ed decided to show me some parts of the area I was unfamiliar with, and we eventually ended up at some lover's lane overlooking the water. After some hugging and kissing, I asked Ed to bring me back to my room. He decided I didn't really want to, and it took a half-hour of persuasion before Ed drove me to my room. It was a typical male-female first-date situation, I thought. I guess I could not blame him for at least trying. Besides, I really liked Ed. He seemed to be everything I would want a boyfriend to be: good looking, intelligent, hard-working, responsible, and witty.

For two weeks after that, he called me every day, and we sat next to one another in class. All my girlfriends loved Ed, and their approval made me like him even more. A vacation came up soon after that; instead of staying home the whole week, I returned to the campus early. I was the only person in my room, and there were only two other students, both guys, staying in my hall.

Saturday afternoon I called Ed and spoke to his mother. She seemed like an extremely pleasant woman. No wonder Ed had such good manners. That night, Ed showed up at my room with a rose and a bottle of wine. We went to the movies and had dinner. When we got back, it was one in the morning, and the hall was dark and quiet. The two guys on my hall were out, but it never occurred to me to be worried. I had come to like Ed and I trusted him as much as any other friend of mine.

We took our shoes off and watched television for a while; Ed asked if I'd like to smoke some pot. I rarely ever did, but we were having a good time, I was mellow, so I figured, why not? We shared a joint, and then Ed smoked another whole joint himself. I wasn't affected by it at all, but he said that he felt pretty good. We sat on the bed and continued to watch television. We hugged and kissed, and I felt really comfortable in Ed's arms; I was happy with the thought that I had found someone who could make me feel so secure. Then, when Ed started to unbutton my shirt, I became annoyed and asked him to please stop. He seemed perplexed and could not understand why I was stopping him. I didn't feel I had done anything to lead him on. It isn't as if I had never been intimate with a man before. I didn't consider myself a tease. In fact, I was very reserved with Ed because I knew he would jump at the first positive indication I gave him. He began a discussion on making love with someone you care about—even if it was only the first date. I told him I didn't care if I went out with someone for six months. If I wasn't ready, I would not sleep with him. Then Ed said he had heard stories to the effect that all resident students who lived in dorms "slept around." (Ed was a commuter.) When I told him I was not one of "those" females, he seemed amazed and even upset. I think he took the rejection personally. The situation probably seemed perfect for him: alone after a date with a girl who liked him, whom he also liked.

I went to the bathroom. When I came back, Ed was lying on the bed; he apologized, and then started to undo my blouse again, this time with more force. I couldn't believe what was happening; before I knew it, I was lying on my bed with him with no clothes on. I begged him to leave me alone and began crying. He refused to stop kissing and caressing me. I tried to push him away, but it was impossible—he weighed well over 200 pounds. At this point he was oblivious to anything I did or said; he was in his own world. I knew even if I screamed, no one would hear me. I was afraid if I struggled, he would beat me up. Finally, I relaxed and just let him do what he wanted, begging him to please be careful—I did not want to get pregnant.

When it was over, I became hysterical. All I could think of was that I had become pregnant on top of this nightmare. I was uncontrollably hysterical, and he *still* could not understand why. He had the nerve to ask me if it felt good and told me he would call the next day. He wanted to stay, but I threw him out. After he left, I was physically ill. I threw up twice and couldn't get to sleep at all that night. I wanted to talk to someone, but there wasn't anybody. What could I do—call my mother at 3 A.M. and say, "Mom, I was just raped"? What could she do anyway? What could anyone do? I was not going to subject myself to being interrogated by police officers. I didn't have bruises on my body. No one would believe that Ed could hurt anyone. I felt alone and devastated. I had never felt this way before in my life.

The next day Ed sent me a dozen red long-stemmed roses so I would forgive him for upsetting me so much the night before. I couldn't believe it. I almost threw the flowers at the woman who delivered them, but instead, I put them on my desk and cried on them. It was now Sunday, and every one was returning from the vacation. My roommate saw the roses, put them in water, and paraded them around. All I heard for the rest of the night was how wonderful Ed was and how lucky I was. One of my suitemates said, "Don't let him go, he's such a good catch." I told her she shouldn't be so sure—he wasn't all he was cracked up to be. They thought I was just being fickle. It twisted my insides that they were telling me how wonderful Ed was when I knew what he had done.

When my best friend returned to school and saw me, she immediately knew there was something wrong. One night, a few days later, I poured the whole story out to her. She was very concerned, and it made me feel good to be able to tell someone about the incident. We sat together and both cried. If it had not been for her, I probably never would have told her, because I knew she wouldn't look down on me because of what happened. She agreed with me that the best thing to do was nothing.

The thought of Ed terrified me. He called a few times, and I told him to leave me alone. I stopped going to the class we were in. The next time I went to that class was at the final, and we were scheduled to take it in different rooms. I had no desire to see him or any other guy—ever. To this day, I am wary of any guy I become involved with. I don't even want to be alone in a room with a guy. I don't trust people as much as I used to. It saddens me that I have become this way, but I have to protect myself.

I often have nightmares about that night. I think the fact that I was two years older than he was had something to do with what happened; I think he imagined I was very worldly and sophisticated. He knew I went out with a boyfriend for two years before then, and someone else for three years before him, and he just assumed I would want or need to sleep with him. Sometimes I think he wanted to show me his masculinity. (Just the day before, I had teased him about the gay guys he worked with.) Whatever his reason, I will never understand him, nor will I forgive him. He has slashed a deep scar in my mind that will never heal. No one has ever made me feel so dirty, cheap, humiliated, or suicidal.

I did not report Ed for several reasons. I have heard about the many rapes that take place on the campus, and how nothing ever gets done about them. I did not want this to be publicized if nothing could come of it anyway. I also felt no one would believe me. Ed maintained a good impression. Chances are, people would assume it was just another case of a girl with a crush on him who changed her mind after things got rough. I was also angry with myself for getting into a situation like that. If I had reported it, the police—and just about everyone else, too—would want to know why I had let him in my room in the first place. I really never imagined such a thing could ever happen to me. The thought never entered my mind not to trust Ed. Imagine—I felt safer with him in my room than alone, in that empty dormitory. In spite of my anger and grief, I was still afraid of getting Ed in trouble. How could I even think of protecting someone who hurt me so badly? The fact that I might have been responsible for his imprisonment actually scared me. There are many things about what happened that I will never fully understand. (From the author's files.)

ACCOUNT: STRANGER RAPE

This account was contributed by a woman in her early thirties; she is married and is raising a young son. She manages a small dress store. This account is quite a bit more violent and gruesome than the previous one. However, both involve force and, therefore, violence; both are instances of rape.

I was half-walking, half-jogging down a road lined with a few houses and wooded lots. My car was parked at the side of the road near the intersection of this road and a main street where a few small stores, a post office, and a bar were located. It was dusk. I was very deep in my own thoughts as I made my way down the road. Passing one of the wooded lots, I realized someone was near me in the woods. I immediately sensed danger, and turned back and began running toward my car. As I ran I could hear twigs and branches break in the woods. In a panic, running, I let out a scream. A few feet ahead of me, a huge man, at least 6 feet 5 inches tall, came crashing out of the woods, laughing crazily, and panting. I stopped and began running in the opposite direction, toward a house. I ran smack into another man who had also been hiding in the woods. He wasn't as big as the first man, but he also towered over me. Before I had time to react, the bigger man grabbed me from behind, locking my arms in a bear hug. He held me so hard I thought my ribs would break.

I was lifted and forced back into the woods, thrown on the ground, and punched twice in the face. I kicked at the men and tried to crawl away, but the smaller of the two men jumped on top of me, grabbed my hair in both hands, and slammed my head on the ground several times. I screamed, "All right! All right!" and he stopped. I looked at my attacker and cried out, "Oh, please, God, help me." The one holding me laughed at me and whispered, "Sweet thing, God isn't on this road, not for you, not tonight." I begged him, "Just don't hurt me, please don't hurt me." He slapped me hard across my face with the back of his hand and screamed at me, "Shut up, you filthy cunt!"

He reached down and ripped my blouse and bra right off my body, throwing them at the bigger one who stood watching. He then put his hands around my neck and ordered the big one to pin me down. The big one knelt near my head and wrapped my bra around my neck, just to the point of strangulation. The smaller one ripped my pants off, and then raped me as the other one held the bra tight around my neck. It only lasted a minute or two. After he withdrew, he bit my breasts as hard as he could, drawing blood. I screamed out from the pain and was ordered to keep quiet. The face of the man who bit me was covered with blood.

The big man then asked the other one to hold me; he undid his pants. The smaller one pulled my arms over my head and stood on my hands. If I moved, he would crush my hands under his boots. I was then raped a second time. Then the smaller one yelled, "Let's cut off her tits!" He laughed like a sadistic child who had just thought up a new game to play. The big one replied, "Well, that's a good idea, Bub. Why don't you go back to the truck and get that big Bowie knife." The smaller one got off my hands and ran through the woods to get the knife. "Please, please," I begged the bigger man. He got off me and pulled me to my feet. "Listen, woman," he said, "if you want to see the morning sun, you better run like hell, cuz if Bub comes back with that knife, he's gonna chop you up so your own momma won't know you. Now get on, girl—get on!"

I ran through the woods, back to my car as fast as I have ever run in my life. I locked my doors and drove to the first gas station I could find. The attendant called the police, and they took me to the hospital. I was tested for smears and treated for my wounds. The police were actually very compassionate and understanding. I wasn't the first victim of these two sick men. The police felt frustrated at their inability to find them. For me, it was over. I just wanted to go home and be left alone to lick my wounds. (From the author's files.)

Below, I present two accounts of "victim-precipitated" acts of violence. The first, submitted by a high-school teacher in his late twenties, entailed a one-punch fight in which the initial attacker was on the receiving end of the assault. The second, submitted by a college student in his early twenties, entailed an exchange of hurled beer bottles. In both cases, the violence was an interactional affair. Fortunately, neither episode escalated into serious damage to any of the participants. However, for every homicide that actually takes place, there are literally thousands of exchanges such as these. As to whether such violent or potentially violent interactions escalate into an instance of homicide is often a matter of luck, the presence or absence of onlookers, the ability or inability of one party to escape, or the possession—or lack of it—of a lethal weapon.

ACCOUNT: THE PUNCH

This happened on the streets of New York a couple years ago. I was walking along Bleecker Street in Greenwich Village on a Saturday night with a woman companion. Just about the point at which Bleecker intersects with MacDougal, a youth, maybe 16 years old, stepped out from between two parked cars and blocked our path on the sidewalk. He was taller than I am, maybe close to six feet, but slim—I don't think he weighed 150 pounds. He was visibly drunk. I tried to step around him, but he stepped into my way, shoving me backwards. This happened several times. "Whaddya tryin ta do?" he slurred to me. I calmly explained that I didn't want to get into any trouble, I just wanted to mind my own business and be on my way. His response was to shove me again, again, and again. Each time I tried to step out of his way, and each time he stepped in front of me again, and shoved me backwards. By about the fifth or sixth shove, something in me snapped. By nature, I am a nonviolent man, but every man has a point at which he retaliates, and I finally reached mine. I slipped my arm behind his neck (his reflexes were slowed down by his state of intoxication), forced him to the sidewalk, and shoved his face against it, hard. "Okay" was all he could say, "okay." But like I said, I had set the process of retaliation in motion, and I wasn't able to call a halt to it at that point. I smashed him once in the face, and then straightened up, and began kicking him in his back. "Goddamn punk!" I screamed. "Stop shoving people around!" My companion was by now extremely distraught and rested a hand on my arm, which pulled me out of my rage and back into reality. I left the lad on the sidewalk—he didn't seem to be that badly hurt—and, with my friend, began trotting up Mac-Dougal Street.

What happened was, the kid immediately ran and found a cop—in fact, *three* cops—on the street, and confronted me with them. One cop held each of his arms, and the third one was standing next to them. The two cops were restraining him as he ranted and struggled. There was blood pouring out of his nose, covering the bottom half of his face—which surprised me, because I didn't hit him all that hard. He began flinging his entire body into the air, aiming kicks at my head, with the cops holding his arms; his feet would stop a few inches from my face with each kick. "Nigger lover!" he screamed, "dirty hippie! You bastard—I'll *kill* ya!" he kept screaming. I just stood there, wondering what was going to happen next. The cops who held him took him off somewhere, and the third said to me, "Wait here—we'll be right back." I was left standing on the sidewalk with a crowd gathering around me—the lad's friends, I later found out, mostly teenage youths, several of whom began to grumble at me threatening things that they were going to do with me when they got their hands on me.

My body was so adrenalized that it was almost as if I was *watching* the whole thing, as if it wasn't really happening to me. I even had a wide grin on my face—the irony of me being attacked, and then getting into trouble for retaliating, seemed highly amusing to me at that moment. One kid, maybe 14 or 15 years old, smaller than I am, said something like, "Whaddya think it's *funny* or something?" Once again, I did something stupid. I said, "That's mighty brave of you, kid, saying that, with 15 of your friends standing right behind you." So *another* kid, this one about the same size and age of the one I punched, standing behind the smaller one, yelled, "I'll fight ya myself, just you and me, come on!" He shoved the smaller one out of the way, pushing his way through the crowd, and prepared to deal with me. Here we go again, I thought, and I slipped out of the crowd and, hand in hand with my companion, began trotting up MacDougal Street again, this time being followed by 15 or 20 adolescent boys lusting for my blood. We were going to a concert right up the street, and I got into the lobby of the theater. The kids, naturally, made a row pushing and shoving into the front door. I handed my tickets to the usher, who said, "Take your friends and get out of here!" I said, "My *friends?* They're trying to *kill* me. I *paid* to see this concert!" He slammed the door in my face.

The tall kid hit me on top of my head, a crude, glancing blow, which I didn't even feel, knocking my glasses to the floor. I got on my hands and knees trying to find my glasses, and at that second a cop came into the lobby and escorted the kid away. I recall someone yelling, "They've got the kid in custody. Wait here—the cops want to talk to you." I thought to myself, wait a minute, didn't I come in here? Didn't we just go through this whole thing a minute ago? No way I was going to talk to any cops at that point. Should I hang around, attract another crowd, and get into another fight? So once again, I grabbed my companion's hand, slipped through the Saturday night crowd, crossed Sixth Avenue, and went home to my apartment. (From the author's files.)

ACCOUNT: THROWING BEER BOTTLES

It was June, and I was heading for a graduation party in the next town. I was driving in the right lane when I noticed a car behind me catching up very fast. Out of a whim to slow the speeding car down, I increased my own speed until I was parallel to a slower car in the left-hand lane. For a few minutes I drove in this fashion, not letting the car behind me pass, slowing him down. Then I increased my speed so the car could pass the slower one. As the car sped by me, I noticed it was a station wagon with about six teenagers in it.

All of a sudden, I heard a "thump" and a "crash." I looked across to the station wagon to see the teenagers throwing empty beer bottles at my car. One bottle hit the car while two others smashed on the road in front of the car, showering glass fragments all over the windshield. I swerved the car left and right, dodging the broken glass for fear of getting a blowout. Meanwhile, the station wagon, with its laughing occupants, sped down the road.

When I brought my car under control, I was furious. Those bottles could have caused me to have a serious accident. I knew I could not let them get away with what they did. I felt a need for vengeance. I passed the exit I should have taken and pursued them. It was only when I pulled up alongside the station wagon that I realized that I couldn't do anything: there were six of them against me. I would have just given up my desire for revenge, but the smirking faces of those six teenagers was more than I could bear. I had to get my revenge.

It was at this point that I realized I had a six-pack of beer with me that I had brought for the party. I knew then what I had to do. It was not like me to waste good beer but that didn't stop me from taking a bottle out of the six-pack and throwing it at the station wagon. It smashed against the side of their car, and I turned onto an exit that forked to the right. Somehow, the station wagon cut over and managed to make the exit, too, and started heading after me. This began a cat-and-mouse chase down the road.

Where once there was total anger, now there was total fear. I felt cornered, with only the thought of escape. I stepped on the gas and drove like a madman, 80 mph down a road I had never been on before. If I couldn't pass a car on the left, I passed it on the right shoulder of the road. Suddenly, I came to a traffic light and signaled to turn right. A van was sitting in the right lane so I was forced to cut through a gas station on the corner. At my next turn, I noticed the station wagon was only a block behind me. An idea hit me to turn off my lights to prevent the occupants of the station wagon from seeing me, since the streets were very dark. The trick worked, and the station wagon missed the street I was on. I turned around and backtracked my way out of town. I was still very shaken and kept looking over my shoulder, thinking that at any second the station wagon would reappear.

When I finally arrived at the party and told my friends about what happened, they were amazed, because they knew me to be a very passive guy. I could hardly believe the story myself, because it was something I wouldn't normally do. I was surprised that my emotions would force me to take on such a risk that would endanger myself and others as well. For the first time in my life, I became aware of hostile emotions I had that I thought were totally alien to me. (From the author's files.)

ACCOUNT: A STABBING

Q: OK, I know this happened a long time ago [23 years ago]. And it's a very painful memory.

A: Yeah, I know, it's a very painful memory.

Q: But I really appreciate your opening up to me. Well, I think this should enlighten some people. . . . Maybe you can re-create what happened, right from the beginning. . . .

A: Briefly, I skipped school, I went down to Greenwich Village. Somebody offered to sell me a nickel bag of grass [five dollars' worth of marijuana].

Q: Now wait. You were on the street.

A: Yeah.

Q: You were walking on the sidewalk, presumably.

A: Yeah.

Q: And somebody, like, just walked up to you?

A: Pretty much. Standing in a doorway. Wanted to know if I wanted to buy a nickel bag of grass. Spanish, I think the guy was Spanish. . . . And [he said], come over here, I'll sell it to you.

Q: How old were you at the time?

A: Seventeen.

Q: And your recollection of how old the gentleman was?

A: In his twenties. [Long pause.] All of a sudden I really don't feel like doing this, but I said I would.

Q: I'm sorry.

A: Yeah. [Long pause.]

Q: He said—he took you someplace or what?

A: We stepped into a doorway of some building.

Q: And you said—what?

A: I got five dollars, there was five dollars' worth of grass, I wanted to smoke it before I went home that day. We went behind the stairs in this building. And he pulled a knife. He asked for all my money and I gave him all the paper money I had. [Long pause.] He made sexual advances. God! I don't want to talk about this!

Q: OK. I'm sorry. [The tape recorder is turned off, then turned back on.]

A. He grabbed me.

Q: OK.

A: And he had a knife. And he stuck it into me, but not far enough to actually cut me. He grabbed me and started molesting me. Rubbed his hands around the front of my trousers. Dropped the knife.

Q: He dropped the knife?

A: Yeah. I said, I gave you my money, what do you want? Leave me alone! He didn't say anything more. . . . I remember what kind of knife it was. AK-55, a German knife with a locking blade. . . . And a great saxophone player named King Curtis had just been killed by some junkies in Lennox Terrace in Harlem. And I tried to get away from him, and he was holding onto me. And the knife was on the floor, I picked it up and stuck it in him.

Q: How many times?

A: Just the once. We had been studying anatomy in school. And I remember that if I held the knife sideways, it would pass between the ribs, and if I stuck it *in* and *up*, it would probably puncture the pericardium and it would kill him.

Q: So you were actually *conscious* of how you stabbed him?

A: Yeah. I remember that. I remember that I wanted to kill him.

Q: And so you stuck the knife in his chest. And then what happened?

A: He coughed. There wasn't much blood. There was a little bit on his jacket and a little bit on mine. It was cold. April, I think it was. I had just been accepted to college. And [at school] they weren't being too particular about us skipping out of school. . . . I took the knife out of him and threw it away.

Q: Where?

A: The East River. Walked all the way across to the East River and threw it in the East River.

Q: So you left him there, slumped on the floor?

A: Yeah. Underneath the stairwell. Behind the stairs, by the garbage cans.

Q: How did you know he wasn't just injured?

A: [Long pause.] I guess I didn't at the time.

Q: What were you feeling afterward?

A: It's funny, because the feelings afterward are much more clear because the whole thing itself, as they always say, happened so fast. . . . The feelings afterward were, I was scared, I took off, I got home, there was nobody home, I changed. . . .

Q: Now wait. You ran to the East River.

A: I walked to the East River.

Q: You walked to the East River.

A: I ran to the corner and walked the rest of the way. Threw the knife as far out into the river as I could.

Q: Where did this take place?

A: [Tells me the location.]

Q: That's all the way on the *West* side.

A: Yeah. I walked all the way over to the East side.

Q: Wow. OK.

A: I got home. There was some blood on some parts of me. I changed every piece of clothing that I had and took all the clothes that I was wearing and threw them away in different garbage cans [in the neighborhood where he lived].

Q: Hmm. How did you feel afterwards?

A: I felt scared. And I felt, you know, wired up. And frightened. I thought I was going to get caught by the police. . . . But actually, that faded kind of quickly after a few days. I got the impression that the cops weren't too concerned about having a scumbag like this taken off the street. After a while, I felt no different from the way somebody would feel about shooting a dog that had attacked your daughter or something like that.

Q: Anything else?

A: My guess is, probably a lot of male ego was involved. It's probably the sort of thing where a certain amount of homophobia is involved. And you know, I hadn't had sex with a girl yet by this point. . . . At the time, it bothered me. . . .

Q: It bothered you in what sense?

A: You know, take your hands off me, leave me alone! It was a creepy feeling. [Long pause.]

Q: It's still hard for you to talk about it.

A: Yeah. The sort of thing you bury.

Q: OK. You want me to stop it?

A: Yeah.

chapter 11

PROPERTY CRIME

Two major types of crimes are *violent crime*, also known as crimes against the person, and *property crime*. We've looked at violent crime, but in the United States (as in most places), property crimes are eight to 10 times as common as violent crimes. By definition, a property crime entails one or more perpetrators taking a physical object of value (mainly money or property) away from its legal owner. Just about all of us have stolen at some time in our lives; rip-offs of one kind or another seem to be the American way. Larceny, it can be said, is "in the American heart" (McCaghy and Capron, 1994, p. 198). This does not mean that everyone who steals—that is, nearly all of us—can be lumped together and studied as a homogeneous category; in fact, roughly 5 to 7 percent of the population commit some 70 percent of all of the serious property crime (Wolfgang, Figlio and Sellin, 1972; Wolfgang, Thornberry, and Figlio, 1987; Tracy, Wolfgang, and Figlio, 1990). Most of us steal very little and very infrequently, while a very few of us steal a great deal, and frequently. Likewise, some thefts involve direct, face-to-face confrontation and force, violence, or the threat of violence, while others are nonviolent and involve stealth. Much (although not all) property crime and most violent crime make up what is colloquially known as "street" crime. Both entail personal loss or a physical attack *by* specific perpetrators *against* specific victims. In addition, another dimension is crucial: Some acts of thievery are done with a pen and not a weapon. *White-collar crimes* do not entail the physical removal of things of value from their rightful owner, but usually involve the tampering of records of some kind: account ledgers, advertising messages, quality control standards, and so on. White-collar crimes are regarded by criminologists as belonging in a completely separate category from street crimes against property, such as burglary and motor vehicle theft. (We'll look at white-collar crimes in Chapter 12.) With many white-collar crimes, even victims may not be aware that thievery has taken place, so subtle, indirect, complex, and diffuse are their effects; such a crime may be detected only by the expert, such as an accountant or a banker. Personal victimization is also difficult to detect; often, we may not be able to point to specific, concrete victims of white-collar crimes. On the other hand, street crimes are much more visible and are almost always known about—if only to the victim—when they occur. Street property crime results in detec-

tion and arrest significantly more often than is true with white-collar crime; for the latter, detection and arrest are extremely infrequent, relatively speaking.

There are many ways of classifying the realm of property theft, the physical removal of things of value from the possession of their legal owner. First, there is ordinary, "conventional" *street crime*, of which robbery, burglary, motor vehicle theft, and some types of larceny-theft are major representatives. Second, there is *shoplifting*, the thievery of merchandise from stores by customers and would-be customers; shoplifting is classified as an example of larceny-theft. And third, there is *employee pilferage*: the inside job conducted by employees of a company or other establishment who steal items of value from their place of employment. Most employee pilferage is also classified as larceny-theft.

Theft flourishes in societies in which some members do not care a great deal about the deprivations they cause to their fellow citizens. Stealing is high in societies in which the collective conscience has broken down, in which the social community has become a fiction. Theft is common because some among us want certain things and just how they acquire them matters less than simply having them. They steal because they are successful at convincing themselves that "it really isn't so bad," that "no one will miss it," or "it's covered by insurance," or "I need it more than they do," or "they're bigger thieves than I am." Basically, some people are able to steal because those from whom they steal have become impersonal, faceless, almost nonhuman to them.

This isn't true everywhere. In societies in which a strong sense of collective identity prevails—in small hunting and gathering societies and small villages in agricultural societies—theft is uncommon. Where we care nearly as deeply about the well-being of our fellow man and woman as we do our own, we are unwilling to rip them off. The impulse to steal from one another has not always prevailed in American society. It varies directly with impersonality; we have become something of "a nation of strangers." Alex Haley, author of *Roots*, which traces his ancestry back to Africa, comments in a *Playboy* interview (January 1977) on this society's transition from a communal to an individualistic nation and its attendant impact on theft. He contrasts his early childhood in Henning, Tennessee, to contemporary life in Los Angeles. Since

Definitions of Property Crimes

Robbery is defined by the Federal Bureau of Investigation (FBI) as "the taking or attempting to take anything of value from the care, custody, or control of a person or persons by force or threat of violence and/or putting the victim in fear." In 1994, nearly four out of 10 robberies that took place in the United States that were reported to the police (39 percent) were weaponless or *strong-arm* robberies, that is, no weapon was used against the victim aside from the strength or apparent strength of the perpetrator. In roughly the same proportion (42 percent), a firearm was used to threaten or intimidate the victim; in a tenth of all reported robberies (10 percent), a knife or some other stabbing or cutting instrument was used; and in the remainder, some other weapon was used. In 1994, 618,817 robberies were reported to the police. The National Crime Victimization Survey (formerly referred to as the National Crime Survey) estimates that only half of all robberies are reported to the police, and that roughly 1.2 million persons were victimized by a robbery each year in the first half of the 1990s. Since victimization surveys sample private households, they do not include commercial establishments in their studies; the 1.2 million figure does not include robberies of stores, banks, and so on, of which roughly 150,000 have taken place each year. Commercial robberies, unlike the robberies of individual persons or households, are *almost always* reported to the police. The FBI estimates that $496 million was taken through robbery in the United States in 1994. This averages out to $801 per robbery.

Burglary is "the unlawful entry of a structure to commit a felony or theft. The use of force to gain entry is not required to classify an offense as burglary." Two out of three burglaries were residential in nature; the remainder were of nonresidential structures, mainly commercial establishments. In nearly seven out of 10 cases (67 percent), forcible entry was involved; in a quarter (25 percent), unlawful entry was involved without forcible entry; the remainder entailed attempted burglary. In 1994, just under three million burglaries (2.7 million) were reported to the police; the national victimization surveys estimated that over 4.7 million American households were the target of burglaries in 1992; commercial burglaries, of course, add to this total. The FBI estimates losses by burglary victims at $3.6 billion, with an average dollar loss per burglary of $1,311.

Motor vehicle theft is "the theft or attempted theft of a motor vehicle, including the stealing of automobiles, trucks, buses, motorcycles, motorscooters, snowmobiles, etc." This definition "excludes the taking of a motor vehicle for temporary use by those persons having lawful access." Roughly eight out of 10 of the motor vehicles stolen in 1994 (79 percent) were cars; 16 percent were trucks or buses, and the remainder were all other types. One out of 130 registered vehicles in America was stolen in 1994. The recovery rate was 61 percent. Over 1.5 million vehicles were stolen in the United States in 1994, the vast majority of which were reported. (In fact, the victimization picture is a bit more complex than this: The NCVS estimated that two million cases of motor vehicle theft took place in the United States in 1992, of which 1.2 million were described as "completed.") The estimated value of all vehicles stolen in the United States in 1994 was $7.6 billion, $4,940 per vehicle.

Larceny-theft is "the unlawful taking, carrying, leading, or riding away of property from the possession or constructive possession of another." It includes practically all property crimes not included in the other categories: purse snatching and chain snatching (when not accompanied by force, violence, or the threat of violence), pickpocketing, thefts from coin machines, shopliftings, thefts from buildings to which the offender has legitimate access, thefts of vehicle parts, and thefts of bicycles. In order to qualify as a larceny-theft, no force, violence, or fraud must take place. In addition, a theft entailing a burglary is classified as a burglary—not a larceny-theft. Larceny-theft does not include embezzlement, "con" or confidence games, forgery, or passing worthless checks. Motor vehicle theft is also excluded from larceny-theft inasmuch as it is classified as a separate crime. In other words, larceny-theft is a grab-bag or miscellaneous category. In the United States in 1994, 7.9 million larceny-thefts were reported to the police; the crime victimization surveys indicated that nearly three times as many persons reported that someone in their household had been a victim of a larceny-theft of some kind during the previous year. The FBI does not issue a total dollar value lost to larceny-theft, since it is both an extremely diverse and a hugely under-reported crime.

The total number of property crimes reported to the police in the United States has declined significantly during the 1990s. From 1990 to 1994, the total number of offenses declined by 4 percent and the rate per 100,000 inhabitants declined 8 percent; between 1993 and 1994, the number of offenses declined almost 1 percent and the rate declined almost 2 percent. Criminologists attribute this decline to an aging "baby boom" population, to a decline in crack use in the inner cities, and more vigilant law enforcement. However, many experts warn of increases in property crime in the late 1990s and into the early twenty-first century, pointing to a more criminally active youth population.

Source: Federal Bureau of Investigation, 1994; Bastian, 1992, 1994.

he grew up, Haley explains, the American family has diminished in size and has been geographically separated. As families moved from the country to the city, from family units with three generations under the same roof to singles and couples living with and for themselves, from grandparents passing on family traditions to their grandchildren to parents leaving their children in the care of baby sitters, we have also moved from leaving doors unlocked because theft virtually never occurred to triple-locking all doors and windows. Somewhere along the line, Haley wistfully adds, a *sense of community* has been lost. While the past "golden age" of community and the family has been exaggerated by many observers—the past wasn't nearly as safe nor as idyllic as most of us think (Coontz, 1992)—both the sense of community membership and identity and relative freedom from theft were far greater in the past, and in small-town America, than is true today, especially in large cities.

Most homicides occur because we care about how others regard us, how we appear in their eyes. We kill the people we care about *because* we care deeply about how they feel about us; we care so much, in fact, that, when they anger us, we cannot simply walk away from them; we must wipe away the humiliation they have caused us by inflicting violence upon them. But theft is quite a different type of crime. The choice is not honor in the face of dishonor, which is usually the way killers see their dilemma: Kill or be humiliated. In contrast, with theft, the choice is between goods and services and all they will bring, as opposed to doing without them. The honor we seek—and the dishonor we seek to avoid—in killing another is specifically one that is bestowed among intimates, or at least, acquaintances who are part of a shared subculture. Yet because we live in a materialistic society, the honor that goods and services bestow travels everywhere. "Money talks," we say, and so does all that it will buy. And where impersonal commodities are valued almost above any other value, the stage is set for a *predatory* or "rip-off" society. In a sense, then, a great deal of violence, especially homicide, has its roots in intimacy, whereas most property crime has its roots in the opposite social condition—impersonality.

STUDYING CRIMINAL BEHAVIOR

How do we assemble information that dictates what we know about criminal behavior, property crimes included? How do we find out how often crime is committed, who commits it, and who its victims are? Criminologists use three principal methods to study criminal behavior. The first is official police data, of which the Uniform Crime Reports, collected, tabulated, and published by the Federal Bureau of Investigation (FBI), is the standard source. The second method used by criminologists is made up of *victimization surveys*, of which the National Crime Victim Survey is the most often relied on. And the third method of studying crime is conducting *self-report surveys*, which ask people directly if they have engaged in certain types of crimes (O'Brien, 1985; Livingston, 1996, pp. 53–76; Adler, Mueller, and Laufer, 1995, pp. 27–40). While other techniques—such as experiments and participant observation studies—are used for certain purposes, only these three are regarded as even remotely valid for determining crime rates. However, each of these three has methodological flaws and limitations.

Each year, nearly all of the more than 16,000 city, county, and state law enforcement agencies in the United States tabulate the crimes and arrests that take place in their jurisdictions and send the results to the Federal Bureau of Investigation in Washington. The FBI combines and tallies these figures and publishes the results in a yearly volume entitled the Uniform Crime Reports (UCR). As we might expect, there are many serious problems with using the UCR's figures as an accurate reflection of the total volume of crime that takes place in the United States. Probably the most serious of these problems is that of *underreporting*. Not all people who are victims of a crime report that fact to the police; a number of studies (Shim and DeBerry, 1988, p. 5; Bastian, 1994, p. 123) found that when compared with victimization data, only a third of crime victims (37 percent in one study, 39 percent in another) report crime to the police. At the same time, violent crimes are significantly more likely to be reported (50 percent) than property crimes (29 percent), and more serious offenses are more likely to be reported than less serious ones (Bastian, 1994, p. 123). Rape is a partial exception. Rape is both a violent and a serious crime, and it is often not reported, as we saw in the previous chapter. Still, the UCR tabulated over 102,000 reported rapes for 1994, and the National Crime Victimization Survey (NCVS) tallied 174,000, which means that even for this often unreported crime, a *majority* of women who reported rape to an interviewer also reported it to the police. However, it is also possible that many women who were raped did not state that fact to a NCVS interviewer. In the last chapter, we saw that by using a far broader definition of rape, the National Women's Study estimated that 683,000 women were sexually assaulted in 1990 in the United States. Motor vehicle theft is *typically* reported, since the vehicle is usually insured, and insurance companies require a police report for reimbursement. Criminal homicide or murder, as we saw in Chapter 10, is almost always reported. Even though the victim can't complain (in the case of murder, the victim is dead!), the police usually find the body and typically surmise that a murder did, in fact, take place. The police statistics are fairly accurate for murder, motor vehicle theft, and commercial robberies (the last of these, again, because of insurance requirements). For crimes where there is no clear-cut victim and no complainant, such as drug possession and sale, or homosexual acts in states where they are against the law, official police statistics are completely worthless as a reflection of their frequency.

The Bureau of Justice Statistics sponsors a crime victimization survey. Formerly referred to as the National Crime Survey (NCS), the National Crime Victimization Survey (NCVS) is conducted periodically, usually every six months; in the survey, members of over 60,000 households are interviewed about whether they have been the victim of a crime during a stipulated period of time. Typically, a higher proportion of individuals are more willing to report having been the victim of a crime to an interviewer than they are to report that crime to the police. In addition, the National Crime Victimization Survey only asks about crimes against individuals and households, or more specifically, individuals who live in the sampled households; it excludes crimes against commercial establishments. (And keep in mind the fact that some crimes, such as burglary, are committed against a household, while others, such as robbery, are committed against an individual.) Thus, the two data sources are not strictly comparable. Even though there are some methodological problems with the national victimization surveys, most criminologists agree that, as an estimate of criminal activity, they are substantially more accurate and valid than official police statistics (O'Brien, 1985, pp. 49–56). What we know is that nearly three times as many crime victims say they have been a victim of a crime in a victimization survey than report that crime to the police.

Table 11.1 shows the total number of property crimes that took place in the United States in 1994

Table 11.1 Number and Rate of Property Crimes, Uniform Crime Reports versus National Crime Victimization Survey

	Uniform Crime Reports, 1994	
	Number	Rate/100,000
Robbery	618,817	237.7
Burglary	2,712,156	1,041.8
Vehicle Theft	1,539,097	591.2
Larceny Theft	7,876,254	3,025.4

	National Crime Victimization Survey, 1992	
	Number	Rate/100,000
Robbery	1,225,510	590
Burglary	4,757,420	4,890*
Vehicle Theft	1,219,510**	1,250
Household Larceny	8,101,150	8,320
Personal Larceny	6,217,360	6,260

*Note: While robbery is based on number of individuals (age 12 and older) in the population, burglary is based on number of households.
**Motor Vehicle Theft figures are based on completed thefts; motor vehicle thefts that are attempted but not completed are deleted.
Source: Bastian, 1994.

A Rational View of Crime: Routine Activities Theory

If we were to ask a cross section of the American public for an explanation of why property crime occurs, the chances are that we'd get theories that focus more or less exclusively on either individual or social factors: poverty, income distribution, ineffective social control, poor childhood socialization, community breakdown, a lack of respect for law and order, and so on. It is unlikely that many of these common-sensical explanations would focus on the factors or variables with which *routine activities* theory deals. Routine activities theory argues that for a criminal act to take place, the following elements are necessary: first, *motivated offenders*, persons who have the will and the the desire to commit a crime; second, *suitable targets*, that is, money or portable property worth stealing; and third, an absence of *capable guardians*, that is, no one who is watching over that property to ensure against theft. If all three of these factors are present, the likelihood that a crime will take place is increased; if any one of them is absent, crime cannot occur (Cohen and Felson, 1979).

Routine activities theory grants that the will and desire to steal varies from one person or category of persons to another. However, the advocates of this theory do not consider this variable to be of much interest. There will always be a plentiful supply of motivated offenders, they say. Instead, they focus on the existence of movable property worth stealing and the presence or absence of guardians to protect that property. Notice that they do not *deny* that motivated offenders are part of the crime picture. They simply assume that there will always be enough of them for crime to continue to flourish.

Common sense would draw a *negative* relationship between affluence and crime, that is, the wealthier a society is, the lower its crime rate will be, since so many people in the population will be satisfied with their standard of living and material possessions. Wealthy people simply have less *need* to steal, this popular explanation would hold. Routine activities theory argues precisely the opposite: that affluence and property crime are *positively* related. The more affluent a society, the higher its crime rate will be. Why? What affluence does is to increase the total volume of property and hence, the "suitable targets" for theft, and in turn, the rate of property crime. Since World War II, the average per capita standard of living in the United States—and correspondingly, the total volume of money and movable property—has increased many times. Over the past

two generations or so, Americans simply have a great deal more money and *stuff* to steal. Hence, the rate of property crime has increased, since opportunities to commit property crime have increased (Gould, 1969).

In addition, over the past half-century, the social organization of American society has altered, making homes, places where money and movable property are kept, more vulnerable to theft. Today, as compared with the past, "capable guardianship" of suitable targets has declined. Since 1950 or so, the proportion of women, especially married women who have children in school and who work has increased several times. What this means is that a higher percentage of houses are left unguarded during the day, making them more vulnerable to burglary and theft from "motivated offenders." In addition, again, over the past four or five decades, fewer Americans live in households with several generations, or persons who are unrelated to one another, living under the same roof. Today's households are smaller than in the past. This also increases the likelihood that no one will be home during the day. This increases the likelihood that American households will be vulnerable to, and will become a target for, property crime (Cohen and Felson, 1979).

This approach assumes that opportunities for crime influence—indeed, determine—the commission of criminal acts. And opportunities are influenced by the routine comings and goings of guardians of property. Opportunities can also be influenced by environmental design: how houses are built, where they are located, who can monitor them, how secure their doors and windows are, and so on. If this theory is correct, this means that the crime rate can be lowered without changing the society in any drastic or fundamental fashion or the persons who live in the society. Simply by reducing opportunities for crime, the crime rate will go down. The space in which property is located can be made more *defensible* (Newman, 1972); crime targets can be *hardened*, that is, made less vulnerable to crime, simply through intelligent, conscious design. The political implications of routine activities theory are conservative, since it does not propose a reform of society's injustices or inequities as a solution to crime. Indeed, if the theory is correct, affluent segments of the society can seal themselves off from crime through environmental design, while the poorer become ever more vulnerable to it.

What do you think of routine activities theory as an explanation of criminal activity?

as tabulated by these two data sources: the Uniform Crime Reports and the National Crime Victimization Survey. As can be seen, for robbery and burglary, there is an underreporting to the police of roughly one-third, for larceny-theft, it is about 50 percent; in contrast, nearly 90 percent of all motor vehicle thefts are reported.

Self-report surveys represent a third method of studying crime. Here, samples of respondents are asked about crimes, offenses, or delinquent acts they themselves have committed. Common sense tells us that hardly anyone will tell the truth when asked about having committed crimes for which they could be arrested. But here, as in so many other instances, common sense is wrong, at least, mostly wrong. Surprisingly, most people are quite willing to admit their own participation in criminal activity. They tend to tell the truth to the best of their ability, as long as they are certain there will be no harmful consequences in telling the truth. People admit to many more crimes than the police record in their official statistics. When a researcher checks what people say they did against the objective evidence of the same offense—arrests, convictions, incarcerations, hospital treatment, clinic records, and so on—the respondent tells the truth in an extremely high proportion of the cases. (See, for example, Inciardi, 1986, p. 121, 1992; Johnson et al., 1985, pp. 208–209.) However, unlike the Uniform Crime Reports and the National Crime Victimization Surveys, self-report surveys are not standardized, are not part of a single coordinated, centralized, ongoing research enterprise, and cannot be used to determine frequency, incidence, or rates of criminal behavior. In addition, the samples on which self-report surveys are based tend to be considerably smaller than those for victimization surveys; they are almost never national or as large-scale in scope. Hence, self-report surveys concentrate on considerably *less* serious crimes. More serious crimes tend to be rarer, and thus, show up with far less frequency in studies based on relatively small samples; as they are conducted currently, self-report surveys are not of much use for estimating the *frequency* of crimes such as murder, rape, and robbery. What they are good for is establishing *relationships* and *correlations* between *certain kinds* of criminal behavior and various sociological characteristics, and from them, attempting to determine the causes of criminal behavior. What they are *not* good for is determining how often the most serious crimes are committed in the United States each year (O'Brien, 1985, pp. 65ff.).

THE SEVERITY OF CRIME

How serious are murder, robbery, rape, burglary, or common theft? A sample of 60,000 Americans were asked to rank dozens of crimes in terms of seriousness. Table 11.2 gives the seriousness score of some representative property crimes and crimes of violence. In this survey, an offense that is given a seriousness score of 20 is regarded as twice as serious as one with a score of 10, which in turn, is seen as twice as serious as one with a score of five. Notice that this is a study of the *subjective* seriousness of crimes, not their "objective" seriousness; it is how seriously crimes are *regarded* by the public. (These two dimensions may overlap, of course, assuming that we had a way of measuring objectivity.) What does this survey tell us about the "subjective" seriousness of crime?

First, we notice that *crimes of violence are rated as significantly more serious than property crimes.* People rate crimes in which victims are killed or injured as vastly more serious than crimes in which victims merely lose money or property. The nine crimes in Table 11.2 with the highest severity score are all crimes of violence, and the 11 crimes with the lowest scores are all strictly property crimes.

Second, robbery or the theft of money or property, which involves victim confrontation where force, violence, or the threat of violence is used, is regarded as more serious than stealing that involves no such element. Even though technically, violence and physical harm may not have occurred, the very threat of, or potential for, violence in a given act of robbery causes most people to regard such acts as more serious than those where no such threat or potential exists. Robbing a victim of $10 at gunpoint is seen as more serious (9.4) than picking someone's pocket (3.3). Nonviolent crimes in which property is stolen—that is, those involving no force, violence, or threat of violence—are seen as much less serious than violent property crimes. Even those offenses which merely took place in the presence of others—threat or no threat—were regarded as more serious than those which occurred when the offender was completely alone. Stealing $1,000 worth of merchandise from a department store counter was ranked as more serious (7.6) than

Table 11.2 How People Rank the Severity of Crime

Severity Score	Offense
72.1	A person plants a bomb in a public building. The bomb explodes and 20 people are killed.
52.8	A man forcibly rapes a woman. As a result of physical injuries, she dies.
43.2	A person robs a victim at gunpoint. The victim struggles and is shot to death.
35.7	A person stabs a victim to death.
30.0	A man forcibly rapes a woman. Her physical injuries require hospitalization.
25.8	A man forcibly rapes a woman. No other physical injury occurs.
24.8	A person intentionally shoots a victim with a gun. The victim requires hospitalization.
21.0	A person robs a victim of $1,000 at gunpoint. The victim is wounded and requires hospitalization.
18.0	A person stabs a victim with a knife. The victim requires hospitalization.
17.7	A person, armed with a gun, robs a bank of $100,000 during business hours. No one is physically hurt.
16.8	A person, using force, robs a victim of $1,000. The victim is hurt and requires hospitalization.
15.5	A person breaks into a bank at night and steals $100,000.
11.9	A person intentionally injures a victim. The victim is treated by a doctor and hospitalized.
10.9	A person steals property worth $10,000 from outside a building.
10.3	A person threatens to harm a victim unless the victim gives him money. The victim gives him $1,000 and is not harmed.
9.7	A person breaks into a department store, forces open a safe, and steals $1,000.
9.7	A person breaks into a display case in a department store and steals $1,000 worth of merchandise.
9.7	A person robs a victim of $1,000 at gunpoint. No physical harm occurs.
9.7	A person breaks into a home and steals $1,000 worth of merchandise.
9.4	A person robs a victim of $10 at gunpoint. No physical harm occurs.
8.5	A person intentionally injures a victim. The victim is treated by a doctor but is not hospitalized.
8.0	A person steals an unlocked car and sells it.
8.0	A person, using force, robs a victim of $1,000. No physical harm occurs.
7.6	A person steals $1,000 worth of merchandise from a department store counter.
7.3	A person beats a victim with his fists. The victim is hurt but does not require medical treatment.
7.3	A person breaks into a department store and steals merchandise worth $1,000.
6.9	A person steals property worth $1,000 from outside a building.
6.6	A person does not have a weapon. He threatens to harm a victim unless the victim gives him money. The victim gives him $10 and is not harmed.
6.6	A person steals $1,000 of merchandise from an unlocked car.
4.9	A person snatches a handbag containing $10 from a victim on the street.
4.4	A person steals an unlocked car and later abandons it undamaged.
4.4	A person picks a victim's pocket of $100.
3.6	A person steals property worth $100 from outside a building.
3.3	A person breaks into a department store, forces open a cash register, and steals $10.
3.3	A person picks a victim's pocket of $10.
3.1	A person breaks into a home and steals $100.
2.2	A person steals $10 worth of merchandise from a department store counter.
1.7	A person steals property worth $10 from outside a building.

Source: Klaus and Kalish, 1984.

How Often Are Perpetrators Arrested?

For the purposes of the Uniform Crime Report, a law enforcement agency "clears" or "solves" a crime "when at least one person is arrested, charged with the commission of the offense, and turned over to the court for prosecution" regardless of whether the persons arrested are convicted, and regardless of whether they actually committed the crime. The percentage of crimes "cleared" by arrest, therefore, is not a foolproof measure of crimes literally "solved" by the police. At the same time, the assumption that the actual perpetrator has been caught when someone is arrested is usually (although far from always) justified. False arrests take place, of course, and sometimes perpetrators plead guilty to offenses they did not commit to "clear the books" for the police in a plea-bargaining deal. In addition, a crime which took place one year may be cleared the next and hence counted as not cleared the year it took place. The offender may die before being arrested. Consequently, his or her crime will never be cleared. Still, clearance rates represent a very *rough* measure of how often crimes are "solved."

As we might expect, the clearance rate is hugely variable according to the type of crime committed. Two factors are crucial here: One is how *serious* the offense is and the second is whether the victim and the offender *know* each other. For crimes of violence, the clearance rate is fairly high; this is especially the case for murder, the most serious of all crimes tabulated by the FBI. In 1994, the clearance rate for murder was 64 percent. Still, one might wonder, given the extreme seriousness of murder, why fully a third of offenders escaped detection. Moreover, clearance rates for murder are *lower* in large cities (since murders are more likely to take place between strangers) and lower today than was true in the past. In 1952, New York City's clearance rate for murder was 90 percent; today, it is only 59 percent. Considering the fact that some 10 to 15 percent of murder arrests do not result in a criminal indictment, and 10 to 15 percent result in an indictment and a dismissal or acquittal, well

over half of all big-city killers are "getting away with murder" (Pooley, 1992). For aggravated assault, the clearance rate for 1994 was 56 percent. In spite of what some feminists claim, rape is not an unusually underprosecuted crime; over half of all rapes that are reported to the police, or 52 percent, result in arrest. (As we know, arrest is no guarantee of conviction, however.) As we've seen, the type of rape that is most likely to be reported, "aggravated" rape, is also most likely to result in arrest and criminal prosecution.

How do clearance rates of the property crimes stack up against those of crimes of violence? Not very well. This is largely because property crime offenders are not usually known to victims and, in addition, property crimes have a lower priority for both victims and the criminal justice system. For robbery—a property crime as well as a crime of violence (and a crime that usually takes place between and among strangers)—the clearance rate was only 24 percent in 1994. Since only a bit more than half of all robberies are reported to the police, we can conclude that the police really solve only one robbery case out of eight. The clearance rate for burglary (13 percent), larceny-theft (20 percent), and motor vehicle theft (14 percent) is even more anemic than it is for robbery. Considering the fact that larceny-theft is reported in only a quarter of all cases, perhaps one offender in 20 is apprehended; for burglary, this is roughly 7 percent. Since property crimes are those of stealth in which the perpetrator is not known to the victim, detection and arrest are obviously extremely problematic. Robbery, the only crime that is also a crime of violence, entails confrontation between the victim and the perpetrator; in principle, the victim should be able to identify the offender. The problem is that robbery not only takes place between strangers, it is also overwhelmingly a big-city crime and hence typically one in which the offender remains anonymous to both the victim and law enforcement.

Source: Federal Bureau of Investigation, 1995.

breaking into a department store and stealing merchandise worth the same amount of money (7.3). This ranking might not seem to make much sense, since the second entails committing burglary in addition to theft—and therefore is legally more serious—while the first merely represents an act of theft. However, when we realize that the first

takes place in the presence of others, while the second takes place where the perpetrator is alone, the ranking becomes understandable.

Third, a weapon, and more specifically the *type* of weapon used, weighs heavily in the public's consideration of seriousness. Crimes entailing the use of a gun are ranked as more serious than those in which a knife is used, which in turn, are ranked as more serious than those in which a lead pipe is used, which again, were ranked as more serious than those in which no weapon is involved. The use of a weapon, and a potentially more lethal weapon, indicates to the public that the perpetrator is more committed in his intention to commit a serious crime and less concerned about the consequences of his action. The fact that victims are more likely to be injured in weaponless robberies (although those few who are injured with weapons are more likely to be seriously injured—and killed) is irrelevant in the public's evaluation of seriousness.

Fourth, the amount of money stolen plays a significant role in the public's judgment of seriousness. For instance, a person stealing $10,000 worth of property from outside a building is given a seriousness score of 10.9; a person stealing $100 from outside a building is scored only 3.6; and a person stealing only $10 worth of property is scored 1.7. Breaking into a home and stealing $1,000 is rated as more serious (9.7) than breaking into a home and stealing $100 (3.1). Although this generalization seems to appeal to common sense, it did not appear to be supported in an earlier survey of the seriousness of crimes (Rossi et al., 1974). Moreover, the relationship between the amount of money or property taken and perceived seriousness—other things being equal, of course—is far from perfect.

And last, the more the perpetrator has to do to commit a given offense the more seriously the act is regarded by the public—again, other things being more or less equal. Breaking into a display case and stealing $1,000 (9.7) is seen as a more serious offense than stealing merchandise worth the same amount of money from a store counter (7.6). Stealing a locked car is seen as more serious than stealing an unlocked car. A person breaking into a house and stealing merchandise worth $1,000 is regarded as more serious (9.7) than someone stealing property worth $1,000 from outside a building (6.9). The crime is seen as less serious when the perpetrator acts on an opportunity that presents itself than when the perpetrator has to make a more active effort to do the same thing (Klaus and Kalish, 1984).

MOTIVES FOR STEALING

The street thieves tabulated in the pages of the Uniform Crime Reports run the gamut from the rankest amateur who steals from time to time to buy things he or she sees others enjoying to the professional who earns a comfortable livelihood exclusively from stealing. For both, stealing seems to be a *rational* activity: It is a means to an end that many of us seek, although the means used are somewhat unconventional. Other benefits that may be derived from stealing ("kicks," fun, excitement, and so on) tend to be secondary to the monetary ones. A nation with high rates of theft, as Merton's anomie theory argues, is one that:

1. Emphasizes material values;
2. Manifests great material differences between rich and poor;
3. Prominently displays the possessions of the affluent;
4. Portrays the possessions of the affluent as attainable for everyone;
5. Deemphasizes the means of attaining these possessions;
6. Makes it difficult, if not nearly impossible, for substantial numbers of the members of that nation to obtain these possessions legally.

It is these features that almost guarantee that a society or nation will have high rates of theft. They make for a "rip-off" society, a "society organized for crime" (Messner and Rosenfeld, 1994, pp. 1–18).

Among the tugs and pulls inducing people to attempt thievery as a means of earning money, certainly two stand out as most prominent. The first would be the choice between poverty and cash. In a nation with high unemployment rates in many neighborhoods, with a Black unemployment rate twice that for whites, and with an unemployment rate for teenagers over three times that for adults, many people are induced to steal because they literally have no other means of earning money at all. In the neighborhood studied by anthropologist Philippe Bourgois, "El Barrio," or East Harlem in New York, 40 percent of all households earned no legally declared wages or salary at all; it is Bourgois's contention that its residents *had no choice* but to resort to a variety of activities in the "underground" economy—among them, stealing (1995, p. 8). Even receiving welfare, or holding a minimum wage job, means not being able to move about in the world with dignity or comfort. Indeed, minimum wage jobs put substantially less in one's pocket than many illegal activites. Clearly, poverty has to be counted as a major inducement to commit property crime. We have a great deal of theft in this society because the economy does not guarantee enough people a decent livelihood, because our economy is incapable of distributing income in an even remotely equitable fashion. But remember, it is not poverty alone that does it; theft tends to be rare in some nations of the world in which people are *the most* impoverished. This may be because the rule of the rich is far more tyrannical than is true here and it may be because the poor do not dream that they could, through simple acts of theft, acquire some of what the rich have. Whatever the causes, a cross-national comparison of property crime would enrich our understanding of the factors that contribute to theft and why it is so much more common in some societies than in others.

The second factor that induces people to steal is that most jobs which are available to a poor, uneducated young person are not very interesting or rewarding; in fact, most are boring, alienating, even demeaning. So the choice for some of us is not between poverty and cash, but between working at a regular job that pays little and that one despises and doing something that is illegal but is less humiliating, or at least that doesn't consume eight or 10 hours a day. Stealing from others involves being one's own boss, choosing one's working hours, and doing jobs one decides to do. It is difficult to imagine more persuasive inducements.

Let's listen to what a professional armed robber has to say about what led him to pick up a revolver and earn a livelihood using it.

I've never had any trouble getting a job. Anybody can work, but of course I don't dig working. I mean, not that type of manual work. And then when we talked it over and decided that in order to get the amount of money we wanted in the shortest time, that crime was the way to get it. And crime, we feel, is just like any other business. In other words, there's setbacks in crime and there's deficits, just like you run a business and there's a chance that you might burn down or you might go bankrupt or your employee might have embezzled everything you got without the insurance to cover it, and it's the same way with crime. Of course the penalty for going bankrupt in crime is much stiffer, but at the same time your material gain is much more than it is in a regular business (Jackson, 1974, pp. 44–45).

A journalist, James Willwerth, talked to, followed around, and hung out with a young man, Jones, who made a living of mugging people on the street, usually with a knife, sometimes with a gun, occasionally with his fists. Willwerth wrote a "portrait of a mugger" from the information he gathered:

Jones is a violent man; he knows the streets may kill him. He looks over his shoulder every moment of his life. He hates the tension of this, while knowing it comes with the life he chooses to lead. For the streets allow him to run away from himself, and from the demands, and limitations of ghetto life. The alternative is a job; years of dreary work and grinding semi-poverty. The people uptown have good-paying jobs, houses and cars and good clothes. It doesn't happen to anyone in Jones's neighborhood. The way to get over is to stay in the street. If you stay alive, you can be anything—sooner or later the "big sting" comes your way and you can have all the women, clothes, cars, and penthouses you need, right? In the meantime, keep moving. . . . When Jones works regularly [at mugging], he says he makes more than a hundred dollars a day . . . it is tax free. . . . "Fear is just another emotion" [Jones explains]. "You are taught from birth you will be punished if you do something wrong. Dig it: pulling a rip is against the law and you are taught fear of the law. But you say, if this can help *me*, it's right . . . I won't lie to you. What I do is wrong. . . . *But man, it gives me life*" (Willwerth, 1976, pp. 23, 32, 46).

FACTORS IN PROPERTY CRIME

Socioeconomic status (SES), including social class, income, education, and occupation, are very strongly correlated with the crimes under discussion. (Of course, highly educated, affluent people have less risky ways of stealing than burglary and robbery, and we discuss them in the next chapter on white-collar crime.) In fact, this relationship is so strong and so well documented (Braithwaite, 1981; Clelland and Carter, 1980; Elliott and Huizinga, 1983) that it seems futile to deny it, as some observers have (Tittle, Villemez, and Smith, 1982; Tittle and Meier, 1990). Overwhelmingly, the poor rather than the affluent are much more likely to steal in conventional ways, that is, in the ways that are discussed in this chapter, along the lines of the property crimes tallied by the FBI. Although members of the middle class do engage in conventional property crimes, they are significantly less likely to do so than members of the lower and working classes; moreover, they are strikingly less likely to engage in *serious* property crimes, especially robbery, and less likely to engage in property crime on a regular, routine, repetitive basis.

It is less the factor of a society's absolute poverty level that influences its rate of property crimes than its *income distribution*. With all due respect to the differing definitions of the crimes we've been discussing that are applied worldwide, an international comparison of crime rates bears this out. (For one such comparison, see Kalish, 1988.) In societies with a fairly equitable income distribution, such as Sweden, Norway, Denmark, and the Netherlands, property crimes are relatively uncommon. On the other hand, property crimes are much more frequent in the United States, with its far less equitable income distribution, and may be even more common in many extremely poor Third World countries, such as Brazil, Colombia, Nigeria, and Jamaica.

One factor that tempers this relationship is that one necessary and obvious ingredient of property crime is *the existence of property in the first place.* It makes sense that in a society in which privately owned goods are extremely scarce, there is little to steal. Ironically, it could be that one major cause of property crime is *general societal affluence:* The greater the abundance of material goods the members of a society have, the more there is to steal, and thus, the higher the rate of property crime (Gould, 1969). Few crimes demonstrate this better than motor vehicle theft. Where there are many cars, there are many cars to steal, and thus auto theft is more common; in societies with few cars, few cars will be stolen. Which leads us to a crucial methodological question: Should the rate of theft be calculated on the basis of the total population or the total number of cars? If it is based on the entire population, China, a country with many people and few cars, will have a minuscule rate of motor vehicle theft by virtue of that fact alone. Of course, the argument that theft is based on the possession of property cannot be pushed too far, since the rates of property crime in nations in which material want is practically nonexistent (for example, Kuwait, Brunei, the United Arab Emirates, and Switzerland), whether calculated on the basis of population *or* property owned, are undoubtedly extremely low, while those of the poorer nations of the Third World are far higher.

In addition to the role of socioeconomic status in the *commission* of property crime, we might also investigate the role of SES in property crime *victimization*. If it is the members of the lower and working classes who are more likely to commit property crimes, is this also true for the victims of these crimes? As we've seen for violent crimes, especially murder, as a general rule, victims are likely to possess the same social class characteristics as perpetrators; is this also true for property crime? The answer is yes and no; it all depends on the crime. As we can see from Table 11.3, the relationship between household income (one measure of SES) and the likelihood of being a victim of property theft varies enormously according to the crime in question. Income bears a positive relationship with victimization for some property crimes, that is, the *higher* the income, the greater the likelihood of victimization. On the other hand, there is a negative relationship with some other crimes, that is, the *lower* the income, the greater the criminal victimization. This is not random, accidental variation; the reason for this variation is that the category, "property crime," is made up of activities with very different dynamics.

In one victimization survey (Bastian, 1992), members of poor households were twice as likely to have been victims of robbery than members of affluent households; for burglary, this was one-and-one-half times. For personal theft (such as purse-snatching and pocket-picking), it was the opposite: Members of more affluent households were nearly twice as likely to have been victimized than members of poor households. For household theft, having things stolen directly from one's apartment or house without illegal entry—no relationship existed: Poor and affluent households were just as likely to have been victims of this particular type of crime.

Although these relationships might seem contradictory, they become understandable when the relationship of particular *types* of crime to income and socioeconomic status is made clear. Robbery is partly a crime of violence; consequently, it is likely to be more common in poorer neighborhoods in which the rates of violence are high. As we've seen in Chapter 10, violence is *negatively* correlated with SES, including income, that is, the *lower* the SES, the *higher* the rate of violent acts. The relationship of income to personal and motor vehicle theft is mostly due to the fact that members of affluent households simply have more to steal. Clearly, households whose members own more cars, and more desirable cars, are more likely to be victims of auto theft than households whose members have few, or no, desirable cars, or no cars at all. On the street (which is where "personal" thefts take place), where poor and affluent mingle, it is the affluent who are more likely to become targets of theft. It is

Table 11.3 Income and Victimization (Victimization Rate/1,000)

	Under $7,500	$7,500–$14,999	$15,000–$24,999	$25,000–$49,999	$50,000 or more
Robbery	1.3	1.3	.9	.8	.6
Burglary	6.7	5.5	4.5	4.2	3.9
Personal	7.9	8.5	9.8	11.5	14.3
Household	7.6	7.8	7.9	7.8	7.9
Vehicle	.9	1.7	1.7	1.9	2.3

Personal = personal theft, or theft from one's person (pocket-picking, purse-snatching, and so on).
Household = thefts from a household (excluding burglary).
Vehicle = motor vehicle theft.
Source: Bastian, 1992.

the well-heeled (or apparently well-heeled) from whom the enterprising thief is likely to take a purse, a wallet, or a chain.

The seemingly contradictory relationship between income and criminal victimization reveals that property criminals are moved by at least two contradictory impulses: *propinquity*, or their physical, ecological, geographical, and social *nearness* to potential victims, and the *affluence* of potential victims, that is, the offender's potential *reward* from enacting a given episode of crime. It is easier to steal from people living in neighborhoods with which one is familiar than from those who live in unfamiliar neighborhoods. In fact, one may be distinctly *unwelcome* in more affluent neighborhoods, where one may be unfamiliar. Residents and law enforcement may take steps to exclude, reject, harass, or otherwise discourage the poor, especially minority interlopers. But it also makes sense to steal from persons who have more money or goods than from those who have less. Thieves who steal vehicles and personal items from others on the street are clearly more attracted to affluence than by propinquity, while robbers and burglars seem to be moved more by propinquity than by affluence.

Age is an excellent predictor of property crime, indeed, of crime in general. The age distribution of crime "represents one of the brute facts of criminology"; it is seen by many criminologists as "invariant across societal and cultural conditions" (Hirschi and Gottfredson, 1983, pp. 552, 554; Gottfredson and Hirschi, 1990, pp. 124–144). The rate of property crimes rises very sharply after the age of 10 or so, reaches a peak in the late adolescent years, and declines fairly steeply throughout the twenties and thirties. Since the Industrial Revolu-

tion in the early 1700s, this relationship has held pretty much everywhere, and does not diminish with the introduction of any other explanatory variables or factors. Exactly what causes this relationship is hotly debated by the experts (Greenberg, 1979, 1985; Hirschi and Gottfredson, 1983, 1985; Gottfredson and Hirschi, 1990; Gove, 1985). Is it the social position of adolescents—for instance, that they earn less money than adults, or that they are less likely to have assumed adult responsibilities, such as marriage and parenthood—that causes this relationship? Or is it the inherent condition of adolescence itself that causes it, for instance, physical, physiological, or maturational characteristics? No clear-cut answer has been provided by researchers, and it is likely that this issue will be debated for some time.

Sex or *gender* is also powerfully related to crime. As we know, arrest figures are not perfect reflections of the crime rate; perpetrators who are caught may be significantly different from those who are not. Still, characteristics of arrestees do provide at least a partial glimpse of the general characteristics of offenders. In 1994, nine out of 10 arrested robbers (91 percent), burglars (90 percent), and motor vehicle thieves (88 percent) were male. Only for larceny-theft (which includes shoplifting) were a sizeable proportion of all arrestees female (33 percent). Clearly, being male has a great deal to do with committing property crimes, as it does with committing crime generally. So much is this the case that two criminologists flatly state: "If you were asked to use a single trait to predict which children . . . would become criminals, you would make fewer mistakes if you chose sex status as the trait and predicted criminality for [all] the males and noncriminality for [all] the females. The prediction would be wrong in many cases. . . . But you would be wrong in more cases if you used any other single trait, such as age, race, family background, or personality characteristic" (Sutherland and Cressey, 1978, p. 130).

Is it the social position of men versus women that causes this relationship, or is it some invariant property of men and women, such as size, strength, or physiology? Once again, the literature offers no clear-cut answer, with proponents on both sides of the controversy (Gove, 1985; Balkan and Berger, 1979; Gottfredson and Hirschi, 1990, pp. 144–149), although the evidence for the existence of the relationship itself is overwhelming.

ROBBERY

Most people use the term "robbery" very loosely. They say, for example, "My apartment was robbed yesterday." To criminologists, robbery has a very specific meaning. Robbery entails *victim confrontation*; it is a theft involving force, violence, or the threat of violence. As we saw, in 1994, a bit over 600,000 robberies were reported to the police in the United States (Table 11.1). There is some controversy among criminologists as to whether robbery is a property crime or a crime of violence; clearly, it has some elements of both. In fact, it is the one crime that is *both* a property crime—since the perpetrator takes money or goods from the victim—*and* a crime of violence—since the perpetrator uses force, violence, or the threat of violence. As we saw, four out of 10 of all robberies entail the use of firearms, one out of eight entail the use of a knife, and four out of 10 were strong-arm or weaponless robberies.

Because of the confrontational nature of the offense and because both robber and victim might be injured in the course of the offense, robberies are much less common than other property offenses. Few who contemplate the crime have the daring and recklessness to face a victim and demand property or cash; most thieves prefer stealth and secrecy. One need only compare the roughly 1.2 million noncommercial robberies that the National Crime Victimization Survey revealed in 1992 with the 4.7 million household burglaries and 20 or so million household and personal thefts to realize that robbery is a *vastly* less common offense than the other forms of property crime. The fact is that most

offenders simply do not wish to engage in robbery; it is a dangerous, high-risk activity. Of course, a minority of offenders do engage in robbery, but this minority is very atypical of property crime offenders in general.

According to the FBI, more than half of all robberies reported in 1994 (55 percent) took place on the street or on a highway; one in 10 (11 percent) occurred in a residence; one in five (21 percent) were robberies of a bank, a convenience store, a gas or service station, or a "commercial house." As we saw, the total financial take for all robberies reported to the police in the United States in 1994 was $496 million—not much of a haul for such a well-publicized crime. Cash or property worth an average of $801 per incident was taken, although bank robbers ($3,551 per incident) did better than robbers of convenience stores ($387 per incident).

As we saw before, the clearance or arrest rate for robbery was 24 percent in 1994. Although this might seem low, consider that if a typical robber steals only $801 per offense, and assuming his crime is reported half the time, and he is arrested only a quarter of the time his crime is reported, he will earn barely $6,000 for each arrest. (Of course, consider two additional facts: One, the more that is stolen, the greater the likelihood that the incident will be reported; and two, commercial robberies are *almost always* reported.) Stated this way, robbery doesn't seem like a very promising way to make a living. Naturally, the FBI's statistics include a great many young, inept, unprofessional robbers who do not plan their jobs and who are very likely to get caught, and relatively few older, professional robbers who do plan their jobs carefully. Robbery may very well be a lucrative career for a small professional elite, but for the average robber, it represents an extremely risky and nonlucrative means of earning a decent income. Its appeal is that it yields a fairly substantial amount of cash in a very short period of time.

Robbery is overwhelmingly a big-city offense (See Table 11.4). The likelihood of being a victim of a robbery in a big city is *stupendously* greater than in a small town or a rural area. In 1994, the robbery rate for rural areas was 18.6 per 100,000 in the population; in cities with a population of a million or more, the robbery rate was 876.9 per 100,000—*over 45 times as high!* Moreover, the robbery rate for nearly every category increased as community size increased; mid-sized cities also followed this trend with respect to their robbery

Table 11.4 Robbery Rate in the United States by Size of Community, 1994

Size of Community	Robbery Rate/100,000
1,000,000 or more	876.9
500,000–999,999	562.9
250,000–499,999	653.8
100,000–249,999	370.6
50,000–99,999	233.6
25,000–49,999	154.0
10,000–24,999	97.7
under 10,000	69.2
Rural	18.6

Note: Suburban jurisdictions eliminated from table because of their variability in population size and proximity to urban areas.
Source: Adapted from FBI, 1995, pp.196–197.

rates. It is unlikely that there is any crime that increases so sharply in concert with community size as robbery does. The reason should be obvious: Since robbery is a crime that entails victim confrontation, the victim typically sees—and can identify—the perpetrator. In a smaller community, the likelihood of identification is vastly greater than in a larger one. What big cities offer to the robber is *anonymity*. The other two violent criminal offenses that entail victim confrontation—rape and aggravated assault—also increase with community size, but not nearly so sharply. Assault is usually a crime that takes place between intimates, and it is almost never planned; thus anonymity rarely figures into the perpetrator's calculations as to when, where, and with whom to commit the offense. And rapists rely on the victim not to report the offense to the police, an assumption to some degree valid for acquaintance rape but increasingly less so for stranger rapes. Clearly, anyone who wants to understand robbery must understand big-city life.

In most cases, then, the robbery victim is confronted by a stranger. In a victimization survey of robbery victims (Harlow, 1987) this was true in just under seven out of 10 cases of robbery by a single offender (69 percent) and just over eight of 10 cases involving multiple offenders (82 percent). For single offenders, not quite one in 10 (9 percent) was a casual acquaintance, just under one in eight (12 percent) was well-known to the victim but was not a relative; 4 percent of all single rob-

bery offenses entailed one *spouse* robbing another (usually a husband robbing a wife), and 2 percent entailed other relatives robbing one another.

The fairly high proportion of acquaintances and relatives—including spouses—among the victims and perpetrators of robbery might seem to contradict my point about the crime being one in which anonymity is an essential ingredient. What these statistics show us, however, is that robbery is not a completely homogeneous category. In fact, the robberies between relatives and acquaintances are less likely to be reported to the police than robberies that take place among strangers, because they often represent disputes between parties over the legitimate ownership of money or a given article of property. For instance, two friends may have made a twenty-dollar bet, which the loser refuses to honor; to force the loser to pay up, the winner may simply take what he sees as rightfully his—by force. Or a separated couple may have an argument about who owns a television set or compact disc player; one night, the husband may come to the wife's apartment and simply take the item—again, by force. Such offenses will not be reported to the police, but may be reported to an interviewer in a victimization survey. Because such offenses are not uncommon—although in the minority among all robberies—our point about robbery and anonymity must be modified, albeit only slightly. The original point still holds, however: Robbery *tends to be* a crime between strangers, in which the offender is not usually known to the victim. As a consequence, it is a crime *vastly* likely to take place in large cities than in small towns and rural areas.

Who is victimized by robbery? In the 1940s, Hans von Hentig (1948), a German criminologist, launched the study of the relationship between criminals and their victims. Hentig argued that much of what victims *do* or *are* leads to their victimization; crime is a product of an *interaction* between offender and victim. The field of "victimization" was born. The earliest victimization studies were heavily influenced by Freudian psychology, which argued that victims *yearned*, and were in some way *responsible*, for their victimization; such an assumption came to be dubbed "blaming the victim" (Ryan, 1976). However, current criminologists are much more careful to make a distinction between *blame* and *cause* (Felson, 1991). Victims may be selected by offenders in part because of what they do or who they are, but they should not be *blamed* for their victimization. *Blame* is a heavily value-laden term, whereas *cause* is a more objective term denoting a readily determinable sequence of events. For instance, young women are more likely to be the victims of sexual assaults than older women—this is a causal, not a moral, statement—but younger women must not be *blamed* for being raped. Poorer households are more likely to be burglarized than more affluent households, but again, to assign blame to their criminal victimization is both causally suspect and a confusion of analytically separate dimensions.

What do the victimization surveys tell us about robbery? Which categories in the population are most likely to be victimized by robberies? In 1992, males were twice as likely as females to be robbery victims with rates of 8.1 per 1,000 and 3.9 per 1,000 in the population, respectively (Bastian, 1994, p. 26). Of all age categories, teenagers (age 16 to 19) were most likely to be robbery victims, 15.4 per 1,000, while the elderly, age 65 and older, were least likely, in fact, roughly one-tenth as likely as teenagers, 1.5 per 1,000 (pp. 27–29). The rate of robbery victimization for African-Americans, 15.6 per 1,000, was over three times as high as for whites, which was 4.7 per 1,000 (p. 35). Lower-income persons are more likely to be robbed than are the more affluent. In one victimization survey (Bastian, 1992), members of families earning less than $7,500 annually were over twice as likely to be victims of a robbery during the previous year (13 per 1,000) than were members of families earning more than $50,000 (6 per 1,000).

One of the reasons why robbery is so important to criminologists is that typically, it is a much more serious crime than the other property offenses; it is a far better predictor of an offender's overall rate of involvement in crime. Given its relative rarity and the strong inhibitions most potential offenders have against forcing, or attempting to force, a person to hand over money or property, it tells us a great deal about someone who overcomes those inhibitions and does the deed. An offender who robs is highly likely, statistically speaking, to have previously engaged in a number of other types of offenses. On the other hand, someone who engages in larceny-theft, for example, or even burglary, is significantly less likely to have engaged in other offenses. In other words, robbery is a very powerful *indicator* or *measure* of someone's involvement in or commitment to criminal behavior; it is a good predictor of future criminal activity in general.

Although robbery is technically a property crime *and* a crime of violence, most of the time, the concrete violence is more potential than actual. Usually, the robber *threatens* his victims with harm rather than actually harming them. However, victims are harmed a fair proportion of the time—a minority, but a significant minority nonetheless. In a summary of a number of victimization surveys, victims were injured in 33 percent of all robberies; of these, they required hospital care in 15 percent of the cases, and in 2 percent, robbery victims required hospitalization at least overnight (Harlow, 1987, p. 7). As we've seen, in 1994, according to the FBI, 4,071 murders were committed while the offender was committing a felony, such as a rape, a burglary, or a robbery, of which half (2,072) were committed in the course of a robbery. In other words, in 1994, robbery-murders made up almost exactly 10 percent all murders that took place in the United States, a total of 23,000. The likelihood of being injured varies with the nature of the weapon. As a general rule, robberies committed with a gun are the *least* likely to result in injury, and strong-arm or weaponless robberies are the *most* likely to result in injury. Though the victim, statistically speaking, is unlikely to be killed during the course of a robbery (out of roughly a million personal robberies and perhaps 150,000 robberies of commercial and financial establishments in the U.S. in 1994, as we saw, 2,000 resulted in the death of a victim—two-tenths of 1 percent of all robberies), it is also true that if the perpetrator uses a gun, death is more likely than for any other type of robbery, strong-arm included (Wright, Rossi, and Daly, 1983, p. 208; Conklin, 1972; Cook and Nagin, 1979). The use of a weapon and the occurrence of injury strongly influence whether a robbery will be reported to the police. In one victimization study, 45 percent of all strong-arm robberies, 54 percent of all robberies in which a knife was used, and 73 percent of those in which a gun was used were reported to the police. Only 49 percent of noninjury, 61 percent of minor injury, and 76 percent of serious injury robberies were reported (Harlow, 1987, p. 9).

Who is the robber? The statistics on arrest compiled by the Uniform Crime Reports for 1994 paint the following portrait of the robber. We already know he is overwhelmingly male, 91 percent, according to the UCR. Over six in 10 of all arrested robbers (61 percent) were Black; only a third (38 percent) were white. And he is young: 64 percent were under the age of 25, 50 percent were under the age of 21, 32 percent were under the age of 18,

Is Robbery a Crime of Passion?

Are robbers rational, calculating criminals who take profit and loss into account and decide to stick up victims because that is how they can make the most money with the least risk and effort to themselves? Jack Katz (1988, pp. 164–194) argues that "doing stickup" is something akin to a crime of passion, that rational calculation of monetary gain and loss in the form of jail and prison terms are beside the point.

As we saw, on an arrest-by-arrest basis, robbery is not a very rational means of making a living. In 1994, the average take for reported robbery was $801 per incident. Most armed robberies are reported to the police (while most strong-arm robberies that do not result in injury are not), and nearly all robberies of commercial and financial establishments are reported. Police statistics show that roughly one-quarter of robberies result in (or are "cleared" by) arrest. As we saw, robbers earn an average of perhaps $6,000 before being arrested. In most jurisdictions, two armed robbery convictions will result in imprisonment and, on average, a three-year prison stint. Even considering the fact that a certain proportion of cases will be dismissed or result in acquittals, taking all things into consideration, robbery does not seem like a very good way to make a living. If we assume that the robber is engaged mainly in a rational pursuit of cash, his behavior (I say "his," since, as we saw, over 90 percent are male) is likely to be seen as totally incomprehensible. The monetary take for armed robbery does not seem to warrant the activity, based on even a moderately hard-nosed "cost-benefit analysis." One could earn more flipping hamburgers at McDonald's and live for that time in comparative freedom. Clearly, robbers are not in it solely for the money.

Of course, flipping hamburgers for four dollars an hour is hard work, at least, it takes a very long time to earn much money doing it. Still, we have to add to this equation the fact that robbery is a "hard" crime, entailing a considerable risk of injury to both victim and offender. From a strictly rational standpoint, robbery seems a dangerous, difficult, and not especially lucrative way of making a living. Indeed, most of us are aware of this fact, since, as we saw, robbery is one of our rarer crimes—far more common in the United States than in most countries of the world, but relative to street crime, extremely uncommon. The 1.2 million robberies annually estimated by victimization surveys, and the 150,000 or so commercial robberies reported to the police, compared with the 4.7 million burglaries and the 20 million or so

larceny-thefts—and this doesn't count almost all shoplifting and employee thefts—leads us to appreciate the rarity of the crime and the fact that it is committed by a very distinctive type of person.

Katz argues that the robber has much more in mind when engaging in stickups than money; a commitment to robbery "must transcend rational considerations" (p. 179). "In virtually all robberies," Katz declares, "the offender . . . fantasizes or manufactures *an angle of moral superiority* over the intended victim. . . . Even before he launches the offense, the would-be stickup man has succeeded in making a fool of his victim" (pp. 169, 174). The victim is humiliated, put in fear, made to look like a "sucker," a fool, a "chump"; the offender has successfully dominated his victim and in so doing has transformed himself into a superior, more righteous person. He has triumphed in a struggle of domination.

The fact that robberies are so rarely planned—they are mostly "spur of the moment" affairs—seems irrational to most of us, because that increases their danger and the likelihood that the offenders will get caught. But for the committed robber, that is part of its appeal. He wants to be "open to whatever might seduce him" (p. 204), "prepared for anything" (p. 219). The chaos that the robbery generates in the lives of those who live with it—victims, law enforcement, and offenders alike—is embraced rather than shunned; it is, Katz says, the robber's own creation. His survival in such a hellish, brutish struggle for domination is proof of the fierceness of his will. It demonstrates that he has managed to "transcend the control of the system" (p. 231). The stickup man, by choosing to act in a harsh environment—who has, in fact, *created* the harshness of the environment—has succeeded in demonstrating that he is a "hardman."

More generally, Katz argues, when we grasp the subjective or emotional interpretation of the experience advanced by the actor, we find that crime and deviance have a sensual, magical, creative appeal that is lacking in most conventional, law-abiding acts. The "central problem" for the criminologist and sociologist of deviance, Katz argues, "is to understand the emergence of distinctive sensual dynamics" (p. 4). Doing evil, he writes, is motivated by a quest for moral transcendence, righteousness in the face of challenge, boredom, humiliation, or chaos. Deviance has authenticity, Katz believes, an attractiveness that uplifts, excites, and purifies. To understand crime as a strictly rational enterprise, as the need to wallow in self-flagellation, as the manifestation of a mental disorder, or as the enactment of straightforward cultural or subcultural dictates, is to miss the point spectacularly. Deviance is the existential pursuit of passion, a "ludic" (or game-like) undertaking, with clear-cut winners and losers, a fevered, out-of-one's- head experience, a world of beauty, accessible only to the righteous, the daring, the members of a kind of soulful elite (see Goode, 1990).

and an astonishing 9 percent were under the age of 15. The problem with these statistics, as anyone might guess, is that they represent *arrested* robbers, not robbers in general; we suspect that robbers who aren't caught will differ in important ways from those who are. For instance, almost certainly the younger, less experienced robber is more likely to be caught than the older, wiser, more cautious, more professional, and more experienced robber.

One way of verifying this suspicion is to compare the FBI's arrest figures with the *perceived offender characteristics* supplied by robbery victims in the victimization surveys of the National Crime Victimization Surveys. The two sources of data generally agree with one another on robbers' characteristics, with some minor inconsistencies. In nine out of 10 robbery victimizations (89 percent), the offenders were male; in 5 percent of all cases, they were female; and in 4 percent, the victim was robbed by both male and female offenders, that is, at least one male and one female were said by victims to have committed the crime. Clearly, there is nearly perfect agreement between the FBI's statistics on arrest and victims' reports with respect to age. In about half of all robbery victimizations, the offenders were identified as Black (51 percent); in a third, they were white (36 percent); in 4 percent, they were members of some other racial category; in 4 percent, the offenders formed a "salt-and-pepper" team of mixed-race offenders; the rest of the victims weren't sure of the race of the offenders. Here, there is less than perfect agreement: Nearly 10 percent more *arrested* robbers were Black than were robbers identified in victimization surveys. In four out of 10 of all cases of robbery (41 percent), offenders were described as 20 years old or younger; in another four out of 10, they were identified as 21 or older; and in not quite one in 10, they were described as being of mixed ages (Harlow, 1987, p. 2). Here, the correspondence between arrest and victimization figures is fairly close.

In a nutshell, the portrait we received from the FBI's figures on arrest and the characteristics identified in victimization surveys is that relative to their numbers in the population, robbers tend to be young, male, and Black—and, of course, overwhelmingly urban.

Clearly, any explanation of robbery focusing on the offender must make use of at least two factors: *daring* and *poverty*. Robbery is not a crime for the fainthearted; it entails a great deal of risk, both to the victim and to the perpetrator. Robbers therefore tend to be (unrealistically) confident that they won't be injured or caught. Such misplaced confidence is more characteristic of males than females, of the young than of the older.

The race of robbery offenders is probably largely a function of a combination of the economic position of Blacks in the United States and the fact that African-Americans live in large cities. Black family income is roughly 55 to 60 percent of that of whites, and Black unemployment is twice as high. Moreover, although a growing proportion of Blacks earn incomes that increasingly approximate those of whites, a substantial proportion of the African-American population is seemingly permanently stuck in the "underclass" (Wilson, 1987; Auletta, 1982). In addition, since 1973, the poor have been getting poorer and the rich have been getting richer; hence, over the past two decades or more, the economic situation of the "underclass," of whom a disproportion number are inner-city minority members, is not only stagnating, but deteriorating (Cassidy, 1995). Added to the economic picture is the demographic factor: African-Americans are much more urban than whites. Nearly three out of 10 whites (29 percent) live in a rural area, whereas only 15 percent of Blacks, half the white figure, live in rural areas. At the other end of the scale, a quarter of all whites in the United States live in central cities (25 percent); for African-Americans, this is more than twice as high—57 percent (Bogue, 1985, p. 115). The combination of a lower per capita income and a far more urban residence makes it almost predictable that Blacks will have a higher rate of robbery than whites. In addition, there is the factor of age; while only 30 percent of the white population is under the age of 20, 40 percent of the Black population is that young. Since the African-American population is so much younger than the white population, this factor alone would tend to boost its robbery rate.

"RESPECTABLE" PROPERTY CRIME: SHOPLIFTING

Technically, shoplifting falls under the FBI's classification scheme as a form of larceny-theft. However, it possesses many features that are distinct. Consequently, it should be discussed separately from what are widely referred to as "street" crimes. What distinguishes the robber, the burglar, the petty thief, and the other "street" criminals from the ordinary, run-of-the-mill shoplifter? Both steal, and yet we perceive them to be radically different species of social animals. (Read the shoplifting account at the end of this chapter; do you consider this young woman a deviant, a criminal who should serve jail or prison time?) One crucial point I'd like to emphasize: Shoplifting is very far from small potatoes when it comes to the total monetary value that is stolen. The National Coalition to Prevent Shoplifting estimates the yearly value of goods shoplifted by customers at $8 billion; the National Retail Survey conducted in 1991 estimated that just under 2 percent of its gross retail sales were lost to "inventory shrinkage" (McCaghy and Capron, 1994, pp. 190–191). This total rivals that for all categories of reported property crimes, which the FBI estimated at $14 billion, and it is more than 10 times the total take for robbery.

Perhaps the most significant fact about shoplifting is that most of us do not regard it as a "real" crime. The majority of shoplifters do not regard themselves as criminals, and they are not so regarded by their nonshoplifting peers. Shoplifters generally take low-value items. Although they may do it often, they do not make a career out of shoplifting and do not earn enough doing it to support themselves. They have no connections with people who do steal for a living, and hold no values, beliefs, or practices that contrast with the rest of us, other than shoplifting itself. The kind of stealing that most retail store thieves engage in requires no skill. Shoplifters stem from all walks of life. They are teenagers, homemakers, stable working-class men and women, professionals, white-collar workers, the elderly on small, fixed incomes, in

short, shoplifters could be just about anyone. Shoplifters are conventional people for the most part, and shoplifting borders on being conventional behavior. Stigma does not adhere to persons who steal low-value items once in a while, even regularly, from stores. "Everybody does it," we say to ourselves, and that's just about the end of the matter; we hold ourselves blameless. "Just don't get caught," we warn.

As I said, shoplifting belongs to that miscellaneous, grab-bag category the FBI calls "larceny-theft." Stealing from stores is not merely widespread, it is routine. Commercial security—personnel and equipment to protect retail business establishments from theft—is one of the nation's fastest-growing industries. "Inventory shrinkage" in large cities has been estimated at *8 percent* of sales (Barmash, 1973). Another study, which took place in Spokane, Washington, found that roughly the same proportion, one shopper out of twelve, was a shoplifter (Ray, 1987). In a study in New York City, it was discovered that one out of 10 randomly observed customers in a retail store took some item of value without paying for it (Hellman, 1970). Moreover, the risk of apprehension is extremely low, which is one of the reasons why its incidence is so high; one British study found that only one out of 100 shoplifters was detected stealing (Buckle and Farrington, 1984).

Not only is shoplifting common, it borders on being respectable; it has group support. This is especially the case among teenagers. They join one another on shoplifting "expeditions," ripping off items of value for amusement and personal gain. There is peer pressure for others to join in, should anyone express reluctance to do so. Moreover, the activity is an adjunct to other pleasurable activities—socializing, fantasizing, "hanging out," meeting members of the opposite sex. In this respect, it is not unlike seeing a movie, going to the beach, driving around in a car, or standing around on street corners. Meeting other teenagers to go to stores and steal—particularly in large shopping centers like suburban malls—does not appear to represent a form of deviant behavior to most of them. This is, in fact, what is so fascinating about it. More than anything else, it manifests adherence to several basic conventional, mainstream values, such as sociability, materialism, and hedonism. For the most part, when adults steal from stores, they do so far less in the company of others, and in all likelihood, derive less excitement from it, but like teenagers, other conventional values seem to be present. "It is ironic," one sociologist writes, "that good citizens should be part of the crime problem, but all that distinguishes them from criminals is the degree of violence used" (McCaghy, 1976, p. 165).

Shoplifters come in two basic varieties: the *booster* and the *snitch* (Cameron, 1964). Boosters steal primarily for the purpose of resale; snitches are amateurs and steal mainly for personal use of the items they take. Boosters steal as a means of earning a living or augmenting what they already make. They take more expensive items, those that are more readily converted to cash; obviously, they are more likely to steal repeatedly; and they tend to be more cautious and less deterred by security measures when they steal. Representatives of stores make a clear distinction between amateurs and professionals: The greater the value of the item stolen, the greater the likelihood that they will report the theft to the police. In one study, there were over three times as many referrals by store representatives to the police for the theft of valuable items as for the theft of less valuable ones (Hindelang, 1974). In over 6,000 cases of shoplifters apprehended in drug and grocery stores, only 13 percent of those who had taken small-value items were reported to the police, but 40 percent who had taken large-value items were reported. In addition, the *nature* of the goods stolen influenced the store's decision to report the theft to the police: Items that could be readily resold—especially meat, liquor, and cigarettes—more often elicited reporting this behavior to the police (Hindelang, 1974). This action is clearly designed to punish the habitual professional thief, the "booster."

The earlier studies on the issue of whether the ancillary characteristics of offenders made a difference in their offenses being reported to the police supported the "labeling" perspective. In Cameron's classic study (1964), sex and race were intimately related to offenders being referred to the police. Only 10 percent of the apprehended women were reported, but over a third (35 percent) of the men received this treatment. The disparity along racial lines was even more glaring; while only a tenth of all non-Blacks were reported to the police (11 percent), this was true of well over half of all Blacks (58 percent). Clearly, prejudice of a high order of magnitude was at work here. Recall that the labeling theory of reactions to deviance holds that contingencies, or characteristics not directly related to

the offense, powerfully shape how conventional authorities sanction the offender. Cameron's study seems to bear out this general argument.

However, consider the fact that Cameron's study was conducted between 1943 and 1949, a period when racial prejudice was considerably higher than it is today. (African-Americans were not even allowed to try on clothes in Chicago department stores until the 1940s!) Consequently, her generalizations concerning the relationship between offenders' characteristics and being reported to the police may not hold today. In a typed addendum to a study which showed that "hippie-appearing" shoplifters were more likely to be reported to store representatives than more conventional-looking shoplifters, the authors acknowledge that their study's findings may have been applicable only to the Vietnam War era (Steffensmeier and Terry, 1973). Later studies do not reveal the ancillary characteristics of race, age, or sex to have any impact on the reporting of shoplifters to the police. Almost exactly the same proportion of Blacks (28 percent) as whites (25 percent) were reported; almost exactly the same percentage of males (26 percent) as females (25 percent) were reported; and almost exactly the same proportion of adolescents (21 percent) as middle-aged adults were reported. Only the *value* of the item stolen and the item's *resalability* influenced whether the crime was reported. This researcher concluded that "the characteristics of the offense, more than the characteristics of the offender, are associated with decisions to take official action" (Hindelang, 1974, p. 592). Another study (Cohen and Stark, 1974) corroborated these findings, the one difference being that an unemployed shoplifter was always referred to the police, whereas in this study an employed shoplifter had a 50-50 chance of being released.

"RESPECTABLE" PROPERTY CRIME: EMPLOYEE PILFERAGE

Even more "respectable" and conventional than shoplifting by the amateur is what is referred to as *employee pilferage*. The National Retail Survey referred to above estimated that while a quarter of all "inventory shrinkage" (26 percent) resulted from shoplifting, substantially more, more than a third (38 percent) was due to theft by employees. Moreover, employees steal not just from retail stores, but from all workplace locales: hospitals, factories, ships and docks, construction sites, trucking companies, offices, the armed services and other governmental agencies, and even schools, colleges, and universities. Two criminologists opine that with respect to monetary value, employee pilferage "is one of the most costly, if not the most costly, offense by individuals in the United States" (McCaghy and Capron, 1994, p. 263).

And yet, employee pilferage attracts relatively little attention from criminologists and sociologists. Criminological studies on money-making street crimes probably outnumber those on employee pilferage by a ratio of perhaps more than 100 to 1. Employees rationalize and justify their participation in theft on the job by saying: "It's a corporation—it's not like taking from one person"; "The company doesn't mind, they've got plenty, they're not losing anything"; "They expect it, they've already figured it in"; "Everyone's doing it"; "The insurance company pays for it" (Barlow, 1993, pp. 234–235). And the general public feels considerably more threat from street crime than from employee pilferage. In fact, perpetrators of the latter crime actually *are* the general public; why should they feel threatened?

Shoplifting and employee pilferage are instances in which the organization and ultimately the public are the victims. Analyses of employee theft hold that it *boosts morale*, it compensates the worker for low wages, and it acts as an *unofficial reward system* (McCaghy, 1976, p. 181). It is, some observers believe, a system of "controlled larceny" (Zeitlin, 1971). Employers typically know of the thievery (although they usually do not know specifically *who* is engaged in it) and are aware that it boosts employee morale. It compensates for low wages and alienating, boring jobs. It is therefore not only tolerated by employers (up to a point, of course, at times, it may become rampant and harmful to the firm), but it may also be considered a worthwhile price to pay for a valuable device for controlling and pacifying employees. By tolerating theft, employers can continue paying employees low wages and do not have to worry so much about their workers hating their jobs. Employee theft, therefore, supports the status quo and may serve to retard meaningful change on the job. The ultimate victim of this thievery is not the organization from which items are stolen, of course, but the public. Losses are recovered by a rise in prices, a lowering of the quality of goods, or a curtailment of services. Radical manifestos written in the 1960s

and 1970s, such as Abbie Hoffman's *Steal This Book*, that urged stealing as a revolutionary act failed to point out that the business community loses considerably less than the consumer does from theft. In an economy controlled and administered by capitalists, steps are taken to ensure that the business community does not suffer significantly from criminal behavior. Losses are passed on to the consumer and the general public. And meanwhile, some crimes may actually profit the business community by producing more pliable workers.

SUMMARY

Much of the crime picture entails property crime: a perpetrator illegally taking something of value from its rightful owner. While stealing is widespread in the population, the vast majority of all serious property crime is committed by an extremely small proportion of Americans. Property crime includes *burglary* (the illegal entry into a structure to commit a crime); *motor vehicle theft*; and an all-purpose, grab-bag category that is referred to as *larceny-theft*. In addition, *robbery* (taking property by force, violence, the threat of violence, or putting the victim in fear) is both a property crime and a crime of violence. In contrast to property crime, *white-collar crime* usually does not involve the physical removal of property; instead, it entails the illegal alteration of records or documents. Criminologists treat white-collar crime as a separate category. *Shoplifting* and *employee pilferage* are two types of property crime that are seen by the public as not especially deviant or criminal. A significant characteristic of property crime is that it is impersonal; it takes place because citizens have become indifferent to depriving the victim of something they want. In this respect, it contrasts sharply with crimes of violence.

Criminologists make use of a variety of research materials to determine the nature of crime generally and property crime specifically. Three of the most important are the Uniform Crime Reports, victimization surveys, and self-report surveys. Each year, the Federal Bureau of Investigation (FBI) combines and tallies information on crimes known to the police from 16,000 separate jurisdictions around the country, roughly 97 percent of the population; these are referred to as the Uniform Crime Reports. One problem with this source of data is *underre-*

porting: Roughly two-thirds of all victims do not report crimes committed against them to the police. Hence, the Uniform Crime Reports leave *most* crimes out of the picture. Still, the more serious the offense, the greater the likelihood that it will be reported. With some crimes, such as murder, motor vehicle theft, and commercial robbery, reporting is nearly complete; with others (such as drug offenses), the "dark figure" of hidden crime is immense.

The federal government sponsors a periodic survey of crime victimization; members of a sample of households are asked if they have been victims of designated offenses in the past six months or a year. More citizens report having been victimized by crimes to a researcher than report those crimes to the police. Most criminologists regard victimization surveys as more accurate, valid, and complete than the Uniform Crime Reports. Lastly, criminologists also make use of self-report surveys to study crime systematically and empirically. Common sense tells us that respondents will lie about their criminal involvement. Surprisingly, when asked about their involvement in criminal activities, most respondents have been found to be telling the truth, to the best of their ability. There is one qualification: Respondents must be made to understand that they are anonymous, their answers are confidential, and their revelations will not get them into trouble in any way. For the most part, the problem with self-report surveys is not truthfulness, but sampling. Since surveys are expensive, their samples tend to be fairly small; hence, questions are usually asked concerning fairly common (and trivial) offenses, while more serious crimes (such as robbery and murder) are too rare to appear frequently in surveys.

Surveys have been conducted on how seriously crimes are regarded by the public. Crimes against persons, also referred to as crimes of violence, are regarded as significantly more serious than property crimes, especially if death or injury occurs. Robbery, which entails victim confrontation and force, violence, or the threat of violence, is regarded as more serious than nonviolent property crime, such as burglary or simple theft. A crime in which a weapon is used, especially a gun, is regarded as more serious than one in which no weapon is used. With property crime, the greater the value of that which is stolen, the more seriously the crime is regarded. And lastly, the more effort the perpetra-

tor has to make to commit the crime, the more seriously the public regards it.

The motives for property crime are diverse, but among them, poverty combined with the ready availability of symbols and manifestations of affluence in the society must be regarded as central. Both low income (an individual variable) and a society's income distribution (a societal variable) must be regarded as central in the etiology of property crime, although important qualifications are necessary. Property crime victimization shows a complex relationship with socioeconomic status (SES). With some crimes, such as robbery, it is the poor who are most likely to be victimized, while the affluent are least likely. On the other hand, some other property crimes, such as personal theft and motor vehicle theft, display a positive relationship with income and SES, that is, the affluent are most likely to be victimized and the poor are least likely. The relationship between property crime and age seems to be fairly invariant in all industrialized countries: Crime rises sharply after the age of 10, reaches a peak late in adolescence, and declines during the twenties and thirties. Sex or gender, likewise, is strongly related to criminal activity, in fact, it is the factor or variable that is most closely related. Roughly 90 percent of all arrestees on the charge of robbery, burglary, and motor vehicle theft are male. Only for larceny-theft, which includes shoplifting, are as many as a third of all suspects female.

Robbery is perhaps the most sociologically interesting of all property crimes; it is both a property crime and a crime of violence. Only half of all robberies in the United States are reported to the police. According to current victimization surveys, roughly 1.2 million robberies take place in the United States each year, making it the least frequently committed of all major categories of property crime. Robbery is a risky, difficult, dangerous criminal endeavor, and is engaged in by an unusual type of perpetrator. Robbery, perhaps more than any other crime, and certainly more than any other type of property crime, is predictive of a serious and committed criminal way of life. Since robbers depend on victims not recognizing them, robbery tends to flourish in a context of anonymity, which usually means in large urban centers. The robbery rate in big cities is nearly 50 times that which prevails in rural areas. In only a minority of robberies are the perpetrator and the victim acquainted. A very low proportion of these cases are reported to the police; often, they involve disputes between intimates as to the ownership of money or property. Robbery victimization is roughly parallel to that of violent crime generally: Males, the young, and the poor are most likely to be victims of robbery. A small minority of robberies (two-tenths of 1 percent) result in criminal homicide. Looked at the other way around, roughly one homicide in 10 results from a robbery—a sizeable proportion. Strong-arm or weaponless robbery is more likely to result in injury to the victim than robberies which entail a weapon, but when the perpetrator has a gun, the victim's chances of being killed are significantly higher than if the assailant has no weapon. A disproportionate percentage of robbers are young, inner-city minority males; poverty, urban residence, and youth are all related to the dynamics of committing robbery.

Shoplifting and employee pilferage are often referred to as "respectable" property crimes, since they are so common, so few perpetrators have a criminal identity, and so much of the public regards them as not seriously deviant or criminal. Still, these two crimes result in a total monetary loss greater than all the more conventional "street" crimes added together. Employee pilferage is sometimes rgarded as a form of "controlled larceny" in which employees feel that they are compensating for low wages and boring work by stealing. Both have a great deal of group or peer normative support.

ACCOUNT: SHOPLIFTING

The contributor of this account is a 20-year-old college student.

It all began the day before Christmas as I was doing my holiday shopping in New York [City]. I went into a few stores and purchased some gifts, when I noticed that my bag was open. I searched frantically for my wallet—only to find that it was gone. I had been robbed! I went out onto the street and looked at all of the faces around me trying to figure out who had stolen my wallet. I was so angry that I wanted to scream out, *"Who stole my wallet?!"*, but I didn't because I was afraid. Then I remembered that the $80 I had saved for holiday shopping was in that wallet. All my money was now gone, and I wouldn't be able to give my family or friends any gifts. I stood there feeling hurt and scared. Soon I began to get cold, and so I wandered into a department store. I noticed a beautiful sweater that would have looked terrific on my boyfriend. I really wanted to give him something for Christmas, but without any money, I wouldn't be able to. In an instant, I realized that if someone stole from me, why can't I steal too?

That's when it began. I got a shopping bag from a cashier and put my gloves, hat, and scarf into the shopping bag so it didn't look so empty. When I felt that no one was looking, I casually slipped the sweater into the shopping bag. I thought to myself, this isn't so hard, and I felt satisfied. But then I became aware of the fact that the sweater cost $20, but the thief who stole my wallet took $80. This just didn't seem very fair. I felt I had to take something else to compensate for the rest of the money that was taken. So I picked up a shirt and slowly slipped it into my bag. I thought to myself, "I did it again." I had stolen $35 worth of merchandise—not enough to get even, but enough to feel satisfied for the time being. Then I rushed out of the store.

Outside I felt relieved. I felt a sense of accomplishment, as if I had done something wonderful, like getting an "A" on an exam or being praised for something I had done. But how could I feel this way? I had done something wrong, something illegal—a sin. Then I realized I didn't care. Anyone in my position would have done the same thing. I felt that I had found revenge on society for stealing my money, for taking what was rightfully mine. I had done the same thing they had done to me; it was "an eye for an eye, a tooth for a tooth." How could anyone condemn me—I was only getting even. After I reached $80, I would stop. Then I would be even.

As time went on, I didn't really feel that I had gotten even. I had stolen $35 worth of merchandise, and they took $80 from me. Therefore, I still had $45 to go. As time went on, I felt less and less guilty. I even started to feel proud of the fact that I had gotten away with it; I had tricked society. It now seemed much easier to steal than to pay for something I wanted. The next time, I stole a bottle of perfume for my Mom by slipping it under my sweater. It seemed so much easier this time, so natural. The more I stole the more I enjoyed the excitement. The idea of getting caught both scared and fascinated me. My heart beat rapidly, my palms would sweat; when I did it, I could only think about getting out of the store as soon as possible. The moment I left the store, I felt relieved and totally relaxed. A sense of total satisfaction came over me. It was like an emotional high.

At some point, I realized that I had reached the $80. I had gotten even with society and had reached my goal. But I still didn't feel the sense of relief I needed. I vowed that I would stop stealing, but whenever I saw something I wanted I thought, why not take it? It takes so long to make money and so little time to spend it. I found that I enjoyed stealing and felt that I wasn't going to stop. This all changed when my brother caught me stealing. We went shopping, and he wanted to purchase a pair of sunglasses. I told him I would get them for him as a present. I went over to the counter and slipped them into my bag, looking around to see if anyone was looking. I thought, great—I did it again. Then I casually walked out of the store. Later, in the car on the way home, my brother said that he saw me stealing the sunglasses. He said that he was ashamed of me and couldn't understand why I had to steal when I could always get money from home. I felt disgusted with myself. I hated myself for making my brother feel ashamed of me. I told him that I would promise never to do it again if he would never repeat this incident to anyone. He agreed.

Afterward, I felt as if someone had lifted a huge burden from my shoulders. I have never lied to my brother, and I wasn't going to start now. I never want to see that hurt look in my brother's face again. It has been a year since I shoplifted anything, and I'm glad that I haven't. I now feel better about myself. However, that exciting thrill of taking something is gone. I can never feel that way again. I still have some trouble when I see something I really want and can't afford; I still say to myself, why not take it? But I feel that I can fight that desire. I feel much better about myself and my life now than I did when I was stealing. (From the author's files.)

chapter **12**

WHITE-COLLAR AND CORPORATE CRIME

"Postal Worker Embezzled $3.5 Million," "A New Insider-Trading Case Hits Major Business Figures," "Texan Gets Five Years In Big S&L Collapse," "U.S. Charges $25 Million Gone in Fraud." These headlines announce a type of crime that is very different from what usually comes to mind when we hear or read about it. This is *white-collar crime*. Will we recognize one when we see it? And, more generally, can we construct a clear definition of the general concept? *White-collar crime* is one of the very few terms coined by a sociologist that has entered into the vocabulary of the mass media as well as the general public. Where did the term come from? And to what exactly does it refer? Who is the perpetrator in a white-collar "crime"? And what consequences might it have? Perhaps most important for our purposes: Is white-collar crime really a form of deviance at all? If it isn't, why are we studying it? If it is, what *makes* it deviant behavior?

White-collar crime is not a classic, clear-cut case of deviance. *In some respects*, it is a form of deviant behavior; in other respects, it is *not*. In the sense that audiences designate corporate actions which harm people physically and take money out of their pockets as serious crimes (Friedrichs, 1996, pp. 48–50), they are a form of deviance. To the extent that illegal white-collar actions are likely to result in prosecution and a jail or prison sentence, they are deviant. To the extent that a conviction and a jail or prison sentence for a white-collar crime is stigmatizing, *personally discrediting*, that it *taints* the character of the offender (for instance, if friends and loved ones regard mention of it in an obituary inappropriate, a "smear"), then clearly, it is a form of deviance. To the extent that there are social circles in this society made up of persons who define executive misdeeds as serious wrongdoing, and attempt to legitimate that view in the society as a whole, then they are indeed a form of deviance *in those circles*.

On the other hand, to the extent that harmful corporate crime is seen as serious but does *not* result in jury conviction of offenders or stiff prison sentences (Friedrichs, 1996, p. 60), then it is not deviant. To the extent that social circles define such actions as acceptable, and characterize their prosecution a "witch hunt," then clearly, in those circles, such actions are *not* deviant. Just because white-collar actions are unethical, harm people, and are formally against the law, does not automatically make them deviant *to the relevant audiences*. Just because we, or persons very much like us, don't like the behavior of executives can't magically make their behavior deviant. *Are corporate misdeeds condemned by the public?* Are they commonly *prosecuted* by the criminal justice system? Can corporate wrongdoers get into *trouble* as a result of their actions? If the answer is yes, then absolutely, they are deviant. If it's no, then they are not. What we see, instead, is an ambivalent case. White-collar crime has one foot in conventionality and one in deviance. This is one of the reasons why it is so interesting.

White-collar crime is wrongdoing in high, or at least moderately high, places. We do not expect the executive, the bank clerk, the physician or lawyer to engage in crime, or to be prosecuted, convicted, and sent to prison. Most of us have a conception of crime that *precludes* the respectability of the offender. "Crime" is what street people—or at least poor people—do. There is, as many observers have pointed out, a certain *incongruity* in seeing an affluent, 60-year-old banker in handcuffs and a prison uniform, being marched off to a prison cell, to serve time with murderers, rapists, and burglars. Many of us can understand the motives of poor, powerless criminals, who steal out of desperation or commit violence as a result of anger and frustration. The crimes of the rich and the powerful are puzzling to us, however; if someone can earn a sizeable income legally, why try to earn even more in an illegal fashion? Why risk one's current material comfort and freedom simply to gain an edge over one's competitors? Is it greed? To many casual observers, white-collar crime doesn't make a great deal of sense.

The fact is that white-collar crime is similar to all *instrumental* actions, that is, those that are designed to achieve a certain goal; under certain circumstances, achievement of the goal assumes far greater importance than the means by which the goal is attained (Merton, 1938). One major *subtype* of deviant behavior takes place when the actor resorts to *illegitimate* means to achieve a *legitimate* goal. If the likelihood of detection is extremely low, resorting to *legal* or *legitimate* means to attain that goal is actually quite *irrational*, since typically, they are less efficient and less effective. Following legal procedures usually ties the corporate actor down to rules, regulations, and restrictions that may actually prevent or frustrate the achievement of desired goals. In the corporate world, we are forced to ask: "Given the great rewards and low risks of detection, why do so many businesspeople adopt the 'economically irrational' course of obeying the law?" (Braithwaite, 1985, p. 6).

But note: The same logic is not unique to the business world, nor even to capitalist society. Students often cheat on exams because it gets them what they want—a higher grade; shoppers may shoplift clothes, again, because it permits them to have what they cannot otherwise afford; many of us lie because, once again, in so doing, we attain what we desire—respect, admiration, or getting out of a sticky situation. When legitimate or conventional avenues make the attainment of a goal difficult or impossible, many of us, whether as individual or as corporate actors, will resort to illegitimate or deviant avenues. But the conditions that create the impulse to deviate are widespread, not confined to business dealings. "Some organizations seek profits, others seek survival, still others seek to fulfill government-imposed quotas, others seek to service a body of professionals who run them, some seek to win wars, and some seek to serve a clientele. Whatever the goals might be, it is the emphasis on them that creates trouble" (Gross, 1978, p. 72). In other words, it is not the worm in the apple that is the problem here—it is the apple itself.

EDWIN SUTHERLAND'S INNOVATION

In December 1939, at the annual meeting of the American Sociological Society (later, the American Sociological Association), Edwin Sutherland, president of the society, delivered a talk entitled "The White-collar Criminal"; a year later, it was published in the *American Sociological Review* (1940); six years later, his argument was elaborated and supported by some preliminary results of an empirical study (1945); 10 years after his talk, he published the results of his research in the form of a book (1949); and decades later, an "uncut" version was published (1983) containing the names of the corporations that were in violation of the law. In his original talk, Sutherland made the following points.

First, white-collar crime is *real* crime. It is "real" crime according to three criteria. One, it is "in violation of the criminal law" (1940, p. 12). Two, it entails the loss of enormous sums of money, several times greater in value than the sums stolen by ordinary, conventional street crime. And three, white-collar crime damages social relations, creates distrust, and "lowers morale and produces social disorganization on a large scale"; in this respect, it is far more harmful than street crime.

Second, Sutherland argued, in spite of the fact that white-collar crime is "real" crime, it is not treated as such. White-collar criminals are treated differently from lower-class street criminals because the upper classes, who commit white-collar crimes, have more influence over legislatures, law enforcement, and the administration of justice. They are administratively segregated from lower-class street criminals, dealt with in the administrative and civil courts, in short, treated as a less serious category of offenders. (For this distinction, see the following section on civil, administrative, and criminal law.) As the Marxists and conflict theorists argue, the criminal law reflects the interests of the most powerful segments or classes in a society (Chambliss, 1964). This does not, however, make white-collar offenders any the less criminal Sutherland argued. As a result of their influence and social status, white-collar criminals do not see themselves as "real" criminals, nor does the public, nor, said Sutherland, do criminologists.

Third, criminological theories of crime causation are inadequate, indeed, fatally flawed, because they focus more or less entirely on street crimes, such as robbery, murder, and rape, which are committed largely by lower-class and working-class persons. Any adequate theory must account for or explain all analytically homogeneous classes of phenomena it purports to explain. It cannot exclude some of them on the basis of arbitrary criteria. The difference between white-collar and street crime is the class composition of their perpetrators, not the nature of crime itself. Since variables such as poverty, broken homes, and psychopathy and sociopathy, are not characteristic of the upper classes, they cannot account for crime in general, and hence, must be rejected as invalid.

Fourth, a theory that explains *all* crime is necessary, not just lower-class crime. And fifth, Sutherland argued, the theory of differential association, which we looked at in Chapter 4, does explain all crime.

Edwin Sutherland did not consider himself a reformer or a muckraker. In fact, what he was most interested in reforming was the field of criminology. His interest was *theoretical*: He felt that the theories of crime that prevailed at that time were invalid because they could not explain a major type of criminal behavior. White-collar crime was ignored, he felt, because of the social standing of its perpetrators. As he saw it, only his theoretical position could account for all crime, white-collar crime included.

Sutherland's argument that the illegal business practices of the rich and powerful were "true" crimes was not completely original with him. In fact, his thesis advisor at the University of Chicago, Charles Henderson, wrote of "new and colossal kinds of crime" committed by the "social classes of the highest culture," which included "debauching of . . . councils, legislatures, and bribery of the press and public officials" (1901, p. 250). Edward A. Ross, another early sociologist, wrote of the "criminaloid" persons who profited from unethical, even wicked, illegal practices (1907). Sutherland adapted and used the term in his 1934 edition of his criminology text which referred to the "white-collar criminaloid." But it was Sutherland who coined the term "white-collar crime" and who put the phenomenon on the intellectual map.

Sutherland's investigation of white-collar crime "altered the study of crime throughout the world in fundamental ways" (Geis and Goff, 1983, p. ix). The immediate impact of the introduction of the concept of white-collar crime was to encourage a whole generation of young scholars to do research on the subject, scholars such as Frank Hartung (1950), Marshall Clinard (1952), and Donald Cressey (1953). In the long run, it stimulated an immense flood of research; indeed, it can be said that Sutherland's talk, delivered some six decades ago, virtually created an entire subfield of criminology. White-collar crime is studied in countries the world over (Geis and Goff, 1983, pp. xi–xii); this makes sense because scholars now recognize that at the highest levels, it is not only an international but a *transnational* phenomenon (Michalowski and Kramer, 1987). Very few ideas in any field have the kind of impact that Sutherland's has had. One summary of the 100 most often cited authors in the field of criminology indicated that Sutherland's book made the single most important contribution to the field (Wolfgang, Figlio, and Thornberry, 1978). Sutherland's contribution was so great, opined one criminologist, that if there were a Nobel Prize awarded in criminology, Sutherland would have received it for his work on white-collar crime (Mannheim, 1965, p. 470). Today, virtually all criminology textbooks devote a chapter or at least a major section to white-collar crime or its equivalent. In addition, it has had a major impact on the study of deviant behavior; all of the recent, full-length deviance textbooks include a chapter that is a direct product of Sutherland's innovation, whether it is referred to as: white-collar crime (Thio, 1995), corporate crime (Ward, Carter, and Perrin, 1994), "deviance and organizations" (McCaghy and Capron, 1994), economic and political criminality (Clinard and Meier, 1995), corporate deviance and state or governmental deviance (Curra, 1994), elite deviance (Little, 1994), or "formal deviance: civil wrongs and administrative violations" (Heitzeg, 1996). This textbook is no exception.

The reception of white-collar crime has not always been smooth or lacking in controversy, however. In 1947, lawyer-sociologist Paul Tappan attacked Sutherland's idea that white-collar crime is "real" crime and that white-collar "criminals" are real criminals (Tappan, 1947). Tappan took the notion "innocent until proven guilty" literally; he argued that it makes no sense to refer to offenders who were not convicted in a court of law *as criminals*. We have to wait until offenders are actually *convicted* before we can call them criminals, whether or not they wear a white collar. In a parallel vein, the behavior in which a given corporate actor engages cannot be referred to as a crime unless that act *results* in conviction. (We notice a parallel here with the "extreme," or hard, reactivist definition, which was discussed in Chapters 2 and 5.) Responding to this criticism, Sutherland argued that behavior does not have to result in a conviction to be called a "crime." He said, concerning a given action, that the informed observer should have "a reasonable expectancy of conviction if tried in a criminal court" (1949, p. 6). "An unlawful act is not defined as criminal by the fact that it is punished," he continued, "but by the fact that it is punishable" (p. 35). (Here, we see a strong parallel with our "soft," or "moderate," reactivist definition of deviance, spelled out in Chapter 5.) The decision of a court is no more necessary to determine an act's objective status, he declared, than is true in determining the property of chemicals or biological phenomena (p. 30). While Tappan's critical comments are often cited in the field of criminology, hardly any scholars nowadays see his objections as fatal to the concept of white-collar crime. One of the very rare exceptions is Gwynn Nettler, who argues that white-collar offenses represent behavior whose "wrongness . . . is disputed"; he claims that it is "a sore issue whether, and when" violations of laws designed to govern business practices are "real crimes" (1984, p. 122).

In addition to the admittedly few outright skeptics and critics of Sutherland's thesis, it must be emphasized that interest in and research on the idea of white-collar crime as "real" crime has gone through cycles of attention and indifference. From Sutherland's initial talk on the subject until the early 1960s, research interest remained fairly lively (considering the fact that the *total volume* of research in both sociology and criminology was vastly smaller in the 1940s and 1950s than is true today). In 1968, Gilbert Geis published an anthology which drew together the bulk of the accumulated research in this fledgling field of white-collar crime studies (Geis, 1968). Between the 1960s and the 1970s, a lull seemed to have fallen over the field. Only a third of the second edition of Geis's anthology on white-collar crime had been published since its first edition, and though the publications listed in its references had doubled, most had originally appeared in law journals (Geis and Meier, 1977; Geis, Meier, and Salinger, 1995, p. 7). In contrast, after the mid to late 1970s, there was a tremendous resurgence in interest in and research on the subject. While the first two editions contained virtually everything "of scholarly merit," by 1995, this was no longer possible; the early trickle had become a flood. The white-collar crime idea is now a fixture in our intellectual landscape; it provides a beacon for a veritable industry of research on a major form of criminal and deviant behavior (Rosoff, Pontell, and Tillman, 1996).

In addition to white-collar crime's occasional doubters and critics, and the up-and-down cycle of interest in and indifference to the idea, there is a third fly in the soup. The fact is that Sutherland's ideas have not been adopted lock, stock, and barrel by the field of criminology. In fact, as Sutherland originally formulated it, the concept of white-collar crime is now almost universally recognized to be deeply flawed, conceptually muddy, even self-contradictory in key respects. In his pioneering talk, Sutherland avoided a formal definition, stating vaguely that he was interested in "crime in relation to business." He got no closer to a consistent, systematic definition in a later article (1945). In his book, the product of a major empirical study of corporate offenses, published a decade later (1949, 1983), Sutherland offered the following definition: "White-collar crime may be defined approximately as a crime committed by a person of respectability and high social status in the course of his occupation" (1949, p. 9). But in a footnote on the same page, he adds that his term "is used to refer principally to business managers and executives" (p. 9). Yet, if we were to follow the definition strictly, why *should* the definition apply "principally" to managers and executives? For that matter, what does "principally" mean? That we can include some, but not all, nonmanagers and nonexecutives? If so, according to what criteria? Why not include bank tellers and accountants—occupants of respectable positions—who embezzle from the firms for which they work? Moreover, Sutherland betrayed his concept with his examples, which included shoe sales personnel, appliance repairers, and even ordinary citizens who cheat on their income taxes. Another locus of conceptual confusion concerns Sutherland's characterization of "crime." At one point, he argues that white-collar crime is "real" crime because "in all cases" it is "in violation of the criminal law" (p. 12). But in other places, Sutherland insisted that the criminal law is written by the powerful classes and hence, we must "supplement" our examination of the criminal law by including administrative and civil law, which do not provide for penal sanctions. How can we properly refer to a type of law as criminal if it is not included in the criminal law? Some observers see a contradiction here.

But in spite of Sutherland's conceptual imprecision, his white-collar crime idea remains influential. He left an intellectual legacy of which very few scholars or researchers can boast. If he did not clarify the concept for later generations, at the very least he put his finger on a phenomenon of enduring importance.

WHAT IS CRIMINAL LAW?

The term "law" is often used very loosely. We often say, "There oughta be a law," when we find something that someone does annoying. Actually, if we wish to be precise about it, there are several very distinct *types* of law, each with different functions and consequences. Let's distinguish among them, beginning with one with which we won't be dealing at all.

For the most part, sociologists don't think of *natural law* as a form of law at all because its very existence is contrary to what we know about deviance and crime. Eighteenth- and early nineteenth-century scholars who studied crime believed that a body of universal, absolute principles existed which spelled out actions that were—or should have been— punished everywhere and at all times. These *innately criminal* acts presumably violated "natural law." If these laws are meant to be *universal*, one problem is that anthropologists can't agree on what they are, so variable are the codes and customs of different societies the world over. In principle, no society on earth permits the wanton killing of its own members. However, exceptions have often been made (in the past, in some societies, monarchs killed powerless citizens almost at will), and perpetrators often went unpunished. The incest taboo is nearly universal, but again, there are exceptions, and punishment is far from consistent. If these laws are meant to be *absolute* rather than simply universal, no one has figured out a means by which this can be determined. Almost without exception, contemporary criminologists and students of deviance have given up on the notion of natural law.

Civil law is a set of rules and principles that spells out the rights, duties, and obligations of persons and other private parties toward one another. (For the purpose of the civil court, a corporation or even the government may be *regarded* as a "private party.") More specifically, it stipulates conditions under which one party has harmed or wronged another. A harm or wrong in civil law is referred to as a *tort*. In a civil court, the wronged or aggrieved party (the plaintiff) seeks *compensation* or *restitution* from the offending party (the defendant). This is what happens in a lawsuit, the plaintiff "sues" the defendant. Four points are crucial in civil law. First, the wrong is a harm inflicted by *one party against another*; it does not entail a wrong against the state or the people as a whole. Second, the aggrieved party seeks *restitution*, that is, to recover what he or she has suffered or lost. This usually entails monetary payment equivalent to what was lost by the injured party, such as the value of a car, a salary, or a lost limb. Under unusual circumstances, in an especially grievous case, the civil court may levy a punitive fine against the defendant. Third, civil law does not and cannot call for the *arrest* of a defendant who is being sued, nor can an unfavorable ruling against a defendant in civil court result in sending that party to *jail* or *prison*. And fourth, for the most part, civil law is *case* law, that is, it is based mainly on precedent, in other words, concrete decisions that judges have made in actual cases.

Administrative law governs the powers and duties of governmental agencies, which oversee and pass judgment on the doings of a variety of parties whose dealings can affect the public. Administrative law sets standards regarding occupational safety, product safety, what may and may not be sent out over the airwaves, which chemicals may be sold as prescription drugs and which ones may be sold over the counter, public transportation, such as airline regulations, restrictions regarding the trucking industry, air and water pollution, and so on. Again, administrative law does not call for arrest; though the administrative court may levy fines against an offending party, usually a business corporation, but it may not send any party to jail or prison. These fines may be (but usually are not) considerable—in principle, a million dollars a day could be levied—and hence, may act as punitive fines. Since the administration of President Ronald Reagan (1981–1989), however, federal budgets and staff for administrative agencies have been cut back. Interestingly, as a result of the unwillingness of many of these agencies to take action, citizens and activist groups have sued some of them in *civil* court in order to take more aggressive action against corporate offenders (Coleman, 1994, p. 158).

Lastly, we have the realm of *criminal law*. A crime, or a violation of the criminal law, is regarded as an offense against the state, the people, and the society as a whole, not merely a specific injured party. The criminal courts represent the only adjudicating body (aside from the military courts) that has the power to imprison a defendant in the event of conviction. (It may also levy punitive fines.) In civil or tort law, it is the injured party (along with enterprising lawyers) who initiates legal proceedings. With criminal law, it is the state that initiates the legal process. (Although this process usually begins with a citizen complaint.) More specifically, the criminal law is the only legal realm which can entail arrest. *Common law* is a hodgepodge of customs and traditions that have not been formally enacted into law by legislatures. Medieval common law guided judges in rendering a decision in a trial. In modern societies, much common law is eventually enacted into formal or legislative criminal law. Hence, criminal law that has its roots in common law is frequently, although loosely, referred to as "common law," even though it is the product of a decision by a legislature. Common law originated in the customs of the people. Perhaps a better term for violations of such legal statutes is "primal crimes" (Cohen, 1988, pp.

236ff.). In sum, the four central facts about criminal law (including much "common" law) are these: One, a violation of criminal law is seen as an offense against *the state*, not merely a specific injured party. Two, the *state* initiates criminal proceedings, including investigation, against a suspect (although, again, private, wronged citizens will lodge a complaint with a state agency, namely, the police); under criminal law, unlike civil and administrative law, the state has the power to *arrest* a suspect and to *imprison* or *incarcerate* a convicted defendant. Three, the state seeks specifically to inflict a *punitive sanction* or to punish the defendant, not merely to recover damages against an injured party. And four, unlike civil law, criminal law is enacted by a legislature and written down in a book of statutes; leeway by a judge's interpretation is fairly narrow.

A recent event underscored the crucial difference between criminal and, in this case, civil law. A student enrolled in a sociology of crime course asked me how it was possible for O.J. Simpson to be sued in *civil* court for the murders of his former wife, Nicole Brown Simpson and her friend, Ron Goldman, after being acquitted in a *criminal* case. I said, it's simple. First of all, the *rules of evidence* in a criminal case are *much* stricter than is true for a civil case. In a *criminal* case, a defendant must be deemed guilty "beyond a reasonable doubt"; in a *civil* case, a plaintiff (the party who sues the defendant) can be awarded compensation if the "preponderance of the evidence" suggests that the defendant harmed the plaintiff. In addition, evidence that may be admitted in civil court may *not* be admissible in criminal court. The rules governing criminal proceedings are quite formal and rigid, whereas they are much more relaxed for civil cases. Hence, in principle—even on the basis of the very same evidence—a defendant who has been found "not guilty" in a criminal case can be judged culpable in a civil case and ordered to pay damages to the plaintiff.

Let's keep in mind that *many* white-collar actions are *literally* criminal. Some of the savings and loan looters were arrested, convicted, and forced to serve jail or prison time. Michael Milken and Ivan Boesky, two Wall Street traders convicted for securities fraud, were *criminally* prosecuted and incarcerated—for absurdly brief sentences, it is true, given the magnitude of their thefts, but, again, they were convicted of *criminal* offenses. *Most* discussions of white-collar crime ignore or blur the

distinction between criminal law on the one hand and administrative and civil law on the other. As we saw, the distinction was of almost no importance whatsoever to Sutherland, who, argued that since corporate representatives have such a powerful hand in shaping the criminal law, they are unlikely to criminalize their own behavior. For the most part, Sutherland's argument has been accepted by contemporary observers. To most white-collar crime experts, the fact that white-collar offenses are not technically encompassed by the authority of the criminal law does not mean that they are not "crimes" in a looser sense. In many cases, prosecutors know that a crime has taken place (in the behavioral sense); however, given the problems of the burden of proof in the criminal courts, they will use the civil or administrative courts to prosecute them (Pontell, 1984).

While it is crucial to keep the most relevant differences between the criminal, civil, and administrative law in mind (arrest and incarceration perhaps paramount among them), there are persuasive reasons for blurring these distinctions. Many corporate actions, while not technically criminal, are *very much like* crimes. In effect, they may even be treated *as* crimes. Two reasons especially stand out.

First of all, let it be said that one arm of the criminal law is the *punitive fine*. Fines are rarely used in connection with most street crimes; the fact is that most street criminals do not have enough money to make a fine meaningful. But the criminal law *does* have provisions for fining convicted defendants, and it is a punitive measure, that is, it is used to *punish* the defendant. Precisely the same is true of civil law. A civil court can award a plaintiff punitive damages *in addition to* compensation or restitution. This will be done if the defendant is deemed flagrantly blameworthy, malicious, negligent, or if his or her actions are seen as intentionally harmful.

This points to the second reason why we can blur the legal distinction between criminal and civil law: Increasingly, the civil courts are being used for punitive purposes. What is the civil case initiated by the Goldman family against O.J. Simpson but an attempt to *substitute* civil for criminal law? Convinced that he murdered Ron Goldman, frustrated that he was not convicted in a criminal case, Goldman's family sought to punish Simpson in a civil case. As Friedrichs says, while criminal law has always been an instrument of social control, civil law, initially a means of compensating harmed or wronged private parties, is now increasingly seen *as a means of social control;* the two courts serve some of the same functions (1996, pp. 263–264). This has had an impact on corporate actors, of course; one of the *principal deterrents* to business practices that are harmful and/or regarded as unethical is the fear of lawsuits (Coleman, 1994, p. 158). Of course, let's keep in mind that *only a very tiny proportion* of all civil cases entail the features I just discussed. The overwhelming majority involve disputes between parties that have *nothing to do* with harmful or unethical corporate actions: automobile accidents, a failure to live up to a contract, property disputes, squabbles over inheritance, charges of libel and slander, and so on. But *some* corporate actions *do* result in court proceedings and judgments that function, in effect, very much like the criminal law. Hence, we may have to be at least somewhat tolerant about blurring the distinction between criminal and other kinds of law.

On the other hand, we have to consider the fact that federal and state regulators who work for administrative agencies that deal with issues such as industrial pollution, consumer protection, occupational safety, and so on *do not regard themselves* as law enforcement officers or agents of the criminal justice system at all. According to Braithwaite (1985), they are "mystified" by the criminologist's expectation that they will police, arrest, and incarcerate offenders. While they do not regard themselves as "captives" of the industries whose activities they oversee, they reject criminal prosecution as the avenue by which to achieve results, even when they see illegal deeds being committed. Instead, Braithwaite argues, they seek kinder, gentler, and less punitive methods: cajoling, persuading, compromising, denying or revoking licenses, fining, alerting customers and the general public, creating adverse publicity, negotiating, bluffing, exerting pressure, and so on. Regulators are far more interested in achieving *compliance* than in using the law as a means of deterrence (Reiss, 1983, 1984). Hence, Braithwaite argues, the field of criminology should "rethink" both its expectation of criminal prosecution and its view that administrative agencies are little more than an adjunct to big business. It is time, he says, to examine just what it is that regulatory agencies "actually do."

To summarize: Are civil and administrative law equivalent to criminal law? Not exactly. *Under certain circumstances* they may be used for punitive purposes. But the fact is that *most* of what civil and administrative courts do is very far removed from what the criminal courts do. It would be hasty and glib to argue that they *always* or *necessarily* serve a punitive function. On the other hand, they *sometimes* do so. These realms overlap. Are civil and administrative violations "crimes"? Not exactly, but *sometimes* the civil and administrative courts act to punish offenders in much the same way the criminal courts do. Hence, under certain circumstances, civil and administrative wrongs can be seen as *analogous* to crimes.

DEFINING WHITE-COLLAR CRIME

As Geis and Meier say, Sutherland's confusion and imprecision "left the door wide open for a barrage of speculative attempts to refine and redefine white-collar crime" (1977, p. 254). Later observers have done no better than Sutherland in devising a consistent definition. In a way, the situation is even muddier than when Sutherland wrote because the efforts of many more observers has resulted in many more—and contradictory—definitions. One observer called the concept of white-collar crime "a mess" (Geis, 1974, p. 283). Another wrote that the concept "is in a state of disarray" (Wheeler, 1983, p. 1655). Geis and Meier, editors of a standard anthology on the subject, refer to defining white-collar crime as "an intellectual nightmare" (1977, p. 25). Two sociologists and criminologists refer to defining white-collar crime as "a lion's den from which no tracks return" (Hirschi and Gottfredson, 1989, p. 363). Is it possible to bring some conceptual clarification to our examination of white-collar crime?

Some experts believe that the term should be applied exclusively to high-level corporate crime, and that embezzlement *against* a corporation *by* middle- or lower-level employees should *not* be included (Clinard and Yeager, 1980, p. 13). In contrast, other experts argue exactly the opposite, that Sutherland's definition was too narrow; they wish to expand the concept to include a wide range of occupational offenses regardless of power, respectability, and affluence, including farmers who water down milk, repairers who make unnecessary repairs on television sets, and so on (Newman, 1958, Quinney, 1964). One observer and critic of Sutherland's original formulation even goes so far as to argue that the concept of white-collar crime should drop the criterion that it take place in the course or context of the offender's occupation.

Instead, he argues, white-collar crime should be any illegal or criminal act "committed by non-physical means and by concealment and guile, to obtain money or property . . . , or to obtain personal or business advantage" (Edelhertz, 1970, p. 3). For the most part, the field has not agreed with most of these suggestions, and retains a narrower focus for white-collar crime as encompassing upper-level occupational crime. Still, substantial conceptual imprecision remains.

Defining Crime

One major issue which continues to muddy the conceptual waters is the same imprecision of which Sutherland was guilty: whether or not a given action has to be illegal or technically *criminal* to be considered a white-collar crime. We've already pointed out the distinction between criminal and other kinds of law. At the very least, we would assume that a "crime" must be a violation of *some* legal statutes and must call for a punitive sanction of some kind, if not a jail or prison sentence, then at least a punitive fine. How can an action be referred to as a white-collar "crime" if no legal provision exists for leveling punitive fines against the violator? Does this make sense? Some observers think so. The author of what is one of the most popular texts in the field argues that we should include as white-collar crime "unethical behavior that is not against current law" (Coleman, 1994, p. 5). Most expert observers of white-collar and corporate crime disagree, it must be said.

As to whether or not such a generous definition of corporate crime makes sense depends on *how* we define crime in the first place. Following our moderate reactivist or constructionist approach, what a crime "is" may be different according to what type of definition we adopt. We could adopt one of a number of very different definitions of crime. First, there is the strictly *legalistic* definition, which defines a crime by what's written in a jurisdiction's criminal statutes. This definition ignores the fact that many laws are not enforced; they have become "dead letters." Second, we could go to the opposite extreme and adopt the strictly *juristic* definition favored by Sutherland's critic Paul Tappan and argue that a crime exists *only* when a conviction has been obtained against an offender. This definition ignores the fact that many offenders literally "get away with murder" and a host of other crimes as well. Third, we could adopt what seems

to me to make the most sense, a *probabalistic* definition of crime: behavior that is *likely* to result in arrest and prosecution. Fourth, we could follow the lead of two sociologists who argue that crime can be defined as force and fraud in pursuit of the satisfaction of self-interest (Gottfredson and Hirschi, 1990) regardless of a crime's legal status. Fifth, if we were to adopt a definition of crime that is based on *harm*, then clearly many acts that are not illegal would nonetheless be "crimes" because they harm people, let's say, a politician starting a war and a tobacco company selling cigarettes. Sixth, we could adopt a definition of crime which is based on how *unethical* behavior is, or how much it violates human rights. The problem is that we'd have to devise a definition that spells out what constitutes unethical behavior or a human rights violation, one that has widespread acceptance. The list of possible definitions of crime could be expanded at much greater length. The point is that definitions vary from one observer to another; the "crimes" we are permitted to examine *as* white-collar crime depends on what our definition of crime is in the first place.

The definition of crime that makes the most sense to me is that it is first and foremost a *legal* concept, it is defined by a legal code, a set of formally spelled-out statutes enacted by a legislature. And second, that legal code should define a set of actions that stand a certain likelihood of generating *formal prosecution*. This means that if the appropriate legal authorities were to encounter evidence that these actions have taken place, there is a significant chance that they would initiate an investigation which stands a high likelihood of resulting in legal action. But again, as I pointed out above, we have to remind ourselves that often, civil and administrative law *stand in for* criminal law. So, as Sutherland said, we have to "supplement" a strictly legal interpretation of what a crime is with a broader conceptualization, which looks at the purposes to which the law and the courts are put. Certain actions may result in proceedings that are, strictly speaking, not within the domain of the criminal law, but that harbor a *punitive* function.

Dimensions

In a review of Lloyd Warner's *The Social Life of a Modern Community* (Warner and Lunt, 1941), C. Wright Mills stated: "If you define a concept along one line, then you can study other items that vary with it. But if you define it so as to make it a sponge word, letting it absorb a number of variables, then you cannot ask questions . . . concerning the relations of the analytically isolatable items which it miscellaneously harbors" (1963, p. 43, 1942). In other words, if you dump or mix factors or variables together, it becomes impossible to find out how, or whether, or to what extent, they are related. For instance, one might define illness as a product of a lack of communication with God, and insist that the evidence that one is ill *demonstrates* that lack of communication. In this case, since one dimension has been defined *in terms of* the other, their empirical relationship can never be demonstrated. Unfortunately, some researchers in the field of white-collar crime make exactly this blunder. (Oddly enough, some of them claim to be working in the tradition of C. Wright Mills!)

The definition of white-collar crime as a legal concept has a whole series of implications that have to be spelled out in a certain amount of detail. We've already spelled them out for deviance in general. One problem is that most white-collar crime specialists do not make any of them clear. *First*, deviance and crime *are not the same thing*, as we saw in Chapter 3 (Quinney, 1965). Certain acts may be against the law—a violation of the criminal code—but *not* widely regarded as reprehensible. In short, they are *not* deviant. Likewise, as I explained in Chapter 3, certain acts may be *deviant but not criminal*. (Shaving your head bald and painting it blue, for example.) *Second*, acts may be formally against the law, but the law may be rarely if ever enforced; that is, no one is arrested for violating the law. Adultery is against the law in nearly half of the states of the United States. Yet arrest for this "crime" is practically nonexistent. Certain acts are crimes in the *formal* sense but not in terms of *enforcement*. There are *degrees of difference* between and among different illegal actions with respect to the likelihood of arrest and legal prosecution. Behavior which is illegal but that almost never results in arrest may be referred to as "formally illegal" actions.

Third, and related to point two, our reactivist definition points to the possibility that some acts may be violations of a formal code but are not deviant in the *reactivist* sense. Such actions, as we saw in Chapter 2, are deviant "objectively," or in the *normative* sense. But *reactively*, they may not be deviant at all, that is, they may result in no negative reaction or condemnation even when they are

discovered. As we've already seen, the normative and the reactive definitions of deviance yield a very different (although overlapping) roster of behaviors designated as deviant. *Fourth*, as we've already seen in Chapters 2 and 3, the *harm* that behavior causes must be distinguished from both deviance and crime. Some harmful acts are neither widely regarded as reprehensible (as we've seen, such as selling tobacco cigarettes or starting wars) nor are they against the law. Harm, deviance, and crime are *independent but overlapping* phenomena. And *fifth*, the *philosophical* and *political* judgments about behaviors that are made by intellectuals, civil rights leaders, moralists, reformers, social critics, muckrakers, and the like—such as whether they are a "violation of human rights," unethical, or an example of "the higher immorality"—again, are *completely independent* of their deviant and criminal status. Moralist X, muckraker Y, or social critic Z can deem, let's say, business executives having a three martini lunch as an unethical practice (Simon, 1996, p. 289), but if the general public does not regard it as worthy of condemnation, and the law does not stipulate that it is against the law, then it is neither deviant nor a crime. As Braithwaite says, those who choose to use the violation of human rights, "or some other imaginative definition" of deviance and crime, "will deserve to be ignored for indulging their personal moralities in a social science that has no relevance for those who do not share that morality" (1985, p. 15).

A major issue for us, as students of deviance, is the *empirical overlap* between deviance and crime. Their very conceptual independence allows us to examine the circumstances under which they overlap, as well as when they don't. That is, certain actions may be *widely regarded* as immoral and unethical—they may be deviant—and yet, they may *not* be defined as crimes by the legal code. Knowing that this discrepancy exists causes us to ask *how* and *why* laws are passed. Do certain social classes or circles have more influence over the passage of laws than others? Do they protect their own interests in passing certain laws and blocking others from being passed? If they are passed, are these laws enforced? Defining crime and deviance independently of one another permits us to ask questions such as these; mixing crime and deviance together does not. The obverse is also true, and much more likely to be the case: Certain actions may be against the law—although rarely enforced—but not widely condemned, that is, not instances of deviance. Again, they must be defined independently so that we can determine their *empirical* relationship. As sociologists of deviance, we are interested in the degree of overlap between social and public definitions of deviance and technical illegality, as well as the overlap between both of these and legal prosecution. As we saw in Chapter 3, certain actions may be *illegal but not deviant*, and *deviant but not criminal*. The what's, why's, how's, and wherefore's of this relationship represent a fascinating issue for any student of deviance.

The same applies to the relationship between crime and "violations of human rights," and between crime and harm as well. Again, presuming that some of us were to agree on a definition for the violation of human rights (*How many* of us have to agree? And *whose* opinion counts more than others?), the fact that certain such actions are in fact *not* against the law should be intriguing. We are led to ask why. Elite influence over the legislative process is an intrinsic part of the crime-defining process; it is a fact we have to take into account in understanding how and why certain laws are passed. Pretending that this process has not occurred by declaring actions that are *not* violations of the criminal code to be crimes because they are supposedly a violation of certain human rights is an idealistic fantasy. The same applies to the relationship between crime and *harm*. Why are certain harmful actions *not* criminalized? Why are some relatively benign actions or behaviors against the law? To throw them together—in short, to use harm as a criterion for a definition of crime—makes it impossible to ask about the empirical connection *between* these two dimensions, as Mills pointed out in a different connection. One of the more fascinating issues in this field is why harm, crime, deviance, and the violation of human rights *are* as independent as they are. Again, only by *defining* them separately can we understand how and why certain criminal codes and moral and ethical standards come into being. The fact is that the criminal law is not a simple reflection of the harm that actions inflict or the degree to which they violate human rights.

As most labeling or constructionist observers would see it, the most vexing problem with defining crime by whether an act is unethical, or a violation of human rights, is that *even a definition of what constitutes murder is not universally agreed upon*. It is one thing to get intellectuals to agree on what constitutes violations of human rights (Simon,

1996, p. 289); it is quite another to examine how these definitions play out at the grass roots, in real life. A killing on one side of a border is regarded as the work of a hero and a martyr, while on the other, it is a dastardly deed, an act of savage and inhumane butchery (Cowell, 1994; Greenberg, 1995). To base one's definition of white-collar crime—a set of actions whose ethical status is *far* more complex and difficult to determine than murder—on what are supposedly universally agreed-upon criteria seems naive in the extreme. Let's emphasize this point most emphatically: White-collar crime is a *construct*, not an essentialistic reality; its reality depends on a judgment that is made by the relevant parties.

Ironically, a substantial proportion of formally illegal white-collar offenses committed in the United States do *not* violate basic human rights, even if we were to get widespread agreement on exactly what that entails. If we were to use the "human rights" criterion, we'd have to *exclude* many genuinely criminal acts from the sphere of white-collar crime. By this statement I mean that most white-collar crimes violate a set of statutes whose violation is determined by technical and often somewhat arbitrary criteria. Exactly *how much* industrial pollution constitutes a violation? We cannot pull numbers out of the air or determine them according to some widely agreed upon standards (if such standards were to exist in the first place). These standards are determined by industrial chemists and physicians, not by intellectuals, and they vary by jurisdiction. Exactly *how much* exaggeration is permitted to advertisers who are selling their products before they engage in "illegal" advertising? Again, there are no universal standards to decide the issue; this is something that is worked out by a variety of parties, including representatives of governmental agencies, advertisers, market researchers, psychologists, and so on, and again, the answer will vary from one set of observers to another.

What criminologists who adopt a *universalistic* and *nonlegal* standard in defining white-collar crime fail to understand is that once again, the reality of white-collar crime is *constructed*, it does not exist as an essentialistic reality, floating in the cosmos somewhere. To base a definition of white-collar crime on a violation of what are supposedly universal, "internationally agreed upon principles of human rights" (Simon, 1996, p. 289) is to base one's definition on shifting sands. To put the matter another way, Western intellectuals may be able to agree on what these human rights are, and they may be able to define *some* white-collar acts as crimes. But they *cannot* spell out the *vast majority* of cases which are judged to be white-collar crimes in empirical instances. The problem with this conceptualization is that it is not only naive and sloppy, but ironically, too narrow. *Most* white-collar crimes would fall outside this concept, since again, they are not so much violations of human rights as the result of *judgments* made by corporate executives to pursue a given line of action (for instance, permitting a certain level of contamination to escape into the air) which is contrary to *other* judgments, which are made by government officials (such a level of contamination is contrary to the statutes).

Essentialism, Constructionism, Double Standards, and Conceptual Scope

Painted on a broader canvas, many researchers in the field of white-collar crime studies are *essentialists* (Simon, 1996; Coleman, 1994), while most scholars of deviance are *constructionists*. This means that white-collar crime is often defined *objectively* in reference to some absolute criterion (human rights and harm being two of them). The assumption is made that all reasonable observers will agree on what these criteria mean and whether examples in the material world fit them or not. In contrast, I insist that we will *not* get nearly universal agreement on what certain abstract definitions mean and whether certain actions fit them. Certainly, asking a sample of Israelis what constitutes a "human rights violation" in the Middle East will yield very different answers from those elicited from a sample of Palestinians. In addition, absolutists usually apply their definition extremely *selectively*; they ignore certain categories of actions that would qualify under their definition but do not fit their ideological biases. For instance, many humanistically inclined and left-leaning sociologists insist that they are concerned about violations of human rights when they study "elite deviance." However, when their work is examined closely, it is clear that many are interested only in violations of human rights in Western capitalist nations, particularly the United States. While Simon claims to be interested in "political prisoners" (1996, pp. 243–247) and "official violence" (pp. 247–253), he never considers the *vastly* greater abuses of power in non-Western regimes than in the United States. For

instance, consider the fact that recent evidence (Wu, 1992, 1995–96, 1996) indicates that there are roughly *ten million* prisoners in China who live under brutally harsh conditions and are forced to engage in slave labor to contribute to the nation's foreign exchange. Is this a human rights violation? Is the killing of Kurds by the Iraqi government a human rights violation? Apparently not, for neither instance is mentioned in this context (Coleman, 1994; Simon, 1996). Somehow, human rights abuses such as these never seem to qualify. We must be wary of definitions that claim to be based on a certain criterion, but practice a double standard as to what to include and what to leave out.

To make things even more confusing, different observers refer to their domain under study in a hugely variable fashion. As I said above, all criminology textbooks include a chapter or a major section on white-collar crime or some equivalent. The problem is that each refers to the subject in a somewhat different way, for instance: "organizational" (Adler, Mueller, and Laufer, 1995), "economic" (Barthol, 1995), "occupational," (Barlow, 1993; Clinard, Quinney, and Wildeman, 1994), "respectable" (Sheley, 1995; Coleman, 1995), "upperworld" (Geis, 1981; Blumberg, 1981), and "corporate" crime (DeKeseredy and Schwartz, 1996). Most authors in the field focus on white-collar *crime* (or some analogous concept), while some address white-collar or "elite" *deviance* (Simon, 1996; Ermann and Lundman, 1996) or some equivalent. In other words, each defines the domain of the field—and hence, white-collar crime itself—in different ways. One text on white-collar crime includes employee pilferage (Coleman, 1994, pp. 16–18); most do not. Are crimes committed by high-level political officials which do not entail dealings with the business world to be regarded as white-collar crimes? Two experts say no (Clinard and Yeager, 1980); most disagree, and regard the actions of politicians as an integral part of the world of white-collar crime. (It must be said that though Sutherland mentioned government crimes in passing, 1949, pp. 8–9, he did not discuss the issue systematically or in any detail.) One discussion in a text on "elite deviance" includes actions that offend his, or some other observers', sensibilities, including the high salaries of executives, their "three-martini lunches," and social inequality (Simon, 1996, p. 289). Most observers would see such inclusions as moralistic and judgmental. In short, even *the delineation of the subject matter* of this field is in contention, variable from one observer to another, totally lacking in clarity, and so fuzzy as to be almost without value.

A Definition of White-Collar Crime

What's the solution to this conceptual confusion? Do we abandon the project altogether, and ignore white-collar crime as a form of deviance? Do we lay down a single definition and rigidly stick to it, dismissing out of hand realms of behavior that fall outside its scope, perhaps ignoring a great deal of interesting realms of behavior that don't quite fit? Or do we "give up the illusion that white-collar crime can—or even should—have a single meaning or definition"? (Friedrichs, 1996, p. 10). In my view, the third of these options makes the most sense. We should recognize that although some definitions may be more useful than others for our purposes, no coherence and consistency will ever be achieved in such a controversial field. We will tread lightly through the various definitions, accept the fact that each spells out a sphere or domain that overlaps extremely imperfectly with others, ignore some that fall too far outside our scope of interest, but not insist on a clear, logically consistent, uniform, or standard definition.

In sum, for our purposes, a white-collar crime is *an illegal action that is committed by the occupant of high occupational status in the course of his or her professional activity.* Exactly how "high" the occupational status in question must be to qualify need not concern us; clearly, we are not referring to manual laborers, but we are including bank clerks. This definition *excludes* "common" or conventional crimes; an executive who murders his wife (or her husband) has committed a crime of violence, not a white-collar crime. It also excludes theft and pilferage from the job; this is larceny-theft, an Index Crime category in the Uniform Crime Reports. And it excludes acts that someone may see as unethical but are not against the law, such as Simon's "three-martini lunches." And it excludes acts that are harmful but are neither deviant nor criminal, such as manufacturing and selling tobacco cigarettes. That is that I reject definitions based on *moralistic* but not legalistic criteria. If an act is not a violation of a legal code and does not call for a punitive sanction, that is, a jail or prison sentence or at least a punitive fine, then, to me it cannot be a white-collar *crime*. (But again, remember that civil and administrative courts can impose puni-tive sanctions against offenders.) It is irrelevant to our definition that actions may violate moral or ethical standards which have been laid down by "leading social critics, muckrakers, and social scientists" or violate the principles "on which the Judeo-Christian, as well as many other non-Western ethical systems, are founded: namely, the Golden Rule" (Simon, 1996, p. 289). (Remember, Simon focuses on elite *deviance*, not specifically white-collar crime.) However, the fact that some business practices may violate certain *definitions* or *constructions* of proper conduct, while not a criterion of our definition, is nonetheless a crucial and interesting topic.

WHITE-COLLAR CRIME: AN OVERVIEW

What are the qualities and characteristics that make white-collar crime distinctive and unique? What sets it apart from other types of crime and deviance? How does it especially contrast with common, run-of-the-mill street crimes? What makes it an analytic, theoretical, and conceptual entity unto itself? We already know what defines white-collar crime: It must be *illegal*, it must be *sanctionable*—that is, call for a jail or prison sentence, or at the very least a punitive fine—and it must be committed by occupants of relatively *high-ranking* positions *in the course of* their occupational activities. The last of these defining criteria means that *of necessity* and *by definition*, white-collar crime is committed by people who occupy the higher rungs of the occupational ladder. Occupants of lower- and working-class occupations *cannot* commit white-collar crimes. Even embezzlement, a relatively lowly white-collar crime, is committed by persons who work in occupations that rank in the top half of the class structure. These are necessary *defining* features; they are the criteria that *make* an act a white-collar crime. There are also some *correlative* features of white-collar crime, aspects of it that are a *product* of its essential defining criteria. What are they? Imagine describing white-collar crime to someone who knows nothing about the phenomenon; what would our description look like? Let's look at eight of the most essential features of white-collar crime.

First, as to the nature of the behavior itself: White-collar crime tends to be made up of *complex*, *sophisticated*, and relatively *technical* actions. Imagine witnessing or watching a videotape of a robbery or a murder; most of the time, we'd be able to unambiguously identify the act *as* a crime. In contrast, white-collar crime—and this applies especially to corporate crime—would not be so readily identified. How do we know a white-collar crime when we see one? We watch a videotape of a burglary, we know a burglary is in progress. In contrast, a videotape of a white-collar crime would result in a more ambiguous judgment from an audience. It might even take an expert—an accountant, for example, an industrial chemist, a physician, or a government official—to determine its illegal status. The way that a corporate crime is committed is complex and interactional. At a board meeting of executives, a proposal is made and discussed. Memos are exchanged; decisions are made, policies are put into practice. Much of the time, it is not clear whether a crime in fact took place. Even experts may have trouble deciding. Even *victims* may not know that they have been victimized. Of course, the criminal status of some actions are more clear-cut than others, but the nature of most white-collar criminal actions is far less clear-cut than for most street crimes. This is because these actions tend to be complex, sophisticated, and technical. In contrast, the meaning of most street crime is more direct, straightforward, and unambiguous.

Second, white-collar crime tends to be *intermingled with legitimate behavior*. Illegal advertising claims are made in the context of a legal, legitimate advertising industry; some exaggeration is considered acceptable and is legal. But how much is too much? Monopolistic restraints of trade are carried out in a capitalistic business environment in which all corporations attempt to capture a larger share of the market; most of such attempts are legal and are considered good business practice, while some are illegal and "go too far." Even embezzlement is enacted within the context of ordinary, routine workaday activities, such as entering numbers into an accountant's ledger. While *some* traditional street crimes are also "intermingled with legitimate behavior" (date rape, for example, is a product of extremely aggressive courtship practices), most is not. It is difficult to imagine, let's say, with what legitimate behavior a robbery or a burglary is "intermingled." With street crime, the crime act is illegal *in its totality*.

A third characteristic of white-collar crime is that *victimization tends to be diffuse*. Harm is not always conceptualized or identifiable as such because it is usually spread out over a substantial number of victims. Again, this represents a sharp contrast with street crime. A rape harms a specific woman; a robbery, a specific store; a murder, obviously, the deceased victim. But with white-collar crimes, harm is usually spread out thinly among many victims. Monopolistic practices may result in us being charged, let's say, $1,000 more for the purchase of a new car, a quarter more for a half-gallon of milk, $2 more for a pair of jeans. Even where there is physical harm, victimization can usually be measured in terms of *statistical odds* and *chances* rather than in a direct, one-to-one fashion. Pollution hardly ever kills or harms everyone exposed to it. Instead, it increases our *likelihood* of getting sick and dying prematurely. For instance, if a given factory pollutes the air in a given area at a given level for a given period of time, the 10,000 people living nearby have a one in 100 lifetime chance of contracting a certain form of cancer as opposed to a one in 200 chance. The harm that embezzlement inflicts is usually more direct, but even there, the loss is almost always insured and hence, is spread out over many policyholders.

A fourth characteristic of white-collar crime is that the monetary sums that are involved tend to be large. The total amount of money stolen by a single extremely successful white-collar criminal in a single year is usually considerably greater than, for example, the take of *all* of the robberies in the country in that same year. As we saw in the chapter on property crime, the FBI estimates that $500 million was stolen in all robberies in the United States last year; this is roughly the same sum of the *fines* the government levied against convicted stock swindler Michael Milken. The Savings and Loan scandal resulted in the "disappearance" of well in excess of $300 *billion*, 70 to 80 percent of which was a product of illegal acts. Since the money was insured, it will be the government—and ultimately the American taxpayer—who will foot the bill. The per capita cost? Roughly $1,500 for every man, woman, and child in the United States. John McNamara, a Long Island entrepreneur and car dealer, admitted to obtaining *billions* of dollars from General Motors in loans for nonexistent vans, of which $422 million remains unreturned. Sums such as these simply *cannot* be stolen by ordinary thieves. Illegal price fixing may add as much as $250 *billion* a year to the cost of the products we purchase. A single price-fixing case brought by the Federal Trade Commission against a single manufacturer, Levi Strauss, resulted in a

$225 million savings to customers—roughly $2 per pair of jeans (Simpson, 1993, p. 241). The average monetary harm caused by cases of corporate offenders sentenced in federal court in the late 1980s was over half a million dollars (Cohen, 1989). It is *only* for white-collar crime that thefts entailing sums in the hundreds of millions and the billions of dollars are possible.

There are two reasons why white-collar crime is so much more lucrative than ordinary burglaries, robberies, and larcenies. The first is that street criminals have to steal money in the form of a *physical object*, and hundreds of millions of dollars are rarely found in the same place at the same time; even when it is, it is usually inaccessible except to trusted employees. In contrast, white-collar criminals steal by *manipulating symbols*, which means that they can steal money that they don't even have to pick up and carry away, indeed, that doesn't even have to *exist* in the form of a physical object. There is a second reason why so much more can be stolen by the thief in the white collar than the street criminal: Street crime tends to be a "one shot deal," a single theft involving a specific sum of money. In contrast, white-collar crime is usually made up of a *number* of *interrelated* actions that extend over a period of time—months, years, even decades.

A fifth characteristic of white-collar crime is that it is *rarely* prosecuted; when prosecuted, and if a conviction is obtained, penalties tend to be *extremely* light. With respect to prosecution, evidence indicating that they have taken place is not as clear-cut as with street crime. Police officers do not patrol business suites looking for white-collar crimes that are being committed. Indeed, because of the complexity of white-collar crime, how would the police even *know* when one is being committed? (In addition, business suites are private property and hence, the police cannot enter them until crimes are reported.) Relative to their incidence, arrests are very rarely made; the ratio of violations (were this known) to arrests almost certainly approaches and may even surpass that for crimes which entail no complainant, such as drug possession and sale. In addition, even if evidence does indicate criminal behavior, arrest is rare and business executives are rarely convicted for their crimes; conviction, when it does occur, is *extremely* unlikely to lead to a lengthy prison sentence. This is especially striking in view of the amount of money that is stolen, as we saw in the introduction to this chapter. John MacNamara, whose multi-billion-dollar theft was men-

tioned above, was sentenced to a five-year term (chances are, he will serve half of its length). Is this commensurate with the magnitude of his theft? The United States Sentencing Commission found that for white-collar crimes prosecuted by federal courts between 1984 and 1987, sentences against convicted corporations tended to be extremely light; nearly half entailed a fine of $5,000 or less, 80 percent were fined $25,000 or less, and even probation against executives was imposed less than one-fifth of the time. Jail or prison time tends to be almost nonexistent (Shenon, 1989).

Although a few stiff "showcase" sentences against white-collar criminals have been handed down, these are almost always overturned or reduced on appeal or as a result of cooperation with the government in prosecuting related cases. In November 1990, financier Michael Milken received a 10-year sentence (and, as we saw, a $600 million fine) for fraud and racketeering, that is, taking part in an illegal insider stock-trading network. In January 1993, he was released after serving 22 months, part of it in a halfway house. Even where physical harm, including death, results from white-collar crimes, lengthy prison sentences almost never prevail. In 1985, three executives were convicted of murder, manslaughter, and reckless endangerment in the death of a worker; they were sentenced to a 25-year term. The worker's job entailed working with cyanide and, in the judgment of the court, was criminally hazardous. However, these executives did not go to prison as a result of their conviction; they were permitted to remain free pending an appeal. In 1990, an appeals court overturned their conviction and found them not guilty (Greenhouse, 1985; Anonymous, 1990).

Sixth, for the most part, white-collar crime does not fit our stereotype of "real" crime; it is rarely condemned to the same degree that streeet crime is, and there is very little public stigma attached to white-collar crime. When harmful corporate actions are listed on rosters of actions of which the public is asked to evaluate the seriousness, for white-collar crimes, condemnation tends to be commensurate with harm. The public regards white-collar crime in which injury occurs as *serious* crime. However, when members of the public are asked to act in the capacity of jurors and pass judgment on and sentence white-collar suspects, they tend to be extremely lenient toward them. In other words, as Friedrichs says, although the public is perfectly willing to see white-collar crime as having serious

Are All White-Collar Criminals Rich and Powerful?

The characterization of white-collar criminals as rich and powerful has been challenged by Weisburd et al. (1991), who examined a cross section of offenders convicted in federal court of a variety of white-collar crimes, including securities fraud, antitrust violations, bank embezzlement, and postal, tax, and credit fraud. This study found that these offenders did not fit the usual portrait of white-collar criminals as occupying high-status positions. True, given the fact that they are *white-collar* offenders, by definition, they were not manual laborers. But a remarkably high proportion occupied the very lowest rungs of the white-collar status hierarchy. Many were unemployed at the time of their arrest or held fairly humble jobs, did not have a college education, and did not own their own homes. A higher proportion were members of racial and ethnic minorities and were in their twenties and thirties than most studies indicate. At the time of the arrests that led to their convictions, offenders were twice as likely to have had a past criminal record than the national average (although this was, obviously, less likely to be the case than for convicted offenders of conventional street crimes). The authors (p. 190) conclude that most white-collar offenders are ordinary people who got into financial difficulty and saw their way out of it through illegal and fraudulent measures. They were "struck by the banal, mundane quality of the vast majority of criminals" in their sample (pp. 45–46); the majority of their crimes "have an undramatic, local or regional quality," a "common, familar ring." Business fraud, say the authors, is "as familiar in their business context as are street crimes in poor communities" (p. 46).

The findings of Weisburd's study have enormous implications. There are several possible explanations for their departure from the usual picture of white-collar criminals as typically rich and powerful. The first and least interesting is that because of inequities in law enforcement, it is the "small fry" who get caught, while the "big fish" get away. This explanation sounds plausible, although in need of qualification. At the very least, it seems likely that the "big fish" are more capable of insulating themselves from prosecutorial scrutiny. In any case, according to one study, when it comes to *conviction*, as opposed to *prosecution*, in studies of decisions made by juries, the higher the socioeconomic status of the offender, the stiffer the sentence juries vote for (Wheeler, Weisburd, and Bode, 1982). While a criminal conviction is not the same thing as a

criminal investigation, and a jury is not the same thing as law enforcement, this study does suggest that populist sentiment may work to penalize the "big fish" and perhaps let some "small fry" go free. Not all studies agree with this generalization (see Rosoff, 1989; Rosoff, Pontell, and Tillman, 1996), the point should be clear: Legally, the cards are not always stacked against the "small fry"; some factors work in the opposite direction.

Braithwaite (1985) suggests that some of the reasons why the "small fry" are more likely to get ensnared by law enforcement's net can be located at the feet of the operation of business, not inequities in law enforcement. That is, top management puts pressure on middle management to achieve corporate goals, often without investigating just *how* these goals are to be achieved. Middle management is caught in a bind: Goals must be achieved, but often this can be accomplished *only* by cutting corners. Top management does not *have* to "get their hands dirty" by directly ordering subordinates to break the law. However, their subordinates know that the *only* way to be successful is to dump toxic waste, bribe officials, or ignore safety regulations. "It is not difficult," Braithwaite writes, for top executives "to structure their affairs so that all of the pressure to break the law surface at a lower level of their own organization or a subordinate organization" (p. 6).

A third, more banal, and almost certainly true explanation for the strong representation of "small fry" in federal white-collar *convictions* is there are simply more small-time white-collar *criminals*, that is, there are more people occupying small-time white-collar *positions*. Even if higher-ups committed criminal acts to the same or a significantly greater degree, there would be far fewer of them at the criminal court dockets simply because there are far fewer of them, period. The business world is shaped something like an immense pyramid, with very few "big fish" at the top and a great many "small fry" at the bottom. It would be remarkable if there were many "big fish," since they are so rare to begin with. Weisburd's work emphasizes the point that the conclusions of a study depend in part on the sample one draws, and the sample, in turn, depends on the definition the researcher uses to define the relevant behavior. Conceptual precision and clarity are absolutely central here.

A fourth explanation for the "small fry" phenomenon observed by Weisburd et al. is suggested by their conclusions. White-collar criminals are motivated by two factors: economic difficulty and greed. While both tempt the occupant of white-collar positions to engage in illegal behavior, economic difficulty is the more pressing and immediate inducement. High-level corporate executives, while they may be tempted to break the law by greed, less often feel the sting of financial disaster than is true of persons occupying the lower reaches of the business world. Small-time businesses tend to operate at the margins, precarious and undercapitalized, they tend to wade into ventures that are ignored by more well-funded organizations. Hence, such entrepreneurs are more likely to feel the hot breath of failure at their backs, and thus, to feel the need to bail out

by cutting corners, bending or breaking the rules, taking risks that stewards of more secure operations would not feel are necessary. Hence, they appear in courts of law in greater numbers. Braithwaite (1985), admitting that the data are thin, argues the contrary, that it is "excess," not "necessity," that generates the motive for corporate and other white-collar crime. Other observers (Friedrichs, 1996, p. 223; Coleman, 1992; Shover and Bryant, 1993; Simpson, 1993) argue the reverse: that the executives of companies that are in trouble financially are more likely to engage in illegal business actions. Perhaps, one day, more detailed and systematic studies will settle the issue.

consequences, this does not always translate into being willing to impose harsh sentences on offenders or support legislation calling for such sentences (1996, pp. 47–50). To put the matter another way, as we've seen, in some ways, there is some question about whether white-collar crime even *qualifies* as a form of deviance.

Seventh, the media tend not to cover white-collar crime in as complete or detailed a fashion as is the case with street crime. True, there have been a few notable exceptions in recent years: It's hard to ignore the theft of billions of dollars. The fact is that white-collar crimes tend to be complex and technical; they are difficult to explain and understand, they are intrinsically unexciting, and there is virtually no way to present them on television in an even remotely dramatic fashion. They do not make "good copy," as members of the media say, they do not provide dramatic "sound bites." They do not lend themselves to juicy, sensationalistic stories that get page-one coverage and a prominent place on the six o'clock news. When they do get space in newspapers, they tend to be buried in back pages, usually in the financial rather than the hard news section. In order for a story on white-collar crime to appear on television news, one of three conditions have to prevail: one, as I said, the sums stolen have to be huge, two, a scandal is connected with the theft, or three, the accused is prominent. For the most part, the public finds news stories of corporate misdeeds boring. It is rare that we have the financial training even to understand the nature of white-collar offenses; for most of us, there is little intrinsic *drama* in these stories. The shotgun robbery of a downtown bank, complete with hostages and a standoff with the police—now, that's

a story! The gangland execution of a mob figure while he's eating a plate of linguine—that grabs our attention! A daring jewel heist from a famous store captures our fancy and interest. We need not invoke conspiracies among the rich and powerful to account for this; the fact is that for most of us, white-collar crimes just don't make good news. Most of us would turn the channel or the page if confronted with such a story. With rare exceptions, we are just not as interested in such stories as we are in reports of meat-and-potatoes, nuts-and-bolts street crime, which most of us find exciting and entertaining.

And eighth, as a result of its lack of correspondence to a crime stereotype and its lack of stigma, white-collar criminals, even after being convicted, rarely think of themselves as "real" criminals. To say they "rationalize" away their involvement in "real" crime is not the point. They use a "vocabulary of motives" that permits them to see themselves in a respectable, law-abiding light; they tend to "deny the guilty mind" and insist that though their actions may have been technically illegal, they did not *intend* to commit a crime. While white-collar criminals use a somewhat different explanation or "vocabulary," depending on the crime in question, they are "nearly unanimous in denying [the] basic criminality" of their illegal actions (Benson, 1985, p. 591). While some persons convicted of street crimes and their defenders will insist that they "didn't do it," white-collar criminals and their defenders take a different tack: They insist that even though they engaged in the action of which they were accused, what they did *wasn't a crime*. In many quarters, Ivan Boesky and Michael Milken, convicted of securities fraud, are heroes; they lecture at major universities, sell videotapes which give tips on how to become rich, and inspire books whose authors insist that they were "persecuted" by a "conspiracy," a "reign of terror" bent on "destroying" a "financial revolution" (Fischel, 1995).

A TYPOLOGY OF WHITE-COLLAR CRIMES

Given that Sutherland's original formulation has spawned a wide variety of concepts that overlap only extremely imperfectly with white-collar crime, and given that even definitions of white-collar crime vary from one scholar and researcher to another, it should come as no surprise that the *types* of behaviors that have been delineated and discussed by the field vary as well. At the same time, everything is *not* up for grabs; there is variation to be sure, but a *measure* of agreement exists as well. To put the matter another way, certain acts are *highly likely* to be regarded as white-collar crimes by the field, while others are *unlikely* to be so regarded (Katz, 1979). In other words, some actions are *high consensus* white-collar crimes, while others are *low consensus* white-collar crimes. Which actions are discussed most frequently as instances of white-collar crime? And how might we divide up the white-collar crime pie? How do we distinguish *among* the most important representatives of this large and variously defined category?

There are many possible ways of dividing up white-collar crimes, on the basis of who engages in them, who their victims are, the sphere or realm in which they take place, and so on. It makes sense to begin by distinguishing among the *realms* in which the crimes we examine take place, business and government most notably. And within the world of business dealings, we'd have to distinguish among the following crimes: (1) Crimes that are enacted *against* a corporation; (2) crimes that are enacted *on behalf of* a corporation; (3) crimes that are enacted against clients by incumbents of a particular *profession* who are *independent* of corporate entities, who are acting on their own behalf. Recently—largely a consequence of the Savings and Loan debacle of the 1980s—a fourth type of white-collar crime has been identified and discussed: (4) crimes that are enacted *against* yet *on behalf of* a corporation (Calavita and Pontell, 1993). And lastly, (5) crimes that take place within the

governmental sphere constitute another broad category of white-collar crimes. (Some crimes, of course, entail behavior that may be located in *both* economic and governmental spheres, for instance, the bribery *of* a public official *by* a business executive.) Government crimes can be divided into those which are crimes in the very *literal* sense of the word, that is, which if discovered are likely to result in criminal prosecution, and those that are crimes in a *broad*, figurative, or *metaphorical* sense, that is, that either would be prosecuted in a jurisdiction other than where they take place, or as judged by another jurisdiction's criminal statutes, or would be prosecuted in no real-life jurisdiction, but violate some basic principle a given observer holds (once again, for example, our "human rights" violations). A good, and certainly one of the most famous, example of a literal governmental crime is the 1970s "Watergate" scandal under President Richard Nixon's administration, in which a number of employees of the Committee to Re-elect the President (CREEP) burglarized the Democratic National Committee, located in the Watergate building in Washington. The burglars (or "plumbers," as they were referred to) and several members of Nixon's White House staff received prison sentences, and Nixon was forced to resign the presidency in disgrace.

Let's briefly examine the following types of white-collar crimes: *embezzlement* (crimes *by* an employee *against* a corporation); *collective embezzlement* (crimes *against yet on behalf of* a corporation); *corporate crime* (crimes *on behalf of* a corporation); *professional* crime (crimes on behalf of the occupant of a particular profession); and *governmental* crimes. They by no means exhaust all manner and variety of white-collar crime, but they do spell out those that receive the most attention in the field and, in all likelihood, those that have the most substantial impact on our society.

White-Collar Crime Against a Corporation: Embezzlement

Embezzlement is the theft *by* a white-collar employee *from* a corporation. Embezzlers "are persons who use their positions of financial trust to acquire an employer's money for their own use" (McCaghy and Capron, 1994, p. 266). The financial loss to American corporations through embezzlement is estimated to be in the neighborhood of

$27 billion a year—*vastly* more than the sum stolen by armed robbers (Thompson et al., 1992). The violation of financial trust is crucial here in explaining their greater take: White-collar employees are granted access to a symbolic realm (that is, documentary records) that makes theft which entails the manipulation of symbols possible. This realm makes *hugely* greater sums available than is true of physical sums of money that happen to be in the same place at the same time, let's say, that is stored in a specific bank vault or transported by a specific armored car. (Some analysts argue that one day, the modern world will have a "cashless" economy, in which the theft of money in physical form will be impossible because it won't exist.) In addition, as I said earlier, simple theft tends to be a "one shot deal," whereas embezzlement tends to take place in a number of transactions over an extended period of time, which makes the theft of larger sums possible.

The classic study of embezzlement was conducted by Donald Cressey, Sutherland's student and coauthor (1953). Cressey argued that three conditions make embezzlement possible and likely. First, persons in a position of financial trust must conceive of themselves as having a *nonshareable problem*, that is, financial difficulties they feel they cannot divulge to anyone. While such a problem could take almost any form, Cressey argued that they usually center around status and respectability; trusted employees feel shame as a result of incurring gambling debts, for instance, or humiliation that their salaries are so low, which makes it impossible for them to maintain reasonably affluent lifestyles (p. 43). A second condition that causes embezzlement is the recognition that funds entrusted to the employees'care can be used to relieve the financial problem (p. 83), that they can use their position and training to withdraw money and use it to purchase what is necessary to solve the nonshareable problem. And third, to violate a financial trust, these trusted employees have to use a "vocabulary of adjustment" which enables them to see themselves as respectable persons, even though they are stealing. They have to claim that they are merely "borrowing" the money, or that everyone steals when they get in a tight spot, or that their troubles are a lot greater than the next person's, or that "business is business," and so on (Cressey, 1965, p. 14). Since stealing is incompatible with their respectable self-image, they have to explain away the negative implications of stealing. Once they do that, the last barrier to embezzlement

is removed. Not all subsequent research has verified Cressey's formulation (Nettler, 1974b), but it is clear that the combination of *financial trust*, *respectability*, and *vocabularies of motive* take us a long way in explaining embezzlement.

Crime By and Against a Corporation: Collective Embezzlement

In 1982, President Ronald Reagan signed the Garn-St. Germain Act; the bill deregulated the savings and loan institutions, also known as "thrifts," which specialize in lending money to persons to finance the purchase of their homes. Too many federal regulations, President Reagan believed, were preventing thrifts from earning a profit and putting money to work in today's economy. The Garn-St. Germain bill "would fix all that," Reagan promised (Pizzo, Fricker, and Muolo, 1992, p. 1). By 1980, America's savings and loans had a negative net worth of $17.5 billion; 85 percent were losing money. Something had to be done, the bill's supporters claimed.

The Garn-St. Germain bill, along with related thrift deregulation measures instituted in the early 1980s, included a number of central provisions:
- Previously, federal insurance on deposits in savings and loans covered accounts up to $40,000; after deregulation, accounts up to $100,000 were insured.
- Previously, only 15 percent of the assets of thrifts could be invested in nonresidential (that is, commercial) real estate; after deregulation, this ceiling was raised to 40 percent.
- Previously, thrift institutions had to have 400 stockholders, with no single stockholder owning more than 25 percent of the total stock; after deregulation, a single shareholder could own an entire savings and loan institution.
- Previously, thrifts were required to make loans on property in their own designated market area; after deregulation, thrifts could make real estate loans anywhere.
- Instead of requiring traditional down payments of 20 percent, thrifts could permit loans on which borrowers put up not a dime of their own money, on which the thrifts provided 100 percent financing.
- To borrow money to purchase a thrift, entrepreneurs were now allowed to put up noncash assets as collateral, such as undeveloped land.
- In addition, since the savings and loan bills

were designed to deregulate, President Reagan assumed that there would be less business to regulate. Consequently, he reduced the number of federal regulators and examiners whose job it was to monitor and audit the dealings of thrifts.

For a short period of time after the bill was signed, the savings and loans appeared to be booming. Between 1983 and 1984, on paper, the thrift industry grew by $300 billion. In 1983, Empire Savings, for instance, a thrift located in Texas, held only $20.7 million in assets; in 1984, it recorded assets of $320 million. Sleepy little savings and loans, almost all of whose business in the past had been lending money to individuals for the purchase of private homes, became deeply involved in lending money for developing and even owning hotels, shopping malls, "mushroom and windmill farms, tanning beds, Arabian horses, Wendy's restaurants, hot-tub spas—or invest in junk bonds and the futures markets. The sky was the limit and it could all be done with federally insured deposits" (p. 13).

Unfortunately, deregulation attracted a breed of entrepreneurs whose intention was not to *build* but to *drain* savings and loans of their resources and then move on to the next get-rich-quick scheme. In the early 1980s, savings and loans became known in banking circles as "money machines"; the industry was not so much deregulated as *unregulated* (p. 14). By early 1987, it was widely recognized that the deregulation bills had inflicted catastrophic damage on the industry. By that year, nearly a third of savings and loan institutions were either insolvent or on the brink of insolvency. In 1989, Reagan's successor, George Bush, announced a plan to bail out the savings and loans which would cost $200 billion over the next decade, and a total of $360 billion over three decades. That comes to roughly $1,500 for every man, woman, and child living in the United States. Of the missing money, perhaps half had been stolen outright. Billions simply "drifted off into the ozone never to be seen again" (p. 5). The entire savings and loan industry "teetered on the edge of collapse" (p. 5). And yet very few of the savings and loan plunderers went to jail and very little of the stolen money was ever recovered.

The savings and loan scandal was probably the largest monetary theft in history. The total amount of money stolen was *six to seven hundred times* that which is taken in *all* the robberies that occur in the United States each year. How could so much have been stolen? How were the thefts accom-

plished? How could a president have been so catastrophically wrong about the impact of a bill he signed? What happened?

The fact is that the bill failed to take into account the human factor of greed. It made the assumption that the entrepreneurs who borrowed money from savings and loans, and the officers of the thrift institutions themselves, were honest and could be trusted to conduct business on the honor system. Although most people are fairly honest, a certain number of dishonest people will always be attracted to financial endeavors when they know that they are not accountable for their actions. In effect, the savings and loan deregulation measures of the early 1980s constituted an invitation to the daring and unethical to steal.

Most of the money disappeared in the following way. First, a borrower approaches a savings and loan institution for a loan, putting up, say, a parcel of undeveloped land as collateral. Through a variety of tricks and gimmicks I'll explain shortly, the land is assessed at ten times its market value. The loan is secured, and the money is lent, but it is used in a variety of nonproductive ways, including the private pleasure of borrowers and investments that have little chance of paying off. Partly because of the recession and the real estate bust that hit the country in the early to mid 1980s, the investment for which the loan was secured did not pay off: A mall that was built does not attract enough retailers, the junk bond market collapsed, too few buyers purchased a house in a huge development, too much of the loan was siphoned off to permit the capitalization of the project. Whatever the reason, the loan payments cannot be met, and the thrift has to foreclose on the loan and seize the collateral. Yet, because the collateral is insufficient to cover the loan, the savings and loan never recovers the true value of the loan. Several dozen such defaults can bankrupt a savings and loan institution.

Just a few of the many larcenous schemes and scams that were a direct result of the deregulation of the savings and loan institutions include:

- *Scraping:* "When swindlers take out a large loan to develop a property, they often steal some of the loan proceeds by using such methods as double invoicing. . . . If they scrape off too much, the project will go bankrupt, and they often did" (p. 375).
- *Walking Money:* "That amount of a loan that exceeds the value of the property securing it, so named because walk is what the borrower does,

leaving the lender with an overencumbered piece of property" (p. 375).

• *Land Flip:* "In order to inflate a property's value well above its actual worth in order to justify the largest possible loan, swindlers would engage in a number of sham sales of the property, each time raising the sales price. No real cash ever changed hands during these sham sales. The only purpose of the sale was to record a new deed, each time reflecting a new, higher price. . . . Once the desired value was reached the borrower would get a loan for that amount and later default on it, leaving the lender stuck with a grossly overencumbered property" (p. 373).

• *Kissing the Paper:* "When a borrower was too financially weak to qualify for a large loan, he would pay someone with a strong financial statement to join him as a partner in a project. Using that person's financial statement, the borrower would then get his loan. Once the loan was made the borrower would 'buy out' his partner with a portion of the loan proceeds, thereby relieving that person of any future financial liability. The buyout was actually the partner's fee for allowing the weak borrower to use his financial strength to get the loan" (p. 373).

• *Bust-out:* "A mob term used to describe a scam designed to extract large sums of money from an unsuspecting company or financial institution. The mob has used bust-outs for decades to gut small firms of their assets. After deregulation they began busting out thrifts as well" (p. 370).

The savings and loan deregulation debacle made a small number of dishonest individuals a great deal of money and left a considerably larger number of individuals saddled with debt. It bankrupted hundreds of savings and loan institutions across the country, and threatened the entire thrift industry. It is very likely that the American taxpayer will eventually pick up the $360 billion bill to pay for these monstrous thefts. The swindles resulting from the savings and loan deregulation of the early 1980s probably represents the largest financial theft in history (Pizzo, Fricker, and Muolo, 1992).

Consider a small "rogue's gallery" of savings and loan case histories.

• Michael Rapp swindled more than $8.4 million from a New York savings and loan institution and $7.5 million from a Florida financial institution. Initially sentenced to 15 years imprisonment for the New York theft and 32 years for the Florida crimes, plus a $1.75 million fine, on appeal, Rapp ended up serving five-and-a-half years in prison and, so far, has paid none of his pared-down $100,000 fine.

• Herman Beebe was charged with a loan fraud which resulted in a loss of more than $30 million from 16 Lousiana and Texas financial institutions. Beebe was a friend of President Reagan, Louisiana Governor Edwin Edwards, and judge Edmund Reggie, Senator Edward Kennedy's father-in-law. His fine: $375,000; his sentence: a year and a day, of which he actually served 10 months.

• In 1984, John Molinaro purchased a California savings and loan institution. Within two years, he had siphoned off all its assets. After federal authorities closed the institution, Molinaro was apprehended trying to obtain a passport under a false name; a notebook was found in his possession which indicated that he was about to leave for a Caribbean island, where he had stashed $3.5 million. Molinaro was charged with defrauding his S&L of $30 million. His sentence: 12 years in prison; actual time served: three-and-a-half years. Although authorities recovered $4 million of his ill-gotten gains, he has paid back none of his $6.7 million punitive fine (Pizzo and Muolo, 1993).

The savings and loan scandal is an excellent example of "heads I win, tails you lose"—*collective embezzlement*, that is, crime *by* a corporation yet *on behalf of* a corporation (Calavita and Pontell, 1990). It entails the officers *of* a corporation looting that same corporation. The "corporation" might appear to be the financial institution itself, but as it turns out, the officers who run and profit from the corporation *constitute* the corporation. The institution's small investors and depositors are simply unwitting instruments—dupes—in the creation of a dummy or "shell" corporation that is set up only to be drained of its assets. In the long run, the loser is the taxpayer since, as I explained, these savings and loan institutions were federally insured.

Professional Crime

All occupations that are classified as professions require advanced, usually graduate, training, and all practitioners possess a specialized skill that is not accessible to the general public. Moreover, all are governed by an ethical code which places service above self-interest; all have a system of licensing which permits only the qualified (and, presumably, the ethical) to practice. And all deal with clients—paying customers who look to the professional for help. Pharmacists, lawyers, physicians, and accountants are expected to render honest and fair service to their clients. The professions stand at the top of the occupational prestige hierarchy; their practitioners are respected members of their community. We are shocked and disappointed when we learn of professionals who engage in criminal activities—schemes which line their own pockets at the expense of persons they are obligated to serve. Perhaps the most common form of professional crime is fraud. Physicians sometimes submit fraudulent claims for reimbursement; pharmacists sometimes bill the government for more drugs than they deliver; lawyers sometimes bilk clients out of an inheritance; accountants divert funds from clients into their own hands. What makes professional crime different from corporate crime is that it is undertaken on behalf of the individual professional for personal gain, not for a larger entity such as a corporation. And almost always, the victim is the client (although the client is sometimes the government). Although business executives are expected to obey the law, they are also expected to make money for the firm, and this may entail skirting or bending the law. Moreover, they owe their primary loyalty to the firm for which they work, not to the general public, their customers, or their employees. Hence, their illegal actions seem understandable to most of us, at least they are not shocking unless they involve a blatant disregard for human life.

Most of us expect the professional to be different. We hold the surgeon, the divorce or inheritance lawyer, the pharmacist, to a higher standard. At the very least, we expect them to place their primary loyalty with their clients. When we go to professionals for help, we place our trust in them; they have a great deal of control over our affairs and the autonomy to conduct them. Moreover, they are governed by a code of ethics, which is not true of the business world. In the business world, the bottom line is profit. In the world of the professions, many of us still believe the bottom line ought to be service to clients. We assume that the prestige granted to members of the professions is warranted, that they deserve the respect we grant them and the pay they receive. When members of the professions commit white-collar crime, they rattle the very foundation of the stratification and reward system in society.

One of the early systematic investigations of professional crime was conducted by Quinney

(1963). His study investigated how the social structure of one profession—that of retail pharmacist—might explain criminal behavior that takes place in that profession. The specific offense that was examined was the violation of laws and regulations governing the compounding and mixing of prescriptions. Quinney found that prescription violation is strongly related to the pharmacist's occupational orientation. Pharmacists oriented toward professional role expectations are more bound by both formal (i.e., legal) and informal (i.e., occupational) controls. Pharmacists more oriented toward a business role, which stresses the merchandising aspects of the job, are less bound by either form of control and are primarily interested in monetary gain. It was found that three-quarters of those categorized as business-oriented had been officially detected as prescription violators, while none of those classified as profession-oriented were known violators. In other words, "for each pharmacist, orientation to a particular role more than to another provides a perspective to which violation may seem appropriate" (Quinney, 1963, p. 184).

It is estimated that 85 percent of all surgical operations performed in the United States are discretionary or elective, that is, they do not involve emergencies or life-threatening or life-prolonging circumstances (Bunker, 1976). Of these operations, it is believed that roughly 15 percent are unnecessary, at an annual cost to patients of some $4 billion (Meier and Geis, 1979). D'Espo (1962) contends that at least 15 percent of all hysterectomies (the surgical removal of the uterus) are performed in the absence of pathology. Lanza-Kaduce investigated this allegation and concluded that unnecessary surgery is a regularly occurring phenomenon, attributable in part to differences in training and operating philosophies among doctors. He notes: "The proportion of operations of questionable necessity is sizeable, and the cost of this professional misconduct in terms of mortality, morbidity, and money is substantial" (1980, p. 344).

Freidson (1970b) offers a political explanation that focuses on economic factors and occupational self-interest as most responsible for unnecessary surgery. In fact, the highest surgery rates in the population have been reported among low-income patients with insurance coverage (Anderson and Feldman, 1956). In one case, an opthalmologist was convicted of performing unneeded cataract surgery on indigent patients to collect Medicaid fees; he totally blinded one woman when he operated needlessly on her (Welkos, 1984).

Medicaid is a government-funded health benefit program designed to provide medical care for the needy. The fee-for-service structure of the program, in which a third party insurer pays all charges, has created a new class of professional white-collar criminal. A number of providers have succumbed to the temptation to overcharge, bill for patients never seen, double-bill, prolong treatment, and perform worthless services. Policing and enforcement have been selective at best, and it is certain that a huge number of undetected illegal practices exists. The professional status of providers, notably physicians, makes it relatively easy to cover up offenses. Some government officials believe that as much as $40 billion is lost annually to fraudulent and abusive practices in the nation's health care programs. Investigations have reported cases in which bills have been submitted for X-rays done without film, daily psychotherapy sessions totalling more than 24 hours, and hysterectomies performed on male patients (Jesilow, Pontell, and Geis, 1993).

Why do doctors engage in Medicaid fraud? Many physicians are unhappy with what they regard as low reimbursement rates (often half their customary charges) and the red-tape paperwork the program requires. Some physicians cheat to "make back" what they feel they should earn. In other instances, doctors see the program as a "game" which, if played well, can provide a lucrative source of extra income. A study of Medicaid fraud, which included a number of interviews with convicted violators (Pontell, Jesilow, and Geis, 1984a), quotes one physician as saying: "If you know how to play the game, you can stay out of trouble and you can milk the program." Researchers suggest that the behavior which enables a physician to engage in fraud is probably at least partially learned from others in the profession, and that professional values may effectively neutralize the doctor's conflicts of conscience (Pontell, Jesilow, and Geis, 1984b). Very few of the professional deviants who were interviewed displayed any remorse for their wrongdoing, preferring instead to attack the program and its officials as the cause of their violations. A similar reaction was manifested by clinical psychologists (Geis et al., 1985). We've already encountered this deviance "neutralization" process among delinquents (Sykes and Matza, 1957), prostitutes (Jackman et al., 1963), and rapists (Scully and Marolla,

1984), and we'll see it again among white-collar criminals generally (Benson, 1985). Other studies (Pontell, Jesilow, and Geis, 1982; Jesilow, Pontell, and Geis, 1985; Jesilow, Pontell, and Geis, 1993) suggest that occupational norms may support an attitude on the part of some professionals that they are "above the law."

A theoretically revealing finding from Medicaid fraud studies focuses on psychiatrists. While psychiatrists represent only 8 percent of all physicians, more than twice that figure (roughly 20 percent) of the physicians suspended from Medicaid because of fraudulent practices are psychiatrists (Geis et al., 1985). Are psychiatrists simply less honest than other physicians? Or are they specifically targeted for prosecution? Almost all physicians bill the Medicaid program for specific services rendered, including examinations, tests, X-rays, injections, and surgeries. The question of fraud focuses primarily on whether the claimed services were actually carried out. Psychiatrists represent one notable exception, Here, the bill includes not simply a service, but a service rendered over a specific period of time. Most states compute their payment rates for psychiatrists by 50-minute sessions. By clocking movement in and out of offices, or by verifying the times with the patients themselves, investigators can readily determine if the actual time periods conform to those that have been billed. Psychiatrists, then, are especially easy *enforcement targets*. Unlike most other types of medical crime, investigators need not deal with complex legal or professional issues and enforcement problems. The fact is that checking psychiatric bills requires little technical expertise beyond an ability to tell time. Thus, it is likely that the relatively easy detection of offenses among psychiatrists, a rarity in white-collar crime, is responsible for their overrepresentation among fraud cases—not necessarily any greater dishonesty on their part.

These three examples—prescription violations, unnecessary surgery, and Medicaid fraud—obviously do not encompass the entire range of professional deviance. There are many other types of offenses involving professionals. However, several recurrent threads run through our examples. To begin with, a state of tension exists between the *service* and the *business* dimensions of the professions. Society expects its professionals to be honest, dedicated, and client-oriented; at the same time, professionals expect to enjoy high socioeconomic status, respect, and most of all, affluence. These expectations need not be incompatible, but they pave the way for possible conflicts. It is entirely possible that under certain circumstances and with certain professionals, the second set of expectations will undermine the first.

Perhaps the most promising theoretical explanation of professional deviance focuses on the manner in which professionals are socialized and organized. In the case of physicians, a look at the way in which medical students are trained (Becker et al., 1961) suggests that "idealism" invariably gives way to "cynicism" during the process of a medical education. Shoemaker reports a measurable incidence of cheating among premedical students, a practice which students are generally able to justify. "Any advantage you can get, take," explains one future doctor (1984, p. 94). As we've seen, Sutherland (1949) believed that professional behaviors are learned as a result of association with fellow professionals. Within each profession, there is a strong demand for autonomy. The result is a "circle the wagons" mentality in reaction to outside regulation and to the external policing of deviant behavior.

A major controversy within the field of criminology centers around the "exceptionalism" of white-collar crime: Do we need a separate and different explanation for white-collar crime? Or can we account for crime in general—all crime—with a single explanation? A focus on deviance perpetrated by professionals highlights a well-educated group of elite persons whose violations cannot in any way be attributed to the difficulties created by poverty, personal pathology, community breakdown, inadequate socialization, or similar explanations that apply much better to more traditional or conventional kinds of crimes. Since becoming a professional requires so much training, skill, and responsibility, it is entirely likely that explanations that rely on impulsiveness and poor self-control are inadequate (Gottfredson and Hirschi, 1990, pp. 180-201). Professional criminals and deviants are almost certainly more impulsive than professionals who are law-abiding, ethical, and traditional. But professional criminals and deviants are also almost certain to be a good deal less impulsive than a substantial proportion of persons who were unwilling to submit themselves to the rigor and discipline of professional training. Professional white-collar crime is often an easy, undemanding, and efficacious means of obtaining a self-interested goal. This much is true. But the process of obtain-

ing professional training does not fit this description; to explain professional white-collar crime, we have to account for the conjunction of these two very different impulses and behaviors, and so far, no criminologist has been able to do so to the satisfaction of the field. We'll examine this issue in a bit more detail in the section, "Why White-Collar Crime?"

Crime By a Corporation: Corporate Crime

Crime committed *by* and *on behalf of* a corporation entails executives and executive officers engaging in illegal actions that are intended to further the interests of that corporation; they are actions taken *on behalf of* the corporation. (These illegal actions may *also* benefit the careers of the individual corporate actors, but that is a different matter.) This type of crime clearly contrasts with individual embezzlement, which is undertaken *against* the corporation *on behalf of* a given employee or several employees. In embezzlement, the victim is the corporation. In corporate crime, the victim, or potential victim, is the *general public* (in the case of illegal pollution), the *consumer* (in the case of price fixing or the sale of illegally unsafe products), the *employee* (such as illegally unsafe working conditions), the *government* (for instance, illegal tax avoidance), or a *competitor* (two firms forming a price-fixing conspiracy against a third).

The issue which I raised above, namely, according to *which* or *whose* code is a given corporate action illegal or deviant, is especially crucial because of the *global reach* of multinational corporations. Are harmful company actions that are *not* illegal in the host country but *would be* in the corporations's home country "crimes"? And which country's normative system is used as the code by which we determine its deviant status? This dilemma is especially acute, as is usually the case, when the multinational is based in a rich, powerful country (such as the United States, Japan, or France) and the host country is a poor, relatively weak Third World nation. (To make things even more complicated, what if the multinational corporation engaged in actions in a Third World country that *would not* be regarded as a crime by observers of a certain political stripe if it *were* committed by a company that was run by citizens of the Third World country?) Some observers pretend that these definitional problems do not exist, but if we are being rigorous and systematic, they have to be addressed.

Framers, practitioners, and observers of the criminal law regard *mens rea*, or the possession of a "guilty mind," a necessary, defining quality of a crime: The offender must have had the *intention* to engage in certain actions and caused their harmful consequences. There are exceptions to this rule, however. It is true that nearly all street crime, just about all forms of embezzlement—both individual and collective—and many (although far from all) government crimes have one key quality in common: They entail the *conscious* and *intentional* inflicting of harm on victims. The robber *means* to deprive the victim of money or property; the rapist *intends* to force sexual penetration upon his victim; embezzlers *act* so as to take money from an organization of some kind.

This is not always or even usually true of corporate crime. In fact, for the majority of corporate crimes, this intention to do harm to a victim is absent. Instead, corporate executives expose parties to a certain measure of *risk*. Whether this risk is acceptable or unacceptable, legal or illegal, is a matter of interpretation. Some corporate actors *knowingly* expose other parties to risks that those parties, and the law, would regard as unacceptable, while other corporate actors do so in the *absence* of such awareness. But nearly all take risk into account and weigh their actions accordingly (Short, 1990). All executives would prefer that the actions they take on behalf of their corporations cause no one any harm. But in the real world, this is not possible. On the one hand, no work site, no product, no industrial waste can be made completely safe; some level of risk is "an inevitable feature of modern existence" (Friedrichs, 1996, p. 17); if corporate risk were to be eliminated altogether, all business activity would cease to exist (Perrow, 1984, p. 311). For instance, no automobile can ever be manufactured in which the likelihood of injury or death is zero. On the other hand, some work sites, products, or waste products are so *blatantly* unsafe, the risk so *immense*, that harm is nearly certain; some corporate actors can be said to *deliberately* expose potential victims to unnecessary, substantial, and avoidable risk.

How does the observer make a judgment that the risk was unacceptable and the action that brought it on is a crime? How do we assess risk? According to what criteria? And *who* assesses it? Do persons who are themselves exposed to the risk of harm assess its magnitude and the acceptability of that exposure? (In effect, they often do, in civil cases, but only *after* the damage has been done, not at the decision-making stage.) One problem is that people assess risk in an extremely inaccurate fashion, exaggerating the likelihood of certain types of harm and minimizing others (Friedrichs, 1996, p. 15; Erikson, 1990; Slovic, Fischoff, and Lichtenstein, 1980; Slovic, Layman, and Flynn, 1991). On the other hand, in determining the culpability of corporate actions, do we rely on corporate actors to assess what constitutes "acceptable risk"? Clearly, we do not, for it is members of the general public who sit on juries in civil trials, not hand-picked panels of corporation executives, who are likely to decide on the basis of what's good for the corporation, not what's good for the customer, the public, or the worker.

There is a second risk the corporate actor calculates in addition to the risk of harm to customers, the public, and employees. This is the likelihood of *accountability*, in the case of the criminal law, the risk of arrest and prosecution, in the case of civil and administrative law, the risk of lawsuits and punitive fines. Corporate offenses *very* rarely result in criminal prosecution, and administrative agencies rarely slap corporations with huge fines. But torts do result in a *great many* civil trials and, occasionally, extremely large settlements. In fact, today, product liability is the largest field of civil law (Priest, 1990). Here, quite clearly, we see the inhibitory impact of civil law: It forces executive actors to consider in their cost-benefit analysis the cost of harmful consequences of their operations or products in the form of substantial settlements.

Let's be clear about this: We live in a capitalist society. Corporations are not philanthropic organizations; they are designed and run to earn a profit. So far, all government experiments based on a socialist economy, or any markedly noncapitalist alternative, have either collapsed or been seriously compromised. (Moreover, decision makers in socialist societies have taken parallel risks on a basis other than that of profit.) To a corporation, what counts is the "bottom line." This means that their executives make decisions based almost exclusively on *cost-benefit analysis:* They weigh potential costs against earnings to determine possible or likely profit. To earn a profit, they make decisions to engage, or not to engage, in certain business ventures that may or may not pay off. Business ventures may be costly in various ways. Some may entail huge expenditures and offer little potential reward. Still others are likely to result in extremely unfavorable and irreparable public relations, and hence, be costly in indirect ways. Others are highly certain to result in criminal prosecution, while still others are so likely to cause damage to customers that extremely expensive lawsuits, along with the possibility of bankruptcy, loom on the horizon. Corporations do not avoid certain actions for the public good or as a service to humanity; they do so because they would be unprofitable.

Ford Motor Company's decision not to install a safety feature on the Pinto gas tank resulted in numerous gas-tank ruptures in accidents and hence, a great deal of extremely bad publicity. In reaching their decision, executives calculated how much the car's tendency to explode upon impact would cost them in increased lawsuits versus how much it would cost the company to install a safer gas tank—in a nutshell, "cost-benefit analysis." This decision was instrumental in the deaths of more than 50 unfortunate Pinto owners, and the serious injuries of hundreds, possibly thousands more, as well as the payment of some $100 million in civil cases. As it turns out, Ford executives underestimated the cost of their action to the company. Horrifying as it may sound, that calculation of cost and benefit is the *basis* of all business in a profit-oriented economy. In fact, as we've seen, risky choices are built into *all* technology, completely *independent* of the type of economy. In a socialist economy, risks are taken for "the people" (or the state), and in a capitalist economy, they are taken to earn a profit for a corporation.

Before looking at a few cases of corporate crime, let's address one crucial issue: *Who is the corporate actor?* It is often stated that corporate crimes are distinct, different from practically all others in that they are, *by their very nature,* enacted by a collectivity rather than individual persons. Decisions are arrived at in consultation with higher-ups and approved or initiated at the top. It is the *corporation* that acts, as a whole, not scattered, isolated actors, one at a time. Often, after conviction, it is the corporation that is fined, not specific persons working for that corporation. On the other hand, individual corporate actors may be fined and, occasionally sentenced to a term of incarceration. (Clearly, a corporate entity cannot serve a prison sentence!) When the Pennwalt Corporation was convicted and fined more than $1 million for illegally dumping a toxic substance into Puget Sound,

a federal district court judge insisted on seeing the company's top executive in court before he would accept a guilty plea; "Who is the corporation?" the judge asked; "I think the public is entitled to know who's responsible" (Egan, 1989). Suffice it to say that though individual persons act, they always do so within certain social structures. In the case of corporate crime, these social structures are formal organizations or bureaucracies. As to whether persons or organizations are responsible for a given white-collar crime depends on the crime in question. But clearly, structural entities play a larger role as actors in corporate crime than perhaps for any other type of crime. (For a contrary argument, see Cressey, 1988, who argues that a corporate actor is a fiction—only individual executives act.)

The question of who the corporate actor is plays a central role when we attempt to determine the *incidence* or *rate* of corporate crime. If the corporation is considered as the actor (and if the entire period of its existence is considered as well), then clearly, *most* (and in Sutherland's pioneering study, *all*) corporations are guilty of committing corporate crimes at least once, since at least some executives have made decisions that turned out to be illegal. Hence, their *rate* of corporate crime would be enormous. However, if all the executives are included in the total number of actors (and if a year-by-year tally is made), it is possible that the rates of white-collar crime would be quite low. Most observers who argue that white-collar crime is rampant have not devoted much thought to determine its rate relative to the number of persons who are in a position to commit it. Sutherland's study was based on *corporations* as the unit of analysis, but his explanation for white-collar crimes took place within them: differential association theory, which was fundamentally *individualistic,* an obvious *contradiction* (Gottfredson and Hirschi, 1990, pp. 188, 191).

An example of the inability to understand the difference between corporate and individual actors is provided by Simon (1996, p. 338), who states that during a recent 10-year span, at least 11 percent of the nation's 1,000 largest corporations were convicted of at least one illegal action. "Imagine," Simon says, "if the same proportion of the adult population of the U.S. had been convicted of an illegal offense and sentenced to prison, 12 million inmates would be crowded into the nation's already over-crowded prison system." (Incidentally, most convictions are for misdemeanors, which do not carry a prison sentence, and even a small minority of convicted felons, perhaps one in eight, actually serves any prison time at all. And 11 percent of approximately 200 million adult Americans is 22 million, not 12 million.) The fact is that again, Simon confuses criminal convictions obtained against a *corporation*, taken as a whole, with criminal convictions obtained against *individuals in the population*. In a corporation of 100,000 executives, let's say 10 in a single division (or one one-hundredth of 1 percent) is responsible for a given criminal act; on the other hand, a conviction against the corporation would mean that the entire corporation is counted in the tally. Clearly, this would be an invalid and sloppy calculation.

Perhaps the classic case of corporate crime is provided by what is now referred to as "the Great Electrical Conspiracy." Starting at about the end of World War II and continuing throughout the 1950s, all the corporations manufacturing and selling heavy electrical equipment were involved in an illegal price-fixing scheme. These corporations ran from the biggest giants in the field, such as General Electric and Westinghouse, to small and less well-known manufacturers. Actually, not just one but 20 separate conspiracies were operating simultaneously, since most of the electrical manufacturing companies were decentralized into semi-autonomous departments. Prices were fixed on equipment such as circuit breakers, huge transformers, turbine generators, switch gears, and insulators. Most of the equipment was not sold to the public but to organized entities or agencies such as city governments, power and light companies, and federal agencies. Executives held private meetings, agreed on prices, and arbitrarily divided up the market. In so doing, they violated the Sherman Anti-Trust Act. They had formed a cartel and were guilty of collusion, conspiracy, price fixing, and bid rigging. They submitted price bids to their customers in sealed envelopes, but it was all a hoax. There was no competition at all; the prices had been agreed upon in advance by the offending companies. Each took turns in submitting the winning bid. As is apt to happen, someone got his signals crossed. In the fall of 1959, representatives of the Tennessee Valley Authority complained to the Department of Justice that they had received identical bids from several supposed competitors. The Justice Department decided to investigate the case. The investigation provided the evidence necessary for criminal prosecution.

The Sherman Anti-Trust Act was designed to discourage the formation of monopolies because they represented "restraints of trade." The act was established to protect the ideal of a "free market system." A truly competitive market could be bad for business, since competitors would have to cut profit margins by cutting prices to attract customers away from the competition. By regulating the market through working arrangements with competitors, a corporation would have more leeway for setting profitable prices; in this way, the market would be divided up among competitors and everyone would be happy—except the customer, of course. One problem is that customers are usually not even aware of such collusive schemes. Executives of electrical corporations entered into the arrangement because they felt that their profits were not high enough. In the words of one: "The market was getting in chaotic condition." Conspiring with other manufacturers, said the president of one electrical company, "is the only way business can be run. It is free enterprise," he added, with no apparent irony intended. True competition, these executives felt, would narrow profit margins and put some manufacturers out of business. Bid rigging kept marginal companies in business and prevented a monopolistic market, or so went their explanation for their illegal activities. "Getting together with their competitors" became a way of life for them (Geis, 1967).

The prevailing estimate as to how much money was involved in these transactions is roughly $1.7 billion in sales annually, for about 10 or 12 years. The amount of money unnecessarily paid as a result of the price-rigging scheme runs into the millions of dollars, and perhaps as high as a billion dollars (in 1960 dollars). This was money that was stolen from the public's pocket. It represented money that all consumers and taxpayers paid over and above what they would have paid had more honest business practices prevailed. It represents real money, just as money stolen in a bank robbery is real, except for the fact that in corporate crime, the sums are vastly huger. Whenever a municipal government was overcharged a quarter of a million dollars for a turbine, its taxpayers had to make up the difference. Whenever a light and power company bought a generator for 10 percent more than it was worth under competitive bidding, its customers paid more for the energy that they consumed. As in other forms of white-collar crime, the fact that each individual customer lost a small amount, to many observers, made the practice seem less evil.

It was found that the conspirators were not much different from ordinary criminals in some of the techniques that they employed. They were secretive about their activities and optimistic that they wouldn't be caught. They minimized telephone calls to and from their offices, using public phones most of the time. They even had fake names and special codes to identify business transactions. Also, as with common criminals, they rationalized their behaviors. A number of the electrical executives said that their actions, while "technically illegal," actually served to "stabilize prices." They shifted the blame to the market structure rather than accepting it themselves. The lack of punitiveness of the judiciary and the companies themselves toward the offenders also sheds light on the nature and dynamics of corporate crime. One judge said of the defendants: "They were torn between conscience and an approved corporate policy, with the rewarding objective of promotion, comfortable security, and large salaries. They were the organization or company man, the conformist who goes along with his superiors and finds balm for his conscience in additional comforts and security of his place in the corporate setup" (Geis, 1967, p. 147).

General Electric fired its offending executives, but Westinghouse did not for four reasons:

First, . . . the men involved had not sought personal aggrandizement. "While their actions cannot in any way be condoned, these men did not act for personal gain, but in the belief, misguided though it may have been, that they were furthering the company's interest"; second, "the punishment incurred by them already was harsh" and "no further penalties would serve any useful purpose"; third, "each of these individuals is in every sense a reputable citizen, a respected and valuable member of the community and of high moral character"; and fourth, there was virtually no likelihood that the individuals would repeat their offense (Geis, 1967, p. 146).

Eventually, 45 executives working for 29 corporations were indicted for criminal conspiracy. Almost all of the corporate defendants admitted their guilt by entering a plea of *nolo contendere*, or "no contest." Seven of them received jail sentences—of 30 days (and 24 were convicted but received suspended sentences). The companies themselves were slapped with criminal fines totalling roughly $2 million, which was paid mostly by General Electric and Westinghouse. Considering the huge sums of money involved in the conspiracy, the criminal penalties meted out seem insignif-

icant in comparison. Geis estimated that the $400,000 fine that was levied against General Electric would be equivalent to a man earning an income of $175,000 receiving a $3 parking ticket (1967, p. 142).

The offenders did not see what they did as criminal. "Sure, collusion was illegal," explained a GE executive, "but it wasn't unethical. . . . These competitor meetings were just attended by a group of distressed individuals who wanted to know where they were going." When a federal attorney asked a Westinghouse executive, "Did you know that these meetings with competitors were illegal?" the reply was, "Illegal? Yes," he explained, "but not criminal. I assumed that criminal action meant damaging someone and we did not do that." An Allis-Chalmers officer was asked: "Why did you go to the meetings?" He answered, "I thought it was part of my duty to do so." Another added, "Meeting with competitors was just one of the many facets of responsibility that was delegated to me." So ingrained was the practice that when convicted, these executives saw themselves as scapegoats, sacrificial lambs. The whole industry—in fact, all of business generally, not just the manufacturers of electrical equipment—made use of collusion, monopolistic control, informal regulation of the market, these executives argued. Why should we be the fall guys? they asked, outraged by their convictions. One executive, who had managed to garner a substantial amount of support for his cause from the community, "got, frankly, madder than hell" when he found out that he would not be paid while he served his brief jail sentence—a sum of $11,000. "We did not fix prices," one president of a small company explained. "I am telling you that all we did was recover costs." A sales manager of the ITE Curcuit Breaker Company put the matter this way: "The spirit of such meetings only appeared to be correcting a horrible price level situation; there was not an attempt to actually damage customers." One executive who refused to go along with the arrangement was replaced; he was described as "getting us into trouble with competition."

At least three of the basic elements that are common to most forms of deviance are lacking in this case: The offenders did not see themselves as committing deviant acts, nor did they see themselves as deviants; second, the public did not view their actions as grossly reprehensible, nor did they feel that they were, in fact, deviants; and third, the formal agencies of social control, in this case, the judges, did not penalize them severely for their actions, at least in relation to their magnitude. The offending executives received a large volume of supportive letters, telegrams, and phone calls; their thrust was "you didn't do anything wrong, and your conviction is grossly unfair." A defense lawyer claimed that the judge "did not understand what it would do to his client, this fine man, to be put behind bars with common criminals." A judge suspended the sentence of another executive by saying that he didn't think that this was the type of offense that probation lent itself to or was designed for. And Westinghouse's defense of its convicted executives certainly summarizes a widespread feeling concerning the respectability of the executives.

As a final note, it should be pointed out that the heavy electrical equipment conspiracy cases received only sparce media coverage. A bank robbery, even when it involves little or no concrete violence, generally makes the headlines if it involves a substantial sum of money. "The Great Electrical Conspiracy" involved sums of up to $1 billion, a massive prosecution effort on the part of federal authorities, and incarceration for some of the corporate executives. Yet the newspaper industry did not consider these events particularly newsworthy. Stories tended to emphasize the individual executives, divorced from any industry or organizational context. Their acts were considered isolated and idiosyncratic rather than related to company and industry-wide practices.

If nothing else, the electrical conspiracy shows support for Sutherland's contentions concerning white-collar crime: that criminal behavior is learned from associates. While data on white-collar, especially corporate, crime are much more difficult to obtain than for most crimes, every time one is prosecuted, light is shed on the phenomenon. The electrical conspiracy highlights the nature and dynamics of corporate crime, and helps us understand the transgressions of powerful individuals and organizations.

Government Crime

Above, I delineated two types of political or government crimes. The first is criminal according to a *strict* or *narrow* interpretation of the definition, that is, such actions must be against the law in jurisdictions in which they take place. I cited the example of the Watergate scandal, enacted during the first Nixon administration, which centered around the "dirty tricks" of the Committee to Re-elect the President (CREEP), committed against Nixon's Democratic opponents. The second, broader type—political crimes not in the literal but the *broader, more metaphorical sense*—is a bit trickier to spell out. Perhaps here, more than for any other type of crime, whether white-collar or any other type, we have to recognize that what constitutes a crime as spelled out in one jurisdiction may not be a crime in another. (To make matters even more complicated, we have to distinguish between the legal code *as it is written* and the power of elites to avoid prosecution, and hence, render a legal code impotent.) Killings during warfare, for example, are often defined as crimes by one side and as legitimate actions by the enemy. For instance, was the war in Vietnam a "crime"? Not according to the legal code of the United States, and not according to its client state, South Vietnam. (And independently, we'd also have to consider how the *populations* of each country defined such actions. Did they consider them criminal? Deviant? Unethical?) But it was *regarded* as a crime by the government of North Vietnam, which waged a war to expel the American military presence from the country and unify North and South Vietnam. Is the killing of tens of thousands of Kurds by Iraqi government troops a "crime"? Not to the Iraqi government, but it *is* so regarded by representatives of many countries outside Iraq. What about the slaughter of the Tutsi by the Hutu, or the Hutu by the Tutsi, in Rwanda? (And in a politically unstable situation, who exactly is "the government"?) In considering governmental crime that is not technically illegal, we are not abandoning our constructionist approach for an objectivist or absolutist definition, we are simply recognizing that different nations (and observers) construct crime differently.

This "metaphorical" or figurative type of crime assumes special importance when two nations engage in conflict to ensure that the definition of each is institutionalized; when one nation defeats another in a war, acts that were previously legal can be *redefined* as a crime. The killing of millions of Jews and other non-German ethnic categories, political prisoners, dissidents, and mentally "unfit" persons that took place in Nazi Germany were not regarded as crimes to many of the higher authorities of the Third Reich. (Some disagreed, although not openly; most did not.) With the defeat of Germany in World War II, the Nuremburg Trials (invoking universal human rights) *defined* them as crimes according to standards that existed in Western democracies *prior* to these trials. It was the legal determination of allied authorities that rendered Nazi killings as crimes—not the fact that they were violation of human rights. To be even more precise, it was the *invocation* of human rights that allied authorities used to render the judgments that Nazi killings were crimes. Again, with political and governmental crimes, we have to be careful to *whose* legal code we are paying attention. Or, for that matter, whether we are referring to actions as "crimes" that are not spelled out in any legal code whatsoever.

This distinction between *literal* and *figurative* (or "metaphorical") political crimes—the latter being acts that are crimes in the loose sense because they violate a certain code of ethics or morality—is crucial because it goes to the heart of *motivation* and hence, causality. Acts that are contemplated by political authorities which have a certain likelihood of prosecution are the product of an entirely different set of dynamics from those which have little or no such likelihood. When we ask, for example, why the Watergate "plumbers" engaged in "dirty tricks" for Richard Nixon, we have to consider that they calculated the likelihood of getting caught. For them, their action's *literal* illegal status is crucial. On the other hand, when Saddam Hussein considers whether and how to crush the Kurdish rebellion—for instance, by leveling their villages or killing them with poison gas—he does not have to consider the issue of legal prosecution. The fact that human rights groups or political leaders from around the world condemn the killing of Kurds is irrelevant (except insofar as it may lead to political, economic, or military consequences, such as a foreign invasion or an oil embargo). Again, by failing to make the distinction between literal and figurative crimes, we become incapable of understanding the dynamics of how such actions come into being. If we are constructing a theory which attempts to account for political crime, we must make this distinction.

When all the qualifications have been registered, we reach the conclusion that a category of actions can be identified which are widely regarded by observers as political and governmental "crimes"; they are seen as deviant, lawless, unethical, unacceptable, and immoral. Different observers will disagree, of course, but some actions receive widespread nominations for lawlessness and wrongdoing. They don't always result in criminal prosecution—in fact, they very rarely do. But they do result in some measure of citizen outrage and public condemnation, media attention and criticism, and occasionally, official investigation the termination of political careers, or once in a while, embarrassing international repurcussions. But keep in mind the fact that the objective or concrete *harm* caused by governmental and political wrongdoing is *independent* of these reactions. Government actions that cause relatively little harm often produce widespread and intense condemnation; others that result in huge, almost unimaginable harm may pass by with little notice. Many political actions undertaken in Third World countries that result in hundreds of thousands, even millions of deaths, receive very little attention, let alone condemnation, in the West. The fact that Chairman Mao's rigid and brutal collectivization program resulted in the deaths of 20 to 40 million Chinese rarely receives so much as acknowledgement in the West; the slaughter of tens, possibly hundreds of thousands of East Timorians, the death of three-quarters of a million residents of Rwanda and Burundi, aided and abetted by ethnic groups in power, the killing of a million Cambodians by the Kmer Rouge—these and other catastrophic and devastating government actions have received a minuscule fraction of the attention and outrage, let's say, of President Richard Nixon's Watergate follies.

Eitzen and Timmer (1985) have identified several forms or types of what they refer to as "government lawlessness." Four that seem to fit in with what is widely regarded as white-collar crime include: (1) the use of citizens as unwitting or unwilling guinea pigs; (2) the abuse of power by government agencies; (3) secrecy, lying, and deception; and (4) corruption and bribery.

The Use of Citizens as Unwitting or Unwilling Guinea Pigs.

The notion of illegal human experiments usually conjures up images of the horrors of Nazi Germany. The scope and scale of the atrocities that took place during the Third Reich were *vastly* more immense than anything that has been undertaken by the American government. Still, there are documented instances of government-run experiments that practically all of us would regard as dangerous, deviant, unacceptable, and criminal as well. One case, particularly notorious in its contempt and disregard for human life, was the infamous "bad blood" study conducted by the U.S. Public Health Service. Beginning in 1932, physicians in Macon County, Alabama began observing 400 Black males who had contracted syphillis. The experiment did not infect them with the disease, but the physicians, knowing that the subjects had contracted it, did not tell them that they were infected; instead, they were told they were suffering from a condition that was vaguely described as "bad blood." Proper diagnosis was withheld from them in order to study the consequences of not treating the disease. This human experiment went on for *40 years*—during which time, the subjects received no medical treatment whatsoever, nor did their wives, who inevitably contracted the disease, nor did their children, who were born with congenital syphillis (Jones, 1981).

Another notorious instance of the American government using naive subjects as human gunea pigs was a 1953 experiment conducted by the Central Intelligence Agency (CIA), in which LSD was slipped into the drinks of unknowing subjects. One man experienced such a severe psychotic reaction to the hallucinogen that he jumped to his death from a hotel window two days later. The CIA covered up the facts of this case for 22 years—even from the victim's family (Bowart, 1978). Similarly, the Freedom of Information Act has also revealed that the CIA tested experimental "knockout" drugs and other incapacitating substances on terminal cancer patients who had no idea that they were being used as human guinea pigs (Lee, 1982).

Abuse of Power by Government Agencies. Many instances of government lawlessness have been perpetrated by agencies such as the Federal Bureau of Investigation (FBI), the CIA, and the Internal Revenue Service (IRS) under the guise of national security. Illegal domestic surveillance offers a prime example. Beginning with the "red scare" of the 1950s and peaking during the antiwar and civil rights protests of the late 1960s and early 1970s, it is now known that the government opened hundreds of thousands of first-class letters and collected secret dossiers on perhaps half a million Americans. Moreover, many of these targets were harassed and persecuted for their political beliefs or activities.

For instance, in an effort to discredit a particular political activist, the husband of an officer in ACTION, a St. Louis civil rights organization, received a handwritten note which read: "Look man, I guess your old lady doesn't get enough action at home or she wouldn't be shucking and jiving with our black men in ACTION, you dig? Like all she wants to integrate is the bedroom and we black sisters ain't gonna take no second best from our men. So lay it on her man or get the hell off Newstead [Street]." The couple soon separated, and the local FBI agent-in-charge wrote to headquarters: "This matrimonial stress and strain should cause her to function much less effectively in ACTION" (Eitzen and Timmer, 1985). Another example: In 1970, actress Jean Seberg helped raise money for the Black Panthers organization. According to documents released by the FBI in 1979, the FBI tried to discredit Seberg by planting the rumor that the father of her unborn baby was a prominent Black Panther leader. This false story may have precipitated a miscarriage, bouts with mental illness and even, possibly, her eventual suicide (Eitzen and Timmer, 1985, p. 347).

Secrecy, Lying, and Deception. The government has frequently tried to withhold information from Congress, the courts, or its citizens. While some of this occurs in the name of "national security," when it takes the form of outright lying by government officials, it can become an act of lawlessness. This has occurred numerous times in the case of illegal interventions in the sovereignty of other countries—Guatemala in the 1950s, Cuba in the 1960s, and Cambodia in the 1970s, to cite only three instances. In the last of these cases, the death certificates of Americans who died in Cambodia were falsified by the government to read that they had died elsewhere (Wise, 1973).

As I mentioned earlier, one of the most blatant cases—and in all probability, the most famous case—of government crimes of deception are those known collectively as "Watergate."

Watergate revealed that under President [Richard] Nixon a kind of totalitarianism had already come to America, creeping in, not like Carl Sandburg's fog, on little cat's feet, but in button-down shirts, worn by handsome young advertising and public relations men carrying neat attaché cases crammed with $100 bills. Men who were willing to perjure themselves to stay on the team, to serve their leader . . . men determined to preserve their own political power at any cost. It came in the form of the ladder against the bedroom window, miniature transmitters in the ceiling, wiretaps, burglaries, enemies lists, tax audits, and psychiatric profiles (Wise, 1973, pp. x–xi).

A partial list of Watergate-related crimes includes (from Eitzen and Timmer, 1985, pp. 343ff.):

1. Burglars financed by the Committee to Re-Elect the President (CREEP) broke into and bugged the headquarters of the Democratic National Committee in the Watergate apartment complex. These burglars, after capture, were paid "hush money" and promised executive clemency to protect the White House.
2. Burglars also broke into the office of the psychiatrist of Daniel Ellsberg, the man who leaked the notorious "Pentagon Papers" to the press. While the case was still at trial, the White House reportedly offered the judge the directorship of the FBI.
3. The president ordered secret wiretaps of his own aides, several journalists, and even his own brother. He also had secret microphones planted in his offices to record every conversation. When he was forced to provide transcripts of the secret tapes, they were edited.
4. The director of the FBI destroyed vital legal evidence at the suggestion of White House aides.
5. The attorney general was involved in the planning of the Watergate break-in and even suggested at one meeting that CREEP employ prositutes at the Democratic National Convention as another means of gathering information.
6. CREEP employees participated in a "dirty tricks" campaign to discredit Democratic challengers. These tricks included the publication and distribution of letters purporting to come from Senator Edmund Muskie to the effect that Senator "Scoop" Jackson was a homosexual, and a letter, with the forged initials of Senator Hubert Humphrey, which denigrated the popular African-American congresswoman Shirley Chisholm.
7. The White House requested tax audits of administration opponents.

In 1987, another major example of government deception became the focus of national attention and criticism: the congressional investigation and public hearings regarding the "Iran-Contra Affair." As with Watergate, this scandal reflected a complex web of political intrigue, spawned in the White House basement and slowly reaching up to the very highest levels of the executive branch, including the Oval Office. At issue were a number of serious accusations and dramatic revelations. It turns out that the United States sold some 200 tons of arms, including two missile systems, to the hostile nation of Iran in May, 1985. The apparent goal of these sales was to obtain the release of American hostages held in Lebanon under the control of Iranian leadership. President Ronald Reagan initially admitted that a "really minuscule" quantity of arms had been sold to Iran, but later conceded the full extent of the sale.

United States government officials authorized two additional indirect shipments of American arms from Israel to Iran in August and November of 1985. The CIA provided transportation for the November shipment, and the United States replaced the Israeli arms that were shipped. President Reagan initially denied knowledge of this arrangement to the presidential commission he had appointed to investigate the charges, but later retracted his denial. Again, the sale violated American arms export laws. The nature of the deal and its illegality were withheld from the American public for over a year.

Presidential aide Oliver North, a Marine colonel, allegedly prepared a cover-up report indicating that the arms shipments were authorized. The report was then revised to suggest that American officials believed that only oil-drilling equipment was involved. This version was later changed again, when the director of the CIA testified before Congress. As we have learned from the Watergate scandal, attempting to cover up illegal acts and lying to Congress are crimes. North was later fired for diverting profits from the Iranian arms sale to the Contras, a now-defunct rebel army that attempted to overthrow the then pro-Soviet government of Nicaragua. Additional allegations charged that North had used part of the profits to purchase personal items. The misuse of government funds or the unauthorized diversion of profits from U.S. arms sales are also illegal. As a footnote to this sordid affair, let it be said that in some quarters, Colonel North is regarded as a hero, not a villain or a deviant. However, perhaps the prevailing public mood on Iran-Contra can best be appreciated by considering the fact that in 1994, Oliver North spent $20 million in campaign funds in his bid to become a senator from the state of Virginia—and lost.

Corruption and Bribery. Personal corruption and bribery of and by political officials represents another major type of government white-collar crime. Like other white-collar offenders, officials who engage in such practices tend not to see themselves as criminals or deviants. Likewise, in the majority of such instances, penalties for such crimes have ranged from nonexistent to lenient. For example, in 1975 the Securities and Exchange Commission accused Gulf Oil Corporation of funnelling more than $10 million into a Bahamian subsidiary for use as illegal political contributions. Gulf's Washington lobbyist instructed the head of the Bahamian firm to disburse large amounts of cash to selected political candidates. Most prominent among them was the minority leader of the United States Senate, who was reportedly given $100,000. Congress chose not to investigate the matter when the senator decided to retire a few months later. Only one, far less powerful, member of Congress was indicted in the payoff; after pleading guilty, he was fined $200 (Sobel, 1977).

Perhaps the best-known and most controversial recent case of political bribery was Operation ABSCAM. ABSCAM ("Arab Scam") began in 1978, when the FBI undertook an investigation of racketeering and influence peddling among public officials. For the next year and a half, undercover agents approached persons suspected of political corruption and informed them that oil-rich Arab sheiks would offer money in exchange for political favors. These bogus middlemen met with political figures in and around Washington, and paid out considerable sums in cash. The meetings and conversations were videotaped. Several public officials were indicted and convicted. Although this "sting" operation has been widely criticized for its use of entrapment tactics, the tapes did offer dramatic evidence of the potential for corruption in the United States Congress.

WHY WHITE-COLLAR CRIME?

Sutherland's original purpose for studying white-collar crime was *theoretical:* He wished to demonstrate that the usual explanations of criminal behavior—specifically, poverty and social and individual pathology—were inadequate and false because they were inapplicable to white-collar and, especially corporate, crime. For instance, how can unemployment explain crime generally if most white-collar criminals are able to engage in their offenses *only* when they are employed? How can poverty account for all or even most crime when white-collar criminals earn considerably more than the national average? Is white-collar crime so sufficiently different from conventional street crime that we need a special explanation? Sutherland did

not think so; he believed that only the theory of differential association, which we examined in Chapter 4, was adequate to account for crime generally, white-collar crime included. A person engages in white-collar crime, Sutherland argued, to the extent that the weight of definitions favorable to the commission of crime promulgated among that person's intimate associations exceeds definitions that are unfavorable (1983, p. 240).

Most contemporary observers believe that Sutherland's differential association cannot explain all white-collar crime. Many crimes do not require association with peers who define criminal acts in favorable terms; they can be, and often are, devised independently by the offender (Cressey, 1953; Clinard, 1952). Moreover, there is much more to explaining the white-collar crime picture than differential association. Certainly larger *structural* factors come into play such as general societal variables and the corporate climate of tolerance for wrongdoing. In addition, more individual or *micro* factors are likely to play a role. So, again, why white-collar crime?

It should be immediately obvious that the simple and common-sensical explanation, *greed*, is not an adequate explanation of white-collar crime. (Interestingly, greed is hardly ever proposed by criminologists as an explanation of white-collar crime.) How could we compare one corporate or white-collar actor with another with respect to our variable, greed? Are some greedier than others? And how would we know? Greed is one of those explanations that appeals to common sense that actually doesn't take us very far.

Likewise, to argue that capitalist society is corrupt, materialistic, the cause of white-collar and corporate crime (Gordon, 1971; Coleman, 1987), again, is not an adequate theory, since it does not explain why *some* occupants of white-collar positions are offenders and others are *not*. Moveover, no one who proposes such a theory has ever bothered to determine, in a systematic and empirical fashion, just how much white-collar crime takes place in noncapitalist societies. It is entirely likely that the analagous actions in a socialist system—cutting corners, bending the rules, endangering workers' lives, producing shoddy and dangerous products, polluting the environment, making false propagandistic claims—are every bit as common as white-collar crimes under capitalism (Braithwaite, 1988). Consider the catastrophe at Chernobyl, which was attributed to factors that would be referred to as "crimes" had they taken place in the United States. It is entirely likely that the argument which makes capitalism the "cause" of white-collar crime is not even advanced for explanatory purposes. Instead of testing the hypothesis, its proponents, in all likelihood, wish to score some propagandistic points of their own.

Gottfredson and Hirschi (1990, pp. 180ff.; Hirschi and Gottfredson, 1987) agree with Sutherland in that one theory explains all crime—but disagree as to what that theory is. Since Sutherland's time, there has been a movement in criminology toward seeing white-collar crime as a special case, requiring a very different set of factors to account for it. On the surface, white-collar crime would seem to require very different characteristics from those that typify most street crimes. Street crime is enacted more by teenagers than older persons, the poor and unemployed rather than the affluent and employed, members of racial and ethnic minorities rather than whites, the previously arrested rather than persons without a record, and so on. But white-collar crime tends to be enacted more by persons in their thirties and older, the affluent and the employed, whites, and persons without criminal records. There seems to be a contradiction here; we have two entirely different sets of actors who seem to engage in two entirely different types of crimes. Hence, the same theory cannot account for them both.

Gottfredson and Hirschi disagree. They agree with Wheeler, Weisburd, and their colleagues (Wheeler, Weisburd, and Bode, 1982; Wheeler et al., 1988; Weisburd et al., 1990) that most researchers have characterized the universe of white-collar criminals inaccurately. Most writers who comment on white-collar crime seem to confuse it with *corporate* crime. In fact, most white-collar criminals are petty, low-level offenders ("small fry") who engage in illegal practices because they find themselves in a financial jam and need to cut corners to survive. The high-level executive making decisions that drag corporations into illegal behavior (the "big fish") tend to be extremely small in number as well as atypical and unrepresentative. Even more important, Gottfredson and Hirschi argue that *the very same factors* that cause street crime *also* cause white-collar crime. Recall their definition of crime: force or fraud used in pursuit of a goal. It does not matter what that goal is; what causes a person to use force or fraud? Someone who is lacking in self-control, someone who

seeks to obtain a goal the easy and most immediately effective way, someone without concern for risk or possible long-term consequences. And what factor or variable produces low self-control? Ineffective child rearing; "discipline, supervision, and affection tend to be missing" in the homes and families of persons who are impulsive and seek immediate gratification (1990, p. 97).

Clearly, there are structural reasons why corporate executives cannot be teenagers, are less likely to be represented among minorities, are unlikely to be poverty-stricken, and so on. Hence, clearly, white-collar and corporate criminals cannot be an exact replication of street criminals in every way, since the population that is in a position to *commit* a white-collar or corporate crime in the first place is not representative of the population as a whole. But *among* persons with white-collar and corporate positions, Gottfredson and Hirschi say, *precisely* the same factors and variables that are correlated with street crime also correlate with white-collar crime. White-collar offenders are more likely to be younger, minority members, and less affluent than is true of white-collar persons who are *not* offenders; they are also overwhelmingly male. What explains white-collar crimes such as embezzlement and fraud are the same things that explain violent and property offenses: low impulse control and a desire for immediate gratification, caused by inadequate socialization.

Consider, for example, embezzlement. Strictly as a form of employee theft, it might be regarded as indistinguishable from a carpenter's on-the-job theft of lumber or a mechanic's theft of a wrench (Gottfredson and Hirschi, 1990, p. 189). The two are not identical, of course; the only question is whether the differences between them are significant enough to warrant a separate analytic and theoretical category. Embezzlers have been described as the "real stars" of employee thieves (McCaghy and Capron, 1994, p. 266). But more than the size of the sums is at work here. The fact is that embezzlement is a far more *sophisticated* act than the simple theft of property. It entails the falsification of written records *in addition to* the simple removal of property, which anyone is capable of doing. By its very nature, *all* crime entails the violation of a certain measure of trust (for instance, we trust others not to commit violence against us). However, the trust extended to the white-collar worker who deals with financial transactions is qualitatively greater than the trust we grant to potential violators of traditional crimes, such as robbery, rape, and murder.

What makes white-collar crimes distinctive, however, is that they entail a category of *trained specialists* being granted access to a *symbolic domain* which can be manipulated for illicit profit. What Gottfredson and Hirschi miss in equating *physical blue-collar crimes* with *symbolic white-collar crimes* is that the very factor that causes the former (that is, impulsiveness leading to immediate gratification) makes access to the latter difficult. It takes a certain measure of training and trustworthiness—which means *inhibiting* immediate self-gratification—to be *permitted* the level of trust that would make white-collar crimes possible. To put it another way, the *same* level of impulsiveness which would lead to street crime *makes white-collar crime impossible*. This is a crucial theoretical difference between ordinary blue-collar theft and white-collar occupational crime such as embezzlement. This applies *even more strongly* to more sophisticated, technical, complex, and interactional white-collar crimes such as corporate crime. While white-collar criminals may very well be more impulsive than law-abiding white-collar employees, clearly far more is at work here, since they have achieved sufficient self-control to be granted positions of trust in the first place. It is fascinating, incidentally, to consider the fact that *the very same reason* why Hirschi abandoned his social control theory (which I explained in Chapter 4) explains why his theory on white-collar crime is inadequate. In putting forth self-control theory, he is now arguing that the social control he thought was so crucial in 1969 *cannot* operate for persons lacking in self-control because such persons hardly ever *achieve* those positions in which social control can operate in the first place. The capacity of a "stake in conformity" in controlling behavior is irrelevant because persons without self-control could never achieve that stake in conformity to begin with. In other words, a lack of self-control *precedes* and *obliterates* the operation of social control. Persons who lack self-control could never sustain a satisfying marriage, purchase a house, obtain a higher education, land or keep a well-paying job, and so on, because it takes a measure of self-control to do these things in the first place. Thus, oddly enough, Hirschi's rejection of his own earlier theory helps explain his mistaken view of white-collar crime. It is difficult to imagine that any researcher could be satisfied with the same

explanation for two such radically different crimes as blue-collar theft and white-collar crime.

Even more damning to Gottfredson and Hirschi's argument that the same factor of impulsiveness and lack of self-control explain white-collar crime as well as street crime is the fact that these researchers *do not even have their hands on white-collar crime* when they make their comparisons. They base their theory of white-collar crime on the data supplied by the Uniform Crime Reports on fraud, forgery, and embezzlement. The problem is that most criminologists agree that the persons arrested for the first two of these crimes do *not* fit the field's definition of white-collar criminals—that is, persons of high socioeconomic status engaging in illegal actions in the course of their occupations. The majority of arrests for fraud and forgery are not occupationally related; they involve passing bad checks, con games, obtaining services through fraud, credit card fraud, welfare fraud, and falsifying an identification. Only 2 percent of arrests for fraud and forgery are occupationally related (Steffensmeier, 1989). Hence, Gottfredson and Hirschi's sample of supposed white-collar criminals is in no way reflective of white-collar crime in general. They seemed to have stacked their argument: They devise a theory based on the idea that white-collar criminals commit crime for the same reason that street criminals do—and then they select persons whom they see as white-collar criminals who are very *similar* to street criminals. Two problems are that these offenders are *not* white-collar criminals and that they've left *out* of the picture the *vast majority* of white-collar criminals who are very *dissimilar* to street criminals. (Gottfredson and Hirschi also make the obviously absurd claim that the *age distribution* of street criminals and white-collar criminals are similar.) Even more "far-fetched," in Gilbert Geis's estimation (1995, p. 218) is Gottfredson and Hirschi's claim that a lack of self-control could explain so sophisticated a crime as antitrust conspiracy, a corporate offense enacted largely by white, college-educated, middle-aged males. Clearly, a more specialized explanation of white-collar crime generally and embezzlement specifically is necessary.

Hence, most observers would argue that Gottfredson and Hirschi have not explained white-collar and corporate crime very adequately. However, at the same time, Simpson (1993) argues that we should not automatically throw out micro, individualistic, or social-psychological explanations for white-collar crime. There are differences among corporate actors, she argues; some *are* more willing to take risks, engage in reckless, illegal, harmful, unethical actions. There are two problems here: One, we don't have adequate data to test the proposition, and two, there is a great deal more to the white-collar crime picture than individual personality flaws. There are *structural* and *institutional* reasons why white-collar and corporate crime takes place. We don't have to look at how ethical individual executives are; instead, we have to understand the social arrangements within which they operate.

At least three structural factors should be mentioned: first, *industry-wide* factors; second, *organizational* factors; and third, the *economic* and *legal* climate that prevails at a given time.

Some industries are *criminogenic*, that is, they are organized in such a way that in order to survive, persons who work in them literally *must* commit criminal acts. Farberman (1975) argues that the used car business is just such a criminogenic industry. Automobile manufacturers set the profit margin on new cars at such a low level that dealers have to resort to a variety of practices to stay alive. Used car dealers have to pay under-the-counter bribe money to obtain the used cars that are traded in to new car dealerships. Of course, this has to be in cash; recorded transactions create a paper trail that can be discovered by authorities. Hence, the dealer needs a source of ready cash. Usually this comes from the "short sale": recording the sale at a much lower price than the car cost, charging the customer much lower taxes, and receiving the rest in untaxed cash. This saves the customer and the dealer taxes, and places a substantial quantity of cash in the dealer's hands so that he can bribe new car dealerships. Again, these illegal dealings are not caused by the unethical characters in the used car business, but because of the structure of the business itself. These practices are accepted and encouraged because business cannot be conducted in any other way.

The criminal price-fixing schemes in which large electrical equipment manufacturers were involved in the 1950s were conducted in an industry-wide climate of tolerance and acceptance. Collusion, price-fixing, and oligopolistic practices were "an established way of life" in the industry (Geis, 1973, p. 109). Quite literally, any executive who refused to go along with the scheme *could not* have transacted business in the industry. Breaking the law industry-wide was simply the way things were done.

Clinard and Yeager (1980, p. 58) found that roughly four out of 10 corporations, out of the top 500 in the country, were not charged with any wrongdoing during the period of time under investigation. In other words, some corporations are more legal and ethical in their business practices than others. The *organizational environment* of certain corporations is not conducive to wrongdoing or illegal corporate practices. In contrast, the "culture of a corporation" (Stone, 1975, p. 236) in other firms is conducive to the commission of illegal practices. Corporate executives need not demand that subordinates break the law; all they have to do is to stress results over proper procedure, stress that attaining goals is more important than the means by which they are attained, and that profits are more important than legality. When asked what led to corporate misdeeds, executives said that the ethic promulgated by superiors was decisive; when superiors "did not wish to know how results were obtained as long as they achieved the desired outcome" (Clinard and Yeager, 1980, p. 59; Brenner and Molander, 1977, p. 60)), the chance of illegal behavior was maximized. In other words, breaking the law can become normative within a specific corporate structure, and the blame must be placed at the top of the executive pyramid. As the president of one firm said, "by example and holding a tight rein a chief executive . . . can set the level of ethical or unethical practices in his organization. This influence can spread throughout the organization." Another high-ranking executive pointed out that in order to take place, price fixing and kickbacks must be "congenial to the corporation." Said a board chairman: "Some corporations . . . tolerate corruption" (Woodmansee, 1975, p. 52).

The economic and legal climate, too, must be regarded as a factor influencing illegal white-collar behavior. Certainly the relaxed restrictions on the savings and loan industry—what conservative politicians refer to as *deregulation*, or "getting the government off our backs"—literally encouraged a frenzy of fraudulent criminal behavior during the 1980s. Moreover, enforcement of the laws changes with the political climate; under conservative administrations regulatory agencies are less vigilant in enforcing statutes against pollution, worker safety, discrimination, and monopolistic practices, and so on (Simpson, 1993, pp. 245–255). As a result, less corporate behavior was deemed prosecutable and hence, by definition, there was less of it. Above, I've already pointed out the possibility that temporary economic downturns might result in more corporate crime: It is entirely possible that firms that are on the edge of being driven out of business may resort to unethical and illegal practices to survive. The worse the economy is, the greater the likelihood that such practices will be widespread. (For the two sides of this issue, see Braithwaite, 1985, and Friedrichs, 1996, p. 223.)

Clearly, a single explanation for white-collar and corporate crime is inadequate. The more entangled the actor is in an organizational structure, the greater the likelihood that structural factors come into play. It is entirely possible that we can account for embezzlement largely with an individualistic explanation; perhaps Gottfredson and Hirschi's self-control theory is relevant here. But corporate actions are so highly dependent on the structures within which actors are implicated that it is inconceivable that individualistic factors give us much explanatory purchase. Unfortunately, a "one size fits all" theory will not take us very far in this most decidedly structural—and sociological—realm. To make much sense of corporate crime, we need an eclectic approach, and that entails looking at several levels of explanation, relying on a number of factors, and making use of multiple theories.

SUMMARY AND CONCLUSIONS

The study of corporate and other white-collar crime was born in *muckraking*, that is, exposing the ills of a corrupt and harmful system, and *reformism*, or the desire to improve existing conditions. The earliest works in this genre include Lincoln Steffens, *The Shame of the Cities* (1904), Ida Tarbell, *The History of the Standard Oil Co.* (1904), and Upton Sinclair, *The Jungle* (1906). Muckraking and reformism are noble and admirable impulses, and should be encouraged, for there is much that should and could be improved in any society, our own included. In principle, they need not contradict a relentless pursuit of the facts of the case. In fact, at its best, muckraking is a just and noble enterprise.

In practice, however, muckrakers and reformers often fail to do their job; it is one thing to point out flaws in a system, it is quite another to understand what *sustains* an unfair, unjust system. If things are as bad as the muckraker says, what keeps it going—and what's going to make it next to impossible to reform the system? Muckrakers rarely explain. The muckrakers of a century ago were successful in their mission not merely because their cause was just, but because conditions were right for reform. And today? If the analyses of our contemporary muckrakers concerning the corporate and government world are correct, and there are indeed deep-seated structural and economic reasons that sustain white-collar crime and deviance, *what will the mechanism for change be?* By what process is reform going to take place? What will *accomplish* the transformation? Are the college students and instructors who read their books—or at least, the ones who are persuaded by their arguments—going to hold a meeting with the most powerful politicians and chief executives of the largest corporations in the country (one at a time or all at once?) and explain the wisdom of reform? Are they going to explain that the necessary reforms will take immense profits out of the pockets of big business (as well as the politicians who support it) and that these executives will be fired if they agree to any of the reformers' sweeping suggestions, and that the politicians who support them will indeed be voted out of office, but it's really all for the best? Are these reformers seriously suggesting that such a scenario is possible? Are the very real material conditions that produced the conditions they describe, analyze, and critique going to vanish in a puff of smoke once they are elaborated to an academic audience of a few hundred instructors and a few thousand undergraduates? With most muckrakers, there is a contradiction between the tough-minded realism of their descriptions, analyses, and criticism, and the silly, simple-minded idealism of their solutions. For instance, Simon (1996, p. 329) suggests that American multinational corporations be taxed so heavily that they will be forced to cease investing abroad. American multinational corporations earn half their profits abroad; how is such a suggestion going to be carried out? And with what economic impact, both on the United States and the countries in which such corporations invest? And would such a proposal be accompanied by a parallel one which attempted to discourage the sale of overseas products in the United States? Such proposals are so naive and unrealistic—and biased—that they discredit the arguments on which they are based and, even more generally, taint the entire study of corporate crime.

Contrary to the bias displayed in the work of some naive reformers and muckrakers, however, I maintain that it *is* possible to study white-collar crime and deviance—wrongdoing in high or at least moderately high, places—in a rigorous, systematic, and empirical fashion. White-collar crime shares a characteristic of all instrumental actions: It is designed to achieve a specific, concrete goal. Under certain circumstances, the attainment of the goal becomes more important than the means by which that goal is attained. In other words, white-collar crime involves cutting corners, bending the rules, skirting the restrictions, violating the rules— all for the purpose of getting something the actor wants. In most cases, *deviant* means are more effective in achieving those goals than methods that follow accepted practice. In such cases, many actors regard following the more restrictive and less effective rules as *irrational*.

The concept "white-collar crime" was launched by sociologist and criminologist Edwin Sutherland in 1939, in a presidential address before the American Sociological Society. Sutherland argued that white-collar crime was *real* crime; neglected by criminologists, he proposed that it become a target for serious study. He insisted that the then-current explanations of crime based on poverty and pathology were inadequate, since they did not explain the behavior of white-collar criminals. Sutherland's talk put white-collar crime on the map. The introduction of white-collar crime was one of those extremely rare contributions that has had a major impact on the field. Thousands of studies on the subject have been conducted, and a virtual library of articles and books has accumulated. Today, no coverage of criminal behavior is complete without a consideration of white-collar crime.

Unfortunately, Sutherland was insufficiently clear about just what he meant by white-collar crime. At times, he included rather lowly and decidedly blue-collar workers in his examples, and often he included actions that were not crimes by even the most generous definition. Later investigators have done no better in clarifying the scope of the concept. Some insist that it include only corporate crimes—that is, those undertaken *by* and *on behalf of* a corporation. Others insist that it include all nonviolent property crimes. Still others argue that it include all crimes committed in the course of an occupation, regardless of its rank, status, or prestige, including simple theft from the job. Certain observers wish to include actions they and others

with similar views consider wrong or unethical. The lack of clarity becomes evident when we consider the fact that although all criminology textbooks contain a chapter on white-collar crime, very few of them cover the same terrain.

To me, the definition that makes the most sense is that white-collar crime is an illegal action that is committed by the occupant of high occupational status in the course of his or her professional activity. This includes embezzlement by bank clerks (committed by an employee against the corporation), white-collar crimes committed by professionals, corporate crime, and a wide range of government crimes. It includes only actions that have a certain likelihood of punitive sanctioning— that is, arrest and criminal prosecution, or at least a punitive fine in a civil or administrative court. It excludes actions that a moralistic standard considers wrong but that never result in official action.

White-collar crime is both similar to and different from ordinary street crime. It tends to be made up of complex, sophisticated, relatively technical actions. Observers witnessing a white-collar crime in action are unlikely to recognize it as such, whereas this is very rarely true of ordinary street crimes. Even victims may be unaware of their victimization. Second, white-collar crime tends to be intermingled with legitimate occupational behavior; with most street crime, in contrast, the criminal act is illegal in its totality. Third, in white-collar crime, victimization tends to be diffuse; harm is spread out thinly over a large number of victims. Fourth, the monetary sums that white-collar crime entails tend to be substantial—at the top of the pyramid, many individual instances involve vastly greater sums than all street crimes added together in a given year. Fifth, criminal prosecution tends to be much more selective and much less vigorous than is true of street crime, and the very rare criminal sentences that are handed down tend to be light. Sixth, most Americans have a hard time thinking of white-collar crime as "real" crime; it does not fit our stereotype of what a crime is. Even when the public regards certain white-collar crimes as serious, this rarely translates into stiff prison sentences by juries. Seventh, the media rarely gives white-collar crime the same attention that dramatic, sensationalistic street crimes receive; the fact is that most of us find detailed reports of corporate doings uninteresting— and to most of us, news is largely entertainment. And last, white-collar offenders, even after being convicted, rarely think of themselves as "real" criminals or deviants. Most do not think of their offenses as crimes.

I have located five different types of white-collar crimes. First, individual embezzlement—crimes *against* a corporation *by* an employee. Second, collective embezzlement—crimes *by* a corporation *against* a corporation, the looting of a firm by the executives of that firm. Third, professional white-collar crime—mostly fraud by physicians, lawyers, and other professionals against their clients. Fourth, corporate crime—acts by a corporation against the public, customers, employees, competitors, or the government. And fifth, government crime—illegal actions by representatives of the government against citizens or against other regimes.

Why white-collar crime? It is clear that we cannot rely on a single explanation. Individualistic explanations ignore structural factors. While personality variables cannot be dismissed as a possible cause of white-collar misdeeds, they are more likely to be relevant for individualistic crimes, such as embezzlement. In the opinion of most criminologists, they are useless for corporate misdeeds. Here, we need to look at industry-wide factors, organizational factors, and legal, political, and economic factors. Unifactoral explanations must inevitably fail here; we need a broad, eclectic approach.

ACCOUNT: WHITE-COLLAR CRIME

Below, we have the transcript of an interview I conducted with a lawyer whose license had been suspended for a white-collar crime. The offense of which he was originally accused was "structuring," and the charge on which he was eventually convicted was "conspiracy to defraud the Internal Revenue Service." The nature of these charges becomes clear in his explanations. The lawyer is designated as "A" and I am, of course, the interviewer ("Q").

Q: Rather than have me ask specific questions, why don't you just tell me what happened.
A: OK. The ultimate charge was "conspiracy to defraud the Internal Revenue Service." My secretary has been working in this office even before I started—I was the sole practitioner. One secretary, one attorney. I trusted her completely, gave her the right to sign checks and everything else. She was, I thought, top-notch and beyond question trustworthy. And I can't really blame *her*. I mean, obviously, I bear all of the blame for this. From time to time, I would have some

clients who needed to borrow money, usually for a real estate transaction. And I had some other clients who from time to time would lend money. And I would prepare a mortgage and a note and that would enable these people to buy a house or a lot or whatever. Well, I had a situation where a client would borrow money. He was buying property in another state and ultimately was going to sell his house here. But he hadn't sold it yet, and he needed to complete the transaction there. My secretary came to me—of course, she knew all of this—and she said that her cousin and her cousin's husband would lend the money. Later, she arrived in the office with $60,000. And this is where my stupidity took over. I was under the impression that if a person deposits more than $10,000 in cash into a bank account, he had to notify the Internal Revenue Service.
Q: That was my impression, too.
A: A lot of people have that impression. That's as far as I knew. Number one, that's wrong, and number two, there's a lot more to it. I now know the actual facts are, if you deposit more than $10,000 in a bank account, the bank has a form, and the *bank* fills out this form. It's called a "currency transaction report." I thought I could avoid all of this aggravation by depositing this in seven transactions, six of $9,500, and then the balance in the seventh. And that's exactly what I did. And that was fine. It was deposited over however many days, I went to the bank every single day, five days a week, the money was fully deposited, nobody did anything. And a week—ten days later, the check was written so that my client could buy the property. He signed the mortgage on his house here, and everything was fine. A couple months later, again, my secretary said that her brother-in-law now wanted to borrow some money. And again, the same thing, that'll be fine, we'll put a mortgage on the property. This was $50,000. And again, she shows up with it in cash. And it's in a small suitcase. Obviously, alarms should have gone off and didn't. Again, same thing. Deposited in the exact same way. The deal closed, no problems. Further period of time passed. I would say another two to three months. And it now developed that the cousin and her husband wanted to buy a piece of property for themselves, now, in Arizona. And wanted me to represent them. I *never talked* to these people. At the time, I don't know that I had ever *met* them. But I explained to my secretary that I am not admitted to practice law in Arizona. I would be very happy to give them whatever expertise I had in real estate. I think I know the procedure there, but I can't be an Arizona attorney. She relayed that message to them, they supposedly came back and said, we want you to give us whatever advice you can, we feel much more comfortable with you than picking a stranger in Arizona. The cousin's husband was an interstate trucker. Supposedly transporting produce

from California to the East Coast. He lived in New York City, he had a number of trucks going back and forth. He had a Spanish surname, and he was from Colombia.

Q: Fascinating.

A: I said, OK, we will do this. Give me the name of the title company and some various information and I will start to handle it. A few days later, his brother, I believe, arrived at the office with a *large* suitcase. And the purchase of this property was $191,000. And supposedly, there was $191,000 in this suitcase. I said, wow, OK. OK, now again, all communication was made through the secretary and the cousin. At this point, I had not had any direct contact with—their names were Helen and Richard. Never had any contact with them. And I made it perfectly clear that, number one, I was not going to count this money, and that I am not responsible for it. If somebody breaks into my office at night and steals the whole thing, I do not want to be responsible for it. OK. I started to deposit this money.

Q: In bundles of $9,500?

A: Yes. I was informed that Richard was going to put it in a safe in the office. So that's fine. And he almost immediately did so. The money was then put into the safe. Deposited *daily*, you know, with all the transactions in the bank. This one also went fine. You can do the math as to how many days it takes. It took a long time. Went fine. When the full amount had been deposited, I got in touch with the title company in Arizona. Arrangements were made to wire the money to the title company who was acting as the escrow agent. The transaction went fine. And the title closed and there were no problems. A further period of months passed. And there were a couple of small transactions. When I say small, maybe $20-25,000, which, again, the same procedure was used. And again, no problems with the bank, no problems with the Internal Revenue Service.

Q: You were dealing with only one bank?

A: Only one bank. Yeah. And went usually five days a week. I guess it was about a year after the first transaction, I was informed by my secretary that they now intended to buy a house in California. And the purchase price of this house was $235,000.

Q: Who's they? Her cousin?

A: Richard and Helen. Yeah. The same people who bought the house in Arizona. And I frankly was not paying too much attention to this thing. I had never kept a running balance of all of these transactions. I said, fine, we'll do exactly the same thing.

Q: Were you getting fees on these transactions?

A: I charged them a $350 fee for preparing the note and mortgage on the Arizona house, which is standard, if anything, it's a very reasonable fee. I charged a $2,500 fee for handling the real estate aspect of the Arizona property, but I never collected it. With the

California property, I again started these deposits. Started to deposit the money. I had $205,000 deposited in the bank account for this transaction. Out of a total of $235,000. Again, I never counted it, but that was supposedly what he had given me. Then, at this point, my wife and I went on vacation. And while I was on vacation, the telephone rings, it's my secretary, calling to say that the Internal Revenue Service had been to the office and had left her with a piece of paper saying that they were seizing the account. And I was literally laughing. The secretary—she talked to my wife, not me—but she was literally crying about how upset she was over this. And when I heard about it, to show how naive I was, I was laughing. I'm saying, look, this is not a problem for me. You'd better tell Richard that *he* may have a problem. But as soon as I get home, I will notify the Internal Revenue Service that none of this is my money. And that if they have any questions about it, they should contact Richard. I got home and I saw the piece of paper that they left concerning this and realized that this was no longer a trivial matter, that this was serious. And at that point, I obtained an attorney. At first, the seizure was strictly a *civil* matter. My attorney contacted the U.S. attorney who was in charge of this case. And explained to her that we were more than willing to cooperate in any respect, but in order to resolve the civil aspects of the case, we also need to resolve the *criminal* action that they may be contemplating. She said, I'm only handling the civil aspects, I can't tell you what's going on in the criminal action. Months passed, nothing was done. They moved the case to a more nearby federal court. The case was assigned to a federal prosecutor who has a terrible reputation. He's very hard-nosed, but we have to deal with him. He made arrangements to meet with me, my lawyer, a U.S. attorney, the IRS investigator, and the chief U.S. attorney in that court, and we all sat down. And I told my story. The, quote, hard-nosed U.S. attorney apparently didn't believe it. Months and months passed. We went in one day, and my attorney was informed that the U.S. attorney has refused to make any deals. That he will allow me to plead guilty to "structuring." And that under the federal sentencing guidelines, I will be sentenced to 13 months in prison.

Q: What exactly is "structuring"?

A: OK, I subsequently learned that in addition to the *bank* filling out this form and not the customer, that it is also illegal for anyone to *structure* the deposits so that the amounts appear to be less that $10,000 when the overall amount deposited is more than $10,000.

Q: I didn't know that.

A: I'm glad you said that because not only I didn't know that, but I've talked to a number of attorneys and they didn't know either. The one thing that was very upsetting to me was that the *bank* didn't know this. I had been dealing with this bank for many, many years. I had a very close relationship with the branch vice-president, the tellers, they have referred me clients over the years. And in the middle of the California transaction, the head teller came to me and said, look, this is silly, why don't you go ahead and deposit the whole thing at one time? And I said, well, I don't want to get involved with the Internal Revenue Service. I've got enough problems without dealing with them. And she gave me the *form*. That's when I learned that it's a form that the bank is supposed to fill out. I read through the instructions on it, and it *clearly* says this form is filled out when a cash deposit is more than $10,000. And made no mention of the fact that there is this crime of "structuring." So I said, look, you know, this form says that we don't have to fill this out. And she didn't say anything else. It was *almost a joke*, when I walked into the bank. One of the tellers would see me come in, and would literally duck behind the counter, saying, oh my God, here he comes again, I don't want to be responsible for counting this money.

Q: How did the IRS get wind of this?

A: Well, we're getting to that. [Laughs.] Shortly after the head teller gave me the form, within, say, a week, I was making another deposit, and she said the branch vice-president would like to see me. So I went in to talk to her. And, you know, we were on a first-name basis. And she explained that the bank had recently gotten itself into some very serious trouble with the Internal Revenue Service over this type of thing. I said, OK, what would you like me to do? And she said, we're going to fill out these forms. I said, OK, *you* know that of course it's not my money. And I had told this to the various tellers. So I said, you have all the information in your records to fill out this form, do what you have to do, you know it's not my money. Within days of that conversation, the account was seized. And supposedly, the bank had some person in their main office whose job it was to look for cash deposits. And if it looks suspicious, they notify the Internal Revenue Service. And that's how I got trapped.

Fortunately, the U.S. attorney who said that he wasn't going to make any deals with me, he was taken off the case. And it was assigned to another U.S. attorney, a woman who had just come in from California, who turned out to be very nice, very understanding. I met with her and we went over again all of these facts, and she believed me. Subsequently, she offered a plea to one count of "conspiracy to defraud the Internal Revenue." Which my attorney thought would go better with the bar association than structuring. Because in the back of our minds, we were worried about what the bar association was ultimately going to do. And she offered a letter that shows the defendant has cooperated in their investigation and has ren-

dered valuable assistance to them. Which frees the judge from the sentencing guidelines, so that he can now sentence somebody to a much lesser sentence. That is the thing my attorney was desperately trying to get all along, otherwise, the guidelines say that the judge had no choice, he would have to sentence me to a prison term of 13 months.

Q: That was the 13 months you talked about earlier?

A: Yeah. Again, it dragged out and dragged out. We signed a plea agreement. Meanwhile, they arrested Richard, Helen, Richard's brother, and my secretary. And there was a travel agent who I didn't know at all at the time, who apparently had been doing some things with cash. They arrested a number of people. Now, the first transaction, I think it was May 1990. When we were on vacation when I got the call, I think it was August of 1991. I entered my plea, it must have been 1993, that I pleaded guilty. And the sentencing was then put off, put off, put off. I was ultimately sentenced in January or February 1994. I had to do 300 hours of community service, pay a $40,000 fine, and I was subject to three month's house detention. A three-year probation was put off until I completed the other things. Within two months, the bar had suspended me, they had issued their interim suspension. I was confined to the house for three months, which was no punishment for me, but it punishes the family. I was able to leave the house, I believe they gave me from seven o'clock in the morning until seven o'clock at night. Clearly, if I wanted to flee the jurisdiction, I could have been halfway around the world by the time they would have known about it. It did nothing but inconvenience the family, it did nothing to me, the criminal. As soon as possible, I completed my 300 hours of the community service. And we went back into court. The three-year probation was immediately lifted. By that time, probably 11 months had passed since the sentencing. Everybody agreed that we'll change it to a one-year probation, which will be up in a matter of weeks. And that ended all of my exposure to the criminal justice system. I had completed everything that was required of me by then. But of course, I was at that point interimly suspended from the practice of law. I was interimly suspended in March. The hearing wasn't actually conducted until April of the following year, 1994. The return date of the motion was September 1995. And the court did not render their decision until February 1996. And their decision was to suspend me from the practice of law for two years. For whatever reason, the decision was, he is suspended effective immediately. In other words, I thought I had *already* served the suspended period—and I *had* been suspended since just after the sentencing—and then my license was suspended for an *additional* two years. My attorney thought they had made a mistake. He argued that surely you can't want to suspend this individual for a total of, really, four years. The decision came back, oh, maybe a month ago, no, motion denied. So, in February 1998, I could apply for reinstatement. And that is my tale of woe.

Q: That's an interesting story. So, now what are you doing at this time?

A: I've done some income tax work. I've done some work for a builder who's selling big pieces of property. And I represent him at closings, but I can't prepare deeds or anything like that. And basically, we are living off investments. You know, we were very fortunate. We have the wherewithall to support the family. Without that, I don't know what I could have done. The suspension effectively ended any of the legal work that I was doing. The practice of law is such that, the work you do, usually you don't get paid for for some period of time. So that there was some overlap of income coming in which carried us for quite a while. And, as I said, then we've been living on investments.

Q: Do you know what happened to Richard and Helen?

A: They were both ultimately sentenced to prison time.

Apparently, absolutely nothing happened to my secretary. She was pregnant at the time of her arrest. And I believe that because of her circumstances, they decided, well, we'll leave her alone. For whatever it's worth, she insisted all along that this was all legitimate. That they make this money on the trucking, that everything was aboveboard. It's easy to blame someone else, but clearly I was the one who did what I did.

Q: Do you know if any of that was drug money?

A: I know it now, yeah. Yeah. Certainly once the arrests were made, I was 100 percent convinced now that that was drug money. I have a copy of their sentencing minutes. Their attorney tried to blame me completely. He made his little speech to the judge, but obviously it didn't work. Yeah, they're in prison.

Q: Do you know what kind of time they got?

A: I think Richard got eight years. I think his brother got three years. And his wife got a shorter term, but it was not something that I would want to spend.

Q: Right. Well, this is really fascinating. Thank you.

chapter 13

MENTAL ILLNESS

"The schizophrenic is a perfect machine of self-destruction." Elizabeth Swados (1991)

Traci is 19. She batters her body black and blue and rubs the skin off her arms and legs, leaving them covered with scars. As a child, she inserted a key into an electrical socket, burning her hand. She has "horrible wounds up and down her body," her mother says. She has run away many times; each time she returns, she says she has been raped. At the age of 17, while being admitted to a mental hospital, she hugged her teddy bear and chanted, "Mommy, Mommy," over and over again. After she was released, Traci went home and took 100 Tylenol tablets; walking into the next room, she handed her mother the glass of water she used to wash down the pills. She was rushed to the hospital and her stomach was pumped. "I like hurting myself," she explains. "I don't know why I do it. But I don't feel the pain" (Talan, 1995, p. B4).

Michael breezed through Yale, receiving a bachelor's degree in three years. But in his twenties, he became, in his own words, a "flaming schizophrenic." After working at his first job, he became convinced that his phone lines were tapped. He quit the job, left abruptly, and settled into his home town. He became convinced that the musicians with whom he played were part of a cult. Soon after, he imagined that neighbors were ringing bells outside his bedroom window on a deathwatch until dawn. Institutionalized, he became convinced that "at any moment," the psychiatrists in the hospital "would surgically cut me to death without any anesthesia." Administered antipsychotic drugs and placed in a halfway house, Michael's hallucinations and paranoia "became manageable." He was offered a job as a cashier at Macy's; instead, he decided to attend Yale Law School, which had accepted him before his illness. Acquiring a reputation for being something of a genius among a number of faculty and students, he acted as editor of *The Yale Law Review* in his senior year. Discussing his condition with a reporter, he says, "I feel that I'm pawing through walls of cotton and gauze when I talk to you now. . . . I'm using 60 or 70 percent of my effort just to maintain the proper reality contact with the world" (Foderaro, 1995, p. B4). Michael wants to work as a law professor, but is afraid his mental condition will discourage schools from hiring him.

Valerie Fabrikant, an engineering Ph.D., left Russia, settled in Canada, and began working as a research assistant for the chair of the department of mechanical engineering at Concordia, a small university in Montreal. He convinced the professor that he be allowed to work on his own research rather than the professor's. Fabrikant was extremely prolific, managing to publish dozens of articles in a few short years. Nearly all of them listed the professor and the dean of the faculty of engineering as coauthors, even though they did little or no work on them. Although supported by "soft" or research funds, Fabrikant received several promotions. The professor who hired him stepped down from his position as chair of the department under a cloud of allegations of bookkeeping irregularities. A year later, Fabrikant was informed that his contract would be renewed for only one year, after which time, he would be terminated. He was "thunderstruck. . . . He was forty-eight years old, had a young wife who couldn't work because of ill health, two small children, and no job prospects" (Wolfe, 1995, p. 57). He began secretly taping conversations with colleagues and administrators, threatening to take the matter of his chair's and his dean's noncollaborations to court. In response, the dean offered Fabrikant a two-year contract. Clearly the threat worked. "It was time to go after bigger game—real job security. Tenure." (p. 57).

Fabrikant asked an administrator to permit him to transfer to another department. He said that "the only way to get what you want . . . is to buy a gun and shoot a lot of people" (p. 57). She became frightened and discussed the matter with the university "conflict-resolution specialist," whom Fabrikant led to believe he already had a gun and that he planned to shoot his two coauthors; he threatened to take an administrator hostage as well. For a time, the administration kept him under surveillance. A psychiatrist judged Fabrikant to be suffering from a personality disorder. Three tenure-track positions opened up at Concordia; Fabrikant asked the chair for one of them. He also sent out 700 applications for positions elsewhere. If he didn't get one of these jobs, he announced, he might have to settle things "the American way," gesturing as if firing a gun. In spite of these threats, the department recommended Fabrikant for one of the tenure-track jobs. An administrator tried to convince the department to reverse the recommendation, but the faculty stuck by its decision. He was even awarded the department's largest merit increase. He responded by making a fresh demand: to use a grant to be excused from teaching. The new chair was outraged and rejected the proposal. Fabrikant reacted with his own self-righteous anger.

Department meetings were held to discuss Fabrikant's case. He was caught lurking outside a meeting room while the department discussed his case; he was escorted from the building. A department personnel committee recommended that Fabrikant not be renewed because of his threats, harassment, blackmail, and allegations. No specifics were given; Fabrikant challenged the committee to come up with details. The department backed down and granted Fabrikant a one-year renewal. He launched an E-mail campaign, portraying himself as a martyr and the administration and members of his department as villains. Fabrikant took a course in the use of handguns, obtained a gun permit, and purchased a pistol. He was told to stop making allegations against members of Concordia's university community. Fabrikant began contacting the media with his allegations. He launched a lawsuit against his coauthors, once again repeating the claim that they had made no contributions to the coauthored papers. When course assignments were made, he objected to the courses he had to teach. He walked into the chair's office demanding that the secretary sign a form approving his legal right to carry a handgun. A meeting of administrators was held; they decided to request Fabrikant's immediate suspension. The university's rector rejected the request. Instead, Fabrikant was offered severance pay of two years' salary; he demanded 10. The university counteroffered with three; he demanded 13. At that point, the negotiations were broken off.

Shortly thereafter, Fabrikant walked onto the ninth floor of the building where the engineering faculty was located. He entered his office, where the president of the Concordia faculty association handed him a letter spelling out the conditions under which he could use the association's office. Fabrikant shot him three times; the man slumped to the floor and bled to death, still clutching the letter. A colleague called out from a nearby office. Fabrikant crossed the hall and shot and killed him. He then shot the chair's secretary, who was fleeing; she was wounded in the thigh. The chair of the department of electrical engineering was discussing a matter with one of Fabrikant's colleagues. He shot the first man, who died several days later; in a scuffle, his colleague managed to get the gun away, then he turned to tend to his mortally wounded friend. But Fabrikant had several more guns in his

briefcase; locating one, he shot and killed another colleague. He then took a colleague and a security guard hostage and demanded to talk to a television reporter, which he did for an hour. When he put the gun he was holding down to adjust the phone, the professor kicked it away, and the security guard overpowered him. None of the faculty members he killed had anything to do with Fabrikant's problems in his department.

In spite of the fact that everyone agreed that Fabrikant suffered from a personality disorder, he was judged competent to stand trial for murder. He was convicted and sentenced to life imprisonment, with no possibility of parole for 25 years. Today, Fabrikant sits in prison, believing himself to be a martyr; he likens himself to a battered wife who kills her husband to protect her own life. Accusing "the authorities of persecuting him, and working on his research," he is "assisted by a former graduate student who is convinced that Fabrikant is a misunderstood genius and who feels honored to serve him in any way he can" (Wolfe, 1995, p. 64).

We all know someone who seems odd, bizarre, who acts in a totally inappropriate fashion. A stroll down many streets in the nation's larger cities will reveal men and women who look disheveled and who scream or mutter incomprehensible phrases to no one in particular. Some people are so fearful of lurking, unmentionable forces that they are literally incapable of walking out of their front door. Others are unable to hold a conversation anyone else would regard as intelligible. Still others are so depressed that they lie curled up in a fetal position for hours or days—or even weeks, or more—on end. Some make it a point to be abusive and offensive to practically everyone they meet, insulting them, physically striking them, engaging in actions that seem almost designed to shock, hurt, or outrage others at every opportunity. Persons we may have read about hear voices from another planet commanding them to kill, to become dictator of the world, or deliver an urgent message to the residents of North America. Some people are convinced that their dentist has implanted an electronic receiver in a filling in their teeth that is sending bizarre messages into their brains. Some people wear a perpetual, peculiar smile, and seem to exist in "their own little world."

In everyday language, we have terms for such persons. "He's whacko," we say. "She's out of her mind," "He's a nut," "She's completely cracked," "He's a weirdo," "She's a sicko," or "He's off his rocker," we declare, pointing to the people who display what we regard as manifestations of a mind that's "not right." More formally, the condition such people suffer from is referred to as *mental illness* or, more broadly, *mental disorder*.

What is mental illness? In what way can a mind be said to be "ill"? What is a mental "disorder"? How can a mind be said to be "disordered"? Is mental illness or disorder an instance of deviance? If so, in what specific ways?

WHAT IS MENTAL DISORDER?

Defining mental disorder is not as easy or as straightforward a task as might appear at first glance. As we've seen, even defining deviant behaviors that manifest themselves in *specific* actions, such as murder, homosexuality, drug use, and prostitution, proves to be an extremely thorny matter. Mental disorder presents a much more formidable definitional problem because, first of all it is not a type of behavior as such; instead, it is seen as a mental condition that presumably manifests itself in certain behaviors, thought patterns, and verbal utterances. Second, even the behavior supposedly associated with it cannot be pinned down to any one type of actions with much precision. (Of course, certain specific *categories* of mental disorder have more clear-cut symptoms than others, but mental disorder *generally* does not.) Rather, mental disorder is a condition that exhibits itself in a *wide range* of behaviors. Consequently, no general definition of the phenomenon can be completely satisfactory.

Let's begin with a fairly obvious distinction: Mental *disorder* encompasses a wide range of conditions or supposed conditions, while mental *illness* is a much more specific category; although itself a fairly broad category, mental illness is clearly a *subcategory*, or one specific *type*, of mental disorder. All mental illnesses are disorders, but not all mental disorders are illnesses. Clearly, clinical depression is both a disorder and an illness. However, mental retardation, or the possession of a measurably low intelligence, is *not* a form of mental illness, at least as the term is most commonly understood—but it *is* clearly a disorder or *malfunction* of the mind. The same is true of autism, Tourette's Syndrome, dyslexia, stuttering, hyperkenesis, and a number of other disorders that are not mental illnesses as such. Throughout, I'll be

using these two terms, "disorder" and "illness," more or less interchangeably, but their conceptual distinction should be clear. When I refer to mental disorder, I'll be referring mainly to mental illness, such as schizophrenia and clinical depression. On the other hand, if I refer to mental illness, I do not necessarily mean to include any of the non-illness disorders such as retardation or dyslexia. In this chapter, I will not discuss the various "non-illness" disorders in any detail. Most discussions mean mental *illness* when they use the term mental *disorder*.

The American Psychiatric Association issues a standard reference work entitled the *Diagnostic and Statistical Manual of Mental Disorders*; its first edition (referred to as DSM-I) appeared in 1952, it was thoroughly revised in 1968 (DSM-II) and 1980 (DSM-III), partially revised in 1987 (DSM-III-R), and thoroughly revised again in 1994 (DSM-IV). We might expect DSM-IV to be a good place to find a coherent framework for understanding mental disorder. In this expectation we would be sorely disappointed. DSM-IV does not so much *define* mental disorder as *enumerate* a range of mental disorder*s*. In fact, this "manual" of mental disorders is descriptive, atheoretical, inductive, and lacking in any explanatory framework. It provides a long list of symptoms the clinician is likely to encounter in therapeutic practice, and leaves matters at that; DSM-IV (as with two of its predecessors) offers what one observer referred to as a "Chinese menu" (Thio, 1995, p. 256). In fact, so useless is the *Diagnostic and Statistical Manual of Mental Disorders* as a means of understanding mental disorder generally that two critics write that it "applies no coherent standard of what constitutes a mental disorder"; "few clinicians actually use it as a basis for psychotherapy." Instead, they say, its popularity is guaranteed "because insurance companies use it to determine reimbursement for psychiatric services" (Kirk and Kutchins, 1994). It is the stranglehold that the American Psychiatric Association has over the field of mental health, not the utility of its diagnostic and statistical manual, that determines DSM-IV's widespread use, these critics argue. Not all observers agree, of course; there exists a lively controversy over the utility of DSM-IV.

With all its shortcomings, DSM-IV does offer a sketchy definition of mental disorder. Each of the disorders enumerated in the manual "is conceptualized as a clinically significant behavioral or psychological syndrome or pattern that occurs in an individual and that is associated with present distress (e.g., a painful symptom) or disability (i.e., impairment in one or more important areas of functioning) or with a significantly increased risk of suffering, death, pain, disability, or an important loss of freedom" (APA, 1994, p. xxi). The manual stresses that such suffering is not the manifestation of a mental disorder if it is in response to a temporary event, such as the loss of a loved one. Moreover, the manual stresses, mere *deviant behavior*—for example, political, religious, or sexual activities or beliefs that run counter to the norms—is *not* to be included as a mental disorder *unless* such behavior is a "symptom of a dysfunction in the individual" (p. xxii). *By itself*, the manual stresses, political radicalism, religious heterodoxy—or atheism—or homosexuality does *not* indicate a mental disorder. (Although such beliefs and practices do not *preclude* that the individual is suffering from a disorder either.) In addition, the manual states, different cultures, subcultures, and ethnic groups have somewhat different customs. Hence, the clinician must make sure to avoid making judgments of psychopathology that ignore the "nuances of an individual's cultural frame of reference" (p. xxiv). For instance, in some societies, bereavement for the death of a loved one may include seeing visions of the deceased. If the patient has grown up in such a society, this experience may be well within the boundaries of what is considered normal.

There are 300 disorders listed in DSM-IV, far too numerous to enumerate, let alone describe in any detail here. (The number has been expanded from the 100 that were listed in its original edition.) There are those that are "usually first diagnosed in infancy, childhood, or adolescence," such as mental retardation, learning disorders, autism, attention deficit disorders, and Tourette's Syndrome. There are "delirium, dementia, and amnesiac and other cognitive disorders," including Alzheimer's and Parkinson's syndromes. The list includes all the "substance-related disorders," that is, abuse of and intoxication and dependence on a variety of psychoactive substances (including caffeine and nicotine). Schizophrenia "and other psychotic disorders" are listed, as are mood disorders, both simple depression and bipolar disorders (manic-depression). A variety of other syndromes follow: anxiety disorders (panic disorder, agoraphobia, obsessive-compulsion, etc.); somatophorm

disorders (such as hypocondriasis); sexual and gender identity disorders, including sexual dysfunctions (a lack of sexual desire, male impotence, an inability to achieve orgasm), "paraphilias" (exhibitionism, fetishism, masochism, sadism, voyeurism); eating disorders, sleeping disorders, impulse-control disorders, and personality disorders. (See the boxed insert on p. 392, which summarizes some of the most common disorders.) This represents a remarkably diverse and miscellaneous grab-bag of mental disorders. DSM-IV represents little more than a listing of syndromes, as I said, and a description of a wide range of disorders the clinician is likely to encounter. But it has no internal logic, and it is atheoretical. That is, it *sidesteps* the issue of etiology or causality—that is, what it is that generates disorders in general or these disorders in particular.

Most of us recognize that there are *degrees* of mental disorder. This dimension is commonsensically captured in the distinction between *neurosis* and *psychosis*. (But keep in mind the fact that the distinction may *also* be qualitative, or one of kind, *as well as* one of degree.) Most people think of the neurosis as less serious than the psychosis. We all recognize that there are neurotics in our midst; we ourselves may even be one of them. Many of us engage in behavior that is regarded as eccentric, excessive, annoying, compulsive, and unacceptable. Neuroses often entail anxiety that is from a "rational" point of view excessive, even needless. (This is why tranquilizers such as Valium are effective against many disorders, because they depress anxiety.) Other neurotic disorders entail a compulsion—a ritualistic action which is repeated without apparent aim, for instance, washing nonexistent germs from one's hands over and over again for hours on end. To the man and woman on the street, neurotics engage in a wide range of unusual and annoying behaviors. Someone who has to take six showers a day, is excessively tight with money, is overly compulsive, neat, and tidy, has an uncontrollable fear of spiders, can't go outside without swallowing a Valium, feels the need to insult or demean others, or vomits or breaks out in a rash upon taking multiple-choice exams, would probably be referred to as a neurotic by most of us. Nonetheless, in most ways, neurotics maintain contact with reality; while psychotics have lost contact with reality, neurotics recognize reality but can't accept certain aspects of it. Consequently, neurotics can function in most areas of life—get an education, hold down a job, carry on meaningful relationships. In contrast, psychotics can very rarely function in any area of life, at least not without medication. Hence, popularly, we tend to reserve the concept of the psychosis for those cases that are considerably more serious, and vastly less common than the neurosis. Again, without medication, the psychotic's condition, unlike the neurotic's, is almost always a barrier to academic and occupational achievement and social relationships, including marriage and family. In addition, although the outbreak of a psychosis is frequently grounds for institutionalization in a mental hospital, that of a neurosis almost never is. DSM-IV does not mention psychosis or the psychotic, and the term "neurosis" does not appear in its index. Still, the neurosis-psychosis distinction captures most laypeople's thinking about the dimensional quality of mental disorders. Moreover, *each* of the disorders listed must be regarded as a matter of degree.

Clearly then, there are no assumptions among experts that mental disorders can be sharply and cleanly separated from the condition of mental health. Mental disorder is not a "completely discrete entity with absolute boundaries dividing it from other mental disorders or from no mental disorder" (APA, 1994, p. xxii). In reality, most experts argue, extreme or "textbook" cases can be detected by encountering the most florid or stereotypical symptoms such as those enumerated in the *Diagnostic and Statistical Manual or Mental Disorders*. Clinicians are emphatic in insisting that the fact that mental disorder is a continuum or dimension does *not* mean that therefore most of these disorders cannot be diagnosed, or do not exist. One observer criticizes "the idea that if it is difficult to make a distinction between two neighboring points on a hypothetical continuum, no valid distinctions can therefore be made even at the extremes of the continuum. There are thus persons who would argue that the existence of several variations of gray precludes a distinction between black and white" (Rimland, 1969, p. 716). This reasoning is invalid, argues this critic. "While I will agree that some patients in mental hospitals are saner than nonpatients, and that it is sometimes hard to distinguish between deep unhappiness and psychotic depression, I do *not* agree that the difficulty sometimes encountered in making the distinction between normal and abnormal necessarily invalidates all such distinctions" (p. 717). In short, most clinicians feel "the fact that some distinctions are difficult to make, such as deciding whether sundown is day or night, does not mean that it is impossible to distinguish between noon and midnight" (Davison and Neale, 1994).

Some Common Mental Disorders Listed in DSM-IV

In the fourth edition of its *Diagnostic and Statistical Manual of Mental Disorders* (DSM-IV), the American Psychiatric Association (1994) spells out the most common symptoms for 300 mental disorders. Some of them are fairly rare, while others are more common. Here are descriptions of several of the most common mental disorders.

Schizophrenia. Schizophrenia is considered a *thought* or *cognitive* disorder. While no single set of symptoms alone is indicative, among other things it tends to be characterized by distortions of perception, that is "distortions or exaggerations of inferential thinking (delusions), perception (hallucinations), language and communication (disorganized speech), and behavioral monitoring (grossly disorganized or catatonic behavior)" (pp. 274–275). Delusions are "erroneous beliefs that usually involve a misinterpretation of perceptions of experiences" (p. 275). Often, such delusions entail a feeling of being persecuted; "the person believes he or she is being tormented, followed, tricked, spied on, or subject to ridicule" (p. 275). Often, the person believes that words in songs, books, newspapers, and other media sources refer directly to him or her. DSM-IV cautions that "bizarreness" is difficult to determine, given the cultural component to beliefs; nonetheless, many schizophrenics' beliefs are bizarre in that they "are clearly implausible and not understandable and do not derive from ordinary life experiences" (p. 275). An example would be the belief that someone has removed all the person's internal organs and replaced them without leaving any traces. Hallucinations, common with schizophrenia, most commonly entail voices separate from the person's own thoughts; "pejorative or threatening" voices are most common. Speech is usually disorganized, with words jumbled, one upon the other ("word salad"), and thought associations frequently incomprehensible to the listener.

Mood Disorders. While a wide range of mood disorders are specified by DSM-IV, two stand out as frequently encountered by clinicians: *depression*, or "major depressive disorder" (a "unipolar" depressive disorder), and *bipolar* disorder. Clinical depression is diagnosed by a period of two or more weeks during which there seems to be a total loss in pleasure "in nearly all activities" (p. 320). This is usually accompanied by a feeling of worthlessness, deep guilt, an inability to concentrate, recurrent thoughts of death or suicide, decreased energy, a loss of appetite, and/or an inability to sleep. The person suffering from depression is typically described as feeling sad, hopeless, and discouraged. Irritability or extreme crankiness sometimes accompanies depression, along with agitation. The person often neglects previously pleasurable activities and describes himself or herself as "not caring anymore." A lack of interest in or desire for sex is also frequently experienced. Fatigue is common; even minimal exertions, such as getting out of bed in the morning or putting on clothes, will be described as exhausting. The person will often blame himself or herself for past failures. While all of these symptoms may be found in clinically normal persons, in a major depressive episode, they become so pronounced that the person is unable to function in a wide range of necessary activities.

In *bipolar* disorders, the above depressive episodes are alternated with periods of extreme and abnormally elevated, expansive, and giddy euphoria. Symptoms include "inflated self-esteem or grandiosity, decreased need for sleep. .., flight of ideas, distractibility..., psychomotor agitation, and excessive involvement in pleasurable activities with a high potential for painful consequences" (p. 328). When the person's wishes are frustrated, irritability and anger characteristically follow. Delusions are common. The person will often make serious pronouncements or undertake projects on subjects on which he or she has no special expertise: writing a novel, running the United Nations, conducting a symphony orchestra, inventing a perpetual motion machine. The person usually has little need for sleep, feeling alert and full of energy after going days without sleep. Manic speech "is usually pressured, loud, rapid, and difficult to interrupt. . . . Individuals may talk nonstop, sometimes for hours on end, without regard for others' wishes to communicate" (p. 328). Poor judgment and an unrealistic optimism will frequently lead to "an imprudent involvement in pleasurable activities" (p. 329), for instance, casual sex with strangers, shopping sprees that cannot be paid for, reckless driving. To others, the person will seem "out of control."

Personality Disorders. DSM-IV lists 10 specific personality disorders, including the following: "paranoid personality disorder," or "a pattern of distrust and suspiciousness such that others' motives are interpreted as malevolent"; "antisocial personality disorder," or "a pattern of disregard for, and violation of, the rights of others"; "histrionic personality disorder," or "a pattern of excessive emotionality and attention seeking"; "narcissistic personality disorder," or "a pattern of grandiosity, need for admiration, and lack of empathy"; "dependent personality disorder," or "a pattern of submissive and clinging behavior related to an excessive need to be taken care of"; and "obsessive-compulsive personality disorder," or "a pattern of preoccupation with orderliness, perfectionism, and control" (p. 629). Only when these personality traits "are inflexible and maladaptive and cause significant functional impairment or subjective distress" do they constitute personality disorders, says DSM-IV (p. 630). The personality disorder that is most likely to come to the attention of authorities is the "antisocial personality disorder," which not infrequently manifests itself in violence.

Substance-Related Disorders. These are the disorders that are "related to the taking of a drug of abuse" (p. 175), "despite significant substance-related problems" (p. 176). While the precise symptomology varies according to the nature and effects of the drug in question, some common features include dependence, tolerance (a need to increase the dosage to achieve the desired effects), withdrawal upon discontinuing the use of the drug, an inability to remain abstinent after withdrawal, persistent unsuccessful attempts to give up the drug, investing an inordinate amount of time, energy, and emotion in obtaining the substance in question, giving up important activities as a consequence of use, and continuing to use despite the harm the drug causes (p. 181). Several of the drugs listed cause acute intoxication, which may be accompanied by "belligerence, mood lability [extreme mood swings], cognitive impairment, impaired judgment, [and] impaired social or occupational functioning" (p. 183).

Sexual and Gender Disorders. "Sexual dysfunctions" are characterized by a lack of sexual desire or incapacity for arousal, including erectile impotence for men and an inability to achieve orgasm for women. "Paraphilias" are characterized by "recurrent, intense sexual urges, fantasies, or behaviors that involve unusual objectives, activities, or situations," that cause severe distress or impairment in other important areas of life. They include exhibitionism, fetishism, pedophilia (the erotic attraction to children), voyeurism, masochism and sadism. "Gender identity disorders" are characterized by strong and persistent "cross-gender identification" combined with a "persistent discomfort with one's assigned sex" (p. 493).

Disorders First Diagnosed before Adulthood. DSM-IV lists a wide range of disorders that are "usually first diagnosed in infancy, childhood, or adolescence" (pp. 37–121). They include mental retardation (a measured IQ of 70 or below); various learning disorders (academic achievement substantially below age level); autism (impaired development in social interaction and communication, and markedly restricted activities and interests); hyperactivity (severe and maladaptive inattentiveness); conduct disorder (a persistent pattern of behavior which entails a violation of either the rights of others and/or basic rules of conduct); Tourette's Disorder (uncontrollable and compulsively repetitive physical and/or verbal tics, such as yelps, barks, snorts, clicks, grunts, squatting, retracing one's steps, and twirling).

DSM-IV does not use the term "mental illness." However, clearly only some of the 300 disorders it lists would colloquially be referred to as a mental "illness"; certainly schizophrenia and, if sufficiently severe, depression and manic-depression, and some of the personality disorders. (On the other hand, most of us know someone who displays a fairly mild version of these disorders. Where to draw the line between a serious and a less serious condition, between a person who is "neurotic" and one who is clearly mentally "ill," is not an easy task.) In contrast, most of us would not refer to the other disorders as a mental *illness*. Is someone who is dependent on cigarettes (APA, 1994, pp. 242–247), coffee (pp. 212–215), or marijuana (pp. 215–221) *mentally ill?* Almost certainly not. Is dyslexia, hyperactivity, Tourette's Syndrome, autism, or mental retardation a mental illness? Again, very few of us would say so; they are disorders of the mind, but are not "illnesses" as we popularly understand the term. Most of us associate mental illness with extreme thought (schizophrenia) or mood (depression) disorders. Once again, the American Psychiatric Association does not use the term mental "illness," and prefers to focus on disorders, malfunctions, dysfunctions, and disabilities of the mind in a wide range of respects. Nonetheless, in the lay or popular mind, the conceptualization of mental illness as distinct from intellectual dysfunction retains a strong measure of influence.

MODELS OF MENTAL ILLNESS

Two questions have to be answered in order to characterize the various approaches to or models of mental disorder. The first is: *How is the reality of mental disorder defined?* And the second is: *What causes mental disorder?* To distinguish among the various perspectives, theories, or "models" of mental disorder, let's look at a concrete example.

In 1722, John Hu, a Chinese convert to Christianity, accompanied a Jesuit missionary to France; only two Chinese before him had ever visited that country. By European standards, Hu behaved oddly. During his first ride in a coach, he jumped from the moving vehicle, rushed over to a clump of blackberry bushes, and gorged himself on the fruit. Acquiring a fine, coffee-colored suit, he promptly gave it to a beggar. And once, he marched through the streets of Paris, banging on a drum and waving a flag with the message, "Men and women should be kept in their separate spheres" written on it. After too many such incidents, the French authorities committed Hu to an insane asylum where he remained for three years (Spence, 1988).

How would the question of Hu be approached? Is it possible to refer to mental illness across such vast cultural and national boundaries? Was Hu sane or insane? Is it even possible to make such a judgement? If we can, and if he was insane, what was the cause? If he was not, why was he institutionalized? If we cannot make such a judgment in the first place, why was one made in his case? Different models of mental disorder answer these questions in different ways.

In answer to the question of how the reality of mental disorder is defined, I do not refer to the sort of formal definition such as that proposed by the American Psychiatric Association. Instead, I would ask a more basic and general question: *Wherein does its reality lie?* On this question, expert observers can be divided into two camps, the same two that have approached all the phenomena we've looked at so far: *essentialists* and *constructionists*.

To the essentialists, what is important is not the

label but the *condition*. What they look at is the *concrete reality* of mental illness. Mental illness is a condition that can be determined by means of objective tests or indicators. Determining what mental illness is is much like picking an apple off a tree or a rock from the ground; it is "there" to be discovered by the expert or specialist, with an objective reality all its own. It does not matter what a society *calls* the condition or how it is *reacted to* or *treated*—it has a concrete reality *independent* of these judgments and reactions. At different times and in different societies, the condition may very well have been misdiagnosed, just as in earlier times, porpoises might have been thought a type of fish. But regardless of how it is regarded at a given time or in a given society, its reality remains intact nonetheless. Moreover, it is *caused* by specific conditions in the material world; those conditions may be social, biological, or psychological—but we can determine what brings this condition into the world. With enough medical and psychiatric knowledge, we can cure or treat mental disorders—we can make sick people healthy.

In contrast, *constructionists* see the reality of mental illness in the label, the reaction, the judgment, the definition, in a set of practices; they are far more concerned with *the social enterprise of mental illness labeling and treatment* than the condition itself. To the constructionist, what counts is *how what is seen* as mental illness is *judged and treated* by professionals and laypersons. What social constructionists look at and study is a certain *discourse*, a narrative—in short, what we *do* and *say* about what we refer to as mental disorder and those persons we refer to as the mentally ill. Whether there is a concrete reality "there" in the material world that we refer to as mental disorder is a secondary or even irrelevant question; what's important is *how judgements of mental illness are made*.

Hu's unfortunate encounter with European society highlights these two perspectives toward mental illness. The strict *essentialistic* model would argue that what counts most is Hu's condition, not how it was diagnosed. *However* Hu was treated by the psychiatric establishment in eighteenth-century France, he either *was or was not* mentally ill. Some essentialists would say that Hu's behavior was so bizarre, so floridly disordered and dysfunctional, that the contemporary clinician cannot but see him as mentally ill. The cultural differences between France and China, however great they were in the eighteenth century, do not explain Hu's peculiar behavior. Hu was hospitalized because *he really was crazy*. It didn't matter that he was only one of three Chinese who had ever visited France at the time; it didn't matter that the French were unacquainted with the rules of proper Chinese conduct, or that Hu was unacquainted with the rules of proper French conduct. The behavior that caused the French to hospitalize Hu would have caused him to be hospitalized everywhere—or, at least, *should have*. Hu would have been regarded as mentally disordered in all cultures, China included; culture had nothing to do with his condition. The process of differential labeling of mental conditions is uninteresting, nonproblematic, and more or less straightforward. Some other essentialists might have argued that it is entirely possible that eighteenth-century French psychiatry was so crude and error-prone that Hu was *misdiagnosed*. Perhaps the condition of mental illness was not fully understood then and hence, Hu's misdiagnosis. But as societies cast off ignorance and superstition, there will be a fuller understanding of what mental illness is and how to diagnosis it. What *counts* is the objective facts of Hu's disorder, not how it has been diagnosed in different societies.

In contrast, the social constructionist would say what is most important about the question of Hu was that he was treated by eighteenth-century French psychiatry in a certain way. These are the facts of the case, not Hu's putative or supposed "condition." The reason why this is so crucial is that definition of mental disorder is culture-bound; what is called crazy in one society or social context may be seen as perfectly normal in another. Hu's behavior was regarded as a sign of mental illness simply because the French expected the man to act the way the French acted; when he acted quite differently, he was labeled crazy. The constructionist would examine the enterprise of *defining* and *dealing with* Hu and all others defined and dealt with as mentally ill in eighteenth-century France, as *itself* a subject to be investigated, *not as* an approximation or a departure from an "accurate" or scientifically valid definition of mental illness. For constructionism, the most interesting question is *not* whether psychiatrists are scientifically accurate when they define and treat the mentally ill. Instead, they look at these definitions and treatments as interesting in and of themselves. Why one judgment rather than another? How and why do judgments vary from one society to another, from one professional to another, from one time period to another? Would Hu be regarded as insane today? Would he be hospitalized? How do popular and expert views of mental illness differ from those of physical illness? How does the public view the mentally ill? Why do certain treatment modalities come into and fall out of vogue? Why is mental illness so much more stigmatizing than physical illness? Is the psychiatric establishment acting as a means of social control? These and other concerns animate the constructionist. The "soft" or "moderate" constructionist puts condition in the background and emphasizes judgments; the "hard" or "strict" or "radical" constructionist argues that *all* judgments, including those made by psychiatrists, are by their very nature equally subjective and problematic—in effect, that *there is no such thing* as mental illness aside from the label.

The answer to our second question, what *causes* mental disorder, discusses a related although analytically distinct dimension—*etiology*. Social constructionists are not especially interested in the question of causality; if mental disorder is socially constructed rather than an objectively identifiable condition, then it cannot be said to be "caused" by factors external to these social definitions. In contrast, etiology is the essentialist's *primary* concern. As we might expect, we have a variety of etiological theories of mental disorder. Some observers are eclectic, of course, and believe that different explanations can account for different sorts of disorders, or that a *combination* of factors can explain mental disorders generally or a specific disorder. Other observers are more monolithic and argue for a *single* theory or explanation, either for a given condition or for all disorders generally. As we've seen with other phenomena, there are almost as many explanations as there are experts. Still, three rough, broad theories or explanations of mental disorder can be identified: the sociological, the psychological or psychodynamic, and the biological. Within each broad category, there are a host of variations. Thus, the biological theory might have argued that Hu suffered from pathological genes, or a hormonal imbalance, or a neurological disorder. The psychological theory might have looked into Hu's childhood experiences, especially with his family, or what rewards and punishments he experienced through his life. Social theories might have looked at the stress he suffered as a member of a certain social category. One variant of the sociological theory, the labeling perspective, might have

argued that, having been *labeled* as crazy, Hu actually *went* crazy after his institutionalization.

Essentialistic Approaches to Mental Illness

As we've seen, the essentialist approach defines mental disorder as an objectivistic condition that can be located in the real world, in the concrete behavior or verbalizations of persons who are disordered. Such behaviors or verbalizations are clear-cut signs or manifestations of a disordered mind, in much the same way that the height of a column of mercury on a thermometer indicates or measures temperature. As I said with respect to the question of Hu, we can define mental disorder and lay our hands on it in much the same way we can pick an apple off a tree. True, defining and locating mental disorder is a bit more complicated, difficult, and intellectually challenging than picking an apple, but the principle is the same: The essential reality of "appleness," as with the reality of mental disorder, is an objective fact, identifiable by pointing to specific properties that the fruit possesses to all observers. In the same way, to identify mental disorder, we would point to specific properties that persons designated by the label manifest, that is, concrete, real-world behavior or verbalizations. Of course, mental disorder manifests itself in somewhat different ways in different societies, but there is an *inner* or *common core* to all mental disorder everywhere. A severe schizophrenic in Zambia would be a severe schizophrenic in Thailand, Panama, or Norway. What counts is not social definitions or constructs of the condition but the nature of the condition itself (Murphy, 1976).

The hardest or most extreme version of the essentialistic approach is often referred to as the *medical* model. It argues that mental disorder is very much like a medical disease; a disease of the mind is very much like a disease of the body. The bizarre and inappropriate behaviors exhibited by mentally disordered persons are symptoms of an underlying or internal pathology of some kind. Mental patients present *symptoms*, those symptoms can be *categorized*, and the sane are *clearly distinguishable* from the insane (Rosenhan, 1973, p. 250). More colloquially: "Some people *are* more crazy than others; we can tell the difference; and calling lunacy a name does not *cause* it" (Nettler, 1974, p. 894). The medical model emphasizes the *intrapsychic* forces in mental illness, that is, it is an internal *condition* within the psyche of the disordered person. Once someone has "become" mentally disordered, that condition will manifest itself in *any and all* situations and contexts, at least until psychiatric intervention treats or cures that person. Much as a physical disease is internal to the sufferer, likewise, a mental disorder is a disease that is "in" the insane.

Essentialists are interested in and study the *epidemiology* and the *etiology* of mental disorder. "Epidemiology" refers to how mental disorders are distributed in categories in the population; "etiology" refers to explanations of the *causes* of mental disorder. Essentialists would argue that there is a "true" rate or incidence mental illness in a given population and a given society. They investigate whether men or women have higher rates of mental disorders, and more specifically *which* disorders. Are married or unmarried men and women more likely to become mentally ill? Blacks or whites? Urban or rural dwellers? How is socioeconomic status or social class related to mental disorder—again, to *which* disorders? Are lower class people crazier because lower class life is more stressful than middle-class life? Or because if you're crazy, it's very difficult to become successful? These and other questions are asked by epidemiologists who regard mental disorder as a concretely real phenomenon with essentialistic qualities. Essentialists hold that there exists a pregiven entity or syndrome that researchers can define, identify, locate, lay their hands on, and eventually explain or account for. Mental disorder is not merely a label or a social construction. *It does not matter* how the disorder is socially defined—the reality exists *independent* of that definition. The application of the label and the treatment of persons so labeled are not the most interesting things about it or even interesting at all. The most interesting thing about mental disorder is what it is, its dynamics, how it works, what causes it—and how we may cure it and restore the mentally ill to mental health.

Epidemiology is usually seen as being in the service of etiology. The goal of studying how diseases are distributed in the population, many experts feel, is so that an explanation of illness can be devised and tested. Someone with an essentialistic orientation sees the primary task of anyone who studies mental illness as devising a valid theory or account of etiology: *What causes it?* Again, whether this theory is sociological, psychological, or biological does not determine the essentialist's model.

The sociologist of mental illness would argue that mental illness is caused, at least in large part by social factors: stress, for instance, brought on by lower class status, gender membership, or racial and ethnic prejudice. Most sociologists agree that social factors combine with genetic, neurological, hormonal, and/or psychological factors. Certain persons who are *genetically predisposed* could experience socially induced stressful conditions, which push them over the edge into mental illness. Still, these sociological etiologists would say, social factors are *crucial* in the causal dynamics leading to mental illness. Again, simply because a theory is sociological does not mean that it is any the less essentialistic: Even sociological theories of mental disorder hold that mental illness is an identifiable clinical entity. What counts is how the condition is caused, how it came about, what brought it on. And what does not count, what is not interesting or problematic—or at least is of secondary significance—is the creation and application of the label. The enterprise of mental health diagnosis and treatment is crucial only insofar as it relates specifically to the success of treatment outcomes. It is important to know which treatments work and which ones don't, but it isn't important to study treatment as an intellectually or theoretically problematic dynamic in its own right, as a phenomenon to be explained and understood for its own sake.

The strict medical model argues that mental illness is largely or always a manifestation of abnormal biophysical functioning—brain damage, a chemical imbalance, pathological genes, neurological malfunction, and so on (Torrey, 1994). This school suggests that certain environmental factors, such as stress or early childhood experiences, have little etiological significance. At most, they may act as "triggering" mechanisms that exacerbate an already established susceptibility to mental illness. Consequently, any legitimate and effective therapy for psychic disorder must be physical in nature, such as drugs, electroshock therapy, or surgical intervention. The strict medical model has been gaining adherents in recent years. Electroshock therapy has been making a comeback in the past decade, while the use of psychoactive drugs has almost literally overtaken all other forms of therapy since their introduction in the 1950s. (In contrast, surgery, such as pre-frontal lobotomies, has been almost completely discredited as a treatment for mental disorder.) At the other end of the spectrum, psychoanalysis, the "talk" therapy introduced by Sigmund Freud, has plummeted in popularity since the 1950s; in some professional circles, it has been completely discredited (Gruenbaum, 1993; Esterson, 1993; Crews, 1995; Webster, 1995; Torrey, 1994).

Just as biological and genetic theories of mental illness, which hold that sociological factors are of secondary importance, could be seen as "hard" essentialistic theories, psychological and sociological theories could be seen as "soft" essentialistic theories. Both agree that the clinical entity, mental illness or mental disorder, is concretely real, that diagnoses tap or measure something in the real world. Both agree that mental disorder represents a genuine malfunction or dysfunction, a true or real disorder above and beyond the mere label or diagnosis itself. But these approaches—the biological on the one hand and the psychological and the sociological on the other—part company on the *cause* of mental disorders. Psychological and sociological theories emphasize that they are caused by the patient's experiences, not by an inherent or inner biological or chemical condition. That is, they stress *nurture*, or environment, rather than *nature*. A mentally ill person may have nothing physically wrong, yet as a result of his or her experiences, still have a disordered mind. Since physical, biological, or congenital theories posit causes that are more indwelling, more inherent, the only way that mental disorders can be cured or treated is by changing the very physical factors that caused them. This means surgical, chemical, hormonal, genetic, or electrical treatment. Merely changing the conditions of the patient's life, or attempting to cure by means of "talk" therapies, will not change that pathological mental patient's condition. Still, these approaches or theories agree that because the condition is concretely real, researchers can identify and explain it and, possibly, eventually, treat and cure it. The sociological and psychological theories of mental disorder argue that certain experiences exist in some persons' lives that cause or influence them to "go crazy." And being crazy can be measured by means of certain concretely real objective criteria or indicators. So the psychological and sociological essentialists don't differ on this particular point with the biological essentialists: Mental illness is concretely real; it is not simply a label.

Before, I introduced the term, the "medical" model. The medical model sees mental disorder as a condition that is internal to, or "in," the mental patient, just as cancer is "in" a medical patient.

Once a person "has" a mental illness, it manifests itself under any and all conditions. The medical model is the most *extreme* version of essentialism. However, not all essentialistic models of mental disorder conform strictly to the medical model. Many sociologists and some psychologists believe that mental illness will manifest itself more under certain conditions than others. For example, some persons who are vulnerable or susceptible to mental disorder may be perfectly normal or healthy under certain conditions—for instance, those that are less stressful, or when they have a social support network. Essentialists who adhere to the non-medical model stress that mental disorder may be a *temporary* condition, one that is not solely "in" the individual, one that is as much dependent on the social environment in which the individual interacts as on the individual's internal condition. Again, non-medical essentialists retain the idea of mental disorder as a real "thing" in the material world as well as a disorder. But they see its appearance as much more heavily dependent on external factors than do proponents of the strict medical model. Biogenetic and biochemical theories of mental illness most definitely adopt a medical model; mental disorder is a condition "in" the individual, again, that manifests itself pretty much everywhere. Psychoanalysis, too, adopts a medical model, although it could be seen as a "softer" version, since mental illness can be treated by means of a form of therapy that does not entail physical or strictly medical intervention. Once someone has gone through certain pathological childhood experiences one will remain mentally ill until treatment intervenes. Thus, though psychoanalysis holds that the environment *causes* mental disorder, once it has been set in motion, it manifests itself pretty much regardless of the environment.

Constructionism

A social constructionist model would argue that whether or not there is a "common thread" or "common core" to mental illness is not especially interesting or intellectually problematic. What counts is the enterprise of mental illness, what is said and done about persons who are defined as mentally ill. One major reason why this is such a crucial question is that diagnoses differ in societies around the world; hence, the reality of mental disorder varies along with them. Definitions of mental disorder are culture-bound; what is labeled crazy in one society or social context may be seen as perfectly normal in another—or possessed, extraordinary, saintly, inspired by the holy spirit.

The constructionists regard mental disorder as socially defined, both by the general public and the psychiatric profession. In other words, as with deviance, constructionists do not think that mental disorder can be defined "objectively" by focusing on the common thread that all disorders share. Instead, they argue, what mental disorder "is" is how it is seen, judged, reacted to, treated, and evaluated in a given society. There exists a mental illness *enterprise* or, in the words of Michel Foucault, a mental illness *discourse:* the psychiatric, legal, and social machinery designed to deal with persons designated as mentally ill, the writing, the research, the diagnostic manuals, the mental health industry and the drug industry built around administering medication to the mentally ill, not to mention public attitudes focusing on mental illness, the popular beliefs, stereotypes, prejudices, legend and folklore, media attention, and so on. Thus, what mental disorder *is* is what we *say* and *do* about persons designated as mentally disordered. Mental disorder has no "essential" reality beyond these social constructions, this "discourse," these reactions, the social enterprise surrounding it.

The constructionist model of mental disorder argues the following points: one, that *it is a form of deviance*, two, its reality is *called into being* by the labeling process, and three, that the application of the label is influenced at least in part by a variety of *extrapsychiatric* factors or variables. The mentally ill are derogated and stigmatized, excluded from full social acceptance; the process of judging persons *to be* mentally ill makes their behavior or mental states sociologically relevant (although, of course, such judgments do not *create* the condition in the first place); and these judgments are influenced by a number of factors *in addition to* the severity of their condition. In a nutshell, these are the basic assumptions of the constructionist approach to mental disorder. It is not a theory which attempts to explain *why* some people are or become mentally ill (see the labeling theory that follows); instead, it is an approach or framework, or set of "sensitizing concepts" which help to understand one major aspect of the phenomenon.

One observer argued that mental patients suffer not so much from mental illness but from *contingencies*. Whether someone becomes a patient in a mental hospital, for instance, depends as much on the person's social and economic status, the visibility of the offense committed, his or her proximity to the hospital, the treatment facilities that are available, and so on (Goffman, 1961, pp. 134–135). Another sociologist, not associated with the labeling or constructionist school, argues that "the diagnosis, categorization, and labeling of mental illnesses are themselves profoundly social acts and that other social factors besides the behavior itself affect the informal and formal processes whereby persons are judged to have a mental pathology" (Akers, 1985, p. 314). One study (Simon and Zussman, 1983) examined a legal case involving the victims of a flood who were suing a coal company for creating conditions that made it possible for the flood to ravage a community. The plaintiffs claimed "psychic damages" as one of the harmful consequences of the flood. Countering their argument, the defendants, representatives of the coal company, argued that the flood had no such impact. Two sets of psychiatrists, one hired by the defense and the other by the plaintiffs, examined 42 flood victims. Not surprisingly, the defense's psychiatrists found little evidence of psychopathology, while the plaintiff's found considerable psychic impairment. If mental disorder were as closely analogous to physical illness as the medical model argues, such extreme discrepancies would seem hardly possible.

Consider the fact that, in the first edition of the *Diagnostic and Statistical Manual of Mental Disorders* (1952), homosexuality was deemed an instance of a "sociopathic personality disturbance." In the second, it was listed as belonging under the category, "sexual deviance." In 1973, under pressure from movement activists and militants, the American Psychiatric Association decided that in and of itself, homosexuality was not a disturbance; it represented a disorder only if it created conflict and generated the wish to change one's sexual orientation. In the third edition (1980) this was further modified to apply only to persons for whom such a wish was a "persistent concern"; the APA referred to this condition as "ego-dystonic homosexuality." In the revised third edition (1987, p. 426), an explanation as to why this condition was dropped was offered ("it suggests to some that homosexuality was considered a disorder"). In the fourth edition (1994), there is no mention of homosexuality whatsoever as a disorder of any kind. It is difficult to imagine such contortions taking place for a physical state or condition.

The influence of extrapsychiatric factors is in large part due to the vagueness of psychiatric diagnosis. Although certainly more precise and reliable today than in the past, diagnoses of mental disorder are considerably less so than are strictly medical diagnoses, that is, those concerning strictly physical conditions. It is clear that agreement among psychiatrists as to patients' conditions is high only when they present "classic" or "archetypical" symptoms. In contrast, agreement is low among patients who present symptoms that are less clear-cut and more ambiguous. In fact, the majority of cases psychiatrists see are less classic and more ambiguous in their symptomology (Townsend, 1980, pp. 270–272). A summary of the reliability of psychiatric diagnoses found it to be high only when the categories were extremely broad or the symptoms extremely and clear-cut; where the categories were specific or detailed or the symptoms less than clear-cut, disagreement between and among psychiatrists was high (Edgerton, 1969, pp. 68–69). Two commentators conclude that "art far outweighs science" in psychiatric judgments (Stoller and Geertsma, 1963, p. 65). An author of a textbook on psychiatric methodology states that expert judgments on mental disorder "are of a social, cultural, economic and sometimes legal nature" (Loftus, 1960, p. 13).

In one study (Kendall et al., 1971), videotapes of diagnostic interviews with patients were shown to a large number of psychiatrists in the United States and Great Britain. Those patients presenting "classic, textbook" symptoms generated almost unanimous agreement as to psychiatric condition. However, patients manifesting less than clear-cut symptoms touched off less than unanimity in diagnosis. One patient was deemed schizophrenic by 85 percent of the American psychiatrists, but only 7 percent of the British; another was judged to be schizophrenic by 69 percent of the Americans, but only 2 percent of the British. Clearly, the American concept of schizophrenia is much broader than is the British. It is difficult to imagine such disparities in the diagnosis of a strictly medical disease, such as cancer or tuberculosis.

In examining *informal* mental disorder labeling around the world, even greater variation prevails. Cross-culturally, certain terms or labels are applied everywhere to persons "who are thought to be conducting themselves in a manner that is inappropriate, abnormal, or unreasonable for persons in that culture who occupy a similar social position; that is, to persons who can provide no otherwise acceptable explanation for their conduct" (Edgerton, 1969, p. 50). Every culture has a label that indicates some version of mental disorder or illness. How are these labels applied? A summary of the available anthropological literature points to two conclusions. First, the recognition and labeling of persons "who are both severely and chronically psychotic" typically occurs with a high degree of consensus "because persons such as these are typically so dramatically, and enduringly, far beyond the pale of everyday rationality" (p. 51). And second, most people who act strangely or "crazily" do not do so in an extreme or chronic fashion; consequently, being labeled for these persons is a complex matter, influenced by a wide range of contingencies. As to whether someone is or is not regarded socially and publicly as psychotic is open to *negotiation* (pp. 51, 65)—that is decided in a give-and-take interaction between two or more parties on the basis of factors unrelated to objective psychiatric conditions.

Thus, the constructionist is more likely to be concerned with the dynamics of mental illness labeling than etiological issues. What factors are related to being labeled as mentally ill? Is it psychiatric condition alone? Or do extrapsychiatric factors play a role in this process? And how prominent is this role? The medical model would hold that psychiatric diagnoses (although not popular or public labels) are an accurate reflection of the patient's "objective" condition. The constructionist and labeling approach argues that this process of mental illness labeling is considerably less rational than the medical model holds, that factors other than severity of psychiatric symptoms influence diagnoses and the decision to admit and discharge patients. (However, labeling theorists do *not* claim that this process is random, that persons are singled out randomly or capriciously, that patients do not differ in any appreciable way from the population at large.) This process is guided by a number of contingencies, they argue. There is, in other words, "a clear tendency for admission and discharge of mental patients to be related more to social than to psychiatric variables" (Krohn and Akers, 1977, p. 341). Sociocultural factors, such as family desires and living arrangements, adequate patient resources outside the mental hospital, cultural conceptions, region of the country, and the danger the patient represents to others can be determinants of psychiatric case outcomes (Townsend, 1978; Krohn and Akers, 1977).

Thus, constructionism argues that *independent*

of etiology, independent of the *consequences* of labeling, and even to some degree independent of the "objective" *validity* of psychiatric diagnoses, the sociologist is obliged to study *the social organization of the labeling process* that *leads to* a judgment or diagnosis of mental disorder. This issue was expressed decades ago by Edwin Lemert, an important precursor of labeling theory; almost half a century ago, Lemert stated: "One of the more important sociological questions here is not what causes human beings to develop such symptoms as hallucinations and delusions, but, instead, what is done about their behavior which leads the community to reject them, segregate them, and otherwise treat them as . . . insane" (1951, p. 387). Thus, regardless of what "causes" homosexuality, there is a social organization of the condemnation of homosexuality; regardless of the etiology of obesity, again, in this society, the obese are stigmatized and condemned. *What is made* of homosexuality, obesity, and mental illness? What factors influence this reaction? These are some of the central concerns of the social constructionist who studies deviance. As a qualification: "Hard" constructionists see *all* views of mental illness as constructions, including those held by psychiatrists, and sidestep the issue of whether any one of them is more valid or accurate than any other. In contrast, "soft" constructionists would argue that the reality of mental illness is not *solely* a construction, and would grant that some constructions strike closer to the empirical reality of mental illness than others.

Labeling Theory

A theory that has always been treated as a variant of the constructionist model, but which harbors a strong essentialistic component, is the labeling theory of mental illness. It may sound confusing to stress the essentialistic strains in labeling theory, since I discussed labeling theory as a constructionist approach in Chapter 5. But the fact is, as with Lemert's theory of secondary deviation, the labeling theory of mental illness emphasizes the causal dynamics or etiological factors underlying mental illness, *not* the nature and dynamics of the social construction of mental illness. To be more specific, it argues that mental disorder *is* concretely real, a material phenomenon in the real world. (Remember, Lemert's theory of secondary deviation emphasizes that it is *being labeled* that often strengthens one's commitment to a deviant role

and further deviant behavior.) Thomas Scheff, the primary proponent of the labeling theory of mental illness takes this mechanism a step or two further. Being labeled as crazy for engaging in mildly eccentric, slightly bizarre behavior results in *really*, *actually*, and *concretely going crazy*. The definition becomes a *self-fulfilling prophecy*. One learns to act out the symptomology of mental illness as a result of being exposed to the definitions that are prevalent in a given society; behaving like a crazy person is how one is supposed to act if one has been defined *as* a crazy person. Hence, engaging in odd, eccentric, unconventional behavior for which there is no ready label—"residual deviance"—results in being *labeled* crazy which, in turn, results in acting the way a crazy person is *supposed* to act, which eventually results in actually *going* crazy. But note: The labeling theory argues that there really is such a thing as being crazy; although the label creates the condition, *the condition becomes concretely real*.

It should be emphasized that although the two approaches have often been confused, Scheff's labeling theory of mental illness and the more general labeling theory of Becker and his associates are substantially different approaches. Although for Scheff the *initial* process of labeling *is* a social construction, the process of labeling actually *produces* an identifiable condition all can point to and identify as "true" mental illness. In other words, Scheff is not quite a true constructionist, since his primary concern is etiological. In contrast, labelists' concerns are much more heavily concentrated on constructionist matters and far less on issues of causality. Becker and the other labeling theorists never *intended* their theory to be an explanation of deviance in the sense of accounting for its origin or etiology (Becker, 1973, pp. 178–179; Kitsuse, 1972, p. 235). Nor did it insist that the process of labeling always and inevitably results in an intensification of a commitment to deviance, the deviant role, or deviant behavior; this is an empirical question and must be studied in individual cases (Becker, 1963, pp. 34-35, 1973, p. 179). For Scheff, in contrast, the whole point is to devise a theory accounting for the origin of mental illness. Note that Walter Gove, a critic of Scheff's "harder" version of labeling theory of mental illness, *supports* "a softer" version of labeling theory "that is not concerned with specific predictions [of causality] but is concerned with how social institutions function and how such functioning is related to our understanding of mental illness as a social category and as a social career" (1989). I am inclined to agree.

To reiterate, then, for Scheff, the *initial* process of labeling *is* a social construction. That is, "normals" label eccentricity or "residual deviance" *as* mental illness. Clearly, to the extent that this process is arbitrary and not based on scientific or real-world criteria, Scheff adopts a constructionist approach. Why are eccentrics being labeled as crazy? Is it because of their condition? Clearly not; a variety of extra-psychiatric social and cultural factors rule this process. However, *once the labeling process has been launched* and the person who is labeled as crazy begins to take on a crazy role, a very real condition of mental illness begins to take over. What was *defined* as real *becomes* real. Thus, Scheff has one foot in constructionism and one foot in essentialism, more specifically in etiology.

Thomas Scheff clearly states that he is *not* a constructionist (personal communication). His theory is *etiological*; it is an attempt to explain the origin of mental illness (1966, 1984). To Scheff, the *how* and *why* of the social construction of mental illness is secondary; what counts is its power to generate behavior and a condition the psychiatric profession knows as mental illness. Hence, he must be regarded at least as much an essentialist as a constructionist. It must be said that labeling theory, in the form stated by Thomas Scheff, has very few followers among clinicians; it is of interest almost exclusively to a very small circle of sociologists. Today, the overwhelming majority of psychiatrists adopt some version of the biomedical model. Still, it has received, and continues to receive, a great deal of attention in the sociological study of deviance. Therefore, let's look at Scheff's theory in a bit more detail.

Scheff distinguishes between *residual rule-breaking* and mental illness. Residual rule-breaking is made up of all those activities, feelings, or experiences, that first, entail a violation of social norms, second, do not fall within a specific categorical realm (such as crime, drunkenness, sexual "perversion," and so on), for which society has no specific, explicit label, and third, make up what is regarded as a sign or manifestation of mental illness. In other words, by "acting weird" (residual rule-breaking), one could be regarded as "crazy." Scheff's theory can be broken down into nine parts. First, rule-breaking has many *sources* or *causes*—temporary stress, food or sleep deprivation, drug ingestion, and so on. Second, many persons engage in residual rule-breaking; however, very few are categorized as crazy, either informally, by the lay public, by people one knows, or formally, by the psychiatric profession. There are many more persons in the general population, Scheff argues, who engage in residual rule-breaking without being labeled than those who do so and are designated as mentally ill. In other words, the rule-breaking in which most of us engage is unrecognized, ignored, or rationalized. And third, most rule-breaking is of *transitory significance*. For the most part, if others don't make a big deal out of someone acting weird, eventually the behavior will go away (1966, pp. 40–51).

Yet, there are some persons who do have a mentally ill "*career*." That is, they continue to act "weird"; acting crazy does not go away. How are they different from the rest of us? Scheff's fourth point about labeling and mental illness is that *stereotyped imagery of mental disorder is learned in early childhood*; it is part of our culture's "lore" about mental illness. And fifth, it is continually *reaffirmed* in ordinary social interaction. In other words, we all learn and know what a crazy person is and does; this is part of our cultural tradition, and is woven into how we are treated, and how we treat others, when certain symptoms are displayed. Sixth, someone who is labeled as a mentally ill person—for whatever reason—will be *rewarded* for playing that role, and seventh, *punished* if he or she attempts to return to normalcy or conventional behavior. Eighth, in a crisis, when someone who engages in residual rule-breaking is publicly labeled as a crazy person, he or she is highly *suggestible* and will often readily accept the proffered role of being insane. In fact, Scheff argues, ninth, among residual rule-breakers, being labeled as mentally ill is the *single most important cause* of having a "career" in mental illness. In other words, if others (friends, relatives, the general public, psychiatrists and other mental health professionals) call one crazy when one is vulnerable, one will continue to act crazy, and this label will intensify one's commitment to crazy behavior and a crazy role (1966, pp. 64–93; 1984).

The Modified Labeling Approach

Gove (1975a, 1975b, 1979a, 1980a, 1982a) argues that the labeling theory of mental illness is empirically wrong. Gove argues that mental patients are unable to function in the real world not because they have been stigmatized but because they are mentally ill; the mentally disordered have a debilitating disease that cripples their capacity to function normally and effectively. Moreover, Gove argues, the process by which the psychiatric profession singles out someone as mentally ill is not significantly influenced by sociological or other extra-psychiatric variables. Instead, this process is almost exclusively determined by the nature and severity of the illness. Labeling, the medical model argues, is neither capricious or arbitrary nor is it based on such hierarchical factors as race, sex, socioeconomic status, or power. Persons who are sick tend to be labeled as such; in turn, those who are well are extremely unlikely to be labeled as sick.

With respect to *informal*, as opposed to professional, far from being eager to label someone as mentally ill, the general public is extremely reluctant to do so and, moreover, does not hold particularly strong, negative, or stigmatizing feelings about the mentally ill. (See also Clausen, 1981.) This is especially true for intimates—spouses, children, parents, close friends—of the mentally ill, who avoid labeling until the disturbed person's behavior becomes intolerable. Lastly, hospitalization and other treatment intervention, far from making the patient's condition worse as the labeling approach claims, most often results in an amelioration of his or her symptoms. In short, a genuine healing process does seem to take place. Gove, the most outspoken and persistent of the critics of the labeling theory of mental illness, argues that these generalizations are so well founded empirically that he states flatly: "For all practical purposes, the labeling explanation of mental illness is of historical interest only" (1979a, p. 301).

Which model is correct? Which one approximates empirical reality most closely? To begin with, we need not be forced into an either-or, black-or-white position. It is possible that there is some middle ground here; labeling theory may be correct on some points, while its critics may be right with respect to some others. In fact, what has come to be referred to as a "soft" or *modified* labeling theory approach fits the facts of mental illness most faithfully (Link et al., 1989). The modified labeling approach would accept certain aspects of the medical model without denying the importance of the labeling process.

First, mentally disordered persons, while they do have difficulty in their everyday lives because of their psychiatric condition, also suffer serious debilitation and demoralization as a consequence of stigma and labeling. Everyone who grows up in this society, including the disordered, is aware of the negative image of the mentally ill. Persons who suffer from a mental disorder anticipate negative treatment from others, and these beliefs taint their interaction with "normals" and with mental health professionals (Thoits, 1985; Link, 1987; Link et al., 1989). Often, the expectations others have of the disordered person's behavior will actually call forth the very behavior that confirms those expectations (Link and Cullen, 1989; Jones, 1986).

We've already examined a basic proposition of labeling theory under the umbrella of constructionism, which overlaps heavily with it. (Constructionism is concerned with how judgments of reality and imputations of deviance are made and put into practice; labeling theory is, in addition, concerned with the *consequences* of such judgments and imputations.) That is, there is a certain measure of arbitrariness when in applying psychiatric labels it comes to psychiatric condition. As we saw, American psychiatrists are far more likely to apply the label of schizophrenia to patients than are British psychiatrists (Kendall et al., 1971); in a civil case which centered around psychic damages to plaintiffs, psychiatrists for the defense found no psychic damage, while psychiatrists for the plaintiffs found considerable psychic damage (Simon and Zussman, 1983); in fact, a wide range of extra-psychiatric factors have been found to influence psychiatric judgments (Krohn and Akers, 1977; Townsend, 1978; 1980). While this must be tempered by the qualification that as seriousness of the condition increases, the uniformity of the psychiatric judgment increases correspondingly, it cannot be stressed too much that *most* of the judgments that psychiatrists make are of patients with a less rather than more serious condition. Hence, it is clear that extra-psychiatric contingencies do play a major role in psychiatric labeling.

The labeling approach is clearly wrong when it comes to treatment outcomes. Enough valid, reliable studies have been conducted on treatment outcomes to demonstrate that psychiatric intervention is more likely to be beneficial to the patient than harmful. Far from entrenching the mental patient more deeply in the mentally ill role, treatment does appear to have some positive effects (Smith, Glass, and Miller, 1980; Landman and Dawes, 1982). Some of these effects are not profound, and many do not persist over time; nonetheless, "it would be difficult for societal reaction theorists to argue that the effects of [psychiatric] labeling are uniformly negative" (Link and Cullen, 1989). Not only is psychiatric intervention more likely to move the patient out of rather than more deeply into disordered behavior, but also, undetected, untreated mentally disordered conditions often persist over long periods of time (Fischer et al., 1979), refuting "the labeling theory notion that symptoms are transient in the absence of labeling" (Link and Cullen, 1989).

In short, although it is difficult to deny the impact of the objective nature of mental disorder, at the same time, stigma, labeling, and societal reaction remain potent and crucial sociological factors to be taken into account in influencing the condition of the mentally disordered. Attempting to prove or disprove the strict labeling or the strict medical model *in toto* seems a futile exercise. More refined attempts to test these models will find that both have a great deal to offer; in short, a "modified" labeling theory approach seems to be the most productive model in understanding mental disorder (Link et al., 1989).

FAMILIES OF THE MENTALLY ILL: LABELING BY INTIMATES

Deviant roles or labels vary enormously according to how swiftly or slowly they are assigned to others and how skimpy or well documented the evidence must be for such an assignment to take place. Alcoholism and mental illness are similar in that they are roles or labels that are very slowly assigned to someone, and then only after great and protracted efforts at denial and the accumulation of many episodes that might point in these directions. Generally speaking, the more intimate the relationship between the potentially labeled person and conventional others, the greater the effort to deny the condition and the greater the evidence necessary to pin a label on that person. This is in part because "closeness permits one to see qualities other than the flaw" (Kreisman and Joy, 1974, p. 39). Still, some labels are slower to be attached than others; perhaps of all labels, as I said, alcoholism and mental illness require the most evidence by intimates and family members to be attached. In this sense, they could be referred to as varieties of *conventional deviance*.

In contrast, homosexuality is swiftly assigned—

to others at any rate—and typically on skimpy evidence (Robins, 1975, p. 30). There is usually no overt behavior for nondeviant adults that can be labeled by anyone *as* homosexuality that is even remotely *like* homosexuality except homosexuality itself. (This is done in prisons, by street hustlers, and by bisexuals, but these scenes are already defined by conventionals as deviant.) Locker room camaraderie, homosociality, masculine competition, athletic contests, macho efforts to demonstrate one's manhood all tend to be kept within socially defined and acceptable limits. They very rarely resemble actual homosexuality to anyone except a psychoanalyst. But each concrete act of same-gender sexual contact would be seen *as* a homosexual act by a nonparticipant, conventional outsider.

In contrast, "normals" tend to refuse to assign a label of "mentally ill" to intimate deviant actors until their behavior has become blatantly public and onerously troublesome. Most of the persons who would be regarded by a substantially proportion of clinicians and therapists as mentally ill are at some time during their lives never professionally diagnosed as such. Most are not so regarded by their peers and intimates, and do not come to see themselves as much. (Eccentric, perhaps, a bit strange, maybe, but not mentally ill.) There is, in other words, a huge number of "hidden" mentally disordered persons at large in the general population. But the more trouble a person causes others, the less power and resources that person has and the more power significant others have. The more bizarre that person's behavior and/or ideas seem to others within a particular cultural system, the greater the likelihood that others will perceive his or her behavior as a manifestation of mental illness. Likewise, the more visible a person's behavior, the greater is that likelihood. The greater the harm that person's behavior causes to others, again, the greater that likelihood is. The greater the departure from expected, normal social relations a person's interactions with others manifest, the greater the likelihood that person will eventually be seen as mentally ill. The greater the cost of the failure to fulfill one's social obligations, the higher the likelihood of this outcome, too. And the more that the individual's interpretations of reality depart from accepted cultural standards, the greater the chances of the imputation of psychosis.

For instance, schizophrenia, which manifests itself in mental states defined as bizarre, is more readily defined as mental illness than clinical depression, whose symptoms seem less peculiar. People do not cause trouble, nor do they exhibit a "strange" way of thinking or acting, simply because they are psychotic. People must be *experienced* as trouble, or *regarded* as strange, by others. What is experienced as trouble or as strange in one place may not be in another. Moreover, one disordered condition may cause more trouble than another. Certainly the various character disorders that result in violent behavior lead to a swifter designation by others of mental disorder than those that do not. There is certainly a central nucleus of behavior that would be experienced as troublesome just about everywhere, thinking that would seem strange in almost every setting. But some variation in community tolerance is exhibited for nearly all behavior that would eventually be regarded as clinically psychotic.

All phenomena have to be mentally conceptualized before they can be understood. We see behavior around us all the time; it does not "make sense" until we sort it out with the assistance of some notions of how the world is ordered. Most of us do not "see" mental illness as such because we look at behavior, for the most part, in terms of misleading stereotypes. And we do not "see" the psychosis of intimates for other reasons as well: We are genuinely motivated not to do so.

In a study of the wives of men who were eventually committed to mental institutions, the basic question was asked, "How were the disorders of illness interpreted and tolerated?" How did these men "come to be recognized by other family members as needing psychiatric help?" The concern of the researchers was with "the factors which led to the reorganization of the wife's perception of her husband from a *well* man to a man who is mentally sick" (Yarrow et al., 1955, p. 12). The answer is that when and how "behavior becomes defined as problematic appears to be a highly individual matter." The subjective beginnings of this perception, these authors write, "are seldom localized in a single strange or disturbing reaction on the husband's part but rather in the piling up of behavior and feelings" (p. 16). The husband's behavior must be, they say, "*organized as a problem*" (emphasis mine). The wife's initial reactions to her husband's strange and troublesome behavior float around in a sea of "fog and uneasiness." Eventually, she begins to "see" that something is wrong. Why? "In some instances, it is when the wife can no longer manage her husband . . . ; in others, when she cannot explain

his behavior." Her "level of tolerance for his behavior," they speculate, "is a function of her specific personality needs and vulnerabilities, her personal and family value systems and the social supports and prohibitions regarding the husband's symptomatic behavior" (p. 18). In other words, being regarded as mentally ill is variable and not dependent solely on one's "symptoms," but on a host of secondary or contingent factors. If these factors are present, one's intimates will "see" one's mental illness; if they are absent, they may very well *not* regard one as mentally ill. Note, however, this is not the same thing as saying that the designation, mentally ill, is assigned randomly, since all the persons in this study who were designated as mentally ill displayed the appropriate symptomology. Contingent factors can delay or speed up the recognition of mental illness, but, in most cases, they cannot create such a judgment out of whole cloth.

There are several factors that "make it difficult for the wife to recognize and accept"—in other words, to regard or *label*—"the husband's behavior in a mental-emotional-psychiatric framework. Many cross-currents seem to influence this process." One is the husband's behavior itself; it is, the authors write, a "fluctuating stimulus. . . . He is not worried and complaining all of the time. His delusions and hallucinations may not persist. His hostility toward the wife may be followed by warm attentiveness. She has, then, the problem of deciding whether his 'strange' behavior is significant. The greater saliency of one or the other of his responses at any moment of time depends in some degree upon the behavior sequence which has occurred most recently" (Yarrow et al., 1955, p. 21). The nature and quality of the relationship between husband and wife also impinge on her judgment; their ability to communicate with one another also influences how she sees his behavior and what she thinks of it. In addition, it is threatening to the wife to look upon her husband as "crazy": It is possible for her to draw the conclusions that she is, somehow, *responsible* for it, clearly, a painful thought. In addition, she may visualize the next few years as the wife of a crazy person, and reject, suppress, and fight against the image because, again, it is too painful to consider.

These women adopted several coping strategies to deal with the anxiety stirred up by such a consideration. One was *normalization:* The husband's behavior "is explained, justified, or made acceptable by seeing it also in herself or by assuring herself that the particular behavior occurs again and again among persons who are not ill" (p. 22). A second coping mechanism is to *attenuate* the seriousness of the behavior momentarily—to discount partly or underplay the degree of strangeness of it. She may also *balance* acceptable with unacceptable behavior, to see both "strange" and "normal" behavior displayed by her husband and come up with the conclusion that he is not seriously disturbed. A last line of defense is outright *denial* that her husband could be emotionally ill (p. 23).

Looking at the other side of the coin, three sociologists studying the *husband's* perceptions of his *wife's* disturbing, bizarre behavior conclude: "Becoming a mental patient is not a simple and direct outcome of 'mental illness.' . . . Persons who are, by clinical standards, grossly disturbed, severely impaired in their functioning, and even overly psychotic, may remain in the community for long periods without being 'recognized' as 'mentally ill.' . . . It is clear that becoming a patient is a socially structured event." There is a "monumental capacity of family members. . . . to overlook, minimize, and explain away the evidence of profound disturbance in an intimate." With regard to mental illness specifically, there is a "high tolerance for deviance" in many families. An informal judgment of a family member as mentally ill is suppressed in the minds of the others until the problems they encounter become "unmanageable" (Sampson et al., 1962).

The dynamics of this denial process are instructive because they contradict the "hard" labeling position, as Gove (1975a) points out. While Scheff correctly argues that most "residual rule-breaking" is denied (1966, p. 51), as we might expect from knowing the dynamics of mental illness labeling among intimates, he further assumes that *if* it is denied, ignored, or rationalized *it will go away*. Here we have persons who are *not* labeled by others—who, in fact, *deny* the intimate's mental disorder—who nonetheless go on to manifest increasingly more serious symptoms. The condition seems to have arisen *independent* of labeling—by intimates, at any rate. Hospitalization eventually took place in these studies in spite of the absence of the initial absence of labeling. Although Scheff denies the significance of these studies (1974a, 1974b), his argument remains unconvincing. The denial of mental illness by intimates shows us that labeling cannot possibly be a cause of disordered symptoms, nor does it appear to stabilize a person's illness "career." The labeling process is certainly an aspect of the mental illness picture, but it does not seem to play the role that the "hard" labeling model insists it plays.

On Being Sane in Insane Places

"If sanity and insanity exist, how shall we know them?" Psychologist and law professor David Rosenhan decided to answer the question by having eight normal or "sane" persons, including himself, take part in an experiment. A "varied group" of people included three psychologists, a psychiatrist, a pediatrician, a painter, a full-time homemaker, and a graduate student; three were women, five were men. They "gained secret admission" to 12 different mental hospitals around the country by complaining of hearing hallucinatory voices which said "empty," "hollow," and "thud." All but one were admitted with a diagnosis of schizophrenia. (That one was diagnosed as a manic-depressive.) Once admitted, the pseudopatients acted normally, that is, did not simulate any symptoms of mental illness or abnormality. No psychiatric staff detected that these pseudopatients were normal; they were hospitalized for an average of 19 days, and were released with a diagnosis of schizophrenia "in remission," that is, without signs of mental illness. Rosenhan's conclusion is that psychiatry "cannot distinguish the sane from the insane" (1973). Clearly, his view is extremely critical of the medical and psychiatric approaches toward mental illness and it supports some version of the constructionist or labeling theory.

Rosenhan's study has received a great deal of attention, the bulk of it favorable. A review of 31 psychology textbooks published only three years after the experiment was published found that 15 cited the article, 12 of them favorably (Spitzer, 1976). In addition, most of the articles that appeared in medical, mental health, and psychology journals commenting on the experiment had positive things to say. The media, too, gave the Rosenhan study a great deal of attention and overwhelmingly favorable coverage, in large part, said one critic, because "it said something that many were delighted to hear." This single study, this critic stated, "is probably better known to the lay public than any other study in the area of psychiatry in the last decade" (Spitzer, 1976, p. 459).

Not all the attention paid to "On Being Sane in Insane Places" has been favorable, however. *The Journal of Abnormal Psychology* devoted its volume 33, April 1976 issue to comments on Rosenhan's piece; most were critical. Robert Spitzer (1975, 1976), a psychiatrist and co-preparer of and consultant to several editions of the American Psychiatric Association's *Diagnostic and Statistical Manual of Mental Disorders*, is perhaps the most articulate and outspoken of Rosenhan's critics. He sees the experiment and the article which summarized it as "pseudoscience presented as science"—prompting a diagnosis of "logic, in remission" (1975, p. 442). Why?

"One hardly knows where to begin," says Spitzer (1975, p. 443). The study "immediately becomes confused" on terminology. As Rosenhan should know (he is a professor of both psychology and the law), the terms "sane" and "insane" are legal, not psychiatric concepts. The central issue for the law (inability to distinguish right from wrong) "is totally irrelevant" to the study, which is concerned with whether psychiatrists can detect a psychiatric condition. But let's assume that Rosenhan is referring to mental disorder, not "insanity." The fact is that the pseudopatient *simulated mental illness* in gaining admission to a mental hospital. Said another critic, "If I were to drink a quart of blood and . . . come to the emergency room of any hospital vomiting blood," the chances are, I would be labeled and treated as having a bleeding peptic ulcer." But "I doubt that I could argue convincingly that medical science does not know how to diagnose that condition" (Kety, 1974, p. 959). The fact is that these pseudopatients claimed to present symptoms of schizophrenia, and that is how they were diagnosed. What reason did the admitting psychiatrists have to doubt the genuineness of the stated symptoms?

For Rosenhan, the fact that no one detected the pseudopatients as "sane" and they were released with a diagnosis of "in remission" was significant; this means, he said, that in the judgment of the hospital, they were neither sane, nor had they been sane at any time. Spitzer argues exactly the reverse: that the fact that these patients were discharged "in remission" indicates that the psychiatric profession is able to detect mental disorder. The fact is that the diagnosis "in remission" indicates that patients are free from any signs of mental illness, which characterizes these cases in a nutshell. It is an *extremely rare* diagnosis, appearing, in one hospital, only once in 100 discharges; in a check of 12 hospitals, 11 *never* used the diagnosis, and in the remaining hospital, in only seven percent of its discharges. Says Spitzer, "we must marvel" at the fact that in Rosenhan's study, the 11 psychiatrists who discharged the pseudopatients "all acted so rationally as to use at discharge . . . a category that is so rarely used with real schizophrenic patients" (1975, p. 445). *Not one* use any of the descriptions that were available to them that would have demonstrated Rosenhan's point far more effectively: "still psychotic," "probably still hallucinating but denies it now," "loose associations," or "inappropriate affect" (p. 445).

Spitzer admits that "there are serious problems with psychiatric diagnosis, as there are with other medical diagnosis" (p. 451). However, diagnosis is *not* so poor "that it cannot be an aid in the treatment of the seriously disturbed psychiatric patient" (p. 451). But, this critic of Rosenhan's experiment says, a correct interpretation of "On Being Sane in Insane Places" contradicts the author's conclusions. "In the setting of a psychiatric hospital," argues Spitzer, "psychiatrists are remarkably able to distinguish the 'sane' from the 'insane'" (p. 451).

THE EPIDEMIOLOGY OF MENTAL ILLNESS

Epidemiology is the study of the distribution of diseases in the population. Psychiatry makes the assumption that the distribution of mental disorders can be determined in much the same way as can the distribution of physical diseases. The field of psychiatric epidemiology is based on the idea that there is, or can be, a "true" rate or prevalence of mental disorder, just as there is a "true" rate of cancer or AIDS. Clearly, this is an essentialist assumption, that is, that mental disorder is a concrete entity on whose reality all reasonable and informed observers can agree. The constructionist, in contrast, seeing mental disorder as a socially determined judgment, does not make the assumption that a "true" rate or prevalence of mental illness can be determined. Instead, constructionists are interested in how mental disorder is conceptualized and defined, how certain categories in the population come to be *designated* as having higher or lower rates of mental disorder, and what extra-psychiatric factors influence rates of institutionalization.

All epidemiologists agree that measuring mental disorder in the population, or in certain segments of the population, is problematic. The issue of how mental disorder is diagnosed and determined for the purposes of an epidemiological study has filled a substantial number of very fat tomes. The rate of admissions to mental hospitals has been used as one measure or index of mental disorder in the population and categories in the population. However, we all recognize that there are many factors which make it likelier that some persons, and persons in certain categories, will end up in a mental hospital than others, holding mental condition constant. Some conditions cause a great deal of trouble for others, while for other conditions, the mentally disordered person suffers in isolation; clearly, the first is more likely to be hospitalized than the second. Some people live among groups and categories who consider mental hospitalization a viable option only under extreme circumstances; others look to institutionalization much more quickly and readily, upon signs of relatively minor abnormality or dysfunction. The point is that there is a huge noninstitutionalized segment of the population who *would be* diagnosed as mentally disordered were they to be evaluated by a psychiatrist. Because of problems such as these, another measure of mental disorder has been developed: a diagnostic interview schedule, which presumably can determine mental condition in a sample of respondents. Over the years, different interview schedules have been used, and somewhat different findings have been obtained. Still, many experts believe that over time, these research instruments are becoming increasingly accurate. Currently, a huge ongoing study, the Epidemiological Catchment Area Program survey, is measuring mental health and disorder in a random sample of the non-institutionalized population at large (Kessler et al., 1994).

A large number of studies have been conducted that have reached conclusions concerning the differential proneness of the groups and categories in the population to mental illness or disorder. Most sociologists believe that specific social processes are related to mental disorder and that these processes are more characteristic of certain groups than others. What characteristics are most important? How do members of these social categories fare with respect to mental health and disorder? Perhaps the most basic and often-studied characteristics studied by psychiatric epidemiologists have been *sex* or *gender*, *marital status*, and *socioeconomic status*.

Gender: Men versus Women

It is not clear that there is a consistent relationship between sex or gender and a crude, unidimensional, undifferentiated measure of mental illness. Reviews of the literature (for instance, Dohrenwend and Dohrenwend, 1976) have revealed that some studies find that women have higher rates of mental disorder than men, while others show that men have higher rates. This is the case for two reasons.

When it comes to *surveys* of the general population, women have somewhat higher rates of mental disorder. One nationally representative study of households across the United States conducted jointly by the National Institutes of Health and the National Center for Health Statistics identified 1.94 million females and 1.32 million males as having serious mental illnesses (Center for Mental Health Services, 1992); rates of mental disorder were 20.6 million for females and 15.5 million for males. The Epidemiological Catchment Area Project survey mentioned above, which was focused on five urban centers, found rates of mental disorder of 16.6 million for females and 14.0 million for males (Reiger et al., 1988). A later study using the same research instrument, based on a more nationally representative sample, reached the same conclusion (Kessler et al., 1994). "An impressive body of evidence is now developing that holds that the number of females in the general population with mental disorders exceeds the number of males at any given period" (Cockerham, 1996, p. 160).

On the other hand, males are significantly more likely to be *admitted to mental hospitals* than females. Moreover, the ratio of males to females is increasing over time. For instance, in 1900 there were 110 males admitted to state mental hospitals for every 100 females; by 1975, this had risen to 183, and it remained between 172 and 186 between the late 1970s and the 1990s. In 1990, there were 146.6 male admissions per 100,000 males in the population and 80.3 female admissions per 100,000 females in the population (Center for Mental Health Services, 1994; Cockerham, 1996, p. 162). It is entirely possible that both essentialists and constructionists would have something to say on the subject. In fact, experts believe that this disparity is due to the conjunction of the specific *type* of mental disorder from which males are more likely to suffer (an essentialistic phenomenon) and professional stereotyping (a constructionist phenomenon). While men are strikingly more likely to fall victim to antisocial personality disorders, women are far more likely to suffer from a mood disorder, especially depression. Each of these disorders manifests itself in a strikingly different way. More specifically, the antisocial personality is highly likely to cause havoc in the lives of others—for instance, in the form of aggressiveness and violence—while depressive mood disorders are more likely to result in withdrawal and isolation. Someone who causes disruptive social and interpersonal trouble is more likely to be institutionalized than someone who withdraws.

To be plain about it, the mental disorder of men, even holding severity of disorder constant, is regarded as more disabling, threatening, and dangerous to the society than is that of women (Gove, 1972; Rushing, 1979a, 1979b). Women are regarded as more cooperative and compliant and more readily influenced by the hospital staff and, therefore, are more likely to be released (Doherty, 1978). Some researchers also feel that the social roles men and women and boys and girls are forced to play impacts on their mental health—or lack of it. Males are expected to be more aggressive, independent, and adventurous; consequently, the disorders they manifest (again, antisocial tendencies, especially toward violence) reflect that role expectation. Females are socialized to be passive, dependent, and lacking in confidence; they, too, exhibit this tendency, in extreme form, in their characteristic disorder, depression (Gove and Herb, 1974, p. 259).

It is hypothesized that there is something of a "double standard" among clinicians in the diagnosis, hospitalization, and release of mental patients with respect to gender (Cockerham, 1996, pp. 171–173; Gallagher, 1995, p. 283). Psychiatrists and clinical psychologists seem to have a lower standard of mental health for women than for men. They are more likely to diagnose mental disorder for men, other things being equal; a woman's condition would have to be more severe to warrant hospitalization, and a man's less severe, to warrant release. In addition to the nature of the symptoms (disruption and violence versus withdrawal and isolation), one hypothesis that has been put forth to explain this observed regularity is that in a sexist or patriarchal society, males are expected to perform in a society to more exacting standards. Being a man in a very achievement-oriented society is incompatible with being mentally disordered; the penalties for stepping out of line are swift and strong. On the other hand, where women are rele-gated to an inferior and dependent role, their performance in that role is met with more indulgence and leeway. It is felt by both clinicians and the general public, male and female, that a mildly psychically impaired woman can perform in an imperfect fashion and still "get by." Ironically, these sexist values result in a higher rate of mental illness labeling for men, supposedly the more powerful social category, and less for women, who are generally less powerful. As sex roles become more equalitarian, one would expect these gender disparities in diagnosis, hospitalization, and release to diminish and eventually disappear.

Marital Status

Another dimension that has been studied extensively to determine its relationship with or impact on mental health and illness is *marital status*. Among men, a very consistent finding emerges from the many studies that have been conducted: Single, never-married men are strikingly more likely to score high on every available measure of mental disorder than are married men; separated and divorced men rank somewhere in between. Two hypotheses have been advanced to account for the observed relationship. The first is that men who are married and stay married are more stable, psychologically healthy, and conventional than men who never marry—and therefore, they are less mentally disordered. The experience of marriage itself, these observers argue, has little or nothing to do with this regularity: It is only that *the kind of man* who marries who exhibits relatively few personality problems, while the man who does *not* marry is far *more likely* to exhibit those same problems. Getting married entails a certain degree of social competence to attract a spouse; men with severe mental problems are not considered desirable partners and thus, will be socially avoided by women (Rushing, 1979b). "The more symptomatic and/or ineffective an individual, the less likely [it is that] he will find a marital partner . . . , and the more likely [it is that] he will spend extended periods in the hospital" (Turner and Gartrell, 1978, p. 378). It is, in other words, "the inadequate man who is left over after the pairing has taken place" (Gallagher, 1995, p. 292).

A second hypothesis is that marriage confers a kind of immunity on a man: Married men have fewer mental problems than do bachelors because the experience of being married is conducive to a man's mental health, security, and well-being. "Marriage does not prevent economic and social problems from invading life," two researchers argue, "but apparently can help fend off the psychological assaults that such problems otherwise create" (Pearlin and Johnson, 1977, p. 714). Bachelors are more socially isolated from others; they lack the social supports and resources that married men have at their disposal. Hence, they are more likely to be psychologically vulnerable and fall victim to mental disorders. Again, whether this is a question of social selection or differential experiences, the tendency for single men to exhibit strikingly more, and more serious, symptoms of mental disorder is well documented in the literature (Cockerham, 1996, pp. 173–176; Gallagher, 1995, pp. 289–293).

This generalization does not hold in the same way for women. Some studies show single women to have the same rates of mental disorder as married women (Warheit et al., 1976), while other studies show married women to have *higher* rates of disorders (Gove, 1979b). In short, the special protection that supposedly extends to men seems to offer no special protection for women. It is even possible that the opposite is the case: Some observers argue that marriage is a stressful, anxiety-provoking, oppressive, exploitative institution, incompatible with the mental health of women (Bernard, 1982). Men have all the advantages in marriage, they feel, and thus profit from the experience; in contrast, women suffer as a result of being married because marriage is more demanding on them. It is frustrating, unsatisfying, and lacking in gratification for them (Gove, 1972). It is also possible that the social selection process that operates so strongly for men does so far less for women. That is, sexual stereotyping rejects mentally impaired men far more strongly than women (Phillips, 1964); a man who is mentally ill is seen by all women as an undesirable partner, while a woman who displays certain mental disorders may still be considered marriageable. In any case, the differences are far less strong among women than men. The evidence seems to favor few differences between married and unmarried women in mental health and illness (Warheit et al., 1976), yet the remarkable difference in the impact of marriage on mental health between men and women should strike the observer forcefully. While it is probably a bit too rash to state that in terms of mental health, marriage is good for men and bad for women, the evidence does at least suggest it may be good for men and of considerably less consequence for women. In a less patriarchal society, marriage will become more equalitarian and, possibly, equally good for both sexes.

Socioeconomic Status

Of all sociological variables, the relationship between social class or socioeconomic status (SES) and mental illness has probably been the most frequently studied. The most commonly used indicators measuring socioeconomic status are income, occupational prestige, and education. The higher someone ranks in any one or all three of these dimensions, the higher is his or her socioeconomic status or social "class," sociologists hold. Mental disorder is very closely related to socioeconomic status: The higher the SES, the lower the rate of mental disorder; the lower the SES, the higher the rate of mental disorder (Kessler et al., 1994; Cockerham, 1996, pp. 138–155; Gallagher, 1995, pp. 261–280). This holds regardless of the specific measure or indicator of SES that is used—occupational prestige, income, or education. People at the bottom of the class ladder are far more likely to suffer from psychiatric distress, especially schizophrenia, than those at the top. There are a few mental disorders that are more common toward the top of the class structure, such as obsessive-compulsive neuroses and some mood disorders, but the most serious illnesses, especially schizophrenia, are most common toward the bottom of the class structure. In dozens of studies, conducted in countries on three continents, the relationship between mental illness and SES has been studied; almost without exception, these studies find schizophrenia significantly and strikingly more likely in the lower socioeconomic strata. This generalization has been verified empirically by studies stretching back more than half a century (Faris and Dunham, 1939; Hollingshead and Redlich, 1958; Srole et al., 1962; Leighton et al., 1963).

Why should this strong inverse relationship between psychopathology and SES exist? There are at least four possible explanations.

The first stresses *types* of disorder. The kinds of disorder exhibited by lower-status persons are more likely to come to the attention of authorities than the kinds of disorders exhibited by middle- and upper-status persons. Lower-status persons are less likely to attribute their problems to a psychiatric condition, since they are more likely to feel that some stigma adheres to consultation with a "shrink" or being committed to a mental hospital. Hence, they are less likely to seek out psychiatric assistance voluntarily. Lower-status persons are most likely to come to the attention of psychiatric authorities as a result of referral by the police or a social worker. In contrast, upper- and middle-status persons are more likely to be referred by relatives or a private physician. A great deal of lower-status mental disorders, especially among men, manifest themselves in the form of "antisocial" behavior, particularly violence, which is likely to attract the attention of agents of formal social control such as the police. This explanation does not say that lower SES persons are more mentally disordered than middle- and upper-SES persons overall so much as it focuses on how certain conditions, differentially distributed by social class, intersect with the social structure.

The second is the constructionist explanation. Some observers have argued that this strong inverse relationship between SES and mental disorder may be due to class bias and the labeling process. Middle-class psychiatrists find lower-class behavior troublesome and are more likely to label it disordered than the behavior of middle-class persons (Wilkinson, 1975). There is something of a built-in bias in psychiatric diagnosis against lower-class subculture and lower-class persons. Mental health is judged by a middle-class yardstick; lower-class values and behavior are more likely to be regarded as disordered by the psychiatric profession, composed, as it is, of persons who are toward the middle or near the top of the social class ladder. It seems almost unarguable that class bias plays a role in psychiatric diagnosis. Nonetheless, this explanation cannot be the whole story, since much of the behavior of the psychiatrically disordered is deemed undesirable by members of *all* social classes. Characteristically, the lower-class person comes to psychiatric attention as a result of being troublesome to, and being reported by, other lower-class persons.

A third hypothesis attempting to explain why mental disorder is more heavily located at the bottom reaches of the SES continuum focuses on the greater *stress* experienced by persons located there. Economic deprivation, poverty, occupational instability, and unemployment are strongly related to psychological impairment (Liem and Liem, 1978). As a result of having to deal with an economically deprived existence and coping with this depriva-

tion, the lower-status person suffers a higher level of emotional stress and consequently is more vulnerable to a psychiatric breakdown (Kessler, 1979). The pressure of daily living under deprived circumstances becomes overwhelming; problems that cannot be solved mount, become unmanageable, and force the person into a break with reality (Cockerham, 1996, p. 154). There is a great deal of evidence supporting the "social stress" hypothesis of mental illness.

A fourth hypothesis that attempts to explain the strong inverse relationship between SES and mental disorder is the *social selection* or the *drift* hypothesis. This theory argues that social class is a *consequence* rather than a *cause* of mental illness. The mentally disordered are incapable of achieving a higher position on the SES hierarchy *because* they are mentally disordered (Dunham, 1965). Members of the lower class who are mentally disordered are either stuck there or have drifted there because their mental disorder prevents them from achieving a higher position. Their disorder retards their social mobility (Harkey, Miles, and Rushing, 1976). The social stress and the drift hypotheses are not necessarily contradictory or mutually exclusive; one could operate in a given case, and the other in another case. However, though there is some validity to both the stress and the drift theories, it is likely that social class contributes more to mental disorder than mental disorder contributes to social class (Fox, 1990; Link et al., 1986; Cockerham, 1996, p. 151).

CHEMICAL TREATMENT OF MENTAL ILLNESS

By the 1950s, it had become clear to psychiatrists who worked with mental patients that conventional therapy was not working; in the treatment of the most serious mental disorders, especially schizophrenia, psychiatrists "functioned mainly as administrators and custodians" (Berger, Hamburg, and Hamburg, 1977, p. 264). In 1952 in France, and in the United States in 1954, a drug was first used that seemed to show some promise in reducing the most blatant, florid, and troublesome symptoms of institutionalized schizophrenic mental patients. Bearing the chemical name chlorpromazine and the trade name Thorazine, it belonged to a major type of psychoactive drugs that are regarded as having an *antipsychotic* effect. Antipsychotics do not produce a high or intoxication, they are not used recreationally, and are not sold illegally on the street. Nearly all the use of the antipsychotics is legal, licit prescription use for the purpose of controlling mental illness. Antipsychotics in addition to Thorazine include Mellaril, Compazine, Stelazine, and Haldol.

It is likely that experts would say that the two most dramatic changes that have taken place in the United States since the 1950s with respect to mental illness are the degree to which antipsychotics are administered to the mentally disordered and, correlatively, the number of patients who are in residence in mental hospitals. There is some controversy concerning the role that antipsychotics have played in depopulating the mental hospitals; some observers argue that the antipsychotics were less a cause than an opportunity (Gronfein, 1985), while others hold to a more directly pharmacological explanation (Pollack and Taube, 1975, p. 49). Regardless of the exact mechanism, the fact is that in 1955, there were nearly 560,000 patients in residence in public mental hospitals; this figure dropped almost every year until, by the 1990s, it was 80,000. This decline is not due to the number of *admissions* to mental hospitals, which actually increased from 178,000 in 1955 to 385,000 in 1970, and then declined to about 255,000 in 1992. The fact is that length of stay has declined sharply, from six months in 1955 to 15 days in 1992. (Data are supplied by the National Institute of Mental Health.) As a result of much quicker discharges, mental hospitals are emptying out. Regardless of the precise timing and the causal mechanism of this change, it is impossible to argue that it could have come about in the absence of the administration of antipsychotics to schizophrenic mental patients. Roughly 85 percent of all patients in public mental hospitals are being administered some form of antipsychotic medication.

When the drug was initially introduced, Thorazine was described as having the following effects on agitated, manic, schizophrenic patients: The drug, an observer wrote, "produces marked quieting of the motor manifestations. Patients cease to be loud and profane, the tendency to hyperbolic [that is, exaggerated] association is diminished, and the patient can sit still long enough to eat and take care of normal physiological needs" (Goldman, 1955). The emotional withdrawal, hallucinations, delusions, and other patterns of disturbed thinking, paranoid, belligerence, hostility, and "blunted affect"

of patients are significantly reduced (Veteran's Administration, 1970, p. 4). As a result of the use of the antipsychotics, patients exhibit fewer and less dramatic symptoms of psychosis, become more manageable, and as a result, have permitted hospitals to discontinue or reduce such ineffective or dangerous practices as hydrotherapy and lobotomies. And, as a result of the administration of these drugs, hospitals have, in the words of one observer, been transformed from "zoo-smelling, dangerous bedlams into places fit for human beings to live and, at times, recover from psychosis" (Callaway, 1958, p. 82). By inducing a more "normal" psychological condition in patients, it has been possible to release them into the community as outpatients, with only minimal treatment and care in after-care facilities. This process is referred to as *deinstitutionalization*; unfortunately, what this has produced is a huge population of mentally ill homeless people who are subject to virtually no supervision or treatment whatsoever. (See the boxed insert on deinstitutionalization.)

Studies have shown that roughly three-quarters of all acute schizophrenics demonstrate significant improvement following the administration of antipsychotic drugs, and between 75 to 95 percent of patients relapse if their medication is discontinued (Ray and Ksir, 1996, p. 189). The use of the antipsychotic drugs is regarded as not only effective for most mental patients, but it is the least expensive of all treatment modalities. However, it should be added that although these drugs do reduce the most bizarre symptoms of schizophrenia, they are not a "cure" for mental illness. They calm the agitated, disturbed patient; the symptoms of mental illness are reduced, and patients are no longer as troublesome to others as they once were: They do not manifest their former signs of craziness. Antipsychotics permit the patient to behave in a more socially acceptable fashion; the patient's problems do not surface so painfully or disturbingly. Surely that represents progress of a sort. However, it is a stopgap measure rather than a genuine cure; no mental health specialist can be satisfied until a more substantial and more permanent treatment modality has been developed. Unfortunately, there is no prospect of this for the foreseeable future.

It is not known just why the antipsychotic drugs have this calming effect on mental patients. In any case, psychiatry has not been successful in treating seriously ill patients by means of any of its more conventional "talking" cures, such as psychoanalysis (which, in addition, is hugely resource-intensive, time-consuming, and extremely protracted). Using the antipsychotics at least keeps patients out of trouble and out of the way of "normals," and enables some to function in important social roles, such as education, marriage, and occupation. Some observers see the use of antipsychotics as a "revolution" in the field of psychiatry (Gove, 1975a, p. 245). Others (Townsend, 1980, p. 272) are more cautious and see the change not as a genuine treatment, but merely as the suppression of troublesome, disruptive behavior.

The antipsychotics are not addictive and very rarely result in lethal overdoses. However, there are some serious side effects that are experienced by many patients with the administration of these drugs, including abnormal, involuntary, and sometimes bizarre movements of the tongue, lips, and cheeks, facial tremors, rigidity, and a shuffling gait. These symptoms can be treated with a separate type of drug, the anti-Parkinsonian drugs. Patients also complain of feeling "doped up. " At higher, often therapeutic doses their responses are often sluggish, they tend to be less acute mentally than usual, display less interest in external stimuli, including other people, and are slower in arousal and response. Thus, the reduction of the socially and culturally bizarre and unacceptable behavior and thinking of mental patients is bought at a not inconsiderable price.

Deinstitutionalization

In 1961, the Joint Commission on Mental Illness submitted a report which criticized warehousing mental patients in huge, dehumanizing, impersonal, and ineffective publicly funded asylums. The report suggested that smaller facilities should be maintained in local communities which care for the mentally ill on a more personal and humane basis. In 1963, President John F. Kennedy signed federal legislation into law mandating local community care facilities for the mentally ill (Mechanic, 1989). Any complex and large-scale change is likely to be a product of many actors and a variety of motives. Still, the desire to improve the lives of mental patients must be counted among the original reasons for deinstitutionalization—releasing the mentally ill from large hospitals into the community. In addition, some politicians reasoned, these asylums were extremely expensive to maintain (not to mention ineffective). Thus, community care facilities would save the taxpayer a great deal of money. And thirdly, as we saw, starting in the mid-1950s, psychiatric medicine possessed an inexpensive and seemingly effective treatment modality at its disposal: psychotropic drugs. Thus, as we've seen, within a few short years, the mental hospitals were practically emptied of patients. By the mid-1970s, only the most untreatable patients remained in public mental hospitals.

Unfortunately, things did not go as these early idealists planned. The war in Vietnam (which United States troops entered in 1961 and departed from in 1975) drained an almost unimaginably huge proportion of resources from the public coffers. And President Richard Nixon (1969–1974) proved to be hostile to the idea of community mental health; in 1972, he announced plans to phase out federal support for its programs. Though partially restored, Presidents Ronald Reagan (1981–1989) and George Bush (1989–1993) continued to put the axe to federal support for local halfway houses and treatment centers.

The upshot of these cuts was that the mentally ill were often released into the community with little more than a vial of pills and a prescription for more. Some lived with relatives (many of whom were eventually ejected), while others were simply on their own. A high proportion gravitated to low-income areas in the community where disorganization and violence are common. Hundreds of thousands became homeless. (Experts estimate that roughly one-third of America's homeless are released former mental patients.) Half of all mental patients released into the community are reinstitutionalized within a year. While the majority of released mental patients prefer living in the community, even under adverse conditions, to life in a mental ward, the fact is that most do not receive the kind of care they need—the kind of care that was envisioned in the idealistic sixties. Meanwhile, city streets have become "open mental wards" (Goleman, 1986). We see the mentally ill on the streets of our cities—and even in smaller communities—wandering into traffic, looking wild-eyed and disheveled, screaming incomprehensible phrases to no one in particular. They have been dumped there, transferred from the asylum to the streets, the victims of massive budget cuts. The system has failed to help them; they are "a silent witness to the heartlessness and befuddlement that has created no better alternative for them" than the street (Goleman, 1986, p. C1).

DEVIANCE AND MENTAL DISORDER: AN OVERVIEW

Mental disorder has both parallels and dissimilarities with other forms of deviant behavior which we encountered in earlier chapters, such as drug use, homicide, and homosexuality. (Some forms of deviance are also regarded as "behavioral disorders," such as drug dependence.) On one hand, both deviance and mental disorder represent a departure from the normative order. Being regarded as mentally abnormal by others is usually a result of breaking the rules of the society; one behaves in a way that is considered odd, eccentric, bizarre, and/or troublesome. One says things that others regard as "crazy," one interacts with others in ways that make them feel uncomfortable. So, to the extent that behavioral manifestations of mental illness result in normative violations, the disruption of smooth social relations, and attracting a socially undesirable label, clearly they represent a form or type of deviant behavior.

Public attitudes toward the mentally ill are more complicated than they are toward the deviant. Although the mentally disordered may do what are regarded as "immoral" things, this is not necessary to any definition of mental illness. Toward the deviant, the dominant emotion is often outrage, anger, hostility. In contrast, the mentally ill attract a feeling more like condescension and pity. Most conventional persons wish to punish the deviant, but keep the mentally ill out of sight and out of mind. The deviant is feared more for the harm we think he or she can do to us, to society as a whole, or to our version of truth or morality. In contrast, we do not take the mentally ill person's version of reality as a threat to our own, but he or she is feared for reminding us of what we could become. Deviants are seen through two contradictory principles: They are sick and act out of compulsive motives, and they are immoral, act out of free will, and are responsible for their actions. In contrast, the mentally ill person is seen as lacking a free will and hence, not responsible for his or her actions.

In addition, deviance is nearly always located in specific actions, that is, in clearly locatable behavioral and attitudinal spheres. One is not *a* deviant generally; few people even use the term. One is a deviant in a specific area of life—sex, drug use, politics, harming others, and so on. The label of mental illness is almost unique in that it is free-floating, eminently generalizable. One is considered mentally ill not because of having done anything in a delimited area of life, but because one has done many things in many areas that are supposedly manifestations of a psychiatric disorder, dysfunction, or disorganization. This is true of practically no other form of deviant behavior.

The major thrust of psychiatric writings published in past decades has been in the direction of adopting the medical model of mental illness, that is, regarding it as perfectly analogous to, or literally and concretely, a manifestation of a physical pathology. The implication of this model is that the mental patient should be treated in much the same way as the sufferer of a physical disease, both by clinicians and the lay public. The social stigma that adhered to the mental patient in the past is regarded in some quarters as an archaic remnant of the past. Being regarded as crazy, this view holds, does not cause others to view the person as deviant but instead will "redefine the deviance in a fairly positive way." Commitment to a mental hospital "tends to shift the person's label from that of being obnoxious and intolerable to that of being mentally ill and in need of help" (Gove, 1975a, p. 245). Insofar as this is true, *mental illness is not a form of deviance.* To the extent that the public sees mental disorder on a par with physical illness, qualitatively no different from, and attracting no more stigma than contracting cancer, and regards the mentally ill as not responsible for their actions, it is not a form of deviance. But remember, earlier in this century, the cancer patient suffered some degree of stigma, and even today, certain diseases, such as AIDS and leprosy are considered loathsome, so physical disease is not always exclusively physical. Even for some physical diseases, the sufferer is seen in some social circles as a deviant.

But consider this: Being physically ill in our society does harbor a dimension of deviance. By that I mean that it represents a departure from being self-reliant, taking care of one's obligations; it is a failure to be healthy, productive, and "normal" (Parsons, 1951, pp. 428–479; Freidson, 1970b, pp. 205–223). Illness, then, is a violation of a number of strongly held values. To a degree, being mentally disordered will always be regarded as a form of deviance in the *same* sense that physical illness is. Falling down on the job, being unable to cope, failing to meet one's obligations, and disrupting interpersonal relations will always be despised in a society that values performance and achievement. Being mentally ill emphasizes one's incapacity and incompetence. As such, it will always be looked down upon.

SUMMARY

Of all deviant phenomena, mental disorder comprises the most diverse and miscellaneous category. Mental illness is a condition that characteristically manifests itself in actions, mental patterns, or speech utterances that are deemed bizarre and deranged by both clinicians and the lay public. Even the behaviors associated with this condition are vastly more diverse than any other deviant behavioral category, however broad it may be, that we have discussed so far.

In the fourth edition of its *Diagnostic and Statistical Manual of Mental Disorders*, the American Psychiatric Association (1994) defines mental disorder as a syndrome or condition that is associated with distress, disability, or an increased risk of "suffering, death, pain, disability, or an important loss of freedom." Three hundred disorders are listed; however, DSM-IV does not provide a framework or a theoretical model for disorders, but a listing of them and a description for each of the symptoms that the clinician is likely to encounter in practice. Schizophrenia (a thought disorder entailing hallucinations, delusions, and disorganized speech) and mood disorders (particularly depression) are two of the most commonly encountered and most often studied mental disorders.

Experts approach the subject of mental disorder through the lens of several different perspectives. *Essentialism* is the view that mental disorder is a real, concrete "thing" the observer can identify, locate, and explicate, much as one can pick an apple off a tree. Essentialists examine issues such as etiology (a study of the causes of mental disorder), epidemiology (a study of how mental disorder is distributed in the population), and the effectiveness of treatment. "Strict," "hard," or "radical" essentialism sees mental disorder as the manifestation of a disease, much like cancer; in its most extreme form, essentialism regards the condition as an actual, literal disease, that is, a product of biophysical pathology. *Constructionism*, in contrast, focuses not on the condition but on how it is regarded, thought about, talked about, and dealt with. Here, treatment is looked at not as a means to a cure but as a social enterprise which is itself to be explained and understood. The "hard," "strict,"

or "radical" constructionists deny the existence of mental disorder in the real or concrete world and focus exclusively on judgments of and reactions to a "putative" or so-called condition. Softer or more moderate constructionists either set aside the question of the reality of mental disorder, or agree that it exists and make comparisons between such judgments and reactions and the condition itself. Constructionists emphasize contingency (factors other than condition influence judgments about mental disorder), stigma (judgments of mental disorder are stigmatizing), and the conceptual creation of mental disorder through labels.

Labeling theory is a perspective distinct from constructionism. While constructionism focuses on the *conceptual* creation of mental disorder through judgments and reactions, labeling theory focuses on its *literal* creation through these processes. It is a perspective that argues that being labeled and treated *as* mentally ill is the primary *cause* of mental illness. Labeling theory straddles essentialism and constructionism, in that the *initial* or *primary* judgments about mental condition are made to some degree independent of "true" mental condition; they act to *create* a true mental disorder. In the past decade or so, a "modified" labeling perspective has arisen which adopts bits and pieces of the approach but not all of its particulars. It emphasizes the stigma of being labeled as mentally ill, the contingency involved in applying such labels, and the fact that treatment is often effective.

Families of the mentally disordered typically attempt to "normalize" or explain away the symptoms of a mentally disordered member. Mental disorder has sometimes been referred to as "conventional" deviance in that it takes a great deal of evidence and many episodes of disordered behavior by a family member, entailing substantial trouble and suffering, before a spouse, parents, or children will regard him or her as mentally disordered and in need of treatment.

Some sociologists study the epidemiology of mental disorder. Three of the most often studied characteristics that correlate with mental illness are gender, marital status, and socioeconomic status.

While women are more likely to be diagnosed as mentally ill on surveys, men are much more likely to be institutionalized. It is possible that the precise conditions that men are more likely to manifest (for instance, character or personality disorder, which often leads to violence) cause more trouble for others and result in more official intervention and hence, psychiatric labeling and commitment. In contrast, the conditions that are more prevalent among women (for instance, depression) often result in withdrawal and isolation and hence, no official notice.

Married men are significantly less likely to be disordered than single men. This may be because marriage offers a kind of immunity or psychological protection for them; they receive support in times of trouble. It may also be because men who are mentally disordered can't get married, since they make undesirable marital partners. With women, the picture is not so clear-cut. Many studies show no differences in mental disorder between married and single women, and some studies actually show married women to have higher rates of disorder than single women. It could be that marriage is more stressful for women than for men, or it could be that disordered women are deemed not nearly so undesirable as marital partners by men than disordered men are by women.

Socioeconomic status (SES) is almost certainly the single social characteristic that correlates most strongly with mental disorder. Studies conducted in the past and those conducted today, and studies around the world as well as in the United States agree: The lower the SES, the higher the rate of mental disorder, most specifically, schizophrenia, regarded as one of the most common, and perhaps the most serious, of all the disorders. Why? At least four explanations come to mind. Personality disorder, which is common among lower-SES men, frequently results, as we saw, in official and therapeutic intervention, whereas the disorders most characteristic of middle- and upper-middle status persons are less troublesome and intrusive to the society. Second, labeling may play a role: Middle-class psychiatrists may be quicker to judge pathology in lower-class persons, particularly males. Third, lower-class life is more stressful than middle-class life and hence, more likely to lead to a psychiatric breakdown. And fourth, the mental condition of the mentally disordered *precedes* achievement on the social class ladder and inhibits that achievement; hence, they "drift" into the lower class.

In 1954, psychoactive chemicals began to be used on a widespread basis to treat the mentally ill. That year, there were over half a million patients in publicly funded mental hospitals, and their average length of stay was six months. While the use of drugs was not the only cause, it was certainly instrumental in emptying out insane asylums. Today, there are only 80,000 patients, and their average length of stay is two weeks. Antipsychotic drugs make schizophrenic patients less agitated, more manageable, and their symptoms less bizarre. They also produce a number of undesirable side-effects. The "deinstitutionalization" of these patients has resulted in relatively little medical care for many of them, and a very high proportion of those who lack family or social supports become homeless and live on the street, often neglecting to take their medication. They have been "dumped" there in large part because society is unwilling to pay for their shelter and an adequate system of halfway houses or treatment facilities that would alleviate the problem of the huge numbers of mentally ill homeless street people.

ACCOUNT: ENCOUNTER WITH MENTAL ILLNESS

The contributor of this account is a 40-year-old college professor.

One year I was a member of the Graduate Committee of my department. Our job was to review the applications of candidates applying for admission to graduate school in our department. One application caught my eye; let's call him John Spencer. John had excellent grades from a first-rate undergraduate institution, and his Graduate Record Exams were top-notch. The thing was, he attended college off and on. He was in his thirties and had spent 10 years or so of his adult life in mental institutions. In the essay he wrote accompanying his application, he said he didn't want to be stigmatized for having been institutionalized. Reading it, I could only agree; I argued that we should admit him. He will make an excellent student, I said; we shouldn't be guilty of discriminating against him for his past problems. Well, the rest of the committee seemed to be persuaded, and we admitted him. He enrolled in our graduate program the following fall.

John was quiet for a couple of months. And then things started to happen. He took one course with an especially tough professor who handed back a paper he had written with critical comments all over it. John read the comments and flew into a rage right in the classroom. He ripped the paper in half, threw it into the trash, and grabbed the professor by the shoulders, screaming "What right do you have to judge me, you smug, self-righteous bastard?!" The other students in the class were horrified, but they managed to separate John from the professor and escorted him away so that he could cool down.

That clued everyone into the fact that John was not in complete control. I doubt if very many people in the department knew his psychiatric past before then, but many of them found out about it after. I guess people started becoming a bit leery of him. One of John's problems was that the medication he took for his illness made him stupid if he took too much of it, but if he took too little, he was smart, but crazy. The precise dose at which he was both smart and sane was extremely difficult to find and maintain. Anyway, a few weeks went by. John was in the habit of attaching himself socially to any one who was the least bit attentive to him or who didn't reject him. Usually they were women. He'd call them incessantly and eventually annoy them and alienate them to the point that they didn't want to have anything to do with him, and then he'd have to search out a new victim.

His latest companion was a fellow graduate student, a woman, and, like him, she was in her thirties. Her name was Katherine. One day, he asked her for a certain article, and she stuck it in his mailbox at school. It had the word "deviant" in the title. He pulled it out of his mailbox and read the title. Perhaps he got it into his head that somehow, Katherine called him a deviant, who knows? A few minutes later, he was in the hallway talking with a professor. Katherine rounded a corner a few feet away from where John was talking with the professor and began walking toward him. He spotted her, ran over to her, and punched her in the jaw; she slumped to the floor, unconscious. Everyone in the vicinity got very nervous and excited and escorted him away from the area. Matters had suddenly be come very serious.

Katherine insisted, for her safety, that John be kept away from the department. All the members of the department had numerous meetings with the campus psychologist and psychiatrist to determine the wisest policy to follow with respect to John's outbursts. The department wished to keep John in the graduate program, but without upsetting any of the other students, who understandably didn't want to be assaulted for some obscure reason. We sent him a memorandum that spelled out the conditions under which he could remain a student in our program. Some of them sound like simple rules for everyday behavior. The memo read approximately along the following lines.

1. You will take courses on a tutorial basis. The course discussions will be confined strictly to academic matters. You will receive individual instruction from each professor teaching your courses; you will meet with them in a room in the library.
2. You are not to come onto the floor where the department is.
3. You are not to go to the computing center, unless you are doing a specific assignment for a course: if so, you must clear it with the individual instructor.
4. You are not to attend meetings or colloquia sponsored by the department.

5. You are not to yell or scream in public places; you are not to curse, harass, or threaten any student or faculty; you are not to hit or strike any student or faculty member.
6. You are to see Dr. McTavish and Dr. Eidelman on a regular basis (as they define this regularity). You are to keep all appointments with them and take any medication they prescribe.
7. Violation of any of these regulations is grounds for dismissal from the program.

At the conclusion of one of our many meetings concerned with the subject of John Spencer, this one with the head of the campus psychological services, a fellow faculty member turned to me—the fellow who was responsible for John being admitted to the program to begin with—and asked, "Nu, Mr. Labeling Theorist?"* I shrugged my shoulders and said, "The man's crazy—what can I say?"

Unfortunately, the procedures and rules we laid down didn't work. John was unable to control his behavior, and he eventually admitted himself to a mental hospital a few weeks after this memo was sent to him. He never returned to the program. (From author's files.)

ACCOUNT: TWO BRIEF PSYCHOTIC EPISODES

The author of this account is a health professional in his late thirties.

Let me explain what it was like, going crazy. I didn't actually go crazy—I just had a couple of psychotic episodes. My experience with insanity—though it isn't called that any more, is it? These two times I knew I was cracking up, freaking out—going crazy. No matter what it's *called*, I felt as if I was going crazy. There were two times. And in each case, it lasted a few hours, no more. The first time, I was stoned on grass. After that, for over a year, I didn't touch marijuana at all. But I still freaked out again, totally straight, a year or so later, so it wasn't the pot. There was something else, and I have no idea what it was. The first time was soon after my thirty-third birthday. I wasn't raised a Christian, but any damn simpleton is aware that Jesus was nailed to the cross at the age of thirty-three. And the feeling I had at the time was

*"Nu?" is a Jewish expression that means "So? What do you have to say about this?" Labeling theory is a perspective that holds that nothing is wrong in itself; behavior is wrong only when it is defined as such—this definition often results in intensifying the behavior in question. The implication of the question was that a labeling theorist would not regard anything John did as wrong in itself, it was only the reactions of the department that made his behavior wrong.

that I was *mortal*, that I was going to die—inevitably. If not that year, then the next or—some time. Even if I lived to be a hundred—or a thousand—one day, I was going to die, my consciousness, my very *existence*, my *being*, would be obliterated from the universe. It was as inevitable as the setting of the evening sun, and there was no way on God's green earth to stop it. It would have helped if I believed in an afterlife, but I can't, it's such a fanciful, silly idea. My realization of the truth of my impending death was no longer merely on the intellectual level—it was on a gut, emotional level as well. I mean, I *felt* it, I really, *really* felt it—I didn't just think it. I knew it in my bones, in my brain cells, in the marrow of my being. It's hard to imagine an insight as terrifying as that. Horrifying—that's what it was.

The first time, I was with a woman friend and, as I said, we were smoking a few joints. We were taking a bubble bath at the time, that's when it happened. This monstrous, slimy *thing* just crawled up my back and took over. It invaded every pore of my body, it took over everything, all of me—it *was* me, totally. It just squatted there, leering and drooling at me, sinking its sharp claws into my flesh. The feeling was, it had the quality of a chemical reaction. I was crazy and I had no control over it. It was a fear, a feeling of utter, total terror—the Great Fear. All I could do was to curl up into a little ball and tell my friend to let me pull out of it. I wasn't going to be in working order for a few hours—I'd appreciate it if she would just humor me and babble and be innocuous and unobtrusive and not too demanding for a while so that I could gradually try to get wrapped up again. Well, she wasn't all that sympathetic. She said something really

stupid which, as I look back on it now, I realize that it could have freaked me out even more—like, "I think your seeds have dried up," something like that. But it didn't—whatever it was was purely chemical. It came, it settled in for a while, and it went away, regardless of what happened in the real world. It just took over—a real horror show. Imagine the most horrifying moment of your life dragged out for four or five hours, with no possibility of turning it off.

Well, as I said, it happened a year or so later, again, out of the blue, with no warning, another freak-out. Again, it lasted for four or five hours. I took a few doses of a downer I had by prescription and managed to fall asleep after a while, and when I woke up the next morning, I felt more or less normal. A transient psychosis. Twice in my life. Here today, gone tomorrow. I have no explanation for it, but, having experienced it, I know with absolute certitude that mental illness is a chemical disorder. It just settles into your body, and that's it. If you're lucky, it comes upon you and goes away, like most diseases. If you're not, it stays for as long as you live. Sometimes, you can be treated with a chemical—a drug—and most of the symptoms will go away. Sometimes, you can't. Life experiences have nothing to do with it—Freud was wrong. I'm sure of it—most of the time, it's strictly chemical. In my case, it sure as hell was. I never want to have to go through that again. I can really empathize with what the mentally ill go through. Being crazy is scary business, really scary. Imagine what it must be like to have to deal with that monster every day of your life, every moment of your existence. I shudder just thinking about it.

chapter 14

IDEOLOGICAL, ETHICAL, AND MORAL IMPLICATIONS OF STUDYING DEVIANCE

In the Preface to *Elite Deviance* (1996, p. xv), sociologist David Simon states that "scientific objectivity and questions about values are interrelated and cannot . . . be divorced from each other." In considering the interrelations between values, ideology, and morality on the one hand and "scientific objectivity" on the other, we might want to consider this statement. What does it mean? How would agreement with it show up in a researcher's and scholar's writing? What would such work look like if the statement were accepted by the author? What would it look like if the author did not accept it as true? Is the author arguing that muckraking and moralizing excuse any and all manner of factual distortion? Does it mean we have to lie if we see something that doesn't agree with our values? Does it mean that we can sweep facts under the rug because they don't agree with our values?

Simon (1996, pp. 1–2, 16, 255–259, 272, 309, 310) argues that the assassination of President John F. Kennedy was the result of a high-level government conspiracy and cover-up. No contrary evidence is presented, although it exists in abundance (Posner, 1993). Again, does holding certain "values" allow us to feel good about arguing in such a one-sided fashion? As we saw, such a flabby cliché enables us to claim that a substantial number of "political prisoners" are incarcerated in American prisons, while we can overlook the fact that China imprisons eight to 10 million inmates, working at slave labor, most of them incarcerated for political reasons (Wu, 1992, 1995–96, 1996). Ironically, Simon's position on ignoring prison abuses in China is very much in agreement with the ideological position held by corporate America, of which Simon is so critical, since there are huge profits to be made in China; by pointing out such abuses, trade agreements American corporations might make with China are endangered. In contrast, parties who favor exposing such conditions are human rights organizations, backed by the American labor movement, the latter interested in the issue because much Chinese commerce is based on slave prison labor, an unfair advantage in competition with American goods. The issue highlights a crucial point I'll emphasize shortly: the *constructed* nature of political arguments.

At the same time, it is naive to imagine that studying deviance—or any form of social behavior—is a world removed from political and ethical considerations. Whenever we do something, whether it is purchasing a certain brand of deodorant or pursuing a specific career, we are forced to think about its impact on our fellow citizens. Studying the behavior of persons who engage in behavior that is widely condemned may influence the lives of the people we study, for better or for worse. The way we look at that behavior, the way we go about conducting our investigation, what we say about our subjects, the conclusions we reach, can impact, positively or negatively, on whom we are studying. We entangle ourselves in painful ethical, political, and ideological dilemmas when we do social research generally, and research on the topic of deviance specifically.

Several years ago, in a course entitled "alcoholism and drug abuse," I was discussing the epidemiology or social distribution of alcohol consumption. I mentioned that in the United States, Irish-Americans have a higher than average rate of alcoholism and, in comparison with other nations of Europe, Ireland has a significantly higher than average rate of alcoholism. And from the back of this very large class, a student spoke up—he didn't raise his hand, but just spoke up—asking me why I was "perpetuating negative stereotypes" about the Irish. The implication of his question was that I harbored a special prejudice against the Irish. I replied by saying that first of all, half my ancestors are Irish; my father's ancestors came from the Emerald Isle. I was, in fact, proud of my Irish ancestry—why should I hold a prejudice against the land of my own ancestors? Why would I want to denigrate a people with whom I share a substantial portion of my own ancestral heritage? Secondly, I said, the point of this course is to tell the truth. The evidence points to what I just said. If you have systematic evidence that says otherwise, I'd like to see it, but it looks as if my statement is accurate—the Irish *do* tend to drink more than citizens and members of other nations and ethnic categories. Stereotypes are not necessarily false; they may contain a grain of truth. My feeling is, I continued, we have an obligation to pursue the facts wherever they may lead, even if they offend some people who might want a different version of reality. The undergraduate who asked the question later apologized for implying that I harbored a special wish to denigrate the Irish; he explained that he had felt personally offended by my discussion, since he was of Irish ancestry himself. Still, I had to insist on the independence of the validity of facts and our feelings *about* them.

Was I being naive in believing that literal, concrete truth is more important than public image? Was my student being too sensitive concerning what he took to be an insult to his ethnicity? *Should* an insult have been perceived in what I said? Is there a difference between literal truths, truths with a small "t," and larger truths—political and ideological truths?

Once, in a deviance course, I read an account by a prostitute of an experience she had with a customer. The customer had a recognizably Jewish name. After class, a student asked me why I had "given" the man a Jewish name; why didn't I call him Jones or Smith? I said I hadn't "given" the man any name—I had used the name the writer supplied which, in turn, was presumably based on the name the prostitute gave the writer. She felt I had the obligation to disguise the man's ethnicity; by permitting a Jewish name to be used, she said, I had implied that Jews are often customers of prostitutes.

Another time, also in my deviance course, I read an account of a Lebanese father murdering his daughter because she had "flirted with boys" (Goode, 1978, p. 26; de Onis, 1973). After the class, two students, who told me that they were born in a Middle Eastern country, asked me why I had read the account. (I also read accounts from the United States, Italy, and Portugal.) I said that they had happened and they were relevant to deviance, that is, they represented reactions to a certain form of behavior. They said they didn't believe the veracity of the account. Somewhat taken aback, I asked why the *Times* would publish such a news story if its editors knew that it wasn't true. They replied that the *Times* was prejudiced against the Arab world.

There are several lessons in these examples. First, political motives may be *read into* many assertions, writing, and research where they are, in fact, actually absent. Second, deciding to tell the truth straight can often embroil one in political controversy. And third, ethnicity and nationality are often the focus of ideological and political controversy; they make up, I concluded, a subject about which many observers are extremely touchy.

I am a supporter of Amnesty International, which is dedicated to helping political prisoners the world over. In the 1980s, several friends of mine informed me that they refused to support this organization because it was as dedicated to exposing brutality against political prisoners in the former Soviet Union, which they saw as a socialist society, as it was to that in capitalist and Third World nations. I strongly disagreed. My feeling was, and remains,

that imprisoning dissenters for political reasons has no place in a decent, humane society, regardless of any other political messages that might be read into raising objections to such a practice. To fail to raise a voice against injustice in the Soviet Union because that might be interpreted as support for the injustices in the United States struck me then, and still strikes me, as perverse and twisted logic.

Consider the following development. Anastasia Karakasidou, an anthropologist, conducted a study of ethnicity in Greece; she wrote a 300-page manuscript, entitled *Fields of Wheat, Rivers of Blood*, and submitted it to the Cambridge University Press. The expert review panel whose members read the book praised it and urged publication. In December 1995, Dr. Karakasidou received some surprising news: Cambridge University Press had rejected the manuscript for publication. The reasons? The book was too controversial. It argued that many residents of Macedonia, a province of the former Republic of Yugoslavia, a region which some nationalistic Greeks consider part of Greece, speak a Slavic language and consider themselves culturally and ethnically as Slavs, not Greeks. The book would offend ultra-rightist, nationalistic Greeks, and, Cambridge felt, endanger Cambridge's employees in Athens. In addition, some observers believed, it would also risk Cambridge's publishing ventures in Greece. (This tale has a happy ending: In February 1996, the University of Chicago Press offered Dr. Karakasidou a contract to publish her book.) Clearly, Macedonians either *do* or *do not* regard themselves ethnically as Slavs, they either *do* or *do not* speak a Slavic language. But, once again, Cambridge University Press was anticipating that political and ideological *implications* would be read into Dr. Karakasidou's book—implications, moreover, which she was unlikely to regard as central (Lyall, 1996).

This does represent a genuine dilemma, however: What if what one says actually *does* hurt a social category, a group? Moreover, what if this group or category is relatively powerless, one that has been victimized in the past—and may be further victimized by what one says? What should the responsible scholar or researcher do? What one decides to do in a case like this represents a painful dilemma that has to be resolved. And these examples illustrate the fact that many recent ideological and political controversies have revolved around race and ethnicity as well as sex and gender. "Are you denigrating my group, my people, my category?" seems to be the theme of a great deal of recent political and ideological discussion. At the same time, objectively true facts can *slant the truth* by presenting a one-sided view. In fact, research can be used more or less explicitly for ideological purposes. Consider the following.

Archaeology, presumably a field that is concerned with telling the truth about the past, may be used for political and ideological purposes. Narrating archaeological truth, however, may entail highlighting some truths and ignoring others. For instance, when Americans think about the history of this continent, most usually ignore the fact that Native Americans have been living here for tens of thousands of years. They speak of American history as if the continent were completely unpopulated when Europeans arrived on these shores. The fact is that some North American sites are considerably older than many of those in the Middle East. But it is in the Middle East that the political motives behind archaeological research are most evident. In Israel, most Jewish sites are two thousand or more years old; Palestinian sites tend to be, of course, less ancient. Sociologist Nachman Ben-Yehuda explained to me, in private communication, what the implications are for doing archaeological research there. When excavating an ancient site, Israeli archaeologists often scrape away and discard or set aside the Palestinian layer to enable them to expose, study, and preserve the Jewish layer. This results in a great deal of lost information. I naively asked Ben-Yehuda why Israeli archaeologists don't simply train Palestinians to study ancient remains; they could then hand the Palestinian artifacts over to them for study, keep the Israeli remains, and no information would be lost. Ben-Yehdua said that I didn't understand. This practice has a political purpose: to legitimate the land of Israel for the Jews. If Jewish settlement can be shown to have existed two or more thousand years ago, it establishes the legitimacy of the Jewish state. If Palestinian archaeologists were to publish studies on *Palestinian* remains, this would legitimate the area for Palestine, because it would establish that they, too, have ancient roots in the area. In fact, if the matter were *the other way around*, Palestinian archaeologists would dig up and preserve Palestinian artifacts and dispose of or ignore Jewish remains. Clearly, in the Middle East, a science, archaeology, has become a handmaiden to politics.

The journalist Janet Malcolm wrote a book attacking journalistic objectivity (1990). In effect, Malcolm accuses journalists of being assassins and traitors. Malcolm says: "The writer, like the murderer, needs a motive." (I assume she includes herself as a representative writer.) I would like to paraphrase that to read: "The sociologist of deviance, like the murderer, needs a motive." I don't mean by this that I endorse it completely as an empirically true statement. I mean that the *belief* that political motives are behind intellectual work has *come to be accepted as true* by a substantial proportion of sociologists including—possibly especially—sociologists of deviance. Hence, it is part of the *constructed landscape* of the field of deviance. Political motives are *attributed* to sociologists generally and sociologists of deviance specifically, motives which they don't necessarily or always hold. Observers *construct* a political analysis or narrative of certain views based in part on current political and ideological lore concerning what certain positions are supposed to mean. It's a little like a particular *code* which has cultural and linguistic meaning. It is widely believed *that* everyone has political motives for doing one or another study of deviance, *that* a particular study will, by its very nature, support one or another political position. And a certain position on a given question *by definition* indicates where one stands politically and ideologically. These beliefs are part of the commentary and debate *about* deviance. Hence, these beliefs must be examined.

One of the things that constructionism does for anyone who thinks about politics and ideology is that it *particularizes* and *historicizes* politics and ideology. That is, it makes them relative to time and place. At a given point in time, many political activists see their ideology as *right* and *true* in much the same way that mathematicians regard adding two and two and getting a total of four as being right and true: A self-evident proposition that only the wrong-headed, stupid, and ignorant see otherwise. But the interesting point is that ideologies change over time; ideologists construct their arguments differently at different times. Ideology twists and turns, it flip-flops over time. Certain positions *come to be seen* as wrong that earlier were regarded as right. And later on, once again, they may be seen as right. A position that is identified with a particular ideology at one time may later be incorporated by a rival ideological position. This is clearly a question of *the social construction of reality* and not a matter of essential truth.

For instance, to environmentalists in the 1970s, wood stoves were good; they represented the use of a natural, renewable resource for fuel. In the 1980s and 1990s, wood stoves came to be seen as bad, since they release tens of thousands of times more particulates into the atmosphere than oil or gas heat. In the 1950s and early 1960s, the cutting edge of the civil rights movement saw integration as good, positive—something to be fought for. In contrast, in the 1980s and 1990s, the most avant guard or "radical" political position among African-American intellectuals and leaders has shifted to separatism, Afrocentrism, and Black nationalism. In the early days of the AIDS crisis, homosexual spokespersons dismissed the threat of AIDS as a scare hoked up by heterosexuals to control and contain the free expression of homosexual sex. Later, the heterosexual power structure was criticized for not paying *enough* attention to AIDS because its victims were "deviants"—homosexuals and drug addicts. In the 1970s and early 1980s, an anti-crime position was identified with conservatism. It was regarded as a thinly disguised form of racism. Today, there is a growing awareness that the victims of crime are disproportionately poor and Black; thus, a number of African-American leaders and liberal and leftist politicians and intellectuals are adopting what was previously seen as a conservative position—being tough on crime. In the spring of 1994, Reverend Jesse Jackson delivered a speech at an African-American church whose main point was that Black-on-Black crime kills more victims *each year* than all the murders and lynchings by the Ku Klux Klan in its entire history. A decade ago, this statement would have been thought heresy, anathema, the wrong thing to say at that time. In the 1950s and 1960s, free speech was a liberal and radical issue; free speech was urged for unpopular ideologies, such as socialism, communism, and atheism—which conservatives wished to silence. In the 1980s and 1990s, liberals and radicals have joined in the attempt to silence free speech because *too much* freedom is regarded as threatening to relatively powerless categories, such as women, Blacks, and homosexuals.

The point is that ideologies change. Now, these changes in position are made or were made in part as a response to real-life or material conditions. Wood stoves *do* pollute the environment; Afrocentric values *are* likely to be undermined by integration and assimilation; homosexuals *are* being killed by AIDS; crime *does* hurt poor and Black victims; and so on. But just because a specific fact is true does not mean that a given political ideology

will recognize it as true. The fact is that in each era, during each historical time period, a given position is *identified* with a certain ideology. A good ideologist or follower of a given ideology is seen as having an *obligation* to hold a specific position. But, as I said, these positions change over time. They are *constructed* by a movement's or an ideology's leadership or its rank-and-file, in part as a result of changing conditions, in part as a result of the accumulation of information, in part as a result of prodding or feedback from the rank-and-file.

These twists and turns should give us pause. They tell us that political position is not simply a matter of eternal right and wrong—that is, who has the better or more correct political or ideological position. It's not always a question of which position should we, as responsible sociologists, adopt, but rather, how are these arguments constructed? How do they come to be *seen* as correct by a certain constituency or following? *Why* are they constructed one way at one time and in a very different way at another time? For our purposes right now, it's not very productive to think that political ideologies we or others hold correspond to—or depart from—some essential, absolute truths that exist out there somewhere in the universe. It is probably more productive to think of them as constructed entities that are held by actors occupying a particular position on a social and political stage, useful and possibly effective *to* certain audiences *for* certain purposes *at* a particular time.

There are at least three positions that might be adopted on the relationship of ideology to empirical research. The first might be referred to as the "naive positivistic" approach; it is possible that, as Stephen Cole says in his book *Making Science*, this position is held in its pure form by *no* practicing scientists at this or possibly any time (1992). This is the "value free" position: That values, beliefs, ideology, and politics on the one hand and the examination of empirical reality on the other are two utterly separate and independent realms. The scientist—social or natural—can set aside his or her values and study the material and social world "objectively," as it *really* and *truly* is. Anyone allowing his or her values to contaminate his or her views of reality is not worthy to be referred to as a scientist. Even though, as I said, in its purest form, hardly anyone accepts this view, it is nonetheless useful to think of a continuum, with this belief at one extreme end.

At the extreme opposite end of this continuum is

the position of the ideologically and politically "engaged" scientist—the "engaged ideologue." The individual who holds this position argues that the two realms, values and empirical fact, are inseparable. There's no use in trying to separate them; it's impossible. There's no such thing as values without facts, no such thing as facts without values. (This certainly characterizes David Simon's statement, quoted at the beginning of this chapter.) From top to bottom, from side to side, science is shot through with values. We see the world through ideologically tinted glasses. We might as well accept this basic fact, latch onto ideologically good values, and do research that *verifies* and *upholds* the good and *challenges* and *undermines* the bad. What counts is our political position and our efforts to maximize positive values in the world. Sociological work should be evaluated in terms of its political implications. In fact, to the purely ideologically engaged social scientist, it is the *only* meaningful criterion by which research should be evaluated. Good work is that which maximizes good values and helps bring about correct change. Bad work is that which threatens these values and helps keep bad conditions as they are. Said one Marxist criminologist—who may not agree with these words today—nearly a generation ago: "Social theory . . . is to serve the working class in the struggle for a socialist society. As bourgeois social theory serves the capitalist class under capitalism, socialist social theory serves the working class under socialism and assists in the transition to socialism. . . . The only purpose in knowing the world is to change it" (Quinney, 1979, pp. 419–422).

I'd like to suggest a third position, one that is very different from those of the "naive positivist" and the "engaged ideologue." It is mine, and, I believe, that of Howard S. Becker, author of "Whose Side Are We On?" (1967), as well. This position holds that *of course* political ideology influences the research one does. Ideology influences a number of scientific or research-related factors. It influences *selection of topics*, what Robert K. Merton calls "foci of attention." A scientist who studies how to make better bombs is not someone who is likely to hold ideological views that support pacifism. More generally, even holding that knowledge is good, that it's better to know than not to know—that it's better to spend time finding out what the answers are to certain questions rather than, let's say, making a lot of money—again, is an expression of values. Why is it more important to know

certain things—such as patterns of stylistic expressions in a medieval Flemish poet—than others, for instance, worldwide changes in income distribution over the past two decades. This does not mean that the findings a social or natural scientist comes up with are false simply because they are motivated by a certain political position. In fact, the empirical truth or falsity of a particular position is *independent* of the political motives behind it. But it *does* mean that certain political positions *allow* or *motivate* scientists to study certain phenomena.

Ideology also influences *whose views* we privilege, that is, *whose interpretation of reality* we focus on or examine when we study a given scene or institution. Do we "privilege" or pay exclusive attention to the way in which the police see and interpret the world—or how criminals see and interpret it? How mental patients define things? Or how psychiatrists define things? If we have more of an "underdog" view of things, politically, we may end up focusing on how the underdogs view reality and soft-pedal or underplay how the "top dogs" define it. As Becker says, questioning (or even supporting) a given *hierarchy of credibility*—whose word we believe—is likely to be seen as taking a political stand. Whether "top dog" or "underdog," each political position or social location holds a certain view of how things are, how they work. Even making factually true statements, as we saw, has political consequences; everyone making them must be aware of what these consequences are likely to be. We cannot be naive about the implications of our findings, the generalizations we make, the conclusions our work reaches. We may give support to an ideology with which we do not agree, but the specific facts we come up with may seem to support that position. As a sociologist, a social scientist, what do we do? As a politically committed individual, what do we do? We can't find the answer in a methodology textbook. The answer comes from values and ideology, not science. The currently fashionable theoretical position identified as "postmodernism" argues for *decentering* intellectual work—privileging the voices of previously passive and silenced parties, such as women and racial minorities.

Politics or ideology may also influence to *which of the many facts before us* we choose to pay attention. Clearly, we can't pay attention to all of them; we have to be selective. Which ones do we examine? And what sort of view do they impart to scene under investigation? A few years ago, "60 Minutes" broadcast an interesting story. It seems a small-town newspaper published an obituary of a local businessman and entrepreneur. The man had, a few years before his death, committed embezzlement and had served a brief prison sentence for his crime. In his obituary, the editor of the newspaper mentioned that fact. The townspeople were outraged. They said that mention of the crime had no place in an obituary; it should not have been mentioned. An obituary should be a eulogy, they felt, containing only positive statements about the deceased. They accused the editor of smearing and demeaning the deceased. The editor responded by saying that the deceased's embezzlement and incarceration were important and basic facts about his life. They happened; the editor was simply reporting the facts as they took place. Nobody in the town claimed that the man did not commit the crime or that he had not served a prison sentence. Everybody agreed about what the facts were. It was the *reporting* of the facts that were in contention. The lesson should be clear: Telling the facts straight may have political and ideological implications.

There is what might be referred to as the "dirty linen" view of studying a group or category: Don't wash our dirty linen before the rest of the world; it makes us look bad. Some scientists have reacted sharply and critically to investigations of scientific wrongdoing; many physicians believe that they should close ranks and defend a physician accused of wrongdoing. Some members of certain racial or ethnic groups, likewise, believe that no statement that could be construed as negative or critical should be made about their category. Sociologists have to be aware of these feelings when they investigate a scene. They should not be shocked or surprised when what they say meets with outrage, hostility, or condemnation. Again, which facts one reports have important ideological consequences.

Some sociologists believe that certain topics shouldn't be studied at all, that certain forms of deviant behavior are too *reprehensible* to study. Clearly, this is an aspect of the "nuts and sluts" line of reasoning launched by Gouldner (1968) and Liazos (1972) a generation or more ago. Instead, they seem to be arguing, we should study *dignified* forms of deviance—for instance, revolutionaries who attempt to overthrow an exploitative system (Piven, 1981), or corporate criminals, major deviants who *oppress*, or deviants who fight *against* oppression. While "nuts and sluts" deviants do exist, these critics argue, they have received altogether too much attention for the good of the field; we should turn

our attention to loftier, more uplifting, and politically instructive wrongdoers, they say. Complained Alvin Gouldner, when the Society for the Study of Social Problems gave an award to a study of homosexuals: "And look at what we get: papers on 'Watch Queens' diddling one another in public toilets! When we gave the C. Wright Mills award for such trivia, one had to suspect it was all over for the Society" (Aurbach et al., 1976, p. 41).

Politics or ideology may also influence how we go about doing a study. A study conducted by Laud Humphreys (1970, 1975) generated an immense controversy over whether his study of "tearooms"—public urinals in which anonymous homosexual encounters took place—was ethical or not. Many observers objected to his particular "snooping" style of research. Humphreys wrote down the license plate numbers of cars parked near the tearooms he studied; he then found out the addresses of the drivers and interviewed them, under the guise of conducting a "public health survey," a year or so later. Is that ethical? Should sociologists be *allowed* to do such research? The publication of Humphreys's book, *Tearoom Trade*, brought a diversity of views into the public arena. Some sociologists argue that all deception (or "disguised observation") in social research is unethical (Erikson, 1967); others argue that deception is necessary because certain valuable but sensitive information cannot be obtained in any other way (Douglas, 1976, Goode, 1996b). No one has a definitive answer to these questions, but it's something every student of deviance must keep in mind when considering political, ideological, and ethical issues in social research.

All in all, there are many different ways that ideology and values can impact upon sociological and scientific research. But Becker insists that even though values and ideology intrude at a variety of points in the research process, one point at which they should *not* intrude is *getting the facts straight*, what reporters call "getting it right." Whatever our ideological position, Becker says, our research should always meet the standards of good scientific work. We should *not* say that something is true when our work reveals—and we know darn well—that it isn't. Our gaze should not be so diverted by our values that we are incapable of seeing what's there, or forced to see what isn't. Just because we are sympathetic to a particular value or belief shouldn't mean that we will never be able to come up with a finding that challenges it. Do we have the courage to accept a fact that is contrary to our ideological views? What do we do when we come across a "pebble in our shoe"—an uncomfortable finding that irritates and disconcerts our politics, our private beliefs? Do we pretend it doesn't exist? Or do we accept it and try to deal with it?

One example should suffice. I am an opponent of nuclear power; I participated in a demonstration against a nuclear plant, Shoreham, going on-line. I think nuclear power is a risky and dirty source of energy that should not be used. I'm also afraid of nuclear accidents, which have far more serious and devastating consequences than those that take place in conventional power plants. And I am afraid of what we are going to do with nuclear waste, which can contaminate the soil, and life on earth, for multiple centuries beyond its disposal. At the same time, I have read technical reports on the likelihood of a nuclear disaster, and I recognize that the odds of a serious accident in a nuclear power plant are extremely slim. Experts argue that the public—myself included—exaggerates the risk of nuclear contamination. They say that studies have shown that most people fear nuclear threats out of proportion to their actual potential for harm. Nuclear accidents take place *extremely* rarely, they say, and those that do happen, very rarely contaminate. The possibility of contamination is *vastly* less likely than the public thinks (Perrow, 1984; Slovic, Layman, and Flynn, 1991; Erikson, 1990). Moreover, I am aware that much of the popular opposition to nuclear energy is based on the fear that a plant will *explode*, much like an atomic bomb—a possibility that is so remote as to be next to impossible. I am also aware that American plants are far safer than those in Russia and Third World nations. In short, I can face these "objectively true" facts *in spite of* my politically and ideologically grounded opposition to nuclear energy; the facts do not change my position, and my position does not prevent me from facing the facts.

But the point is that my position on nuclear energy is *independent* of the risk involved. I am able to face the fact of the statistical likelihood of nuclear contamination in spite of my political views. I can see the validity in the conclusions that have been reached in studies on risk and harm, in spite of the fact that I think that the nuclear industry should be shut down. I am able to look the facts squarely in the face in spite of the fact that they do not support my ideological view. I am not so biased that I am forced to claim that the researchers, sci-

entists, and experts who come up with low estimates of risk are dupes of a nuclear industry that only wants to risk poisoning us in order to fatten their profits. I'm not that naive—or biased.

Being able to face uncomfortable facts is part of being a researcher in any field. I agree with Becker: If one is *only* going to come up with or believe in facts that support one's private ideology, then in my view, one cannot call oneself a legitimate sociologist or researcher. One ought to be able to accept facts that are inconvenient for or inconsistent with one's own ideological and political position. One ought to be brave enough to recognize that certain facts are likely to be true even though they may undermine one's cherished values or beliefs.

Richard Felson, in "Blame Analysis" (1991), attacks the validity of one of the more cherished views in American sociology: that victims should not be blamed for their plight (Ryan, 1976). Felson makes a distinction between *blame* and *cause*. Blame is *an attribution of moral responsibility*, while cause is a deterministic concept which belongs in the scientific, not the moral, realm. Someone takes an airplane flight and the plane crashes; this passenger is injured. The fact that he took that particular flight is part of the causal sequence that led to his being injured in the accident; if he had not taken that flight, he would not have been injured in it. Of course, he is not *responsible* for being injured in the crash—he cannot be *blamed* for his injuries. But his injuries were caused, in part, by his taking that particular flight. To many observers, Felson's argument sounds cruel, but its logic is impeccable. Too often, he says, cause and blame have been confused; all too often, when researchers discuss "causes" of certain actions, conditions, or outcomes, they are accused of "blaming the victim." It is not good social science, Felson says, and it is a practice that ought to be discontinued. Of course, we must recognize that "blaming the victim" is a perfectly valid criticism of *some* arguments, for some do "blame" the victim. But it is not a valid criticism of arguments in which cause and effect are carefully separated from moral responsibility.

A key concept intertwined in the debate over distinguishing "cause" and "blame" and its political and ideological implications is *agency*. Agency refers to a mental construct on the part of an observer that the person or persons, the members of a particular category of class of persons under observation, *have* or *lack* the free will to enact behavior deemed unethical. That is, there must be an effort on the part of the observer to *deny* agency to actors deemed victims and to *assert* agency for persons who are deemed victimizers. Put this way, it almost seems as if we've taken a major weapon in the ideological struggle out of the hands of combatants. But the fact is that agency is a construct, not a reality, a philosophical and not a sociological concept.

A couple of examples should suffice. In *Cocaine: White Gold Rush in Peru*, Edmundo Morales (1989) argues that the sale of cocaine is causing such a huge influx of "narco-dollars" into Peru that the entire social structure of vast areas is being destroyed. People, whose only previous mode of transportation was walking, are now purchasing Toyota 4Runners in villages that lack even paved roads. Law enforcement is being corrupted, women are being turned into prostitutes, crime and violence are everywhere, inflation is rampant. Morales argues that since Peru is a poor, weak country, we can't blame drug dealing on Peruvians. In contrast, the United States is a rich, powerful country; hence, the locus of blame is to be put at the feet of the United States. It's the Americans who are responsible for getting drug abusers to stop taking cocaine, which will stop the dealing, which will stop the social disintegration described by Morales. Interestingly, Morales inverts the usual equation in asserting agency to drug users and addicts (or at least the country in which they live) while denying agency to dealers, at least those in Peru. Most often (at least among liberals and reformers), addicts are said to *lack* agency—acting in the absence of a free will, out of an addiction, a compulsion, in need of treatment. In contrast, dealers, being victimizers and corrupters, most decidedly *possess* agency, and are said to be in need of punishment, not treatment.

The same argument that agency determines blame may also be found in an otherwise truly remarkable and candid book, Philippe Bourgois's *In Search of Respect* (1995), an anthropological account of crack dealing, and cocaine and heroin use, in the Puerto Rican *barrio* or neighborhood of Manhattan. His subjects and informants engaged in all manner of deviant activities—rape, domestic violence, attempted murder, robbery, and burglary; drug use and dealing seem almost the least of their crimes. But again, Bourgois seems to absolve them from blame, arguing that it is the collapse of the economy, especially in the inner city, and especially at the bottom economic rungs, that is responsible

for their crimes. They are the victims, they are the oppressed and the exploited, they must not be blamed for their crimes. The real crime is primarily the economy, in which the rich are getting richer and the poor are getting poorer, and secondarily the drug laws, which come down harder on the poor and the powerless. Redistribute the economic pie, bring jobs into *El Barrio*, decriminalize cocaine and heroin—and you'll find his informants to be humane, decent, and law-abiding, Bourgois argues. (Interestingly, the author never explains why some residents of the neighborhood he studied transcend their difficult surroundings while others do not.) Clearly, *agency* is crucial here in constructing a plausible account of attributions of deviance.

An African-American journalist affiliated with the Nation of Islam, Salim Muwakil, introduced a crucial concept that is relevant here: *candor with context*. Candor is, of course, being honest and empirically accurate about what one sees—seeing what's there, not seeing what isn't, telling it straight, getting it right, reporting the facts of the matter. (In this respect, Bourgois's book is astoundingly candid and honest.) But that's not enough, Muwakil says. *Context* is just as important. He says that a number of Black journalists have attempted to deny or ignore Black-on-Black crime. That's naive, he argues; that lacks candor. Black-on-Black crime is a reality, a fact of American life that must be addressed. But at the same time, he says, we have to understand where this phenomenon comes from, what manner of social structure produces it. Crime grows out of a specific social and economic structure or context. And tracing out the causal dynamics of Black-on-Black crime, he argues, is simultaneously a critique of contemporary American society. While not absolving African-Americans, who victimize other African-Americans, of responsibility for their actions, Muwakil places it in context. Again, what is the role of agency? Wherein does blame lie? Is blame even a sociological concept? And where do we, as observers and analysts of this society stand in this drama? I'm suggesting that the answers, if they exist, aren't that clear or straightforward.

In contrast to the nonattribution of blame to actors considered to lack agency, some critics wish to introduce the political dimension into the study of deviance by *asserting* agency. Why don't sociologists of deviance study deviants who *fight back*, who are "defiant," who "make a scene" (Gouldner, 1968, p. 107), who resist domination, who "resist the rules of their society," who have an impact on "the social arrangements within which they live," who "win political victories," who are "rule break- ers who . . . change the world," who break the rules and, in so doing, "not only make history" but do so in ways that *reflect* history (Piven, 1981, pp. 491, 500, 502, 503). Instead, sociologists of deviance, or so this politically engaged line of argu- ment asserts, focus on "nuts and sluts"—deviants who slink around at the margins of the society but who do not act upon the society. They are impo- tent rule-breakers; they do not challenge the struc- tures of social and economic domination (p. 503).

Such forms of politically relevant deviance are, indeed, interesting. In repressive societies, a truly remarkable and insightful line of inquiry might very well be challenges to the status quo. Certainly, political deviants qualify as a major subgroup which exhibits deviant behavior. Such an enterprise, unfor- tunately, has not been undertaken much by the field. The biases of the field of the sociology of deviance are, indeed, worth taking a look at. But there are two absolutely crucial qualifications that must be made if we are to take this suggestion seriously.

The first is that *most* persons who enact deviant behavior are *not* challenging the status quo when they do so. Most are *not* openly defiant or rebel- lious. In fact, as the very author of this challenge to the field has herself written, most people are not defiant, they do not take part in social movements that attempt to change the society, most people, in fact, are fairly passive politically (Piven and Cloward, 1977, p. 6). Even most people who devi- ate from the norms simply wish to be left alone to do their thing (even if "their thing" is ripping others off!). Thus, it is inaccurate to portray deviants *in general* as persons who would change history. On the other hand, *some* deviants—a tiny minority— *do* wish to change the course of history, and their very challenges *may* reveal interesting and important principles about the workings of the social system. However, unfortunately, although there have been many excellent studies of revolutions, social move- ments, and other forces and phenomena that have challenged the status quo and changed the course of history. hardly any sociologists have looked at these phenomena *as deviant behavior.*

There is a second qualification we must register before we open our inquiry to include political "movers and shakers" in the full spectrum of deviants. Once stated, it seems obvious, but it does not seem to be clear to the critics who frame these and other politically motivated critiques of the field.

If we are to cast political deviants into the role of rebellious heroes because they wish to bring down the status quo, we must keep in mind that chal- lenges to that status quo come from an immense variety of quarters. Some stem from a political posi- tion that the progressive and radical framers of cri- tiques of the field would *themselves* find repugnant. There seems to be a left-wing bias that makes the assumption that *any and all* challenges to the exist- ing social and economic order represent progres- sive causes, those of which they would approve. This is far from the case.

The bombers who destroyed the federal building in Oklahoma City in 1995 consider themselves opponents of the status quo they wish so desper- ately to change. They are "defiant" deviants, deviants who want to make history, "movers and shakers" of the social order. Indeed, the racist, white supremacist, separatist, anti-Semitic, militant resis- tance organizations with which these bombers are affiliated wish to make radical political changes. Some of their numbers wish to expel all Jews from the country, arguing that Washington is "ZOG"— a Zionist Occupational Government. Many of them want to see Blacks shipped "back" to Africa, a con- tinent on which most African-Americans have never set foot. Many of them want to eliminate all gov- ernment above the county level. They want to see the United States withdraw from the United Nations—indeed, many believe that the UN is poised to invade and take over the United States. They believe that their programs represent a *resis- tance* to the existing, entrenched power structure. (Consider the fact that a neo-Nazi record company is called "Resistance Records.") Their ideology and programs are fascinating, and elaborating them in great detail need not detain us at this point. But the point should be clear: *No one* who adopts a polit- ically engaged position on the sociology of deviance approves of *any* of these programs. Yet *all* of them make the naive assumption that oppo- sition to the status quo represents, *by its very nature,* a progressive position. Such a view represents a poverty-stricken imagination. It fails to recognize that opposition to the existing political and eco- nomic structure *may* rest on extremely elitist, reac- tionary, racist, and nonprogressive grounds. These critics are taking certain aspects of the status quo, of which they approve, *for granted,* while naively assuming that any other critic will attack specifi- cally those of which they disapprove. To quote George and Ira Gershwin, "It ain't necessarily so."

REFERENCES

Abel, Ernest L. 1987. "Drugs and Homicide in Erie County, New York." *International Journal of the Addictions*, 22 (February): 195–200.

Abel, Ernest L., and Phillip Zeidenberg. 1985. "Age, Alcohol and Violent Death: A Post Mortem Study." *Journal of Studies on Alcohol*, 46 (3): 228–231.

Abel, Gene G., Judith V. Becker, Edward B. Blanchard, and Armen Djenderdjian. 1978. "Differentiating Sexual Aggressives with Penile Measures." *Criminal Justice and Behavior*, 5 (December): 315–322.

Abel, Gene G., Judith V. Becker, and Linda J. Skinner. 1980. "Aggressive Behavior and Sex." *Psychiatric Clinics of North America*, 3 (April): 133–151.

Abrahamsen, David. 1960. *The Psychology of Crime*. New York: John Wiley & Sons.

Adam, Barry. 1978. *The Survival of Domination: Inferiorization and Everyday Life*. New York: Elsevier.

Adams, Nathan M. 1981. "Portait of a Pimp. " *Reader's Digest*, April, pp. 94–98.

Adler, Freda. 1975. *Sisters in Crime: The Rise of the New Female Criminal*. New York: McGraw-Hill.

Adler, Freda. 1979. "The Interaction Between Women's Emancipation and Female Criminality: A Cross-Cultural Perspective." In Freda Adler and Rita James Simon (eds.), *The Criminology of Deviant Women*. Boston: Houghton Mifflin, pp. 407–418.

Adler, Freda, and William S. Laufer (eds.). 1995. *The Legacy of Anomie Theory*. New Brunswick, N.J.: Transaction.

Adler, Freda, Gerhard O.W. Mueller, and William S. Laufer. 1995. *Criminology* (2nd ed.). New York: McGraw-Hill.

Adler, Jerry, with John McCormick. 1985. "Chicago's Unsilent Scream." *Newsweek*, January 14, p. 25.

Adler, Patricia A., and Peter Adler (eds.). 1994. *Constructions of Deviance: Social Power, Context, and Interaction*. Belmont, Calif.: Wadsworth.

Agnew, Robert. 1985. "Social Control Theory and Delinquency: A Longitudinal Test." *Criminology*, 23 (February): 47–61.

Agnew, Robert. 1995. "The Contribution of Social-Psychological Strain Theory to the Explanation of Crime and Delinquency." In Freda Adler and William S. Laufer (eds.), *The Legacy of Anomie Theory*. New Brunswick, N.J.: Transaction, pp. 113–137.

Akers, Ronald L. 1968. "Problems in the Sociology of Deviance: Social Definitions and Behavior." *Social Forces,* 46 (June): 455–465.

Akers, Ronald L. 1985. *Deviant Behavior: A Social Learning Approach* (3rd ed.). Belomont, Calif.: Wadsworth.

Akers, Ronald L. 1991. "Self-Control as a General Theory of Crime." *Journal of Quantitative Criminology*, 7: 201–211.

Alexander, Jeffrey (ed.). 1985. *Neofunctionalism*. Newbury Park, Calif.: Sage.

Altman, Lawrence K. 1994. "Obstacle-Strewn Road to Rethinking the Numbers on AIDS." *The New York Times*, March 1, p. C3.

American Psychiatric Association. 1994. *Diagnostic and Statistical Manual of Mental Disorders* (4th ed.). Washington, D.C.: APA.

Amir, Menachem. 1971a. "Forcible Rape." *Sexual Behavior*, 1 (November): 24–36.

Amir, Menachem. 1971b. *Patterns in Forcible Rape*. Chicago: University of Chicago Press.

Anderson, Nels. 1923. *The Hobo*. Chicago: University of Chicago Press.

Anderson, Odin W., and Jacon B. Feldman. 1956. *Family Medical Costs and Voluntary Health Insurance: A Nationwide Survey*. New York: McGraw-Hill.

Angier, Natalie. 1991. "Zone of Brain Linked to Men's Sexual Orientation." *The New York Times*, August 30, pp. A1, D18.

Angier, Natalie. 1992. "Scientists, Finding Second Idiocyncracy in Homosexuals' Brains, Suggest Orientation Is Physiological." *The New York Times*, August 1, p. 7.

Angier, Natalie. 1993. "Report Suggests Homosexuality Is Linked to Genes." *The New York Times*, July 16, pp. A1, D21.

Anonymous.1990. "Job-Related Murder Convictions of 3 Executives Are Overturned." *The New York Times*, January 20, p. 10.

Anonymous. 1995. "Men with Other Options May Seek Prostitutes for Non-Fuss, No-Muss Relationship. " *The Sun* (Baltimore), July 3, p. 8D.

APA. *See* American Psychiatric Association.

Ardrey, Robert. 1961. *African Genesis*. New York: Dell.

Armor, David J., J. Michael Polich, and Harriet B. Stampul. 1976. *Alcoholism and Treatment*. Santa Monica, Calif.: RAND Corporation.

Ashley, Richard. 1975. *Cocaine: Its History, Uses, and Effects*. New York: St. Martin's Press.

Atwater, Lynn. 1982. *The Extramarital Connection: Sex, Intimacy, and Identity*. New York: Irvington.

Auletta, Ken. 1982. *The Underclass*. New York: Random House.

Aurbach, Herbert A., et al. 1976. "SSSP as the Organization of a Social Movement: Comments and Suggestions." *Social Problems*, 24 (1): 37–53.

Austin, Roy L. 1982. "Women's Liberation and Increases in Minor, Major, and Occupational Offenses." *Criminology*, 20 (November): 407–430.

Babchuk, Nicholas, and Bruce Keith. 1995. "Introducing the Discipline: The Scholarly Content of Introductory Texts." *Teaching Sociology*, 23 (Jule): 215–225.

Bachman, Ronet. 1994. *Violence Against Women: A National Crime Victimization Survey Report*. Washington, D.C.: U.S. Department of Justice, Bureau of Justice Statistics.

Bailey, Michael, and Richard Pillard. 1991. "Are Some People Born Gay?" *The New York Times*, December 17, p. A21.

Baker, Robert A. 1992. *Hidden Memories*. Buffalo, N.Y.: Prometheus Books.

Balkan, Sheila, and Ronald J. Berger. 1979. "The Changing Nature of Female Delinquency." In Claire B. Koop and Martha Kirkpatrick (eds.), *Becoming Female: Perspectives on Development*. New York: Plenum Press, pp. 207–227.

Ball, John C., and and John C. Urbaitis. 1970. "Absence of Major Medical Complications Among Chronic Opiate Addicts." In John C. Ball and Carl D. Chambers (eds.), *Epidemiology of Opiate Addiction in the United States*. Springfield, Ill.: Charles C Thomas, pp. 301–306.

Ball, Richard A., and J. Robert Lilly. 1982. "The Menace of Margarine: The Rise and Fall of a Social Problem." *Social Problems*, 29 (June): 488–498.

Barbaree, Howard E. 1990. "Stimulus Control of Sexual Arousal: Its Role in Sexual Assault." In W.L. Marshall, D.R. Laws, and Howard E. Barbaree (eds.), *Handbook of Sexual Assault*. New York: Plenum Press, pp. 115–142.

Barbararee, Howard E., and William L. Marshall. 1991. "The Role of Male Sexual Arousal in Rape: Six Models." *Journal of Consulting and Clinical Psychology*, 59 (5): 621–630.

Barlow, Hugh D. 1993. *Introduction to Criminology* (6th ed.). New York: HarperCollins.

Barmash, Isadore. 1973. "Pilferage Abounds in the Nation's Stores." *The New York Times*, October 28, p. 9.

Baron, Larry, and Murray A. Straus. 1989. *Four Theories of Rape in American Society: A State-Level Analysis*. New Haven, Conn.: Yale University Press.

Baron, Robert A., and Paul A Bell. 1977. "Sexual Arousal and Aggression by Males: Effects of Type and Erotic Stimuli and Prior Provocation." *Journal of Personality and Social Psychology*, 35 (2): 79–87.

Barringer, Felicity. 1991. "The Sting of AIDS, the Scorn of Strangers." *The New York Times*, February 9, pp. 1, 10.

Barry, Kathleen. 1984. *Female Sexual Slavery*. New York: New York University Press.

Barry, Kathleen. 1995. *Prostitution of Sexuality*. New York: New York University Press.

Bart, Pauline B. 1975. "Rape Doesn't End with a Kiss." *Viva*, June, pp. 39–42, 100–102.

Bart, Pauline B. 1991. Review of Lee Ellis, *Theories of Rape: Inquiries into the Causes of Sexual Aggression*. New York: Hemisphere, 1989, in *Contemporary Sociology*, 20 (March): 268–270.

Barthol, Curt R. 1995. *Criminal Behavior: A Psychosocial Approach* (4th ed.). Englewood Cliffs, N.J.: Prentice Hall.

Bass, Ellen, and Laura Davis. 1988. *The Courage to Heal: A Guide for Women Survivors of Child Sexual Abuse*. New York: Harper & Row.

Bastian, Lisa D. 1992. "Crime and the Nation's Households, 1992." *Bureau of Justice Statistics Bulletin*, July, pp. 1–7.

Bastian, Lisa D. 1994. *Criminal Victimization in the United States: 1973–92 Trends*. Washington, D.C.: U.S. Department of Justice, Bureau of Justice Statistics.

Bastian, Lisa D., and Marshall M. DeBerry. 1994. *Criminal Victimization in the United States, 1992*. Washington, D.C.: U.S. Department of Justice, Bureau of Justice Statistics.

Baunach, Phyllis Jo. 1985. "Jail Inmates 1983." *Bureau of Justice Statistics Bulletin*, November, pp. 1–7.

Beauchamp, William. 1983. "The 2nd AIDS Epidemic." *The New York Times*, August 7, p. E21.

Beauvoir, Simone De. 1953. *The Second Sex* (trans. & ed. H.M. Parshley). New York: Alfred Knopf.

Beck, Melinda, et al. 1985. "America's Abortion Dilemma." *Newsweek*, January 14, pp. 20–25.

Becker, Gary S. 1968. "Crime and Punishment: An Economic Approach." *Journal of Political Economy*, 76 (April): 169–217.

Becker, Howard S. 1953. "Becoming a Marijuana User." *American Journal of Sociology*, 59 (November): 235–242.

Becker, Howard S. 1955. "Marijuana Use and Social Control." *Social Problems*, 3 (July): 35–44.

Becker, Howard S. 1963. *Outsiders: Studies in the Sociology of Deviance*. New York: Free Press.

Becker, Howard S. (ed.). 1964. *The Other Side: Perspectives on Deviance*. New York: Free Press.

Becker, Howard S. 1967. "Whose Side Are We On?" *Social Problems*, 14 (Winter): 239–247.

Becker, Howard S. 1973. "Labelling Theory Reconsidered." In Howard S. Becker, *Outsiders: Studies in the Sociology of Deviance* (expanded ed.). New York: Free Press, pp. 177–212.

Becker, Howard S. 1981. Review of Walter R. Gove (ed.), *The Labelling of Deviance: Evaluating a Perspective* (2nd ed.). Newbury Park, Calif.: Sage, in *Society*, May-June, pp. 73–74.

Becker, Howard S., Blance Geer, Everett C. Hughes, and Anselm

L. Strauss. 1961. *Boys in White: Student Culture in Medical School*. Chicago: University of Chicago Press.

Bell, Alan P., and Martin S. Weinberg. 1978. *Homosexualities: A Study of Diversity Among Men and Women*. New York: Simon & Schuster.

Bell, Arthur. 1976. "The Bath House Gets Respectable." *The Village Voice*, September 27, pp. 19–20.

Bell, Daniel. 1961. "Crime as an American Way of Life: A Queer Ladder of Social Mobility." In *The End of Ideology: On the Exhaustion of Political Ideas in the Fifties* (rev. ed.). New York: Collier Books, pp. 127–150.

Benson, Michael L. 1985. "Denying the Guilty Mind: Accounting for Involvement in a White-Collar Crime." *Criminology*, 23 (November): 589–599.

Ben-Yehuda, Nachman. 1980. "The European Witch Craze of the 14th to 17th Centuries: A Sociologist's Perspective." *American Journal of Sociology*, 86 (July): 1–31.

Ben-Yehuda, Nachman. 1985. *Deviance and Moral Boundaries: Witchcraft, the Occult, Science Fiction, Deviant Sciences and Scientists*. Chicago: University of Chicago Press.

Ben-Yehuda, Nachman. 1986. "The Sociology of Moral Panics: Toward a New Synthesis." *The Sociological Quarterly*, 27 (4): 495–513.

Ben-Yehuda, Nachman. 1990a. *The Politics and Morality of Deviance: Moral Panics, Drug Abuse, Deviant Science, and Reversed Stigmatization*. Albany: State University of New York Press.

Ben-Yehuda, Nachman. 1990b. "Positive and Negative Deviance: More Fuel for a Controversy." *Deviant Behavior*, 11 (3): 221–243.

Berendt, John. 1995. "High-Heel Neil." *The New Yorker*, January 16, pp. 38—45.

Berger, Peter L. 1963. *Invitation to Sociology*. Garden City, N.Y.: Doubleday-Anchor.

Berger, Philip B., Beatrix Hamburg, and David Hamburg. 1977. "Mental Health: Progress and Problems." In John H. Knowles (ed.), *Doing Better and Feeling Worse: Health in the United States*. New York: Norton, pp. 261–276.

Berk, Richard A., Alec Campbell, Ruth Klapp, and Bruce Western. 1992. "The Deterrent Effect of Arrest in Incidents of Domestic Violence: A Bayesian Analysis of Four Field Experiments." *American Sociological Review*, 57 (October): 698–709.

Bernard, Jesse. 1982. *The Future of Marriage* (2nd ed.). New Haven, Conn.: Yale University Press.

Best, Joel (ed.). 1989a. *Images of Issues: Typifying Contemporary Social Problems*. New York: Aldine de Gruyter.

Best, Joel. 1989b. "Dark Figures and Child Victims: Statistical Claims About Missing Children." In Joel Best (ed.), *Images of Issues: Typifying Contemporary Social Problems*. New York: Aldine de Gruyter, pp. 21–37.

Best, Joel. 1989c. "Afterword: Extending the Constructionist Perspective: A Conclusion and an Introduction." In Joel Best (ed.), *Images of Issues: Typifying Contemporary Social Problems*. New York: Aldine de Gruyter, pp. 243–253.

Best, Joel. 1990. *Threatened Children: Rhetoric and Concern about Child Victims*. Chicago: University of Chicago Press.

Best, Joel. 1993. "But Seriously Folks: The Limitations of the Strict Constructionist Interpretation of Social Problems." In James A. Holstein and Gale Miller (eds.), *Social Constructionism: Debates in Social Problems Theory*. New York: Aldine de Gruyter, pp. 129–147.

Best, Joel (ed.). 1995. *Images of Issues: Typifying Contemporary Social Problems* (2nd ed.). New York: Aldine De Gruyter.

Bettleheim, Bruno. 1971. "The Roots of Radicalism." *Playboy*, March, pp. 106ff.

Bieber, Irving, et al. 1962. *Homosexuality: A Psychoanalytic Study of Male Homosexuals*. New York: Basic Books.

Black, Donald J. (ed.). 1984. *Toward a General Theory of Social Control*. Orlando: Academic Press.

Black, Donald J., and Albert J. Reiss, Jr. 1970. "Police Control of Juveniles." *American Sociological Review*, 35 (February): 63–77.

Bland, Roger, and Helene Orn. 1986. "Family Violence and Psychiatric Disorder." *Canadian Journal of Psychiatry*, 31 (March): 129–137.

Blane, Howard T., and Kenneth E. Leonard (eds.). 1987. *Psychological Theories of Drinking and Alcoholism*. New York: Giolford Press.

Bleuel, Hans Peter. 1974. *Sex and Society in Nazi Germany* (trans.. J. Maxwell Brownjohn). New York: Bantam Books.

Blumberg, Abraham S. (ed.). 1981. *Current Perspectives on Criminal Behavior: Essays in Criminology* (2nd ed.). New York: Alfred Knopf.

Blume, E. Sue. 1990. *Secret Survivors: Uncovering Incest and Its Aftereffects in Women*. New York: John Wiley & Sons.

Blumer, Herbert. 1969. *Symbolic Interactionism*. Englewood Cliffs, N.J.: Prentice Hall.

Blumer, Herbert. 1971. "Social Problems as Collective Behavior." *Social Problems*, 18 (Winter): 298–306.

Boffey, Philip M. 1982. "Panel Clears 2 in Scientific Fraud in Alcoholism Study." *The New York Times*, November 5, p. A12.

Boffey, Philip M. 1983. "Controlled Drinking Gains as a Treatment in Europe." *The New York Times*, November 22, pp. C1, C7.

Boffey, Philip M. 1984. "Panel Finds No Fraud by Alcohol Researchers." *The New York Times*, September 11, p. C8.

Boffey, Philip M. 1988a. "Spread of AIDS Abating, but Deaths Will Soar." *The New York Times*, February 14, pp. 1, 36.

Boffey, Philip M. 1988b. "Researchers List Odds of Getting AIDS in Heterosexual Intercourse." *The New York Times*, April 22, pp. A1, A18.

Bogue, Donald J. 1985. *The Population of the United States: Historical Trends and Future Predictions*. Chicago: University of Chicago Press.

Bohlen, Celestine. 1988. "Domestic Violence Arrests Quadruple in New York City." *The New York Times*, February 14, pp. 1, 36.

Boland, Barbara, Catherine H. Conley, Paul Mahanna, Lynn Warner, and Ronald Sones. 1990. *The Prosecution of Felony Arrests, 1987*. Washington, D.C.: U.S. Department of Justice, Bureau of Justice Statistics.

Bordua, David J. 1967. "Recent Trends: Deviant Behavior and Social Control." *Annals of the American Academy of Political and Social Science*, 369: 149–163.

Bourgois, Philippe. 1995. *In Search of Respect: Selling Crack in El Barrio*. New York: Cambridge University Press.

Bourque, Linda Brookover. 1989. *Defining Rape*. Durham, N.C.: Duke University Press.

Bowart, William H. 1978. *Operation Mind Control: Our Government's War Against Its Own People*. New York: Dell.

Boyatzis, Richard E. 1975. "The Predisposition Toward Alcohol-Related Interpersonal Aggression in Men." *Journal of Studies in Alcohol*, 36 (September): 1196–1207.

Bracey, Dorothy Heid. 1979. *"Baby Pros": Profiles of Juvenile Prostitutes*. New York: John Jay Press.

Braithwaite, John. 1981. "The Myth of Social Class and Criminality Revisited." *American Sociological Review*, 46 (February): 36–57.

Braithwaite, John. 1985. "White-Collar Crime." *Annual Review of Sociology*, 11: 1–21.

Braithwaite, John. 1988. "White Collar Crime, Competition, and Capitalism: Comment on Coleman." *American Journal of Sociology*, 94 (November): 627–634.

Braithwaite, John. 1989. *Crime, Shame, and Reintegration*. Cambridge, England: Cambridge University Press.

Braithwaite, John, and Valerie Braithwaite. 1980. "The Effect of Income Inequality and Social Democracy on Homicide." *British Journal of Criminology*, 20 (January): 45–53.

Brasley, Patrick. 1988. "Arrests Up in Family Violence." *Newsday*, December 11, Part II, p. 21.

Brecher, Edward M., et al. 1972. *Licit and Illicit Drugs*. Boston: Little, Brown.

Brenner, S.N., and E.A. Molander. 1977. "Is the Ethics of Business Changing?" *Harvard Business Review*, 55 (January-February): 59–70.

Brodie, H. Keith. 1973. "The Effects of Ethyl Alcohol in Man." In National Commission on Marihuana and Drug Abuse, *Drug Use in America: Problem in Perspective*, Vol. I. Washington, D.C.: U.S. Government Printing Office, pp. 6–59.

Bronner, Simon J. 1990. *Piled Higher and Deeper: The Folklore of Campus Life*. Little Rock, Ark.: August House.

Brooke, James. 1996. "Lawsuit Tests Lethal Power of Words." *The New York Times*, February 16, p. A12.

Browne, Angela. 1987. *When Battered Women Kill*. New York: Free Press.

Brownmiller, Susan. 1975. *Against Our Will: Women, Men, and Rape*. New York: Simon & Schuster.

Brownmiller, Susan, and Dolores Alexander. 1992. "How We Got Here: From Carmita Wood to Anita Hill." *Ms.*, January-February, pp. 70–71.

Broznan, Nadine. 1991. "Anti-Gay Violence Rises in 6 Cities, a Study Finds." *The New York Times*, March 7, p. B3.

Brunvand, Jan Harold. 1981. *The Vanishing Hitchhiker: American Urban Legends and Their Meanings*. New York: W.W. Norton.

Brunvand, Jan Harold. 1984. *The Choking Doberman and Other "New" Urban Legends*. New York: W.W. Norton.

Brunvand, Jan Harold. 1986. *The Mexican Pet: More "New" Urban Legends and Some Old Favorites*. New York: W.W. Norton.

Brunvand, Jan Harold. 1989. *Curses! Broiled Again!* New York: W.W. Norton.

Brunvand, Jan Harold. 1993. *The Baby Train and Other Lusty Urban Legends*. New York: W.W. Norton.

Buckle, Abigail, and David P. Farrington. 1984. "An Observational Study of Shoplifting." *British Journal of Criminology*, 24 (1): 63–73.

Buckner, H. Taylor. 1971. *Deviance, Reality, and Change*. New York: Random House.

Buder, Leonard. 1977. "Half of 1976 Murder Victims Had Police Records." *The New York Times*, August 28, pp. 1, 34.

Bunker, John P. 1976. "Risks and Benefits in Surgery." *Surgery in the United States*, (pamphlet).

Burg, B.R. 1984. *Sodomy and the Pirate Tradition: English Sea Rovers in the Seventeenth-Century Caribbean*. New York: New York University Press.

Burgess, Robert L., and Ronald L. Akers. 1966. "A Differential Reinforcement Theory of Criminal Behavior." *Social Problems*, 14 (Fall): 128–147.

Burnham, David. 1973. "Crime Rates in Precincts and Census Data Studied." *The New York Times*, October 16, 45, 51.

Burrough, Bryan. 1986. "The Embezzler." *The Wall Street Journal*, September 19, p. 1.

Bursik, Robert J., and Harold G. Grasmick. 1993. *Neighborhoods and Crime: The Dimensions of Effective Community Control*. New York: Lexington Books.

Buss, Dale. 1993. "Ways to Curtain Employee Theft." *Nation's Business*, April, pp. 36, 38.

Butterfield, Fox. 1991. "Role of a Man and $13 Million In Rhode Island's Bank Crisis." *The New York Times*, January 4, pp. A1, A14.

Butterfield, Fox. 1992a. "Medical Board Takes Up Bizarre Case at Harvard." *The New York Times*, March 31, p. A14.

Butterfield, Fox. 1992b. "Therapy in Suicide Case Defended by Psychiatrist." *The New York Times*, April 1, p. A16.

Butterfield, Fox. 1994. "Historical Study of Homicide and Cities Surprises the Experts." *The New York Times*, October 23, p. 16.

Byck, Robert (ed.). 1974. *Cocaine Papers by Sigmund Freud*. New York: Stonehill.

Byron, Christopher. 1992. "Drug Problems." *New York*, June 15, pp. 18–19.

Byron, Peg. 1985. "What We Do When We Talk About Dildos." *The Village Voice*, March 5, pp. 48–49.

Cahalan, Don, and Robin Room. 1974. *Problem Drinking among American Men*. New Brunswick, N.J.: Rutgers Center for Alcohol Studies.

Cahnman, Werner J. 1968. "The Stigma of Obesity." *The Sociological Quarterly*, 9 (Summer): 283–299.

Calavita, Kitty. 1983. "The Demise of the Occupational Safety and Health Administration: A Case Study in Symbolic Interaction." *Social Problems*, 30 (April): 437–448.

Calavita, Kitty, and Henry N. Pontell. 1990. "'Heads I Win, Tails You Lose': Deregulation, Crime, and Crisis in the Savings and Loan Industry." *Crime and Delinquency*, 36 (July): 309–341.

Calavita, Kitty, and Henry N. Pontell. 1993. "Savings and Loan Fraud as Organized Crime: Towards a Conceptual Typology of Corporate Illegality." *Criminology*, 31 (November): 519–548.

Califia, Pat. 1994. *Public Sex: The Culture of Radical Sex*. Pittsburgh, Pa.: Cleis Press.

Callaway, Enoch, III. 1958. "Institutional Use of Ataractic Drugs." *Modern Medicine, 1958 Annual*, Part I (January 1–June 15): 26–29.

Cameron, Mary Owen. 1964. *The Booster and the Snitch*. New York: Free Press.

Carpenter, John A., and Nicholas P. Armenti. 1972. "Some Effects of Ethanol on Human Sexual and Aggressive Behavior." In Benjamin Kissin and Henri Begleiter (eds.), *The Biology of Alcoholism*, Vol. 2, *Physiology and Behavior*. New York: Plenum Press, pp. 509–543.

Carnes, Patrick. 1983. *Out of the Shadows: Understanding Sexual Addiction*. Minneapolis, Minn.: CompCare.

Cass, Vivienne C. 1979. "Homosexual Identity Formation: Testing a Theoretical Model." *Journal of Homosexuality*, 4 (3): 219–235.

Cass, Vivienne C. 1984. "Homosexual Identity Formation: Testing a Theoretical Model." *Journal of Sex Research*, 20 (2): 143–167.

Cassidy, John. 1995. "Who Killed the Middle Class?" *New Yorker*, October 16, pp. 113–124.

Cavan, Ruth S. 1928. *Suicide*. Chicago: University of Chicago Press.

Center for Mental Health Services. 1992. *Mental Health, United States, 1992*. Washington, D.C.: U.S. Government Printing Office.

Center for Mental Health Services. 1994. *Mental Health, United States, 1994*. Washington, D.C.: U.S. Government Printing Office.

Chambliss, William J. 1964. "A Sociological Analysis of the Law of Vagrancy." *Social Problems*, 12 (Summer): 67–77.

Chambliss, William J. 1973. "The Saints and the Roughnecks." *Society*, 11 (December): 24–31.

Chambliss, William J. 1976. "Functional and Conflict Theories of Crime." In William J. Chambliss and Milton Mankoff (eds.), *Whose Law? What Order? A Conflict Approach to Criminology*. New York: John Wiley & Sons, pp. 1–28.

Chancer, Lyn. 1989. "Abortion Without Apology." *The Village Voice*, April 11, pp. 37–38, 40.

Chappell, Duncan, and Susan Singer. 1977. "Rape in New York City: A Study of Material in Police Files and Its Meaning." In Duncan Chappell, Robley Geis, and Gilbert Geis (eds.), *Forcible Rape: The Crime, the Victims, and the Offender*. New York: Columbia University Press, pp. 245–271.

Chasnoff, Ira J., et al. 1989. "Temporary Patterns of Cocaine Use in Pregnancy." *Journal of the American Medical Association*, 261 (March 24–31): 1741–1744.

Church, George J., et al. 1988. "Thinking the Unthinkable." *Time*, May 30, pp. 12–19.

Clark, Russell D., III, and Elaine Hatfield. 1981. "Gender Differences in Receptivity to Sexual Offers." Unpublished article. Department of Psychology, Florida State University, Tallahassee.

Clarke, Matt, et al. 1985. "AIDS." *Newsweek*, August 12, pp. 20–27.

Clarke, Ronald V., and Marcus Felson (eds.). 1993. *Routine Activity and and Rational Choice*. New Brunswick, N.J.: Transaction.

Clausen, John A. 1981. "Stigma and Mental Disorder: Phenomena and Terminology." *Psychiatry*, 44 (November): 287–296.

Clelland, Donald, and Timothy J. Carter. 1980. "The New Myth of Class and Crime." *Criminology*, 18 (November): 319–336.

Clinard, Marshall B. 1952. *The Black Market: A Study of White Collar Crime*. New York: Rinehart.

Clinard, Marshall B. 1964a. *Anomie and Deviant Behavior: A Discussion and Critique*. New York: Free Press.

Clinard, Marshall B. 1964b. "The Theoretical Implications of Anomie and Deviant Behavior." In Marshall B. Clinard (ed.), *Anomie and Deviant Behavior: A Discussion and Critique*. New York: Free Press, pp. 1–56.

Clinard, Marshall B., and Robert F. Meier. 1995. *Sociology of Deviant Behavior* (9th ed.). Ft. Worth, Tex.: Harcourt Brace.

Clinard, Marshall B., Richard Quinney, and John Wildeman. 1994. *Criminal Behavior Systems: A Typology* (3rd ed.). Cincinnati, Ohio: Anderson.

Clinard, Marshall B., and Peter C. Yeager. 1980. *Corporate Crime*. New York: Free Press.

Cloward, Richard. 1959. "Illegitimate Means, Anomie, and Deviant Behavior." *American Sociological Review*, 24 (April): 167–177.

Cloward, Richard, and Lloyd E. Ohlin. 1960. *Delinquency and Opportunity: A Theory of Juvenile Gangs*. New York: Free Press.

Clymer, Adam. 1986. "One Issue That Seems to Defy a Yes or a No." *The New York Times*, February 23, p. 22E.

Cockerham, William C. 1995. *Sociology of Mental Disorder* (3rd ed.). Englewood Cliffs, N.J.: Prentice Hall.

Cohen, Albert K. 1955. *Delinquent Boys: The Subculture of the Gang*. New York: Free Press.

Cohen, Albert K. 1966. *Deviance and Control*. Englewood Cliffs, N.J.: Prentice Hall.

Cohen, Bernard. 1980. *Deviant Street Networks: Prostitution in New York City*. Lexington, Mass.: Lexington Books.

Cohen, Lawrence E., and Marcus Felson. 1979. "Social Change and Crime Rate Trends: A Routine Activity Approach." *American Sociological Review*, 44 (August): 588–608.

Cohen, Lawrence E., Marcus Felson, and Kenneth C. Land. 1980. "Property Crime Rates in the United States: A Macrodynamic Analysis, 1947–1977." *American Journal of Sociology*, 86 (July): 90–118.

Cohen, Lawrence E., and Rodney Stark. 1974. "Discriminatory Labeling and the Five-Fingered Discount: An Empirical Analysis of Differential Shoplifting Dispositions." *Social Problems*, 11 (January): 25–39.

Cohen, Maimon, M., Michelle J. Marinello, and Nathan Back. 1967. "Chromosomal Damage in Human Leukocytes Induced by Lysergic Acid Diethylamide." *Science*, 155 (17 March): 1417–1419.

Cohen, Mark A. 1989. "Corporate Crime and Punishment: A Study of Social Harm and Sentencing Practice in the Federal Courts, 1984–1987," *American Criminal Law Review*, 26: 605–660.

Cohen, Stanley. 1972. *Folk Devils and Moral Panics*. New York: St. Martin's Press.

Cohen, Stanley. 1985a. *Visions of Social Control*. Cambridge, England: Polity Press.

Cohen, Stanley. 1985b. Review of Donald Black (ed.), "Toward a General Theory of Social Control." Orlando, Fla.: Academic Press, 1984, in *American Journal of Sociology*, 91 (November): 714–717.

Cohen, Stanley. 1988. *Against Criminology*. New Brunswick, N.J.: Transaction.

Cohen, Stanley, and Andrew Scull (eds.). 1983. *Social Control and the State: Historical and Comparative Essays*. New York: St. Martin's Press.

Cole, Stephen. 1975. "The Growth of Scientific Knowledge: Theories of Deviance as a Case Study." In Lewis A. Coser (ed.), *The Idea of Social Structure: Papers in Honor of Robert K. Merton*. New York: Harcourt Brace Jovanovich, pp. 175–220.

Cole, Stephen. 1992. *Making Science: Between Nature and Society*. Cambridge, Mass.: Harvard University Press.

Cole, Stephen, and Harriet Zuckerman. 1964. "Inventory of Empirical and Theoretical Studies of Anomie." In Marshall B. Clinard (ed.), *Anomie and Deviant Behavior: A Discussion and Critique*. New York: Free Press, pp. 243–311.

Coleman, James William. 1987. "Toward an Integrated Theory of White Collar Crime." *American Journal of Sociology*, 93 (September): 406–439.

Coleman, James William. 1992. "The Theory of White Collar Crime: From Sutherland to the 1990s." In Kip Schlegel and

David Weisburd (eds.), *White Collar Crime Reconsidered.* Boston: Northeastern University Press, pp. 53–77.

Coleman, James William. 1994. *The Criminal Elite: The Sociology of White Collar Crime* (3rd ed.). New York: St. Martin's Press.

Coleman, James William. 1995. "Respectable Crime." In Joseph F. Sheley (ed.), *Criminology: A Contemporary Handbook.* Belmont, Calif.: Wadsworth, pp. 249–269.

Coles, Claire D. 1992. "Effects of Cocaine and Alcohol Use in Pregnancy on Neonatal Growth and Neurobehavioral Status." *Neurotoxicology and Teratology,* 14 (January-February): 1–11.

Conklin, John E. 1972. *Robbery and the Criminal Justice System.* New York: Lippincott.

Conklin, John E. 1995. *Criminology* (5th ed.). Boston: Allyn & Bacon.

Connell, Noreen, and Cassandra Wilson (eds.). 1974. *Rape: The First Source-Book for Women.* New York: New American Library.

Conover, Patrick W. 1976. "A Reassessment of Labeling Theory: A Constructive Response to Criticism." In Lewis A. Coser and Otto Larsen (eds.), *The Uses of Controversy in Sociology.* New York: Free Press, pp. 228–249.

Cook, Philip J., and Daniel Nagin. 1979. *Does the Weapon Matter?* Washington, D.C.: Institute for Law and Society.

Cook, Shirley J. 1970. "The Social Background of Narcotics Legislation." *Addictions,* 17 (Summer): 14–29.

Coombes-Orme, Terri, John R. Taylor, Ellen Bates Scott, and Sandra Holmes. 1983. "Violent Death among Alcoholics: A Descriptive Study." *Journal of Studies on Alcohol,* 44 (6): 938–949.

Coontz, Stephanie. 1992. *The Way We Never Were: American Families and the Nostalgia Trap.* New York: Basic Books.

Coser, Lewis A. 1956. *The Functions of Social Conflict.* New York: Free Press.

Covington, Jeanette. 1995. "Racial Classiciation in Criminology: The Reproduction of Radicalized Crime," *Sociological Forum,* 10 (4): 547–568.

Cowell, Alan. 1994. "Israeli's Death: Atrocity or Act of War?" *The New York Times,* October 17, p. A11.

Cowley, Geoffrey, et al. 1990. "The Promise of Prozac." *Newsweek,* March 26, pp. 38–41.

Cowley, Geoffrey, et al. 1991. "A Prozac Backlash." *Newsweek,* April 1, pp. 64–67.

Cowley, Geoffrey. 1994. "The Culture of Prozac." *Newsweek,* February 7, pp. 41–42.

Cressey, Donald R. 1953. *Other People's Money.* New York: Free Press.

Cressey, Donald R. 1960. "Epidemiology and Individual Conduct: A Case From Criminology." *Pacific Sociological Review,* 3 (Fall): 47–58.

Cressey, Donald R. 1965. "The Respectable Criminal." *Transaction,* 3 (March–April): 12–15.

Cressey, Donald R. 1988. "Poverty of Theory in Corporate Crime Research." *Advances in Criminological Theory,* 1 (1): 31–56.

Crews, Frederick. 1995. *The Memory Wars: Freud's Legacy in Dispute.* New York: New York Review.

Curra, John. 1994. *Understanding Social Deviance: From the Near Side to the Outer Limits.* New York: HarperCollins.

Curran, Daniel J., and Claire M. Renzetti. 1994. *Theories of Crime.* Boston: Allyn & Bacon.

Currie, Elliot P. 1968. "Crimes without Criminals: Witchcraft and Its Control in Renaissance Europe." *Law and Society Review,* 3 (August); 7–32.

Currie, Elliott P. 1985. *Confronting Crime: An American Challenge.* New York: Pantheon Books.

Currie, Elliott P. 1993. *Reckoning: Drugs, the Cities, and the American Future.* New York: Hill & Wang.

Currie, Elliott P., and Jerome H. Skolnick. 1984. *America's Problems: Social Issues and Public Policy.* Boston: Little, Brown.

Cushman, John H., Jr. 1992. "Top Military Officers Object to Lifting Homosexual Ban." *The New York Times,* November 14, pp. 9.

Cuskey, Walter R., Lisa H. Berger, and Arthur H. Richardson. 1978. "The Effects of Marijuana Decriminalization on Drug Use Patterns." *Contemporary Drug Problems,* 7 (Winter): 491–532.

Dai, Bingham. 1937. *Opium Addiction in Chicago.* Shanghai: Commercial Press.

Daly, Kathleen. 1995. *Gender, Crime, and Punishment.* New Haven, Conn.: Yale University Press.

Daly, Kathleen, and Meda Chesney-Lind. 1988. "Feminism and Criminology." *Justice Quarterly,* 5 (December): 497–538.

Daly, Martin, and Margo Wilson. 1988. *Homicide.* New York: Aldine de Gruyter.

Dank, Barry M. 1971. "Coming Out in the Gay World." *Psychiatry,* 34 (May): 180–197.

Danner, Mark. 1994. *The Massacre at El Mozote.* New York: Vintage Books.

Davidson, Gerald C., John M. Neale. 1994. *Abnormal Psychology: An Experimental Clinical Approach* (6th ed.). New York: John Wiley & Sons.

Davis, Kingsley. 1937. "The Sociology of Prostitution." *American Sociological Review,* 2 (October): 744–755.

Davis, Kingsley. 1949. *Human Behavior.* New York: Macmillan.

Davis, Kingsley. 1971. "Prostitution." In Robert K. Merton and Robert Nisbet (eds.), *Contemporary Social Problems.* New York: Harcourt Brace Jovanovich, pp. 341–351.

Davis, Kingsley. 1976. "Sexual Behavior." In Robert K. Merton and Robert Nisbet (eds.), *Contemporary Social Problems.* New York: Harcourt Brace Jovanovich, pp. 219–261.

Davis, Kingsley, and Wilbert E. Moore. 1945. "Some Principles of Stratification." *American Sociological Review,* 10 (April): 242–249.

Davis, Murray S. 1971. "That's Interesting! Towards a Phenomenology of Sociology and a Sociology of Phenomenology." *Philosophy of the Social Sciences,* 1: 309–344.

Davis, Nanette J. 1971. "The Prostitute: Developing a Deviant Identity." In James M. Henslin (ed.), *Studies in the Sociology of Sex.* New York: Appleton-Century-Crofts, pp. 297–322.

Davis, Nanette J. 1980. *Sociological Construction of Deviance: Perspectives and Issues in the Field* (2nd ed.). Dubuque, Iowa: William C. Brown.

Davis, Nanette J., and Bo Anderson. 1983. *Social Control: The Production of Deviance in the Modern State.* New York: Irvington.

Davis, Nanette J., and Clarice Stasz. 1990. *Social Control: The Production of Deviance in the Modern State.* New York: McGraw-Hill.

Davison, Bill. 1967. "The Hidden Evils of LSD." *The Saturday Evening Post,* August 12, pp. 19–23.

DeFleur, Melvin L., and Richard Quinney. 1966. "A Reformulation of Sutherland's Differential Association Theory and a Strategy for Empirical Verification." *Journal of Research in Crime and Delinquency*, 3 (January): 1–11.

DeKeseredy, Walter S., and Martin D. Schwartz. 1996. *Contemporary Criminology*. Belmont, Calif.: Wadsworth.

DeLindt, Jan, and Wolfgang Schmidt. 1971. "Alcohol Use and Alcoholism." *Addictions*, 18 (Summer): 1–14.

Delph, Edward William. 1978. *The Silent Community: Public Homosexual Encounters*. Newbury Park, Calif.: Sage.

D'Espo, D. Anthony. 1962, "Hysterectomy When the Uterus is Grossly Normal." *American Journal of Obstectrics and Gynecology*, 83 (January): 113–121.

Dishotsky, Norman I., William D. Loughman, Robert E. Mogar, and Wendell R. Lipscomb. 1971. "LSD and Genetic Damage." *Science*, 172 (April 30): 431–440.

Ditton, Jason. 1979. *Controlology: Beyond the New Criminology*. London: Macmillan Press.

Dodge, David L. 1985. "The Over-Negativized Conceptualization of Deviance: A Programmatic Exploration." *Deviant Behavior*, 6 (1): 17–37.

Doherty, Edmund G. 1978. "Are Different Discharge Criteria Used for Men and Women Psychiatric Inpatients?" *Journal of Health and Social Behavior*, 19 (March): 107–116.

Dohrenwend, Bruce P., and Barbara Snell Dohrenwend. 1974. "Social and Cultural Influences on Psychopathology." *Annual Review of Psychology*, 25: 417–452.

Dohrenwend, Bruce P., and Barbara Snell Dohrenwend. 1976. "Sex Differences and Psychiatric Disorder." *American Journal of Sociology*, 81 (May): 1447–1454.

Doll, Lynda, et al. 1987. "Self-Reported Change in Sexual Behaviors in Gay and Bisexual Men from the San Francisco City Clinic Cohort." Paper presented at the Third International Conference on AIDS, Washington, D.C., June.

Donnerstein, Edward. 1981. Pornography and Violence Against Women: Experimental Studies." *Annals of the New York Academy of Sciences*, 347 (Part VII): 277–288.

Donnerstein, Edward, Daniel Linz, and Steven Penrod. 1987. *The Question of Pornography: Research Findings and Policy Implications*. New York: Free Press.

Douglas, Jack D. 1970. (ed.). *Deviance and Respectability: The Social Construction of Moral Meanings*. New York: Basic Books.

Douglas, Jack D. 1976. *Investigative Social Research: Individual and Team Field Research*. Newbury Park, Calif. Sage.

Douglas, Jack D., and Frances C. Waksler. 1982. *The Sociology of Deviance: An Introduction*. Boston: Little, Brown.

Dover, K.J. 1978. *Greek Homosexuality*. New York: Vintage Books.

Downes, David. 1979. "Praxis Makes Perfect: A Critique of Critical Criminology." In David Downes and Paul Rock (eds.), *Deviant Interpretations*. London: Martin Robertson, pp. 1–16.

Downes, David, and Paul Rock (eds.). 1979. *Deviant Interpetations*. London: Matrin Robertson.

Downes, David, and Paul Rock. 1988. *Understanding Deviance: A Guide to the Sociology of Crime and Rule Breaking* (2nd ed.). Oxford, United Kingdom: Clarendon Press.

Drake, St. Clair, and Horace R. Cayton. 1945. *Black Metropolis. A Study of Negro Life in a Northern City*. New York: Harcourt Brace.

Dullea, Georgia. 1988. "Gay Couples' Wish to Adopt Grows, Along with Increasing Resistance." *The New York Times*, February 7, p. 26.

Dunford, Franklyn, David Huizinga, and Delbert S. Elliott.

1990. "The Role of Arrest in Domestic Assault: The Omaha Police Experiment." *Criminology*, 28 (May): 183–206.

Dunham, H. Warren. 1964. "Anomie and Mental Disorder." In Marshall B. Clinard (ed.), *Anomie and Deviant Behavior: A Discussion and Critique*. New York: Free Press, pp. 128–157.

Dunham, H. Warren. 1965. *Community and Schizophrenia: An Epidemiological Analysis*. Detroit: Wayne State University Press.

Dunlap, David W. 1995. "Opponents of Gay Topics Press Crusade." *The New York Times*, October 11, p. B7.

Dunlap, David W. 1996. "Fearing a Toehold for Gay Marriage, Conservatives Rush to Bar the Door." *The New York Times*, March 6, p. A13.

Durkheim, Emile. 1933. *The Division of Labor in Society* (trans.. George Simpson). New York: Macmillan (orig. pub. 1893).

Durkheim, Emile. 1938. *The Rules of the Sociological Method* (trans. Sarah A. Solovay and John H. Mueller, ed. George E.G. Catlin). Chicago: University of Chicago Press (orig. pub. 1895).

Durkheim, Emile. 1951. *Suicide: A Study in Sociology* (trans. John A. Spaulding and George Simpson; ed. George Simpson). New York: Free Press (orig. pub. 1897).

Duster, Troy. 1970. *The Legislation of Morality: Law, Drugs, and Moral Judgement*. New York: Free Press.

Duster, Troy. 1995. "The New Crisis of Legitimacy in Controls, Prisons, and Legal Structures." *The American Sociologist*, 26 (Spring): 20–29.

Dutton, Donald G. 1994. *The Domestic Assault of Women: Psychological and Criminal Justice Perspectives* (2nd ed.). Vancouver: University of British Columbia Press.

Dworkin, Andrea. 1981. *Pornography: Men Possessing Women*. New York: Perigee.

Dworkin, Andrea. 1982a. "Why So-Called Radical Men Love and Need Pornography." In Laura Lederer (ed.), *Take Back the Night: Women on Pornography*. New York: Bantam Books, pp. 141–147.

Dworkin, Andrea. 1982b. "For Men, Freedom of Speech: For Women, Silence, Please." In Laura Lederer (ed.), *Take Back the Night: Women on Pornography*. New York: Bantam Books, pp. 255–258.

Dworkin, Andrea. 1982c. "Pornography and Grief." In Laura Lederer (ed.), *Take Back the Night: Women on Pornography*. New York: Bantam Books, pp. 286–291.

Dworkin, Andrea. 1987. *Intercourse*. New York: Free Press.

Dzeich, Billie Wright, and Linda Weiner. 1984. *The Lecherous Professor: Sexual Harassment on Campus*. Boston: Beacon Press.

Eckholm, Erik. 1992. "AIDS, Fatally Steady in the U.S., Accelerates Worldwide." *The New York Times*, June 28, p. E5.

Edelhertz, Herbert. 1970. *The Nature, Impact, and Prosecution of White Collar Crime*. Washington, D.C.: National Institute of Law Enforcement and Criminal Justice.

Edgerton, Robert B. 1967. *The Cloak of Competence: Stigma in the Lives of the Mentally Retarded*. Berkeley: University of California Press.

Edgerton, Robert B. 1969. "On the Recognition of Mental Illness." In Robert B. Edgerton (ed.), *Perspectives in Mental Illness*. New York: Holt, Reinhart & Winston, pp. 49–72.

Edgerton, Robert B. 1976. *Deviance: A Cross-Cultural Perspective*. Menlo Park, Calif.: Cummings.

Egan, Timothy. 1988. "Gay Ex-Soldier Wants to Return to the Army." *The New York Times*, February 12, p. A18.

Egan, Timothy. 1989. "Putting a Face on Corporate Crime." *The New York Times*, July 14, p. B8.

Egan, Timothy. 1996. "Critics Say Coroner Puts His Morality Before the Facts," *The New York Times*, March 31, p. 14.

Eichenwald, Kurt. 1995. "A City's Savior? Not Quite." *The New York Times*, April 12, pp. D1, D4.

Eitzen, D. Stanley. 1983. *Social Problems* (2nd ed.). Boston: Allyn & Bacon.

Eitzen, D. Stanley. 1984. "Teaching Social Problems: Implications of the Objectivist-Subjectivist Debate." *SSSP Newsletter*, 16 (Fall): 10–12.

Eitzen, D. Stanley, and Doug A. Timmer. 1985. *Criminology: Crime and Criminal Justice*. New York: John Wiley & Sons.

Elliott, Delbert S., and Suzanne S. Ageton. 1980. "Reconciling Race and Class Differences in Self-Reported and Official Estimates of Delinquency." *American Sociological Review*, 45 (February): 95–110.

Elliott, Delbert S., and David Huizinga. 1983. "Social Class and Delinquent Behavior in a National Youth Panel: 1976–1980." *Criminology*, 21 (May): 149–177.

Ellis, Bill. 1988. "The Varieties of Alien Experience." *The Skeptical Inquirer*, 12 (Spring): 263–269.

Ellis, Kate, et al. (eds.). 1988. *Caught Looking: Feminism, Pornography, and Censorship*. Seattle, Wash.: Real Comet Press.

Ellis, Lee. 1989. *Theories of Rape: Inquiries into the Causes of Sexual Aggression*. New York: Hemisphere.

Empey, Lamar T. 1982. *American Delinquency: Its Meaning and Construction* (2nd ed.). Homewood, Ill.: Dorsey Press.

Epstein, Steven. 1987. "Gay Politics, Ethnic Identity: The Limits of Social Constructionism." *Socialist Review*, 17 (3–4): 9–54.

Ericson, Richard V., Patricia M. Baranek, and Janet B.L. Chan. 1987. *Visualizing Deviance: A Study of News Organization*. Toronto: University of Toronto Press.

Ericson, Richard V., Patricia M. Baranek, and Janet B.L. Chan. 1989. *Negotiating Control: A Study of News Sources*. Toronto: University of Toronto Press.

Ericson, Richard V., Patricia M. Baranek, and Janet B.L. Chan. 1991. *Representing Order: Crime, Law, and Justice in the News Media*. Toronto: University of Toronto Press.

Erikson, Kai T. 1962. "Notes on the Sociology of Deviance." *Social Problems*, 9 (Spring): 9–21.

Erikson, Kai T. 1964. "Notes on the Sociology of Deviance." In Howard S. Becker (ed.), *The Other Side: Perspectives on Deviance*. New York: Free Press, pp. 307–314.

Erikson, Kai T. 1966. *Wayward Puritans: A Study in the Sociology of Deviance*. New York: John Wiley & Sons.

Erikson, Kai T. 1967. "A Comment on Disguised Observation in Sociology." *Social Problems*, 14 (Spring): 366–373.

Erikson, Kai T. 1990. "Toxic Reckoning: Business Faces a New Kind of Fear." *Harvard Business Review*, 68 (January-February): 118–126.

Ermann, M. David, and Richard J. Lundman (eds.). 1996. *Corporate and Government Deviance: Problems of Organizational Behavior in Contemporary Society* (5th ed.). New York: Oxford University Press.

Esterson, Allen. 1993. *Seductive Mirage: An Exploration of the Work of Sigmund Freud*. Chicago: Open Court Press.

Estrich, Susan. *Real Rape*. 1987. Cambridge, Mass.: Harvard University Press.

Evans-Pritchard, E.E. 1970. "Sexual Inversion Among the Azande." *American Anthropologist*, 72 (October): 1428–1433.

Ewing, Charles Patrick. 1987. "Prepared Statement." Paper presented to the Select Committee on Children, Youth and Families, U.S. House of Representatives, Washington, D.C., September 16.

Falwell, Jerry (ed.). 1981. *The Fundamentalist Phenomenon: The Resurgence of Conservative Christianity*. Garden City, N.Y.: Doubleday-Galilee.

Farberman, Harvey A. 1975. "A Criminogenic Market Structure." *The Sociological Quarterly*, 16 (Autumn): 438–457.

Faris, Robert E., and H. Warren Dunham. 1939. *Mental Disorders in Urban Areas*. Chicago: University of Chicago Press.

Farley, Lin. 1978. *Sexual Shakedown: The Sexual Harassment of Women on the Job*. New York: Warner.

Farr, John. 1976. "Making Love in Public Places." *Hustler*, June, pp. 18–19.

Feagin, Joe R. 1982. *Social Problems: A Critical Power-Conflict Perspective*. Englewood Cliffs, N.J.: Prentice Hall.

Feagin, Joe R., and Robert Parker. 1990. *Building American Cities: The Urban Real Estate Game* (2nd ed.). Englewood Cliffs, N.J.: Prentice Hall.

Felson, Marcus. 1987. "Routine Activities and Crime Prevention in the Developing Metropolis," *Criminology*, 25 (November): 911–931.

Felson, Richard B. 1991. "Blame Analysis: Accounting for the Behavior of Protected Groups." *The American Sociologist*, 22 (Spring): 5–23.

Ferracuti, Franco, Renato Lazari, and Marvin E. Wolfgang. 1973. "The Subculture of Violence in Sardinia." In Walter C. Reckless, *The Crime Problem* (5th ed.). New York: Appleton-Century-Crofts, pp. 212–215.

Finestone, Harold. 1964. "Cats, Kicks, and Color." In Howard S. Becker (ed.), *The Other Side: Perspectives on Deviance*. New York: Free Press, pp. 281–297.

Finkelhor, David. 1979. *Sexually Victimized Children*. New York: Free Press.

Finkelhor, David, and Kersti Yllo. 1985. *License to Rape: Sexual Abuse of Wives*. New York: Free Press.

Fischel, Daniel. 1995. *Payback: The Conspiracy to Destroy Michael Milken and His Financial Revolution*. New York: Harper Business.

Fischer, Anita, Janos Marton, E. Joel Millman, and Leo Srole. 1979. "Long-Range Influences on Mental Health: The Midtown Longitudinal Study, 1954–1974." In Roberta Simmons (ed.), *Research in Community and Mental Health*, Vol. 1. Greenwich, Conn.: JAI Press, pp. 305–333.

Fishman, Mark. 1978. "Crime Waves as Ideology." *Social Problems*, 25 (June): 531–543.

Foderaro, Lisa W. 1995. "A Voyage to Bedlam and Part Way Back." *The New York Times*, November 9, pp. B1, B4.

Fonseca, Isabel. 1995. "Among the Gypsies." *New Yorker*, September 25, pp. 84–97.

Ford, Clelland S., and Frank A. Beach. 1951. *Patterns of Sexual Behavior*. New York: Harper & Row.

Forrest, Jacqueline Darroch, and Susheela Singh. 1990. "Sexual and Reproductive Behavior of American Women, 1982–1988." *Family Planning Perspectives*, 22 (September-October): 206–215.

Forward, Susan, and Craig Buck. 1978. *Betrayal of Innocence: Incest and Its Devastation*. Los Angeles: Tarcher.

Fosdick, Raymond B., and Albert L. Scott. 1933. *Toward Liquor Control*. New York: Harper & Brothers.

Foucault, Michel. 1967. *Madness and Civilization: A History of Insanity in the Age of Reason* (trans. Richard Howard). New York: Mentor.

Foucault, Michel. 1979. *Discipline and Punish* (trans. Alan Sheridan). New York: Vintage Books.

Fox, John W. 1990. "Social Class, Mental Illness, and Social Mobility: The Social Selection-Drift Hypothesis for Serious Mental Illness." *Journal of Health and Social Behavior*, 21 (September): 260–267.

Franklin, H. Bruce. 1993. *M.I.A. or Mythmaking in America*. New Brunswick, N.J.: Rutgers University Press.

Freedman, Rita Jackway. 1986. *Beauty Bound*. Lexington, Mass.: Lexington Books.

Freidson, Eliot. 1966. "Disability as Deviance." In Marvin B. Sussman (ed.), *Sociology and Rehabilitation*. Washington, D.C.: American Sociological Association pp. 71–99.

Freidson, Eliot. 1970a. *Professional Dominance: The Social Structure of Medical Care*. Chicago: Aldine.

Freidson, Eliot. 1970b. *Profession of Medicine: A Study of the Sociology of Applied Knowledge*. New York: Dodd, Mead.

Freud, Sigmund. 1961. *Civilization and its Discontents* (trans. & ed., James Strachey). New York: W.W. Norton.

Friedman, Joel, Marcia Mobilia Boumil, and Barbara Ewert Taylot. 1992. *Sexual Harassment*. Deerfield Beach, Fla.: Health Communications.

Friedman, Wolfgang. 1964. *Law in a Changing Society*. Harmondsworth, England: Penguin Books.

Friedrichs, David O. 1996. *Trusted Criminals: White Collar Crime in Contemporary Society*. Belmont, Calif.: Wadsworth.

Fuller, Richard C., and Richard R. Myers. 1941. "Some Aspects of a Theory of Social Problems." *American Sociological Review*, 6 (February): 24–32.

Gabriel, Trip. 1994. "Heroin Finds a New Market Along Cutting Edge of Style." *The New York Times*, May 8, pp. 1, 22.

Gagnon, John H. 1971. "Physical Strength, Once of Significance." *Impact of Science on Society*, 21 (1): 31–42.

Gagnon, John H., and William Simon (eds.). 1967. *Sexual Deviance*. New York: Harper & Row.

Gagnon, John H., and William Simon. 1973. *Sexual Conduct: The Social Sources of Human Sexuality*. Chicago: Aldine.

Gallagher, Bernard J., III. 1995. *The Sociology of Mental Illness* (3rd ed.). Englewood Cliffs, N.J.: Prentice Hall.

Galliher, John F. (ed.). 1991. *Deviant Behavior and Human Rights*. Englewood Cliffs, N.J.: Prentice Hall.

Garb, Maggie. 1989. "Abortion Foe Gives Birth to a Syndrome." *In These Times*, February 22–March 1, pp. 3, 22.

Garland, David. 1985. *Punishment and Welfare: A History of Penal Strategies*. Aldershot, England: Gower.

Garland, David. 1990. *Punishment and Modern Society: A Study in Social Theory*. Clendon Press.

Garland, David, and Peter Young (eds.). 1983. *The Power to Punish: Contemporary Penalty and Social Analysis*. London: Heinemann Educational Books.

Gebhard, Paul H., John H. Gagnon, Wardell Pomeroy, and Cornelia V. Christenson. 1965. *Sex Offenders: An Analysis of Types*. New York: Harper & Row.

Geertz, Clifford. 1973. *The Interpretation of Cultures: Selected Essays*. New York: Basic Books.

Geis, Gilbert. 1967. "White Collar Crime: The Great Electrical Conspiracy." In Marshall B. Clinard and Richard Quin-

ney (eds.), *Criminal Behavior Systems: A Typology*. New York: Holt, Reinhart & Winston, pp. 139–163.

Geis, Gilbert (ed.). 1968. *White Collar Criminal: The Offender in Business and the Professions*. New York: Atherton Press.

Geis, Gilbert. 1973. "Deterring Corporate Crime." In Ralph Nader and Mark J. Green (eds.), *Corporate Power in America*. New York: Grossman, pp. 182–197.

Geis, Gilbert. 1974. "Avocational Crime." In Daniel Glaser (ed.), *Handbook of Criminology*. New York: Rand McNally, pp. 272–298.

Geis, Gilbert. 1981. "Upperworld Crime." In Abraham S. Blumberg (ed.), *Current Perspectives on Criminal Behavior: Essays in Criminology*. New York; Alfred Knopf, pp. 179–198.

Geis, Gilbert. 1984. "White Collar and Corporate Crime." In Robert F. Meier (ed.), *Major Forms of Crime*. Newbury Park, Calif.: Sage, pp. 137–166.

Geis, Gilbert. 1995. "White-Collar Crime." In Alex Thio and Thomas Calhoun (eds.), *Readings in Deviant Behavior*. New York: HarperCollins, pp. 213–221.

Geis, Gilbert, and Colin Goff. 1983. "Introduction." To Edwin H. Sutherland, *White Collar Crime: The Uncut Version*. New Haven, Conn.: Yale University Press, pp. ix–xxxiii.

Geis, Gilbert, Paul Jesilow, Henry N. Pontell, and Mary Jane O'Brien. 1985. "Fraud and Abuse of Government Medical Benefits Programs by Psychiatrists." *American Journal of Psychiatry*, 142 (February): 231–234.

Geis, Gilbert, and Robert F. Meier (eds.). 1977. *White Collar Crime: Offenses in Business, Politics, and the Professions* (rev. ed.). New York: Free Press.

Geis, Gilbert, Robert F. Meier, and Laurence M. Salinger (eds.). 1995. *White Collar Crime: Classic and Contemporary Views* (3rd ed.). New York: Free Press.

Geis, Gilbert, et al. 1985b. "Peculating Psychiatrists: Fraud and Abuse Against Medicaid." *Professional Psychology: Research and Practice*, 16 (6): 823–832.

Gelles, Richard J. 1976. "Abused Wives: Why Do They Stay?" *Journal of Marriage and the Family*, 38 (November): 659–668.

Gelles, Richard J. 1979. *Family Violence*. Beverly Hills, Calif.: Sage.

Gelles, Richard J. 1987. *Family Violence* (2nd ed.). Newbury Park, Calif.: Sage.

Gelles, Richard J., and Murray A. Straus. 1988. *Intimate Violence: The Causes and Consequences of Abuse in the American Family*. New York: Simon & Schuster.

Gelman, Davie, et al. 1985. "The Social Fallout from an Epidemic." *Newsday*, August 12, pp. 28–29.

Gelsthorpe, Loraine, and Allison Morris. 1988. "Feminism and Criminology in Britain." *British Journal of Criminology*, 28 (Spring): 223–240.

Gentry, Cynthia. 1991. "Pornography and Rape: An Empirical Analysis." *Deviant Behavior*, 12 (July-September): 277–288.

Gibbons, Don C. 1992. *Society, Crime, and Criminal Behavior* (6th ed.). Englewood Cliffs, N.J.: Prentice Hall.

Gibbons, Don C., and Joseph F. Jones. 1975. *The Study of Deviance: Perspectives and Problems*. Englewood Cliffs, N.J.: Prentice Hall.

Gibbs, Jack P. 1966. "Conceptions of Deviant Behavior.: The Old and the New." *Pacific Sociological Review*, 9 (Spring): 9–14.

Gibbs, Jack P. 1972. "Issues in Defining Deviant Behavior." In Robert A. Scott and Jack D. Douglas (eds.), *Theoretical*

Perspectives on Deviance. New York: Basic Books, pp. 39–68.

Gibbs, Jack P. 1981. *Norms, Deviance, and Social Control: Conceptual Matters*. New York: Elsevier.

Gibbs, Jack P. 1989. *Control: Sociology's Central Notion*. Urbana: University of Illinois.

Gibbs, Jack P. 1995. "Major Notions and Theories in the Sociology of Deviance." In Alex Thio and Thomas C. Calhoun (eds.), *Readings in Deviant Behavior*. New York: Harper-Collins, pp. 64–83.

Gieringer, Dale. 1990. "How Many Crack Babies?" *The Drug Policy Letter*, March/April, pp. 4–6.

Giesbrecht, Norman, et al. 1989. *Drinking and Casualties: Accidents, Poisonings and Violence in an International Perspective*. London: Tavistock/Routledge.

Gillespie, Cynthia K. 1989. *Justifiable Homicide: Battered Women, Self-Defense, and the Law*. Columbus, Ohio: Ohio State University Press.

Gillies, Hunter. 1976. "Homicide in the West of Scotland." *British Journal of Psychiatry*, 128 (February): 105–127.

Ginsburg, George L., et al. 1972. "The New Impotence." *Archives of General Psychiatry*, 26 (March): 218–220.

Glasser, Ira. 1975. "The Yellow Star and the Pink Triangle." *The New York Times*, September 10, p. 45.

Glassner, Barry. 1982. "Labeling Theory." In M. Michael Rosenberg, Robert A. Stebbins, and Allan Turowitz (eds.), *The Sociology of Deviance*. New York: St. Martin's Press, pp. 71–89.

Goffman, Erving. 1959. *The Presentation of Self in Everyday Life*. Garden City, N.Y.: Doubleday-Anchor.

Goffman, Erving. 1961. *Asylums*. Garden City, N.Y.: Doubleday-Anchor.

Goffman, Erving. 1963. *Stigma: Notes on the Management of Spoiled Identity*. Englewood Cliffs, N.J.: Prentice Hall/Spectrum.

Gold, Herbert. 1976. "The Therapist Will See You Now, Big Boy." *Oui*, February, pp. 81–82, 88ff.

Goldberg, Carey. 1995. "Sex Slavery, Thailand to New York." *The New York Times*, September 11, pp. B1, B6.

Goldman, Douglas. 1955. "Treatment of Psychotic States with Chlorpromazine." *Journal of the American Medical Association*, 157 (April 19): 1274–1278.

Goldstein, Avram. 1994. *Addiction: From Biology to Drug Policy*. New York: W.H. Freeman.

Goldstein, Jeffrey H. 1986. *Aggression and Crimes of Violence* (2nd ed.). New York: Oxford University Press.

Goldstein, Paul J. 1985. "The Drugs/Violence Nexus: A Tripartite Conceptual Framework." *Journal of Drug Issues*, 15 (Fall): 493–506.

Goldstein, Paul J., Henry H. Brownstein, Patrick J. Ryan, and Patricia A. Bellucci. 1989. "Crack and Homicide in New York City, 1988: A Conceptually Based Event Analysis." *Contemporary Drug Problems*, 16 (Winter): 651–687.

Goleman, Daniel. 1984. "Violence Against Women in Films Is Found to Alter Attitudes of Men." *The New York Times*, August 28, pp. 19, 20.

Goleman, Daniel. 1986. "To Expert Eyes, City Streets Are Open Mental Wards." *The New York Times*, November 4, pp. C1, C3.

Goleman, Daniel. 1990. "Homophobia: Scientists Find Clues To Its Roots." *The New York Times*, July 10, pp. C1, C11.

Goleman, Daniel. 1991a. "Sexual Harassment: It's About Power, not Lust." *The New York Times*, October 22, pp. C1, C12.

Goleman, Daniel. 1991b. "New Studies Map the Mind of the Rapist." *The New York Times*, December 10, pp. C1, C10.

Gonzales, Laurence. 1985. "Why Drug Enforcement Doesn't Work." *Playboy*, September, pp. 113–114, 148, 194ff.

Goode, Erich. 1970. *The Marijuana Smokers*. New York: Basic Books.

Goode, Erich. 1975. "On Behalf of Labeling Theory." Social Problems, 22 (June): 570–583.

Goode, Erich. 1978. *Deviance: An Interactionist Approach*. Englewood Cliffs, N.J.: Prentice Hall.

Goode, Erich. 1981a. "Deviance, Norms, and Social Reaction." *Deviant Behavior*, 3 (October-December): 46–53.

Goode, Erich. 1981b. "Comments on the Homosexual Role." *Journal of Sex Research*, 17 (February): 54–65.

Goode, Erich. 1988. "False Identity." In Erich Goode, *Sociology* (2nd ed.). Englewood Cliffs, N.J.: Prentice Hall, pp. 90–91.

Goode, Erich. 1989. "The American Drug Panic of the 1980s: Social Construction or Objective Threat?" *Violence, Aggression, and Terrorism*, 3 (4): 327–344.

Goode, Erich. 1990. "Crime Can Be Fun: The Deviant Experience." *Contemporary Sociology*, 19 (January): 5–12.

Goode, Erich. 1991. "Positive Deviance: A Viable Concept?" *Deviant Behavior*, 12 (3): 289–309.

Goode, Erich. 1992. *Collective Behavior*. Ft. Worth, Tex.: Harcourt Brace.

Goode, Erich. 1993. *Drugs in American Society* (4th ed.). New York: McGraw-Hill.

Goode, Erich. 1994. "Round Up the Usual Suspects: Crime, Deviance, and the Limits of Constructionism." *The American Sociologist*, 25 (Winter): 90–104.

Goode, Erich. 1996a. "The Stigma of Obesity." In Erich Goode (ed.), *Social Deviance*. Boston: Allyn & Bacon, pp. 332–340.

Goode, Erich. 1996b. "The Ethics of Deception in Social Research: A Case Study." *Qualitative Sociology*. 19 (1): 11–33.

Goode, Erich. 1997. *Between Politics and Reason: The Drug Legalization Debate*. New York: St. Martin's Press.

Goode, Erich, and Nachman Ben-Yehuda. 1994a. "Moral Panics: Culture, Politics, and Social Construction." *Annual Review of Sociology*, 20: 149–171.

Goode, Erich, and Nachman Ben-Yehuda. 1994b. *Moral Panics: The Social Construction of Deviance*. London: Blackwell.

Goode, Erich, and Lynn Haber. 1977. "Sexual Correlates of Homosexual Experience: An Exploratory Study of College Women." *Journal of Sex Research*, 13 (February): 12–21.

Goode, Erich, and Richard R. Troiden. 1979. "Heterosexual and Homosexual Activity Among Gay Males." *Deviant Behavior*, 1 (October-December): 37–55.

Goode, William J. 1973. *Explorations in Social Theory*. New York: Oxford University Press.

Goodman, Richard A., et al. 1986. "Alcohol Use and Interpersonal Violence: Alcohol Detected in Homicide Victims." *American Journal of Public Health*, 76 (February): 144–149.

Goodman, Richard A., et al. 1991. "Alcohol and Fatal Injuries in Oklahoma." *Journal of Studies on Alcohol*, 52 (2): 156–161.

Gootman, Roberta, and Reina Mekelburg. 1973. "Silky the Pimp Counts His Money." *Gallery*, September, pp. 32, 108.

Gora, Joann Gennaro. 1982. *The New Female Criminal: Empirical Reality or Social Myth?* New York: Praeger.

Gordon, David M. 1971. "Class and the Economics of Crime."

The Review of Radical Political Economics, 3 (Summer): 50–75.

Gorer, Geoffrey. 1966. "Man Has No Killer Instinct." *The New York Times Magazine*, November 27, pp. 47, 82, 92–93ff.

Gorer, Geoffrey. 1967. *Himalayan Village: An Account of the Lepcha of Sikkim* (2nd ed.), New York: Basic Books.

Gottfredson, Michael R., and Travis Hirschi (eds.). 1987. *Positive Criminology*. Newbury Park, Calif.: Sage.

Gottfredson, Michael R., and Travis Hirschi. 1990. *A General Theory of Crime*. Stanford, Calif.: Stanford University Press.

Gould, Leroy C. 1969. "The Changing Structure of Property Crime in an Affluent Society." *Social Forces*, 48 (1): 50–59.

Gould, Stephen Jay. 1981. *The Mismeasure of Man*. New York: W.W. Norton.

Gouldner, Alvin W. 1968. "The Sociologist as Partisan: Sociology and the Welfare State." *The American Sociologist*, 3 (May): 103–116.

Gouldner, Alvin W. 1970. *The Coming Crisis of Western Sociology*. New York: Basic Books.

Gove, Walter R. 1970a. "Societal Reactions as an Explanation of Mental Illness: An Evaluation." *American Sociological Review*, 35 (October): 873–884.

Gove, Walter R. 1970b. "Who Is Hospitalized? A Critical Evaluation of Some Sociological Studies of Mental Illness." *Journal of Health and Social Behavior*, 11 (December): 294–303.

Gove, Walter R. 1972. "The Relationship Between Sex Roles, Marital Status, and Mental Illness." *Social Forces*, 51 (September): 34–44.

Gove, Walter R. 1975a. "The Labelling Theory of Mental Illness: A Reply to Scheff." *American Sociological Review*, 40 (April): 242–248.

Gove, Walter R. 1975b. "The Labelling Perspective: An Overview." In Walter R. Gove (ed.), *The Labelling of Deviance*. New York: John Wiley & Sons/Halstead/Sage, pp. 35–81.

Gove, Walter R. 1979a. "The Labelling Versus the Psychiatric Explanation of Mental Illness: A Debate that Has Become Substantially Irrelevant (Reply to Comment by Horwitz)." *Journal of Health and Social Behavior*, 20 (September): 89–93.

Gove, Walter R. 1979b. "Sex, Marital Status, and Psychiatric Treatment: A Research Note." *Social Forces*, 58 (September): 89–93.

Gove, Walter R. (ed.). 1980a. *The Labelling of Deviance: Evaluating a Perspective*. Newbury Park, Calif.: Sage.

Gove, Walter R. 1980b. "Labelling and Mental Illness: A Critique." In Walter R. Gove (ed.), *The Labelling of Deviance: Evaluating a Perspective*. Newbury Park, Calif.: Sage, pp. 307–327.

Gove, Walter R. (ed.). 1982a. *Deviance and Mental Illness*. Newbury Park, Calif.: Sage.

Gove, Walter R. 1982b. "Labelling Theory's Explanation of Mental Illness: An Update of Recent Evidence." *Deviant Behavior*, 3 (July-September): 307–327.

Gove, Walter R. 1985. "The Effect of Age and Gender on Deviant Behavior: A Biosocial Perspective." In Alice S. Rossi (ed.), *Gender and the Life Course*. New York: Aldine de Gruyter, pp. 115–144.

Gove, Walter R. 1989. "On Understanding Mental Illness and Some Insights to Be Gained from the Labelling Theory of Mental Illness." Unpublished paper.

Gove, Walter R., and Terry Fain. 1973. "The Stigma of Mental Hospitalization: An Attempt to Evaluate Its Consequences." *Archives of General Psychiatry*, 28 (April): 494–500.

Gove, Walter R., and Terry R. Herb. 1974. "Stress and Mental Illness Among the Young: A Comparison of the Sexes." *Social Forces*, 53 (December): 256–265.

Gove, Walter R., and Michael Hughes. 1989. "A Theory of Mental Illness: An Attempted Integration of Biological, Psychological, and Social Variables." In Steven F. Messner, Marvin D. Kron, and Allen E. Liska (eds.), *Theoretical Integration in the Study of Deviance and Crime: Problems and Prospects*. Albany: State University of New York Press, pp. 61–76.

Gove, Walter R., Maurizia Tovo, and Michael Hughes. 1985. "Involuntary Psychiatric Hospitalization: A Review of the Statutes Regulating the Social Control of the Mentally Ill." *Deviant Behavior*, 6 (3): 287–318.

Grant, Bridget F., John Noble, and Henry Malin. 1986. "Decline in Liver Cirrhosis Mortality and Components of Change." *Alcohol Health and Research World*, 10 (Spring): 66–69.

Gray, Diana. 1973. "Turning Out: A Study of Teenage Prostitution." *Urban Life and Culture*, 1 (January): 401–425.

Gray, Paul. 1993. "The Assault on Freud." *Time*, November 29, pp. 47–51.

Greeley, Andrew M., William C. McCready, and Gary Thielson. 1980. *Ethnic Drinking Subcultures*. New York: Praeger.

Green, Mark, and Norman Waitzman. 1981. *Business War on the Law: An Analysis of the Benefits of Federal Health/Safety Enforcement*. Washington: Ralph Nader.

Greenberg, David F. 1976. "Delinquency and the Age Structure of Society." In Sheldon L. Messenger amd Egon Bittner (eds.), *Criminology Review Yearbook*. Beverly Hills Calif.: Sage, pp. 586–620.

Greenberg, David F. 1979. "Delinquency and the Age Structure of Society." In Sheldon L. Messenger and Egon Bittner (eds.), *Criminology Review Yearbook*. Beverly Hills, Calif.: Sage, pp. 586–620.

Greenberg, David F. 1985. "Age, Crime, and Social Explanation." *American Journal of Sociology*, 91 (July): 1–21.

Greenberg, David F. 1988. *The Construction of Homosexuality*. Chicago: University of Chicago Press.

Greenberg, Joel. 1995. "Shared Hate: Jews and Arabs Mark Mosque Slayings." *The New York Times*, February 17, p. A3.

Greenhouse, Linda. 1986. "High Court, 5–4, Says States Have the Right to Outlaw Private Homosexual Acts: Privacy Law and History." *The New York Times*, July 1, pp. A1, A19.

Greenhouse, Steven. 1985. "3 Executives Convicted of Murder for Unsafe Workplace Conditions." *The New York Times*, June 15, p. 1, 29.

Griffin, Richard T. 1976. "Grandma Was a Junkie." *Penthouse*, February, pp. 80ff.

Griffin, Susan. 1971. "Rape: The All-American Crime." *Ramparts*, September, pp. 26–35.

Griffin, Susan. 1981. *Pornography and Silence: Culture's Revenge Against Nature*. New York: Harper Colophon.

Grinspoon, Lester, and James B. Bakalar. 1976. *Cocaine: A Drug and Its Social Evolution*. New York: Basic Books.

Grinspoon, Lester, and James B. Bakalar. 1979. *Psychedelic Drugs Reconsidered*. New York: Basic Books.

Gronfein, William. 1985. "Psychotropic Drugs and the Origins of Institutionalization." *Social Problems*, 32 (June): 437–454.

Gross, Edward. 1978. "Organizational Crime: A Theoretical

Perspective." In Norman Denzin (ed.), *Studies in Symbolic Interaction*. Greenwich, Conn.: JAI Press, pp. 55–88.

Groth, Nicholas, with H. Jean Birnbaum. 1979. *Men Who Rape: The Psychology of the Offender*. New York: Plenum Press.

Gruenbaum, Adolph. 1993. *Validation in the Clinical Theory of Psychoanalysis*. International Universities Press.

Gusfield, Joseph R. 1963. *Symbolic Crusade: Status Politics and the American Temperance Movement*. Urbana: University of Illinois Press.

Gusfield, Joseph R. 1967. "Moral Passage: The Symbolic Process in Public Designations of Deviance." *Social Problems*, 15 (Fall): 175–188.

Gusfield, Joseph R. 1981. *The Culture of Public Problems: Drinking-Driving and the Symbolic Order*. Chicago: University of Chicago Press.

Gutis, Philip A. 1987. Homosexual Parents Winning Some Custody Cases." *The New York Times*, January 21, pp. C1, C16.

Haberman, Paul W., and Michael M. Baden. 1974. "Alcoholism and Violent Death." *Quarterly Journal of Studies on Alcohol*, 33, Part A (March): 221–231.

Haberman, Paul W., and Michael M. Baden. 1978. *Alcohol, Other Drugs, and Violent Death*. New York: Oxford University Press.

Hagan, John. 1980. "The Legislation of Crime and Delinquency: A Review of Theory, Method, and Research." *Law and Society Review*, 14 (Spring): 603–628.

Hagan, John. 1991. *The Disreputable Pleasures: Crime and Deviance in Canada* (3rd ed.). Toronto: McGraw-Hill Ryerson.

Hall, Jerome. 1952. *Theft, Law, and Society* (2nd ed.). Indianapolis, Ind.: Bobbs-Merrill.

Hall, Susan. 1972. *Gentleman of Leisure*. New York: New American Library.

Hall, Susan. 1974. *Ladies of the Night*. New York: Pocket Books.

Hamer, Dean, and Peter Copeland. 1995. *The Science of Desire: The Search for the Gay Gene and the Biology of Behavior*. New York: Simon & Schuster.

Hamill, Pete. 1988. "Facing Up to Drugs: Is Legalization the Solution?" *New York*, August 15, pp. 21–27.

Hamilton, Jon. 1995. "AIDS: Where Are We Now?" *American Health*, May, pp. 53–57.

Harkey, John, David L. Miles, and William A. Rushing. 1976. "The Relationship Between Social Class and Functional Status: A New Look at the Drift Hypothesis." *Journal of Health and Social Behavior*, 17 (September): 194–204.

Harlow, Caroline Wolf. 1987. "Robbery Victims." *Bureau of Justice Statistics Special Report*, April, pp. 1–10.

Harman, Leslie D. 1985. "Acceptable Deviance as Social Control: The Cases of Fashion and Slang." *Deviant Behavior*, 6 (1): 1–15.

Harrington, Michael. 1962. *The Other America*. New York: Macmillan.

Hartung, Frank. 1950. "White Collar Offenses in the Wholesale Meat Industry in Detroit." *American Journal of Sociology*, 56 (July): 25–32.

Hatfield, Elaine, and Susan Sprecher. 1986. *Mirror, Mirror . . . The Importance of Looks in Everyday Life*. Albany: State University of New York Press.

Hawkins, E.R., and Willard Waller. 1936. "Critical Notes on the Cost of Crime." *Journal of Criminal Law, Criminology, and Police Science*, 26 (January): 679–694.

Hawkins, Richard, and Gary Tiedeman. 1975. *The Creation of Deviance: Interpersonal and Organizational Determinants*. Columbus, Ohio: Charles E. Merrill.

Hayes, Constance L. 1988. "Teen-Agers Attack Pair Seen as Gay." *The New York Times*, August 24, pp. B1, B4.

Hayes, Constance L. 1990. "Anti-Gay Attacks Increase and Some Fight Back." *The New York Times*, September 3, pp. 23, 26.

Health, Education, and Welfare, U.S. Department of. 1971. *Alcohol and Health*, First Special Report. Washington, D.C.: U.S. Goverment Printing Office.

Health and Human Services, U.S. Department of. 1987. *Alcohol and Health*, Sixth Special Report to the U.S. Congress. Rockville Md.: National Institute on Alcohol Abuse and Alcoholism, HHS.

Health and Human Services, U.S. Department of. 1990. *Alcohol and Health*, Seventh Special Report to the U.S. Congress. Rockville, Md.: Alcohol, Drug Abuse, and Mental health Administration, HHS.

Health and Human Services, U.S. Department of. 1991a. *Annual Emergency Room Data 1990*. Rockville, Md.: Alcohol, Drug Abuse, and Mental Health Administration, HHS.

Health and Human Services, U.S. Department of. 1991b. *Annual Medical Examiner Data 1990*. Rockville, Md.: Alcohol, Drug Abuse, and Mental Health Administration.

Health and Human Services, U.S. Department of. 1993. *Alcohol and Health*, Eighth Special Report to the U.S. Congress. National Institute on AlcoholAbuse and Alcoholism, HHS.

Health and Human Services, U.S., Department of. 1994a. *Alcohol and Health*, Eighth Special Report to the U.S. Congress. Rockville, Md.: National Institute on Alcohol Abuse and Alcoholism, HHS.

Health and Human Services, U.S. Department of. 1994b. *1993 Preliminary Estimates of Drug-Related Emergency Department Episodes*. Rockville, Md.: Substance Abuse and Mental Health Services Administration.

Health and Human Services, U.S. Department of. 1995a. *National Household Survey on Drug Abuse: Main Findings 1993*. Rockville, Md.: Substance Abuse and Mental Health Services, HHS.

Health and Human Services, U.S. Department of. 1995b. *National Household Survey on Drug Abuse: Population Estimates 1994*. Rockville, Md.: Substance Abuse and Mental Health Services, HHS.

Health and Human Services, U.S. Department of. 1995c. *Annual Medical Examiner Data 1993*. Rockville, Md.: Substance Abuse and Mental Health Services, HHS.

Heather, Nick, and Ian Robertson. 1981. *Controlled Drinking*. London: Methuen.

Heckert, Druann Maria. 1989. "The Relativity of Positive Deviance: The Case of the French Impressionists." *Deviant Behavior*, 10 (2): 131–144.

Heidensohn, Frances. 1968. "The Deviance of Women: A Critique and an Enquiry." *British Journal of Sociology*, 12 (2): 160–175.

Heidensohn, Frances. 1985. *Women and Crime*. New York: New York University Press.

Heitzeg, Nancy A. 1996. *Deviance: Rulemakers and Rulebreakers*. St. Paul, Minn.: West.

Hellman, Peter. 1970. "One in Ten Shoppers Is a Shoplifter." *The New York Times Magazine*, March 15, pp. 34–35ff.

Henderson, Charles R. 1901. *Introduction to the Study of Dependent, Defective, and Delinquent Classes* (2nd ed.). Boston: D.C. Heath.

Henry, Jules. 1941. *Jungle People*. Richmond, Va.: Augustin.

Henry, William A., III. 1994. "Pride and Prejudice." *Time*, June 27, pp. 55–59.

Hentoff, Nat. 1990. "The Most Violently Attacked Community in America." *The Village Voice*, September 25, pp. 24–25.

Herdt, Gilbert. 1981. *Guardians of the Flute: Idioms of Masculinity*. New York: McGraw-Hill.

Herdt, Gilbert. 1987. *The Sambia: Ritual and Gender in New Guinea*. New York: Holt, Rinehart & Winston.

Herdt, Gilbert. 1988. "Cross-Cultural Forms of Homosexuality and the Concept 'Gay.'" *Psychiatric Annals*, 18 (1): 37–39.

Herman, Judith Lewis. 1992. *Trauma and Recovery*. New York: Basic Books.

Herman, Judith Lewis, and Lisa Hirschman. 1977. "Father-Daughter Incest: A Feminist Theoretical Perspective." *Signs: Journal of Women in Culture and Society*, 2 (Summer): 735–756.

Herman, Judith Lewis, with Lisa Hirschman. 1981. *Father-Daughter Incest*. Cambridge, Mass.: Harvard University Press.

Hicks, Robert D. 1991. *In Pursuit of Satan: The Police and the Occult*. Buffalo, N.Y.: Prometheus Books.

Hilton, Michael E. 1989. "How Many Alcoholics Are There in the United States?" *British Journal of Addiction*, 84 (May): 459–460.

Hilts, Philip J. 1990. "New Study Says AIDS Bias Grows Faster Than Disease." *The New York Times*, June 17, p. 20.

Hilts, Philip J. 1992. "Touched by AIDS, Minister Finds Doors Shut." *The New York Times*, September 8, pp. A1, D14.

Himmelstein, Jerome L. 1983. *The Strange Career of Marihuana: Politics and Ideology of Drug Control*. Westport, Conn.: Greenwood Press.

Hinch, Ronald. 1983. "Marxist Criminology in the 1970s: Clarifying the Clutter." *Crime and Social Justice*, 13 (Summer): 65–74.

Hinch, Ronald. 1984. *An Analysis of Class, State, and Crime: A Contribution of Critical Criminology*. Hamilton, Ontario: Ph.D. dissertation, Department of Sociology, McMaster University.

Hindelang, Michael J. 1974. "Decisions of Shoplifting Victims to Invoke the Criminal Justice Process." *Social Problems*, 21 (April): 580–593.

Hirschi, Travis. 1969. *Causes of Delinquency*. Berkeley: University of California Press.

Hirschi, Travis. 1973. "Procedural Rules and the Explanation of Crime." *Social Problems*, 21 (Fall): 159–173.

Hirschi, Travis, and Michael R. Gottfredson. 1983. "Age and the Explanation of Crime." *American Journal of Sociology*, 89 (November): 552–584.

Hirschi, Travis, and Michael R. Gottfredson. 1985. "Age and Crime, Logic and Scholarship: Comment on Greenberg." *American Journal of Sociology*, 91 (July): 22–27.

Hirschi, Travis, and Michael Gottfredson. 1987. "Causes of White-Collar Crime," *Criminology*, 25 (November): 949–974.

Hirschi, Travis, and Michael R. Gottfredson, 1989. "The Significance of White Collar Crime for a General Theory of Crime," *Criminology*, 27 (August): 359–371.

Hirschi, Travis, and Hanan C. Selvin. 1966. "False Criteria of Causality in Delinquency Research." *Social Problems*, 13 (Winter): 254–268.

Hirschi, Travis, and Hanan C. Selvin. 1967. *Delinquency*

Research: An Appraisal of Analytic Methods. New York: Free Press.

Hoffman, Martin. 1968. *The Gay World*. New York: Basic Books.

Hoffman, Richard J. 1980. "Some Cultural Aspects of Greek Homosexuality." *Journal of Homosexuality*, 5 (Spring): 217–226.

Hoigard, Cecilie, and Liv Finstad. 1992. *Backstreets: Prostitution, Money, and Love*. University Park: Pennsylvania State University Press.

Hollander, Xaviera. 1972. *The Happy Hooker*. New York: Dell.

Hollingshead, August B., and Frederick C. Redlich. 1958. *Social Class and Mental Illness*. New York: John Wiley & Sons.

Holstein, James A., and Gale Miller (eds.). 1993. *Reconsidering Social Constructionism: Debates in Social Problems Theory*. New York: Aldine de Gruyter.

Hooker, Evelyn. 1965. "An Empirical Study of Some Relationships Between Sexual Patterns and Gender Identity in Male Homosexuals." In John Money (ed.), *Sex Research: New Developments*. New York: Holt, Rinehart & Winston, pp. 24–52.

Hornblower, Margot. 1993. "The Skin Trade." *Time*, June 21, pp. 45–51.

Horney, Karen. 1935. "The Problem of Feminine Masochism." *Psychoanalytic Review*, 12 (3): 241–257.

Horney, Karen. 1973. "The Problem of Feminine Masochism." In Jean Baker Miller (ed.), *Psychoanalysis and Women*. Baltimore: Penguin Books, pp. 21–38.

Horwitz, Allan V. 1990. *The Logic of Social Control*. New York: Plenum Press.

Hough, Michael. 1987. "Offenders' Choice of Target: Findings From Victim Surveys." *Journal of Qualitative Criminology*, 3: 355–369.

Hudson, Henry E. (chair). 1986. *Attorney General's Commission on Pornography: Final Report*. Washington, D.C.: U.S. Government Printing Office.

Humphreys, Laud. 1970. *Tearoom Trade: Impersonal Sex in Public Places*. Chicago: Aldine.

Humphreys, Laud. 1972. *Out of the Closets: The Sociology of Homosexual Liberation*. Englewood Cliffs, N.J.: Prentice Hall/Spectrum.

Humphreys, Laud. 1975. *Tearoom Trade: Impersonal Sex in Public Places* (rev. ed.). New York: Aldine.

Hyman, Herbert H. 1953. "The Value Systems of Different Classes." In Reinard Bendix and Seymour Martin Lipset (eds.), *Class Status, and Power*. New York: Free Press, pp. 426–442.

Inciardi, James A. 1986. *The War on Drugs: Heroin, Cocaine, Crime, and Public Policy*. Mountain View, Calif.: Mayfield.

Inciardi, James A. 1987. "Beyond Cocaine: Basuco, Crack, and Other Coca Products." *Contemporary Drug Problems*, 14 (Fall): 461–492.

Inciardi, James A. 1989. "Trading Sex for Crack Among Juvenile Drug Users: A Research Note." *Contemporary Drug Problems*, 16 (Winter): 689–700.

Inciardi, James A. 1992. *The War on Drugs II: Heroin, Cocaine, Crime, and Public Policy* (2nd ed.). Mountain View, Calif.: Mayfield.

Inciardi, James A., Ruth Horowitz, and Anne E. Pottieger. 1993. *Street Kids, Street Drugs, Street Crime: An Examination of Drug Use and Serious Delinquency in Miami*. Belmont, Calif.: Wadsworth.

Isbell, Harris. 1966. "Medical Aspects of Opiate Addiction." In

John A. O'Donnell and John C. Ball (eds.), *Narcotic Addiction*. New York: Harper & Row, pp. 62–75.

Jackman, Norman R., et al. 1963. "The Self-Image of the Prostitute." *The Sociological Quarterly*, 4 (Spring): 150–161.

Jackson, Bruce (ed.). 1974. *In the Life: Versions of the Criminal Experience*. New York: New American Library.

Jacobs, David M. 1992. *Secret Life: Firsthand Accounts of UFO Abductions*. New York: Simon & Schuster.

Jacobs, James B. 1989. *Drunk Driving: An American Dilemma*. New York: University of Chicago Press.

James, Jennifer, and Jane Meyerding. 1977. "Early Sexual Experiences and Prostitution." *American Journal of Psychiatry*, 134 (December): 1381–1385.

Janeway, Elizabeth. 1981. "Incest: A Rational Look at the Oldest Taboo." *Ms.*, November, pp. 61–64, 78, 81, 109.

Janowitz, Morris. 1978. *The Last Half Century*. Chicago: University of Chicago Press.

Jensen, Eric L., Jurg Gerber, and Ginna M. Babcock. 1991. "The New War on Drugs: Grass Roots Movement or Political Construction?" *Journal of Drug Issues*, 21 (3): 651–667.

Jesilow, Paul, Henry N. Pontell, and Gilbert Geis. 1985. "Medical Criminals: Physicians and White Collar Offenses." *Justice Quarterly*, 2 (June): 149–165.

Jesilow, Paul, Henry N. Pontell, and Gilbert Geis. 1993. *Prescription for Profit: How Doctors Defraud Medicaid*. Berkeley: University of California Press.

Johnson, Allan Griswold. 1980. "On the Prevalence of Rape in the United States." *Signs: Journal of Women in Culture and Society*, 6 (1): 136–146.

Johnson, Anne M., et al. 1992. "Sexual Lifestyle and HIV Risk." *Nature*, 360 (3 December): 410–412.

Johnson, Anne M., et al. 1994. *Sexual Attitudes and Lifestyles*. Oxford, England: Blackwell Scientific Publications.

Johnson, Bruce D., et al. 1985. *Taking Care of Business: The Economics of Crime by Heroin Abusers*. Lexington, Mass.: Lexington Books.

Johnson, Dirk. 1996. "Gay-Rights Movement Ventures Beyond Urban America." *The New York Times*, January 21, p. 12.

Johnson, Stuart, Lorne Gibson, and Rick Linden. 1978. "Alcohol and Rape In Winnipeg, 1966–1975." *Journal of Studies on Alcohol*, 39 (November): 1887–1894.

Johnston, David. 1991. "Illegal Drug Sales in Nation Put at $40 Billion." *The New York Times*, June 20, p. A20.

Johnston, Lloyd D. 1980. "Marijuana Use and the Effects of Marijuana Decriminalization." Unpublished testimony delivered at the Hearings on the Effects of Marijuana, held by the Subcommittee on Criminal Justice, Judiciary Committee, U.S. Senate, Washington, D.C., January 6.

Johnston, Lloyd D., Patrick M. O'Malley, and Jerald G. Backman. 1994a. *National Survey Results on Drug Use from The Monitoring the Future Study, 1975–1993*, Vol. I, Secondary School Students. Rockville, Md.: National Institute on Drug Abuse, HHS.

Johnston, Lloyd D., Patrick M. O'Malley, and Jerald G. Backman. 1994b. *National Survey Results on Drug Use from The Minotoring the Future Study, 1975–1993*, Vol. II, College Students and Young Adults. Rockville, Md.: National Institute on Drug Abuse, HHS.

Johnston, Lloyd D., Patrick M. O'Malley, and Jerald G. Bachman. 1995. *National Survey Results on Drug Use from The Monitoring the Future Study, 1975–1994*. Rockville, Md.: National Institute on Drug Abuse, HHS.

Jones, Edward E. 1986. "Interpreting Interpersonal Behavior: The Effects of Expectancies." *Science*, 234 (October 3): 41–46.

Jones, Edward E., et al. 1984. *Social Stigma: The Psychology of Marked Relationships*. New York: W.H. Freeman.

Jones, Helen C., and Paul W. Lovinger. 1985. *The Marijuana Question and Science's Search for an Answer*. New York: Dodd, Mead.

Jones, James H. 1981. *Bad Blood*. New York: Free Press.

Jones, Russell A. 1977, *Self-Fulfilling Prophecies: Social, Psychological, and Physiological Effects of Expectancies*. Hillsdale, N.J.: Lawrence Erlbaum.

Jones, Trevor, Brian MacLean, and Jock Young. 1986. *The Islington Crime Survey: Crime, Victimization, and Policing in Inner-City London*. Aldershot, England: Gower.

Julien, Robert M. 1995. *A Primer of Drug Action* (7th ed.). New York: W.H. Freeman.

Kagay, Michael R. 1990. "Deficit Raises as Much Alarm as Illegal Drugs, Poll Finds." *The New York Times*, July 25, p. A9.

Kalish, Carol B. 1988. "International Crime Rates." *Bureau of Justice Statistics Special Report*, May, pp. 1–11.

Kalvin, Harry, and Hans Zeisel. 1966. *The American Jury*. Boston: Little, Brown.

Kantor, Glenda Kaufman, and Murray A. Straus. 1987. "The 'Drunken Bum' Theory of Wife Beating." *Social Problems*, 34 (June): 213–230.

Kapferer, Jean-Noel. 1990. *Rumors: Uses, Interpretations, and Images* (trans. Bruce Fink). New Brunswick, N.J.: Transaction.

Kaplan, Jane Rachel (ed.). 1980. *A Woman's Conflict: The Special Relationship Between Women and Food*. New Brunswick, N.J.: Prentice Hall.

Karlen, Arno. 1971. *Sexuality and Homosexuality*. New York: W.W. Norton.

Karpel, Craig. 1975. "Ten Great Places to Have Semipublic Sex." *Penthouse*, October, pp. 123–126, 148.

Katz, Jack. 1979. "Concerted Ignorance: The Social Construction of a Cover-up. " *Urban Life: A Journal of Ethnographic Research*, 8 (October): 295–316.

Katz, Jack. 1988. *Seductions of Crime: Moral and Sensual Attractions of Doing Evil*. New York: Basic Books.

Katz, Jonathan. 1995. *The Invention of Heterosexuality*. New York: Dutton.

Kelly, Delos H. (ed.). 1993. *Deviant Behavior: A Text-Reader in the Sociology of Deviance*. New York: St. Martin's Press.

Kempton, Murray. 1992. "A New Colonialism." *The New York Review*, November 19, p. 39.

Kendall, R.E., et al. 1971. "Diagnostic Criteria of American and British Psychiatrists." *Archives of General Psychiatry*, 25 (August): 123–130.

Kerr, Peter. 1986. "Anatomy of an Issue: Drugs, the Evidence, the Reaction." *The New York Times*, November 17, pp. A1, B6.

Kerr, Peter. 1988. "The Unspeakable Is Debated: Should Drugs Be Legalized?" *The New York Times*, May 15, pp. 1, 15.

Kessler, Ronald C. 1979. "Stress, Social Status, and Psychological Distress." *Journal of Health and Social Behavior*, 20 (September): 259–272.

Kessler, Ronald C., et al. 1994. Lifetime and 12-Month Prevalence of DSM-III Psychiatric Disorders in the United States." *Archives of General Psychiatry*, 51 (1): 8–19.

Kety, Seymour S. 1974. "From Rationalization to Reason." *American Journal of Psychiatry*, 131 (September): 957–963.

Kimball, Roger. 1993. Review of David Halle, *Inside Culture: Art and Class in the American Home*, Chicago: University of Chicago Press, in *The Times Literary Supplement*, June 10, p. 29.

Kimmel, Michael. 1993. "Does Pornography Cause Rape?" *Violence Update*, 3 (June): 1–2, 4, 8.

King, Carl F. 1968. "Police Discretion and the Judgment That a Crime Has Been Committed." *University of Pennsylvania Law Review*, 117 (December): 227–322.

Kinsey, Alfred C., Wardell B. Pomeroy, and Clyde E. Martin. 1948. *Sexual Behavior in the Human Male*. Philadelphia: W.B. Saunders.

Kinsey, Alfred C., Wardell B. Pomeroy, Clyde E. Martin, and Paul H. Gebhard. 1953. *Sexual Behavior in the Human Female*. Philadelphia: W.B. Saunders.

Kirk, Stuart A., and Herb Kutchins. 1994. "Is Bad Writing a Mental Disorder?" *The New York Times*, June 20, p. A17.

Kitsuse, John I. 1962. "Societal Reactions to Deviant Behavior: Problems of Theory and Method." *Social Problems*, 9 (Winter): 247–257.

Kitsuse, John I. 1972. "Deviance, Deviant Behavior, and Deviants: Some Conceptual Problems." In William J. Filstead (ed.), *An Introduction to Deviance: Readings in the Process of Making Deviants*. Chicago: Markham, pp. 233–243.

Kitsuse, John I. 1975. "The New Conception of Deviance and Its Critics." In Walter R. Gove (ed.), *The Labelling of Deviance: Evaluating a Perspective*. New York: John Wiley & Sons/Halstead/Sage, pp. 273–284.

Kitsuse, John I. 1980. "The New Conception of Deviance and its Critics." In Walter R. Gove (ed.), *The Labelling of Deviance: Evaluating a Perspective*. Newbury Park, Calif.: Sage, pp. 381–393.

Kitsuse, John I., and Joseph W. Schneider. 1989. Preface." In Joel Best (ed.), *Images of Issues: Typifying Contemporary Social Problems*. New York: Aldine de Gruyter, pp. xi–xiii.

Kitsuse, John I., and Malcolm Spector. 1973. "Toward a Sociology of Social Problems: Social Conditions, Value-Judgments, and Social Problems." *Social Problems*, 20 (Spring): 407–419.

Kitsuse, John I., and Malcolm Spector. 1975. "Social Problems and Deviance: Some Parallel Issues." *Social Problems*, 22 (June): 584–594.

Klassen, Albert D., Colin J. Williams, and Eugene E. Levitt. 1989. *Sex and Morality in the U.S.: An Empirical Enquiry Under the Auspices of the Kinsey Institute*. Middletown, Conn.: Wesleyan University Press.

Klaus, Patsy A., and Carol B. Kalish. 1984. "The Severity of Crime." *Bureau of Justice Statistics*, January, pp. 1–5.

Klein, Dorie. 1973. "The Etiology of Female Crime: A Review of the Literature." *Issues in Criminology*, 8 (Fall): 3–30.

Klemmack, Susan H., and David L. Klemmack. 1976. "The Social Definition of Rape." In Marcia J. Walker and Stanley L. Brodsky (eds.), *Sexual Assault*. Lexington, Mass.: D. C. Heath, pp. 135–147.

Knopf, Terry Ann. 1975. *Rumors, Race, and Riots*. New Brunswick, N.J.: Transaction.

Kobler, John. 1973. *Ardent Spirits: The Rise and Fall of Prohibition*. G.P. Putnam's Sons.

Kolata, Gina. 1990. "Under Pressure and Stigma, More Doctors Shun Abortion." *The New York Times*, January 8, pp. A1, B8.

Kolata, Gina. 1992a. "Maker of Sleeping Pill Hid Data on Side Effects, Researchers Say." *The New York Times*, January 20, pp. A1, B7.

Kolata, Gina. 1992b. "Finding a Bad Night's Sleep with Halcion." *The New York Times*, January 20, p. B7.

Kolata, Gina. 1995. "New Picture of Who Will Get AIDS Is Crammed With Addicts." *The New York Times*, February 28, p. C3.

Kolb, Laurence, and A.G. DuMez. 1924. "The Prevalence and Trend of Drug Addiction in the United States and Factors Influencing It." *Public Health Reports*, 39 (May 23): 1179–1204.

Kolbert, Elizabeth. 1987. "Youths' Buying of Alcohol Fell in '86." *The New York Times*, February 13, p. B2.

Kolbert, Elizabeth. 1991. "Sexual Harassment at Work Is Pervasive, Survey Suggests." *The New York Times*, October 11, pp. A1, A17.

Kolko, Gabriel. 1963. *The Triumph of Conservativism*. New York: Free Press.

Kornbluth, Jesse. 1992. *Highly Confident: The Crime and Punishment of Michael Milken*. New York: William Morrow.

Kornhauser, Ruth. 1978. *Social Sources of Delinquency: An Appraisal of Analytic Models*. Chicago: University of Chicago Press.

Koss, Pary P., and Kenneth E. Leonard. 1984. "Sexually Aggressive Men: Empirical Findings and Theoretical Implications." In Neil M. Malamuth and Edward Donnerstein (eds.), *Pornography and Sexual Aggression*. Orlando, Fla.: Academic Press, pp. 213–232.

Koss, Mary P., and Cheryl J. Oros. 1982. "Sexual Experiences Survey: A Research Instrument Investigating Sexual Aggression and Victimization." *Journal of Consulting and Clinical Psychology*, 50 (3): 455–457.

Kossy, Donna. 1994. *Kooks: A Guide to the Outer Limits of Human Belief*. Portland, Oregon: Feral House.

Kramer, Peter D. 1993. *Listening to Prozac*. New York & London: Penguin Books.

Kramer, Ronald C. 1984. "Corporate Criminality: The Development of an Idea." In Ellen Hochstedler (ed.), *Corporations as Criminals*. Beverly Hills, Calif. Sage, pp. 13–37.

Kreisman, Dolores, and Virginia D. Joy. 1974. "Family Response to Mental Illness of a Relative: A Review of the Literature." *Schizophrenia Bulletin*, 10 (Fall): 34–57.

Krim, Seymour. 1961. "Making It!" In Seymour Krim, *Views of a Nearsighted Canoneer*. New York: Excelsior Press, pp. 32–38.

Kristof, Nicholas D. 1990. "China Using Electrodes To 'Cure' Homosexuals." *The New York Times*, January 29, p. A2.

Krohn, Marvin D., and Ronald L. Akers. 1977. "An Alternative View of the Labeling Versus Psychiatric Perspectives on Societal Reaction to Mental Illness." *Social Forces*, 56 (December): 341–361.

Lacayo, Richard. 1989. "Whose Life Is It?" *Time*, May 1, pp. 20–24.

LaFree, Gary. 1989. *Rape and Criminal Justice: The Social Construction of Sexual Assault*. Belmont, Calif.: Wadsworth.

Lambert, Bruce. 1988. "AIDS Among Prostitutes Not as Prevalent as Believed, Studies Show." *The New York Times*, September 20, pp. B1, B5.

Landman, Janet T., and Robyn Dawes. 1982. "Psychotherapy

Outcome: Smith and Glass' Conclusions Stand Up Under Scrutiny." *Psychological Bulletin*, 57: 504–516.

Lang, John S., with Ronald A. Taylor. 1986. "America on Drugs." *U.S. News & World Report*, July 28, pp. 48–49.

Langan, Patrick, and Christopher A. Innes. 1986. "Predicting Domestic Violence Against Women." *Bureau of Justice Statistics Special Report*, August, pp. 1–5.

Langley, Roger, and Richard G. Levy. 1977. *Wife Beating: The Silent Crisis*. New York: Dutton.

Langone, John. 1985. "AIDS." *Discover*, December, pp. 28–53.

Langone, John. 1988. *AIDS: The Facts*. Boston: Little, Brown.

Lanza-Kaduce, Lonn. 1980. "Deviance Among Professionals: The Case of Unnecessary Surgery." *Deviant Behavior*, 1 (April-September): 333–359.

Laumann, Edward O., John H. Gagnon, Robert T. Michael, and Stuart Michaels. 1994. *The Social Organization of Sexuality: Sexual Practices in the United States*. Chicago: University of Chicago Press.

Lawson, Anette. 1988. *Adultery: An Analysis of Love and Betrayal*. New York: Basic Books.

Lea, John, and Jock Young. 1984. *What Is to Be Done About Law and Order?* Harmondsworth, England: Penguin Books.

Lederer, Laura (ed.). 1982. *Take Back the Night: Women on Pornography*. New York: Bantam Books.

Lee, Alfred McClung, and Norman Daymond Humphrey. 1943. *Race Riot*. New York: Dryden Press.

Lee, Martin A. 1982. "CIA: Carcinogen." *The Nation*, 235 (18): 675.

Leerson, Charles, with Bob Cohn. 1986. "A Gay Conservative Tells His Story." *Newsweek*, August 18, p. 18.

Leigh, Barbara C., Mark T. Temple, and Karen F. Trocki. 1993. "The Sexual Behavior of US Adults: Results from a National Survey." *American Journal of Public Health*, 83 (10): 1400–1408.

Leighton, D.C., et al. 1963. *The Character of Danger: Psychiatric Symptoms in Selected Communities*. New York: Basic Books.

Lemert, Edwin M. 1951. *Social Pathology: A Systematic Approach to the Study of Sociopathic Behavior*. New York: McGraw-Hill.

Lemert, Edwin M. 1953. "An Isolation and Closure Theory of Naive Check Forgery." *Journal of Criminal Law, Criminology, and Police Science*, 44 (September-October): 296–307.

Lemert, Edwin M. 1958. "The Behavior of the Systematic Check Forger." *Social Problems*, 6 (Fall): 141–149.

Lemert, Edwin M. 1964a. "Social Structure, Social Control, and Deviation." In Marshall B. Clinard (ed.), *Anomie and Deviant Behavior: A Discussion and Critique*. New York: Free Press, 57–97.

Lemert, Edwin M. 1964b. "The Behavior of the Systematic Check Forger." In Howard S. Becker (ed.), *The Other Side: Perspectives on Deviance*. New York: Free Press, pp. 211–224.

Lemert, Edwin M. 1972. *Human Deviance, Social Problems, and Social Control* (2nd ed.). Englewood Cliffs, N.J.: Prentice Hall.

Lemert, Edwin M. 1974. "Beyond Mead: The Societal Reaction to Deviance." *Social Problems*, 21 (April): 457–467.

Lender, Mark Edward, and James Kirby Martin. 1987. *Drinking in America: A History* (rev. ed.). New York: Free Press.

Leonard, Eileen B. 1982. *Women, Crime, and Society: A Critique of Theoretical Criminology*. New York: Longman.

LeVay, Simon. 1995. *The Sexual Brain*. Cambridge, Mass.: MIT Press/Bradford.

Levi, Ken. 1981. "Becoming a Hit Man: Neutralization in a Very Deviant Career." *Urban Life*, 10 (April): 47–63.

Levin, Max. 1968. "The Meaning of Sex and Marriage." *Bride and Home*, Autumn Preview, pp. 102–103, 156, 166–168.

Levine, Harry Gene. 1983. "The Committee of Fifty and the Origins of Alcohol Control." *Journal of Drug Issues*, 13 (Winter): 95–116.

Levine, Harry Gene. 1985. "The Birth of American Alcohol Control: Prohibition, the Power Elite, and the Problem of Lawlessness." *Contemporary Drug Problems*, 12 (Spring): 63–115.

Levine, Harry Gene. 1989. "Preface." In John J. Rumbarger, *Profits, Power, and Prohibition: Alcohol Reform and the Industrializing of America 1800–1930*. Albany: State University of New York Press, pp. vix–xvi.

Levine, Harry Gene, and Craig Reinarman. 1992. "From Prohibition to Regulation: Lessons from Alcohol Policy for Drug Policy." *The Milbank Quarterly*, 69 (3): 1–34.

Levine, Martin P., and Richard R. Troiden. 1988. "The Myth of Sexual Compulsivity." *Journal of Sex Research*, 25 (August): 347–363.

LeVine, Robert A. 1959. "Gusii Sex Offenses: A Study in Social Control." *American Anthropologist*, 61 (December): 965–990.

Levitt, Eugene E., and Albert D. Klassen. 1974. "Public Attitutdes Toward Homosexuality." *Journal of Homosexual*, 1 (Fall): 29–43.

Lewin, Tamar. 1991. "A Case Study of Sexual Harassment and the Law." *The New York Times*, October 11, p. A17.

Lewontin, R.C. 1995. "Sex, Lies, and Social Science." *The New York Review*, April 20, pp. 24–29.

Liazos, Alexander. 1972. "The Poverty of the Sociology of Deviance: Nuts, Sluts, and Preverts." *Social Problems*, 20 (Summer): 103–120.

Liazos, Alexander. 1982. *People First: An Introduction to Social Problems*. Boston: Allyn & Bacon.

Lief, Harold I. 1977. "Current Thinking on Homosexuality." *Medical Aspects of Human Sexuality*, 11 (November): 110–111.

Liem, Ramsay, and Joan Liem. 1978. "Social Class and Mental Illness Reconsidered: The Role of Economic Stress and Social Support." *Journal of Health and Social Behavior*, 19 (June): 139–156.

Lindesmith, Alfred R. 1947. *Opiate Addiction*. Bloomington, Ind.: Principia Press.

Lindesmith, Alfred R. 1965. *The Addict and the Law*. Bloomington, Ind.: Indiana University Press.

Lindesmith, Alfred R. 1968. *Addiction and Opiates*. Chicago: Aldine.

Lindesmith, Alfred R., and John H. Gagnon. 1964. "Anomie and Drug Addiction." In Marshall B. Clinard (ed.), *Anomie and Deviant Behavior: A Discussion and Critique*. New York: Free Press, pp. 158–188.

Lingeman, Richard R. 1974. *Drugs From A to Z* (2nd ed.). New York: McGraw-Hill.

Link, Bruce G. 1987. "Understanding Labeling Effects in the Area of Mental Disorders: An Assessment of the Effects of Expectations of Rejection." *American Sociological Review*, 52 (February): 96–112.

Link, Bruce G., Howard Andrews, and Francis T. Cullen. 1992. "The Violent and Illegal Behavior of Mental Patients Reconsidered." *American Sociological Review*, 57 (June): 275–292.

Link, Bruce G., and Frances T. Cullen. 1989. "The Labeling Theory of Mental Disorder: A Review of the Evidence." In James Greenly (ed.), *Mental Illness in Social Context*. Detroit: Wayne State University Press.

Link, Bruce G., Francis T. Cullen, Elmer Struening, Patrick Shrout, and Bruce P. Dohrenwend. 1989. "A Modified Labeling Theory Approach to Mental Disorders: An Empirical Assessment." *American Sociological Review*, 54 (June): 400–423.

Link, Bruce G., Bruce P. Dohrenwend, and Andrew E. Skodol. 1986. "Socioeconomic Status and Schizophrenia: Noisome Occupational Characteristics as a Risk Factor." *American Sociological Review*, 51 (April): 242–258.

Linsky, Arnold A., and Murray A. Straus. 1986. *Social Stress in the United States: Links to Regional Patterns in Crime and Illness*. Dover, Mass.: Auburn House.

Little, Craig B. 1995. *Deviance and Control: Theory, Research, and Social Policy* (3rd ed.). Itasca, Ill.: F.E. Peacock.

Livingston, Jay. 1996. *Crime and Criminology* (2nd ed.). Upper Saddle River, N.J.: Prentice Hall.

Lofland, John. 1969. *Deviance and Identity*. Englewood Cliffs, N.J.: Prentice Hall.

Loftus, Elizabeth. 1979. *Eyewitness Testimony*. Cambridge, Mass.: Harvard University Press.

Loftus, Elizabeth, and Katherine Ketcham. 1994. *The Myth of Repressed Memory: False Memories and Allegations of Child Abuse*. New York: St. Martin's Press.

Loftus, T.A. 1960. *Meaning and Methods of Diagnosis in Clinical Psychiatry*. Philadelphia: Lea & Febinger.

Lombroso, Cesare, and William Ferro. 1916. *The Female Offender*. New York: Appleton.

London, Robb. 1990. "Gay Groups Turn to State Courts to Win Rights." *The New York Times*, December 21, p. B6.

Longino, Helen E. 1982. "Pornography, Oppression and Freedom: A Closer Look." In Laura Lederer (ed.), *Take Back the Night: Women on Pornography*. New York: Bantam Books, pp. 26–41.

Lowman, John, Margaret Jackson, T.S. Palys, and Shelly Gavigan (eds.). 1986. *Regulating Sex*. Burnaby, British Columbia: School of Criminology, Simon Fraser University.

Lowman, John, Robert J. Menzies, and T.S. Palys (eds.). 1987. *Transcarceration: Essays in the Sociology of Social Control*. Gower, England: Aldershot.

Lumby, Malcolm E. 1976. "Homophobia: The Quest for a Valid Scale." *Journal of Homosexuality*, 2 (Fall): 39–47.

Lundsgaarde, Henry P. 1977. *Murder in Space City: A Cultural Analysis of Houston Homicide Patterns*. New York: Oxford University Press.

Lyall, Sarah. 1996. "Fearing Reprisal, Publisher Drops Book on Greece." *The New York Times*, February 17, p. 3.

Lynch, Michael J., and W. Byron Groves. 1995. "In Defense of Comparative Criminology: A Critique of General Theory and the Rational Man." In Freda Adler and William S. Laufer (eds.), *The Legacy of Anomie Theory*. New Brunswick, N.J.: Transaction, pp. 367–392.

Lynn, Barry W. 1986. *Polluting the Censorship Debate: A Summary and Critique of the Final Report of the Attorney General's Commission on Pornography*. Washington, D.C.: American Civil Liberties Union.

MacAndrew, Craig, and Robert B. Edgerton. 1969. *Drunken Comportment*. Chicago: Aldine.

Mack, John E. 1995. *Abduction: Human Encounters with Aliens*. New York: Ballantine Books.

MacKinnon, Catherine A. 1979. *Sexual Harassment of Working Women*. New Haven, Conn.: Yale University Press.

MacKinnon, Catherine A. 1987. *Feminism Unmodified: Discourses on Life and Law*. Cambridge, Mass.: Harvard University Press.

MacKinnon, Catherine A. 1993. *Only Words*. Cambridge, Mass.: Harvard University Press.

Maddox, George L., Kurt W. Back, and Veronica R. Liederman. 1968. "Overweight as Social Deviance and Disability." *Journal of Health and Social Behavior*, 9 (December): 287–298.

Maitland, Leslie. 1976. "Rape Study Details the How, the Why, and the Who." *The New York Times*, July 29, pp. 25, 32.

Malamuth, Neil M. 1981. "Rape Proclivity Among Males." *Journal of Social Issues*, 37 (4): 138–157.

Malamuth, Neil M., and James V.P. Check. 1981. "The Effects of Mass Media Exposure on Acceptance of Violence Against Women: A Field Experiment." *Journal of Research in Personality*, 15 (December): 436–446.

Malamuth, Neil M., James V.P. Check, and John Briere. 1986. "Sexual Arousal in Response to Aggression: Ideological, Aggressive, and Sexual Correlates." *Journal of Personality and Social Psychology*, 50 (2): 330–340.

Malamuth, Neil M., Christopher L. Heavey, and Daniel Linz. 1992. "Predicting Men's Antisocial Behavior Against Women: The Interaction Model of Sexual Aggression." In Gordon C. Nagayama Hall (ed.), *Sexual Aggression: Issues in Etiology and Assessment, Treatment, and Policy*. New York: Hemisphere, pp. 63–97.

Malamuth, Neil M., and Barry Spinner. 1980. "A Longitudinal Content Analysis of Sexual Violence in the Best-Selling Erotic Magazines." *Journal for Sex Research*, 16 (August): 226–237.

Malcolm, Andrew H. 1987. "Nation Is Gaining on Drunken Driving." *The New York Times*, March 23, pp. A1, A15.

Malcolm, Janet. 1990. *The Journalist and the Murderer*. New York: Vintage.

Malinowski, Bronislaw. 1926. *Crime and Custom in Savage Society*. London: Routledge & Kegan Paul.

Maltby, Karin. 1982. "Review Committee Clears Sobells on Scientific Misconduct Charges." *The Journal* (Addiction Research Foundation, Toronto), December 1, p. 2.

Manis, Jerome. 1974. "The Concept of Social Problems: Vox Poluli and Sociological Analysis." *Social Problems*, 21 (Winter): 305–315.

Manis, Jerome. 1976. *Analyzing Social Problems*. New York: Praeger.

Mankoff, Milton. 1971. "Societal Reaction and Career Deviance: A Marxist Critique." *The Sociological Quarterly*, 12 (Spring): 204–218.

Mankoff, Milton. 1980. "A Tower of Babel: Marxist Criminologists and Their Critics." In James A. Inciardi (eds.). *Radical Criminology: The Coming Crisis*. Newbury Park, Calif.: Sage, pp. 139–148.

Mann, Coramae Richey. 1984. *Female Crime and Delinquency*. Birmingham: University of Alabama.

Mann, Coramae Richey. 1993. *Unequal Justice: A Question of Color*. Bloomington: Indiana University Press.

Mann, Coramae Richey. 1996. *When Women Kill*. Albany: State University of New York Press.

Mann, Peggy. 1985. *Marijuana Alert*. New York: McGraw-Hill.

Mannheim, Herman. 1965. *Comparative Criminology*. London: Routledge & Kegan Paul.

Manning, Peter K. 1975. "Deviance and Dogma: Comments on the Labelling Perspective." *British Journal of Criminology*, 15 (January): 1–20.

Marcuse, Herbert. 1966. *Eros and Civilization: A Philosophical Inquiry into Freud*. Boston: Bracon Press.

Margolick, David. 1994. "Rapist Isn't Exiled Far Enough for a Community in Wilderness." *The New York Times*, March 27, p. 18.

Markle, Gerald E., and Ronald J. Troyer. 1979. "Smoke Gets in Your Eyes: Cigarette Smoking as Deviant Behavior." *Social Problems*, 26 (June): 611–625.

Marks, Peter. 1995. "Dealer's Plea in G.M. Fraud May Be Bargain of His Life." *The New York Times*, January 20, pp. A1, B6.

Marshall, Donald S. 1971. "Sexual Behavior in Mangaia." In Donald S. Marshall and Robert C. Suggs (eds.), *Human Sexual Behavior: Variations in the Ethnographic Spectrum*. New York: Basic Books, pp. 103–162.

Martin, Del. 1976. *Battered Wives*. San Francisco: Glide Foundation.

Massa, Robert. 1991. "The Way We Wear Our Genes." *The Village Voice*, December 24, p. 49.

Masters, William H., and Virginia E. Johnson. 1966. *Human Sexual Response*. Boston: Little, Brown.

Masters, William H., and Virginia E. Johnson. 1970. *Human Sexual Inadequacy*. Boston: Little, Brown.

Masters, William H., and Virginia E. Johnson. 1979. *Homosexuality in Perspective*. Boston: Little, Brown.

Masters, William H., Virginia E. Johnson, and Robert C. Kolodny. 1988. *Crisis: Heterosexual Behavior in the Age of AIDS*. New York: Grove Press.

Matthews, Roger, and Jock Young (eds.). 1986. *Confronting Crime*. Newbury Park, Calif.: Sage.

Matza, David. 1969. *Becoming Deviant*. Englewood Cliffs, N.J.: Prentice Hall.

Mauss, Armand L. 1975. *Social Problems as Social Movements*. Philadelphia: Lippencott.

McAuliffe, William E., and Robert A. Gordon. 1974. "A Test of Lindesmith's Theory of Addiction: The Frequency of Euphoria Among Long-Term Addicts." *American Journal of Sociology*, 79 (January): 795–840.

McAuliffe, William E., and Robert A. Gordon. 1980. "Reinforcement and the Combination of Effects: Summary of a Theory of Opiate Addiction." In Dan J. Lettieri et al. (eds.), *Theories on Drug Abuse*. Rockville, Md.: National Institute on Drug Abuse, pp. 137–141.

McCaghy, Charles H. 1967. "Child Molesters: A Study of Their Career as Deviants." In Marshall B. Clinard and Richard Quinney (eds.), *Criminal Behavior Systems: A Typology*. New York: Holt, Rinehart & Winston, pp. 75–88.

McCaghy, Charles H. 1968. "Drinking and Disavowal: The Case of Child Molesters." *Social Problems*, 16 (Summer): 43–49.

McCaghy, Charles H. 1976. *Deviant Behavior: Crime, Conflict, and Interest Groups*. New York: Macmillan.

McCaghy, Charles H., and Timothy A. Capron. 1994. *Deviant Behavior: Crime, Conflict, and Interest Groups* (3rd ed.). New York: Macmillan.

McCormack, Thelma. 1978. "Machismo in Media Research: A Critical Review of Research on Violence and Pornography." *Social Problems*, 28 (February): 244–255.

McCoy, Clyde B., and James A. Inciardi. 1995. *Sex, Drugs, and the Continuing Spread of AIDS*. Los Angeles: Roxbury.

McCoy, H. Virginia, Christine Miles, and James A. Inciardi. 1995. "Survival Sex: Inner-City Women and Crack-Cocaine," in James A. Inciardi and Karen McElrath (eds.), *The American Drug Scene: An Anthology*. Los Angeles: Roxbury, pp. 172–177.

McIntosh, Mary. 1968. "The Homosexual Role." *Social Problems*, 16 (Fall): 182–192.

McQuiston, John T. 1995. "Lesbian Banns Divide Church, and a Minister Loses His Job." *The New York Times*, August 2, p. B4.

Mechanic, David. 1989. *Mental Health and Social Policy* (3rd ed.). Englewood Cliffs, N.J.: Prentice Hall.

Medea, Andrea, and Kathleen Thompson. 1974. *Against Rape*. New York: Farrar, Straus & Giroux.

Meier, Robert F. 1982. "Perspectives on the Concept of Social Control." *Annual Review of Sociology*, 8: 35–55.

Meier, Robert F., and Gilbert Geis. 1979. "The White Collar Offender." In Hans Toch (ed.), *The Psychology of Crime and Criminal Justice*. New York: Holt, Reinhart & Winston, pp. 428–445.

Mendelsohn, Beniamin. 1963. "The Origin of the Doctrine of Victimology." *Excerpta Criminologica*, 3 (May-June): 239–244.

Mendelson, Jack H., and Nancy Mello. 1985. *Alcohol Use and Abuse in America*. Boston: Little, Brown.

Merson, Michael. 1995. "What Can Be Done?" *The UNESCO Courier*, June, pp. 10–13.

Merton, Robert K. 1938. "Social Structure and Anomie." *American Sociological Review*, 3 (October): 672–682.

Merton, Robert K. 1948. "The Self-Fulfilling Prophecy." *Antioch Review*, 7 (Summer): 193–210.

Merton, Robert K. 1949. *Social Theory and Social Structure*. New York: Free Press.

Merton, Robert K. 1957. *Social Theory and Social Structure* (rev. & expanded ed.). New York: Free Press.

Merton, Robert K. 1968. *Social Theory and Social Structure* (enlarged ed.). New York: Free Press.

Merton, Robert K. 1971. "Social Problems and Sociological Theory." In Robert K. Merton and Robert Nisbet (eds.), *Contemporary Social Problems* (3rd ed.). New York: Harcourt Brace Jovanovich, pp. 793–845.

Merton, Robert K. 1976. "Introduction: The Sociology of Social Problems." In Robert K. Merton and Robert Nisbet (eds.), *Contemporary Social Problems* (4th ed.). New York: Harcourt Brace Jovanovich, pp. 5–43.

Merton, Robert K., and Robert Nisbet (eds.). 1976. *Contemporary Social Problems* (4th ed.). New York: Harcourt Brace Jovanovich.

Messenger, John C. 1971. "Sex and Repression in an Irish Folk Community." In Donald S. Marshall and Robert C. Suggs (eds.), *Human Sexual Behavior: Variations in the Ethnographic Spectrum*. New York: Basic Books, pp. 3–37.

Messner, Steven F., and Richard Rosenfeld. 1994. *Crime and the American Dream*. Belmont, Calif.: Wadsworth.

Miall, Charlene E. 1986. "The Stigma of Involuntary Childlessness." *Social Problems*, 33 (April): 268–282.

Michael, Robert T., John H. Gagnon, Edward O. Laumann, and

Gina Kolata. 1994. *Sex in America: A Definitive Survey.* Boston: Little, Brown.

Michalowski, Raymond J., and Ronald C. Kramer. 1987. "The Space Between the Laws: The Problem of Corporate Crime in a Transnational Context." *Social Problems*, 34 (February): 34–53.

Michigan, University of, News and Information Services. 1995. "Drug Use Rises Again in 1995 Among American Teens." News Release, December 15.

Miller, Gale, and James A. Holstein (eds.). 1993. *Constructivist Controversies: Issues in Social Problems Theory.* New York: Aldine de Gruyter.

Miller, James. 1992. "Beyond Good and Evil: Michel Foucault's Death Valley Days and Leather Bar Nights." *Lingua Franca*, November-December, pp. 34–43.

Miller, James. 1993. *The Passion of Foucault.* New York: Simon & Schuster.

Miller, Jody. 1995. "Sex Tourism in Southeast Asia." In Alex Thio and Thomas S. Calhoun (eds.), *Readings in Deviant Behavior.* New York: HarperCollins, pp. 278–283.

Miller, Judith Droitcour, and Ira H. Cisin. 1980. *Highlights from the National Survey on Drug Abuse: 1979.* Rockville, Md.: National Institute on Drug Abuse.

Miller, Walter B. 1958. "Lower Class Culture as a Generating Milieu of Gang Delinquency." *Journal of Social Issues*, 14 (3): 5–19.

Millett, Kate (ed.). 1973. *The Prostitution Papers.* New York: Avon.

Millman, Marcia. 1975. "She Did It All for Love: A Feminist View of the Sociology of Deviance." In Marcia Millman and Rosabeth Kantor Moss (eds.), *Another Voice: Feminist Perspectives on Social Life and Social Science.* Garden City, N.Y.: Doubleday-Anchor, pp. 251–279.

Mills, C. Wright. 1942. "The Social Life of a Modern Community," review of W. Lloyd Warner and Paul S. Lunt, *The Social Life of a Community.* New Haven, Conn.: Yale University Press, 1941, in *American Sociological Review*, 7 (April): 263–271.

Mills, C. Wright. 1943. "The Professional Ideology of Social Pathologists." *American Journal of Sociology*, 49 (September): 165–180.

Mills, C. Wright. 1963. *Power, Politics, and People: The Collected Essays of C. Wright Mills* (ed. Irving Louis Horowitz). New York: Ballantine Books.

Minai, Naila. 1981. *Women in Islam: Tradition and Transition in the Middle East.* New York: Seaview Press.

Miron, J.A., and J. Zweibel. 1991. "Alcohol Consumption During Prohibition." *American Economic Association Papers and Proceedings*, 81 (2): 242–247.

Modell, Jack C. and James M. Mountz. 1990. "Drinking and Flying—The Problem of Alcohol Use by Pilots." *New England Journal of Medicine*, 323 (August 16): 455–461.

Molony, Carol. 1988. "The Truth About the Tasaday: Are They a Primitive Tribe—Or a Modern Hoax?" *The Sciences*, September-October, pp. 12–20.

Montgomery, Ruth. 1988. *Aliens Among Us.* New York: G.P. Putnam's Sons.

Morales, Edmundo. 1989. *Cocaine: White Gold Rush in Peru.* Tucson: University of Arizona Press.

Morgan, John P. 1991. "Prohibition Is Perverse Policy: What Was True in 1933 Is True Now." In Melvyn B. Kraus and Edward P. Lazear (eds.), *Searching for Alternatives: Drug Control Policy in the United States.* Stanford, Calif.: Hoover Institution Press, pp. 405–423.

Morgan, Robin. 1982. "Theory and Practice: Pornography and Rape." In Laura Lederer (ed.), *Take Back the Night: Women on Pornography.* New York: Bantam Books, pp. 125–140.

Morris, Nomi, et al. 1993. "The Skin Trade." *Time*, June 21, pp. 45–51.

Moskowitz, Herbert, and Marcelline Burns. 1990. "Effects of Alcohol on Driving Performance." *Alcohol Health and Research World*, 14 (1): 12–14.

Moynihan, Daniel Patrick. 1993. "Defining Deviancy Down." *The American Scholar*, 62 (Winter 1993): 25–33.

Murphy, Jane M. 1976. "Psychiatric Labeling in Cross-Cultural Perspective." *Science*, 191 (12 March): 1019–1028.

Musto, David F. 1973. *The American Disease: Origins of Narcotic Control.* New Haven, Conn.: Yale University Press.

Musto, David F. 1987. *The American Disease: Origins of Narcotic Control* (expanded. ed.). New York: Oxford University Press.

Mydans, Seth. 1988. "20th Century Lawsuit Asserts Stone-Age Identity." *The New York Times*, October 29, p. 4.

Mydans, Seth. 1992. "Christian Conservatives Counting Gains in Local Votes." *The New York Times*, November 21, pp. 1, 9.

Nadelmann, Ethan A. 1988. "The Case for Legalization." *The Public Interest*, no.92 (Summer): 3–31.

Nadelmann, Ethan A. 1989. "Drug Prohibition in the United States: Costs, Consequences, and Alternatives." *Science*, 245 (September 1): 939–947.

Naffin[e], Ngaire. 1981. "Theorizing About Female Crime." In Satyanshu K. Mukherjee and Jocelynne A. Scutt (eds.), *Women and Crime.* North Sydney: George Allen & Unwin Australia, pp. 70–91.

Naffine, Ngaire. 1987. *Female Crime: The Construction of Women in Criminology.* London: Allen & Unwin.

Nance, John. 1975. *The Gentle Tasaday.* New York: Harcourt Brace Jovanovich.

National Institute on Drug Abuse (NIDA). 1986. "Highlights of the 1985 National Household Survey on Drug Abuse." Rockville, Md.: National Institute on Drug Abuse.

Nelson, Steve, and Menachem Amir. 1975. "The Hitchhike Victim of Rape: A Research Report." In Israel Drapkin and Emilio Viano (eds.), *Victimology: A New Focus.* Lexington, Mass.: Lexington Books, pp. 47–65.

Nettler, Gwynn. 1970. *Explanations.* New York: McGraw-Hill.

Nettler, Gwynn. 1974a. "On Telling Who's Crazy." *American Sociological Review*, 39 (December): 893–894.

Nettler, Gwynn. 1974b. "Embezzlement Without Problems." *British Journal of Criminology*, 14 (January): 70–77.

Nettler, Gwynn. 1982. *Killing One Another.* Cincinnati, Ohio: Anderson.

Nettler, Gwynn. 1984. *Explaining Crime* (3rd ed.). New York: McGraw-Hill.

Neuspiel, D.R., et al. 1991. "Maternal Cocaine Use and Infant Behavior." *Neurotoxicology and Teratology*, 13 (March-April): 229–233.

Newman, Donald J. 1958. "Public Attitudes Toward a Form of White Collar Crime." *Social Problems*, 4 (Winter): 228–232.

Newman, Graeme. 1976. *Comparative Deviance: Perception and Law in Six Cultures.* New York: Elsevier.

Newman, Oscar. 1972. *Defensible Space: Crime Prevention Through Urban Design.* New York: Macmillan.

NIDA (*see* National Institute on Drug Abuse).

Niebuhr, Gustav. 1996. "Open Attitude on Homosexuality Makes Pariahs of Some Churches." *The New York Times*, February 8, pp. A1, B13.

Nimmons, David. 1994. "Sex and the Brain." *Discover*, March, pp. 64–71.

Nix, Crystal. 1986. "For Police, Domestic Violence Is No Longer Low Priority." *The New York Times*, December, pp. B1, B3.

Norman, Michael, 1983. "Homosexuals Struggle Amid Life Style Shifts." *The New York Times*, June 16, pp. A1, A18.

Nye, F. Ivan. 1958. *Family Relationships and Delinquent Behavior.* New York: John Wiley & Sons.

O'Brien, John E. 1975. "Violence in Divorce-Prone Families." In Suzanne K. Steinmetz and Murray A. Straus (eds.), *Violence in the Family*. New York: Dodd, Mead, pp. 65–75.

O'Brien, Robert and Sidney Cohen. 1984. *The Encyclopedia of Drug Abuse*. New York: Facts on File.

O'Brien, Robert E. 1985. *Crime and Victimization Data*. Newbury Park, Calif.: Sage.

Ofshe, Richard, and Ethan Watters. 1994. *Making Monsters: False Memories, Psychotherapy, and Sexual Hysteria*. New York: Charles Scribner's Sons.

Oliver, William. 1994. *The Violent Social World of Black Men*. New York: Lexington Books.

Onis, Juan de. 1973. "Honor Killing Fought in Beirut." *The New York Times*, March 5, p. 8.

Orcutt, James D. 1983. *Analyzing Deviance*. Homewood, Ill.: Dorsey Press.

Oreskes, Michael. 1990. "Drug War Underlines Fickleness of Public." *The New York Times*, September 6, p. A22.

Paige, Karen Ericksen. 1977. "Sexual Pollution: Reproductive Sex Taboos in American Society." *Journal of Social Issues*, 33 (2): 144–165.

Palys, T.S. 1986. "Testing the Common Wisdom: The Social Content of Video Pornography." *Canadian Psychology*, 27 (July): 22–35.

Park, Robert E. 1926. "The Urban Community as a Spacial Pattern and a Moral Order." In Ernest W. Burgess (ed.), *The Urban Community*. Chicago: University of Chicago Press, pp. 3–18.

Park, Robert E., and Ernest W. Burgess. 1921. *Introduction to the Science of Sociology*. Chicago: University of Chicago Press.

Parker, Robert Nash, with Linda-Anne Rebhun. 1995. *Alcohol and Homicide: A Deadly Combination of Two American Traditions*. Albany: State University of New York Press.

Parrott, Andrea, and Steven Allen. 1984. "Acquaintance Rape: Seduction or Crime? When Sex Becomes a Crime." Paper presented at the Eastern Regional Society for the Scientific Study of Sex, April 6–8.

Parsons, Talcott. 1951. *The Social System*. New York: Free Press.

Pate, Anthony M., and Edwin E. Hamilton. 1992. "Formal and Informal Deterrents to Domestic Violence: The Dade County Spouse Assault Experiment." *American Sociological Review*, 57 (October): 691–697.

Pearlin, Leonard I., and Joyce S. Johnson. 1977. "Marital Status, Life-Strains, and Depression." *American Sociological Review,* 42 (October): 704–715.

Peckham, Morse. 1969. *Art and Pornography: An Experiment in Explanation*. New York: Basic Books.

Pendery, Mary L., Irving M. Maltzman, and L. Jolyon West. 1982. "Controlled Drinking by Alcoholics? New Findings and a Reevaluation of a Major Affirmative Study." *Science*, 217 (9 July): 169–175.

Pernanen, Kai. 1991. *Alcohol in Human Violence*. New York: Guilford Press.

Perrine, M.W. Bud. 1990. "Who Are the Drinking Drivers? The Spectrum of Drinking Drivers Revisited" *Alcohol Health and Research World*, 14 (1): 26–35.

Perrow, Charles. 1984. *Normal Accidents: Living with High-Risk Technologies*. New York: Basic Books.

Petersen, Robert C. (ed.). 1980. *Marijuana Research Findings: 1980*. Rockville, Md.: National Institute on Drug Abuse.

Petras, James W. 1973. *Sexuality and Society*. Boston: Allyn & Bacon.

Petrunik, Michael. 1980. "The Rise and Fall of 'Labelling Theory': The Construction and Deconstruction of a Sociological Strawman." *Canadian Journal of Sociology*, 5 (3): 213–233.

Peyser, Marc. 1992. "A Cheater's Guide to High Marks (and Big $)." *Newsweek*, January 6, p. 45.

Pfohl, Stephen J. 1977. "The 'Discovery' of Child Abuse." *Social Problems*, 24 (February): 310–323.

Pfohl, Stephen J. 1994. *Images of Deviance and Social Control: A Sociological History* (2nd ed.). New York: McGraw-Hill.

Pfuhl, Erdwin H., and Stuart Henry. 1993. *The Deviance Process* (3rd ed.). New York: Aldine.

Phillips, Derek L. 1964. "Rejection of the Mentally Ill: The Influence of Behavior and Sex," *American Sociological Review*, 29 (October): 755–763.

Pines, Ayala M., and Mimi H. Silbert. 1983. "Early Sexual Exploitation as an Influence in Prostitution." *Social Work*, 28 (July-August): 285–289.

Piven, Frances Fox. 1981. "Deviant Behavior and the Remaking of the World." *Social Problems*, 28 (June): 489–508.

Piven, Francis Fox, and Richard A. Cloward. 1977. *Poor People's Movement: Why They Succeed, How They Fail*. New York: Random House.

Pizzo, Stephen P., Mary Fricker, and Paul Muolo. 1992. *Inside Job: The Looting of America's Savings and Loans*. New York: McGraw-Hill.

Pizzo, Stephen P., and Paul Muolo. 1993. "Take the Money and Run: A Rogue's Gallery of Some Lucky S.& L. Thieves." *The New York Times Magazine*, May 9, pp. 26, 56, 60.

Plant, Richard. 1986. *The Pink Triangle: The Nazi War Against Homosexuality*. New York: New Republic/Holt.

Plummer, Kenneth. 1975. *Sexual Stigma: An Interactionist Account*. London: Routledge & Kegan Paul.

Plummer, Kenneth. 1979. "Misunderstanding Labelling Perspectives." In David Downes and Paul Rock (eds.), *Deviant Interpretations*. London: Martin Robertson, pp. 85–121.

Plummer, Kenneth. 1981a. "Building a Sociology of Homosexuality." In Kenneth Plummer (ed.), *The Making of the Modern Homosexual*. Totowa, N.J.: Barnes & Noble, pp. 17–29.

Plummer, Kenneth. 1981b. "Homosexual Categories: Some Research Problems in the Labeling Perspective on Homosexuality." In Kenneth Plummer (ed.), *The Making of the Modern Homosexual*. Totowa, N.J.: Barnes & Noble, pp. 53–75.

Plummer, Kenneth. 1982. "Symbolic Interactionism and Sexual Conduct: An Emergent Perspective." In Mike Brake (ed.), *Human Sexual Relations: Towards a Redefinition of Politics*. New York: Pantheon Books, pp. 223–241.

Plummer, Ken. 1984. "Sexual Diversity: A Sociological Perspective." In Kevin Howells (ed.), *The Psychology of Sexual Diversity*. Oxford: Basil Blackwell, pp. 221–253.

Plummer, Ken. 1995. *Telling Sexual Stories: Power, Change and Social Worlds*. London: Routledge.

Pogrebin, Mark R., Eric D. Poole, and Amos Martinez. 1992. "Psychotherapists' Accounts of Their Professional Misdeeds." *Deviant Behavior*, 13 (3): 229–252.

Polich, J. Michael, David J. Armor, and Harriet Braiker. 1980. *The Course of Alcoholism: Four Years After Treatment*. Santa Monica, Calif.: RAND Corporation.

Polk, Kenneth. 1991. Review of Michael R. Gottfredson and Travis Hirschi, *A General Theory of Crime*, Stanford, Calif.: Stanford University Press, 1990, in *Crime and Delinquency*, 37: 275–279.

Pollack, Earl, and Carl A. Taube. 1975. "Trends and Projections in State Hospital Use." In Jack Zusman and Elmer Bertsch (eds.), *The Future Role of the State Hospital*. Lexington, Mass.: D.C. Heath, pp. 31–55.

Pollak, Ott. 1950. *The Criminality of Women*. Philadelphia: University of Pennsylvania Press.

Pollner, Melvin. 1974. "Sociological and Common-Sense Models of the Labelling Process." In Roy Turner (ed.), *Ethnomethodology: Selected Readings*. Baltimore: Penguin Books, pp. 27–40.

Polsky, Ned. 1969. *Hustlers, Beats, and Others*. Garden City, N.Y.: Doubleday-Anchor.

Ponse, Barbara. 1978. *Identities in the Lesbian World: The Social Construction of Self*. Westport, Conn.: Greenwood Press.

Pontell, Henry N. 1984. *A Capacity to Punish: The Ecology of Crime and Punishment*. Bloomington: Indiana University Press.

Pontell, Henry N., Paul Jesilow, and Gilbert Geis. 1982. "Policing Physicians: Practitioner Fraud and Abuse in a Government Medical Program." *Social Problems*, 30 (October): 117–125.

Pontell, Henry N., Paul Jesilow, and Gilbert Geis. 1984a. *Practitioner Fraud and Abuse in Medical Benefit Programs*. Final Report Submitted to the National Institute of Justice, U.S. Department of Justice.

Pontell, Henry N., Paul Jesilow, and Gilbert Geis. 1984b. "Practitioner Fraud and Abuse in Medical Benefit Programs: Government Regulation and Professional White Collar Crime." *Law and Policy*, 6 (October): 405–426.

Pool, Robert. 1993. "Evidence for Homosexuality Gene." *Science*, 261 (16 July): 291–292.

Pooley, Eric. 1992. "Getting Away With Murder: The Cops Don't Catch Half the City's Killers," *New York*, September 28, pp. 27–33.

Popper, Karl. 1953. *The Logic of Scientific Discovery*. New York: Basic Books.

Popper, Karl. 1963. *The Open Society and Its Enemies*. New York: Harper Torchbooks.

Posner, Gerald. 1993. *Case Closed: Lee Harvey Oswald and the Assassination of JFK*. New York: Doubleday/Anchor Books.

Priest, G.L. 1990. "The New Legal Structure of Risk Control." *Daedalus*, 119: 207–228.

Prus, Robert, and Styllianos Irini. 1980. *Hookers, Rounders, and Desk Clerks: The Social Organization of the Hotel Community*. Salem, Wisc.: Sheffield.

Quindlen, Anna. 1990. "Hearing the Cries of Crack." *The New York Times*, October 7, p. E19.

Quinney, Richard. 1963. "Occupational Structure and Criminal Behavior: Prescription Violations by Retail Pharmacists." *Social Problems*, 11 (Fall): 179–185.

Quinney, Richard. 1964. "The Study of White-Collar Crime: Toward a Reorientation in Theory and Research." *Journal of Criminal Law, Criminology, and Police Science*, 55 (2): 208–214.

Quinney, Richard. 1965. "Is Criminal Behaviour Deviant Behaviour?" *British Journal of Criminology*, 5 (April): 132–142.

Quinney, Richard. 1970. *The Social Reality of Crime*. Boston: Little, Brown.

Quinney, Richard (ed.). 1974a. *Criminal Justice in America: A Critical Understanding*. Boston: Little, Brown.

Quinney, Richard. 1974b. *Critique of Legal Order: Crime Control in Capitalist Society*. Boston: Little, Brown.

Quinney, Richard. 1977. *The Problem of Crime: A Critical Introduction to Criminology* (2nd ed.). New York: Harper & Row.

Quinney, Richard. 1979. *Criminology* (2nd ed.). Boston: Little, Brown.

Quinney, Richard. 1980. *Class, State, and Crime* (2nd ed.). New York: Longman.

Quinney, Richard. 1986. *Mystery in the Land: A Journey East*. SSSP Newsletter, 17 (Winter): 25–29.

Quinney, Richard, and John Wildeman. 1977. *The Problem of Crime: A Critical Introduction to Criminology* (2nd ed.). Harper & Row.

Quinney, Richard, and John Wildeman. 1991. *The Problem of Crime: A Peace and Social Justice Perspective* (3rd ed.). Mountain View, Calif.: Mayfield.

Rada, Richard T. 1975. "Alcoholism and Forcible Rape." *American Journal of Psychiatry*, 123 (April): 444–446.

Rada, Richard T. 1976. "Alcoholism and the Child Molester." *Annals of the New York Academy of Science*, 273 (May 28): 492–496.

Randall, Susan, and Vicki McNickle Rose. 1984. "Forcible Rape." In Robert F. Meier (ed.), *Major Forms of Crime*. Newbury Park, Calif.: Sage, pp. 47–72.

Ravenholt, R.T. 1984. "Addiction Morality in the United States: Tobacco, Alcohol and Other Substances." *Population and Developmental Review*, 10 (December): 697–724.

Ravo, Nick. 1987. "Drinking Age Is Said to Fall for Students." *The New York Times*, December 21, pp. A1, B15.

Ray, Jo-Ann. 1987. "Every Twelfth Shopper: Who Shoplifts and Why?" *Social Casework*, 68: 234–239.

Ray, Marsh B. 1964. "The Cycle of Abstinence and Relapse Among Heroin Addicts." In Howard S. Becker (ed.), *The Other Side: Perspectives on Deviance*. New York: Free Press, pp. 163–177.

Ray, Oakley, and Charles Ksir. 1996. *Drugs, Society, and Human Behavior* (7th ed.). St. Louis: Times Mirror/Mosby.

Reckless, Walter C. 1926. "The Distribution of Commercialized Vice in the City: A Sociological Analysis." In Ernest W. Burgess (ed.), *The Urban Community*. Chicago: University of Chicago Press, pp. 192–205.

Reckless, Walter C. 1933. *Vice in Chicago*. Chicago: University of Chicago Press.

Reckless, Walter C. 1950. *The Crime Problem*. New York: Appleton-Century-Crofts.

Reckless, Walter C. 1973. *The Crime Problem* (5th ed.). New York: Appleton-Century-Crofts.

Rector, Frank. 1981. *The Nazi Extermination of Homosexuals.* New York: Stein & Day.

Rediker, Marcus. 1987. *Between the Devil and the Deep Blue Sea: Merchant Seamen, Pirates and the Anglo-American World, 1700–1750.* New York & Cambridge, United Kingdom: Cambridge University Press.

Reiger, Darrel A., et al. 1988. "One-Month Prevalence of Mental Disorders in the United States Based on Five Epidemiologic Catchment Area Sites." *Archives of General Psychiatry,* 45 (November): 977–986,

Reinarman, Craig. 1994. "The Social Construction of Drug Scares." In Patricia A. Adler and Peter Adler (eds.), *Constructions of Deviance: Social Power, Context, and Interaction.* Belmont, Calif.: Wadsworth, pp. 92–104.

Reinarman, Craig, and Harry G. Levine. 1995. "The Crack Attack: America's Latest Drug Scare." In Joel Best (ed.), *Images of Issues: Typifying Contemporary Social Problems* (2nd ed.). New York: Aldine de Gruyter, pp. 147–186.

Reiss, Albert J., Jr. 1961. "The Social Integration of Queers and Peers." *Social Problems,* 9 (Fall): 102–120.

Reiss, Albert J, Jr. 1964. "The Social Integration of Queers and Peers." In Howard S. Becker (ed.), *The Other Side: Perspectives on Deviance.* New York: Free Press, pp. 181–210.

Reiss, Albert J. Jr. 1983. "The Policing of Organizational Life." In Maurice Punch (ed.), *Control in the Police Organization.* Cambridge, Mass.: MIT Press, pp. 78–97.

Reiss, Albert J., Jr. 1984. "Selecting Strategies of Social Control Over Organizational Life." In Keith Hawkins and John M. Thomas (eds.), *Enforcing Regulations.* Boston: Kluwer-Nijhoff, pp. 23–35.

Reiss, Ellen (ed.). 1986. *The Esthetic Realism of Eli Siegel and the Change From Homosexuality.* New York: Definition Press.

Reuben, David R. 1969. *Everything You Always Wanted to Know About Sex But Were Afraid to Ask.* New York: David McKay.

Richardson, Gale A. 1991. "Maternal and Neonatal Effects of Moderate Cocaine Use During Pregnancy." *Neurotoxicology and Teratology,* 13 (June-August): 455–460.

Richardson, Gale A., and Nancy L. Day. 1994. "Detrimental Effects of Prenatal Cocaine Exposure: Illusion or Reality?" *Journal of the American Academy of Child and Adolescent Psychiatry,* 33 (January): 28–34.

Richardson, James T., Joel Best, and David G. Bromley (eds.). 1991. *The Satanism Scare.* Aldine de Gruyter.

Rimland, Bernard. 1969. "Psychogenesis Versus Biogenesis: The Issues and the Evidence." In Stanley C. Plog and Robert B. Edgerton (eds.), *Changing Perspectives in Mental Health.* New York: Holt, Reinhart & Winston, pp. 702–735.

Roberts, Cathy. 1989. *Women and Rape.* New York: New York University Press.

Robertson, Roland, and Laurie Taylor. 1973. *Deviance, Crime, and Socio-Legal Control.* London: Martin Robertson.

Robins, Lee N. 1975. "Alcoholism and Labeling Theory." In Walter R. Gove (ed.), *The Labelling of Deviance.* New York: John Wiley & Sons/Halstead/Sage, pp. 21–33.

Robinson, Lillian S. 1993. "Touring Thailand's Sex Industry." *The Nation,* November 1, pp. 492–497.

Rock, Paul. 1980. "Has Deviance a Future?" In Hubert M. Blalock (ed.), *Sociological Theory and Research: A Critical Appraisal.* New York: Free Press, 290–303.

Rodmell, Sue. 1981. "Men, Women, and Sexuality: A Feminist Critique of the Sociology of Deviance." *Women's Studies International Quarterly,* 4 (2): 145–155.

Rohter, Larry. 1986. "Friend and Foe See Homosexual Defeat." *The New York Times,* July 1, p. A19.

Room, Robin G.W., and Gary Collins (eds.). 1983. *Alcohol and Disinhibition: Nature and Meaning of the Link.* Rockville, Md.: U.S. Department of Health and Human Services.

Rorabaugh, W.A. 1979. *The Alcoholic Republic: An American Tradition.* New York: Oxford University Press.

Rose, Harold M., and Paula D. McClain. 1990. *Race, Place and Risk: Black Homicide in Urban America.* Albany: State University of New York Press.

Rosenbaum, Rob. 1995. "The Great Ivy League Nude Posture Photo Scandal." *The New York Times Magazine,* January 15, pp. 26–31, 40, 46, 55–56.

Rosenblum, Karen E. 1975. "Female Deviance and the Female Sex Role: A Preliminary Investigation." *British Journal of Sociology,* 26 (2): 169–185.

Rosenhan, David L. 1973. "On Being Sane in Insane Places." *Science,* 179 (January 19): 250–258.

Rosenthal, Andrew. 1992. "Bush Tries to Recoup from Harsh Tones on 'Values.'" *The New York Times,* September 21, pp. A1, A14.

Rosenthal, Marilynn. 1971. "Where Rumor Raged." *Transaction,* 8 (February): 34–43.

Rosnow, Ralph L. 1988. "Rumor as Communication: A Contextualist Approach." *Journal of Communication,* 38 (Winter): 12–28.

Rosnow, Ralph L. 1991. "Inside Rumor: A Personal Journey." *American Psychologist,* 46 (May): 484–496.

Rosnow, Ralph L., and Gary Alan Fine. 1976. *Rumor and Gossip: The Social Psychology of Hearsay.* New York: Elsevier.

Rosoff, Stephen M. 1989. "Physicians as Criminal Defendants: Specialty, Sanctions, and Status Liability." *Law and Human Behavior,* 15: 231–235.

Rosoff, Stephen M., Henry N. Pontell, and Robert Tillman. 1996. *Profit Without Honor: White-Collar Crime in America.* Upper Saddle River, N.J.: Prentice Hall.

Ross, Edward A. 1901. *Social Control: A Survey of the Foundations of Order.* New York: Macmillan.

Ross, Edward A. 1907. "The Criminaloid." *Atlantic Monthly,* 99 (January): 44–50.

Ross, Susan M., and Leonard E. Ross. 1990. "Pilots' Knowledge of Blood Alcohol Levels and the 0.04% Blood Alcohol Concentration Rule." *Aviation, Space, and Environmental Medicine,* 61 (May): 412–417.

Rossi, Peter, et al. 1974. "The Seriousness of Crimes: Normative Structure and Individual Differences." *American Sociological Review,* 39 (April): 224–237.

Rotenberg, Mordechai. 1974. "Self-Labeling: A Missing Link in the 'Societal Reaction Theory of Deviance.'" *The Sociological Quarterly,* 15 (April): 335–355.

Rubin, Gayle. 1984. "Thinking Sexuality." In Carole S. Vance (ed.), *Pleasure and Danger: Exploring Female Sexuality.* Boston: Routledge & Kegan Paul, pp. 267–319.

Rubington, Earl, and Martin S. Weinberg (eds.). 1995. *The Study of Social Problems: Seven Perspectives.* New York: Oxford University Press.

Rubington, Earl, and Martin S. Weinberg (eds.). 1996. *Deviance: The Interactionist Perspective* (6th ed.). New York: Macmillan.

Rule, Sheila. 1990. "British Homosexuals Report Rise in Attacks." *The New York Times*, August 19, p. 6.

Rumbarger, John J. 1989. *Profits, Power, and Prohibition: Alcohol Reform and the Industrializing of America, 1800–1930*. Albany: State University of New York Press.

Rushing, William. 1978. "Status Resources: Societal Reactions and Type of Mental Hospitalization." *American Sociological Review*, 43 (August): 521–533.

Rushing, William A. 1979a. "The Functional Importance of Sex Roles and Sex-Related Behavior in Societal Reactions to Residual Deviants." *Journal of Health and Social Behavior*, 20 (September): 208–217.

Rushing, William A. 1979b. "Marital Status and Mental Disorder: Evidence in Favor of a Behavioral Model." *Social Forces*, 58 (December): 540–556.

Russell, Diana E.H. 1975. *The Politics of Rape: The Victim's Perspective*. New York: Stein & Day.

Russell, Diana E.H. 1982a. "The Prevalence and Incidence of Forcible Rape and Attempted Rape of Females." *Victimology: An International Journal*, 7 (1–4): 81–93.

Russell, Diana E.H. 1982b. *Rape in Marriage*. New York: Collier Books.

Russell, Diana E.H. 1986. *The Secret Trauma: Incest in the Lives of Girls and Women*. New York: Basic Books.

Russell, Diana E.H., and Nancy Howell. 1983. "The Prevalence of Rape in the United States Revisited." *Signs: Journal of Women in Culture and Society*, 8 (Summer): 688–695.

Russell, Katheryn. 1992. "Development of a Black Criminology and the Role of the Black Criminologist." *Justice Quarterly*, 9 (December): 667–683.

Ryan, William. 1976. *Blaming the Victim* (2nd ed.). New York: Vintage Books.

Sacco, Vincent F. (ed.). 1988. *Deviance: Conformity and Control in Canadian Society*. Scarborough, Ontario: Prentice Hall Canada.

Sagarin, Edwin. 1975. *Deviants and Deviance: An Introduction to the Study of Disvalued People and Behavior*. New York: Praeger.

Saghir, Marcel T., and Eli Robins. 1973. *Male and Female Homosexuality*. Baltimore: Williams & Wilkins.

Sampson, Harold, Sheldon L. Messenger, and Robert D. Towne, et al. 1962. "Family Processes and Becoming a Mental Patient." *American Journal of Sociology*, 68 (July): 88–96.

Sampson, Harold, Sheldon L. Messenger, and Robert D. Towne, et al. 1964. "The Mental Hospital and Marital Family Ties." In Howard S. Becker (ed.), *The Other Side: Perspectves on Deviance*. New York: Free Press, pp. 139–162.

Sanday, Peggy Reeves. 1990. *Fraternity Gang Rape: Sex, Brotherhood, and Privilege on Campus*. New York: New York University Press.

Sandwijk, P.P., P.D.A. Cohen, and S. Musterd. 1991. *Licit and Illicit Drug Use in Amsterdam*. Amsterdam: Institute for Social Geography.

Sapolsky, Barry S. 1984. "Arousal, Affect, and the Aggression-Moderating Effect of Erotica." In Neil M. Malamuth and Edward Donnerstein (eds.), *Pornography and Sexual Aggression*. Orlando, Fla.: Academic Press, pp. 85–113.

Scheff, Thomas J. 1966. *Being Mentally Ill: A Sociological Theory*. Chicago: Aldine.

Scheff, Thomas J. 1974a. "The Labelling Theory of Mental Illness." *American Sociological Review*, 39 (June): 444–452.

Scheff, Thomas J. 1974b. "Reply to Nettler." *American Sociological Review*, 39 (December): 894–895.

Scheff, Thomas J. 1975. "Reply to Clancey and Gove." *American Sociological Review*, 40 (April): 252–257.

Scheff, Thomas, J. 1979. "Reply to Comment by Horwitz." *Journal of Health and Social Behavior*, 20 (September): 305–306.

Scheff, Thomas J. 1984. *Becoming Mentally Ill: A Sociological Theory* (2nd ed.). New York: Aldine de Gruyter.

Schmalz, Jeffrey. 1988. "AIDS Issue Lingers in Florida Town." *The New York Times,* October 7, p. A16.

Schmalz, Jeffrey. 1992. "Gay Rights and AIDS Emerging as Divisive Issues in Campaign." *The New York Times*, August 20, pp. A1, A21.

Schneider, Joseph W. 1985. "Social Problems Theory." *Annual Review of Sociology*, 11: 209–229.

Schneider, Joseph W., and John I. Kitsuse (eds.). 1985. *Studies in the Sociology of Social Problems*. Norwood, N.J.: Ablex.

Schoenborn, Charlotte A., Shannon L. Marsh, and Ann M. Hardy. 1994. "AIDS Knowledge and Attitudes for 1992." *Advance Data*, from Vital and Health Statistics of the Centers for Disease Control and Prevention/National Center for Health Statistics, no.243 (February 23): 1–15.

Schuckit, Marc A. 1984. *Drug and Alcohol Abuse: A Clinical Guide to Diagnosis and Treatment* (2nd ed.). New York: Plenum Press.

Schuckit, Marc A. 1985. "Overview: Epidemiology of Alcoholism." In Marc A. Schuckit (ed.), *Alcohol Patterns and Problems*. New Brunswick, N.J.: Rutgers University Press, pp. 1–42.

Schultes, Richard Evans, and Albert Hofmann. 1979. *Plants of the Gods: Origins of Hallucinogenic Use*. New York: Alfred van der Marck Editions.

Schur, Edwin M. 1971. *Labeling Deviant Behavior: Its Sociological Implications*. New York: Harper & Row.

Schur, Edwin M. 1979. *Interpreting Deviance: A Sociological Introduction*. New York: Harper & Row.

Schur, Edwin M. 1980. *The Politics of Deviance: Stigma Contests and the Uses of Power* Englewood Cliffs, N.J.: Prentice Hall/Spectrum.

Schur, Edwin M. 1984. *Labeling Women Deviant: Gender, Stigma, and Social Control*. New York: Random House.

Schwartz, Richard D., and Jerome H. Skolnick. 1964. "Two Studies of Legal Stigma." In Howard S. Becker (ed.), *The Other Side: Perspectives on Deviance*. New York: Free Press, pp. 103–117.

Schwendinger, Herman, and Julia Schwendinger. 1975. "Defenders of Order or Guardians of Human Rights?" In Ian Taylor, Paul Walton, and Jock Young (eds.), *Critical Criminology*. London: Routledge & Kegan Paul, pp. 113–146.

Schwendinger, Herman, and Julia Schwindinger. 1983. *Rape and Inequality*. Newbury Park, Calif.: Sage.

Scott, Joseph E., and Steven J. Cuvelier. 1987a. "Sexual Violence in Playboy Magazine: A Longitudinal Analysis." *Archives of Sexual Behavior*, 16 (4): 279–288.

Scott, Joseph E., and Steven J. Cuvelier. 1987b. "Sexual Violence in Playboy Magazine: A Longitudinal Content Analysis." *The Journal of Sex Research*, 25 (November): 534–539.

Scott, Robert A. 1969. *The Making of Blind Men: A Study of Adult Socialization*. New York: Russell Sage.

Scull, Andrew. 1977. *Decarceration: Community Treatment*

and the Deviant—A Radical View. Englewood Cliffs, N.J.: Prentice Hall.

Scull, Andrew. 1984a. *Decarceration: Community Treatment and the Deviant—A Radical View* (2nd ed.). Cambridge, England: Polity Press.

Scull, Andrew. 1984b. "Competing Perspectives on Deviance." *Deviant Behavior,* 5 (3): 275–289.

Scull, Andrew. 1988. "Deviance and Social Control." In Neil J. Smelser (ed.), *Handbook of Sociology.* Newbury Park, Calif.: Sage, pp. 667–693.

Scully, Diana. 1990. *Understanding Sexual Violence: A Study of Convicted Rapists.* Boston: Unwin Hyman.

Scully, Diana, and Joseph Marolla. 1984. "Convicted Rapists' Vocabulary of Motive: Excuses and Justifications." *Social Problems,* 31 (June): 530–544.

Scully, Diana, and Joseph Marolla. 1985. "Riding the Bull at Gilley's: Convicted Rapists Describe the Rewards of Rape." *Social Problems,* 32 (February): 251–263.

Seidlin, Mindell, et al. 1988. "Prevalence of HIV Infection in New York Call Girls." *Journal of Acquired Immune Deficiency Syndromes,* 1: 150–154.

Seinfels, Peter. 1988. "Methodists Vote to Retain Policy Concerning Homosexual Behavior." *The New York Times,* May 3, p. A22.

Shaw, Clifford R. 1929. *Delinquency Areas.* Chicago: University of Chicago Press.

Shaw, Clifford R. 1930. *The Jack-Roller: A Delinquent Boy's Story.* Chicago: University of Chicago Press.

Shaw, Clifford R. 1931. *The Natural History of a Delinquent Career.* Chicago: University of Chicago Press.

Shaw, Clifford R., and Henry D. McKay. 1942. *Juvenile Delinquency and Urban Areas.* Chicago: University of Chicago Press.

Sheehy, Gail. 1973. *Hustling: Prostitution in Our Wide-Open Society.* New York: Delacorte Press.

Sheley, Joseph F. 1995. *Criminology: A Contemporary Handbook* (2nd ed.). Belmont, Calif.: Wadsworth.

Shenon, Philip. 1989. "The Case of the Criminal Corporation." *The New York Times,* January 15, p. 28E.

Shenon, Philip. 1990a. "Cocaine Epidemic May Have Peaked." *The New York Times,* September 2, p. 32.

Shenon, Philip. 1990b. "War on Drugs Remains Top Priority, Bush Says." *The New York Times,* September 6, p. A22.

Shenon, Philip. 1996a. "AIDS Epidemic, Late to Arrive, Now Explodes in Populous Asia." *The New York Times,* January 21, pp. 1, 8.

Shenon, Philip. 1996b. "Homosexuality Still Questioned By the Military." *The New York Times,* February 27, pp. 1, 20.

Sheppard, Nathaniel, Jr. 1979. "Episcopal Bishops Vote to Reject the Ordination of Homosexuals." *The New York Times,* September 18, p. A20.

Sherman, Lawrence W., and Richard A. Berk. 1984. "The Specific Deterrent Effect for Domestic Assault." *American Sociological Review,* 49 (April): 261–272.

Sherman, Lawrence W., and Douglas A. Smith. 1992. "Crime, Punishment, and Stake in Conformity: Legal and Informal Control of Domestic Violence." *American Sociological Review,* 57 (October): 680–690.

Sherman, Lawrence W., et al. 1991. "From Initial Deterrence to Longterm Escalation: Short Custody Arrest for Poverty Ghetto Domestic Violence." *Criminology,* 29 (November): 821–850.

Shibutani, Tamotsu. 1966. *Improvised News: A Sociological Theory of Rumor.* Indianapolis, Ind.: Bobbs-Merrill.

Shilts, Randy. 1987. *And the Band Played On: Politics, People, and the AIDS Epidemic.* New York: St. Martin's Press.

Shim, Kelly H., and Marshall M. DeBerry. 1988. "Criminal Victimization, 1987." *Bureau of Justice Statistics Bulletin,* October, pp. 1–6.

Shoemaker, Donald J. 1984. *Theories of Delinquency: An Examination of Explanations of Delinquent Behavior.* New York: Oxford University Press.

Short, James F., Jr. 1964. "Gang Delinquency and Anomie." In Marshall B. Clinard (ed.), *Anomie and Deviant Behavior: A Discussion and Critique.* New York: Free Press, pp. 98–127.

Short, James F., Jr. 1984. "The Social Fabric of Risk: Toward the Social Transformation of Risk Analysis." *American Sociological Review,* 49 (December): 711–725.

Short, James F., Jr. 1990. "Hazards, Risk, and Enterprise: Approaches to Science, Law, and Social Policy." *Law and Society Review,* 24 (1): 179–198.

Shover, Neal, and Kevin M. Bryant. 1993. "Theoretical Explanations of Corporate Crime." In Michael B. Blankenship (ed.), *Understanding Corporate Criminality.* New York: Garland, pp. 141–176.

Shupe, Lloyd M. 1954. "Alcohol and Crime: A Study of the Urine Alcohol Concentration Found in 882 Persons Arrested During or Immediately After the Commission of a Felony." *Journal of Criminal Law, Criminology, and Police Science,* 44 (January-February): 661–664.

Simmons, Jerry L. 1965. "Public Stereotypes of Deviants." *Social Problems,* 13 (Fall): 223–232.

Simmons, Jerry L. 1969. *Deviants.* Santa Barbara, Calif.: Glendessary Press.

Simon, David R. 1996. *Elite Deviance* (5th ed.). Boston: Allyn & Bacon.

Simon, Jesse, and Jack Zussman. 1983. "The Effect of Contextual Factors on Psychiatrists' Perception of Illness: A Case Study." *Journal of Health and Social Behavior,* 24 (2): 186–198.

Simon, Rita James. 1975a. *Women and Crime.* Lexington, Mass.: D.C. Heath.

Simon, Rita James. 1975b. *The Contemporary Woman and Crime.* Rockville, Md.: National Institute of Mental Health.

Simon, Rita James, and Jean Landis. 1991. *The Crimes Women Commit, the Punishments They Receive.* Lexington, Mass.: Lexington Books.

Simon, William. 1973. "The Social, the Erotic, and the Sensual: The Complexities of Erotic Scripts." *Nebraska Symposium on Motivation,* 21: 61–82.

Simon, William, and John H. Gagnon. 1984. "Sexual Scripts." *Society,* 22 (November-December): 53–60.

Simon, William, and John H. Gagnon. 1986. "Sexual Scripts: Permanence and Change." *Archives of Sexual Behavior,* 15 (2): 97–120.

Simons, Marlise. 1994. "The Littlest Prostitutes." *The New York Times Magazine,* January 16, pp. 30–35.

Simpson, Sally S. 1989. "Feminist Theory, Crime, and Justice." *Criminology,* 27 (November): 605–631.

Simpson, Sally S. 1993. "Corporate Crime." In Craig Calhoun and George Ritzer (eds.), *Introduction to Social Problems.* New York: McGraw-Hill.

Single, Eric W. 1981. "The Impact of Marijuana Decriminalization." In Yedy Israel et al. (eds.), *Research Advances in*

Alcohol and Drug Problems. New York: Plenum Press, pp. 405–424.

Skogan, Wesley G. 1986. "Fear of Crime and Neighborhood Change." In Albert J. Reiss, Jr. and Michael Tonry (eds.), *Communities and Crime*. Chicago: University of Chicago Press, pp. 203–229.

Skogan, Wesley G. 1990. *Disorder and Decline: Crime and the Spiral of Decay in American Neighborhoods*. New York: Free Press.

Skolnick, Jerome H., et al. 1969. *The Politics of Protest*. New York: Simon & Schuster.

Slade, Margot. 1994. "Law Firms Reigning In Sex-Harassing Partners." *The New York Times*, February 25, p. A19.

Slovic, Paul, Baruch Fischoff, and Sarah Lichtenstein. 1980. "Risky Assumptions." *Psychology Today*, June, pp. 44–48.

Slovic, Paul, Mark Layman, and James H. Flynn. 1991. "Risk, Perception, Trust, and Nuclear Waste: Lessons From Yucca Mountain." *Environment*, 33 (April): 28–30.

Small, Shirley J. [Cook]. 1978. "Canadian Narcotics Legislation, 1908–1923: A Conflict Model Interpretation." In William K. Greenaway and Stephen L. Brickey (eds.), *Law and Social Control in Canada*. Scarborough, Ontario: Prentice Hall of Canada, pp. 28–42.

Smart, Carol. 1976. *Women, Crime, and Criminology: A Feminist Critique*. London: Routledge & Kegan Paul.

Smith, Don D. 1976. "The Social Content of Pornography." *Journal of Communication*, 26 (Winter): 16–24.

Smith, Dusky Lee. 1973. "Symbolic Interactionism: Definitions of the Situation From Becker and Lofland." *Catalyst*, no.7 (Winter): 62–75.

Smith, Mary Lee, Gene Glass, and Thomas Miller. 1980. *The Benefits of Psychotherapy*. Baltimore: Johns Hopkins University Press.

Smith, S.M., et al. 1989. "Alcohol and Fatal Injuries: Temporal Patterns." *American Journal of Preventative Medicine*, 5 (5): 296–302.

Snitow, Ann, Christine Stansell, and Sharon Thompson (eds.). 1983. *Powers of Desire: The Politics of Sexuality*. New York: Monthly Review Press.

Snyder, Charles R. 1964. "Inebriety, Alcoholism, and Anomie." In Marshall B. Clinard (ed.), *Anomie and Deviant Behavior: A Discussion and Critique*. New York: Free Press, pp. 189–212.

Sobel, Lester. 1977. *Corruption in Business*. New York: Facts on File.

Sobell, Mark B., and Linda C. Sobell. 1978. *Behavioral Treatment of Alcohol Problems: Individualized Therapy and Controlled Drinking*. New York: Plenum Press.

Sobell, Mark B., and Linda C. Sobell. 1984. "The Aftermath of Heresy: A Response to Pendery et al.'s (1982) Critique of 'Individualized Behavior Therapy for Alcoholics.'" *Behavior Research and Therapy*, 22 (4): 413–440.

Socarides, Charles W. 1978. *Homosexuality*. New York: Jason Aronson.

Solzhenitsyn, Aleksander I. 1974. *The Gulag Archipelago, 1918–1956: An Experiment in Literary Investigation, I–II* (trans. Thomas Whitney). New York: Harper & Row.

Solzhenitsyn, Aleksander I. 1975. *The Gulag Archipelago, 1918–1956: An Experiment in Literary Investigation, III–IV* (trans. Thomas Whitney). New York: Harper & Row.

Spector, Malcolm, and John I. Kitsuse. 1973. "Social Problems: A Re-formulation." *Social Problems*, 21 (Fall): 145–159.

Spector, Malcolm, and John I. Kitsuse. 1977. *Constructing Social Problems*. Menlo Park, Calif.: Cummings.

Spence, Jonathan D. 1988. *The Question of Hu*. New York: Alfred Knopf.

Spira, Alfred, et al. 1992. "AIDS and Sexual Behavior in France." *Nature*, 360 (3 December): 407–409.

Spira, Alfred, et al. 1993. *Les Comportments Sexuels en France*. Paris: La Documentation Francais.

Spitzer, Robert L. 1975. "On Pseudoscience in Science, Logic in Remission, and Psychiatric Diagnosis: A Critique of Rosenhan's 'On Being Sane in Insane Places.'" *Journal of Abnormal Psychiatry*, 84 (5): 442–452.

Spitzer, Robert L. 1976. "More on Pseudoscience in Science and the Case for Psychiatric Diagnosis: A Critique of D.L. Rosenhan's 'On Being Sane in Insane Places' and 'The Contextual Nature of Psychiatric Diagnosis.'" *Archives of General Psychiatry*, 33 (April): 459–470.

Spitzer, Stephen. 1975. "Toward a Marxist Theory of Deviance." *Social Problems*, 22 (June): 638–651.

Spitzer, Stephen. 1987. "Security and Control in Capitalist Societies: The Fetishism of Security and the Secret Thereof." In John Lowman, Robert J. Menzies, and T.S. Palys (eds.), *Transcarceration: Essays in the Sociology of Social Control*. Aldershot, England: Gower, pp. 43–58.

Srole, Leo, et al. 1962. *Mental Health in the Metropolis: The Midtown Manhattan Study*. New York: McGraw-Hill.

Srole, Leo, et al. 1978. *Mental Health in the Metropolis: The Midtown Manhattan Study* (rev. & enlarged ed.). New York: New York University Press.

Stanley, Alessandra. 1991. "The Symbols Spawned by a Killing." *The New York Times*, November 18, pp. B1, B4.

Steffensmeier, Darrell J. 1978. "Crime and the Contemporary Woman." *Social Forces*, 57 (December): 566–584.

Steffensmeier, Darrell J. 1989. "On the Causes of White-Collar Crime: An Assessment of Hirschi and Gottfredson's Claims." *Criminology*, 27 (August): 345–358.

Steffensmeier, Darrell J., and Michael J. Cobb. 1981. "Sex Differences in Urban Arrest Patterns, 1934–1979." *Social Problems*, 29 (October): 37–50.

Stein, Peter (ed.). 1992. *Forms of Desire: Sexual Orientation and the Social Constructionist Controversy*. New York: Routledge, Chapman & Hall.

Steinem, Gloria. 1982. "Erotica and Pornography: A Clear and Present Difference." In Laura Lederer (ed.), *Take Back the Night: Women on Pornography*. New York: Bantam Books, pp. 21–25.

Stoller, Robert J., and R.H. Geertsma. 1963. "The Consistency of Psychiatrists' Clinical Judgments." *Journal of Nervous and Mental Disease*, 137 (January): 58–66.

Stone, Christopher. 1975. *Where the Law Ends: The Social Control of Corporate Behavior*. New York: Harper & Row.

Straus, Murray A., Richard J. Gelles, and Suzanne K. Steinmetz. 1980. *Behind Closed Doors: Violence: Violence in the American Family*. Garden City, N.Y.: Doubleday.

Straus, Robert. 1976. "Alcoholism and Problem Drinking." In Robert K. Merton and Robert Nisbet (eds.), *Contemporary Social Problems* (4th ed.). New York: Harcourt Brace Jovanovich, pp. 181–217.

Suchar, Charles S. 1978. *Social Deviance: Perspectives and Prospects*. New York: Holt, Reinhart & Winston.

Sullivan, Walter. 1980. "Violent Pornography Elevates Aggression, Researchers Say." *The New York Times*, September 30, pp. C1, C3.

Summers, Anne. 1981. "Hidden From History: Women Victims of Crime." in Satyanshu K. Mukherjee and Jocelynne A. Scutt (eds.), *Women and Crime*. North Syndey: George Allen & Unwin Australia, pp. 22–30.

Sumner, Colin. 1994. *The Sociology of Deviance: An Obituary*. London: Open University Press.

Sutherland, Edwin H. 1939. *Principles of Criminology* (3rd ed.). Philadelphia: Lippincott.

Sutherland, Edwin H. 1940. "The White Collar Criminal." *American Sociological Review*, 5 (February): 1–12.

Sutherland, Edwin H. 1945. "Is 'White Collar Crime' Crime?" *American Sociological Review*, 10 (April): 132–139.

Sutherland, Edwin H. 1949. *White Collar Crime*. New York: Dryden.

Sutherland, Edwin H. 1983. *White Collar Crime: The Uncut Version*. New Haven, Conn.: Yale University Press.

Sutherland, Edwin H., and Donald R. Cressey. 1978. *Criminology* (10th ed.). Philadelphia: Lippencott.

Sutter, Alan G. 1966. "The World of the Righteous Dope Fiend." *Issues in Criminology*, 2 (Fall): 177–222.

Swados, Elizabeth. 1991. "The Story of a Street Person." *The New York Times Magazine*, August 18, pp. 18, 44–45.

Sykes, Gersham M., and David Matza. 1957. "Techniques of Neutralization: A Theory of Delinquency." *American Sociological Review*, 22 (December): 664–670.

Sykes, Gresham M., and and Frances T. Cullen. 1992. *Criminology* (2nd ed.). Ft. Worth, Tex.: Harcourt Brace Jovanovich.

Szasz, Thomas. 1976. *Heresies*. Garden City, N.Y.: Doubleday-Anchor.

Talan, Jamie. 1995. "Both Sides Now." *Newsday*, August 16, Part 2, pp. B4–B5, B14.

Tannenbaum, Frank. 1938. *Crime and the Community*. New York: Ginn.

Tappan, Paul. 1947. "Who Is the Criminal?" *American Sociological Review*, 12 (February): 96–102.

Tart, Charles T. 1971. *On Being Stoned: A Psychological Study of Marijuana Intoxication*. Palo Alto: Science & Behavior Books.

Tavris, Carol. 1993. "Beware the Incest-Survivor Machine." *The New York Times Book Review*, January 3, pp. 1, 16–17.

Taylor, Ian, Paul Walton, and Jock Young. 1973. *The New Criminology: For a Social Theory of Deviance*. London: Routledge & Kegan Paul.

Taylor, Ian, Paul Walton, and Jock Young (ed.). 1975. *Critical Criminology*. London: Routledge & Kegan Paul.

Taylor, John. 1991. "Men on Trial II." *New York*, December 16, pp. 30–36.

Taylor, John. 1992. "Family Therapy: Bush and the Hyperextended GOP Family." *New York,* August 31, pp. 22–26.

Taylor, Stuart, Jr. 1986. "High Court, 5-4, Says States Have the Right to Outlaw Private Homosexual Acts: Division Is Bitter." *The New York Times*, July 1, pp. A1, A19.

Temin, Carolyn Engel. 1973. "Discriminatory Sentencing of Women Offenders: The Case for ERA in a Nutshell." *The American Criminal Law Review*, 11 (Winter): 355–373.

Terry, Charles E., and Mildred Pellens. 1928. *The Opium Problem*. New York: Bureau of Social Hygiene.

Thio, Alex. 1973. "Class Bias in the Sociology of Deviance." *The American Sociologist*, 8 (February): 1–12.

Thio, Alex. 1995. *Deviant Behavior* (4th ed.). New York: HarperCollins.

Thoits, Peggy. 1985. "Self-Labeling Processes in Mental Illness: The Role of Emotional Distance." *American Journal of Sociology*, 91 (September): 221–249.

Thompson, Terri, David Hage, and Robert F. Black. 1992. "Crime and the Bottom Line." *U.S. World & News Report*, April 13, pp. 55–58.

Thrasher, Frderick M. 1927. *The Gang*. Chicago: University of Chicago Press.

Tinklenberg, Jared R. 1973. "Drugs and Crime." In National Commission on Marihuana and Drug Abuse, *Drug Use in America: Problem in Perspective*, Vol. I. Washington, D.C.: U.S. Government Printing Office, pp. 242–299.

Tinklenberg, Jared R., et al. 1981. "Drugs and Criminal Assaults by Adolescents: A Replication Study." *Journal of Psychoactive Drugs*, 13 (July-September): 277–287.

Tittle, Charles R., and Robert F. Meier. 1990. "Specifying the SES/Delinquency Relationship. " *Criminology*, 28 (May): 271–299.

Tittle, Charles R., Wayne J. Villmez, and Douglas A. Smith. 1982. "One Step Forward, Two Steps Back: More on the Class/Criminality Controversy." *American Sociological Review*, 47 (June): 435–438.

Toby, Jackson. 1957. "Social Disorganization and Stake in Conformity: Complementary Factors in the Predatory Behavior of Young Hoodlums." *Journal of Criminal Law, Criminology, and Police Science*, 48 (1): 12–17.

Toby, Jackson. 1974. "The Socialization and Control of Deviant Motivation." In Daniel Glaser (ed.), *Handbook of Criminology*. Chicago: Rand McNally, pp. 85–100.

Tomlinson, Kenneth Y. 1981. "You'll Be a Hooker—Or Else!" *Reader's Digest*, February, pp. 147–152.

Tonry, Michael. 1995. *Malign Neglect: Race, Crime, and Punishment in America*. New York: Oxford University Press.

Torrey, E. Fuller, with Ann E. Bowler, Edward H. Taylor, and Irving I. Gottesman. 1994. *Schizophrenia and Manic-Depressive Disorder: The Biological Roots of Mental Illness as Revealed by the Landmark Study of Identical Twins*. New York: Basic Books.

Toufexis, Anastasia. 1991. "Innocent Victims." *Time*, May 13, pp. 56–60.

Toufexis, Anastasia. 1994. "When Is Crib Death a Cover for Murder?" *Time*, April 11, pp. 63–64.

Townsend, John Marshall. 1978. *Cultural Conceptions of Mental Illness*. Chicago: University of Chicago Press.

Townsend, John Marshall. 1980. "Psychiatry Versus Societal Reaction: A Critical Analysis." *Journal of Health and Social Behavior*, 21 (September): 268–278.

Tracy, Paul E., Marvin E. Wolfgang, and Robert M. Figlio. 1990. *Delinquency Careers in Two Birth Cohorts*. New York: Plenum Press.

Traub, Stuart H., and Craig B. Little (eds.). 1994. *Theories of Deviance* (4th ed.). Itasca, Ill.: F.E. Peacock.

Trebay, Guy. 1990. "In Your Face!" *The Village Voice*, August 14, pp. 34–39.

Troiden, Richard R. 1977. *Becoming Homosexual: Research on Acquiring a Gay Identity*. Ph.D. dissertation, Department of Sociology, State University of New York at Stony Brook.

Troiden, Richard R. 1979. "Becoming Homosexual: A Model of Gay Identity Acquisition." *Psychiatry*, 42 (February): 362–373.

Troiden, Richard R. 1988. *Gay and Lesbian Identity: A Sociological Analysis*. Dix Hills, N.Y.: General Hall.

Troutman, Philip. 1965. *Velasquez*. London: Spring Books.

Troyer, Ronald J., and Gerald E. Markle. 1983. *Cigarettes*. New Brunswick, N.J.: Rutgers University Press.

Troyer, Ronald J., and Gerald E. Markle. 1984. "Coffee Drinking: An Emerging Problem?" *Social Problems*, 31 (April): 403–416.

Tunnell, Kenneth D. 1992. *Choosing Crime: The Criminal Calculus of Property Offenders*. Chicago: Nelson/Hall.

Turk, Austin T. 1980. "Analyzing Official Deviance: For Nonpartisan Conflict Analyses in Criminology." In James A, Inciardi (ed.), *Radical Criminology: The Coming Crisis*. Newbury Park, Calif.: Sage, pp. 249–264.

Turnbull, Colin. 1961. *The Forest People*. New York: Simon & Schuster.

Turner, Carleton E. 1980. "Chemistry and Metabolism." In Robert C. Petersen (ed.), *Marijuana Research Findings: 1980*. Rockville, Md.: National Institute on Drug Abuse, pp. 81–97.

Turner, Patricia A. 1993. *I Heard It Through the Grapevine: Rumor in African-American Culture*. Berkeley: University of California Press.

Turner, R. Jay, and John W. Gartrell. 1978. "Social Factors in Psychiatric Outcome: Toward a Resolution of Interpretive Controversies." *American Sociological Review*, 43 (June): 368–382.

Tyre, Peg. 1989. "Holy War: On the Front Lines with Operation Rescue." *New York*, April 24, pp. 49–51.

Unnever, James D. 1987. Review of James M. Byrne and Robert J. Sampson (eds.), *The Social Ecology of Crime*, New York: Springer-Verlag, 1986, in *Contemporary Sociology*, 16 (November): 845–846.

Valentine, Charles A. 1968. *Culture and Poverty: Critique and Counter-Proposals*. Chicago: University of Chicago Press.

Vance, Carole (ed.). 1984. *Pleasure and Danger: Exploring Female Sexuality*. Boston: Routledge & Kegan Paul.

Van den Berghe, Pierre L. 1978. *Man in Society: A Biosocial View* (2nd ed.). New York: Elsevier.

Van Hasselt, Vincent B., Randall L. Morrison, and Alan S. Bellack. 1985. "Alcohol Use in Wife Abusers and Their Spouses." *Addictive Behaviors*, 10 (2): 127–135.

Van Stolk, Mary. 1972. *The Battered Child in Canada*. Toronto: McClelland & Stewart.

Veteran's Administration. 1970. *Drug Treatment in Psychiatry*. Washington, D.C.: U.S. Government Printing Office.

Victor, Jeffrey S. 1989. "A Rumor–Panic About a Dangerous Satanic Cult in Western New York," *New York Folklore*, 15 (1-2): 23–49.

Victor, Jeffrey S. 1990. "Satanic Legends as Contemporary Legend." *Western Folklore*, 49 (January): 51–82.

Victor, Jeffrey S. 1993. *Satanic Panic: The Creation of a Contemporary Legend*. Chicago: Open Court.

Victor, Jeffrey S. 1995. "The Dangers of Moral Panics: What Skeptics (And Everyone Else) Needs to Know." *Skeptic*, 3 (3): 44–51.

Virkkunen, Matti. 1974. "Alcohol as a Factor Precipitating Aggression and Conflict Behavior Leading to Homicide." *British Journal of Addiction*, 69 (June): 149–154.

Vold, George B., and Thomas J. Bernard. 1986. *Theoretical Criminology* (3rd ed.). Oxford University Press.

Von Hentig, Hans. 1948. *The Criminal and His Victim*. New Haven, Conn.: Yale University Press.

Voss, Harwin L., and John R. Hepburn. 1968. "Patterns in Criminal Homicide in Chicago." *Journal of Criminal Law, Criminology, and Police Science*, 59 (December): 499–508.

Wald, Matthew L. 1986. "Battle Against Drunken Driving Should Focus on Alcoholics, Experts Say." *The New York Times*, January 3, p. 5.

Walfish, Steven, and William R. Blount. 1989. "Alcohol and Crime: Issues and Directions for Future Research." *Criminal Justice and Behavior*, 16 (September): 370–386.

Walker, Lenore E. 1979. *The Battered Woman*. New York: Harper & Row.

Wallace, Joyce. 1989. "AIDS in Prostitutes." In Pearl Ma and Donald Armstrong (eds.), *AIDS and Infections of Heterosexual Men*. Boston: Butterworths, pp. 285–295.

Waller, Willard. 1936. "Social Problems and the Mores." *American Sociological Review*, 1 (December): 922–932.

Wallis, Claudia, et al. 1985. "AIDS: A Growing Threat." *Time*, August 12, pp. 40–47.

Warburton, Clark. 1932. *The Economic Results of Prohibition*. New York: Columbia University Press.

Ward, David A., Timothy J. Carter, and Robin D. Perrin. 1994. *Social Deviance: Being, Behaving, and Branding*. Boston: Allyn & Bacon.

Warheit, George J., Charles E. Holzer, III, Roger A. Bell, and Sandra A. Avery. 1976. "Sex, Marital Status, and Mental Health: A Reappraisal." *Social Forces*, 55 (December): 459–470.

Warner, Michael. 1992. "From Queer to Eternity: An Army of Theorists Cannot Fail." *The Village Voice*, Voice Literary Supplement, June, pp. 18–19.

Warner, W. Lloyd, and Paul S. Lunt. 1941. *The Social Life of a Modern Community*. New Haven, Conn.: Yale University Press.

Warren, Carol A.B. 1974. *Identity and Community in the Gay World*. New York: John Wiley & Sons.

Warren, Carol A.B., and John M. Johnson. 1972. "A Critique of Labeling Theory from the Phenomenological Perspective." In Robert A. Scott and Jack D. Douglas (eds.), *Theoretical Perspectives on Deviance*. New York: Basic Books, pp. 69–92.

Warren, E.J., Jr. 1978. "The Economic Approach to Crime." *Canadian Journal of Criminology*, 10: 437–449.

Watson, Traci, and Joseph P. Shapiro. 1995. "Is There a 'Gay Gene'?" *U.S. News & World Report*, November 13, pp. 93–95.

Weber, Max. 1958. *The Protestant Ethic and the Spirit of Capitalism* (trans. Talcott Parsons). New York: Charles Scribner's Sons (orig. pub. 1904).

Webster, Richard. 1995. *Why Freud Was Wrong: Sin, Science, and Psychoanalysis*. Basic Books.

Weeks, Jeffrey, Kenneth Plummer, and Mary McIntosh. 1981. "Postscript: 'The Homosexual Role' Revisited." In Kenneth Plummer (ed.), *The Making of the Modern Homosexual*. Totowa, N.J.: Barnes & Noble, pp. 44–49.

Weil, Andrew T. 1972. *The Natural Mind: A New Way of Looking at Drugs and the Higher Consciousness*. Boston: Houghton Mifflin.

Weinberg, Martin S., and Colin J. Williams. 1974. *Male Homosexuals*. New York: Oxford University Press.

Weisburd, David, Stanton Wheeler, Elin Waring, and Nancy Bode. 1991. *Crimes of the Middle Classes: White-Collar Offenders in the Federal Courts*. New Haven, Conn.: Yale University Press.

Weitzman, Lenore. 1970. *Social Suicide: A Study of Missing Persons*. PhD. Dissertation, Department of Sociology, Columbia University.

Weitzman, Lenore. 1981. "Social Suicide." In Samuel E. Wallace and Albin Eser (eds.), *Suicide and Euthanasia: The Rights of Personhood.* Knoxville: University of Tennessee Press, pp. 10–23.

Welkos, Robert. 1984. "Doctor Involved in Blindings Is Given a 4-Year Term." *Los Angeles Times*, April 27.

Wellings, Kaye, Julia Field, Anne Johnson, and Jane Wadsworth. 1994. *Sexual Behaviour in Britain: The National Survey of Sexual Attitudes and Lifestyles.* New York: Penguin.

Wells, John Warren. 1970. *Tricks of the Trade.* New York: New American Library.

Welte, John W., and Ernest L. Abel. 1989. "Homicide: Drinking By the Victim." *Journal of Studies on Alcohol,* 50 (3): 197–201.

Wheeler, Stanton. 1960. "Sex Offenses: A Sociological Critique." *Law and Contemporary Society,* 25 (Spring): 258–278.

Wheeler, Stanton. 1983. "White Collar Crime: History of an Idea." In Sanford H. Kadish (ed.), *Encyclopedia of Crime and Justice.* New York: Free Press, pp. 1652–1656.

Wheeler, Stanton, Kenneth Mann, and Austin Sarat. 1988. *Sitting in Judgment: The Sentencing of White Collar Criminals.* New Haven, Conn.: Yale University Press.

Wheeler, Stanton, David Weisburd, and Nancy Bode. 1982. "Sentencing the White Collar Criminal: Rhetoric and Reality." *American Sociological Review,* 47 (October): 641–659.

Wheeler, Stanton, David Weisburd, E. Waring, and Nancy Bode. 1988. "White Collar Crimes and Criminals." *American Criminal Law Review,* 25: 331–358.

Whitam, Frederick L. 1977. "The Homosexual Role: A Reconsideration." *The Journal of Sex Research,* 13 (February): 1–13.

Whitam, Frederick L. 1983. "Culturally Invariable Properties of Male Homosexuality: Tentative Conclusions from Cross-Cultural Research." *Archives of Sexual Behavior,* 12 (June): 207–226.

Whitam, Frederick L., and Ronin M. Mathay. 1986. *Male Homosexuality in Four Societies: Brazil, Guatemala, the Philippines, and the United States.* New York: Praeger.

White, Byron R.. 1986. "Excerpts from the Court Opinion on Homosexuality." *The New York Times*, July 1, pp. A18.

Whyte, Martin King. 1990. *Dating, Mating, and Marriage.* New York: Aldine de Gruyter.

Whyte, William F. 1943. *Street-Corner Society: The Social Structure of an Italian Slum.* Chicago: University of Chicago Press.

Wiatroski, Michael D., David B. Griswold, and Mary K. Roberts. 1981. "Social Control Theory and Delinquency." *American Sociological Review,* 46 (October): 525–541.

Wieczorek, W.F., J.W. Welte, and E.L. Abel. 1990. "Alcohol, Drugs, and Murder: A Study of Convicted Homicide Offenders." *Journal of Criminal Justice,* 18 (3): 217–227.

Wikler, Abraham. 1968. "Drug Addiction: Organic and Physiological Aspects." *International Encyclopedia of the Social Sciences.* New York: Macmillan, pp. 290–298.

Wilkins, Leslie T. 1964. *Social Deviance: Social Policy, Action, and Research.* London: Tavistock.

Wilkinson, Gregg S. 1975. "Patient-Audience Social Status and the Social Construction of Psychiatric Disorder: Toward a Differential Frame of Reference Hypothesis." *Journal of Health and Social Behavior,* 16 (March): 28–38.

Williams, Gerald D., David A. Clem, and Mary C. Dufour. 1994. *Apparent Per Capita Alcohol Consumption: National, State,* *and Regional Trends, 1977–1992.* Bethesda, Md.: National Institute on Alcohol Abuse and Alcoholism.

Williams, Joyce E., and Willard A. Nielsen, Jr. 1979. "The Rapist Looks at His Crime." *Free Inquiry Into Creative Sociology,* 7 (November): 128–132.

Willis, Ellen. 1983. "Feminism, Moralism, and Pornography." In Ann Snitow et al. (eds.), *Powers of Desire: The Politics of Sexuality.* New York: Monthly Review Press, pp. 460–467.

Willwerth, James. 1976. *Jones: Portrait of a Mugger.* New York: Fawcett.

Wilson, Edward O. 1975. *Sociobiology: The New Synthesis.* Cambridge, Mass.: Harvard University Press.

Wilson, Edward O. 1978. *On Human Nature.* Cambridge, Mass.: Harvard University Press.

Wilson, Edward O. 1984. *Biophilia.* Cambridge, Mass.: Harvard University Press.

Wilson, James Q., and Richard J. Herrnstein. 1985. *Crime and Human Nature.* New York: Simon & Schuster.

Wilson, Margo I., and Martin Daly. 1992. "Who Kills Whom in Spouse Killings? On the Exceptional Sex Ratio of Spousal Homicides in the United States." *Criminology,* 30 (May): 189–215.

Wilson, Wiliam Julius. 1987. *The Truly Disadvantaged: The Inner City, the Underclass, and Public Policy.* Chicago: University of Chicago Press.

Winick, Charles. 1964. "Physician Narcotic Addicts." In Howard S. Becker (ed.), *The Other Side: Perspectives on Deviance.* New York: Free Press, pp. 261–279.

Wise, David. 1973. *The Politics of Lying.* New York: Vintage Books.

Wolfe, Morris. 1995. "A Clear and Present Danger: How One Professor Overwhelmed a Montreal University." *Lingua Franca,* May/June, pp. 54–64.

Wolfgang, Marvin E. 1958. *Patterns in Criminal Homicide.* Philadelphia: University of Pennsylvania Press.

Wolfgang, Marvin E. 1981. "Foreword." In James J. Collins, Jr. (ed.), *Drinking and Crime: Perspectives on the Relationships Between Alcohol Consumption and Criminal Behavior.* New York: Guilford Press, pp. xi–xii.

Wolfgang, Marvin E., and Franco Ferracuti. 1967. *The Subculture of Violence.* London: Tavistock.

Wolfgang, Marvin E., Robert M. Figlio, and Thorsten Sellin. 1972. *Delinquency in a Birth Cohort.* Chicago: University of Chicago Press.

Wolfgang, Marvin E., Robert M. Figlio, and Terence P. Thornberry. 1978. *Evaluating Criminology.* New York: Elsevier.

Wolfgang, Marvin E., Terence P. Thornberry, and Robert M. Figlio. 1987. *From Boy to Man, From Delinquency to Crime.* Chicago: University of Chicago Press.

Wolman, Baron. 1973. "A House Is not a Home in Nevada," *Gallery,* September, pp. 33–34, 105–107, 111–112.

Wooden, Wayne S., and Jay Parker. 1982. *Men Behind Bars: Sexual Exploitation in Prison.* New York: Plenum Press.

Woodmansee, John. 1975. *The World of a Giant Corporation: A Report from the GE Project.* Seattle: North Country.

Woolgar, Steve, and Dorothy Pawluch. 1985. "Ontological Gerrymandering: The Anatomy of Social Problems Explanations." *Social Problems,* 32 (February): 214–227.

Wright, Charles. 1984. *Constructions of Deviance in Sociological Theory: The Problem of Commensurability.* Landham, Md.: University Press of America.

Wright, James D., and Peter H. Rossi. 1986. *Armed and Con-*

sidered Dangerous: A Survey of Felons and their Firearms. New York: Aldine de Gruyter.

Wright, James D., Peter H. Rossi, and Kathleen Daly. 1983. *Under the Gun: Weapons, Crime, and Violence in America.* New York: Aldine de Gruyter.

Wu, Harry. 1992. *Laogai: The Chinese Gulag.* Boulder, Colo.: Westview Press.

Wu, Harry, 1995–96. "Forced Labor in China." *American Educator,* Winter, pp. 37–43.

Wu, Harry, 1996. *Laogai: The Chinese Gulag* (2nd ed.). Boulder, Colo.: Westview Press.

Wyatt, Gail Elizabeth, Michael D. Newcomb, and Monika H. Riederle. 1993. *Sexual Abuse and Consensual Sex: Women's Developmental Patterns and Outcomes.* Newbury Park, Calif.: Sage.

Yarrow, Marian Radke, et al. 1955. "The Psychological Meaning of Mental Illness in the Family." *Journal of the Social Issues,* 11 (December): 12–24.

Yearwood, Lennox, and Thomas S. Weinberg. 1979. "Black Organizations, Gay Organizations, Sociological Parallels." In Martin P. Levine (ed.). *Gay Men.* New York: Harper & Row, pp. 301–316.

Yin, Peter P. 1980. "Fear of Crime Among the Elderly: Some Issues and Suggestions." *Social Problems,* 27 (April): 492–504.

Young, Wayland. 1966. *Eros Denied: Sex in Western Society.* New York: Grove Press.

Zador, Paul L. 1991. "Alcohol-Related Relative Risk of Fatal Driver Injuries in Relation to Driver Age and Sex." *Journal of Studies on Alcohol,* 52 (4): 302–310.

Zausner, Michael. 1986. *The Streets: A Factual Portrait of Six Prostitutes as Told in Their Own Words.* New York: St. Martin's Press.

Zeitlin, Lawrence R. 1971. "A Little Larceny Can Do a Lot for Employee Morale." *Psychology Today,* June, pp. 22–26, 64.

Zimring, Franklin E., Satyanshu K. Mukherjee, and Barrik van Winkle. 1983. "Intimate Violence: A Study of Interpersonal Homicide in Chicago." *University of Chicago Law Review,* 50 (Spring): 910–930.

Zinberg, Norman E. 1984. *Drug, Set, and Setting: The Basis for Controlled Intoxicant Use.* New Haven, Conn.: Yale University Press.

Zola, Irving Kenneth. 1964. "Observations on Gambling in a Lower Class Culture." In Howard S. Becker (ed.), *The Other Side: Perspectives on Deviance.* New York: Free Press, pp. 247–260.

Zorbaugh, Harvey W. 1929. *The Gold Coast and the Slum.* Chicago: University of Chicago Press.

INDEXES

AUTHOR INDEX

SUBJECT INDEX